understanding
Business

THIRTEENTH EDITION

William G. Nickels
UNIVERSITY OF MARYLAND

James M. McHugh
ST. LOUIS COMMUNITY COLLEGE AT FOREST PARK

Susan M. McHugh
APPLIED LEARNING SYSTEMS

UNDERSTANDING BUSINESS

Published by McGraw Hill LLC, 1325 Avenue of the Americas, New York, NY 10121. Copyright © 2022 by
McGraw Hill LLC. All rights reserved. Printed in Singapore. No part of this publication
may be reproduced or distributed in any form or by any means, or stored in a database or retrieval system,
without the prior written consent of McGraw Hill LLC, including, but not limited to, in any network or
other electronic storage or transmission, or broadcast for distance learning.

Some ancillaries, including electronic and print components, may not be available to customers outside the
United States.

This book is printed on acid-free paper.

3 4 5 6 7 8 9 MPM 24 23 22 21

ISBN 978-1-266-04322-2
MHID 1-266-04322-5

Cover image: *sollia/shutterstock*

The Internet addresses listed in the text were accurate at the time of publication. The inclusion of a website does
not indicate an endorsement by the authors or McGraw Hill LLC, and McGraw Hill LLC does not guarantee the
accuracy of the information presented at these sites.

mheducation.com/highered

DEDICATION

To our families—Marsha, Joel, Carrie,
Claire, Casey, Dan, Molly, Michael,
Patrick, and Quinn. Thank you
for making everything worth doing and
giving us the support to do it well!

AND

To the team that made this edition
possible, especially the instructors and
students who gave us such valuable
guidance as we developed the text
and package.

Bill Nickels is emeritus professor of business at the University of Maryland, College Park. He has over 30 years' experience teaching graduate and undergraduate business courses, including introduction to business, marketing, and promotion. He has won the Outstanding Teacher on Campus Award four times and was nominated for the award many other times. He received his MBA degree from Western Reserve University and his PhD from Ohio State University. Bill has written a marketing communications text and two marketing principles texts in addition to many articles in business publications. He has taught many seminars to businesspeople on subjects such as power communications, marketing, nonbusiness marketing, and stress and life management. His son, Joel, is a professor of English at the University of Miami (Florida).

Jim McHugh holds an MBA degree from Lindenwood University and has had broad experience in education, business, and government. As chair of the Business and Economics Department of St. Louis Community College–Forest Park, Jim coordinated and directed the development of the business curriculum. In addition to teaching several sections of Introduction to Business each semester for nearly 30 years, Jim taught in the marketing and management areas at both the undergraduate and graduate levels. Jim enjoys conducting business seminars and consulting with small and large businesses. He is actively involved in the public-service sector and served as chief of staff to the St. Louis County Executive.

Susan McHugh is a learning specialist with extensive training and experience in adult learning and curriculum development. She holds an MEd degree from the University of Missouri and completed her coursework for a PhD in education administration with a specialty in adult learning theory. As a professional curriculum developer, she has directed numerous curriculum projects and educator training programs. She has worked in the public and private sectors as a consultant in training and employee development. While Jim and Susan treasure their participation in writing projects, their greatest accomplishment is their collaboration on their three children. Casey is carrying on the family's teaching tradition as an adjunct professor at Washington University. Molly and Michael are carrying on the family writing tradition by contributing to the development of several supplementary materials for this text.

Photos: McGraw Hill

THE **GOLD** ★★★★ STANDARD

In Preparing Future-Ready Learners

Congratulations. You've made an excellent selection. Welcome to the preeminent teaching and learning experience ever created for Introduction to Business classes.

Our experienced and diverse authors and long-tenured editorial team have created a product that meets the needs of nearly all classrooms, no matter the size, teaching modality, or learning objectives. The content is unmatched in depth, breadth, currency, and relevancy, and is presented in an extremely readable format for students with all learning styles. A wealth of technology solutions engages students, enriches learning, furthers understanding, and simplifies instructors' assessment processes. Course supplements tightly align with chapter concepts and enhance retention, making instructors of all experience levels Grade-A rock stars. And unparalleled support from our digital faculty consultants helps ensure you and your students benefit from the full experience of what is now the gold standard in Introduction to Business classes. Nickels/McHugh/McHugh, *Understanding Business,* 13th Edition does more than teach—it prepares students to create real impact on the world.

1. The Gold Standard in Relevancy and Currency

Real-world case studies—across nearly all industries and company sizes—ensure your students are apprised of the most current challenges businesspeople face today. From COVID-19 and unemployment to USMCA and artificial intelligence, you have access to numerous relevant samples that tie directly into chapter lessons. Plus with the option to take advantage of the ***From the News to the Classroom blog***, understandingbiz.com, you can enrich the learning experience with content that is updated multiple times each week and includes abstracts of relevant news stories, videos tied to chapter topics, and critical thinking questions that streamline your prep time and help create an ultra-current course.

2. The Gold Standard in Results-Driven Technology

Interactive learning tools increase teaching effectiveness and learning efficiency by facilitating a stronger connection between the course material and the modern student.

Where the Science of Learning Meets the Art of Teaching *McGraw-Hill Connect* is the leading online assignment and assessment solution that connects students with the tools and resources they need to achieve success. It also allows instructors to quickly and easily choose the content and assignments that will best emphasize the learning objectives they prefer to cover. The result is a customized course, rich with engaging presentations and activities that prepare students for the business world.

The First and Only Adaptive Reading Experience *SmartBook 2.0* creates a dynamic reading experience and personalizes content for each student, helping students master and retain foundational concepts. Tracking each student's progress, it automatically assesses comprehension levels and delivers the content required to reinforce topics needing more attention. This continuously adaptive learning path is proven to accelerate learning and strengthen memory recall, all while providing instructors a turnkey tool that ensures students stay on track.

Bridging the Gap between Theory and Real Life Having knowledge is the first step—and understanding how to apply that knowledge is what determines a person's success in the working world. That's why we provide an array of application exercises that are as educational as they are engaging. *Click-and-Drag* exercises reinforce key models and processes, and demonstrate application-level knowledge. *Video Cases* allow students to observe and analyze key concepts as they are utilized by companies and organizations they know and recognize. *Case analyses* expose students to real-world scenarios and engage their critical-thinking and analysis skills. New to this edition, 15-minute *Application-Based Activities* put students in the role of business professionals, allowing them to make decisions and learn from the results.

3. The Gold Standard in Teaching Resources

Whether it's your first or fortieth year teaching, you can benefit from a wealth of assessments and class-tested resources that simplify your evaluation process and enrich the learning experience.

Assessment Tools:

- **NEW SmartBook 2.0** personalizes learning to individual student needs, continually adapting to pinpoint knowledge gaps and focus learning on topics that need the most attention. With SmartBook 2.0, learning is more productive and the guesswork is taken out of what to study in a no-fail environment. As a result, students are better prepared for class and coursework.
- **NEW Writing Assignment Premium** evaluates, scores, and gives feedback on student responses to provided prompts.
- **NEW Application-Based Activities** are highly interactive, automatically graded exercises that immerse students in a business environment, analyze the situation, and apply their knowledge to a real-world scenario.
- **Business Plan Prep Activities** guide students in creating a basic business plan.
- **Chapter quizzes** are pre-built to cover all chapter learning objectives.
- **Test bank** that is by far the largest and most accurate collection of questions on the market, including over 300 questions per chapter, makes testing student knowledge a simple and efficient process.
- **Application exercises** challenge students to demonstrate their knowledge of key concepts and terms by applying them to a variety of business-world scenarios.
- **Video assignments** help explain difficult concepts and show business concepts in action in companies large and small.
- **Instructor's Manual** includes tools to improve retention and engagement, while helping save the instructor's time.

	SmartBook 2.0	iSeeit! Videos	Click and Drags	Video Cases/Case Analyses	Manager's Hot Seat Videos	Application-Based Activities	Business Plan Prep Activities	Writing Assignment Premium
CREATE (Higher Order Thinking Skills)							✓	✓
EVALUATE						✓	✓	✓
ANALYZE				✓	✓	✓	✓	✓
APPLY		✓	✓	✓	✓	✓	✓	✓
UNDERSTAND	✓	✓	✓	✓	✓	✓	✓	✓
REMEMBER (Lower Order Thinking Skills)	✓	✓	✓	✓	✓	✓	✓	✓

- ***From the News to the Classroom*** blog, understandingbiz.com, is updated multiple times each week, featuring abstracts of relevant news stories, video tied to chapter topics, and critical-thinking questions that streamline your prep time and help create an ultra-current course.
- **PowerPoint presentations** include integrated polling questions that improve student engagement.
- **Video library** with teaching guides includes:

  - **Company case videos** produced specifically to expound on chapter learning objectives via real-world business situations across a broad range of industries, sizes, and geographic locations, allowing students to contextualize the chapter's content.
  - **Manager's Hot Seat videos** offer short cases that show real business professionals confronting a variety of workplace challenges.
  - **iSeeit! animated video explanations** clarify some of the most important topics and can be accessed within the eBook.

4. The Gold Standard in Support, Service, and Solutions

We want you to get the most out of our products, and we do everything possible to help provide your students an exceptional learning experience. From the first to the last day of the semester, we support you with:

- Learning technology representatives
- Digital faculty consultants
- Student ambassadors
- Implementation consultants
- Technical support
- Integration with your learning management system

- Content your way/customizable content/a robust library of cross-disciplinary content
- Student progress-tracking
- Accreditation and assurance of learning ready
- Fully automated lecture capture via Tegrity®

Our team of digital faculty consultants and extensive toolbox of support programs ensure you receive the full value of all this product has to offer.

The Bottom Line

The business world is constantly changing, and your classroom needs to keep up. With Nickels/McHugh/McHugh, *Understanding Business,* 13th Edition, both you and your students can experience *the Gold Standard* in Introduction to Business classes.

Changes to the New Edition

Users of *Understanding Business* have always appreciated the currency of the material and the large number of examples from companies of all sizes and industries (e.g., service, manufacturing, nonprofit, and profit) in the United States and around the world. A glance at the Chapter Notes will show you that almost all of them are from 2019 or 2020. Accordingly, the latest business practices and other developments affecting business include:

- Equifax data breach
- Inclusion and creating a sense of *belonging* in the workplace
- The rise of Gen Z's economic influence
- Baby Boomer brain drain/retaining older workers
- US–Mexico–Canada Agreement (USMCA)
- Brexit
- Real unemployment rate (vs. standard unemployment rate)
- Effects of artificial intelligence on unemployment
- Tightening of Cuban trade and travel
- Right to Disconnect laws
- Business Roundtable Statement on the Purpose of a Corporation
- Cloud architects
- Small Business Reorganization Act of 2019 (SBRA)
- 5G
- Artificial intelligence
- Machine learning
- COVID-19
- Green bonds
- Negative interest rates
- LAN
- WAN
- Blockchain
- Web 3.0
- And much, much more

McGraw-Hill Customer Experience Group Contact Information

At McGraw-Hill Education, we understand that getting the most from new technology can be challenging. That's why our services don't stop after you purchase our products. You can e-mail our Product Specialists 24 hours a day to get product training online. Or you can search our knowledge bank of Frequently Asked Questions on our support website. For Customer Support, call **800-331-5094** or visit www.mhhe.com/support. One of our Technical Support Analysts will be able to assist you in a timely fashion.

ACKNOWLEDGMENTS

Our executive portfolio manager Meredith Fossel led the talented team at McGraw-Hill Education. We appreciate her dedication to the success of the project and her responsiveness to the demands of the market. Anne Leung served as our senior product developer and kept everyone on task and on schedule. Molly and Michael McHugh helped revise the text and contributed many of the new boxes and profiles. Matt Diamond created the new fresh, open interior design and extraordinary cover. Traci Vaske and Jen Blankenship carried out the extensive research for photos that was necessary to effectively reflect the concepts presented in the text. Lead project manager, Christine Vaughan, did a splendid job of keeping the production of the text on schedule. Bruce Gin expertly supervised Connect production.

Many dedicated educators and content experts made extraordinary contributions to the quality and utility of this teaching and learning package. For this edition, Diana Murphy and her team at Editors Inc. did a superb job of creating a useful and current Instructor's Manual, Test Bank, and PowerPoints. We also recognize the efforts of those who contributed to the creation of Connect materials: Stacy Martin at Southwestern Illinois College. We are grateful to our SmartBook team, in particular to Judy Bulin at Monroe Community College, who tirelessly worked to review and perfect the probes and feedback and respond to student queries, along with Kathleen Borbee. Thank you to Kelly Luchtman and team at Lightfellow for the fabulous new videos they produced. Thank you to the Digital Faculty Consultants who have helped train and support so many of their fellow instructors in the Introduction to Business course, as well as assist them in successfully implementing Connect into their courses: Chris Finnin, Drexel University; Tim Rogers, Ozarks Technical Community College; Allison Smith, West Kentucky Community and Technical College; and Ruth White, Bowling Green State University. We would like to give special thanks to Tim Rogers for his dedication to this project, including the hard work he did revising the student study guide.

Our outstanding marketing manager, Nicole Young, and marketing director, Natalie King, were up to the challenge of guiding the text to continued market leadership. With the assistance of the market's finest sales professionals, they led the text to record highs. We want to thank the many instructors who contributed to the development of *Understanding Business.*

Reviewers

We would like to thank the following instructors for sharing with us their opinions, input, and advice—all of which contributed to the development of each edition:

For this edition we thank:

David M. Baird, *Indiana University Southeast*

Kali Bard, *Crowder College*

Richard Barnhart, *Grand Rapids Community College*

Jessie Bellflowers, *Fayetteville Technical Community College*

Bob Dodd, *College of Lake County*

Erik Ford, *University of Oregon*

Terri Gonzales-Kreisman, *Delgado Community College*

Patrick Greek, *Macomb Community College*

John Guess, *Delgado Community College*

Francis A. Hatstat, *Bellevue College*

Venkat Krishnamurthy, *College of Lake County*

Susan Jennings Lantz, *West Virginia University*

Catherine E. Levitt, *College of the Desert*

Paula Y. Mooney, *Georgia Southern University*

Alexandra Moran, *Purdue University Northwest*

Annette D. Rakowski, *Bergen Community College*

Varun Ramberran, *Miami Dade College*

Greg Rapp, *Portland Community College*

Levi Richard, *Citrus Community College*

Tim Rogers, *Ozarks Technical College*

Storm Russo, *Valencia College*

Freddie Sandifer Jr., *Tarrant County College Northeast Campus*

Phyllis T. Shafer, *Brookdale Community College*

Dennis M. Sheridan, *Fayetteville Technical Community College*

Keith Shishido, *Santa Monica College*

Joe Tungol, *College of DuPage*

Michael Wiggins, *Georgia Southern University*

For previous editions we thank:

Nikolas Adamou, *Borough of Manhattan Community College*

Rebecca Adams, *Kansas State University*

Cathy Adamson, *Southern Union State Community College*

Ashraf Almurdaah, *Los Angeles City College*

Gary Amundson, *Montana State University–Billings*

Kenneth Anderson, *Borough of Manhattan Community College*

Kenneth Anderson, *Mott Community College*

Lydia Anderson, *Fresno City College*

Narita Anderson, *University of Central Oklahoma*

Roanne Angiello, *Bergen Community College*

Brenda T. Anthony, *Tallahassee Community College*

Chi Anyansi-Archibong, *North Carolina A&T State University*

Maria Aria, *Camden County College*

Michael Atchison, *University of Virginia–Charlottesville*

Michael Aubry, *Cuyamaca College*

Andrea Bailey, *Moraine Valley Community College*

Sandra Bailey, *Ivy Tech Community College of Indiana*

Scott Bailey, *Troy University*

Wayne Ballantine, *Prairie View A&M University*

Frank Barber, *Cuyahoga Community College*

Ruby Barker, *Tarleton State University*

Rosalia (Lia) Barone, *Norwalk Community College*

Barbara Barrett, *St. Louis Community College–Meramec*

Barry Barrett, *University of Wisconsin–Milwaukee*

Richard Bartlett, *Columbus State Community College*

Denise Barton, *Wake Technical Community College*

Lorraine Bassette, *Prince George's Community College*

Robb Bay, *College of Southern Nevada–West Charleston*

Jim Beard, *University of Arkansas–Fort Smith*

Amy Beattie, *Champlain College*

Charles Beavin, *Miami Dade College North*

Charles Beem, *Bucks County Community College*

Cathleen Cogdill, *Northern Virginia Community College*

Lori Bennett, *Moorpark College*

Robert Bennett, *Delaware County Community College*

Ellen Benowitz, *Mercer Community College*

Michael Bento, *Owens Community College*

George H. Bernard, *Seminole State College of Florida*

Patricia Bernson, *County College of Morris*

Harry V. Bernstein, *Essex County College, Newark, New Jersey*

Marilyn Besich, *Montana State University–Great Falls*

William Bettencourt, *Edmonds Community College*

Robert Blanchard, *Salem State College*

Mary Jo Boehms, *Jackson State Community College*

James Borden, *Villanova University*

Michael Bravo, *Bentley College*

Dennis Brode, *Sinclair Community College*

Kathy Broneck, *Pima Community College*

Harvey Bronstein, *Oakland Community College*

Deborah Brown, *North Carolina State University–Raleigh*

Aaron A. Buchko, *Bradley University*

Jerri Buiting, *Baker College–Flint*

Laura Bulas, *Central Community College–Hastings*

Judy Bulin, *Monroe Community College*

Barry Bunn, *Valencia Community College–West Campus*

Bill Burton, *Indiana Wesleyan University*

Paul Callahan, *Cincinnati State Technical and Community College*

William Candley, *Lemoyne Owen College*

Nancy Carr, *Community College of Philadelphia*

Ron Cereola, *James Madison University*

Bonnie Chavez, *Santa Barbara City College*

Susan Cisco, *Oakton Community College*

Margaret (Meg) Clark, *Cincinnati State Technical and Community College*

Savannah Clay, *Central Piedmont Community College*

David Clifton, *Ivy Tech Community College of Indiana*

C. Cloud, *Phoenix College*

Paul Coakley, *Community College of Baltimore County*

Doug Cobbs, *JS Reynolds Community College*

Cathleen H. Cogdill, *Northern Virginia Community College*

Brooks Colin, *University of New Orleans*

Debbie Collins, *Anne Arundel Community College*

Patrick Conroy, *Delgado Community College*

Andrew Cook, *Limestone College*

Bob Cox, *Salt Lake Community College*

Susan Cremins, *Westchester Community College*

Julie Cross, *Chippewa Valley Tech College*

Geoffrey Crosslin, *Kalamazoo Valley Community College*

Douglas Crowe, *Bradley University*

James Darling, *Central New Mexico Community College*

John David, *Stark State College of Technology*

Peter Dawson, *Collin County Community College*

Joseph Defilippe, *Suffolk County Community College–Brentwood*

Tim DeGroot, *Midwestern State University*

Len Denault, *Bentley College*

Frances Depaul, *Westmoreland County Community College*

Donna DeVault, *Fayetteville Technical Community College*

Sharon Dexter, *Southeast Community College–Beatrice*

John Dilyard, *St. Francis College*

Barbara Dinardo, *Owens Community College*

Bob Dodd, *College of Lake County*

George Dollar, *St. Petersburg College*

Glenn Doolittle, *Santa Ana College*

Ron Dougherty, *Ivy Tech Community College of Indiana*

Michael Drafke, *College of DuPage*

Rosario (Bud) Drago, *Villanova University*

Joseph Dutka, *Ivy Tech Community College of Indiana*

Karen Eboch, *Bowling Green State University*

Brenda Eichelberger, *Portland State University*

Kelvin Elston, *Nashville State Tech Community College*

Robert Ettl, *Stony Brook University*

Nancy Evans, *Heartland Community College*

Mary Ewanechko, *Monroe Community College*

Michael Ewens, *Ventura College*

Hyacinth Ezeka, *Coppin State University*

Bob Farris, *Mt. San Antonio College*

Karen Faulkner, *Long Beach City College*

Gil Feiertag, *Columbus State Community College*

Joseph Flack, *Washtenaw Community College*

Lucinda Fleming, *Orange County Community College*

Jackie Flom, *University of Toledo*

Andrea Foster, *John Tyler Community College*

Michael Foster, *Bentley College*

Leatrice Freer, *Pitt Community College*

Alan Friedenthal, *Kingsborough Community College*

MaryBeth Furst, *Howard Community College*

Charles Gaiser, *Brunswick Community College*

Wayne Gawlik, *Joliet Junior College*

Ashley Geisewite, *Southwest Tennessee Community College*

Katie Ghahramani, *Johnson County Community College*

Debora Gilliard, *Metropolitan State College–Denver*

Ross Gittell, *University of New Hampshire*

James Glover, *Community College of Baltimore County–Essex*

Constance Golden, *Lakeland Community College*

Doug Greiner, *University of Toledo–Scott Park*

Toby Grodner, *Union County College*

John Guess, *Delgado Community College*

Lisa E. Hadley, *Southwest Tennessee Community College*

Peggy Hager, *Winthrop University*

Clark Hallpike, *Elgin Community College*

Geri Harper, *Western Illinois University*

Britt Hastey, *Los Angeles City College*

Frank Hatstat, *Bellevue Community College*

Spedden Hause, *University of Maryland–University College*

Karen H. Hawkins, *Miami Dade College*

Travis Hayes, *Chattanooga State Technical Community College*

Jack Heinsius, *Modesto Junior College*

Charlane Held, *Onondaga Community College*

Nancy Hernandez, *Howard College*

James Hess, *Ivy Tech Community College of Indiana*

Steve Hester, *Southwest Tennessee Community College*

William Hill, *Mississippi State University*

Nathan Himelstein, *Essex County College*

Paula Hladik, *Waubonsee Community College*

David Ho, *Metropolitan Community College*

Douglas Hobbs, *Sussex County Community College*

Linda Hoffman, *Ivy Tech Community College–Fort Wayne*

Maryanne Holcomb, *Antelope Valley College*

Mary Carole Hollingsworth, *Georgia Perimeter College*

Russell E. Holmes, *Des Moines Area Community College*

Scott Homan, *Purdue University–West Lafayette*

Stacy Horner, *Southwestern Michigan College*

Dennis Hudson, *University of Tulsa*

Jo Ann Hunter, *Community College Allegheny County in Pittsburgh*

Kimberly Hurns, *Washtenaw Community College*

Victor Isbell, *University of Nevada–Las Vegas*

Deloris James, *University of Maryland–University College*

Pam Janson, *Stark State College of Technology*

William Jedlicka, *Harper College*

Carol Johnson, *University of Denver*

Russell Johnson, *Utah Valley University*

Gwendolyn Jones, *The University of Akron*

Kenneth Jones, *Ivy Tech Community College of Indiana*

Marilyn Jones, *Friends University*

Michael Jones, *Delgado Community College*

Dmitriy Kalyagin, *Chabot College*

Jack Kant, *San Juan College*

Janice M. Karlen, *La Guardia Community College*

Jimmy Kelsey, *Seattle Central Community College*

Robert Kemp, *University of Virginia–Charlottesville*

David Kendall, *Fashion Institute of Technology*

Kristine Kinard, *Shelton State Community College*

Sandra King, *Minnesota State University–Mankato*

Mary Beth Klinger, *College of Southern Maryland*

Andrzej Kobylanski, *San Joaquin Delta College*

Jon Krabill, *Columbus State Community College*

John Kurnik, *Saint Petersburg College*

Jeff LaVake, *University of Wisconsin–Oshkosh*

Robert Lewis, *Davenport University*

Byron Lilly, *DeAnza College*

Beverly Loach, *Central Piedmont Community College*

Boone Londrigan, *Mott Community College*

Ladonna Love, *Fashion Institute of Technology*

Ivan Lowe, *York Technical College*

Yvonne Lucas, *Southwestern College*

Robert Lupton, *Central Washington University*

Megan Luttenton, *Grand Valley State University*

Elaine Madden, *Anne Arundel Community College*

Lawrence Maes, *Davenport University*

Niki Maglaris, *Northwestern College*

James Maniki, *Northwestern College*

James W. Marco, *Wake Technical Community College*

Martin Markowitz, *College of Charleston*

Theresa Mastrianni, *Kingsborough Community College*

Fred Mayerson, *Kingsborough Community College*

Lee McCain, *Valencia College*

Stacy McCaskill, *Rock Valley College*

Vershun L. McClain, *Jackson State University*

Gina McConoughey, *Illinois Central College*

Patricia McDaniel, *Central Piedmont Community College*

Pam McElligott, *St. Louis Community College–Meramec*

Tom McFarland, *Mt. San Antonio College*

Grace McLaughlin, *University of California, Irvine*

Bill McPherson, *Indiana University of Pennsylvania*

Michelle Meyer, *Joliet Junior College*

Catherine Milburn, *University of Colorado–Denver*

Ginger Moore, *York Technical College*

Sandy Moore, *Ivy Tech Community College of Indiana*

Jennifer Morton, *Ivy Tech Community College of Indiana*

Peter Moutsatson, *Central Michigan University*

Rachna Nagi-Condos, *American River College*

Darrell Neron, *Pierce College*

Mihai Nica, *University of Central Oklahoma*

Charles Nichols, *Sullivan University*

Frank Novakowski, *Davenport University*

Mark Nygren, *Brigham Young University–Idaho*

Paul Okello, *Tarrant County College*

David Oliver, *Edison Community College*

Faviana Olivier, *Bentley College*

John Olivo, *Bloomsburg University of Pennsylvania*

Teresa O'Neill, *International Institute of the Americas*

Cathy Onion, *Western Illinois University*

Susan Ontko, *Schoolcraft College*

Joanne Orabone, *Community College of Rhode Island*

Glenda Orosco, *Oklahoma State University Institute of Technology*

Javier Osorio, *Seminole State College*

Christopher O'Suanah, *J. S. Reynolds Community College*

Karen E. Overton, *Houston Community College Houston*

Daniel Pacheco, *Kansas City Kansas Community College*

Esther Page-Wood, *Western Michigan University*

Lauren Paisley, *Genesee Community College*

James Papademas, *Wright Community College, Chicago*

John Pappalardo, *Keene State College*

Ron Pardee, *Riverside Community College*

Jack Partlow, *Northern Virginia Community College*

Dyan Pease, *Sacramento City College*

Jeff Pepper, *Chippewa Valley Tech College*

Sheila Petcavage, *Cuyahoga Community College Western–Parma*

Roy Pipitone, *Erie Community College*

Lana Powell, *Valencia Community College–West Campus*

Dan Powroznik, *Chesapeake College*

Litsa Press, *College of Lake County*

Sally Proffitt, *Tarrant County College–Northeast*

Vincent Quan, *Fashion Institute of Technology*

Michael Quinn, *James Madison University*

Anthony Racka, *Oakland Community College*

Larry Ramos, *Miami-Dade Community College*

Greg Rapp, *Portland Community College–Sylvania*

Robert Reese, *Illinois Valley Community College*

David Reiman, *Monroe County Community College*

Gloria Rembert, *Mitchell Community College*

Levi Richard, *Citrus College*

Clinton Richards, *University of Nevada–Las Vegas*

Patricia Richards, *Westchester Community College*

Steve Riczo, *Kent State University*

Susan Roach, *Georgia Southern University*

Sandra Robertson, *Thomas Nelson Community College*

David Robinson, *University of California–Berkeley*

Catherine Roche, *Rockland Community College*

Tim Rogers, *Ozark Technical College*

Sam Rohr, *University of Northwestern Ohio*

Pamela Rouse, *Butler University*

Carol Rowey, *Community College of Rhode Island*

Jeri Rubin, *University of Alaska–Anchorage*

Storm Russo, *Valencia Community College*

Mark Ryan, *Hawkeye Community College*

Richard Sarkisian, *Camden County College*

Andy Saucedo, *Dona Ana Community College–Las Cruces*

James Scott, *Central Michigan University*

Janet Seggern, *Lehigh Carbon Community College*

Sashi Sekhar, *Purdue University–Calumet-Hammond*

Pat Setlik, *Harper College*

Swannee Sexton, *University of Tennessee–Knoxville*

Phyllis Shafer, *Brookdale Community College*

Richard Shortridge, *Glendale Community College*

Denise M. Simmons, *Northern Virginia Community College*

William Spangler, *Duquesne University*

Rieann Spence-Gale, *Northern Virginia Community College*

Clifford Stalter, *Chattanooga State Technical Community College*

Kurt Stanberry, *University of Houston–Downtown*

Desiree Stephens, *Norwalk Community College*

Louise Stephens, *Volunteer State Community College*

Martin St. John, *Westmoreland County Community College*

Edith Strickland, *Tallahassee Community College*

John Striebich, *Monroe Community College*

David Stringer, *DeAnza College*

Ron Surmacz, *Duquesne University*

William Syvertsen, *Fresno City College*

Scott Taylor, *Moberly Area Community College*

Marguerite Teubner, *Nassau Community College*

Rod Thirion, *Pikes Peak Community College*

Jim Thomas, *Indiana University Northwest*

Deborah Thompson, *Bentley College*

Evelyn Thrasher, *University of Massachusetts–Dartmouth*

Jon Tomlinson, *University of Northwestern Ohio*

Bob Trewartha, *Minnesota School of Business*

Bob Urell, *Irvine Valley College*

Dan Vetter, *Central Michigan University*

Andrea Vidrine, *Baton Rouge Community College*

Daniel Viveiros, *Johnson & Wales University*

Jean Volk, *Middlesex County College–Edison*

William J. Wardrope, *University of Central Oklahoma*

Joann Warren, *Community College of Rhode Island–Warwick*

David Washington, *North Carolina State University*

R. Patrick Wehner, *Everest University*

Sally Wells, *Columbia College*

Mildred Wilson, *Georgia Southern University*

Karen Wisniewski, *County College of Morris*

Greg Witkowski, *Northwestern College*

Colette Wolfson, *Ivy Tech Community College of Indiana*

Deborah Yancey, *Virginia Western Community College*

Mark Zarycki, *Hillsborough Community College, Tampa*

Nancy E. Zimmerman, *The Community College of Baltimore County*

Lisa Zingaro, *Oakton Community College*

Mark Zorn, *Butler County Community College*

This edition continues to be the market's gold standard due to the involvement of these committed instructors and students. We thank them all for their help, support, and friendship.

Bill Nickels

Jim McHugh

Susan McHugh

Instructors: Student Success Starts with You

Tools to enhance your unique voice

Want to build your own course? No problem. Prefer to use our turnkey, prebuilt course? Easy. Want to make changes throughout the semester? Sure. And you'll save time with Connect's auto-grading too.

65%
Less Time Grading

Laptop: McGraw Hill; Woman/dog: George Doyle/Getty Images

Study made personal

Incorporate adaptive study resources like SmartBook® 2.0 into your course and help your students be better prepared in less time. Learn more about the powerful personalized learning experience available in SmartBook 2.0 at **www.mheducation.com/highered/connect/smartbook**

Affordable solutions, added value

Make technology work for you with LMS integration for single sign-on access, mobile access to the digital textbook, and reports to quickly show you how each of your students is doing. And with our Inclusive Access program you can provide all these tools at a discount to your students. Ask your McGraw Hill representative for more information.

Padlock: Jobalou/Getty Images

Solutions for your challenges

A product isn't a solution. Real solutions are affordable, reliable, and come with training and ongoing support when you need it and how you want it. Visit **www.supportateverystep.com** for videos and resources both you and your students can use throughout the semester.

Checkmark: Jobalou/Getty Images

Students: Get Learning that Fits You

Effective tools for efficient studying

Connect is designed to make you more productive with simple, flexible, intuitive tools that maximize your study time and meet your individual learning needs. Get learning that works for you with Connect.

Study anytime, anywhere

Download the free ReadAnywhere app and access your online eBook or SmartBook 2.0 assignments when it's convenient, even if you're offline. And since the app automatically syncs with your eBook and SmartBook 2.0 assignments in Connect, all of your work is available every time you open it. Find out more at **www.mheducation.com/readanywhere**

> *"I really liked this app—it made it easy to study when you don't have your textbook in front of you."*
>
> - Jordan Cunningham,
>   Eastern Washington University

Calendar: owattaphotos/Getty Images

Everything you need in one place

Your Connect course has everything you need—whether reading on your digital eBook or completing assignments for class, Connect makes it easy to get your work done.

Learning for everyone

McGraw Hill works directly with Accessibility Services Departments and faculty to meet the learning needs of all students. Please contact your Accessibility Services Office and ask them to email accessibility@mheducation.com, or visit **www.mheducation.com/about/accessibility** for more information.

Top: Jenner Images/Getty Images, Left: Hero Images/Getty Images, Right: Hero Images/Getty Images

BRIEF CONTENTS

CONTENTS

PART 2

Business Ownership: Starting a Small Business   112

CHAPTER 6

Entrepreneurship and Starting a Small Business 142

PART 3

Business Management: Empowering Employees to Satisfy Customers 170

CHAPTER 7

Management and Leadership 170

PART 4

Management of Human Resources:
Motivating Employees to Produce Quality
Goods and Services 244

CHAPTER 10
Motivating Employees 244

CHAPTER 11
Human Resource Management: Finding and
Keeping the Best Employees 272

CHAPTER 12

Dealing with Employee–Management Issues 306

PART 5

Marketing: Developing and Implementing Customer-Oriented Marketing Plans 332

CHAPTER 13

Marketing: Helping Buyers Buy 332

CHAPTER 14

Developing and Pricing Goods and Services   358

CHAPTER 15

Distributing Products   384

CHAPTER 20
Money, Financial Institutions, and the Federal Reserve   522

BONUS CHAPTERS

A

Working within the Legal Environment   548

understanding
Business

THIRTEENTH EDITION

Getting Ready for This Course and Your Career

Top 10 Reasons to Read This Introduction
(even if it isn't assigned)

10 What the heck—you already bought the book, so you might as well get your money's worth.

9 You don't want the only reason you get a raise to be that the government has increased the minimum wage.

8 Getting off to a good start in the course can improve your chances of getting a higher grade, and your Uncle Ernie will send you five dollars for every A you get.

7 Your friends say that you've got the manners of a troll and you want to find out what the heck they're talking about.

6 How else would you find out a spork isn't usually one of the utensils used at a business dinner?

5 You don't want to experience the irony of frantically reading the "time management" section at three o'clock in the morning before a test.

4 Like the Boy Scouts, you want to be prepared.

3 It must be important because the authors spent so much time writing it.

2 You want to run with the big dogs someday.

And the number one reason for reading this introductory section is . . .

1 It could be on a test.

Learning the Skills You Need to Succeed Today and Tomorrow

Your life is full. You're starting a new semester, perhaps even beginning your college career, and you're feeling pulled in many directions. Why take time to read this introduction? We have lightheartedly offered our top 10 reasons, but the real importance of this section is no joking matter.

Its purpose, and that of the entire text, is to help you learn principles, strategies, and skills for success that will serve you not only in this course but also in your career and your life. Whether you learn them is up to you. Learning them won't guarantee success, but not learning them—well, you get the picture.

This is an exciting and challenging time. Success in any venture comes from understanding basic principles and knowing how to apply them effectively. What you learn now could help you be a success—for the rest of your life. Begin applying these skills now to gain an edge on the competition. READ THIS SECTION BEFORE YOUR FIRST CLASS and make a great first impression! Good luck. We wish you the best.

Bill Nickels　　　　**Jim McHugh**　　　　**Susan McHugh**

Lorraine Boogich/Getty Images

The rewards of college are well worth the effort for graduates, who can expect to earn much more than high school graduates over the course of their careers. Businesses like graduates too, because the growing needs of a global workplace require knowledgeable workers to fill the jobs of the future. What other benefits do you see from earning a college degree?

Using This Course to Prepare for Your Career

Since you've signed up for this course, we're guessing you already know the value of a college education. Those who earn a four-year college degree are half as likely to be unemployed and will earn about $32,000 more each year than those who have only a high school diploma. That adds up to over $1 million more over a lifetime.[1] Thus, what you invest in a college education is likely to pay you back many times. That doesn't mean there aren't good careers available to noncollege graduates. It just means that those with an education are more likely to have higher earnings over their lifetimes.

The value of a college education is more than just a larger paycheck. Other benefits include increasing your ability to think critically and communicate your ideas to others, improving your ability to use technology, and preparing yourself to live in a diverse and competitive world. Knowing you've met your goals and earned a college degree also gives you the self-confidence to work toward future goals.

Many college graduates in the last generation held seven or eight different jobs (often in several different careers) in their lifetime. Today, Millennials are changing jobs just as rapidly; most jump jobs four times in the first decade after graduation. A key reason why many say they leave their jobs is because today's jobs need to be reinvented every four years.[2] Many returning students are changing their careers and their plans for life. In fact, more than half of all part-time college students are older than 25.[3]

You too may want to change careers someday. It can be the path to long-term happiness and success. That means you'll have to be flexible and adjust your strengths and talents to new opportunities. Today companies are looking for skills that machines lack, including creativity, interpersonal skills, and fine motor control. Learning has become a lifelong job. It's not going to be just what you know now that counts, but what you learn in the future and how you adapt your skills to add value to yourself, your job, and your company.[4]

FIGURE P.1 NEW
CAREERS

THESE CAREERS DIDN'T EXIST 10 YEARS AGO:	
• App Developer	• Big Data Analyst/Data Scientist
• Social Media Manager	• Sustainability Manager
• Uber Driver	• YouTube Content Creator
• Driverless Car Engineer	• Drone Operator
• Cloud Computing Specialist	• Millennial Generational Expert

Source: World Economic Forum, weforum.org, accessed March 2020.

If you're typical of many college students, you may not have any idea what career you'd like to pursue. That isn't necessarily a big disadvantage in today's fast-changing job market. After all, many of the best jobs of the future don't even exist today. Figure P.1 lists 10 careers that didn't exist 10 years ago. There are no perfect or certain ways to prepare for the most interesting and challenging jobs of tomorrow. Rather, you should continue your college education, develop strong technology skills, improve your verbal and written communication skills, and remain flexible and forward thinking while you explore the job market.

One of the objectives of this class, and this book, is to help you choose an area in which you might enjoy working and have a good chance to succeed. You'll learn about economics, global business, ethics, entrepreneurship, management, marketing, accounting, finance, and more. At the end of the course, you should have a much better idea which careers would be best for you and which you would not enjoy.

But you don't have to be in business to use business principles. You can use marketing principles to get a job and to sell your ideas to others. You can use your knowledge of investments to make money in the stock market. You'll use your management skills and general business knowledge wherever you go and in whatever career you pursue—including government agencies, charities, and social causes.

Assessing Your Skills and Personality

The earlier you can do a personal assessment of your interests, skills, and values, the better it can help you find career direction. Hundreds of schools use software exercises like the System for Interactive Guidance and Information (SIGI) and DISCOVER to offer self-assessment exercises, personalized lists of occupations based on your interests and skills, and information about different careers and the preparation each requires. Visit your college's placement center, career lab, or library soon and learn what programs are available for you. Of course, there are career assessment tools online, but many are as accurate as a Magic 8 ball. You can find reviews of online assessments at livecareer.com/quintessential/online-assessment-review. While no test can give you a definitive answer about what the perfect career for you is, the assessments can point you to career paths that you may not have considered before.

Self-assessment will help you determine the kind of work environment you'd prefer (technical, social service, or business); what values you seek to fulfill in a career (security, variety, or independence); what abilities you have (creative/artistic, numerical, technological, or sales); and what job characteristics matter to you (income, travel, or amount of job pressure versus free time, potential for advancement).

Using Professional Business Strategies Right Now

Here are two secrets to success you can start practicing now: *networking* and *keeping files on subjects important to you.*

Networking is building a personal array of people you've met, spoken to, or corresponded with who can offer you advice about and even help with your career options.[5] Start with the names of your professors, both as employment references and as resources about fields of interest to you. Add additional contacts, mentors, and resource people, and keep the notes you make when talking with them about careers including salary information and courses you need to take.

All students need a way to retain what they learn. An effective way to become an expert on almost any business subject is to set up your own information system. You can store data on your computer, tablet, and cell phone (back up these files!), you can establish a comprehensive filing system on paper, or you can use a combination of the two. Few college students take the time to make this effort; those who don't lose much of the information they read in college or thereafter.

Keep as many of your textbooks and other assigned readings as you can, as well as your course notes. Read a national newspaper such as *The Wall Street Journal, The New York Times, Barron's,* or *USA Today.* Read your local

John M Lund Photography Inc./Getty Images

newspaper to stay current on what's happening in your community. Each time you read a story that interests you, save a paper copy or add a link to the story online in your electronic file, under a topic heading like *careers, small business, marketing, economics,* or *management.* Don't rely on just one Internet site for information (and be wary of *Wikipedia*)! Get familiar with a variety of sources and use them.

Start a file for your résumé. In it, keep a copy of your current résumé along with reference letters and other information about jobs you may have held, including projects accomplished and additions to your responsibilities over time, plus any awards or special recognition you may have received. Soon you'll have a tremendous amount of information to help you prepare a polished résumé and answer challenging job interview questions with ease.

Watching television shows about business, such as *Nightly Business Report* and Jim Cramer's *Mad Money* and other programs on CNBC, can help you learn the language of business and become more informed about current happenings in business and the economy. Try viewing some of these shows or listening to similar shows online, and see which ones you like best. Take notes and put them in your files. Keep up with business news in your area so that you know what jobs are available and where. You may also want to join a local business group to begin networking with people and learning the secrets of the local business scene. Many business groups and professional business societies readily accept student members.

 *Networking provides you with an array of personal contacts on whom you can call for career advice and help. Have you begun creating your network yet? Are you part of someone else's?*

Learning to Behave Like a Professional

There's a reason good manners never go out of style. As the world becomes increasingly competitive, the gold goes to teams and individuals with that extra bit of polish. The person who makes a good impression will be the one who gets the job, wins the promotion, or clinches the deal. Good manners and professionalism are not difficult to acquire; they're second nature to those who achieve and maintain a competitive edge.

Not even a great résumé or designer clothes can substitute for poor behavior, including verbal behavior, in an interview. Say "please" and "thank you" when you ask for something. Certainly make it a point to arrive on time, open doors for others, stand when an older person enters the room, and use a polite tone of voice. You may want to take a class in etiquette or read a book on etiquette to learn the proper way to eat in a nice restaurant, what to do at a formal party, when and how to text/e-mail business associates properly, and so on. Of course, it's also critical to be honest, reliable, dependable, and ethical at all times.

Some rules are not formally written anywhere; instead, every successful businessperson learns them through experience. If you follow these rules in college, you'll have the skills for success when you start your career. Here are the basics:

Pepsco Studio/Shutterstock

Many businesses have adopted business casual as the proper work attire, but others still require traditional clothing styles. How does your appearance at work affect both you and your company?

1. **Making a good first impression.** An old saying goes, "You never get a second chance to make a good first impression." You have just a few seconds to make an impression. Therefore, how you dress and how you look are important. Take your cue as to what is appropriate at any specific company by studying the people there who are most successful. What do they wear? How do they act?

2. **Focusing on good grooming.** Be aware of your appearance and its impact. Wear appropriate, clean clothing and a few simple accessories. Revealing shirts, nose rings, and tattoos may not be appropriate in a work setting. Be consistent, too; you can't project a good image by dressing well a few times a week and then showing up looking like you're getting ready to mow a lawn.

    Many organizations have adopted "business casual" guidelines, but others still require traditional attire, so find out what the organization's policies are and choose your wardrobe accordingly. Casual doesn't mean sloppy or shabby. Wrinkled clothing, shirttails hanging out, and hats worn indoors are not usually appropriate. For women, business casual attire includes simple skirts and pants, no jeans (unless approved by the company), cotton shirts, sweaters (not too tight), blazers, and low-heeled shoes or boots. Men may wear khaki trousers, jeans (only if approved by the company), sport shirts with collars, sweaters or sport jackets, and casual loafers or lace-up shoes.

3. **Being on time.** When you don't come to class or work on time, you're sending this message to your teacher or boss: "My time is more important than your time. I have more important things to do than be here." In addition to showing a lack of respect to your teacher or boss, lateness rudely disrupts the work of your colleagues or concentration of your classmates.

    Pay attention to the corporate culture. Sometimes you have to come in earlier than others and leave later to get that promotion you desire. To develop good work habits and get good grades, arrive in class on time and avoid leaving (or packing up to leave) early.

4. **Practicing considerate behavior.** Listen when others are talking—for example, don't check your cell phone for messages, read the newspaper, or eat in class. Don't interrupt others when they are speaking; wait your turn. Eliminate profanity from your vocabulary. Use appropriate body language by sitting up attentively and not slouching. Sitting up has the added bonus of helping you stay awake! Professors and managers alike get a favorable impression from those who look and act alert.

5. **Practicing good text/e-mail etiquette.** The basic rules of courtesy in face-to-face communication also apply to text and e-mail exchanges. Introduce yourself at the beginning of your first e-mail message. Next, let your recipients know how you got their names and e-mail addresses. Then proceed with your clear but succinct message, and always be sure to type full words (*ur* is not the same thing as *your*). Finally, close the e-mail with a signature. Do not send an attachment unless your correspondent has indicated he or she will accept it. Ask first! You can find much more information about proper Internet etiquette, or netiquette, online—for example, at NetManners.com.

6. **Practicing good cell phone manners.** Your Introduction to Business class is not the place to be arranging a date for tonight. Turn off the phone during class or in a business meeting unless you are expecting a critical call. If you are expecting such a call, let your professor know before class. Turn off your ringer and put the phone on vibrate. Sit by the aisle and near the door. If you do receive a critical call, leave the room before answering it. Apologize to the professor after class and explain the situation.

7. **Practicing safe posting on social media.** Be careful what you post on your Facebook page or any other social media. Although it may be fun to share your latest adventures with your friends, your boss or future boss may not appreciate your latest party pictures. Be aware that those pictures may not go away even if you delete them from your page. If anyone else downloaded them, they are still out there waiting for a recruiter to discover. Make sure to update your privacy settings frequently. It's a

good idea to separate your list of work friends and limit what that group can view. Also be aware that some work colleagues aren't interested in becoming your followers or Facebook friends. To avoid awkwardness, wait for work associates to reach out to you first. Make sure you know your employer's policy on using social media on company time. Obviously, they will probably frown on using it for personal use on company time, but there may be rules about sharing technical matter, company information, and so on. Be mindful that social media accounts time-stamp your comments.

8. **Being prepared.** A businessperson would never show up for a meeting without having read the appropriate materials and being prepared to discuss the topics on the agenda. For students, acting like a professional means reading assigned materials before class, having written assignments ready to be turned in, asking and responding to questions in class, and discussing the material with fellow students.

9. **Learning local customs.** Just as traffic laws enable people to drive more safely, business etiquette allows people to conduct business with the appropriate amount of consideration. Sharpen your competitive edge by becoming familiar with its rules. If you travel internationally, learn the proper business etiquette for each country you visit.[6] Customs differ widely for such everyday activities as greeting people, eating, giving gifts, presenting and receiving business cards, and conducting business in general. In Japan, businesspeople typically bow instead of shaking hands, and in some Arab countries it is insulting to sit so as to show the soles of your shoes. Honesty, high ethical standards, and reliability and trustworthiness are important for success in any country.

10. **Behaving ethically.** Having a reputation for integrity will enable you to be proud of who you are and contribute a great deal to your business success. Unethical behavior can ruin your reputation, so think carefully before you act. When in doubt, don't! Ethics is so important to success that we include discussions about it throughout the text.

recep-bg/Getty Images

Behavior that's taken for granted in other countries might be unusual in the United States. In some cultures bowing is a form of greeting to show respect. How can you learn the appropriate business etiquette for the countries in which you do business?

Doing Your Best in College

The skills you need to succeed in life after college are the same ones that will serve you well in your studies. Career, family, and hobbies all benefit from organizational and time management skills you can apply right now. Here are some tips for improving your study habits, taking tests, and managing your time.

Study Hints

For the remainder of your college career, consider studying to be your business. Though you may hold another job while enrolled in this class, you're in school because you want to advance yourself. So until you get out of school and into your desired occupation, studying is your business. And like any good businessperson, you aim for success. Follow these strategies:

1. **Go to class.** It's tempting to cut a class on a nice day or when there are other things to do. But nothing is more important to doing well in school than going to class every time. If possible, sit in the front near the instructor. This will help you focus better and avoid distractions in the room. If your class is online, follow the same procedures as if in a classroom. Do not miss class information, listen attentively, and participate according to your instructor's recommendations.

2. **Listen well.** It's not enough to show up for class if you use the time for a nap. Make eye contact with the instructor. In your mind, form a picture of what he or she is

discussing. Include your existing knowledge and past experiences in your picture. This ties new knowledge to what you already know.

3. **Take careful notes.** Make two columns in your notebook, laptop, or tablet. On one side write down important concepts, and on the other examples or more detailed explanations. Use abbreviations and symbols whenever possible and wide spacing to make the notes easier to read. Edit your notes after class to make sure you fully understand what was discussed in class or online. Rereading and rewriting help store the information in your long-term memory. Learn the concepts in your courses the same way you learn the words to your favorite song: through repetition and review.

4. **Find a good place to study.** Find a place with good lighting and a quiet atmosphere. Some students do well with classical music or other music without lyrics playing in the background. Keep your study place equipped with extra supplies such as mobile devices, pens, pencils, calculator, folders, and paper so you don't have to interrupt studying to hunt for them.

5. **Read the text using a strategy such as "survey, question, read, recite, review" (SQ3R).**

   a. *Survey* or scan the chapter first to see what it is all about. This means looking over the table of contents, learning objectives, headings, photo essays, and charts so you get a broad idea of the content. The summaries at the end of each chapter in this text provide a great overview of the concepts in the chapter. Scanning will provide an introduction and help get your mind in a learning mode.

   b. Write *questions,* first by changing the headings into questions. For example, you could change the heading of this section to "What hints can I use to study better?" Read the questions that appear throughout each chapter in the Test Prep sections to give yourself a chance to recall what you've read.

   c. *Read* the chapter to find the answers to your questions. Be sure to read the boxes in the chapter as well. They offer extended examples or discussions of the concepts in the text. You've probably asked, "Will the material in the boxes be on the tests?" Even if your instructor chooses not to test over them directly, they are often the most interesting parts of the chapter and will help you retain the chapter concepts better.

   d. *Recite* your answers to yourself or to others in a study group. Make sure you say the answers in your own words so that you clearly understand the concepts. Research has shown that saying things is a more effective way to learn them than seeing, hearing, or reading about them. While often used in study groups, recitation is also good practice for working in teams in the work world.

   e. *Review* by rereading and recapping the information. The chapter summaries are written in a question-and-answer form, much like a classroom dialogue. They're also tied directly to the learning objectives so that you can see whether you've accomplished the chapter's objectives. Cover the written answers and see whether you can answer the questions yourself first.

6. **Use flash cards.** You'll master the course more easily if you know the language of business. To review the key terms in the book, write any terms you don't know on index cards and go through your cards between classes and when you have other free time.

7. **Use Connect Introduction to Business** (if your professor has recommended it for your course). Connect's online features include SmartBook 2.0, Application-Based Activities, exercises, and videos.

The SQ3R study system recommends that you "survey, question, read, recite, and review" to stay up-to-date with assignments and shine in class every day. Have you adopted this system?

Dragon Images/Shutterstock

8. **Go over old exams, if possible.** If old exams are not available from your professor, ask how many multiple-choice, true/false, and essay questions will be on your test. It's acceptable to ask your professor's former students what kind of questions are given and what material is usually emphasized. It is unethical, though, to go over exams you obtain illegally.

9. **Use as many of your senses in learning as possible.** If you're an auditory learner—that is, if you learn best by hearing—record yourself reading your notes and answering the questions you've written. Listen to the tape while you're dressing in the morning. You can also benefit from reading or studying aloud. If you're a visual learner, use pictures, charts, colors, and graphs. The videos that accompany this text illustrate the concepts discussed in the chapters. If you're a kinesthetic learner, you remember best by doing, touching, and experiencing. Doing the Developing Career Skills exercises at the end of each chapter will be a big help.

Test-Taking Hints

Often students will say, "I know this stuff, but I'm just not good at taking multiple-choice (or essay) tests." Other students find test taking relatively easy. Here are a few test-taking hints:

1. **Get plenty of sleep and have a good meal.** It's better to be alert and awake during an exam than to study all night and be groggy. If you keep up with your reading and your reviews on a regular basis, you won't need to pull an all-nighter. Proper nutrition also plays an important part in your brain's ability to function.

2. **Bring all you need for the exam.** Sometimes you'll need No. 2 pencils, erasers, and a calculator. Ask beforehand and follow cell phone policies.

3. **Relax.** At home before the test, take deep, slow breaths. Picture yourself in the testing session, relaxed and confident. Reread the chapter summaries. Get to class early to settle down. If you start to get nervous during the test, stop and take a few deep breaths. Turn the test over and write down information you remember. Sometimes this helps you connect the information you know to the questions on the test.

4. **Read the directions on the exam carefully.** You don't want to miss anything or do something you're not supposed to do.

5. **Read all the answers in multiple-choice questions.** Even if there is more than one correct-sounding answer to a multiple-choice question, one is clearly better. Read them all to be sure you pick the best. Try covering up the choices while reading the question. If the answer you think of is one of the choices, it is probably correct. If you are still unsure of the answer, start eliminating options you know are wrong. Narrowing the choices to two or three improves your odds.

6. **Answer all the questions.** Unless your instructor takes off more for an incorrect answer than for no answer, you have nothing to lose by guessing. Also, skipping a question can lead to inadvertently misaligning your answers on a scan sheet. You could end up with all your subsequent answers scored wrong!

7. **Read true/false questions carefully.** All parts of the statement must be true or else the entire statement is false. Watch out for absolutes such as *never, always,* and *none.* These often make a statement false.

8. **Organize your thoughts before answering essay questions.** Think about the sequence in which to present what you want to say. Use complete sentences with correct grammar and punctuation. Explain or defend your answers.

9. **Go over the test at the end.** Make sure you've answered all the questions, your name is on the exam, and you've followed all directions.

Time Management Hints

The most important management skill you can learn is how to manage your time. Now is as good an opportunity as any to practice time management. Here are some hints other students have learned—often the hard way:

1. **Write weekly goals for yourself.** Make certain your goals are realistic and attainable. Write the steps you'll use to achieve each goal. Reward yourself when you reach a goal.

2. **Keep a "to do" list.** It's easy to forget things unless you write them down or list them on your phone. Jot down tasks as soon as you know of them. That gives you one less thing to do: remembering what you have to do.

3. **Prepare a daily schedule.** Use a commercial printed or electronic daily planner or create your own. Write the days of the week across the top of the page. Write the hours of the day from the time you get up until the time you go to bed down the left side. Draw lines to form columns and rows and fill in all the activities you have planned in each hour. Hopefully, you will be surprised to see how many slots of time you have available for studying.

4. **Prepare for the next day the night before.** Having everything ready to go will help you make a quick, stress-free start in the morning.

5. **Prepare weekly and monthly schedules.** Use a calendar to fill in activities and upcoming assignments. Include both academic and social activities so that you can balance your work and fun.

6. **Space out your work.** Don't wait until the last week of the course to write all your papers and study for your exams. If you do a few pages a day, you can write a 20-page paper in a couple of weeks with little effort. It is really difficult to push out 20 pages in a day or two.

7. **Defend your study time.** Study every day. Use the time between classes to go over your flash cards and read the next day's assignments. Make it a habit to defend your study time so you don't slip.

8. **Take time for fun.** If you have some fun every day, life will be full. Schedule your fun times along with your studying so that you have balance.

"Time is money," the saying goes. Some, however, would argue that time is more valuable than money. If your bank account balance falls, you might be able to build it back up by finding a better-paying job, taking a second job, or even selling something you own. But you have only a limited amount of time and there is no way to make more. Learn to manage your time well, because you can never get it back.

Keeping a daily schedule is only one of the many strategies that will help you manage your time. You should also keep a running list of goals and tasks you need to do each week. In what other ways can you defend your study time?

Rawpixel Ltd/Alamy Stock Photo

Making the Most of the Resources for This Course

College courses and textbooks are best at teaching you concepts and ways of thinking about business. However, to learn firsthand how to apply those ideas to real business situations, you need to explore and interact with other resources. Here are seven basic resources for the class in addition to the text:

andresr/Getty Images

1. **The professor.** One of the most valuable facets of college is the chance to study with experienced professors. Your instructor is a resource who's there to answer some questions and guide you to answers for others. Many professors get job leads they can pass on to you and can provide letters of recommendation too. Thus it's important to develop a friendly relationship with your professors.

2. **The supplements that come with this text.** Connect Introduction to Business online course material (if your professor has recommended it for your course) will help you review and interpret key material and give you practice answering test questions. Even if your professor does not assign these materials, you may want to use them anyhow. Doing so will improve your test scores and help you compete successfully with the other students.

3. **Outside readings.** One secret to success in business is staying current. Review and become familiar with the following magazines and newspapers during the course and throughout your career: *The Wall Street Journal, Forbes, Barron's, Bloomberg Businessweek, Fortune, The Economist, Hispanic Business, Harvard Business Review, Black Enterprise, Fast Company,* and *Entrepreneur.* You may also want to read your local newspaper's business section and national news magazines such as *Time* and *Newsweek.* You can find them in your school's learning resource center or the local public library. Some are also available online free.

4. **Your own experience and that of your classmates.** Many college students have had experience working in business or nonprofit organizations. Hearing and talking about those experiences exposes you to many real-life examples that are invaluable for understanding business. Don't rely exclusively on the professor for all the answers and other exercises in this book. Often there is no single "right" answer, and your classmates may open up new ways of looking at things for you.

    Part of being a successful businessperson is learning how to work with others. Some professors encourage their students to work together and build teamwork as well as presentation and analytical skills. Students from other countries can help you learn about different cultures and different approaches to handling business problems. There is strength in diversity, so seek out people different from you to work with on teams.

5. **Outside contacts.** Who can tell you more about what it's like to start a career in accounting than someone who's doing it now? One of the best ways to learn about different businesses is to visit them in person. The world can be your classroom.

    When you go shopping, think about whether you would enjoy working in and managing a store. Think about owning or managing a restaurant, an auto body shop, a health club, or any other establishment you visit. If something looks interesting, talk to the employees and learn more about their jobs and the industry. Be constantly on the alert to find career possibilities, and don't hesitate to talk with people about their careers. Many will be pleased to give you their time and honest opinions.

Your college professors are among the most valuable resources and contacts you'll encounter as you develop your career path. How many of your professors have you gotten to know so far?

6. **The Internet.** The Internet offers more material than you could use in a lifetime. Throughout this text we present information and exercises that require you to use the Internet. Information changes rapidly, and it is up to you to stay current.

7. **The library or learning resource center.** The library is a great complement to the Internet and a valuable resource. Work with your librarian to learn how to best access the information you need.

Getting the Most from This Text

Many learning aids appear throughout this text to help you understand the concepts:

1. **List of Learning Objectives at the beginning of each chapter.** Reading through these objectives will help you set the framework and focus for the chapter material. Since every student at one time or other has found it difficult to get into studying, the Learning Objectives are there to provide an introduction and to get your mind into a learning mode.

2. **Getting to Know and Name That Company features.** The opening stories will help you *get to know* professionals who successfully use the concepts presented in the chapters. Listen to what they say in the short "Let's Talk Business" bubble above their picture. The Name That Company feature at the beginning of each chapter challenges you to identify a company discussed in the chapter.

3. **Photo essays.** The photos offer examples of the concepts in the chapter. Looking at the photos and reading the photo essays (captions) before you read the chapter will give you a good idea of what the chapter is all about.

4. **Self-test questions.** Periodically, within each chapter, you'll encounter set-off lists of questions called Test Prep. These questions give you a chance to pause, think carefully about, and recall what you've just read.

5. **Key terms.** Developing a strong business vocabulary is one of the most important and useful aspects of this course. To assist you, all key terms in the book are highlighted in boldface type. Key terms are also defined in the margins, and page references to these terms are given at the end of each chapter. A full glossary is located in the back of the book. You should rely heavily on these learning aids in adding new terms to your vocabulary.

6. **Boxes.** Each chapter contains a number of boxed extended examples or discussions that cover major themes of the book: (a) ethics (Making Ethical Decisions); (b) small business (Spotlight on Small Business); (c) global business (Reaching beyond Our Borders); (d) social media (Connecting through Social Media); and (e) contemporary business issues (Adapting to Change). They're interesting to read and provide key insights into important business issues; we hope you enjoy and learn from them.

7. **End-of-chapter summaries.** The chapter summaries are directly tied to the chapter Learning Objectives so that you can see whether you've accomplished the chapter's objectives.

8. **Critical Thinking questions.** The end-of-chapter questions help you relate the material in the text to your own experiences.

9. **Putting Principles to Work exercises.** These exercises direct you to dynamic outside resources that reinforce the concepts introduced in the text. You might want to bookmark some of the websites you'll discover.

10. **Developing Career Skills exercises.** To really remember something, it's best to do it. That's why Developing Career Skills sections at the end of each chapter suggest small projects that help you use resources, develop interpersonal skills, manage information, understand systems, and sharpen technology skills.

11. **Career Exploration exercise.** At the end of each chapter, we offer a brief list of potential careers that deal with the concepts presented in the chapter and encourage you to find out more about them in the *Occupational Outlook Handbook.*

12. **Video cases.** These cases feature companies, processes, practices, and managers that bring to life the key concepts in the chapter and give you real-world information to think over and discuss.

If you use the suggestions we've presented here, you'll actively participate in a learning experience that will help you greatly in this course and your chosen career. The most important secret to success may be to enjoy what you're doing and do your best in everything. To do your best, take advantage of all the learning aids available to you.

NOTES

1. Abigail Hess, "82% of College Grads Believe Their Bachelor's Degree Was a Good Investment—but Most Would Make This One Change," *CNBC,* cnbc.com, February 27, 2020; Derek Newton, "Despite What You Hear, College Pays Off," *Forbes,* forbes.com, February 27, 2020; Nariman Farvardin, "Is Your Higher Ed Institution Providing Students the Best ROI?," *University Business,* universitybusiness.com, February 18, 2020.
2. Kathryn Dill, "Millennials Show Loyalty to Employers," *The Wall Street Journal,* February 18, 2020; Brianna Wiest, "What to Ask Yourself before You Make a Career Change in Your 20s," *Forbes,* forbes.com, March 9, 2020.
3. U.S. Census Bureau, census.gov, accessed March 2020.
4. May Rostom, "Do You Have What It Takes? Five Soft Skills That You Need in 2020," *Entrepreneur,* entrepreneur.com, February 23, 2020; Arianne Cohen, "The Best Way

to Change Your Job Is to Focus on Your Personality," *Bloomberg Businessweek,* bloomberg.com, February 12, 2020; Jennifer Liu, "The 3 Most Important Skills Workers Need to Learn in 2020, according to Business Leaders," *CNBC,* cnbc.com, March 3, 2020.
5. "The Importance of Networking in Business (Tips Included)," *Indeed Career Guide,* indeed.com, February 14, 2020; Alison Doyle, "How to Use Networking to Find a Job," *The Balance Careers,* thebalancecareers.com, February 20, 2020; Kourtney Whitehead, "4 Tips to Stay Committed and Manage Job Search Stress," *Forbes,* forbes.com, February 16, 2020.
6. Irina Suciu, "Understanding and Overcoming Cultural Differences," *Performance Magazine,* performancemagazine.org, February 26, 2020; Rashan Dixon, "3 Steps to a Successful International Expansion," *Entrepreneur,* entrepreneur.com, March 5, 2020.

1

Taking Risks and Making Profits within the Dynamic Business Environment

---

LEARNING OBJECTIVES *After you have read and studied this chapter, you should be able to*

LO 1–1 Describe the relationship between profit and risk, and show how businesses and nonprofit organizations can raise the standard of living for all.

LO 1–2 Explain how entrepreneurship and the other factors of production contribute to the creation of wealth.

LO 1–3 Analyze the effects of the economic environment and taxes on businesses.

LO 1–4 Describe the effects of technology on businesses.

LO 1–5 Demonstrate how businesses can meet and beat competition.

LO 1–6 Analyze the social changes affecting businesses.

LO 1–7 Identify what businesses must do to meet global challenges, including war and terrorism.

LO 1–8 Review how past trends are being repeated in the present and what those trends mean for tomorrow's college graduates.

Tristan Walker, Founder of Walker & Company

For entrepreneur Tristan Walker, one of the most frustrating parts of his daily life was finding the right razor for his coarse, curly facial hair. "The need here was really the fact that I could not shave," said Walker. "Why are there no products that really understood the fact that I have curly hair?"

Besides failing to find the razor he needed, Walker also couldn't believe that companies would ignore such a large portion of the market. "People of color spend more money on this stuff than anyone else," said Walker. "So I said, 'I'm going to respect those things before anybody else does, and really create a long-term view around celebrating this beautiful community and culture.'" That long-term view turned into Walker & Company, a lifestyle brand dedicated to providing Black men with top-quality personal care products. When he first launched the company, Walker claimed he wanted to create the "Procter & Gamble for people of color." And after years of solid sales and growth, in 2018 Walker & Company grew large enough to attract the attention of the actual Procter & Gamble. Although the consumer goods conglomerate purchased the brand for millions of dollars, Walker remains in charge so he can continue the company's mission. "We want this company and its purpose to still be around 150 years from now," said Walker.

Of course, building a company with such lofty goals isn't easy. In order to realize his vision, Walker needed expertise and connections, and the willingness to do plenty of hard work. While Walker has always been motivated to work hard, he didn't have access to any high-level business connections when he was growing up. "I'm from Jamaica, Queens, New York, born and raised in the projects on welfare," said Walker. "And the necessity of not wanting to live that life really got me where I am today." After excelling at his studies as well as sports, a basketball coach advised Walker to apply to an elite boarding school. Walker took his advice and received a full scholarship to the prestigious Hotchkiss School. This led to his enrollment at Stony Brook University where he earned a degree in economics.

Walker's drive and impeccable educational background landed him a job on Wall Street after graduation. However, he quickly grew tired of the hectic pace of the financial industry and decided to look at business graduate schools far out of state. That's when he learned about Silicon Valley, the famed tech hub in California's San Francisco Bay Area. He enrolled in nearby Stanford University to take advantage of the region's abundance of tech-related resources. "I was 24 when I came to Stanford," said Walker. "The other 24-year-olds here were not only making millions of dollars but fundamentally changing the world. Why did I not have any idea this place existed?" After graduating in 2008, Walker joined the newly launched location-based search company Foursquare. Although Walker made only a $1,000 stipend for his first months as head of business development, he played a vital role in expanding the company through partnerships with other brands.

When he left Foursquare in 2012, he joined Andreessen-Horowitz as the venture capital firm's "entrepreneur-in-residence." This gave him the resources to develop and launch Walker & Company. The business is centered around a shaving brand called Bevel. Unlike other major shaving brands that use multiple blades for their razors, Bevel sticks to a single-blade system that helps prevent bumps. Walker & Company also sells a line of hair care products called Form, which it initially had trouble promoting due to lack of resources. Now that the company is part of Procter & Gamble, though, it can take advantage of the conglomerate's multibillion-dollar marketing budget. Walker & Company will also have access to P&G's $2 billion research and development budget, allowing it to keep innovating for years to come.

The business environment is constantly changing, and along with those changes come opportunities. The purpose of this chapter and this textbook is to introduce you to the dynamic world of business and to some of the people who thrive in it. Businesspeople like Tristan Walker contribute much to the communities they serve, and they also make a good living doing so. That's what business is all about.

Sources: Jason Del Rey, "Procter & Gamble Has Acquired the Startup Aiming to Build the Procter & Gamble for People of Color," *Vox,* vox.com, December 12, 2018; J.J. McCorvey, "Tristan Walker Announces Acquisition by Procter & Gamble, Will Remain as CEO and Move Company to Atlanta," *Fast Company,* fastcompany.com, December 12, 2018; David Gelles, "Tristan Walker on the Roman Empire and Selling a Start-Up to Procter & Gamble," *The New York Times,* December 12, 2018; J.J. McCorvey, "Atlanta's Black Tech Founders Are Changing Entrepreneurship in America. Can They Avoid Silicon Valley's Mistakes?," *Fast Company,* fastcompany. com, August 5, 2019; Derek Hambrick, "Tristan Walker on the Cutting Edge of Disruption," *Emory Business,* emorybusiness.com, August 13, 2019; "Tristan Walker on Building Walker & Company Brands," National Retail Federation Foundation, nrffoundation.org, accessed January 2020.

Let's talk business!
bit.ly/LetsTalkBusiness1

Matt Edge/The New York Times/Redux

business
Any activity that seeks to provide goods and services to others while operating at a profit.

goods
Tangible products such as computers, food, clothing, cars, and appliances.

services
Intangible products (i.e., products that can't be held in your hand) such as education, health care, insurance, recreation, and travel and tourism.

LO 1–1 Describe the relationship between profit and risk, and show how businesses and nonprofit organizations can raise the standard of living for all.

Business and Wealth Building

Success in business depends on consistently adapting to changes in the market. A **business** is any activity that seeks to provide goods and services to others while operating at a profit. To earn that profit, you provide desired goods, jobs, and services to people or other businesses. **Goods** are *tangible* products such as computers, food, clothing, cars, and appliances. **Services** are *intangible* products (i.e., products that can't be held in your hand) such as education, health care, insurance, recreation, and travel and tourism. Once you have developed the right goods and services, based on consumer wants and needs, you need to reach those consumers using whatever media they prefer, including social media, online advertising, TV, and more.

Although you don't need to have wealth as a primary goal, one result of successfully filling a market need is that you can make money for yourself, sometimes a great deal, by giving customers what they want. Sam Walton of Walmart began by opening one store in Arkansas and, over time, became one of the richest people in the United States. Now his heirs are some of the richest people in the United States.[1]

There are over 22.1 million millionaires in the United States.[2] Maybe you will be one of them someday if you start your own business. An **entrepreneur** is a person who risks time and money to start and manage a business.

When Aaron Krause couldn't find buyers at auto body shops for his polymer foam product, he tossed it in a box labeled "scrap" and forgot about it. A few years later, Krause dug out his old invention to clean some patio furniture and discovered it worked surprisingly well on his lounge chairs as well as his dirty dishes. He redesigned the foam into a smiling face, branded it Scrub Daddy, and took it onto the ABC show Shark Tank. Scrub Daddy is the most successful product to appear on Shark Tank to date. What risks and rewards did Krause face when starting his business?

Scrub Daddy Inc.

Revenues, Profits, and Losses

Revenue is the total amount of money a business takes in during a given period by selling goods and services. **Profit** is the amount of money a business earns above and beyond what it spends for salaries and other expenses needed to run the operation. A **loss** occurs when a business's expenses are more than its revenues. If a business loses money over time, it will likely have to close, putting its employees out of work. Over 175,000 businesses in the United States close each year.[3]

As noted, the business environment is constantly changing. What seems like a great opportunity one day may become a huge failure when the economy changes. Starting a business may thus come with huge risks. But huge risks often result in huge profits. We'll explore that concept next.

Matching Risk with Profit

Risk is the chance an entrepreneur takes of losing time and money on a business that may not prove profitable. Profit, remember, is the amount of money a business earns *above and beyond* what it pays out for salaries and other expenses. For example, if you were to start a business selling hot dogs from a cart in the summer, you would have to pay for the cart rental. You would also have to pay for the hot dogs and other materials, and for someone to run the cart while you were away. After you paid your employee and yourself, paid for the food and materials you used, paid the rent on the cart, and paid your taxes, any money left over would be profit.

Keep in mind that profit is over and above the money you pay yourself in salary. You could use any profit to rent or buy a second cart and hire other employees. After a few summers, you might have a dozen carts employing dozens of workers.

Not all enterprises make the same amount of profit. Usually those that take the most risk may make the most profit. There is high risk, for example, in making a new kind of automobile. It's also risky to open a business in an inner city, because insurance and rent are usually higher than in suburban areas, but reduced competition makes substantial profit possible. Big risk can mean big profits.

Standard of Living and Quality of Life

Entrepreneurs such as Sam Walton (Walmart), Bill Gates (Microsoft), Jeff Bezos (Amazon), and Sara Blakely (Spanx) not only became wealthy themselves; they also provided employment for many other people. Walmart is currently the nation's largest private employer, with Amazon coming in second.[4]

Businesses and their employees pay taxes that the federal government and local communities use to build hospitals, schools, libraries, playgrounds, roads, and other public facilities. Taxes also help keep the environment clean, support people in need, and provide police and fire protection. Thus, the wealth businesses generate and the taxes they pay help everyone in their communities. A nation's businesses are part of an economic system that contributes to the standard of living and quality of life for everyone in the country (and, potentially, the world). How has the economic recovery and growth over the past 10 years affected the standard of living and quality of life in your part of the world?

The term **standard of living** refers to the amount of goods and services people can buy with the money they have. Prices for goods and services in some locations are higher than in others, so people in those places can't buy as much with the same amount of money. Often, goods cost more in one country than in another because of higher taxes and stricter government regulations. Finding the right level of taxes and regulation is important in making a country or city prosperous. We'll explore those issues in more depth in Chapter 2. At this point, it is enough to understand that the United States enjoys a high standard of living largely because of the wealth created by its businesses.

The term **quality of life** refers to the general well-being of a society in terms of its political freedom, natural environment, education, health care, safety, amount of leisure, and rewards that add to the satisfaction and joy that other goods and services provide. Maintaining a high quality of life requires the combined efforts of businesses, nonprofit organizations, and government agencies. Remember, there is more to quality of life than simply making money.

entrepreneur
A person who risks time and money to start and manage a business.

revenue
The total amount of money a business takes in during a given period by selling goods and services.

profit
The amount of money a business earns above and beyond what it spends for salaries and other expenses.

loss
When a business's expenses are more than its revenues.

risk
The chance an entrepreneur takes of losing time and money on a business that may not prove profitable.

standard of living
The amount of goods and services people can buy with the money they have.

quality of life
The general well-being of a society in terms of its political freedom, natural environment, education, health care, safety, amount of leisure, and rewards that add to the satisfaction and joy that other goods and services provide.

FIGURE 1.1 A BUSINESS AND ITS STAKEHOLDERS
Often the needs of a firm's various stakeholders will conflict. For example, paying employees more may cut into stockholders' profits. Balancing such demands is a major role of business managers.

Source: John Mackey and Raj Sisodia, *Conscious Capitalism* (Boston, MA: Harvard Business Review Press, 2013).

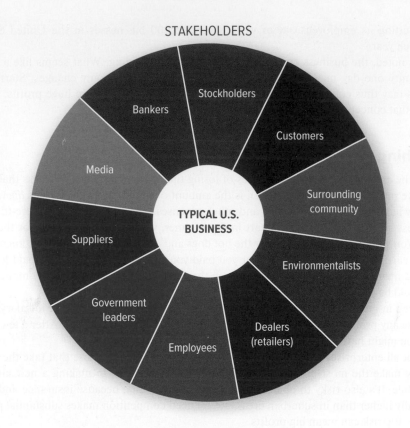

STAKEHOLDERS

Stockholders
Customers
Surrounding community
Environmentalists
Dealers (retailers)
Employees
Government leaders
Suppliers
Media
Bankers

TYPICAL U.S. BUSINESS

Responding to the Various Business Stakeholders

stakeholders
All the people who stand to gain or lose by the policies and activities of a business and whose concerns the business needs to address.

outsourcing
Contracting with other companies (often in other countries) to do some or all of the functions of a firm, like its production or accounting tasks.

Stakeholders are all the people who stand to gain or lose by the policies and activities of a business and whose concerns the business needs to address. They include customers, employees, stockholders, suppliers, dealers (retailers), bankers, people in the surrounding community, the media, environmentalists, competitors, unions, critics, and elected government leaders (see Figure 1.1).[5]

A primary challenge for organizations of the 21st century will be to recognize and respond to the needs of their stakeholders.[6] For example, the need for the business to make profits may be balanced against the needs of employees to earn sufficient income or the need to protect the environment. Ignore the media, and they might attack your business with articles that hurt sales. Oppose the local community, and it may stop you from expanding.

Staying competitive may call for outsourcing. **Outsourcing** means contracting with other companies (often in other countries) to do some or all of the functions of a firm, like its production or accounting tasks. Outsourcing has had serious consequences in some states where jobs have been lost to overseas competitors. We discuss outsourcing in more detail in Chapter 3.

The other side of the outsourcing coin is *insourcing.* Many foreign companies are setting up design and production facilities here in the United States. For example, Korea-based Hyundai designs cars in California, operates engineering headquarters in Detroit, Michigan, and produces cars in Montgomery, Alabama.[7] Japanese automaker Honda has been producing cars in the United States for over 40 years, and opened its 12th U.S. manufacturing plant in 2016.[8] Some information technology firms have begun to bring jobs back to the United States because it can save time in decision-making processes which leads to saving money.[9] Insourcing creates many new U.S. jobs and helps offset those jobs being outsourced.

It may be legal and profitable to outsource, but is it best for all the stakeholders? Business leaders must make outsourcing decisions based on all factors. Pleasing stakeholders is not easy and often calls for trade-offs.

connect

▶ **iSeeit!** Need help understanding the roles of stakeholders? Visit your Connect eBook to view a video for a brief animated explanation.

Barbara Gindl/Getty Images

Using Business Principles in Nonprofit Organizations

Despite their efforts to satisfy their stakeholders, businesses cannot do everything needed to make a community all it can be. Nonprofit organizations—such as public schools, civic associations, charities like the United Way and the Salvation Army, and groups devoted to social causes—also make a major contribution to the welfare of society. A **nonprofit organization** is an organization whose goals do not include making a personal profit for its owners or organizers. Nonprofit organizations often do strive for financial gains, but they use them to meet their social or educational goals rather than for personal profit.

nonprofit organization
An organization whose goals do not include making a personal profit for its owners or organizers.

Your interests may lead you to work for a nonprofit organization. That doesn't mean, however, that you shouldn't study business in college. You'll still need to learn business skills such as information management, leadership, marketing, and financial management. The knowledge and skills you acquire in this and other business courses are useful for careers in any organization, including nonprofits. We'll explore entrepreneurship right after the Test Prep.

TESTPREP

- What is the difference between *revenue* and *profit*?
- What is the difference between *standard of living* and *quality of life*?
- What is *risk*, and how is it related to *profit*?
- What do the terms *stakeholders, outsourcing,* and *insourcing* mean?

LO 1–2 Explain how entrepreneurship and the other factors of production contribute to the creation of wealth.

The Importance of Entrepreneurs to the Creation of Wealth

There are two ways to succeed in business. One is to rise through the ranks of a large company. The advantage of working for others is that somebody else assumes the company's

Rawpixel.com/Shutterstock

To create wealth for its citizens, a country requires more than natural resources. It needs the efforts of entrepreneurs and the skill and knowledge to produce goods and services. How can government support entrepreneurship and the spread of knowledge?

factors of production

The resources used to create wealth: land, labor, capital, entrepreneurship, and knowledge.

entrepreneurial risk and provides you with benefits like paid vacation time and health insurance. It's a good option, and many people choose it.

The other, riskier, but often more exciting, path is to become an entrepreneur. The national anthem, "The Star Spangled Banner," says that the United States is the "land of the free and the home of the brave." Part of being free is being able to own your own business and reap the profits from it. But freedom to succeed also means freedom to fail, and many small businesses fail each year. It takes a brave person to start one. As an entrepreneur, you don't receive any benefits such as paid vacation time, day care, a company car, or health insurance. You have to provide them for yourself! But what you gain—freedom to make your own decisions, opportunity, and possible wealth—is often worth the effort. Before you take on the challenge, you should study successful entrepreneurs to learn the process. You can talk to them personally and read about them in Chapter 6, as well as in other books, magazines (e.g., *Entrepreneur, Fast Company,* and *Inc.*), and online (e.g., Small Business Administration at sba.gov).

The Five Factors of Production

Have you ever wondered why some countries are relatively wealthy and others poor? Economists have been studying the issue of wealth creation for many years. They began by identifying five **factors of production** that seemed to contribute to wealth (see Figure 1.2):

1. *Land* (or natural resources). Land and other natural resources are used to make homes, cars, and other products.

2. *Labor* (workers). People have always been an important resource in producing goods and services, but many people are now being replaced by technology.

3. *Capital.* This includes machines, tools, buildings, or whatever else is used in the production of goods. It might not include money; money is used to buy factors of production but is not always considered a factor by itself.

4. *Entrepreneurship.* All the resources in the world have little value unless entrepreneurs are willing to take the risk of starting businesses to use those resources.

5. *Knowledge.* Information technology has revolutionized business, making it possible to quickly determine wants and needs and to respond with desired goods and services.

FIGURE 1.2 THE FIVE FACTORS OF PRODUCTION

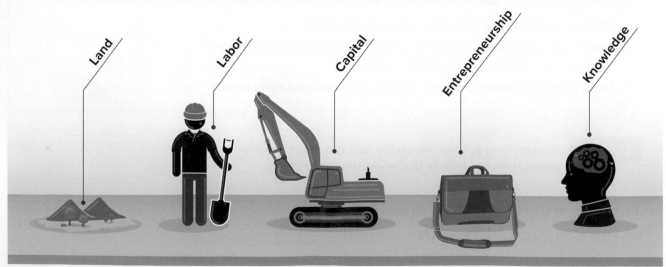

Source: Drucker Institute, druckerinstitute.com, April 2017.

Traditionally, business and economics textbooks emphasized only four factors of production: land, labor, capital, and entrepreneurship. But the late management expert and business consultant Peter Drucker said the most important factor of production in our economy is and always will be *knowledge*.[10]

What do we find when we compare the factors of production in rich and poor countries? Some poor countries have plenty of land and natural resources. Russia, for example, has vast areas of land with many resources such as timber and oil, but it is not considered a rich country (yet). Therefore, land isn't the critical element for wealth creation.

Most poorer countries, such as Mexico, have many laborers, so it's not labor that's the primary source of wealth today. Laborers need to find work to make a contribution; that is, they need entrepreneurs to create jobs for them. Furthermore, capital—machinery and tools—is now fairly easy for firms to find in world markets, so capital isn't the missing ingredient either. Capital is not productive without entrepreneurs to put it to use.

What makes rich countries rich today is a combination of *entrepreneurship* and the effective use of *knowledge*. Entrepreneurs use what they've learned (knowledge) to grow their businesses and increase wealth. Economic and political freedom also matter.

The business environment either encourages or discourages entrepreneurship. That helps explain why some states and cities in the United States grow rich while others remain relatively poor. In the following section, we'll explore what makes up the business environment and how to build an environment that encourages growth and job creation.

?TESTPREP

- What are some of the advantages of working for others?
- What benefits do you lose by being an entrepreneur, and what do you gain?
- What are the five factors of production? Which ones seem to be the most important for creating wealth?

The Business Environment

The **business environment** consists of the surrounding factors that either help or hinder the development of businesses. Figure 1.3 shows the five elements in the business environment.

1. The economic and legal environment.
2. The technological environment.
3. The competitive environment.
4. The social environment.
5. The global business environment.

Businesses that create wealth and jobs grow and prosper in a healthy environment. Thus, creating the right business environment is the foundation for social benefits of all kinds, including good schools, clean air and water, good health care, and low rates of crime. Businesses normally can't control their environment, but they need to monitor it carefully and do what they can to adapt as it changes.

business environment
The surrounding factors that either help or hinder the development of businesses.

iSeeit! Need help understanding the impact of today's dynamic business environment? Visit your Connect eBook to view a video for a brief animated explanation.

LO 1–3 Analyze the effects of the economic environment and taxes on businesses.

The Economic and Legal Environment

People are willing to start new businesses if they believe the risk of losing their money isn't too great. The economic system and the way government works with or against businesses can have a strong impact on that level of risk. For example, a government can minimize

FIGURE 1.3 TODAY'S DYNAMIC BUSINESS ENVIRONMENT

GLOBAL BUSINESS ENVIRONMENT

The Economic and Legal Environment
1. Freedom of ownership
2. Contract laws
3. Elimination of corruption
4. Tradable currency
5. Minimum taxes and regulation

The Technological Environment
1. Information technology
2. Databases
3. Bar codes
4. The Internet

BUSINESS MANAGEMENT AND JOB CREATION

The Competitive Environment
1. Customer service
2. Stakeholder recognition
3. Employee service
4. Concern for the environment

The Social Environment
1. Diversity
2. Demographic changes
3. Family changes

GLOBAL COMPETITION

FREE TRADE

THE QUALITY IMPERATIVE

spending and keep taxes and regulations to a minimum—policies that tend to favor business. Much of the debate in recent elections has focused on whether to raise or cut taxes, how to control government spending, and whether to cut regulations.

One way for government to actively promote entrepreneurship is to allow private ownership of businesses. In some countries, the government owns most businesses, and there's little incentive for people to work hard or create profit. Around the world today, however, some governments are selling those businesses to private individuals to create more wealth. One of the best things the governments of developing countries can do is to minimize interference with the free exchange of goods and services. (You can read more about the various economic systems in different countries in Chapter 2.)

The government can further lessen the risks of entrepreneurship by passing laws that enable businesspeople to write enforceable contracts. In the United States, the Uniform Commercial Code, for example, regulates business agreements such as contracts and warranties so that firms know they can rely on one another. In countries that don't yet have such laws, the risks of starting a business are that much greater. (You can read more about business laws in Bonus Chapter A.)

The government can also establish a currency that's tradable in world markets. That is, the currency lets you buy and sell goods and services anywhere in the world when it is easily exchanged for that of the other countries where you do business. If the Chinese did not want to trade their yuan for the U.S. dollar, for instance, it's hard to imagine how Coca-Cola or Disney would be able to sell their products and services there. (You can read more about currency in Chapters 3 and 20).

Tuul & Bruno Morandi/Getty Images

Finally, the government can help minimize corruption in business and in its own ranks. Where governments are corrupt, it's difficult to build a factory or open a store without a government permit, which is obtained largely through bribery of public officials. Among businesses themselves, unscrupulous leaders can threaten their competitors and unlawfully minimize competition.

Many laws in the United States attempt to minimize corruption. Nonetheless, corrupt and illegal activities at some companies do negatively affect the business community and the economy as a whole. The news media widely report these scandals. Ethics is so important to the success of businesses and the economy as a whole that we feature stories about ethics in most chapters and devote Chapter 4 to the subject.

Governments from different countries can work together to create an environment that allows entrepreneurship to thrive. For example, in 2015 the United Nations adopted what it calls Sustainable Development Goals (SDGs) that list specific targets for ending poverty and improving the lives of the disadvantaged in the next 15 years. The ultimate goal is to move toward prosperity by partnering governments, businesses, and nonprofits in order to solve problems at the ground level in developing countries.

LO 1–4 **Describe the effects of technology on businesses.**

The Technological Environment

Since prehistoric times, humans have felt the need to create tools that make work easier. Few technological changes have had a more comprehensive and lasting impact on businesses, however, than information technology (IT). IT has completely changed the way people communicate with one another. Advertisers and other businesspeople have created ways of using these tools to reach their suppliers and customers. Even politicians have harnessed the power of the Internet to advance their causes.[11] IT is such a major force in business today that we discuss its impact on businesses throughout the entire text.

How Technology Benefits Workers and You Technology means everything from phones to computers, mobile devices, medical imaging machines, robots, the Internet, social media, and the various software programs and apps that make business processes more effective, efficient, and productive.[12] *Effectiveness* means producing the desired result.

technology
Everything from phones to computers, mobile devices, medical imaging machines, robots, the Internet, social media, and the various software programs and apps that make business processes more effective, efficient, and productive.

ADAPTING TO CHANGE

Creating Sustainability through a Circular Economy

plantchicago.org

There's no denying that people around the world create a lot of waste. Each year, more than 52 million tons of food end up in landfills with an additional 10 million tons remaining unharvested on farms. Less than 1 percent of the material used to produce clothing gets recycled into new apparel. The vast majority of plastic doesn't get recycled either, with much of it ending up in garbage dumps or incinerators. Besides squandering resources, the world's waste also pollutes the environment and contributes to rising greenhouse gas emissions.

To combat this problem of global proportions, some entrepreneurs have launched companies that depend on a circular economy to succeed. *Circular economy* refers to reusing, redistributing, refurbishing, and recycling products instead of dumping them in landfills—in other words, keeping products in the value circle. The aim is to produce no waste as every material is either recycled or reused

Plant Chicago

in some capacity. For example, the Chicago-based firm Bubbly Dynamics refurbishes vacant industrial buildings and transforms them into sustainable business incubators. At one site called The Plant, indoor farms irrigated with rainwater and power generated by solar panels helps more than 20 companies thrive without creating unnecessary waste. The

Plant's largest tenant is a brewery that produces about 20,000 pounds of compost per month, providing plenty of fertilizer for the facility's farmers.

Other circular economy–driven companies include Earth Angel, a Brooklyn start-up that recycles waste generated by film and television productions based in New York. The company donates mattresses and used clothing to humanitarian agencies while redistributing old scenery to independent theaters and filmmakers. Socially minded enterprises like Earth Angel and Bubbly Dynamics hope other companies will follow their lead and adopt similarly sustainable business practices in the near future. Not only would it help the environment, but it could also be good for business.

Sources: Anne Kadet, "The 'Circular Economy' Rolls into New York City," *The Wall Street Journal,* June 18, 2019; Eduardo Garcia, "Where's the Waste? A 'Circular' Food Economy Could Combat Climate Change," *The New York Times,* September 21, 2019; Anne Field, "Building a Circular Economy: A Society Where 'There's No Concept of Waste,'" *Forbes,* forbes.com, October 31, 2019; "What Is a Circular Economy?," Ellen Arthur Foundation, ellenarthurfoundation.org, accessed January 2020.

Efficiency means producing goods and services using the least amount of resources. The Adapting to Change box discusses how some businesses strive to become so effective and efficient that they create no waste.

productivity

The amount of output you generate given the amount of input (e.g., hours worked).

Productivity is the amount of output you generate given the amount of input, such as the number of hours you work. The more you can produce in any given period, the more money you are worth to companies. The problem with productivity today is that workers are so productive that fewer are needed.[13]

Technology affects people in all industries. For example, a farmer can use his computer to compare data from the previous year's harvest with drone or satellite photos of his farm that show which crops are flourishing. He can check the latest grain prices and use the website newAgTalk.com to converse with other farmers from all over the world. He can also save money on chemicals by bidding for bulk fertilizer on FarmTrade.com, an online agricultural exchange. High-tech equipment tells him how and where to spread fertilizer and seed, tracks yields yard by yard, and allows him to maintain high profit margins.[14] Of course, more tech often means fewer workers. Is that a good or bad thing for farmers?

e-commerce

The buying and selling of goods over the Internet.

The Growth of E-commerce **E-commerce** is the buying and selling of goods online. There are two major types of e-commerce transactions: business-to-consumer (B2C) and business-to-business (B2B). As important as the Internet has been to online retailers in the consumer market, it has become even more important in the B2B market, where businesses sell goods and services to one another, such as IBM selling consulting services to a local bank. E-commerce has become so important that we discuss it in many chapters throughout the text.

Using Technology to Be Responsive to Customers

A major theme of this text is that those businesses most responsive to customer wants and needs will succeed. Technology can help businesses respond to customer needs in many ways. For example, businesses use bar codes to identify products you buy and their size, quantity, and color. The scanner at the checkout counter identifies the price but can also put all your purchase information into a **database**, an electronic storage file for information.

Databases enable stores to carry only the merchandise their local customers want. But because companies routinely trade database information, many retailers know what you buy and from whom you buy it. Thus they can send you online ads or catalogs and other direct mail advertising offering the kind of products you might want based on your past purchases. We discuss many of the other ways businesses use technology to be responsive to consumers throughout the text.

Unfortunately, the legitimate collection of personal customer information also opens the door to identity theft. **Identity theft** is the obtaining of individuals' personal information, such as Social Security and credit card numbers, for illegal purposes. For example, in 2017 Equifax, one of the credit bureaus charged with protecting consumers from identity theft and fraud, was hacked itself. The data breach exposed the personal information of 147 million people. Equifax agreed to spend up to $425 billion to help people affected by the breach.[15]

Experts advise us to create new passwords for each account so that if the password on one account is stolen, the hackers can't access the rest of your accounts too. They also recommend storing them in a password manager, and activating two-factor authentication, which is an additional layer of security, when possible.[16] The Federal Trade Commission says millions of U.S. consumers are victims of identity theft each year. Cybersecurity will continue to be a major concern of governments, business, and consumers.[17]

Many people are concerned about how technology might be used to invade the privacy of their phone or e-mail conversations or even to track their movement through facial recognition technology used in stores, casinos, on cruise ships, and in other public places.[18] You can read more about security and privacy issues and how businesses use technology to manage information in Bonus Chapter B.

Bob Croslin/Getty Images News/Getty Images

LO 1–5 Demonstrate how businesses can meet and beat competition.

The Competitive Environment

Competition among businesses has never been greater. Some have found a competitive edge by focusing on *quality*. The goal for many companies is zero defects—no mistakes in making the product. However, even achieving a rate of zero defects isn't enough to stay competitive in world markets. Companies now have to offer both high-quality products and good value—that is, outstanding service at competitive prices.

Competing by Exceeding Customer Expectations

Today's customers want not only good quality at low prices but great service as well. Every manufacturing and service organization in the world should have a sign over its door telling its workers that the customer is king. Business has become more customer-driven, not management-driven as often occurred in the past. Successful organizations must now listen more closely to customers to determine their wants and needs, and then adjust the firm's products, policies, and practices accordingly. We will explore these ideas in more depth in Chapter 13.

database
An electronic storage file for information.

identity theft
The obtaining of individuals' personal information, such as Social Security and credit card numbers, for illegal purposes.

empowerment
Giving frontline workers the responsibility, authority, freedom, training, and equipment they need to respond quickly to customer requests.

demography
The statistical study of the human population with regard to its size, density, and other characteristics such as age, race, gender, and income.

In 2020 people around the world joined protests against institutionalized racism and police violence. The movement placed a renewed focus on racial bias in many areas of life, including business. What can companies do to create diverse and inclusive workplaces?

Competing by Restructuring and Empowerment To meet the needs of customers, firms must give their frontline workers—for example, office clerks, front-desk people at hotels, and salespeople—the responsibility, authority, freedom, training, and equipment they need to respond quickly to customer requests. They also must allow workers to make other decisions essential to producing high-quality goods and services. The process is called **empowerment**, and we'll be talking about it throughout this book.

As many companies have discovered, it sometimes takes years to restructure an organization so that managers can and will give up some of their authority and employees will assume more responsibility. We'll discuss such organizational changes in Chapter 8.

LO 1–6   Analyze the social changes affecting businesses.

The Social Environment

Demography is the statistical study of the human population with regard to its size, density, and other characteristics such as age, race, gender, and income. In this text, we're particularly interested in the demographic trends that most affect businesses and career choices. The U.S. population is going through major changes that are dramatically affecting how people live, where they live, what they buy, and how they spend their time. Furthermore, tremendous population shifts are leading to new opportunities for some firms and to declining opportunities for others. For example, there are many more retired workers than in the past, creating new markets for all kinds of goods and services.

Managing Diversity

Diversity means much more than recruiting and retaining minority and female employees. Diversity efforts include older adults, people with disabilities, people with different sexual orientations, atheists, religious people, extroverts, introverts, married people, and single people. It also means dealing sensitively with workers and cultures around the world.[19] Managing diversity involves creating a workplace that promotes inclusion and belonging. *Inclusion* is about having a voice that is heard. *Belonging* is about feeling part of a community.[20]

Mark Kerrison/In Pictures/Getty Images

Legal and illegal immigrants have had a dramatic effect on many regions, and will continue to do so as the government debates immigration reform.[21] Businesses, schools, and hospitals have been especially affected.[22] Some local governments are making efforts to adapt, including changing signs, brochures, websites, and forms to include other languages. Has your city experienced such changes? What are some of the impacts you've noticed? How has the debate about changing immigration policies affected your community?

The Increase in the Number of Older Citizens People aged 75 and over are currently the richest demographic group in the United States.[23] Therefore they represent a lucrative market for companies involved with food service, transportation, entertainment, education, lodging, and so on. By 2030 the percentage of the population 65 or older will be over 20 percent; by 2050 it will more than double.[24] What do these changes mean for you and for businesses in the future? Think of the products and services that middle-aged and older people will need—medicine, nursing homes, assisted-living facilities, adult day care, home health care, transportation, recreation, and the like—and you'll see opportunities for successful businesses of the 21st century. Don't rule out computer games and online services. Businesses that cater to older consumers will have the opportunity for exceptional growth in the near future. The market is huge.

stockbroker/123RF

On the other hand, retired people will be draining the economy of wealth. Social Security has become a major issue.[25] The pay-as-you-go system (in which workers today pay the retirement benefits for today's retirees) operated just fine in 1940, when 42 workers supported each retiree; but by 1960, there were only 5 workers per retiree, and today, as members of the Baby-Boom generation (born between 1946 and 1964) retire, that number is 2.8 and is projected to drop to 2.2 by 2036.[26] In addition, the government has been spending some of the accumulated Social Security money instead of leaving it all in the Social Security account.

Soon, less money will be coming into Social Security than will be going out. The government will have to do something to make up for the shortfall: raise taxes, reduce Social Security benefits (e.g., raise the retirement age at which people qualify for payments), reduce spending elsewhere (e.g., in other social programs like Medicare or Medicaid), or borrow on the world market.

In short, paying Social Security to older citizens in the future will draw huge amounts of money from the working population. That is why there is so much discussion in the media today about what to do to save Social Security.

The Increase in the Number of Single-Parent Families

It is a tremendous task to work full-time and raise a family. Thus, the growth of single-parent households has also had a major effect on businesses. Whereas only 7 percent of parents were single in 1950, today a third of the children in the United States live with a single parent.[27] Single parents, including those forced by welfare rules to return to work after a certain benefit period, have encouraged businesses to implement programs such as family leave (giving workers time off to attend to a sick child or elder relative) and flextime (allowing workers to arrive or leave at selected times). You will read about such programs in more detail in Chapter 11.

The Rise of Gen Z's Economic Influence

Generation Z (those born after the mid-1990s) will soon be the largest group of consumers in the world, accounting for as much as $143 billion in spending power in the United States alone. Designing products and services to meet the broad tastes of this demographic is critical to the success of many companies. In order to reach these consumers, marketers have to use a variety of tools to capture their attention and engage them. The Connecting through Social Media box discusses how a few companies are using social media to connect with Gen Zers.

Ariel Skelley/Getty Images

The Lucrative Challenge of Connecting with Gen Z Online

The Internet has always existed for Generation Z. As a result, this tech-savvy generation spends a ton of time on social media, especially platforms like Instagram, YouTube, and TikTok. Although reaching young people online can be a challenge for companies, the potential rewards for doing so are too significant to ignore given the size of this demographic group. And while social media will play a major role in this group's future purchasing decisions, they may not use it in the ways that some would expect.

For instance, while it might seem logical to assume that Gen Zers do all their shopping online, studies show that they love the experience of brick-and-mortar stores and malls. While they're out shopping, they are constantly on their smartphones seeking deals on social media.

As the social network of choice for many influencers,

Paul Bradbury/Getty Images

Facebook-owned Instagram has become an incredibly powerful force in branding. Experts expect it will stay that way since the platform has more than 1 billion active users. In fact, social networks like Instagram and

YouTube have grown so big that tech developers have largely stopped trying to create new apps to compete with them. Instead, many of today's social media start-ups focus on creating tools that can then be used on major platforms. For example, John Barnett worked as a developer at Snapchat and Instagram before founding his own company called Chroma Stories, an app that helps users make visual "stories" on social media. "We're focused on helping people create for whatever platform they're on, if it's Facebook, Instagram, Snap, WhatsApp, Pinterest, Twitter," said Barnett. Like the members of Generation Z themselves, modern companies will need to be similarly versatile in order to appeal to young consumers.

Sources: Craig Giammona and Tiffany Kary, "What Gen Z Wants," *Bloomberg Businessweek,* April 29, 2019; Jordyn Holman, Tiffany Kary, and Kim Bhasin, "A New Crop of Mall Rats," *Bloomberg Businessweek,* April 29, 2019; Katherine Bindley, "Catching Gen Z Requires a Big Fish: Instagram," *The Wall Street Journal,* September 28, 2019; Kathryn Lundstrom, "How to Reach Gen Z in 2020—Beyond Authenticity," *Adweek,* adweek.com, January 2, 2020.

LO 1–7 **Identify what businesses must do to meet global challenges, including war and terrorism.**

The Global Environment

The global environment of business is so important that we show it as surrounding all other environmental influences (see again Figure 1.3). Two important issues here are the growth of global competition and the negotiation of trade agreements among nations.

World trade, or *globalization,* has grown due to the development of efficient distribution systems (we'll talk about these in Chapter 15) and technological advances such as online communication systems. Globalization has greatly improved living standards around the world. China and India have become major U.S. competitors. Shop at Walmart and most other U.S. retail stores, and you can't help but notice the number of "Made in China" stickers you see. Call for computer help, and you are as likely to be talking with someone in India as someone in the United States.

World trade has its benefits and costs. You'll read much more about its importance in Chapter 3 and in the Reaching beyond Our Borders boxes throughout the text. This chapter's Reaching beyond Our Borders box on the next page discusses how Coca-Cola adapted its products to meet the needs of its global markets.

War and Terrorism War and terrorism have drained trillions of dollars a year from the U.S. economy.[28] Some companies—like those that make bullets, tanks, and uniforms—have benefited greatly. Others, however, lost workers to the armed forces, and still others have grown more slowly as money was diverted to the war effort. The threat of more wars and terrorism leads the government to spend even more money on spying and the military. Such expenditures are subject to much debate. The increased unrest in the world adds great uncertainty. This uncertainty is considered by some to be the biggest risk in business. It is difficult to plan when there are so many unknown factors such as how changes in military policy will affect the economy.[29]

How Global Changes Affect You As businesses expand to serve global markets, new jobs will be created in both manufacturing and service industries. Global trade also means global competition. The students who will prosper will be those prepared for the markets of tomorrow. Rapid changes create a need for continuous learning, so be prepared to continue your education throughout your career. You'll have every reason to be optimistic about job opportunities in the future if you prepare yourself well.

The Ecological Environment Few issues have captured the attention of the international business community more than climate change. **Climate change** is the movement of the temperature of the planet up or down over time. There are some who remain unconvinced of the dangers of global warming.[30] However, most scientists and many of the world's largest firms—including General Electric, Coca-Cola, Shell, Nestlé, DuPont, Johnson & Johnson, British Airways, and Shanghai Electric—say the evidence for climate change is overwhelming. Saving energy and producing products that cause less harm to the environment, such as solar energy, is called **greening**.

climate change
The movement of the temperature of the planet up or down over time.

greening
The trend toward saving energy and producing products that cause less harm to the environment.

?TEST**PREP**

- What are four ways the government can foster entrepreneurship?
- What are the differences among effectiveness, efficiency, and productivity?
- What is *empowerment*?
- What are some of the major issues affecting the economy today?

LO 1–8 Review how past trends are being repeated in the present and what those trends mean for tomorrow's college graduates.

The Evolution of U.S. Business

Businesses in the United States have become so productive that they need fewer workers than ever before to produce goods. If global competition and improved technology are

Coca-Cola's Global Offerings Expand Far beyond Soda

coca-colacompany.com

Koktaro/Shutterstock

For more than a century, Coca-Cola's immense branding power has centered on its signature soft drink. But the company's namesake is far from the only beverage in its enormous roster of products. In fact, Coca-Cola owns hundreds of drink brands that cater to the diverse needs of markets around the world. The company carefully researches local tastes and incorporates these flavors into beverages that appeal to a variety of global consumers.

One such drink is Mazza Chunky, an Indian fruit juice that includes chunks of mango. Coca-Cola researchers thought of the idea when they noticed that many people in the country liked to drink mango pulp straight from the fruit. Keeping an eye on local trends also led to products like a sesame-and-walnut drink in China, as well as a Brazilian line of whey shakes. Some flavors that perform well in global markets are eventually introduced to American consumers. For instance, in 2019 the company launched Coca-Cola Energy in countries like Germany, the United Kingdom, Spain, and many others. The drink was such a success that Coca-Cola introduced it to the United States less than a year later.

Quickly bringing new products to market has become a top priority for the company as it continues to expand its global offerings. In the past, Coca-Cola spent at least a year developing a drink before it launched. These days, though, the company can finish the process in as little as four months. By dedicating so many resources to new-product development, Coca-Cola has built a worldwide empire of soft drinks that should only grow larger in the years to come.

Sources: Eric Bellman and Jennifer Maloney, "Coca-Cola Launched 500 Drinks Last Year. Most Taste Nothing Like Coke," *The Wall Street Journal,* August 23, 2018; Jasmine Wu, "Coca-Cola to Launch Coke-Branded Energy Drink in US, in a Bid for More Growth," *CNBC,* cnbc.com, October 1, 2019; Coca-Cola Company, coca-colacompany.com, accessed January 2020.

putting skilled people out of work, should we be concerned about the prospect of high unemployment rates and low incomes? Where will the jobs be when you graduate? These important questions force us all to look briefly at the U.S. economy and its future.

Progress in the Agricultural and Manufacturing Industries

The United States has experienced strong economic development since the 1800s. The agricultural industry led the way, providing food for the United States and much of the world. Cyrus McCormick's invention of the harvester in 1834, other inventions such as Eli Whitney's cotton gin, and modern improvements on such equipment did much to make large-scale farming successful. Technology has made modern farming so efficient that the number of farmers has dropped from about 33 percent of the population to less than 1 percent today. However, average farm size is now about 430 acres versus 150 acres in the past.[31]

Agriculture is still a major industry in the United States. What has changed is that the millions of small farms that existed previously have been replaced by some huge farms, some merely large farms, and some small but highly specialized farms. The loss of farmworkers over the past century is not a negative sign. It is instead an indication that U.S. agricultural workers are the most productive in the world.

Most farmers who lost their jobs during the 19th and 20th centuries went to work in factories springing up around the country. Manufacturers, like farms, began using new technology, new tools, and machines to become more productive. Eventually the consequence in manufacturing, as in farming, was the elimination of many jobs.

baranozdemir/Getty Images

Again, the loss to society is minimized if the wealth created by increased productivity and efficiency creates new jobs elsewhere—and that's exactly what has happened over the past 50 years. Many workers in the industrial sector found jobs in the growing service sector. Most of those who can't find work today are people who need retraining and education to become qualified for jobs that now exist or will exist in the near future, such as building wind farms or making electric automobiles. We'll discuss the manufacturing sector and production in more detail in Chapter 9.

Progress in Service Industries

In the past, the fastest-growing industries in the United States produced goods like steel, automobiles, and machine tools. Today, the fastest-growing firms provide services in areas such as law, health, telecommunications, entertainment, and finance.

Since the mid-1980s, the service sector has generated almost all the increases in employment. Together, services employ about 85 percent of workers in the United States.[32] Chances are very high that you'll work in a service job at some point in your career. Figure 1.4 lists many service-sector jobs; look it over to see where the careers of the future are likely to be. Retailers like Nordstrom Rack are part of the service sector. Each new retail store can create managerial jobs for college graduates.

Another bit of good news is that there are *more* high-paying jobs in the service sector than in the goods-producing sector. High-paying service-sector jobs abound in health care, accounting, finance, entertainment, telecommunications, architecture, law, software engineering, and more.[33] Projections are that some areas of the service sector will grow rapidly, while others may have much slower growth. The strategy for college graduates is to remain flexible, find out where jobs are being created, and move when appropriate.

Progress in the Information Age

Despite the growth in the service sector we've described above, the service era is giving way to a new era. We're in the midst of an information-based global and technical revolution that is altering all sectors of the economy: agricultural, industrial, and service. In the Information Age, a significant portion of a company's value is based on its intellectual capital. *Intellectual capital* includes employee knowledge and skills that can be used to create new products, attract new customers, and increase profits.[34]

The new or enhanced products and services created by intellectual expertise in areas such as the technical and scientific fields encourage innovation in the economy as a whole. For example, universities and companies engaging in research and development may develop new software and search engines that can be passed on to workers in more traditional fields. Doctors can use the new technology to offer improved treatments such as robot-assisted surgeries. Farmers can use the new software applications to manage their farm crops. Schools can provide students with digital study aids and online courses.[35]

Agriculture is one of the largest and most important industries in the United States. Technology has increased productivity and made farmers more efficient, allowing for larger farms. This trend has helped reduce the increase in price of some foods for consumers, but has also reduced the number of small, family-run farms. Does the new technology also help smaller farms compete? If so, how?

FIGURE 1.4 WHAT IS THE SERVICE SECTOR?

There's much talk about the service sector, but few discussions actually list what it includes. Here are examples of businesses in the service sector.

Examples of Businesses in the Service Sector						
Amusement and Recreation Services						
Amusement parks	Ice skating rinks	Bowling alleys	Pool halls	Botanical gardens	Infotainment	Carnivals
Race tracks	Circuses	Golf courses	Symphony orchestras	Restaurants	Fairs	Video rentals
Business Services						
Collection agencies	Management services	Equipment rental	Trash collection	Computer programming	Exterminating	Research & development labs
Window cleaning	Tax preparation	Web design	Commercial photography	Accounting	Commercial art	Ad agencies
Public relations	Consulting	Detective agencies	Interior design	Stenographic services	Employment agencies	
Legal Services						
Lawyers	Paralegals	Notary public				
Educational Services						
Schools	Libraries	Online schools	Computer schools			
Health Services						
Chiropractors	Nursery care	Dentists	Physicians	Medical labs	Dental labs	
Motion Picture Industry						
Production	Distribution	Theaters	Drive-ins			
Social Services						
Job training	Elder care	Family services	Child care			
Automotive Repair Services and Garages						
Transmission repair	Tire retreading	Exhaust system shops	Truck rental	Auto rental	Paint shops	Parking lots
Car washes						
Financial Services						
Banking	Real estate agencies	Investment firms (brokers)	Insurance			
Personal Services						
Photographic studios	Shoe repair	Tax preparation	Laundries	Funeral homes	Linen supply	
Beauty shops	Child care	Health clubs	Diaper service	Carpet cleaning		
Lodging Services						
Hotels, rooming houses, and other lodging places	Sporting and recreation camps	Trailer parks and campsites for transients				
Cultural Institutions						
Noncommercial museums	Art galleries	Botanical and zoological gardens				
Selected Membership Organizations						
Civic associations	Business associations					
Miscellaneous Services						
Tele-communications	Architectural	Engineering	Utilities	Lawn care	Vending	Delivery
Surveying	Septic tank cleaning	Radio and television	Sharpening	Reupholstery	Watch	Welding

Your Future in Business

It's exciting to think about the role you'll play in business. You may be a leader who will implement the changes and accept the challenges of world competition based on world quality standards. This book will introduce you to some of the concepts that make such leadership possible, not just in business but also in government agencies and nonprofit organizations. Business can't prosper in the future without the cooperation of government and social leaders throughout the world.

?TEST**PREP**

- What major factor caused people to move from farming to manufacturing and from manufacturing to the service sector?
- What does the future look like for tomorrow's college graduates?

SUMMARY

LO 1–1 Describe the relationship between profit and risk, and show how businesses and nonprofit organizations can raise the standard of living for all.

- **What is the relationship of businesses' profit to risk assumption?**

  Profit is money a business earns above and beyond the money that it spends for salaries and other expenses. Businesspeople make profits by taking risks. *Risk* is the chance an entrepreneur takes of losing time and money on a business that may not prove profitable. A loss occurs when a business's costs and expenses are higher than its revenues.

- **Who are stakeholders, and which stakeholders are most important to a business?**

  Stakeholders include customers, employees, stockholders, suppliers, dealers, bankers, the media, people in the local community, environmentalists, and elected government leaders. The goal of business leaders is to try to recognize and respond to the needs of these stakeholders and still make a profit.

LO 1–2 Explain how entrepreneurship and the other factors of production contribute to the creation of wealth.

- **What are the advantages and disadvantages of entrepreneurship?**

  Working for others means getting benefits like paid vacations and health insurance. Entrepreneurs take more risks and lose those benefits. They gain the freedom to make their own decisions, more opportunity, and possible wealth.

- **What are the five factors of production?**

  The five factors of production are land, labor, capital, entrepreneurship, and knowledge. Of these, the most important are entrepreneurship and knowledge. Entrepreneurs are people who risk time and money to start and manage a business. What makes rich countries rich today is a combination of *entrepreneurship* and the effective use of *knowledge*.

LO 1–3 Analyze the effects of the economic environment and taxes on businesses.

- **What can governments in developing countries do to reduce the risk of starting businesses and thus help entrepreneurs?**

The government may allow private ownership of businesses, pass laws that enable businesspeople to write contracts that are enforceable in court, establish a currency that's tradable in world markets, help lessen corruption in business and government, and keep taxes and regulations to a minimum. From a business perspective, lower taxes mean lower risks, more growth, and thus more money for workers and the government.

LO 1–4 Describe the effects of technology on businesses.

- **How has technology benefited workers, businesses, and consumers?**

Technology enables workers to be more effective, efficient, and productive. *Effectiveness* means doing the right thing in the right way. *Efficiency* means producing items using the least amount of resources. *Productivity* is the amount of output you generate given the amount of input (e.g., hours worked).

LO 1–5 Demonstrate how businesses can meet and beat competition.

- **What are some ways in which businesses meet and beat competition?**

Some companies have found a competitive edge by focusing on making high-quality products, all the way to zero defects. Companies also aim to exceed customer expectations. Often that means *empowering* frontline workers by giving them more training and more responsibility and authority.

LO 1–6 Analyze the social changes affecting businesses.

- **How have social changes affected businesses?**

Diversity has come to mean much more than recruiting and keeping minority and female employees. Diversity efforts now include older adults, people with disabilities, people with different sexual orientations, atheists, religious people, extroverts, introverts, married people, and single people. Managing diversity means dealing sensitively with workers and cultures around the world. Providing Social Security benefits to older citizens in the future will draw huge amounts of money from the working population. That is why there is so much discussion about Social Security in the media today.

LO 1–7 Identify what businesses must do to meet global challenges, including war and terrorism.

- **Which countries are creating the greatest competitive challenges?**

China and India are two major competitors.

- **What will be the impacts of future wars and terrorism?**

Some businesses, such as those in the defense industry, may prosper. Others, such as tourism, may suffer. One way to minimize world tensions is to help less-developed countries become more prosperous.

LO 1–8 Review how past trends are being repeated in the present and what those trends mean for tomorrow's college graduates.

- **What is the history of our economic development in the United States, and what does it tell us about the future?**

Agricultural workers displaced by improved farm technology went to work in factories. Improved manufacturing productivity and increased competition from foreign firms contributed to the development of a service economy in the United States. The service era is now giving way to an information-based global revolution that will affect all sectors of the economy. The secret to long-term success in such an economy is flexibility and continuing education to be prepared for the opportunities that are sure to arise.

- **What job opportunities for college graduates exist in the service sector?**

  Check over Figure 1.4, which outlines the service sector. That is where you are most likely to find the fast-growing firms of the future.

KEY TERMS

business 4	factors of production 8	profit 4
business environment 9	goods 4	quality of life 5
climate change 17	greening 17	revenue 4
database 13	identity theft 13	risk 5
demography 14	loss 4	services 4
e-commerce 12	nonprofit organization 7	stakeholders 6
empowerment 14	outsourcing 6	standard of living 5
entrepreneur 4	productivity 12	technology 11

CRITICAL THINKING

Imagine you are thinking of starting a restaurant in your community. Answer the following questions:

1. Who will be the various stakeholders of your business?

2. What are some of the things you can do to benefit your community other than providing jobs and tax revenue?

3. How will you establish good relationships with your suppliers? With your employees?

4. Do you see any conflict between your desire to be as profitable as possible and your desire to pay employees a living wage?

5. Which of the environmental factors outlined in this chapter might have the biggest impact on your business? How?

PUTTING PRINCIPLES TO WORK

PURPOSE

To learn what changes are occurring in the business environment today and how those changes are affecting businesses.

EXERCISE

1. Go to the National Taxpayers Union website (ntu.org). Search for "Who Pays Income Taxes?" Study the tables showing what percentage of taxes the various income groups pay. Do you think that everyone pays their fair share? What percentage of taxes does the top 1 percent of earners pay? What about the top 5 percent? The lowest 50 percent? How do such tax rates affect incentives to become a successful entrepreneur?

2. Go to the Census Bureau's website (census.gov) and learn what the population of the United States is at this moment. While at the site, you may want to look up the population in your town or city. Explore what other data is available at this site. What trends seem most important to you and to businesspeople in general?

3. Do a Google search for "business blogs" and check out some of the available results. Go to one of the blogs that seems interesting to you and write a brief paragraph about it—including such things as who sponsors it, who contributes the posts, and what other features it has—and how it may help a student in an introductory business course.

DEVELOPING CAREER SKILLS

KEY: ● **Team**   ★ **Analytic**   ▲ **Communication**   ▣ **Technology**

 1. Poll the class and determine which students believe that climate change is primarily caused by humans and which believe that other factors, such as climate cycles or sun spots, are the primary cause. Discuss what students can do to minimize human effects on the environment regardless of the primary causes of climate change. Are there any negative consequences to trying to minimize humans' impact on the environment?

 2. Imagine you are a local businessperson who has to deal with the issue of outsourcing. You want to begin with the facts. How many, if any, jobs have been lost to outsourcing in your area? Are there any foreign firms in your area that are creating jobs (insourcing)? You will need to go online to find the data you need.

★ 3. What indicates that you and other people in the United States have a high standard of living? What are some signs that maintaining such a high standard of living may have a negative impact on quality of life? Does everyone in the United States enjoy a high standard of living? If not, how does this impact their quality of life?

 4. Use Yelp to find five businesses that provide services in your area. List those businesses and, for each, describe how social trends, such as building a diverse workforce, might affect them. Be prepared to explain your descriptions to your team or the whole class, as your instructor directs.

 5. Form into teams of four or five and discuss the technological and e-commerce revolutions. How often do students shop for goods and services online? What have been their experiences? What other technology do they use (smartphones, tablets, laptops, etc.)? Discuss what life, school, and work would be like without these devices.

CAREER EXPLORATION

At the end of each chapter, we offer a brief list of potential careers that deal with the concepts present in the chapter. Since this first chapter is an overview of all the different fields of business, we thought we'd concentrate on identifying a few careers in the sector with the most jobs: services. Find out about the tasks performed, skills needed, pay, and opportunity outlook in these careers in the *Occupational Outlook Handbook (OOH)* at bls.gov.

- **Lodging manager**—ensures that guests on vacation or business travel have a pleasant experience at a hotel, motel, or other type of establishment with accommodations and that the business is run efficiently and profitably.

- **Meeting and event planner**—coordinates all aspects of events and professional meetings, including arranging meeting locations, transportation, and other details.

- **Interior designer**—selects and specifies colors, furniture, and other materials to create useful and stylish interiors for buildings.

- **Network and computer systems administrator**—responsible for the day-to-day operation of computer networks.

VIDEO CASE   *Building a Shopping Community of People*

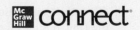

If you have the inspiration and tenacity to become an entrepreneur, the service industry offers great possibilities. Services are now the largest area of growth in the United States. A great idea and hard work can lead to great success. In 2007, Manish Chandra realized that the move to environmental sustainability and advances in technology could shift the fashion industry away from its traditional focus of selling new products toward providing a service centered on exchanging gently used clothing. He knew that people all across America often ask the same question:

"What do I do with clothing I no longer wear?" Chandra developed and founded Poshmark, a social commerce platform that boasts 60 million users who list 38 million products daily.

Like other successful entrepreneurs, Chandra was able to start Poshmark and expand it rapidly thanks to the business environment in the United States. To be successful, businesses must navigate factors that impact the five key business environments in the U.S. economy: the social environment, the technological environment, the economic and legal environment, the competitive environment, and the global environment. Even though businesses cannot control these environments, they must be quick to adapt to changes in key environments that affect them.

For instance, changes in the social environment in the United States had a significant impact on Poshmark since its launch in 2010. Building a community-centric organization was a key shift in online retailing, Changing demographics and values of Millennials and Gen Z consumers fit perfectly with Poshmark's business model. The advent of mobile technology vastly expanded the market opportunities for the company, and the growth of the circular economy also provided a major benefit. The circular economy encourages reusing and recycling products rather than discarding them in a landfill. This shift in social perspective assisted Poshmark in being at the forefront of the movement away from fast fashion toward a sustainable method of consumption.

The expanding technological environment, especially mobile technology, contributed heavily to the success of Poshmark. Without the tremendous growth of technology, Poshmark would not be feasible. Chandra credits the introduction of iPhone 4 in 2010 as a turning point in Poshmark's growth. The iPhone 4 was introduced with a great camera that expanded the ease of use and viability of Poshmark's business plan. Shoppers could now take photos in real time, then merchandise and market their items to others. The vibrant mobile platform developed by Poshmark allowed customers to place orders instantly. Packaging assistance offered by the company simplified the delivery of clothing items.

The economic and legal environment in the United States is very favorable for businesses like Poshmark. The government supports private ownership of businesses by providing a stable currency and a legal system that enforces contracts, keeps regulations to a minimum, and avoids bureaucratic roadblocks that hinder businesses. Transportation and distribution in the United States make shipment of products easy and efficient. However, companies like Poshmark must make sure to follow any laws and regulations that apply to their industry.

When the company first entered the market, competition was limited. That's not the case today. With competitors such as thredUP, Etsy, the RealReal, and others offering stiff competition, Poshmark knows it faces daily challenges to its community of "poshers." That's a key reason why the company moved from operating purely online to establishing a presence in the real world. Poshmark hosts a number of real-life community programs such as "Posh Parties" where poshers can exchange their experiences and offer marketing tips to fellow sellers. The company's two-day conference called "Posh Fest" has grown every year and sells out. Even though Poshmark holds the advantage of being in business the longest, the company must still work hard every day to keep its 60 million users happy and loyal.

In business today, every company needs to consider the global environment. Poshmark has not made major efforts to expand its business beyond the United States and Canada. Still, Poshmark's ease of operation and openness of its app makes global expansion in the future very possible. Clearly, advances in communication and the Internet make it possible for the company to build a presence overseas.

In the years since its founding, Poshmark has had a tremendous impact on the fashion industry and has been very profitable. Going forward, the company must remain committed to connecting people through its app as well as socially with its events. By responding to the challenges of the business environment and improving the experience for shoppers, Poshmark plans to be part of the U.S. business landscape for the long term.

THINKING IT OVER

1. Which of the five environmental factors are most critical to Poshmark's continued success and stability?

2. How did iPhone 4 provide the boost Poshmark needed to expand its business model in the online market?

3. How do "Posh Parties" and "Posh Fest" help expand Poshmark's business and build the loyalty of Poshmark customers?

NOTES

1. *Forbes,* forbes.com, accessed January 2020.
2. "Global Wealth 2019," Boston Consulting Group, bcg.com, accessed January 2020.
3. U.S. Bureau of Labor Statistics, bls.gov, accessed January 2020.
4. Nick Routley, "Walmart Nation," *Visual Capitalist,* visualcapitalist.com, January 24, 2019.
5. Terin Miller, "What Is a Stakeholder and Why Is It Important for Business?," *TheStreet,* thestreet.com, February 10, 2019; Mona Mortazavi, "2 Key Tools for Stakeholder Analysis," *PMWorld 360 Magazine,* pmworld360.com, accessed January 2020.
6. Michelle Chapman, "Top US CEOs Rethink the Meaning of Shareholder Value," *St. Louis Post-Dispatch,*

August 20, 2019; Brian O'Connell, "A New Era in Corporate Responsibility," Society for Human Resource Management, shrm.org, January 4, 2020.

7. Hyundai, hyundai.com, accessed January 2020.

8. Honda, honda.com, accessed January 2020.

9. Ayan Pramanik, "Insourcing Threat Looms Large over IT Services Providers," *The Economic Times,* economictimes.indiatimes.com, May 9, 2019; Jared Council, "Target and Lowe's Tech Execs Credit Talent, Culture for Insourcing Success," *The Wall Street Journal,* wsj.com, January 13, 2020.

10. Drucker Institute, drucker.institute, accessed January 2020.

11. John Harris, "Elections Used to Bring Us Solutions," *The Guardian,* theguardian.com, November 4, 2019; "Tech Platforms, on the Hook to Clean Up Political Advertising, Take Different Approaches," *Marketplace,* marketplace.org, January 2, 2020.

12. Peter High, "Lessons from the Man Who Is Revolutionizing the Grocery Business," *Forbes,* January 14, 2019; Morris Panner, "How Mobile Medical Services Are Improving Health Care," *Forbes,* January 16, 2019.

13. Robert D. Atkinson, "Higher Productivity Is Good for Workers," *National Review,* July 25, 2019; Eduardo Porter, "Tech Is Splitting the U.S. Work Force in Two," *The New York Times,* nytimes.com, February 4, 2019; Carl Benedikt Frey, "The High Cost of Impeding Automation," *The Wall Street Journal,* October 25, 2019.

14. Norman Mayersohn, "How High Tech Is Transforming One of the Oldest Jobs: Farming," *The New York Times,* nytimes.com, September 6, 2019; "Agriculture Technology," National Institute of Food and Agriculture, nifa.usda.gov, accessed January 2020.

15. Alvaro Puig, "Equifax Data Breach Settlement: What You Should Know," Federal Trade Commission, consumer.ftc.gov, July 22, 2019; Kathleen Howley, "Equifax Victims: You're Not Getting Your $125," *HousingWire,* housingwire.com, January 2, 2020.

16. Thorin Klosowski, "The Best Two-Factor Authentication App," *The Wirecutter,* thewirecutter.com, October 25, 2019; Ed Bott, "The 6 Life-Changing Tech Habits You Need This Year," *ZDNet,* zdnet.com, January 1, 2020.

17. Joyce M. Rosenberg, "No Target Proves Too Small for Cybercriminals," *St. Louis Post-Dispatch,* September 8, 2019; "Indian Researcher Finds Starbucks API Key Exposed Online," *CISO Mag,* ciso.com, January 2, 2020.

18. Nicole Martin, "The Major Concerns around Facial Recognition Technology," *Forbes,* forbes.com, September 25, 2019; Associated Press, "School District's Facial Recognition Raises Privacy Concern," *The New York Times,* nytimes.com, January 3, 2020.

19. Sandy Cross and Porter Braswell, "A Data-Driven Approach to Hiring More Diverse Talent," *Harvard Business Review,* hbr.org, December 10, 2019.

20. Jena McGregor, "First There Was 'Diversity.' Then 'Inclusion.' Now H.R. Wants Everyone to Feel Like They 'Belong,' *The Washington Post,* washingtonpost.com, December 30, 2019.

21. Janet Adamy and Paul Overberg, "Immigration's Impact on Nation Grows," *The Wall Street Journal,* April 18, 2019; Sol Trujillo, "Latino Workers Save America from Stagnation," *The Wall Street Journal,* September 26, 2019.

22. Dieter Holger, "The Business Case for More Diversity," *The Wall Street Journal,* October 28, 2019; "Immigration Impact," American Immigration Council, americanimmigrationcouncil.org, accessed January 2020.

23. Dayana Yochim, "What's Your Net Worth, and How Do You Compare to Others?," *MarketWatch,* marketwatch.com, January 29, 2019; Federal Reserve, federalreserve.gov, accessed January 2020.

24. U.S. Census Bureau, census.gov, accessed January 2020.

25. Kate Davidson, "Red Ink Seen for Social Security by 2020," *The Wall Street Journal,* April 23, 2020.

26. "Fast Facts & Figures about Social Security," Social Security Administration, ssa.gov, accessed January 2020.

27. "National Single Parent Day: One-Parent Families Are on the Rise in the US," *The Guardian,* theguardian.com, March 21, 2019.

28. "National Defense Budget Estimates for FY 2020," Office of the Undersecretary of Defense (Comptroller), comptroller.defense.gov, accessed January 2020.

29. "The Effects of Uncertainty on Economic Outcomes," The Federal Reserve Bank of St. Louis, stlouisfed.org, July 9, 2019; Will England, Taylor Telford, and Thomas Heath, "Oil Prices Spike, Dow Dives after U.S. Airstrike Kills Top Iranian Military Leader," *The Washington Post,* washingtonpost.com, January 3, 2020.

30. Amy Remeikis, "Rupert Murdoch Says 'No Climate Change Deniers Around'—but His Writers Prove Him Wrong," *The Guardian,* December 14, 2019; Spencer Bokat-Lindell, "So You Want to Convince a Climate Change Skeptic," *The New York Times,* nytimes.com, January 2, 2020.

31. U.S. Department of Agriculture, "Farms and Land in Farms," nass.usda.gov, accessed January 2020.

32. "The Growing Importance of the Services Sector," The Federal Reserve Bank of Kansas City, kansascityfed.org, accessed January 2020.

33. Euny Hong, "25 Highest Paid Occupations in the U.S. for 2019," *Investopedia,* investopedia.com, November 19, 2019; Quentin Fottrell, "Here Is the No. 1 Highest Paid, Fastest-Growing Job in Every U.S. State," *MarketWatch,* marketwatch.com, January 1, 2020.

34. James Chen, "Intellectual Capital," *Investopedia,* investopedia.com, April 29, 2019.

35. Will Kenton, "Knowledge Economy," *Investopedia,* investopedia.com, April 14, 2019.

2

Understanding Economics and How It Affects Business

Mariana Mazzucato, Economist

In the last few decades, many major economic thinkers have pushed to reduce the government's influence over the business world. According to the economist Mariana Mazzucato, however, the state has played a crucial role in the development of all sorts of innovations. From breakthroughs in aeronautics and engineering to world-changing technology like the Internet, government funding and research have provided many private companies with vital support. "The more I looked, the more I realized: state investment is everywhere," said Mazzucato.

Her mission is to transform the economic role of governments from regulators and fixers of market failures to innovators and drivers of market growth. Mazzucato wants to confront big issues like climate change, income inequality, and ocean pollution by combining the powers of the private and public sectors. She works closely with politicians in the United States and Europe to develop sweeping reforms that draw on her vast knowledge of world economics. Although Mazzucato is committed to capitalism, she maintains that the current system doesn't do enough to maximize the potential of all stakeholders. "History tells us that innovation is an outcome of a massive collective effort," said Mazzucato. "And if we want to solve the world's biggest problems, we better understand that."

Born in Rome to Italian parents and raised in New Jersey, Mazzucato's nuclear physicist father taught her at an early age how to look at the world with skepticism. "A critical eye was the first thing my dad instilled in me, mainly just from watching him swear at the TV," said Mazzucato. Her inquisitive nature served her well in school. After graduating from Princeton High School, she earned degrees in history and international relations from Tufts University. She then moved on to the New School for Social Research in New York where she obtained a master's degree and a PhD in economics. Once she completed her formal education, Mazzucato taught at prestigious institutions like New York University, London Business School, and the University of Edinburgh. Along with her teaching duties, she also published articles and books that studied the relationship between government research and innovation in the private sector. Mazzucato argues that state agencies should be structured as "mission-oriented" organizations that solve problems and take risks, allowing them to become true engines of innovation.

She cites the Apollo space program as a prime example of this strategy. In order to land a manned spacecraft on the moon, NASA created more than 300 programs that studied rocket science as well as subjects like electronics, medicine, and nutrition. These collaborations between government agencies and private companies produced more than 1,800 spin-off products ranging from freeze-dried food to integrated circuit technology. Mazzucato also describes the iPhone as another marvel of cooperation between private and state organizations. While the Department of Defense created microprocessors and LCD displays, researchers at the University of Delaware developed the touchscreen. "Steve Jobs has rightly been called a genius for the visionary products he conceived and marketed, [but] this story creates a myth about the origin of Apple's success," said Mazzucato. "Without the massive amount of public investment behind the computer and internet revolutions, such attributes might have led only to the invention of a new toy."

Mazzucato's insights are becoming increasingly valuable to world leaders who want to increase innovation and prosperity around the globe. Along with advising U.S. presidential candidates as well as members of British parliament, she also works with the European Union to combat the planet's most pressing issues. "That's what I want: to bring about change," said Mazzucato.

As you'll find out in this chapter, economics is all about the direct effect that economic systems can have on the wealth and well-being of countries throughout the world. You will learn about the strengths and weaknesses of different economic systems and what makes some countries rich and others poor. We will especially cover the free-market system that the United States depends on and the challenges it could face in the future. By the end of this chapter, you should be well aware of the relationship of economics to business success.

Sources: Eshe Nelson, "One of the World's Most Influential Economists Is on a Mission to Save Capitalism from Itself," *Quartz,* quartz.com, July 22, 2019; João Medeiros, "This Economist Has a Plan to Fix Capitalism. It's Time We All Listened," *Wired UK,* wired.co.uk, October 8, 2019; Kate Lederer, "Meet the Leftish Economist with a New Story about Capitalism," *The New York Times,* November 26, 2019; marianamazzucato.com, accessed January 2020.

Let's talk business!
bit.ly/LetsTalkBusiness2

name that company

GROWTH OF U.S. GDP can be influenced by productivity of the nation's workforce. It can also be impacted by the misfortunes of major U.S. companies. When this company was forced to stop production of its 737 MAX airliner, the company, as well as suppliers and airlines that fly the 737, saw their growth severely impacted. Name that company. (Find the answer in the chapter.)

LO 2-1   Explain basic economics.

How Economic Conditions Affect Businesses

Compared to, say, Mexico, the United States is a relatively wealthy country. Why? Why is South Korea comparatively wealthy while North Korea continues to suffer economically, with power outages still a part of daily life?[1] Such questions are part of the subject of economics. In this chapter, we explore the various economic systems of the world and how they either promote or hinder business growth, the creation of wealth, and a higher quality of life for all.

A major part of the United States' business success is due to an economic and social climate that allows most businesses to operate freely. People are free to start a business anywhere, and just as free to fail and start again. That freedom motivates people to try until they succeed because the rewards are often so great. Any change in the U.S. economic or political system has an influence on business success. For example, an increase or decrease in government regulations has an economic effect due to the costs of adhering to the regulations. Some experts believe that less regulation is better for businesses; others believe more regulations are necessary. The optimal level of government regulation is a constant topic of debate.[2]

Global economics and global politics also have a major influence on businesses in the United States. For example, the revenue of major U.S. industrial companies such as Caterpillar depend heavily on the global market, especially China. In fact, 59 percent of Caterpillar's revenue comes from outside the United States.[3] Clearly, to understand business

The economic contrast shown here is remarkable. Business is booming in Seoul, South Korea (as shown in the photo on the right). But North Korea, a communist country, is not doing well, as the picture on the left shows. What do you think accounts for the dramatic differences in the economies of these two neighboring countries?

Ng Han Guan/AP Images

Gw. Nam/Getty Images

you must also understand basic economics and politics.[4] This is especially true of new college graduates looking for jobs.

What Is Economics?

Economics is the study of how society chooses to employ resources to produce goods and services and distribute them for consumption among various competing groups and individuals. There are two major branches of economics: **macroeconomics** looks at the operation of a nation's economy as a whole (the whole United States), and **microeconomics** looks at the behavior of people and organizations in markets for particular products or services. A question in macroeconomics might be: What should the United States do to lower its national debt?[5] Macroeconomic topics in this chapter include gross domestic product (GDP), the unemployment rate, and price indexes. A question in microeconomics might be: Why do people buy smaller cars when gas prices go up? Such questions seem easier to answer.

Some economists define economics as the study of the allocation of *scarce* resources. They believe resources need to be carefully divided among people, usually by the government. However, there's no way to maintain peace and prosperity in the world by merely dividing the resources we have today among the existing nations. There aren't enough known resources to do that. **Resource development** is the study of how to increase resources (say, by getting oil and gas from shale and tar sands) and create conditions that will make better use of them (like recycling and conservation).

Businesses can contribute to an economic system by inventing products that greatly increase available resources. For example, they can discover new energy sources (natural gas for autos); new ways of growing food (hydroponics); and new ways of creating needed goods and services such as nanotechnology, 3D printing, and 4D technology (moving 3D, with time as the fourth dimension). Mariculture, or raising fish in pens out in the ocean, could lead to more food for everyone and more employment. In fact, many believe that aquaculture is the only way we can stop the overfishing that is depleting the world's fish population.[6]

economics
The study of how society chooses to employ resources to produce goods and services and distribute them for consumption among various competing groups and individuals.

macroeconomics
The part of economics study that looks at the operation of a nation's economy as a whole.

microeconomics
The part of economics study that looks at the behavior of people and organizations in particular markets.

resource development
The study of how to increase resources and to create the conditions that will make better use of those resources.

The Secret to Creating a Wealthy Economy

Imagine the world when kings and other rich landowners had most of the wealth, and the majority of the people were peasants. The peasants had many children, and it may have seemed a natural conclusion that if things went on as usual there would soon be too many people and not enough food and other resources. Economist Thomas Malthus made this argument in the late 1700s and early 1800s, leading the writer Thomas Carlyle to call economics "the dismal science."[7]

Violetastock/Getty Images

The latest world statistics, however, show population growing more slowly than expected. In fact, it is predicted that the population will stop growing at all by the end of the century.[8] In some industrial countries—such as Japan, Germany, Italy, Russia, and the United States—population growth may be so slow that eventually there will be too many older people and too few young people to care for them.[9] In the developing world—India, South Africa—on the other hand, population is climbing steadily and may lead to greater poverty and more economic unrest.[10] The Adapting to Change box discusses significant global population shifts that are expected over the next 25 years. Such studies about the effects of population growth on the economy are part of macroeconomics.

New ways of producing goods and services add resources to the economy and create more employment. Fish farms, for instance, create both food and jobs. Can you think of other innovations that can help increase economic development?

World Population Could Go from Boom to Bust

census.gov/popclock

According to the United Nations (UN), the global population will grow to nearly 10 billion people by 2050. This upcoming increase of more than 2 billion humans will have a major impact on resources and could lead to significant lifestyle changes in many countries. But while the world will have to grapple with the effects of population growth in the next few decades, it might not be much of an issue after that.

Experts at the UN estimate that the global population will peak at 10.9 billion people by the end of the century. Unlike previous forecasts, researchers no longer expect the world's population to continue growing without end. Instead, declining birth rates across the globe suggest that the number of humans on the planet should stabilize by 2100. For instance, the global fertility rate fell from 3.2 births per woman in 1990 to 2.5 in 2015. The UN predicts that number will fall to 2.2 by 2050, just above the rate needed to ensure that generations can be replaced without decline. Analysts claim that the increasingly urbanized world population is partly responsible for the drop in birth rates. With 55 percent of the globe now living in cities, people are more likely to have just a couple of kids rather than large families with four or five children.

As a result, older people will likely make up a large portion of the population for years to come. This could potentially lead to future economic difficulties if there is a lack of young people to replace the aging workforce. The UN says that immigration could become very important to many countries as they look to attract new workers that can take the place of older generations.

Goodboy Picture Company/Getty Images

Sources: Darrell Bricker and John Ibbitson, "Forget Overpopulation. The World Could Soon Face a Population Bust," *Los Angeles Times,* February 24, 2019; Rick Gladstone, "The Globe Is Going Gray Fast, U.N. Says in New Forecast," *The New York Times,* June 17, 2019; "Demographic Density: What Will the World Be Like in 2050?," *The Wall Street Journal,* wsj.com, accessed January 2020.

Some macroeconomists believe that a large population, especially an educated one, can be a valuable resource. You've probably heard the saying "Give a man a fish and you feed him for a day, but teach a man to fish and you feed him for a lifetime." You can add to that: "Teach a person to start a fish farm, and he or she will be able to feed a village for a lifetime." *The secret to economic development is contained in this last statement.* Business owners provide jobs and economic growth for their employees and communities as well as for themselves.

The challenge for macroeconomists is to determine what makes some countries relatively wealthy and other countries relatively poor, and then to implement policies and programs that lead to increased prosperity for everyone in all countries. One way to begin understanding this challenge is to consider the theories of Adam Smith.

Adam Smith and the Creation of Wealth

Rather than believing fixed resources had to be divided among competing groups and individuals, Scottish economist Adam Smith envisioned creating more resources so that everyone could become wealthier. Smith's book *An Inquiry into the Nature and Causes of the Wealth of Nations* (often called simply *The Wealth of Nations*) was published in 1776.

Smith believed *freedom* was vital to the survival of any economy, especially the freedom to own land or property and to keep the profits that result from working the land or running a business. He believed people will work long and hard if they have incentives for doing so—that is, if they know they'll be rewarded.[11] As a result of those efforts, the economy will prosper, with plenty of food and all kinds of products available to everyone. Smith's ideas were later challenged by Malthus and others who believed economic conditions would only get worse, but Smith, not Malthus, is considered the "father" of modern economics.

How Businesses Benefit the Community

In Adam Smith's view, businesspeople don't necessarily deliberately set out to help others. They work primarily for their own prosperity and growth. Yet as people try to improve their own situation in life, Smith said, their efforts serve as an "invisible hand" that helps the economy grow and prosper through the production of needed goods, services, and ideas. Thus, the phrase **invisible hand** is used to describe the process that turns self-directed gain into social and economic benefits for *all*.

How do people working in their own self-interest produce goods, services, and wealth for others? The only way farmers can become wealthy is to sell some of their crops to others. To become even wealthier, they have to hire workers to produce more food. So the farmers' self-centered efforts to become wealthy lead to jobs for some and food for almost all. Think about that process for a minute, because it is critical to understanding economic growth in the United States and other free countries. The same principles apply to everything from clothing to houses to iPhones.

Smith assumed that as people became wealthier, they would naturally reach out to help the less fortunate in the community. That has not always happened. In fact, today the poverty rate in the United States remains high and there is a great disparity between the amount of money the wealthy have and the amount of money poor people have.[12] This "inequality" is the central concern of many political, religious, and social leaders today.[13] Many businesspeople are becoming more concerned about social issues and their obligation to return to society some of what they've earned. The Giving Pledge, a philanthropic initiative started by billionaires Bill Gates and Warren Buffett, encourages the world's wealthiest individuals and families to donate the majority of their wealth to support causes related to poverty, health issues,

invisible hand

A phrase coined by Adam Smith to describe the process that turns self-directed gain into social and economic benefits for all.

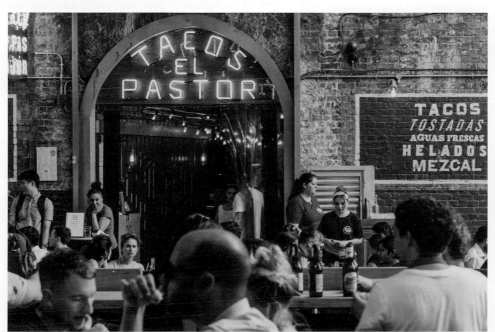

Alena Kravchenko/Alamy Stock Photo

According to Adam Smith's theory, business owners are motivated to work hard because they know they will earn, and keep, the rewards of their labor. When they prosper, as the owner of this restaurant has, they are able to add employees and grow, indirectly helping the community and the larger economy grow in the process. What might motivate you to start your own business?

and education.[14] Still, the economic question remains: What can and should we do about poverty and unemployment in the United States and around the world?

As we mentioned in Chapter 1, it is important for businesses to be ethical as well as generous. Unethical practices undermine the whole economic system.

?TESTPREP

- What is the difference between macroeconomics and microeconomics?
- What is better for an economy than teaching a man to fish?
- What does Adam Smith's term *invisible hand* mean? How does the invisible hand create wealth for a country?

LO 2–2 Explain what capitalism is and how free markets work.

Understanding Free-Market Capitalism

Basing their ideas on free-market principles such as those of Adam Smith, businesspeople in the United States, Europe, Japan, Canada, and other countries began to create more wealth than ever before. They hired others to work on their farms and in their factories, and their nations began to prosper as a result. Businesspeople soon became the wealthiest people in society.

However, great disparities in wealth remained or even increased. Many businesspeople owned large homes and fancy carriages while most workers lived in humble surroundings. Nonetheless, there was always the promise of better times. One way to gain wealth was to start a successful business of your own. Of course, it wasn't that easy—it never has been. Then and now, you have to accumulate some money to buy or start a business, and you have to work long hours to make it grow. But the opportunities are there.

capitalism

An economic system in which all or most of the factors of production and distribution are privately owned and operated for profit.

The economic system that has led to wealth creation in much of the world is known as capitalism. Under **capitalism** all or most of the factors of production and distribution—such as land, factories, railroads, and stores—are owned by individuals. They are operated for profit, and businesspeople, not government officials, decide what to produce and how much, what to charge, and how much to pay workers. They also decide whether to produce goods in their own countries or have them made in other countries. No country is purely capitalist, however. Often the government gets involved in issues such as determining minimum wages, setting farm prices, and lending money to some failing businesses—as it does in the United States. But capitalism is the *foundation* of the U.S. economic system, and of the economies of England, Australia, Canada, and most other industrialized nations.

Capitalism, like all economic systems, has its faults.[15] For example, income inequality is a major issue that concerns many today.[16] However, John Mackey, CEO of Whole Foods, believes that "conscious capitalism," that is, capitalism based on businesses that serve all major stakeholders, not just stockholders, is the best system in the world. Marc Benioff, CEO of Salesforce, concurs and uses the term *compassionate capitalism.* He believes that not just businesses but also stakeholders—from customers to environmentalists—should share in the benefits of capitalism.[17]

state capitalism

A combination of freer markets and some government control.

Some countries have noticed the advantages of capitalism and have instituted what has become known as state capitalism. **State capitalism** is a combination of freer markets and some government control. China, for example, has had rapid growth as a result of state capitalism—that is, freer markets and less government control even though the country is controlled by the Communist Party.[18]

Under free-market capitalism, people have four basic rights:

1. *The right to own private property.* This is the most fundamental of all rights under capitalism. Private ownership means that individuals can buy, sell, and use land, buildings, machinery, inventions, and other forms of property. They can also pass on property to their children. Would farmers work as hard if they didn't own the land and couldn't keep the profits from what they earned?

2. *The right to own a business and keep all that business's profits.* Recall from Chapter 1 that profits equal revenues minus expenses (salaries, materials, taxes). Profits act as important incentives for business owners.

3. *The right to freedom of competition.* Within certain guidelines established by the government, individuals are free to compete with other individuals or businesses in selling and promoting goods and services.

4. *The right to freedom of choice.* People are free to choose where they want to work and what career they want to follow. Other choices people are free to make include where to live and what to buy or sell.

One benefit of the four basic rights of capitalism is that people are willing to take more risks than they might otherwise. President Franklin Roosevelt believed four additional freedoms were essential to economic success: freedom of speech and expression, freedom to worship in your own way, freedom from want, and freedom from fear. Do you see the benefits of these additional freedoms?

Now let's explore how the free market works. What role do consumers play in the process? How do businesses learn what consumers need and want? These questions and more are answered next.

How Free Markets Work

A free market is one in which decisions about what and how much to produce are made by the market—by buyers and sellers negotiating prices for goods and services. You and I and other consumers send signals to tell producers what to make, how many, in what color, and so on. We do that by choosing to buy (or not to buy) certain products and services.

Photography by Virginia Harold

After years of planning and saving, Jessica Douglass (left) purchased a building with plenty of room to grow and started a business called Flowers and Weeds. The right to own private property and the right to own a business and keep its profits are two of the fundamental rights that exist in the economic system called free-market capitalism. Would either of these rights be viable without the other?

For example, if all of us decided we wanted T-shirts supporting our favorite baseball team, the clothing industry would respond in certain ways. Manufacturers and retailers would increase the price of those T-shirts, because they know people are willing to pay more for the shirts they want. They would also realize they could make more money by making more of those T-shirts. Thus, they have an incentive to pay workers to start earlier and end later. Further, the number of companies making T-shirts would increase. How many T-shirts they make depends on how many we request or buy in the stores or online. Prices and quantities will continue to change as the number of T-shirts we buy changes.

The same process occurs with most other products. The *price* tells producers how much to produce. If something is wanted but isn't available, the price tends to go up until someone begins making more of that product, sells the ones already on hand, or makes a substitute. As a consequence, there's rarely a long-term shortage of goods in the United States.

How Prices Are Determined

In a free market, *prices are not determined by sellers;* they are determined by buyers and sellers negotiating in the marketplace. For example, a seller may want to receive $50 for a T-shirt, but the quantity buyers demand at that high price may be quite low. If the seller lowers the price, the quantity demanded is likely to increase. How is a price determined that is acceptable to both buyers and sellers? The answer is found in the microeconomic concepts of supply and demand. We shall explore both next.

The Economic Concept of Supply

supply

The quantity of products that manufacturers or owners are willing to sell at different prices at a specific time.

Supply refers to the quantities of products manufacturers or owners are willing to sell at different prices at a specific time. Generally speaking, the amount supplied will increase as the price increases because sellers can make more money with a higher price.

Economists show this relationship between quantity supplied and price on a graph. Figure 2.1 shows a simple supply curve for T-shirts. The price of the shirts in dollars is shown vertically on the left of the graph. The quantity of shirts sellers are willing to supply is shown horizontally at the bottom of the graph. The various points on the curve indicate how many T-shirts sellers would provide at different prices. For example, at a price

The economic concept of demand measures the quantities of goods and services that people are willing to buy at a given price. All else equal, the lower the price, the higher the demand will be. Do you think there would be this many customers rushing to shop on Black Friday if it wasn't for those low-price/low-quantity deals?

Nelson Antoine/Shutterstock

of $5 a shirt, a T-shirt vendor would provide only 5 shirts, but at $50 a shirt the vendor would supply 50 shirts. The supply curve indicates the relationship between the price and the quantity supplied. All things being equal, the higher the price, the more the vendor will be willing to supply.

The Economic Concept of Demand

Demand refers to the quantity of products that people are willing to buy at different prices at a specific time. Generally speaking, the quantity demanded will increase as the price decreases. Again, we can show the relationship between price and quantity demanded in a graph. Figure 2.2 shows a simple demand curve for T-shirts. The various points on the graph indicate the quantity demanded at various prices. For example, at $45, buyers demand just 5 shirts, but at $5, the quantity demanded would increase to 35 shirts. All things being equal, the lower the price, the more buyers are willing to buy.

demand
The quantity of products that people are willing to buy at different prices at a specific time.

The Equilibrium Point, or Market Price

You might realize from Figures 2.1 and 2.2 that the key factor in determining the quantities supplied and demanded is *price*. If you were to lay the two graphs one on top of the other, the supply curve and the demand curve would cross where quantity demanded and quantity supplied are equal. Figure 2.3 illustrates that point. At a price of $15, the quantity of T-shirts demanded and the quantity supplied are equal (25 shirts). That crossing point is known as the *equilibrium point* or *equilibrium price*. In the long run, that price will become the market price. **Market price**, then, is determined by supply and demand. It is the price toward which the market will trend.

Proponents of a free market argue that, because supply and demand interactions determine prices, there is no need for the government to set prices. If quantity supplied exceeds quantity demanded, the resulting surplus signals sellers to lower the price. If shortages develop because the quantity supplied is less than quantity demanded, it signals sellers

market price
The price determined by supply and demand.

 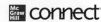 **connect**

▶ **iSeeit!** Need help understanding supply and demand? Visit your Connect eBook to view a video for a brief animated explanation.

FIGURE 2.1 THE SUPPLY CURVE AT VARIOUS PRICES

The supply curve rises from left to right. Think it through. The higher the price of T-shirts goes (the vertical axis), the more sellers will be willing to supply.

FIGURE 2.2 THE DEMAND CURVE AT VARIOUS PRICES

This is a simple demand curve showing the quantity of T-shirts demanded at different prices. The demand curve falls from left to right. It is easy to understand why. The lower the price of T-shirts, the higher the quantity demanded.

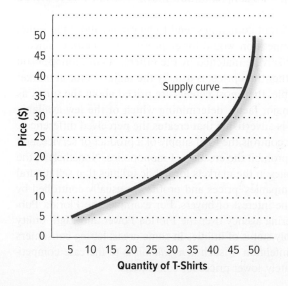

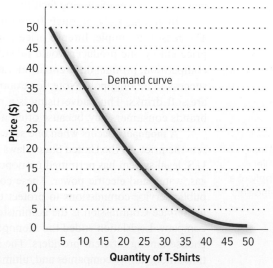

FIGURE 2.3 THE EQUILIBRIUM POINT
The place where quantity demanded and quantity supplied meet is called the equilibrium point. When we put both the supply and demand curves on the same graph, we find that they intersect at a price where the quantity supplied and the quantity demanded are equal. In the long run, the market price will tend toward the equilibrium point.

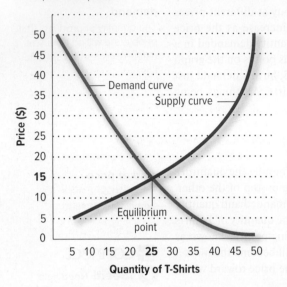

perfect competition
The degree of competition in which there are many sellers in a market and none is large enough to dictate the price of a product.

monopolistic competition
The degree of competition in which a large number of sellers produce very similar products that buyers nevertheless perceive as different.

oligopoly
A degree of competition in which just a few sellers dominate the market.

monopoly
A degree of competition in which only one seller controls the total supply of a product or service, and sets the price.

to increase the price. Eventually, supply will again equal demand if nothing interferes with market forces.

The Making Ethical Decisions box raises an interesting question about when pricing may be a bit out of control and what to do about it. In countries without a free market, there is no mechanism to reveal to businesses (via price) what to produce and in what amounts, so there are often shortages (not enough products) or surpluses (too many products). In such countries, the government decides what to produce and in what quantity, but without price signals it has no way of knowing what the proper quantities are. Furthermore, when the government interferes in otherwise free markets, such as when it subsidizes farm goods, surpluses and shortages may develop. Competition differs in free markets, too. We shall explore that concept next.

Competition within Free Markets

Economists generally agree there are four different degrees of competition: (1) perfect competition, (2) monopolistic competition, (3) oligopoly, and (4) monopoly.

Perfect competition exists when there are many sellers in a market and none is large enough to dictate the price of a product. Sellers' products appear to be identical, such as agricultural products like apples, corn, and potatoes. However, there are no true examples of perfect competition. Today, government price supports and drastic reductions in the number of farms make it hard to argue that even farming represents perfect competition.

Under **monopolistic competition** a large number of sellers produce very similar products that buyers nevertheless perceive as different, such as hot dogs, sodas, laptop computers, and T-shirts. Product differentiation—the attempt to make buyers think similar products are different in some way—is a key to success. Think about what that means. Through advertising, branding, and packaging, sellers try to convince buyers that their products are different from competitors', though they may be very similar or even interchangeable. The fast-food industry, with its pricing battles among hamburger offerings and the like, offers a good example of monopolistic competition.

An **oligopoly** is a degree of competition in which just a few sellers dominate a market, as we see in tobacco, gasoline, automobiles, aluminum, and aircraft. One reason some industries remain in the hands of a few sellers is that the initial investment required to enter the business often is tremendous. Think, for example, of how much it would cost to start a new airplane manufacturing facility.

In an oligopoly, products from different companies tend to be priced about the same. The reason is simple: Intense price competition would lower profits for everyone, since a price cut by one producer would most likely be matched by the others. As in monopolistic competition, product differentiation, rather than price, is usually the major factor in market success in an oligopoly. Note, for example, that most cereals are priced about the same, as are soft drinks. Thus, advertising is a major factor determining which of the few available brands consumers buy, because often it is advertising that creates the perceived differences.

A **monopoly** occurs when one seller controls the total supply of a product or service, and sets the price. In the United States, laws prohibit the creation of monopolies. Nonetheless, the U.S. legal system has permitted monopolies in the markets for public utilities that sell natural gas, water, and electric power. These companies' prices and profits are usually controlled by public service commissions to protect the interest of buyers. For example, the Florida Public Service Commission is the administering agency over the Florida Power and Light utility company. Legislation ended the monopoly status of utilities in some areas, letting consumers choose among different providers. The intention of such *deregulation* is to increase competition among utility companies and, ultimately, lower prices for consumers.

Your company, a large pharmaceutical firm, acquired a drug called Relivoform when it bought a generic drugmaker. The purchased company was the market's leading supplier of the drug, and it was by far its most profitable product. Relivoform is a major chemotherapy drug important in the treatment of liver cancer. It costs $300 per treatment, and many patients rely on it to control the spread of their cancer.

Currently, your company has many new drugs in development costing the company millions in research and testing. It may be years before the Food and Drug Administration approves the new drugs and you can get them into the market. Your finance committee has recommended increasing the price of Relivoform to $3,000 per treatment to help alleviate the development costs of new drugs. Since your company now controls the distribution of the drug (even though it's a generic), you doubt any competitors could immediately impact your market. When word leaked out that Relivoform's price may increase 10-fold, the

fluxfoto/Getty Images

public reacted with rage, accusing your firm of favoring profits over patients' needs. Will you follow your committee's recommendation and raise the price? What are your alternatives? What might be the consequences of each?

Benefits and Limitations of Free Markets

One benefit of the free market is that it allows open competition among companies. Businesses must provide customers with high-quality products at fair prices with good service. If they don't, they lose customers to businesses that do. Do government services have the same incentives?

The free market—with its competition and incentives—was a major factor in creating the wealth that industrialized countries now enjoy. Free-market capitalism, more than any other economic system, provides opportunities for poor people to work their way out of poverty. Capitalism also encourages businesses to be more efficient so they can successfully compete on price and quality. Would you say that the United States is increasing or decreasing the emphasis on capitalism? Why?

Yet, even as free-market capitalism has brought prosperity to the United States and to much of the rest of the world, it has brought inequality as well. Business owners and managers usually make more money and have more wealth than lower-level workers.[19] Yet people who are older, disabled, or sick may not be able to start and manage a business, and others may not have the talent or the drive. What should society do about such inequality?

Unfortunately, one of the dangers of free markets is that some people let greed dictate how they act. Criminal and ethics charges brought against some big businesses in banking, accounting, telecommunications, and pharmaceuticals indicate the scope of the potential problem. Some businesspeople have deceived the public about their products; others have deceived stockholders about the value of their stock, all in order to increase executives' personal assets.

Clearly, some government laws and regulations are necessary to protect businesses' stakeholders and make sure people who cannot work get the basic care they need. To overcome some of capitalism's limitations, some countries have adopted an economic system called socialism. It, too, has its good and bad points. We explore these after you review the following Test Prep questions.

- What are the four basic rights that people have under free-market capitalism?
- How do businesspeople know what to produce and in what quantity?
- How are prices determined?
- What are the four degrees of competition, and what are some examples of each?

socialism
An economic system based on the premise that some, if not most, basic businesses should be owned by the government so that profits can be more evenly distributed among the people.

brain drain
The loss of the best and brightest people to other countries.

Socialism has been more successful in some countries than in others. This photo shows Denmark's clean and modern public transportation system. In Greece, overspending caused a debt crisis that forced the government to impose austerity measures that many Greeks oppose. What other factors might lead to slower growth in socialist countries?

LO 2–3   **Compare socialism and communism.**

Understanding Socialism

Socialism is an economic system based on the premise that some, if not most, basic businesses (e.g., steel mills, coal mines, and utilities) should be owned by the government so that profits can be more evenly distributed among the people. Entrepreneurs often own and run smaller businesses, and individuals are often taxed relatively steeply to pay for social programs. The top federal personal income tax rate in the United States, for example, was 37 percent recently, but in some socialist countries the top rate can be as much as 61 percent.[20] Whereas U.S. shoppers pay sales taxes ranging from over 10 percent in Chicago to zero in Delaware, some socialist countries charge a similar value-added tax of 15 to 20 percent or more.[21] Socialists acknowledge the major benefit of capitalism—wealth creation—but believe that wealth should be more evenly distributed than occurs in free-market capitalism. They believe the government should carry out the distribution and be much more involved in protecting the environment and providing for the poor.

The Benefits of Socialism

The major benefit of socialism is supposed to be social equality. Ideally it comes about because the government takes income from wealthier people, in the form of taxes, and redistributes it to poorer people through various government programs. Free education through college, free health care, and free child care are some of the benefits socialist governments, using the money from taxes, may provide to their people. Workers in socialist countries usually get longer vacations, work fewer hours per week, and have more employee benefits (e.g., generous sick leave) than those in countries where free-market capitalism prevails.

Oliver Foerstner/Shutterstock

The Negative Consequences of Socialism

Socialism promises to create more equality than capitalism, but it takes away some of businesspeople's incentives. For example, when socialist Francois Hollande became president of France, the top tax rate reached 75 percent, with many citizens paying over 70 percent. This caused many innovators, creative thinkers, doctors, lawyers, business owners, and others who earned a lot of money to leave France. This loss of the best and brightest people to other countries is called a **brain drain**.

Imagine an experiment in socialism in your own class. Imagine that after the first exam, those with grades of 90 and above have to give some of their points to those who make 70 and below so that everyone ends up with grades in the 80s. Would those who got 90s study as hard for the second exam? What about those who got 70s? Can you see why workers may not work as hard or as well if they all get the same benefits regardless of how hard they work?

Socialism also tends to result in fewer inventions and less innovation, because those who come up with new ideas usually don't receive as much reward as they would in a capitalist system. Communism may be considered a more intensive version of socialism. We shall explore that system next.

Understanding Communism

Communism is an economic and political system in which the government makes almost all economic decisions and owns almost all the major factors of production. It intrudes further into the lives of people than socialism does. For example, some communist countries have not allowed their citizens to practice certain religions, change jobs, or move to the town of their choice.

One problem with communism is that the government has no way of knowing what to produce, because prices don't reflect supply and demand as they do in free markets. The government must guess what the people need. As a result, shortages of many items, including food and clothing, may develop. Another problem is that communism doesn't inspire businesspeople to work hard because the incentives are not there. Communist countries such as North Korea and Cuba are suffering severe economic depression. People in North Korea suffer continued economic hardships, with food shortage common.[22] In Cuba, people suffer a lack of goods and services readily available in most other countries.[23] Therefore, communism is slowly disappearing as an economic form. Today, only China, North Korea, Vietnam, Laos, and Cuba are communist countries.

Eric Feferberg/AFP/Getty Images

communism
An economic and political system in which the government makes almost all economic decisions and owns almost all the major factors of production.

Starting in the 1990s, Russia made the major change from communism toward a viable market economy. Still, there are few laws in place that help promote small businesses, and an active black market remains for many goods. This "shadow economy" represents as much as 20 percent of the country's GDP. Why are black markets bad for economic growth?

LO 2–4 Analyze the trend toward mixed economies.

The Trend toward Mixed Economies

The nations of the world have largely been divided between those that followed the concepts of capitalism and those that adopted the concepts of communism or socialism. We can now further contrast the two major economic systems as follows:

1. **Free-market economies** exist when the market largely determines what goods and services get produced, who gets them, and how the economy grows. *Capitalism* is the popular term for this economic system.

2. **Command economies** exist when the government largely decides what goods and services will be produced, who gets them, and how the economy will grow. *Socialism* and *communism* are variations on this economic system.

Although all countries actually have some mix of the two systems, neither free-market nor command economies have resulted in optimal economic conditions. Free-market mechanisms don't seem to respond enough to the needs of those who are poor, elderly, or disabled. Some people also believe that businesses in free-market economies have not done enough to protect the environment. Over time, free-market countries, such as the United States, have adopted many social and environmental programs such as Social Security, welfare, unemployment compensation, and various clean air and water acts.

Socialism and communism haven't always created enough jobs or wealth to keep economies growing fast enough. Thus, communist governments are disappearing, and some

free-market economies
Economic systems in which the market largely determines what goods and services get produced, who gets them, and how the economy grows.

command economies
Economic systems in which the government largely decides what goods and services will be produced, who will get them, and how the economy will grow.

mixed economies
Economic systems in which some allocation of resources is made by the market and some by the government.

socialist governments have been cutting back on social programs and lowering taxes on businesses and workers to generate more business growth and more revenue.

The trend, then, has been for mostly capitalist countries (like the United States) to move toward socialism (e.g., more government involvement in health care), and for some socialist countries to move toward capitalism (more private businesses, lower taxes). All countries, therefore, have some mix of the two systems. Thus, the long-term global trend is toward a blend of capitalism and socialism. The net effect is the emergence throughout the world of mixed economies.

Mixed economies exist where some allocation of resources is made by the market and some by the government. Most countries don't have a name for such a system. If free-market mechanisms allocate most resources, the leaders call their system capitalism. If the government allocates most resources, the leaders call it socialism. Figure 2.4 compares the various economic systems.

Like most other nations of the world, the United States has a mixed economy. The U.S. government is the largest employer in the country, which means there are more workers in the public sector (government) than in any of the major businesses (e.g., Walmart, General Electric) in the United States.[24] Do you think the government will continue to grow or decline in the coming years?

TESTPREP

- What led to the emergence of socialism?
- What are the benefits and drawbacks of socialism?
- What countries still practice communism?
- What are the characteristics of a mixed economy?

LO 2–5 Describe the economic system of the United States, including the significance of key economic indicators (especially GDP), productivity, and the business cycle.

Understanding the U.S. Economic System

The following sections will introduce the terms and concepts that you, as an informed student and citizen, will need to understand in order to grasp the issues facing government and business leaders in the United States.

Key Economic Indicators

Three major indicators of economic conditions are (1) the gross domestic product (GDP), (2) the unemployment rate, and (3) price indexes. Another important economic indicator is the increase or decrease in productivity. When you read business literature, you'll see these terms used again and again. Let's explore what they mean.

gross domestic product (GDP)
The total value of final goods and services produced in a country in a given year.

Gross Domestic Product Gross domestic product (GDP), which we mentioned briefly in Chapter 1, is the total value of final goods and services produced in a country in a given year. Both domestic and foreign-owned companies can produce the goods and services included in GDP, as long as the companies are located within the country's boundaries. For example, production values from Japanese automaker Honda's factory in Ohio are included in U.S. GDP. Revenue generated by Ford's factory in Mexico is included in Mexico's GDP, even though Ford is a U.S. company.

Almost every discussion about a nation's economy is based on GDP. If growth in GDP slows or declines, businesses may feel many negative effects. A major influence on the growth of GDP is the productivity of the workforce—that is, how much output workers create with a given

FIGURE 2.4 COMPARISONS OF KEY ECONOMIC SYSTEMS

	CAPITALISM* (United States)	SOCIALISM (Sweden)	COMMUNISM (North Korea)	MIXED ECONOMY (Germany)
Social and Economic Goals	Private ownership of land and business. Liberty and the pursuit of happiness. Free trade. Emphasis on freedom and the profit motive for economic growth.	Public ownership of major businesses. Some private ownership of smaller businesses and shops. Government control of education, health care, utilities, mining, transportation, and media. Very high taxation. Emphasis on equality.	Public ownership of all businesses. Government-run education and health care. Emphasis on equality. Many limitations on freedom, including freedom to own businesses and to assemble to protest government actions.	Private ownership of land and business with government regulation. Government control of some institutions (e.g., mail). High taxation for defense and the common welfare. Emphasis on a balance between freedom and equality.
Motivation of Workers	Much incentive to work efficiently and hard because profits are retained by owners. Workers are rewarded for high productivity.	Capitalist incentives exist in private businesses. Government control of wages in public institutions limits incentives.	Very little incentive to work hard or to produce quality goods or services.	Incentives are similar to capitalism except in government-owned enterprises, which may have fewer incentives.
Control over Markets	Complete freedom of trade within and among nations. Some government control of markets.	Some markets are controlled by the government and some are free. Trade restrictions among nations vary and include some free-trade agreements.	Total government control over markets except for illegal transactions.	Some government control of trade within and among nations (trade protectionism).
Choices in the Market	A wide variety of goods and services is available. Almost no scarcity or over-supply exists for long because supply and demand control the market.	Variety in the marketplace varies considerably from country to country. Choice is directly related to government involvement in markets.	Very little choice among competing goods.	Similar to capitalism, but scarcity and oversupply may be caused by government involvement in the market (e.g., subsidies for farms).
Social Freedoms	Freedom of speech, press, assembly, religion, job choice, movement, and elections.	Similar to mixed economy. Governments may restrict job choice, movement among countries, and who may attend upper-level schools (i.e., college).	Very limited freedom to protest the government, practice religion, or change houses or jobs.	Some restrictions on freedoms of assembly and speech. Separation of church and state may limit religious practices in schools.

*The United States is a mixed economy based on a foundation of capitalism.

amount of input. GDP can also be affected by the fortunes of major U.S. firms. For example, when Boeing was forced to stop production of the 737 MAX, the cost to the company, as well as many of its suppliers, was severely impacted. Airlines such as Southwest also suffered revenue losses due to the grounding of the aircraft. Such losses have a negative effect on GDP.[25]

The level of U.S. economic activity is actually larger than the GDP figures show, because those figures don't take into account illicit activities in the underground economy such as sales of illegal drugs, off-the-books transactions, and unauthorized gambling.[26] The high GDP in the United States is what enables its citizens to enjoy a high standard of living.

gross output (GO)

A measure of total sales volume at all stages of production.

Although the country relies on GDP data, the accuracy of the data (at least in the short run) is questionable. Starting in the spring of 2014, the United States Bureau of Economic Analysis at the Commerce Department reports a statistic called gross output (GO). **Gross output (GO)** is a measure of total sales volume at all stages of production. GO is almost twice the size of GDP and is considered a better indicator of the business cycle and more consistent with economic growth theory.[27] It shows that consumer spending is the effect, not the cause, of prosperity.

unemployment rate

The percentage of civilians at least 16 years old who are unemployed and tried to find a job within the prior four weeks.

The Unemployment Rate
The **unemployment rate** refers to the percentage of civilians at least 16 years old who are unemployed *and tried to find a job within the prior four weeks.* The unemployment rate was over 7 percent in 2013 and was down to 3.5 percent in early 2020. The COVID-19 pandemic resulted in a dramatic rise in unemployment to 14.7 percent in mid-2020 (see Figure 2.5).[28] Most economists consider a rate of 4 or 5 percent to be functionally full employment. However, many argue that the standard unemployment statistics don't accurately measure the pain being felt by those who have been unemployed for a long time or those who have simply given up looking for a job. For this reason, they believe the real unemployment rate gives a more accurate picture of unemployment. The *real unemployment rate* is comprised of those included in the standard unemployment rate plus those who are underemployed, discouraged, and marginally attached (those who have looked for a job within the last *year*). The real unemployment rate is typically double the standard rate.[29] Some believe that government benefits (i.e., unemployment benefits) may lead to more unemployment. Do you agree?

Figure 2.6 describes the four types of unemployment: frictional, structural, cyclical, and seasonal. The United States tries to protect those who are unemployed because of recessions (defined later in the chapter), industry shifts, and other cyclical factors. Which type of unemployment seems to be the most serious to the economy?

inflation

A general rise in the prices of goods and services over time.

Inflation and Price Indexes
Price indexes help gauge the health of the economy by measuring the levels of inflation, disinflation, deflation, and stagflation. **Inflation** is a general rise in the prices of goods and services over time. The official definition is "a persistent increase in the level of consumer prices or a persistent decline in the purchasing power of money, caused by an increase in available currency and credit beyond the proportion of goods and services."[30] Thus, it is also described as "too many dollars chasing too few goods." Go back and review the laws of supply and demand to see how that works. Rapid

FIGURE 2.5 U.S. UNEMPLOYMENT RATE 1989–2020

FIGURE 2.6 FOUR TYPES
OF UNEMPLOYMENT

Frictional unemployment

Frictional unemployment refers to those people who have quit work because they didn't like the job, the boss, or the working conditions and who haven't yet found a new job. It also refers to those people who are entering the labor force for the first time (e.g., new graduates) or are returning to the labor force after significant time away (e.g., parents who reared children). There will always be some frictional unemployment because it takes some time to find a first job or a new job.

Structural unemployment

Structural unemployment refers to unemployment caused by the restructuring of firms or by a mismatch between the skills (or location) of job seekers and the requirements (or location) of available jobs (e.g., coal miners in an area where mines have been closed).

Cyclical unemployment

Cyclical unemployment occurs because of a recession or a similar downturn in the business cycle (the ups and downs of business growth and decline over time). This type of unemployment is the most serious.

Seasonal unemployment

Seasonal unemployment occurs where demand for labor varies over the year, as with the harvesting of crops.

FIGURE 2.6 FOUR TYPES OF UNEMPLOYMENT

inflation is scary. If the prices of goods and services go up by just 7 percent a year, they will double in about 10 years. The Reaching beyond Our Borders box highlights several examples of inflation out of control—way out of control.

Disinflation occurs when price increases are slowing (the inflation rate is declining). That was the situation in the United States throughout the 1990s. **Deflation** means that prices are declining. It occurs when countries produce so many goods that people cannot afford to buy them all (too few dollars are chasing too many goods). While declining prices might sound good, it's an indication that economic conditions are deteriorating.[31] **Stagflation** occurs when the economy is slowing but prices are going up anyhow.[32]

The **consumer price index (CPI)** consists of monthly statistics that measure the pace of inflation or deflation. The government can compute the cost of goods and services, including housing, food, apparel, and medical care, to see whether or not they are going up or down.[33] Today, however, the government is relying more on the measure of **core inflation**. That means the CPI minus food and energy costs. Since the cost of food and energy can have temporary price shocks, the inflation measures reported (core inflation) are actually lower than real costs. The CPI is important to you because some wages and salaries, rents and leases, tax brackets, government benefits, and interest rates are based on that data.

The **producer price index (PPI)** measures the change in prices at the wholesale level. It tracks price changes in nearly all industries in the goods-producing sectors of the U.S. economy.[34] Other indicators of the economy's condition include housing starts, retail sales, and changes in personal income. You can learn more about such indicators by reading business periodicals, listening to business broadcasts on radio and television, and exploring business sites online.

Productivity in the United States

An increase in productivity means a worker can produce more goods and services than before in the same time period, usually thanks to machinery, technology, or other equipment. Productivity in the United States has risen because computers and other technology

disinflation
A situation in which price increases are slowing (the inflation rate is declining).

deflation
A situation in which prices are declining.

stagflation
A situation when the economy is slowing but prices are going up anyhow.

consumer price index (CPI)
Monthly statistics that measure the pace of inflation or deflation.

core inflation
CPI minus food and energy costs.

producer price index (PPI)
An index that measures the change in prices at the wholesale level.

How a Stack of Cash Can Become Worthless

How would you react if prices for everyday goods like food and toiletries doubled every 19 days? It's probably difficult to even imagine, but that's what happened toward the end of 2018 in Venezuela due to extreme hyperinflation.

Hyperinflation is when the price of goods and services rises by 50 percent a month. It often starts when a country's government prints more money to pay for excess spending. In Venezuela, the inflation rate climbed from 63 percent in 2014 to 481 percent in 2016. Then in 2018, the International Monetary Fund estimated that the country's annual inflation rate shot up by a whopping 1.37 million percent. Venezuela's currency, the Bolivar, collapsed so low that cash to pay for goods and services was being weighed instead of counted. As a result, more than 3 million Venezuelans have left the country in recent years as they struggle to afford even basic items.

Venezuela is not the first country to suffer the ravages of hyperinflation. German hyperinflation was a classic example after World War I, when prices were doubling every three days. Pictures of Germans pushing wheelbarrows full of cash to buy a loaf of bread were common. Zimbabwe had hyperinflation from 2004 to 2009. Its economy faced an inflation rate of 98 percent a day, with prices doubling every 24 hours. To prevent anything like this from happening in the United States, the Federal Reserve maintains the money supply and carefully sets interest rates so that inflation stays under control.

Sources: Siobhán O'Grady, Chris Alcantara, and Armand Emamdjomeh, "Venezuela's Crisis in 5 Charts," *The Washington Post*, washingtonpost.com, January 26, 2019; "Venezuela: All You Need to Know about the Crisis in Nine Charts," *BBC*, bbc.com, February 4, 2019; Virginia López Glass, "Nothing Can Prepare You for Life with Hyperinflation," *The New York Times*, February 12, 2019.

Manaure Quintero/Bloomberg/Getty Images

have made production faster and easier. The higher productivity is, the lower the costs are of producing goods and services, and the lower prices can be. Therefore, businesspeople are eager to increase productivity. Remember, however, that high productivity through computers and robots can lead to high unemployment. Until recently, automation affected primarily factory and clerical jobs. Today, with the rising use of artificial intelligence, even highly skilled, white-collar workers will be vulnerable.[35]

Now that the U.S. economy is a service economy, productivity is an issue because service firms are so labor-intensive. Spurred by foreign competition, productivity in the manufacturing sector is rising rapidly. In the service sector, productivity is growing more slowly because service workers have fewer new technologies available than there are for factory workers. However, that may change if the use of artificial intelligence grows as predicted.

Productivity in the Service Sector

One problem with the service industry is that an influx of machinery and technology may add to the quality of the service provided but not to the output per worker. For example, you've probably noticed how many computers there are on college campuses. They add to the quality of education but don't necessarily boost professors' productivity. The same is true of some equipment in hospitals, such as CAT scanners, PET scanners, and MRI scanners. They improve patient care but don't necessarily increase the number of patients doctors can see. In other words, today's productivity measures in the service industry fail to capture the increase in quality created by new technology.

Clearly, the United States and other countries need to develop new measures of productivity for the service economy that include quality as well as quantity of output. Despite growing productivity improvement, the economy is likely to go through a series of ups and downs, much as it has over the past several years. We'll explore that process next.

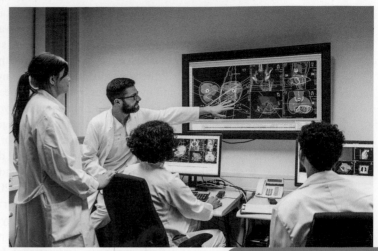

Tom Werner/Digital Vision/Getty Images

The Business Cycle

Business cycles are the periodic rises and falls that occur in economies over time. Economists look at a number of business cycles, from seasonal cycles that occur within a year to cycles that occur every 48–60 years.

Economist Joseph Schumpeter identified the four phases of long-term business cycles as boom–recession–depression–recovery:

1. An *economic boom* is just what it sounds like—business is booming.

2. **Recession** is two or more consecutive quarters of decline in the GDP. In a recession prices fall, people purchase fewer products, and businesses fail. A recession brings high unemployment, increased business failures, and an overall drop in living standards.

3. A **depression** is a severe recession, usually accompanied by deflation. Business cycles rarely go through a depression phase. In fact, while there were many business cycles during the 20th century, there was only one severe depression (1930s).

4. A *recovery* occurs when the economy stabilizes and starts to grow. This eventually leads to an economic boom, starting the cycle all over again.

One goal of economists is to predict such ups and downs. That is very difficult to do. Business cycles are identified according to facts, but we can explain those facts only by using theories. Therefore, we cannot predict with certainty. But one thing is certain: Over time, the economy will rise and fall as it has done lately.

Since dramatic swings up and down in the economy cause all kinds of disruptions to businesses, the government tries to minimize such changes. It uses fiscal policy and monetary policy to try to keep the economy from slowing too much or growing too rapidly.[36]

> **LO 2–6**   Contrast fiscal policy and monetary policy, and explain how each affects the economy.

Stabilizing the Economy through Fiscal Policy

Fiscal policy refers to the federal government's efforts to keep the economy stable by increasing or decreasing taxes or government spending. When the government employs fiscal policy it is following the basic economic theory of John Maynard Keynes.[37] **Keynesian economic theory** is the theory that a government policy of increasing spending and cutting taxes could stimulate the economy in a recession.[38]

It can be difficult to measure productivity in the service sector. New technology can improve the quality of services without necessarily increasing the number of people served. A doctor can make more-accurate diagnoses with scans, for instance, but still can see only so many patients in a day. How can productivity measures capture improvements in the quality of service?

business cycles
The periodic rises and falls that occur in economies over time.

recession
Two or more consecutive quarters of decline in the GDP.

depression
A severe recession, usually accompanied by deflation.

fiscal policy
The federal government's efforts to keep the economy stable by increasing or decreasing taxes or government spending.

Keynesian economic theory
The theory that a government policy of increasing spending and cutting taxes could stimulate the economy in a recession.

The first fiscal policy tool is taxation. Theoretically, high tax rates tend to slow the economy because they draw money away from the private sector and put it into the government. High tax rates may discourage small-business ownership because they decrease the profits businesses can earn and make the effort less rewarding. It follows, then, that low tax rates will theoretically give the economy a boost. When you count all fees, sales taxes, state taxes, and more, taxes on the highest-earning U.S. citizens could exceed 50 percent. Is that figure too high or not high enough in your opinion? Why?

national debt

The sum of government deficits over time.

The second fiscal policy tool is government spending on highways, social programs, education, infrastructure (e.g., roads, bridges, and utilities), defense, and so on. Such spending, however, can increase the national deficit.[39] The national deficit is the amount of money the federal government spends beyond what it collects in taxes for a given fiscal year.[40] The deficit was almost $600 billion in 2016. It ballooned to over $800 billion in 2018 and was $1.1 trillion in 2020.[41] Economists attribute this increased deficit to less money coming in due to recent tax cuts and more money going out due to retiring Baby Boomers and health care costs.[42] Such deficits increase the national debt. The **national debt** is the sum of government deficits over time. The national debt is now more than $26 trillion (see Figure 2.7).[43] If the government takes in more revenue than it spends (i.e., tax revenues exceed expenditures), there is a national *surplus*. That is not likely to happen soon.

FIGURE 2.7 THE NATIONAL DEBT

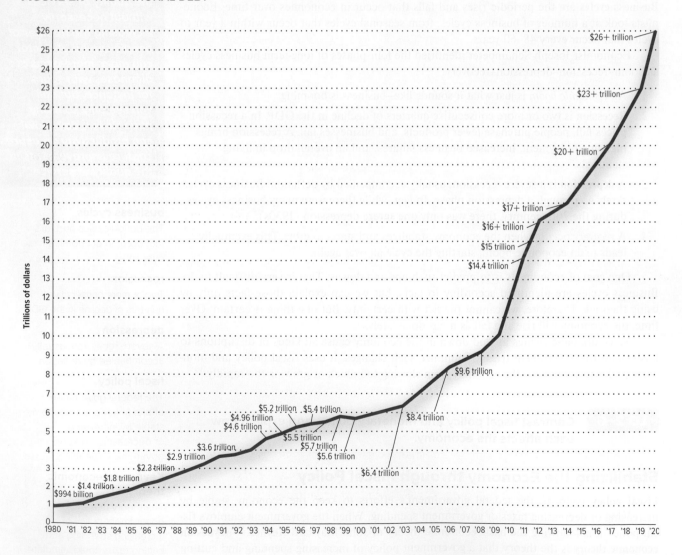

One way to lessen deficits is to cut government spending. Many presidents and those in Congress have promised to make the government "smaller," that is, to reduce government spending—unfortunately, that doesn't happen very often. Entitlements such as Social Security, Medicare, and Medicaid take a large portion of the federal budget and there always seems to be a need for new social programs each year. Thus the deficits continue and add to the national debt. Some people believe that government spending helps the economy grow. Others believe that the money the government spends comes out of the pockets of consumers and businesspeople, and thus slows growth. What do you think?

Using Monetary Policy to Keep the Economy Growing

Have you ever wondered what organization adds money to or subtracts money from the economy? The answer is the Federal Reserve Bank (the Fed). The Fed is a semiprivate organization that is not under the direct control of the government but does have members appointed by the president. We will discuss the Fed in detail when we look at banking in Chapter 20. Now we simply introduce monetary policy and the role of the Fed in controlling the economy. **Monetary policy** is the management of the money supply and interest rates by the Federal Reserve Bank. The Fed's most visible role is the raising and lowering of interest rates. When the economy is booming, the Fed tends to raise interest rates. This makes money more expensive to borrow. Businesses thus borrow less, and the economy slows as businesspeople spend less money on everything they need to grow, including labor and machinery. The opposite is true when the Fed lowers interest rates. Businesses tend to borrow more, and the economy is expected to grow. Raising and lowering interest rates should help control the rapid ups and downs of the economy.

The Fed also controls the money supply. A simple explanation of this function is that the more money the Fed makes available to businesspeople and others, the faster the economy is supposed to grow. To slow the economy (and prevent inflation), the Fed lowers the money supply.

To sum up, there are two major tools for managing the economy of the United States: fiscal policy (using government taxes and spending) and monetary policy (the Fed's control over interest rates and the money supply). The goal is to keep the economy growing so that more people can rise up the economic ladder and enjoy a higher standard of living and quality of life.

Scott Heins/Stringer/Getty Images

The financial crisis beginning in 2008 caused much anguish among Wall Street workers and people in general. How effective was the government's response?

monetary policy
The management of the money supply and interest rates by the Federal Reserve Bank.

TESTPREP

- Name the three economic indicators and describe how well the United States is doing based on each indicator.
- What's the difference between a recession and a depression?
- How does the government manage the economy using fiscal policy?
- What does the term *monetary policy* mean? What organization is responsible for monetary policy?

SUMMARY

LO 2–1   Explain basic economics.

What is economics?

Economics is the study of how society chooses to employ resources to produce goods and services and distribute them for consumption among various competing groups and individuals.

What are the two branches of economics?

There are two major branches of economics: *macroeconomics* studies the operation of a nation's economy as a whole, and *microeconomics* studies the behavior of people and organizations in particular markets (e.g., why people buy smaller cars when gas prices go up).

How can we be assured of having enough resources?

Resource development is the study of how to increase resources and create the conditions that will make better use of them.

How does capitalism create a climate for economic growth?

Under capitalism, businesspeople don't often deliberately set out to help others; they work mostly for their own prosperity and growth. Yet people's efforts to improve their own situation in life act like an *invisible hand* to help the economy grow and prosper through the production of needed goods, services, and ideas.

LO 2–2   Explain what capitalism is and how free markets work.

What is capitalism?

Capitalism is an economic system in which all or most of the means of production and distribution are privately owned and operated for profit.

Who decides what to produce under capitalism?

In capitalist countries, businesspeople decide what to produce, how much to pay workers, and how much to charge for goods and services. They also decide whether to produce certain goods in their own countries, import those goods, or have them made in other countries.

What is state capitalism?

State capitalism is a combination of freer markets and some government control.

What are the basic rights people have under capitalism?

The four basic rights under capitalism are (1) the right to own private property, (2) the right to own a business and to keep all of that business's profits after taxes, (3) the right to freedom of competition, and (4) the right to freedom of choice. President Franklin D. Roosevelt felt that other freedoms were also important: the right to freedom of speech and expression, the right to worship in your own way, and freedom from want and fear.

How does the free market work?

The free market is one in which buyers and sellers negotiating prices for goods and services influence the decisions about what gets produced and in what quantities. Buyers' decisions in the marketplace tell sellers what to produce and in what quantity. When buyers demand more goods, the price goes up, signaling suppliers to produce more. The higher the price, the more goods and services suppliers are willing to produce. Price is the mechanism that allows free markets to work.

LO 2–3   Compare socialism and communism.

What is socialism?

Socialism is an economic system based on the premise that some businesses should be owned by the government.

What are the advantages and disadvantages of socialism?

Socialism intends to create more social equity. Workers in socialist countries usually receive more education, health care, and other benefits and also work fewer hours, with longer vacations. The major disadvantage of socialism is that because of high taxes, it lowers the incentive to start a business or to work hard. Socialist economies tend to have a higher unemployment rate and a slower growth rate than capitalist economies.

How does socialism differ from communism?

Under communism, the government owns almost all major production facilities and dictates what gets produced and by whom. Communism is also more restrictive when it comes to personal freedoms, such as religious freedom.

LO 2–4 Analyze the trend toward mixed economies.

What is a mixed economy?

A *mixed economy* is part capitalist and part socialist. Some businesses are privately owned, but taxes tend to be high to distribute income more evenly among the population.

What countries have mixed economies?

The United States has a mixed economy, as do most other industrialized countries.

What are the benefits of mixed economies?

A mixed economy has most of the benefits of wealth creation that free markets bring plus the benefits of greater social equality and concern for the environment that socialism promises.

LO 2–5 Describe the economic system of the United States, including the significance of key economic indicators (especially GDP), productivity, and the business cycle.

What are the key economic indicators in the United States?

Gross domestic product (GDP) is the total value of final goods and services produced in a country in a given year. The *unemployment rate* refers to the percentage of civilians at least 16 years old who are unemployed and tried to find a job within the most recent four weeks. The *consumer price index (CPI)* measures changes in the prices of about 400 goods and services that consumers buy.

What is gross output?

Gross output (GO) is a measure of total sales volume at all stages of production.

What are the four phases of business cycles?

In an *economic boom,* businesses do well. A *recession* occurs when two or more quarters show declines in the GDP, prices fall, people purchase fewer products, and businesses fail. A *depression* is a severe recession. *Recovery* occurs when the economy stabilizes and starts to grow.

LO 2–6 Contrast fiscal policy and monetary policy, and explain how each affects the economy.

What is fiscal policy?

Fiscal policy consists of government efforts to keep the economy stable by increasing or decreasing taxes or government spending.

What is the importance of monetary policy to the economy?

Monetary policy is the management of the money supply and interest rates. When unemployment gets too high, the Federal Reserve Bank (the Fed) may put more money into the economy and lower interest rates. That is supposed to provide a boost to the economy as businesses borrow and spend more money and hire more people.

KEY TERMS

brain drain 40	free-market economies 41	monopoly 38
business cycles 47	gross domestic	national debt 48
capitalism 34	product (GDP) 42	oligopoly 38
command economies 41	gross output (GO) 44	perfect competition 38
communism 41	inflation 44	producer price
consumer price	invisible hand 33	index (PPI) 45
index (CPI) 45	Keynesian economic	recession 47
core inflation 45	theory 47	resource
deflation 45	macroeconomics 31	development 31
demand 37	market price 37	socialism 40
depression 47	microeconomics 31	stagflation 45
disinflation 45	mixed economies 42	state capitalism 34
economics 31	monetary policy 49	supply 36
fiscal policy 47	monopolistic competition 38	unemployment rate 44

CRITICAL THINKING

In 2002, the U.S. Supreme Court ruled that cities could have school voucher programs that give money directly to parents, who could then choose among competing schools, public or private. The idea was to create competition among schools. Like businesses, schools were expected to improve their services (how effectively they teach) to win students from competitors. The result would be improvement in all schools, private and public, to benefit many students.

1. Do you believe economic principles, like competition, apply in both private and public organizations? Be prepared to defend your answer.

2. Are there other public functions that might benefit from more competition, including competition from private firms?

3. Many people say that businesspeople do not do enough for society. Some students choose to go into the public sector instead of business because they want to help others. However, businesspeople say that they do more to help others than nonprofit groups do because they provide jobs for people rather than giving them charity. Furthermore, they believe businesses create all the wealth that nonprofit groups distribute.

   a. How can you find some middle ground in this debate to show that both business-people and those who work for nonprofit organizations contribute to society and need to work together more closely to help people?

   b. How could you use the concepts of Adam Smith to help illustrate your position?

PUTTING PRINCIPLES TO WORK

PURPOSE

To familiarize you with the sources of economic information that are important to business decision makers.

EXERCISE

Imagine that your boss asked you to help her to prepare the company's sales forecast for the coming two years. In the past, she felt that trends in the nation's GDP, U.S. manufacturing, and employment in Illinois were especially helpful in forecasting sales. She would like you to do the following:

1. Go to the Bureau of Economic Analysis website (bea.gov) and locate the gross domestic product data. Compare the annual figure for the last four years. What do the figures indicate for the next couple of years?

2. At the Bureau of Labor Statistics website (bls.gov) under "Industries" in the "Topics" box, click on "Industries at a Glance" to find the information about the manufacturing industry. What is the employment trend in manufacturing over the last four years?

3. Return to the Bureau of Labor Statistics home page (bls.gov) and use the Search feature to find trends in employment for the state of Illinois. Look around the website to see what other information is available. Plot the trend in employment in Illinois over the last four years. On your own, discuss what economic changes may have influenced that trend.

4. Based on the information you have gathered, write a brief summary of what may happen to company sales over the next couple of years.

DEVELOPING CAREER SKILLS

KEY: ● **Team**   ★ **Analytic**   ▲ **Communication**   ▣ **Technology**

1. In teams, develop a list of the advantages of living in a capitalist society. Then develop lists headed "What are the disadvantages?" and "How could such disadvantages be minimized?" Describe why a person who is poor in a socialist country might reject capitalism and prefer a socialist state. ●▲★

2. Show your understanding of the principles of supply and demand by looking at the oil market today. Go online and search for a chart of oil prices for the last few years. Why does the price of oil fluctuate so greatly? What will happen as more and more people in China and India decide to buy automobiles? What would happen if most U.S consumers decided to drive electric cars? ▣★

3. This exercise will help you understand socialism from different perspectives. Form three groups. Each group should adopt a different role in a socialist economy: One group will be the business owners, another group will be workers, and another will be government leaders. Within your group discuss and list the advantages and disadvantages to you of lowering taxes on businesses. Then have each group choose a representative to go to the front of the class and debate the tax issue with the representatives from the other groups. ●▲★

4. Draw a line and mark one end "Free-Market Capitalism" and the other end "Central Planning." Mark where on the line the United States is now. Explain why you marked the spot you chose. Students from other countries may want to do this exercise for their own countries and explain the differences to the class. ▲★

5. Break into small groups. In your group discuss how the following changes have affected people's purchasing behavior and attitudes toward the United States and its economy: the wars in Iraq and Afghanistan, the increased amount spent on homeland security, the government involvement in banking and other industries, and the growth of the Internet. Have a group member prepare a short summary for the class. ●▲★

CAREER EXPLORATION

If you are interested in pursuing a major in economics, here are a few careers to consider after graduation. Find out about the tasks performed, skills needed, pay, and opportunity outlook in these fields in the *Occupational Outlook Handbook (OOH)* at bls.gov.

- **Economist**—studies the production and distribution of resources, goods, and services by collecting and analyzing data, researching trends, and evaluating economic issues.

- **Statistician**—applies mathematical or statistical theory and methods to collect, organize, interpret, and summarize numerical data to provide useful information.

- **Marketing research analyst**—studies market conditions and helps companies understand what products people want, who will buy them, and at what price.

- **Actuary**—analyzes the financial costs of risk and uncertainty and uses mathematics, statistics, and financial theory to assess the risk that an event will occur.

VIDEO CASE   *Kiva: Giving Poor Entrepreneurs a Chance*

Economics impacts people and businesses around the world. Whether or not you are free to start and own a business, how you get financing to launch the business, and how the government supports or interferes with your business depends on what type of economic system exists in your country. In capitalist countries like the United States, individuals are free to start their own companies and find limited interference from the government. In communist countries like North Korea, the government either owns the business or exerts a strong hand in business operations.

Globally, small businesses often drive local economies. Unfortunately, billions of people in the world make $2 a day or less. In fact, a billion people make less than $1 a day. It's not surprising, then, that aspiring entrepreneurs in developing countries have a hard time starting and growing businesses. In such places, a loan of $100 or $200 can make a huge difference in getting a business started. However, access to even such small amounts of capital is often impossible for would-be entrepreneurs to obtain. That's where microloans from organizations such as Kiva come in.

Kiva is an organization founded in 2005 that provides loans to budding entrepreneurs in developing countries so they can invest in a business. Those investments often lead to community growth and employment and help the owners themselves to prosper on a moderate scale. The loans are small and referred to as microcredit or microfinancing. Kiva uses a crowdfunding approach to its microfinancing where visitors to their website can browse through pictures and profiles of people from 80 different countries around the world. When they find a business and entrepreneur they like, they can lend $25 or more to the business. Borrowers must pay back the money, and when it's repaid, lenders can withdraw the money from Kiva's system or lend it to another entrepreneur. As they become successful, entrepreneurs can borrow more and keep their business growing.

Kiva crowdfunds several thousand loan requests each week. It helps over a million people in over 80 countries, giving them the opportunity to change their lives for the better. This video highlights some of those people but primarily explains how freedom and a little money can combine to create huge differences in people's lives and their country's quality of life.

Kiva carefully considers several factors before it commits to lending money in a particular country. It first checks to see that the government will allow businesses to receive money and pay it back to lenders from another country. It then looks at how many microfinance institutions are already operating in the country. If the market seems too crowded or saturated, Kiva will not get involved. Finally, Kiva looks for a strong network of field partners (local nonprofit, nongovernmental enterprises) who know the community and can identify legitimate borrowers and distribute the loans to them. Kiva strongly believes lending is a better approach to helping overcome poverty than giving donations. By supporting entrepreneurs, they help grow businesses and the economy by hiring local people.

In developing its mission, Kiva follows the principles set out by Adam Smith who stressed that wealth comes from freedom—the ability to keep the profits from what you do. When people try to maximize profits, they have to hire other people to help them do the work. This provides jobs for others and wealth for the entrepreneur. And, like an invisible hand, the whole community benefits from the entrepreneurs' desire to earn a profit.

Kiva has shown through small loans how important entrepreneurs, freedom, opportunity, and a little bit of money are to economic growth and prosperity. You are hopefully encouraged by this video to participate in helping poor people around the world. You can do this by contributing time and money to organizations like Kiva. You can join the Peace Corps or other groups designed to assist less-developed countries. Microcredit will not single-handedly solve the economic problems throughout the world, but it's a good start.

THINKING IT OVER

1. Discuss why many people believe that capitalism gives entrepreneurs the best opportunity to be successful.

2. Why do people in developing countries have such a difficult time getting out of poverty?

3. Why would an entrepreneur in the United States need a microloan from Kiva?

NOTES

1. Choe Sang-Hun, "North Korea's State-Run Economy Falters under Sanctions, Testing Elite Loyalty," *The New York Times,* April 18, 2019; Elliot Waldman, "Do Dire Economic Conditions in North Korea Threaten Kim's Legacy?," *USA Today,* July 2, 2019; Michael O'Hanlon, "Why America Should Strike an Interim Deal with North Korea," Brookings Institution, brookings.edu, January 2, 2020.

2. Karen Appold, "Top 6 Challenges Healthcare Executives Will Face in 2020," *Managed Health Care Executive,* managedhealthcareexecutive.com, January 4, 2020.

3. Caterpillar, caterpillar.com, accessed January 2020.

4. Mark Hendrickson, "2020: The Centenary of the Most Important Breakthrough in the History of Economics," *The Epoch Times,* theepochtimes.com, January 2, 2020.

5. Chad Pergram, "How the Growing National Debt Seems to Be Fading from Concern in DC," *Fox News,* foxnews.com, January 3, 2020.

6. Abigail Curtis and Brent Schanding, "For the Maine Coast, 2019 Was the Year of the Fish," *Bangor Daily News,* bangordailynews.com, January 1, 2020.

7. Joseph Epstein, "Economics Is Dismal, but Is It Science?," *The Wall Street Journal,* September 4, 2019.

8. Anthony Cilluffo and Neil G. Ruiz, "World's Population Is Projected to Nearly Stop Growing by the End of the Century," Pew Research Center, pewresearch.org, June 17, 2019; William H. Frey, "The 2010s May Have Seen the Slowest Population Growth in U.S. History," Brookings Institution, brookings.edu, January 2, 2020.

9. Dudley L. Poston Jr., "Three Ways the U.S. Will Change in the 2020s," *Intellectual Takeout,* intellectualtakeout.org, January 2, 2020.

10. *CIA Fact Book,* cia.gov, accessed January 2020.

11. Vernon Smith, "Adam Smith's Refreshing Idea of Justice," *The Wall Street Journal,* July 9, 2019; Grant Freeland, "Keep Your New Year's Resolutions by Using Behavioral Economics," *Forbes,* forbes.com, January 6, 2020.

12. AnnaMaria Andriotis, Ken Brown, and Shane Shifflett, "Record Debt Swamps Middle-Class Families," *The Wall Street Journal,* August 3, 2019; Jeanna Smialek, "The Business of Equality," *Bloomberg Businessweek,* March 25, 2019; "Americans Increasingly Concerned about Gap between Rich and Poor," *FOX13 Salt Lake City,* fox13now.com, January 9, 2020.

13. Justin Lahart, "Income Inequality Holds Back U.S. Economy," *The Wall Street Journal,* September 11, 2019; Phil Gramm and John F. Early, "The Truth about Income Inequality," *The Wall Street Journal,* November 4, 2019.

14. The Giving Pledge, givingpledge.org, accessed January 2020.

15. Randall Lane, "Reimagining Capitalism," *Forbes,* March 31, 2019.

16. Juliana Menasce Horowitz, Ruth Igielnik, and Rakesh Kocchar, "Trends in Income and Wealth Inequality," Pew Research Center, pewsocialtrends.org, January 9, 2020.

17. Courtney Seiter, "5 Work Culture Trends We're Looking Out for in 2020," Buffer, open.buffer.com, January 13, 2020.

18. Jeremy Page, "The Birth of State Capitalism," *The Wall Street Journal,* June 1–2, 2019; James Pethokoukis, "America Dreams of Chinese State Capitalism," American Enterprise Institute, aei.org, January 12, 2020.

19. Michael Pettis, "Inequality's Endgame," *Barron's,* April 22, 2019; Darren Walker, "Saving Capitalism," *Fast Company,* fastcompany.com, November 2019; Gerard Baker, "To Fix Capitalism, We May Need More Capitalism," *The Wall Street Journal,* May 4–5, 2019; "Can Capitalism Be Fixed by Making Companies More Just?," *Harvard Business Review,* hbr.org, January 7, 2020.

20. Amy Fontinelle, "Which Countries Have High Taxes on High Incomes?," *Investopedia,* investopedia.com, January 18, 2020.

21. Janelle Cammenga, "State and Local Sales Tax Rates, 2020," Tax Foundation, taxfoundation.org, January 15, 2020.

22. Benjamin Katzeff Silberstein, "The North Korean Economy in 2019," *38 North,* 38north.org, January 16, 2020.

23. Marc Frank and Nelson Acosta, "Cuban Economy Still Afloat Despite U.S. Sanctions," Reuters, reuters.com, December 20, 2019; Jessica Donati, "U.S. Adds New Restrictions on Cuba Travel," *The Wall Street Journal,* wsj.com, January 10, 2020.

24. U.S. Department of Labor, dol.gov, accessed January 2020.

25. "Marketwatch," *CNBC,* January 24, 2020.

26. Jo Craven McGinty, "The Wages of Sin Would Give Boost to GDP," *The Wall Street Journal,* December 7–8, 2019; Gillian Tett, "Should America's GDP Data Include Drug Dealing?," *Financial Times,* ft.com, January 8, 2020.

27. "Real Gross Output of General Government," Federal Reserve Bank of St. Louis, fred.stlouisfed.org, accessed January 2020.

28. "Monthly Unemployment Rate in the United States from December 2018 to December 2019," Statista, statista.com, accessed January 2020.

29. Kimberly Amadeo, "Real Unemployment Rate with Calculations," *Investopedia,* investopedia.com, January 10, 2020; Kimberly Amadeo, "Current US Unemployment Rate Statistics and News," *The Balance,* thebalance.com, January 10, 2020.

30. Donald Rapp, *Bubbles, Booms, and Busts: The Rise and Fall of Financial Assets* (New York: Springer, 2014).

31. Adam Hayes, "Why Is Deflation Bad for the Economy?," *Investopedia,* October 28, 2019; Jim Chappelow, "Deflation," *Investopedia,* investopedia.com, August 29, 2019; Elaine Godfrey, "Progressives Warn of a Great Deflation," *The Atlantic,* theatlantic.com, January 18, 2020.

32. Jim Chappelow, "What Is Stagflation?," *Investopedia,* investopedia.com, May 21, 2019; Paul R. LaMonica, "The Fed's Worst Nightmare Could Be around the Corner," *CNN Business,* cnn.com, September 30, 2019.

33. U.S. Bureau of Labor Statistics, bls.gov, accessed January 2020; "Fed's Preferred Measure of Inflation Isn't Giving the Complete Picture," *The Wall Street Journal,* September 30, 2019; David Harrison, "U.S. Economists Shift to Big Data," *The Wall Street Journal,* May 1, 2019; U.S. Bureau of Labor Statistics, bls.gov, accessed January 2020.

34. Christina Majaski, "What Is the Producer Price Index (PPI)?" September 24, 2019; "U.S. Producer Prices Post Biggest Drop in over Two Years," *CNBC,* January 15, 2019; U.S. Bureau of Labor Statistics, bls.gov, accessed January 2020.

35. "The Effect of AI across the US and How to Adjust," *IndustryWeek,* industryweek.com, January 25, 2019; "Robots Stole Blue Collar Jobs, Now AI Is Coming for White Collar Workers," *Voice of America,* voxnews.com, January 2, 2020.

36. Cristina Lindblad and David Rocks, "Why Are Economists So Bad at Predicting Recessions?," *Bloomberg Businessweek,* April 1, 2020.

37. Madsen Pirie, "The Legacy of John Maynard Keynes," Adam Smith Institute, adamsmith.org, June 5, 2019.

38. Will Kenton, "Keynesian Economics," *Investopedia,* investopedia.com, accessed January 2020.

39. Shawn Tully, "America's Disastrous New Normal: A Booming Economy and Soaring Deficits," *Fortune,* January 5, 2019; Jim Tankersley, "Budget Deficit Topped $1 Trillion in 2019," *The New York Times,* nytimes.com, January 13, 2020.

40. "Deficit vs. Debt: What's the Difference?," Peter G. Peterson Foundation, pgpf.org, accessed January 2020.

41. Kimberly Amadeo, "Current US Federal Budget Deficit," *The Balance,* thebalance.com, January 10, 2020.

42. Jim Tankersley and Emily Cochrane, "Budget Deficit on Path to Surpass $1 Trillion under Trump," *The New York Times,* nytimes.com, August 21, 2019; Ben Ritz, "2019 Was Officially Trump's First Trillion-Dollar Deficit," *Forbes,* forbes.com, January 13, 2019.

43. Lydia DePillis, "US National Debt Rises $2 Trillion under Trump," *CNN,* January 4, 2019; Jeffry Bartash, "U.S. on Track to Add $12 Trillion to National Debt by 2029 Unless Washington Changes Course," *MarketWatch,* January 28, 2019; Troy Adkins, "What the National Debt Means to You," *Investopedia,* investopedia.com, accessed January 2020; "U.S. Debt Clock," usdebtclock.org, accessed January 2020.

3

Doing Business in Global Markets

LEARNING OBJECTIVES »

After you have read and studied this chapter, you should be able to

LO 3–1 Discuss the importance of the global market and the roles of comparative advantage and absolute advantage in global trade.

LO 3–2 Explain the importance of importing and exporting, and understand key terms used in global business.

LO 3–3 Illustrate the strategies used in reaching global markets, and explain the role of multinational corporations.

LO 3–4 Evaluate the forces that affect trading in global markets.

LO 3–5 Debate the advantages and disadvantages of trade protectionism.

LO 3–6 Discuss the changing landscape of the global market and the issue of offshore outsourcing.

Tim Cook, CEO of Apple Computer

As the maker of such landmark products as the iPhone and iPad, Apple ranks as one of the most successful companies in world history. But a few years before it began earning tens of billions from smartphones and tablets, Apple nearly folded under the pressure of an increasingly competitive tech sector. Thanks to the efforts of globally minded managers like Tim Cook, though, Apple bounced back and grew into the giant that we all know today.

Tim Cook's personal road to success started in the small town of Robertsdale, Alabama, where his mother worked at a pharmacy and his father served as foreperson of a shipyard. Along with his two brothers, Cook got a job as soon as he was old enough to do so. He delivered newspapers, worked at a restaurant, and even joined his mother at the drugstore. Cook applied this strong work ethic to his education as well. An all-star student, he graduated second in his high school class and was voted "most studious" by his classmates. From there Cook went on to Auburn University where he earned a bachelor's degree in engineering. He continued his education at Duke University's Fuqua School of Business and graduated in the top 10 percent of his class.

After earning his MBA, Cook accepted a job at IBM and embarked on his career in computer technology. He rose through the ranks over the years and eventually advanced to the position of North American fulfillment director, where he managed manufacturing and distribution of personal computers in both North and Latin America. Cook left IBM after 12 years to become chief operating officer (COO) at a computer retailer before moving on to Compaq, a major computer maker. Soon after taking this new position, however, Apple cofounder and CEO Steve Jobs reached out to Cook and offered him a job. Although it may seem strange today, choosing between the two companies was a tough decision in 1998. After all, Apple had not earned a profit in years while analysts predicted Compaq would soon become a major force in tech. (HP bought Compaq in 2002 for $25 billion.) But Cook was sold once he spoke with Jobs in person. "No more than five minutes into my initial interview with Steve, I wanted to throw caution and logic to the wind and join Apple," said Cook.

He certainly had his work cut out for him. Almost immediately after taking the position of senior vice president for worldwide operations, Cook began closing Apple factories and distribution centers around the globe. He replaced these expensive facilities with contract manufacturers that both cost less and increased the efficiency of the company's supply chain. In fact, many experts say that Cook's streamlining of the supply chain was just as important for Apple as the innovative designs of the iPod or iPhone. In 2007 he received a promotion to COO where he managed worldwide sales and operations. Following the death of Jobs in 2011, Cook took over as chief executive officer (CEO).

Apple has grown substantially under Cook's leadership. Along with launching the Apple Watch in 2015, he also oversaw the company's purchase of Beats Electronics for $3 billion. By 2018, Apple became the first American public company to earn a trillion-dollar valuation. Still, Cook will face many challenges as he works to keep Apple on top in the long term. Perhaps most importantly, the company needs to make a greater impact on consumers in global markets like China and India. If the past is any indication, though, Cook should be up to the task.

Tim Cook is an example of a successful global businessperson who's proven it doesn't matter who you are or where you came from if you have the will and determination to succeed. He understands cultural and economic differences, and knows how to adapt Apple to global changes successfully. This chapter explains the opportunities and challenges businesspeople like Tim Cook face every day in dealing with the dynamic environment of global business.

Sources: Michael Finch II, "Tim Cook—Apple CEO and Robertsdale's Favorite Son—Still Finds Time to Return to His Baldwin County Roots," AL.com, February 24, 2014; Evan Niu and Dylan Lewis, "Inside Apple and Tim Cook's Operational Brilliance," *The Motley Fool*, themotleyfool.com, June 2, 2016; Matt Weinberger, "The Rise of Apple CEO Tim Cook, the Most Powerful Business Leader in the World," *Business Insider*, businessinsider.com, August 24, 2016; Jack Nicas, "5 Reasons You Wouldn't Want to Be in Tim Cook's Shoes Right Now," *The New York Times*, January 4, 2019; Elizabeth Gurdus, "Tim Cook Teases New Apple Services to Come in 2019," *CNBC*, cnbc.com, January 8, 2019; Lisa Eadicicco, "Apple CEO Tim Cook's Best Advice for College Graduates in 2019," *Business Insider*, businessinsider.com, June 22, 2019; "Don't Be Surprised to See Investors Start Musing on a Potential Eventual Successor to Apple CEO Tim Cook," *MacDaily News*, macdailynews.com, January 3, 2020.

Let's talk business!
bit.ly/LetsTalkBusiness3

Justin Sullivan/Getty Images

LO 3–1 Discuss the importance of the global market and the roles of comparative advantage and absolute advantage in global trade.

The Dynamic Global Market

Have you dreamed of traveling to cities like Paris, London, Rio de Janeiro, or Tokyo? Today, most companies doing business globally believe it is important for their employees to have experience working in other countries. The reason is not surprising—although the United States is a market of over 328 *million* people, there are over 7.7 *billion* potential customers in the 195 countries that make up the global market.[1] That's too many people to ignore! (See Figure 3.1 for a map of the world and important statistics about world population.)

Today, U.S. consumers buy hundreds of billions of dollars' worth of goods from Canada, Mexico, and China.[2] Costco opened its first store in Shanghai and was greeted by such huge numbers of Chinese shoppers that traffic needed to be shut down.[3] Walmart and PepsiCo have expanded and built up business in South Africa.[4] Major League Baseball is broadcast in 189 countries in 17 languages.[5] The National Basketball Association (NBA)

FIGURE 3.1 WORLD POPULATION BY CONTINENT

As shown on this map, 59.64 percent of the world's population lives in Asia while only 4.73 percent lives in North America.

Source: "Continent and Region Populations 2020," World Population Review, worldpopulationreview.com, accessed February 2020.

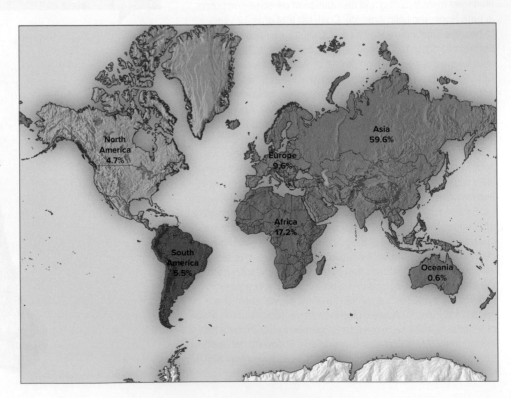

Martin Leitch/Icon Sportswire/Getty Images

It may not be what the rest of the world calls "football," but American football is attracting an audience outside the United States. London's Wembley Stadium has been home to the NFL's International Series since 2007, and the league recently signed an agreement for 10 more years. What cultural factors must U.S. sports franchises overcome in order to increase popularity abroad?

and the National Football League (NFL) played regular season games in London and Mexico in 2019.[6] NBC paid $1 billion to telecast England's Barclays Premier Soccer League in the United States through 2022.[7] U.S. film stars Robert Downey Jr., Tom Hanks, and Meryl Streep draw crowds to movie theaters around the globe.

Because the global market is so large, it is important to understand the language used in global trade. For example, **importing** is buying products from another country. **Exporting** is selling products to another country. As you might suspect, competition among exporting nations is intense. The United States is the largest importing nation in the world and is the second-largest exporting nation, behind China.

This chapter will familiarize you with global business and its many challenges. As competition in global markets intensifies, the demand for students with training in global business is almost certain to keep growing.

importing
Buying products from another country.
exporting
Selling products to another country.

Why Trade with Other Nations?

No nation, not even a technologically advanced one like the United States, can produce all the products its people want and need. Even if a country did become self-sufficient, other nations would seek to trade with it to meet the needs of their own people. Some nations, like Venezuela and the Democratic Republic of the Congo, have an abundance of natural resources but limited technological know-how. Other countries, such as Japan and Switzerland, have sophisticated technology but few natural resources. Global trade enables a nation to produce what it is most capable of producing and buy what it needs from others in a mutually beneficial exchange

FIGURE 3.2 THE PROS AND CONS OF FREE TRADE

PROS	CONS
• The global market contains over 7.7 billion potential customers for goods and services.	• Domestic workers (particularly in manufacturing-based jobs) can lose their jobs due to increased imports or production shifts to low-wage global markets.
• Productivity grows when countries produce goods and services in which they have a comparative advantage.	• Workers may be forced to accept pay cuts from employers, who can threaten to move their jobs to lower-cost global markets.
• Global competition and less-costly imports keep prices down, so inflation does not curtail economic growth.	• Moving operations overseas because of intense competitive pressure often means the loss of service jobs and growing numbers of white-collar jobs.
• Free trade inspires innovation for new products and keeps firms competitively challenged.	• Domestic companies can lose their comparative advantage when competitors build advanced production operations in low-wage countries.
• Uninterrupted flow of capital gives countries access to foreign investments, which help keep interest rates low.	

free trade
The movement of goods and services among nations without political or economic barriers.

comparative advantage theory
Theory that states that a country should sell to other countries those products that it produces most effectively and efficiently, and buy from other countries those products that it cannot produce as effectively or efficiently.

absolute advantage
The advantage that exists when a country has a monopoly on producing a specific product or is able to produce it more efficiently than all other countries.

relationship. This happens through the process called free trade. **Free trade** is the movement of goods and services among nations without political or economic barriers. It has become a hotly debated concept.[8] Figure 3.2 offers some of the pros and cons of free trade.

The Theories of Comparative and Absolute Advantage

Countries exchange more than goods and services, however. They also exchange art, sports, cultural events, medical advances, space exploration, and labor. Comparative advantage theory, suggested in the early 19th century by English economist David Ricardo, was the guiding principle that supported the idea of free economic exchange.[9] **Comparative advantage theory** states that a country should sell to other countries those products it produces most effectively and efficiently, and buy from other countries those products it cannot produce as effectively or efficiently. The United States has a comparative advantage in producing goods and services, such as software development and engineering services. In contrast, it lacks a comparative advantage in growing coffee or making shoes; thus, we import most of the shoes and coffee we consume. By specializing and trading, the United States and its trading partners can realize mutually beneficial exchanges.

A country has an **absolute advantage** if it can produce a specific product more efficiently than all other countries. Absolute advantage does not last forever; global competition causes absolute advantages to fade. Today there are very few instances of absolute advantage in global markets.

LO 3–2   Explain the importance of importing and exporting, and understand key terms used in global business.

Getting Involved in Global Trade

Job seekers interested in working in global business often think they are limited to major companies like Boeing, Caterpillar, or IBM, which have large multinational accounts. However, real global job potential may be with small businesses. In the United States, only 1 percent of the 30 million small businesses export, yet they account for about one-third of the total U.S. exports.[10] With the support of the U.S. Department of Commerce, U.S. small-business exporting has increased significantly in the past decade, but not quite to the level many would like.

Getting started globally is often a matter of observing, being determined, and taking risks. In a classic story, several years ago a U.S. traveler in an African country noticed there was no ice available for drinks or for keeping foods fresh. Research showed there was no ice factory for hundreds of miles, yet the market seemed huge. The man returned to the United States, found some investors, and returned to Africa to build an ice-making plant. The job was tough; much negotiation was necessary with local authorities (much of which was done by local citizens and businesspeople who knew the system). But the plant was eventually built, and this forward-thinking entrepreneur gained a considerable return on his idea, while the people gained a needed product.

Importing Goods and Services

Students attending colleges and universities abroad often notice that some products widely available in their countries are unavailable or more expensive elsewhere. By working with producers in their native countries, finding some start-up financing, and putting in long hours of hard work, many have become major importers while still in school.

Howard Schultz, chair emeritus of Starbucks, found his opportunity while traveling in Milan, Italy.[11] Schultz was enthralled with the ambience, the aroma, and especially the sense of community in the Italian neighborhood coffee and espresso bars that stretched across the country. He felt such gathering places would be great in the United States. Schultz bought the original Starbucks coffee shop in Seattle and transformed it according to his vision. Americans soon became aware of what a grande latte was all about. In 2018, 35 years after his trip to Italy, Schultz saw his dream of opening Starbucks in Italy happen. The company opened its first store in Milan.[12]

Sean P. Aune/Shutterstock

Exporting Goods and Services

Who would think U.S. firms could sell beer in Germany, home of the first state "beer purity" law (called the *Reinheitsgebot*) and maker of so many classic beers? Well, some of Munich's most famous beer halls and store shelves offer U.S. beers like Samuel Adams Boston Lager. U.S. brewer Sierra Nevada is collaborating with Germany's Bitburger Brewery to produce its Oktoberfest beer.[13] If this surprises you, imagine selling sand in the Middle East. Pool owners in Abu Dhabi purchase a special kind of sand used in swimming pool filters that sells well there.

The fact is, you can sell just about any good or service used in the United States to other countries—and sometimes the competition is not nearly so intense as it is at home. For example, you can sell snowplows to Saudi Arabians, who use them to clear sand off their driveways. Airbnb started in San Francisco as a community marketplace for people looking to book and list accommodations in the Bay Area. The company has since grown to a $31 billion company that serves 500 million guests by expanding booking listings in over 100,000 cities worldwide.[14] Company cofounder Brian Chesky believed that people wanted to connect with the people and the culture where they were staying, not just have a room to sleep in. Chesky's philosophy and creative social media strategy were significant in helping Airbnb transform the hospitality industry. The Connecting through Social Media box highlights how social media strategy in global business is vital to companies, global success.

Exporting also provides a terrific boost to the U.S. economy. C. Fred Bergsten, director emeritus of the Peterson Institute for International Economics, states that the U.S. economy was $1 trillion a year richer because of its integration with the world economy.[15] He also estimates that every $1 billion in additional U.S. exports generates over 7,000 jobs at home. Overall, exports represent about 12 percent of U.S. GDP and account for 11.5 million jobs. But selling in global markets and adapting products to global customers are by no means easy tasks. We discuss key forces that affect global trading later in this chapter.

If you are interested in learning more about exporting, go to the International Trade Administration (export.gov) and click on "Learn How to Export." More advice is available

Although Funko's Pop! line of toys aren't very lifelike, that hasn't stopped these big-headed figurines from becoming a global sensation. Funko's toys usually take on the appearance of famous fictional characters or pop culture icons, giving them widespread appeal to collectors around the world. As a result, each year Funko earns tens of millions from sales of its Pop! toys. Does a career in the global collectibles market seem appealing to you?

Global Consumers Increasingly Listen to Influencers

To stay competitive in today's global business environment, companies of all sizes are looking to improve the effectiveness of their social media marketing. Experts estimate that more than 3 billion people around the world spend at least two hours per day on social networks like Instagram, YouTube, and Facebook. These digital platforms allow consumers to discover and share information about brands by word of mouth, which can influence between 20 and 50 percent of all purchasing decisions. But in the ever-evolving world of social media networking, word of mouth needs to extend beyond the recommendations of friends and family.

That's where online influencers come in. These powerful personalities have social media followings that number in the millions, giving them enormous power over their legions of fans.

Lancton/Camera Press/Redux

In fact, recent research indicates that half of consumers turn to influencers for purchasing guidance while almost 40 percent bought a product as a direct result of an influencer. To reach these enormous audiences, savvy brands are paying billions to promote their products on the feeds of famous social media figures. Some influencers become so powerful that they launch their own branded products. For example, the YouTuber Zoe Sugg markets her line of candles, lotions, and accessories to an audience of nearly 12 million subscribers. Influencers like these will likely continue to have a major impact on both marketing and product development in the years to come.

Sources: "How Do Social Media Influencers Impact Global Business?," *Aperian Global,* aperianglobal.com, accessed February 2020; Joanna Carter, "Social Media Marketing Trends 2020," *Smart Insights,* smartinsights.com, accessed February 2020; Ortenca Aliaj, "Social Media Influencers Named as Stock Market Listing Factor," *Financial Times,* January 11, 2020; Deepa Prahalad and Ananthanarayanan V, "4 Questions to Boost Your Social Media Marketing," *Harvard Business Review,* January 17, 2020.

---

balance of trade

The total value of a nation's exports compared to its imports over a particular period.

trade surplus

A favorable balance of trade; occurs when the value of a country's exports exceeds that of its imports.

trade deficit

An unfavorable balance of trade; occurs when the value of a country's imports exceeds that of its exports.

balance of payments

The difference between money coming into a country (from exports) and money leaving the country (for imports) plus money flows from other factors such as tourism, foreign aid, military expenditures, and foreign investment.

at websites such as those sponsored by the U.S. Department of Commerce (doc.gov), the Bureau of Export Administration (bea.gov), the Small Business Administration (sba.gov), and the Small Business Exporters Association (sbea.org).

Measuring Global Trade

In measuring global trade, nations rely on two key indicators: balance of trade and balance of payments. The **balance of trade** is the total value of a nation's exports compared to its imports measured over a particular period. A *favorable* balance of trade, or **trade surplus**, occurs when the value of a country's exports exceeds that of its imports. An *unfavorable* balance of trade, or **trade deficit**, occurs when the value of a country's exports is less than its imports. It's easy to understand why countries prefer to export more than they import. If I sell you $200 worth of goods and buy only $100 worth, I have an extra $100 available to buy other things. However, I'm in an unfavorable position if I buy $200 worth of goods from you and sell you only $100.

The **balance of payments** is the difference between money coming into a country (from exports) and money leaving the country (for imports) plus money flows coming into or leaving a country from other factors such as tourism, foreign aid, military expenditures, and foreign investment. The goal is to have more money flowing into the country than out—a *favorable* balance of payments. Conversely, an *unfavorable* balance of payments exists when more money is flowing out of a country than coming in.

In the past, the United States exported more goods and services than it imported. However, since 1975 it has bought more goods from other nations than it has sold and thus has a trade deficit. Today, the United States runs its highest trade deficit with China.[16] Nonetheless, the United States remains one of the world's largest *exporting* nations even though it exports a much lower *percentage* of its products than other countries, such as China, Germany, and Japan. (Figure 3.3 lists the major trading countries in the world and the leading U.S. trading partners.)

In supporting free trade, the United States, like other nations, wants to make certain global trade is conducted fairly. To ensure a level playing field, countries prohibit unfair trade practices such as dumping. **Dumping** is selling products in a foreign country at lower prices than those charged in the producing country. This predatory pricing tactic is sometimes used to reduce surplus products in foreign markets or to gain a foothold in a new market. Some governments may even offer financial incentives to certain industries to sell goods in global markets for less than they sell them at home. China and Brazil, for example, have been penalized for dumping steel in the United States.[17] U.S. laws against dumping are specific and require foreign firms to price their products to include 10 percent overhead costs plus an 8 percent profit margin.

Now that you understand some of the basic terms used in global business, we can look at different strategies for entering global markets. First, let's assess your understanding so far by doing the Test Prep.

iSeeit! Need help understanding balance of trade? Visit your Connect eBook to view a video for a brief animated explanation.

dumping
Selling products in a foreign country at lower prices than those charged in the producing country.

TESTPREP

- What are two of the main arguments favoring the expansion of U.S. businesses into global markets?
- What is comparative advantage, and what are some examples of this concept at work in the United States?
- How are a nation's balance of trade and balance of payments determined?
- What is meant by the term *dumping* in global trade?

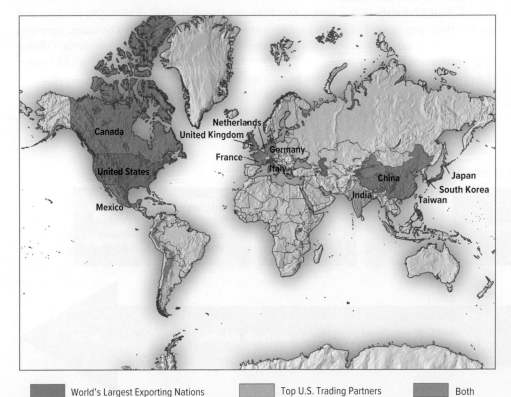

FIGURE 3.3 THE LARGEST EXPORTING NATIONS IN THE WORLD AND THE LARGEST U.S. TRADE PARTNERS

World's Largest Exporting Nations   Top U.S. Trading Partners   Both

LO 3–3   Illustrate the strategies used in reaching global markets, and explain the role of multinational corporations.

Strategies for Reaching Global Markets

Businesses use different strategies to compete in global markets. The key strategies include licensing, exporting, franchising, contract manufacturing, international joint ventures and strategic alliances, foreign subsidiaries, and foreign direct investment. Each provides different economic opportunities, along with specific commitments and risks. Figure 3.4 places the strategies on a continuum showing the amount of commitment, control, risk, and profit potential associated with each strategy. Take some time to look over the information in Figure 3.4 before you continue.

Licensing

licensing

A global strategy in which a firm (the licensor) allows a foreign company (the licensee) to produce its product in exchange for a fee (a royalty).

A firm (the licensor) may decide to compete in a global market by **licensing** the right to manufacture its product or use its trademark to a foreign company (the licensee) for a fee (a royalty). A company with an interest in licensing generally sends company representatives to the foreign company to help set up operations. The licensor may also assist or work with a licensee in such areas as distribution, promotion, and consulting.

A licensing agreement can benefit a firm in several ways. First, the firm can gain revenues it would not otherwise have generated in its home market. Also, foreign licensees often must purchase start-up supplies, materials, and consulting services from the licensing firm. Coca-Cola has entered into global licensing agreements with over 225 licensees that have extended into long-term service contracts that sell over 1.9 billion servings of the company's products each day.[18] Service-based companies are also active in licensing. For example, Tokyo Disneyland, the first Disney theme park opened outside the United States, is operated by Oriental Land Company under a licensing agreement with the Walt Disney Company. In fact, Disney is the largest licensor of consumer products globally, with almost $55 billion of licensed products.[19]

A final advantage of licensing is that licensors spend little or no money to produce and market their products. These costs come from the licensee's pocket. Therefore, licensees generally work hard to succeed. However, licensors may also experience problems. Often a firm must grant licensing rights to its product for an extended period, 20 years or longer. If a product experiences remarkable growth in the foreign market, the bulk of the revenues belong to the licensee. Perhaps even more threatening is that the licensing firm is actually selling its expertise. If a foreign licensee learns the company's technology or product

FIGURE 3.4 STRATEGIES FOR REACHING GLOBAL MARKETS

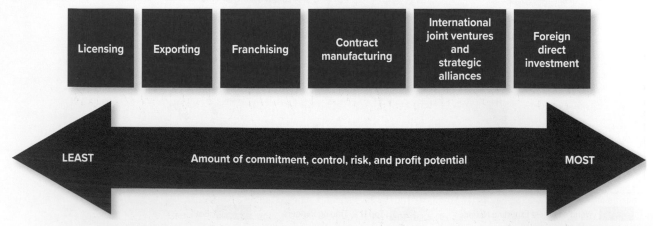

Naumova Ekaterina/Shutterstock

secrets, it may violate the agreement and begin to produce a similar product on its own. If legal remedies are not available, the licensing firm may lose its trade secrets, not to mention promised royalties.

Exporting

To meet increasing global competition, the U.S. Department of Commerce created Export Assistance Centers (EACs). EACs provide hands-on exporting assistance and trade-finance support for small and medium-sized businesses that wish to directly export goods and services.[20]

U.S. firms that are still hesitant can engage in *indirect* exporting through specialists called export-trading companies (or export-management companies) that assist in negotiating and establishing trading relationships. An export-trading company not only matches buyers and sellers from different countries but also deals with foreign customs offices, documentation, and even weights and measures conversions to ease the process of entering global markets. It also can assist exporters with warehousing, billing, and insuring. If you are considering a career in global business, export-trading companies often provide internships or part-time opportunities for students.

Franchising

Franchising is a contractual agreement whereby someone with a good idea for a business sells others the rights to use the business name and sell a product or service in a given territory in a specified manner. Franchising is popular domestically and globally. (We discuss it in depth in Chapter 5.) Major U.S. franchisors such as Subway, Holiday Inn, and KFC have many global units operated by foreign franchisees, but global franchising isn't limited to large franchisors. For example, Snap Fitness, of Chanhassen, Minnesota, has a chain of gym and fitness center franchises in over 2,500 locations in 26 countries.[21] Physique 57, a small, emerging high-end female-centric boutique fitness center in New York, has opened franchises in Abu Dhabi, Bangkok, Manila, and Riyadh.[22] Rocky Mountain Chocolate Factory, a Colorado-based producer of premium chocolates, has franchisees in Canada, Japan, South Korea, and the Philippines as well as the United Arab Emirates where chocolate is considered a gourmet luxury.[23] Foreign franchisors have also experienced success in the

A World of Options under the Arches

mcdonalds.com

For decades, McDonald's has been the undisputed king of global food franchising. Every day the fast-food chain serves tens of millions of customers at more than 36,000 restaurants located in over 100 countries.

So how did McDonald's become such a global powerhouse? It certainly didn't get there through hamburgers alone. Since it first began expanding overseas, McDonald's has been careful to include regional tastes on its menus along with the usual Big Mac and fries. For instance, during the winter, Japanese customers can order the Gracoro Burger, a sandwich that features a fried shrimp and macaroni patty topped with beef sauce. German locations offer the McNurnburger, which consists of three bratwurst sausages served on a bun with mustard and onions. Customers in the Philippines can even order a fried chicken leg with a side of McSpaghetti, one of the country's most popular McDonald's combos.

Danny Ye/Shutterstock

Other global items cater to a nation's specific customs and dietary restrictions. In India, McDonald's pays respect to religious sentiments by not including any beef or pork on its menu. This has led to popular items like the Maharaja Mac, which switches out the Big Mac's beef patties for chicken, as well as the McSpicy Paneer, a fried cheese sandwich that has become a major hit with Indian customers.

But not every move that McDonald's makes on the global stage is a success. In 2019, a European Union court ruled that the company lost the trademark rights to "Big Mac" after McDonald's tried to stop an Irish fast-food chain from selling a similar sandwich. The company could face more challenges like this in the future as it continues adapting and expanding further into the global market.

Sources: "McDonald's Loses 'Big Mac' Trademark Case to Irish Chain Supermac's," Reuters, reuters.com, January 15, 2019; M. Paramita Lin, "The Fried Paneer Sandwich Has Become a Cult Fast-Food Hit," *The Takeout,* thetakeout.com, January 16, 2019; Kenzie Osborne, "Top 25 International McDonald's Menu Items We Want in North America, Ranked," *TheRecipe,* therecipe.com, January 25, 2019; Anay Katyal and Meredith Cash, "15 McDonald's Fast-Food Items Everyone Should Try from around the World," *Insider,* insider.com, February 28, 2019; McDonald's, mcdonalds.com, accessed February 2020.

U.S. market. Japan's Kumon Math & Reading Centers and Australia's Cartridge World have found long-term success with American consumers.

Franchisors have to be careful to adapt their product or service to the countries they serve. Domino's Pizza makes an average of 3 million pizzas a day and has over 16,500 stores in 85 countries outside the United States.[24] Unfortunately, the toppings on those pizzas vary from country to country. In India, where the company operates over 1,200 stores, curry is a must. Japanese customers often prefer seafood and fish on their pizza, with squid and sweet mayonnaise pizza a favorite. Dunkin' Brands's donut holes might look the same in its 11,300 stores in 36 countries across the globe, but local taste preferences are anything but the same.[25] For example, in the company's donut shops in China, the donut of choice is dry pork and seaweed. Read the Adapting to Change box that highlights another global franchise champion, McDonald's.

Contract Manufacturing

contract manufacturing
A foreign company's production of private-label goods to which a domestic company then attaches its brand name or trademark; part of the broad category of outsourcing.

In **contract manufacturing** a foreign company produces private-label goods to which a domestic company then attaches its own brand name or trademark. For example, contract manufacturers make circuit boards and components used in computers, printers, smartphones, medical products, airplanes, and consumer electronics for companies such as Dell, Apple, and IBM. Foxconn is the world's largest contract manufacturer and makes such well-known products as the iPhone and Microsoft's Xbox One. Nike has 525 contract factories around the world that manufacture all its footwear and apparel. The medical devices industry also makes heavy use of contract manufacturing. Medical device contract manufacturing grew to a $96 billion market in 2018 and is expected to grow to $208 billion by 2026.[26] Worldwide contract manufacturing is estimated to be an almost $300 billion industry.

Jukov studio/Shutterstock

Contract manufacturing enables a company to experiment in a new market without incurring heavy start-up costs such as building a manufacturing plant. If the brand name becomes a success, the company has penetrated a new market with relatively low risk. A firm can also use contract manufacturing temporarily to meet an unexpected increase in orders, and, of course, labor costs are often very low. Contract manufacturing falls under the broad category of *outsourcing,* which we will discuss in depth later in this chapter.

Tired of studying and want a quick snack? How about a piping hot pizza topped with eel, mussels, cream cheese, and olives like this one? International chains serve pies like these around the globe in order to appeal to different tastes. How can franchises ensure their products are appropriate for global markets?

International Joint Ventures and Strategic Alliances

A **joint venture** is a partnership in which two or more companies (often from different countries) join to undertake a major project. Joint ventures are often mandated by governments such as China as a condition of doing business in their country. For example, Disney and state-owned Shanghai Shendi Group's $5.5 billion joint venture created the first Disneyland theme park in Mainland China (Disney has operated in Hong Kong since 2005), which opened in 2016.[27]

Joint ventures are developed for many different reasons. Marriott International and AC Hotels in Spain entered a joint venture over 10 years ago to create AC Hotels by Marriott to increase their global footprint and future growth. Joint ventures can also be truly unique. A joint venture called Verb Surgical involves pharmaceutical giant Johnson & Johnson and Alphabet (parent company of Google) to develop robotic surgery technology.[28] A classic joint venture 20 years ago between the University of Pittsburgh's Medical Center and the Italian government brought a new medical transplant center to Sicily.[29] Joint ventures can even involve two competing companies joining forces. German auto giant BMW and Japanese carmaker Toyota teamed together to create the new 2020 Toyota Supra and the BMW Z4 sports cars.[30] The benefits of international joint ventures are clear:

joint venture
A partnership in which two or more companies (often from different countries) join to undertake a major project.

1. Shared technology and risk.

2. Shared marketing and management expertise.

3. Entry into markets where foreign companies are often not allowed unless goods are produced locally.

The drawbacks of joint ventures are not so obvious but are important. One partner can learn the other's technology and business practices and then use what it has learned to its own advantage. Also, a shared technology may become obsolete, or the joint venture may become too large to be as flexible as needed. Sometimes partners may choose to break ties for various reasons. For example, Fuji/Xerox, a joint venture between Fujifilm and Xerox that existed for 57 years, ended in 2019 after attempts for a full merger failed.[31]

The global market has also fueled the growth of strategic alliances. A **strategic alliance** is a long-term partnership between two or more companies established to help each company build competitive market advantages. Unlike joint ventures, strategic alliances don't share costs, risks, management, or even profits. Such alliances provide broad

strategic alliance
A long-term partnership between two or more companies established to help each company build competitive market advantages.

Friso Gentsch/picture alliance/Getty Images

The United States has been and remains a popular spot for foreign direct investment. Global automobile manufacturers like Volkswagen, Toyota, and Honda have spent millions of dollars building facilities in the United States. Would you consider a Volkswagen made at the company's plant in Chattanooga, Tennessee, to be an American car or a German car?

foreign direct investment (FDI)

The buying of permanent property and businesses in foreign nations.

foreign subsidiary

A company owned in a foreign country by another company, called the *parent company.*

multinational corporation

An organization that manufactures and markets products in many different countries and has multinational stock ownership and multinational management.

sovereign wealth funds (SWFs)

Investment funds controlled by governments holding large stakes in foreign companies.

access to markets, capital, and technical expertise. Thanks to their flexibility, strategic alliances can effectively link firms from different countries and firms of vastly different sizes. U.S. retail giant Walmart and Japanese e-commerce services firm Rakuten formed a strategic alliance to open Walmart's first e-commerce store in Japan, the Walmart Rakuten Ichiba Store. The alliance combines Walmart's expertise in delivering high-quality products with Rakuten's strength in online commerce and its knowledge of Japanese consumers.[32]

Foreign Direct Investment

Foreign direct investment (FDI) is the buying of permanent property and businesses in foreign nations. The most common form of FDI is a **foreign subsidiary**, a company owned in a foreign country by another company, called the *parent company.* The subsidiary operates like a domestic firm, with production, distribution, promotion, pricing, and other business functions under the control of the subsidiary's management. The subsidiary also must observe the legal requirements of both the country where the parent firm is located (called the *home country*) and the foreign country where the subsidiary is located (called the *host country*).

The primary advantage of a subsidiary is that the company maintains complete control over any technology or expertise it may possess. The major shortcoming is the need to commit funds and technology within foreign boundaries. Should relationships with a host country falter, the firm's assets could be *expropriated* (taken over by the foreign government). Swiss-based Nestlé has many foreign subsidiaries and over 2,000 brands it markets. The consumer-products giant spent billions of dollars acquiring foreign subsidiaries such as Gerber Baby Foods, Ralston Purina, Chef America (maker of Hot Pockets), Libby Foods, and Dreyer's and Häagen-Dazs Ice Cream (which it sold in 2020) in the United States as well as Perrier in France. Nestlé employs over 308,000 people in 86 countries and has operations in almost every country in the world.[33]

Nestlé is a **multinational corporation**, one that manufactures and markets products in many different countries and has multinational stock ownership and management. Multinational corporations are typically extremely large corporations like Nestlé, but not all large global businesses are multinationals. For example, a corporation could export everything it produces, deriving 100 percent of its sales and profits globally, and still not be a multinational corporation. Only firms that have *manufacturing capacity* or some other physical presence in different nations can truly be called multinational. Figure 3.5 lists the 10 largest multinational corporations in the world.

A growing form of foreign direct investment is the use of **sovereign wealth funds (SWFs)**, investment funds controlled by governments holding investment stakes in foreign companies. SWFs from the United Arab Emirates, Singapore, and China have purchased interests in many U.S. companies. Norway, with a population of 5 million people, is the world's richest SWF, with assets of over $1 trillion.[34] The size of SWFs ($7 trillion globally) and government ownership made some fear they might be used for achieving geopolitical objectives, by gaining control of strategic natural resources, or obtaining sensitive technologies. Thus far this has not been a problem. In fact during the Great Recession in 2008, SWFs injected billions of dollars into struggling U.S. companies such as Citigroup and Morgan Stanley.

Entering global business requires selecting an entry strategy that best fits your business goals. The different strategies we've discussed reflect different levels of ownership, financial commitment, and risk. However, this is just the beginning. You should also be aware of market forces that affect a business's ability to thrive in global markets. After the Test Prep, we'll discuss them.

COMPANY	REVENUE (in billions)	COUNTRY
1 Walmart	$500	U.S.
2 State Grid	$349	China
3 Sinopec Group	$327	China
4 China National Petroleum	$326	China
5 Royal Dutch Shell	$312	Netherlands
6 Toyota Motor	$265	Japan
7 Volkswagen	$260	Germany
8 BP	$245	Great Britain
9 Exxon Mobil	$244	U.S.
10 Berkshire Hathaway	$242	U.S.

FIGURE 3.5 THE LARGEST MULTINATIONAL CORPORATIONS IN THE WORLD

Source: *Fortune,* fortune.com, accessed January 2020.

?TEST**PREP**

- What are the advantages to a firm of using licensing as a method of entry in global markets? What are the disadvantages?
- What services are usually provided by an export-trading company?
- What is the key difference between a joint venture and a strategic alliance?
- What makes a company a multinational corporation?

LO 3–4 Evaluate the forces that affect trading in global markets.

Forces Affecting Trading in Global Markets

The hurdles to success are higher and more complex in global markets than in domestic markets. Such hurdles include dealing with differences in sociocultural forces, economic and financial forces, legal and regulatory forces, and physical and environmental forces. Let's analyze each of these market forces to see how they challenge even the most established and experienced global businesses.

Sociocultural Forces

The word *culture* refers to the set of values, beliefs, rules, and institutions held by a specific group of people. Culture can include social structures, religion, manners and customs, values and attitudes, language, and personal communication. If you hope to get involved in global trade, it's critical to be aware of the cultural differences among nations. Unfortunately, while the United States is a multicultural nation, U.S. businesspeople are often accused of *ethnocentricity,* an attitude that your own culture is superior to other cultures.

In contrast, many foreign companies are very good at adapting to U.S. culture. Think how effectively German, Japanese, and Korean carmakers have adapted to U.S. drivers' wants and needs. In 2019, 6 of the top-10-selling cars and trucks in the United States were from Japan. German discount grocery chain Aldi continues expanding in the United States and now has over 1,900 locations with plans to expand to 2,500 by 2022.[35] Lidl, another German discount grocery chain, entered the U.S. market two years ago and has approximately

100 U.S. locations.[36] Despite worldwide acceptance, the United States has not conformed to the metric system of measurement. Liberia and Myanmar are the only other nations that do not use the metric system. Let's look at other hurdles U.S. businesses face in adapting to social and cultural differences in global markets.

Religion is an important part of any society's culture and globally can have a significant impact on business operations. In order to be successful, it's imperative global companies are aware of religious implications in making business decisions. For example, Islam prohibits eating pork and Hindus do not consume beef. Such religious restrictions are very important for companies like Domino's and Pizza Hut to follow, especially in countries such as Saudi Arabia and India. McDonald's learned the importance of respecting religious beliefs over 25 years ago at the World Cup. The company reprinted the flag of Saudi Arabia on its food bags. Muslims were offended with the flag on its packaging because the flag's design contained the Muslim Shahada (the Muslim declaration of faith). Offended Muslims believed their holy writ should never be wadded up and thrown away. The company learned a valuable lesson from this experience that understanding religious implications in the global market is critical.

In a similar classic story, a U.S. manager in Islamic Pakistan toured a new plant under his control. While the plant was in full operation, he went to his office to make some preliminary production forecasts. Suddenly all the machinery in the plant stopped. The manager rushed out, suspecting a power failure, only to find his production workers on their prayer rugs. Upon learning that Muslims are required to pray five times a day, he returned to his office and lowered his production estimates.

Understanding sociocultural differences is also important in managing employees. In some Latin American countries, workers believe managers are in positions of authority to make decisions concerning the well-being of the workers under their control. Consider the U.S. manager working in Peru who was unaware of this cultural characteristic and believed workers should participate in managerial functions. He was convinced he could motivate his workers to higher levels of productivity by instituting a more democratic decision-making style. Workers began quitting in droves. When asked why, they said the new manager did not know his job and was asking the workers what to do. All stated they wanted to find new jobs, since this company was doomed due to its incompetent management.

Even today, many U.S. companies still fail to think globally, not understanding that something like the color used in packaging can have different meanings in different cultures. A sound philosophy is: *Never assume what works in one country will work in another.* Intel, Nike, IBM, Apple, KFC, and Walmart have developed brand names with widespread global appeal and recognition, but even they often face difficulties. To get an idea of problems companies have faced with translations of advertising globally, take a look at Figure 3.6.

Economic and Financial Forces

Economic differences can muddy the water in global markets. In Qatar, annual per capita income is over $130,000, the highest in the world. In the economically strapped Central African Republic, per capita income is barely over $700, the lowest in the world.[37] It's difficult for us to imagine buying chewing gum by the stick. Yet this behavior is commonplace in economically depressed nations like Haiti, where customers can afford only small quantities. You might suspect with over 1.3 billion potential customers, India would be one of the world's largest markets for Coca-Cola. Unfortunately, Indians consume only 5 percent of what the United States consumes due to low per capita income. The same is true in the booming beauty and personal care market in India. Since Indians are accustomed to buying in very small quantities, cosmetic giants Estée Lauder and L'Oréal sell primarily small, sample sizes of shampoo, skin treatments, and hair color due to low incomes.[38]

Financially, Mexicans shop with pesos, Chinese with yuan (also known as renminbi), South Koreans with won, Japanese with yen, and U.S. consumers with dollars. Among currencies, globally the U.S. dollar is considered a dominant and stable currency. However, it

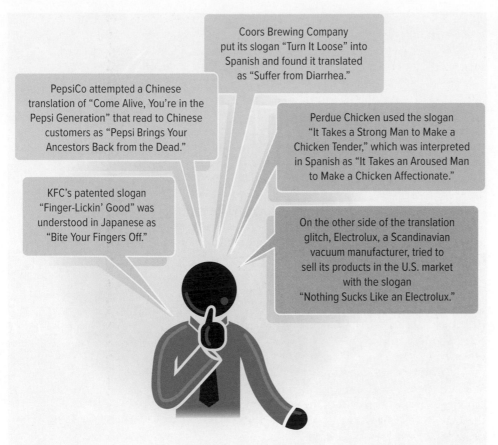

FIGURE 3.6 OOPS, DID
WE SAY THAT?
A global marketing strategy
can be very difficult to
implement. Look at the
problems these well-known
companies encountered in
global markets.

doesn't always retain the same market value. In a global transaction today, a dollar may be exchanged for eight pesos; tomorrow you may get seven. The **exchange rate** is the value of one nation's currency relative to the currencies of other countries. Changes in a nation's exchange rates have effects in global markets. A *high value of the dollar* means a dollar is trading for more foreign currency than previously. Therefore, foreign products become cheaper because it takes fewer dollars to buy them. However, U.S.-produced goods become more expensive because of the dollar's high value. Conversely, a *low value of the dollar* means a dollar is traded for less foreign currency—foreign goods become more expensive because it takes more dollars to buy them, but U.S. goods become cheaper to foreign buyers because it takes less foreign currency to buy them.

Global financial markets operate under a system called *floating exchange rates,* which means that currencies "float" in value according to the supply and demand for them in the global market for currency. This supply and demand is created by global currency traders who develop a market for a nation's currency based on the country's perceived trade and investment potential.

Changes in currency values can cause many problems globally. For instance, labor costs for multinational corporations like Unilever, General Electric, Nestlé, and Nike can vary considerably as currency values shift, causing them to sometimes juggle production from one country to another. The same is true for medium-sized companies like H.B. Fuller, a global industrial adhesives provider from St. Paul, Minnesota, which has 4,600 employees in 43 countries. Like its larger counterparts, H.B. Fuller uses currency fluctuations to its advantage in dealing with its global markets.

Currency valuation problems can be especially harsh on developing economies. At times a nation's government will intervene and readjust the value of its currency, often to increase the export potential of its products. **Devaluation** lowers the value of a nation's currency relative to others. Venezuela devalued its currency in 2014 to try to alleviate mounting economic problems. Unfortunately, the move did little to solve the country's problems.

exchange rate
The value of one nation's currency relative to the currencies of other countries.

devaluation
Lowering the value of a nation's currency relative to other currencies.

When the dollar is "up," foreign goods and travel are a bargain for U.S. consumers. When the dollar trades for less foreign currency, however, foreign tourists often flock to U.S. cities to enjoy relatively cheaper vacations and shopping trips. Do U.S. exporters profit more when the dollar is up or when it is down?

Marc Dozier/The Image Bank Unreleased/Getty Images

Inflation in Venezuela hit 1.37 million percent in 2018 (see Chapter 2).[39] Even though the government continues to raise the minimum wage, a month's worth of work still can't buy two pounds of beef.[40] Sometimes, due to a nation's weak currency, the only way to trade is *bartering,* the exchange of merchandise for merchandise or service for service with no money traded.

countertrading

A complex form of bartering in which several countries may be involved, each trading goods for goods or services for services.

Countertrading is a complex form of bartering in which several countries each trade goods or services for other goods or services. Let's say a developing country such as Jamaica wants to buy vehicles from Ford Motor Company in exchange for bauxite, a mineral compound that is a source of aluminum ore. Ford does not need Jamaican bauxite, but it does need compressors. In a countertrade, Ford may trade vehicles to Jamaica, which trades bauxite to another country, say India, which exchanges compressors with Ford. All three parties benefit and avoid some of the financial problems and currency constraints in global markets. Estimates are that countertrading accounts for over 20 percent of all global exchanges, especially with developing countries.[41]

Legal and Regulatory Forces

In any economy, the conduct and the direction of business are firmly tied to the legal and regulatory environment. In global markets, no central system of law exists, so different systems of laws and regulations may apply in different places. This makes conducting global business difficult as businesspeople navigate a sea of laws and regulations that are often inconsistent. Antitrust rules, labor relations, patents, copyrights, trade practices, taxes, product liability, child labor, prison labor, and other issues are governed differently country by country. The Making Ethical Decisions box raises ethical questions about selling products in a global market with a different legal system.

As the top manager of Sweet Dreams, a maker of children's sleepwear, you received notification from the U.S. Consumer Product Safety Commission (CPSC) that the fabric you use in your girls' nightgowns has been deemed unsafe. The commission conducted a study of the product after a child was seriously burned while wearing a nightgown that burst into flames when she ventured too close to a gas stove. The CPSC ruled the material used did not have sufficient flame-retardant capabilities to meet U.S.

kdshutterman/Getty Images

standards. Your company was instructed to immediately remove the product from store shelves and issue a product recall.

This is a tough blow for the company since the nightgowns are popular and sell well in the market. Plus, you have a large supply of the product in your warehouse that now is just taking up space. A big financial loss for the company is likely.

Your sales manager reminds you that many countries do not have such strict product laws as the United States. He suggests the product could be exported to a country with less stringent product safety rules. Exporting the product to another country would solve your inventory and profit concerns, but you wonder about sending a product deemed unsafe in the United States to children in another market. What are the consequences of each alternative? What will you do?

U.S. businesses must follow U.S. laws and regulations in conducting business globally, although legislation such as the Foreign Corrupt Practices Act of 1978 can create competitive disadvantages. This law prohibits "questionable" or "dubious" payments to foreign officials to secure business contracts.[42] That runs contrary to practices in some countries (generally developing countries), where corporate or government bribery is not merely acceptable but perhaps the only way to secure a lucrative contract. The Organization for Economic Cooperation and Development (OECD) and Transparency International have led a global effort to fight corruption and bribery in global business, with limited success.[43] Figure 3.7 shows a partial list of countries where bribery or other unethical business practices are most common.

The cooperation and sponsorship of local businesspeople in a foreign market can help a company penetrate the market and deal with laws, regulations, and bureaucratic barriers in their country.

Physical and Environmental Forces

Physical and environmental forces certainly affect a company's ability to conduct global business. Some developing countries have such primitive transportation and storage systems that international distribution is ineffective, if not impossible, especially for perishable food. Add unclean water, the lack of effective sewer systems, and unacceptable air pollution levels, and you can see the intensity of the problem.

Technological differences also influence the features and feasibility of exportable products. For example, residential electrical systems in many developing countries do not match those of U.S. homes, in kind or capacity. Computer and Internet use in many developing countries has improved due to the adoption of cloud services but still lags behind developed nations due to consumers' inability to afford even low-priced laptops. Facts like these make for a tough environment for business in general and for e-commerce in particular. Economic development is also severely impacted. After the Test Prep, we'll explore how another force, trade protectionism, affects global business.

FIGURE 3.7 COUNTRIES RATED HIGHEST ON CORRUPT BUSINESS

1. Somalia
2. Syria
3. South Sudan
4. Yemen
5. North Korea
6. Sudan
7. Guinea-Bissau
8. Equatorial Guinea
9. Afghanistan
10. Libya

Source: Transparency International, 2019.

?TEST**PREP**

- What are four major hurdles to successful global trade?
- What does *ethnocentricity* mean, and how can it affect global success?
- How would a low value of the dollar affect U.S. exports?
- What does the Foreign Corrupt Practices Act prohibit?

LO 3–5 Debate the advantages and disadvantages of trade protectionism.

---

trade protectionism
The use of government regulations to limit the import of goods and services.

tariff
A tax imposed on imports.

import quota
A limit on the number of products in certain categories that a nation can import.

embargo
A complete ban on the import or export of a certain product, or the stopping of all trade with a particular country.

Trade Protectionism

As we discussed in the previous section, sociocultural, economic and financial, legal and regulatory, and physical and environmental forces are all challenges to global trade. What is often a much greater barrier to global trade, however, is trade protectionism. **Trade protectionism** is the use of government regulations to limit the import of goods and services. Advocates of protectionism believe it allows domestic producers to survive and grow, producing more jobs. Other countries use protectionist measures because they are wary of foreign competition in general. To understand how protectionism affects global business, let's briefly review a little bit of global economic history.

Business, economics, and politics have always been closely linked. Economics was once referred to as *political economy,* indicating the close ties between politics (government) and economics. In the 17th and 18th centuries, businesspeople and government leaders endorsed an economic policy called *mercantilism.* The idea was for a nation to sell more goods to other nations than it bought from them; that is, to have a favorable balance of trade. According to mercantilists, this resulted in a flow of money to the country that sold the most globally. The philosophy led governments to implement **tariffs**, taxes on imports, making imported goods more expensive to buy.

There are two kinds of tariffs: protective and revenue. *Protective tariffs* (import taxes) raise the retail price of imported products so that domestic goods are more competitively priced. These tariffs are meant to save jobs for domestic workers and keep industries—especially infant industries that have companies in the early stages of growth—from closing down because of foreign competition. *Revenue tariffs* are designed to raise money for the government. For example, tariffs on imports coming into the United States are collected by the Customs and Border Protection on behalf of the U.S. Commerce Department. Keep in mind that this tax is paid by the *importer.* This means that if the United States imposes a tariff on foreign goods, it is the U.S. companies that buy the foreign goods must pay the tariff bill.[44]

Some workers believe that too many U.S. jobs have been lost due to the growing number of imported products. Should governments protect their industries by placing tariffs on imported products? Why or why not?

An **import quota** limits the number of products in certain categories a nation can import.[45] The United States has import quotas on a number of products, including sugar and beef, to protect U.S. companies and preserve jobs. The United States also prohibits the export of specific products. Antiterrorism laws and the U.S. Export Administration Act of 1979 prohibit exporting goods such as high-tech weapons that could endanger national security. An **embargo** is a complete ban on the import or export of a certain product, or the stopping of all trade with a particular country. In 2019, the United States imposed an embargo against Venezuela. This action places them on par with

Jeff Swensen/Getty Images

Iran, Syria, North Korea, and Cuba as countries that are subjects of a U.S. embargo.[46] The embargo against Cuba has existed since 1962. In 2016, some trade restrictions were lifted and diplomatic relations restored. However, in 2017, diplomatic relations again soured making it unclear what the future holds for the U.S. embargo against Cuba.[47]

Some *nontariff barriers* are not as specific or formal as tariffs, import quotas, and embargoes but can be just as detrimental to free trade. For example, India imposes a number of restrictive standards like import licensing, burdensome product testing requirements, and lengthy customs procedures that inhibit the sale of imported products. China omits many American-made products from its government catalogs that specify what products may be purchased by its huge government sector. Other trade barriers detail exactly how a product must be sold in a country or may insist on local content requirements that require that some part of a product be produced domestically.

Would-be exporters might view such trade barriers as good reasons to avoid global trade, but overcoming constraints creates business opportunities. Next, we'll look at organizations and agreements that attempt to eliminate these trade barriers.

The World Trade Organization

In 1948, government leaders from 23 nations formed the **General Agreement on Tariffs and Trade (GATT)**, a global forum for reducing trade restrictions on goods, services, ideas, and cultural programs. In 1986, the Uruguay Round of the GATT convened to renegotiate trade agreements. After eight years of meetings, 124 nations voted to lower tariffs an average of 38 percent worldwide and to expand new trade rules to areas such as agriculture, services, and the protection of patents.

The Uruguay Round also established the **World Trade Organization (WTO)** to mediate trade disputes among nations. The WTO, headquartered in Geneva, is an independent entity of 164 member nations whose purpose is to oversee cross-border trade issues and global business practices.[48] Trade disputes are presented by member nations, with decisions made within a year, rather than languishing for years as in the past; member nations can appeal a decision.

The WTO has not solved all global trade problems. In fact, the WTO has not reached any significant trade accord since the Doha Round of negotiations ended in 2015. Recently, the organization has come under heavy criticism from the United States. The United States has even blocked appointing new members to the WTO's appellate body that is the ultimate authority on trade disputes.[49] Without its ability to intervene in trade wars, it is possible the organization may cease to exist. Since its inception, a wide gap has persisted between developing nations (80 percent of the WTO membership) and industrialized nations like the United States.

Common Markets

A **common market** (also called a *trading bloc*) is a regional group of countries with a common external tariff, no internal tariffs, and coordinated laws to facilitate exchange among members. The European Union (EU), Mercosur, the Association of Southeast Asian Nations (ASEAN) Economic Community, and the Common Market for Eastern and Southern Africa (COMESA) are common markets.

The EU began in the late 1950s as an alliance of six trading partners (then known as the Common Market and later the European Economic Community). Today it is a group of 27 nations (see Figure 3.8) with a combined population of over 477 million and a GDP of $18.4 trillion.[50] Though the EU is represented as a unified body in the WTO, the economies of five members (Germany, France, Italy, Spain, and the Netherlands) account for the majority of the EU's GDP.

In 1999, the EU took a significant step by adopting the euro as a common currency. The euro helped EU businesses save billions by eliminating currency conversions. Nineteen member nations now use the euro as their common currency. In 2016, the UK voted to leave the EU (an action called Brexit, a combination of the words *Britain* and *exit*). The UK became

General Agreement on Tariffs and Trade (GATT)
A 1948 agreement that established an international forum for negotiating mutual reductions in trade restrictions.

World Trade Organization (WTO)
The international organization that replaced the General Agreement on Tariffs and Trade, and was assigned the duty to mediate trade disputes among nations.

common market
A regional group of countries that have a common external tariff, no internal tariffs, and a coordination of laws to facilitate exchange; also called a *trading bloc*. An example is the European Union.

FIGURE 3.8 MEMBERS OF THE EUROPEAN UNION
Current EU members are highlighted in yellow. Countries that have applied for membership are in orange.

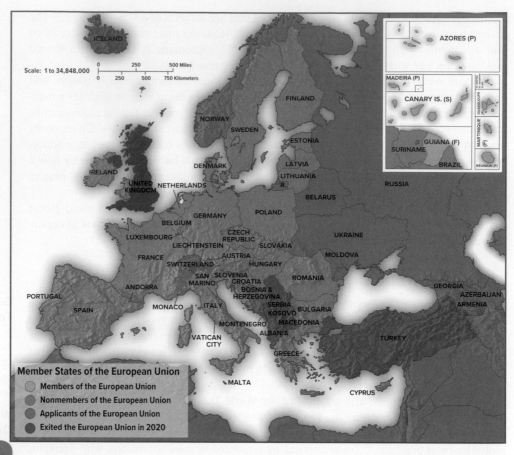

Member States of the European Union
- Members of the European Union
- Nonmembers of the European Union
- Applicants of the European Union
- Exited the European Union in 2020

On January 31, 2020, the United Kingdom officially left the European Union after voting to withdraw from the economic bloc four years earlier. This monumental departure ended more than forty years of economic and political cooperation between the UK and the Continent. Do you think it was a good decision for the UK to leave the EU?

Olivier Hoslet/Pool/AFP/Getty Images

the first nation to withdraw from the EU when it formally left in 2020.[51] This isn't the first problem the EU has confronted. Financial difficulties in member nations Italy, Portugal, Spain, and especially Greece required financial bailout assistance. Going forward, the EU faces many challenges. Still, leading members consider economic integration among member nations as the best strategy to compete globally against major global competitors like the United States and China.

Mercosur unites Brazil, Argentina, Paraguay, Uruguay, and associate members Bolivia, Chile, Colombia, Ecuador, Peru, and Suriname in a trading bloc that encompasses almost 307 million people. Venezuela was a former member but was suspended from the Mercosur in 2016. The EU and Mercosur finalized a trade agreement in 2019 that, if ratified by the EU, would create the largest free-trade agreement in the world.[52]

The ASEAN Economic Community was established in 1967 in Thailand to create economic cooperation among its five original members (Indonesia, Malaysia, the Philippines, Singapore, and Thailand). ASEAN has expanded to include Brunei, Cambodia, the Lao People's Democratic Republic, Myanmar, and Vietnam, creating a trade association with a population of approximately 650 million and a GDP of almost $2.9 trillion.[53] The African Continental Free Trade Area (AfCFTA) is the largest free-trade area in the world in terms of member nations. The AfCFTA brings together all 55 member states of the African Union with a market of over 1.2 billion people, a growing middle class, and a combined GDP of $3.4 trillion. The addition of Africa's largest economy, Nigeria, in 2019 promises to spark economic expansion for the continent in 2020.[54]

NAFTA and United States–Mexico–Canada Agreement (USMCA)

The **North American Free Trade Agreement (NAFTA)** created a free-trade area among the United States, Canada, and Mexico. The agreement was widely controversial and often criticized since its passage in 1993. Opponents warned of the loss of U.S. jobs and capital. Supporters predicted NAFTA would open a vast new market for U.S. exports and create jobs and market opportunities in the long term.

NAFTA's key objectives were to (1) eliminate trade barriers and facilitate cross-border movement of goods and services, (2) promote conditions of fair competition, (3) increase investment opportunities, (4) provide effective protection and enforcement of intellectual property rights (patents and copyrights), (5) establish a framework for further regional trade cooperation, and (6) improve working conditions in North America, particularly in Mexico.

In 2018, leaders from the United States, Mexico, and Canada signed a new trade deal that revised NAFTA known as the **United States–Mexico–Canada Agreement (USMCA).** The new agreement was ratified in 2020.[55] At the time of this writing, the three countries still needed to meet a list of requirements before the agreement could go into effect.

Under NAFTA, attempts to boost job growth, fight poverty, improve environmental controls, and close the wage gap between Mexico and the United States largely failed. Illegal immigration also remained a major problem between the two nations.[56] The USMCA attempts to remedy these past shortcomings and create more balanced and reciprocal trade in the following areas: (1) creating a more level playing field for U.S. workers including improved rules for automobiles, trucks, and other products; (2) providing benefits to American farmers, ranchers, and other agribusiness by modernizing and strengthening food and agricultural trade in North America; (3) supporting a modern economy through new protections for U.S. intellectual property and opportunities for trade in U.S. services, and (4) introducing new rules covering digital trade, anticorruption, and good regulatory practices. It also includes a chapter devoted to ensuring that small and medium-sized enterprises benefit from the agreement.[57] Time will tell if USMCA achieves these lofty goals.

North American Free Trade Agreement (NAFTA)
Agreement that created a free-trade area among the United States, Canada, and Mexico.

United States–Mexico–Canada Agreement (USMCA)
Free-trade agreement among the United States, Mexico, and Canada that replaced NAFTA in an effort to create more balanced and reciprocal trade.

Central American Free-Trade Agreements

The United States has remained committed to free trade. For example, CAFTA, the Central American Free Trade Agreement, created a free-trade zone with Costa Rica, the Dominican Republic, El Salvador, Guatemala, Nicaragua, and Honduras that has worked well since being signed in 2006. The United States also has free-trade agreements with 12 other nations including South Korea and Australia.[58]

Common markets and free-trade areas will be debated far into the future. While some economists resoundingly praise such efforts, others are concerned the world could divide into major trading blocs that will exclude poor and developing nations. There is also a fear that protectionist policies are growing. After the Test Prep, we'll look at the future of global trade and address the issue of outsourcing.

?TESTPREP

- What are the advantages and disadvantages of trade protectionism and of tariffs?
- What is the primary purpose of the WTO?
- What is the key objective of a common market like the European Union?

LO 3–6   Discuss the changing landscape of the global market and the issue of offshore outsourcing.

The Future of Global Trade

Global trade opportunities grow more interesting and more challenging each day. After all, over 7.7 billion potential customers are attractive. However, terrorism, nuclear proliferation, rogue states, income inequality, trade wars, and other issues cast a dark shadow on global markets. Let's conclude this chapter by looking at issues certain to influence global markets, and perhaps your business career.

With more than 1.4 billion people and incredible exporting prowess, China has transformed the world economic map. China is the world's largest exporter and the second-largest economy. Not long ago, foreign direct investment in China was considered risky and not worth the risk. In 2018, China attracted $136 billion in foreign direct investment. Today, over 400 of the *Fortune* 500 companies (the world's largest companies) have invested in China. China has been the largest motor vehicle market in the world since 2009.[59] Walmart began operations in China in 1996 and now has over 400 stores, with plans to open more. Some economists even predict China will overtake the United States as the world's largest economy within the 2020s.[60]

Many view China as a free trader's dream, where global investment and entrepreneurship will lead to wealth. However, concerns remain about China's one-party political system, human rights abuses, currency issues, increasing urban population growth, trade restrictions, and aging population. China's underground economy still generates significant product piracy and counterfeiting, although the country has been more responsive to these problems since its admission to the WTO. With the global economy continuing to grow, China will be a key driver of the world economy along with the United States, the EU, and Japan.

While China attracts most of the attention in Asia, India's population of over 1.36 billion presents a tremendous opportunity. With nearly 50 percent of its population under the age of 25, India's working-age population will continue to grow while the United States, China, and the EU face declining and aging populations in the 2020s. In fact, India is expected to surpass China as the world's most populated country in 2024. India has seen strong growth in information technology and biotechnology, and its pharmaceutical business is expected

China's economy is booming, and a highly educated middle class with money to spend is emerging, especially in the cities. Many observers believe China will continue its growth and play a major role in the global economy. Are U.S. firms prepared to compete?

Tuul & Bruno Morandi/Getty Images

to grow to $55 billion in 2020. The government is trying to transform the country's image as a difficult place to do business, but difficult trade laws and an inflexible bureaucracy are continuing challenges.[61] Many economists hope for better times for India.

Russia and Brazil were projected to be wealthy global economies by 2025. Unfortunately, Russia's economy slowed when world oil prices declined and the government admitted that growth prospects for its economy were not strong for the next two decades. To complicate matters, Russia is plagued by political, currency, and social problems and is considered by Transparency International as the world's most corrupt major economy. Brazil is the largest economy in South America and the seventh-largest economy in the world, with well-developed agriculture, mining, manufacturing, and service sectors. Along with Russia, Brazil was expected to dominate the global market as a supplier of raw materials. Unfortunately, the past few years have been tough times for Brazil's economy, with widespread political corruption, inflation, and slow growth.[62] Still, its growing consumer market of over 200 million people is a prime target for major exporters like the United States and China.

Other areas of opportunity include the developing nations of Asia. Today, South Korea and Vietnam rank fifth and sixth in terms of exports to the United States. Trade with both countries increased significantly due to U.S. trade conflicts with China.[63] The potential of both nations has not gone unnoticed among competing global producers. German giant Adidas, the second-largest athletic gear maker in the world, decided to close its footwear facilities in Ansbach, Germany, and suburban Atlanta, Georgia, and move facilities to a high-tech "speedfactory" in Vietnam where it will test automated production technology for footwear.

Africa has only begun to emerge as a center for global economic growth, with East Africa expected to be the major center of growth. As you can see, business today is truly global, and your role in it is up to you.

The Challenge of Offshore Outsourcing

Outsourcing is the process whereby one firm contracts with other companies, often in other countries, to do some or all of its functions. In the United States, companies have outsourced payroll functions, accounting, and some manufacturing operations for many years. However, the shift to primarily low-wage global markets, called *offshore outsourcing,* remains a major issue in the United States. Take a look at the pros and cons of offshore outsourcing in Figure 3.9.

As lower-level manufacturing became more simplified, U.S. companies such as Levi Strauss and Nike outsourced manufacturing offshore. Today, we have moved beyond the outsourcing of manufactured goods to what economists call the "second wave" of offshore outsourcing, shifting from strict product assembly to design and architecture. Increasing numbers of skilled, educated, middle-income workers in service-sector jobs that require

outsourcing
Contracting with other companies (often in other countries) to do some or all of the functions of a firm, like its production or accounting tasks.

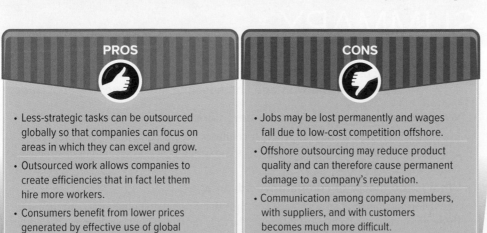

FIGURE 3.9 THE PROS AND CONS OF OFFSHORE OUTSOURCING

PROS

- Less-strategic tasks can be outsourced globally so that companies can focus on areas in which they can excel and grow.
- Outsourced work allows companies to create efficiencies that in fact let them hire more workers.
- Consumers benefit from lower prices generated by effective use of global resources and developing nations grow, thus fueling global economic growth.

CONS

- Jobs may be lost permanently and wages fall due to low-cost competition offshore.
- Offshore outsourcing may reduce product quality and can therefore cause permanent damage to a company's reputation.
- Communication among company members, with suppliers, and with customers becomes much more difficult.

specific training such as accounting, law, finance, risk management, health care, and information technology are seeing their jobs outsourced offshore.

Loss of jobs through offshore outsourcing has been a major concern. Today, IBM has more employees in India than in the United States. However, it's not the only concern. Nations such as China have a spotty safety record in manufacturing toys, food, pet food, and drugs. Boeing experienced problems with batteries and electrical systems on its 787 Dreamliner due to poor-quality components outsourced from its supply chain. Some medical providers are shifting surgical procedures to nations such as India to save costs. Eastern Europe, India, China, and other emerging Asian nations are the most popular locations for offshore outsourcing.

As technical talent grows around the globe, offshore outsourcing will likely increase and be challenged. To stay competitive, education and training will be critical for U.S. workers to preserve the skill premium they possess today and to stay ahead in the future.

Globalization and Your Future

Whether you aspire to be an entrepreneur, a manager, or some other type of business leader, think globally in planning your career. By studying foreign languages, learning about foreign cultures, and taking business courses (including a global business course), you can develop a global perspective on your future. As you progress through this text, keep two things in mind: globalization is real, and economic competition promises to intensify.

Also keep in mind that global market potential does not belong only to large, multinational corporations. Small and medium-sized businesses have a world of opportunity in front of them. In fact, these firms are often better prepared to leap into global markets and react quickly to opportunities than are large businesses. Finally, don't forget the potential of franchising, which we examine in more detail in Chapter 5.

TESTPREP

- What are the major threats to doing business in global markets?
- What key challenges must China face before becoming the major global economic leader?
- What are the two primary concerns associated with offshore outsourcing?

SUMMARY

LO 3-1 Discuss the importance of the global market and the roles of comparative advantage and absolute advantage in global trade.

- **Why should nations trade with other nations?**

  (1) No country is self-sufficient, (2) other countries need products that prosperous countries produce, and (3) natural resources and technological skills are not distributed evenly around the world.

- **What is the theory of comparative advantage?**

  The theory of comparative advantage contends that a country should make and then sell those products it produces most efficiently but buy those it cannot produce as efficiently.

- **What is absolute advantage?**

  Absolute advantage exists if a country produces a specific product more efficiently than any other country. There are few examples of absolute advantage in the global market today.

LO 3-2 Explain the importance of importing and exporting, and understand key terms used in global business.

- **What kinds of products can be imported and exported?**

  Though it is not necessarily easy, just about any product can be imported or exported.

- **What terms are important in understanding world trade?**

  Exporting is selling products to other countries. *Importing* is buying products from other countries. The *balance of trade* is the relationship of exports to imports. The *balance of payments* is the balance of trade plus other money flows such as tourism and foreign aid. *Dumping* is selling products for less in a foreign country than in your own country. See the Key Terms list after this Summary to be sure you know the other important terms.

LO 3-3 Illustrate the strategies used in reaching global markets, and explain the role of multinational corporations.

- **What are some ways in which a company can engage in global business?**

  Ways of entering global trade include licensing, exporting, franchising, contract manufacturing, joint ventures and strategic alliances, and direct foreign investment.

- **How do multinational corporations differ from other companies that participate in global business?**

  Unlike companies that only export or import, multinational corporations also have manufacturing facilities or other physical presence in global markets.

LO 3-4 Evaluate the forces that affect trading in global markets.

- **What are some of the forces that can discourage participation in global business?**

  Potential stumbling blocks to global trade include sociocultural forces, economic and financial forces, legal and regulatory forces, and physical and environmental forces.

LO 3-5 Debate the advantages and disadvantages of trade protectionism.

- **What is trade protectionism?**

  Trade protectionism is the use of government regulations to limit the import of goods and services. Advocates believe it allows domestic producers to grow, producing more jobs. The key tools of protectionism are tariffs, import quotas, and embargoes.

- **What are tariffs?**

  Tariffs are taxes on foreign products. Protective tariffs raise the price of foreign products and protect domestic industries; revenue tariffs raise money for the government.

- **What is an embargo?**

  An embargo prohibits the importing or exporting of certain products to a particular country.

- **Is trade protectionism good for domestic producers?**

  That is debatable. Trade protectionism offers pluses and minuses.

- **Why do governments continue such practices?**

  The theory of mercantilism started the practice of trade protectionism and it has persisted, though in a weaker form, ever since.

LO 3-6 Discuss the changing landscape of the global market and the issue of offshore outsourcing.

- **What is offshore outsourcing? Why is it a major concern for the future?**

  Outsourcing is the purchase of goods and services from outside a firm rather than providing them from inside the company. Today, many businesses are outsourcing manufacturing and services offshore. Many fear that growing numbers of jobs in the United States will be lost due to offshore outsourcing and that the quality of products produced could be inferior.

KEY TERMS

absolute advantage 60

balance of payments 62

balance of trade 62

common market 75

comparative advantage
  theory 60

contract
  manufacturing 66

countertrading 72

devaluation 71

dumping 63

embargo 74

exchange rate 71

exporting 59

foreign direct
  investment (FDI) 68

foreign subsidiary 68

free trade 60

General Agreement on
  Tariffs and Trade
  (GATT) 75

importing 59

import quota 74

joint venture 67

licensing 64

multinational corporation 68

North American Free
  Trade Agreement
  (NAFTA) 77

outsourcing 79

sovereign wealth
  funds (SWFs) 68

strategic alliance 67

tariff 74

trade deficit 62

trade protectionism 74

trade surplus 62

United States–Mexico–
  Canada Agreement
  (USMCA) 77

World Trade Organization
  (WTO) 75

CRITICAL THINKING

1. About 95 percent of the world's population lives outside the United States, but many U.S. companies, especially small businesses, still do not engage in global trade. Why not? Do you think more small businesses will participate in global trade in the future? Why or why not?

2. Countries like the United States that have a high standard of living are referred to as *industrialized nations*. Countries with a lower standard of living and quality of life are called *developing countries* (or sometimes *underdeveloped* or *less-developed countries*). What factors often prevent developing nations from becoming industrialized nations?

3. What can businesses do to prevent unexpected problems in dealing with sociocultural, economic and financial, legal and regulatory, and physical and environmental forces in global markets?

4. How would you justify the use of revenue or protective tariffs in today's global market?

PUTTING PRINCIPLES TO WORK

PURPOSE

To compare the shifting exchange rates of various countries and to predict the effects of such exchange shifts on global trade.

EXERCISE

One of the difficulties of engaging in global trade is the constant shift in exchange rates. How much do exchange rates change over a 30-day period? Research this by choosing five currencies (say, the euro, the British pound, the Japanese yen, the Mexican peso, the Saudi Arabian riyal) and looking at their exchange rates relative to the U.S. dollar for the past month. The rates are available online at Yahoo! Finance (finance.yahoo.com/currency-converter). Choose a company and describe what effects the currency shifts you noted might have on this company's trade with each of the countries or areas whose currency you chose.

DEVELOPING CAREER SKILLS

KEY: ● **Team**   ★ **Analytic**   ▲ **Communication**   ▣ **Technology**

1. Find out firsthand the global impact on your life. How many different countries' names appear on the labels in your clothes? How many languages do your classmates speak? List the ethnic restaurants in your community. Are they family-owned or corporate chains?   ▲

2. Call, e-mail, or visit a local business that imports foreign goods (perhaps a wine or specialty foods importer). Ask the owner or manager about the business's participation in global trade, and compile a list of the advantages and disadvantages he or she cites. Compare notes with your classmates about their research.   ▲ ★

3. Visit four or five public locations in your community such as schools, hospitals, city/county buildings, or airports. See how many signs are posted in different languages (don't forget the restrooms) and look for other multilingual information, such as brochures or handouts. Do any of the locations fly flags from different nations? In what other ways do they recognize the diversity of employees or students? What does your search tell you about your community?   ★

4. Suppose Representative I. M. Wright delivers a passionate speech at your college on tariffs. He argues tariffs are needed to   ▲ ★

   a. Protect our young and struggling industries.
   b. Encourage consumers to buy U.S.-made products because it's patriotic.
   c. Protect U.S. jobs and wages.
   d. Achieve a favorable balance of trade and balance of payments.

   Do you agree with Representative Wright? Evaluate each of his major points and decide whether you consider it valid. Be sure to justify your position.

5. Form an imaginary joint venture with three classmates and select a product, service, or idea to market to a specific country. Have each team member select a key global market force in that country (sociocultural, economic and financial, legal and regulatory, or physical and environmental) to research. Have each report his or her findings. Then, as a group, prepare a short explanation of whether the market is worth pursuing or avoiding.   ● ▲ ★

CAREER EXPLORATION

If you are interested in pursuing a career in international business, here are a few to consider. Find out about the tasks performed, skills needed, pay, and opportunity outlook in these fields in the *Occupational Outlook Handbook (OOH)* at bls.gov.

■ **Customs broker**—acts as a liaison between the federal government and import/export firms; handles the logistics of moving products across borders.

■ **Translator**—converts information from one language into another language.

■ **Wholesale and manufacturing sales representative**—sells goods for wholesalers or manufacturers to businesses, government agencies, and other organizations in global markets.

■ **Buyer and purchasing agent**—buys products and services for organizations to use or resell; evaluates suppliers, negotiates contracts, and reviews the quality of products.

VIDEO CASE

McGraw Hill connect   *Domino's Wild World of Pizza*

Mention the word *Domino's* and you probably think of pizza delivery. The company that started in a small store in Ypsilanti, Michigan, built its business by promising a tasty, hot pizza delivered directly to your location. Today, Domino's is the largest pizza delivery chain in the world with locations in over 80 global markets. While you might think pizza is the same throughout the world, regional tastes and customs can be very different. Domino's success has been based on its ability to spread its offerings to many varied customers.

Brian Trier, vice president of the Americas and International Marketing, explains the strategy Domino's uses when it enters a new market. "So, the first thing we do when we go into a new market is try to answer important questions such as: What's the local regional tastes? What do they enjoy eating? How exactly do they eat? Do they eat in groups? Do they eat by themselves? What time of the day do folks eat?" These are the questions and challenges that must be accommodated and addressed if Domino's expects to succeed in global markets.

Another major issue Domino's must address in targeting global markets is the availability of an acceptable supply chain. In fact, according to Trier, it's the company's number-one challenge. "We must make sure there is availability and acceptable quality in the local regional markets. If the right products are not available, or of the quality that's acceptable, the company must limit the products they can offer. It's also critical that the quantity of the product that's needed is available."

A good example of a global opportunity that required careful adaptation was the company's move into India. Traditionally, the Indian diet was primarily vegetarian, but meat consumption was becoming more common. In accepting the meat challenge, Domino's began offering both pork and chicken pepperoni with its pizza. It was very careful, however, to make sure consumers could easily identify the pizza ingredients. The company also found that India had very significant regional differences between the north and south related to spices as well as vegan and nonvegan. The company found that it was important to have stickers on the front of the pizza boxes, red for a nonvegan product and green for a vegan product, to make sure a customer opens the right box.

Tailoring menu items to fit the needs of specific geographic locations and cultures was fairly straightforward. However, tailoring the company's marketing approach was a bit more challenging. For example, Domino's produced a soap-opera series in South Korea to introduce customers to the journey into Domino's. A couple met along the way, found the path to Domino's, got married, and continued their life together at Domino's Pizza. Asian cultures like South Korea's were difficult for Domino's since most Asians are not consumers of bread and cheese products. Knowing that fact, the company took its time to educate customers concerning pizza and its great taste. Domino's did this by first introducing a number of chicken and rib products, along with lasagna and salad to supplement pizza.

The country of Turkey presented another challenge. Turkish consumers wanted a good deal of meat on their pizza and fewer vegetables. The meat was also expected to be high quality. Therefore, pizza in Turkey is served with a heavy layer of meat cut in a way consumers see it as a high-quality product they would grill at their own homes.

Pizza is a surprisingly translatable meal served around the globe. Domino's recognizes it is first and foremost a pizza company built on high-quality products and an established delivery system. However, the company clearly understands the need to be flexible in dealing with the wide variances that exist in markets around the world. According to Trier, "adapting a product to local markets is perhaps the most critical factor to any business hoping to build a market in the global marketplace." Domino's practices this principle very well.

THINKING IT OVER

1. What major factors affect Domino's or any other major company in dealing in global markets?

2. Why does Domino's carefully research supply chain potential before it decides to enter a global market?

3. What delivery problems could Domino's face in dealing with various global markets?

NOTES

1. *World Atlas,* worldatlas.com, accessed January 2020; U.S. Census Bureau, census.gov, accessed February 2020.
2. Ken Roberts, "Mexico Is Now Top Trade Partner, Ahead of China, Canada," *Forbes,* April 26, 2019; Statista, statista. com, accessed January 2020.
3. James T. Areddy, "China's New Costco Draws Crowd," *The Wall Street Journal,* August 28, 2019; Andria Cheng, "Think the Fervor around Costco's First Store in China Is Fleeting? Think Again," *Forbes,* August 28, 2019; "First-Ever Costco Thrives in China," *Investor's Business Daily,* investors.com, January 9, 2020.
4. Walmart, corporate.walmart.com, accessed October 2019; Alexandra Wexler, "PepsiCo Makes Push into Africa," *The Wall Street Journal,* July 21, 2019; Philip Georgiadis, "PepsiCo Plots Expansion in Africa with $1.7 Billion Deal," *Financial Times,* July 19, 2019; Janice Kew, "Walmart's South Africa

Firm Plans Job Cuts in Profit Slump," *Bloomberg,* bloomberg. com, January 13, 2020; Trefis Team, "How Important Is Europe & Sub-Saharan Africa for PepsiCo's Growth?," NASDAQ, nasdaq.com, January 13, 2020.
5. Major League Baseball International, mlb.com, accessed January 2020.
6. Kevin Patra, "NFL Unveils Dates, Times for 2019 International Games," NFL, nfl.com, April 17, 2019; NBA, global.nba.com, accessed January 2020.
7. Ian Thomas, "NBC Sports Plots Plan to Deepen Premier League Reach in U.S.," Front Office Sports, frntofficesports.com, August 9, 2019; John Ourand, "Sky Deal Gives NBC Higher-Quality Premier League Games," *Business Journal,* bizjournals.com, August 7, 2019.
8. Scott Lincicome, "The Case for Free Trade," *National Review,* nationalreview.com, May 2, 2019: Patricia M. Goff,

"Trade and Culture: The Ongoing Debate," *International Journal of Cultural Policy,* July 30, 2019; Fred P. Hochberg, "Let Trump Have His Trade Wars," *USA Today,* usatoday.com, January 17, 2020.

9. Kimberly Amadeo, "Comparative Advantage Theory and Examples," *The Balance,* thebalance.com, May 30, 2019; Jim Chappelow, "Who Was David Ricardo?," *Investopedia,* July 14, 2019; Tim Worstall, "Comparative Advantage Is Indeed Difficult," Adam Smith Institute, adamsmith.org, January 8, 2020.

10. "Facts & Data on Small Business and Entrepreneurship," Small Business & Entrepreneurship Council, sbecouncil. org, accessed January 2020.

11. Starbucks Coffee Company, starbucks.com, accessed January 2020.

12. Benjamin Romano, "Starbucks Reveals Opulent Store in Milan, the Culmination of Howard Schultz's Italian Dream," *The Seattle Times,* September 7, 2018; Claudia Romeo, "Inside Italy's Only Starbucks That's the Biggest in Europe and Serves Pizza and Cocktails," *Insider,* insider.com, August 6, 2019; "The Italian Market Potential for Coffee," Centre for the Promotion of Imports, cbi.eu, accessed January 2020.

13. Michael Gubisch, "Sierra Nevada to Restart Dornier 328 Production in Germany," *Flight Global,* flightglobal.com, August 15, 2019; "Sierra Nevada Collaborates with Bitburger Brewery on Oktoberfest Beer," B*evNET,* bevnet. com, May 8, 2019; Todd Alstrom, "The Year in Beer," *BeerAdvocate,* beeradvocate.com, January 13, 2020.

14. "2020 Airbnb Update," Airbnb, news.airbnb.com, January 21, 2020.

15. C. Fred Bergsten, "Current Trade Policies and the US Economy," Peterson Institute for International Economics, piie.com, June 19, 2019.

16. Natasha Bach, "Trump's Plan to Reduce Trade Deficit Falters as It Hits an All-Time High Instead," *Fortune,* March 6, 2019; Jim Tankersley and Ana Swanson, "In Blow to Trump, America's Trade Deficit in Goods Hits Record $891 Billion," *The New York Times,* March 6, 2019; Jeff Cox, "US Trade Deficit Falls More Than Expected to Hit Lowest Level since Trump Took Office," *CNBC,* cnbc.com, January 7, 2020.

17. "US Imposes New Anti-Dumping Duties on Chinese Mattresses, Beer Kegs," *CNBC,* cnbc.com, May 29, 2019; "U.S. Department of Commerce Initiates Antidumping Duty and Countervailing Duty Investigations of Imports of Forged Steel Fluid End Blocks from China, Germany, India, and Italy," U.S. Commerce Department, commerce.gov, January 9, 2020.

18. "The Coca-Cola System," The Coca-Cola Company, coca-colacompany.com, accessed January 2020.

19. Etan Vlessing, "Disney Consumer Products Hits $54.7 Bn in Retail Sales as Top Global Licensor of 2018," *The Hollywood Reporter,* hollywoodreporter.com, August 8, 2019; Amy Watson, "Disney—Statistics & Facts," Statista, statista.com, September 26, 2019.

20. U.S. Commercial Service, export.gov, accessed January 2020; U.S. Small Business Administration, sba.gov, accessed January 2020.

21. "15 Years of Fit," Snap Fitness, snapfitness.com, accessed January 2020.

22. Maria Aspan, "Why the Founders of Physique 57 Are Determined to Bring Their New York Fitness Boutique to Saudi Arabia," *Inc.,* March/April 2019.

23. Rocky Mountain Chocolate Factory, rmcf.com, accessed January 2020.

24. Domino's, biz.dominos.com, accessed January 2020.

25. Dunkin Brands, dunkindonuts.com, accessed January 2020.

26. "Medical Device Contract Manufacturing Update— Winter 2018–2019," Duff & Phelps, duffandphelps.com, accessed January 2020.

27. "For Disney, Its Shanghai Resort Is a Local Company," CBS News, *cbsnews.com,* April 26, 2018; Patrick Frater, "Disney to Open 'Zootopia' Land at Shanghai Theme Park," *Variety,* January 22, 2019; Brittani Tuttle, "Celebrate the Year of the Mouse with Spring Festival at Shanghai Disney Resort," *Attractions Magazine,* January 9, 2020.

28. "Did Johnson & Johnson Just Spit in Alphabet's Face?," *OrthoFeed,* orthofeed.com, February 16, 2019; Michelle Tindera, "Alphabet's Verb Surgical's CEO Exits, Health Robotics Startup Has Not Named a Replacement," *Forbes,* January 18, 2019.

29. University of Pittsburgh Medical Center Italy, upmcitaly. it, accessed January 2020; Paul J. Gough, "UPMC Plans Second Hospital in Sicily," *Pittsburgh Business Times,* January 8, 2019.

30. Paul A. Eisenstein, "Behind the Scenes: How Toyota and BMW Teamed Up to Develop New Z4 and Supra, *The Detroit Bureau,* May 13, 2019; Edward Loh, "Why Toyota's Supra-Z4 Partnership with BMW Makes Sense," *MotorTrend,* January 14, 2019; Curtis Moldrich and Jake Groves, "New Toyota Supra," *Car* magazine, carmagazine. co.uk, January 14, 2020.

31. Carol Lombardo, "Xerox to Sell Stake in Joint Venture to Fujifilm for about $2.3 Billion," *The Wall Street Journal,* November 5, 2019; O'Ryan Johnson, "Fujifilm to End 58-Year-Old Xerox Joint Venture in March 2021," The Channel Company, crn.com, January 7, 2020.

32. "First Walmart E-Commerce Store in Japan Officially Opens on Rakuten Ichiba," Rakuten, rakutentoday.com, February 15, 2019.

33. Nestlé SA, nestle.com, accessed January 2020.

34. "Top 83 Largest Sovereign Wealth Fund Rankings by Total Assets," Sovereign Wealth Fund Institute, swfinstitute.org, accessed January 2020.

35. Nathaniel Meyersohn, "How a Cheap, Brutally Efficient Grocery Chain Is Upending America's Supermarkets," *CNN Business,* cnn.com, May 17, 2019; Jaewon Kang, "Grocers Feel Heat from Two Overseas Rivals," *The Wall Street Journal,* October 16, 2019; Mike Troy, "Aldi Will Begin 2020 with Nearly 2000 Stores," *Store Brands,* November 12, 2019; "Aldi History," Aldi, corporate.aldi.us, accessed January 2020.

36. Eric Mandel, "Lidl to Invest $100M, Create 270 Jobs for Georgia Regional Distribution Center," *Atlanta Business Chronicle,* bizjournals.com, January 3, 2020; *Lidl,* lidl.com, accessed June 2020.

37. Jonathan Gregson, "The World's Richest and Poorest Countries," *Global Finance,* February 14, 2019; "Countries with the Lowest Incomes," *World Atlas,* accessed January 2020.

38. Jamie Matusow, "Innovation and Sustainability Drive L'Oréal's Packaging," *Beauty Packaging,* January 30, 2017; Varuni Khosla and Rasul Bailay, "Indian Cosmetics Industry: Mini on Mind for Beauty Conscious," *The Economic Times,* economictimes.indiatimes.com, accessed January 2020.

39. Siobhan O'Grady, "Venezuela's Crisis in Six Charts," *The Washington Post,* January 26, 2019; Antonio Maria Delgado, "Venezuela Had a Brutal Year. The Outlook for 2019 Isn't Any Better, Experts Say,"

Miami Herald, January 1, 2019; Steve Hanke, "Venezuela's Hyperinflation Hits 80,000 Percent per Year in 2018," *Forbes,* January 1, 2019.

40. Max de Haldevang, "Inflation Causes Maduro to Raise Minimum Wage 67% but a Month of Work Still Can't Buy 1 Kg of Beef," *Quartz,* qz.com, January 11, 2020.

41. World Trade Organization, wto.org, accessed January 2020.

42. Austen Hufford, "3M Probes Potential Anti-bribery Violations," *The Wall Street Journal,* July 29, 2019; U.S. Securities & Exchange Commission, sec.gov, accessed January 2020; Josh Wingrove, "White House Considers Changes to Law Banning Overseas Bribes," *Bloomberg,* January 17, 2020.

43. Organization for Economic Cooperation and Development, oecd.org, accessed January 2020; Transparency International, transparency.org, accessed January 2020.

44. Jeanna Smialek and Ana Swanson, "American Consumers, Not China, Are Paying for Trump's Tariffs," *The New York Times,* nytimes.com, January 6, 2020; Michael Hiltzik, "Trump's China Trade Deal Doesn't Even Get Us Back to Square One, Despite Immense Cost," *Los Angeles Times,* latimes.com, January 15, 2020; Gina Heeb, "Americans Have Paid an Extra $46 Billion in Tariffs Since the Start of the China Trade War," *Business Insider,* businessinsider.com, January 9, 2020; Rochelle Toplensky, "Tariffs Cost U.S. Consumers," *The Wall Street Journal,* January 15, 2020.

45. Kwanwoo Jun and William Mauldin, "U.S Dusts Off Quota Rules," *The Wall Street Journal,* May 13, 2019; "Quota Bulletin," U.S. Customs and Border Protection, cbp.gov, accessed January 2020.

46. Vivian Salama, "U.S. Expands Sanctions against Venezuela into an Embargo," *The Wall Street Journal,* August 5, 2019; Michael Crowley and Anatoly Kurmanaev, "Trump Imposes New Sanctions on Venezuela," *The New York Times,* August 6, 2019; Anthony Faiola, "Madera Says He Is Still in Control in Venezuela, Ready for Direct Talks with the U.S.," *The Washington Post,* January 18, 2020.

47. Council on Foreign Relations, cfr.org, accessed January 2020; Mimi Whitefield, "Trump Officials Say Cuba Meddles in Venezuela, but Havana Almost Ignored in Threat Report," *Miami Herald,* miamiherald.com, February 1, 2019; Nora Gamez Torres, "Trump Readies New Sanctions on Cuba," *Miami Herald,* miamiherald.com, December 30, 2019; Conor Finnegan, "US Further Restricts Air Travel to Cuba to Increase Pressure," *ABC News,* abcnews.go.com, January 10, 2020.

48. World Trade Organization, wto.org, accessed January 2020.

49. Ana Swanson, "Trump Cripples WTO While Trade War Rages," *The New York Times,* December 8, 2019; Jacob M. Schlesinger, "Will the U.S. Bring Down the WTO?," *The Wall Street Journal,* December 1, 2019; Doug Palmer, "Trump's 2020 Trade Vision," *Politico,* politico.com, January 6, 2020.

50. "World Economic Outlook Database, April 2020," International Monetary Fund, IMF.org, accessed April 2020.

51. Benjamin Mueller, "What Is Brexit? A Simple Guide to Why It Matters and What Happens Next," *The New York Times,* January 30, 2019; Giles Turner, "Data Sharing Adds to the List of Brexit Challenges for UK and EU: Quick Take," *The Washington Post,* February 15, 2019; Tariro Mzezewa, "How Brexit Will Affect Travel to the UK and Europe," *The New York Times,* January 16, 2020.

52. Claire Felter, Danielle Renwick, and Andrew Chatzky, "Mercosur: South America's Fractious Trade Block," Council on Foreign Relations, cfr.org, July 10, 2019; "EU-Mercosur Trade Deal Could Be Ready by Late 2020 in Best Case," Reuters, August 28, 2019; Associated Press, "Belgium Region 'Totally Opposes' Mercosur Trade Pact," *International Business Times,* ibt.com, January 20, 2020.

53. ASEAN Economic Community, asean.org, accessed January 2020.

54. Grace Shao, "What You Should Know about Africa's Massive, 54-Country Trade Bloc," *CNBC,* cnbc.com, July 11, 2019; David Meyer, "The Largest Free Trade Deal in Nearly a Quarter-Century Seeks to Make Africa a Single Market," *Fortune,* May 25, 2019; NAN, "Nigeria Undergoing Reforms for AfCFTA," *The Guardian,* January 6, 2020.

55. Niv Elis, "Grassley Signs USMCA, Sending It to Trump's Desk," *The Hill,* thehill.com, January 22, 2020; Ana Swanson and Jim Tankersley, "Trump Just Signed USMCA. Here's What's in the New NAFTA," *The New York Times,* January 28, 2020; Michael Collins, "Trump Signs Revised Trade Deal with Mexico, Canada, but Shuts Democrats Out of Celebration," *USA Today,* January 28, 2020.

56. Kimberly Amadeo, "NAFTA Pros and Cons," *The Balance,* thebalance.com, December 14, 2019; John Burnett, "$11 Billion and Counting," National Public Radio, npr.org, January 19, 2020.

57. "United States–Mexico–Canada Trade Fact Sheet," Office of United States Trade Representative, ustr.gov, accessed February 2020.

58. Department of Commerce, International Trade Administration, trade.gov, accessed January 2020.

59. Robert Ferris, "China Annual Auto Sales Fall for First Time in about Two Decades with More Pain on the Way," *CNBC,* cnbc.com, January 3, 2019; Yilei Sun and Brenda Goh, "Auto Industry Cautious as China Starts 2020 with a Forecast of a 2% Sales Decline," Reuters, January 12, 2020.

60. David Fickling, "China Could Outrun the U.S. Next Year. Or Never," *Bloomberg,* bloomberg.com, March 8, 2019; Alexandra Stevenson, "China's Improving Economic Data Mask Deeper Problems," *The New York Times,* January 16, 2020.

61. Erich Bellman and Rajesh Roy, "India Sees Opportunity to Lure Big Companies from China," *The Wall Street Journal,* October 21, 2019; Newley Purnell, "Bezos Vows $1 Billion for Amazon in India," *The Wall Street Journal,* January 16, 2020.

62. "Brazil," *The Economist,* country.eiu.com/brazil, accessed October 2019; "Brazil: Much Work Needs to Be Done," *Deloitte,* deloitte.com, accessed January 2020.

63. Karen Waksman, "Top Countries Exporting to the U.S.," *The Balance Small Business,* thebalancesmb.com, December 11, 2019; Christian Smith, "Taiwan and South Korea Move to Expand Their Tech Influence as US-China Trade War Drags On," *CNBC,* cnbc.com, January 11, 2020

4

Demanding Ethical and Socially Responsible Behavior

LEARNING OBJECTIVES >> *After you have read and studied this chapter, you should be able to*

LO 4–1 Explain why obeying the law is only the first step in behaving ethically.

LO 4–2 Ask the three questions you need to answer when faced with a potentially unethical action.

LO 4–3 Describe management's role in setting ethical standards.

LO 4–4 Distinguish between compliance-based and integrity-based ethics codes, and list the six steps in setting up a corporate ethics code.

LO 4–5 Define *corporate social responsibility,* and compare corporations' responsibilities to various stakeholders.

LO 4–6 Analyze the role of U.S. businesses in influencing ethical behavior and social responsibility in global markets.

GETTING TO KNOW

Matt Damon and Gary White, Cofounders of Water.org

In the classic poem "The Rime of the Ancient Mariner" Samuel Taylor Coleridge laments the fate of sailors dying of thirst while drifting at sea: "Water, water, everywhere, nor any drop to drink." Of course, these days not many people in developed nations give much thought to the availability of this seemingly abundant resource. While water is easily accessible in the United States, that's not the case in many other places. In fact, 663 million people across the world still don't have access to safe water, and one out of three people (2.4 billion) doesn't have a toilet.

Besides damaging the health and well-being of billions of people, lack of clean water also creates a tremendous obstacle to economic growth. In many impoverished countries, women and school-age children must search for and collect clean water for their families. Experts estimate that young girls and women spend 200 million hours every day gathering clean water from sources far away from their homes. This burden prevents young girls from attending school and achieving a future beyond their current life.

"The potential it robs people of, right?," said actor and cofounder of the nonprofit Water.org Matt Damon. "If you are a little girl who now can't go to school because you are in charge of water collection for your family, and you are spending your entire day scavenging for water, what kind of outcome can you expect for your life? Certainly you are not going to live up to your potential." When Damon first became aware of this issue, he used his resources and influence to form a nonprofit called H2O Africa. Then he met Gary White, an entrepreneur and engineer who had been running his own clean water organization for more than two decades. In 2009, the two partnered up to form Water.org, a nonprofit that helps families access microloans to fund their own water operations.

Families helped by the organization typically need $200 to $300 to buy a filtration system, toilet, or water-catching tank. When Water.org first launched, however, its microfinance partners found it difficult to keep up with the enormous demand. This frustrated Damon and White who recognized they could aid more families if they generated more capital into the microfinance system. So in order to secure money for equipment, Water.org sought funding from major companies like Bank of America, Target, IKEA Foundation, and many others.

Rather than simply soliciting donations, though, Damon and White formed a separate nonprofit called WaterEquity to invest in various enterprises. The organization is raising over $50 million and offers investors an annual return of 3.5 percent, a rate that's lower than what could generally be achieved through

a private equity fund. Rather than pass on all the profits to investors, Water.org provides that money to millions of underprivileged people. "We take those funds and invest them in enterprises that serve the poor in terms of their water and sanitation needs," said White.

Using this business model, Water.org's goal is to provide 4.6 million people with clean water and sanitation over the course of seven years. The organization has already provided more than 16 million people with water relief, the vast majority of whom have paid back their initial microloans. "These loans pay back between 97 and 99 percent," said Damon. And as more consumers push companies toward social responsibility, the worthy goals of Water.org will likely remain appealing to the organization's corporate funders for years to come.

For ethical entrepreneurs like Matt Damon and Gary White, receiving feedback and cooperation and seeing results is the best part of their business. In this chapter, we explore the responsibility of businesses to their stakeholders: customers, investors, employees, and society. We look at the responsibilities of individuals as well. After all, companies like Water.org depend on the responsible behavior and commitment of everyone involved in the business mission.

Sources: "Beckie Strum, "Water Solutions: How a Hollywood A-lister Teamed Up with a Social Entrepreneur on a Mission to End the Global Water Crisis," PENTA, March 2019; Devin Thorpe, "Matt Damon's Water Charity Takes Impact Investing Plunge," Forbes, December 19, 2018; Catherine Clifford, "Matt Damon: A Million People a Year Die 'Completely Needlessly' from Lack of Clean Water," CNBC, CNBC. com, March 22, 2018; Barbara Booth, "Matt Damon's Water Crusade Has Helped 16 Million People So Far," CNBC, CNBC.com, January 24, 2019; water.org, accessed February 2020; Water Equity, waterequity.org, accessed February 2020.

Let's talk business!
bit.ly/LetsTalkBusiness4

Rick Kern/Getty Images

LO 4–1 Explain why obeying the law is only the first step in behaving ethically.

Ethics Is More Than Legality

In the early 2000s, the U.S. public was shocked to learn that Enron, the giant energy trading company, had created off-the-books partnerships to unlawfully hide its debts and losses. The Enron disgrace was soon followed by more scandals at major companies such as World-Com, Tyco International, and Lehman Brothers (see Figure 4.1 for a summary of a few of the largest corporate scandals). Greedy borrowers and lenders alike were among those who brought the real estate, mortgage, and banking industries to the edge of a financial crisis that threatened the entire United States and world economies in 2008.[1]

Given the ethical lapses prevalent today, how can we restore trust in the free-market system and in leaders in general? First, those who have broken the law should be punished accordingly. New laws making accounting records more transparent (easy to read and understand) and businesspeople and others more accountable for their actions may also help. But laws alone don't make people honest, reliable, or truthful. If they did, crime would disappear.

In 2016, the Consumer Financial Protection Bureau fined Wells Fargo $185 million for creating more than 1.5 million fake accounts and 500,000 fraudulent credit cards in customers' names without their knowledge. This brought widespread attention to a number of other scandals associated with the financial services firm, which has resulted in Wells Fargo paying out billions of dollars in lawsuit settlements.

View_Point/Shutterstock

FIGURE 4.1 EXAMPLES OF THE LARGEST CORPORATE SCANDALS

Company	What Happened	Result
Enron Corp	Former CEO Kenneth Lay, CFO Andrew Fastow, and CEO Jeffrey Skilling were found guilty of committing accounting fraud by moving billions of dollars of debt off Enron's balance sheet which artificially inflated the company's stock and bond prices. The executives sold millions of dollars' worth of stock just before the fraud became public while the company's pension regulations prohibited regular employees from selling their stock.	The executives who bankrupted the company made millions while employees and other small investors lost $74 billion. Lay died prior to his sentencing. Fastow served a 4-year sentence, which ended in 2011. Skilling originally received a 24-year sentence, but in 2013 he struck a deal to reduce his sentence by 10 years in exchange for giving $42 million to the victims of the Enron fraud. Skilling was released in February 2019.
WorldCom	WorldCom's intentional accounting irregularities (not disclosing debt and falsely counting revenue that was not received) made the company look almost $11 billion more profitable than it was. This led to the loss of 30,000 jobs and $180 billion in losses to investors.	CEO Bernie Ebbers served 13 years of a 25-year sentence. He was released in December 2019 due to deteriorating health and died February 2, 2020. Enron's and WorldCom's collapses led to new regulations and legislation to promote the accuracy of financial reporting for publicly held companies. The 2002 Sarbanes-Oxley Act increased the consequences for destroying, altering, or fabricating financial records, and for trying to defraud shareholders.
Tyco	CEO Dennis Kozlowki and CFO Mark Swartz stole $150 million through unapproved loans and fraudulent stock sales and inflated company income $500 million.	Kozlowski and Swartz were sentenced to 8–25 years. Tyco had to pay $2.9 billion to investors. Kozlowski was released in 2012 after serving almost 7 years and Swartz was released in 2014 after serving 8 years.
Freddie Mac	The federally backed mortgage-lending giant intentionally misstated and understated $5 billion in earnings.	President/COO David Glenn, chair/CEO Leland Brensel, and former CFO Vaughn Clarke were fired.
Lehman Brothers	The global financial services firm hid over $50 billion in loans as sales.	The company was forced into the largest bankruptcy in U.S. history which helped spark the worldwide financial crisis. The SEC didn't prosecute due to lack of evidence.
Bernie L. Madoff Investment Securities	Bernie Madoff tricked investors out of $64.8 billion in the largest-ever Ponzi scheme. Madoff paid investors returns out of their own money or the money of other investors instead of out of profits.	Madoff was sentenced to 150 years plus $170 billion in restitution.

Sources: Adam Hayes, "The Rise and Fall of WorldCom," *Investopedia,* investopedia.com, January 11, 2020; Michael W. Peregrine, "Bernie Ebbers and Board Oversight of the Office of Legal Affairs," *Harvard Law School Forum on Corporate Governance,* corpgov.law.harvard.edu, January 11, 2020; Katharine Q. Seelye and Daniel Victor, "Bernard J. Ebbers, WorldCom Chief Jailed in Fraud, Dies at 78," *The New York Times,* nytimes.com, February 3, 2020.

One danger in writing new laws to correct behavior is that people may begin to think that any behavior that is within the law is also acceptable. The measure of behavior then becomes "Is it legal?" A society gets into trouble when people consider only what is illegal and not also what is unethical. Ethics and legality are two very different things. Although following the law is an important first step, behaving ethically requires more than that. Ethics reflects people's proper relationships with one another: How should we treat others? What responsibility should we feel for others? Legality is narrower. It refers to laws we have written to protect ourselves from fraud, theft, and violence. Many immoral and unethical acts fall well within our laws. For example, gossiping about your neighbor or sharing something told to you in confidence is unethical, but not illegal.

Ethical Standards Are Fundamental

ethics

Standards of moral behavior; that is, behavior accepted by society as right versus wrong.

We define **ethics** as society's accepted standards of moral behavior; that is, behaviors accepted by society as right rather than wrong. Many Americans today have few moral absolutes. Many decide situationally whether it's OK to steal, lie, or text and drive. They seem to think that what is right is whatever works best for the individual—that each person has to work out for himself or herself the difference between right and wrong. Such thinking may be part of the behavior that has led to scandals in government and business.

This isn't the way it always was. When Thomas Jefferson wrote that all men have the right to life, liberty, and the pursuit of happiness, he declared it to be a self-evident truth. Going back even further in time, the Ten Commandments were not called the "Ten Highly Tentative Suggestions."

In the United States, with so many diverse cultures, you might think it is impossible to identify common standards of ethical behavior. However, among sources from many different times and places—such as the Bible, Aristotle's *Ethics,* the Koran, and the *Analects* of Confucius—you'll find the following common statements of basic moral values: Integrity, respect for human life, self-control, honesty, courage, and self-sacrifice are right. Cheating, cowardice, and cruelty are wrong. Furthermore, all the world's major religions support a version of what some call the Golden Rule: Do unto others as you would have them do unto you.[2]

LO 4–2 Ask the three questions you need to answer when faced with a potentially unethical action.

Ethics Begins with Each of Us

It is easy to criticize business and political leaders for moral and ethical shortcomings. Both managers and workers often cite low managerial ethics as a major cause of U.S. businesses' competitive woes. But employees also frequently violate safety standards and goof off during the workweek. U.S. adults in general are not always as honest or honorable as they should be. Even though volunteerism is at an all-time high according to the U.S. Census Bureau, three of every four citizens do not give any time to the community in which they live because they think it will take too much time or they don't think they are qualified.[3]

Plagiarizing material from the Internet, including cutting and pasting information from websites without giving credit, is the most common form of cheating in schools today. To fight this problem, many instructors now use services like Turnitin, which scans students' papers against more than 40 billion online sources to provide evidence of copying in seconds. Turnitin now includes the ability to determine if a paper was written by the student who submitted it or if it was actually written by someone else.[4]

In a recent study, an alarming 51 percent of high school students admitted that they had cheated on tests in the last year.[5] Studies have found a strong relationship between academic dishonesty among undergraduates and dishonesty at work.[6] In response, many schools are establishing heavier consequences for cheating and requiring students to perform a certain number of hours of community service to graduate. Do you think such policies make a difference in student behavior?

Choices are not always easy, and the obvious ethical solution may have personal or professional drawbacks. Imagine that your supervisor has asked you to do something you feel is unethical. You've just taken out a mortgage on a new house to make room for your first baby, due in two months. Not carrying out your supervisor's request may get you fired. What should you do? Sometimes there is no easy alternative in such *ethical dilemmas* because you must choose between equally unsatisfactory alternatives.

Some days at work you are tempted to spend most of the time playing games on your computer, watching videos, texting, sending e-mails to friends, or reading a book or magazine on your devices. What is the problem in this situation? What are your alternatives? What are the consequences of each alternative? Which alternative will you choose? Is your choice ethical?

It can be difficult to balance ethics and other goals, such as pleasing stakeholders or advancing in your career. According to management writer Ken Blanchard and religious leader Norman Vincent Peale, it helps to ask yourself the following questions when facing an ethical dilemma:[7]

1. *Is my proposed action legal?* Am I violating any law or company policy? Whether you're thinking about having a drink and driving home, gathering marketing intelligence, designing a product, hiring or firing employees, getting rid of industrial waste, or using a questionable nickname for an employee, think about the legal implications. This is the most basic question in business ethics, but it is only the first.

2. *Is it balanced?* Am I acting fairly? Would I want to be treated this way? Will I win everything at the expense of another? Win–lose situations often become lose–lose situations and generate retaliation from the loser. Not every situation can be completely balanced, but the health of our relationships requires us to avoid major imbalances over time. An ethical businessperson has a win–win attitude and tries to make decisions that benefit all.

3. *How will it make me feel about myself?* Would I feel proud if my family learned of my decision? My friends? Could I discuss the proposed situation or action with my supervisor? The company's clients? Will I have to hide my actions? Has someone warned me not to disclose them? What if my decision were announced on the evening news? Am I feeling unusually nervous? Decisions that go against our sense of right and wrong make us feel bad—they erode our self-esteem. That is why an ethical businessperson does what is proper as well as what is profitable.

Individuals and companies that develop a strong ethics code and use the three questions above have a better chance than most of behaving ethically. The Making Ethical Decisions box gives you a chance to think about how you might make an ethical decision in the workplace. The Connecting through Social Media box features a story about a mother who found a way to help others sell no-longer-needed items online and instantly donate the sale proceeds to charities of their choice.

? TESTPREP

- What is ethics?
- How do ethics and legality differ?
- When faced with ethical dilemmas, what questions can you ask yourself that might help you make ethical decisions?

Creating an Online Garage Sale for a Good Cause

When Meghan Winegrad was cleaning out her St. Louis–area home of unwanted stuff, she asked her sons what they should do with their old items. Rather than drop it off at a thrift store, they decided to create a sale on Facebook and donate the proceeds to charity. "No one was bargaining or haggling, and the items sold really fast," said Winegrad. "People always followed through and picked up. That's really rare. I thought, 'I can't be the only person who wants to do this.'"

This successful sale gave Winegrad the idea to launch Generopolis, an online platform that allows people to sell stuff in support of local nonprofits. After creating an account on the site, users list the items they're selling

Twoellis/Getty Images

along with the charity they want to benefit. They can then share a link to their Generopolis sale through the social network of their choice. Before she started her company, Winegrad carefully researched the market and found that no other service offered a way to earmark sales for charities. She

also discovered that Generopolis could be especially appealing to today's young people, who have different expectations for donating to philanthropic organizations than past generations. "They want to be hands-on, not just write a check," said Winegrad. "I wanted to make giving accessible for everybody. It's a noncash model that creates cash."

Sources: "Generopolis: Spring Cleaning for a Good Cause Made Easy," *KMOV,* kmov.com, March 23, 2019; Colleen Schrappen, "Web Startup Provides New Platform for Nonprofit Giving," *The St. Louis Post-Dispatch,* June 1, 2019.

LO 4–3   Describe management's role in setting ethical standards.

Managing Businesses Ethically and Responsibly

Ethics is caught more than it is taught. That is, people learn their standards and values from observing what others do, not from hearing what they say. This is as true in business as it is at home. Organizational ethics begins at the top, and the leadership and example of strong managers can help instill corporate values in employees.

Trust and cooperation between workers and managers must be based on fairness, honesty, openness, and moral integrity. The same applies to relationships among businesses and between nations. A business should be managed ethically for many reasons: to maintain a good reputation; to keep existing customers and attract new ones; to avoid lawsuits; to reduce employee turnover; to avoid government intervention in the form of new laws and regulations controlling business activities; to please customers, employees, and society; and simply to do the right thing.

Some managers think ethics is a personal matter—either individuals have ethical principles or they don't. These managers believe that they are not responsible for an individual's misdeeds and that ethics has nothing to do with management. But a growing number of people think ethics has everything to do with management. Individuals do not usually act alone; they need the implied, if not the direct, cooperation of others to behave unethically in a corporation.

For example, several years ago there were reports of cell phone service sales representatives who actually lied to get customers to extend their contracts—or even extended their contracts without the customers' knowledge. Some phone reps intentionally hung up on callers to prevent them from canceling their contracts. Why did these sales reps sometimes resort to overly aggressive tactics? Because poorly designed incentive programs rewarded them for meeting certain goals, sometimes doubling or tripling their salaries with incentives. Did their managers say directly, "Deceive the customers"? No, but the message was clear. Overly ambitious goals and incentives can create an environment in which unethical actions like this can occur.[8]

LO 4–4   Distinguish between compliance-based and integrity-based ethics codes, and list the six steps in setting up a corporate ethics code.

Setting Corporate Ethical Standards

More and more companies have adopted written codes of ethics. Figure 4.2 offers Hershey's as a sample. Although these codes vary greatly, they can be placed into two categories: compliance-based and integrity-based (see Figure 4.3). **Compliance-based ethics codes** emphasize preventing unlawful behavior by increasing control and penalizing wrongdoers. **Integrity-based ethics codes** define the organization's guiding values, create an environment that supports ethically sound behavior, and stress shared accountability.

Here are six steps many believe can improve U.S. business ethics:[9]

1. Top management must adopt and unconditionally support an explicit corporate code of conduct.

2. Employees must understand that expectations for ethical behavior begin at the top and that senior management expects all employees to act accordingly.

3. Managers and others must be trained to consider the ethical implications of all business decisions.

4. An ethics office must be set up with which employees can communicate anonymously. **Whistleblowers** (insiders who report illegal or unethical behavior) must feel protected from retaliation. The Sarbanes-Oxley Act protects whistleblowers

compliance-based ethics codes
Ethical standards that emphasize preventing unlawful behavior by increasing control and by penalizing wrongdoers.

integrity-based ethics codes
Ethical standards that define the organization's guiding values, create an environment that supports ethically sound behavior, and stress a shared accountability among employees.

whistleblowers
Insiders who report illegal or unethical behavior.

FIGURE 4.2 OVERVIEW OF THE HERSHEY COMPANY'S CODE OF ETHICS

Note: This is an overview of Hershey's code of ethics. To see the company's complete ethics code, go to hersheypa.com/assets/pdf/code-of-conduct.pdf.
Richard Watkins/Alamy Stock Photo

CODE *of* ETHICS

We have each made a commitment to operate ethically and to lead with integrity. This commitment is embedded in the Hershey values. Our Code of Ethical Business Conduct ("Code") shows us how to uphold this commitment as we interact with the various groups that have a stake in our Company's success.

• **Our Commitment To Consumers:** We maintain the trust consumers place in our brands, providing the best products on the market and adhering to honest marketing practices.

• **Our Commitment To The Marketplace:** We deal fairly with our business partners, competitors and suppliers, acting ethically and upholding the law in everything we do.

• **Our Commitment To Stockholders:** We act honestly and transparently at all times, maintaining the trust our stockholders have placed in us.

• **Our Commitment To The Global Community:** We comply with all global trade laws, protecting our natural resources and supporting the communities where we live, work and do business.

FIGURE 4.3
STRATEGIES FOR ETHICS MANAGEMENT
Integrity-based ethics codes move beyond legal compliance to create a "do-it-right" climate that emphasizes core values such as honesty, fair play, good service to customers, a commitment to diversity, and involvement in the community. These values are ethically desirable, but not necessarily legally mandatory.

	Features of compliance-based ethics codes	Features of integrity-based ethics codes
Ideal	Conform to outside standards (laws and regulations)	Conform to outside standards (laws and regulations) and chosen internal standards
Objective	Avoid criminal misconduct	Enable responsible employee conduct
Leaders	Lawyers	Managers with aid of lawyers and others
Methods	Education, reduced employee discretion, controls, penalties	Education, leadership, accountability, decision processes, controls, and penalties

by requiring all public corporations to allow employee concerns about accounting and auditing to be submitted confidentially and anonymously. The act also requires reinstatement and back pay to people who were punished by their employers for passing on information about fraud to authorities. (We cover Sarbanes-Oxley in more detail in Chapter 17.) In 2010 the Dodd-Frank Wall Street Reform and Consumer Protection Act was signed into law (read more detail about Dodd-Frank in Chapter 17). The law includes a "bounty" provision that allows corporate whistleblowers who provide information that leads to a successful enforcement action to collect 10–30 percent of the total penalty for violations that exceed $1 million. The largest award was $50 million to an anonymous whistleblower (and, yes, it is taxable).[10]

5. Outsiders such as suppliers, subcontractors, distributors, and customers must be told about the ethics program. Pressure to put aside ethical considerations often comes from the outside, and it helps employees resist such pressure when everyone knows what the ethical standards are.

6. The ethics code must be enforced with timely action if any rules are broken. When it was discovered that the Houston Astros had violated the rules of Major League Baseball and stolen signals in the 2017 World Series, team owner Jim Crane immediately fired both the manager and general manager of the team.[11] That is the most forceful way to communicate to all employees that the code is serious.

This last step is perhaps the most critical. No matter how well intended a company's ethics code, it is worthless if not enforced. Enron had a written code of ethics. By ignoring it, Enron's board and management sent employees the message that rules could be shelved when inconvenient. In contrast, Johnson & Johnson's (J&J) response to a cyanide poisoning crisis in the 1980s shows that enforcing ethics codes can enhance profit. Although not legally required to do so, the company recalled its Tylenol products and won great praise and a reputation for corporate integrity. Today, J&J's integrity is being challenged by many court cases brought by about 16,800 plaintiffs claiming the company's talcum powder caused their cancers. While J&J lost some of these cases and has been ordered to pay more than $5 billion (in 2020, an appeals court reduced that figure by half). Some of the verdicts have been thrown out. In other cases, J&J won verdicts or there were hung juries. At the time of this writing, there are several more cases pending and the U.S. Department of Justice and the Securities and Exchange Commission have open investigations concerning possible asbestos contamination of J&J talc-based products.[12] How has the company's decision to continue to fight these cases affected its reputation for corporate integrity?

An important factor in enforcing an ethics code is selecting an ethics officer. The most effective ethics officers set a positive tone, communicate effectively, and relate well

Mark Wilson/Getty Images

Harry Markopolos is a forensic accountant who spent nearly a decade uncovering evidence that Bernie Madoff operated his wealth management company as a gigantic Ponzi scheme. Although Markopolos frequently notified the Securities and Exchange Commission about his findings, the federal agency failed to act until Madoff's sons revealed the full extent of his scam to the FBI. What motivates whistleblowers like Harry Markopolos?

to employees at every level. They are equally comfortable as counselors and investigators and can be trusted to maintain confidentiality, conduct objective investigations, and ensure fairness. They can demonstrate to stakeholders that ethics is important in everything the company does.

?TEST**PREP**

- What are compliance-based and integrity-based ethics codes?
- What are the six steps to follow in establishing an effective ethics program in a business?

LO 4–5 Define *corporate social responsibility,* and compare corporations' responsibilities to various stakeholders.

Corporate Social Responsibility

Just as you and I need to be good citizens, contributing what we can to society, corporations need to be good citizens as well. **Corporate social responsibility (CSR)** is the concern businesses have for the welfare of society, not just for their owners. CSR goes well beyond being ethical. It is based on a commitment to integrity, fairness, and respect.

You may be surprised to know that not everyone thinks that CSR is a good thing. Some critics of CSR believe that a manager's sole role is to compete and win in the marketplace. The late U.S. economist Milton Friedman made the famous statement that the

corporate social responsibility (CSR)
A business's concern for the welfare of society.

corporate philanthropy
The dimension of social responsibility that includes charitable donations.

corporate social initiatives
Enhanced forms of corporate philanthropy directly related to the company's competencies.

corporate responsibility
The dimension of social responsibility that includes everything from hiring minority workers to making safe products.

corporate policy
The dimension of social responsibility that refers to the position a firm takes on social and political issues.

only social responsibility of business is to make money for stockholders. He thought doing anything else was moving dangerously toward socialism. Other CSR critics believe that managers who pursue CSR are doing so with other people's money—which they invested to make more money, not to improve society. In this view spending money on CSR activities is stealing from investors.[13]

CSR defenders, in contrast, believe that businesses owe their existence to the societies they serve and cannot succeed in societies that fail.[14] Firms have access to society's labor pool and its natural resources, in which every member of society has a stake. Even Adam Smith, the "father" of capitalism, believed that self-interested pursuit of profit was wrong and that benevolence was the highest virtue. CSR defenders acknowledge that businesses have deep obligations to investors and should not attempt government-type social responsibility projects. However, they also argue that CSR makes more money for investors in the long run. Studies show that companies with good ethical reputations attract and retain better employees, draw more customers, and enjoy greater employee *loyalty.*[15]

The social performance of a company has several dimensions:

- **Corporate philanthropy** includes charitable donations to nonprofit groups of all kinds. A recent study of 250 of the largest companies in the world found they contribute approximately $26 billion a year to philanthropic efforts.[16] Some make long-term commitments to one cause, such as McDonald's Ronald McDonald Houses for families whose critically ill children require treatment away from home. The Bill & Melinda Gates Foundation is by far the nation's largest philanthropic foundation, with assets of more than $50 billion.[17]

- **Corporate social initiatives** include enhanced forms of corporate philanthropy. Corporate social initiatives differ from traditional philanthropy in that they are more directly related to the company's competencies. For example, three of the largest global logistics and transportation companies, Agility, UPS, and Maersk, work together to support humanitarian efforts during large-scale natural disasters. Their emergency relief teams go anywhere in the world to provide support in aviation, warehousing, transportation, reporting, and communications.[18]

- **Corporate responsibility** includes essentially everything that has to do with acting responsibly within society—for example, treating employees fairly and ethically. This is especially true of businesses that operate in other countries with different labor laws than those in the United States.

- **Corporate policy** refers to the position a firm takes on social and political issues. For example, Patagonia's corporate policy includes this statement: "A love of wild and beautiful places demands participation in the fight to save them, and to help reverse the steep decline in the overall environmental health of our planet. We donate our time, services and at least 1% of our sales to hundreds of grassroots environmental groups all over the world who work to help reverse the tide."[19]

The problems corporations cause get so much news coverage that people tend to get a negative view of their impact on society. But businesses make positive contributions too. Few people know, for example, that a Google program called Google.org Fellowship allows employees to take up to six months to work for a nonprofit organization while earning their full Google salary and benefits.[20] IBM and Wells Fargo Bank have similar programs.

In fact, many companies allow employees to give part-time help to social agencies of all kinds. For example, Fidelity Investments partnered with Common Impact to start Tech Impact Week as a way to solve some of the local nonprofit organizations' information technology–related challenges. The annual hackathon involves nearly 450 Fidelity technologists helping more than 65 nonprofit organizations solve IT problems. When the Fidelity volunteers identify cases that require longer-term support, they provide four to six months of free consulting services.[21] NetworkforGood.org, 1-800-Volunteer.org, and VolunteerMatch.org are web-based services that link volunteers with nonprofit and public-sector organizations around the country. Volunteers enter a zip code or indicate the geographic area in which they'd like to work, and the programs list organizations that could use their help.

Bruce R. Bennett/Zuma Press/Newscom

These Publix employees are planting a garden at a homeless shelter during Publix Serves Day, an annual event where the grocery chain partners with more than 135 nonprofit organizations to help communities across the Southeastern United States. Do companies have responsibilities to the communities in which they operate beyond obeying the laws?

The majority of Millennials surveyed said they would take a reduced salary to work for a socially responsible company.[22] Let's look at the concept of social responsibility through the eyes of the stakeholders to whom businesses are responsible: customers, investors, employees, and society in general. (See Figure 4.4 for examples of companies' social responsibility efforts.)

Responsibility to Customers

President John F. Kennedy proposed four basic rights of consumers: (1) the right to safety, (2) the right to be informed, (3) the right to choose, and (4) the right to be heard. These rights will be achieved only if businesses and consumers recognize them and take action in the marketplace.

A recurring theme of this book is the importance of pleasing customers by offering them real value. Since three of five new businesses fail, we know this responsibility is not as easy to meet as it seems. One sure way of failing to please customers is to be less than honest with them. The payoff for socially conscious behavior, however, can be new customers who admire the company's social efforts—a powerful competitive edge. Consumer behavior studies show that, all else being equal, a socially conscious company is likely to be viewed more favorably than others. In fact, a recent Nucleus Research survey showed that consumers surveyed were willing to pay 6 percent more for goods from socially responsible companies.[23]

Given the value customers place on social efforts, how do companies make customers aware of such efforts? One tool many companies use to raise awareness of their social responsibility efforts is social media. The primary value of using social media to communicate CSR efforts is that it allows companies to reach broad and diverse groups; allows them to connect directly with customers in a low-cost, efficient way; and enables them to interact with specific groups more easily than through more traditional efforts. One very important group who most often says knowing a company is socially conscious influences their purchases and whose purchasing decisions are shaped by social media is Gen Z (those born after 2000). Think about this: The two-billion-strong Gen Z makes up 40 percent of the global market and has an estimated purchasing power of $44 billion ($600 billion if you consider their influence on their parents' purchases).[24]

It's not enough for companies to brag about their social responsibility efforts; they must live up to the expectations they raise or face the consequences. When herbal tea maker Celestial Seasonings ignored its advertised image of environmental stewardship by poisoning prairie

FIGURE 4.4 EXAMPLES OF CORPORATE SOCIAL RESPONSIBILITY EFFORTS

COMPANY	SOCIAL RESPONSIBILITY EFFORTS
Starbucks	When the South American coffee crops were dying from coffee-leaf rust, Starbucks's R&D farm developed rust-resistant coffee plants. The company improved the lives of coffee growers by giving away the superior seeds to more than a million farmers and workers across seven countries and three continents.
Harmless Harvest	The San Francisco–based coconut water brand uses only coconuts that are ethically harvested, processed, and packaged.
Zipline International	Zipline uses drones to distribute medical supplies to clinics hindered by impassable roads and limited storage facilities. The company is 100 percent focused on serving the neediest health care systems and has turned away customers asking it to deliver other goods.
PepsiCo, Panera, McDonald's, Nestlé	These are just a few of the food companies that are providing healthier food and drink options by doing such things as switching to cage-free eggs; adopting stricter antibiotics policy; removing preservatives; reducing fat, sugar, and sodium; and adding more minerals and nutrients.
GlaxoSmithKline	The pharmaceutical company delivers health care to those who are underserved. GSK no longer files drug patents in the lowest-income regions of the world in order to make drugs more accessible. It reinvests 20 percent of any profits it makes in the least-developed countries into training health workers and building medical infrastructure.
General Electric	GE invested $17 billion in research and development of clean technology such as the Digital Wind Farm which can boost a wind farm's energy production by 20 percent.
Mastercard	The credit company is making it easier for charities to get help to the people who really need it quickly. Mastercard distributes cards similar to gift cards that are loaded with points redeemable for groceries, medicine, shelter, building materials, or business supplies. The cards can be made and distributed in a day or two, compared with the weeks needed to create and send paper vouchers.
Coca-Cola	The soft drink company has helped 1.2 million women in 60 countries become entrepreneurs by partnering with governments and nonprofit organizations to create market-specific entrepreneurship programs.
Intel	The technology giant is helping build a workforce capable of keeping up with the digital revolution. Intel's Teach program helps K–12 teachers integrate technology in classrooms and build critical STEM (science, technology, engineering, and math) skills.

Sources: Starbucks, starbucks.com, accessed February 2020; Harmless Harvest, harmlessharvest.com, accessed February 2020; Zipline International, flyzipline.com, accessed February 2020; PepsiCo, pepsico.com, accessed February 2020; Panera, panera.com, accessed February 2020; McDonald's, mcdonalds.com, accessed February 2020; Nestlé, nestle.com, accessed February 2020; GlaxoSmithKline, gsk.com, accessed February 2020; General Electric, ge.com, accessed February 2020; Mastercard, mastercard.com, accessed February 2020; Coca-Cola, coca-colacompany.com, accessed February 2020; Intel, intel.com, accessed February 2020.

dogs on its property several years ago, it incurred customers' wrath. Customers prefer to do business with companies they trust and, even more important, don't want to do business with those they don't trust. Companies earn customers' trust by demonstrating credibility over time; they can lose it at any point. For example, when it was disclosed that venerable Wells Fargo's unattainable sales quotas led employees to open millions of accounts in customers' names without their knowledge, the company was fined $180 million and 5,300 employees were fired. The CEO was forced to resign in 2016, and in 2020, bank regulators fined him $17.5 million and banned him from ever working in banking again. However, the biggest loss to the company by far was trust: The positive perception of the company plummeted from 60 percent before the scandal to 24 percent. Hundreds of thousands of customers dropped the company.[25] What will Wells Fargo have to do to attract new ones?

Responsibility to Investors

Ethical behavior doesn't subtract from the bottom line; it adds to it. In contrast, unethical behavior, even if it seems to work in the short term, does financial damage. Those cheated are the shareholders themselves. For example, in just 11 business days in June 2002, 44 CEOs left U.S. corporations amid accusations of wrongdoing, and the stock prices of their companies plummeted.

Many investors believe that it makes financial as well as moral sense to invest in companies that plan ahead to create a better environment. By choosing to put their money into companies whose goods and services benefit the community and the environment, investors can improve their own financial health while improving society's.[26]

A few investors, however, have chosen unethical means to improve their financial health. For example, **insider trading** uses private company information to further insiders' own fortunes or those of their family and friends. In 2011, one of the biggest insider trading cases in history went to trial in New York. Billionaire Raj Rajaratnam was convicted of masterminding an insider trading ring that made his Galleon Group hedge fund $64 million richer. Of course, he didn't do this all by himself. More than three dozen former traders, executives, and lawyers pled guilty or faced charges that they helped Rajaratnam trade illegally on more than 35 stocks, including Intel, Hilton, IBM, and eBay. Rajaratnam was sentenced to 11 years in prison and lost appeals in 2013 and 2018. In 2019 he was released from prison 2 years early and will serve the remainder of his sentence in home confinement.[27]

Insider trading isn't limited to company executives and their friends. In a classic example, before it was publicly known that IBM was going to take over Lotus Development, an IBM secretary told her husband, who told two co-workers, who told friends, relatives, business associates, and even a pizza delivery person. A total of 25 people traded illegally on the insider tip within a six-hour period. When the deal was announced publicly, Lotus stock soared 89 percent. One of the inside traders, a stockbroker who passed the information to a few customers, made $468,000 in profits. The U.S. Securities and Exchange Commission (SEC) filed charges against the secretary, her husband, and 23 others. Four defendants settled out of court by paying penalties of twice their profits. Prosecutors are increasingly pursuing insider trading cases to ensure that the securities market remains fair and equally accessible to all.[28] A recent Supreme Court ruling made it easier to prosecute some insider trading cases. The court ruled that people who share inside information with others who profit from it are guilty of insider trading even if they themselves don't profit.[29]

After the deluge of insider trader cases was made public in the early 2000s, the SEC adopted a new rule called Regulation FD (for "fair disclosure"). The rule doesn't specify what information can and cannot be disclosed. It simply requires companies that release any information to share it with everybody, not just a few select people. In other words, if companies tell anyone, they must tell everyone—at the same time.

Some companies have misused information for their own benefit at investors' expense. When WorldCom admitted to accounting irregularities misrepresenting its profitability, investors who had purchased its stock on the basis of the false financial reports saw share prices free-fall from the midteens in January 2002 to less than a dime the following July. The pain was even greater for long-term investors, who had bought the stock at around $60 three years earlier.

insider trading
An unethical activity in which insiders use private company information to further their own fortunes or those of their family and friends.

In 2014 a judge sentenced former hedge fund trader Mathew Martoma to nine years in prison for overseeing one of the largest insider trading schemes in history. While working as a portfolio manager at SAC Capital, Martoma made a series of illegal trades that earned the company $275 million. The hedge fund's founder Steven Cohen managed to avoid jail time but was forced to pay a record $1.8 billion fine.

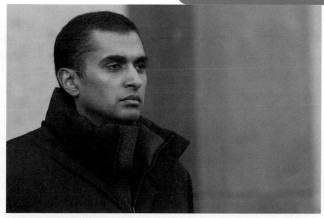
Spencer Platt/Getty Images

Responsibility to Employees

It's been said that the best social program in the world is a job. Businesses have a responsibility to create jobs if they want to grow. Once they've done so, they must see to it that hard work and talent are fairly rewarded. Employees need realistic hope of a better future, which comes only through a chance for upward mobility. One of the most powerful influences on a company's effectiveness and financial performance is responsible human resource management. We'll discuss this in Chapter 11.

Paul Kane/Stringer/Getty Images

The wage and benefit packages offered by warehouse retailer Costco are among the best in hourly retail. Even part-time workers are covered by Costco's health plan. Increased benefits reduce Costco employee turnover to less than a third of the industry average. Why do you think Costco is so successful at keeping its employees?

If a company treats employees with respect, those employees usually will respect the company as well. Mutual respect can make a huge difference to a company's profit. In their book *Contented Cows Still Give Better Milk,* Bill Catlette and Richard Hadden compared "contented cow" companies with "common cow" companies. The companies with contented employees outgrew their counterparts by four to one for more than 10 years. They also outearned the "common cow" companies by nearly $40 billion and generated 800,000 more jobs. Catlette and Hadden attribute this difference in performance to the commitment and caring the outstanding companies demonstrated for their employees.[30]

One way a company can demonstrate commitment and caring is to give employees salaries and benefits that help them reach their personal goals. The wage and benefit packages offered by warehouse retailer Costco are among the best in hourly retail. Even part-time workers are covered by Costco's health plan, and the workers pay less for their coverage than at other retailers such as Walmart. Increased benefits reduce employee turnover, which at Costco is less than a third of the industry average.[31] Replacing employees costs between 50 and 200 percent of their annual salaries depending on the job and employee skills. So retaining workers is good for business as well as morale.[32]

Getting even is one of the most powerful incentives for good people to do bad things. Few disgruntled workers are desperate enough to commit violence in the workplace, but a great number relieve their frustrations in subtle ways: blaming mistakes on others, not accepting responsibility, manipulating budgets and expenses, making commitments they intend to ignore, hoarding resources, doing the minimum needed to get by, and making results look better than they are.

The loss of employee commitment, confidence, and trust in the company and its management can be costly indeed. Employee fraud costs U.S. businesses approximately $7 billion according to the Association of Certified Fraud Examiners.[33]

Responsibility to Society and the Environment

More than 10 percent of U.S. workers in the private sector receive salaries from nonprofit organizations that receive funding from others, that in turn receive their money from businesses.[34] Foundations, universities, and other nonprofit organizations own billions of shares in publicly held companies. As stock prices of those firms increase, businesses create more wealth to benefit society.

Businesses are also partly responsible for promoting social justice. Many companies believe they have a role in building communities that goes well beyond simply "giving back." To them, charity is not enough. Their social contributions include cleaning up the environment, building community toilets, providing computer lessons, caring for older people, and supporting children from low-income families.

As concern about climate change increased, the green movement emerged in nearly every aspect of daily life. What makes a product green? Some believe that a product's carbon footprint (the amount of carbon released during production, distribution, consumption, and disposal) defines how green it is. Many variables contribute to a product's carbon footprint. The carbon footprint of a package of, say, frozen corn includes not only the carbon released by the fertilizer to grow the corn but also the carbon in the fertilizer itself, the gas used to run the farm equipment and transport the corn to market, the electricity to make the plastic packages and power the freezers, and so on.

No specific guidelines define the carbon footprints of products, businesses, or individuals or outline how to communicate them to consumers. PepsiCo presents carbon information with a label on bags of cheese-and-onion potato chips, for example, that

EnVogue_Photo/Alamy Stock Photo

Since Patagonia's founding in 1973, the outdoor apparel brand has strived to make quality goods in an ethical manner. From closely vetting its suppliers to promoting fair labor practices in factories, Patagonia believes that businesses should have a positive impact on the world. What do you think?

says "75 grams of CO_2." Simple enough, but what does it mean? (We don't know either.) Researchers are trying to devise a simpler way of communicating carbon footprint information to consumers.[35]

The green movement has provided consumers with lots of product choices. However, making those choices means sorting through the many and confusing claims made by manufacturers. The noise in the marketplace challenges even the most dedicated green activists, but taking the easy route of buying what's most readily available violates the principles of the green movement.

Environmental efforts may increase a company's costs, but they also allow the company to charge higher prices, increase market share, or both. Ninety percent of Millennials say they are willing to pay more for products with environmentally friendly ingredients. Green products have been steadily increasing market share, from 19.7 percent in 2014 to 22.3 percent in 2017, and to an estimated 25 percent in 2021.[36]

Not all environmental strategies are financially beneficial, however. In the early 1990s, tuna producer StarKist responded to consumer concerns about dolphins in the eastern Pacific dying in nets set out for yellowfin tuna. The company announced it would sell only skipjack tuna from the western Pacific, which do not swim near dolphins. Unfortunately, customers were unwilling to pay a premium for dolphin-safe tuna and considered the taste of skipjack inferior. Nor was there a clear environmental gain: For every dolphin saved in the eastern Pacific, thousands of immature tuna and dozens of sharks, turtles, and other marine animals died in the western Pacific fishing process.

The green movement can have a positive impact on the U.S. labor force. Emerging renewable-energy and energy-efficiency industries currently account for 9 million jobs and by 2030 may create as many as 40 million more in engineering, manufacturing, construction, accounting, and management, according to a green-collar job report by the American Solar Energy Society.[37]

Environmental quality is a public good; that is, everyone gets to enjoy it regardless of who pays for it. The challenge for companies is to find the public goods that will appeal to their customers. Many corporations are publishing reports that document their net social contribution. To do that, a company must measure its positive social contributions and subtract its negative social impacts. We discuss that process next.

RAINFOREST
ACTION NETWORK

Courtesy of Rainforest Action Network

The goal of the Rainforest Action Network, an environmental activist group, is to show companies that it is possible to do well by doing good. It conducts public campaigns designed to put consumer pressure on companies that refuse to adopt responsible environmental policies. RAN has helped convince dozens of corporations including Home Depot, Citigroup, Boise Cascade, and Goldman Sachs to change their practices.

social audit

A systematic evaluation of an organization's progress toward implementing socially responsible and responsive programs.

Social Auditing

Can we measure whether organizations are making social responsibility an integral part of top management's decision making? The answer is yes, and the term that represents that measurement is *social auditing.*

A **social audit** is a systematic evaluation of an organization's progress toward implementing socially responsible and responsive programs. One of the major problems of conducting a social audit is establishing procedures for measuring a firm's activities and their effects on society. What should a social audit measure? Many consider workplace issues to include areas such as the environment, product safety, community relations, military weapons contracting, international operations and human rights, and respect for the rights of local people.

It remains a question whether organizations should add up positive actions like charitable donations and pollution control efforts, and then subtract negative effects like layoffs and overall pollution created, to get a net social contribution. Or should they just record positive actions? What do you think? However they are conducted, social audits force organizations to consider their social responsibility beyond the level of just feeling good or managing public relations.

In addition to social audits conducted by companies themselves, five types of groups serve as watchdogs to monitor how well companies enforce their ethical and social responsibility policies:

1. *Socially conscious investors* insist that a company extend its own high standards to its suppliers. Social responsibility investing (SRI) is on the rise, with about $12 trillion invested in SRI funds in the United States already.[38]

2. *Socially conscious research organizations,* such as Ethisphere, analyze and report on corporate social responsibility efforts.[39]

3. *Environmentalists* apply pressure by naming companies that don't abide by environmentalists' standards. After months of protests coordinated by the San Francisco–based Rainforest Action Network (RAN), JPMorgan Chase & Co. adopted guidelines that restrict its lending and underwriting practices for industrial projects likely to have a negative impact on the environment. RAN activists first go after an industry leader, like JPMorgan, then tackle smaller companies. "We call it, 'Rank 'em and spank 'em,'" says RAN's executive director.[40]

4. *Union officials* hunt down violations and force companies to comply to avoid negative publicity.

5. *Customers* make buying decisions based on their social conscience. Many companies surveyed are adjusting their environmental and social responsibility strategies because of the number of customers that factor these into their buying decisions.

As you can see, it isn't enough for a company to be right when it comes to ethics and social responsibility—it also has to convince its customers and society that it's right.

?TESTPREP

- What is corporate social responsibility, and how does it relate to each of a business's major stakeholders?
- What is a social audit, and what kinds of activities does it monitor?

LO 4–6   Analyze the role of U.S. businesses in influencing ethical behavior and social responsibility in global markets.

International Ethics and Social Responsibility

Ethical problems and issues of social responsibility are not unique to the United States. Influence-peddling or bribery charges have been brought against top officials in Japan, South Korea, China, Italy, Brazil, Pakistan, and the Democratic Republic of the Congo. What is new about the moral and ethical standards by which government leaders are being judged? They are much stricter than in the past. Top leaders are now being held to higher standards.

Many U.S. businesses also demand socially responsible behavior from their international suppliers, making sure they don't violate U.S. human rights and environmental standards. Clothing manufacturer PVH (makers of such brands as Calvin Klein and Tommy Hilfiger) will cancel orders from suppliers that violate its ethical, environmental, and human rights code. Dow Chemical expects suppliers to conform to tough U.S. pollution and safety laws rather than just to local laws of their respective countries. McDonald's denied rumors that one of its suppliers grazes cattle on cleared rain-forest land but wrote a ban on the practice anyway.

In contrast are companies criticized for exploiting workers in less-developed countries. Nike, the world's largest athletic shoe company, has been accused by human rights and labor groups of treating its workers poorly while lavishing millions of dollars on star athletes to endorse its products. Cartoonist Garry Trudeau featured an anti-Nike campaign in his popular syndicated series *Doonesbury.*

Nike worked hard to improve its reputation. Nike monitors efforts to improve labor conditions in its 700 contract factories that are subject to local culture and economic conditions. The company released the names and locations of its factories, both as a show of transparency and to encourage its competitors to work on improving conditions as well. While Nike's efforts had little impact at first, conditions have improved in many of its suppliers' factories. However, even though factory workers earn more than the 20 cents an hour they were paid for the 70 to 80 hours a week they worked years ago, today they still receive less than 25 percent of a living wage while working 48 to 60 hours or more a week. Keep in mind that many other major companies share these factories with Nike and pay the same low wages for long hours. [41]

Why has Nike's monitoring program not been as successful as the company hoped? One reason is that in emerging economies, government regulations tend to be weak, which leaves companies to police their suppliers. That's a major task for a company like Nike, which produces 98 percent of its shoes in hundreds of factories in many different countries. Another reason is that as a buyer, Nike has different degrees of leverage. This leverage is based on how long Nike has worked with a supplier or how much of the factory's revenue depends on Nike alone.

The fairness of requiring international suppliers to adhere to U.S. ethical standards is not as clear-cut as you might think. For example, a gift in one culture can be a bribe in another. Is it always ethical for companies to demand compliance with the standards of their own countries? What about countries where child labor is accepted and families depend on children's salaries for survival? Should foreign companies doing business in the United States expect U.S. companies to comply with their ethical standards? Since multinational corporations span different societies, should they conform to any society's standards? Why are some U.S. retailers applauded for not importing goods made in Chinese prisons when there are many prison-based enterprises in the United States? None of these questions are easy to answer, but they suggest the

Nike has outsourced the manufacture of its products to plants in other countries and has weathered much criticism for operating in low-wage nations where child labor is common. The company has taken many corrective measures, including working with other companies and advocacy groups on a set of common labor standards and factory guidelines. Can a successful firm overcome past ethical errors?

Imagine China/Newscom

The extension of corporations' reach into communities across the globe has led to many questions: For which communities are the companies responsible? Are domestic operations more important than foreign ones? Should the interests of employees be put first, or is the company's image the main priority?

Here's an example of how corporate ethics can clash with cultural ethics. Joe, the oldest son of a poor South American cloth peddler, managed to move to the United States, earn an engineering degree, and get a job with a large telecommunications company. After five years, Joe seemed to have bought into the company culture and was happy to be granted a transfer back to his home country. He was told that the company expected him to live there in a safe and presentable home of his choice. To help him afford such a residence, his employer agreed to reimburse him a maximum of $2,000 a month for the cost of his rent and servants. Each month Joe submitted rental receipts for exactly $2,000. The company later found out that Joe was living in what was, by Western standards, a shack in a dangerous area of town. Such a humble home could not have cost more than $200 a month. The company

David R. Frazier Photolibrary, Inc./Alamy Stock Photo

was concerned for Joe's safety as well as for the effect his residence would have on its image. The human resource manager was also worried about Joe's lack of integrity, given he had submitted false receipts for reimbursement.

Joe was upset with what he considered the company's invasion of his privacy. He argued he should receive the full $2,000 monthly reimbursement all employees received. He explained his choice of housing by saying he was making

sacrifices so he could send the extra money to his family and put his younger siblings through school. This was especially important since his father had died and his family had no one else to depend on. He tried to make the company understand that for him to do anything less than send the money to his family would be defiling the honor of his late father.

Often it is difficult to understand what others perceive as ethical. Different situations often turn the clear waters of "rightness" downright muddy. Joe was trying to do the honorable thing for his family. Yet the company's wish to have its higher-level people live in safe housing is not unreasonable, given the dangerous conditions of the city in which Joe lived. The policy of housing reimbursement supports the company's intent to make its employees' stay in the country reasonably comfortable and safe, not to increase their salaries. If Joe worked in the United States, where he would not receive a housing supplement, it would be unethical for him to falsify expense reports in order to receive more money to send to his family. In South America, though, the issue is not so clear.

complexity of social responsibility in international markets. (See the Reaching beyond Our Borders box for an example of an ethical culture clash.)

In the 1970s, the Foreign Corrupt Practices Act (discussed in Chapter 3) sent a chill throughout the U.S. business community by criminalizing the act of paying foreign business or government leaders to get business. Many U.S. executives complained that this law put their businesses at a competitive disadvantage when bidding against non-U.S. companies, since foreign companies don't have to abide by it.

To identify some form of common global ethics and fight corruption in global markets, partners in the Organization of American States signed the Inter-American Convention

Against Corruption.[42] The United Nations adopted a formal condemnation of corporate bribery, as did the European Union and the Organization for Economic Cooperation and Development. The International Organization for Standardization (ISO) published a standard on social responsibility called ISO 26000, with guidelines on product manufacturing, fair pay rates, appropriate employee treatment, and hiring practices.[43] These standards are advisory only and will not be used for certification purposes. The formation of a single set of international rules governing multinational corporations is unlikely in the near future. In many places "Fight corruption" remains just a slogan, but even a slogan is a start.

?TEST**PREP**

- How are U.S. businesses demanding socially responsible behavior from their international suppliers?
- Why is it unlikely that there will be a single set of international rules governing multinational companies soon?

SUMMARY

LO 4–1 Explain why obeying the law is only the first step in behaving ethically.

How is legality different from ethics?

Ethics goes beyond obeying laws to include abiding by the moral standards accepted by society. Ethics reflects people's proper relationships with one another. Legality is more limiting; it refers only to laws written to protect people from fraud, theft, and violence.

LO 4–2 Ask the three questions you need to answer when faced with a potentially unethical action.

How can we tell if our business decisions are ethical?

We can put our business decisions through an ethics check by asking three questions: (1) Is it legal? (2) Is it balanced? and (3) How will it make me feel?

LO 4–3 Describe management's role in setting ethical standards.

What is management's role in setting ethical standards?

Managers often set formal ethical standards, but more important are the messages they send through their actions. Management's tolerance or intolerance of ethical misconduct influences employees more than any written ethics codes.

LO 4–4 Distinguish between compliance-based and integrity-based ethics codes, and list the six steps in setting up a corporate ethics code.

What's the difference between compliance-based and integrity-based ethics codes?

Whereas compliance-based ethics codes are concerned with avoiding legal punishment, integrity-based ethics codes define the organization's guiding values, create an environment that supports ethically sound behavior, and stress a shared accountability among employees.

LO 4–5 Define *corporate social responsibility,* and compare corporations' responsibilities to various stakeholders.

- **What is corporate social responsibility?**

  Corporate social responsibility (CSR) is the concern businesses have for society.

- **How do businesses demonstrate corporate responsibility toward stakeholders?**

  Businesses demonstrate responsibility to stakeholders by (1) satisfying *customers* with goods and services of real value; (2) making money for *investors;* (3) creating jobs for *employees,* maintaining job security, and seeing that hard work and talent are fairly rewarded; and (4) creating new wealth for *society,* promoting social justice, and contributing to making the businesses' own environment a better place.

- **How are a company's social responsibility efforts measured?**

  A corporate social audit measures an organization's progress toward social responsibility. Some people believe the audit should add together the organization's positive actions and then subtract the negative effects to get a net social benefit.

LO 4–6 Analyze the role of U.S. businesses in influencing ethical behavior and social responsibility in global markets.

- **How can U.S. companies influence ethical behavior and social responsibility in global markets?**

  Many U.S. businesses are demanding socially responsible behavior from their international suppliers by making sure their suppliers do not violate U.S. human rights and environmental standards. Companies such as PVH and Dow Chemical will not import products from companies that do not meet their ethical and social responsibility standards.

KEY TERMS

compliance-based
  ethics codes 95
corporate philanthropy 98
corporate policy 98
corporate responsibility 98

corporate social
  initiatives 98
corporate social
  responsibility (CSR) 97
ethics 92

insider trading 101
integrity-based ethics
  codes 95
social audit 104
whistleblowers 95

CRITICAL THINKING

Think of a situation that tested your ethical behavior. For example, maybe your best friend forgot about a term paper due the next day and asked if he could copy a paper you wrote for another instructor last semester.

1. What are your alternatives, and what are the consequences of each?

2. Would it have been easier to resolve the dilemma if you had asked yourself the three questions listed in the chapter? Try answering them now and see whether you would have made a different choice.

PUTTING PRINCIPLES TO WORK

PURPOSE

To demonstrate the level of commitment one business has to social responsibility.

EXERCISE

According to household products and personal care company Seventh Generation, corporate responsibility is in its DNA as it considers the effects of its actions on the next seven generations. It strives to limit the effect of all aspects of its products on the environment, from development to their production, purchase, use, and disposal. Visit the company's website at seventhgeneration.com. Then answer the following questions:

1. What is the social mission of Seventh Generation?

2. How is Seventh Generation involved in improving the Vermont community?

3. How does Seventh Generation communicate the company's social mission to its customers?

DEVELOPING CAREER SKILLS

KEY: ● **Team**   ★ **Analytic**   ▲ **Communication**   ▣ **Technology**

1. What sources have helped shape your personal code of ethics and morality? What influences, if any, have ever pressured you to compromise those standards? Think of an experience you had at work or school that tested your ethical standards. How did you resolve your dilemma? Now that time has passed, are you comfortable with the decision you made? If not, explain what you would do differently. ★▲

2. Do a little investigative reporting of your own. Go online and search for a public interest group in your community. Identify its officers, objectives, sources and amount of financial support, and size and characteristics of membership. List some examples of its recent actions and/or accomplishments. You should be able to choose from environmental groups, animal protection groups, political action committees, and so on. Visit the website of the local chamber of commerce, the Better Business Bureau, or local government agencies for help.

3. You're the manager of a coffeehouse called the Morning Cup. One of your best employees desires to be promoted to a managerial position; however, the owner is grooming his slow-thinking son for the job. The owner's nepotism may hurt a valuable employee's chances for advancement, but complaining may hurt your own chances for promotion. What do you do? ★

4. Go to the website of a local corporation and search for its written ethics code. Would you classify its code as compliance-based or integrity-based? Explain.

5. What effects have the new laws protecting whistleblowers had on the business environment? Go online or to the library to research individuals who reported their employers' illegal and/or unethical behavior. Did the companies change their policies? If so, what effect have these policies had on the companies' stakeholders? What effect did reporting the problems have on the whistleblowers themselves?

CAREER EXPLORATION

Of course ethical behavior is important on every career path. However, if you are interested in pursuing a career that is more focused on helping people, society, and the environment, here are a few to consider. Find out about the tasks performed, skills needed, pay, and opportunity outlook in these fields in the *Occupational Outlook Handbook (OOH)* at bls.gov.

- **Compliance officer**—examines, evaluates, and investigates conformity with laws and regulations.

- **Green job**—job that produces goods or provides services that benefit the environment or conserve natural resources. Search in the *OOH* for careers in water conservation, sustainable forestry, biofuels,

geothermal energy, environmental remediation, solar power, recycling, and so on.

- **Social and community service manager**—coordinates and supervises social service programs and community organizations; manages staff members who provide social services to the public.

- **Fundraising manager**—organizes events and campaigns to raise money and other donations for an organization; increases awareness of an organization's work, goals, and financial needs.

- **Social worker**—helps people solve and cope with problems in their everyday lives.

VIDEO CASE   *Conscious Marketing at Gluten Free Bars*

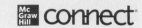

The economist Milton Friedman once said that a company's only responsibility is to make a profit for its shareholders. For many years, these words served as a guiding principle for countless businesses. But today, a focus on corporate social responsibility (CSR) has shifted business leaders toward addressing the needs of all stakeholders, not just stockholders. CEOs from major U.S. companies have developed a new definition of corporate purpose that emphasizes investing in employees, supporting communities, dealing ethically with suppliers, and offering fair prices. Many firms depend on "conscious marketing" in order to make consumers aware of these values.

Conscious marketing revolves around four key concepts: having a higher purpose, embracing stakeholders, creating a conscious company culture, and making ethical decisions. Gluten Free Bars (GFB), a maker of certified gluten-free snacks, has been an advocate of conscious marketing since launching in 2010. According to founder Elliott Rader, the company works hard to make sure that both its employees and suppliers are happy and fulfilled. GFB takes its role so seriously that soon after launching it became a certified "B corp," or benefit corporation.

As a B corp, GFB must consider how its actions impact not only shareholders but also customers, employees and their families, supply chain partners, government agencies, the environment, and the community at large. GFB's motto is "We Win Together"—meaning that if the company does well, so does everybody else. The company provides benefits like health care, 401(k), and generous vacation time and sick days. GFB is also dedicated to giving second chances to people with criminal records. In fact, almost 40 percent of GFB's employees were formerly incarcerated.

Being a conscious marketer also means developing a sustainable supply chain. GFB works with local food sources and nearby manufacturers to keep its carbon footprint low. Under its Zero Waste Production initiative, all of the company's waste is either recycled, reused, or composted. As much as 9 out of every 10 pounds of waste produced by GFB gets recycled, and the company is always working to make further improvements to this system.

Gluten Free Bars hopes its model will inspire other American companies to do their part in making the world a better place. GFB's leadership remains committed to its socially conscious missions and pledges to keep the interests of its stakeholders at the forefront. The company's founder says that customers trust the products GFB makes and care about who's producing them, where they're coming from, and how they're sourced. As more businesses develop CSR strategies, it could be hard to survive by following Milton Friedman's old advice.

THINKING IT OVER

1. Should companies consider all stakeholders or strictly shareholders when making business decisions? Why?

2. How does "conscious marketing" benefit companies like Gluten Free Bars?

3. Would you be more inclined to purchase products from a company certified as a B corp?

NOTES

1. Jeff Cox, "More Cracks Are Appearing in the Market for Loans That Helped Cause the Financial Crisis," *CNBC,* cnbc.com, January 29, 2019; Kimberly Amadeo, "2008 Financial Crisis: The Causes and Costs of the Worst Crisis Since the Great Depression," *The Balance,* thebalance.com, January 22, 2020.
2. "The Golden Rule (aka Ethics of Reciprocity)," *Religious Tolerance,* religioustolerance.org, accessed February 2020.
3. David Lazarus, "You Can Deduct Charitable Donations. Why No Tax Benefit for Volunteering?," *Los Angeles Times,* latimes.com, January 24, 2020.
4. Turnitin, turnitin.com, accessed February 2020.
5. "Cheating in College: The Numbers and Research," Best College Reviews, bestcollegereviews.org, accessed February 2020.
6. Trevor S. Harding, Donald D. Carpenter, Cynthia J. Finelli, and Honor J. Passow, "Does Academic Dishonesty Relate to Unethical Behavior in Professional Practice? An Exploratory Study," CiteSeerX, accessed February 2020.
7. Kenneth Blanchard and Norman Vincent Peale, *The Power of Ethical Management* (New York: William Morrow, 1996).
8. Allison Tringale, "Be Sure Rewards System Motivate Valued Behavior," *bizTIMES,* telegraphherald.com, January 9, 2020.
9. Tony Prophet, "Ethics and Technology in the Fourth Industrial Revolution," World Economic Forum, weforum.org, January 21, 2019; Shana Lynch, "Are You an Ethical Leader?," *Stanford Business,* gsb.stanford.edu, October 18, 2019; Patrick Quinlan, "Building an Ethics-First Employee Culture Is Crucial for All Leaders," *Forbes,* forbes.com, accessed February 2020.
10. U.S. Securities and Exchange Commission, sec.gov, accessed February 2020.
11. Jason Gay, "A Trashy Scandal for Baseball," *The Wall Street Journal,* January 16, 2020; Dave Sheinin, "A.J. Hinch and Jeff Luhnow Fired by Astros after MLB Suspension, Fine in Sign-Stealing Scandal," *The Washington Post,*

January 13, 2020; Tyler Kepner, "The Rise and Fall of the Houston Astros," *The New York Times,* January 18, 2020.

12. Peter Loftus, "For First Time, J&J CEO Testifies in a Talcum-Powder Court Case," *The Wall Street Journal,* wsj. com, January 27, 2020; Peter Loftus, "Missouri Court Cuts Talc-Powder Verdict Against J&J to $2.1 Billion," *The Wall Street Journal,* wsj.com, June 23, 2020.

13. Andrew Ross Sorkin, "World's Biggest Investor Tells C.E.O.s Purpose Is the 'Animating Force' for Profits," *The New York Times,* nytimes.com, January 17, 2019; Mark R. Kramer, "The Backlash to Larry Fink's Letter Shows How Far Business Has to Go on Social Responsibility," *Harvard Business Review,* January 31, 2019; Art Carden, "'The Essential Milton Friedman' Shows a Great Mind at Work," *Forbes,* forbes.com, January 16, 2020; Deborah D'Souza, "Stakeholder Capitalism," *Investopedia,* investopedia.com, January 22, 2020.

14. Doug Sundheim and Kate Starr, "Making Stakeholder Capitalism a Reality," *Harvard Business Review,* hbr. org, January 22, 2020; Addisu Lashitew, "Stakeholder Capitalism Arrives at Davos," Brookings Institution, brookings.edu, January 21, 2020.

15. Kate Bloomgarden, "Corporate Responsibility Is Taking On a New Meaning," *Fortune,* fortune.com, January 2, 2019; Kevin Xu, "How to Make Your Corporate Social Responsibility Come from Within," *Forbes,* forbes.com, February 4, 2019; Magda B. L. Donia, "Employees Want Genuine Corporate Responsibility, Not Greenwashing," *The Conversation,* theconversation.com, January 29, 2020.

16. Timothy J. McClimon, "Corporate Giving by the Numbers," *Forbes,* forbes.com, January 16, 2020.

17. Bill & Melinda Gates Foundation, gatesfoundation.org, accessed February 2020.

18. Logistics Cluster, logcluster.org, accessed February 2020.

19. Jeff Beer, "Uphill," *Fast Company,* November 2019; Patagonia, patagonia.com, accessed February 2020.

20. Danielle Abril, "Google Is Paying Employees for Six Months of Charity Work," *Fortune,* fortune.com, January 16, 2019; Alyssa Dinberg, "Podcast: Enhancing Public Services with the Google.org Fellowship," Engaging Local Government Leaders, elgl.org, January 17, 2020.

21. Danielle Holly, "Building Social Sector Capacity through a Day of Skilled Service," *Stanford Social Innovation Review,* ssir.org, February 1, 2019.

22. Valerie Bolden-Barrett, "Companies to Act as 'Stewards of Society' through CSR Programs," *HR Dive,* hrdive.com, February 9, 2019; Adele Peters, "Most Millennials Would Take a Pay Cut to Work at an Environmentally Responsible Company," *Fast Company,* fastcompany.com, February 14, 2019.

23. "The ROI of Philanthropy: Consumers Willing to Spend 6% More for Products from Socially Responsible Companies," *MarketWatch,* marketwatch.com, November 12, 2018; Susan Ward, "What Is Green Marketing?," *The Balance Small Business,* thebalancesmb.com, January 22, 2020.

24. "The Ultimate Guide to Marketing to Gen Z in 2019," *Campaign Monitor,* campaignmonitor.com, accessed February 2020.

25. Kevin Wack, "Wells Fargo Bends to Critics in Its Latest Response to Scandals," *American Banker,* americanbanker.com, January 30, 2019; Michael Hiltzik, "That Wells Fargo Accounts Scandal Was Even Worse Than You Can Imagine," *Los Angeles Times,* latimes.com, January 27, 2020.

26. Kristin Stoller, "Here's How to Invest in a Socially Responsible Way," *Forbes,* forbes.com, June 25, 2019; "SRI Basics," The Forum for Sustainable and Responsible Investment, ussif.org, accessed February 2020.

27. Natalie Sachmechi, "Behind Bars: Billionaires and Ex-Billionaires Who Have Served Time," *Forbes,* forbes.com, January 25, 2020.

28. Peter J. Henning, "Insider Trading Remains a Fixture for Securities Enforcement," *The New York Times,* nytimes. com, January 1, 2019; Sarah E. Aberg and Bochan Kim, "United States v. Blaszczak: Second Circuit Ruling Creates Opening for Significant Increase in Insider Trading Prosecutions," *The National Law Review,* natlawreview. com, January 31, 2020.

29. "What Exactly Is Insider Trading—and How Do You Avoid It?," *MarketWatch,* marketwatch.com, February 13, 2019; Wilbmer Hale, "The Second Circuit Clears the Path for Insider Trading Convictions Absent a Dirks Personal Benefit," *JDSupra,* jdsupra.com, January 8, 2020; Stephen L. Ascher, Anthony S. Barkow, Anne Cortina Perry, and Charles D. Riely, "Second Circuit Allows Insider Trading to Be Proven without Personal Benefit," *Lexology,* lexology.com, January 10, 2020.

30. Bill Catlette and Richard Hadden, *Contented Cows Still Give Better Milk* (Jacksonville, FL: Contented Cow Partners, 2012); Contented Cow Partners, contentedcows. com, accessed February 2020.

31. "Service Jobs Should Be—and Can Be—Middle-Class Jobs," *Harvard Business Review,* hbr.org, August 30, 2019; Jake Rossen, "14 Secrets of Costco Employees," *Mental Floss,* mentalfloss.com, January 27, 2020.

32. John Hall, "The Cost of Turnover Can Kill Your Business and Make Things Less Fun," *Forbes,* forbes.com, May 9, 2019; "How to Calculate Employee Turnover Rate," PayScale, payscale.com, January 29, 2020; "Why Employee Turnover Is the Single Most Revealing HR Metric," Paycor, paycor.com, January 20, 2020.

33. Association of Certified Fraud Examiners, acfe.com, accessed February 2020; "Why Employee Fraud Has Double the Impact on Small Business," security.org, accessed February 2020.

34. Steve Dubb, "Nonprofit Workforce Study Finds Strengths in Growth, Pay, and Resilience," *Nonprofit Quarterly,* nonprofitquarterly.org, February 7, 2019; Kori Kanayama, "Why Nonprofit Staff Wages Are as Important as CEO Salaries," *Nonprofit Quarterly,* nonprofitquarterly.org, January 27, 2020.

35. Nonprofit Quarterly, nonprofitquarterly.org, "Communications Footprint," Carbon Footprint, carbonfootprint.com, accessed February 2020.

36. Susan Ward, "What Is Green Marketing?," *The Balance Small Business,* thebalancesmb.com, January 22, 2020.

37. American Solar Energy Society, ases.org, accessed February 2020.

38. The Forum for Sustainable and Responsible Investment, ussif.org, accessed February 2020.

39. Ethisphere, ethisphere.com, accessed February 2020.

40. Rainforest Action Network, ran.org, accessed February 2020.

41. Andy Burt, "J.Crew Group Selects Sustainable Denim Supplier. Is It a Natural Fit?," *Supply Chain Dive,* supplychaindive.com, January 31, 2019; Samantha Putterman, "Post about Nike Factory Workers Uses Outdated Numbers for Pay, Hours," PolitiFact, politifact. com, November 22, 2019.

42. Organization of American States, oas.org, accessed February 2020.

43. "ISO 26000 Social Responsibility," International Organization of Standardization, iso.org, accessed February 2020.

5

How to Form a Business

LEARNING OBJECTIVES »

After you have read and studied this chapter, you should be able to

LO 5–1 Compare the advantages and disadvantages of sole proprietorships.

LO 5–2 Describe the differences between general and limited partners, and compare the advantages and disadvantages of partnerships.

LO 5–3 Compare the advantages and disadvantages of corporations, and summarize the differences among C corporations, S corporations, and limited liability companies.

LO 5–4 Define and give examples of three types of corporate mergers, and explain the role of leveraged buyouts and taking a firm private.

LO 5–5 Outline the advantages and disadvantages of franchises, and discuss the opportunities for diversity in franchising and the challenges of global franchising.

LO 5–6 Explain the role of cooperatives.

Alli Webb, Founder of Drybar

Like many American adolescents, Alli Webb always seemed to have trouble getting her curly hair under control. "I'd look at Cindy Crawford or Christie Brinkley and think, how is their hair so perfect?" said Webb. "I spent many, many hours in my bathroom trying to figure that out." Soon she discovered a solution to her problem: blowouts, or a salon treatment where the client's hair is simultaneously styled and blow-dried. Although this relaxing procedure tamed Webb's hair, she also noticed that upscale salons overcharged for blowouts while low-cost chains did not offer great experiences. This left a gap in the market that Webb eventually filled with Drybar, her $100 million blowout-based business with more than 125 locations.

Before she built Drybar, Webb trained as a hairstylist in New York and worked in one of the city's top salons. After getting married in 2003, Webb moved to California and planned to become a stay-at-home mother. She never lost her passion for hairstyling, though, and within five years she launched a mobile blowout business in Los Angeles called Straight-at-Home. Webb acted as sole proprietor of the company, visiting every client at home and charging $40 for blowouts. As her reputation grew and her client base expanded beyond a one-woman show, she decided it was time to expand the business and move into her own shop.

While Webb had plenty of experience with hair, she didn't know much about opening a proper store. Fortunately, her husband Cameron worked in marketing and provided vital branding expertise. Webb also wanted to bring in her business-savvy brother Michael but feared he would say no after the two had clashed on a previous venture. "We were fighting like cats and dogs, we were both so young and inexperienced and stupid," said Webb. Rather than scare her brother off, this experience made the siblings realize what things would work and what things wouldn't with the new business. So with her husband and brother on board as partners, Webb was ready to launch Drybar. "Despite the fact that they are both bald, they got it and were in!" said Webb.

The team opened their first Drybar location in the affluent L.A. neighborhood of Brentwood and quickly had a line of customers stretching out the door. Webb originally estimated that the store would provide about 30 to 40 blowouts a day. Instead, on an average day, Drybar performed as many as 80 blowouts. "For six months, I couldn't hire stylists fast enough," said Webb. Not only were customers attracted by the affordable blowouts, but they also loved the store's unique design that made it seem more like a bar than a salon. The partners realized that they needed to expand soon or else run the risk of losing market share to imitators. To fund this expansion, the trio raised $2.5 million from family and friends and also started to offer franchising opportunities to interested clients. Drybar then became a limited liability company (LLC) and made the decision to take on additional investors.

After considering many potential backers, Webb and the team accepted a $16 million investment from Castanea Partners, a Boston-based private equity firm with experience in cosmetics. As Drybar rapidly expanded, Castanea recommended that the company hire a CEO who had experience managing large organizations. Although she was reluctant to share control with an outsider, Webb soon changed her mind after meeting John Heffner. With executive positions at major companies like Procter & Gamble and Unilever on his résumé, Heffner has helped Webb expand the scope of Drybar's brand. Along with its core business of blowout salons, the company also offers an assortment of products from dry shampoo to lightweight blow-dryers. And with more than 3,000 people now employed by Drybar, Webb stresses the importance of making the right connections at all levels of business: "Recognize your strengths and bring in people who know the things you don't."

Just like Alli Webb, all business owners must decide for themselves which form of business is best for them. Whether you dream of starting a business for yourself, going into business with a partner, forming a corporation, or someday being a leading franchisor, it's important to know that each form of ownership has its advantages and disadvantages. You will learn about them all in this chapter.

Source: Jane Larkworthy, "Alli Webb Has Opened over a Hundred Drybars," The Cut, thecut.com, June 26, 2018.

Let's talk business!
bit.ly/LetsTalkBusiness5

▶ **iSeeit!** Need help understanding forms of business ownership? Visit your Connect eBook to view a video for a brief animated explanation.

sole proprietorship
A business that is owned, and usually managed, by one person.

partnership
A legal form of business with two or more owners.

corporation
A legal entity with authority to act and have liability separate from its owners.

Basic Forms of Business Ownership

Hundreds of thousands of people have started new businesses in the United States. In fact, approximately 400,000 are started each year.[1] Chances are, you've thought of owning your own business or know someone who has.

How you form your business can make a tremendous difference in your long-term success. The three major forms of business ownership are (1) sole proprietorships, (2) partnerships, and (3) corporations. Each has advantages and disadvantages that we'll discuss.

A business owned, and usually managed, by one person is called a **sole proprietorship**. Many people do not have the money, time, or desire to run a business on their own. When two or more people legally agree to become co-owners of a business, the organization is called a **partnership**.

Sole proprietorships and partnerships are relatively easy to form, but there are advantages to creating a business that is separate and distinct from the owners. This is a **corporation**, a legal entity with authority to act and have liability apart from its owners. The almost 5 million corporations in the United States make up only 20 percent of all businesses, but they earn 81 percent of total U.S. business receipts (see Figure 5.1).

Keep in mind that just because a business starts in one form of ownership, it doesn't have to stay in that form. Many companies start out in one form, then add (or drop) a partner or two, and eventually become corporations, limited liability companies, or franchisors. Let's begin our discussion by looking at the most basic form of ownership—the sole proprietorship.

FIGURE 5.1 FORMS OF BUSINESS OWNERSHIP
Although corporations make up only 20 percent of the total number of businesses, they earn 81 percent of the total receipts. Sole proprietorships are the most common form (72 percent), but they earn only 6 percent of the receipts.
Source: U.S. Census Bureau.

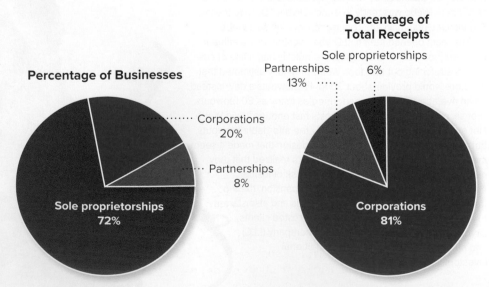

Percentage of Businesses

Corporations 20%

Partnerships 8%

Sole proprietorships 72%

Percentage of Total Receipts

Sole proprietorships 6%

Partnerships 13%

Corporations 81%

LO 5–1	Compare the advantages and disadvantages of sole proprietorships.

Sole Proprietorships

Advantages of Sole Proprietorships

Sole proprietorships are the easiest kind of businesses to explore in your quest for an interesting career. Every town has sole proprietors you can visit and talk with about the joys and frustrations of being in business on their own. Most will mention the benefits of being their own boss and setting their own hours. Other advantages include:

1. *Ease of starting and ending the business.* All you have to do to start a sole proprietorship is buy or lease the needed equipment (a saw, a laptop, a tractor, a lawn mower) and put up some announcements saying you are in business. You may have to get a permit or license from the local government, but often that is no problem. It is just as easy to get out of business; you simply stop. There is no one to consult or disagree with about such decisions.

2. *Ability to be your own boss.* Working for others simply does not have the same excitement as working for yourself—at least, that's the way sole proprietors feel. You may make mistakes, but they are your mistakes—and so are the many small victories each day.

3. *Pride of ownership.* People who own and manage their own businesses are rightfully proud of their work. They deserve all the credit for taking the risks and providing needed goods or services.

4. *Leaving a legacy.* Owners can leave an ongoing business for future generations.

5. *Retention of company profits.* Owners not only keep the profits earned but also benefit from the increasing value as the business grows.

6. *No special taxes.* All the profits of a sole proprietorship are taxed as the personal income of the owner, and the owner pays the normal income tax on that money. However, owners do have to pay the self-employment tax (for Social Security and Medicare). They also have to estimate their taxes and make quarterly payments to the government or suffer penalties for nonpayment.

Stuart Ramson/Invision/AP/Shutterstock

Evan, better known as EvanTubeHD, started making toy unboxing videos on YouTube when he was a little kid. Now a teenager with more than 6 million subscribers, Evan creates viral content with his whole family and earns more than $1 million per year from ads and sponsorships. Do you have a passion you would like to pursue as a business?

Disadvantages of Sole Proprietorships

Not everyone is equipped to own and manage a business. Often it is difficult to save enough money to start a business and keep it going. The costs of inventory, supplies, insurance, advertising, rent, computers, utilities, and so on may be too much to cover alone. There are other disadvantages:

1. *Unlimited liability—the risk of personal losses.* When you work for others, it is their problem if the business is not profitable. When you own your own business, you and the business are considered one. You have **unlimited liability**; that is, any debts or damages incurred by the business are your debts and you must pay them, even if it means selling your home, your car, or whatever else you own. This is a serious risk, and undertaking it requires not only thought but also discussion with a lawyer, an insurance agent, an accountant, and others.

2. *Limited financial resources.* Funds available to the business are limited to what the one owner can gather. Since there are serious limits to how much money one person can raise, partnerships and corporations have a greater probability of obtaining the financial backing needed to start and equip a business and keep it going.

unlimited liability
The responsibility of business owners for all of the debts of the business.

Hero Images Inc./Alamy Stock Photo

Being the sole proprietor of a company, like a flower shop, means making a major time commitment to run the business, including constantly seeking out new customers and looking for reliable employees when the time comes to grow. If you were a sole proprietor, what would you need to do if you wanted to take a week's vacation?

3. *Management difficulties.* All businesses need management; someone must keep inventory, accounting, and tax records. Many people skilled at selling things or providing a service are not so skilled at keeping records. Sole proprietors often find it difficult to attract qualified employees to help run the business because often they cannot compete with the salary and benefits offered by larger companies.

4. *Overwhelming time commitment.* Though sole proprietors say they set their own hours, it's hard to own a business, manage it, train people, and have time for anything else in life when there is no one with whom to share the burden. The owner of a store, for example, may put in 12 hours a day at least six days a week—almost twice the hours worked by a nonsupervisory employee in a large company. Imagine how this time commitment affects the sole proprietor's family life. Many sole proprietors will tell you, "It's not a job, it's not a career, it's a way of life."

5. *Few fringe benefits.* If you are your own boss, you lose the fringe benefits that often come with working for others. You have no paid health insurance, no paid disability insurance, no pension plan, no sick leave, and no vacation pay. These and other benefits may add up to 30 percent or more of a worker's compensation.

6. *Limited growth.* Expansion is often slow since a sole proprietorship relies on its owner for most of its creativity, business know-how, and funding.

7. *Limited life span.* If the sole proprietor dies, is incapacitated, or retires, the business no longer exists (unless it is sold or taken over by the sole proprietor's heirs).

Talk with a few local sole proprietors about the problems they've faced in being on their own. They are likely to have many interesting stories about problems getting loans from the bank, problems with theft, and problems simply keeping up with the business. These are reasons why many sole proprietors choose to find partners to share the load.

?TEST**PREP**

- Most people who start businesses in the United States are sole proprietors. What are the advantages and disadvantages of sole proprietorships?
- Why would unlimited liability be considered a major drawback to sole proprietorships?

general partnership
A partnership in which all owners share in operating the business and in assuming liability for the business's debts.

limited partnership
A partnership with one or more general partners and one or more limited partners.

general partner
An owner (partner) who has unlimited liability and is active in managing the firm.

LO 5–2 Describe the differences between general and limited partners, and compare the advantages and disadvantages of partnerships.

Partnerships

A partnership is a legal form of business with two or more owners. There are several types: (1) general partnerships, (2) limited partnerships, and (3) master limited partnerships. In a **general partnership** all owners share in operating the business and in assuming liability for the business's debts. A **limited partnership** has one or more general partners and one or more limited partners. A **general partner** is an owner (partner) who has unlimited liability and is active in managing the firm. Every partnership must have at least one general partner. A **limited partner** is an owner who invests money in the business but does not have any management responsibility or liability for losses beyond his or her investment. **Limited liability** means that the limited partners' liability for the debts of the business is *limited* to the amount they put into the company; their personal assets are not at risk.

One form of partnership, the **master limited partnership (MLP)**, looks much like a corporation (which we discuss next) in that it acts like a corporation and is traded on the stock exchanges like a corporation, but is taxed like a partnership and thus avoids the corporate income tax.[2] Master limited partnerships are limited to the oil, real estate, and gas industries. For example, Sunoco Inc. formed the MLP Sunoco Logistics Partners (SXL) to acquire, own, and operate a group of crude oil and refined-product pipelines and storage

Pop the Cork Wine Tours

facilities. Income received by SXL is not taxed before it is passed on to investors as dividends as it would be if SXL were a corporation.[3]

Another type of partnership was created to limit the disadvantage of unlimited liability. A **limited liability partnership (LLP)** limits partners' risk of losing their personal assets to the outcomes of only their own acts and omissions and those of people under their supervision. If you are a limited partner in an LLP, you can operate without the fear that one of your partners might commit an act of malpractice resulting in a judgment that takes away your house, car, retirement plan, even your collection of vintage *Star Wars* action figures, as would be the case in a general partnership. However, in many states this personal protection does not extend to contract liabilities such as bank loans, leases, and business debt the partnership takes on; loss of personal assets is still a risk if these are not paid. In states without additional contract liability protections for LLPs, the LLP is in many ways similar to an LLC (discussed later in the chapter).

All states except Louisiana have adopted the Uniform Partnership Act (UPA) to replace earlier laws governing partnerships. The UPA defines the three key elements of any general partnership as (1) common ownership, (2) shared profits and losses, and (3) the right to participate in managing the operations of the business.

Advantages of Partnerships

Often, it is much easier to own and manage a business with one or more partners. Your partner may be skilled at inventory control and accounting, while you do the selling or servicing. A partner can also provide additional money, support, and expertise as well as cover for you when you are sick or on vacation. Figure 5.2 suggests several questions to ask yourself when choosing a partner.

Partnerships usually have the following advantages:

1. *More financial resources.* When two or more people pool their money and credit, it is easier to pay the rent, utilities, and other bills incurred by a business. A limited partnership is specially designed to help raise money. As mentioned earlier, a limited partner invests money in the business but cannot legally have management responsibility and has limited liability.

2. *Shared management and pooled/complementary skills and knowledge.* It is simply much easier to manage the day-to-day activities of a business with carefully chosen partners. Partners give each other free time from the business and provide different

Chuck and La Tanya Eiland took their love of travel and wine and turned it into a business with Pop the Cork, a company that organizes tours of Georgia's wine country. What are the potential advantages and disadvantages of becoming business partners with a spouse or family member?

limited partner
An owner who invests money in the business but does not have any management responsibility or liability for losses beyond the investment.

limited liability
The responsibility of a business's owners for losses only up to the amount they invest; limited partners and shareholders have limited liability.

master limited partnership (MLP)
A partnership that looks much like a corporation (in that it acts like a corporation and is traded on a stock exchange) but is taxed like a partnership and thus avoids the corporate income tax.

limited liability partnership (LLP)
A partnership that limits partners' risk of losing their personal assets to only their own acts and omissions and to the acts and omissions of people under their supervision.

FIGURE 5.2
QUESTIONS TO ASK WHEN CHOOSING A BUSINESS PARTNER

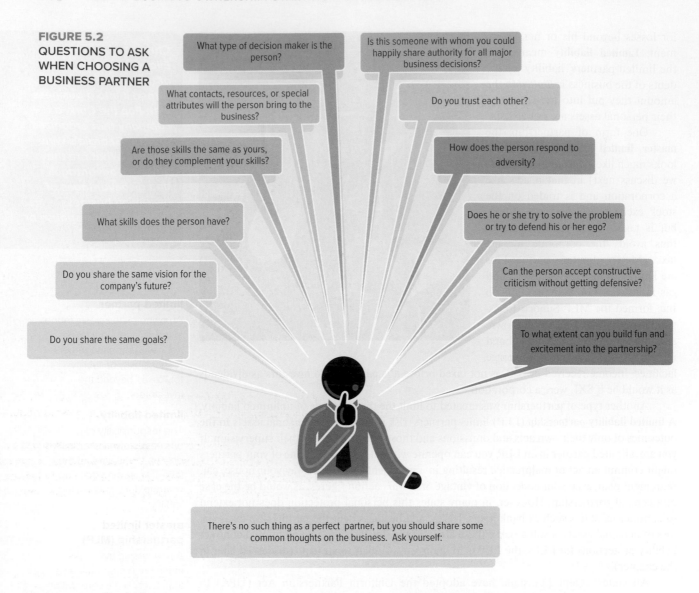

What type of decision maker is the person?

Is this someone with whom you could happily share authority for all major business decisions?

What contacts, resources, or special attributes will the person bring to the business?

Do you trust each other?

Are those skills the same as yours, or do they complement your skills?

How does the person respond to adversity?

What skills does the person have?

Does he or she try to solve the problem or try to defend his or her ego?

Do you share the same vision for the company's future?

Can the person accept constructive criticism without getting defensive?

Do you share the same goals?

To what extent can you build fun and excitement into the partnership?

There's no such thing as a perfect partner, but you should share some common thoughts on the business. Ask yourself:

skills and perspectives. Some people find that the best partner is a spouse. Many husband-and-wife teams manage restaurants, service shops, and other businesses.[4]

3. *Longer survival.* Partnerships are more likely to succeed than sole proprietorships because being watched by a partner can help a businessperson become more disciplined.[5]

4. *No special taxes.* As with sole proprietorships, all profits of partnerships are taxed as the personal income of the owners, who pay the normal income tax on that money. Similarly, partners must estimate their taxes and make quarterly payments or suffer penalties for nonpayment.

Disadvantages of Partnerships

Anytime two people must agree, conflict and tension are possible. Partnerships have caused splits between relatives, friends, and spouses. Let's explore the disadvantages of partnerships:

1. *Unlimited liability.* Each *general* partner is liable for the debts of the firm, no matter who was responsible for causing them. You are liable for your partners' mistakes as well as your own. Like sole proprietors, general partners can lose their homes, cars, and everything else they own if the business loses a lawsuit or goes bankrupt.

2. *Division of profits.* Sharing risk means sharing profits, and that can cause conflicts. There is no set system for dividing profits in a partnership, and they are not always divided evenly. For example, if one partner puts in more money and the other puts in more hours, each may feel justified in asking for a bigger share of the profits.

3. *Disagreements among partners.* Disagreements over money are just one example of potential conflict in a partnership. Who has final authority over employees? Who hires and fires employees? Who works what hours? What if one partner wants to buy expensive equipment for the firm and the other partner disagrees? All terms of the partnership should be spelled out in writing to protect all parties and minimize misunderstandings.[6] The Making Ethical Decisions box offers an example of a difference of opinions between partners.

4. *Difficulty of termination.* Once you have committed yourself to a partnership, it is not easy to get out of it. Sure, you can just quit. However, questions about who gets what and what happens next are often difficult to resolve when the partnership ends. Surprisingly, law firms often have faulty partnership agreements and find that breaking up is hard to do. How do you get rid of a partner you don't like? It is best to decide such questions up front in the partnership agreement. Figure 5.3 gives you ideas about what to include in partnership agreements.

The best way to learn about the advantages and disadvantages of partnerships is to interview several people who have experience with them. They will give you insights and hints on how to avoid problems.

One fear of owning your own business or having a partner is the fear of losing everything you own if someone sues the business or it loses a lot of money. Many businesspeople try to avoid this and the other disadvantages of sole proprietorships and partnerships by forming corporations. We discuss this basic form of business ownership in the following section.

FIGURE 5.3 HOW TO FORM A PARTNERSHIP

It's not hard to form a partnership, but it's wise for each prospective partner to get the counsel of a lawyer experienced with such agreements. Lawyers' services are usually expensive, so would-be partners should read all about partnerships and reach some basic agreements before calling a lawyer.

For your protection, be sure to put your partnership agreement in writing. The Model Business Corporation Act recommends including the following in a written partnership agreement:

- The name of the business. Many states require the firm's name to be registered with state and/or county officials if the firm's name is different from the name of any of the partners.
- The names and addresses of all partners.
- The purpose and nature of the business, the location of the principal offices, and any other locations where business will be conducted.
- The date the partnership will start and how long it will last. Will it exist for a specific length of time, or will it stop when one of the partners dies or when the partners agree to discontinue?
- The contributions made by each partner. Will some partners contribute money, while others provide real estate, personal property, expertise, or labor? When are the contributions due?
- The management responsibilities. Will all partners have equal voices in management, or will there be senior and junior partners?

- The duties of each partner.
- The salaries and drawing accounts of each partner.
- Provision for sharing of profits or losses.
- Provision for accounting procedures. Who'll keep the accounts? What bookkeeping and accounting methods will be used? Where will the books be kept?
- The requirements for taking in new partners.
- Any special restrictions, rights, or duties of any partner.
- Provision for a retiring partner.
- Provision for the purchase of a deceased or retiring partner's share of the business.
- Provision for how grievances will be handled.
- Provision for how to dissolve the partnership and distribute the assets to the partners.

Background image: Aha-Soft/Shutterstock

Imagine that you and your partner own a construction company. You receive a bid from a subcontractor that you know is 20 percent too low. Such a loss to the subcontractor could put him out of business. Accepting the bid will certainly improve your chances of winning the contract for a big shopping center project. Your partner wants to take the bid and let the subcontractor suffer the consequences of his bad estimate. What do you think you should do? What will be the consequences of your decision?

TEST PREP

- What is the difference between a limited partner and a general partner?
- What are some of the advantages and disadvantages of partnerships?

LO 5–3 Compare the advantages and disadvantages of corporations, and summarize the differences among C corporations, S corporations, and limited liability companies.

Corporations

Many corporations—like General Electric, Microsoft, and Walmart—are big and contribute substantially to the U.S. economy. However, it's not necessary to be big to incorporate. Incorporating may be beneficial for small businesses as well.

conventional (C) corporation

A state-chartered legal entity with authority to act and have liability separate from its owners.

A **conventional (C) corporation** is a state-chartered legal entity with authority to act and have liability separate from its owners—its *stockholders*. Stockholders are not liable for the debts or other problems of the corporation beyond the money they invest in it by buying ownership shares, or stock, in the company. They don't have to worry about losing their house, car, or other property because of some business problem—a significant benefit. A corporation not only limits the liability of owners but often enables many people to share in the ownership (and profits) of a business without working there or having other commitments to it. Corporations may choose whether to offer ownership to outside investors or remain privately held. (We discuss stocks in Chapter 19.) Figure 5.4 describes various types of corporations.

Advantages of Corporations

Most people are not willing to risk everything to go into business. Yet for a business to grow, prosper, and create economic opportunity, many people have to be willing to invest money in it. One way to solve this problem is to create an artificial being, an entity that exists only in the eyes of the law—a corporation. Let's explore some of the advantages of corporations:

1. *Limited liability.* A major advantage of corporations is the limited liability of their owners. Remember, limited liability means that the owners of a business are responsible for its losses only up to the amount they invest in it.

2. *Ability to raise more money for investment.* To raise money, a corporation can sell shares of its stock to anyone who is interested. This means that millions of people can own part of

FIGURE 5.4 CORPORATE TYPES
Corporations can fit in more than one category.

You may find some confusing types of corporations when reading about them. Here are a few of the more widely used terms:

- *Alien corporations* do business in the United States but are chartered (incorporated) in another country.

- *Domestic corporations* do business in the state in which they are chartered (incorporated).

- *Foreign corporations* do business in one state but are chartered in another. About one-third of all corporations are chartered in Delaware because of its relatively attractive rules for incorporation. A foreign corporation must register in states where it operates.

- *Closed (private) corporations* have stock that is held by a few people and isn't available to the general public.

- *Open (public) corporations* sell stock to the general public. General Motors and ExxonMobil are examples of public corporations.

- *Quasi-public corporations* are chartered by the government as an approved monopoly to perform services to the general public. Public utilities are examples of quasi-public corporations.

- *Professional corporations* are owned by those who offer professional services (doctors, lawyers, etc.). Shares in professional corporations aren't publicly traded.

- *Nonprofit (or not-for-profit) corporations* don't seek personal profit for their owners.

- *Multinational corporations* operate in several countries.

major companies like IBM, Apple, and Coca-Cola, and smaller corporations as well. If a company sells 10 million shares of stock for $50 a share, it will have $500 million available to build plants, buy materials, hire people, manufacture products, and so on. Such a large amount of money would be difficult to raise any other way. Corporations can also borrow money by obtaining loans from financial institutions like banks. They can also borrow from individual investors by issuing bonds, which involves paying investors interest until the bonds are repaid sometime in the future. You can read about how corporations raise funds through the sale of stocks and bonds in Chapter 19.

3. *Size.* "Size" summarizes many of the advantages of some corporations. Because they can raise large amounts of money to work with, big corporations can build modern factories or software development facilities with the latest equipment. They can hire experts or specialists in all areas of operation. They can buy other corporations in different fields to diversify their business risks. In short, a large corporation with numerous resources can take advantage of opportunities anywhere in the world. But corporations do not have to be large to enjoy the benefits of incorporating. Many doctors, lawyers, and individuals, as well as partners in a variety of businesses, have incorporated. The vast majority of corporations in the United States are small businesses.

4. *Perpetual life.* Because corporations are separate from those who own them, the death of one or more owners does not terminate the corporation.

5. *Ease of ownership change.* It is easy to change the owners of a corporation. All that is necessary is to sell the stock to someone else.

6. *Ease of attracting talented employees.* Corporations can attract skilled employees by offering benefits like stock options (the right to purchase shares of the corporation for a fixed price).

7. *Separation of ownership from management.* Corporations are able to raise money from many different owners/stockholders without getting them involved in management.

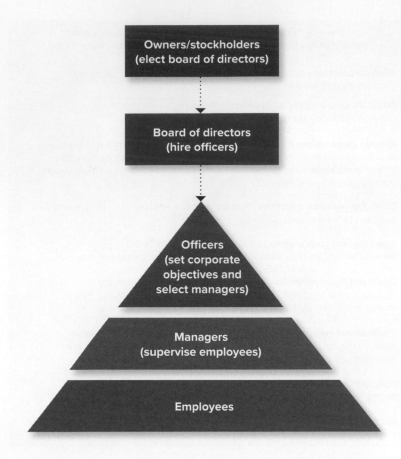

The corporate hierarchy in Figure 5.5 shows how the owners/stockholders are separate from the managers and employees. The owners/stockholders elect a board of directors, who hire the officers of the corporation and oversee major policy issues.[7] The owners/stockholders thus have some say in who runs the corporation but have no real control over the daily operations.

Disadvantages of Corporations

There are so many sole proprietorships and partnerships in the United States that there must be some disadvantages to incorporating. Otherwise, everyone would do it. The following are a few of the disadvantages:

1. *Initial cost.* Incorporation may cost thousands of dollars and require lawyers and accountants. There are less costly ways of incorporating in certain states (see the following subsection), but many people do not have the time or confidence to go through this procedure without the help of a potentially expensive lawyer.

2. *Extensive paperwork.* The paperwork needed to start a corporation is just the beginning. A sole proprietor or partnership may keep rather broad accounting records. A corporation, in contrast, must keep detailed financial records, the minutes of meetings, and more. As noted in Figure 5.4, many firms incorporate in Delaware or Nevada because these states' business-oriented laws make the process easier than it is in other states.

3. *Double taxation.* Corporate income is taxed twice. First the corporation pays tax on its income before it can distribute any, as *dividends,* to stockholders. Then the stockholders pay income tax on the dividends they receive. States often tax corporations more heavily than other enterprises, and some special taxes apply only to corporations.

4. *Two tax returns.* An individual who incorporates must file both a corporate tax return and an individual tax return. Depending on the size of the corporation, a

How B Corps Help Society While Earning Profits

Over the decades, many top companies have been guided by the principle that their ultimate goal is to increase value for shareholders. For benefit corporations, however, the purpose of business is to do good as well as earn profits. These mission-based companies are certified by an organization called B Lab that determines how well they meet a set of socially and environmentally beneficial goals. In order to qualify, potential "B corps" must dedicate substantial resources both towards staff and society as a whole.

At Bigelow Tea, for example, sustainability and employee benefits like profit sharing and 401(k) matching have been priorities for generations. Along with achieving zero-waste-to-landfill status, the family-owned company also powers its Connecticut headquarters with nearly 900 solar panels. In 2018

karandaev/Getty Images

Bigelow became a certified B corp in order to ensure that the company remained committed to its founding principles. "We were very excited to discover that by doing the things that had been written into our

mission statement more than 30 years ago, we were already meeting the requirements," said CEO Cindi Bigelow. Sales even ticked up the year after the company received its certification, but Bigelow insists that "we didn't become a B corp to increase sales."

Instead, the company earns more than $200 million in annual revenue while also providing for its employees and pursuing worthy causes. B Lab estimates that more than 60,000 certified B corps around the world operate in similar ways, including major brands like Patagonia, Ben & Jerry's, and Kickstarter. The number of B corps could continue to increase as more consumers call on companies to provide material benefits for all stakeholders, not just shareholders.

Source: Bigelow Tea, bigelowtea.com, accessed February 2020.

corporate return can be quite complex and require the assistance of a certified public accountant (CPA).

5. *Size.* Size may be one advantage of corporations, but it can be a disadvantage as well. Large corporations sometimes become too inflexible and tied down in red tape to respond quickly to market changes, and their profitability can suffer.

6. *Difficulty of termination.* Once a corporation has started, it's relatively difficult to end.

7. *Possible conflict with stockholders and board of directors.* Conflict may brew if the stockholders elect a board of directors who disagree with management.[8] Since the board of directors chooses the company's officers, entrepreneurs serving as managers can find themselves forced out of the very company they founded. This happened to Travis Kalanick, one of the founders of Uber, and Steve Jobs, a founder of Apple (Jobs of course returned to the company later).[9]

Many businesspeople are discouraged by the costs, paperwork, and special taxes corporations must pay. However, many others believe the advantages of incorporation outweigh the hassles. See the Adapting to Change box for an example of a benefit corporation, a new type of nonprofit corporation.

Individuals Can Incorporate

Not all corporations are large organizations with hundreds of employees and thousands of stockholders. Truckers, doctors, lawyers, plumbers, athletes, and small-business owners of all kinds can also incorporate. Normally, individuals who incorporate do not issue stock to

FIGURE 5.6 HOW TO INCORPORATE

The process of forming a corporation varies somewhat from state to state. The articles of incorporation are usually filed with the secretary of state's office in the state in which the company incorporates. The articles contain:

- The corporation's name.
- The names of the people who incorporated it.
- Its purposes.
- Its duration (usually perpetual).
- The number of shares that can be issued, their voting rights, and any other rights the shareholders have.
- The corporation's minimum capital.
- The address of the corporation's office.
- The name and address of the person responsible for the corporation's legal service.
- The names and addresses of the first directors.
- Any other public information the incorporators wish to include.

Before a business can so much as open a bank account or hire employees, it needs a federal tax identification number. To apply for one, get an SS-4 form from the IRS.

In addition to the articles of incorporation listed, a corporation has bylaws. These describe how the firm is to be operated from both legal and managerial points of view. The bylaws include:

- How, when, and where shareholders' and directors' meetings are held, and how long directors are to serve.
- Directors' authority.
- Duties and responsibilities of officers, and the length of their service.
- How stock is issued.
- Other matters, including employment contracts.

outsiders; therefore, they do not share all the advantages and disadvantages of large corporations (such as size and more money for investment). Their major advantages are limited liability and possible tax benefits. Although you are not required to file for incorporation through a lawyer, it is usually wise to consult one. In addition to lawyers' fees, the secretary of state's office charges a fee for incorporating a business, varying by state from a low of $50 in Arkansas to a high of $725 in Nevada.[10] Like the fee, the length of time it will take to actually have your business incorporated will vary by state. The average time is approximately 30 days from the date of application. Figure 5.6 outlines how to incorporate.

S Corporations

S corporation

A unique government creation that looks like a corporation but is taxed like sole proprietorships and partnerships.

An **S corporation** is a unique government creation that looks like a corporation but is taxed like sole proprietorships and partnerships. (The name comes from the fact that the rules governing them are in Subchapter S of Chapter 1 of the Internal Revenue Code.) The paperwork and details of S corporations are similar to those of conventional (C) corporations. S corporations have shareholders, directors, and employees, and the benefit of limited liability, but their profits are taxed only as the personal income of the shareholders—thus avoiding the double taxation of C corporations.

Avoiding double taxation is reason enough for approximately 4.7 million U.S. companies to operate as S corporations.[11] Yet not all businesses can become S corporations. In order to qualify, a company must:[12]

1. Have no more than 100 shareholders. (All members of a family count as 1 shareholder.)

2. Have shareholders that are individuals or estates, and who (as individuals) are citizens or permanent residents of the United States.

3. Have only one class of stock. (You can read more about the various classes of stock in Chapter 19.)

4. Derive no more than 25 percent of income from passive sources (rents, royalties, interest).

An S corporation that loses its S status may not operate under it again for at least five years. The tax structure of S corporations isn't attractive to all businesses. For one thing, the benefits change every time the tax rules change. The best way to learn all the benefits or shortcomings for a specific business is to go over the tax advantages and liability differences with a lawyer, an accountant, or both.[13]

Limited Liability Companies

A **limited liability company (LLC)** is similar to an S corporation, but without the special eligibility requirements. LLCs were introduced in Wyoming in 1977, and were recognized by the Internal Revenue Service as a partnership for federal income tax purposes in 1988. An LLC can submit a form to the IRS if it chooses to be treated as a corporation.[14] By 1996, all 50 states and the District of Columbia recognized LLCs.

The number of LLCs has risen dramatically since 1988, when there were fewer than 100 filings to operate them. Today, more than half of new business registrations in some states are LLCs.[15]

Why the drive toward forming LLCs? Advantages include:

1. *Limited liability.* Personal assets are protected. Limited liability was previously available only to limited partners and shareholders of corporations.

2. *Choice of taxation.* LLCs can choose to be taxed as partnerships or as corporations. Partnership-level taxation was previously a benefit normally reserved for partners or S corporation owners.

3. *Flexible ownership rules.* LLCs do not have to comply with ownership restrictions as S corporations do. Owners can be a person, partnership, or corporation.

4. *Flexible distribution of profits and losses.* Profits and losses don't have to be distributed in proportion to the money each person invests, as in corporations. LLC members agree on the percentage to be distributed to each member.

5. *Operating flexibility.* LLCs do have to submit articles of organization, which are similar to articles of incorporation, but they are not required to keep minutes, file written resolutions, or hold annual meetings. An LLC also submits a written operating agreement, similar to a partnership agreement, describing how the company is to be operated.

Of course, LLCs have their disadvantages as well. These include:

1. *No stock.* LLC ownership is nontransferable. LLC members need the approval of the other members in order to sell their interests in the company. In contrast, regular and S corporation stockholders can sell their shares as they wish.

2. *Fewer incentives.* Unlike corporations, LLCs can't deduct the cost of fringe benefits for members owning 2 percent or more of the company. And since there's no stock, they can't use stock options as incentives to employees.

3. *Taxes.* LLC members must pay self-employment taxes—the Medicare/Social Security taxes paid by sole proprietors and partnerships—on their profits. In contrast, S corporations pay self-employment tax on owners' salaries but not on the entire profits.

4. *Paperwork.* While the paperwork required of LLCs is not as great as that required of corporations, it is more than required of sole proprietors.

Splash/PetZen/GoPet/Newscom

PetZen Products LLC offers doggie treadmills to help pudgy pets get back their puppy figures. What are the advantages and disadvantages of LLCs?

limited liability company (LLC)

A company similar to an S corporation but without the special eligibility requirements.

The start-up cost for an LLC varies. Online legal services such as LegalZoom (legalzoom.com) can file the necessary paperwork for as little as $79 plus the state filing fee.[16] Figure 5.7 summarizes the advantages and disadvantages of the major forms of business ownership.

FIGURE 5.7 COMPARISON OF FORMS OF BUSINESS OWNERSHIP

	SOLE PROPRIETORSHIP	PARTNERSHIPS		CORPORATIONS		
		General Partnership	Limited Partnership	Conventional Corporation	S Corporation	Limited Liability Company
Documents Needed to Start Business	None; may need permit or license	Partnership agreement (oral or written)	Written agreement; must file certificate of limited partnership	Articles of incorporation, bylaws	Articles of incorporation, bylaws, must meet criteria	Articles of organization and operating agreement; no eligibility requirements
Ease of Termination	Easy to terminate: just pay debts and quit	May be hard to terminate, depending on the partnership agreement	Same as general partnership	Hard and expensive to terminate	Same as conventional corporation	May be difficult, depending upon operating agreement
Length of Life	Terminates on the death of owner	Terminates on the death or withdrawal of partner	Same as general partnership	Perpetual life	Same as conventional corporation	Varies according to dissolution dates in articles of organization
Transfer of Ownership	Business can be sold to qualified buyer	Must have other partner(s)' agreement	Same as general partnership	Easy to change owners; just sell stock	Can sell stock, but with restrictions	Can't sell stock
Financial Resources	Limited to owner's capital and loans	Limited to partners' capital and loans	Same as general partnership	More money to start and operate; may sell stocks and bonds	Same as conventional corporation	Same as partnership
Risk of Losses	Unlimited liability	Unlimited liability	Limited liability	Limited liability	Limited liability	Limited liability
Taxes	Taxed as personal income	Taxed as personal income	Same as general partnership	Corporate, double taxation	Taxed as personal income	Varies
Management Responsibilities	Owner manages *all* areas of the business	Partners share management	Can't participate in management	Separate management from ownership	Same as conventional corporation	Varies
Employee Benefits	Usually fewer benefits and lower wages	Often fewer benefits and lower wages; promising employee could become a partner	Same as general partnership	Usually better benefits and wages, advancement opportunities	Same as conventional corporation	Varies, but are not tax-deductible

TEST**PREP**

- What are the major advantages and disadvantages of incorporating a business?
- What is the role of owners (stockholders) in the corporate hierarchy?
- If you buy stock in a corporation and someone gets injured by one of the corporation's products, can you be sued? Why or why not?
- Why are so many new businesses choosing a limited liability company (LLC) form of ownership?

LO 5–4 Define and give examples of three types of corporate mergers, and explain the role of leveraged buyouts and taking a firm private.

Corporate Expansion: Mergers and Acquisitions

What's the difference between mergers and acquisitions? A **merger** is the result of two firms joining to form one company. It is similar to a marriage, joining two individuals as one family. An **acquisition** is one company's purchase of the property and obligations of another company. It is more like buying a house than entering a marriage.

There are three major types of corporate mergers: vertical, horizontal, and conglomerate. A **vertical merger** joins two firms operating in different stages of related businesses. A merger between a soft drink company and an artificial sweetener maker would ensure the merged firm a constant supply of an ingredient the soft drink manufacturer needs. It could also help ensure quality control of the soft drink company's products.

A **horizontal merger** joins two firms in the same industry and allows them to diversify or expand their products. A soft drink company and a mineral water company that merge can now supply a variety of beverage products.

A **conglomerate merger** unites firms in completely unrelated industries in order to diversify business operations and investments. A soft drink company and a snack food company would form a conglomerate merger. Figure 5.8 illustrates the differences among the three types of mergers.

Mergers between large competitors must prove to the Federal Trade Commission (FTC) that the new combined company does not limit competition unfairly.[17] For example, in 2016 Staples and Office Depot had to abandon their plans to merge when a judge ruled that the merger would mean diminished competition and higher prices for large national businesses that buy office supplies in bulk.[18] In 2020 the FTC blocked the sale of shaving upstart Harry's to Schick-maker Edgewell. The shaving market is dominated by just two companies, Edgewell and Gillette, which were forced to lower prices when Harry's entered the market online and later entered brick-and-mortar stores. The FTC judged that allowing one of these giants to swallow Harry's would harm the competition and innovation that the small disrupter spurred.[19]

Rather than merge or sell to another company, some corporations decide to maintain, or in some cases regain, control of a firm internally. By *taking a firm private,* management or a group of stockholders obtains all the firm's stock for themselves by buying it back from the other stockholders. Burger King, Dell, Krispy Kreme, and Panera Bread are examples of firms that have been taken private.[20]

Suppose employees believe they may lose their jobs, or managers believe they could improve corporate performance if they owned the company. Does either group have an opportunity of taking ownership of the company? Yes—they might attempt a leveraged

merger
The result of two firms forming one company.

acquisition
One company's purchase of the property and obligations of another company.

vertical merger
The joining of two companies involved in different stages of related businesses.

horizontal merger
The joining of two firms in the same industry.

conglomerate merger
The joining of firms in completely unrelated industries.

FIGURE 5.8 TYPES OF MERGERS

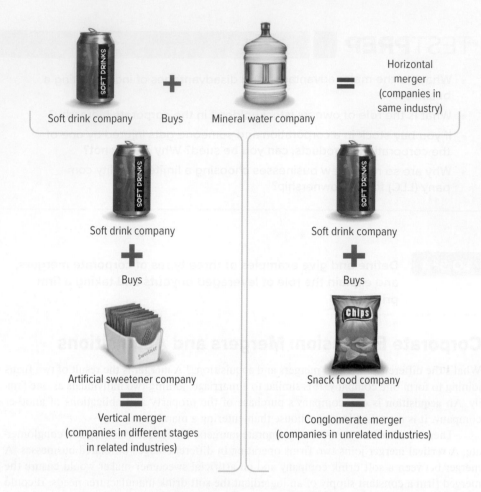

Soft drink company   Buys   Mineral water company   =   Horizontal merger (companies in same industry)

Soft drink company
+
Buys
Artificial sweetener company
=
Vertical merger (companies in different stages in related industries)

Soft drink company
+
Buys
Snack food company
=
Conglomerate merger (companies in unrelated industries)

leveraged buyout (LBO)
An attempt by employees, management, or a group of investors to purchase an organization primarily through borrowing.

buyout. A **leveraged buyout (LBO)** is an attempt by employees, management, or a group of private investors to buy out the stockholders in a company, primarily by borrowing the necessary funds. The employees, managers, or investors now become the owners of the firm. LBOs have ranged in size from $50 million to $34 billion and have involved everything from small family businesses to giant corporations like Hertz Corporation, the former Toys "R" Us, Chrysler, and the former RJR Nabisco. In November 2019, investment firm KKR approached drugstore giant Walgreens Boots Alliance about a potential $70 billion take-private transaction. If successful, the deal would be the largest LBO in history.[21]

Today, business acquisitions are not limited to U.S. buyers. Foreign companies have found the fastest way to grow is often to buy an established operation that can enhance their technology

In 2019, Disney purchased the film and TV assets held by 21st Century Fox for more than $71 billion, giving the entertainment giant the rights to valuable properties like The Simpsons. What type of merger is this: vertical, horizontal, or conglomerate?

Art of Drawing/Alamy Stock Photo

Photo 12/Alamy Stock Photo

or expand the number of brands they offer. Number two brewer Miller Brewing Company was acquired by London-based SAB. Belgium's InBev purchased the largest U.S. brewer, Anheuser-Busch and its Budweiser and Bud Light brands, for $52 billion. In 2018, the German drug company Bayer paid $63 billion to take control of agrochemical company Monsanto.[22]

> **LO 5–5**   Outline the advantages and disadvantages of franchises, and discuss the opportunities for diversity in franchising and the challenges of global franchising.

Franchises

In addition to the three basic forms of business ownership, there are two special forms: franchises and cooperatives. Let's look at franchises first. A **franchise agreement** is an arrangement whereby someone with a good idea for a business (the **franchisor**) sells the rights to use the business name and sell a product or service (the **franchise**) to others (the **franchisees**) in a given territory.

Some people, uncomfortable with the idea of starting their own business from scratch, would rather join a business with a proven track record through a franchise agreement. A franchise can be formed as a sole proprietorship, a partnership, or a corporation. The U.S. Census Bureau estimates that 1 out of every 10 businesses in the United States is a franchise.[23] Some of the best-known franchises are McDonald's, Jiffy Lube, 7-Eleven, WW International (formerly called Weight Watchers), and Holiday Inn.

According to the International Franchise Association, the more than 733,000 franchised businesses operating in the United States create approximately 7.6 million jobs that produce a direct and indirect economic impact of $674 billion in the U.S. economy.[24] The most popular businesses for franchising are restaurants (fast-food and full-service) and gas stations with convenience stores. McDonald's, the largest restaurant chain in the United States in terms of sales, is often considered the gold standard of franchising. Health and fitness clubs, financial services, hotels and motels, and automotive centers are also popular franchised businesses.[25] See Figure 5.9 for some tips on evaluating franchises.

Advantages of Franchises

Franchising has penetrated every aspect of U.S. and global business life by offering products and services that are reliable, convenient, and competitively priced. Franchising clearly has some advantages:

1. *Management and marketing assistance.* Compared with someone who starts a business from scratch, a franchisee usually has a much greater chance of succeeding because he or she has an established product to sell, help choosing a location, and assistance in all phases of promotion and operation. It's like having your own store but with full-time consultants when you need them. Franchisors usually provide intensive training. For example, McDonald's sends all new franchisees and managers to Hamburger University in Chicago, Illinois, and six other campuses worldwide.[26]

   Some franchisors help their franchisees with local marketing efforts rather than having them depend solely on national advertising. Franchisees also have a network of fellow franchisees facing similar problems who can share their experiences.

2. *Personal ownership.* A franchise operation is still your business, and you enjoy as much of the incentives and profit as any sole proprietor would. You are still your own boss, although you must follow more rules, regulations, and procedures than with your own privately owned business. The Spotlight on Small Business box features an example of a growing franchise that is attracting new franchisees.

3. *Nationally recognized name.* It is one thing to open a gift shop or an ice cream store. It is quite another to open a new Hallmark store or a Baskin-Robbins. With an

franchise agreement
An arrangement whereby someone with a good idea for a business sells the rights to use the business name and sell a product or service to others in a given territory.

franchisor
A company that develops a product concept and sells others the rights to make and sell the products.

franchise
The right to use a specific business's name and sell its products or services in a given territory.

franchisee
A person who buys a franchise.

Benjamin Rasmussen

Dan Remus and Jef Strauss founded the canine-cleaning company Wag 'N Wash when they were concerned about leaving their Dalmatian Geni at home all day. They began franchising a few years later and now have locations in nine states, with more on the way. While launching a single store costs an average of $340,000, franchisees can eventually earn more than $1.3 million annually. What type of service franchise might appeal to you as a business owner?

FIGURE 5.9 BUYING A FRANCHISE

Since buying a franchise is a major investment, be sure to check out a company's financial strength before you get involved. Watch out for scams too. Scams called *bust-outs* usually involve people coming to town, renting nice offices, taking out ads, and persuading people to invest. Then they disappear with the investors' money. For example, in San Francisco a company called T.B.S. Inc. sold distributorships for in-home AIDS tests. It promised an enormous market and potential profits of $3,000 for an investment of less than $200. The "test" turned out to be nothing more than a mail-order questionnaire about lifestyle.

A good source of information about evaluating a franchise deal is the handbook *Investigate before Investing*, available from International Franchise Association Publications.

Checklist for Evaluating a Franchise

The Franchise

Did your lawyer approve the franchise contract you're considering after he or she studied it paragraph by paragraph?

Does the franchise give you an exclusive territory for the length of the franchise?

Under what circumstances can you terminate the franchise contract and at what cost to you?

If you sell your franchise, will you be compensated for your goodwill (the value of your business's reputation and other intangibles)?

If the franchisor sells the company, will your investment be protected?

The Franchisor

How many years has the firm offering you a franchise been in operation?

Does it have a reputation for honesty and fair dealing among the local firms holding its franchise?

Has the franchisor shown you any certified figures indicating exact net profits of one or more going firms that you personally checked yourself with the franchisee? Ask for the company's disclosure statement.

Will the firm assist you with

    A management training program?

    An employee training program?

    A public relations program?

    Capital?

    Credit?

    Merchandising ideas?

Will the firm help you find a good location for your new business?

Has the franchisor investigated you carefully enough to assure itself that you can successfully operate one of its franchises at a profit both to itself and to you?

You, the Franchisee

How much equity capital will you need to purchase the franchise and operate it until your income equals your expenses?

Does the franchisor offer financing for a portion of the franchising fees? On what terms?

Are you prepared to give up some independence of action to secure the advantages offered by the franchise? Do you have your family's support?

Does the industry appeal to you? Are you ready to spend much or all of the remainder of your business life with this franchisor, offering its product or service to the public?

Your Market

Have you made any study to determine whether the product or service that you propose to sell under the franchise has a market in your territory at the prices you'll have to charge?

Will the population in the territory given to you increase, remain static, or decrease over the next five years?

Will demand for the product or service you're considering be greater, about the same, or less five years from now than it is today?

What competition already exists in your territory for the product or service you contemplate selling?

Sources: U.S. Department of Commerce, *Franchise Opportunities Handbook;* Steve Adams, "Buying a Brand," *Patriot Ledger* (Quincy, MA), March 1, 2008.

established franchise, you get instant recognition and support from a product group with established customers around the world.

4. *Financial advice and assistance.* Two major problems for small-business owners are arranging financing and learning to keep good records. Franchisees often get valuable assistance and periodic advice from people with expertise in these areas. In fact, some franchisors, including Jiffy Lube, and UPS Stores, provide financing to potential franchisees they feel will be valuable parts of the franchise system.[27]

5. *Lower failure rate.* Historically, the failure rate for franchises has been lower than that of other business ventures. However, franchising has grown so rapidly that many weak franchises have entered the field, so you need to be careful and invest wisely.

stumpyshh.com

While chucking an axe at a big hunk of wood might not seem like an ideal first date activity, Brendan Wehmann claims that he sees new couples all the time at his Stumpy's Hatchet House franchise in Tampa, Florida. "It's something fun and different," said Wehmann. Founded in New Jersey, Stumpy's has opened more than 30 franchises across the country where people can join their friends for a game that's like darts, only with hatchets instead. Customers rent rooms by the hour and take turns tossing axes individually while the rest of the party stands away in a safe zone. Although Stumpy's offers some snacks and soft drinks, people

Jewel Samad/AFP/Getty Images

can also bring their own food and alcoholic beverages to enjoy.

The four founders of Stumpy's came up with the idea one day when they were barbecuing by the New Jersey coast. After cutting wood for the chiminea, they

began to toss an axe against the remnants of a big tree that had fallen during Hurricane Sandy. It became a regular outdoor activity that eventually led to the founding of Stumpy's in 2016. The company started franchising soon after due to the venture's relatively simple setup. Along with its modest franchise fee of $35,000, Stumpy's also has plenty of room to grow since many Americans have never gone hatchet-tossing before. "I always say to people, when was the last time you did something for the first time? And that's what Stumpy's is," said cofounder Trish Oliphant. "I think this is America's next bowling."

Source: Matthew Rocco, "How Stumpy's Turned Hatchet-Throwing Into a Fast-Growing Business," *Fox Business*, foxbusiness.com, August 28, 2018.

Disadvantages of Franchises

There are, however, some potential pitfalls to franchising. Check out any franchise arrangement with present franchisees and discuss the idea with an attorney and an accountant. Disadvantages of franchises include the following:

1. *Large start-up costs.* Most franchises demand a fee for the rights to the franchise. Start-up costs for a Cruise Planners franchise begin at $2,000, but if it's a Dunkin' franchise you're after, you'd better have a lot more dough—approximately $1.6 million.[28]

2. *Shared profit.* The franchisor often demands either a large share of the profits in addition to the start-up fees or a percentage commission based on sales, not profit. This share is called a *royalty.* For example, if a franchisor demands a 10 percent royalty on a franchise's net sales, 10 cents of every dollar the franchisee collects (before taxes and other expenses) must be paid to the franchisor.[29]

3. *Management regulation.* Management "assistance" has a way of becoming managerial orders, directives, and limitations. Franchisees feeling burdened by the company's rules and regulations may lose the drive to run their own business.[30] Often franchisees will band together to resolve their grievances with franchisors rather than fighting their battles alone. For example, the KFC National Council & Advertising Cooperative, which represents all U.S. KFC franchisees, sued KFC to gain control of advertising strategies. The franchisees were angry over Yum! Brands's (owner of KFC) decision to implement an ad strategy that emphasized a shift to grilled chicken rather than fried chicken. The campaign centered around the slogan "Unthink KFC," which was exactly what customers did. Sales plummeted 7 percent

that quarter and franchisees had to throw away up to 50 percent of their grilled chicken supplies.

4. *Coattail effects.* What happens to your franchise if fellow franchisees fail? The actions of other franchises have an impact on your future growth and profitability. Due to this *coattail effect,* you could be forced out of business even if your particular franchise has been profitable. For example, the customer passion for high-flying franchisor Krispy Kreme sank as the market became flooded with new stores and the availability of the product at retail locations caused overexposure. McDonald's and Subway franchisees complain that due to the company's relentless growth, some new stores have taken business away from existing locations, squeezing franchisees' profits per outlet.

5. *Restrictions on selling.* Unlike owners of private businesses, who can sell their companies to whomever they choose on their own terms, many franchisees face restrictions on the resale of their franchises. To control quality, franchisors often insist on approving the new owner, who must meet their standards.[31]

6. *Fraudulent franchisors.* Most franchisors are not large systems like McDonald's and Subway. Many are small, rather obscure companies that prospective franchisees may know little about. Most are honest, but complaints to the Federal Trade Commission have increased about franchisors that delivered little or nothing of what they promised. For example, new restaurant franchise Burgerim grew from zero to 1,200 franchise licenses in just four years. Many of the franchisees were inexperienced and underfinanced. Unfortunately when the company couldn't handle the growth, it collapsed and the owner fled the country, leaving franchisees with unfinished stores and heavy loan debt.[32] Before you buy a franchise, make certain you check out the facts fully and remember the old adage "You get what you pay for."

Diversity in Franchising

A lingering issue in franchising is the number of women who own franchises. While women own about half of all U.S. companies and are opening businesses at double the rate of men, their ownership of franchises is only about 35 percent. However, that statistic doesn't tell the whole story; female franchise ownership has grown significantly from only 24 percent a decade ago.[33]

Women aren't just franchisees anymore; they're becoming franchisors as well. If they face difficulty getting financing for growing their businesses, turning to franchisees to help carry expansion costs can help. For example, top-rated franchise companies like Auntie Anne's, Decorating Den, and Build-A-Bear Workshops were started by women.

Franchisors are also becoming more focused on recruiting minority franchisees. Today there are more than four million minority-owned businesses in operation, employing almost 5 million people and generating nearly $591 billion in annual revenue.[34] Minority business owners started more than 50 percent of the 2 million new businesses in the United States in the last 10 years.[35] In order to draw talented entrepreneurs like these to franchising, initiatives like DiversityFran by the International Franchise Association work to build awareness of franchising opportunities within minority communities. The U.S. Commerce Department's Federal Minority Business Development Agency also provides aspiring minority business owners with training in how to run franchises. Some franchisors support minority ownership programs as well. For example, Dunkin' Brands's Diversity in Franchising Initiative offers financing and development support to minorities and military veterans.[36]

Today more than 30 percent of franchises are owned by African Americans, Latinos, Asians, and

Artists of all skill levels can bring a bottle of wine and join their friends for a relaxing, creative evening at Painting with a Twist. Michelle Lewis enjoyed her first visit so much that she partnered with her sister Donna to open a franchise in Detroit in 2009 followed by two more locations a couple of years later. What is the appeal of franchising to entrepreneurs like Michelle and Donna Lewis?

Donna and Michelle Lewis, Painting with a Twist, Detroit

Native Americans. Less than 19 percent of non-franchise businesses are minority owned.[37] Franchising opportunities seem perfectly attuned to the needs of aspiring minority businesspeople. Minorities may choose franchising over sole proprietorship because they have limited access to business connections and support. For example, after Michelle Lewis spent an evening at a Painting with a Twist studio, a paint-and-sip franchise where guests paint "masterpieces" as they sip wine, she quit her job as an architect and bought a franchise. She admits that she was concerned about not having what it takes to be a business owner. But after receiving the guidance she needed to be successful, she now owns three Painting with a Twist franchises and employs 30 people.[38]

Home-Based Franchises

Home-based businesses offer many obvious advantages, including relief from the stress of commuting, extra time for family activities, and low overhead expenses. One disadvantage is the feeling of isolation. Compared to home-based entrepreneurs, home-based franchisees feel less isolated. Experienced franchisors often share their knowledge of building a profitable enterprise with other franchisees.

Home-based franchises can be started for as little as $2,000. Today you can be a franchisee in areas ranging from cleaning services to tax preparation, child care, pet care, or cruise planning.[39] Before investing in a home-based franchise it is helpful to ask yourself the following questions: Are you willing to put in long hours? Can you work in a solitary environment? Are you motivated and well organized? Does your home have the space you need for the business? Can your home also be the place you work? It's also important to check out the franchisor carefully.

E-commerce in Franchising

The Internet has changed franchising in many ways. Most brick-and-mortar franchises have expanded their businesses online and created virtual storefronts to deliver increased value to customers. Setting up a website is one of the best ways for a franchisee to increase sales quickly. However, many franchisors prohibit franchisee-sponsored websites because conflicts can erupt if the franchisor creates its own website. Sometimes franchisors send "reverse royalties" to franchisees who believe their sales were hurt by the franchisor's online sales, but that doesn't always bring about peace. Before buying a franchise, read the small print regarding online sales.

Using Technology in Franchising

Franchisors often use technology, including social media, to extend their brands and meet the needs of both their customers and their franchisees. For example, Candy Bouquet International, Inc., of Little Rock, Arkansas, offers franchises that sell candies in flowerlike arrangements. Franchisees have brick-and-mortar locations to serve walk-in customers, but they also are provided leads from the company's main website. All franchisees are kept up-to-date daily on company news via e-mail, and they use a chat room to discuss issues and product ideas with each other. Candy Bouquet International now has 300 locations around the globe.[40]

Franchising in Global Markets

Franchising today is truly a global effort. U.S. franchisors are counting their profits in euros, yuan, pesos, won, krona, baht, yen, and many other currencies. McDonald's has more than 36,000 restaurants in over 100 countries serving an estimated 69 million customers each day.[41]

Because of its proximity and shared language, Canada is the most popular target for U.S.-based franchises. Franchisors are finding it surprisingly easier now to move into China, South Africa, the Philippines, and the Middle East. Plus it's not just the large franchises like Subway and Marriott Hotels making the move. Newer, smaller franchises are going global as well. Auntie Anne's sells hand-rolled pretzels in more than 25 countries including

Indonesia, Malaysia, the Philippines, Singapore, Venezuela, and Thailand.[42] In 2005, 29-year-old Matthew Corrin launched Freshii, a sandwich, salad, and soup restaurant with fresh affordable food in trendy locations. He already has almost 500 locations in 17 countries.[43]

What makes franchising successful in global markets is what makes it successful in the United States: convenience and a predictable level of service and quality. Franchisors, though, must be careful and do their homework before entering into global franchise agreements.[44]

Three questions to ask before forming a global franchise are: Will your intellectual property be protected? Can you give proper support to global partners? Are you able to adapt to franchise regulations in other countries? If the answer is yes to all three questions, global franchising creates great opportunities. It's also important to remember that adapting products and brand names to different countries creates challenges. In France, people thought a furniture-stripping franchise called Dip 'N Strip was a bar that featured strippers.

Just as McDonald's and Subway have exported golden arches and sub sandwiches worldwide, foreign franchises see the United States as a popular target. Japanese franchises like Kumon Learning Centers and Australian franchises like Cartridge World are very active in the United States. Other franchises are hoping to change our tastes here.[45]

Pikoso.kz/Shutterstock

Although KFC is famous around the world for its fried chicken, in India the Colonel must also appeal to the nation's millions of vegetarians with meatless options like the plant-based burger pictured here. Do you think a sandwich like this would be successful with KFC customers in the United States.?

LO 5–6 Explain the role of cooperatives.

Cooperatives

Some people dislike the notion of owners, managers, workers, and buyers being separate individuals with separate goals, so they have formed cooperatives, a different kind of organization to meet their needs for electricity, child care, housing, health care, food, and financial services. A **cooperative (co-op)**, is owned and controlled by the people who use it—producers, consumers, or workers with similar needs who pool their resources for mutual gain. In many rural parts of the country, for example, the government sells wholesale power to electric cooperatives at rates 40 to 50 percent below the rates nonfederal utilities charge. Electric cooperatives serve 42 million U.S. consumer-members in 47 states—or 12 percent of the population.[46]

cooperative (co-op)
A business owned and controlled by the people who use it—producers, consumers, or workers with similar needs who pool their resources for mutual gain.

Worldwide, more than 1 billion people are members of cooperatives.[47] Members democratically control these businesses by electing a board of directors that hires professional management. Some co-ops ask consumer-members to work for a number of hours a month as part of their membership duties. You may have one of the country's 4,000 food co-ops near you. If so, stop by and chat to learn more about this growing aspect of the U.S. economy. If you are interested in knowing more about cooperatives, visit the National Cooperative Business Association's website at ncba.coop.

Another kind of cooperative in the United States is formed to give members more economic power as a group than they have as individuals. The best example is a farm cooperative. The goal at first was for farmers to join together to get better prices for their food products. Eventually the idea expanded, and farm cooperatives now buy and sell fertilizer, farm equipment, seed, and other products in a multibillion-dollar industry. Cooperatives have an advantage in the marketplace because they don't pay the same kind of taxes corporations pay.

Cooperatives are still a major force in agriculture and other industries today. Some top co-ops have familiar names such as Land O'Lakes, Sunkist Growers, Ocean Spray, Blue Diamond, Associated Press, Ace Hardware, Riceland Foods, and Welch's.

Which Form of Ownership Is for You?

You can build your own business in a variety of ways. You can start your own sole proprietorship, partnership, corporation, LLC, or cooperative—or you can buy a franchise and be part of a larger corporation. There are advantages and disadvantages to each. Before you decide which form is for you, evaluate all the alternatives carefully.

The miracle of free enterprise is that the freedom and incentives of capitalism make risks acceptable to many people who go on to create the great corporations of America. You know many of their names and companies: Steve Jobs (Apple Computer), Sam Walton (Walmart), Levi Strauss (Levi Strauss & Co), Henry Ford (Ford Motor Company), Thomas Edison (General Electric), Bill Gates (Microsoft), and so on. They started small, accumulated capital, grew, and became industrial leaders. Could you do the same?

TEST**PREP**

- What are some of the factors to consider before buying a franchise?
- What opportunities are available for starting a global franchise?
- What is a cooperative?

SUMMARY

LO 5–1 Compare the advantages and disadvantages of sole proprietorships.

- **What are the advantages and disadvantages of sole proprietorships?**

  The advantages of sole proprietorships include ease of starting and ending, ability to be your own boss, pride of ownership, retention of profit, and no special taxes. The disadvantages include unlimited liability, limited financial resources, management difficulties, overwhelming time commitment, few fringe benefits, limited growth, and limited life span.

LO 5–2 Describe the differences between general and limited partners, and compare the advantages and disadvantages of partnerships.

- **What are the three key elements of a general partnership?**

  The three key elements of a general partnership are common ownership, shared profits and losses, and the right to participate in managing the operations of the business.

- **What are the main differences between general and limited partners?**

  General partners are owners (partners) who have unlimited liability and are active in managing the company. Limited partners are owners (partners) who have limited liability and are not active in the company.

- **What does *unlimited liability* mean?**

  Unlimited liability means that sole proprietors and general partners must pay all debts and damages caused by their business. They may have to sell their houses, cars, or other personal possessions to pay business debts.

- **What does *limited liability* mean?**

  Limited liability means that corporate owners (stockholders) and limited partners are responsible for losses only up to the amount they invest. Their other personal property is not at risk.

- **What is a master limited partnership?**

  A master limited partnership is a partnership that acts like a corporation but is taxed like a partnership.

- **What are the advantages and disadvantages of partnerships?**

  The advantages include more financial resources, shared management and pooled/complementary skills and knowledge, longer survival, and no special taxes. The disadvantages include unlimited liability, division of profits, disagreements among partners, and difficulty of termination.

LO 5–3 Compare the advantages and disadvantages of corporations, and summarize the differences among C corporations, S corporations, and limited liability companies.

- **What is the definition of a corporation?**

  A corporation is a state-chartered legal entity with authority to act and have liability separate from its owners.

- **What are the advantages and disadvantages of corporations?**

  The advantages include limited liability, ability to raise more money for investment, size, perpetual life, ease of ownership change, ease of attracting talented employees, and separation of ownership from management. The disadvantages include initial cost, extensive paperwork, double taxation, two tax returns, size, difficulty of termination, and possible conflict with stockholders and board of directors.

- **Why do people incorporate?**

  Two important reasons for incorporating are special tax advantages and limited liability.

- **What are the advantages of S corporations?**

  S corporations have the advantages of limited liability (like a corporation) and simpler taxes (like a partnership). To qualify for S corporation status, a company must have fewer than 100 stockholders (members of a family count as 1 shareholder), its stockholders must be individuals or estates and U.S. citizens or permanent residents, it must have only one class of stock, and the company cannot derive more than 25 percent of its income from passive sources.

- **What are the advantages of limited liability companies?**

  Limited liability companies have the advantage of limited liability, choice of being taxed as partnerships or corporations, flexible ownership rules, flexible distribution of profits and losses, and operating flexibility.

LO 5–4 Define and give examples of three types of corporate mergers, and explain the role of leveraged buyouts and taking a firm private.

- **What is a merger?**

  A merger is the result of two firms forming one company. The three major types are vertical mergers, horizontal mergers, and conglomerate mergers.

- **What are leveraged buyouts, and what does it mean to take a company private?**

  Leveraged buyouts are attempts by managers and employees to borrow money and purchase the company. Individuals who, together or alone, buy all the stock for themselves are said to take the company private.

LO 5–5 Outline the advantages and disadvantages of franchises, and discuss the opportunities for diversity in franchising and the challenges of global franchising.

- **What is a franchise?**

  An arrangement to buy the rights to use the business name and sell its products or services in a given territory is called a franchise.

- **What is a franchisee?**

  A franchisee is a person who buys a franchise.

- **What are the benefits and drawbacks of being a franchisee?**

  The benefits include getting management and marketing assistance, the pride of personal ownership, a nationally recognized name, financial advice and assistance, and lower failure rate.

- **What is the major challenge to global franchises?**

  It is often difficult to transfer an idea or product that worked well in the United States to another culture. It is essential to adapt to the region.

LO 5–6 Explain the role of cooperatives.

- **What is the role of a cooperative?**

  Cooperatives are organizations owned by consumer-members. Some people form cooperatives to acquire more economic power than they would have as individuals. Small businesses often form cooperatives to gain more purchasing, marketing, or product development strength.

KEY TERMS

acquisition 127

conglomerate merger 127

conventional (C) corporation 120

cooperative (co-op) 134

corporation 114

franchise 129

franchise agreement 129

franchisee 129

franchisor 129

general partner 116

general partnership 116

horizontal merger 127

leveraged buyout (LBO) 128

limited liability 117

limited liability company (LLC) 125

limited liability partnership (LLP) 117

limited partner 116

limited partnership 116

master limited partnership (MLP) 117

merger 127

partnership 114

S corporation 124

sole proprietorship 114

unlimited liability 115

vertical merger 127

CRITICAL THINKING

Imagine you are considering starting your own business.

1. What kinds of products or services will you offer?

2. What talents or skills do you need to run the business?

3. Do you have all the skills and resources to start the business, or will you need to find one or more partners? If so, what skills would your partners need to have?

4. What form of business ownership would you choose—sole proprietorship, partnership, C corporation, S corporation, or LLC? Why?

PUTTING PRINCIPLES TO WORK

PURPOSE

To explore franchising opportunities and to evaluate the strengths and weaknesses of a selected franchise.

EXERCISE

Go to Be the Boss (betheboss.com).

1. Use the search tool to find a franchise that has the potential of fulfilling your entrepreneurial dreams. Navigate to the profile of the franchise you selected. Explore the franchise's website if a link is available. Refer to the questions listed in Figure 5.9 in this chapter and assess the strengths and weaknesses of your selected franchise.

2. Did your search give you enough information to answer most of the questions in Figure 5.9? If not, what other information do you need, and where can you obtain it?

DEVELOPING CAREER SKILLS

KEY: ● **Team**   ★ **Analytic**   ▲ **Communication**   ▣ **Technology**

● ▣ ▲ ★   1. Research businesses in your area and identify sole proprietorships, partnerships, corporations, and franchises. Arrange interviews with managers using each form of ownership and get their impressions, hints, and warnings. (If you are able to work with a team of fellow students, divide the interviews among team members.) How much does it cost to start? How many hours do they work? What are the specific benefits? Share the results with your class.

● ▲ ★   2. Have you thought about starting your own business? What opportunities seem attractive? Choose someone in the class whom you might want for a partner or partners in the business. List all the financial resources and personal skills you will need to launch the business. Then make separate lists of the personal skills and the financial resources that you and your partner(s) might bring to your new venture. How much capital and what personal skills will be needed beyond those you already have? Develop an action plan for needed capital.

▲ ★   3. Let's assume you want to open one of the following new businesses. What form of business ownership would you choose for each? Why? Explain your choices to the rest of the class.

   a. Video game rental store.
   b. Wedding planning service.
   c. Software development firm.
   d. Online bookstore.

▣ ★   4. Successful businesses continually change hands. Methods of change discussed in this chapter include mergers, acquisitions, taking a firm private, and using leveraged buyouts. Search for an article online that illustrates how one of these methods changed an organization. What led to the change? How did this change affect the company's stakeholders? What benefits did the change provide? What new challenges were created?

▣ ★   5. Find information online about a business cooperative (e.g., Welch's, Land O'Lakes, Sunkist). Research how it was formed, who can belong to it, and how it operates.

CAREER EXPLORATION

Whether you choose to structure your business as a sole proprietorship, partnership, corporation, or LLC, you can operate in any industry you like. Here are a few with low start-up costs to consider. Find out about the tasks performed, skills needed, and opportunity outlook in these fields in the *Occupational Outlook Handbook (OOH)* at bls.gov.

- **Graphic design service**—creates visual concepts to communicate ideas that inspire, inform, and attract consumers; develops the overall layout and production design for various applications such as advertisements, brochures, magazines, and corporate reports.

- **Lawn care service**—makes sure the grounds of houses, businesses, and parks are attractive, orderly, and healthy.

- **Information technology support service**—provides help and advice to people and organizations using computer software or equipment.

- **Pet care service**—feeds, grooms, bathes, and exercises pets and other nonfarm animals.

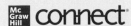

Domino's Still Rolling in the Dough

Every year more than a half-million new businesses are launched in the United States. Of those aspiring businesses, roughly 1 out of 10 are franchises. Today, franchising has clearly found its place in virtually every form of business including health clubs, hotels, gas stations, and of course, restaurants. In 1960, brothers Tom and Jim Monaghan opened DomiNick's Pizza in Ypsilanti, Michigan, as a partnership. After 8 months, Jim decided the pizza business was not for him and he sold his share of the business to his brother for a used Volkswagen Beetle. It was hard to imagine then that Tom Monaghan's sole proprietorship pizza business would grow from DomiNick's to Domino's and create a franchise empire with more than 13,000 stores in 80 countries on 6 continents.

Starting any business from scratch is a difficult, risky, and time-consuming effort. After opening a new restaurant, it can take many years to develop the correct product line and build a loyal customer base. With over 50 years' experience, an established product, and a respected brand name, Domino's has already built its reputation in the market. That's the key reason why many aspiring businesspeople seek to open a Domino's franchise rather than attempting to open a restaurant on their own. With a brand like Domino's, a franchisee can hit the market full speed ahead with a proven business model and product offerings that are tried and tested.

Proven franchise systems such as Domino's also offer franchisees valuable training as well as management and marketing assistance. Domino's knows that for the company to succeed, it's vital that its franchisees be successful. Valuable company promotions, including advertising, in-store displays, and coupon programs, let franchisees focus on running their businesses without having to worry about developing expensive promotions to attract customers. Since location is such a crucial component in a restaurant's success, Domino's assists franchisees with securing the proper location for their businesses.

While the United States remains the company's largest market, over 5,000 Domino's Pizza locations can be found around the globe. While the menus may be different, and some of the toppings a bit unique to U.S. tastes, Domino's remains dedicated to its single-brand image, quality control, and same core strategy. All aspects from uniforms, store layouts, training programs, supplier approval systems, and ordering systems remain the same. But even though Domino's remains committed to its successful system and business model, the company is always open to adapting its product to meet the wants and needs of its consumers. This is especially true in global markets where consumer tastes and expectations can be very different.

Today, as technology changes many aspects of business, Domino's has provided franchisees with innovative ordering platforms including Facebook Messenger, Apple Watch, Amazon Echo, Twitter, and a text message with a pizza emoji. To ensure the efficiency of its technology system, Domino's Tracker follows a pizza order from when it arrives in the store to when it heads out the door for delivery.

The franchise system has been called the greatest business model ever developed. Domino's has had pizza delivery drivers and pizza makers become part of the Domino's family of franchisees and live the dream of this great business model.

THINKING IT OVER

1. Why do franchises like Domino's have a lower business failure rate than businesses started from scratch?

2. How is a franchise different from a partnership?

3. What important questions should you ask before becoming a franchisee in a company like Domino's?

NOTES

1. Small Business Administration, sba.com, accessed February 2020.
2. James Chen, "Master Limited Partnership," *Investopedia,* investopedia.com, August 28, 2019; Ned Piplovic, "7 Best MLP Stocks to Buy Now," *DividendInvestor,* dividendinvestor.com, January 16, 2020.
3. Sunoco, sunoco.com, accessed February 2020.
4. Internal Revenue Service, irs.gov, accessed February 2020; John Hall, "How Love Can Be One of the Biggest Drivers of Business Success," *Forbes,* forbes.com, February 9, 2020.
5. Bureau of Labor Statistics, bls.gov, accessed February 2020.
6. Sam Ashe-Edmunds, "Importance of Partnership Agreement," *Small Business Chronicle,* smallbusiness.chron.com, accessed February 2020.
7. Joshua Kennon, "The Role and Duties of a Corporate Board of Directors," *The Balance,* thebalance.com,

accessed February 2020; Terry Lane, "How Does a Corporation Board of Directors Work?," *Houston Chronicle,* chron.com, accessed February 2020.

8. Alejandro Cremades, "How to Manage a Board of Directors," *Forbes,* forbes.com, January 14, 2019; Sean Ross, "How Do a Corporation's Shareholders Influence Its Board of Directors?," *Investopedia,* investopedia.com, February 4, 2020.

9. Nicolas Vega, "Uber Founder Travis Kalanick Missing Out on Stock Surge," *New York Post,* nypost.com, February 7, 2020.

10. "State Filing Fees," Incorporate Fast Inc., incorporatefast.com, accessed February 2020.

11. S Corporation Association, s-corp.org, accessed February 2020.

12. U.S. Internal Revenue Service, irs.gov, accessed February 2020.

13. "Choose Your Business Structure," *Entrepreneur,* entrepreneur.com, accessed February 2020.

14. U.S. Internal Revenue Service, irs.gov, accessed February 2020.

15. U.S. Internal Revenue Service, irs.gov, accessed February 2020.

16. LegalZoom, legalzoom.com, accessed February 2020.

17. Talia Lakritz, "14 Companies You Didn't Realize Disney Owns," *Insider,* insider.com, January 28, 2020; "Federal Antitrust Enforcers Release Long-Awaited Vertical Merger Guidelines for Public Comment," Buchanan, Ingersoll, & Rooney, bipc.com, January 14, 2020.

18. Sanford Stein, "Does Staples Rebranding Foretell the Fall of Another Retailer to Private Equity?," *Forbes,* forbes.com, April 10, 2019; "Stemberg, Thomas," encyclopedia.com, December 29, 2019.

19. Susan Heavey and Diane Bartz, "U.S. Seeks to Stop Schick-Maker Edgewell from Buying Shaving Upstart Harry's," Reuters, reuters.com, February 3, 2020.

20. Rachel Farrow, "4 Companies That Went from Public to Private," *Yahoo! Finance,* finance.yahoo.com, February 7, 2019; Laura Anthony, "Number of Public Companies Decline, Cash-Heavy Private Equity Firms Poised for Even More Buyouts in 2020," PR Newswire, prnewswire.com, January 13, 2020; Jordan Valinsky, "Krispy Kreme Is Expanding in New York City," *Gwinnett Daily Post,* gwinnettdailypost.com, February 3, 2020.

21. Andrew Nussbaum, Steve Cohen, and Karessa Cain, "Private Equity—Year in Review and 2020 Outlook," *Harvard Law School Forum on Corporate Governance,* corpgov.law.harvard.edu, February 8, 2020.

22. Trevor Williams, "Anheuser-Busch Invests $85M in Cartersville Expansion," *Global Atlanta,* globalatlanta.com, January 13, 2020; "Bayer-Monsanto: Power of Two," *Business Today,* businesstoday.in, January 25, 2020.

23. U.S. Census Bureau, census.gov, accessed February 2020.

24. International Franchise Association, franchise.org, accessed February 2020.

25. "2019 Top Fastest Growing Franchises," *Entrepreneur,* entrepreneur.com, accessed October 2019.

26. McDonald's, corporate.mcdonalds.com, accessed February 2020.

27. "Rankings of the Best Franchises," *Franchise Rankings,* franchiserankings.com, January 17, 2020.

28. *Entrepreneur,* entrepreneur.com, accessed February 2020.

29. Andrew Seid, "The Basics of Franchise Royalty Payments," *The Balance,* thebalance.com, April 13, 2019; Mark Siebert, "How Franchisees and Franchisors Can Master Their Relationship," *Entrepreneur,* entrepreneur.com, January 14, 2020.

30. Minda Zetlin, "Subway Franchisees Claim They're Being Forced to Give Up Their Stores," *Inc.,* inc.com, June 29, 2019; Alice Tuffery, "5 Tips for Avoiding Franchise Conflict," *Point Franchise,* pointfranchise.co.uk, January 17, 2020.

31. Matthew McCreary, "5 Things You Need to Know before Investing in a Chick-fil-A Franchise," *Entrepreneur,* entrepreneur.com, January 13, 2020.

32. Johnathan Maze, "As Burgerim Grew, Protection for Franchisees Fell Short," *Restaurant Business,* restaurantbusinessonline.com, January 22, 2020.

33. Anne Stych, "Women Increasingly Turn to Franchises to Own Their Own Business," *Bizwomen,* bizjournals.com, December 3, 2019; Eric Stites, "More Women Are Embracing Franchise Business Ownership, but There's More Work to Be Done," *Forbes,* forbes.com, January 31, 2020.

34. "Women and Minority Entrepreneurship," U.S. Committee on Small Business and Entrepreneurship, sbc.senate.gov, accessed February 2020.

35. "Minority Entrepreneurs," U.S. Senate Committee on Small Business and Entrepreneurship," sbc.senate.gov, accessed February 2020.

36. "NAACP Partners with Dunkin' Brands to Promote Diversity in Franchising," NAACP, naacp.org, accessed February 2020.

37. International Franchise Association, franchise.org, accessed February 2020.

38. Dalvin Brown, "Franchises Help African Americans 'Level the Playing Field,'" *USA Today,* usatoday.com, February 11, 2020.

39. "Home Based Business Franchises," Franchise Services Group, franchiseservicesgroup.com, accessed February 2020.

40. Candy Bouquet, candybouquet.com, accessed February 2020.

41. McDonald's, mcdonalds.com, accessed February 2020.

42. Auntie Anne's, auntieannesfranchising.com, accessed February 2020.

43. Freshii, freshii.com, accessed February 2020.

44. Ross Gilfillan, "The Top Fitness Franchises in Southeast Asia," Global Franchising, globalfranchising.com, accessed February 2020.

45. Jeff Elgin, "Buying a Foreign-Based Franchise," *Entrepreneur,* entrepreneur.com, accessed February 2020.

46. National Rural Electric Cooperative Association, electric.coop, accessed February 2020.

47. International Cooperative Alliance, ica.coop, accessed February 2020.

6

Entrepreneurship and Starting a Small Business

LEARNING OBJECTIVES >> *After you have read and studied this chapter, you should be able to*

LO 6–1 Explain why people take the risks of entrepreneurship; list the attributes of successful entrepreneurs; and describe entrepreneurial teams, intrapreneurs, and home- and web-based businesses.

LO 6–2 Discuss the importance of small business to the American economy, and summarize the major causes of small-business failure.

LO 6–3 Summarize ways to learn about how small businesses operate.

LO 6–4 Analyze what it takes to start and run a small business.

LO 6–5 Outline the advantages and disadvantages small businesses have in entering global markets.

Joel Clark, Cofounder and CEO of Kodiak Cakes

Many entrepreneurs depend on their families for encouragement as well as investment as they work hard to launch a business. But few brands are as much of a family project as Kodiak Cakes. In the 1980s, Penny Clark created a whole-grain pancake mix that was a big hit with both of her kids. So she started packaging it in sandwich bags and sent her son Joel out into the neighborhood with a little red wagon full of mix to sell. Flash-forward a few decades later and now Joel Clark is CEO of Kodiak Cakes, a packaged foods brand that earns more than $100 million in annual sales.

Of course, it wasn't easy to take Kodiak from a hobby to a multimillion-dollar enterprise. Although Clark's mother sold the homemade pancake mix for only about a year, her dedication inspired her sons to pick up where she left off. In 1995, Joel's older brother Jon changed the recipe so that customers would need to add only water to create the perfect pancake batter. Joel helped out by selling the mix door-to-door to local retailers in between his studies at the University of Utah. After a couple of years running the business part-time, however, Jon wanted to move on to a career with more stability. He handed over the reins to Joel, who spent a frantic seven years operating the business on the side while he earned an MBA and worked a number of other jobs. Finally in 2004, Joel quit his side gigs and started focusing on Kodiak full-time.

By 2007 the company was earning $800,000 in annual revenue, but it wasn't enough to make the business sustainable. "It was so many years of bootstrapping, and just trying to hang in there and keep it alive and keep it going," said Joel. "And we didn't really have any money to put into it, so it just kind of had to grow on its own." As he struggled to support both his family and the company at the same time, Joel stepped down as CEO and licensed the Kodiak brand to an outside firm. He landed an executive job at a health care company but still kept a close watch on his old business. After learning that the new operators raised prices, though, Joel exercised his right to cancel the deal within the first year and returned to the CEO position. "I had already spent 11 years on the business; I couldn't watch this," said Joel. "I jumped back into it—I was going to see it through to the end whether it worked or whether it failed."

But just because Joel was back in charge didn't mean that Kodiak's problems suddenly vanished. To stay afloat, he borrowed $250,000 from his father, Richard, who had also been working with the company since Joel turned it into a full-time enterprise. Shortly after this investment, the company hired a chief operating officer named Cameron Smith, a young student at the University of Utah who reminded Joel of himself. Smith suggested that the company appear on the ABC show *Shark Tank* as a way to solve Kodiak's cash flow problems. Joel had never heard of the program but soon spent hours binge-watching it as entrepreneurs tried to woo the show's panel of big-time investors. "Cameron and I watched a ton of episodes and would write down all the questions we ever heard, so we would role-play each other for hours and go over and over different questions and how we would answer them," said Joel. "And I think that was one of the best things we did, because we walked out onto the show feeling prepared."

Although they were more than ready to sell the sharks on their business, things didn't exactly go as planned once the cameras started rolling. The pair talked up the high-protein content of Kodiak's pancake mix and how it appealed to the nation's growing number of health-conscious consumers. The sharks wouldn't bite, though, dismissing their product as a "commodity" and offering only investments that came with enormous ownership stakes. Joel and Cameron rejected the sharks' deals and walked away that day empty-handed. But sales skyrocketed when their appearance aired in 2014 and they impressed viewers with their persuasive pitch. Within a year, sales rose from $3.6 million to $6.7 million. Now the company's annual sales exceed more than $100 million, driven by popular brands like Kodiak's Protein Power Cakes as well as dozens of other products. And while Joel faced a lot of hardships along the way, he credits his entrepreneurial passion for seeing him through. "Sometimes the obstacles are great and logic would say, you should quit," said Joel. "But passion can overcome that. It has to."

Entrepreneurs like Joel Clark take big risks in order to reap big rewards. As you read about such risk takers in this chapter, maybe you'll be inspired to become an entrepreneur yourself.

Sources: Sarah Berger, "This Family Business Was a 'Shark Tank' Reject — Now It's Bringing in $100 Million a Year with the Best-Selling Pancake Mix at Target," *CNBC*, cnbc.com, August 8, 2018; Emily Canal, "This Startup Didn't Get a Deal on 'Shark Tank,' and That Helped Save It from Bankruptcy," *Inc.*, inc.com, April 3, 2018; Virginia Nell Rainey, "Kodiak Cakes Moves beyond Pancakes," *Park City Magazine*, parkcitymag.com, June 19, 2019; Kodiak Cakes, kodiakcakes.com, accessed July 2020.

Let's talk business!
bit.ly/LetsTalkBusiness6

Courtesy of Kodiak Cakes

name that company

THE FOUNDER OF THIS COMPANY opened a candy company in Chicago, but it failed. He tried again in New York and failed again. But he didn't give up, and today his company is one of the largest candy companies in the world. Name that company. (Find the answer in the chapter.)

entrepreneurship
Accepting the risk of starting and running a business.

Wacky grocer Jungle Jim Bonaminio may put on a wizard suit and roller-skate through his Jungle Jim's International Market, but he's serious when it comes to his business. Instead of competing on price against big firms like Walmart, Jungle Jim's competes on product variety. For example, a case holding 1,500 kinds of hot sauce rests beneath an antique fire engine. Why do you think customers might remain loyal to Jungle Jim's?

The Job-Creating Power of Entrepreneurs in the United States

Today most new graduates know it's unlikely they will get a job in a large corporation and stay 30 years. For those who want more control over their destinies, working in or starting a small business makes sense. **Entrepreneurship** is accepting the risk of starting and running a business.

One of the major issues in the United States continues to be the need to create more jobs. You can begin to understand the job-creating power of entrepreneurs when you look at some of the great U.S. entrepreneurs from the past and the present. The history of the United States is the history of its entrepreneurs. Consider just a few of the many who have helped shape the U.S. economy:

- DuPont, which manufactures thousands of products under such brand names as Teflon and Lycra, was started in 1802 by French immigrant Éleuthère Irénée du Pont de Nemours. Some 18 shareholders provided $36,000 in start-up money.
- Avon, the familiar beauty products retailer, started in 1886 with $500 David McConnell borrowed from a friend.
- George Eastman launched photographic giant Kodak in 1880 with a $3,000 investment.
- Procter & Gamble, now a multinational marketer of household products, was formed in 1837 by William Procter, James Gamble, and a total of $7,000 in capital.
- Ford Motor Company began with an investment of $28,000 by Henry Ford and 11 associates.
- Amazon began with investments by founder Jeff Bezos's family and friends. Bezos's parents invested $300,000, a huge portion of their retirement account. Today they are billionaires.

These stories have much in common. One or a couple of entrepreneurs had a good idea, borrowed some money from friends and family, and started a business. That business now employs thousands of people and helps the country prosper.

The United States has plenty of entrepreneurial talent. Names such as Mark Zuckerberg (Facebook), Michael Dell (Dell Inc.), Bill Gates (Microsoft), Howard Schultz (Starbucks), Jack Dorsey (Twitter), and Chad Hurley

Courtesy of Jungle Jim Bonaminio

Student Start-ups

Although most entrepreneurs wait until they finish their education to make the jump into their own businesses, some aspiring entrepreneurs choose to buck the trend. Here are just a few examples of young entrepreneurs who found success in their college years:

Matt Czarnecki, Bennett Byerley, and André Monteiro started Verb Energy in their dorm kitchen at Yale University where they wanted to make delicious snacks that could help them stay awake during long study sessions. After experimenting with about 127 recipes, they settled on a stable of core flavors that each contain a kick of organic green tea with as much caffeine as an espresso.

Fatimah Hussein and Jamie Glover founded Asiya in order to make a line of sports hijabs that Muslim women could wear for any athletic activity. Hussein came up with the idea at her local community center and went on to design prototype headscarves with help from the University of Minnesota. Glover joined the venture while she was a graduate student at the Carlson School of Management so that Asiya could reach communities outside of its home state.

Logan Rae and Kim Hruda teamed up at Florida Atlantic University to create Bacon Boxes, a tasty start-up that specializes in boxes and bouquets of bacon roses. Making these unique gifts had just been a hobby for the two college students until they sent a bacon bouquet to a friend in a busy office. The hungry workers couldn't take their eyes off the elegant display of cured meats and soon the orders started pouring in.

Austin Webb, Brac Webb, and Austin Lawrence developed a start-up called RoBotany at Carnegie Mellon University where they grew organic vegetables in indoor vertical farms. After incubating at the university, they rebranded as Fifth Season and started a new farm among a bunch of abandoned steel mills south of Pittsburgh. The company heavily depends on automation, artificial intelligence, and other high-tech elements in order to plant and harvest the best produce possible.

ASIYA Modest Activewear

Sources: Stephanie Ritenbaugh, "Building a High-Tech Indoor Farm in the Steel Town of Braddock," *Pittsburgh Post-Gazette*, post-gazette.com, October 21, 2019; Ruqaya Izzidien, "Fatimah Hussein Is America's Sports Hijab Pioneer," *Outside*, outsideonline.com, June 6, 2018; Jeff Kart, "Verb Energy Bars Want to Replace Your Coffee," *Forbes*, forbes.com, September 13, 2018; Bacon Boxes, baconboxes.com, accessed February 2020; Asiya, asiyasport.com, accessed February 2020; Fifth Season, fifthseasonfresh.com, accessed February 2020.

and Steve Chen (YouTube) have become as familiar as those of the great entrepreneurs of the past. The Spotlight on Small Business box highlights several young entrepreneurs who started businesses while still in school.

LO 6–1 Explain why people take the risks of entrepreneurship; list the attributes of successful entrepreneurs; and describe entrepreneurial teams, intrapreneurs, and home- and web-based businesses.

Why People Take the Entrepreneurial Challenge

Taking the risks of starting a business can be scary and thrilling at the same time. One entrepreneur described it as almost like bungee jumping. You might be scared, but if you watch six other people do it and they survive, then you're more likely to do it yourself. Here are some reasons people are willing to take the entrepreneurial risk:[1]

- *Opportunity*. The opportunity to share in the American Dream is a tremendous lure. Many people, including those new to this country, may not have the skills for today's complex organizations, but they do have the initiative and drive to work the long hours demanded by entrepreneurship. The same is true of many corporate managers who

Nunbelievable

Kuda Biza and Bryan Janeczko founded Nunbelievable Cookies in 2019 as a way to take a bite out of world hunger. For every dozen cookies that the company sells, it donates two meals to soup kitchens across the United States. Do you think more entrepreneurs should use their businesses to directly support charitable causes?

leave corporate life (by choice or after downsizing) to run businesses of their own. Others, including an increasing number of Millennials, women, minorities, older people, and people with disabilities, find that starting their own businesses offers them more opportunities than working for others.

- *Profit.* Profit is another important reason to become an entrepreneur. Bill Gates, who cofounded Microsoft, is one of the richest persons in the United States and one of the richest people in the world.

- *Independence.* Many entrepreneurs simply do not enjoy working for someone else. They want to be the ones to make the decisions that lead to their success or failure. They want to be free to roam, create, work, and delegate.

- *Challenge.* Some people believe that entrepreneurs are excitement junkies who thrive on risk.

Entrepreneurs take moderate, calculated risks; they don't just gamble. In general, though, entrepreneurs seek achievement more than power.

What Does It Take to Be an Entrepreneur?

Would you succeed as an entrepreneur? You can learn about the managerial and leadership skills needed to run a firm. However, you may not have the personality to assume the risks, take the initiative, create the vision, and rally others to follow your lead. Such personality traits are harder to learn or acquire than academic skills are. A list of entrepreneurial attributes to look for in yourself includes:[2]

- *Self-directed.* You should be self-disciplined and thoroughly comfortable being your own boss. You alone will be responsible for your success or failure.

- *Self-nurturing.* You must believe in your idea even when no one else does, and be able to replenish your own enthusiasm. When Walt Disney suggested the possibility of a full-length animated feature film, *Snow White,* the industry laughed. His personal commitment and enthusiasm caused the Bank of America to back his venture. The rest is history.

- *Action-oriented.* Great business ideas are not enough. Most important is a burning desire to realize, actualize, and build your dream into reality.

- *Highly energetic.* It's your business, and you must be emotionally, mentally, and physically able to work long and hard. Employees have weekends and vacations; entrepreneurs often work seven days a week and don't take vacations for years. Working 18-hour days in your own business can be exhausting, but most entrepreneurs think it is better than working long hours for someone else.

- *Tolerant of uncertainty.* Successful entrepreneurs take only calculated risks (if they can help it). Still, they must be able to take *some* risks. Remember, entrepreneurship is not for the squeamish or those bent on security. You can't be afraid to fail. Many well-known entrepreneurs failed several times before achieving success. The late football coach Vince Lombardi summarized the entrepreneurial philosophy when he said, "We didn't lose any games this season, we just ran out of time twice." New entrepreneurs must be prepared to run out of time a few times before they succeed.

Turning Your Passions and Problems into Opportunities

While many entrepreneurs' business ideas are inspired by their passions, many see business opportunities where others see only problems. For example, Celtel's founder Mo Ibrahim saw the opportunity to bring mobile phones to the over 1 billion people in Africa who had never even used a phone much less owned one, whereas large telecommunication companies saw only poor peasants and logistical hurdles. Celtel soon became Africa's largest cell phone provider. Ibrahim sold the company for $3.4 billion.[3]

Most entrepreneurs don't get ideas for products and services from some flash of inspiration. The source of innovation is more like a *flashlight*. Imagine a search party walking in the dark, shining lights, looking around, asking questions, and looking some more. "That's how most creativity happens," says business author Dale Dauten. "Calling around, asking questions, saying 'What if?' till you get blisters on your tongue."

To look at problems and/or passions and see opportunities in them, ask yourself these questions: What do I want, but can never find? What product or service would improve my life? What really irritates me, and what product or service would help?

Keep in mind, however, that not all ideas are opportunities. If your idea doesn't meet anyone else's needs, the business won't succeed. You may have a business idea that is a good opportunity if:

- It fills customers' needs.

- You have the skills and resources to start a business.

- You can sell the product or service at a price customers are willing and able to pay—and still make a profit.

- You can get your product or service to customers before your window of opportunity closes (before competitors with similar solutions beat you to the marketplace).

- You can keep the business going.

If you'd like to take a survey to find out if you might have the entrepreneurial spirit in your blood, visit bdc.ca and search for "Entrepreneurial Potential Self-Assessment."[4]

Entrepreneurial Teams

An **entrepreneurial team** is a group of experienced people from different areas of business who join to form a managerial team with the skills to develop, make, and market a new product. A team may be better than an individual entrepreneur because team members can combine creative skills with production and marketing skills right from the start. Having a team also can ensure more cooperation and coordination later among functions in the business.

While Steve Jobs was the charismatic folk hero and visionary of Apple Computers, it was Steve Wozniak who invented the first personal computer model and Mike Markkula who offered business expertise and access to venture capital. The key to Apple's early success was that it was built around this "smart team" of entrepreneurs. The team wanted to combine the discipline of a big company with an environment in which people could feel they were participating in a successful venture. The trio of entrepreneurs recruited seasoned managers with similar desires. Everyone worked together to conceive, develop, and market products.[5]

Entrepreneurship within Firms

Entrepreneurship in a large organization is often reflected in the efforts and achievements of **intrapreneurs**, creative people who work as entrepreneurs within corporations. The idea is to use a company's existing resources—human, financial, and physical—to launch new products and generate new profits.

At 3M, which produces a wide array of products from adhesives like Scotch tape to nonwoven materials for industrial use, managers are expected to devote 15 percent of their work time to thinking up new products or services.[6] You know those bright-colored Post-it Notes people use to write messages on just about everything? That product was developed by Art Fry, a 3M employee.[7] He needed to mark the pages of his hymnal with something that wouldn't damage the book or fall out. He came up with the idea of the self-stick, repositionable paper slips. The labs at 3M produced a sample, but distributors were unimpressed, and market surveys were inconclusive. Nonetheless, 3M kept sending samples to office staff

entrepreneurial team
A group of experienced people from different areas of business who join together to form a managerial team with the skills needed to develop, make, and market a new product.

intrapreneurs
Creative people who work as entrepreneurs within corporations.

Gianfranco Chicco/EyeEm/Getty Images

When you come up with a winning idea, stick with it. That's certainly been the motto of 3M, the maker of Post-it Notes. The company encourages intrapreneurship among its employees by requiring them to devote at least 15 percent of their time to think about new products. How has this commitment to innovation paid off for 3M and its employees?

Vladimir Vladimirov/Getty Images

Music teachers often operate independently and teach a limited number of pupils at any given time. Despite the small scale of their businesses, music teachers can have a big impact on the artistic development of their clients. Can you see why music teachers could be considered micropreneurs?

micropreneurs

Entrepreneurs willing to accept the risk of starting and managing the type of business that remains small, lets them do the kind of work they want to do, and offers them a balanced lifestyle.

of top executives. Eventually, after a major sales and marketing program, the orders began pouring in, and Post-it Notes became a big winner. The company continues to update the product; making it from recycled paper is one of many innovations. Post-it Notes have gone international as well—the notepads sent to Japan are long and narrow to accommodate vertical writing. You can even use Post-it Notes electronically—the Post-it Software Notes program or the Post-it app allow you to type messages onto brightly colored notes and store them on memo boards, embed them in documents, or send them through e-mail.[8]

Other examples of intrapreneurial ventures include Lockheed Martin's first U.S. fighter jet in 1943 and the Stealth fighter in 1991; Apple's Mac; Google's Gmail, Google News, and Google AdSense; General Motors's Saturn; 3M's Scotch Pop-Up Tape; and Sony's PlayStation.[9]

Micropreneurs and Home-Based Businesses

Not everyone who starts a business wants to grow a mammoth corporation. Some are interested in maintaining a balanced lifestyle while doing the kind of work they want to do. Such business owners are called **micropreneurs**. While other entrepreneurs are committed to the quest for growth, micropreneurs know they can be happy even if their companies never appear on a list of top-ranked businesses.

Many micropreneurs are home-based business owners. More than half of all small businesses are run from owners' homes.[10] Micropreneurs include consultants, video producers, architects, and bookkeepers. Many with professional skills such as graphic design, writing, and translating have found that one way of starting a freelance business is through websites such as Upwork and Freelancer that link clients and freelancers. The sites post job openings and client feedback and serve as secure intermediaries for clients' payments.

Many home-based businesses are owned by people combining career and family. Don't picture just moms with young children; nearly 60 percent are men.[11] Here are more reasons for the growth of home-based businesses:

- Computer technology has leveled the competitive playing field, allowing home-based businesses to look and act as big as their corporate competitors. Fast broadband connections, smartphones, and other technologies are so affordable that setting up a business takes a much smaller initial investment than it once did.

- Corporate downsizing has led many to venture out on their own. Meanwhile, the work of the downsized employees still needs to be done, and corporations are outsourcing much of it to smaller companies.

- Social attitudes have changed. Whereas home-based entrepreneurs used to be asked when they were going to get a "real" job, they are now likely to be asked for how-to-do-it advice.

- Newer tax laws have loosened restrictions on deducting expenses for home offices.

Working at home has its challenges, of course. Here are a few:

- *Getting new customers.* Getting the word out can be difficult because you don't have a retail storefront.

- *Managing time.* You save time by not commuting, but it takes self-discipline to use that time wisely.

- *Keeping work and family tasks separate.* It's great to be able to throw a load of laundry in the washer in the middle of the workday if you need to, but you have to keep such distractions to a minimum. It also takes self-discipline to leave your work at the office if the office is at home.

Many businesses can be started at home. Listed below are businesses that have low start-up costs and don't require an abundance of administrative tasks:

- Personal Creations — artwork and handmade items that can be sold on sites such as Etsy, eBay, and Amazon.

- In-home services — tutoring, landscaping, snow shoveling, house cleaning, pet sitting, babysitting, web designing, personal training, home organizing, etc.

- Repair or skill-based services — tailoring, plumbing, home repairs, painting, etc.

- Consulting — advising businesses in areas in which you have an expertise such as technology, marketing, search engine optimization, or social media management.

- Resale — buying goods and reselling them (i.e., reselling items online that you buy in garage or estate sales).

- Shared-economy opportunities — Uber driver or Airbnb host.

Look for a business that meets these important criteria: (1) The job is something you truly enjoy doing; (2) you know enough to do the job well or you are willing to spend time learning it while you have another job; and (3) you can identify a market for your product or service.

FIGURE 6.1 POTENTIAL HOME-BASED BUSINESSES

Sources: Lesley Spencer Pyle, "Businesses You Can Start at Home," *Entrepreneur,* entrepreneur.com, accessed March 2020; Mindy Lilyquist, "Home Businesses Ideas That Really Pay," *The Balance,* November 24 2019; "20 Business Ideas for Stay-at-Home Parents," *Entrepreneur,* January 31, 2019; John Rampton, "50 Work-From-Home Jobs Paying As Much or a Lot More Than the Average American Salary," *Entrepreneur,* entrepreneur.com, accessed March 2020.

- *Abiding by city ordinances.* Government ordinances restrict the types of businesses allowed in certain parts of the community and how much traffic a home-based business can attract to the neighborhood.

- *Managing risk.* Home-based entrepreneurs should review their homeowner's insurance policy, since not all policies cover business-related claims. Some even void the coverage if there is a business in the home.

Home-based entrepreneurs should focus on finding opportunity instead of accepting security, getting results instead of following routines, earning a profit instead of earning a paycheck, trying new ideas instead of avoiding mistakes, and creating a long-term vision instead of seeking a short-term payoff. Figure 6.1 lists ideas for potentially successful home-based businesses, and Figure 6.2 highlights clues for avoiding home-based business scams. You can find a wealth of online information about starting a home-based business at *Entrepreneur*'s website (entrepreneur.com).

You've probably seen many ads selling home-based businesses. You may have even received unsolicited e-mail messages touting the glory of particular work-at-home opportunities. Beware of work-at-home scams! Here are a few clues that tell you a home business opportunity is a scam:

1. The ad promises that you can earn hundreds or even thousands of dollars a week working at home.

2. No experience is needed.

3. You need to work only a few hours a week.

4. There are loads of CAPITAL LETTERS and exclamation points!!!!!

5. You need to call a 900 number for more information.

6. You're asked to send in some money to receive a list of home-based business opportunities.

7. You're pressured to make a decision NOW!!!!

Do your homework before investing in a business opportunity. Call and ask for references. Contact the Better Business Bureau (bbb.org), county and state departments of consumer affairs, and the state attorney general's office. Conduct an Internet search and ask people in forums or on social networking sites if they've dealt with the company. Visit websites such as Friends In Business (friendsinbusiness.com) to find advice on specific online scams. Most important, don't pay a great deal of money for a business opportunity until you've talked to an attorney.

FIGURE 6.2 WATCH OUT FOR SCAMS

JGI/Tom Grill/Getty Images

Each year more than 2 million American couples get married. And for many of these soon-to-be newlyweds, TheKnot. com is an invaluable resource for planning the big day. From sharing gift registries to creating detailed schedules, the website helps ease the stress that inevitably comes with getting ready for a wedding. What does the site offer that other wedding planners don't?

Online Businesses

A multitude of small businesses sell everything online from staplers to refrigerator magnets to wedding dresses. In 2019, online retail sales in the United States reached over $365 billion, or approximately 12 percent of all retail sales.[12] Online sales are projected to climb to $600 billion by 2024.[13]

Online businesses have to offer more than the same merchandise customers can buy at stores—they must offer unique products or services. For example, Marc Resnik started his online distribution company after waking up one morning laughing about his business idea. Now ThrowThings.com makes money for him—he's shipped products to more than 44 countries. Although the company's offerings seem like a random collection of unrelated items, everything it sells can be thrown. You can buy promotional products in the "Throw Your Name Around!" section, ventriloquist dummies in the "Throw Your Voice!" section, and sporting equipment in the "Things to Throw!" section. Stranger products include fake vomit ("Throw Up!") and a $3.50 certificate that says you wasted your money ("Throw Your Money Away!"). Resnik doesn't sell very many of those certificates, but he does sell more dummies than anyone else in the United States. About two-thirds of the company's revenue comes from the promotional products section, which allows customers to add logos to thousands of products. Why is Resnik's business so successful? As one frequent customer said, it's because of Resnik's exceptional service and quick turnaround time.[14]

An online business isn't always a fast road to success. It can sometimes be a shortcut to failure. Hundreds of high-flying sites crashed after promising to revolutionize the way we shop. That's the bad news. The good news is that you can learn from someone else's failure and spare yourself some pain. And, of course, you can learn from their successes as well.

One of the disadvantages of online businesses is that it is easy for copycats to find your successful products, copy them, and sell the imitations on other sites (particularly Amazon). The Adapting to Change box talks about how some online businesses fight these imposters in order to prevent lost revenue and to preserve their businesses' reputations.

Encouraging Entrepreneurship: What Government Can Do

Part of the Immigration Act passed by Congress in 1990 was intended to encourage more entrepreneurs to come to the United States. The act created a category of "investor visas" that allows 10,000 people to come to the United States each year if they invest at least $1.8 million (or $900,000 in high unemployment areas) in an enterprise that creates 10 full-time jobs.[15]

Another way to encourage entrepreneurship is **enterprise zones**, specific geographic areas to which governments attract private business investment by offering lower taxes and other government support. These are also sometimes called *empowerment zones* or *enterprise communities*. As part of the 2017 federal tax overhaul, the federal government identified nearly 9,000 opportunity zones in high-poverty areas across the country. Investors qualify for deferred and/or reduced taxes if they invest in companies or projects in these communities.[16]

The government could have a significant effect on entrepreneurship by offering tax breaks to businesses that make investments to create jobs. The Jumpstart Our Business Startups (JOBS) Act of 2012 was enacted in an effort to make it easier for small businesses to raise funds and hopefully create new jobs.[17]

States are becoming stronger supporters of entrepreneurs, and are creating programs that invest directly in new businesses. Often, state commerce departments serve as clearinghouses for such programs. States are also creating incubators and technology centers to reduce start-up capital needs. **Incubators** offer new businesses in the critical stage of early development low-cost offices with basic services such as accounting, legal advice,

enterprise zones
Specific geographic areas to which governments try to attract private business investment by offering lower taxes and other government support.

incubators
Centers that offer new businesses low-cost offices with basic business services.

Small Businesses Struggle to Fight Fakes on Amazon

As the world's largest online marketplace, Amazon is an essential platform for countless small businesses who want to reach as many consumers as possible. Not only are 45 percent of American households members of the company's Prime program, but the e-commerce giant also collects 50 cents for every dollar spent shopping online in the United States.

This enormous customer base makes Amazon impossible for many small businesses to ignore. At the same time, the online retailer also provides copycats with the perfect environment to thrive. Once a product becomes successful enough on Amazon, counterfeiters will often swoop in and sell knockoff versions through third-party vendors that are difficult to trace and shut down. That's what happened to Kevin Williams, cofounder of a company that sells a specialized hose attachment called the Brush Hero. After enjoying a spike in sales following an appearance

BrushHero Copyright 2020

on ABC's *Shark Tank,* Williams noticed a similar uptick in the number of knockoff Brush Heroes on Amazon. Customers soon started to complain about these poor-quality fakes while the product's Amazon rating plummeted as well.

Williams eventually enlisted the services of a sourcing agent in China who discovered five factories making copycat Brush Heroes. He then began the laborious process of shutting

down these operations through a combination of overseas legal wrangling and long phone calls with Amazon representatives. It was almost too much for the start-up's nine-person operation to bear. In fact, many companies do not have the time or resources to take on counterfeiters as a whole. Instead, they can only react to each individual infraction through Project Zero, an Amazon service that allows sellers to delete knockoff product pages themselves. Entrepreneurs like Kevin Williams, however, feel that Amazon should take more responsibility for fakes rather than placing the burden entirely on small-business owners.

Sources: Jeff Bercovici, "Small Businesses Say Amazon Has a Huge Counterfeiting Problem. This 'Shark Tank' Company Is Fighting Back," *Inc.,* inc.com, March/April 2019; Jay Greene, "How Amazon's Quest for More, Cheaper Products Has Resulted in a Flea Market of Fakes," *The Washington Post,* washingtonpost.com, November 14, 2019; Paul Armstrong, "Amazon Primed: US Government Counterfeit Goods Ruling, New Small Business Numbers, + 55m Prime Music Accounts," *Forbes,* forbes.com, January 26, 2020.

and secretarial help. According to a recent study conducted by the International Business Innovation Association (InBIA), 87 percent of incubator graduates remain in business. Approximately one-third of all business incubators have ties to universities.[18] For example, at the St. Louis University food incubator, Salus Center Kitchen, women from a local shelter for victims of domestic abuse gather to make chicken pot pies that they sell to area stores and restaurants, and homeless men learn to make dog treats and food for Fresh Start Dog Food.[19] To learn more about what incubators offer and to find links to incubators in your area, visit the InBIA's website (inbia.org).

A few states offer assistance to qualified candidates under the Self-Employment Assistance (SEA) program. The program allows participants to collect self-employment payments instead of regular unemployment checks while they build their businesses. Participants often get training and counseling as well. Small self-employment checks may not seem like much, but many business owners say they are enough to help them launch

Incubators, such as this one in Washington, DC, offer new businesses low-cost offices with basic business services such as accounting, legal advice, and secretarial help. Do you have such incubators in your area?

Mladen Antonov/AFP/Getty Images

their companies without depleting savings to pay for living expenses until their businesses are strong enough to support them.[20]

The government can also join with private entities to promote entrepreneurship. For example, Startup America was an initiative started in 2011 by the federal government in partnership with the Kauffman Foundation to "celebrate, inspire, and accelerate high-growth entrepreneurship throughout the nation."[21] It is a public and private effort to bring together the country's most innovative entrepreneurs, corporations, universities, foundations, and other leaders to work with federal agencies to increase the number and success of U.S. entrepreneurs. One of the core goals is to empower more Americans not just to get a job, but also to create jobs. Learn more about the resources offered by Startup America at startupamericapartnership.org.

?TESTPREP

- Why are people willing to take the risks of entrepreneurship?
- What are the advantages of entrepreneurial teams?
- How do micropreneurs differ from other entrepreneurs?
- What does the government do to promote entrepreneurship?

LO 6–2   Discuss the importance of small business to the American economy, and summarize the major causes of small-business failure.

Getting Started in Small Business

Let's suppose you have a great idea for a new business, you have the attributes of an entrepreneur, and you're ready to take the leap into business for yourself. How do you start? That's what the rest of this chapter is about.

It may be easier to identify with a small neighborhood business than with a giant global firm, yet the principles of management are similar for each. The management of charities, government agencies, churches, schools, and unions is much the same as the management of small and large businesses. So, as you learn about small-business management, you will take a giant step toward understanding management in general. All organizations demand capital, good ideas, planning, information management, budgets (and financial management in general), accounting, marketing, good employee relations, and good overall managerial know-how. We shall explore these areas as they relate to small businesses and then, later in the book, apply the concepts to large firms and even global organizations.

Small versus Big Business

small business
A business that is independently owned and operated, is not dominant in its field of operation, and meets certain standards of size (set by the Small Business Administration) in terms of employees or annual receipts.

The Small Business Administration (SBA) defines a **small business** as one that is independently owned and operated, is not dominant in its field of operation, and meets certain standards of size in terms of employees or annual receipts (such as under $2.5 million a year for service businesses). A small business is considered "small" only in relationship to other businesses in its industry. A wholesaler may sell up to $22 million and still be considered a small business by the SBA. In manufacturing, a plant can have 500 employees and still be considered small. Let's look at some interesting statistics about small businesses:[22]

- There are over 30 million small businesses in the United States.
- Of all nonfarm businesses in the United States, almost 96 percent are considered small by SBA standards.

- Small businesses account for more than 43 percent of the gross domestic product (GDP).

- Nearly 400,000 tax-paying, employee-hiring businesses are started every year.

- Small businesses employ more than half of all private-sector employees.

- About 80 percent of U.S. workers find their first jobs in small businesses.

As you can see, small business is really a big part of the U.S. economy. How big? Let's find out.

Importance of Small Businesses

Since 65 percent of the nation's new jobs are in small businesses, there's a very good chance you'll either work in a small business someday or start one.[23] In addition to providing employment opportunities, small firms believe they offer other advantages over larger companies—more personal customer service and the ability to respond quickly to opportunities.

Bigger is not always better. Picture a hole in the ground. If you fill it with boulders, there are many empty spaces between them. If you fill it with sand, there is no space between the grains. That's how it is in business. Big businesses don't serve all the needs of the market. There is plenty of room for small companies to make a profit filling those niches.

Small-Business Success and Failure

You can't be naïve about business practices, or you'll go broke. According to the SBA half of new businesses don't last five years.[24] Some people argue that the failure rate is actually much lower than that statistic suggests. When small-business owners closed down one business to start another, for instance, they were included in the "failure" category—even though they hadn't failed at all. Similarly, when a business changed its form of ownership or a sole proprietor retired, it was counted as a failure. The good news for entrepreneurs is that business failures are much lower than traditionally reported.

Figure 6.3 lists reasons for small-business failures, among them managerial incompetence and inadequate financial planning. Keep in mind that when a business fails, it is important that the owners learn from their mistakes. Some entrepreneurs who have suffered flops are more realistic than novice entrepreneurs. Because of the lessons they've

Jeffrey Coolidge/Getty Images

When Roni Di Lullo's dog Midknight had trouble catching a Frisbee due to his squinting, she retrofitted sports goggles to fit his canine face. Midknight became the hit of the dog park, and soon Di Lullo was making pairs for all sorts of interested pet owners. Eventually she contracted with a manufacturer and started a company called Doggles, which now earns $3 million a year selling goggles to doggie fashionistas, veterinary ophthalmologists, and even military canines.

FIGURE 6.3 CAUSES OF SMALL-BUSINESS FAILURE

The following are some of the causes of small-business failure:

- Plunging in without first testing the waters on a small scale.
- Underpricing or overpricing goods or services.
- Underestimating how much time it will take to build a market.
- Starting with too little capital.
- Starting with too much capital and being careless in its use.
- Going into business with little or no experience and without first learning something about the industry or market.
- Borrowing money without planning just how and when to pay it back.
- Attempting to do too much business with too little capital.

- Not allowing for setbacks and unexpected expenses.
- Buying too much on credit.
- Extending credit too freely.
- Expanding credit too rapidly.
- Failing to keep complete, accurate records, so that the owners drift into trouble without realizing it.
- Carrying habits of personal extravagance into the business.
- Not understanding business cycles.
- Forgetting about taxes, insurance, and other costs of doing business.
- Mistaking the freedom of being in business for oneself for the liberty to work or not, according to whim.

FIGURE 6.4 SITUATIONS FOR SMALL-BUSINESS SUCCESS

The following factors increase the chances of small-business success:

- The customer requires a lot of personal attention, as in a salon.
- The product is not easily made by mass-production techniques (e.g., custom-tailored clothes or custom auto-body work).
- Sales are not large enough to appeal to a large firm (e.g., a novelty shop).
- The neighborhood is not attractive because of crime or poverty. This provides a unique opportunity for small grocery stores and laundries.
- A large business sells a franchise operation to local buyers. (Don't forget franchising as an excellent way to enter the world of small business.)
- The owner pays attention to new competitors.
- The business is in a growth industry (e.g., computer services or web design).

learned, they may be more successful in their future ventures. Milton Hershey, for example, tried starting candy businesses in Chicago and New York and failed both times. He could have followed in the footsteps of his father, a dreamer who lacked the perseverance and work ethic to stick to an idea long enough to make it work. Instead Hershey kept trying and eventually built not only the world's largest candy company, but also schools, churches, and housing for his employees.

Steven Spielberg was rejected from film school three times before he got his first chance. Today he's considered one of the greatest directors of our time.[25] Arianna Huffington, cofounder of the *Huffington Post,* put learning from failure this way: "I failed, many times in my life . . . but my mother used to tell me, 'failure is not the opposite of success, it's a stepping stone to success.' So at some point, I learned not to dread failure."[26]

Choosing the right type of business is critical. Many businesses with low failure rates require advanced training to start—veterinary services, dental practices, medical practices, and so on. While training and degrees may buy security, they do not tend to produce much growth—one dentist can fill only so many cavities. If you want to be both independent and rich, you need to go after growth. Often high-growth businesses, such as technology firms, are not easy to start and are even more difficult to keep going.

The easiest businesses to start have the least growth and greatest failure rate (like restaurants). The easiest to keep alive are difficult to get started (like manufacturing). And the ones that can make you rich are both hard to start and hard to keep going (like automobile assembly). See Figure 6.4 to get an idea of the business situations most likely to lead to success.

When you decide to start your own business, think carefully. You're unlikely to find everything you want—easy entry, security, and reward—in one business. Choose those characteristics that matter most to you; accept the absence of the others; plan, plan, plan; and then go for it!

LO 6–3 **Summarize ways to learn about how small businesses operate.**

Learning about Small-Business Operations

Hundreds of would-be entrepreneurs ask the same question: "How can I learn to run my own business?" Here are some hints.

Learn from Others

Investigate your local community college for classes on small business and entrepreneurship; there are thousands of such programs throughout the United States. Many bring together entrepreneurs from diverse backgrounds who form helpful support networks.[27] Talk to others who have already done it. They'll tell you that location is critical and caution you not to be undercapitalized; that is, not to start without enough money. They'll warn you about

Suppose you've worked for two years in a company and you see signs that it is beginning to falter. You and a co-worker have ideas about how to make a company like your boss's succeed.

Rather than share your ideas with your boss, you and your friend are considering quitting your jobs and starting your own company together. Should you approach other co-workers about working for your new venture? Will you try to lure your old boss's customers to your own business? What are your alternatives? What are the consequences of each alternative? What's the most ethical choice?

the problems of finding and retaining good workers.[28] And, most of all, they'll tell you to keep good records and hire a good accountant and lawyer before you start. Free advice like this is invaluable.

Get Some Experience

There is no better way to learn small-business management than by becoming an apprentice or working for a successful entrepreneur. Many small-business owners got the idea for their businesses from their prior jobs. The rule of thumb is: Have three years' experience in a comparable business first.

Back in 1818, Cornelius Vanderbilt sold his own sailing vessels and went to work for a steamboat company so that he could learn the rules of the new game of steam. After learning what he needed to know, he quit, started his own steamship company, and became the first U.S. business owner to accumulate $100 million.

Running a small business part-time, during your off hours or on weekends, can bring the rewards of working for yourself while still enjoying a regular paycheck at another job. It may save you money too, because you're then less likely to make "rookie mistakes" when you start your own business. The Making Ethical Decisions box presents ethical questions about using the knowledge you've gained as an employee to start your own business.

Nancy Newberry

Take Over a Successful Firm

Small-business owners work long hours and rarely take vacations. After many years, they may feel stuck and think they can't get out because they have too much time and effort invested. Thus millions of small-business owners are eager to get away, at least for a long vacation.

This is where you come in. Find a successful businessperson who owns a small business. Tell him or her you are eager to learn the business and would like to serve an apprenticeship; that is, a training period. Say that at the end of the training period (one year or so) you would like to help the owner or manager by becoming assistant manager. Thus you can free the owner to take off weekends and holidays and have a long vacation—a good deal for him or her. For another year or so, work very hard to learn all about the business—suppliers, inventory, bookkeeping, customers, promotion. At the end of two years, make this offer: The owner can retire or work only part-time, and you will take over management of the business. You can establish a profit-sharing plan with the owner plus pay yourself a salary. Be generous with yourself; you'll earn it if you manage the business. You can even ask for 40 percent or more of the profits.

Sharon Anderson Wright spent her teenage years sorting novels, nonfiction, and newspapers at her family's used bookstore. She knew what her customers liked to read and worked closely with her mother to learn the fine details of the business. This experience served her well as she expanded Half Price Books into a national company earning $240 million in annual revenue. How do you think Wright's experience helped the business succeed?

The owner benefits by keeping ownership in the business and making 60 percent of what he or she earned before—without having to work. You benefit by making 40 percent of the profits of a successful firm. This is an excellent deal for an owner about to retire—he or she is able to keep the firm and a healthy profit flow. It is also a clever and successful way to share in the profits of a successful small business without making any personal monetary investment.

If profit sharing doesn't appeal to the owner, you may want to buy the business outright. As more Baby Boomers reach retirement age, there will be an increasing number of businesses for sale.[29] In fact, nearly 10,000 Baby Boomers reach retirement age every day.[30] How do you determine a fair price for a business? Value is based on (1) what the business owns, (2) what it earns, and (3) what makes it unique. Naturally, an accountant will need to help you determine the business's value.

If you fail at your efforts to take over the business through either profit sharing or buying, you can quit and start your own business fully trained.

LO 6–4   Analyze what it takes to start and run a small business.

Managing a Small Business

According to the Small Business Administration, one of the major causes of small-business failures is poor management. Keep in mind, though, that *poor management* covers a number of faults. It could mean poor planning, cash flow management, recordkeeping, inventory control, promotion, or employee relations. Most likely it includes poor capitalization. To help you succeed as a business owner, in the following sections we explore the functions of business in a small-business setting:

- Planning your business.
- Financing your business.
- Knowing your customers (marketing).
- Managing your employees (human resource development).
- Keeping records (accounting).
- Looking for help.

Although all the functions are important in both the start-up and management phases of the business, the first two—planning and financing—are the primary concerns when you start your business. The others are the heart of your operations once the business is under way.

Planning Your Business

Many people eager to start a small business come up with an idea and begin discussing it with professors, friends, and other businesspeople. At this stage the entrepreneur needs a business plan. A **business plan** is a detailed written statement that describes the nature of the business, the target market, the advantages the business will have over competition, and the resources and qualifications of the owner(s). A business plan forces potential small-business owners to be quite specific about the products or services they intend to offer. They must analyze the competition, calculate how much money they need to start, and cover other details of operation. A business plan is also mandatory for talking with bankers or other investors.

Lenders want to know everything about an aspiring business. First, pick a bank that serves businesses the size of yours. Have a good accountant prepare a complete set of financial statements

Rimas Buinevicius first used a wheelchair after fracturing his leg and quickly became aware of the shoulder pain that can result from constant pushing. To reduce the stress on his body, Buinevicius and some partners devised and designed Rowheels, a system that allows users to row rather than push their wheelchairs. Rowheels won the 2012 Wisconsin Governor's Business Plan Competition in the advanced manufacturing category. The company aims to relieve those who suffer from frequent shoulder injuries by providing them with "the world's first truly therapeutic manual wheelchair."

Rowheels, Inc.

OUTLINE OF A COMPREHENSIVE BUSINESS PLAN

A good business plan is between 25 and 50 pages long and takes at least six months to write.

Cover Letter

Only one thing is certain when you go hunting for money to start a business: You won't be the only hunter out there. You need to make potential funders want to read *your* business plan instead of the hundreds of others on their desks. Your cover letter should summarize the most attractive points of your project in as few words as possible. Be sure to address the letter to the potential investor by name. "To whom it may concern" or "Dear Sir or Madam" is not the best way to win an investor's support.

Section 1—Executive Summary

Begin with a two-page or three-page management summary of the proposed venture. Include a short description of the business, and discuss major goals and objectives.

Section 2—Company Background

Describe company operations to date (if any), potential legal considerations, and areas of risk and opportunity. Summarize the firm's financial condition, and include past and current balance sheets, income and cash flow statements, and other relevant financial records (you will read about these financial statements in Chapter 17). It is also wise to include a description of insurance coverage. Investors want to be assured that death or other mishaps do not pose major threats to the company.

Section 3—Management Team

Include an organization chart, job descriptions of listed positions, and detailed résumés of the current and proposed executives. A mediocre idea with a proven management team is funded more often than a great idea with an inexperienced team. Managers should have expertise in all disciplines necessary to start and run a business. If not, mention outside consultants who will serve in these roles and describe their qualifications.

Section 4—Financial Plan

Provide five-year projections for income, expenses, and funding sources. Don't assume the business will grow in a straight line. Adjust your planning to allow for funding at various stages of the company's growth. Explain the rationale and assumptions used to determine the estimates. Assumptions should be reasonable and based on industry/historical trends. Make sure all totals add up and are consistent throughout the plan. If necessary, hire a professional accountant or financial analyst to prepare these statements.

Stay clear of excessively ambitious sales projections; rather, offer best-case, expected, and worst-case scenarios. These not only reveal how sensitive the bottom line is to sales fluctuations but also serve as good management guides.

Section 5—Capital Required

Indicate the amount of capital needed to commence or continue operations, and describe how these funds are to be used. Make sure the totals are the same as the ones on the cash flow statement. This area will receive a great deal of review from potential investors, so it must be clear and concise.

Section 6—Marketing Plan

Don't underestimate the competition. Review industry size, trends, and the target market segment. Sources like the *Rand McNally Commercial Atlas and Marketing Guide* can help you put a plan together. Discuss strengths and weaknesses of the product or service. The most important things investors want to know are what makes the product more desirable than what's already available and whether the product can be patented. Compare pricing to the competition's. Forecast sales in dollars and units. Outline sales, advertising, promotion, and public relations programs. Make sure the costs agree with those projected in the financial statements.

Section 7—Location Analysis

In retailing and certain other industries, the location of the business is one of the most important factors. Provide a comprehensive demographic analysis of consumers in the area of the proposed business as well as a traffic-pattern analysis and vehicular and pedestrian counts.

Section 8—Manufacturing Plan

Describe minimum plant size, machinery required, production capacity, inventory and inventory-control methods, quality control, plant personnel requirements, and so on. Estimates of product costs should be based on primary research.

Section 9—Appendix

Include all marketing research on the product or service (off-the-shelf reports, article reprints, etc.) and other information about the product concept or market size. Provide a bibliography of all the reference materials you consulted. This section should demonstrate that the proposed company won't be entering a declining industry or market segment.

business plan

A detailed written statement that describes the nature of the business, the target market, the advantages the business will have in relation to competition, and the resources and qualifications of the owner(s).

iSeeit! Need help understanding the key aspects of the business plan? Visit your Connect eBook to view a video for a brief animated explanation.

iSeeit! Need help understanding how an entrepreneur can secure financing for a small business? Visit your Connect eBook to view a video for a brief animated explanation.

and a personal balance sheet. Make an appointment before going to the bank, and go to the bank with an accountant and all the necessary financial information. Demonstrate to the banker that you're a person of good character, civic-minded and respected in business and community circles. Finally, ask for *all* the money you need, be specific, and be prepared to personally guarantee the loan.

Writing a Business Plan A good business plan takes a long time to write, but you've got only five minutes, in the *executive summary,* to convince readers not to throw it away. Since bankers receive many business plans every day, the summary has to catch their interest quickly. An outline of a comprehensive business plan follows. There's no such thing as a perfect business plan; even the most comprehensive business plan changes as the new business evolves.[31]

Many software programs can help you get organized. One highly rated business plan program is Business Plan Pro by Palo Alto Software. For a simplified business plan, you may want to check out *Fortune* 500 executive Jim Horan's book *The One Page Business Plan.* The book includes access to interactive exercises, forms, and templates. To see samples of successful business plans for a variety of businesses go to bplans.com/sample_business_plans. You can also learn more about writing business plans on the Small Business Administration website at sba.gov/business-guide/plan/write-your-business-plan-template.

Getting the completed business plan into the right hands is almost as important as getting the right information into the plan. Finding funding requires research. Next we discuss sources of money available to new business ventures. All require a comprehensive business plan. The time and effort you invest before starting a business will pay off many times later. The big payoff is survival.

Financing Your Small Business

An entrepreneur has several potential sources of capital: personal savings; family and business associates; banks and finance institutions; angels, crowdfunding, and venture capitalists; and government agencies such as the Small Business Administration (SBA), the U.S. Economic Development Administration, and the Minority Business Development Agency.[32]

Family and Business Associates The most common source of funding after personal savings is friends and family.[33] You may even want to consider borrowing from a potential supplier to your future business. Helping you get started may be in the supplier's interest if there is a chance you will be a big customer later. This is what Ray Kroc did in the early years of McDonald's. When Kroc didn't have the funds available to keep the company going, he asked his suppliers to help him with the necessary funds. These suppliers grew along with McDonald's. It's usually not a good idea to ask such an investor for money at the outset. Begin by asking for advice; if the supplier likes your plan, he or she may be willing to help you with funding too.

Banks and Finance Institutions Small-business owners often need to do a little extra shopping to find a lender. Many find that smaller community banks are more likely to grant loans than larger regional banks. Since small banks do business in a single town or cluster of towns, they know their customers better. They have more flexibility to make lending decisions based on everything they know about their customers, rather than on a more automated basis as larger banks must.[34]

Community development financial institutions (CDFIs) may be a source of funding for businesses in lower-income communities. CDFIs played a big role in the economic recovery after the Great Recession of 2008. CDFIs succeeded even after the credit bubble of 2008 because they maintained the financial discipline other lenders lacked. They have the incentive to make sure their clients succeed because, if borrowers don't repay their loans, the CDFIs take the hit, not investors. Less than 1 percent of their loans were not paid back in the last three decades.[35] CDFIs don't just loan money. More importantly, they provide business counseling such as helping owners learn how to develop marketing strategies, manage inventory, and improve cash flow.

Angels, Crowdfunding, and Venture Capitalists

Individual investors are also a frequent source of capital for most entrepreneurs. *Angel investors* are private individuals who invest their own money in potentially hot new companies before they go public.

A number of websites match people who want money with those willing to lend it. They include donation-based services (such as GoFundMe and Kickstarter where companies accept small donations in exchange for perks like T-shirts or other memorabilia) and debt-investment sites (such as Funding Circle that offers loans that need to be repaid plus interest). This form of individual investing is called *peer-to-peer (P2P) lending* or *crowdfunding.* A creditworthy borrower often gets such money faster and more easily than going to the bank. And the cost is often less than a bank loan. With hundreds of crowdfunding sites, it can be confusing to know which one is the best fit for you and your prospective business. Reviewing services like CrowdsUnite offer feedback from users of lending sites to help you better understand your options.

The JOBS Act of 2012 allows businesses to raise up to $1 million a year from private investors without making an initial public offering (discussed in Chapter 19). Prior to the JOBS Act, it was illegal for private companies to sell shares in their companies to the public. The JOBS Act allows businesses to use fundraising sites to solicit larger investments in exchange for ownership shares in the business.[36] Many prefer the terms *crowdinvesting* or *equity crowdfunding* for this form of fundraising.

Venture capitalists may finance your project—for a price. Venture capitalists may ask for a hefty stake in your company (as much as 60 percent) in exchange for the cash to start your business. If the venture capitalist takes too large a stake, you could lose control of the business. Since the widespread failure of early web start-ups, venture capitalists have been willing to invest less and expect more return on their investment if the new company is sold.[37] Therefore, if you're a very small company, you don't have a very good chance of getting venture capital. You'd have a better chance finding an angel investor or using crowdfunding.

If your proposed venture does require millions of dollars to start, experts recommend that you talk with at least five investment firms and their clients in order to find the right venture capitalist. You may be able to connect with potential investors through AngelList, an online nonprofit service that helps entrepreneurs and venture capitalists get to know each other.[38] To learn more about how to find venture capitalists, visit the National Venture Capital Association's website (nvca.org).

The Small Business Administration (SBA)

John Lund/Blend Images/Getty Images

Wouldn't it be great if money grew on trees? Unfortunately it doesn't, so prospective entrepreneurs must find other sources of capital such as personal savings, relatives, former employers, banks, finance companies, venture capitalists, and government agencies. What is the most common source of funding after personal savings?

The Small Business Administration (SBA)

The **Small Business Administration** (SBA) is a U.S. government agency that advises and assists small businesses by providing management training and financial advice and loans (see Figure 6.5). The SBA started a microloan demonstration program in 1991. The program provides very small loans (up to $50,000) and technical assistance to small-business owners. It is administered through a nationwide network of nonprofit organizations chosen by the SBA. Rather than award loans based on collateral, credit history, or previous business success, the program judges worthiness on belief in the borrowers' integrity and the soundness of their business ideas.[39]

The SBA reduced the size of its application from 150 pages to 1 page for loans under $50,000. Since government regulations are constantly changing, you may want to go to the SBA's website (sba.gov) for the latest information about SBA programs and other business services.

venture capitalists
Individuals or companies that invest in new businesses in exchange for partial ownership of those businesses.

FIGURE 6.5 TYPES OF SBA FINANCIAL ASSISTANCE

The SBA may provide the following types of financial assistance:

- *Standard 7(a) loans*—loans made by a financial institution that the government will repay if the borrower stops making payments. The maximum individual loan guarantee is capped at $5 million.

- *Microloans*—amounts ranging from $100 to $50,000 to people such as single mothers and public housing tenants.

- *SBA Express*—program that accelerates the SBA response time to 36 hours. Loan limit $350,000.

- *Export Express*—loans made to small businesses wishing to export. The maximum guaranteed loan amount is $500,000.

- *International Trade Loans*—long-term financing to businesses that are expanding because of growing export sales or that have been adversely affected by imports and need to modernize to meet foreign competition. Loan limit $5 million.

- *Community Adjustment and Investment Program (CAIP)*—loans to businesses to create new, sustainable jobs or to preserve existing jobs in eligible communities that have lost jobs due to changing trade patterns with Mexico and Canada following the adoption of NAFTA.

- *504 certified development company (CDC) loans*—loans for purchasing major fixed assets, such as land and buildings for businesses in eligible communities, typically rural communities or urban areas needing revitalization. The maximum guaranteed loan amount is $5 million for meeting the job creation criteria or a community development goal. The business must create or retain one job for every $65,000 ($100,000 for small manufacturers) provided by the SBA.

- *CAPLine loans*—loans to help small businesses meet their short-term and cyclical working capital needs. The maximum CAPLine loan is $5 million.

Small Business Administration (SBA)

A U.S. government agency that advises and assists small businesses by providing management training and financial advice and loans.

Small Business Investment Company (SBIC) Program

A program through which private investment companies licensed by the Small Business Administration lend money to small businesses.

market

People with unsatisfied wants and needs who have both the resources and the willingness to buy.

You may also want to consider requesting funds from the **Small Business Investment Company (SBIC) Program**. SBICs are private investment companies licensed by the SBA to lend money to small businesses. An SBIC must have a minimum of $5 million in capital and can borrow up to $2 from the SBA for each $1 of capital it has. It lends to or invests in small businesses that meet its criteria. Often SBICs are able to keep defaults to a minimum by identifying a business's trouble spots early, giving entrepreneurs advice, and in some cases rescheduling loan payments.

Perhaps the best place for young entrepreneurs to start shopping for an SBA loan is a Small Business Development Center (SBDC). SBDCs are funded jointly by the federal government and individual states, and are usually associated with state and community colleges and universities. SBDCs can help you evaluate the feasibility of your idea, develop your business plan, and complete your funding application—all for no charge.

Obtaining money from banks, venture capitalists, and government sources is very difficult for most small businesses. (You will learn more about financing in Chapter 18.) Those who do survive the planning and financing of their new ventures are eager to get their businesses up and running. Your success in running a business depends on many factors, especially knowing your customers, managing your employees, and keeping good records.

Knowing Your Customers

One of the most important elements of small-business success is knowing the **market**, which consists of consumers with unsatisfied wants and needs who have both resources and willingness to buy. Most of our students have the willingness to own a brand-new Maserati sports car. However, few have the resources necessary to satisfy this want. Would they be a good market for a luxury car dealer?

Once you have identified your market and its needs, you must set out to fill those needs. How? Offer top quality at a fair price with great service. Remember, it isn't enough to get customers—you have to *keep* them. As sales coach Phil Glosserman says, "People buy in order to experience the feelings they get from having their needs met." Sure, your product may meet those needs now. However, if customers tell you they've discovered something they don't like in your product, call them back quickly when you fix it and tell them, "Thanks for the good idea."[40]

One of the greatest advantages small businesses have is the ability to know their customers better and adapt quickly to their ever-changing needs. The only way to know what your customers' needs are is to listen, listen, listen. Don't let your passion and ego get in the way of changing your products or services to fit what customers really want.[41] You will gain more insights about markets in Chapters 13 and 15. Now let's consider effectively managing the employees who help you serve your market.

Mattel/MEG/Newscom

Managing Your Employees

As a business grows, it becomes impossible for an entrepreneur to oversee every detail, even by putting in 60 hours per week. This means that hiring, training, and motivating employees are critical.

It is not easy to find good help when you offer less money, skimpier benefits, and less room for advancement than larger firms do. That's one reason good employee relations are important for small-business management. Employees of small companies are often more satisfied with their jobs than are their counterparts in big business. Why? Quite often they find their jobs more challenging, their ideas more accepted, and their bosses more respectful.[42]

Often entrepreneurs are reluctant to recognize that to keep growing, they must delegate authority to others. Who should have this delegated authority, and how much? This can be a particularly touchy issue in small businesses with long-term employees and in family businesses. As you might expect, entrepreneurs who have built their companies from scratch often feel compelled to promote employees who have been with them from the start—even when they aren't qualified to serve as managers. Common sense tells you this could hurt the business. The idea that you must promote or can't fire people because "they're family" can also hinder growth. Entrepreneurs best serve themselves and the business if they gradually recruit and groom employees for management positions, enhancing trust and support between them. You'll learn more about managing employees in Chapters 7 through 12.

Not all small businesses stay small; some become superstars. For example, Mattel founders Ruth and Elliot Handler started their business in their garage making picture frames. When they discovered that the dollhouse furniture they made with the wood scraps sold better than the frames, they changed their business to focus on dolls. Today, Mattel is a multibillion-dollar business thanks to the success of blockbuster toys like Barbie.

Keeping Records

Small-business owners often say the most important assistance they received in starting and managing their business was in accounting. A businessperson who sets up an effective accounting system early will save much grief later. Accurate recordkeeping enables a small-business owner to follow daily sales, expenses, and profits, as well as helps owners with inventory control, customer records, and payroll.

Many business failures are caused by poor accounting practices that lead to costly mistakes. A good accountant can help you decide whether to buy or lease equipment and whether to own or rent a building. He or she may also help you with tax planning, financial forecasting, choosing sources of financing, and writing requests for funds.

Other small-business owners may tell you where to find an accountant experienced in small business. It pays to shop around for advice. You'll learn more about accounting in Chapter 17.

Looking for Help

Small-business owners have learned, sometimes the hard way, that they need outside consulting advice early in the process. This is especially true of legal, tax, and accounting advice but also of marketing, finance, and other areas. Most small and medium-sized firms cannot afford to hire such experts as employees, so they must turn to outside assistance.

A necessary and invaluable aide is a competent, experienced lawyer who knows and understands small businesses. Lawyers can help with leases, contracts, partnership

Ron Hill Photography, www.ronhillphotography.com

Karen Williams, owner of the Cincinnati-based company Sewendipity Lounge, worked with a SCORE mentor to develop the business side of her sewing studio. The mentor advised her about financing, sales and marketing, human resources, operations, and organizational planning. What was the price tag for all of this valuable advice? $0!

Service Corps of Retired Executives (SCORE)

An SBA office with volunteers from industry, trade associations, and education who counsel small businesses at no cost (except for expenses).

agreements, and protection against liabilities. They don't have to be expensive. In fact, several prepaid legal plans offer services such as drafting legal documents for a low annual rate. Of course, you can find plenty of legal services online. The SBA offers plain-English guides and mini-tutorials that will help you gain a basic understanding of the laws that affect each phase of the life of a small business. Sites like FindForms.com offer search tools that help you find free legal forms from all over the web as well as advice, links, books, and more. Remember, "free" isn't a bargain if the information isn't correct, so check the sources carefully and double-check any legal actions with an attorney.[43]

Make your marketing decisions long before you introduce a product or open a store. An inexpensive marketing research study may help you determine where to locate, whom to select as your target market, and what is an effective strategy for reaching it. Thus a marketing consultant with small-business experience can be of great help to you, especially one who has had experience with building websites and using social media.

Two other invaluable experts are a commercial loan officer and an insurance agent. The commercial loan officer can help you design an acceptable business plan and give you valuable financial advice as well as lend you money when you need it. An insurance agent will explain all the risks associated with a small business and how to cover them most efficiently with insurance and other means like safety devices and sprinkler systems.

An important source of information for small businesses is the **Service Corps of Retired Executives (SCORE)**. This SBA resource partner has more than 10,000 volunteers (many still working in their fields) from industry, trade associations, and education who counsel small businesses at no cost (except for expenses).[44] You can find a SCORE counselor by logging on to score.org. The SBA also offers a free, comprehensive online entrepreneurship course for aspiring entrepreneurs.

Often business professors from local colleges will advise small-business owners free or for a small fee. Some universities have clubs or programs that provide consulting services by master of business administration (MBA) candidates for a nominal fee. The University of Maryland and Virginia Tech have internship programs that pair MBA students with budding companies in local incubator programs. The incubator companies pay half the intern's salary, which is around $20 an hour.[45]

It is also wise to seek the counsel of other small-business owners. Entrepreneur.com offers experienced entrepreneurs and young start-ups an open forum to exchange advice and ideas. Visitors have access to articles on marketing, business planning, incorporation, and financial management. Peer groups within specific industries can give you better insights into the challenges and solutions encountered by other business owners in your field. For example, Gateway Wellness Associates in St. Louis, Missouri, offers office space, resources, and business guidance to therapists and other wellness professionals who want to start their own private practices.[46] Peer advisory organizations that could help you connect with a peer group in your industry include Young Entrepreneurs' Council and Entrepreneurs' Organization.

Other sources of counsel include local chambers of commerce, the Better Business Bureau, national and local trade associations, the business reference section of your library, and many small-business-related websites.

?TESTPREP

- A business plan is probably the most important document a small-business owner will ever create. There are nine sections in the business plan outline shown in the chapter. Can you describe at least five of those sections now?

LO 6–5 Outline the advantages and disadvantages small businesses have in entering global markets.

Going Global: Small-Business Prospects

As we noted in Chapter 3, there are over 328 million people in the United States but more than 7.7 billion people in the world.[47] Obviously, the world market is a much larger, more lucrative market for small businesses than the United States alone. Small and medium-sized business accounted for 99 percent of the growth in exporting firms in recent years. All this exporting is paying off. According to the International Trade Commission small exporting firms account for 98 percent of all exporting firms and 34 percent of all U.S. exporting value.[48]

Technological advances have helped increase small-business exporting. PayPal makes it possible for small businesses to get paid automatically when they conduct global business online. The Internet also helps small businesses find customers without the expense of international travel. It's becoming easier than ever for small businesses to access foreign markets online. In 2019, Chinese e-commerce giant Alibaba Group Holdings Ltd. began to allow small businesses in the United States to sell on Alibaba.com. Up until then, U.S.-based businesses were only able to buy items on the site. Approximately a third of the buyers on Alibaba.com are in the United States while more than 95 percent of the sellers are in China. This plan opened up markets to U.S. merchants in other countries including India, Brazil, and Canada.[49]

Still, many small businesses have difficulty getting started in global business. Why are so many missing the boat to the huge global markets? Primarily because the voyage includes a few major hurdles: (1) financing is often difficult to find, (2) would-be exporters don't know how to get started and do not understand the cultural differences between markets, and (3) the bureaucratic paperwork can threaten to bury a small business.

Beside the fact that most of the world's market lies outside the United States, there are other good reasons for going global. Exporting can absorb excess inventory, soften downturns in the domestic market, and extend product lives. It can also spice up dull routines.

Small businesses have several advantages over large businesses in international trade:

- Overseas buyers often enjoy dealing with individuals rather than with large corporate bureaucracies.
- Small companies can usually begin shipping much faster.
- Small companies can provide a wide variety of suppliers.
- Small companies can give customers personal service and undivided attention because each overseas account is a major source of business to them.

A good place to start finding information about exporting is the Department of Commerce's Bureau of Industry and Security (bis.doc.gov). Other sources include the SBA's Office of International Trade. The SBA's Export Express loan program provides export financing opportunities for small businesses. The program is designed to finance a variety of needs of small-business exporters, including participation in foreign trade shows, catalog translations for use in foreign markets, lines of credit for export purposes, and real estate and equipment for the production of goods or services to be exported.[50]

Global Gumball

Dave Haymond, creator of The Wizard Spiral Gumball Machine, liked to say that his mission was to "help people make money while doing nothing." That's certainly not the case for Global Gumball, which ships the machines to clients around the world. How do the Internet and other technological advancements help Global Gumball serve its global customers?

TESTPREP

- Why do many small businesses avoid doing business globally?
- What are some of the advantages small businesses have over large businesses in selling in global markets?

SUMMARY

LO 6–1 Explain why people take the risks of entrepreneurship; list the attributes of successful entrepreneurs; and describe entrepreneurial teams, intrapreneurs, and home- and web-based businesses.

▪ **What are a few of the reasons people start their own businesses?**

Reasons include profit, independence, opportunity, and challenge.

▪ **What are the attributes of successful entrepreneurs?**

Successful entrepreneurs are self-directed, self-nurturing, action-oriented, highly energetic, and tolerant of uncertainty.

▪ **What have modern entrepreneurs done to ensure longer terms of management?**

They have formed entrepreneurial teams with expertise in the many skills needed to start and manage a business.

▪ **What is a micropreneur?**

Micropreneurs are people willing to accept the risk of starting and managing the type of business that remains small, lets them do the kind of work they want to do, and offers them a balanced lifestyle.

▪ **What is intrapreneuring?**

Intrapreneuring is the establishment of entrepreneurial centers within a larger firm where people can innovate and develop new-product ideas internally.

▪ **Why has there been such an increase in the number of home-based and web-based businesses in the last few years?**

The increase in power and decrease in price of computer technology have leveled the field and made it possible for small businesses to compete against larger companies—regardless of location.

LO 6–2 Discuss the importance of small business to the American economy, and summarize the major causes of small-business failure.

▪ **Why are small businesses important to the U.S. economy?**

Small business accounts for about 43 percent of gross domestic product (GDP). Perhaps more important to tomorrow's graduates, 80 percent of U.S. workers' first jobs are in small businesses.

▪ **What does the *small* in small business mean?**

The Small Business Administration defines a small business as one that is independently owned and operated and not dominant in its field of operation, and that meets certain standards of size in terms of employees or sales (depending on the size of others in the industry).

▪ **Why do many small businesses fail?**

Many small businesses fail because of managerial incompetence and inadequate financial planning. See Figure 6.3 for a list of causes of small-business failure.

LO 6–3 Summarize ways to learn about how small businesses operate.

▪ **What hints would you give someone who wants to learn about starting a small business?**

First, learn from others. Take courses and talk with some small-business owners. Second, get some experience working for others. Third, take over a successful firm. Finally, study the latest in small-business management techniques.

LO 6–4 Analyze what it takes to start and run a small business.

- **What goes into a business plan?**

  See the outline of a business plan in the chapter.

- **What sources of funds should someone wanting to start a new business consider investigating?**

  A new entrepreneur has several potential sources of capital: personal savings; family and business associates; banks and finance institutions; angels, crowdfunding, and venture capitalists; and government agencies and more.

- **What are some of the special problems that small-business owners have in dealing with employees?**

  Small-business owners often have difficulty finding competent employees and grooming employees for management responsibilities.

- **Where can budding entrepreneurs find help in starting their businesses?**

  Help can come from many sources: accountants, lawyers, marketing researchers, loan officers, insurance agents, the SBA, SBDCs, SBICs, peer groups, and even college professors.

LO 6–5 Outline the advantages and disadvantages small businesses have in entering global markets.

- **What are some advantages small businesses have over large businesses in global markets?**

  Foreign buyers enjoy dealing with individuals rather than large corporations because (1) small companies provide a wider variety of suppliers and can ship products more quickly and (2) small companies give more personal service.

- **Why don't more small businesses start trading globally?**

  There are several reasons: (1) financing is often difficult to find, (2) many people don't know how to get started and do not understand the cultural differences in foreign markets, and (3) the bureaucratic red tape is often overwhelming.

KEY TERMS

business plan 158
enterprise zones 150
entrepreneurial team 147
entrepreneurship 144
incubators 150
intrapreneurs 147

market 160
micropreneurs 148
Service Corps of
  Retired Executives
  (SCORE) 162
small business 152

Small Business
  Administration (SBA) 159
Small Business
  Investment Company
  (SBIC) Program 160
venture capitalists 159

CRITICAL THINKING

1. Do you have the entrepreneurial spirit? What makes you think that?

2. Are there any similarities between the characteristics demanded of an entrepreneur and those of a professional athlete? Would an athlete be a good prospect for entrepreneurship? Why or why not? Could teamwork be important in an entrepreneurial effort? Why or why not?

3. Imagine yourself starting a small business. What kind of business would it be? How much competition is there? What could you do to make your business more attractive than those of competitors? Would you be willing to work 60 to 70 hours a week to make the business successful?

PUTTING PRINCIPLES TO WORK

PURPOSE

To assess your potential to succeed as an entrepreneur and to evaluate a sample business plan.

EXERCISE

1. Go to bizmove.com/other/quiz.htm and take the interactive entrepreneurial quiz to find out whether you have the qualities to be a successful entrepreneur.

2. If you have entrepreneurial traits and decide you would like to start your own business, you'll need to develop a business plan. Go to bplans.com/sample_business_plans. cfm and click on Restaurant, Cafe, and Bakery. Review the sample business plan for Internet Cafe. Although the plan may not follow the same format as the business plan outline in the chapter, does it contain all the necessary information listed in the outline? If not, what is missing?

DEVELOPING CAREER SKILLS

KEY: ● **Team** ★ **Analytic** ▲ **Communication** ▣ **Technology**

▣▲ 1. Find issues of *Entrepreneur, Black Enterprise, Fast Company,* and *Inc.* magazines online. Read about the entrepreneurs who are heading today's dynamic new businesses. Write a profile about one.

▲★ 2. Select a small business that looks attractive as a career possibility for you. Talk to at least one person who manages such a business. Ask how he or she started it. Ask about financing; human resource management (hiring, firing, training, scheduling); accounting issues; and other managerial matters. Prepare a summary of your findings, including whether the person's job was rewarding, interesting, and challenging—and why or why not.

▣▲ 3. Contact the Small Business Administration by visiting a local office or the organization's website at sba.gov. Write a brief summary of the services the SBA offers.

▲★ 4. Select a small business in your area or a surrounding area that has failed. List the factors you think led to its failure. Compile a list of actions the business owners might have taken to keep the company in business.

●▲★ 5. Choose a partner from among your classmates and put together a list of factors that might mean the difference between success and failure of a new company entering the business technology industry. Can small start-ups realistically hope to compete with companies such as Microsoft and Intel? Discuss the list and your conclusions in class.

CAREER EXPLORATION

You can start a small business in any industry you like. We've talked about a few throughout the chapter, but here are a few more with low start-up costs to consider. Find out about the tasks performed, skills needed, and opportunity outlook in these fields in the *Occupational Outlook Handbook (OOH)* at bls.gov.

- **Craft and fine artist**—uses a variety of materials and techniques to create art for sale. Craft artists create handmade objects such as pottery, glassware, textiles, and other objects. Fine artists create original works of art such as paintings and sculptures.

- **Web developer**—designs and creates websites; responsible for the look of the site and for its technical aspects, and may create content for the site.

- **General repair service**—paints, makes household repairs, works on plumbing and electrical systems, and so on.

- **Small-engine mechanic**—inspects, services, and repairs motorized power equipment such as outdoor power equipment (lawn mowers, leaf blowers, etc.).

Cousins Maine Lobster: From Small Partnership to Successful Franchisor

If you have a passion for what you do and want to share it with others, there's a chance you could succeed as an entrepreneur. As lifelong residents of Maine, cousins Jim Tselikis and Sabin Lomac were passionate about lobster and knew many people who were lobstermen and lobsterwomen. When Lomac moved to Los Angeles, he quickly started to miss the shellfish from back home. That's when he and his cousin came up with the idea to open a food truck that served authentic Maine lobster rolls in California. Appropriately, they named their company Cousins Maine Lobster.

Today the company brings premium lobster rolls, lobster bisque, and other tasty fare to hungry diners in the Los Angeles area as well as 20 additional cities across the United States. As company cofounder Jim Tselikis explains, Cousins focuses on serving the nation's best lobster while providing superior, Maine-inspired customer service. At the start of things, though, the cousins didn't know anything about business, let alone one as challenging as a food truck. They learned as much as they could about food trucks and picked the brains of everyone they knew for tips about running a business. Finally, they felt confident enough to roll out their first Cousins Maine Lobster truck.

Opening day was a true eye-opener for the cousins as the line for lobster stretched as far as they could see. While both of them knew they had hit on something big, they also discovered just how much they needed to learn if they were going to succeed. For example, prior to opening they had not thought of the logistics and forecasting critical to their business. If they ordered too much lobster, it would spoil and they'd lose money. If they ran out of lobster, customers would leave hungry and the company would lose money once again. They needed an angel to throw them a lifeline.

Fortunately, help came in the form of a shark. Tselikis and Lomac were invited to go on *Shark Tank,* a reality TV show where entrepreneurs pitch their ideas to a panel of investors. Before their appearance, they studied the backgrounds of each "shark" they would face and prepared for questions that could be raised about their business. After a tense negotiation, the cousins secured a deal with real estate tycoon Barbara Corcoran, who offered $55,000 for 15 percent of their business. More importantly, she served as a mentor to the aspiring entrepreneurs and advised them to consider franchising their business.

Franchising allowed them to scale their business by replicating Cousins Maine Lobster food trucks across the country. Franchising, however, caused them to lose some control over their business. They also learned that they needed to choose the right franchisees in order to keep the business sustainable and healthy. Today, caring for employees and franchisees is a vital part of Cousins culture. Both staff and franchisees are empowered to make their own decisions. Cousins Maine Lobster envisions a bright future with rapid expansion. Tselikis and Lomac believe this success will hinge on not compromising on three key things: quality of food, customer service, and treatment of employees and franchisees like family.

THINKING IT OVER

1. What personal characteristics do you think helped Tselikis and Lomac succeed as entrepreneurs?

2. Why did they seek outside help to improve their business? What sort of help did they receive?

3. What are some of the advantages and disadvantages of expanding a business by franchising?

1. Daniel Priestley, "Are Successful Entrepreneurs Born or Made?," *Forbes,* February 11, 2019; Alejandro Cremades, "How to Start a Business," *Forbes,* February 13, 2019; Matt D'Angelo, "101 Reasons Being an Entrepreneur Rocks," *Business News Daily,* businessnewsdaily. com, January 3, 2019; Susan Ward, "The Benefits of Owning Your Own Business," *The Balance Small Business,* thebalancesmb.com, February 4, 2020; Jonathan Long, "60 Reasons Why Entrepreneurship Is Amazing," *Entrepreneur,* entrepreneur.com, accessed February 2020.

2. "10 Traits All Successful Entrepreneurs Share," *Entrepreneur,* entrepreneur.com, accessed February 2020; "Five Qualities of Successful Entrepreneurs,"

Entrepreneur, entrepreneur.com, accessed February 2020; John Boitnott, "Starting a Business Isn't What You Think," *Entrepreneur,* entrepreneur.com, January 22, 2020; "15 Traits of Successful Entrepreneurs," *Atlanta Small Business Network,* myasbn.com, February 6, 2020.

3. "The World's Billionaires," *Forbes,* forbes.com, accessed February 2020.

4. Entrepreneurial Potential Self-Assessment, bdc.ca, accessed October 2019.

5. "Apple Fast Facts," *CNN,* cnn.com, February 3, 2020; Con Reisinger, "Apple Co-Founder Steve Wozniak Is Still Collecting a Salary," *Inc.,* inc.com, February 7, 2020.

6. 3M, 3m.com, accessed March 2020.

7. "9 Things Invented or Discovered by Accident," howstuffworks.com, accessed March 2020.

8. Post-it, post-it.com, accessed March 2020.

9. Jordan Daykin, "Intrapreneurships," *Forbes,* January 8, 2019; "The Intrapreneur," *Investopedia,* investopedia. com, accessed March 2020; Isabel Yang, "The Innovation Game," *Innovation News,* innovationnews.com, February 10, 2020.

10. Small Business Administration, sba.gov, accessed March 2020.

11. U.S. Census Bureau, census.gov, accessed March 2020.

12. N. Sonnichsen, "Retailing Market Value in the U.S. 2015–2020," Statista, statista.com, January 31, 2020.

13. J. Clement, "United States: Retail E-commerce Sales 2017–2024," Statista, statista.com, February 6, 2020.

14. ThrowThings, throwthings.com, accessed March 2020.

15. "EB-5 Immigrant Investor Program," United States Citizenship and Immigration Services, uscis.gov, accessed March 2020.

16. U.S. Department of Housing and Urban Development, hud.gov, accessed March 2020; Ruth Simon and Peter Grant, "Opportunity-Zone Tax Break Off to Slow Start with Investors," *The Wall Street Journal,* October 23, 2019; Tony Nitti and Stephanie Cumings, "Final Tax Opportunity Zone Rules," *Forbes,* forbes.com, February 3, 2020.

17. Gabe Alpert, "Jumpstart Our Business Startups Act (JOBS)," *Investopedia,* investopedia.com, November 13, 2019; U.S. Securities and Exchange Commission, sec.gov, accessed March 2020.

18. International Business Innovation Association, inbia.org, accessed October 2019.

19. Salus Center Kitchen, slu.edu, accessed March 2020.

20. Self-Employment Assistance Center, sea.workforcegps. org, accessed March 2020.

21. Startup America Partnership, startupamericapartnership. org, accessed March 2020.

22. Small Business Administration, sba.gov, accessed March 2020; U.S. Census Bureau, census.gov, accessed March 2020; Chamber of Commerce, chamberofcommerce. org, accessed March 2020; Kimberly Amadeo, "Small Businesses and Their Impact on the Economy," *The Balance,* thebalance.com, February 7, 2020; National Small Business Association, nsba.biz, accessed March 2020.

23. Small Business Administration, sba.gov, accessed March 2020.

24. Small Business Administration, sba.gov, accessed March 2020; U.S. Census Bureau, census.gov, accessed March 2020.

25. "Celebs Who Went from Failures to Success Stories," *CBS News,* cbsnews.com, accessed March 2020.

26. Marc Ferris, "Arianna Huffington Speaks at Sarah Lawrence Commencement: Failure Is Not the opposite of Success, It Is the Stepping Stone to Success'" *Huffington Post,* May 20, 2011.

27. "2020 Best Undergraduate Entrepreneurship Programs," *U.S. News & World Report,* usnews.com, accessed March 2020.

28. Ruth Simon, "Small Firms Struggle in Hunt to Find New Workers," *The Wall Street Journal,* February 10, 2020.

29. "How to Buy a Business from a Retiring Baby Boomer," *Entrepreneurs Hub,* entrepreneurshub.com, accessed March 2020.

30. Jeremy Harbour, "Now Is the Perfect Time to Buy a Business. Here's Why," *Forbes,* February 19, 2019; Michael Guta, "Number of Businesses Bought and Sold Hit Record Level in 2018," *Small Business Trends,* January 27, 2019; Ben Carlson, "Will Retiring Baby Boomers Crash the Stock Market?," *Fortune,* Fortune.com, January 23, 2020.

31. Tim Berry, "Updating Your Business Plan," *Entrepreneur,* entrepreneur.com, accessed October 2019.

32. "An Introduction to Small Business Financing," *Funding Circle,* fundingcircle.com, February 6, 2020; Meredith Wood, "Small Business Funding: The 9 Best Options for Financing in 2020," *Fundera,* fundera.com, February 12, 2020; "Best Small Business Loans of 2020," *Money,* money.com, January16, 2020; "Financing & Capital Resources," SCORE, score.org, accessed March 2020.

33. Small Business Administration, sba.gov, accessed March 2020.

34. Rohit Arora, "The Best Places to Get a Small Business Loan in 2019," *Forbes,* forbes.com, October 10, 2019.

35. Community Development Financial Institutions Fund, cdfifund.gov, accessed March 2020.

36. Elvis Picardo, "Invest through Equity Crowdfunding: Risks and Rewards," *Investopedia,* investopedia.com, January 18, 2020.

37. Nathan Heller, "Is Venture Capital Worth the Risk?," *The New Yorker,* newyorker.com, January 20, 2020; Brian Bradley, "Venture Capitalist Ed-Tech Investments Rose Sharply over Last Decade," *Market Brief,* marketbrief. edweek.org, January 31, 2020.

38. AngelList, angel.co, accessed March 2020.

39. Small Business Administration, sba.gov, accessed March 2020.

40. Drew Hendricks, "Why It's Important for Businesses to Respond Quickly to Feedback," *Small Business Trends,* smallbiztrends.com, February 12, 2019.

41. Jim Schleckser, "When You Get the Sale, Stop Talking," *Inc.,* January 22, 2019; Paul Geiger, "Your Best New Customer Strategy for 2020: Learn How They Listen—and Use It," *Forbes,* forbes.com, January 29, 2020; Samuel Thimothy, "How to Use Conversational Marketing to Build Customer Relationships," *Inc.,* inc.com, January 24, 2020.

42. Mary Ellen Slayter, "17 Reasons You Might Want to Work for a Small Business," *Monster,* monster.com, accessed March 2020; Jessica Dickler, "Why Small Businesses Are Banking on Better Benefits," *CNBC,* cnbc.com, January 27, 2020.

43. FindForms.com website, accessed March 2020.

44. Service Corps of Retired Executives, score.org, accessed March 2020.

45. "Cooperative Education and Internship Program," Virginia Tech, career.vt.edu, accessed March 2020.

46. Gateway Wellness Associates, gwa-stl.com, accessed March 2020.

47. "World Population Clock," U.S. Census Bureau, census. gov, accessed March 2020.

48. United States International Trade Commission, usitc.gov, accessed March 2020.

49. Melissa Fares, "Alibaba Welcomes US Small Businesses to Sell Globally on Its Platform," *Business of Fashion,* businessoffashion.com, July 23, 2019.

50. Small Business Administration, sba.gov, accessed March 2020.

7

Management and Leadership

LEARNING OBJECTIVES *After you have read and studied this chapter, you should be able to*

LO 7–1 Describe the changes occurring today in the management function.

LO 7–2 Describe the four functions of management.

LO 7–3 Relate the planning process and decision making to the accomplishment of company goals.

LO 7–4 Describe the organizing function of management.

LO 7–5 Explain the differences between leaders and managers, and describe the various leadership styles.

LO 7–6 Summarize the five steps of the control function of management.

Sheena Wright, CEO of United Way of New York

The organization that became the United Way of New York City started in 1938 after a group of business magnates combined their efforts to fight against poverty during the height of the Great Depression. President Franklin D. Roosevelt applauded the charitable enterprise, saying at its foundation ceremony, "I am so glad that in your great cosmopolitan city, men and women of all races, all creeds, and all faiths have joined in a common effort for the good of all."

Although this remains an excellent description of what UWNYC continues to do for communities across the Big Apple, the organization has changed dramatically since its founding more than 80 years ago. Much of that change can be credited to CEO Sheena Wright, the first woman to lead UWNYC in its history. Since taking the top position in 2012, Wright has totally revamped the organization's mission while also fearlessly confronting everything from hurricanes to illiteracy. "The great thing about United Way is that it's citywide. We touch about a million New Yorkers," said Wright. "We are able to not only identify, fund and co-create significant programs but we're also able to change policy that has an impact on systems and really can cause huge, wide-scale social change."

Making a positive impact through UWNYC is a personal undertaking for Wright, a lifelong New Yorker. Born in the South Bronx, she grew up in a bad neighborhood where her teenage single mother had to stand guard on the stoop so that Wright and her sister could play safely. Despite this rough environment, her mother managed to earn bachelor's and master's degrees while working and raising two children on her own. She also dedicated lots of time to activist organizations like the National Black Leadership Commission on AIDS, which she founded in 1987. "My mom's trajectory was just inspiring," said Wright. "Most people would think that's it, your own life and your own success are over. Through her own striving, she demonstrated to us that no matter what your obstacles, you can persevere and reach your goals."

This shared passion for hard work was apparent in Wright's early commitment to her education. A gifted student, at age 12 Wright enrolled in a prestigious private high school with a full scholarship. She had plenty of athletic talent to match her academic skills, excelling in both cross country and tennis. Before she even got a driver's license, Wright started her studies at Columbia University where she continued to stand out as an all-star student and athlete. She was also a passionate activist who played a vital role in the university's establishment of an African American studies major as well as its complete divestment from apartheid South Africa. Wright went on to Columbia Law School and graduated with job offers from the country's top law firms.

She worked as a corporate lawyer for much of the 1990s, negotiating high-stakes deals with major companies and financial institutions. After spending nearly a decade in corporate law, however, Wright wanted to switch to a more fulfilling profession. "I needed to be doing work that was more closely connected to the community that I came from and helping people who started out with more similar circumstances to mine," said Wright. In 2002, she landed a job as chief operating officer of the non-profit arm of the Abyssinian Baptist Church in Harlem. In this position, Wright worked to secure affordable housing for the community and developed educational programs that helped both young and old. Her efforts eventually caught the attention of United Way New York City, which hired her as CEO in 2012.

Wright's first day at UWNYC was memorable to say the least: Hurricane Sandy had just hit the Northeast and knocked out power across New York. She immediately mobilized hundreds of volunteers who checked on the well-being of residents who were older or disabled living in high-rise apartments. Wright also created the United Way Hurricane Sandy Recovery Fund, which went on to raise more than $10 million. After managing that crisis, she then set her sights on revamping the organization's mission statement. Throughout its history, UWNYC primarily partnered with companies to develop corporate social responsibility programs. With many companies now doing that work in-house, though, Wright transformed UWNYC into an activist organization that develops its own social programs and charitable funds. She is especially proud of ReadNYC, a program that has helped hundreds of children in the South Bronx read at grade level. "If you are doing something important and impactful, it is an obligation for you to shine a light, because it inspires people to do the same," said Wright.

This chapter is all about leadership and management. You will learn about the skills that leaders like Sheena Wright need in order to manage complicated organizations. You will also learn about the basic functions of management and how management differs from leadership. All in all, you should get a better idea of what leaders and managers do and how they do it.

Sources: Lydia Dishman, "The Uphill Battle of United Way NYC's First Female President," *Fast Company*, fastcompany.com, April 19, 2017; "Five Questions with Sheena Wright," *Women and Wealth Magazine*, bbh.com, January 9, 2020; Yelena Shuster, "Trail Blazer," *Columbia College Today*, college.columbia.edu, accessed February 2020; United Way of New York City, unitedwaynyc.org, accessed February 2020.

Let's talk business!
bit.ly/LetsTalkBusiness7

Bryan Bedder/Getty Images for
United Way of New York City

STAFFING AN ORGANIZATION is one of the key challenges managers face in keeping their companies competitive. This company's gourmet chefs cook up lunches, dinners, and snacks for its employees. The company also offers massage therapy and has an on-site gym among other perks. Name that company. (Find the answer in the chapter.)

| LO 7–1 | Describe the changes occurring today in the management function. |

Managers' Roles Are Evolving

Managers must practice the art of getting things done through organizational resources, which include workers, financial resources, information, and equipment. At one time, managers were called "bosses" and their job consisted of telling people what to do, watching over them to be sure they did it, and reprimanding those who didn't. Many managers still behave that way. Perhaps you've witnessed or experienced such behavior; some coaches use this style.

Today, however, most managers tend to be more collaborative. For example, they emphasize teams and team building; they create drop-in centers, team spaces, and open work areas. They may change the definition of *work* from a task you do for a specified period in a specific place to something you do anywhere, anytime. They tend to guide, train, support, motivate, and coach employees rather than tell them what to do.[1] Thus most modern managers emphasize teamwork and cooperation rather than discipline and order giving.[2] They may also open their books to employees to share the company's financials.

Managers of high-tech firms, like Google and Apple, realize that many workers often know more about technology than they do. At first, Google tried to get by with no managers. Soon, however, it found that managers were necessary for communicating strategy, helping employees prioritize projects, facilitating cooperation, and ensuring that processes and systems aligned with company goals.[3]

Rather than telling employees exactly what to do, managers today tend to give their employees enough independence to make their own informed decisions about how best to please customers. How do you think most employees respond to this empowerment on the job?

John Walker/The Fresno Bee/Alamy Stock Photo

What these changes mean for you is that management will demand a new kind of person: a skilled communicator and team player as well as a planner, organizer, motivator, and leader.[4] Future managers will need to be more globally prepared; that is, they need skills such as adaptability, foreign language skills, and ease in other cultures. We'll address these trends in the next few chapters to help you decide whether management is the kind of career you would like. In the following sections, we shall discuss management in general and the functions managers perform.

> **LO 7–2** Describe the four functions of management.

The Four Functions of Management

The following definition of management provides the outline of this chapter: **Management** is the process used to accomplish organizational goals through planning, organizing, leading, and controlling people and other organizational resources (see Figure 7.1).

Planning includes anticipating trends and determining the best strategies and tactics to achieve organizational goals and objectives. One of the major objectives of organizations is to please customers. The trend today is to have *planning teams* to help monitor the environment, find business opportunities, and watch for challenges. *Planning* is a key management function because accomplishing the other functions depends heavily on having a good plan.

Organizing includes designing the structure of the organization and creating conditions and systems in which everyone and everything work together to achieve the organization's goals and objectives. Many of today's organizations are being designed around pleasing the customer at a profit. Thus they must remain flexible and adaptable, because when customer needs change, firms must change with them. When Amazon purchased Whole Foods Market in 2017, it initiated a complete organizational analysis of Whole Foods operations

management
The process used to accomplish organizational goals through planning, organizing, leading, and controlling people and other organizational resources.

planning
A management function that includes anticipating trends and determining the best strategies and tactics to achieve organizational goals and objectives.

organizing
A management function that includes designing the structure of the organization and creating conditions and systems in which everyone and everything work together to achieve the organization's goals and objectives.

FIGURE 7.1 WHAT MANAGERS DO
Some modern managers perform all of these tasks with the full cooperation and participation of workers. Empowering employees means allowing them to participate more fully in decision making.

Planning
- Setting organizational goals.
- Developing strategies to reach those goals.
- Determining resources needed.
- Setting precise standards.

Organizing
- Allocating resources, assigning tasks, and establishing procedures for accomplishing goals.
- Preparing a structure (organization chart) showing lines of authority and responsibility.
- Recruiting, selecting, training, and developing employees.
- Placing employees where they'll be most effective.

Leading
- Guiding and motivating employees to work effectively to accomplish organizational goals and objectives.
- Giving assignments.
- Explaining routines.
- Clarifying policies.
- Providing feedback on performance.

Controlling
- Measuring results against corporate objectives.
- Monitoring performance relative to standards.
- Rewarding outstanding performance.
- Taking corrective action when necessary.

Planning is what helps managers understand the environment in which their businesses must operate. When the COVID-19 pandemic forced restaurants to practice social distancing, food service managers needed to be ready to respond with operational alternatives. What restaurant changes have occurred in your area?

Pedro Talens Masip/Getty Images

connect

▶ **iSeeit!** Need help understanding the four functions of management? Visit your Connect eBook to view a video for a brief animated explanation.

leading

Creating a vision for the organization and guiding, training, coaching, and motivating others to work effectively to achieve the organization's goals and objectives in a timely manner.

controlling

A management function that involves establishing clear standards to determine whether or not an organization is progressing toward its goals and objectives, rewarding people for doing a good job, and taking corrective action if they are not.

which led to organizational changes. For example, Whole Foods had recently introduced its lower-cost store (called 365) to appeal to Millennials with an emphasis on lower prices, technology, and social media integration.[5] After a thorough organizational analysis, Amazon determined it was not necessary to continue the low-cost alternative. Instead, Amazon decided to push technology and social media integration in all its Whole Foods Markets through Amazon Prime Now grocery delivery.

Leading means creating a vision for the organization and communicating, guiding, training, coaching, and motivating others to achieve goals and objectives in a timely manner. The trend is to empower employees, giving them as much freedom as possible to become self-directed and self-motivated. This function was once known as *directing;* that is, telling employees exactly what to do. In many smaller firms, that is still the manager's role. In most large firms, however, managers no longer tell people exactly what to do because knowledge workers and others often know how to do their jobs better than the manager does. Nonetheless, leadership is still necessary to keep employees focused on the right tasks at the right time.

Controlling establishes clear standards to determine whether an organization is progressing toward its goals and objectives, rewarding people for doing a good job, and taking corrective action if they are not. Basically, it means measuring whether what actually occurs meets the organization's goals.

Planning, organizing, leading, and controlling are the heart of management, so let's explore them in more detail. The process begins with planning; we'll look at that right after the Test Prep questions.

?TESTPREP

- What are some of the changes happening in management today?
- What's the definition of *management* used in this chapter?
- What are the four functions of management?

LO 7–3   Relate the planning process and decision making to the accomplishment of company goals.

vision

An encompassing explanation of why the organization exists and where it is trying to go.

Planning and Decision Making

Planning, the first managerial function, is setting the organization's vision, goals, and objectives. Executives find planning to be their most valuable tool. A **vision** is more than a goal; it's a broad explanation of why the organization exists and where it's trying to go. It gives the organization a sense of purpose and a set of values that unite workers in a common destiny. Managing an organization without first establishing a vision is like getting everyone in a rowboat excited about going somewhere, but not telling them exactly where. The boat will just keep changing directions rather than speeding toward an agreed-on goal.

Top management usually sets the vision for the organization and then often works with others in the firm to establish a mission statement. A **mission statement** outlines the organization's fundamental purposes. It should address the following:

mission statement
An outline of the fundamental purposes of an organization.

- The organization's self-concept.
- Its philosophy.
- Its long-term survival needs.
- Its customer needs.
- Its social responsibility.
- The nature of its product(s) or service(s).

The mission statement becomes the foundation for setting specific goals and objectives. **Goals** are the broad, long-term accomplishments an organization wishes to attain. Because workers and management need to agree on them, setting goals is often a team process. **Objectives** are specific, short-term statements detailing *how to achieve* the organization's goals. One of your goals for reading this chapter, for example, may be to learn basic concepts of management. An objective you could use to achieve this goal is to answer the chapter's Test Prep questions and end-of-chapter exercises.

goals
The broad, long-term accomplishments an organization wishes to attain.

objectives
Specific, short-term statements detailing how to achieve the organization's goals.

Planning is a continuous process. A plan that worked yesterday may not be successful in today's market. Most planning also follows a pattern. The procedure you'll follow in planning your life and career is basically the same as the one businesses use. It answers several fundamental questions:

1. *What is the situation now?* What are the success factors affecting the industry participants and how do we compare? What is the state of the economy and other environments? What opportunities exist for meeting people's needs? What products and customers are most profitable? Who are our major competitors? What threats are there to our business? These questions are part of **SWOT analysis**, which analyzes the organization's **s**trengths and **w**eaknesses, and the **o**pportunities and **t**hreats it faces, usually in that order.[6] Opportunities and threats are often *external* to the firm and cannot always be anticipated or controlled.

SWOT analysis
A planning tool used to analyze an organization's **s**trengths, **w**eaknesses, **o**pportunities, and **t**hreats.

Weaknesses and strengths are more often *internal* and therefore more within reach of being measured and fixed. Figure 7.2 lists some of the general issues companies consider when conducting a SWOT analysis: What external success factors affect the industry? How does our firm measure up to other firms? What are our social objectives? What are our personal development objectives? What can we do to survive and prosper during a recession? For more on SWOT analysis, see the Putting Principles to Work exercise at the end of this chapter.

iSeeit! Need help understanding SWOT analysis? Visit your Connect eBook to view a video for a brief animated explanation.

2. *How can we get to our goal from here?* Answering this question is often the most important part of planning. It takes four forms: strategic, tactical, operational, and contingency (see Figure 7.3).

Strategic planning is done by top management and determines the major goals of the organization and the policies, procedures, strategies, and resources it will need to achieve them. *Policies* are broad guidelines for action, and *strategies* determine the best way to use resources. At the strategic planning stage, top managers of the company decide which customers to serve, when to serve them, what products or services to sell, and the geographic areas in which to compete. Take Taco Bell, for example. When the economy slumped, the company created a "value menu" of items like cheese roll-ups and bean burritos with low prices. It also went after the "fourth-meal" (late-night) crowd and introduced several low-calorie, low-fat Fresco items. When the labor market tightened, Taco Bell hosted nearly 600 hiring parties with free food and games to attract potential employees. Some attending were offered jobs on the spot.[7]

strategic planning
The process of determining the major goals of the organization and the policies and strategies for obtaining and using resources to achieve those goals.

FIGURE 7.2 SWOT MATRIX
This matrix identifies potential strengths, weaknesses, opportunities, and threats organizations may consider in a SWOT analysis.

Potential Internal STRENGTHS
- Core competencies in key areas
- An acknowledged market leader
- Well-conceived functional area strategies
- Proven management
- Cost advantages
- Better advertising campaigns

Potential Internal WEAKNESSES
- No clear strategic direction
- Obsolete facilities
- Subpar profitability
- Lack of managerial depth and talent
- Weak market image
- Too narrow a product line

Potential External OPPORTUNITIES
- Ability to serve additional customer groups
- Ability to expand product lines
- Ability to transfer skills/technology to new products
- Falling trade barriers in attractive foreign markets
- Complacency among rival firms
- Ability to grow due to increases in market demand

Potential External THREATS
- Entry of lower-cost foreign competitors
- Rising sales of substitute products
- Slower market growth
- Costly regulatory requirements
- Vulnerability to recession and business cycles
- Changing buyer needs and tastes

In today's rapidly changing environment, strategic planning is becoming more difficult because changes are occurring so fast that plans—even those set for just months into the future—may soon be obsolete. Streaming giant Netflix was forced to increase its original programming when strong competition from Apple, Disney, Comcast, and others changed the on-demand media market.[8] Think of how an amusement park company like Six Flags needs to change its plans depending on the price of gas. When the price of gas soars (and crowds decrease), Six Flags can offer reduced ticket prices in exchange for a gas receipt. When gas prices drop (and crowds increase), pricing can go back to normal.

Even though top managers are responsible for strategic planning, it is important for them to listen to those who might have the best strategic insights—employees. Employees whose ideas about strategy are ignored might get the last laugh. For example, the late Steve Jobs left the company he helped found, Apple, due to product development issues with the company CEO and board. After leaving, Jobs formed NeXT, a computer platform development company, and later acquired a computer graphics division of Lucasfilm that would become Pixar. In 1996, Apple purchased NeXT, a move that brought Jobs back into the company. A year later, he became CEO and helped build Apple into the global powerhouse it is today.[9]

FIGURE 7.3 PLANNING FUNCTIONS
Not all firms bother to make contingency plans. If something changes the market, such companies may be slow to respond. Most organizations do strategic, tactical, and operational planning.

FORMS OF PLANNING

STRATEGIC PLANNING
The setting of broad, long-range goals by top managers

TACTICAL PLANNING
The identification of specific, short-range objectives by lower-level managers

CONTINGENCY PLANNING
The creation of backup plans in case primary plans fail

OPERATIONAL PLANNING
The setting of work standards and schedules

Does AI Mean the End of Managers?

The continued integration of artificial intelligence (AI) (see Bonus Chapter B) into the knowledge economy appears inevitable. This movement is leading companies to think about overhauling long-held beliefs regarding the role of managers. In fact, technology research firm Gartner suggests that AI algorithms could take over almost 70 percent of the routine work currently performed by managers within the next four years. For example, managers often spend a considerable amount of their work time performing tasks such as filling in forms, updating information, and approving workflows. Automating these tasks through AI would allow managers to focus on human strengths in areas such as strategic planning and decision making where machines lack an element of creativity.

Massachusetts Institute of Technology (MIT) economics professor David Autor believes that

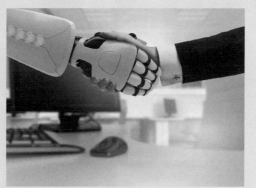

AAUB/Getty Images

middle management positions are particularly vulnerable to the wave of AI implementation. He cites dire prospects specifically for managers in finance and inventory management where considerable time is spent translating data in order to make specific decisions. Other economists predict very dramatic changes in many upper-tier white-collar positions such as accounting and law because of machine advances.

Even though some management positions face a rocky future due to AI advancements, most economists are still upbeat about the future of management. Humans still play a vital role in designing experiments and reviewing data traces in order to plan the evolution of the machines, and there is still a level of reasoning only human strategists can do. A manager's ability to think strategically and intuitively promises to be even more prized in this era of strategic human–machine partnerships.

Sources: Jeremy Khan, "A.I. Is Unstoppable. And A.I. Is Struggling," *Fortune*, January 20, 2020; Alejandro de la Garza, "AI Is about to Spark a Radical Shift in White-Collar Work. But There's Still 'Plenty of Work for People to Do,' "*Time*, January 23, 2020; Sheelah Kolhatkar," Could New Research on AI and White-Collar Jobs Finally Bring about a Strong Policy Response?," *The New Yorker*, January 14, 2020; Maria Aspan, "This Tech Giant Says AI Has Already Helped It Save $1 Billion," *Fortune*, January 24, 2020.

Clearly, some companies are making plans that allow for quick responses to customer needs and requests.[10] The goal is to be flexible and responsive to the market. The Adapting to Change box talks about how artificial intelligence (AI) may change the role of managers in the future.

Tactical planning is the process of developing detailed, short-term statements about what is to be done, who is to do it, and how. Managers or teams of managers at lower levels of the organization normally make tactical plans. Such plans can include setting annual budgets and deciding on other activities necessary to meet strategic objectives. If the strategic plan of a truck manufacturer, for example, is to sell more trucks in the South, the tactical plan might be to fund more research of southern truck drivers' wants and needs, and to plan promotions to reach them.

Operational planning is the process of setting work standards and schedules necessary to implement the company's tactical objectives. Whereas strategic planning looks at the organization as a whole, operational planning focuses on specific supervisors, department managers, and individual employees. The operational plan is the department manager's tool for daily and weekly operations. An operational plan may include, for example, the specific dates for certain truck parts to be completed and the quality specifications they must meet before production.

Contingency planning is the process of preparing alternative courses of action the firm can use if its primary plans don't work out. The economic and competitive environments change so rapidly that it's wise to have alternative plans of action ready in anticipation of

tactical planning
The process of developing detailed, short-term statements about what is to be done, who is to do it, and how it is to be done.

operational planning
The process of setting work standards and schedules necessary to implement the company's tactical objectives.

contingency planning
The process of preparing alternative courses of action that may be used if the primary plans don't achieve the organization's objectives.

Organizations of all kinds need contingency plans for unexpected events. Here, first responders help two men during an emergency drill simulating a chemical weapons attack. What contingency plans are you aware of on your campus or at work?

Philippe Desmazes/AFP/Getty Images

such changes. For example, if an organization doesn't meet its sales goals by a certain date, the contingency plan may call for more advertising or a cut in prices at that time. *Crisis planning* is a part of contingency planning that anticipates sudden changes in the environment. For example, many cities and businesses have developed plans to respond to terrorist attacks or natural disasters such as floods, hurricanes, or tornados. You can imagine how important such plans are to hospitals, airlines, the police, and public transportation authorities.

Instead of creating detailed strategic plans, the leaders of market-based companies (companies that respond quickly to changes in competition or to other environmental changes) often simply set direction. They want to stay flexible, listen to customers, and seize opportunities—expected or not. Think of how stores selling to teenagers must adapt to style changes and creators of video games adapt to changing trends.[11]

The opportunities, however, must fit into the company's overall goals and objectives; if not, the company could lose its focus. Clearly, then, much of management and planning requires decision making.

Decision Making: Finding the Best Alternative

decision making

Choosing among two or more alternatives.

Planning and all the other management functions require decision making. **Decision making** is choosing among two or more alternatives, which sounds easier than it is. In fact, decision making is the heart of all the management functions.

The *rational decision-making model* is a series of steps managers often follow to make logical, intelligent, and well-founded decisions. Think of the steps as the six Ds of decision making:

1. Define the situation.
2. Describe and collect needed information.
3. Develop alternatives.
4. Decide which alternative is best.
5. Do what is indicated (begin implementation).
6. Determine whether the decision was a good one, and follow up.

Managers don't always go through this six-step process. Sometimes they have to make decisions *on the spot*—with little information available. They still must make good decisions in all such circumstances. **Problem solving** is less formal than decision making and usually calls for quicker action to resolve everyday issues. Both decision making and problem solving call for a lot of judgment.

Problem-solving teams are two or more workers assigned to solve a specific problem (e.g., Why aren't customers buying our service contracts?). Problem-solving techniques include **brainstorming**, that is, coming up with as many solutions as possible in a short period of time with no censoring of ideas. Another technique is called **PMI**, or listing all the **p**luses for a solution in one column, all the **m**inuses in another, and the **i**mplications in a third. The idea is to make sure the pluses exceed the minuses.

You can try using the PMI system on some of your personal decisions to get some practice. For example, should you stay home and study tonight? List all the pluses in one column: better grades, more self-esteem, more responsible behavior, and so on. In the other column, put the minuses: boredom, less fun, and so forth. We hope the pluses outweigh the minuses most of the time and that you study often. But sometimes it's best to go out and have some fun, as long as doing so won't hurt your grades or job prospects.

problem solving

The process of solving the everyday problems that occur. Problem solving is less formal than decision making and usually calls for quicker action.

brainstorming

Coming up with as many solutions to a problem as possible in a short period of time with no censoring of ideas.

PMI

Listing all the pluses for a solution in one column, all the minuses in another, and the implications in a third column.

TEST**PREP**

- What's the difference between goals and objectives?
- What does a company analyze when it does a SWOT analysis?
- What are the differences among strategic, tactical, and operational planning?
- What are the six Ds of decision making?

LO 7–4 Describe the organizing function of management.

Organizing: Creating a Unified System

After managers have planned a course of action, they must organize the firm to accomplish their goals. That means allocating resources (such as funds for various departments), assigning tasks, and establishing procedures. A managerial pyramid shows the organization's levels of management (see Figure 7.4). **Top management**, the highest level, consists of the president and other key company executives who develop strategic plans. Job titles and abbreviations you're likely to see often are chief executive officer (CEO), chief operating officer (COO), chief financial officer (CFO), and chief information officer (CIO) or in some companies chief knowledge officer (CKO). The CEO is often also the president of the firm and is responsible for all top-level decisions. The CEO and president are the same person in many of the S&P 500 companies, including big companies such as Ford Motor, Walmart, Amazon, and Procter & Gamble.

CEOs are responsible for introducing change into an organization.[12] The COO is responsible for putting those changes into effect. His or her tasks include structuring work, controlling operations, and rewarding people to ensure that everyone strives to carry out the leader's vision. Many companies today have eliminated the COO function as a cost-cutting measure and have assigned that role to the CEO. Often, the CFO participates in the decision to cut the COO position. The CFO is responsible for obtaining funds, planning budgets, collecting funds, and so on. The CIO or CKO is responsible for getting the right information to other managers so they can make correct decisions. CIOs are more important than ever to the success of their companies, given the crucial role that information technology has come to play in every aspect of business.

top management

Highest level of management, consisting of the president and other key company executives who develop strategic plans.

FIGURE 7.4 LEVELS OF MANAGEMENT

This figure shows the three levels of management. In many firms, there are several levels of middle management. However, firms have eliminated many middle-level managers because fewer are needed to oversee self-managed teams and higher-skilled employees.

middle management

The level of management that includes general managers, division managers, and branch and plant managers who are responsible for tactical planning and controlling.

supervisory management

Managers who are directly responsible for supervising workers and evaluating their daily performance.

technical skills

Skills that involve the ability to perform tasks in a specific discipline or department.

human relations skills

Skills that involve communication and motivation; they enable managers to work through and with people.

Middle management includes general managers, division managers, and branch and plant managers (in colleges, deans and department heads) who are responsible for tactical planning and controlling. Many firms have eliminated some middle managers through downsizing and have given their remaining managers more employees to supervise. Nonetheless, middle managers are still considered very important to most firms.

Supervisory management includes those directly responsible for supervising workers and evaluating their daily performance; they're often known as first-line managers (or supervisors) because they're the first level above workers. This is the first management position you are most likely to acquire after college. (*The First-Time Manager* written by Loren B. Belker, Jim McCormick, and Gary S. Topchik is a good source for individuals assuming their first management job.)

Tasks and Skills at Different Levels of Management

Few people are trained to be good managers. Usually a person learns how to be a skilled accountant or sales representative or production-line worker, and then—because of her or his skill—is selected to be a manager. Such managers tend to become deeply involved in showing others how to do things, helping them, supervising them, and generally being active in the operating task.

The further up the managerial ladder a person moves, the less important his or her original job skills become. At the top of the ladder, the need is for people who are visionaries, planners, organizers, coordinators, communicators, morale builders, and motivators. Figure 7.5 shows that a manager must have three categories of skills:

1. **Technical skills** are the ability to perform tasks in a specific discipline (such as selling a product or developing software) or department (such as marketing or information systems).

2. **Human relations skills** include communication and motivation; they enable managers to work through and with people. Communication can be especially

So You Want to Be a Social Media Manager

buffer.com

Today, three billion people—approximately 40 percent of the world's population—use social media. It's no wonder then that one of the fastest-growing careers today is social media manager. Increasingly, social media have gained importance as they present the face and voice of an organization. If you are interested in becoming a social media manager, do you have the skills it takes? According to social media management site Buffer, you'll need to be curious, adapt quickly, and understand the role that social media play in meeting the organization's goals. You'll also need skills in the following areas:

- Writing
- Graphic and video design
- Public speaking
- Customer service and community engagement
- Behavioral psychology
- Analysis of social media metrics (e.g., likes, comments, shares, etc.) and business metrics (e.g., traffic, leads, revenue, etc.)
- Budgeting
- Ability to build a community, not just an audience

If you are interested in knowing how you can develop these skills, go online to buffer.com/resources/ social-media-manager-job-description. This post identifies many resources that can help you work on the skills that you will need. While you may not be strong in all of these areas, being proficient in a few of them will help make you a great social media manager.

Sources: Lilach Bullock, "The Best Tools for Planning Your Social Media Marketing Strategy," *Forbes*, January 9, 2019; Rob Marvin, "The Best Social Media Management and Analytics Tools for 2019," *PC Magazine*, March 14, 2019; Alex McGeeney, "How You Can Become a Social Media Manager in 2020," *New York Post*, January 3, 2020; Julia Campbell, "5 Habits for Successful Social Media Managers in 2020," *Social Media Today*, socialmediatoday.com, January 8, 2020.

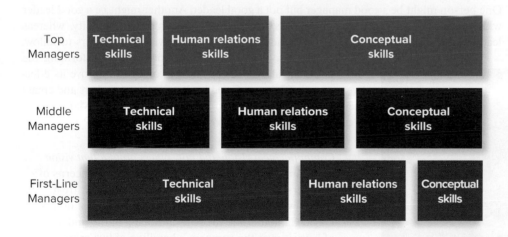

FIGURE 7.5 SKILLS NEEDED AT VARIOUS LEVELS OF MANAGEMENT
All managers need human relations skills. At the top, managers need strong conceptual skills and rely less on technical skills. First-line managers need strong technical skills and rely less on conceptual skills. Middle managers need to have a balance between technical and conceptual skills.

difficult when managers and employees speak different languages. Skills associated with leadership—coaching, morale building, delegating, training and development, and supportiveness—are also human relations skills.

3. **Conceptual skills** let the manager picture the organization as a whole and see the relationships among its various parts. They are needed in planning, organizing, controlling, systems development, problem analysis, decision making, coordinating, and delegating.

Looking again at Figure 7.5, you'll notice that first-line managers need to be skilled in all three areas. However, they spend most of their time on technical and human relations tasks, like assisting operating personnel and giving directions, and less time on conceptual tasks. Top managers, in contrast, need to use few technical skills. Instead, they spend almost

conceptual skills
Skills that involve the ability to picture the organization as a whole and the relationships among its various parts.

all their time on human relations and conceptual tasks. A person who is competent at a low level of management may not be competent at higher levels, and vice versa. Different skills are needed at different levels.[13] Read the Connecting through Social Media box to learn about the skills needed to be a social media manager, one of today's fastest-growing careers.

Staffing: Getting and Keeping the Right People

staffing
A management function that includes hiring, motivating, and retaining the best people available to accomplish the company's objectives.

To get the right kind of people to staff an organization, the firm has to offer the right kind of incentives. For example, Google's gourmet chefs cook up free lunches, dinners, and snacks for employees. The company also offers massage therapy, an on-site gym, and other perks. Would these incentives appeal to you? How important to you is pay relative to other incentives?

Staffing is recruiting, hiring, motivating, and retaining the best people available to accomplish the company's objectives. Today, staffing is critical, especially in the Internet and high-tech areas. At most high-tech companies, like Google, Facebook, and Microsoft, the primary capital equipment is brain power. A firm with innovative and creative workers can sometimes go from start-up to major competitor in just a few years.[14]

Many people are not willing to work at companies unless they are treated well and get fair pay. They also may leave to find a better balance between work and home. Staffing is becoming a greater part of each manager's assignment, and all managers need to cooperate with human resource management to win and keep good workers. Chapter 11 is devoted to human resource issues, including staffing.

LO 7–5 Explain the differences between leaders and managers, and describe the various leadership styles.

Leading: Providing Continuous Vision and Values

One person might be a good manager but not a good leader. Another might be a good leader without being a good manager. Managers strive to produce order and stability, whereas leaders embrace and manage change. Leadership is creating a vision for others to follow, establishing corporate values and ethics, and transforming the way the organization does business in order to improve its effectiveness and efficiency. Good leaders motivate workers and create the environment for them to motivate themselves.[15] Management is carrying out the leader's vision.

Leaders must therefore:

- *Communicate a vision and rally others around that vision.* The leader should be openly sensitive to the concerns of followers, give them responsibility, and win their trust. A successful leader must influence the actions of others. David Calhoun took the reins at Boeing in the middle of a crisis over the company's handling of two crashes involving its 737 MAX plane. He set a new commitment to full transparency at the company to regain confidence in Boeing with consumers, employees, and the Federal Aviation Administration.[16]

- *Establish corporate values.* These include concern for employees, for customers, for the environment, and for the quality of the company's products. When companies set their business goals, they're defining the company's values as well. The number one trait that others look for in a leader is honesty. The second requirement is that the leader be forward looking.

- *Promote corporate ethics.* Ethical behavior includes an unfailing demand for honesty and an insistence that

Tony Hsieh, CEO of Zappos.com, views culture as his company's top priority. He believes that all other aspects of business fall easily into place as long as employees are happy and motivated by their work. Hsieh got rid of middle managers and allowed employees to make more decisions on their own. Do you think you would thrive in a self-managed workplace?

Brad Swonetz/Redux

First-line managers often assist in the decisions made by their department heads. However, the department heads retain full responsibility for the decisions—if a plan succeeds, it's their success; if a plan fails, it's their failure. Now imagine this: As a first-line manager, you have uncovered new information that your department head hasn't seen yet. Your findings indicate that your manager's recent plans are sure to fail. If the plans do fail, the manager will probably be demoted or fired, and you're the most likely candidate to fill the vacancy. Will you give your department head the report or keep it to yourself? What is the ethical thing to do? What might be the consequences of your decision?

everyone in the company gets treated fairly (see the Making Ethical Decisions box). That's why we stress ethical decision making throughout this text. Many businesspeople have made the news by giving away huge amounts to charity, thus setting a model of social concern for their employees and others.

- *Embrace change.* A leader's most important job may be to transform the way the company does business so that it's more effective (does things better) and more efficient (uses fewer resources to accomplish the same objectives).

- *Stress accountability and responsibility.* If there is anything we learned from the financial crisis in 2008 that involved failures of banking managers and other industry and government managers, it is that leaders need to be held accountable and need to feel responsible for their actions. A keyword that emerged from the financial crisis is *transparency.* **Transparency** is the presentation of a company's facts and figures in a way that is clear and apparent to all stakeholders.

All organizations need leaders, and all employees can help lead. You don't have to be a manager to perform a leadership function. That is, any employee can motivate others to work well, add to a company's ethical environment, and report ethical lapses when they occur.

Leadership Styles

Nothing has challenged management researchers more than the search for the best leadership traits, behaviors, or styles. Thousands of studies have tried to identify characteristics that make leaders different from other people. Intuitively, you might conclude the same thing they did: leadership traits are hard to pin down. Some leaders are well groomed and tactful, while others are unkempt and abrasive—yet both may be just as effective.

Just as no one set of traits describes a leader, no one style of leadership works best in all situations. Even so, we can look at a few of the most commonly recognized leadership styles and see how they may be effective (see Figure 7.6):

1. **Autocratic leadership** means making managerial decisions without consulting others. This style is effective in emergencies and when absolute followership is needed—for example, when fighting fires. Autocratic leadership is also effective sometimes with new, relatively unskilled workers who need clear direction and guidance. It is also often successful in sports at the college and professional level. The New England Patriots have won six Super Bowls under the autocratic leadership of Coach Bill Belichick. Nick Saban, head coach at the University of Alabama, has built a football dynasty that has won five national championships under his stern control. What kind of leadership do you see being used most successfully in basketball, football, and other areas?

2. **Participative (democratic) leadership** involves managers and employees working together to make decisions. Employee participation in decisions may not always increase effectiveness, but it usually does increase job satisfaction. Many large

transparency

The presentation of a company's facts and figures in a way that is clear and apparent to all stakeholders.

autocratic leadership

Leadership style that involves making managerial decisions without consulting others.

participative (democratic) leadership

Leadership style that consists of managers and employees working together to make decisions.

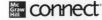

iSeeit! Need help understanding management, leadership, and leadership styles? Visit your Connect eBook to view a video for a brief animated explanation.

FIGURE 7.6 VARIOUS LEADERSHIP STYLES

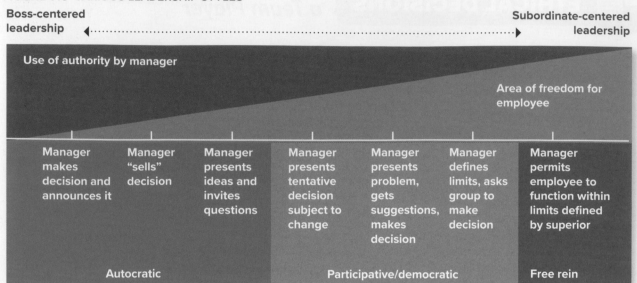

Source: Robert Tannenbaum and Warren Schmidt, "How to Choose a Leadership Pattern," *Harvard Business Review*, May–June 1973.

Jeff Kowalsky/Bloomberg/Getty Images

Alan Mulally, former CEO of Ford Motor Company, managed to lead the U.S. auto giant back to profitability after the Great Recession—without a government bailout. The reason for this success was the leadership style of the most authoritarian CEO that Ford has seen since Henry Ford. When an organization is under extreme pressure, why might autocratic leadership be necessary?

organizations like Google, Apple, IBM, Cisco, and AT&T, and most smaller firms have been highly successful using a democratic style of leadership that values traits such as flexibility, good listening skills, and empathy. Employees meet to discuss and resolve management issues by giving everyone some opportunity to contribute to decisions.

3. In **free-rein leadership** managers set objectives and employees are free to do whatever is appropriate to accomplish those objectives. Free-rein leadership is often the most successful leadership style in certain organizations, such as those in which managers supervise doctors, professors, software developers, engineers, or other professionals. The traits managers need in such organizations include warmth, friendliness, and understanding. More and more firms are adopting this style of leadership with at least some of their employees.

Individual leaders rarely fit neatly into just one of these categories. We can think of leadership as a continuum along which employee participation varies, from purely boss-centered leadership to employee-centered leadership.

Which leadership style is best? Research tells us that it depends largely on what the goals and values of the firm are, who's being led, and in what situations. A manager may be autocratic but friendly with a new trainee, democratic with an experienced employee, and free-rein with a trusted long-term supervisor.

There's no such thing as a leadership trait that is effective in all situations, or a leadership style that always works best. A successful leader in one organization may not be successful in another organization. A truly successful leader has the ability to adopt the leadership style most appropriate to the situation and the employees.[17]

Empowering Workers

Many leaders in the past gave explicit instructions to workers, telling them what to do to meet the goals and objectives of the organization. The term for this process is *directing*. Managers are sometimes reluctant to give up decision-making power. In traditional organizations, directing includes giving assignments, explaining routines, clarifying policies, and providing feedback on performance. Many organizations still follow this model, especially fast-food restaurants and small retail establishments where the employees don't have the skill and experience needed to work on their own, at least at first.

Progressive leaders, such as those in some high-tech firms and Internet companies, empower employees to make decisions on their own. **Empowerment** means giving employees the authority to make a decision without consulting the manager and the responsibility to respond quickly to customer requests. For example, Zappos, an online shoe and clothing retailer, gives its employees wide discretion to do whatever they feel is right to please customers. In firms that implement the concept, the manager's role is less that of a boss and director and more that of a coach, assistant, counselor, or team member.

Enabling means giving workers the education and tools they need to make decisions. Clearly, it's the key to the success of empowerment. Without the right education, orientation, training, coaching, and tools, workers cannot assume the responsibilities and decision-making roles that make empowerment work.

Kauka Jarvi/Shutterstock

Managing Knowledge

"Knowledge is power." Empowering employees means giving them knowledge—that is, the information they need to do the best job they can. Finding the right information, keeping it in a readily accessible place, and making it known to everyone in the firm together constitute the tasks of **knowledge management**.

Today there is no shortage of information to manage. In fact, the amount of data gathered has grown so much that *big data* has become the popular term to describe the vast collection of available information. This data is collected from both traditional sources like sales transactions and digital sources like social media from both inside and outside the company.

The first step to developing a knowledge management system is determining what knowledge is most important. Do you want to know more about your customers? Do you want to know more about competitors? What kind of information would make your company more effective or more efficient or more responsive to the marketplace? Once you've decided what you need to know, you set out to find answers to those questions.

Knowledge management tries to keep people from reinventing the wheel—that is, duplicating the work of gathering information—every time a decision must be made. A company really progresses when each person continually asks, "What do I still not know?" and "Whom should I be asking?" It's as important to know what's *not* working as it is to know what *is* working. Employees and managers have texting, tweeting, and other means of keeping in touch with one another, with customers, and with other stakeholders. The key to success is learning how to process information effectively and turn it into knowledge that everyone can use to improve processes and procedures. The benefits are obvious. See Bonus Chapter B for a more detailed discussion about using technology to manage information.

LO 7-6 Summarize the five steps of the control function of management.

Controlling: Making Sure It Works

The control function measures performance relative to the planned objectives and standards, rewards people for work well done, and takes corrective action when necessary. Thus the control process (see Figure 7.7) provides the feedback that lets managers and workers adjust to deviations from plans and to changes in the environment that have affected performance.

Controlling consists of five steps:

1. Establishing clear performance standards. This ties the planning function to the control function. Without clear standards, control is impossible.

2. Monitoring and recording actual performance or results.

Fast-food restaurant employees often don't have the skill and experience to make empowerment work very well. Instead, their managers generally have to supervise and direct them fairly closely. What do you think are some of the consequences for managers of not being able to empower their staff with decision-making authority?

free-rein leadership
Leadership style that involves managers setting objectives and employees being relatively free to do whatever it takes to accomplish those objectives.

empowerment
Giving frontline workers the responsibility, authority, freedom, training, and equipment they need to respond quickly to customer requests.

enabling
Giving workers the education and tools they need to make decisions.

knowledge management
Finding the right information, keeping the information in a readily accessible place, and making the information known to everyone in the firm.

FIGURE 7.7 THE CONTROL PROCESS

The whole control process is based on clear standards. Without such standards, the other steps are difficult, if not impossible. With clear standards, performance measurement is relatively easy and the proper action can be taken.

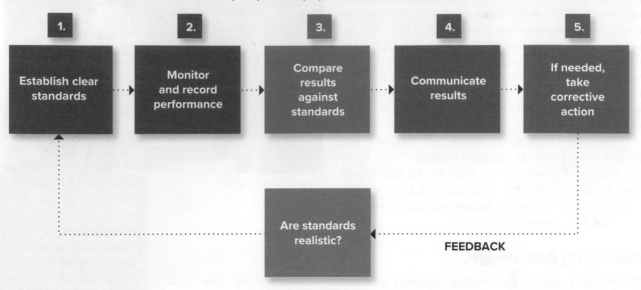

1. Establish clear standards

2. Monitor and record performance

3. Compare results against standards

4. Communicate results

5. If needed, take corrective action

Are standards realistic?

FEEDBACK

One way colleges and universities measure their performance is to track the number of students who complete their degrees or who graduate within a certain number of years. What are some of the factors that could affect the achievement of this performance standard, and how do college administrators take corrective action when necessary?

Syda Productions/Shutterstock

3. Comparing results against plans and standards.

4. Communicating results and deviations to the appropriate employees.

5. Taking corrective action when needed and providing positive feedback for work well done.

For managers to measure results, the standards must be specific, attainable, and measurable. Setting such clear standards is part of the planning function. Vague goals and standards such as "better quality," "more efficiency," and "improved performance" aren't sufficient because they don't describe in enough detail what you're trying to achieve. For example, let's say you're a runner and you have made the following statement: "My goal is to improve my distance." When you started your improvement plan last year, you ran 2.0 miles a day; now you run 2.1 miles a day. Did you meet your goal? Well, you did increase your distance, but certainly not by very much.

A more appropriate statement would be "My goal is to increase my running distance from two miles a day to four miles a day by January 1." It's important to establish a time period for reaching goals. The following examples of goals and standards meet these criteria:

● Cutting the number of finished product rejects from 10 per 1,000 to 5 per 1,000 by March 31.

● Increasing the number of times managers praise employees from 3 per week to 12 per week by the end of the quarter.

● Increasing sales of product X from 10,000 per month to 12,000 per month by July.

One way to make control systems work is to establish clear procedures for monitoring performance. Accounting and finance are often the foundations for control systems because they provide the numbers management needs to evaluate progress.

A Key Criterion for Measurement: Customer Satisfaction

Traditional measures of success are usually financial; that is, they define success in terms of profits or return on investment. Certainly these measures are still important, but they're not the whole purpose of the firm. Other purposes may include pleasing employees, stakeholders, and customers—including both external and internal customers.

External customers include dealers, who buy products to sell to others, and ultimate customers (also known as end users) such as you and me, who buy products for their own personal use. **Internal customers** are individuals and units within the firm that receive services from other individuals or units. For example, the field salespeople are the internal customers of the marketing research people who prepare market reports for them.

One goal today is to go beyond simply satisfying customers to "delighting" them with unexpectedly good products and services. We'll discuss management in more detail in the next few chapters. Let's pause now, review, and do some exercises. Management is doing, not just reading.

external customers
Dealers, who buy products to sell to others, and ultimate customers (or end users), who buy products for their own personal use.

internal customers
Individuals and units within the firm that receive services from other individuals or units.

TESTPREP

- How does enabling help achieve empowerment?
- What are the five steps in the control process?
- What's the difference between internal and external customers?

SUMMARY

LO 7–1 Describe the changes occurring today in the management function.

- **What does management look like today?**

At one time, managers were called bosses, and their job consisted of telling people what to do, watching over them to be sure they did it, and reprimanding those who didn't. Many, if not most, managers still behave that way. Today, however, some managers tend to be more progressive. For example, they emphasize teams and team building; they create drop-in centers, team spaces, and open work areas. They tend to guide, train, support, motivate, and coach employees rather than tell them what to do.

- **What reasons can you give to account for changes in management?**

Leaders of *Fortune* 100 companies today tend to be younger, more of them are female, and fewer of them were educated at elite universities. They know that many of their employees know more about technology and other practices than they do. Therefore, they tend to put more emphasis on motivation, teamwork, and cooperation. Managers in the future are likely to be assuming completely new roles in the firm. Further, they'll be doing more expansion in global markets.

LO 7–2 Describe the four functions of management.

- **What are the primary functions of management?**

The four primary functions are (1) planning, (2) organizing, (3) leading, and (4) controlling.

- **How do you define each of these functions?**

Planning includes anticipating trends and determining the best strategies and tactics to achieve organizational goals and objectives. Organizing includes designing the structure of the organization and creating conditions and systems in which everyone and everything works together to achieve the organization's goals and objectives. Leading means creating a vision for the organization, and communicating, guiding, training, coaching, and motivating others to achieve goals and objectives. Controlling means measuring whether what actually occurs meets the organization's goals.

LO 7–3   Relate the planning process and decision making to the accomplishment of company goals.

● **What's the difference between goals and objectives?**

Goals are broad, long-term achievements that organizations aim to accomplish, whereas objectives are specific, short-term plans made to help reach the goals.

● **What is a SWOT analysis?**

Managers look at the strengths and weaknesses of the firm and the opportunities and threats facing it.

● **What are the four types of planning, and how are they related to the organization's goals and objectives?**

Strategic planning is broad, long-range planning that outlines the goals of the organization. *Tactical planning* is specific, short-term planning that lists organizational objectives. *Operational planning* is part of tactical planning and sets specific timetables and standards. *Contingency planning* is developing an alternative set of plans in case the first set doesn't work out.

● **What are the steps involved in decision making?**

The six Ds of decision making are (1) define the situation; (2) describe and collect needed information; (3) develop alternatives; (4) decide which alternative is best; (5) do what is indicated (begin implementation); and (6) determine whether the decision was a good one, and follow up.

LO 7–4   Describe the organizing function of management.

● **What are the three levels of management in the corporate hierarchy?**

The three levels of management are (1) top management (highest level consisting of the president and other key company executives who develop strategic plans); (2) middle management (general managers, division managers, and plant managers who are responsible for tactical planning and controlling); and (3) supervisory management (first-line managers/supervisors who evaluate workers' daily performance).

● **What skills do managers need?**

Managers must have three categories of skills: (1) technical skills (ability to perform specific tasks such as selling products or developing software), (2) human relations skills (ability to communicate and motivate), and (3) conceptual skills (ability to see organizations as a whole and how all the parts fit together).

● **Are these skills equally important at all management levels?**

Managers at different levels need different skills. Top managers rely heavily on human relations and conceptual skills and rarely use technical skills, while first-line supervisors need strong technical and human relations skills but use conceptual skills less often. Middle managers need to have a balance of all three skills (see Figure 7.5).

LO 7–5   Explain the differences between leaders and managers, and describe the various leadership styles.

● **What's the difference between a manager and a leader?**

A manager plans, organizes, and controls functions within an organization. A leader has vision and inspires others to grasp that vision, establishes corporate values, emphasizes corporate ethics, and doesn't fear change.

● **Describe the various leadership styles.**

Figure 7.6 shows a continuum of leadership styles ranging from boss-centered to employee-centered leadership.

- **Which leadership style is best?**

  The most effective leadership style depends on the people being led and the situation. The challenge of the future will be to empower self-managed teams.

- **What does empowerment mean?**

  Empowerment means giving employees the authority and responsibility to respond quickly to customer requests. Enabling is giving workers the education and tools they need to assume their new decision-making powers.

- **What is knowledge management?**

  Knowledge management is finding the right information, keeping the information in a readily accessible place, and making the information known to everyone in the firm.

> **LO 7–6**   Summarize the five steps of the control function of management.

- **What are the five steps of the control function?**

  Controlling incorporates (1) setting clear standards, (2) monitoring and recording performance, (3) comparing performance with plans and standards, (4) communicating results and deviations to employees, and (5) providing positive feedback for a job well done and taking corrective action if necessary.

- **What qualities must standards possess to measure performance results?**

  Standards must be specific, attainable, and measurable.

KEY TERMS

autocratic leadership 183
brainstorming 179
conceptual skills 181
contingency planning 177
controlling 174
decision making 178
empowerment 185
enabling 185
external customers 187
free-rein leadership 184
goals 175
human relations
  skills 180

internal customers 187
knowledge
  management 185
leading 174
management 173
middle
  management 180
mission statement 175
objectives 175
operational planning 177
organizing 173
participative (democratic)
  leadership 183

planning 173
PMI 179
problem solving 179
staffing 182
strategic planning 175
supervisory
  management 180
SWOT analysis 175
tactical planning 177
technical skills 180
top management 179
transparency 183
vision 174

CRITICAL THINKING

Many students say they would like to be a manager someday. Here are some questions to get you started thinking like a manager:

1. Would you like to work for a large firm or a small business? Private or public company? In an office or out in the field? Give your reasons for each answer.

2. What kind of leader would you be? Do you have evidence to support your choice?

3. Do you see any problems with a participative (democratic) leadership style? Can you see a manager getting frustrated when he or she can't control others?

4. Can someone who's trained to give direction and orders (like a military sergeant) be retrained to be a participative leader? How? What problems may emerge?

PUTTING PRINCIPLES TO WORK

PURPOSE

To perform a simple SWOT analysis.

EXERCISE

Go to marketingteacher.com, locate the list of SWOT analysis examples, and click the link to go to the SWOT for Nike.

1. What are Nike's strengths, weaknesses, opportunities, and threats?

2. Analyze Nike's weaknesses. How do you think the company's strengths might be used to overcome some of its weaknesses?

3. Analyze Nike's opportunities and threats. What additional opportunities can you suggest? What additional threats can you identify?

DEVELOPING CAREER SKILLS

KEY: ● **Team** ★ **Analytic** ▲ **Communication** ▣ **Technology**

★▲ 1. Allocate time to do some career planning with a SWOT analysis of your present situation. Choose one career you are interested in and answer the following questions: What does the marketplace for your chosen career look like today? What skills do you have that will make you a winner in that type of career? What weaknesses might you target to correct? What are the threats to your career choice? What are the opportunities? Prepare a short presentation to the class.

●★▲ 2. Bring several decks of cards to class and have the class break up into teams of four or so members. Each team should then elect a leader. Each leader should be assigned a leadership style and learn how to perform that style: autocratic, participative (democratic), or free rein. Have each team try to build a house of cards by stacking them on top of each other. The team with the tallest house wins. Each team member should report his or her experience under the selected style of leadership.

★▲ 3. In class, discuss the advantages and disadvantages of becoming a manager. Does the size of the business make a difference? What are the advantages of a career in a profit-seeking business versus a career in a nonprofit organization?

★▲ 4. Review Figure 7.6 and discuss managers you have known, worked for, or read about who have practiced each management style. Students from other countries may have interesting experiences to add. Which managerial style did you like best? Why? Which was or were most effective? Why?

★▲ 5. Because of the illegal and unethical behavior of a few managers, managers are often under suspicion for being greedy and dishonest. Discuss the fairness of such charges, and suggest what could be done to improve the opinion of managers among the students in your class.

CAREER EXPLORATION

If you are interested in pursuing a career in management, here are a few to consider. Find out about the tasks performed, skills needed, pay, and opportunity outlook in these fields in the *Occupational Outlook Handbook (OOH)* at bls.gov.

- **Administrative services manager**—plans, directs, and coordinates supportive services of an organization; maintains facilities and supervises activities that include recordkeeping, mail distribution, and office upkeep.

- **Construction manager**—plans, coordinates, budgets, and supervises construction projects from start to finish.

- **Emergency management director**—prepares plans and procedures for responding to natural disasters or other emergencies.

- **Food service manager**—is responsible for the daily operation of restaurants and other establishments that prepare and serve food and beverages.

- **Computer and information technology (IT) manager**—plans, coordinates, and directs computer-related activities in an organization.

 **connect** | *Rosetta Stone: Leader in Language Learning* | **VIDEO CASE**

For nearly 30 years, Rosetta Stone has been one of the nation's most recognized and respected language learning companies. But as Rosetta Stone built a solid reputation over the years, its distribution system grew seriously outdated. The company continued to rely on CDs long after the rest of the world turned to the Internet to reach customers.

Rosetta Stone executives knew they needed a leader who could take the company into the 21st century. Fortunately, they hired Matt Hulett, a successful entrepreneur who later became famous as a turnaround expert. While working at an online entertainment start-up in the days before YouTube, Hulett discovered that many of his creative colleagues knew little about business and management. That's when he started to learn all he could about capital, strategy, and how to apply proper leadership direction. These skills made him the perfect person to become Rosetta Stone's new president of language.

As the leader of the company's consumer products division, Hulett must create a vision for the company and motivate employees to embrace that vision. He is also allowed to make changes if he feels it's in the company's best interest.

For instance, Hulett found that Rosetta Stone was not committing enough resources to the company's largest potential market—individual consumers. In order to shift focus, he employed a three-step process that helped him make big changes. In the first step, Hulett analyzed the company's intended market and decided how to optimize its position. He also found ways to inspire employees so that they would do their best to reach customers.

Second, Hulett studied the company to find out what was unique about it. He discovered that Rosetta Stone's brand was a key component to its success. Although customers loved and respected the company, they wanted modern innovations like subscription models, improved mobile capabilities, and personalization. Along with streamlining the mobile experience, Hulett also suggested using augmented reality to fit the product to the customer's personal needs.

His final step was people. Rather than bringing in new workers to the company, Hulett spent time with current employees and listened to their ideas for improving the product. This relationship building helped put the staff at ease and motivated them to work even harder. As a result, Rosetta Stone eventually built a product that worked just like their customers wanted. By implementing his three steps, Hulett was able to make Rosetta Stone speak everybody's language.

THINKING IT OVER

1. Did it surprise you that, until recently, a company would still be distributing content solely on CDs instead of online? Why do you think it took Rosetta Stone so long to move its language learning services online?

2. Why is it important for managers to keep their employees motivated and satisfied with their work?

3. Describe the process that Matt Hulett employed to turn around Rosetta Stone. Do you think a similar management strategy would work at other companies?

NOTES

1. Rick Wartzman and Kelly Tang, "Adapt and Thrive," *The Wall Street Journal,* March 30, 2020.

2. Victor Lipman, "Four Fundamental Qualities That Can Make You a Stronger Manager in 2019," *Forbes,* January 1, 2019; Chip Cutter, "How to Be a Boss 101," *The Wall Street Journal,* May 12, 2019; "6 Tips for Getting Your Team to Work Together," *Business News Daily,* businessnewsdaily.com, January 21, 2020.

3. Scott Mautz, "Google Tried to Prove Managers Don't Matter," *Inc.,* inc.com, June 17, 2019.

4. Sally Percy, "The Five Most Important Skills for Managers to Develop in 2019," *Forbes,* February 22, 2019; Lisa Lai, "Managing When the Future Is Unclear," *Harvard Business Review,* January 9, 2019; Bas Kohnke, "Five Soft Skills You Need to Be a Better Leader in 2020," *Fast Company,* July 22, 2019; Allana Akhtar and Caroline Hroncich, "20 Soft Skills Every Leader Needs to Be Successful," *Business Insider,* businessinsider.com, January 8, 2020.

5. Matthew Rothstein, "Whole Foods Discontinues Millennial Targeting 365 Brand," Bisnow, bisnow.com, January 16,

2019; Mike Pomranz, "Whole Foods Won't Open Any More '365' Stores," *Food & Wine,* January 14, 2019; Jessica Dumont, "Whole Foods Is Updating Its 365 Private Label Branding," *Grocery Dive,* grocerydive.com, accessed January 16, 2020.

6. Alyssa Gregory, "How to Conduct a SWOT Analysis for Your Small Business," *The Balance Small Business,* thebalancesmb.com, May 9, 2019; Mitchell Grant, "Strength, Weakness, Opportunity, and Threat (SWOT) Analysis," *Investopedia,* investopedia.com, October 19, 2019; Commerce Bank, "Tips for Setting Strong Strategic Goals," *Kansas City Business Journal,* bizjournals.com, January 15, 2020.

7. Fiona Simpson, "You're Invited: Taco Bell to Throw Hiring Parties Nationwide to Scale Recruitment Practices," *Forbes,* April 17, 2019; Danielle Wiener-Bronner, "How Tight Is the Job Market? Taco Bell Is Throwing Hiring Parties," *CNN Business,* cnn.com, accessed January 2020.

8. Steve Kovash, "Netflix Is Feeling the Pressure of the Streaming Wars," *CNBC,* cnbc.com, January 22, 2020; "How Netflix Is Changing the TV Industry," *Investopedia,* investopedia.com, January 15, 2020.

9. Andrew Beattie, "Steve Jobs and the Apple Story," *Investopedia,* investopedia.com, June 30, 2019; Ryan Robinson, "How Steve Jobs Learned to Embrace Failure and Saved Apple," *The Balance Small Business,* thebalancesmb.com, May 30, 2019.

10. Elena Lytkina Botelho and Sanja Koh, "Unexpected Companies Sometimes Produce the Best CEOs," *Harvard Business Review,* January 10, 2020.

11. Anya van Wagtendonk, "The Hidden World and Overlooked Problems of Acting in Video Games," *The Washington Post,* January 8, 2020.

12. Jeanne Sahadi, "The Hazards of Being CEO," *CNN Business,* cnn.com, January 3, 2020; Rachel Feintzeig, "Recession Rises on List of CEO's Fears for 2020," *The Wall Street Journal,* January 3, 2020; Marcel Schwantes, "5 CEOs Share 5 Leadership Tips for a Successful 2020," *Inc.,* January 21, 2020.

13. Joann S. Lublin, "Know-It-All Bosses Have a Lot to Learn," *The Wall Street Journal,* January 10, 2019; Allana Akhtar and Caroline Hroncich, "20 Soft Skills Every Leader Needs to Be Successful," *Business Insider,* businessinsider.com, January 8, 2020; Heather Backstrom, "Three Essential Coaching Skills for Managers," *Forbes,* January 3, 2020.

14. Eric Sherman, "Tesla Faces 'Serious Competition' from a Detroit Start-Up, according to Morgan Stanley," *Fortune,* February 11, 2019; Kevin J. Ryan, "7 Innovative Start-Ups to Watch in 2020," *Inc.,* January 6, 2020; Brett Derricott, "4 Startups to Keep an Eye on in 2020," *CFO,* cfo.com, January 7, 2020.

15. John Hall, "The Best Ways to Inspire Creativity within Your Team," *Forbes,* March 10, 2019; Jim Barnett, "Here's What Happens When Leaders Get Employee Motivation Right," *Forbes,* January 6, 2020.

16. "Boeing's New CEO Takes the Reins with Company Integrity in Doubt," *The Washington Post,* January 13, 2020; "New Boeing CEO Inherits Crisis Created under His Predecessor," Associated Press, January 13, 2020.

17. Hal Gregersen, "To Be a Better Leader, Ask Better Questions," *The Wall Street Journal,* May 14, 2019; Maynard Webb, "Four Tips for Becoming a Better Leader in 2020," *Fast Company,* January 1, 2020; James Friel, "7 Qualities of an Extraordinary Leader," *Entrepreneur,* January 3, 2020.

8

Structuring Organizations for Today's Challenges

LEARNING OBJECTIVES *After you have read and studied this chapter, you should be able to*

LO 8–1 Outline the basic principles of organizational management.

LO 8–2 Compare the organizational theories of Fayol and Weber.

LO 8–3 Evaluate the choices managers make in structuring organizations.

LO 8–4 Contrast the various organizational models.

LO 8–5 Identify the benefits of interfirm cooperation and coordination.

LO 8–6 Explain how organizational culture can help businesses adapt to change.

GETTING TO KNOW

Michele Buck, President and CEO of the Hershey Company

Think of the word *Hershey* and one thing probably comes to mind: chocolate. Since 1894 the Pennsylvania company has thrived on the sweet success of brands like Hershey's Kisses, Reese's Peanut Butter Cups, and many others. But while cocoa-based products have made Hershey into a $25 billion business, the U.S. chocolate market isn't growing like it used to. Despite an overall uptick in snacking, these days many Americans are choosing to reach for healthier options rather than sugary treats.

That's why president and CEO Michele Buck has made it a priority for Hershey to expand its offerings beyond candy. Since taking over the top job in 2017, she has overseen the acquisition of major snack brands like SkinnyPop and Pirate's Booty. Buck says that providing consumers with "better-for-you" brands like these will be essential for Hershey's growth in the future. "Consumers are now snacking more and more than ever before. On some occasions they're looking for treats, and other occasions they're looking for something a little more nutrient dense," said Buck. "As we look at all that's going on in the world around us—our job as leadership is to transform the company and capture that growth."

Buck grew up in Carlisle, Pennsylvania, just a 45-minute drive away from Hershey's headquarters and theme park. She credits her parents with teaching her the importance of hard work and resilience at a young age. "I grew up in a very humble family," said Buck. "My mother lived on a farm with no indoor plumbing. My father was the first in his family to graduate from high school and I learned very early the values and virtues of hard work." These principles served Buck well once she enrolled at Shippensburg University, a central Pennsylvania college where she earned her bachelor's degree. She then worked in government at the Pennsylvania Department of Revenue until she began to wonder what other career opportunities awaited her out in the world. So in the mid-1980s she left her home state and headed to graduate school at the University of North Carolina at Chapel Hill to study business.

After earning her MBA, Buck took the skills she learned from her years of education and applied them to her new job in the Frito-Lay marketing department. This initial experience with food brand management led to more opportunities at companies like Kraft and Nabisco. Throughout the 1990s she led operations on major brands such as Cool Whip, Life Savers, Jell-O, and many others. Her work eventually caught the attention of executives at Hershey who recruited Buck for the position of chief U.S. marketing officer in 2005. Along with overseeing an array of classic brands, she was also given the opportunity to utilize Hershey's research and development team to create new products. Her innovative ideas and collaborative spirit helped Buck climb up the corporate ladder to chief operating officer in 2016 and then president and chief executive officer the year after that.

Taking the top job at Hershey is certainly the most difficult challenge that Buck has faced so far in her career. With 80 percent of revenue currently coming from chocolate sales, she must increase the company's portfolio of non-candy products while also tending to the needs of its core brands. The acquisition of SkinnyPop and Pirate's Booty will help Hershey achieve this balance, but it still has a long way to go before it becomes the "innovative snacking powerhouse" that Buck envisions. "You have to put it all in perspective, things constantly change, and you have to constantly evolve and look at change as an opportunity, not a challenge, as an opportunity," said Buck.

This chapter is about changing and adapting organizations to today's markets, as Michele Buck is doing at Hershey. Most managers never face challenges that big, but there are plenty of opportunities in every firm to use the principles of organizing to manage—and benefit from—change.

Sources: David Gelles, "Hershey's C.E.O. Knows How to Get Americans to Indulge," *The New York Times*, October 10, 2019; Susie Gharib, "Hershey's CEO on Professional Growth and Women in Business," *Fortune*, January 3, 2018; Susie Gharib, "Hershey's CEO Looks to Acquisitions and Innovation to Transform the Company," *Fortune*, October 31, 2017; Lauren Hirsch, "After 124 Years, Hershey Tries to Be More Than Just a Chocolate Company (Again)," *CNBC*, April 24, 2018; "Hershey's Strategy for a Healthy-Snack World," *The Wall Street Journal*, October 2, 2018; Lauren Hirsch, "Not Just a Chocolate Company: Hershey Plots Its Future in Snacking," *CNBC*, April 24, 2018; Marty Swant, "Hershey Is Running Its First Super Bowl Ad in More Than a Decade with a Buy for Take5," *Forbes*, January 28, 2020; "Michele Gross Buck—Executive Profile," *Bloomberg*, bloomberg.com, accessed February 2020.

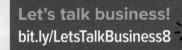

Let's talk business!
bit.ly/LetsTalkBusiness8

Richard Drew/AP Images

name that
company

LO 8-1	Outline the basic principles of organizational management.

Organizing for Success

You may be wondering why so many organizations fail. Adjusting to changing markets is a normal function in a capitalist economy. There will be big winners, like Amazon, Google, and Facebook, and big losers as well. The key to success is remaining flexible enough to adapt to the changing times. Often that means going back to basic organizational principles and rebuilding the firm on a sound foundation. This chapter begins by discussing such basic principles.

Building an Organization from the Bottom Up

The principles of organization apply to businesses of all sizes. Structuring the business, making an appropriate division of labor using job specialization and departmentalization, establishing procedures, and assigning authority are tasks found in most firms. How do these principles operate at your current or most recent job?

No matter the size of the business, the principles of organization are much the same. Let's say you and two friends plan to start a lawn-mowing business. One of the first steps is to organize your business. *Organizing,* or structuring, begins with determining what work needs to be done (mowing, edging, trimming) and then dividing up the tasks among the three of you; this is called a *division of labor.* One of you might have a special talent for trimming bushes, while another is better at mowing. The success of a firm often depends on management's ability to identify each worker's strengths and assign the right tasks to the right person. Many jobs can be done quickly and well when each person specializes. Dividing tasks into smaller jobs is called *job specialization.* For example, you might divide the mowing task into mowing, trimming, and raking.

If your business is successful, you'll probably hire more workers to help. You might organize them into teams or departments to do the various tasks. One team might mow while another uses blowers to clean up leaves and debris. If you're really successful over time, you might hire an accountant to keep records, various people to handle advertising, and a crew to maintain the equipment.

You can see how your business might evolve into a company with several departments: production (mowing and everything related to that), marketing, accounting, and maintenance. The process of setting up individual departments to do specialized tasks is called *departmentalization.* Finally, you'll assign authority and responsibility to people so that you can control the whole process. If something went wrong in the accounting department, for example, you would know who was responsible.

Structuring an organization, then, consists of devising a division of labor (sometimes resulting in specialization); setting up teams or departments to do specific tasks (like production and accounting); and assigning responsibility and authority to people. It also includes allocating

Huntstock/Getty Images

Imagine you have begun a successful lawn-mowing service in your neighborhood. Other lawn-mowing services in the area seem to hire untrained workers, many from other countries. They pay only the minimum wage or slightly more. Often they don't provide safety equipment. Workers don't have ear protection against the loud mowers and blowers. Most don't wear goggles when operating the shredder. Very few wear masks when spraying potentially harmful fertilizers.

You are aware there are many hazards connected with yard work, but safety gear can be expensive and workers often prefer to work without it. You are interested in making as much money as possible, but you also are concerned about the safety and welfare of your workers. You know yard maintenance equipment creates noise pollution, but quiet equipment is expensive.

The corporate culture you create as you begin your service will last a long time. If you emphasize

safety and environmental concern from the start, your workers will adopt your values. On the other hand, you can see the potential for making faster profits by ignoring safety rules and paying little attention to the environment as many of your competitors seem to do. Will you provide the safety equipment? What are the consequences of your decision?

resources (such as funds for various departments), assigning specific tasks, and establishing procedures for accomplishing the organizational objectives. From the start, you have to make ethical decisions about how you'll treat your workers and how you will benefit the community (see the Making Ethical Decisions box).

You may develop an *organization chart* (discussed later in this chapter) that shows relationships among people: who is accountable for the completion of specific work, and who reports to whom. Finally, you'll monitor the environment to see what competitors are doing and what customers are demanding. Then you must adjust to the new realities. For example, a major lawn care company may begin promoting itself in your area. You might have to make some organizational changes to offer even better service at competitive prices. What would you do first if you began losing business to competitors?

LO 8–2   Compare the organizational theories of Fayol and Weber.

The Changing Organization

Never before in the history of business has so much change been introduced so quickly. As we noted in earlier chapters, much change is due to the evolving business environment—more global competition, faster technological change, and pressure to preserve the natural environment.

Equally important to many businesses is the change in customer expectations. Consumers today expect high-quality products and fast, friendly service—at a reasonable cost. Doug Rauch, former president of Trader Joe's, views employees and customers as two wings of a bird: you need both of them to fly. They go together—if you take care of your employees, they'll take care of your customers. When your customers are happier and they enjoy shopping, it also makes your employees' lives happier, so it's a virtuous cycle.[1]

Managing change, then, has become a critical managerial function. That sometimes includes changing the whole organizational structure. For example, technology giant Google restructured its organization into a conglomerate called Alphabet.[2] Alphabet consists of independent units including Google (the search engine and related businesses such as Gmail and YouTube), Waymo (self-driving cars), Verily (health care and disease prevention), DeepMind (artificial intelligence), and several others. These smaller units have more flexibility to listen to customers and adapt accordingly. Such change may occur in nonprofit and government organizations as well as businesses.

Many organizations in the past were designed more to facilitate management than to please the customer. Companies designed many rules and regulations to give managers control over employees. As you'll learn later in this chapter, this reliance on rules is called *bureaucracy.* The government has to wrestle with bureaucracy just as businesses do.[3]

To understand where we are in organizational design, it helps to know where we've been. We'll look at that subject next.

The Development of Organizational Design

Until the 20th century, most businesses were rather small, the processes for producing goods were relatively simple, and organizing workers was fairly easy. Organizing workers is still not too hard in most small firms, such as a lawn-mowing service or a small shop that produces custom-made boats. Not until the 1900s and the introduction of *mass production* (methods for efficiently producing large quantities of goods) did production processes and business organization become so complex. Usually, the bigger the plant, the more efficient production became.

Business growth led to **economies of scale**. This term refers to the fact that companies can reduce their production costs by purchasing raw materials in bulk. Thus, the average cost of goods decreases as production levels rise. The cost of building a car, for example, declined sharply when automobile companies adopted mass production, and GM, Ford, and others introduced their huge factories. Over time, such innovations became less meaningful as other companies copied the processes.

During the era of mass production, organizational theorists emerged. Two influential thinkers were Henri Fayol and Max Weber. Many of their principles are still being used in businesses throughout the world. Let's explore these principles.

Fayol's Principles of Organization   In France, economic theoretician Henri Fayol published his book *Administration industrielle et générale* in 1919. It was popularized in the United States in 1949 under the title *General and Industrial Management.* Fayol introduced such principles as the following:

- *Unity of command.* Each worker is to report to one, and only one, boss. The benefits of this principle are obvious. What happens if two different bosses give you two different assignments? Which one should you follow? To prevent such confusion, each person should report to only one manager. (Later we'll discuss an organizational plan that seems to violate this principle.)

- *Hierarchy of authority.* All workers should know to whom they report. Managers should have the right to give orders and expect others to follow. (As we discussed in Chapter 7, this concept has changed over time, and empowerment is often more important now.)

- *Division of labor.* Functions are to be divided into areas of specialization such as production, marketing, and finance. (This principle too is being modified, as you'll read later, and cross-functional teamwork is getting more emphasis.)

- *Subordination of individual interests to the general interest.* Workers are to think of themselves as a coordinated team. The goals of the team are more important than the goals of individual workers. (This concept is still very much in use.) Have you heard this concept being applied to football and basketball teams? Did you see this principle at work in the latest Super Bowl?

  - *Authority.* Managers have the right to give orders and the power to enforce obedience. Authority and responsibility are related: Whenever authority is exercised, responsibility arises. (This principle is also being modified as managers empower employees.)

  - *Degree of centralization.* The amount of decision-making power vested in top management should vary by circumstances. In a small organization,

economies of scale

The situation in which companies can reduce their production costs if they can purchase raw materials in bulk; the average cost of goods goes down as production levels increase.

Henri Fayol introduced several management principles still followed today, including the idea that each worker should report to only one manager and that managers, in turn, should have the right to give orders for others to follow and the power to enforce them. Which of Fayol's principles have you observed?

Daniel Wren

it's possible to centralize all decision-making power in the top manager. In a larger organization, however, some decision-making power, for both major and minor issues, should be delegated to lower-level managers and employees.

- *Clear communication channels.* All workers should be able to reach others in the organization quickly and easily.
- *Order.* Materials and people should be placed and maintained in the proper location.
- *Equity.* A manager should treat employees and peers with respect and justice.
- *Esprit de corps.* A spirit of pride and loyalty should be created among people in the firm.

Management courses in colleges throughout the world taught Fayol's principles for years, and they became synonymous with the concept of management. Organizations were designed so that no person had more than one boss, lines of authority were clear, and everyone knew to whom to report. Naturally, these principles tended to be written down as rules, policies, and regulations as organizations grew larger.

That process of rule making has often led to rather rigid organizations that haven't always responded quickly to consumer requests. For example, in various cities, the Department of Motor Vehicles (DMV) and auto repair facilities have been slow to adapt to the needs of their customers. So where did the idea of *bureaucracy* come from? We talk about that next.

hierarchy
A system in which one person is at the top of the organization and there is a ranked or sequential ordering from the top down of managers who are responsible to that person.

Max Weber and Organizational Theory Max Weber's book *The Theory of Social and Economic Organizations,* like Fayol's, appeared in the United States in the late 1940s. Weber (pronounced Vay-ber), a German sociologist and economist, promoted the pyramid-shaped organizational structure that became popular in large firms. Weber put great trust in managers and felt the firm would do well if employees simply did what they were told. The less decision making they had to do, the better. Clearly, this is a reasonable way to operate if you're dealing with relatively uneducated and untrained workers. Such was generally the case at the time Weber was writing. Most employees today, however, have considerably more education and technical skills.

Weber's principles of organization resembled Fayol's. In addition, Weber emphasized:

- Job descriptions.
- Written rules, decision guidelines, and detailed records.
- Consistent procedures, regulations, and policies.
- Staffing and promotion based on qualifications.

Weber believed that large organizations demanded clearly established rules and guidelines to be followed precisely. In other words, he was in favor of *bureaucracy.* Although his principles made sense at the time, rules and procedures became so rigid in some companies that they grew counterproductive. Some organizations today still thrive on Weber's theories. United Parcel Service (UPS), for example, maintains strict written rules and decision guidelines. Those rules enable the firm to deliver packages quickly because employees don't have to pause to make decisions—procedures are clearly spelled out for them.[4]

Some organizations that follow Weber's principles are less effective than UPS because they don't allow employees to respond quickly to new challenges. Later, we explore how to make organizations more responsive. First, let's look at some basic terms and concepts.

Max Weber promoted an organizational structure composed of middle managers who implement the orders of top managers. He believed less-educated workers were best managed if supervisors gave them strict rules and regulations to follow and monitored their performance. What industries or businesses today would benefit by using such controls?

Turning Principles into Organizational Design

Following theories like Fayol's and Weber's, managers in the late 1900s began designing organizations so that managers could *control* workers. Many companies are still organized that way, with everything set up in a hierarchy. A **hierarchy** is a system in which one person is at the top of the organization and there is a ranked or sequential ordering from the top down of managers and others who are responsible to that person. Since one person can't keep track of thousands of workers, the top manager needs many lower-level managers to help.

Interfoto/Alamy Stock Photo

FIGURE 8.1 TYPICAL ORGANIZATION CHART
This is a rather standard chart with managers for major functions and supervisors reporting to the managers. Each supervisor manages three employees.

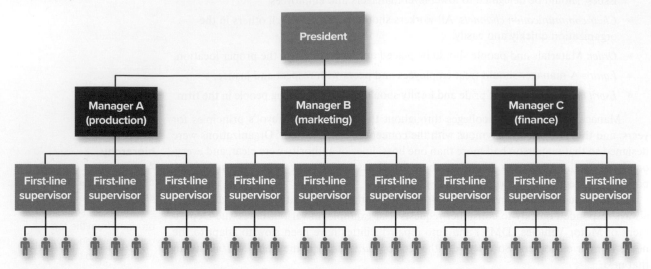

chain of command
The line of authority that moves from the top of a hierarchy to the lowest level.

organization chart
A visual device that shows relationships among people and divides the organization's work; it shows who is accountable for the completion of specific work and who reports to whom.

bureaucracy
An organization with many layers of managers who set rules and regulations and oversee all decisions.

The **chain of command** is the line of authority that moves from the top of the hierarchy to the lowest level. Figure 8.1 shows a typical hierarchy on an organization chart. An **organization chart** is a visual device that shows relationships among people and divides the organization's work; it shows who reports to whom.

Some organizations have a dozen or more layers of management between the chief executive officer (CEO) and the lowest-level employees. If employees want to introduce work changes, they ask a supervisor (the first level of management), who asks his or her manager, who asks a manager at the next level up, and so on. It can take weeks or months for a decision to be made and passed from manager to manager until it reaches employees. At pharmaceutical company Pfizer, for example, there were once 17 layers between the chief executive and the lowest employee.

Max Weber used the word *bureaucrat* to describe a middle manager whose function was to implement top management's orders. Thus, **bureaucracy** came to be the term for an organization with many layers of managers.

When employees in a bureaucracy of any size have to ask managers for permission to make a change, the process may take so long that customers become annoyed. Has this happened to you in a department store or other organization? Since customers want efficient service—and they want it *now*—slow service is simply not acceptable in today's competitive firms.

Some companies are therefore reorganizing to let employees make decisions in order to please customers no matter what.[5] Home Depot has adopted this approach to win more customers from competitors. Nordstrom employees can accept a return from a customer without managerial approval on a case-by-case basis.[6] As you read earlier in this book, giving employees such authority is called *empowerment*. Remember that empowerment works only when employees are given the proper training and resources to respond. Can you see how such training would help first responders in crisis conditions?

?TESTPREP

- What do the terms *division of labor* and *job specialization* mean?
- What are the principles of management outlined by Fayol?
- What did Weber add to the principles of Fayol?

> **LO 8–3** Evaluate the choices managers make in structuring organizations.

Decisions to Make in Structuring Organizations

When designing responsive organizations, firms have to make decisions about several organizational issues: (1) centralization versus decentralization, (2) span of control, (3) tall versus flat organizational structures, and (4) departmentalization.

Choosing Centralized or Decentralized Authority

Centralized authority occurs when decision making is concentrated at the top level of management. For example, Burger King has a globally centralized structure in which most major decisions are made by a core management team. While this organizational structure has the advantage of providing strong global control, it limits the flexibility to immediately respond to regional or local market changes and trends.

McDonald's believes that purchasing, promotion, and other such decisions are best handled centrally too. However, today's rapidly changing markets, added to global differences in consumer tastes, tend to favor some decentralization and thus more delegation of authority. McDonald's restaurants in Austria offer a Chili Donut, in France a Croque McDo (a hot ham-and-cheese sandwich), those in Japan sell rice, and Chinese McDonald's offer taro pie.[7]

Decentralized authority occurs when decision making is delegated to lower-level managers and employees more familiar with local conditions than headquarters management could be. This is particularly true in many large retail stores. Macy's customers in California, for example, demand clothing styles different from what customers in Minnesota or Maine like. It makes sense to delegate to store managers in their 680 stores in various cities the authority to buy, price, and promote merchandise appropriate for each area.[8] Both Home Depot and Lowe's are doing more to cater to local markets. Figure 8.2 lists some advantages and disadvantages of centralized and decentralized authority.

centralized authority
An organizational structure in which decision-making authority is maintained at the top level of management at the company's headquarters.

decentralized authority
An organizational structure in which decision-making authority is delegated to lower-level managers more familiar with local conditions than headquarters management could be.

Choosing the Appropriate Span of Control

Span of control describes the optimal number of employees a manager supervises or should supervise. What is the "right" span of control? At lower levels, where work is standardized, it's possible to implement a broad span of control (15 to 40 workers). For example, one supervisor can be responsible for 20 or more workers assembling computers or cleaning movie theaters. The appropriate span gradually narrows at higher levels of the organization, because work becomes less standardized and managers and workers need more face-to-face communication.

The trend today is to expand the span of control as organizations adopt empowerment, reduce the number of middle managers, and hire more talented and better educated

span of control
The optimum number of subordinates a manager supervises or should supervise.

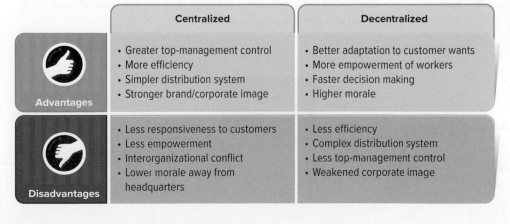

	Centralized	Decentralized
Advantages	• Greater top-management control • More efficiency • Simpler distribution system • Stronger brand/corporate image	• Better adaptation to customer wants • More empowerment of workers • Faster decision making • Higher morale
Disadvantages	• Less responsiveness to customers • Less empowerment • Interorganizational conflict • Lower morale away from headquarters	• Less efficiency • Complex distribution system • Less top-management control • Weakened corporate image

FIGURE 8.2
ADVANTAGES AND DISADVANTAGES OF CENTRALIZED VERSUS DECENTRALIZED AUTHORITY

Friso Gentsch/picture alliance/Getty Images

A broad span of control allows one supervisor to be responsible for many workers whose work tasks are predictable and standardized. In addition to assembly lines, can you think of other management situations that might benefit from a broad span of control? What about in a service industry?

tall organizational structure

An organizational structure in which the pyramidal organization chart would be quite tall because of the various levels of management.

flat organizational structure

An organizational structure that has few layers of management and a broad span of control.

departmentalization

The dividing of organizational functions into separate units.

lower-level employees. Information technology also allows managers to handle more information, so the span can be broader still.

Choosing between Tall and Flat Organizational Structures

In the early 20th century, organizations grew even bigger, adding layer after layer of management to create **tall organizational structures**. As noted earlier, some had as many as 17 levels, and the span of control was small (few people reported to each manager).

Imagine how a message might be distorted as it moved up the organization and back down through managers, management assistants, secretaries, assistant secretaries, supervisors, trainers, and so on. The cost of all these managers and support people was high, the paperwork they generated was enormous, and the inefficiencies in communication and decision making were often intolerable.

More recently, organizations have adopted **flat organizational structures** with fewer layers of management (see Figure 8.3) and a broad span of control (many people report to each manager). Flat structures can respond readily to customer demands because lower-level employees have authority and responsibility for making decisions, and managers can be spared some day-to-day tasks. In a bookstore with a flat organizational structure, employees may have authority to arrange shelves by category, process special orders for customers, and so on.

Large organizations use flat structures to try to match the friendliness of small firms, whose workers often know customers by name. The flatter organizations become, the broader their spans of control, which means some managers lose their jobs. Figure 8.4 lists advantages and disadvantages of narrow and broad spans of control.

Weighing the Advantages and Disadvantages of Departmentalization

Departmentalization divides organizations into separate units. The traditional way to departmentalize is by function—such as design, production, marketing, and accounting. Departmentalization groups workers according to their skills, expertise, or resource use so that they can specialize and work together more effectively. It may also save costs and thus improve efficiency. Other advantages include the following:

1. Employees can develop skills in depth and progress within a department as they master more skills.

2. The company can achieve economies of scale by centralizing all the resources it needs and locate various experts in that area.

3. Employees can coordinate work within the function, and top management can easily direct and control various departments' activities.

FIGURE 8.3 A FLAT ORGANIZATIONAL STRUCTURE

	Broad	Narrow
Advantages	• Reduced costs • More responsiveness to customers • Faster decision making • More empowerment	• More control by top management • More chances for advancement • Greater specialization • Closer supervision
Disadvantages	• Fewer chances for advancement • Overworked managers • Loss of control • Less management expertise	• Less empowerment • Higher costs • Delayed decision making • Less responsiveness to customers

FIGURE 8.4
ADVANTAGES AND DISADVANTAGES OF A NARROW VERSUS A BROAD SPAN OF CONTROL
The flatter the organization, the broader the span of control.

Disadvantages of departmentalization by function include the following:

1. Departments may not communicate well. For example, production may be so isolated from marketing that it does not get needed feedback from customers.

2. Employees may identify with their department's goals rather than the organization's. The purchasing department may find a good value somewhere and buy a huge volume of goods. That makes purchasing look good, but the high cost of storing the goods hurts overall profitability.

3. The company's response to external changes may be slow.

4. People may not be trained to take different managerial responsibilities; rather, they tend to become narrow specialists.

5. Department members may engage in groupthink (they think alike) and may need input from outside to become more creative.

Looking at Alternative Ways to Departmentalize Functional separation isn't always the most responsive form of organization. So what are the alternatives? Figure 8.5 shows five ways a firm can departmentalize. One way is by product. A book publisher might have a trade book department (for books sold to the general public), a textbook department,

Miguel Medina/AFP/Getty Images

After the leather for an upscale Celine handbag has been cut, it moves on to the sewing department where workers like this perform precise needlework before sending the bag on to have buckles and other features attached. What are the advantages and disadvantages of departmentalizing by processes like this?

FIGURE 8.5 WAYS TO DEPARTMENTALIZE
A publisher may want to departmentalize by product, a manufacturer by function, a pharmaceutical company by customer group, a computer company by geographic location, and a leather manufacturer by process. In each case the structure must fit the firm's goals.

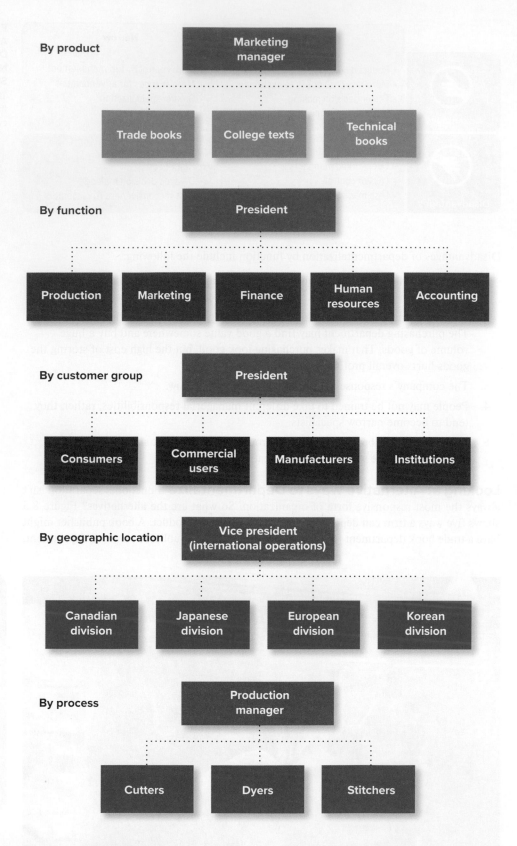

and a technical book department, each with separate development and marketing processes. Such product-focused departmentalization usually results in good customer relations.

Some organizations departmentalize by customer group. A pharmaceutical company might have one department for the consumer market, another that calls on hospitals (the institutional market), and another that targets doctors. You can see how customer groups can benefit from having specialists satisfying their needs.

Some firms group their units by geographic location because customers vary so greatly by region. Japan, Europe, and South America may deserve separate departments, with obvious benefits.

The decision about how to departmentalize depends on the nature of the product and the customers. A few firms find that it's most efficient to separate activities by process. For example, a firm that makes leather coats may have one department cut the leather, another dye it, and a third sew the coat together. Such specialization enables employees to do a better job because they can focus on learning a few critical skills.

Some firms use a combination of departmentalization techniques to create hybrid forms. For example, a company could departmentalize by function, geographic location, and customer groups.

?TEST**PREP**

- Why are organizations becoming flatter?
- What are some reasons for having a narrow span of control in an organization?
- What are the advantages and disadvantages of departmentalization?
- What are the various ways a firm can departmentalize?

LO 8–4   Contrast the various organizational models.

Organizational Models

Now that we've explored the basic choices in organizational design, let's look in depth at four ways to structure an organization: (1) line organizations, (2) line-and-staff organizations, (3) matrix-style organizations, and (4) cross-functional self-managed teams. You'll see that some of these models violate traditional management principles. The business community is in a period of transition, with some traditional organizational models giving way to new structures. Such transitions can be not only unsettling to employees and managers but also fraught with problems and errors.

Line Organizations

A **line organization** has direct two-way lines of responsibility, authority, and communication running from the top to the bottom of the organization, with everyone reporting to only one supervisor. Many small businesses are organized this way. For example, a locally owned pizza parlor might have a general manager and a shift manager. All the general employees report to the shift manager, and he or she reports to the general manager or owner.

A line organization does not have any specialists who provide managerial support. There is no legal department, accounting department, human resource department, or information technology (IT) department. Line organizations follow all of Fayol's traditional management rules. Line managers can issue orders, enforce discipline, and adjust the organization as conditions change.

In large businesses, a line organization may have the disadvantages of being too inflexible, of having few specialists or experts to advise people along the line, and of having lengthy lines of communication. Thus a line organization may be unable to handle complex decisions relating to thousands of products and tons of paperwork. Such organizations usually turn to a line-and-staff form of organization.

line organization
An organization that has direct two-way lines of responsibility, authority, and communication running from the top to the bottom of the organization, with all people reporting to only one supervisor.

Line-and-Staff Organizations

line personnel
Employees who are part of the chain of command that is responsible for achieving organizational goals.

staff personnel
Employees who advise and assist line personnel in meeting their goals.

iSeeit! Need help understanding line vs. staff employees? Visit your Connect eBook to view a video for a brief animated explanation.

To minimize the disadvantages of simple line organizations, many organizations today have both line and staff personnel. **Line personnel** are responsible for directly achieving organizational goals, and include production workers, distribution people, and marketing personnel. **Staff personnel** advise and assist line personnel in meeting their goals, and include those in marketing research, legal advising, information technology, and human resource management.

See Figure 8.6 for a diagram of a line-and-staff organization. One important difference between line and staff personnel is authority. Line personnel have formal authority to make policy decisions. Staff personnel have authority to advise line personnel and influence their decisions, but they can't make policy changes themselves. The line manager may seek or ignore the advice from staff personnel.

Many organizations benefit from expert staff advice on safety, legal issues, quality control, database management, motivation, and investing. Staff personnel strengthen the line positions and are like well-paid consultants on the organization's payroll.

Matrix-Style Organizations

Both line and line-and-staff organizational structures may suffer from inflexibility. Both allow for established lines of authority and communication and work well in organizations with stable environments and slow product development (such as firms selling household appliances). In such firms, clear lines of authority and relatively fixed organizational structures are assets that ensure efficient operations.

Today's economy, however, is dominated by high-growth industries like telecommunications, nanotechnology, robotics, biotechnology, and aerospace, where competition is stiff and the life cycle of new ideas is short. Emphasis is on product development, creativity, special projects, rapid communication, and interdepartmental teamwork. From those changes grew

FIGURE 8.6 A SAMPLE LINE-AND-STAFF ORGANIZATION

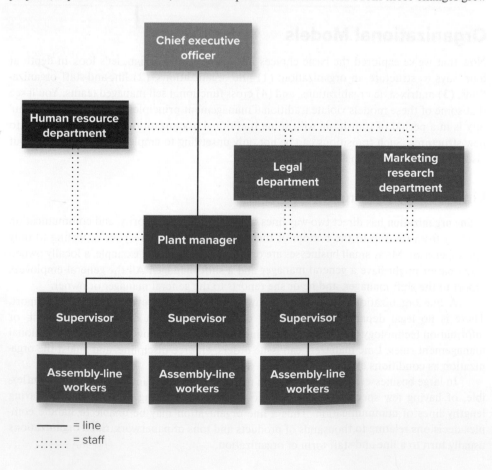

—— = line
······· = staff

FIGURE 8.7 A MATRIX ORGANIZATION
In a matrix organization, project managers are in charge of teams made up of members of several departments. In this case, project manager 2 supervises employees A, B, C, and D. These employees are accountable not only to project manager 2 but also to the head of their individual departments. For example, employee B, a marketing researcher, reports to project manager 2 and to the vice president of marketing.

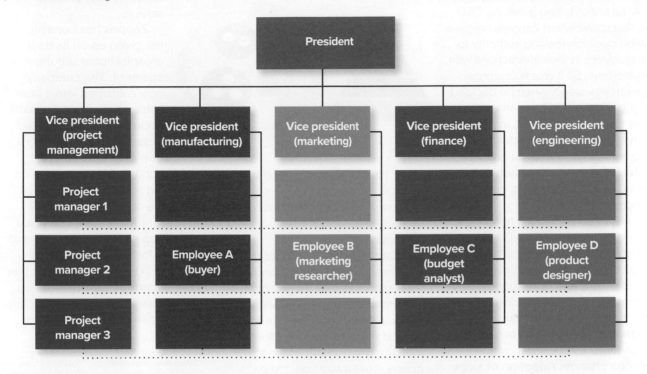

the popularity of the **matrix organization**, in which specialists from different parts of the organization work together temporarily on specific projects, but still remain part of a line-and-staff structure (see Figure 8.7). In other words, a project manager can borrow people from different departments to help design and market new-product ideas.

The matrix structure was developed in the aerospace industry and is now familiar in areas such as banking, management consulting firms, accounting firms, ad agencies, and school systems. Among its advantages:

- It gives managers flexibility in assigning people to projects.
- It encourages interorganizational cooperation and teamwork.
- It can produce creative solutions to product development problems.
- It makes efficient use of organizational resources.

As for disadvantages:

- It's costly and complex.
- It can confuse employees about where their loyalty belongs—with the project manager or with their functional unit.
- It requires good interpersonal skills as well as cooperative employees and managers to avoid communication problems.
- It may be only a temporary solution to a long-term problem.

If you're thinking that matrix organizations violate some traditional managerial principles, you're right. Normally a person can't work effectively for two bosses. Who has the real authority? Whose directive has first priority?

In reality, however, the system functions more effectively than you might imagine. To develop a new product, a project manager may be given temporary authority to "borrow" line personnel from production, marketing, and other line functions. The employees work

matrix organization
An organization in which specialists from different parts of the organization are brought together to work on specific projects but still remain part of a line-and-staff structure.

Unholy Holacracy!

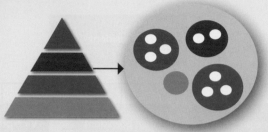

Tony Hsieh has never been bashful about taking a risk. As CEO of Amazon-owned Zappos, he gave wide decision-making authority to employees in their interactions with customers. So it was no surprise, seven years ago, when he decided to upend the traditional management system at Zappos. In lieu of a typical corporate structure with leadership at the top, he adopted a totally decentralized system that featured no job titles, no managers, and no hierarchy.

Hsieh envisioned a holacracy, a radical organizational shift in which authority and decision making were vested in circles of teams spread throughout the company. A circle is a group of "roles" working toward the same purpose that is formed or dissolved as the organization's needs change. Adoption of such a system can be disorienting even for employees who buy into the self-management concept. In fact,

when Hsieh first introduced the change, 18 percent of the company's employees chose to accept a buyout offer.

Zappos discovered that holacracy is a difficult concept to implement. The company, whose reputation was built on exceptional customer service, saw flaws and a lack of focus developing in its biggest market advantage. It was then the decision was made to quietly move away from the parts of holacracy that focused too much on internal issues and redirect employee efforts back to providing

extraordinary customer service.

Zappos has certainly not given up on its trust in organizational self-management. The company now is divided into a marketplace system where the circles act as small businesses that handle their own projects and profit and loss, rather than focusing on managing the inner workings of the whole company. The small businesses are also encouraged to develop new-product lines and services for consumers. While Zappos isn't a pure holacracy, it is still a decentralized organization that encourages entrepreneurship and a sense of self-sovereignty.

Sources: Aimee Groth, "Zappos Has Quietly Backed Away from Holacracy," Yahoo! Finance, finance.yahoo.com, January 29, 2020; Holacracy, holacracy.org, accessed February 2020; Heidi Lynne Kurter, "3 Simple Tips to Building an Untouchable Company Culture Like Zappos, *Forbes*, January 29, 2020.

together to complete the project and then return to their regular positions. Thus, no one actually reports to more than one manager at a time.

A potential real problem with matrix management, however, is that the project teams are not permanent. They form to solve a problem and then break up. There is little chance for cross-functional learning because teams often work together so briefly.

Cross-Functional Self-Managed Teams

cross-functional self-managed teams

Groups of employees from different departments who work together on a long-term basis.

One solution to the temporary nature of matrix teams is to establish *long-lived teams* and empower them to work closely with suppliers, customers, and others to quickly and efficiently bring out new, high-quality products while giving great service.

Cross-functional self-managed teams are groups of employees from different departments who work together on a long-term basis (as opposed to the temporary teams established in matrix-style organizations). *Self-managed* means that they are empowered to make decisions without management approval. The barriers among design, engineering, marketing, distribution, and other functions fall when interdepartmental teams are created. Sometimes the teams are interfirm; that is, the members come from two or more companies.

Cross-functional teams should be empowered and collaborative. They work best when leadership is shared. An engineer may lead the design of a new product, but a marketing expert may take the leadership position once it's ready for distribution. See the Adapting to Change box to learn about how online shoe retailer Zappos attempted to take self-management to a new level.

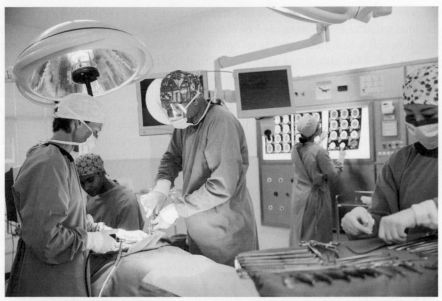

Caiaimage/Robert Daly/Getty Images

You can think of a team of medical specialists in an operating room as a cross-functional, self-managed team. Doctors, nurses, technicians, and anesthesiologists from different departments and areas in the hospital work together to complete successful operations. What kinds of tasks do cross-functional, self-managed teams complete in an office or retail environment?

Going beyond Organizational Boundaries

Cross-functional teams work best when the voice of the customer is brought in, especially in product development tasks. Suppliers and distributors should be on the team as well. A cross-functional team that includes customers, suppliers, and distributors goes beyond organizational boundaries. When suppliers and distributors are in other countries, cross-functional teams may share market information across national boundaries. Government coordinators may assist such projects, letting cross-functional teams break the barriers between government and business.

Cross-functional teams are only one way businesses can interact with other companies. Next we look at others.

TEST**PREP**

- What is the difference between line and staff personnel?
- What management principle does a matrix-style organization challenge?
- What is the main difference between a matrix-style organization's structure and the use of cross-functional teams?

LO 8–5 Identify the benefits of interfirm cooperation and coordination.

Managing the Interactions among Firms

Whether it involves customers, suppliers, distributors, or the government, **networking** uses communications technology and other means to link organizations and allow them to work together on common objectives. Let's explore this concept further.

Transparency and Virtual Organizations

Networked organizations are so closely linked online that each can find out what the others are doing in real time. **Real time** simply means the present moment or the actual time in which

networking
The process of establishing and maintaining contacts with key managers in one's own organization and other organizations and using those contacts to weave strong relationships that serve as informal development systems.

real time
The present moment or the actual time in which something takes place.

an event takes place. The Internet has allowed companies to send real-time data to organizational partners as it is developed or collected. The result is transparency (see Chapter 7), which occurs when a company is so open to other companies that electronic information is shared as if the companies were one. With this integration, two companies can work as closely as two departments in traditional firms.

Can you see the implications for organizational design? Most organizations are no longer self-sufficient or self-contained. Rather, they are part of a vast network of global businesses that work closely together. An organization chart showing what people do within any one organization is simply not complete, because the organization is part of a much larger system of firms. A modern chart would show people in different organizations and indicate how they are networked.

Networked organizational structures tend to be flexible. A company may work with a design expert from another company in Italy for a year and then not need that person anymore. It may hire an expert from a company in another country for the next project. Such a temporary network, made of replaceable firms that join and leave as needed, is a **virtual corporation** (see Figure 8.8). This is quite different from a traditional organizational structure; in fact, traditional managers sometimes have trouble adapting to the speed of change and the impermanence of relationships in networking.[9] We discuss adaptation to change below; first, we describe how organizations use benchmarking and outsourcing to manage their interactions with other firms.

Organizations historically tried to do all functions themselves. Each had its own department for accounting, finance, marketing, production, and so on. As we've noted, today's organizations look to other organizations for help in areas where they do not generate world-class quality.

Benchmarking compares an organization's practices, processes, and products against the world's best. As one example, K2 Skis is a company that makes skis, snowboards, in-line skates, and related products. It studied the compact-disc industry and learned to use ultraviolet inks to print graphics on skis. It went to the aerospace industry to get piezoelectric technology to reduce vibration in its snowboards (the aerospace industry uses the technology for wings on planes). It learned from the cable television industry how to braid layers of fiberglass and carbon and adapted that knowledge to make skis. As another example, CVS Health was cited as a leader in climate change after benchmarking government environmental policy and legislation, best practices of companies that shifted to renewable energy and sustainable packaging, and competitors that invested in low-carbon product innovation.[10]

virtual corporation

A temporary networked organization made up of replaceable firms that join and leave as needed.

benchmarking

Comparing an organization's practices, processes, and products against the world's best.

FIGURE 8.8 A VIRTUAL CORPORATION

A virtual corporation has no permanent ties to the firms that do its production, distribution, legal, and other work. Such firms are flexible enough to adapt to changes in the market quickly.

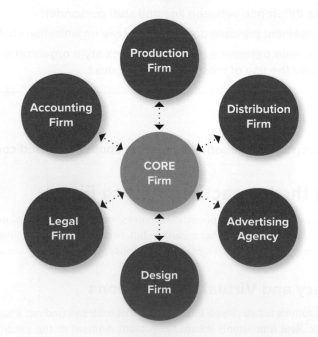

Benchmarking also has a more directly competitive purpose. In retailing, Target may compare itself to Walmart to see what, if anything, Walmart does better. Target will then try to improve its practices or processes to become even better than Walmart.[11] In the fast-food industry, competitors often research market leader Chick-fil-A on benchmarks such as order accuracy, food quality, and cleanliness.[12] Companies today are employing social media benchmarking to compare metrics such as posting times, follower counts and chats, and engagement level compared to key competitors.[13]

TanyaKim/Shutterstock

If an organization can't do as well as the best in, say, shipping, it will try to outsource the function to an organization like UPS or FedEx that specializes in shipping. Outsourcing, remember, means assigning one or more functions—such as accounting, production, security, maintenance, and legal work—to outside organizations. Even small firms are involved in outsourcing. We've already discussed some problems with outsourcing, especially when companies outsource to other countries. Some functions, such as information management and marketing, may be too important to assign to outside firms. In that case, the organization should benchmark the best firms and restructure its departments to try to be equally good. It is important to remember that companies in other countries often outsource their functions to companies in the United States. We call that *insourcing* and it is the source of many jobs.

When a firm has completed its outsourcing process, the remaining functions are its **core competencies**, those functions it can do as well as or better than any other organization in the world. For example, Nike is great at designing and marketing athletic shoes. Those are its core competencies. It outsources manufacturing, however, to other companies that assemble shoes better and less expensively than Nike can.[14]

> *Nike's core competencies are designing and marketing athletic shoes. The company outsources other functions (i.e., manufacturing) to other companies that assemble shoes better and cheaper than Nike could do on its own. What are the advantages of focusing on the company's core competencies? What are the disadvantages?*

core competencies
Those functions that the organization can do as well as or better than any other organization in the world.

LO 8-6   Explain how organizational culture can help businesses adapt to change.

Adapting to Change

Once you have formed an organization, you must be prepared to adapt the structure to changes in the market. That's not always easy to do. Over time, an organization can get stuck in its ways. Employees have a tendency to say, "That's the way we've always done things. If it isn't broken, don't fix it." Managers also get complacent. They may say they have 20 years' experience when in fact they've had one year's experience 20 times.

Introducing change is thus one of the hardest challenges facing any manager. Nonetheless, change is what's happening at General Motors (GM), Tesla, Amazon, Facebook, and other companies eager to become more competitive. If you have old facilities, products, or technology that are no longer efficient, you have to get rid of them. That's exactly what GM and other companies have done.[15]

The Internet created whole new opportunities, not only to sell to customers directly but also to ask them questions and provide them with any information they want. To win market share, companies must coordinate the efforts of their traditional departments and their information technology staff to create friendly, easy-to-manage interactions. Younger people today are called **digital natives** because they grew up with the Internet and cell phones; using high-tech devices is second nature to them. On the other hand, companies often need to retrain older employees to be more tech-savvy. While the ease and immediacy of communication created by technology may be powerful, being constantly connected to work does have its downsides (see the Adapting to Change box).

digital natives
Young people who have grown up using the Internet and social networking.

Companies that are the most successful in adapting to change have these common traits: (1) they listen to customers, (2) they have inspirational managers who drive new ideas throughout the organizations, and (3) they often have had a close call with going out of business.[16] Of course, adapting to change is difficult, but not changing can be disastrous.

My Time Is Your Time

In a very old song likely hummed by your great-grandparents, the late singer Rudy Vallee crooned "My time is your time." No one thought much of those lyrics then, but today many insist these words have become a motto for how many employees feel about their jobs. Since most of us are connected online 24/7, many employees find it difficult to be "off" work. Employees working from home (virtual workers) say they put in more work hours than they do in the office and work is more stressful. Finding a work–life balance is getting more and more difficult.

Many employers expect their workers to be available whenever they are needed. Workers fear if they are not available, it may convince their managers they are not fully committed to their jobs. For those employees disconnected from the job by working from home, over 60 percent say they feel pressured to respond

Andrey_Popov/Shutterstock

to work-related communication around the clock. Unfortunately, research indicates the more hours employees spend working outside of prescribed hours, the more likely they are to be stressed. This stress can negatively affect overall worker performance and job satisfaction.

It's important for managers to remember that technology can be an amazing tool that enables workers to work faster, smarter, and even easier. However, it can also tether employees 24/7 to their jobs. Other countries have passed "right to disconnect" laws

that stop employers from contacting workers by phone or e-mail once they've clocked out. To avoid stress and burnout, many U.S. managers and workers have taken it upon themselves to set boundaries to achieve a work–life balance. For example, those working remotely from home want flexibility in both when and where they work. Agreements have also been reached as to setting time requirements for e-mail messages and phone calls. Younger workers today value free time as much as traditional workplace benefits. Helping build a work–life balance can be the key to retaining them.

Sources: Valerie Bolden-Barrett, "Work-Life Balance Is Non-Existent for Corporate Professionals, Poll Says," *HR Dive*, hrdive.com, January 29, 2020; Gary Burnison, "Have Virtual Workers? Here's What to Tell Them," *CFO*, cfo.com, February 5, 2020; Sandra Hart, "The Differences between America's Working Culture and the Rest of the World," *The National Digest*, thenationaldigest.com, January 25, 2020.

Restructuring for Empowerment

restructuring
Redesigning an organization so that it can more effectively and efficiently serve its customers.

To empower employees, firms often must reorganize dramatically to make frontline workers their most important people. **Restructuring** is redesigning an organization so it can more effectively and efficiently serve its customers.

At one time, workers such as department store clerks and front-desk staff in hotels weren't considered key employees. Instead, managers had the responsibility of directing the work of the frontline people. This process often frustrated both managers and frontline workers who felt their contributions were not appreciated or considered valuable. The organization chart in a typical firm looked much like a pyramid.

inverted organization
An organization that has contact people at the top and the chief executive officer at the bottom of the organization chart.

As service-oriented organizations empowered frontline workers, the traditional organizational structure was literally turned upside down. An **inverted organization** has contact people (like nurses) at the top and top management at the bottom. Management layers are few, and the manager's job is to *assist and support* frontline people, not boss them around.[17] Figure 8.9 illustrates the difference between an inverted and a traditional organizational structure.

Companies based on this organizational structure support frontline personnel with internal and external databases, advanced communication systems, and professional assistance. Naturally, this means frontline people have to be better educated, better trained, and better paid than in the past. It takes a lot of trust for top managers to implement such a system—but when they do, the payoff in customer satisfaction and profits is often well worth the effort.

FIGURE 8.9 COMPARISON OF AN INVERTED ORGANIZATIONAL STRUCTURE AND A TRADITIONAL ORGANIZATIONAL STRUCTURE

In the past, managers also controlled information—and that gave them power and control. In more progressive organizations today, everyone shares information, often through an elaborate database system, and *among* firms as well as *within* them (for a more detailed explanation see Bonus Chapter B). No matter what organizational model you choose or how much you empower your employees, the secret to successful organizational change is to focus on customers and give them what they want.[18]

Creating a Change-Oriented Organizational Culture

Any organizational change is bound to cause some stress and resistance among members. Firms adapt best when their culture is already change-oriented. **Organizational (or corporate) culture** is the widely shared values within an organization that foster unity and cooperation to achieve common goals. Usually the culture of an organization is reflected in its stories, traditions, and myths.

Each McDonald's restaurant has the same feel, look, and atmosphere; in short, each has a similar organizational culture. It's obvious from visiting many McDonald's restaurants that the culture emphasizes quality, service, cleanliness, and value.

An organizational culture can also be negative. Have you ever been in an organization where you feel no one cares about service or quality? The clerks may seem uniformly glum, indifferent, and testy. Their mood pervades the atmosphere, and patrons become unhappy or upset. It may be hard to believe an organization, especially a profit-making one, can be run so badly and still survive. Clearly then, when you search for a job, study the organizational culture to see whether you will thrive in it.

Some of the best organizations have cultures that emphasize service to others, especially customers. The atmosphere reflects friendly, caring people who enjoy working together to provide a good product at a reasonable price. Companies that have such cultures have less need for close supervision of employees. That usually means fewer policy manuals; organization charts; and formal rules, procedures, and controls. The key to a productive culture is mutual trust. You get such trust by giving it. The very best companies stress high moral and ethical values such as honesty, reliability, fairness, environmental protection, and social involvement.[19]

We've been talking as if organizational matters were mostly controllable by management. In fact, the formal structure is just one element of the total organizational system, including its culture. The informal organization is of equal or even greater importance. Let's explore this notion next.

organizational (or corporate) culture
Widely shared values within an organization that provide unity and cooperation to achieve common goals.

The informal organization is the system that develops as employees meet and form relationships. The grapevine, the unofficial flow of information among employees, is the nerve center of the informal organization. How does the informal organization affect the work environment?

Sjale/Getty Images

Managing the Informal Organization

formal organization

The structure that details lines of responsibility, authority, and position; that is, the structure shown on organization charts.

informal organization

The system that develops spontaneously as employees meet and form cliques, relationships, and lines of authority outside the formal organization; that is, the human side of the organization that does not appear on any organization chart.

All organizations have two organizational systems. The **formal organization** details lines of responsibility, authority, and position. It's the structure shown on organization charts. The other system is the **informal organization**, the system that develops spontaneously as employees meet and form cliques, relationships, and lines of authority separate from the formal organization. It's the human side of the organization that doesn't show on any organization chart.

No organization can operate effectively without both types of organization. The formal system is often too slow and bureaucratic to let the organization adapt quickly, although it does provide helpful guides and lines of authority for routine situations.

The informal organization is often too unstructured and emotional to allow careful, reasoned decision making on critical matters. It's extremely effective, however, in generating creative solutions to short-term problems and creating camaraderie and teamwork among employees.

In any organization, it's wise to learn quickly who is important in the informal organization. Following formal rules and procedures can take days. Who in the organization knows how to obtain supplies immediately without the normal procedures? Which administrative assistants should you see if you want your work given first priority? Answers to these questions help people work effectively in many organizations.

The informal organization's nerve center is the *grapevine,* the system through which unofficial information flows between and among managers and employees. Key people in the grapevine usually have considerable influence.

In the old "us-versus-them" system of organizations, where managers and employees were often at odds, the informal system hindered effective management. In more open organizations, managers and employees work together to set objectives and design procedures. The informal organization is an invaluable managerial asset that can promote harmony among workers and establish the corporate culture.

As effective as the informal organization may be in creating group cooperation, it can still be equally powerful in resisting management directives. Employees may form unions, go on strike together, and generally disrupt operations. Learning to create the right corporate culture and work within the informal organization is thus a key to managerial success.

? TESTPREP

- What is an inverted organization?
- Why do organizations outsource functions?
- What is organizational culture?

SUMMARY

LO 8–1 Outline the basic principles of organizational management.

- **What is happening today to American businesses?**

  They are adjusting to changing markets. That is a normal function in a capitalist economy. There will be big winners, like Google and Facebook, and big losers as well. The key to success is remaining flexible and adapting to the changing times.

- **What are the principles of organizational management?**

  Structuring an organization means devising a division of labor (sometimes resulting in specialization), setting up teams or departments, and assigning responsibility and authority. It includes allocating resources (such as funds), assigning specific tasks, and establishing procedures for accomplishing the organizational objectives. Managers also have to make ethical decisions about how to treat workers.

LO 8–2 Compare the organizational theories of Fayol and Weber.

- **What were Fayol's basic principles?**

  Fayol introduced principles such as unity of command, hierarchy of authority, division of labor, subordination of individual interests to the general interest, authority, clear communication channels, order, and equity.

- **What principles did Weber add?**

  Weber added principles of bureaucracy such as job descriptions, written rules and decision guidelines, consistent procedures, and staffing and promotions based on qualifications.

LO 8–3 Evaluate the choices managers make in structuring organizations.

- **What are the four major choices in structuring organizations?**

  Choices to make in structuring and restructuring organizations cover (1) centralization versus decentralization, (2) breadth of span of control, (3) tall versus flat organizational structures, and (4) type of departmentalization.

- **What are the latest trends in structuring?**

  Departments are often replaced or supplemented by matrix organizations and cross-functional teams that decentralize authority. The span of control becomes larger as employees become self-directed. Another trend is to eliminate managers and flatten organizations.

LO 8–4 Contrast the various organizational models.

- **What are the two major organizational models?**

  Two traditional forms of organization are (1) line organizations and (2) line-and-staff organizations. A line organization has clearly defined responsibility and authority, is easy to understand, and provides each worker with only one supervisor. The expert advice of staff assistants in a line-and-staff organization helps in areas such as safety, quality control, computer technology, human resource management, and investing.

- **What are the key alternatives to the major organizational models?**

  Matrix organizations assign people to projects temporarily and encourage interorganizational cooperation and teamwork. Cross-functional self-managed teams have all the benefits of the matrix style and are long term.

LO 8–5 Identify the benefits of interfirm cooperation and coordination.

■ **What are the major concepts involved in interfirm communications?**

Networking uses communications technology and other means to link organizations and allow them to work together on common objectives.

A virtual corporation is a networked organization of replaceable firms that join and leave as needed. Benchmarking tells firms how their performance measures up to that of their competitors in specific functions. The company may then *outsource* to companies that perform its weaker functions more effectively and efficiently. The functions that are left are the firm's *core competencies.*

■ **What is an inverted organization?**

An inverted organization places employees at the top of the hierarchy; managers are at the bottom to train and assist employees.

LO 8–6 Explain how organizational culture can help businesses adapt to change.

■ **What is organizational culture?**

Organizational (or corporate) culture consists of the widely shared values within an organization that foster unity and cooperation to achieve common goals.

■ **What is the difference between the formal and informal organization of a firm?**

The formal organization details lines of responsibility, authority, and position. It's the structure shown on organization charts. The informal organization is the system that develops spontaneously as employees meet and form cliques, relationships, and lines of authority outside the formal organization. It's the human side of the organization. The informal organization is an invaluable managerial asset that often promotes harmony among workers and establishes the corporate culture. As effective as the informal organization may be in creating group cooperation, it can still be equally powerful in resisting management directives.

KEY TERMS

benchmarking 210
bureaucracy 200
centralized authority 201
chain of command 200
core competencies 211
cross-functional self-managed teams 208
decentralized authority 201
departmentalization 202
digital natives 211

economies of scale 198
flat organizational structure 202
formal organization 214
hierarchy 199
informal organization 214
inverted organization 212
line organization 205
line personnel 206
matrix organization 207

networking 209
organizational (or corporate) culture 213
organization chart 200
real time 209
restructuring 212
span of control 201
staff personnel 206
tall organizational structure 202
virtual corporation 210

CRITICAL THINKING

Now that you have learned some of the basic principles of organization, pause and think about where you have already applied such concepts yourself or when you have been part of an organization that did.

1. Did you find a division of labor necessary and helpful?
2. Were you assigned specific tasks or left on your own to decide what to do?
3. Were promotions based strictly on qualifications, as Weber suggested? What other factors may have been considered?
4. What problems seem to emerge when an organization gets larger?
5. What organizational changes might you recommend to the auto companies? The airline industry? Technology firms? Fast-food restaurants?

PURPOSE

To construct a simple organization chart.

EXERCISE

An organization chart maps the relationships among people working in an organization and illustrates who reports to whom. Go to smartdraw.com. Use the site's drawing tools to create an organization chart for a company with the following employees:

1. CEO who is in charge of the entire company.

2. Marketing director, production director, and chief financial officer (CFO) who report directly to the CEO.

3. The marketing director oversees four marketing managers, the production manager directs three frontline managers, and the CFO directs three supervisors.

4. Each manager/supervisor oversees multiple workers. For simplicity, include only three workers under each manager/supervisor on your chart.

PUTTING PRINCIPLES TO WORK

KEY: ● **Team** ★ **Analytic** ▲ **Communication** **Technology**

DEVELOPING CAREER SKILLS

1. There is no better way to understand the effects of having many layers of management on communication accuracy than the game of Message Relay. Choose seven or more members of the class and have them leave the classroom. Then choose one person to read the following paragraph and another student to listen. Call in one of the students from outside and have the "listener" tell him or her what information was in the paragraph. Then bring in another student and have the new listener repeat the information to him or her. Continue the process with all those who left the room. Do not allow anyone in the class to offer corrections as each listener becomes the storyteller in turn. In this way, all the students can hear how the facts become distorted over time. The distortions and mistakes are often quite humorous, but they are not so funny in organizations such as Ford, which once had 22 layers of management.

   Here's the paragraph:

   Dealers in the midwestern region have received over 130 complaints about steering on the new Commander and Roadhandler models of our minivans. Apparently, the front suspension system is weak and the ball joints are wearing too fast. This causes slippage in the linkage and results in oversteering. Mr. Berenstein has been notified, but so far only 213 of 4,300 dealers have received repair kits.

2. Describe some informal groups within an organization with which you are familiar at school or work. What have you noticed about how those groups help or hinder progress in the organization? ★

3. Imagine you are working for Kitchen Magic, an appliance manufacturer that produces dishwashers. A competitor introduces a new dishwasher that uses sound waves not only to clean even the worst burned-on food but also to sterilize dishes and silverware. You need to develop a similar offering fast, or your company will lose market share. Write an e-mail to management outlining the problem and explaining your rationale for recommending use of a cross-functional team to respond quickly. ▲

4. Divide the class into teams of five. Each team should imagine your firm, a producer of athletic shoes, has been asked to join a virtual network. How might you minimize the potential problems of joining? Begin by defining a virtual corporation and listing its advantages and disadvantages. Each team should report its solutions to the class.

● ★ ▲   5. A growing number of work groups, including management, are cross-functional and self-managed. To practice working in such an organization, break into groups of five or so students, preferably with different backgrounds and interests. Each group must work together to prepare a report on the advantages and disadvantages of working in teams. Many of the problems and advantages of cross-functional, self-managed teams should emerge in your group as you try to complete this assignment. Each group should report to the class how it handled the problems and benefited from the advantages.

CAREER EXPLORATION

If you are interested in pursuing a major in organizational strategy and management, here are a few careers to consider. Find out about the tasks performed, skills needed, pay, and opportunity outlook in these fields in the *Occupational Outlook Handbook (OOH)* at bls.gov.

- **Top executive**—works in nearly every industry in both large and small businesses and nonprofit organizations, ranging from companies in which

there is only one employee to firms with thousands of employees.

- **Management analyst**—proposes ways to improve an organization's efficiency.
- **Change management consultant**—specializes in measuring the impact of change in an organization and applying strategies to implement changes within the organization.

VIDEO CASE *Freshii's Winning Organization*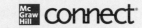

Freshii has been described as the "new generation of quick-service dining." The company was founded in 2005 by 23-year-old Matthew Corrin and has expanded to over 300 locations worldwide. Today, it is the fastest-growing restaurant franchise in the world and receives over 4,000 franchise applications every year. Freshii specializes in fresh, healthy, customizable food options such as burritos, wraps, soups, salads, and frozen yogurt. As a rapidly expanding company with locations around the world, it has a growing operation to watch over and a very specific mission to uphold: to change the way the world eats by making fresh food convenient and affordable.

To achieve its goals, Freshii needed to establish an organizational structure that supports the mission of the company and clarifies the role of each organizational member. There are different types of organizational structures. It's very important that a company select the specific type of organizational structure that fits the objectives and culture of the particular company. To meet its goals, Freshii adopted a flat organizational structure.

Company founder Matthew Corrin's dream was to make it easier for people to eat healthier and live better lives. With this goal in mind, he felt it was essential to team up with like-minded franchisees and members of his administrative team that shared his objectives. By using a flat structure, the company removes excess layers of management that can often slow or completely stall important communication and decisions. At Freshii, all employees (even interns) are considered company partners and stakeholders in the company. The firm's lean corporate team is empowered to execute on all elements

of their area of expertise and make a significant impact on business operations.

The flat organizational structure works very well with the corporate culture at Freshii. Its motivated, like-minded workforce lives by the company core value of "Talk Is Cheap. Execution Sets You Apart." At Freshii, team members are encouraged and empowered to step up and excel in their jobs and see their suggestions move forward from initial idea to full implementation. Corporate staff members are not restricted by a formal organization chart or title. Team members work together at standing desks in a shared space where personal interaction flows easily among every level and department within the company. The corporate team also practices what its corporate mission preaches about fitness and health by holding companywide competitions where team members display the healthy lifestyle they promote.

Freshii leadership has encouraged its franchisees to embrace the same culture and employee structure used at the corporate headquarters in their own stores. The franchise stores have responded by maintaining lean and efficient operations with employees on board that share the company's core values. The headquarters staff stays in continuous communication with the franchisees by sharing corporate ideas with them as well as listening and implementing suggestions proposed by franchisees. It's safe to conclude that a flat and lean organizational structure was appropriate, and has worked well for Freshii.

Today, Freshii continues to expand into new markets around the world. Despite that challenge going forward, it's managed to keep what's unique about its organizational culture and pure about its mission: helping people eat healthier and live better lives.

THINKING IT OVER

1. Organizations like Freshii follow some of the principles of Henri Fayol, such as the *esprit de corps*. What is *esprit de corps* and how is it developed at Freshii?

2. Is the decision making at Freshii centralized or decentralized? What does that mean for the company's operations?

3. Do you think the corporate culture at Freshii is somewhat resistant to change or accepting of change? Why?

NOTES

1. Ann Smarty, "3 Ways to Build a Happier Team," *Small Business Trends,* smallbiztrends.com, January 3, 2019; Daria Leshchenko, "Four Strategies for Working with Difficult Customers," *Forbes,* February 26, 2019; "A Better Customer Experience in the Feedback Economy," *Forbes,* January 23, 2020; Shep Hyken, "Transform the Customer Experience," *Forbes,* January 19, 2020.

2. Rakesh Sharma, "Why Google Became Alphabet," *Investopedia,* investopedia.com, accessed January 2020.

3. "The Organization of the Bureaucracy," *US History,* ushistory.org, accessed February 2020.

4. Liz Gold, "Advantages & Disadvantages of Bureaucratic Organizational Structure," *BizFluent,* bizfluent.com, January 22, 2019; Brooke Sutherland, "FedEx, UPS, and Amazon Dodge a Holiday Logistical Nightmare," *Bloomberg Business,* bloomberg.com, January 13, 2020.

5. Phil Geldart, "How to Empower Your Employees to Be More Customer-Centric," *Entrepreneur,* January 18, 2020; "Workforce Engagement as Business Strategy," *IndustryWeek,* industryweek.com, accessed February 2020.

6. Rich Duprey, "Nordstrom Local Now Accepts Returns from Kohl's and Macy's," *The Motley Fool,* fool.com, September 12, 2019; Rachel Tashjian, "Can Nordstrom Become Your Next Grail Destination?," *GQ,* gq.com, January 29, 2020.

7. McDonald's, mcdonalds.com, accessed February 2020.

8. Macy's Inc., macysinc.com, accessed February 2020.

9. Susan Ward, "A Definition of Virtual Business," *The Balance,* thebalance.com, August 1, 2019; "Virtual Company," *PC Magazine,* pcmag.com, accessed February 2020.

10. "Climate Change Policy Statement," CVS Health, cvshealth.com, accessed February 2020.

11. Will Healy, "How Target Compares to Its 3 Main Rivals," *The Motley Fool,* fool.com, January 24, 2020; Sara Castellanos, "Target CIO Helped It Find Its Tech Groove," *The Wall Street Journal,* January 22, 2020.

12. "What We Can All Learn from Chick-fil-A," Reddit, reddit.com, accessed February 2020; Aine Cain, "McDonald's Franchisees Say in a Survey That Chick-fil-A Is the Biggest Chain Holding Them Back from Winning the Chicken Category," *Business Insider,* businessinsider.com, January 23, 2020.

13. "Know What's Working on Social Media: 27 Paid and Free Social Media Analytics Tools," Buffer, buffer.com, accessed February 2020.

14. "Michelle Seidel, "How Are Nike Shoes Produced?," *BizFluent,* bizfluent.com, accessed February 2020.

15. Kalea Hall, "GM Picks Lordstown Site for $2.3 Billion Battery Plant," *Detroit News,* January 14, 2020; Andrew J. Hawkins, "GM Will Spend $2.2 Billion to Build Electric and Autonomous Vehicles at Detroit Plant," *The Verge,* theverge.com, January 27, 2020.

16. Dave Roos, "Ten Companies That Reinvented Themselves," *Money,* money.howstuffworks.com, accessed February 2020.

17. Scott Gaddis, "Flip the Leadership Pyramid, and Reap Organizational Rewards," *IndustryWeek,* June 25, 2019; Rob Markey, "Are You Undervaluing Your Customers?," *Harvard Business Review,* January–February 2020.

18. Jeremy Korst and Kimberly Whitler, "Why the Best Tech Firms Keep Customers Front-of-Mind," *Harvard Business Review,* January 10, 2020; Michael Hinshaw, "14 Ways to Enable Digital Customer Experience Transformation," *Forbes,* January 7, 2020.

19. Gregg Ward, "Organizational Culture in the Age of Burnout: What Every Leader Should Know," *Forbes,* January 16, 2020; Dorie Clark, "Navigating a New Job with a Very Difficult Culture," *Harvard Business Review,* January 15, 2020; Greg Kihlstrom, "How Do You Measure Company Culture?," *Forbes,* January 10, 2020.

9

Production and Operations Management

LEARNING OBJECTIVES »

After you have read and studied this chapter, you should be able to

LO 9–1 Describe the current state of U.S. manufacturing and what manufacturers have done to become more competitive.

LO 9–2 Describe the evolution from production to operations management.

LO 9–3 Identify various production processes, and describe techniques that improve productivity, including computer-aided design and manufacturing, flexible manufacturing, lean manufacturing, mass customization, robotics, and 3D printing.

LO 9–4 Describe operations management planning issues including facility location, facility layout, materials requirement planning, purchasing, just-in-time inventory control, and quality control.

LO 9–5 Explain the use of PERT and Gantt charts to control manufacturing processes.

Shahid Khan, CEO of Flex-N-Gate

At just 16 years old, Shahid Khan moved to Champaign, Illinois, ready to live the American Dream. However, the young Pakistani immigrant quickly lost his confidence when he discovered an enormous blizzard had hit his new midwestern home. To make matters worse, the dorms at the University of Illinois hadn't opened yet, forcing Khan to pay $3 for a room and a meal at the local YMCA. With precious little money to his name, he began to worry about how he would survive the next four years at college.

But his fears disappeared the next morning when he discovered a notice for a dishwashing job in the YMCA kitchen. With a starting salary of $1.20 per hour, Khan was shocked that he could recoup his losses from the previous night so quickly. "It's like, wow," said Khan. "If you put the $1.20 per hour in terms of Pakistan, you're making more than 99 percent of the people over there. I'm breathing oxygen for the first time."

Khan channeled this enthusiasm into his work both at school and beyond. After graduating with a degree in engineering, he took a job overseeing production for a local aftermarket auto parts business named Flex-N-Gate. At first Khan couldn't believe the inefficient manufacturing methods the company used to make its bumpers. In some instances, employees welded as many as 15 different parts together to make one bumper. Employing his engineering expertise, Khan gradually refined the process to make it less complicated. His hard work paid off in the form of a revolutionary new product: a bumper stamped from a single piece of steel that managed to slim down the rear end of a truck.

After seven years in the aftermarket business, though, Kahn realized that the value-focused industry didn't provide much room for innovation. If he wanted his product to succeed, he knew he had to sell directly to automakers. So in 1978 Khan started his own company armed with little more than a PO box and a small-business loan. Within two years he earned enough money to buy Flex-N-Gate from his old boss, giving him additional revenue streams as well as an established brand name. While business boomed at first, sales eventually ground to a halt when Khan's biggest client, General Motors, gave his bumper design to its large-scale suppliers.

Other entrepreneurs would have reacted with anger to such a slight, but Khan kept on the bright side. "It really was the right thing for them," said Khan. "We had no business going from making 200 bumpers a day to making 40,000." Plus, his dealings with GM put him in contact with executives at Isuzu, one of Japan's biggest auto companies. So Khan traveled to Japan in the early 1980s in a last-ditch effort to win clients. His timing couldn't have been better. Japanese car companies had been preparing to enter the American market but required more domestic suppliers to fuel their growth. Khan fit this need perfectly thanks to his manufacturing experience and his game-changing bumper design. Soon Flex-N-Gate was manufacturing parts for Toyota, Isuzu, and Mazda. As these brands grew into some of the biggest names on the American market, Khan's company grew right along with them. By 2011, two-thirds of cars and trucks sold in America used Flex-N-Gate parts. And since Khan is the sole shareholder, all profits from the company's sales go to him. He's now worth about $7 billion.

In 2012 he used some of that immense wealth to purchase the Jacksonville Jaguars, fulfilling a personal dream to own an NFL franchise. Although the Jaguars haven't exactly been Super Bowl contenders in recent years, Khan is confident that someday the team will become another one of his comeback stories.

By setting Flex-N-Gate on the path to productivity, Shahid Khan made a fortune while creating thousands of jobs. It has also earned him great respect in the auto industry. In this chapter you'll learn about how other company leaders thrive and survive in the production and operations sector. You'll also find out why the United States is generally moving from a production-based economy to a service economy.

Sources: Jerry Brewer, "Jaguars Owner Shahid Khan Proves to Be the Exception in More Ways Than One among NFL Owners," *The Washington Post*, January 12, 2018; "Shahid Khan," *Forbes*, forbes.com, accessed February 2020; Brian Solomon, "Shahid Khan: The New Face of the NFL and the American Dream," *Forbes*, forbes.com, September 5, 2012; Amy Lamare, "The Incredible Rags-to-Riches Story of Billionaire Jacksonville Jaguars Owner Shahid Khan," *Celebrity Net Worth*, celebritynetworth.com, accessed January 2020; "Shahid Khan—Owner," Jaguars, jaguars.com, accessed February 2020.

Let's talk business!
bit.ly/LetsTalkBusiness9

name that **company**

LOCATING A FACILITY IS A BIG DECISION. This company conducted an extensive search for a second North American headquarters that entailed $5 billion in construction and 50,000 high-tech jobs. Cities across the country began a high-stakes competition to land the facility. Name that company. (Find the answer in the chapter.)

LO 9–1 Describe the current state of U.S. manufacturing and what manufacturers have done to become more competitive.

Manufacturing and Services in Perspective

Let's begin with a brief look back at manufacturing in the United States several decades ago. In 1953 American industry reached its postwar peak as factories employed about 30 percent of the workforce.[1] By 1979, nearly 20 million people worked in manufacturing.[2] Since then, however, the number of Americans employed by factories has steadily dropped year after year. Approximately 12.82 million people worked in manufacturing in 2019.[3] However, that same year the value of products made in the United States reached a record high. In other words, there's never been a more productive time for American manufacturing than the present.[4]

So how has output been able to increase while the number of factory workers continues to fall? Thanks to advancements in technology and automation, American factories can operate efficiently without large amounts of human labor. Whereas robots have been performing manufacturing tasks for decades, past models were so big and dangerous that people could rarely be in the same room with them.[5] Now many factory employees work side by side with robots that can learn from and collaborate with their human colleagues.[6]

These advancements have drastically changed the types of jobs available at today's factories. In the past, workers needed little more than a high school diploma to land a well-paying job on an assembly line. As automation increased, though, robots began performing these repetitive tasks. For some perspective on this shift to automated labor: In 1980 factories needed 25 people to produce $1 million worth of manufacturing output. Today, it takes only 6 people.[7] Employees in these positions, however, must have advanced skills in order to be hired and succeed. So rather than relying on low-skill assembly-line workers, modern factories depend on engineers and software developers to operate their cutting-edge equipment and technology.[8]

Due to these changes, American industry will likely never employ as many people as it did in the 1950s. Today's economy overwhelmingly depends on services rather than manufacturing. More than 70 percent of U.S. GDP is consumer spending and about 80 percent of jobs are now in the service sector.[9] This includes professions like lawyers, doctors, and teachers as well as business services like accounting, finance, and management consulting. Manufacturers today must compete with companies in lucrative fields such as technology development when recruiting top talent. In fact, many American factories have struggled to fill positions as engineers and computer experts

Unlike their colossal predecessors, many modern factory robots can safely work side by side with humans. Do you think that manufacturing could someday be driven entirely by automated labor?

Kinwun/Getty Images

Will Bats, Bombs, and Regulations Stall Tesla's German Production Venture?

tesla.com

Elon Musk, CEO of Tesla, was dancing on the factory floor when his company pulled off what many thought was an impossible feat—opening up a new auto plant in China in less than a year and a half. Building a car plant in such time is unheard of in production circles. But Musk has no thought of basking in the limelight—his next mission is building a new car plant in Germany in a comparable time frame to the one that opened in Shanghai. The expansion in Germany would affirm Tesla as an established global automaker and put the company on the path to producing 1 million vehicles a year.

Unfortunately, during the initial phase of construction at the German site, seven unexploded bombs from World War II were unearthed, which caused an unexpected stall in the plant's production. Each of the explosives weighed 110 pounds. The company was told that finding unexploded devices in Germany was not uncommon. Estimates are

Anton Violin/Alamy Stock Photo

that 300,000 tons of unexploded devices are scattered throughout the country. The company was told that defusing the explosives would not slow down production significantly.

However, Tesla's plans were again derailed by a unique speed trap that was not remotely anticipated. The company was informed that a colony of bats on their land had to be removed before they could even break ground on the new project. The colonies of the winged mammals occupy a 382-acre patch of pine forest that is protected under German

environmental law. Tesla must relocate the bats and clear the woods within just a few months, because the felling of trees must stop before birds and other animals come to nest in the spring. If Tesla misses the deadline, it could delay production of the plant by several months. The company has promised to both relocate the bats and plant a new tree elsewhere for every tree that is removed. Gruenheide mayor Arne Christiani insists that these are rules everyone must meet. Tesla is no exception. What the company accomplished in China will be difficult to duplicate in Germany.

Sources: Stefan Nicola, "Tesla's German Plant Faces Deadline over Breeding Wildlife," *Bloomberg,* January 20, 2020; Martin Lerma, "Tesla Discovered 7 Bombs from WWII at the Site of Its New German Factory," Yahoo! Lifestyle, yahoo.com, accessed February 2020; "Tesla's German Factory Gets off to an Explosive Start," *Reuters Technology News,* January 23, 2020; William Boston and Tom Higgins, "Tesla Sees Hurdles at German Factory," *The Wall Street Journal,* January 21, 2020.

migrated to the tech industry.[10] Global expansion has been even more difficult in many instances. The Reaching beyond Our Borders box looks at how American manufacturer Tesla has experienced multiple problems in its attempt to build an auto plant in Germany.

Manufacturers and Service Organizations Become More Competitive

Although American industry is more productive than ever, it faces increased competition from all over the world. U.S. producers must compete with China and Germany's mighty manufacturing firms as well as expanding enterprises in South Korea, Vietnam, and India.[11] Many foreign manufacturers depend on U.S. technology and concepts to increase effectiveness and efficiency. But plenty of innovation happens overseas as well, meaning that American manufacturers must keep up with the latest production techniques no matter where they are developed.

Service providers will also need to step up their game as the sector becomes increasingly crowded. However, improving the efficiency of services isn't as easy it sounds. After all, would you choose a hair stylist just because he or she can give you the quickest haircut possible? Instead, companies in the service sector must focus on providing customers with quality care and attention. They also need to maintain close relationships with their suppliers and other companies in order to satisfy customer needs. Finally, like their counterparts in manufacturing, service providers must continuously improve if they want to maintain their competitive edge.

This chapter explores these and other operations management techniques in both the service and manufacturing sectors. We'll begin by going over a few key terms.

LO 9–2   Describe the evolution from production to operations management.

From Production to Operations Management

production

The creation of finished goods and services using the factors of production: land, labor, capital, entrepreneurship, and knowledge.

production management

The term used to describe all the activities managers do to help their firms create goods.

operations management

A specialized area in management that converts or transforms resources (including human resources) into goods and services.

Production is the creation of finished goods and services using the factors of production: land, labor, capital, entrepreneurship, and knowledge (see Chapter 1). Production has historically meant *manufacturing,* and the term **production management** has described the activities that helped firms create *goods.* (As we discussed in the previous section, though, in recent decades the U.S. economy has been largely driven by services rather than manufacturing.)

Operations management is a term that is used in both manufacturing and service organizations. **Operations management** is a specialized area in management that converts or transforms resources, including human resources like technical skills and innovation, into goods and services. It includes inventory management, quality control, production scheduling, follow-up services, and more. In automobile plants such as Tesla or Ford, operations management transforms raw materials, human resources, parts, supplies, paints, tools, and other resources into automobiles. It does this through the processes of fabrication and assembly.

In a service-based setting like a college or university, operations management takes inputs—such as information, professors, supplies, buildings, offices, and computer labs and systems—and creates services that transform students into educated people. It does this through processes like teaching and explanation.

Some organizations—such as factories, farms, and mines—produce mostly goods. Others—such as hospitals, schools, and government agencies—produce mostly services. Some produce a combination of goods and services. For example, an automobile manufacturer not only makes cars but also provides services such as repairs, financing, and insurance. At Wendy's you get goods such as hamburgers and fries, but you also get services such as order taking, order filling, food preparation, and cleanup.

Operations Management in the Service Sector

Operations management in the service industry is all about creating a good experience for those who use the service. In a Hilton hotel, for example, operations management includes smooth-running elevators, fine restaurants, comfortable beds, and a front desk that processes people quickly. It may also include fresh-cut flowers in lobbies and dishes of fruit in every room.

Along with these classic amenities, Hilton must also stay innovative so it can cater to the ever-changing needs of its guests. Most business travelers today expect in-room WiFi as well as updated work centers that provide all the resources of a modern office. Hilton provides these services and also develops new features that often become standard in their hotels. One example is keyless room entry. Rather than give guests a keycard they can easily lose, Hilton created a system that allows guests to use their smartphone to enter their room. Robots today are increasingly commonplace in hotels and other businesses. Hilton introduced a project called Connie, a two-foot-tall front-desk robot that can answer guests' basic questions such as dining recommendations and directions.[12]

Service businesses have also tripled the use of artificial intelligence (AI) in the last three years. For example, Hilton

Companies are constantly discovering new ways of automating that eliminate the need for human labor. This robo-waiter delivers plates of pasta in the first restaurant in Italy to use automated servers. Which would you rather have your food served by: a human or a robot?

Stefano Mazzola/Shutterstock

Thomas Barwick/Getty Images

uses an AI-backed interview platform in its recruiting process, and Domino's uses an AI tool to supervise pizza makers in Australia and New Zealand. Management consulting firm McKinsey & Company estimates by 2030, 70 percent of businesses will be using some type of AI.[13]

In short, pleasing customers by anticipating their needs has become the quality standard for companies like Hilton and Domino's as it has for other service businesses. But knowing customer needs and satisfying them are two different things. Operations management acts as a bridge between these concepts, allowing companies to turn their ideas into actual goods and services. Next we'll explore production processes and what companies are doing to keep the United States competitive in that area.

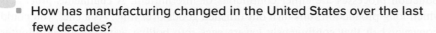

?TESTPREP

- How has manufacturing changed in the United States over the last few decades?
- What must American companies do to remain competitive?
- How does operations management differ between the manufacturing and service sectors?

LO 9–3 Identify various production processes, and describe techniques that improve productivity, including computer-aided design and manufacturing, flexible manufacturing, lean manufacturing, mass customization, robotics, and 3D printing.

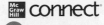

iSeeit! Need help understanding the transformation process for goods and services? Visit your Connect eBook to view a video for a brief animated explanation.

Production Processes

Common sense and some experience have already taught you a lot about production processes. For instance, you know what it takes to write a term paper or prepare a dinner. You need money to buy the materials, you need a place to work, and you need to be organized to get the task done. The same is true of the production process in industry. It uses basic inputs to produce outputs (see Figure 9.1). Production adds value, or utility, to materials or processes.

FIGURE 9.1 THE PRODUCTION PROCESS
The production process consists of taking the factors of production (land, etc.) and using those inputs to produce goods, services, and ideas. Planning, routing, scheduling, and the other activities are the means to accomplish the objective—output.

INPUTS	PRODUCTION CONTROL	OUTPUTS
Land	Planning	Goods
Labor	Routing	Services
Capital	Scheduling	Ideas
Entrepreneurship	Dispatching	
Knowledge	Follow-up	

form utility
The value producers add to materials in the creation of finished goods and services.

process manufacturing
That part of the production process that physically or chemically changes materials.

Bakers add form utility to materials by transforming basic ingredients like milk, flour, and sugar into special customized cakes. Can you see how the production of such cakes involves both process manufacturing and assembly processes?

Pat Canova/Alamy Stock Photo

Form utility is the value producers add to materials in the creation of finished goods and services, such as by transforming silicon into computer chips or putting services together to create a vacation package. Form utility can exist at the retail level as well. For example, a butcher can produce a specific cut of beef from a whole cow, or a baker can make a specific type of cake from basic ingredients. We'll be discussing utility in more detail in Chapter 15.

Manufacturers use several different processes to produce goods. Andrew S. Grove, the late former CEO and chair of computer chip manufacturer Intel, used this analogy to explain production:

> *Imagine that you're a chef . . . and that your task is to serve a breakfast consisting of a three-minute soft-boiled egg, buttered toast, and coffee. Your job is to prepare and deliver the three items simultaneously, each of them fresh and hot.*[14]

Grove says this task encompasses the three basic requirements of production: (1) to build and deliver products in response to the demands of the customer at a scheduled delivery time, (2) to provide an acceptable quality level, and (3) to provide everything at the lowest possible cost.

Let's use the breakfast example to understand process and assembly. **Process manufacturing** physically or chemically changes materials. For example, boiling physically changes an egg. Similarly, process manufacturing turns sand into glass or computer chips. The **assembly process** puts together components (eggs, toast, and coffee) to make a product (breakfast). Cars are made through an assembly process that puts together the frame, engine, and other parts.

Production processes are either continuous or intermittent. A **continuous process** is one in which long production runs turn out finished goods over time. As a chef, you could have a conveyor belt that continuously lowers eggs into boiling water for three minutes and then lifts them out. A three-minute egg would be available whenever you wanted one. A chemical plant and steel mill, for example, are run on a continuous process.

It usually makes more sense when responding to specific customer orders to use an **intermittent process**. Here the production run is short (one or two eggs) and the producer adjusts machines frequently to make different products (like the oven in a bakery or the toaster in a diner). Manufacturers of custom-designed furniture would use an intermittent process.

Today many manufacturers use intermittent processes. Computers, robots, and flexible manufacturing processes allow firms to turn out custom-made goods almost as fast as mass-produced goods were once produced. We'll discuss how they do that in more detail in the next few sections as we explore advanced production techniques and technology.

The Need to Improve Production Techniques and Cut Costs

The ultimate goal of operations management is to provide high-quality goods and services instantaneously in response to customer demand.

As we stress throughout this book, traditional organizations were simply not designed to be so responsive to the customer. Rather, they were designed to make goods efficiently (inexpensively). The idea behind mass production was to make a large number of a limited variety of products at very low cost.

Over the years, low cost often came at the expense of quality and flexibility. Furthermore, suppliers didn't always deliver when they said they would, so manufacturers had to carry large inventories of raw materials and components to keep producing. Such inefficiencies made U.S. companies vulnerable to foreign competitors who were using more advanced production techniques and less expensive labor.

As a result of new global competition, companies have had to make a wide variety of high-quality custom-designed products at low cost. Clearly, something had to change on the production floor to make that possible. Several major developments have made U.S. companies more competitive: (1) computer-aided design and manufacturing, (2) flexible manufacturing, (3) lean manufacturing, (4) mass customization, (5) robotics, and (6) 3D printing.

Computer-Aided Design and Manufacturing

One development that has changed production techniques is the use of computers to design products. Called **computer-aided design (CAD)**, businesses ranging from construction companies to carmakers to video game designers depend on 3D modeling software to create new products.[15]

The next step was to bring computers directly into the production process with **computer-aided manufacturing (CAM)**. CAD/CAM, the use of both computer-aided design and computer-aided manufacturing, makes it possible to custom-design products to meet the needs of small markets with very little increase in cost. A manufacturer programs the computer to make a simple design change, and that change is readily incorporated into production. In the clothing industry, a computer program establishes a pattern and cuts the cloth automatically, even adjusting to a specific person's dimensions to create custom-cut clothing at little additional cost.

In food service, CAM supports on-site, small-scale, semiautomated, sensor-controlled baking in fresh-baked cookie shops to make consistent quality easy to achieve. 3D printers are among the latest CAM technology. With 3D printing, a product is made layer by layer until it appears, almost by magic, as a finished good.

CAD can greatly improve productivity for businesses. In the past CAD machines couldn't talk to CAM machines directly. Today, however, software programs unite CAD and CAM: The result is **computer-integrated manufacturing (CIM)**. When companies use CIM, computers control the entire production process. The software is expensive, but it can drastically reduce the time needed to program machines to increase production.

Flexible Manufacturing

Flexible manufacturing means designing machines to do multiple tasks so they can produce a variety of products. Allen-Bradley uses flexible manufacturing to build motor starters. Orders come in daily, and within 24 hours the company's machines and robots manufacture, test, and package the starters—which are untouched by human hands. Allen-Bradley's machines are so flexible that managers can include a special order, even a single item, in the assembly without slowing down the process. Toyota uses flexible manufacturing at one of its newer factories where capacity can be increased or decreased without affecting production costs. If the company needs to change capacity, it can be done in a weekend.[16]

assembly process
The part of the production process that puts together components.

continuous process
A production process in which long production runs turn out finished goods over time.

intermittent process
A production process in which the production run is short and the machines are changed frequently to make different products.

computer-aided design (CAD)
The use of computers in the design of products.

computer-aided manufacturing (CAM)
The use of computers in the manufacturing of products.

computer-integrated manufacturing (CIM)
The uniting of computer-aided design with computer-aided manufacturing.

flexible manufacturing
Designing machines to do multiple tasks so that they can produce a variety of products.

3D CAD tools allow these designers to create high-tech, double-layered face mask prototypes without constantly sewing and trying on potential new models. What advantages might this technology offer to smaller manufacturing companies?

Emanuele Cremaschi/Getty Images

lean manufacturing
The production of goods using less of everything compared to mass production.

Lean Manufacturing

Lean manufacturing is the production of goods using less of everything than in mass production: less human effort, less manufacturing space, less investment in tools, and less engineering time to develop a new product. A company becomes lean by continuously increasing its capacity to produce high-quality goods while decreasing its need for resources.

Technological improvements are largely responsible for the increase in productivity and efficiency of U.S. plants. That technology made labor more productive but also presented other challenges. After all, employees can get frustrated by innovations (e.g., they must learn new processes), and companies must constantly train and retrain employees to stay competitive. One way companies stay competitive is by making products that are more individualistic. The next section discusses how that happens.

Mass Customization

mass customization
Tailoring products to meet the needs of a large number of individual customers.

To *customize* means to make a unique product or provide a specific service to specific individuals.[17] Although it once may have seemed impossible, **mass customization**, which means tailoring products to meet the needs of a large number of individual customers, is now practiced widely. The National Bicycle Industrial Company in Japan made 18 bicycle models in more than 2 million combinations, each designed to fit the needs of a specific customer. A popular trend today involves foldable bikes made to customer specifics. Brompton is the industry standard for folding bikes. It takes various measurements from the buyer and sends the data to the factory, where robots handle the bulk of the assembly.[18]

More and more companies are learning to customize their products. The fashion start-up Proper Cloth uses software called Smart Sizes to custom-design shirts for online shoppers.[19] Nature Made Vitamins creates customized vitamin packs to suit individual needs. For those with more of a sweet tooth, you can even buy custom-made M&M's in colors of your choice.[20]

Mass customization exists in the service sector as well. Some insurance companies use the latest computer software and hardware to sell customized risk-management plans to companies. Vanguard offers personalized retirement plans to fit each individual's wants and needs. Health clubs offer unique fitness programs for individuals, travel agencies provide vacation packages that vary according to individual choices, and some colleges allow students to design their own majors. It is much easier to custom-design service programs than to custom-make goods, because there is no fixed tangible good to adapt. Each customer can specify what he or she wants, within the limits of the service organization—limits that seem to be ever-widening.

Robotics

Industrial robotics can work 24 hours a day, seven days a week with great precision. Mass customization is no problem for them. (At least, no one has heard them complain.) Robots have completely changed manufacturing by improving productivity while also reducing the number of jobs available to humans.[21] Along with assembly-line jobs in factories, robots have begun to take over in service businesses as well. It's very possible that in the near future robots will be pervasive in airports handling tasks such as check-in, security, and concierge services.[22] Even Wall Street financial analysts have had to start competing for jobs with AI-enabled robots (see Chapter 19).[23] In other words, in many cases, robots are slowly but surely either helping people perform better or replacing them completely. Robotic technology will likely take over productivity, but humans will continue to produce value by thinking and acting creatively.[24] The Adapting to Change box looks at what is happening right now as the use of robots grows in the workplace.

3D printing isn't just for prototypes. This 85-foot concrete bridge in Shanghai was printed in several stages and then connected together, providing both an affordable and safe crossing option for pedestrians. Can you think of any other structures that could be 3D printed?

Imagine China/Newscom

3D Printing

One of the most exciting production processes to emerge in recent years has been 3D printing. During this advanced procedure, also

Meet Your New Workmate: R2D2

Ringo Chiu/ZUMA Wire/Alamy Stock Photo

Workers have long complained about boring, repetitive tasks they are expected to perform as part of their jobs. Cheer up! Help is on the way. Robots excel at straightforward, repetitive tasks that tend to be mundane and boring for humans. This increasingly sophisticated generation of robots is capable of completing a wide range of tasks, including data entry and jobs that require little or no interaction with human beings. They don't excel in situations that are unpredictable or require emotional intelligence.

The food industry has been a prime candidate for using robots to improve efficiencies. Walmart, for example, is experimenting using a backroom robotic system for gathering groceries that are bagged for later consumer pickup or delivery. At CaliBurger, a fast-food burger joint, a robot appropriately named "Flippy" is flipping burgers and frying fries at

its restaurants around the country as well as baseball's Dodger Stadium. The company estimates "Flippy" flips up to 2,000 burgers a day at its locations. Caffeine seekers at Cafe X in San Francisco and San Jose are served coffee prepared by the company's robot barista.

Health care has also made the move to robots. Laser eye surgery is now almost completely performed using robotic technology under the direction of a doctor. Johns Hopkins and other medical centers use robotic-assisted technology to give doctors better control and more precise vision in treating diseases such as kidney disorders and prostate cancer.

Do robotic advances mean the end of flesh-and-blood workers is near? Hardly! As the ability of robots to do specific tasks increases, workers will be able to expand their use and interact positively with them. Today, workers and robots are working alongside each other in both business and social situations. For example, Charmin introduced a new bathroom aide called RollBot that can be summoned with your phone to deliver a fresh roll of toilet paper when needed.

Sources: Nicholas Upton, "Can a Robot Rule the Restaurant? Cali Group Says Yes," *Franchise Times,* January 23, 2020; Megan Cerello, "Robots: Now Coming to a Workplace Near You," *CBS News,* January 9, 2020; Sarah Nassauer, "Robots Help with Walmart's Groceries," *The Wall Street Journal,* January 9, 2020; Alicia Kelso, "'We're Stepping on the Gas': Miso Robotics Unveils a Restaurant Prototype That's Cheaper Than Flippy," *Forbes,* January 28, 2020.

known as additive manufacturing, a product is created one layer at a time by a nozzle similar to those found in inkjet printers. 3D printing has grown rapidly over the past five years driven by rapid technological developments. Expectations are that 3D printing could grow to a market reaching \$35 billion by 2024.[25] Most companies use 3D printing to create prototype models or molds for other industrial projects due to their significantly reduced costs. But experts claim that it won't be long until 3D printing revolutionizes the production of all sorts of items.[26] In fact, 3D printing firm Carbon3D has already contracted with Adidas to make rubberlike midsoles for athletic shoes and with sports-gear firm Riddell to make customized helmet padding for football players. The world's first 3D-printed concrete bridge was installed in a park near Madrid, Spain.[27]

Using Sensing, Measurement, and Process Control

Most advanced manufacturing techniques are driven by computers working with vast amounts of data. Such data controls sensors that measure humidity, global positioning trackers (that fix location), or calipers that measure a material's thickness. Products can be tracked from the beginning of production to the point of delivery. The moment anything goes wrong, a sensor can detect it immediately and notify someone to make the needed changes.[28] Companies are also using nanomanufacturing. A nanometer is one billionth of a meter, so nanomanufacturing means being able to manipulate materials on a molecular or even atomic scale.[29]

?TESTPREP

- What is form utility?
- Define and differentiate the following: *process manufacturing, assembly process, continuous process,* and *intermittent process.*
- What do you call the integration of CAD and CAM?
- What is mass customization?

LO 9–4 Describe operations management planning issues including facility location, facility layout, materials requirement planning, purchasing, just-in-time inventory control, and quality control.

Operations Management Planning

facility location
The process of selecting a geographic location for a company's operations.

Operations management planning helps solve many of the problems in the service and manufacturing sectors. These include facility location, facility layout, materials requirement planning, purchasing, inventory control, and quality control. The resources used may be different, but the management issues are similar.

Facility Location

Facility location is a major decision for manufacturers and other companies. The decision involves taking into account the availability of qualified workers; access to transportation, suppliers, and customers; and local regulations including zoning and taxes. How has the growth of commerce on the Internet affected company location decisions?

Facility location is the process of selecting a geographic location for a company's operations. In keeping with the need to focus on customers, one strategy is to find a site that makes it easy for consumers to use the company's services and to communicate about their needs. Flower shops and banks have placed facilities in supermarkets so that their products and services are more accessible than in freestanding facilities. Starbucks has also set up operations in supermarkets and Target stores. You can find a McDonald's inside some Walmart stores or even in gas stations.

Of course, the ultimate convenience is never having to leave home to get something. That's why services like online banking and online shopping have become so popular. E-commerce uses Facebook and other social media to make transactions even easier. For brick-and-mortar retailers to beat such competition, they have to choose good locations and offer outstanding service. Study the location of service-sector businesses—such as hotels, banks, health clubs, hospitals, and supermarkets—and you'll see that the most successful are conveniently located. Facility location selection can be a detailed process. Amazon conducted an extensive search for a second North America headquarters that entailed $5 billion of construction and employment of 50,000 high-tech workers. Cities across the country began a high-stakes competition to land the online retailer for their community. The company finally settled on Crystal City in Arlington, Virginia.[30]

Facility Location for Manufacturers

Geographic shifts in production sometimes result in pockets of unemployment in some geographic areas and tremendous growth in others. For instance, the decline of auto manufacturing caused the economy of Detroit to decline for many years. At the same time, the rise of the tech industry turned Silicon Valley into one of the wealthiest places in the world.

B Brown/Shutterstock

Why would companies spend millions of dollars to move their facilities from one location to another? They consider labor costs; availability of resources, including labor; access to transportation that can reduce time to market; proximity to suppliers; proximity to customers; crime rates; quality of life for employees; cost of living; and the need to train or retrain the local workforce.

Even though labor is becoming a smaller percentage of total cost in highly automated industries, availability of low-cost labor or the right kind of skilled labor remained a key reason many producers moved their plants to Malaysia, China, India, Mexico, Vietnam, and other countries. In general, U.S. manufacturing firms tend to pay more and offer more benefits than firms elsewhere in the world.

Inexpensive resources are another major reason for moving production facilities. Companies usually need water, electricity, wood, coal, and other basic resources. By moving to areas where these items are inexpensive and plentiful, firms can significantly lower not only the cost of buying such resources but also the cost of shipping finished products. Often the most important resource is people, so companies tend to cluster where smart and talented people are, such as Silicon Valley.

Time to market is another decision-making factor. As manufacturers attempt to compete globally, they need sites that allow products to move quickly, at the lowest costs, so they can be delivered to customers fast. Access to highways, rail lines, waterways, and airports is thus critical. Information technology (IT) is also important to quicken response time, so many firms seek countries with the most advanced information systems.

Another way to work closely with suppliers to satisfy customers' needs is to locate production facilities near supplier facilities. That cuts the cost of distribution and makes communication easier.

Many businesses build factories in foreign countries to get closer to their international customers. That's a major reason the Japanese automaker Honda builds cars in Ohio and the German company Mercedes builds them in Alabama. When U.S. firms select foreign sites, they consider whether they are near airports, waterways, and highways so that raw and finished goods can move quickly and easily.

Businesses also study the quality of life for workers and managers. Are good schools nearby? Is the weather nice? Is the crime rate low? Does the local community welcome new businesses? Do the chief executive and other key managers want to live there? Sometimes a region with a high quality of life is also an expensive one, which complicates the decision. In short, facility location has become a critical issue in operations management. The Making Ethical Decisions box looks at the difficult decisions companies must make when it comes to locating.

Interfirm Operations Management

Many rapidly growing companies do very little production themselves. Instead, they outsource engineering, design, manufacturing, and other tasks to companies such as Flex and Sanmina that specialize in those functions. They create new relationships with suppliers online, making operations management an *interfirm* process in which companies work closely together to design, produce, and ship products to customers.

Manufacturing companies are developing online strategies that will enable them and others to compete more effectively in the future. These changes are having a dramatic effect on operations managers as they adjust from a one-firm system to an interfirm environment. So rather than a relatively stable system that companies can solely control, they must now deal with an environment that is constantly changing and evolving.

Facility Location in the Future

Information technology (IT)—that is, computers, software, WiFi, e-mail, voice mail, texting, and so forth—is giving firms and employees increased flexibility to choose locations while staying in the competitive mainstream. **Telecommuting**, working from home via computer, is a major trend in business. Companies that no longer need to locate near sources of labor will be able to move to areas where land is less expensive and the quality of life may be

telecommuting
Working from home via computer and modem.

facility layout

The physical arrangement of resources (including people) in the production process.

materials requirement planning (MRP)

A computer-based operations management system that uses sales forecasts to make sure that needed parts and materials are available at the right time and place.

higher. Plus, it's never been easier to stay in touch either by computer or phone thanks to videoconferencing apps like Skype, Zoom, and Webex.[31]

Another big incentive to locate in a particular city or state is the tax situation there and degree of government support. Some states and local governments have higher taxes than others, yet many compete fiercely by offering companies tax reductions and other support, such as zoning changes and financial aid, so they will locate there. The state of New York, for example, offers entrepreneurs the opportunity to operate tax-free for 10 years.

Facility Layout

Facility layout is the physical arrangement of resources, including people, to most efficiently produce goods and provide services for customers. Facility layout depends greatly on the processes that are to be performed. For services like retail, the layout is usually designed to help the consumer find and buy things. Other service-oriented organizations, such as hospitals, use layouts that improve efficiency, just as manufacturers do. After all, the right facility layout can greatly reduce a factory's costs in the long term.

Many companies are moving from an *assembly-line layout,* in which workers do only a few tasks at a time, to a *modular layout,* in which teams of workers combine to produce more complex units of the final product. There may have been a dozen or more workstations on an assembly line to complete an automobile engine in the past, but all that work might be done in one module today.

When working on a major project, such as a bridge or an airplane, companies use a *fixed-position layout* that allows workers to congregate around the product to be completed.

A *process layout* is one in which similar equipment and functions are grouped together. The order in which the product visits a function depends on the design of the item. This allows for flexibility. The igus manufacturing plant in Cologne, Germany, can shrink or expand in a flash. Its flexible design keeps it competitive in a fast-changing market. Because the layout of the plant changes so often, some employees use scooters in order to more efficiently provide needed skills, supplies, and services to multiple workstations. A fast-changing plant needs a fast-moving employee base to achieve maximum productivity. Figure 9.2 illustrates typical layout designs.

Materials Requirement Planning

Materials requirement planning (MRP) is a computer-based operations management system that uses sales forecasts to make sure needed parts and materials are available at the

This open office plan helps employees maintain social distance in a post-coronavirus world. By limiting the number of people in each room and providing plenty of space between desks, employees can collaborate while staying safely apart. Do you think open office plans are an effective way to keep workers safe and productive?

Cushman & Wakefield

PRODUCT LAYOUT (also called Assembly-Line Layout)
Used to produce large quantities of a few types of products.

FIGURE 9.2 TYPICAL LAYOUT DESIGNS

PROCESS LAYOUT
Frequently used in operations that serve different customers' different needs.

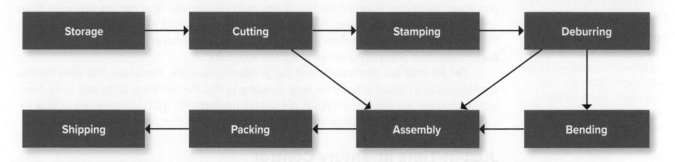

CELLULAR or MODULE LAYOUT
Can accommodate changes in design or customer demand.

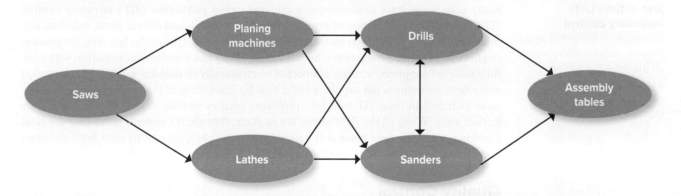

FIXED-POSITION LAYOUT
A major feature of planning is scheduling work operations.

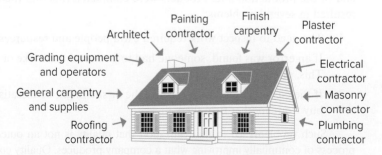

right time and place. **Enterprise resource planning (ERP),** a newer version of MRP, combines the computerized functions of all the divisions and subsidiaries of the firm—such as finance, human resources, and order fulfillment—into a single integrated software program that uses a single database. The result is shorter time between orders and payment, less staff needed to do ordering and order processing, reduced inventories, and better customer service. For example, the customer can place an order, either through a customer service representative or online, and immediately

enterprise resource planning (ERP)
A newer version of materials requirement planning (MRP) that combines the computerized functions of all the divisions and subsidiaries of the firm—such as finance, human resources, and order fulfillment—into a single integrated software program that uses a single database.

purchasing
The function in a firm that searches for quality material resources, finds the best suppliers, and negotiates the best price for goods and services.

see when the order will be filled and how much it will cost. The representative can instantly see the customer's credit rating and order history, the company's inventory, and the shipping schedule. Everyone else in the company can see the new order as well; thus when one department finishes its portion, the order is automatically routed via the ERP system to the next department. The customer can see exactly where the order is at any point by logging in to the system.

Purchasing

Purchasing is the function that searches for high-quality material resources, finds the best suppliers, and negotiates the best price for quality goods and services. Some manufacturers purchase from many suppliers so that if one can't deliver, the firm can get materials from someone else. Others, however, develop close relationships with just a few suppliers so that they can secure affordable prices in the long term. Which strategy do you think works best: purchasing from many suppliers or just a few suppliers?

The Internet has also transformed the purchasing function. Businesses that once needed connections to a certain industry can now go online to find the best items at the best price. Similarly, a company wishing to sell supplies can use the Internet to find all the companies looking for such supplies. The time and dollar cost of purchasing items has thus been reduced tremendously.

Just-in-Time Inventory Control

just-in-time (JIT) inventory control
A production process in which a minimum of inventory is kept on the premises and parts, supplies, and other needs are delivered just in time to go on the assembly line.

One major cost of production is the expense of holding parts, motors, and other items in storage for later use. Storage not only subjects items to obsolescence, theft, and damage but could also require construction and maintenance of costly warehouses. To cut such costs, many companies have implemented a concept called **just-in-time (JIT) inventory control**. JIT systems keep a minimum of inventory on the premises—and deliver parts, supplies, and other needs just in time to go on the assembly line. To work effectively, however, the process requires an accurate production schedule (using ERP) and excellent coordination with carefully selected suppliers, who are connected electronically so they know what will be needed and when. Sometimes the suppliers build new facilities close to the main producer to minimize distribution time. JIT runs into problems such as weather delays when suppliers are farther away. When all the right pieces are in place, though, JIT systems make sure the right materials are at the right place at the right time at the cheapest cost to meet both customer and production needs. That's a key step in modern production innovation.

Quality Control

quality
Consistently producing what the customer wants while reducing errors before and after delivery to the customer.

Maintaining **quality** means consistently producing what the customer wants while reducing errors before and after delivery. In the past, firms often conducted quality control at the end of the production line. Products were completed first and then tested for quality. This resulted in several problems:

1. The need to inspect work required extra people and resources.

2. If an error was found, someone had to correct the mistake or scrap the product. This, of course, was costly.

3. If the customer found the mistake, he or she might be dissatisfied and might even buy from another firm thereafter.

Six Sigma quality
A quality measure that allows only 3.4 defects per million opportunities.

statistical quality control (SQC)
The process some managers use to continually monitor all phases of the production process to ensure that quality is being built into the product from the beginning.

Such problems led to the realization that quality is not an outcome; it is a never-ending process of continually improving what a company produces. Quality control should thus be part of the operations management planning process rather than simply an end-of-the-line inspection.

Companies have turned to the use of modern quality-control standards such as Six Sigma. **Six Sigma quality**, which sets a benchmark of just 3.4 defects per million opportunities, detects potential problems to prevent their occurrence. That's important to a company that makes 4 million transactions a day, like some banks.

Statistical quality control (SQC) is the process some managers use to continually monitor all phases of the production process and ensure quality is being built into the product from the beginning. **Statistical process control (SPC)** is the process of testing statistical samples of product components at each stage of production and plotting the test results on a graph. Managers can thus see and correct any deviation from quality standards. Making sure products meet standards all along the production process reduces the need for a quality-control inspection at the end because mistakes are caught much earlier in the process. SQC and SPC thus save companies much time and money.

Some companies use a quality-control approach called the Deming cycle (after the late W. Edwards Deming, the "father" of the movement toward quality). Its steps are Plan, Do, Check, Act (PDCA). Again, the idea is to find potential errors *before* they happen.

Along with quality products, U.S. businesses are serious about providing top customer service. But even though physical goods can be designed and manufactured to near perfection, there's no similar process that can be applied to services. For instance, a jeweler can develop a method of making gold rings that ensures a flawless end product every time. However, there is no such guarantee of quality when designing and providing a service experience like a dance lesson or a cab drive through New York City. In those instances, it's hard to predict how some customers will react to even the most professional service providers.

Nestlé Purina was awarded a Baldrige. What's that?

It's like Best in Show, but for businesses.

Nestlé Purina Petcare Company wishes to thank our associates, customers, and business partners for helping us be our best. We are honored to be the first consumer package goods company to receive the Malcolm Baldrige National Quality Award for organizational performance excellence, and share our success with the community.

PURINA. Your Pet, Our Passion.

Courtesy of Nestlé Purina PetCare Company

The Baldrige Awards

A standard was set for overall company quality with the introduction of the Malcolm Baldrige National Quality Awards, named in honor of a former U.S. secretary of commerce. Companies can apply for these awards in each of the following areas: manufacturing, services, small businesses, nonprofit/government, education, and health care.

To qualify, an organization has to show quality in key areas such as leadership, strategic planning, customer and market focus, information and analysis, human resource focus, process management, and business results. Major criteria for earning the award include whether customer wants and needs are being met and whether customer satisfaction ratings are better than those of competitors. As you can see, the focus is shifting away from just making quality goods and services to providing top-quality customer service in all respects.

ISO 9001 and ISO 14001 Standards

The International Organization for Standardization (ISO) is a worldwide federation of national standards bodies from more than 170 countries that set global measures for the quality of individual products.[32] ISO is a nongovernmental organization established to promote the development of world standards to facilitate the international exchange of goods and services. (*ISO* is not an acronym. It comes from the Greek word *isos*, meaning "oneness.") **ISO 9001** is the common name given to quality management and assurance standards.

The standards require that a company determine what customer needs are, including regulatory and legal requirements, and make communication arrangements to handle issues such as complaints. Other standards cover process control, product testing, storage, and delivery.

What makes ISO 9001 so important is that the European Union (EU) demands that companies that want to do business with the EU be certified by ISO standards. Some major U.S. companies are also demanding that suppliers meet these standards. Several accreditation agencies in Europe and the United States will certify that a company meets the standards for all phases of its operations, from product development through production and testing to installation.

ISO 14001 is a collection of the best practices for managing an organization's impact on the environment. As an environmental management system, it does not prescribe a performance level. Requirements for certification include having an environmental policy,

Nestlé Purina PetCare, a company headquartered in St. Louis, received the Malcolm Baldrige National Quality Award in the manufacturing category. What quality criteria do you think the award was based on?

statistical process control (SPC)
The process of taking statistical samples of product components at each stage of the production process and plotting those results on a graph. Any variances from quality standards are recognized and can be corrected if beyond the set standards.

ISO 9001
The common name given to quality management and assurance standards.

ISO 14001
A collection of the best practices for managing an organization's impact on the environment.

having specific improvement targets, conducting audits of environmental programs, and maintaining top management review of the processes.

Certification in both ISO 9001 and ISO 14001 would show that a firm has a world-class management system in both quality and environmental standards. In the past, firms assigned employees separately to meet each set of standards. Today, ISO 9001 and 14001 standards have been blended so that an organization can work on both at once. ISO has also compiled social responsibility guidelines to go with the other standards.

TESTPREP

- What are the major criteria for facility location?
- What is the difference between MRP and ERP?
- What is just-in-time inventory control?
- What are Six Sigma quality, the Baldrige Award, ISO 9001, and ISO 14001?

LO 9–5 Explain the use of PERT and Gantt charts to control manufacturing processes.

Control Procedures: PERT and Gantt Charts

Operations managers must ensure products are manufactured and delivered on time, on budget, and to specifications. How can managers be sure all will go smoothly and be completed by the required time? One popular technique for monitoring the progress of production was developed in the 1950s by the U.S. Navy for constructing nuclear submarines: the **program evaluation and review technique (PERT)**. PERT users analyze the tasks to complete a given project, estimate the time needed to complete each task, and compute the minimum time needed to complete the whole project.

The steps used in PERT are (1) analyzing and sequencing tasks that need to be done, (2) estimating the time needed to complete each task, (3) drawing a PERT network illustrating the information from steps 1 and 2, and (4) identifying the critical path. The **critical path** is the sequence of tasks that takes the longest time to complete. We use the word *critical* because a delay anywhere along this path will cause the project or production run to be late.

Figure 9.3 illustrates a PERT chart for producing a music video. The squares indicate completed tasks, and the arrows indicate the time needed to complete each. The path from one completed task to another illustrates the relationships among tasks; the arrow from "set designed" to "set materials purchased" indicates we must design the set before we can purchase the materials. The critical path, indicated by the bold black arrows, shows producing the set takes more time than auditioning dancers, choreographing dances, or designing and making costumes. The project manager now knows it's critical that set construction remain on schedule if the project is to be completed on time, but short delays in dance and costume preparation are unlikely to delay it.

A PERT network can be made up of thousands of events over many months. Today, this complex procedure is simplified by using a computer. Another, more basic strategy manufacturers use for measuring production progress is a Gantt chart. A **Gantt chart** (named for its developer, Henry L. Gantt) is a bar graph, now also prepared by computer, that clearly shows what projects are being worked on and how much has been completed at any given time. Figure 9.4, a Gantt chart for a doll manufacturer, shows that the dolls' heads and bodies should be completed before the clothing is sewn. It also shows that at the end of week 3, the dolls' bodies are ready, but the heads are about half a week behind. Using a Gantt-like computer program, a manager can trace the production process minute by minute to determine which tasks are on time and which are behind, so that adjustments can be made to allow the company to stay on schedule.

program evaluation and review technique (PERT)
A method for analyzing the tasks involved in completing a given project, estimating the time needed to complete each task, and identifying the minimum time needed to complete the total project.

critical path
In a PERT network, the sequence of tasks that takes the longest time to complete.

Gantt chart
Bar graph showing production managers what projects are being worked on and what stage they are in at any given time.

FIGURE 9.3 PERT CHART FOR A MUSIC VIDEO
The minimum amount of time it will take to produce this video is 15 weeks. To get that number, you add the 1 week it takes to pick a star and a song to the 4 weeks to design a set, the 2 weeks to purchase set materials, the 6 weeks to construct the set, the 1 week of rehearsals, and the final 1 week when the video is made. That's the critical path. Any delay in that process will delay the final video.

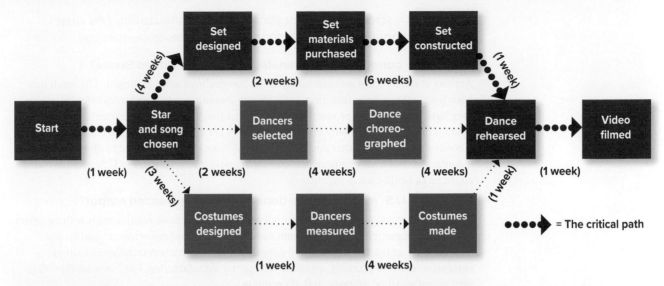

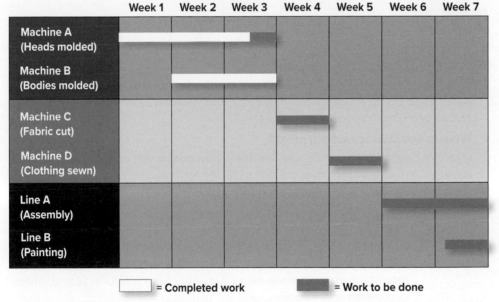

FIGURE 9.4 GANTT CHART FOR A DOLL MANUFACTURER
A Gantt chart enables a production manager to see at a glance when projects are scheduled to be completed and what the status is now. For example, the dolls' heads and bodies should be completed before the clothing is sewn, but they could be a little late as long as everything is ready for assembly in week 6. This chart shows that at the end of week 3, the dolls' bodies are ready but the heads are about half a week behind.

Preparing for the Future

The United States remains a major industrial country, but competition grows stronger each year. Tremendous opportunities exist for careers in operations management as both manufacturing and service companies fight to stay competitive. Students who can see future trends and have the technological and creative skills to work in tomorrow's highly automated factories and modern service facilities will benefit.

? TESTPREP

- Draw a PERT chart for making a breakfast of three-minute eggs, buttered toast, and coffee. Define *critical path*.
- How could you use a Gantt chart to keep track of production?

SUMMARY

LO 9–1 Describe the current state of U.S. manufacturing and what manufacturers have done to become more competitive.

- **What is the current state of manufacturing in the United States?**

Activity in the nation's manufacturing sector has declined since its height. The result has been fewer jobs in manufacturing. Even though manufacturing companies offer fewer jobs, they have become more productive, meaning that they need fewer employees to do the same amount of work. Today many manufacturing jobs are coming back to the United States as labor costs increase in other countries. Much of this chapter is devoted to showing you what manufacturers and service providers can do to revive and reinforce the U.S. economy to continue as world-class competitors.

- **What have U.S. manufacturers done to achieve increased output?**

U.S. manufacturers have increased output by emphasizing close relationships with suppliers and other companies to satisfy customer needs; continuous improvement; quality; site selection; use of the Internet to unite companies; and production techniques such as enterprise resource planning, computer-integrated manufacturing, flexible manufacturing, lean manufacturing, robotics, and 3D printing.

LO 9–2 Describe the evolution from production to operations management.

- **What is production management?**

Production management consists of all the activities managers do to help their firms create goods. To reflect the change in importance from manufacturing to services, the term *production* is often replaced by the term *operations*.

- **What is operations management?**

Operations management is the specialized area in management that converts or transforms resources, including human resources, into goods and services.

- **What kind of firms use operations managers?**

Firms in both the manufacturing and service sectors use operations managers.

LO 9–3 Identify various production processes, and describe techniques that improve productivity, including computer-aided design and manufacturing, flexible manufacturing, lean manufacturing, mass customization, robotics, and 3D printing.

- **What is process manufacturing, and how does it differ from assembly processes?**

Process manufacturing physically or chemically changes materials. Assembly processes put together components.

- **How do CAD/CAM systems work?**

Design changes made in computer-aided design (CAD) are instantly incorporated into the computer-aided manufacturing (CAM) process. The linking of CAD and CAM is computer-integrated manufacturing (CIM).

- **What is flexible manufacturing?**

Flexible manufacturing means designing machines to produce a variety of products.

- **What is lean manufacturing?**

Lean manufacturing is the production of goods using less of everything than in mass production: less human effort, less manufacturing space, less investment in tools, and less engineering time to develop a new product.

- **What is mass customization?**

  Mass customization means making custom-designed goods and services for a large number of individual customers. Flexible manufacturing makes mass customization possible. Given the exact needs of a customer, flexible machines can produce a customized good as fast as mass-produced goods were once made. Mass customization is also important in service industries.

- **How do robotics help make manufacturers more competitive?**

  Industrial robotics can work 24 hours a day, seven days a week, with great precision. Many of the jobs they replace are dirty or so repetitive that robots are necessary, or at least helpful. However, robots are beginning to encroach on white-collar jobs in many professions.

- **What is 3D printing and what is it used for?**

  3D printing (also known as additive manufacturing) is technology that creates a product one layer at a time by a nozzle similar to those found in inkjet printers. Today 3D printing is largely used to create prototype models or molds for other industrial projects, but use is growing in areas such as medical equipment.

LO 9–4   Describe operations management planning issues including facility location, facility layout, materials requirement planning, purchasing, just-in-time inventory control, and quality control.

- **What is facility location and how does it differ from facility layout?**

  Facility location is the process of selecting a geographic location for a company's operations. Facility layout is the physical arrangement of resources, including people, to produce goods and services effectively and efficiently.

- **How do managers evaluate different sites?**

  Labor costs and land costs are two major criteria for selecting the right sites. Other criteria include whether resources are plentiful and inexpensive, skilled workers are available or are trainable, taxes are low and the local government offers support, energy and water are available, transportation costs are low, and the quality of life and of education are high.

- **What relationship do materials requirement planning (MRP) and enterprise resource planning (ERP) have with the production process?**

  MRP is a computer-based operations management system that uses sales forecasts to make sure the needed parts and materials are available at the right time and place. Enterprise resource planning (ERP), a newer version of MRP, combines the computerized functions of all the divisions and subsidiaries of the firm—such as finance, material requirements planning, human resources, and order fulfillment—into a single integrated software program that uses a single database. The result is shorter time between orders and payment, less staff to do ordering and order processing, reduced inventories, and better customer service for all the firms involved.

- **What is just-in-time (JIT) inventory control?**

  JIT requires suppliers to deliver parts and materials just in time to go on the assembly line so they don't have to be stored at the firm's location or in warehouses.

- **What is Six Sigma quality, SQC, and SPC?**

  Six Sigma quality sets standards at just 3.4 defects per million opportunities and detects potential problems before they occur. Statistical quality control (SQC) is the process some managers use to continually monitor all processes in the production process and ensure quality is being built into the product from the beginning. Statistical process control (SPC) tests statistical samples of product components at each stage of the production process and plots the results on a graph so managers can recognize and correct deviations from quality standards.

- **What quality standards do firms use in the United States?**

  To qualify for the Malcolm Baldrige National Quality Award, a company must demonstrate quality in seven key areas: leadership, strategic planning, customer and market focus, information and analysis, human resource focus, process management, and business results. International standards U.S. firms strive to meet include ISO 9001 and ISO 14001. The first is a world standard for quality and the second is a collection of the best practices for managing an organization's impact on the environment.

> **LO 9–5** Explain the use of PERT and Gantt charts to control manufacturing processes.

■ **Is there any relationship between a PERT chart and a Gantt chart?**

Figure 9.3 shows a PERT chart. Figure 9.4 shows a Gantt chart. Whereas PERT is a tool used for planning, a Gantt chart is a tool used to measure progress.

KEY TERMS

assembly process 226
computer-aided design (CAD) 227
computer-aided manufacturing (CAM) 227
computer-integrated manufacturing (CIM) 227
continuous process 226
critical path 236
enterprise resource planning (ERP) 233
facility layout 232
facility location 230
flexible manufacturing 227
form utility 226

Gantt chart 236
intermittent process 226
ISO 9001 235
ISO 14001 235
just-in-time (JIT) inventory control 234
lean manufacturing 228
mass customization 228
materials requirement planning (MRP) 232
operations management 224
process manufacturing 226
production 224

production management 224
program evaluation and review technique (PERT) 236
purchasing 234
quality 234
Six Sigma quality 234
statistical process control (SPC) 235
statistical quality control (SQC) 234
telecommuting 231

CRITICAL THINKING

1. Workers on the manufacturing floor are being replaced by robots and other machines. On the one hand, this lets companies compete with cheap labor from other countries. On the other hand, automation eliminates many jobs. Are you concerned that automation may increase unemployment or underemployment in the United States and around the world? Why or why not?

2. Computer-integrated manufacturing (CIM) has revolutionized the production process. What will such changes mean for the clothing industry, the shoe industry, and other fashion-related industries? What will they mean for other consumer and industrial goods industries? How will you benefit as a consumer?

3. One way to create new jobs in the United States is to increase innovation among new graduates from engineering and the sciences. How can the United States motivate more students to major in those areas?

PUTTING PRINCIPLES TO WORK

PURPOSE

To illustrate production processes.

EXERCISE

Go to youtube.com and search for the video *How It's Made: McDonald's Chicken McNuggets.* You'll see how Tyson makes chicken nuggets for McDonald's.

1. Does Tyson use process manufacturing or the assembly process? Is the production of McDonald's McNuggets an intermittent or continuous production process? Justify your answers.

2. What location factors might go into the selection of a manufacturing site for McDonald's McNuggets?

KEY: ● **Team**　★ **Analytic**　▲ **Communication**　▣ **Technology**

1. Choosing the right location for a manufacturing plant or a service organization is often critical to its success. Form small groups and have each group member pick one manufacturing plant or one service organization in town and list at least three reasons why its location helps or hinders its success. If its location is not ideal, what would be a better one? ●▲★

2. In teams of four or five, discuss the need for better operations management in the airline industry. Have the team develop a report listing (*a*) problems team members have encountered in traveling by air and (*b*) suggestions for improving operations so such problems won't occur in the future. ★▲

3. Discuss some of the advantages and disadvantages of producing goods overseas using inexpensive labor. Summarize the moral aspects, health risks, and ethical dimensions of this practice. ★▲

4. Think of any production facility at your school, such as a sandwich shop, library, or copy center, and redesign the layout (make a pencil sketch) to more effectively serve customers (students) and allow employees to be more effective and efficient. ★▲

5. Think about recent experiences you have had with service organizations and select one in which you had to wait for an unreasonable length of time to get what you wanted. Describe what happens when customers are inconvenienced, and explain how management could make the operation more efficient and customer-oriented. ★▲

CAREER EXPLORATION

If you are interested in pursuing a career in production, here are a few to consider. Find out about the tasks performed, skills needed, pay, and opportunity outlook in these fields in the *Occupational Outlook Handbook (OOH)* at bls.gov.

- **Production, planning and expediting clerk—** coordinates and expedites the flow of work and materials within or between departments according to production schedule.

- **First-line supervisor—**directly supervises and coordinates the activities of production and operating workers, such as inspectors, precision workers,

machine setters and operators, assemblers, fabricators, and plant and system operators.

- **Industrial production manager—**oversees the daily operations of manufacturing and related plants; coordinates, plans, and directs the activities used to create a wide range of goods, such as cars, computer equipment, or paper products.

- **Producer and director—**creates motion pictures, television shows, live theater, commercials, and other performing arts productions.

VIDEO CASE

McGraw Hill connect® *Production in the 21st Century*

We sometimes read or hear about the downfall of U.S. manufacturing and how many people are losing their jobs in manufacturing. It sounds depressing, but the question is, "Has the United States really fallen that far behind other countries in manufacturing capability?" The answer is no. This video highlights how production processes have changed, making production and operations more efficient through innovative operations management.

Every product we buy has been created and distributed through a series of processes that transforms raw materials,

machinery, and labor into goods and services. Operations management is a specialized area of management that focuses on designing, supervising, and improving the transformation process, as well as keeping costs to a minimum. Operations management is responsible for purchasing parts, overseeing suppliers, scheduling production, maintaining inventory and quality control, and performing other duties. Operations management is a key part of service businesses as well, as companies seek to provide great customer service while keeping costs to a minimum.

Originally, goods were mass-produced with little input from customers. As Henry Ford once said, "You can have any color Ford you want, so long as it's black." How things have changed! Today, Ford Motor Company encourages its customers to choose their colors online instead of having to settle for what a dealer has on the lot. While such customization costs more than Henry Ford's one-color strategy, customization is crucial for U.S. producers so they can compete in an expanding global economy. Advances in technology have also given a huge boost to customization and efficiency. Computer-aided design (CAD), which uses precise drawings of a product in both 2D and 3D, coupled with computer-aided manufacturing (CAM) makes it possible to customize even the smallest orders. CAD-CAM also allows manufacturers to make small changes quickly without having to completely redo a production process. Through flexible manufacturing, companies can design machinery that can produce multiple product variations at any time. For example, M&M's can create its candies with the same familiar taste, size, and shape but with multiple colors and special messages.

It's hard to deny the impact that robots have had on the production process. Robotics has made manufacturing more efficient from a production and cost perspective. Today, robotics plays a major role in almost every process in production. It is also a key part of operations management planning. Operations management planning's primary objective is to make decisions regarding key issues such as the location of a production facility. Factors that influence the decision about where to locate a plant are access to resources, proximity to transportation, availability of labor, and quality of life. After location facilities have been determined, the most efficient layout of the facility must be designed.

Supplies and materials sitting idle cost the company money. That's why inventory control is vital to a firm's efficiency and profitability. Many companies have turned to just-in-time inventory control systems to make sure that materials and supplies are available at the right place and time without excess storage costs. The use of enterprise resource planning (ERP) software has helped make the control process even more effective. Through ERP, companies can automatically route an order to scheduling, then production, and on to shipping and billing.

All production and operations strategies are put in place to enhance overall product quality. Therefore, quality control is the final and perhaps most important operations mangement process. If a company does not produce a quality product, it will fail. Traditionally, quality control was conducted after the production of goods. If the goods were found to be deficient, the products were scrapped, often at a high cost. Today, companies conduct quality-control testing throughout the production process, so errors can be identified and corrected immediately to prevent having to be discarded at the end.

Next time you take a cold drink from a can, take a ride on a bike, or read a good book, think about the U.S. companies that make those goods. Think, too, of the opportunities available to tomorrow's college graduates. Often students are not attracted to the manufacturing sector even though many opportunities exist. Think of companies producing emerging products such as solar panels, Lithium-ion batteries, and more. You only have to look around your home, school, or office to see the many products being made today and the many products that will be made in the future using biotechnology, nanotechnology, and so on.

THINKING IT OVER

1. Looking at the future of manufacturing in the United States, do you think U.S. companies are adapting to the challenges of global manufacturing?

2. Why has just-in-time inventory control become a dominant production process used in the automobile industry? Can you name other industries where it would be effective?

3. Why is it important to apply quality-control processes throughout production rather than evaluate products only at the end of the production cycle?

NOTES

1. Andy Kiersz, "20 Jobs Popular in the 1950s That Are Almost Gone Today," *Business Insider,* businessinsider.com, October 10, 2019; "American Identity of Economic Success," Bureau of Labor Statistics, bls.gov, accessed February 2020.
2. Nemanja Stamenkovic, "14 Incredible Statistics on Loss of Manufacturing Jobs," *What to Become,* whattobecome. com, January 20, 2020; "All Employees, Manufacturing," Federal Reserve Bank of St. Louis, fred.stlouisfed.org, accessed February 2020.
3. Kimberly Amadeo, "U.S. Manufacturing: Statistics and Outlook," *The Balance,* thebalance.com, October 22, 2019; "18 Facts about Manufacturing You Need to Know," National Association of Manufacturers, nam.org, accessed February 2020.
4. Justin Lahart, "Manufacturing's Impact Is Bigger Than You Think," *The Wall Street Journal,* October 2, 2019; Chip Cutter, "Americans Are Back at Work Making Stuff," *The Wall Street Journal,* March 1, 2019; "18 Top Facts You Need to Know about Manufacturing," National Association of Manufacturers, nam.org, accessed February 2020.
5. "Timeline of Computer History," Computer History Museum, computerhistory.org, accessed February 2020.
6. Bruce Shutan, "Exploring the Future of Employee-Robot Relations," *EBN,* benefitnews.com, accessed February 2020; Joshua Conrad Jackson, Kurt Gray, and Noah Castello, "Why Having Robot Co-Workers Might Make You Less Prejudiced," *Los Angeles Times,* January 1, 2020; Matt O'Brien, "Working Together Harmoniously?

As Robots Take Over Warehousing, Workers Pushed to Adapt," *St. Louis Post-Dispatch,* January 5, 2020.

7. Fred Dews, "9 Things to Consider about U.S. Manufacturing Jobs," Brookings Institution, brookings.edu, accessed February 2020.

8. Francisco Betti, "How Factories of the Future Are Leading the Way to Innovation in Manufacturing," *Forbes,* forbes.com, January 10, 2020; Daniel Brightmore, "Censornet: Securing the Future of the Manufacturing Industry," *Manufacturing Global,* manufacturingglobal.com, January 14, 2020.

9. Neil Irwin, "Economy in a Nutshell: Manufacturing in Recession. Services Booming," *The New York Times,* January 10, 2020; Alison Doyle, "Best U.S. Industries for Employment," *The Balance,* thebalance.com, accessed February 2020; "Women Outnumber Men in the Paid Workforce for Only the Second Time," *The Washington Post,* January 10, 2020.

10. David Mangot, "Engineering the Hiring of Engineers," *CIO,* cio.com, accessed February 2020; Jennifer Liu, "5 High-Paying, Growing Jobs Didn't Exist a Decade Ago—But They'll Be Booming in the 2020s," *CNBC,* cnbc.com, accessed March 2020.

11. Ralph Jennings, "These Developing Asian Economies Will Grow the Fastest in 2020," *Forbes,* December 31, 2019; Erin Duffy, "Global Manufacturing Industry," Statista, statista.com, accessed February 2020.

12. "Robots Revamping the Travel Industry," *Robotics Tomorrow,* roboticstomorrow.com, accessed February 2020; Greg Nichols, "CES 2020: Is This Robot Concierge the Future of Service Robots?," *ZDNet,* zdnet.com, accessed February 2020.

13. Jason Wingard, "Leading in the 2020s: 3 Emerging Workplace Trends," *Forbes,* January 3, 2020.

14. Andrew S. Grove, *High Output Management* (New York: Knopf Doubleday, 2015).

15. Jayesh Shah, "A Journey from Pendulum to Smart Watches," *Entrepreneur,* March 8, 2019; Alan Zeichick, "Barcelona Startup Creates 3D Models of Diseased Hearts Using High-Performance Cloud Computing," *Forbes,* March 6, 2019; "Mechanical Computer-Aided Design Market Size, Share 2020," *MarketWatch,* marketwatch.com, accessed February 2020.

16. Kayla Matthews, "How Flexible Production Systems Hold the Key to ROI," *Robotics Business Review,* roboticsbusinessreview.com, January 24, 2020.

17. Jim Vinoski, "New Research Shows Customers Already Expect Mass Personalization. Time to Get Ready," *Forbes,* January 20, 2020.

18. "The Best Folding Bikes You Can Buy Right Now," *Bicycling,* bicycling.com, accessed February 2020;

Michelle Arthurs-Brennan, "The Best Folding Bikes," *Cycling Weekly,* January 20, 2020.

19. Katie Lundin, "How to Start a Successful Clothing Brand or Clothing Line from Scratch in 2020: The Definitive Guide," *Crowdspring,* crowdspring.com January 10, 2020; Proper Cloth, propercloth.com, accessed February 2020.

20. "Personalized M&M's," mms.com, accessed February 2020.

21. Robert Seamans, "The Complicated Relationship between Robots and Workers," *Forbes,* January 10, 2020; David Deming, "The Robots Are Coming. Prepare for Trouble," *The New York Times,* January 30, 2020.

22. Kent German and Katie Collins, "Delta Airlines Sees a Future in Robotics," *CNET,* cnet.com, January 7, 2020; Tim Hornyak, "Meet the Robots That May Be Coming to an Airport Near You," *CNBC,* cnbc.com, January 11, 2020.

23. Katie Linsell and Lananh Nguyen, "The End of the Bonus Culture Is Coming to Wall Street," *Bloomberg,* January 13, 2020; Shae Russell, "Taking Advantage of Wall Street's Little Secret: Robots Run the Stock Market," *Daily Reckoning,* dailyreckoning.com, January 22, 2020.

24. Scott Belsky, "Why It's Time to Quit Worrying about Your Productivity," *Wired,* January 9, 2020; Alana Semuels, "Soon a Robot Will Be Writing This Headline," *The New York Times,* January 14, 2020; Lauren Weber, "A Counterintuitive Fix for Robot-Driven Unemployment," *The Wall Street Journal,* January 6, 2020.

25. 3D Printing Industry, 3dprintingindustry.com, accessed February 2020; Greg Nichols, "2020 Predictions: Five Telling Trends in 3D Printing," *ZDNet,* znet.com, January 31, 2020; "What's ahead for 3D Printing in 2020," *IndustryWeek,* January 6, 2020.

26. Michael Petch, "80 Additive Manufacturing Experts Predict the 3D Printing Trends to Watch in 2020," 3D Printing Industry, 3dprintingindustry.com, January 15, 2020.

27. Mark Zastrow, "3D Printing Gets Bigger, Faster and Stronger," *Nature,* nature.com, February 5, 2020.

28. Norbert Sparrow, "The Future of Smart Manufacturing," *Plastics Today,* plasticstoday.com, February 6, 2020.

29. Mark Howard, "Three Ways Nanotechnology Improves Manufacturing," *EHS Today,* ehstoday.com, January 17, 2020.

30. Jon Banister, " Amazon Plans to Begin Work on HQ2 Development This Month," *Bisnow,* bisnow.com, January 15, 2020.

31. Ed Bott, "Best Video Conferencing Services for Business," *ZDNet,* zdnet.com, February 5, 2020.

32. International Organization for Standardization, iso.org, accessed February 2020.

10

Motivating Employees

LEARNING OBJECTIVES **»**

After you have read and studied this chapter, you should be able to

LO 10–1 Explain Taylor's theory of scientific management.

LO 10–2 Describe the Hawthorne studies and their significance to management.

LO 10–3 Identify the levels of Maslow's hierarchy of needs and apply them to employee motivation.

LO 10–4 Distinguish between the motivators and hygiene factors identified by Herzberg.

LO 10–5 Differentiate among Theory X, Theory Y, and Theory Z.

LO 10–6 Explain the key principles of goal-setting, expectancy, and equity theories.

LO 10–7 Show how managers put motivation theories into action through such strategies as job enrichment, open communication, and job recognition.

LO 10–8 Show how managers personalize motivation strategies to appeal to employees across the globe and across generations.

Rose Marcario, CEO of Patagonia

While most American offices keep a closet or two stocked with essential supplies, Patagonia's California HQ is perhaps the only workplace in the country with a storage room full of surfboards. In fact, at any time of day staffers can grab a board, consult the daily wave report written nearby, and then hit the water. If employees don't feel like taming the waves, they can take a 30-mile bike ride through the mountains during lunch. Or if they really want to expand their horizons, they can sign up for a company "field trip" to learn fly-fishing in Wyoming or rock climbing in Yosemite National Park.

Along with these outdoorsy perks, Patagonia employees also enjoy on-site child care, paid vacations, and complete health care coverage. According to CEO Rose Marcario, this generous package of benefits boosts productivity and improves morale for the entire company, not just a few fortunate executives. "We support the whole community, as opposed to a few people who do very, very well and enjoy all the perks," said Marcario. "We've figured it out. Seems to me that the rest of corporate America should be able to figure it out, too."

As the head of a company well known for its commitment to social and environmental causes, Marcario isn't afraid to challenge other American firms to follow Patagonia's lead. Before she joined the outdoor apparel brand, however, Marcario spent years studying business and working in the corporate world. She graduated from the State University of New York (SUNY) Albany with a bachelor's degree in finance and earned an MBA at California State University, Los Angeles. By her early thirties, Marcario was leading the mergers and acquisitions department at a major West Coast investment firm. After that, she became chief financial officer (CFO) at a start-up called General Magic, an Apple spin-off that included a number of soon-to-be stars in Silicon Valley. Marcario later moved on to a private equity firm where she served as executive vice president.

By then, though, she was tired of obsessing over quarterly results and relentlessly meeting the demands of investors. Marcario said that as she grew more successful, "I felt myself more and more divided from my values. I felt like, 'Wow, I'm transforming as a person, but my work isn't reflecting that.'" A practicing Buddhist, Marcario quit her job and spent the next two years meditating and traveling through India and Nepal. "I went through a kind of personal transformation," she said. "Studying Buddhism, just figuring out who I was as a person. . . . If you don't take that to your work and the world, then I don't think that transformation is complete."

When she finally returned home to the United States, Marcario wasn't sure what to do next until a friend mentioned that Patagonia was looking for a CFO. Although she was skeptical about taking another executive job, a phone call with Patagonia founder Yvon Chouinard convinced her that the company was as committed to ecological and social causes as it claimed. Joining the outdoor clothing maker in 2008, Marcario immediately began revamping the company's supply chains to eliminate both financial and environmental waste. She also greatly increased sales by improving Patagonia's e-commerce capabilities. In 2013 she took the top job as CEO where she continued to oversee record growth while also championing causes such as the preservation of national parks.

Marcario is a passionate advocate for on-site child care as well, providing Patagonia employees with some of the most generous parental benefits available. In her mind, removing the stress of paying for day care or babysitters allows staffers to live up to their full potential in both work and in life. "Taking care of our tribe is part of our culture and our commitment to helping our own people live the way they want," said Marcario. In 2020, Marcario announced plans to step down as CEO, and no replacement has been named as of this writing.

In this chapter, you'll learn about the theories and practices that managers like Rose Marcario use in motivating their employees to focus on goals common to them and the organization.

Brigid Schulte, "A Company That Profits as It Pampers Workers," *The Washington Post,* October 25, 2014; Ryan Bradley, "The Woman Driving Patagonia to Be (Even More) Radical," *Fortune,* September 14, 2015; Jeff Beer, "How Patagonia Grows Every Time It Amplifies Its Social Mission," *Fast Company,* February 21, 2018; Rose Marcario, "Patagonia's CEO Explains How To Make On-Site Child Care Pay for Itself," *Fast Company,* August 15, 2016; Jeff Beer, "Patagonia CEO Rose Marcario Is Stepping Down," *Fast Company,* June 10, 2020.

Let's talk business!
bit.ly/LetsTalkBusiness10

Peter Bohler/Redux

name that
company

RECOGNITION IS IMPORTANT to most employees. This company introduced an oddly named, yet prestigious honor. The award was created when an employee solved a problem and the manager grabbed a banana from his lunch. This was the very first Golden Banana Award. Name that company. (Find the answer in the chapter.)

The Value of Motivation

"If work is such fun, how come the rich don't do it?," quipped comedian Groucho Marx. Well, the rich do work—Jeff Bezos didn't make his billions reading books and shopping online. And workers can have fun, if managers make the effort to motivate them.

It's difficult to overstate the importance of workers' job satisfaction. Happy workers can lead to happy customers, and happy customers lead to successful businesses.[1] On the other hand, unhappy workers are likely to leave. When that happens, the company usually loses more than an experienced employee. It can also lose the equivalent of six to nine months' salary to cover the costs of recruiting and training a replacement. Other costs of losing employees are even greater: loss of intellectual capital, decreased morale of remaining workers, increased employee stress, increased employee gossip, decreased customer service, interrupted product development, and a poor reputation.[2]

Jetta Productions/Blend Images LLC

Although it is costly to recruit and train new workers, it's also expensive to retain those who are disengaged. The word *engagement* is used to describe employees' level of motivation, passion, and commitment. Engaged employees work with passion, feel a connection to their company, and are more productive.[3] Disengaged workers have essentially checked out; they give the company their time, but not their energy. Not only do they act out their unhappiness at work, but disengaged employees undermine the efforts of their co-workers. A Gallup survey estimated that actively disengaged workers cost companies around 34 percent of those workers' salaries and the U.S. economy about $350 billion a year in lost productivity.[4]

Many managers today are focusing beyond employee engagement as they realize the importance of facilitating a positive employee experience. *Employee experience* is the level of satisfaction at every step along an employee's path throughout his or her time with a company. It begins at recruitment and continues all the way through to offboarding (see Chapter 11).[5] Every experience job seekers or employees have with the company, their co-workers, and the management team has an influence on their satisfaction. Even a highly engaged employee can have a negative employee experience. For example, an employee who enjoys designing may be very engaged in a design project, but may not be satisfied with the company overall. Such employees will be shopping for a job somewhere else.

Motivating the right people to join the organization and stay with it is a key function of managers. Top-performing managers are usually surrounded by top-performing employees. It is no coincidence that geese fly faster in formation than alone. Although the desire to perform well ultimately comes from within, good managers stimulate people and bring out their natural drive to do a good job. People are willing to work, and work hard, if they feel their work makes a difference and is appreciated.[6]

One important type of motivator is intrinsic (inner) rewards, which include the personal satisfaction you feel for a job well done. People who respond to such inner promptings often enjoy their work and share their enthusiasm with others. Are you more strongly motivated by your own desire to do well, or by extrinsic rewards like pay and recognition?

People are motivated by a variety of things, such as recognition, accomplishment, and status. An **intrinsic reward** is the personal satisfaction you feel when you perform well and complete goals. The belief that your work makes a significant contribution to the organization or to society is a form of intrinsic reward.[7] An **extrinsic reward** is given to you by someone else as recognition for good work. Pay raises, praise, and promotions are extrinsic rewards.

This chapter will help you understand the concepts, theories, and practice of motivation. We begin with a look at some traditional theories of motivation. Why should you learn about these theories? Because sometimes "new" approaches aren't really new; variations of them have been tried in the past. Knowing what has been tried before will help you see what has worked and what hasn't. First, we discuss scientific management and its effect on productivity and then the Hawthorne studies because they created a new interest in worker satisfaction and motivation. Then we look at some assumptions about employees that come from the traditional theorists. You will see the names of these theorists over and over in business literature and future courses: Taylor, Mayo, Maslow, Herzberg, and McGregor. Finally, we'll introduce modern motivation theories and show you how managers apply them.

intrinsic reward
The personal satisfaction you feel when you perform well and complete goals.

extrinsic reward
Something given to you by someone else as recognition for good work; extrinsic rewards include pay increases, praise, and promotions.

LO 10–1 Explain Taylor's theory of scientific management.

Frederick Taylor: The "Father" of Scientific Management

Several 19th-century thinkers presented management principles, but not until the early 20th century did any work with lasting implications appear. *The Principles of Scientific Management* was written by U.S. efficiency engineer Frederick Taylor and published in 1911, earning Taylor the title "father" of scientific management. Taylor's goal was to increase worker productivity to benefit both the firm and the worker. The solution, he thought, was to scientifically study the most efficient ways to do things, determine the single "best way" to perform each task, and then teach others those methods. This approach became known as **scientific management**. Three elements were basic to Taylor's approach: time, methods, and rules of work. His most important tools were observation and the stopwatch. Taylor's thinking lies behind today's measures of how many burgers McDonald's expects its cooks to flip.

scientific management
Studying workers to find the most efficient ways of doing things and then teaching people those techniques.

time-motion studies
Studies, begun by Frederick Taylor, of which tasks must be performed to complete a job and the time needed to do each task.

A classic Taylor story describes his study of men shoveling rice, coal, and iron ore with the same type of shovel. Believing different materials called for different shovels, he proceeded to invent a wide variety of sizes and shapes of shovels and, stopwatch in hand, measured output over time in what were called **time-motion studies**. These were studies of the tasks performed in a job and the time needed for each. Sure enough, an average person could shovel 25 to 35 tons more per day using the most efficient motions and the proper shovel. This finding led to time-motion studies of virtually every factory job. As researchers determined the most efficient ways of doing things, efficiency became the standard for setting goals.

Taylor's scientific management became the dominant strategy for improving productivity in the early 1900s. One follower of

Michael Dwyer/Alamy Stock Photo

UPS tells drivers how to get out of their trucks, how fast to walk, how many packages to pick up and deliver per day, and even how to hold their keys. Can you see how UPS follows the principles of scientific management by teaching people the one "best way" to perform each task?

principle of motion economy

Theory developed by Frank and Lillian Gilbreth that every job can be broken down into a series of elementary motions.

Taylor was Henry L. Gantt, who developed charts by which managers plotted the work of employees a day in advance down to the smallest detail. (See Chapter 9 for a discussion of Gantt charts.) U.S. engineers Frank and Lillian Gilbreth used Taylor's ideas in a three-year study of bricklaying. They developed the **principle of motion economy**, showing how every job could be broken into a series of elementary motions called a *therblig* (*Gilbreth* spelled backward with the *t* and *h* transposed). They then analyzed each motion to make it more efficient.

Scientific management viewed people largely as machines that needed to be properly programmed. There was little concern for the psychological or human aspects of work. Taylor believed that workers would perform at a high level of effectiveness—that is, be motivated—if they received high enough pay.

Some of Taylor's ideas are still in use. Some companies continue to emphasize conformity to work rules rather than creativity, flexibility, and responsiveness. For example, UPS tells drivers how to get out of their trucks (with right foot first), how fast to walk (three feet per second), how many packages to deliver a day (an average of 150 to 175 in off-peak seasons), and how to hold their keys (teeth up, third finger). Drivers use a handheld computer called a Delivery Information Acquisition Device to scan bar codes on packages. This lets a customer check online and know exactly where a package is at any given moment. If a driver is considered slow, a supervisor rides along, prodding the driver with stopwatches and clipboards. UPS has training centers in nine U.S. cities with simulators that teach employees how to properly lift and load boxes, drive their trucks proficiently, and even lessen the risk of slipping and falling when carrying a package.[8]

The benefits of relying on workers to come up with solutions to productivity problems have long been recognized, as we shall discover next.

LO 10–2 Describe the Hawthorne studies and their significance to management.

Elton Mayo and the Hawthorne Studies

One study, inspired by Frederick Taylor's research, began at the Western Electric Company's Hawthorne plant in Cicero, Illinois, in 1927 and ended six years later. Let's see why it is one of the major studies in management literature.

Elton Mayo and his colleagues from Harvard University came to the Hawthorne plant to test the degree of lighting associated with optimum productivity. In this respect, their study was a traditional scientific management study. The idea was to keep records of the workers' productivity under different levels of illumination. But the initial experiments revealed what seemed to be a problem. The researchers had expected productivity to fall as the lighting was dimmed. Yet the experimental group's productivity went up regardless of whether the lighting was bright or dim, and even when it was reduced to about the level of moonlight.

In a second series of 13 experiments, a separate test room was set up where researchers could manipulate temperature, humidity, and other environmental factors. Productivity went up each time; in fact, it increased by 50 percent overall. When the experimenters repeated the original conditions (expecting productivity to fall to original levels), productivity increased yet again. The experiments were considered a

Little did Elton Mayo and his research team from Harvard University know that their work would forever change managers' beliefs about employee motivation. Their research at the Hawthorne plant of Western Electric in Cicero, Illinois (pictured here), gave birth to the concept of human-based motivation by showing that employees behaved differently simply because they were involved in planning and executing the experiments.

Bettmann/Getty Images

total failure at this point. No matter what the experimenters did, productivity went up. What was causing the increase?

In the end, Mayo guessed that some human or psychological factor was at play.[9] He and his colleagues interviewed the workers, asking about their feelings and attitudes toward the experiment. The answers began a profound change in management thinking that still has repercussions today. Here is what the researchers concluded:

- The workers in the test room thought of themselves as a social group. The atmosphere was informal, they could talk freely, and they interacted regularly with their supervisors and the experimenters. They felt special and worked hard to stay in the group. This was a form of motivation for them.

- The workers were included in planning the experiments. For example, they rejected one kind of pay schedule and recommended another, which was adopted. They believed their ideas were respected and felt engaged in managerial decision making. This, too, motivated them.

- No matter the physical conditions, the workers enjoyed the atmosphere of their special room and the additional pay for being more productive. Job satisfaction increased dramatically.

Researchers now use the term **Hawthorne effect** to refer to people's tendency to behave differently when they know they're being studied. The Hawthorne studies' results encouraged researchers to study human motivation and the managerial styles that lead to higher productivity. Research emphasis shifted from Taylor's scientific management toward Mayo's new human-based management.

Mayo's findings led to completely new assumptions about employees. One was that pay is not the only motivator. In fact, money was found to be a relatively ineffective motivator. New assumptions led to many theories about the human side of motivation. One of the best-known motivation theorists was Abraham Maslow, whose work we discuss next.

Hawthorne effect
The tendency for people to behave differently when they know they are being studied.

LO 10–3   Identify the levels of Maslow's hierarchy of needs and apply them to employee motivation.

Motivation and Maslow's Hierarchy of Needs

Psychologist Abraham Maslow believed that to understand motivation at work, we must understand human motivation in general. It seemed to him that motivation arises from need. That is, people are motivated to satisfy unmet needs. Needs that have already been satisfied no longer provide motivation.

Figure 10.1 shows **Maslow's hierarchy of needs**, whose levels are:

Physiological needs: Basic survival needs, such as the need for food, water, and shelter.
Safety needs: The need to feel secure at work and at home.
Social needs: The need to feel loved, accepted, and part of the group.
Esteem needs: The need for recognition and acknowledgment from others, as well as self-respect and a sense of status or importance.
Self-actualization needs: The need to develop to one's fullest potential.

When one need is satisfied, another, higher-level need emerges and motivates us to satisfy it. The satisfied need is no longer a motivator. For example, if you just ate a four-course dinner, hunger would not be a motivator (at least for several hours), and your attention might turn to your surroundings (safety needs) or family (social needs). Of course, lower-level needs (perhaps thirst) may reemerge at any time they are not being met and take your attention away from higher-level needs.

To compete successfully, U.S. firms must create a work environment that includes goals such as social contribution, honesty, reliability, service, quality, dependability, and

Maslow's hierarchy of needs
Theory of motivation based on unmet human needs from basic physiological needs to safety, social, and esteem needs to self-actualization needs.

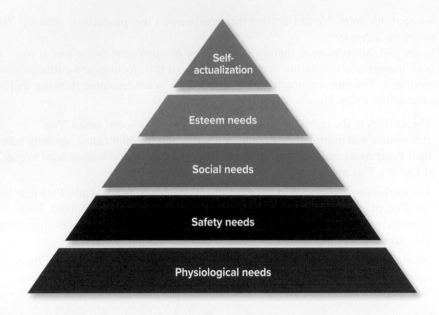

FIGURE 10.1 MASLOW'S HIERARCHY OF NEEDS

Maslow's hierarchy of needs is based on the idea that motivation comes from need. If a need is met, it's no longer a motivator, so a higher-level need becomes the motivator. Higher-level needs demand the support of lower-level needs. This chart shows the various levels of need. Do you know where you are on the chart right now?

Self-actualization

Esteem needs

Social needs

Safety needs

Physiological needs

iSeeit! Need help understanding Maslow's hierarchy? Visit your Connect eBook to view a video for a brief animated explanation.

unity—for all levels of employees. Tony Hsieh, CEO of shoe giant Zappos, thinks about higher-level needs such as meaning (self-actualization) for all employees, including lower-level workers. Hsieh is known to take part in the interview process and even ask, "On a scale of 1 to 10, how weird are you?" This question is designed to not just learn about the candidate but to get an idea of the person's passions. Zappos employees spend 20 percent of their time working on projects outside of their primary roles. This gives meaning to the work of Zappos employees and helps satisfy higher-level needs.[10]

LO 10–4   Distinguish between the motivators and hygiene factors identified by Herzberg.

Herzberg's Motivating Factors

Another direction in managerial theory explores what managers can do with the job itself to motivate employees. In other words, some theorists ask: Of all the factors controllable by managers, which are most effective in generating an enthusiastic work effort?

In the mid-1960s, psychologist Frederick Herzberg conducted the most discussed study in this area. Herzberg asked workers to rank various job-related factors in order of importance relative to motivation. The question was: What creates enthusiasm for workers and makes them work to full potential? The most important factors were:

1. Sense of achievement.
2. Earned recognition.
3. Interest in the work itself.
4. Opportunity for growth.
5. Possibility for advancement.
6. Importance of responsibility.
7. Peer and group relationships.
8. Pay.
9. Supervisor's fairness.
10. Company policies and rules.
11. Status.
12. Job security.
13. Supervisor's friendliness.
14. Working conditions.

Motivators	Hygiene (Maintenance) Factors
(These factors can be used to motivate workers.)	(These factors can cause dissatisfaction, but changing them will have little motivational effect.)
Work itself Achievement Recognition Responsibility Growth and advancement	Company policy and administration Supervision Working conditions Interpersonal relations (co-workers) Salary, status, and job security

FIGURE 10.2
HERZBERG'S MOTIVATORS AND HYGIENE FACTORS
There's some controversy over Herzberg's results. For example, sales managers often use money as a motivator. Recent studies have shown that money can be a motivator if used as part of a recognition program.

Factors receiving the most votes all focused on job content. Workers like to feel as if they contribute to the company (sense of achievement was number 1). They want to earn recognition (number 2) and feel their jobs are important (number 6). They want responsibility (which is why learning is so important) and to earn recognition for that responsibility by having a chance for growth and advancement.[11] Of course, workers also want the job to be interesting. Is this the way you feel about your work?

Workers did not consider factors related to job environment to be motivators. It was interesting to find that one of those factors was pay. Workers felt the *absence* of good pay, job security, and friendly supervisors could cause dissatisfaction, but their presence did not motivate employees to work harder; it just provided satisfaction and contentment. Would you work harder if you were paid more?

Herzberg concluded that certain factors, which he called **motivators**, made employees productive and gave them satisfaction. These factors, as you have seen, mostly related to job content. Herzberg called other elements of the job **hygiene factors** (or maintenance factors). These related to the job environment and could cause dissatisfaction if missing but would not necessarily motivate employees if increased. See Figure 10.2 for a list of motivators and hygiene factors.

Herzberg's motivating factors led to this conclusion: The best way to motivate employees is to make their jobs interesting, help them achieve their objectives, and recognize their achievement through advancement and added responsibility.[12] A review of Figure 10.3 shows the similarity between Maslow's hierarchy of needs and Herzberg's theory.

motivators
In Herzberg's theory of motivating factors, job factors that cause employees to be productive and that give them satisfaction.

hygiene factors
In Herzberg's theory of motivating factors, job factors that can cause dissatisfaction if missing but that do not necessarily motivate employees if increased.

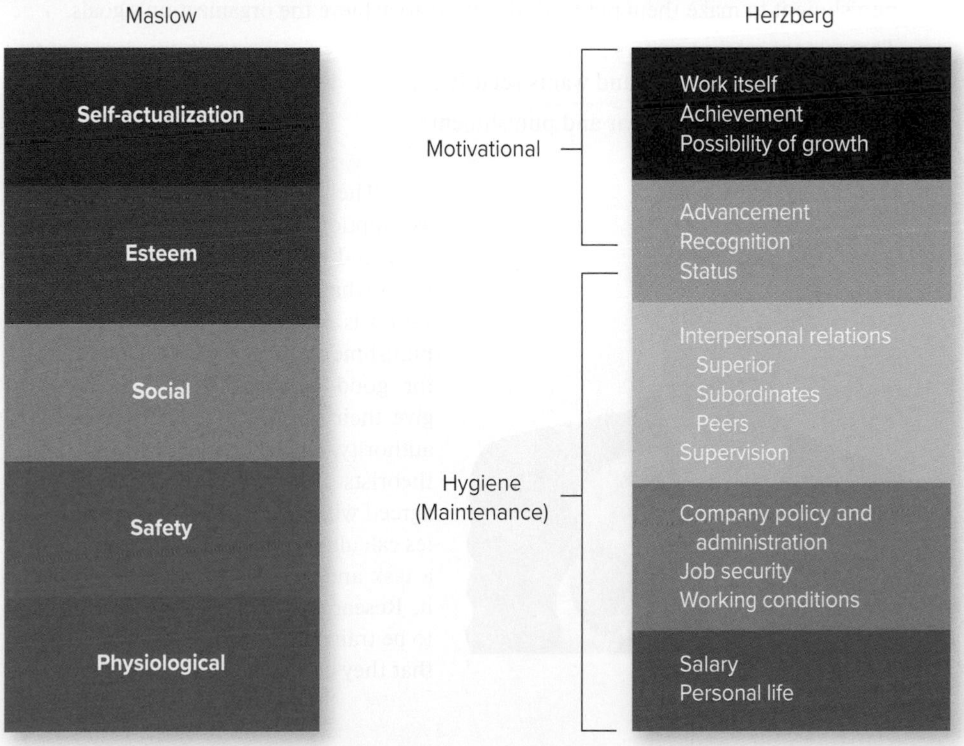

FIGURE 10.3
COMPARISON OF MASLOW'S HIERARCHY OF NEEDS AND HERZBERG'S THEORY OF FACTORS

Maslow:
- Self-actualization
- Esteem
- Social
- Safety
- Physiological

Herzberg:

Motivational:
- Work itself
- Achievement
- Possibility of growth
- Advancement
- Recognition
- Status

Hygiene (Maintenance):
- Interpersonal relations
  - Superior
  - Subordinates
  - Peers
- Supervision
- Company policy and administration
- Job security
- Working conditions
- Salary
- Personal life

Look at Herzberg's motivating factors, identify those that motivate you, and rank them in order of importance to you. Keep them in mind as you consider future jobs and careers. What motivators do your job opportunities offer you? Are they the ones you consider important? Evaluating your job offers in terms of what's really important to you will help you make a wise career choice.

?TESTPREP

- What are the similarities and differences between Taylor's time-motion studies and Mayo's Hawthorne studies?
- How did Mayo's findings influence scientific management?
- Draw a diagram of Maslow's hierarchy of needs. Label and describe the parts.
- Explain the distinction between what Herzberg called motivators and hygiene factors.

LO 10–5 Differentiate among Theory X, Theory Y, and Theory Z.

McGregor's Theory X and Theory Y

The way managers motivate people at work depends greatly on their attitudes toward workers. Management theorist Douglas McGregor observed that managers' attitudes generally fall into one of two entirely different sets of managerial assumptions, which he called Theory X and Theory Y.

Theory X

The assumptions of Theory X management are:

- The average person dislikes work and will avoid it if possible.
- Because of this dislike, workers must be forced, controlled, directed, or threatened with punishment to make them put forth the effort to achieve the organization's goals.
- The average worker prefers to be directed, wishes to avoid responsibility, has relatively little ambition, and wants security.
- Primary motivators are fear and punishment.

> *Theory X managers don't live to make their employees happy. For example, Charlie Ergen, the cofounder and chair of Dish Network, makes employees work long hours and a whole lot of mandatory overtime with few paid holidays. Employees describe the Ergen-created company culture as one of condescension and distrust. Yet the company's earnings have consistently beat market expectations. Would you prefer to work for a Theory X or a Theory Y manager?*

Robert Galbraith/Reuters/Newscom

The natural consequence of these assumptions is a manager who is very busy and watches people closely, telling them what to do and how to do it. Motivation is more likely to take the form of punishment for bad work than reward for good work.[13] Theory X managers give their employees little responsibility, authority, or flexibility. Taylor and other theorists who preceded him would have agreed with Theory X. Time-motion studies calculated the one best way to perform a task and the optimal time to devote to it. Researchers assumed workers needed to be trained and carefully watched to see that they conformed to standards.

Many managers and entrepreneurs still suspect that employees cannot be fully trusted and need to be closely supervised.[14] No doubt you have seen such managers in action. How did they make you feel? Were these managers' assumptions accurate regarding workers' attitudes?

Theory Y

Theory Y makes entirely different assumptions about people:

- Most people like work; it is as natural as play or rest.

- Most people naturally work toward goals to which they are committed.

- The depth of a person's commitment to goals depends on the perceived rewards for achieving them.

- Under certain conditions, most people not only accept but also will seek responsibility.

- People are capable of using a relatively high degree of imagination, creativity, and cleverness to solve problems.

- In industry, the average person's intellectual potential is only partially realized.

- People are motivated by a variety of rewards. Each worker is stimulated by a reward unique to him or her (time off, money, recognition, and so on).

Rather than authority, direction, and close supervision, Theory Y managers emphasize a relaxed managerial atmosphere in which workers are free to set their own objectives, be creative, be flexible, and go beyond the goals set by management. A key technique here is *empowerment*, giving employees authority to make decisions and tools to implement the decisions they make.[15] For empowerment to be a real motivator, management should follow these three steps:

1. Find out what people think the problems in the organization are.

2. Let them design the solutions.

3. Get out of the way and let them put those solutions into action.

Often employees complain that although they're asked to engage in company decision making, their managers fail to actually empower them to make decisions. Have you ever worked in such an atmosphere? How did that make you feel?

Ouchi's Theory Z

One reason many U.S. companies choose a more flexible managerial style is to meet competition from firms in Japan, China, and the European Union. In the 1980s, Japanese companies seemed to be outperforming U.S. businesses. William Ouchi, management professor at the University of California–Los Angeles, wondered whether the reason was the way Japanese companies managed their workers. The Japanese approach, which Ouchi called Type J, included lifetime employment, consensual decision making, collective responsibility for the outcomes of decisions, slow evaluation and promotion, implied control mechanisms, nonspecialized career paths, and holistic concern for employees. In contrast, the U.S. management approach, which Ouchi called Type A, relied on short-term employment, individual decision making, individual responsibility for the outcomes of decisions, rapid evaluation and promotion, explicit control mechanisms, specialized career paths, and segmented concern for employees.

FIGURE 10.4 THEORY Z: A BLEND OF AMERICAN AND JAPANESE MANAGEMENT APPROACHES

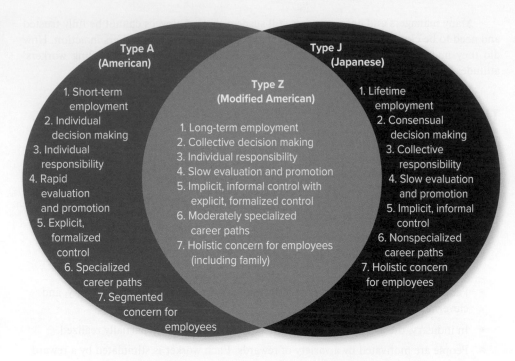

Type A (American)
1. Short-term employment
2. Individual decision making
3. Individual responsibility
4. Rapid evaluation and promotion
5. Explicit, formalized control
6. Specialized career paths
7. Segmented concern for employees

Type Z (Modified American)
1. Long-term employment
2. Collective decision making
3. Individual responsibility
4. Slow evaluation and promotion
5. Implicit, informal control with explicit, formalized control
6. Moderately specialized career paths
7. Holistic concern for employees (including family)

Type J (Japanese)
1. Lifetime employment
2. Consensual decision making
3. Collective responsibility
4. Slow evaluation and promotion
5. Implicit, informal control
6. Nonspecialized career paths
7. Holistic concern for employees

Type J firms are based on the culture of Japan, which includes a focus on trust and intimacy within the group and family. Conversely, Type A firms are based on American culture, which includes a focus on individual rights and achievements. Ouchi wanted to help U.S. firms adopt successful Japanese strategies, but he realized it wouldn't be practical to expect U.S. managers to accept an approach based on the culture of another country. Judge for yourself. A job for life may sound good until you think of the implications: no chance to change jobs and no opportunity to move quickly through the ranks.

Ouchi recommended a hybrid approach, Theory Z (see Figure 10.4). Theory Z includes long-term employment, collective decision making, individual responsibility for the outcomes of decisions, slow evaluation and promotion, moderately specialized career paths, and holistic concern for employees (including family). Theory Z views the organization as a family that fosters cooperation and organizational values.

In recent years, demographic and social changes, fierce global competition, and economic changes have led Japanese managers to reevaluate the way they conduct business.[16]

Electronics giant Hitachi was the first major Japanese company to quit requiring corporate calisthenics. Having everyone start the day with group exercises had symbolized doing the same thing the same way, and reinforced the cultural belief that employees should not take risks or think for themselves. Many managers think such conformity is what hurt Japanese business. Will Japanese managers move toward the hybrid Theory Z in the future? We'll have to wait and see. An appropriate managerial style matches the culture,

Google employees enjoy a variety of perks, from state-of-the-art gyms to free meals to EnergyPods like the one pictured here. These relaxation stations "harness science and NASA technology" to provide employees with refreshing naps at any time of day. Can you think of any other examples of the kind of holistic concern for employees suggested by William Ouchi's Theory Z style of management?

Brooks Kraft LLC/Corbis/Getty Images

FIGURE 10.5 A COMPARISON OF THEORIES X, Y, AND Z

THEORY X	THEORY Y	THEORY Z
1. Employees dislike work and will try to avoid it.	**1.** Employees view work as a natural part of life.	**1.** Employee involvement is the key to increased productivity.
2. Employees prefer to be controlled and directed.	**2.** Employees prefer limited control and direction.	**2.** Employee control is implied and informal.
3. Employees seek security, not responsibility.	**3.** Employees will seek responsibility under proper work conditions.	**3.** Employees prefer to share responsibility and decision making.
4. Employees must be intimidated by managers to perform.	**4.** Employees perform better in work environments that are nonintimidating.	**4.** Employees perform better in environments that foster trust and cooperation.
5. Employees are motivated by financial rewards.	**5.** Employees are motivated by many different needs.	**5.** Employees need guaranteed employment and will accept slow evaluations and promotions.

FIGURE 10.5 A COMPARISON OF THEORIES X, Y, AND Z

situation, and specific needs of the organization and its employees. (See Figure 10.5 for a summary of Theories X, Y, and Z.)

LO 10–6 Explain the key principles of goal-setting, expectancy, and equity theories.

Goal-Setting Theory and Management by Objectives

Goal-setting theory says setting ambitious but attainable goals can motivate workers and improve performance if the goals are accepted and accompanied by feedback, and if conditions in the organization pave the way for achievement. All organization members should have some basic agreement about both overall goals and specific objectives for each department and individual. Therefore, there should be a system to engage everyone in the organization in goal-setting and implementation.

The late management expert Peter Drucker developed such a system in the 1960s. "Managers cannot motivate people; they can only thwart people's motivation because people motivate themselves," he said. Called **management by objectives (MBO)**, Drucker's system of goal-setting and implementation includes a cycle of discussion, review, and evaluation of objectives among top and middle-level managers, supervisors, and employees. It calls on managers to formulate goals in cooperation with everyone in the organization, to commit employees to those goals, and to monitor results and reward accomplishment.[17] Government agencies, like the Department of Defense, use MBO.

MBO is most effective in relatively stable situations when managers can make long-range plans and implement them with few changes. Managers must also understand the difference between helping and coaching employees. *Helping* means working with the employee and doing part of the work if necessary. *Coaching* means acting as a resource—teaching, guiding, and recommending—but not participating actively or doing the task. The central idea of MBO is that employees need to motivate themselves.

Employee input and expectations are important. Problems can arise when management uses MBO as a strategy for forcing managers and workers to commit to goals that are not agreed on together, but are instead set by top management.[18]

goal-setting theory
The idea that setting ambitious but attainable goals can motivate workers and improve performance if the goals are accepted, accompanied by feedback, and facilitated by organizational conditions.

management by objectives (MBO)
Peter Drucker's system of goal-setting and implementation; it involves a cycle of discussion, review, and evaluation of objectives among top and middle-level managers, supervisors, and employees.

Victor Vroom identified the importance of employee expectations and developed a process called expectancy theory. Let's examine this concept next.

Meeting Employee Expectations: Expectancy Theory

expectancy theory
Victor Vroom's theory that the amount of effort employees exert on a specific task depends on their expectations of the outcome.

According to Victor Vroom's **expectancy theory**, employee expectations can affect motivation. That is, the amount of effort employees exert on a specific task depends on their expectations of the outcome. Vroom contends that employees ask three questions before committing their maximum effort to a task: (1) Can I accomplish the task? (2) If I do accomplish it, what's my reward? (3) Is the reward worth the effort? (See Figure 10.6.)

Think of the effort you might exert in class under the following conditions: Suppose your instructor says that to earn an A in the course, you must achieve an average of 90 percent on coursework plus jump eight feet high. Would you exert maximum effort toward earning an A if you knew you could not possibly jump eight feet high? Suppose your instructor said any student can earn an A in the course, but you know this instructor has not awarded an A in 25 years of teaching. If the reward of an A seems unattainable, would you exert significant effort in the course? Better yet, let's say you read online that businesses prefer hiring C-minus students to A-plus students. Does the reward of an A seem worth it? Now think of similar situations that may occur on the job.

Expectancy theory does note that expectation varies from individual to individual. Employees establish their own views of task difficulty and the value of the reward.[19] Researchers David Nadler and Edward Lawler modified Vroom's theory and suggested that managers follow five steps to improve employee performance:[20]

1. Determine what rewards employees value.
2. Determine each employee's desired performance standard.
3. Ensure that performance standards are attainable.
4. Guarantee rewards tied to performance.
5. Be certain that employees consider the rewards adequate.

Treating Employees Fairly: Equity Theory

equity theory
The idea that employees try to maintain equity between inputs and outputs compared to others in similar positions.

Equity theory looks at how employees' perceptions of fairness affect their willingness to perform. It assumes employees ask, "If I do a good job, will it be worth it?" and "What's fair?" Employees try to maintain equity between what they put into the job and what they get out of it, comparing those inputs and outputs to those of others in similar positions. Workers find comparative information through personal relationships, professional organizations, and other sources.[21]

FIGURE 10.6
EXPECTANCY THEORY
The amount of effort employees exert on a task depends on their expectations of the outcome.

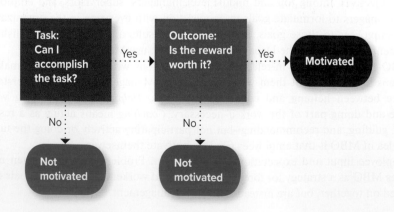

When workers perceive inequity, they will try to reestablish fairness in a number of ways.[22] For example, suppose you compare the grade you earned on a term paper with your classmates' grades. If you think you received a lower grade than someone who put out the same effort as you, you may (1) reduce your effort on future class projects or (2) rationalize the difference by saying, "Grades are overvalued anyway!" If you think your paper received a higher grade than comparable papers, you will probably (1) increase your effort to justify the higher reward in the future or (2) rationalize by saying, "I'm worth it!"

In the workplace, perceived inequity may lead to lower productivity, reduced quality, increased absenteeism, and voluntary resignation.

Remember that equity judgments are based on perception and are therefore subject to error. When workers overestimate their own contributions—as happens often—they feel *any* rewards given out for performance are inequitable. Sometimes organizations try to deal with this by keeping employee salaries secret, but secrecy may make things worse. Employees are likely to overestimate the salaries of others, in addition to overestimating their own contribution. A recent study conducted by the U.S. Bureau of Labor Statistics showed workers often overestimate their own productive hours by 10 percent.[23] The best remedy is generally clear and frequent communication. Managers must communicate as clearly as possible both the results they expect and the outcomes that will occur.[24]

TESTPREP

- Briefly describe the managerial attitudes behind Theories X, Y, and Z.
- Explain goal-setting theory.
- Evaluate expectancy theory. When could expectancy theory apply to your efforts or lack of effort?
- Explain the principles of equity theory.

LO 10–7   Show how managers put motivation theories into action through such strategies as job enrichment, open communication, and job recognition.

Putting Theory into Action

Now that you know what a few theorists have to say about motivation, you might be asking yourself "So what? What do all those theories have to do with what really goes on in my modern workplace?" Fair question. Let's look at how companies put these theories into action through job enrichment, open communication, and job recognition.

Motivating through Job Enrichment

Managers have extended both Maslow's and Herzberg's theories through **job enrichment**, a strategy that motivates workers through the job itself. Work is assigned so that individuals can complete an identifiable task from beginning to end and are held responsible for successful achievement. Job enrichment is based on Herzberg's higher motivators, such as responsibility, achievement, and recognition.[25] It stands in contrast to *job simplification,* which produces task efficiency by breaking a job into simple steps and assigning people to each. Review Maslow's and Herzberg's work to see how job enrichment grew from those theories.

job enrichment
A motivational strategy that emphasizes motivating the worker through the job itself.

Glassblowers like this use a variety of dangerous tools to create vibrant works of art. One of the hallmarks of job enrichment is the worker's ability to perform a complete task from beginning to end. Why do you think this might be more motivating than simply adding a few parts to a product on an assembly line?

Marianne Purdie/Getty Images

Those who advocate job enrichment believe that five characteristics of work are important in motivation and performance:

1. *Skill variety.* The extent to which a job demands different skills.

2. *Task identity.* The degree to which the job requires doing a task with a visible outcome from beginning to end.

3. *Task significance.* The degree to which the job has a substantial impact on the lives or work of others in the company.

4. *Autonomy.* The degree of freedom, independence, and discretion in scheduling work and determining procedures.

5. *Feedback.* The amount of direct and clear information given about job performance.

Variety, identity, and significance contribute to the meaningfulness of the job. Autonomy gives people a feeling of responsibility; feedback contributes to a feeling of achievement and recognition.[26]

job enlargement

A job enrichment strategy that involves combining a series of tasks into one challenging and interesting assignment.

job rotation

A job enrichment strategy that involves moving employees from one job to another.

One type of job enrichment is **job enlargement**, which combines a series of tasks into one challenging and interesting assignment. Maytag, the home appliance manufacturer, redesigned its washing machine production process so that employees could assemble an entire water pump instead of just adding a single part. **Job rotation** also makes work more interesting and motivating by moving employees from one job to another. One problem, of course, is the need to train employees to do several different operations. However, the resulting increase in motivation and the value of having flexible, cross-trained employees usually offsets the costs.

Motivating through Open Communication

Communication and information must flow freely throughout the organization when employees are empowered to make decisions—they can't make them in a vacuum. Procedures for encouraging open communication include the following:[27]

- *Create an organizational culture that rewards listening.* Top managers must create places to talk and show employees that talking with superiors matters—by providing feedback, adopting employee suggestions, and rewarding upward communication—even if the discussion is negative. Employees must have the freedom to say anything they deem appropriate and believe their opinions are valued.

- *Train supervisors and managers to listen.* Most people receive no training in how to listen, in school or anywhere else, so organizations must do such training themselves or hire an expert to do it.

- *Use effective questioning techniques.* We get information through questioning. Different kinds of questions yield different kinds of information. Closed questions that generate yes/no answers don't encourage the longer, more thoughtful responses that open questions do. Appropriate personal questions can create a sense of camaraderie between employee and manager.

- *Remove barriers to open communication.* Separate offices, parking areas, bathrooms, and dining rooms for managers only set up barriers. Other barriers are different dress codes and different ways of addressing one another (like calling workers by their first names and managers by their last). Removing such barriers may require imagination and managers' willingness to give up special privileges.

- *Avoid vague and ambiguous communication.* Passive voice appears weak and tentative. Statements such as "Mistakes were made" leave you wondering who made the mistakes. Hedging is another way managers send garbled messages. Terms like *possibly* and *perhaps* sound wishy-washy to employees who are seeking definitive direction.

- *Make it easy to communicate.* Encouraging organization members to eat together at large lunch tables, allowing employees to gather in conference rooms, having organizational picnics and athletic teams, and so on can help workers at all levels mix with one another.

- *Ask employees what is important to them.* Managers shouldn't wait until the exit interview to ask an employee, "What can I do to keep you?" At that point, it's too late. Instead they should have frequent *stay interviews* to find out what matters to employees and what they can do to keep them on the job.

Applying Open Communication in Self-Managed Teams

Auto companies are often praised for good practices. At Ford Motor Company, for example, a group known as Team Mustang set the guidelines for how production teams should be formed. Given the challenge to create a car that would make people dust off their old "Mustang Sally" records and dance into showrooms, the 400-member team was also given the freedom to make decisions without waiting for approval from headquarters. Everyone worked under one roof in an old warehouse where drafting experts sat next to accountants, engineers next to stylists. Budgetary walls between departments were knocked down too as department managers were persuaded to surrender some control over their employees on the team.

Grzegorz Czapski/Shutterstock

When the resulting Mustang convertible displayed shaking problems, engineers were so motivated to finish on time and under budget that they worked late into the night, sleeping on the floor when necessary. Senior Ford executives were tempted to intervene, but they stuck with their promise not to meddle. Working with suppliers, the team solved the shaking problem and still came in under budget and a couple of months early. The new car was a hit with drivers, and sales soared.

To implement such teams, managers at most companies must reinvent work. This means respecting workers, providing interesting work, developing workers' skills, allowing autonomy, decentralizing authority, and rewarding good work.[28] Let's take a look at some of the ways companies recognize and reward good work.

Recognizing a Job Well Done

A recent survey indicated that the top reason employees voluntarily left their jobs was due to disengagement. However, lack of appreciation did not follow too far behind.[29] Letting people know you appreciate their work is usually more powerful than giving a raise or bonus alone. More and more recent college graduates report salary is not their ultimate motivator. Yes, they needed enough money to cover their basic needs. However, the majority of participants rated career advancement opportunities as well as interesting and challenging work to be the most important things. Clearly, providing advancement opportunity and recognizing achievements are important in attracting and retaining valuable, engaged employees.[30]

Promotions aren't the only way to celebrate a job well done. Recognition can be as simple as noticing positive actions out loud, making employees feel their efforts are worthwhile and valued enough to be noticed. For example: "Sarina, you didn't say much in the meeting today. Your ideas are usually so valuable; I missed hearing them." This comment

In the car business, nothing works quite like the "wow" factor. At Ford, the 400-member Team Mustang group was empowered to create a car that would "wow" everyone on the road. The work team, suppliers, company managers, and even customers worked together to make the Mustang a winner in the very competitive automobile market.

Instant Insight into Employee Engagement

Have you ever wondered what was going on in someone else's head? Managers always want to know. They need to know what keeps employees going, what causes them to disengage, and, ultimately, what makes workers happy. Though they may not be able to read exactly what is in their employees' heads, they now have more tools to help track employee moods.

Artificial intelligence (AI) technology from companies like IBM gives managers the opportunity to ask employees questions, receive employee feedback, and even predict if an employee is planning on quitting. Although some managers may call them "happiness meters," they are much more than that. They help managers monitor moods, yes, but they can also help discover what employees really want and what is important to the workplace culture as

a whole. More importantly, the processed information gets to the manager fast! Gathering useful information used to take teams weeks or months to process but now are completed almost instantly.

Employees may often hide their true feelings on topics, such as how they get along with their manager, but AI can get around that. AI can monitor employee–manager interactions to evaluate whether conversations between the two show engagement or frustration. From here, management can assess better ways to engage the employee or communicate better in the future. Some managers, who had previously assumed their employees wanted enhancements to the games in the break room, found their employees actually craved more responsibilities and greater roles in the strategic planning process. Not knowing

what the employees were looking for almost led to another foosball table. Oops!

Managers won't always know what motivates and engages their employees unless they go digging for it. AI is already helping increase employee engagement. How's that? Managers are learning that employees are looking for expanded roles, greater responsibility, and more recognition. AI gives modern managers the opportunity to remedy a problem or increase an employee's role well before they might lose that employee.

Sources: Maria Aspan, "A.I. Is Transforming the Job Interview—and Everything After," *Fortune,* January 20, 2020; Eric Rosenbaum, "IBM Artificial Intelligence Can Predict with 95% Accuracy Which Workers Are about to Quit Their Jobs," *CNBC,* April 3, 2019; Sam Boykin, "Startup Offers AI Technology to Boost Employee Engagement," *Sacramento Business Journal,* January 31, 2020; Falon Fatemi, "4 Non-Obvious Ways to Use AI to Predict and Prevent Employee Turnover," *Forbes,* January 15, 2020.

lets Sarina know her ideas are appreciated, and she'll be more apt to participate fully in the next meeting.

Here are just a few examples of ways managers have raised employee spirits without raising paychecks:

- A Los Angeles law firm sent 400 employees and their families to Disneyland for the day. FedEx Office did something similar, but it sent high-achieving employees to Disneyland *and* put the company's top executives in those employees' place while they were gone.

- Walt Disney World offers more than 150 employee recognition programs. The Spirit of Fred Award is named after an employee named Fred, who makes each award (a certificate mounted and varnished on a plaque) himself. Fred's name became an acronym for Friendly, Resourceful, Enthusiastic, and Dependable.

Rather than giving out boring certificates or plaques, Hewlett-Packard awards golden bananas to show its appreciation to exceptional employees. What role do you think these awards play in motivating the winners to continue their outstanding performance?

ptashka/Shutterstock

- Maritz Motivation Solutions, in Fenton, Missouri, has a Thanks a Bunch program that gives flowers to a selected employee in appreciation of a job well done. That employee passes the bouquet to someone else who helped. The idea is to see how many people are given the flowers throughout the day. The bouquet comes with thank-you cards that are entered into a drawing for awards like binoculars and jackets.

● Hewlett-Packard (HP) bestows its Golden Banana Award for a job well done. The award started when an engineer burst into his manager's office saying he'd found the solution to a long-standing problem. In his haste to find something to give the employee to show his appreciation, the manager grabbed a banana from his lunch and said, "Well done! Congratulations!" The Golden Banana is now one of the most prestigious honors given to an inventive HP employee.

Giving valued employees prime parking spots, more vacation days, or more flexible schedules may help them feel their work is meaningful and appreciated, but sometimes nothing inspires workers like the prospect of a payout down the road. Companies that offer a small equity stake or stock options often have a good chance of developing loyal employees.

The Adapting to Change box discusses how some organizations utilize "happiness meters" to learn how they can identify and address workplace issues in order to keep employees engaged.

The same things don't motivate all employees. Next we'll explore how employees from different cultures and generations are motivated in different ways.

LO 10–8 Show how managers personalize motivation strategies to appeal to employees across the globe and across generations.

Personalizing Motivation

Managers cannot use one motivational formula for all employees. They have to get to know each worker personally and tailor the motivational effort to the individual. This is further complicated by the increase in global business and the fact that managers now work with employees from a variety of cultural backgrounds. Cultural differences also exist between generations raised in the same country. Let's look at how managers personalize their strategies to appeal to employees across the globe and across generations.

Motivating Employees across the Globe

Different cultures experience motivational approaches differently; therefore, managers study and understand these cultural factors in designing a reward system. In a *high-context culture,* workers build personal relationships and develop group trust before focusing on tasks. In a *low-context culture,* workers often view relationship building as a waste of time that diverts attention from the task. Koreans, Italians, and Saudis tend to be high-context workers who often view their U.S. colleagues as insincere due to their need for data and quick decision making.

The Hershey Company solved a cross-cultural problem with a recognition program for its 21,000 employees in 17 countries, all of whom use a wide variety of languages and currencies. Workhuman (previously Globoforce) revamped and introduced a new rewards program for Hershey called SMILES that automatically adjusts for differences created by cultural preferences, tax laws, and even local standards of living. The points-based system allows for rewards to be redeemed for thousands of products and gift card options, depending on where the employee is based. The system allows for both managers and employees to send SMILES, and in the program's first week almost 9 percent of the entire company was recognized for good work—some employees recognized for the very first time.[31]

Understanding motivation in global organizations and building effective global teams are still new tasks for most companies. Developing group leaders who are culturally astute, flexible, and able to deal with ambiguity is a challenge today's businesses face.

Motivating Employees across Generations

Members of each generation—Baby Boomers (born between 1946 and 1964), Generation X (born between 1965 and 1980), Generation Y, better known as Millennials (born between 1980 and 1995), Generation Z (born 1995–2009), Generation Alpha (born after 2010)—are linked through experiences they shared in their formative years, usually the first 10 years of life. (*Note:* The year spans for Gen X, Y, and Z are widely debated so these dates are approximations.) The beliefs you accept as a child affect how you view risk, challenge, authority, technology, relationships, and economics. When you're in a management position, they can even affect whom you hire, fire, or promote.

In general, Boomers were raised in families that experienced unprecedented economic prosperity, secure jobs, and optimism about the future. Gen Xers were raised in dual-career families with parents who focused on work. As children, they attended day care or became latchkey kids. Their parents' layoffs added to their insecurity about a lifelong job. Millennials were raised by indulgent parents, and most don't remember a time without the Internet and mobile phones. Gen Zers grew up post–9/11, in the wake of the Great Recession and amid countless reports of school violence.

The main constant in the lives of Gen Xers, Millennials, and Gen Zers is inconstancy. Consider the unprecedented change in the past 20 years in every area (i.e., economic, technological, scientific, social, and political). Gen Xers, Millennials, and Gen Zers expect change. It is the absence of change that they find questionable.

How do generational differences among these groups affect motivation in the workplace? Boomer managers need to be flexible with their younger employees, or they will lose them. Gen Xers need to use their enthusiasm for change and streamlining to their advantage. Although many are unwilling to pay the same price for success their parents and grandparents did, their concern about undue stress and long hours doesn't mean they lack ambition. They want economic security as much as older workers, but they have a different approach to achieving it. Rather than focusing on job security, Gen Xers tend to focus on career security instead and are willing to change jobs to find it.

vorDa/Getty Images

Millennials tend to be skeptical, outspoken, and image-driven as well as adaptable, tech-savvy employees with a sense of fun and tolerance. It is important for managers of all ages to be aware that employees of different generations communicate differently. How do you think generational differences will affect this manager and employee?

Gen X managers are responsible for motivating other employees. What kind of managers are they? In general, they are well equipped to motivate people. They usually understand that there is more to life than work, and they think a big part of motivating is letting people know you recognize that fact. Gen X managers tend to focus more on results than on hours in the workplace. They tend to be flexible and good at collaboration and consensus building. They often think in broader terms than their predecessors because the media have exposed them to problems around the world. They also have a big impact on their team members. They are more likely to give them the goals and outlines of the project and leave them alone to do their work.

Perhaps the best asset of Gen X managers is their ability to give employees feedback, especially positive feedback. One reason might be that they expect more of it themselves. One new employee was frustrated because he hadn't received feedback from his boss since he was hired—two weeks earlier. In short, managers need to realize that today's workers demand performance reviews and other forms of feedback more than the traditional one or two times a year.

Today, over 35 percent of the American workforce is Millennials.[32] As a group, they tend to share a number of characteristics: They're often impatient, skeptical, blunt, expressive, and image-driven. Like any other generation, Millennials can transform their characteristics into unique skills. For example, they tend to be adaptable, tech-savvy, able to

The two youngest generations in the workplace, Millennials and Gen Zers, have changed how we communicate day-to-day. Sure, there have always been performance reviews and other ways to assess employee potential. However, never have employers encountered the need for the regular, or even constant, feedback that young professionals have come to expect. Feedback isn't just sought from managers either; employees also seek recognition from their peers.

One of the largest firms that fills that need for companies and employees alike is TINYpulse. Through the company's website or mobile app, employees can get the recognition they are hungry for through "Cheers for Peers." Anyone can send cheers to co-workers and see a live chart of all the kudos going out. A leaderboard shows how many cheers each person received and what he or she did to earn them. This creates a culture in the workplace that is focused on appreciation and teamwork.

Although all the information (except for who is getting cheers) is anonymous, there are many helpful metrics for managers. They can see whether or not the number of cheers being sent to co-workers is rising or falling, receive suggestions through a private message system, and ask quick questions that employees can answer right away. By asking one question at a time instead of a lengthy survey, managers are more likely to receive useful feedback. The app even reminds employees to answer the question if it has been ignored too long.

D. Hurst/Alamy Stock Photo

With tools like TINYpulse, creating a comfortable and openly communicative work environment should be easier to achieve. There's enough anonymity for employees to be honest about how they feel and enough public information for an employee to feel directly recognized.

Sources: Ruzbeh Irani, "Culture Is Just as Important to the Diversified Global Enterprise as to the Startup," *Entrepreneur,* January 13, 2020; Blair Stern, Kris Curtis, and Adam Chapman, "The Dynamic Connection between People and Their Workplace," GeekWire, November 8, 2019; Albert Costill, "What Really Motivates Employees? Research Reveals Secrets," *Business 2 Community,* February 5, 2020; TINYpulse, tinypulse.com, accessed February 2020.

grasp new concepts, practiced at multitasking, efficient, and tolerant.[33] Millennials tend to place a higher value on work–life balance, expect their employers to adapt to them (not the other way around), and are more likely to rank fun and stimulation in their top five ideal-job requirements. What do you think are the most effective strategies managers can use to motivate Millennial workers?

Many Millennials didn't rush to find lifetime careers after graduation. They tended to "job surf" and weren't opposed to living with their parents while they tested out jobs. Some of this career postponement wasn't by choice as much as a result of the state of the economy. The recession of 2008 hurt younger workers more deeply than other workers. In fact, Millennials were less likely to be employed than Gen Xers or Boomers were at the same age. The recession greatly increased the competition for jobs as Millennials struggled to enter the job market, Boomers tried to make up lost retirement savings, and Gen Xers fought to pay mortgages and raise families.

As Millennials assume more responsibilities in the workplace and take on management roles, they sometimes must manage and lead others far older than themselves. How can young managers lead others who may have more experience than they do? Perhaps the three most important things to keep in mind are to be confident, be open-minded, and solicit feedback regularly.[34] Just remember that asking for input and advice is different from asking for permission or guidance. The nearby Connecting through Social Media box highlights a new way for managers to give and receive feedback.

From 2012 to 2020, former T-Mobile CEO John Legere transformed his company from an also-ran in the telecom world into one of the industry's top brands. Along with being a ruthless corporate negotiator, Legere is also known for his animated personality that won the widespread approval of his employees. How do you think lively bosses like Legere develop happy, productive, and loyal employees?

David Becker/Showtime/Getty Images

The oldest Gen Zers are now entering the workplace. As they enter the job market, they create a workplace very generationally diverse. This is the first time in history that the workforce consists of four generations.[35] They are likely to be more cautious and security-minded, but inspired to improve the world. Since they've seen the effects of the economy firsthand, they are more aware of troubling times. A recent survey of Gen Zers shows that they believe school violence/shootings will have the biggest impact on their generation, overriding the invention of social networking and the election of the first Black president. These events make them resilient and pragmatic; they want to confront rather than hide from their problems. Like Millennials, Gen Zers are tech-savvy and are looking to be part of a community within their workplaces. On the other side of that, Gen Zers are interested in more practical benefits like health care and 401(k)s, and are less likely to job hop than Millennials.[36]

It is important for managers of all ages to be aware that employees of different generations communicate differently. Boomers generally prefer to communicate in meetings or conference calls. Gen Xers typically prefer e-mail and will choose meetings only if there are no other options. Millennials most often use technology to communicate, particularly through social media. Gen Zers are starting to trend back toward face-to-face meetings and shy away from phone calls.[37]

In every generational shift, the older generation tends to say the same thing about the new: "They break the rules." The traditionalists said it of the Baby Boomers. Boomers look at Gen Xers and say, "Why are they breaking the rules?" And now Gen Xers are looking at Millennials and Gen Zers and saying, "What's wrong with these kids?" And you know Gen X and Z will be saying the same thing about Generation Alpha someday.

One thing in business is likely to remain constant: Much motivation will come from the job itself rather than from external punishments or rewards. Managers need to give workers what they require to do a good job: the right tools, the right information, and the right amount of cooperation. Motivation doesn't have to be difficult. It begins with acknowledging a job well done—and especially doing so in front of others. After all, as we said earlier, the best motivator is frequently a sincere "Thanks, I really appreciate what you're doing."

?TESTPREP

- What are several steps firms can take to increase internal communications and thus motivation?
- What problems may emerge when firms try to implement participative management?
- Why is it important to adjust motivational styles to individual employees? Are there any general principles of motivation that today's managers should follow?

SUMMARY

LO 10–1 Explain Taylor's theory of scientific management.

- **What is Frederick Taylor known for?**

Human efficiency engineer Frederick Taylor was one of the first people to study management and has been called the "father" of scientific management. He conducted time-motion studies to learn the most efficient way of doing a job and then trained workers in those procedures. He published his book *The Principles of Scientific Management* in 1911. Henry L. Gantt and Frank and Lillian Gilbreth were followers of Taylor.

LO 10–2 Describe the Hawthorne studies and their significance to management.

- **What led to the more human-based managerial styles?**

The greatest impact on motivation theory was generated by the Hawthorne studies in the late 1920s and early 1930s. In these studies, Elton Mayo found that human factors such as feelings of involvement and participation led to greater productivity gains than did physical changes in the workplace.

LO 10–3 Identify the levels of Maslow's hierarchy of needs and apply them to employee motivation.

- **What did Abraham Maslow find human motivation to be based on?**

Maslow studied basic human motivation and found that motivation was based on needs. He said that a person with an unfilled need would be motivated to satisfy it and that a satisfied need no longer served as motivation.

- **What levels of need did Maslow identify?**

Starting at the bottom of Maslow's hierarchy and going to the top, the levels of need are physiological, safety, social, esteem, and self-actualization.

- **Can managers use Maslow's theory?**

Yes, they can recognize what unmet needs a person has and design work so that it satisfies those needs.

LO 10–4 Distinguish between the motivators and hygiene factors identified by Herzberg.

- **What is the difference between Frederick Herzberg's motivator and hygiene factors?**

Herzberg found that whereas some factors motivate workers (motivators), others cause job dissatisfaction if missing but are not motivators if present (hygiene or maintenance factors).

- **What are the factors called motivators?**

The work itself, achievement, recognition, responsibility, growth, and advancement.

- **What are the hygiene (maintenance) factors?**

Company policies, supervision, working conditions, interpersonal relationships, and salary.

LO 10–5 Differentiate among Theory X, Theory Y, and Theory Z.

- **Who developed Theory X and Theory Y?**

Douglas McGregor held that managers have one of two opposing attitudes toward employees. He called them Theory X and Theory Y.

- **What is Theory X?**

  Theory X assumes the average person dislikes work and will avoid it if possible. Therefore, people must be forced, controlled, and threatened with punishment to accomplish organizational goals.

- **What is Theory Y?**

  Theory Y assumes people like working and will accept responsibility for achieving goals if rewarded for doing so.

- **What is Theory Z?**

  William Ouchi based Theory Z on Japanese management styles and stresses long-term employment; collective decision making; individual responsibility; slow evaluation and promotion; implicit, informal control with explicit, formalized control; moderately specialized career paths; and a holistic concern for employees (including family).

LO 10–6 Explain the key principles of goal-setting, expectancy, and equity theories.

- **What is goal-setting theory?**

  Goal-setting theory is based on the notion that setting ambitious but attainable goals will lead to high levels of motivation and performance if the goals are accepted and accompanied by feedback, and if conditions in the organization make achievement possible.

- **What is management by objectives (MBO)?**

  MBO is a system of goal-setting and implementation; it includes a cycle of discussion, review, and evaluation of objectives among top and middle-level managers, supervisors, and employees.

- **What is the basis of expectancy theory?**

  According to Victor Vroom's expectancy theory, employee expectations can affect an individual's motivation.

- **What are the key elements of expectancy theory?**

  Expectancy theory centers on three questions employees often ask about performance on the job: (1) Can I accomplish the task? (2) If I do accomplish it, what's my reward? and (3) Is the reward worth the effort?

- **According to equity theory, employees try to maintain equity between inputs and outputs compared to other employees in similar positions. What happens when employees perceive that their rewards are not equitable?**

  If employees perceive they are underrewarded, they will either reduce their effort or rationalize that it isn't important. If they perceive that they are overrewarded, they will either increase their effort to justify the higher reward in the future or rationalize by saying, "I'm worth it!" Inequity leads to lower productivity, reduced quality, increased absenteeism, and voluntary resignation.

LO 10–7 Show how managers put motivation theories into action through such strategies as job enrichment, open communication, and job recognition.

- **What characteristics of work affect motivation and performance?**

  The job characteristics that influence motivation are skill variety, task identity, task significance, autonomy, and feedback.

- **Name two forms of job enrichment that increase motivation.**

  Job enlargement combines a series of tasks into one challenging and interesting assignment. Job rotation makes work more interesting by moving employees from one job to another.

■ **How does open communication improve employee motivation?**

Open communication helps both top managers and employees understand the objectives and work together to achieve them.

■ **How can managers encourage open communication?**

Managers can create an organizational culture that rewards listening, train supervisors and managers to listen, use effective questioning techniques, remove barriers to open communication, avoid vague and ambiguous communication, and actively make it easier for all to communicate.

LO 10–8 Show how managers personalize motivation strategies to appeal to employees across the globe and across generations.

■ **What is the difference between high-context and low-context cultures?**

In high-context cultures, people build personal relationships and develop group trust before focusing on tasks. In low-context cultures, people often view relationship building as a waste of time that diverts attention from the task.

■ **How are Generation X managers likely to be different from their Baby Boomer predecessors?**

Baby Boomers tend to be willing to work long hours to build their careers and often expect their employees to do likewise. Gen Xers may strive for a more balanced lifestyle and are likely to focus on results rather than on how many hours their teams work. Gen Xers tend to be better than previous generations at working in teams and providing frequent feedback. They usually are not bound by traditions that may constrain those who have been with an organization for a long time and are willing to try new approaches to solving problems.

■ **What are some common characteristics of Millennials and Gen Zers?**

Millennials tend to be adaptable, tech-savvy, able to grasp new concepts, practiced at multitasking, efficient, and tolerant. They often place a higher value on work–life balance, expect their employers to adapt to them, and are more likely to rank fun and stimulation in their top five ideal-job requirements. Gen Zers tend to be more cautious and security-minded but inspired to improve the world. They want to confront rather than hide from problems. Like Millennials, Gen Zers are tech-savvy and are looking to be part of a community within their workplaces. However, Gen Zers are interested in more practical benefits like health care and 401(k)s, and are less likely to job hop than Millennials.

KEY TERMS

equity theory 256	job enlargement 258	motivators 251
expectancy theory 256	job enrichment 257	principle of motion
extrinsic reward 247	job rotation 258	economy 248
goal-setting theory 255	management by	scientific management
Hawthorne effect 249	objectives (MBO) 255	247
hygiene factors 251	Maslow's hierarchy	time-motion studies 247
intrinsic reward 247	of needs 249	

CRITICAL THINKING

Your job right now is to finish reading this chapter. How strongly would you be motivated to do that if you were sweating in a room at 105 degrees Fahrenheit? Imagine your roommate has turned on the air-conditioning. Once you are more comfortable, are you more likely to read? Look at Maslow's hierarchy of needs to see what need would be motivating you at both times. Now recall a situation in your home, school, or work life in which you were feeling particularly motivated to do something. Which of the needs identified by Maslow motivated you then and why?

PUTTING PRINCIPLES TO WORK

PURPOSE

To assess your personality type using the Jung-Briggs Myers typology test and to evaluate how well the description of your personality type fits you.

EXERCISE

Sometimes understanding differences in employees' personalities helps managers understand how to motivate them. Find out about your personality by going to the HumanMetrics website (humanmetrics.com) and take the Jung Typology Test (based on Carl Jung's and Isabel Briggs Myers's approaches to typology). (Disclaimer: The test, like all other personality tests, is only a rough and preliminary indicator of personality.)

1. After you identify your personality type, read the corresponding personality portrait. How well or how poorly does the identified personality type fit?

2. Sometimes a personality test does not accurately identify your personality, but it may give you a place to start looking for a portrait that fits. After you have read the portraits on the website, ask a good friend or relative which one best describes you.

DEVELOPING CAREER SKILLS

KEY: ● **Team**   ★ **Analytic**   ▲ **Communication**   ▣ **Technology**

★ ▲ 1. Talk with several of your friends about the subject of motivation. What motivates them to work hard or not work hard in school and on the job? How important to them is self-motivation as opposed to external reward?

★ 2. Look over Maslow's hierarchy of needs and try to determine where you are right now on the hierarchy. What needs of yours are not being met? How could a company go about meeting those needs and thus motivate you to work more effectively?

★ ▲ 3. One managerial idea is to let employees work in self-managed teams. There is no reason why such teams could not be formed in colleges as well as businesses. Discuss the benefits and drawbacks of dividing your class into self-managed teams for the purpose of studying, doing cases, and so forth.

★ 4. Think of all the groups with which you have been associated over the years—sports groups, friendship groups, and so on—and try to recall how the leaders of those groups motivated the group to action. Did the leaders assume a Theory X or a Theory Y attitude? How often was money a motivator? What other motivational tools were used and to what effect?

★ 5. Herzberg concluded that pay was not a motivator. If you were paid to get better grades, would you be motivated to study harder? In your employment experiences, have you ever worked harder to obtain a raise or as a result of receiving a large raise? Do you agree with Herzberg about the effects of pay?

CAREER EXPLORATION

If you are interested in pursuing a career that involves motivating others, here are a few to consider. Find out about the tasks performed, skills needed, pay, and opportunity outlook in these fields in the *Occupational Outlook Handbook (OOH)* at bls.gov.

- **Coach**—teaches amateur or professional athletes the skills they need to succeed at their sport.

- **Elementary, middle, and high school principal**—manages all school operations, including daily school activities; coordinates curricula; oversees teachers and other school staff; and provides a safe and productive learning environment for students.

- **Sales manager**—directs organizations' sales teams, sets sales goals, analyzes data, and develops training programs for organizations' sales representatives.

*Enriching Employees
at Taco Bell*

VIDEO CASE

Keeping employees motivated and happy is a key to success for many of the world's top companies, including fast-food chains like Taco Bell. From GED prep to educational support to college scholarships, Taco Bell helps its employees achieve their goals in all sorts of ways.

While this level of support might seem strange for a fast-food chain, the company recognizes that today's workers tend to demand more from their employers. Besides collecting a paycheck, young employees also want to develop a healthy balance between their work lives and personal lives. That's why Taco Bell provides both full- and part-time staffers with access to educational resources from their first day forward. For instance, the company fully funds an all-inclusive, start-to-finish GED program specially designed for its employees. Along with receiving unlimited access to study materials and practice tests, the program also provides students with advisors who guide them through every step of the process.

For those who have already earned a high school diploma or GED, the company offers discounted tuition and reimbursements through its Guild Education program. In partnership with 80 online universities and learning institutions, employees can choose from thousands of classes and earn certificates or degrees in many fields. This type of educational programming not only boosts morale and commitment but also provides workers with a sense of intrinsic value.

Employees who are pursuing other goals can apply for the company's Live Más Scholarship program, which grants awards as high as $25,000. Unlike other scholarships, Taco Bell doesn't require test scores or a minimum GPA in order to apply. Instead, the company wants to appeal to students who don't qualify for traditional scholarships. By removing the usual academic requirements, the program receives applications from a wide variety of highly motivated employees.

Taco Bell also encourages managers to seek out and support workers who would benefit the most from its educational programs. In fact, many managers take special pride in this role since they likely received promotions thanks to the guidance of senior leaders. Managers also benefit from leadership programs where they learn all about team building and the fundamentals of management. After all, employees who feel appreciated by their superiors are more likely to stay around for the long term. By taking the interests of its workers to heart, Taco Bell creates positive opportunities for the company as well as its staff.

THINKING IT OVER

1. What are the benefits of Taco Bell's educational initiatives both for employees and the company?

2. How does Taco Bell's Live Más Scholarship differ from traditional scholarship programs?

3. Why do many Taco Bell managers take special pride in supporting workers through the company's educational programs?

NOTES

1. Andrew Chamberlain and Daniel Zhao, "The Key to Happy Customers? Happy Employees," *Harvard Business Review,* August 19, 2019; Shep Hyken, "Keep Your Employees and You'll Keep Your Customers," *Forbes,* forbes.com, February 10, 2019; Phil Geldart, "Does Your Company Culture Lead to Happy Customers?," *Forbes,* forbes.com, January 31, 2020.
2. F. John Reh, "The Cost of High Employee Turnover," *The Balance,* thebalance.com, accessed February 2020; Chris Strub, "45% of Nonprofit Employees to Seek New Jobs by 2025: Report," *Forbes,* February 10, 2020.
3. "Developing and Sustaining Employee Engagement," Society for Human Resource Management, shrm.org, accessed February 2020.
4. Karlyn Borysenko, "How Much Are Your Disengaged Employees Costing You?," *Forbes,* May 2, 2019; Jim Harter, "Dismal Employee Engagement Is a Sign of Global Mismanagement," Gallup, gallup.com, accessed February 2020; Justin Warner, "The ROI of Employee Engagement: Show Me the Money!," *Decision Wise,* January 1, 2020.
5. Ed Rogers, "For Employee Experience Strategies, Think Big and Act Small," *Forbes,* February 10, 2020; Valerie Bolden-Barrett, "LinkedIn: Employee Experience Is Central to Talent Retention, Bottom Line," *HR Dive,* January 24, 2020.
6. "The 100 Best Companies to Work For," *Fortune,* fortune.com, accessed February 2020; "25 Best Places to Work," *Forbes,* forbes.com, accessed February 2020; Pawan Kumar, "5 Ways to Improve Employee Retention in Your Organization," *Thrive Global,* February 5, 2020.
7. Jacinta Jimenez, "The Motivating Manager: Developing Your People through Coaching," *Forbes,* February 6, 2020.
8. "UPS Fact Sheet," UPS, ups.com, accessed February 2020.
9. "Human Relations Movement: How It Changed Management," *Business News Daily,* businessnewsdaily.com, January 16, 2020.
10. Veronika Kero, "How to Answer Zappos CEO Tony Hsieh's Quirky Interview Question," *CNBC,* cnbc.com, January 25,

2019; Anna Verasai, "What Is the Internal Culture Like at Zappos?," *The HR Digest,* March 19, 2018; Susan M. Heathfield, "Find Out How Zappos Reinforces Its Company Culture," *The Balance,* July 30, 2019; Julianna Young, "7 Zappos Amenities That Boost Employee Happiness," Zappos, zappos.com, accessed March 2020.

11. John Hilton, "Why Is Strategic Employee Recognition So Important?," *HR Director,* January 28, 2020.

12. Albert Costill, "What Really Motivates Employees? Research Reveals Secrets," *Business 2 Community,* February 5, 2020.

13. Jurie Rossouw, "Five Signs Fear-Based Leadership Is Holding Your Business Back," *Smart Company,* February 4, 2020.

14. Joe Cecala, "5 Reasons Employees Will Leave Your Company, No Matter How Good the Pay Is," *Thrive Global,* thriveglobal.com, accessed February 2020.

15. Jacinta Jimenez, "The Motivating Manager: Developing Your People through Coaching," *Forbes,* February 6, 2020; Dean Wheeler and Sherna Bhadresa, "Four Ways to Empower Teams and Unlock Potential," *Personnel Today,* February 10, 2020.

16. Andre Andonian, Maya Horii, Naoyuki Iwatani, Michele Raviscioni, et al., "A More Effective Model for Managing Change in Japan Could Accelerate Economic Growth," McKinsey and Company, mckinsey.com, accessed February 2020.

17. Matt Alderton, "What Your Business Can Learn from Peter Drucker," business.com, accessed February 2020.

18. Adam Hayes, "Management by Objectives (MBO)," *Investopedia,* investopedia.com, accessed February 2020.

19. Craig Tanner, "Moneyball Changed Baseball, Is Data Science Changing HR?," *HR Technologist,* January 23, 2020.

20. David Nadler and Edward Lawler, "Motivation—a Diagnostic Approach," *Perspectives on Behavior in Organizations* (New York: McGraw-Hill, 1977).

21. Renzo Costarella, "Is Balance the Answer to the Motivation Equation?," *Business 2 Community,* January 14, 2020; "What Is Equity Theory?," *HRZone,* hrzone.com, accessed February 2020.

22. Robert Tanner, "Equity Theory—Why Employee Perceptions about Fairness Do Matter," *Management Is a Journey,* managementisajourney.com, February 10, 2020.

23. Nick Wolney, "Why Not Being Confident Can Sometimes Be a Good Thing," *Entrepreneur,* January 24, 2020; John P. Robinson, Steven Martin, Ignace Glorieux, and Joeri Minnen, "The Overestimated Workweek Revisited," Bureau of Labor Statistics, bls.gov, accessed February 2020.

24. Andrew Thomas, "10 Communication Habits of Extraordinary Leaders," *Inc.,* inc.com, accessed February 2020.

25. "Job Enrichment: Enhancing Jobs for Greater Motivation," *Mind Tools,* mindtools.com, accessed February 2020.

26. John Lincoln, "Ways to Get People to Do Things They Don't Want to Do," *Thrive Global,* February 10, 2020.

27. "How to Improve Teamwork in the Workplace," Gallup, gallup.com, accessed February 2020; John Boitnott, "How to Know If You're Intimidating Employees (and How to Stop It)," *Entrepreneur,* January 15, 2020; Megan Reitz, Viktor O. Nilsson, Emma Day, and Josh Higgins, "Speaking Truth to Power at Work," Hult Research, hult.edu, accessed February 2020.

28. "The Impact of Teamwork in the Workplace," Gallup, January 22, 2020.

29. Macy Bayern, "64% of Employees May Quit in 2020," *TechRepublic,* January 29, 2020.

30. Pawan Kumar, "5 Ways to Improve Employee Retention in Your Organization," *Thrive Global*, February 5, 2020.

31. Workhuman, workhuman.com, accessed February 2020.

32. Aram Lulla, "The Millennial Managers Are Here: Four Ways Millennials Are Reshaping the Workplace (Again)," *Forbes,* December 3, 2019; Karl Moore, "Dos and Don'ts for Millennials and Zs Managing Boomers," *Forbes,* January 13, 2020.

33. Sally Kane, "The Common Characteristics of Millennial Professionals," *The Balance,* thebalance.com, accessed February 2020.

34. Kevin Kruse, "Top 5 Leadership Development Trends for 2020," *Forbes,* January 15, 2020.

35. Karl Moore, "Dos and Don'ts for Millennials and Zs Managing Boomers," *Forbes,* January 13, 2020.

36. Ashley Stahl, "How Generation-Z Will Revolutionize the Workplace," *Forbes,* September 10, 2019; Eric Johnson, "Gen Z Won't Disrupt the Workforce—They'll Elevate It," *Forbes,* January 17, 2020.

37. "Communicating with Gen Z Employees: The Modern Manager's Guide," *Rise,* risepeople.com, January 15, 2020.

11

Human Resource Management: Finding and Keeping the Best Employees

---

LEARNING OBJECTIVES *After you have read and studied this chapter, you should be able to*

LO 11–1 Explain the importance of human resource management, and describe current issues in managing human resources.

LO 11–2 Illustrate the effects of legislation on human resource management.

LO 11–3 Summarize the five steps in human resource planning.

LO 11–4 Describe methods that companies use to recruit new employees, and explain some of the issues that make recruitment challenging.

LO 11–5 Outline the six steps in selecting employees.

LO 11–6 Illustrate employee training and development methods.

LO 11–7 Trace the six steps in appraising employee performance.

LO 11–8 Summarize the objectives of employee compensation programs, and evaluate pay systems and fringe benefits.

LO 11–9 Demonstrate how managers use scheduling plans to adapt to workers' needs.

LO 11–10 Describe how employees can move through a company: promotion, reassignment, termination, and retirement.

Cynthia Marshall, CEO of the Dallas Mavericks

Starting a new job is never easy, but few people in business have ever faced a challenge as tough as Cynthia Marshall did when she became CEO of the Dallas Mavericks in 2018. Months before she took the position, an in-depth article in *Sports Illustrated* described a toxic company culture that had infected the NBA franchise for more than two decades. An independent report commissioned by the Mavericks soon confirmed the article's allegations of sexual harassment and improper workplace conduct. The report also found that owner Mark Cuban had made "significant errors in judgment," leading him to publicly apologize and donate $10 million to women's advocacy groups.

After recognizing his role in the organization's dysfunction, Cuban reached out to "Cynt" Marshall to take over and right the Mavericks's many wrongs. "I walked in his office and while he greeted me at the door, he just looked broken. I mean, he looked as if he had been crying," said Marshall. "He was disturbed by it all and just said, 'I need you.' Literally the mandate was, 'I need you to come in and transform the culture.'" And that's exactly what Marshall did. Since taking over as CEO, she has improved diversity while also creating an inclusive and accepting work environment for all employees. "I have to do it for the sisterhood," said Marshall. "I have to help create a great place to work."

Marshall has had a lifetime of experience dealing with difficult situations to prepare her for this challenge with the Mavericks. Raised in a high-crime neighborhood in Richmond, California, at a young age her mother moved Marshall and her siblings out of the house after suffering physical abuse by their father. Despite this hard upbringing, Marshall's mother made sure that her kids stayed committed to school and pursued their dreams. "If you asked me right now, I would say I had a great childhood," said Marshall. "Even with the stuff with my father, my mother worked hard. She went to great lengths to make sure we were normal, as normal as could be." Marshall succeeded in high school and potentially saw herself becoming a math teacher in the future. She earned a full scholarship to the University of California, Berkeley, where she obtained degrees in business administration and human resource management while also becoming the school's first Black cheerleader.

After graduation, Marshall joined AT&T as a manager of the telecom's long-distance operations in California. She worked at the company for 36 years, eventually reaching the position of senior vice president of human resources as well as chief diversity officer. During her long tenure with the telecom giant, Marshall had to overcome the prejudices of some of her colleagues while also dealing with several highly stressful events in her personal life. Marshall suffered four miscarriages, lost her six-month-old daughter, and survived stage 3 colon cancer all while working as an executive at one of the nation's largest companies. She credits her faith with helping her continue to face new challenges in her life and career.

It's this unshakable attitude that made Marshall the perfect person to transform the Mavericks's toxic work environment. "I walked into a bad culture," said Marshall.

"I walked into a place where the women were not valued and treated the way I would like to see them treated. Frankly, I think we had a problem with how we respected and treated people of color. It wasn't a very diverse and inclusive environment when I got there. And so we needed to do some things." Within weeks of taking over, she implemented a 100-day plan to revamp the organization's leadership and culture. Along with developing a zero-tolerance policy toward harassment, Marshall also created an agenda for women's issues as well as a 24/7 hotline where employees could anonymously report any potential abuses. Copies of "The Marshall Plan" were sent both to Mavericks staff and fans in an effort to be as transparent as possible.

The team developed a diversity and inclusion strategy that featured several innovative policies. Since initiating these changes, 50 percent of Mavericks executives are women and 47 percent are people of color. Marshall and her colleagues also established employee resource groups; built a network of influencers to create awareness of cultural differences; developed an advisory council made up of influential and diverse business and community leaders; and strengthened supplier diversity by significantly increasing spending with minority, women, and disadvantaged business enterprises.

While Marshall has received lots of praise for improving so many of the Mavericks's issues, she readily admits that she couldn't have done it alone. "I own the fact that we have turned around the culture and I didn't do it by myself," said Marshall. "I brought some folks in with me. We promoted some people. We created a great diverse leadership team."

In this chapter, you'll learn how successful organizations recruit, manage, and make the most of their employees, just like Cynthia Marshall does with the Dallas Mavericks.

Sources: Doyle Rader, "Dallas Mavericks Win NBA Inclusion Leadership Award," *Forbes*, forbes.com, January 17, 2020; Jerry Bembry, "Mavericks' Cynthia Marshall: 'I Want to Do It for the Sisterhood,'" The Undefeated, theundefeated.com, February 27, 2018; Eddie Sefko and Karen Robinson-Jacobs, "She Beat Cancer, Domestic Abuse, and Racial Barriers, but Can She Save the Dallas Mavericks?," *Dallas Morning News*, May 17, 2018; Mary Pilon, "The Dallas Mavericks' New CEO Is Cleaning Up a #MeToo Mess," *Bloomberg Businessweek*, December 20, 2018; Haley Draznin, "The Dallas Mavericks Were Plagued by a Toxic Culture. She Is Turning It Around," *CNN*, cnn.com, November 19, 2019; Dallas Mavericks, mavs.com, accessed February 2020.

Let's talk business!
bit.ly/LetsTalkBusiness11

Ethan Miller/Getty Images

LO 11–1 Explain the importance of human resource management, and describe current issues in managing human resources.

Working with People Is Just the Beginning

Students often say they want to go into human resource management because they want to "work with people." Human resource managers do work with people, but they are also deeply involved in planning, recordkeeping, and other administrative duties. This chapter will tell you what else human resource management is all about.

Human resource management (HRM) is the process of determining human resource needs and then recruiting, selecting, developing, motivating, evaluating, compensating, and scheduling employees to achieve organizational goals (see Figure 11.1). For many years, human resource management was called "personnel" and involved clerical functions such as screening applications, keeping records, processing the payroll, and finding new employees when necessary. The roles and responsibilities of HRM have evolved primarily because of two key factors: (1) organizations' recognition of employees as their ultimate resource and (2) changes in the law that rewrote many traditional practices. Let's explore both.

human resource management (HRM)

The process of determining human resource needs and then recruiting, selecting, developing, motivating, evaluating, compensating, and scheduling employees to achieve organizational goals.

Developing the Ultimate Resource

One reason the role of human resource management has grown is that the shift from traditional manufacturing industries to service and high-tech manufacturing industries requires businesses to hire workers with highly technical job skills. This shift means that many workers must be retrained for new, more challenging jobs. People truly are the ultimate resource. They develop the ideas that eventually become products to satisfy consumers' wants and needs. Take away their creative minds, and leading firms such as Disney, Apple, Procter & Gamble, Google, Facebook, and Amazon would be nothing.

In the past, human resources were plentiful, so there was little need to nurture and develop them. If you needed qualified people, you simply hired them. If they didn't work out, you fired them and found others. Most firms assigned the job of recruiting, selecting, training, evaluating, compensating, motivating, and, yes, firing people to the functional departments that employed them, like accounting, manufacturing, and marketing. Today the job of human resource management has taken on an increased role in the firm since *qualified* employees are much scarcer due to an increase in jobs that require advanced or specialized training, This shortage of qualified workers makes recruiting and retaining people more important and more difficult.[1] What human resource challenges do all managers face? We'll outline a few next.

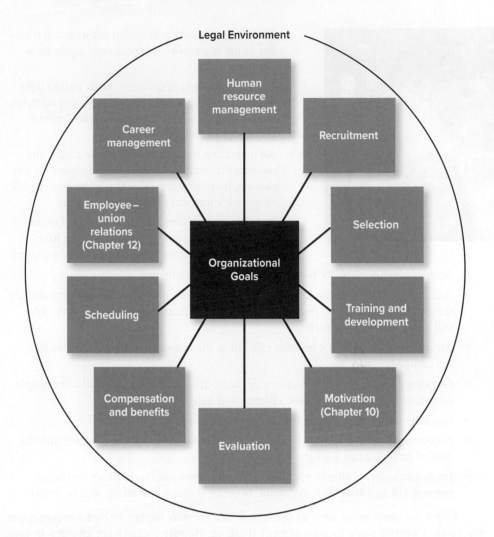

FIGURE 11.1 HUMAN RESOURCE MANAGEMENT
As this figure shows, human resource management is more than hiring and firing personnel. All activities are designed to achieve organizational goals within the laws that affect human resource management. (Note that human resource management includes motivation, as discussed in Chapter 10, and employee–management relations, as discussed in Chapter 12.)

The Human Resource Challenge

Many of the changes that have had the most dramatic impact on U.S. business are those in the labor force. The ability to compete in global markets depends on new ideas, new products, and new levels of productivity—in other words, on people with good ideas. These are some of the challenges and opportunities in human resources:[2]

- Uncertainty in global politics and increased attention on hiring immigrants.

- Technology, such as talent networks, crowdsourcing, and internal social networks.

- Multigenerational workforce. Older Millennials and Gen Xers hold management positions, whereas Gen Zers are entering the workforce and many Baby Boomers are delaying retirement (discussed in more detail later in the chapter).

- Shortages of trained workers in growth areas such as computer technology, biotechnology, robotics, green technology, and the sciences.

- Large numbers of skilled and unskilled workers from declining industries, such as steel and automobiles, who are unemployed or underemployed and need retraining. *Underemployed workers* are those who have more skills or knowledge than their current jobs require or those with part-time jobs who want to work full-time.

- A growing percentage of new workers who are undereducated and unprepared for jobs in the contemporary business environment.

Diane Keough/Moment/Getty Images

U.S. firms face a shortage of workers skilled in areas such as biotechnology and sustainable engineering. What other job markets do you think will grow as companies focus more on environmentally friendly policies? Which ones appeal to you?

- A shortage of workers in skilled construction trades due to the retirement of experienced, aging Baby Boomers.

- The Baby Boomer brain drain. With 10,000 Baby Boomers retiring every year, employers in all fields must plan for and manage how to transfer their knowledge to younger workers.

- An increasing number of both single-parent and two-income families, resulting in a demand for job sharing, maternity and paternity leave, and special career advancement programs for women.

- A shift in employee attitudes toward work. Leisure time has become a much higher priority, as have flextime, working from home, and a shorter workweek.

- An increased demand for temporary and part-time workers.

- A challenge from overseas labor pools whose members work for lower wages and are subject to fewer laws and regulations than U.S. workers. This results in many jobs still being outsourced overseas.

- An increased demand for benefits tailored to the individual yet cost-effective to the company.

- Growing concerns over child care, elder care, drug testing, opportunities for people with disabilities, and workplace violence and bullying.

- Implementation of changing health care regulations.

- A decreased sense of employee loyalty, which increases employee turnover and the cost of replacing lost workers.

- Implementation of human resource information systems (technology that helps manage HR activities such as payroll, benefits, training, recruiting, and so forth).

Given so many issues such as these, you can see why human resource management has taken a central place in management thinking. However, significant changes in laws covering hiring, safety, unionization, equal pay, and affirmative action have also had a major influence. Let's look at their impact on human resource management.

LO 11–2 Illustrate the effects of legislation on human resource management.

Laws Affecting Human Resource Management

Until the 1930s, the U.S. government had little to do with human resource decisions. Since then, legislation and legal decisions have greatly affected all areas of human resource management, from hiring to training to monitoring working conditions (see Figure 11.2). These laws were passed because many businesses did not exercise fair labor practices voluntarily.

One of the more important pieces of social legislation passed by Congress was the Civil Rights Act of 1964. This act generated much debate and was amended 97 times before final passage. Title VII of that act brought the government directly into the operations of human resource management. Title VII prohibits discrimination in hiring, firing, compensation, apprenticeships, training, terms, conditions, or privileges of employment based on race, religion, creed, sex, or national origin. Age was later added to the conditions of the act. In 2020, the Supreme Court ruled that the law applies to sexual orientation and gender identity. The Civil Rights Act of 1964 was expected to stamp out discrimination in the workplace, but specific language in it made enforcement quite difficult. Congress took on the task of amending the law.

In 1972, the Equal Employment Opportunity Act (EEOA) was added as an amendment to Title VII. It strengthened the Equal Employment Opportunity Commission (EEOC),

FIGURE 11.2 EXAMPLES OF GOVERNMENT LEGISLATION AFFECTING HUMAN RESOURCE MANAGEMENT

National Labor Relations Act of 1935. Established collective bargaining in labor–management relations and limited management interference in the right of employees to have a collective bargaining agent.

Fair Labor Standards Act of 1938. Established a minimum wage and overtime pay for working more than 40 hours a week for employees who are not otherwise exempt (i.e., salaried employees earning above a certain amount and those who perform exempt duties such as managers). Amendments expanded the classes of workers covered, raised the minimum wage, redefined regular-time work, raised overtime payments, and equalized pay scales for men and women.

Manpower Development and Training Act of 1962. Provided for the training and retraining of unemployed workers.

Equal Pay Act of 1963. Specified that men and women doing equal jobs must be paid the same wage.

Civil Rights Act of 1964. For firms with 15 or more employees, outlawed discrimination in employment based on sex, race, color, religion, or national origin.

Age Discrimination in Employment Act of 1967. Outlawed employment practices that discriminate against people 40 and older. An amendment outlaws requiring retirement by a specific age.

Occupational Safety and Health Act of 1970. Regulates safety and health conditions in most private industries and some public-sector organizations.

Equal Employment Opportunity Act of 1972. Strengthened the Equal Employment Opportunity Commission (EEOC) and authorized the EEOC to set guidelines for human resource management.

Comprehensive Employment and Training Act of 1973 (CETA). Provided funds for training unemployed workers.

Vocational Rehabilitation Act of 1973. Extended protection to people with any physical or mental disability.

Employee Retirement Income Security Act of 1974 (ERISA). Regulated and insured company retirement plans.

Immigration Reform and Control Act of 1986. Required employers to verify employment eligibility of all new hires including U.S. citizens.

Supreme Court ruling against set-aside programs (affirmative action), 1989. Declared that setting aside 30 percent of contracting jobs for minority businesses was reverse discrimination and unconstitutional.

Older Workers Benefit Protection Act, 1990. Protects older people from signing away their rights to pensions and protection from illegal age discrimination.

Civil Rights Act of 1991. For firms with over 15 employees, extends the right to a jury trial and punitive damages to victims of intentional job discrimination.

Americans with Disabilities Act of 1990 (1992 implementation). Prohibits employers from discriminating against qualified individuals with disabilities in hiring, advancement, or compensation and requires them to adapt the workplace if necessary.

Family and Medical Leave Act of 1993. Businesses with 50 or more employees must provide up to 12 weeks of unpaid leave per year upon birth or adoption of an employee's child or upon serious illness of a parent, spouse, or child.

Americans with Disabilities Amendments Act of 2008 (ADA). Provides broader protection for workers with disabilities and reverses Supreme Court decisions deemed too restrictive. Adds disabilities such as epilepsy and cancer to ADA coverage.

Lilly Ledbetter Fair Pay Act of 2009. Amends the Civil Rights Act of 1964 by changing the start of the 180-day statute of limitations for filing a discrimination suit from the date of the first discriminatory paycheck to the date of the most recent discriminatory paycheck.

which was created by the Civil Rights Act, by giving it rather broad powers. For example, it permitted the EEOC to issue guidelines for acceptable employer conduct in administering equal employment opportunity. The EEOC also mandated specific recordkeeping procedures, and Congress vested it with the power of enforcement to ensure these mandates were carried out. The EEOC became a formidable regulatory force in the administration of human resource management.[3] For example, in an effort to reduce barriers to employment for those with criminal records, the EEOC established enforcement guidance limiting the use of arrest and conviction records in hiring. The *ban-the-box* rule prohibits asking questions about convictions on job applications and initial interviews. Today, 35 states and 150 cities have enacted ban-the-box laws.[4] In 2020, Congress passed the Fair Chance Law

Andersen Ross/The Image Bank/Getty Images

The Americans with Disabilities Act guarantees that all U.S. workers have equal opportunity in employment. This legislation requires businesses to make "reasonable accommodations" on the job for people with disabilities. What required accommodations do you think would be reasonable?

 connect

▶ **iSeeit!** Need help understanding key employment laws? Visit your Connect eBook to view a video for a brief animated explanation.

affirmative action

Employment activities intended to "right past wrongs" by increasing opportunities for minorities and women.

that prohibits the federal government and federal contractors from asking about an applicant's criminal history prior to a conditional job offer.[5]

The EEOC was also empowered to enforce **affirmative action**, which was intended to "right past wrongs" by increasing opportunities for minorities and women. Affirmative action requires that all recruitment, selection, and promotion be handled in a nondiscriminatory manner to create opportunities for minorities and other underrepresented groups. Questions persist about the interpretation of affirmative action. The issue has generated heated debate as well as many lawsuits.[6] The Office of Federal Contract Compliance Programs (OFCCP) ensures that employers comply with nondiscrimination and affirmative action laws and regulations when doing business with the federal government.

The Civil Rights Act of 1991 expanded the remedies available to victims of discrimination by amending Title VII of the Civil Rights Act of 1964. Now victims of discrimination have the right to a jury trial and punitive damages. Human resource managers must follow court decisions closely to see how the law is enforced.

Laws Protecting Employees with Disabilities and Older Employees

As you read earlier, laws prohibit discrimination related to race, sex, or age in hiring, firing, and training. The Vocational Rehabilitation Act of 1973 extended protection to people with any physical or mental disability.

The Americans with Disabilities Act of 1990 (ADA) requires employers to give applicants with physical or mental disabilities the same consideration for employment as people without disabilities. The ADA also protects individuals with disabilities from discrimination in public accommodations, transportation, schools, and all public and private places open to the general public.

In the workplace, the ADA requires making "reasonable accommodations" for employees with disabilities, such as modifying equipment or widening doorways. Most companies have no trouble making structural changes to be accommodating. However, at times such changes can be difficult for some small businesses.[7] Employers used to think that being fair and reasonable meant treating everyone the same, but *accommodation,* in fact, means treating people *according to their specific needs.* That can include putting up barriers to isolate people readily distracted by noise, reassigning workers to new tasks, and making changes in supervisors' management styles. Accommodations are not always expensive; an inexpensive headset can allow someone with cerebral palsy to talk on the phone.

In 2008, Congress passed the Americans with Disabilities Amendments Act, which overturned Supreme Court decisions that had reduced protections for people with certain disabilities such as diabetes, epilepsy, heart disease, autism, major depression, and cancer.[8] In 2011, the EEOC issued regulations that widened the range of disabilities covered by the ADA and shifted the burden of proof of disability in labor disputes from employees to business owners. Enforcement of this law promises to be a continuing issue for human resource management.[9]

The Age Discrimination in Employment Act of 1967 (ADEA) protects individuals aged 40 or older from employment and workplace discrimination in hiring, firing, promotion, layoff, compensation, benefits, job assignments, and training. The ADEA, enforced by the EEOC, applies to employers with 20 or more employees, and protects both employees and job applicants.[10] The ADEA suffered a setback in 2009 when the U.S. Supreme Court ruled that age must be the determining reason for any employment action against older workers and not one of a number of factors in an adverse employment decision.[11] Pending legislation in Congress that would strengthen protections for older workers against age discrimination is currently being debated.[12] The ADEA outlaws mandatory retirement in most organizations. It does, however, allow age restrictions for certain job categories such as airline pilot or bus driver if evidence shows that the ability to perform significantly diminishes with age or that age imposes a danger to society.

Effects of Legislation

Clearly, laws ranging from the Social Security Act of 1935 to the 2008 Americans with Disabilities Amendments Act require human resource managers to keep abreast of laws and court decisions to effectively perform their jobs. Choosing a career in human resource management offers a challenge to anyone willing to put forth the effort. Remember:

- Employers must know and act in accordance with the legal rights of their employees or risk costly court cases.

- Legislation affects all areas of human resource management, from hiring and firing, to training and compensation.

- New court cases and legislation change human resource management continuously; the only way to keep current is to read the business news and stay familiar with emerging issues.

TESTPREP

- What is human resource management?
- What did Title VII of the Civil Rights Act of 1964 achieve?
- What is the EEOC, and what was the intention of affirmative action?
- What does *accommodations* mean in the Americans with Disabilities Act of 1990?

LO 11–3 Summarize the five steps in human resource planning.

Determining a Firm's Human Resource Needs

All management, including human resource management, begins with planning. The five steps in the human resource planning process are:

1. *Preparing a human resource inventory of the organization's employees.* This inventory should include ages, names, education, capabilities, training, specialized skills, and other relevant information (such as languages spoken). It reveals whether the labor force is technically up-to-date and thoroughly trained.

2. *Preparing a job analysis.* A **job analysis** is a study of what employees do who hold various job titles. It's necessary in order to recruit and train employees with the necessary skills to do the job. The results of job analysis are two written statements: job descriptions and job specifications. A **job description** specifies the objectives of the job, the type of work, the responsibilities and duties, working conditions, and the job's relationship to other functions. **Job specifications** are a written summary of the minimal education and skills a person needs to do a particular job. In short, job descriptions are about the *job,* and job specifications are about the *person* who does the job. See Figure 11.3 for a hypothetical job description and job specifications.

3. *Assessing future human resource demand.* Because technology changes rapidly, effective human resource managers are proactive; that is, they forecast the organization's requirements and train people ahead of time or ensure trained people are available and willing to come aboard when needed.[13]

4. *Assessing future labor supply.* The labor force is constantly shifting: getting older, becoming more technically oriented, becoming more diverse. Some workers will be scarcer in the future, like biomedical engineers, cloud architects, and robotic repair workers; and others will be oversupplied, like assembly-line workers.[14]

job analysis
A study of what is done by employees who hold various job titles.

job description
A summary of the objectives of a job, the type of work to be done, the responsibilities and duties, the working conditions, and the relationship of the job to other functions.

job specifications
A written summary of the minimum qualifications required of workers to do a particular job.

iSeeit! Need help understanding job analysis? Visit your Connect eBook to view a video for a brief animated explanation.

FIGURE 11.3 JOB ANALYSIS

A job analysis yields two important statements: job descriptions and job specifications. Here you have a job description and job specifications for a sales representative.

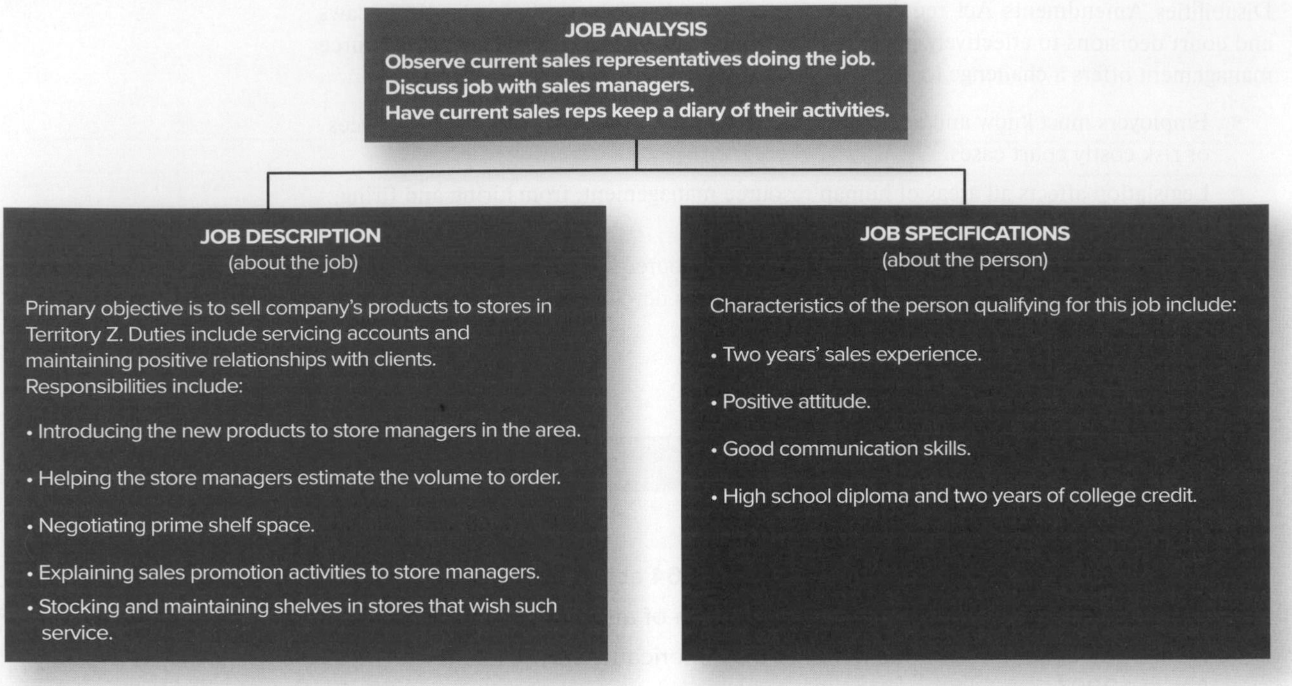

JOB ANALYSIS

Observe current sales representatives doing the job.
Discuss job with sales managers.
Have current sales reps keep a diary of their activities.

JOB DESCRIPTION
(about the job)

Primary objective is to sell company's products to stores in Territory Z. Duties include servicing accounts and maintaining positive relationships with clients. Responsibilities include:

- Introducing the new products to store managers in the area.

- Helping the store managers estimate the volume to order.

- Negotiating prime shelf space.

- Explaining sales promotion activities to store managers.

- Stocking and maintaining shelves in stores that wish such service.

JOB SPECIFICATIONS
(about the person)

Characteristics of the person qualifying for this job include:

- Two years' sales experience.

- Positive attitude.

- Good communication skills.

- High school diploma and two years of college credit.

5. *Establishing a strategic plan.* The human resource strategic plan must address recruiting, selecting, training, developing, appraising, compensating, and scheduling the labor force. Because the first four steps lead up to this one, we'll focus on them in the rest of the chapter.

Some companies use information technology to perform the human resource planning process more efficiently. Human resource information system (HRIS) software uses multiple tools and processes to manage an organization's employees and databases.[15] HRIS (such as Kronos, Salesforce, IBM Kenexa, and Sage) helps businesses of all sizes perform basic HR functions ranging from recruitment to retirement. For example, IBM manages its global workforce of over 350,000 employees with a database that matches employee skills, experiences, schedules, and references with jobs available. If a client in Quebec, Canada, has a monthlong project requiring a consultant who speaks English and French, has an advanced degree in engineering, and has experience with Linux programming, IBM can find the best-suited consultant available and put that person in touch with the client.

LO 11–4 Describe methods that companies use to recruit new employees, and explain some of the issues that make recruitment challenging.

Recruiting Employees from a Diverse Population

recruitment

The set of activities used to obtain a sufficient number of the right people at the right time.

Recruitment is the set of activities for obtaining the right number of qualified people at the right time. Its purpose is to select those who best meet the needs of the organization. You might think a continuous flow of new people into the workforce makes recruiting easy. On the contrary, it's become very challenging. In fact, 45 percent of CEOs surveyed say that attracting and retaining talent is their biggest challenge.[16] Here are several reasons why:

Human resource managers today have the opportunity to recruit people from a wide range of cultural and ethnic backgrounds. What are some of the advantages of a diverse workforce?

Monalyn Gracia/Fancy/age fotostock

- Some organizations have policies that demand promotions from within, operate under union regulations, or offer low wages, which makes recruiting and keeping employees difficult or subject to outside influence and restrictions.

- An emphasis on corporate culture, teamwork, and participative management makes it important to hire people who not only are skilled but also fit in with the culture and leadership style of the company.[17] For example, in order to find out if its new hires fit the company culture, companies such as Macy's, Walmart, and PetSmart use pre-employment testing and simulations.[18] At Disney Pixar, job candidates go through a rigorous screening at an assessment center where they are evaluated for abstract reasoning, verbal reasoning, and situational judgments along with a host of other aptitude-related skills.[19] How the potential employees react and perform determines if they may be working on the next *Toy Story.*

- Sometimes people with the necessary skills are not available; then workers must be hired and trained internally.

Human resource managers can turn to many sources for recruiting assistance (see Figure 11.4). *Internal sources* include current employees who can be transferred or promoted or who can recommend others to hire. Using internal sources is less expensive than recruiting from outside and helps maintain employee morale. However, it isn't always possible to find qualified workers within the company, so human resource managers also use *external sources* such as advertisements, public and private employment agencies, college placement bureaus, management consultants, online sites, professional organizations, referrals, and online and walk-in applications.

Recruiting qualified workers may be particularly difficult for small businesses with few staff members and less-than-competitive compensation to attract external sources. Online sites like Glassdoor, Indeed, and LinkedIn have helped such firms by attracting millions of visitors per day.

> **LO 11–5**   Outline the six steps in selecting employees.

Selecting Employees Who Will Be Productive

Selection is the process of gathering information and deciding who should be hired, under legal guidelines, to serve the best interests of the individual and the organization. Selecting and training employees are extremely expensive processes in some firms. Just think

selection
The process of gathering information and deciding who should be hired, under legal guidelines, for the best interests of the individual and the organization.

FIGURE 11.4 EMPLOYEE SOURCES
Internal sources are often given first consideration, so it's useful to get a recommendation from a current employee of the firm for which you want to work. College placement offices are also an important source. Be sure to learn about such facilities early so that you can plan a strategy throughout your college career.

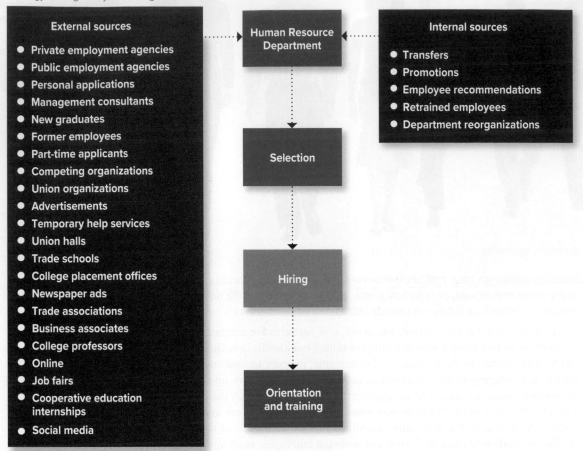

External sources

- Private employment agencies
- Public employment agencies
- Personal applications
- Management consultants
- New graduates
- Former employees
- Part-time applicants
- Competing organizations
- Union organizations
- Advertisements
- Temporary help services
- Union halls
- Trade schools
- College placement offices
- Newspaper ads
- Trade associations
- Business associates
- College professors
- Online
- Job fairs
- Cooperative education internships
- Social media

Human Resource Department

Selection

Hiring

Orientation and training

Internal sources

- Transfers
- Promotions
- Employee recommendations
- Retrained employees
- Department reorganizations

what's involved: advertising or recruiting agency fees, interview time, medical exams, training costs, unproductive time spent learning the job, possible travel and moving expenses, and more. It can cost up to 75 percent of an employee's annual salary to recruit, process, and train even an entry-level worker in some jobs, and more than 150 percent of a year's salary for a top manager.[20]

A typical selection process has six steps:

1. *Obtaining complete application forms.* Although equal employment laws limit the kinds of questions that can appear, applications help reveal the applicant's educational background, work experience, career objectives, and other qualifications directly related to the job.

2. *Conducting initial and follow-up interviews.* A staff member from the human resource department often screens applicants in a first interview. If the interviewer considers the applicant a potential hire, the manager who will supervise the new employee and other employees the applicant might work with may interview the applicant as well. It's important that managers prepare adequately for the interview to avoid selection decisions they may regret. No matter how innocent the intention, interview missteps such as asking about pregnancy or child care could later be evidence if the applicant files discrimination charges.

3. *Giving employment tests.* Organizations often use tests to measure basic competency in specific job skills like welding or firefighting, or to help evaluate applicants' personalities and interests. There are many employment test software options

Today, your social media and digital footprint has become a major part of your public persona. Whatever you say or do online goes into the virtual world and stays there. The online personality you project reflects to potential employers who you really are. Seventy percent of employers say they use social media to screen prospective hires and evaluate a person's fit with a company's culture. Sixty percent eliminated candidates on the basis of what they believed was negative content. What this means to you is that your social media footprint could be a selling tool in your job search—or could end up costing you a job.

Social media background checks have created red flags that can cripple the candidate's chance of being hired. A few of these flags are shown in these statistics: 49 percent of employers say they've eliminated candidates because of provocative or inappropriate photographs or videos; 45 percent because of information about drinking or drug use; and 33 percent because of discriminatory comments about race, religion, gender, and their previous employer.

Make sure to use social media to your advantage. Many companies admit to selecting a candidate because of the professional image they conveyed on social media. Word to the wise is, if you have any reservations about posting something online, the best advice is, don't.

Sources: Lydia Smith, "How to Stop Your Social Media Habits Jeopardizing Your New Job," *Yahoo! Finance,* finance.yahoo.com, February 9, 2020; Sara LaJeunesse, "Social Media Content Matters for Job Candidates, Researchers Find," *Penn State News,* news.psu.edu, February 5, 2020; Alonzo Martinez, "What Employers Should Consider When Drafting a Social Media Policy," *Forbes,* forbes.com, February 6, 2020.

available such as WonScore, HireSelect, and eSkill Pre-employment Test Selection. The tests should always be directly related to the job. Employment tests have been legally challenged as potential means of discrimination. As was noted in the previous section, some companies test potential employees in assessment centers where they evaluate specific skills and perform actual job tasks. Such testing can make the selection process more efficient and will generally satisfy legal requirements.

4. *Conducting background investigations.* Most organizations now investigate a candidate's work record, school record, credit history, and references more carefully than in the past to help identify those most likely to succeed. Background services such as GoodHire and Intelius Review allow prospective employers not only to conduct speedy background checks of criminal records, driving records, and credit histories but also to verify work experience and professional and educational credentials.[21] The Connecting through Social Media box discusses how companies use social media to screen job applicants and weed out those with undesirable traits.

5. *Obtaining results from physical exams.* There are obvious benefits to hiring people who are physically and mentally healthy. However, according to the Americans with Disabilities Act, medical tests cannot be given just to screen out individuals. In some states, physical exams can be given only after an offer of employment has been accepted. In states that allow pre-employment physical exams, they must be given to everyone applying for the same position. Pre-employment testing to detect drug or alcohol abuse has been controversial, especially with the changing laws in many states.[22]

6. *Establishing trial (probationary) periods.* Often an organization will hire an employee conditionally to let the person prove his or her value on the job. After a specified probationary period (perhaps three months or longer), the firm can either permanently hire or discharge that employee on the basis of supervisors' evaluations. Some businesses include co-workers' evaluations as well.

The selection process is often long and difficult, but it is worth the effort to select new employees carefully because of the high cost of replacing them. Being careful helps ensure that new employees meet all requirements, including communication skills, education, technical skills, experience, personality, and health.

Hiring Contingent Workers

contingent workers

Workers who do not have the expectation of regular, full-time employment.

A company with employment needs that vary—from hour to hour, day to day, week to week, season to season, or project to project—may find it cost-effective to hire contingent workers. **Contingent workers** include part-time workers (anyone who works less than 35 hours per week), temporary workers (workers paid by temporary employment agencies), seasonal workers, independent contractors, interns, and co-op students.

Although exact numbers are difficult to gather, the Bureau of Labor Statistics estimates there are approximately 15 million contingent workers in the United States, with the majority under age 25.[23] Some reports estimate that in many companies, approximately 50 percent of the workforce are contingent workers.[24] In fact, hiring contingent workers is so common today that some have called this a *gig economy*. A gig describes a single project or task for which a worker is hired, often through a digital marketplace, to work on demand.[25] Some gigs are types of short-term jobs, and some workers look at gigs such as Uber and Lyft vas self-employment options. When one gig is over, workers who need to earn a steady income must find another. Sometimes, that means juggling multiple jobs at once. There are two key reasons for the rise of the gig economy. Workers want diversity and flexibility in their roles and the ability to showcase their skills; and employers have shifted from "I need to hire a person" to "I need to complete a task."

Companies may hire contingent workers when full-timers are on some type of leave (such as maternity leave), when there is a peak demand for labor or products (like the holiday shopping season), or when quick service to customers is a priority. Companies also tend to hire more contingent workers in an uncertain economy, particularly when they are available and qualified, and when the jobs require minimal training.[26]

Contingent workers receive few benefits; they are rarely offered health insurance, vacation time, or company pensions. They also tend to earn less than permanent workers do. These are the reasons why states, including California and New York, are attempting through legislation to convert contingent workers into permanent employees.[27] Businesses are contesting such laws, insisting that they will deprive contingent workers of the flexibility they have in their jobs. This debate is expected to continue well into the 2020s. Many managers see using temporary workers as a way of weeding out underperforming workers and finding good hires.[28] Experts admit that temps are filling openings in an increasingly broad range of jobs, from unskilled manufacturing and distribution positions to middle management. Increasing numbers of contingent workers are educated professionals such as accountants, attorneys, engineers, and technology specialists.

Retailers often hire contingent (temporary) workers to help them through busy times like the Christmas shopping season. What are the advantages and disadvantages of hiring contingent workers?

Many companies include college students in their contingent workforce plan. Working with temporary staffing agencies, companies have easier access to workers who have already been screened.[29] Of course, temp agencies benefit college students as well. Once the agencies have assessed the workers, their information is entered into their databases. Then when students are coming back in town for vacations or whatever, they can call the agency and ask them to put their names into the system for work assignments. There is no need to spend time searching for openings or running around town for interviews. Companies such as Randstad, a global staffing services giant with over 1,100 branches in the United States, welcome college students primarily

Jane Barlow/PA Images/Getty Images

MAKING ETHICAL DECISIONS

Possible Hire or Indentured Servant?

monster.com/career-advice/career-levels/student-intern

Traditionally, unpaid internships have been a great way for young people to gain hands-on job experience. The trade-off of no financial compensation for practical experience was considered a fair price to pay for valuable insight into the workplace that was not available in a classroom or online. Businesses, in turn, risked nothing financially but could end up benefiting in the long run if an intern showed promise and eventually became a valued paid employee. However, interns often feel that they are being treated more like indentured servants than interns and wonder if they are improving their chances for a rewarding career or simply performing free services for a company.

To distinguish a quality internship from a dead end, simply look at the tasks you're asked to do every day. If your central duties include keeping the coffeepot full, making copies, or running errands, chances are these skills will not translate into valuable experience or a future job. As an intern, you should be exposed to the day-to-day activities of a business and learn why things work as they do in the business world. In quality internships, managers should outline an intern's responsibilities explicitly and provide regular feedback. Even without a regular paycheck, internships can be beneficial as long as the intern is compensated in valuable experience and possible employment.

Is it ethical for companies to use unpaid interns if they know they will not have any jobs to offer at the end of the internship? Why or why not?

AVAVA/iStock/360/Getty Images

because of their technology skills and familiarity with many of the software programs that companies use.[30]

In an era of rapid change and economic uncertainty, some contingent workers have even found that temping can be more secure than full-time employment. College interns, looking for mentoring and experience, can be considered temporary workers. However, when these internships are unpaid, ethical questions could arise (see the Making Ethical Decisions box).

? TESTPREP

- What are the five steps in human resource planning?
- What factors make it difficult to recruit qualified employees?
- What are the six steps in the selection process?
- Who is considered a contingent worker, and why do companies hire such workers?

285

LO 11–6   Illustrate employee training and development methods.

Training and Developing Employees for Optimum Performance

training and development

All attempts to improve productivity by increasing an employee's ability to perform. Training focuses on short-term skills, whereas development focuses on long-term abilities.

orientation

The activity that introduces new employees to the organization; to fellow employees; to their immediate supervisors; and to the policies, practices, and objectives of the firm.

on-the-job training

Training at the workplace that lets the employee learn by doing or by watching others for a while and then imitating them.

The term **training and development** includes all attempts to improve productivity by increasing an employee's ability to perform. A well-designed training program often leads to higher retention rates, increased productivity, and greater job satisfaction. Employers in the United States generally find that money for training is well spent. *Training* focuses on short-term skills, whereas *development* focuses on long-term abilities. Both include three steps: (1) assessing organizational needs and employee skills to determine training needs; (2) designing training activities to meet identified needs; and (3) evaluating the training's effectiveness. As technology and other innovations change the workplace, companies must offer training programs that often are quite sophisticated. Some common training and development activities are employee orientation, on-the-job training, apprenticeships, off-the-job training, vestibule training, job simulation, and management training.

- **Orientation** is the activity that initiates new employees into the organization; to fellow employees; to their immediate supervisors; and to the policies, practices, and objectives of the firm. Orientation programs range from informal talks to formal activities that last a day or more and often include scheduled visits to various departments and required reading of company handbooks.[31] At customer-centric companies like Zappos, every new employee must spend two weeks answering customer calls, two weeks learning in a classroom, and a week shipping boxes in the company's fulfillment center. If the employee does not match the company's expectations, he or she will be discharged.[32]

- **On-the-job training** lets the employee learn by doing, or by watching others for a while and then imitating them, right at the workplace. Salespeople, for example, are often trained by watching experienced salespeople perform (often called *shadowing*). Naturally, this can be either quite effective or disastrous, depending on the skills and habits of the person being observed. On-the-job training is the easiest kind of training to implement when the job is relatively simple (such as clerking in a store) or repetitive (such as collecting refuse, cleaning carpets, or mowing lawns). More demanding or intricate jobs require a more intense training effort. Technology makes cost-effective on-the-job training programs available 24 hours a day. Online systems can monitor workers' input and give them instructions if they become confused about what to do next.

- In **apprentice programs** a trainee works alongside an experienced employee to master the skills and procedures of a craft. Some apprentice programs include classroom training. Trade unions in skilled crafts, such as bricklaying and plumbing, require a new worker to serve as an apprentice for several years to ensure excellence as well as to limit entry to the union. As Baby Boomers retire from skilled trades such as pipefitting, welding, and carpentry, shortages of trained workers are developing.[33] Apprentice programs may be shortened to prepare people for skilled jobs in changing industries such as auto repair and aircraft maintenance that require increased knowledge of computer technology.

- **Off-the-job training** occurs away from the workplace and consists of internal or external programs to develop any of a variety of skills or to foster personal development. Training is becoming more sophisticated as jobs become more sophisticated. Furthermore, training is expanding to include education (through the PhD) and personal development. Subjects may include time management, stress management, health and wellness, physical education, nutrition, and even art and languages.

At FedEx, time is money. That's why the company spends six times more on employee training than the average firm. Does the added expense pay off? You bet. FedEx enjoys a remarkably low 4 percent employee turnover rate. Should other companies follow FedEx's financial commitment to training? Why or why not?

Joe Raedle/Getty Images

Maia Kennedy/Alamy Stock Photo

- **Online training** demonstrates how technology is improving the efficiency of many off-the-job training programs. Online training's key advantage is the ability to provide a large number of employees with consistent content tailored to specific training needs at convenient times. Both nonprofit and profit-seeking businesses make extensive use of online training. Most colleges and universities offer a wide variety of online classes, sometimes called *distance learning.* Technology leaders like Apple, large manufacturers like Timken, and pharmaceutical giant Novartis use the online training tool GlobeSmart to teach employees how to operate in different cultures.[34]

- **Vestibule training** (or *near-the-job training*) is done in classrooms with equipment similar to that used on the job so that employees learn proper methods and safety procedures before assuming a specific job assignment. Computer and robotics training is often completed in a vestibule classroom.

- **Job simulation** is the use of equipment that duplicates job conditions and tasks so that trainees can learn skills before attempting them on the job. It differs from vestibule training in that it duplicates the *exact* combination of conditions that occur on the job. This is the kind of training given to astronauts, airline pilots, army tank operators, ship captains, and others who must learn difficult procedures of the job. Virtual reality is being more widely used in job simulations. For example, in medical facilities, doctors in training practice their skills before working with live patients, and UPS puts drivers in virtual reality simulators as part of the company's basic safety training.[35]

Management Development

Managers often need special training. To be good communicators, they need to learn listening skills and empathy. They also need time management, planning, and human relations skills. **Management development**, then, is the process of training and educating employees to become good managers, and then monitoring the progress of their managerial skills over time. Management development programs are widespread, especially at colleges, universities, and private management development firms. Managers may participate in role-playing exercises, solve various management cases, and attend films and lectures to improve their skills.

Management development is increasingly being used as a tool to accomplish business objectives and face new management challenges.[36] Procter & Gamble, Microsoft, and Goldman Sachs management teams were built with significant investments in their development.[37] Most management training programs include several of the following:

- *On-the-job coaching.* A senior manager assists a lower-level manager by teaching needed skills and providing direction, advice, and helpful feedback.

- *Understudy positions.* Job titles such as *undersecretary* and *assistant* are part of a relatively successful way of developing managers. Selected employees work as assistants to higher-level managers and participate in planning and other managerial

Morsa Images/Getty Images

Informal gatherings like this help professionals make new connections with people in their fields. Why do you think younger workers prefer such informal gatherings?

networking
The process of establishing and maintaining contacts with key managers in one's own organization and other organizations and using those contacts to weave strong relationships that serve as informal development systems.

mentor
An experienced employee who supervises, coaches, and guides lower-level employees by introducing them to the right people and generally being their organizational sponsor.

functions until they are ready to assume such positions themselves.

- *Job rotation.* So that they can learn about different functions of the organization, managers are often given assignments in a variety of departments. Such job rotation gives them the broad picture of the organization they need to succeed.

- *Off-the-job courses and training.* Managers periodically go to classes or seminars for a week or more to hone technical and human relations skills. Major universities like the University of Michigan, MIT, and the University of Chicago offer specialized short courses to assist managers in performing their jobs more efficiently. McDonald's Corporation has its own Hamburger University. Managers and potential franchisees attend six days of classes and complete a course of study equivalent to 36 hours of college business-school credit.[38]

Networking

Networking is the process of establishing and maintaining contacts with key managers in your own and other organizations, and using those contacts to weave strong relationships that serve as informal development systems. Of equal or greater importance may be a **mentor**, a corporate manager who supervises, coaches, and guides selected lower-level employees by introducing them to the right people and generally acting as their organizational sponsor. In most organizations informal mentoring occurs as experienced employees assist less experienced workers. However, many organizations formally assign mentors to employees considered to have strong potential. Companies have found that mentoring programs provide a number of benefits: (1) improved recruiting and retention, (2) more engaged employees, (3) cost savings, and (4) increased skills and better attitudes.[39]

It's also important to remember that networking and mentoring go beyond the business environment. For example, college is a perfect place to begin networking. Associations you nurture with professors, with local businesspeople through internships, and especially with your classmates can provide a valuable network to turn to for the rest of your career.

Diversity in Management Development

Today, more women are working in the paid workforce than men.[40] As more women moved into management, they learned the importance of networking and of having mentors. Unfortunately, women often have more difficulty than men in networking or finding mentors, since most senior managers are male. In 1988, women won a major legal victory when the U.S. Supreme Court ruled it illegal to bar women from certain clubs, long open to men only, where business activity flows and contacts are made. This decision allowed more women to enter established networking systems or, in some instances, create their own. Today, women are members of prestigious clubs such as the Augusta National Golf Club and growing numbers of women are becoming board members at America's largest companies.[41]

Similarly, African American and Hispanic managers learned the value of networking. Both groups have formed pools of capital and new opportunities helping many individuals overcome traditional barriers to success. *Black Enterprise* magazine sponsors several networking forums each year for African American professionals.[42] The Hispanic Alliance for Career Enhancement (HACE) is committed to building career opportunities and career advancement for Hispanics. MJAA is an association that helps Asian American professionals assimilate into U.S. business.

Companies that take the initiative to develop female and minority managers understand three crucial principles: (1) grooming women and minorities for management positions isn't about legality, morality, or even morale but rather about bringing more talent in the door, the key to long-term profitability; (2) the best women and minorities will become harder to attract and retain, so companies that commit to development early have an edge; and (3) having more women and minorities at all levels lets businesses serve their increasingly female and minority customers better. If you don't have a diversity of people working in the back room, how are you going to satisfy the diversity of people coming in the front door?

LO 11–7 Trace the six steps in appraising employee performance.

Appraising Employee Performance to Get Optimum Results

Managers must be able to determine whether their workers are doing an effective and efficient job, with a minimum of errors and disruptions. They do so by using a **performance appraisal**, an evaluation that measures employee performance against established standards in order to make decisions about promotions, compensation, training, or termination. Performance appraisals have six steps:

1. *Establishing performance standards.* This step is crucial. Standards must be understandable, subject to measurement, and reasonable. Both manager and employee must accept them.

2. *Communicating those standards.* It's dangerous to assume that employees know what is expected of them. They must be told clearly and precisely what the standards and expectations are, and how to meet them.

3. *Evaluating performance.* If the first two steps are done correctly, performance evaluation is relatively easy. It is a matter of evaluating the employee's behavior to see whether it matches standards.

4. *Discussing results with employees.* Employees often make mistakes and fail to meet expectations at first. It takes time to learn a job and do it well. Discussing an employee's successes and areas that need improvement can provide managers an opportunity to be understanding and helpful and guide the employee to better performance. The performance appraisal can also allow employees to suggest how a task could be done better.

5. *Taking corrective action.* As part of performance appraisal, a manager can take corrective action or provide feedback to help the employee perform better. The key word here is *perform.* The primary purpose of an appraisal is to improve employee performance if possible.

6. *Using the results to make decisions.* Decisions about promotions, compensation, additional training, or firing are all based on performance evaluations. An effective performance appraisal system is also a way of satisfying legal requirements about such decisions.

Managing effectively means getting results through top performance. That's what performance appraisals are for at all levels of the organization, including at the top where managers benefit from reviews by their employees and peers.

In the *360-degree review,* management gathers opinions from all around the employee, including those under, above, and on the same level, to get an accurate, comprehensive idea of the worker's abilities.

Many companies such as General Electric, Kimberly-Clark, and Coca-Cola are moving away from formal annual reviews toward *continuous performance reviews.* This performance management strategy allows workers to receive and give continuous, real-time feedback via mobile apps that are focused on helping employees meet goals—or leave the company faster. These strategies are particularly welcomed by Millennial workers who demand more feedback, more coaching, and a better idea of their career paths.[43]

performance appraisal

An evaluation that measures employee performance against established standards in order to make decisions about promotions, compensation, training, or termination.

?TESTPREP

- Name and describe four training techniques.
- What is the primary purpose of a performance appraisal?
- What are the six steps in a performance appraisal?

LO 11-8 Summarize the objectives of employee compensation programs, and evaluate pay systems and fringe benefits.

Compensating Employees: Attracting and Keeping the Best

Companies don't just compete for customers; they also compete for employees. Compensation is one of the main tools companies use to attract qualified employees, and one of their largest operating costs. The long-term success of a firm—perhaps even its survival—may depend on how well it can control employee costs and optimize employee efficiency. Service organizations like hospitals, hotels, and airlines struggle with high employee costs since these firms are *labor-intensive* (the primary cost of operations is the cost of labor). Employees in manufacturing firms in the auto and steel industries accepted reductions in wages (called givebacks) to make their firms more competitive. These examples are just a few reasons why compensation and benefit packages require special attention. In fact, some experts believe determining how best to compensate employees is today's greatest human resource challenge.

A carefully managed and competitive compensation and benefit program can accomplish several objectives:

- Attracting the kinds of people the organization needs, and in sufficient numbers.
- Providing employees with the incentive to work efficiently and productively.
- Keeping valued employees from going to competitors or starting competing firms.
- Maintaining a competitive position in the marketplace by keeping costs low through high productivity from a satisfied workforce.
- Providing employees with some sense of financial security through fringe benefits such as health insurance and retirement benefits.

Pay Systems

Many companies still use the pay structure known as the Hay method, devised by Edward Hay. This plan is based on job grades, each of which has a strict pay range. The system is set up on a point basis with three key factors considered: knowledge, problem solving, and accountability.

The most commonly used pay structure today is market-based.[44] Companies that use *market-based pay structures* compensate people relative to the market value of their job, regardless of their level in the organization. Companies research

Competitive compensation and benefit programs can have a tremendous impact on employee efficiency and productivity. Sometimes businesses reward exceptional performance by handing out bonuses. Does your instructor ever award bonuses for exceptional performance in class?

DoxaDigital/Getty Images

FIGURE 11.5 PAY SYSTEMS

Salary

Fixed compensation computed on weekly, biweekly, or monthly pay periods (e.g., $3,600 per month or $900 per week). Salaried employees do not receive additional pay for any extra hours worked.

Hourly wage or daywork

Wage based on number of hours or days worked, used for most blue-collar and clerical workers. Often employees must punch a time clock when they arrive at work and when they leave. Hourly wages vary greatly. The federal minimum wage is $7.25, and top wages go as high as $40 per hour or more for skilled craftspeople. This does not include benefits such as retirement systems, which may add 30 percent or more to the total package.

Piecework system

Wage based on the number of items produced rather than by the hour or day. This type of system creates powerful incentives to work efficiently and productively.

Commission plans

Pay based on some percentage of sales. Often used to compensate salespeople, commission plans resemble piecework systems.

Bonus plans

Extra pay for accomplishing or surpassing certain objectives. There are two types of bonuses: monetary and cashless. Money is always a welcome bonus. Cashless rewards include written thank-you notes, appreciation notes sent to the employee's family, movie tickets, flowers, time off, gift certificates, shopping sprees, and other types of recognition.

Profit-sharing plans

Annual bonuses paid to employees based on the company's profits. The amount paid to each employee is based on a predetermined percentage. Profit sharing is one of the most common forms of performance-based pay.

Gain-sharing plans

Annual bonuses paid to employees based on achieving specific goals such as quality measures, customer satisfaction measures, and production targets.

Stock options

Right to purchase stock in the company at a specific price over a specific period. Often this gives employees the right to buy stock cheaply despite huge increases in the price of the stock. For example, if over the course of his employment a worker received options to buy 10,000 shares of the company stock at $10 each and the price of the stock eventually grows to $100, he can use those options to buy the 10,000 shares (now worth $1 million) for $100,000.

what other firms are paying and decide to pay either the same, more, or less. The market may suggest, for example, that certain, specially trained technology workers should be paid more because there is a high demand and short supply of skilled tech workers.[45]

The way an organization chooses to pay its employees can have a dramatic effect on efficiency and productivity. Managers therefore look for a system that compensates employees fairly. Figure 11.5 outlines some of the most common pay systems. Which do you think is the fairest?

Compensating Teams

Thus far, we've talked about compensating individuals. What about teams? Since you want your teams to be more than simply a group of individuals, would you still compensate them like individuals? Measuring and rewarding individual performance on teams, while at the same time rewarding team performance, is tricky—but it can be done. Professional football players, for example, are rewarded as a team when they go to the playoffs and to the Super Bowl, but they are paid individually as well. Companies are now experimenting with and developing similar incentive systems.

Jay Schuster, coauthor of a study of team pay, found that when pay is based strictly on individual performance, it erodes team cohesiveness and makes the team less likely to meet its goals as a collaborative effort. Skill-based pay and gain-sharing systems are the two most common compensation methods for teams.

Skill-based pay rewards the growth of both the individual and the team. Base pay is raised when team members learn and apply new skills. Baldrige Award winner Eastman Chemical Company rewards its teams for proficiency in technical, social, and business knowledge skills. A cross-functional compensation policy team defines the skills. The drawbacks of skill-based pay are twofold: the system is complex, and it is difficult to relate the acquisition of skills directly to profit gains. The advantages of skill-based pay include improved employee skill development and job satisfaction.[46]

Most *gain-sharing systems* base bonuses on improvements over previous performance.[47] Nucor Steel, one of the largest U.S. steel producers, calculates bonuses on quality—tons of steel that go out the door with no defects. There are no limits on bonuses a team can earn. One of the drawbacks of basing bonuses on improving previous performance is that workers may improve just enough to meet the target, but not by much. Since their target for the next year will be to beat this year's performance, they don't want to risk setting a new goal they won't be able to reach.

It is important to reward individual team players. Outstanding team players—who go beyond what is required and make an outstanding individual contribution—should be separately recognized, with cash or noncash rewards. A good way to compensate for uneven team participation is to let the team decide which members get what type of individual award. After all, if you really support the team process, you need to give teams freedom to reward themselves.

fringe benefits
Benefits such as sick-leave pay, vacation pay, pension plans, and health plans that represent additional compensation to employees beyond base wages.

The employees at DreamWorks Studios who help create hit animated franchises like How to Train Your Dragon *enjoy perks like free breakfast and lunch, afternoon yoga classes, free movie screenings, on-campus art classes, and monthly parties. How might fringe benefits like these affect employee performance?*

Collection Christophel/Alamy Stock Photo

Fringe Benefits

Fringe benefits include sick-leave pay, vacation pay, pension plans, and health plans that provide additional compensation to employees beyond base wages. Benefits in recent years grew faster than wages and can't really be considered "fringe" anymore. In 1929, such benefits accounted for less than 2 percent of payroll; today they can account for over 30 percent.[48] Health care costs have been one of the key reasons for the increase, forcing employees to pay a larger share of their health insurance bill. Employees often will request more benefits instead of salary, in order to avoid higher taxes. This increase in the value of benefits has led to much debate and government investigation.

Fringe benefits can include recreation facilities, company cars, country club memberships, discounted massages, special home-mortgage rates, paid and unpaid sabbaticals, day care services, and executive dining rooms. Increasingly, employees often want dental care, mental health care, wellness programs, elder care, legal counseling, eye care, and even short workweeks.[49] Two newer employee benefits are aimed at Millennials: help paying off student loan debt and low-cost loans.[50]

Understanding that it takes many incentives to attract and retain the best employees, dozens of firms among *Fortune* magazine's "100 Best Companies to Work For" list offer so-called soft benefits. *Soft benefits* help workers maintain the balance between work and family

Keeping Your Global Workforce Happy

shrm.org

Human resource management of a global workforce begins with an understanding of the customs, laws, and local business needs of every country in which the organization operates. Country-specific cultural and legal standards affect a variety of human resource functions. Examples include:

Tinpixels/Getty Images

- *Compensation.* Salaries must be converted to and from foreign currencies. Often employees working globally receive special allowances for relocation, children's education, housing, travel, and other business-related expenses.

- *Health and pension standards.* There are different social contexts for benefits management in other countries. In the Netherlands, the government provides retirement income and health care.

- *Paid time off.* Four weeks of paid vacation is the standard of many European employers. But many other countries lack the short-term and long-term absence policies offered in the United States, including sick leave, personal leave, and family and medical leave. Global companies need a standard definition of *time off.*

- *Taxation.* Each country has different taxation rules, and the payroll department must know and work within each country's regulations.

- *Communication.* When employees leave to work in another country, they often feel disconnected from their home country. Technology can help keep these distant employees in direct contact.

- *Regulatory requirements.* The Fair Labor Standards Act in the United States, the Factory Act in India, and the Labor Law of the People's Republic of China all impact how employees work and their workplace rights.

Global countries and cultures influence human resource management actions at home in the United States. As global expansion continues, HR managers need to stay abreast of overseas cultural and business practices and their impact on the organization and global markets.

Sources: John Winsor, "Mindfully Employ a Global Workforce by Staying Sensitive to Language Identity," *Forbes,* December 31, 2019; Jeanne Meister, "Top 10 HR Trends That Matter Most in the 2020 Workplace," *Forbes,* January 15, 2020; "Strategies to Reskill the Global Workforce," *Yahoo! Finance,* finance.yahoo.com, accessed February 2020.

life that is often as important to hardworking employees as the nature of the job itself. These perks include on-site haircuts and shoe repair, concierge services, and free breakfasts. Freeing employees from errands and chores gives them more time for family—and work. Facebook offers employee benefits many consider second-to-none. The company offers free housing for interns; free meals; an arcade of video games; discounts on automobiles, travel, and hotels; an on-site laundry; and multiple other perks.[51]

At one time, most employees sought benefits that were similar. Today, however, some may seek child care benefits while others prefer attractive pension plans. To address such growing demands, many large firms offer **cafeteria-style fringe benefits**, in which employees can choose the benefits they want up to a certain dollar amount. Such plans let human resource managers equitably and cost-effectively meet employees' individual needs by allowing them choice.[52]

As the cost of administering benefits programs has accelerated, many companies have chosen to outsource this function. Managing benefits can be especially complicated when employees are located in other countries. The Reaching beyond Our Borders box discusses the human resource challenges faced by global businesses. To put it simply, benefits are often as important to recruiting top talent as salary and may even become more important in the future.

cafeteria-style fringe benefits
Fringe benefits plan that allows employees to choose the benefits they want up to a certain dollar amount.

LO 11–9   Demonstrate how managers use scheduling plans to adapt to workers' needs.

Scheduling Employees to Meet Organizational and Employee Needs

Workplace trends and the increasing costs of transportation have led employees to look for scheduling flexibility. Flextime, in-home employment, and job sharing are important benefits employees seek. In fact, large majorities of Millennials and Gen Xers surveyed say they look for jobs that allow flexible work schedules and believe that flexible work hours make them more productive at their jobs.[53]

Flextime Plans

flextime plan

Work schedule that gives employees some freedom to choose when to work, as long as they work the required number of hours.

core time

In a flextime plan, the period when all employees are expected to be at their job stations.

A **flextime plan** gives employees some freedom to choose which hours to work, as long as they work the required number of hours or complete their assigned tasks. The most popular plans allow employees to arrive between 7:00 and 9:00 a.m. and leave between 4:00 and 6:00 p.m. Flextime plans generally incorporate core time. **Core time** is the period when all employees are expected to be at their job stations. An organization may designate core time as 9:00 to 11:00 a.m. and 2:00 to 4:00 p.m. During these hours all employees are required to be at work (see Figure 11.6). Flextime allows employees to adjust to work–life demands. Two-income families find them especially helpful. Companies that use flextime say that it boosts employee productivity and morale.

Flextime is not for all organizations, however. It doesn't suit shift work like fast-food or assembly processes like manufacturing, where everyone on a given shift must be at work at the same time. Another disadvantage is that managers often have to work longer days to assist and supervise in organizations that may operate from 6:00 a.m. to 6:00 p.m. Flextime also makes communication more difficult because certain employees may not be there when others need to talk to them. Furthermore, if not carefully supervised, some employees could abuse the system, causing resentment among others.

compressed workweek

Work schedule that allows an employee to work a full number of hours per week but in fewer days.

Another option that about one in four companies use is a **compressed workweek**. An employee works the full number of hours, but in fewer than the standard number of days. For example, an employee may work four 10-hour days and then enjoy a long weekend, instead of working five 8-hour days with a traditional weekend. There are obvious advantages of compressed workweeks, but some employees get tired working such long hours, and productivity can decline. Others find the system a great benefit, however, and are enthusiastic about it.[54] Nurses often work compressed weeks.

Flexible scheduling isn't always a benefit to employees. The strategy called *on-call scheduling* entails employers calling in or canceling workers with little notice. This practice may violate state laws requiring workers to be paid for a least of a portion of their shifts if they are sent home

FIGURE 11.6 A FLEXTIME CHART
At this company, employees can start work anytime between 6:30 and 9:30 a.m. They take a half hour for lunch anytime between 11:00 a.m. and 1:30 p.m. and can leave between 3:00 and 6:30 p.m. Everyone works an eight-hour day. The blue arrows show a typical employee's flextime day.

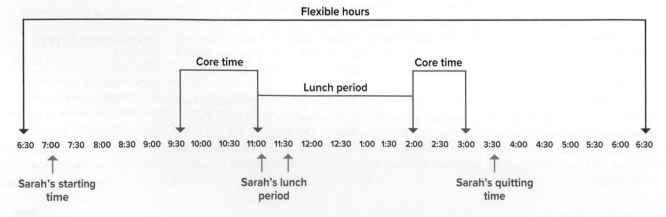

gartner.com

Like many workers, Lasse Rheingans realized that taking time to check Facebook and respond to reply-all e-mails distracted him from his daily work goals. That's why, when he acquired a small tech consulting firm in Bielefeld, Germany, he decided on a radical change. He reduced the normal workday to five hours, from the standard eight, while leaving worker salaries and vacations at the same level. Today, at Rheingans Digital Enabler, 16 employees start work at 8:00 a.m. and leave at 1:00 p.m.

According to Rheingans, employees can produce the same output in a focused 25-hour workweek as they can in a 40-hour week full of disruptions. To accomplish his objective, small talk is

luma_art/Shutterstock

discouraged at work, use of social media is banned, and phones are kept in backpacks. Company e-mail accounts are checked twice a day, and meetings are restricted to 15 minutes. The result: His company produces the same level of output despite the shorter workdays.

Tower Paddle Boards in San Diego, California, began a five-hour workday in 2015. Company CEO Stephan Aarstol said the initial experiment was a success but later limited the five-hour days to summer months. Brian Kropp, chief of research at Gartner Inc., says the five-hour workday makes sense and fits well with the growing trend of companies looking to increase worker flexibility, something they value more than money. Five-hour workdays may also have a benefit in giving small businesses an edge in attracting workers from bigger, more established companies.

Sources: Eric Morath, "Five-Hour Workday Gets Put to the Test," *The Wall Street Journal,* October 24, 2019; Walden Siew, "Experimenting with New Workplace Models," *Employee Benefit News,* benefitnews.com, accessed February 2020; Renato Profico, "To Get More Done in Four-Hour Workdays, Do These Three Things," *Fast Company,* January 15, 2020.

early. Using software that determines hourly staffing needs based on sales and traffic information, chain retailers and restaurants, for example, can adjust the number of workers required quickly during slow or busy times. This flexibility is great for the company but can cause stress on the lives and pay of workers. On-call scheduling makes it a struggle for workers to arrange reliable child care or supplement their incomes with second jobs.[55] The Spotlight on Small Business box looks into an interesting strategy that could make job flexibility even more attractive.

Home-Based Work

Forty-four percent of U.S. workers now work from home at least once per week or more, and the numbers are clearly increasing.[56] Home-based workers can choose their own hours, interrupt work for child care or other tasks, and take time out for personal reasons. Working at home isn't for everyone. It requires discipline to stay focused on the job and not be easily distracted. Yet, even with such challenges, over 50 percent of office workers say they would leave their jobs for one that offered more flexibility, including working from home.[57]

Home-based work can also benefit employers because it can limit absences, increase productivity, and save money. One study found workers were more productive, got more done, worked longer hours, took fewer breaks, and used less sick time than in-office workers. Home-based workers were also happier and quit less than those who went into the office regularly. Such results are causing many companies to adopt remote work policies.[58]

Many companies also offer "hot desking," or sharing a desk with other employees who work at different times. Hot desking can lead to more collaboration since workers get to know more people throughout the organization than they would have at a fixed desk. Companies sharing work space have hot desks that can be rented for the day, week, month, or longer, which allow professionals to get to know and learn from each other. Figure 11.7 outlines the benefits and challenges of home-based work to organizations, individuals, and society.

FIGURE 11.7 BENEFITS AND CHALLENGES OF HOME-BASED WORK

Home-based work (also known as *telecommuting*) offers many benefits and challenges to organizations, individuals, and society as a whole.

BENEFITS	CHALLENGES
To Organization	
• Increases productivity due to fewer sick days, fewer absences, higher job satisfaction, and higher work performance ratings	• Makes it more difficult to appraise job performance
• Broadens available talent pool	• Can negatively affect the social network of the workplace and can make it difficult to promote team cohesiveness
• Reduces costs of providing on-site office space	• Complicates distribution of tasks (should office files, contact lists, and such be allowed to leave the office?)
To Individual	
• Makes more time available for work and family by reducing or eliminating commute time	• Can cause feeling of isolation from social network
• Reduces expenses of buying and maintaining office clothes	• Can raise concerns regarding promotions and other rewards due to being out of sight, out of mind
• Avoids office politics	• May diminish individual's influence within company due to limited opportunity to learn the corporate culture
• Helps balance work and family	
• Expands employment opportunities for individuals with disabilities	
To Society	
• Decreases traffic congestion	• Increases need to resolve zoning regulations forbidding business deliveries in residential neighborhoods
• Discourages community crime that might otherwise occur in bedroom communities	• May reduce ability to interact with other people in a personal, intimate manner
• Increases time available to build community ties	

During the COVID-19 pandemic, it was necessary for many employees to work at home. Working from home requires self-discipline to stay focused on the job and not allow yourself to be distracted. Do you think you have the discipline to be a home-based worker full-time?

martinedoucet/Getty Images

Job-Sharing Plans

Job sharing lets two or more part-time employees share one full-time job. Students and parents with small children, for instance, may work only during school hours, and older workers can work part-time before fully retiring or after retiring. Benefits of job sharing include:

- Employment opportunities for those who cannot or prefer not to work full-time.
- An enthusiastic and productive workforce.
- Reduced absenteeism and tardiness.
- Ability to schedule part-time workers into peak demand periods.
- Retention of experienced employees who might otherwise have retired.

Disadvantages include the need to hire, train, motivate, and supervise at least twice as many people and perhaps prorate some fringe benefits. But firms are finding that the advantages generally outweigh the disadvantages.

LO 11–10 Describe how employees can move through a company: promotion, reassignment, termination, and retirement.

Moving Employees Up, Over, and Out

Employees don't always stay in the position they were hired to fill. They may excel and move up the corporate ladder or fail and move out the door. Employees can also be reassigned or retire. Of course, some choose to move themselves by going to another company.

Promoting and Reassigning Employees

Many companies find that promotion from within the company improves employee morale. It's also cost-effective in that the promoted employees are already familiar with the corporate culture and procedures and don't need to spend valuable time on basic orientation.

In the new, flatter corporate structures (see Chapter 8) there are fewer levels for employees to reach than in the past. Thus they often move *over* to a new position rather than *up*. Such lateral transfers allow employees to develop and display new skills and learn more about the company overall. Reassignment is one way of motivating experienced employees to remain in a company with few advancement opportunities.

During the COVID-19 pandemic, managers had to terminate a great number of employees. Do you think companies rehired these full-time workers as the economy slowly recovered? Why or why not? What alternatives do employers have?

Eric Von Seggern/Shutterstock

Terminating Employees

We've seen that the relentless pressure of global competition, shifts in technology, increasing customer demands for greater value, and uncertain economic conditions have human resource managers struggling to manage layoffs and firings.[59] Even if the economy is booming, many companies are hesitant to hire or rehire workers full-time. Why is that the case? One reason is that the cost of terminating employees is prohibitively high in terms of lost training costs and possible damages and legal fees for wrongful discharge suits. That's why many companies are either using temporary employees or outsourcing certain functions.

At one time the prevailing employment doctrine in the United States was "employment at will." This meant managers had as much freedom to fire workers as workers

FIGURE 11.8 HOW TO AVOID WRONGFUL DISCHARGE LAWSUITS

Consultants offer this advice to minimize the chance of a lawsuit for wrongful discharge:

- Prepare before hiring by requiring recruits to sign a statement that retains management's freedom to terminate at will.
- Don't make unintentional promises by using such terms as *permanent employment.*
- Document reasons before firing and make sure you have an unquestionable business reason for the firing.
- Fire the worst first and be consistent in discipline.
- Buy out potential litigation by offering severance pay in exchange for a signed release from any claims.
- Be sure to give employees the true reasons they are being fired. If you do not, you cannot reveal it to a recruiter asking for a reference without risking a defamation lawsuit.
- Disclose the reasons for an employee's dismissal to that person's potential new employers. For example, if you fired an employee for dangerous behavior and you withhold that information from your references, you can be sued if the employee commits a violent act at his or her next job.

Source: Sean Peek, "How to Legally Fire an Employee," U.S. Chamber of Commerce, uschamber.com, January 31, 2020.

had to leave voluntarily. Most states now limit the at-will doctrine to protect employees from wrongful firing. For example, an employer can no longer fire someone for exposing the company's illegal actions or refusing to violate a law. Employees who are members of a minority or other protected group also may have protections under equal employment law. In some cases, workers fired for using illegal drugs have sued on the grounds that they have an illness (addiction) and are therefore protected by laws barring discrimination under the Americans with Disabilities Act (ADA). Well-intended legislation has in some ways restricted management's ability to terminate employees as it increased workers' rights to their jobs. See Figure 11.8 for advice about how to minimize the chance of wrongful discharge lawsuits.

Retiring Employees

Companies looking to downsize sometimes offer early retirement benefits to entice older (and more expensive) workers to retire. Such benefits can include one-time cash payments, known in some companies as *golden handshakes.* The advantage early retirement benefits have over layoffs or firing is the increased morale of surviving employees. Retiring older workers earlier also increases promotion opportunities for younger employees.

When the number of qualified workers is low, employers must find ways to retain older, experienced workers and/or to transfer their knowledge to younger workers. Many companies offer older employees more flexible, part-time schedules in order to entice them to stay long enough to train their replacements. An increasing number of would-be retirees choose to keep working either because they enjoy it or because they lack the financial resources to retire.[60]

Losing Valued Employees

In spite of a company's efforts to retain them, some talented employees will choose to pursue opportunities elsewhere. Knowing their reasons for leaving can be invaluable in preventing the loss of other good people in the future. One way to learn the reasons is to have an outside expert conduct an *exit interview.* Outsiders can provide confidentiality and anonymity that earns more honest feedback than employees are comfortable giving in face-to-face interviews with their bosses. Online systems can capture, track, and statistically analyze employee exit interview data to generate reports that identify trouble areas. Such programs can also coordinate exit interview data with employee satisfaction surveys to predict which departments should expect turnover to occur.

Offboarding is the process surrounding employee exits. Whether employees are fired, resigning, or retiring, there are things that need to be done before they leave. This includes managing payments, insurance, and benefits; conducting exit interviews; collecting work and documents; and returning anything owned by the company.

Attracting and retaining the best employees is the key to success in the competitive global business environment. Dealing with controversial issues employees have on the job is challenging and never-ending. Chapter 12 discusses such issues.

TESTPREP

- Can you name and describe five alternative compensation techniques?
- What advantages do compensation plans such as profit sharing offer an organization?
- What are the benefits and challenges of flextime? Telecommuting? Job sharing?

SUMMARY

LO 11–1 Explain the importance of human resource management, and describe current issues in managing human resources.

- **What are current challenges and opportunities in the human resource area?**

  Many current challenges and opportunities arise from changing demographics: more women, minorities, immigrants, and older workers in the workforce. Others include a shortage of trained workers and an abundance of unskilled workers, skilled workers in declining industries requiring retraining, changing employee work attitudes, and complex laws and regulations.

LO 11–2 Illustrate the effects of legislation on human resource management.

- **What are some of the key laws?**

  See Figure 11.2 and review the text section on laws.

LO 11–3 Summarize the five steps in human resource planning.

- **What are the steps in human resource planning?**

  The five steps are (1) preparing a human resource inventory of the organization's employees; (2) preparing a job analysis; (3) assessing future demand; (4) assessing future supply; and (5) establishing a plan for recruiting, hiring, educating, appraising, compensating, and scheduling employees.

LO 11–4 Describe methods that companies use to recruit new employees, and explain some of the issues that make recruitment challenging.

- **What methods do human resource managers use to recruit new employees?**

  Recruiting sources are classified as either internal or external. Internal sources include those hired from within (transfers, promotions, reassignments) and employees who recommend others to hire. External recruitment sources include advertisements, public and private employment agencies, college placement bureaus, management consultants, online sites, professional organizations, referrals, and online and walk-in applications.

- **Why has recruitment become more difficult?**

  Legal restrictions complicate hiring and firing practices. Finding suitable employees can be more difficult if companies are considered unattractive workplaces.

LO 11–5 Outline the six steps in selecting employees.

- **What are the six steps in the selection process?**

  The steps are (1) obtaining complete application forms, (2) conducting initial and follow-up interviews, (3) giving employment tests, (4) conducting background investigations, (5) obtaining results from physical exams, and (6) establishing a trial period of employment.

- **What are contingent workers?**

  Contingent workers include part-time workers (anyone who works less than 35 hours per week), temporary workers (workers paid by temporary employment agencies), seasonal workers, independent contractors, interns, and co-op students.

- **Why has there been such an increase in hiring contingent workers?**

  Workers want diversity and flexibility in their roles and the ability to showcase their skills; and employers have shifted from "I need to hire a person" to "I need to complete a task."

LO 11–6 Illustrate employee training and development methods.

- **What are some training activities?**

  Training activities include employee orientation, on- and off-the-job training, apprentice programs, online training, vestibule training, and job simulation.

- **What methods help develop managerial skills?**

  Management development methods include on-the-job coaching, understudy positions, job rotation, off-the-job courses, and training.

- **How does networking fit in this process?**

  Networking is the process of establishing contacts with key managers within and outside the organization to get additional development assistance.

LO 11–7 Trace the six steps in appraising employee performance.

- **How do managers evaluate performance?**

  The steps are (1) establish performance standards; (2) communicate those standards; (3) compare performance to standards; (4) discuss results; (5) take corrective action when needed; and (6) use the results for decisions about promotions, compensation, additional training, or firing.

LO 11–8 Summarize the objectives of employee compensation programs, and evaluate pay systems and fringe benefits.

- **What are common types of compensation systems?**

  They include salary systems, hourly wages, piecework, commission plans, bonus plans, profit-sharing plans, and stock options.

- **What types of compensation are appropriate for teams?**

  The most common are gain-sharing and skill-based compensation programs. Managers also reward outstanding individual performance within teams.

- **What are fringe benefits?**

  Fringe benefits include sick leave, vacation pay, company cars, pension plans, and health plans that provide additional compensation to employees beyond base wages. Cafeteria-style fringe benefits plans let employees choose the benefits they want, up to a certain dollar amount.

LO 11–9 Demonstrate how managers use scheduling plans to adapt to workers' needs.

- **What scheduling plans can adjust work to employees' need for flexibility?**

  Such plans include flextime, compressed workweeks, home-based work, and job sharing.

LO 11–10 Describe how employees can move through a company: promotion, reassignment, termination, and retirement.

- **How can employees move within a company?**

  Employees can be moved up (promotion), over (reassignment), or out (termination or retirement) of a company. They can also choose to leave a company to pursue opportunities elsewhere.

KEY TERMS

affirmative action 278
apprentice programs 286
cafeteria-style fringe benefits 293
compressed workweek 294
contingent workers 284
core time 294
flextime plan 294
fringe benefits 292
human resource management (HRM) 274
job analysis 279
job description 279
job sharing 297
job simulation 287
job specifications 279
management development 287
mentor 288
networking 288
off-the-job training 286
online training 287
on-the-job training 286
orientation 286
performance appraisal 289
recruitment 280
selection 281
training and development 286
vestibule training 287

CRITICAL THINKING

1. Does human resource management interest you as a career? What are your experiences working with human resource professionals?

2. What effects have dual-career families had on the human resource function?

3. What problems can arise when family members work together in the same firm?

4. If you were a human resource manager, how would you address the brain drain that occurs as knowledgeable, older workers retire?

5. Imagine you must fire an employee. What effect might the dismissal have on remaining employees? Explain how you would tell the employee to be fired and your other employees.

PUTTING PRINCIPLES TO WORK

PURPOSE

The two purposes here are to illustrate the types of questions managers typically ask during interviews and to practice answering such questions in a safe environment.

EXERCISE

Go to Monster.com, click on "Career Advice," then "Interview Practice Questions." This list of articles identifies some of the more common questions asked during an interview. Read the articles for advice about how to best answer these common questions. This will give you the opportunity to practice your answers, so that when you do go on an actual interview, you are less likely to fumble for an answer.

DEVELOPING CAREER SKILLS

KEY: ● **Team** ★ **Analytic** ▲ **Communication** ◉ **Technology**

◉ ★ 1. Look for job listings online, at your college, or in your local newspaper and find at least two positions you might like to have when you graduate. List the qualifications specified in each of the ads and identify methods the companies might use to determine how well applicants meet them.

◉ ★ 2. Read several current business periodicals or search online to find information about the latest court rulings on benefits, affirmative action, accommodating disabilities, and other human resource issues. Summarize your findings. Is there a trend in these decisions? If so, what is it, and what will it mean for tomorrow's college graduates?

★ ▲ 3. Recall any on-the-job and off-the-job training sessions you've experienced. Write a brief critique of each. How would you improve them? Share your ideas with the class.

★ ▲ 4. Consider the following occupations: doctor, computer salesperson, computer software developer, teacher, and assembly worker. Identify the method of compensation you think is appropriate for each. Explain your answer.

★ ▲ 5. Choose one of these positions: a human resource manager notifying employees of mandatory drug testing or an employee representative protesting such testing. Write a memorandum supporting your position.

CAREER EXPLORATION

If you are interested in pursuing a career in the field of human resource management, here are a few to consider. Find out about the tasks performed, skills needed, pay, and opportunity outlook in these fields in the *Occupational Outlook Handbook (OOH)* at bls.gov.

- **Training and development manager**—plans, directs, and coordinates programs to enhance the knowledge and skills of an organization's employees; oversees a staff of training and development specialists.
- **Compensation manager**—plans, develops, and oversees programs to determine how much an

organization pays its employees and how employees are paid.

- **Benefits manager**—plans, directs, and coordinates retirement plans, health insurance, and other benefits that an organization offers its employees.
- **Human resource manager**—plans, directs, and coordinates the administrative functions of an organization; oversees the recruiting, interviewing, and hiring of new staff; consults with top executives on strategic planning; and serves as a link between an organization's management and its employees.

Hiring and Developing Employees at Hilton

VIDEO CASE

Organizations can offer great products, have carefully developed strategic plans, and employ dedicated management yet still not be successful in the market if they lack a committed workforce. Employees are literally the lifeblood of any company. This is particularly true for service-based companies where employees are required to deal directly with customers on an everyday basis. Human resource management (HRM) is the process of recruiting, training, and retaining the correct number and specific type of employees a company needs. Effective HRM is challenging for any organization, but it presents a very difficult task for companies like international hotel giant Hilton, which employs over 414,000 team members around the globe.

Conrad Hilton founded the hotel giant in 1919, with the goal of "spreading the light and warmth of hospitality around the world." Since its inception, Hilton has been considered a hospitality pioneer, leading the industry in guest satisfaction as well as employee satisfaction. In 2019, Hilton earned the number one ranking on *Fortune* magazine's list of the "100 Best Companies to Work For in the United States." As a leader in employee satisfaction, Hilton knows that effective HRM starts with recruiting the right employees for the company. Therefore, Hilton extends encouragement and opportunity to anyone who expresses an interest in working for the company. This welcoming attitude is especially admirable at a large company like Hilton.

Hilton looks to fill a very large number of positions serving a wide range of company needs. From room attendants, to managers, to marketing and sales specialists, the company must recruit qualified candidates. Applicants often don't realize the number of career opportunities the company offers. Still, Hilton hires approximately 66,000 new team members each year from the more than 1 million applications it receives. These applicants come from both internal and external sources that include college campus recruiting, word of mouth, or people who know of Hilton and its workplace culture.

Once a person is hired, he or she begins Hilton's numerous training and development programs. Training

and development is critical at Hilton, and training programs are delivered through a variety of formats. The company even has its own learning platform called Hilton University. Learning content can include topics that range from brand training to job skills. The company also has Virtual Instructor Led Training (VILT) that allows employees to connect with specific training from anywhere in the world. Management development training, for example, helps managers build human relations, planning, and listening skills necessary for effective leadership. Managers all the way up to the CEO have learned valuable insights from Hilton's training and development programs.

Hilton realizes that beyond training and development, it needs to build a work environment where employees feel secure. The company offers this through its expansive benefits program. Hilton's "umbrella" program called Thrive includes many programs that aim to support employees' personal needs. For example, Thrive Sabbatical offers team members the opportunity to take a monthlong sabbatical in which they can enrich the lives of others through volunteer activities or take time to pursue their own personal goals or objectives. It also provides adoption assistance and flexible hours for parents who need to pick up children.

Likely thanks to Hilton's forward-thinking human resource efforts, the company will continue to attract dedicated and enthusiastic employees vital to the firm's mission. Like many other successful organizations, Hilton knows that happy employees make for happy customers.

THINKING IT OVER

1. Why is careful recruitment and selection particularly important in a direct service business such as Hilton?

2. What's the major value of Hilton's Virtual Instructor Led Training (VILT) program?

3. Does a benefits program like Thrive@Hilton build employee loyalty? Do employees generally like this type of structure? Why or why not?

NOTES

1. Dinah Wisenberg Brin, "Retailers Faced Staffing Woes during 2019 Holiday Season," Society for Human Resource Management, shrm.org, February 7, 2020; "Blue-Collar Workers Are Now Scarcer Than White-Collar Workers," *IndustryWeek,* industryweek.com, accessed February 2020.

2. James Freeman, "More Job Growth at Small Companies," *The Wall Street Journal,* January 9, 2020; "Ken Martin, "Construction Jobs Are Being Created, but Where Are the Workers?," *Yahoo! Finance*, finance.yahoo.com, January 10, 2020; "14 Ways Leaders Can Prepare for Generation Z's

Entry into the Job Market," *Forbes,* forbes.com, February 6, 2020; Katie Kuehner-Hebert, "AGC Urges Congress to Help Increase Supply of Skilled Workers," *Electrical Contractor*, ecmag.com, January 2020; Steve Boese, "A Look at What HR Leaders Think about HR Technology," *Human Resource Executive,* hrexecutive.com, February 17, 2020.

3. Equal Employment Opportunity Act, eeoc.gov, accessed February 2020.

4. Irene Liu, "Here's Why Fair Chance Hiring Is a Benefit to Employees and Employers," Newswire, newswire.com,

February 6, 2020; "Ban the Box Laws and Second Chance Programs That Help Ex-Offenders Find Work Will Expand in 2020," ESR, esrcheck.com, accessed February 2020.

5. "Fair Chance Act Boosts Job Prospects of Ex-Prisoners," *Newswise,* newswise.com, accessed February 2020; Irene Liu, "Here's Why Fair Chance Hiring Is a Boost for Employees and Employers," *Workforce,* workforce.com, February 6, 2020.

6. Louis Menand, "The Changing Meaning of Affirmative Action," *The New Yorker,* January 20, 2020; Orlando Patterson, "Affirmative Action: The Uniquely American Experience," *The New York Times,* January 30, 2020.

7. Patricia Chaney, "5 Tips for Accommodating Employees with Disabilities in Your Wellness Program," *Anthem: The Benefits Guide,* thebenefitsguide.com, January 8, 2020.

8. Equal Employment Opportunity Commission, eeoc.gov, accessed February 2020.

9. "The Americans with Disabilities Act: Applying Performance and Conduct Standards to Employees with Disabilities," EEOC, eeoc.gov, accessed March 2020.

10. "Age Discrimination in Employment Act of 1967," Society for Human Resource Management, accessed February 2020.

11. Patricia Barnes, "Finally, U.S. House Will Address Disastrous U.S. Supreme Court Ruling on Age Discrimination," *Forbes,* January 13, 2020; Hunter Moyler, "What Wednesday's Supreme Court Case Could Mean for Age Discrimination in the Workplace," *Newsweek,* January 14, 2020.

12. "AARP Applauds U.S. House Vote on Bipartisan Bill to Fight Age Bias," *Yahoo! Finance,* finance.yahoo.com, accessed February 2020; Alan Smith, "House Passes Protecting Older Workers Against Discrimination Act," Society for Human Resource Management, shrm.org, January 16, 2020.

13. Peter Louch, "Workforce Planning Is Essential to High-Performing Organizations," Society for Human Resource Planning, accessed February 2020; Austen Hufford, "Skilled Workers Score Sweeter Perks to Move," *The Wall Street Journal,* January 13, 2020.

14. Jeff Cox, "Manufacturing Jobs Are 'Tough to Fill' and Stand Out as the Weak Spot in the Employment Picture," *CNBC,* cnbc.com, January 10, 2020; Sarah K. White, "The Ten Most In-Demand Tech Jobs in 2020—and How to Hire for Them," *CIO,* cio.com, January 10, 2020.

15. Diane Bogino, "Human Resources and Information Technology: An Odd, Yet Necessary Relationship," *Forbes,* February 28, 2019; Geraldine Grones, "HRIS Systems: What You Need to Know," *HR Director,* hcamag.com, January 23, 2020.

16. Sarah Todd, "CEOs Everywhere Are Stressed about Talent Retention—and Ignoring Obvious Solutions for It," *Yahoo! Finance,* finance.yahoo.com, January 15, 2020; "The Shortlist," McKinsey and Company, mckinsey.com, accessed February 2020; Kate Rogers, "Manufacturers to Spend $26.2 Billion on 'Upskilling' in 2020 to Attract and Keep Workers," *CNBC,* cnbc.com, January 17, 2020.

17. "Three External Factors Driving Corporate Cultural Change Today," *IndustryWeek,* industryweek.com, accessed February 2020; Alison Doyle, "The Definition of Company Culture," *The Balance Careers,* thebalancecareers.com, January 19, 2020; Joann S. Lublin, "Check Out the Culture before a New Job," *The Wall Street Journal,* January 18, 2020.

18. Alison Doyle, "What Are Talent Assessments and How Do Companies Use Them?," *The Balance Careers,* thebalancecareers.com, January 15, 2020.

19. "Ten Major Companies That Use Aptitude Testing," aptitude-test.com, accessed February 2020.

20. Shane McFeeley and Ben Wigert, "This Fixable Problem Cost U.S. Businesses $1 Trillion," Gallup, gallup.com, March 13, 2019; "14 Effective Employee Retention Strategies," Robert Half, roberthalf.com, February 6, 2020.

21. "The Best Background Check Service for 2020," GoodHire, goodhire.com, accessed February 2020; "Best Background Checks Based on In-Depth Reviews," ConsumersAdvocate.org, February 7, 2020.

22. Liza Nagele Piazza, "Workplace Drug Testing: Can Employers Still Screen for Marijuana?," Society for Human Resource Management, shrm.org, January 21, 2020; Lisa Schencker, "Smoking Legal Marijuana Can Still Get You Fired," *Chicago Tribune,* January 10, 2020; Sean Peek, "Is Drug Testing Your Employees Legal?," U.S. Chamber of Commerce, uschamber.com, January 29, 2020.

23. Alison Doyle, "Key Job Facts about the Gig Economy," *The Balance Small Business,* thebalancesmb.com, January 22, 2020; U.S. Bureau of Labor Statistics, bls.gov, accessed February 2020.

24. Richard Eisenberg, "How Well Is the Gig Economy Working for Gig Workers?," *Forbes,* February 18, 2019; "How the Gig Economy Fits into the Future of Work," Wharton, University of Pennsylvania, wharton.upenn.edu, accessed February 2020; Greg Iacurci, "The Gig Economy Has Ballooned by 6 Million People since 2010. Financial Worries May Follow," *CNBC,* cnbc.com, February 4, 2020.

25. "How the Gig Economy Fits Into the Future of Work," Wharton, University of Pennsylvania, wharton.penn.edu, January 16, 2020; Ryan Vet, "What to Expect When Hiring Freelancers from the Gig Economy in 2020," *Forbes,* forbes.com, January 20, 2020.

26. Greg Barber, "This Company Hires Gig Workers—as Employees," *Wired,* January 13, 2020; Tammy Kim, "The Gig Economy Is Coming for Your Job," *The New York Times,* nytimes.com, January 10, 2020.

27. Eli Rosenberg, "Gig Economy Bills Move Forward in Other Blue States after California Clears the Way," *The Washington Post,* January 17, 2020; Rhonda Abrams, "Who's An Employee, Who's a Contractor? California Law Could Change Entrepreneurs' Status," *USA Today,* January 15, 2020; Kate Conger, "California Sues Uber and Lyft, Claiming Workers Are Misclassified," *The New York Times,* August 10, 2020.

28. U.S. Department of Labor, dol.gov, accessed February 2020.

29. Alison Doyle, "Temporary to Permanent Jobs," *The Balance Careers,* thebalancecareers.com, January 21, 2020.

30. Randstad, randstadusa.com, accessed February 2020.

31. Emily Heaslip, "Welcome! Onboarding New Employees Is the Key to Hiring Success," U.S. Chamber of Commerce, uschamber.com, February 6, 2020; John Boitnott, "10 Must-Follow Company-Onboarding Techniques," *Entrepreneur,* entrepreneur.com, February 5, 2020.

32. Steven McDonald, "How to Create a Customer Centric Strategy for Your Business," SuperOffice, superoffice.com, January 20, 2020; Trish Cristopherson, "Memorable Onboarding for New Hires, the Zappos Way," Zappos, zappos.com, January 28, 2020.

33. Ken Martin, "Construction Jobs Are Being Created, but Where Are the Workers?," *Yahoo! Finance,* finance.yahoo.com, January 10, 2020; Steve Brown, "Help Wanted: Builders Still Struggle to Find Workers," *Dallas Morning News,* dallasnews.com, January 22, 2020.

34. GlobeSmart, aperianglobesmart.com, accessed February 2020.

35. Jen Miller, "VR Addresses Healthcare Training Needs to Improve Outcomes," *HealthTech Magazine,* healthtechmagazine.net, January 23, 2020; Jennifer Kite-Powell, "Training a New Generation of Truck Drivers with Virtual Reality," *Forbes,* forbes.com, January 27, 2020.

36. Kevin Kruse, "Top 5 Leadership Development Trends for 2020," *Forbes,* forbes.com, January 15, 2020; Douglas A. Ready, Carol Cohen, David Kuron, and Benjamin Pring, "The New Leadership: Playbook for the Digital Age," *MIT Sloan Management Review,* sloanreview.mit.edu, January 21, 2020.

37. Tomas Chamorro-Premuzic and Jonathan Kirschner, "How the Best Managers Identify and Develop Talent," *Harvard Business Review,* hbr.org, January 12, 2020; Margaret Rogers, "A Better Way to Develop and Retain Top Talent," *Harvard Business Review,* hbr.org, January 20, 2020.

38. Tim Harford, "How McDonald's Revolutionised Business," *BBC,* bbc.com, February 5, 2020; McDonald's, mcdonalds.com.

39. Jill Griffin, "How to Find a Great Mentor," *Forbes,* forbes.com, January 23, 2020; Tamika Tremaglio, "Make Mentoring Matter to You and Those around You," *Washington Business Journal,* bizjournals.com, January 27, 2020; Tracy Brower, "Mentoring Is Worth Your Time. Here's How You Can Be Great at It," *Fast Company,* fastcompany.com, January 30, 2020.

40. Rachel Siegel, "Women Outnumber Men in the American Workforce for Only the Second Time," *The Washington Post,* January 10, 2020; Emma Hinchliffe, "Women Now Outnumber Men in U.S. Workforce," *Fortune,* January 13, 2020; Amara Omeokwe, "Women Overtake Men as Majority of U.S. Workforce," *The Wall Street Journal,* January 10, 2020.

41. J. Anneken Tappe, "Goldman Sachs' New Rule: At Least 1 Woman on the Board or You Can't Go Public," *CNN,* cnn.com, January 23, 2020; Yo-Jud Cheng and Boris Groysberg, "Gender Diversity at the Board Level Can Mean Innovation Success," *MIT Sloan Management Review,* sloanreview.mit.edu, January 22, 2020.

42. Selena Hill, "9 Ways to Reach New Career Levels in 2020," *Black Enterprise,* blackenterprise.com, January 29, 2020.

43. Rachel Montanez, "5 Strategies for Engaging a Workforce Inclusive of Black Millennial Talent," *Forbes,* forbes.com, February 3, 2020; Adam Hickman, "What 'Meaningful Feedback' Means to Millennials," Gallup, gallup.com, January 29, 2020; Stuart Hearn, "Experts Share 5 Proven Methods to Retain Millennials," *Recruiter,* recruiter.com, January 29, 2020; Kathy Miller Perkins, "Millennials: What Do You Want from Your Career in 2020?," *Forbes,* forbes.com, January 20, 2020.

44. "How to Establish Salary Ranges," Paycor, paycor.com, accessed February 2020; "More Organizations Shift to Market-Based Pay Structures," Society for Human Resource Management, shrm.org, accessed February 2020.

45. Eric Hamilton, "It's 2020, Is There Still a Skills Gap in Big Tech?," *Tech Times,* techtimes.com, January 16, 2020; Cynthia Harvey, "IT Careers: 10 Job Skills in High Demand This Year," *InformationWeek,* February 2, 2020.

46. "What Is Compentency-Based Pay?," TalentLyft, talentlyft.com, accessed February 2020; Chris Joseph, "Pros and Cons of Competency-Based Pay Plans," *Chron,* smallbusiness.chron.com, accessed February 2020.

47. "The Decline of 'Piece-Rate' Compensation in Manufacturing," National Bureau of Economic Research, nber.org, February 10, 2020.

48. Matthew Speiser, "Fringe Benefits: What Are They and Should You Offer Them?," Fundera, fundera.com, accessed February 2020; U.S. Bureau of Labor Statistics, bls.gov, accessed February 2020.

49. Kelsey Gee, "Employers Offer to Pay for College," *The Wall Street Journal,* January 3, 2019; Kate Ashford, "6 Awesome Perks and Benefits You Need to Know about before Your Next Job Search," TheMuse, themuse.com, accessed February 2020.

50. Brian O'Connell, "The Business Case for Employee Student Loan Repayment," Society for Human Resource Management, shrm.org, January 25, 2020; "Company Benefits and Perks: Are You Keeping Up?" *Monster Worldwide,* monster.com, accessed February 2020; Kelly Hagan, "20 Companies That Pay Off Employee Student Loans," *The Motley Fool,* fool.com, February 6, 2020.

51. Nick Otto, "7 Companies Offering Facebook-Level Benefits to Attract Talent," *Employee Benefit News,* ebn.com, accessed February 2020.

52. Julia Kagan, "Cafeteria Plan," *Investopedia,* investopedia.com, accessed February 2020; Miriam Caldwell, "How to Make the Most of Your Paycheck," *The Balance Careers,* thebalancecareers.com, accessed February 2020; Susan Heathfield, "Cafeteria-Style Benefits Plans: Employees May Select among a Variety of Nontaxable Options," *Investopedia,* investopedia.com, accessed February 2020.

53. Katie Burke, "5 Factors Shaping the Future of Work in 2020 and Beyond," *Inc.,* inc.com, January 14, 2020; Sonu Batra, "How Flexible Work Culture Can Reinvent Your Workplace," *Employee Benefit News,* benefitnews.com, January 17, 2020; Karl Moore, "Dos and Don'ts for Millennials and Zs Managing Boomers," *Forbes,* January 13, 2020.

54. Andrew Barnes, "Forget Work–Life Balance, and Focus on Productivity. You'll Have More Free Time," *Fast Company,* February 7, 2020; Richard Eisenberg, "Four-Day Workweek, Has Its Time Come?," *Forbes,* February 6, 2020.

55. Rick Bell, "On-Shift Scheduling Doesn't Have to Be a Headache for Managers or Employees," *Workforce,* workforce.com, January 22, 2020.

56. Adam Hickman and Jennifer Robison, "Is Working Remotely Effective? Gallup Research Says Yes," Gallup Workplace, gallup.com, January 24, 2020.

57. Adam Hickman and Jennifer Robison, "Is Working Remotely Effective? Gallup Research Says Yes," Gallup Workplace, gallup.com, January 24, 2020.

58. Sarah White, "Working from Home Can Benefit Employers as Much as Employees," Monster Worldwide, monster.com, accessed February 2020; Adam Hickman and Jennifer Robison, "Is Working Remotely Effective? Gallup Research Says Yes," Gallup Workplace, gallup.com, January 24, 2020.

59. Lauren Weber, "There Will Be Life after the Pink Slip," *The Wall Street Journal,* January 10, 2020; Sean Peek, "How to Legally Fire an Employee," U.S. Chamber of Commerce, uschamber.com, January 31, 2020.

60. Sarah Chaney, "Older Workers Give Economy a Kick," *The Wall Street Journal,* July 1, 2019; Katie Brockman, "The Huge Retirement Risk You Probably Don't Realize You're Facing," *The Motley Fool,* fool.com, January 16, 2020; Gene Marks, "An Increasingly Older Workforce Brings Opportunities, Challenges for Small Employers," *Philadelphia Inquirer,* inquirer.com, January 20, 2020.

12

Dealing with Employee–Management Issues

LEARNING OBJECTIVES »

After you have read and studied this chapter, you should be able to

LO 12–1 Trace the history of organized labor in the United States.

LO 12–2 Discuss the major legislation affecting labor unions.

LO 12–3 Outline the objectives of labor unions.

LO 12–4 Describe the tactics used by labor and management during conflicts, and discuss the role of unions in the future.

LO 12–5 Assess some of today's controversial employee–management issues, such as executive compensation, pay equity, sexual harassment, child care and elder care, drug abuse and drug testing, and violence and bullying in the workplace.

Lily Eskelsen García, President of the National Education Association

As anyone who's spent enough time in a classroom knows, teaching requires plenty of patience, expertise, and communication skills. These abilities also come in handy for leaders like Lily Eskelsen García, president of the National Education Association (NEA). As the head of the largest American labor union, she looks after the interests of more than three million educators in schools across the country.

Eskelsen García became a labor leader after decades of teaching in Utah. But before she began her award-winning classroom career, she worked in a different part of school: the cafeteria. As a young woman in search of work, Eskelsen García hoped to become a teacher's assistant at a day care center or preschool. With little experience, however, the only educational employment she could find was as a "lunch lady." Her main responsibilities were to make salads and wash dishes, but her favorite part of the job was interacting with the kids. Eventually, a director at the school noticed her skills with children and hired her as a teacher's assistant. Eskelsen García flourished in this new job. Along with helping out around the classroom, she also played funny songs on her guitar that impressed both students and co-workers. "It was a kindergarten teacher who tapped me on the shoulder and said, 'You're really good with kids; you should go to college,'" said Eskelsen García. "And I did."

She graduated from the University of Utah with a degree in elementary education and later earned a master's degree in instructional technology. After college, she finally achieved her goal by securing a teaching job. Although Eskelsen García loved to teach, the job had plenty of challenges, including handling large class sizes. Her classrooms contained as many as 40 kids, leaving her emotionally exhausted after trying to keep them under control all day. At one point she considered quitting. But rather than give up, she got help. "So I called my union and said, 'Here is my situation,' and they had a list of things to do: rally at the capital, write to the legislature, call some of these politicians and tell them what it's like, call a press conference," said Eskelsen García. "I was so impressed that they had a plan and I wanted to be a part of that plan, and I became a very active volunteer."

Eskelsen García became even more involved after she was named Utah Teacher of the Year in 1989. She and her union colleagues protested that year against cuts to the state's education budget. When she won the award, radio and TV stations from all over Utah wanted to interview her. Soon she delivered speeches regularly at events and climbed up the leadership ladder at the NEA. After the organization elected her secretary-treasurer in 2002, she became a vocal critic against educational policies that focused heavily on standardized testing. By 2014, Eskelsen García's commitment to quality public education took her all the way to the presidency of the NEA.

In this executive position, she plans to make teaching more diverse and dedicated to students while also advocating for causes such as limiting the use of active shooter drills in schools. In her eyes, preparing children to live their dreams will always be one of the most important jobs in the world. "If anyone wants to talk to me about what a teacher makes I'll tell them: A teacher makes a difference," said Eskelsen García. "And I would encourage anybody who feels they have the talent and temperament to be a teacher to go for it. I can practically guarantee you won't get rich but you will, without a doubt, be the most powerful person in many people's lives."

Education, of course, is not the only industry that must deal with working conditions, labor–management relations, employee compensation, and other work-related issues. This chapter discusses such issues and other employee–management concerns, including executive pay, pay equity, child and elder care, drug testing, and bullying and violence in the workplace.

Sources: Esther J. Cepeda, "From Teacher to Powerful Labor Leader: Lily Eskelsen García's Journey," *NBC News*, March 31, 2016; Damien Willis, "Q&A: NEA President Lily Eskelsen García," *Las Cruces Sun-News*, January 19, 2017; James Call, "Teachers to 'Take on Tallahassee' with a March on the Capitol on Eve of 2020 Florida Session," *Tallahassee Democrat*, tallahassee.com, January 8, 2020; Pat Eaton-Robb, "Teachers Unions Ask Schools to Rethink Shooting Drills," Associated Press, February 11, 2020; "NEA President Profile: Lily Eskelsen García," NEA.org, accessed February 2020.

Let's talk business!
bit.ly/LetsTalkBusiness12

Cheriss May/Alamy Stock Photo

name that company

IN 1955, TWO MAJOR LABOR ORGANIZATIONS saw the benefit of merging together after legislation was passed unfavorable to unions. Today, this organization maintains affiliations with 55 national and international labor unions and has about 12.5 million members. Name that organization. (Find the answer in the chapter.)

Employee–Management Issues

Unfortunately, the relationship between managers and employees isn't always trouble-free. Management's responsibility to produce a profit by maximizing productivity sometimes means making hard decisions, which aren't always popular with employees. Employees have long been concerned about fairness, income equality, and workplace security. Like other managerial challenges, employee–management issues require open discussion, goodwill, and compromise. In this chapter, we will look at several key workplace issues that impact the manager's job and workplace environment: unions, executive compensation, pay equity, sexual harassment, child care, elder care, drug abuse and drug testing, and bullying and violence in the workplace.

> **LO 12–1** Trace the history of organized labor in the United States.

Labor Unions Yesterday and Today

One of the major issues in employee–management relations involves labor unions. Labor (the collective term for nonmanagement workers) is interested in fair and competent management, human dignity, and a reasonable share of the wealth its work generates. A **union** is an employee organization whose main goal is representing its members in employee–management negotiations over job-related issues.

union

An employee organization that has the main goal of representing members in employee–management bargaining over job-related issues.

Workers originally formed unions to protect themselves from intolerable work conditions and unfair treatment, and also to secure some say in the operation of their jobs. As the number of private-sector union members grew, workers gained more negotiating power with managers and more political power. For example, labor unions were largely responsible for the establishment of minimum-wage laws, overtime rules, workers' compensation, severance pay, child-labor laws, job safety regulations, and more. Although labor unions have lost a great deal of the economic and political power they once had, and membership has declined (especially in private unions), they still play a significant role in many sectors in some parts of the country.[1]

We often think of union members as workers in the private sector, such as in construction and manufacturing. In fact, public-sector labor unions (those employees who work for governments, such as teachers, firefighters, police officers, etc.) comprise 7.1 million of the 14.6 million workers in labor unions.[2] Overall union membership in the public sector stands at 34 percent compared to just 6.2 percent in the private sector.[3]

Historians generally agree that today's unions are an outgrowth of the economic transition caused by the Industrial Revolution of the 19th and early 20th centuries. Workers who once toiled in the fields, dependent on the mercies of nature for survival, found themselves relying on the continuous roll of factory presses and assembly lines for their living.

Making the transition from an agricultural economy to an industrial economy was quite difficult. Over time, workers in businesses learned that strength through unity (unions) could lead to improved job conditions, better wages, and job security.

Today's critics of organized labor maintain that few of the inhuman conditions once dominant in U.S. industry exist in the modern workplace. They argue that organized labor is an industry in itself, and protecting workers has become secondary. Some workplace analysts maintain that the current legal system and changing management philosophies minimize the possibility that sweatshops (workplaces of the late 19th and early 20th centuries with unsatisfactory, unsafe, or oppressive labor conditions) could reappear in the United States. Let's look at the history of labor unions to see how we got to where we are today.

Lewis W. Hine/Buyenlarge/Getty Images

The History of Organized Labor

Formal labor organizations in the United States date to the time of the American Revolution. As early as 1792, cordwainers (shoemakers) in Philadelphia met to discuss fundamental work issues of pay, hours, conditions, and job security—pretty much the same issues that dominate labor negotiations today. The cordwainers were a **craft union**, an organization of skilled specialists in a particular craft or trade, typically local or regional. Most craft unions were established to achieve some short-range goal, such as curtailing the use of unpaid convict labor instead of available workers who would need to be paid. Often, after attaining their goal, the union disbanded. This situation changed dramatically in the late 19th century with the expansion of the Industrial Revolution in the United States. The Industrial Revolution brought enormous productivity increases, gained through mass production and job specialization, that made the United States an economic world power. This growth, however, created problems for workers in terms of productivity expectations, hours of work, wages, job security, and unemployment.

Workers were faced with the reality that productivity was vital. Those who failed to produce, or who stayed home because they were ill or had family problems, lost their jobs. Over time, the increased emphasis on production led firms to expand the hours of work. The length of the average workweek in 1900 was 60 hours, but an 80-hour week was not uncommon for some industries. Wages were low, and child labor was widespread. Minimum-wage laws and unemployment benefits were nonexistent, which made periods of unemployment hard on families who earned subsistence wages. The nearby Spotlight on Small Business box highlights the severity of these conditions and the infamous tragedy that resulted.

The first truly national labor organization was the **Knights of Labor**, formed by Uriah Smith Stephens in 1869. The Knights offered membership to all private working people, *including employers,* and promoted social causes as well as labor and economic issues.[4] The organization fell from prominence, however, after being blamed for a bomb that killed eight police officers during a labor rally at Haymarket Square in Chicago in 1886.

A rival group, the **American Federation of Labor (AFL)**, was formed that same year. By 1890, the AFL, under the dynamic leadership of Samuel Gompers, stood at the forefront of the labor movement. The AFL was never one big union, but rather an organization of craft unions that championed fundamental labor issues. It intentionally limited membership to skilled workers (craftspeople), assuming they would have better bargaining power than unskilled workers in obtaining concessions from employers. As a federation, its many individual unions can become members yet keep their separate union status.

Over time, an unauthorized AFL group called the Committee of Industrial Organizations began to organize **industrial unions**, which consisted of unskilled and semiskilled

While the technological achievements of the Industrial Revolution brought countless new products to market and reduced the need for physical labor in many industries, it also put pressure on workers to achieve higher productivity in factory jobs that called for long hours and low pay. Can you see how these conditions made it possible for labor unions to take hold by the turn of the 20th century?

craft union
An organization of skilled specialists in a particular craft or trade.

Knights of Labor
The first national labor union; formed in 1869.

American Federation of Labor (AFL)
An organization of craft unions that championed fundamental labor issues; founded in 1886.

industrial unions
Labor organizations of unskilled and semiskilled workers in mass-production industries such as automobile manufacturing and mining.

The Fire That Changed Labor Laws

On March 25, 1911, a warm spring day in New York City, hundreds of young women (between the ages of 13 to 23) were busy at work at the Triangle Shirtwaist Company when the unthinkable happened. The factory owners got a phone call warning them of a fire. The owners escaped, but the workers were not so fortunate. As the fire raced from the eighth floor to the ninth and then the tenth, the panic-stricken women tried to race to safety. But they found that a crucial door was locked, trapping them in the fire. It was suggested at a later trial that the door was kept locked to prevent theft. In the blaze that lasted about 15 minutes, 146 workers were killed. Many of the workers burned to death, while others jumped to their fate holding hands with their clothes burning. The fire became the touchstone for organized labor and raised support for changes in the workplace.

Prior to the tragedy at Triangle Shirtwaist, workers had struck for

Science History Images/Alamy Stock Photo

higher pay, shorter hours (the average workweek was often 60–80 hours), and safer workplace conditions. Unfortunately public opinion was strongly against them. After the tragedy, the International

Ladies' Garment Workers' Union (now called Workers United) grew in numbers and in public support. Today labor leaders say that the Triangle fire is evidence of why labor unions are crucial to maintain workplace balance in the United States. At a ceremony in New York City commemorating the 100th anniversary of the fire in 2015, labor leaders encouraged workers to not let the modern labor movement die. It's hard to imagine that in the 1950s, unions represented 36 percent of the private-sector workers in the United States, compared to just 6.2 percent today.

Sources: Patrick Kiger, "How the Horrific Tragedy of the Triangle Shirtwaist Fire Led to Workplace Safety Laws," History.com, history.com, accessed March 2020; Glynn Cosker, "How 1911's Triangle Fire Changed U.S. Safety Laws," *EDM Digest*, edmdigest.com, March 25, 2019; Triangle Shirtwaist Factory Fire Memorial, trianglememorial.org, accessed March 2020.

---

workers in mass-production industries such as automobile manufacturing and mining. John L. Lewis, president of the United Mine Workers, led this committee. His objective was to organize both craftspeople and unskilled workers under one banner.

When the AFL rejected his proposal in 1935, Lewis broke away to form the **Congress of Industrial Organizations (CIO)**. The CIO soon rivaled the AFL in membership, partly because of the passage of the National Labor Relations Act (also called the Wagner Act) that same year (see the next section). For 20 years, the two organizations struggled for power. It wasn't until passage of the Taft-Hartley Act in 1947 (see Figure 12.1) that they saw the benefits of a merger. In 1955, the two groups formed the AFL-CIO. The AFL-CIO today maintains affiliations with 55 national and international labor unions and has about 12.5 million members.[5]

Congress of Industrial Organizations (CIO)

Union organization of unskilled workers; broke away from the American Federation of Labor (AFL) in 1935 and rejoined it in 1955.

LO 12–2 Discuss the major legislation affecting labor unions.

Labor Legislation and Collective Bargaining

Much of the growth and influence of organized labor in the United States has depended primarily on two major factors: the law and public opinion. Figure 12.1 outlines five major federal laws with a significant impact on the rights and operations of labor unions. Take a few moments to read it before going on. Note that such laws govern *private* workers.

FIGURE 12.1 MAJOR LEGISLATION AFFECTING LABOR–MANAGEMENT RELATIONS

Norris-LaGuardia Act, 1932

Prohibited courts from issuing injunctions against nonviolent union activities; outlawed contracts forbidding union activities; outlawed the use of yellow-dog contracts by employers. (Yellow-dog contracts were contractual agreements forced on workers by employers whereby the employee agreed not to join a union as a condition of employment.)

National Labor Relations Act (Wagner Act), 1935

Gave employees the right to form or join labor organizations (or to refuse to form or join); the right to collectively bargain with employers through elected union representatives; and the right to engage in labor activities such as strikes, picketing, and boycotts. Prohibited certain unfair labor practices by the employer and the union, and established the National Labor Relations Board to oversee union election campaigns and investigate labor practices. This act gave great impetus to the union movement.

Fair Labor Standards Act, 1938

Set a minimum wage and maximum basic hours for workers in interstate commerce industries. The first minimum wage set was 25 cents an hour, except for farm and retail workers.

Labor–Management Relations Act (Taft-Hartley Act), 1947

Amended the Wagner Act; permitted states to pass laws prohibiting compulsory union membership (right-to-work laws); set up methods to deal with strikes that affect national health and safety; prohibited secondary boycotts, closed shop agreements, and featherbedding (the requiring of wage payments for work not performed by unions). This act gave more power to management.

Labor–Management Reporting and Disclosure Act (Landrum-Griffin Act), 1959

Amended the Taft-Hartley Act and the Wagner Act; guaranteed individual rights of union members in dealing with their union, such as the right to nominate candidates for union office, vote in union elections, attend and participate in union meetings, vote on union business, and examine union records and accounts; required annual financial reports to be filed with the U.S. Department of Labor. One goal of this act was to clean up union corruption.

yellow-dog contract
A type of contract that required employees to agree as a condition of employment not to join a union; prohibited by the Norris-LaGuardia Act in 1932.

collective bargaining
The process whereby union and management representatives form a labor–management agreement, or contract, for workers.

certification
Formal process whereby a union is recognized by the National Labor Relations Board (NLRB) as the bargaining agent for a group of employees.

decertification
The process by which workers take away a union's right to represent them.

The Norris-LaGuardia Act paved the way for union growth in the United States. This legislation prohibited employers from using employment contracts that included provisions such as a yellow-dog contract. A **yellow-dog contract** required employees to agree, as a condition of employment, not to join a union. The National Labor Relations Act (or Wagner Act) passed three years later provided labor unions with clear legal justification to pursue key issues that were strongly supported by Samuel Gompers and the AFL. One of these issues, **collective bargaining**, is the process whereby union and management representatives negotiate a contract for workers. The Wagner Act expanded labor's right to collectively bargain by obligating employers to meet at reasonable times and bargain in good faith with respect to wages, hours, and other terms and conditions of employment.[6]

Union Organizing Campaigns

The Wagner Act established an administrative agency (discussed in Bonus Chapter A), the National Labor Relations Board (NLRB), to oversee labor–management relations. The NLRB consists of five members appointed by the U.S. president and is authorized to investigate and remedy unfair labor practices. It also provides workplace guidelines and legal protection to workers seeking to vote on organizing a union to represent them.[7] **Certification** is the formal process whereby the NLRB recognizes a labor union as the authorized bargaining agent for a group of employees. **Decertification** is the process by which workers can take away a union's right to represent them. After an election, both the union and company have five days to contest the results with the NLRB.

LO 12–3 Outline the objectives of labor unions.

Objectives of Organized Labor over Time

negotiated labor–management agreement (labor contract)

Agreement that sets the tone and clarifies the terms under which management and labor agree to function over a period of time.

The objectives of labor unions shift with social and economic trends. The **negotiated labor–management agreement** (informally referred to as the **labor contract**), sets the tone and clarifies the terms and conditions under which management and the union will function over a specific period. Unions attempt to address their most pressing concerns in the labor contract such as job security, pay, and offshore outsourcing. Negotiations can cover a wide range of work topics, and it can take a long time to reach an agreement. Figure 12.2 lists topics commonly negotiated by management and labor.

FIGURE 12.2 ISSUES IN A NEGOTIATED LABOR–MANAGEMENT AGREEMENT

Labor and management often meet to discuss and clarify the terms that specify employees' functions within the company. The topics listed in this figure are typically discussed during these meetings.

1. Management rights
2. Union recognition
3. Union security clause
4. Strikes and lockouts
5. Union activities and responsibilities
   a. Dues checkoff
   b. Union bulletin boards
   c. Work slowdowns
6. Wages
   a. Wage structure
   b. Shift differentials
   c. Wage incentives
   d. Bonuses
   e. Piecework conditions
   f. Tiered wage structures
7. Hours of work and time-off policies
   a. Regular hours of work
   b. Holidays
   c. Vacation policies
   d. Overtime regulations
   e. Leaves of absence
   f. Break periods
   g. Flextime
   h. Mealtime allotments
8. Job rights and seniority principles
   a. Seniority regulations
   b. Transfer policies and bumping
   c. Promotions
   d. Layoffs and recall procedures
   e. Job bidding and posting
9. Discharge and discipline
   a. Suspension
   b. Conditions for discharge
10. Grievance procedures
    a. Arbitration agreement
    b. Mediation procedures
11. Employee benefits, health, and welfare

Labor unions generally insist that a contract contain a **union security clause** stipulating that employees who reap union benefits either officially join or at least pay dues to the union. After passage of the Wagner Act, unions sought strict security in the form of the **closed shop agreement**, which specified that workers had to be members of a union before being hired for a job. To labor's dismay, the Labor–Management Relations Act (Taft-Hartley Act) outlawed this practice in 1947 (see Figure 12.3).

Today, unions favor the **union shop agreement**, under which workers do not have to be members of a union to be hired but must agree to join within a prescribed period (usually 30, 60, or 90 days). However, under a contingency called an **agency shop agreement**, employers may hire workers who are not required to join the union but must pay a special union fee or regular union dues. Labor leaders believe that such fees or dues are justified because the union represents all workers in collective bargaining, not just its members. However, in 2018, the U.S. Supreme Court ruled that workers who choose not to join a union in public- sector unions cannot be forced to pay union dues.[8]

The Taft-Hartley Act recognized the legality of the union shop but granted individual states the power to outlaw such agreements through **right-to-work laws**. To date, 27 states have passed such legislation (see Figure 12.4). In a right-to-work state, an **open shop agreement** gives workers the option to join or not join a union if one exists. In a right-to-work state, a worker who does not join a union cannot be forced to pay a fee or union dues.[9]

Future contract negotiations will likely focus on evolving workplace issues such as child and elder care, worker retraining, two-tiered wage plans, drug testing, and other such work-related issues. Job security is sure to remain a top union priority due to job losses from offshore outsourcing and free-trade agreements. Unions will continue to support federal changes such as increasing the minimum wage to $15 per hour. Critics of proposals to raise the minimum wage say that if it is raised, many low-skilled workers would be priced out of the market and unemployment will increase.[10] Advocates of the minimum wage increase say that the increase is necessary to protect the "working poor." What do you think?

Resolving Labor–Management Disagreements

The negotiated labor–management agreement becomes a guide to work relations between management and the union. However, it does not necessarily end negotiations between them because there are sometimes differences concerning interpretations of the agreement.

FIGURE 12.3 DIFFERENT FORMS OF UNION AGREEMENTS

Closed shop
The Taft-Hartley Act made this form of agreement illegal. Under this type of labor agreement, employers could hire only current union members for a job.

Union shop
The majority of labor agreements are of this type. In a union shop, the employer can hire anyone, but as a condition of employment, employees hired must join the union to keep their jobs.

Agency shop
Employers may hire anyone. Employees need not join the union, but are required to pay a union fee. A small percentage of labor agreements are of this type.

Open shop
Union membership is voluntary for new and existing employees. Those who don't join the union don't have to pay union dues. Few union contracts are of this type.

union security clause
Provision in a negotiated labor–management agreement that stipulates that employees who benefit from a union must either officially join or at least pay dues to the union.

closed shop agreement
Clause in a labor–management agreement that specified workers had to be members of a union before being hired (was outlawed by the Taft-Hartley Act in 1947).

union shop agreement
Clause in a labor–management agreement that says workers don't have to be members of a union to be hired, but must agree to join the union within a prescribed period.

agency shop agreement
Clause in a labor–management agreement that says employers may hire nonunion workers; employees aren't required to join the union but must pay a union fee.

right-to-work laws
Legislation that gives workers the right, under an open shop, to join or not join a union if it's present.

open shop agreement
Agreement in right-to-work states that gives workers the option to join or not join a union, if one exists in their workplace.

FIGURE 12.4 STATES WITH RIGHT-TO-WORK LAWS

= **Right-to-work states**

grievance

A charge by employees that management isn't abiding by the terms of the negotiated labor–management agreement.

shop stewards

Union officials who work permanently in an organization and represent employee interests on a daily basis.

bargaining zone

The range of options between the initial and final offer that each party will consider before negotiations dissolve or reach an impasse.

mediation

The use of a third party, called a mediator, who encourages both sides in a dispute to continue negotiating and often makes suggestions for resolving the dispute.

 connect

▶ **iSeeit!** Need help understanding mediation vs. arbitration? Visit your Connect eBook to view a video for a brief animated explanation.

arbitration

The agreement to bring in an impartial third party (a single arbitrator or a panel of arbitrators) to render a binding decision in a labor dispute.

For example, managers may interpret a certain clause in the agreement to mean they are free to select who works overtime. Union members may interpret the same clause to mean that managers must select employees for overtime on the basis of seniority. If the parties cannot resolve such controversies, employees may file a grievance.

A **grievance** is a charge by employees that management is not abiding by or fulfilling the terms of the negotiated labor–management agreement as they perceive it. Overtime rules, promotions, layoffs, transfers, and job assignments are generally sources of employee grievances. Handling them demands a good deal of contact between union officials and managers. Grievances, however, do not imply that a company has broken the law or the labor agreement. In fact, the vast majority of grievances are negotiated and resolved by **shop stewards** (union officials who work permanently in an organization and represent employee interests on a daily basis) and supervisory-level managers. However, if a grievance is not settled at this level, formal grievance procedures will begin. Figure 12.5 illustrates the steps a formal grievance procedure could follow.

Mediation and Arbitration

During the contract negotiation process, there's generally a **bargaining zone**, which is the range of options between the initial and final offers that each party will consider before negotiations dissolve or reach an impasse. If labor and management negotiators aren't able to agree on alternatives within this bargaining zone, mediation may be necessary.

Mediation is the use of a third party, called a *mediator,* who encourages both sides in a dispute to continue negotiating and often makes suggestions for resolving the matter. Keep in mind that mediators evaluate facts in the dispute and then make suggestions, not decisions. Elected officials (both current and past), attorneys, and college professors often serve as mediators in labor disputes. The National Mediation Board can provide federal mediators when requested in a labor dispute. Both the National Football League and the National Hockey League used the assistance of a federal mediator before agreeing to new contracts after talks stalled.[11]

A more extreme option used to resolve conflicts is **arbitration**—an agreement to bring in an impartial third party—a single arbitrator or arbitration panel—to render a binding decision in a labor dispute. The arbitrator(s) must be acceptable to both labor and management. You may have heard of professional baseball players filing for arbitration to resolve a contract dispute with their teams or to contest a penalty imposed by the league.[12] Many negotiated labor–management agreements in the United States call for the use of arbitration to end labor disputes. The nonprofit American Arbitration Association is the dominant organization used in dispute resolution.[13]

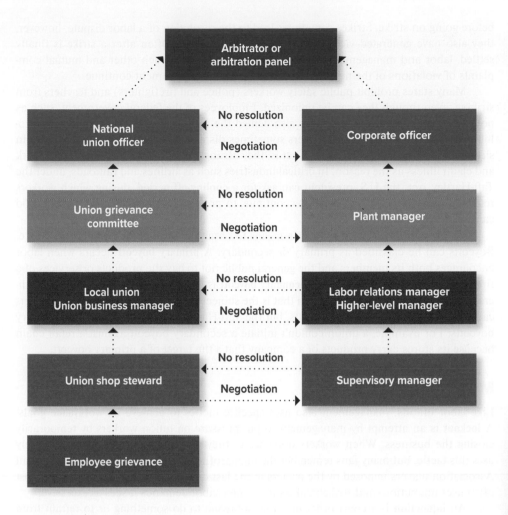

FIGURE 12.5 THE GRIEVANCE RESOLUTION PROCESS
The grievance process may move through several steps before the issue is resolved. At each step, the issue is negotiated between union officials and managers. If no resolution is achieved, an outside arbitrator may be mutually agreed on. If so, the decision by the arbitrator is binding (legally enforceable).

On May 1, 2020, thousands of Amazon employees called on their colleagues to go on strike after accusing the company of providing inadequate protection during the pandemic. The action attracted considerable media attention but did not lead to any immediate changes at the company. Do you think this strike could have been more successful if Amazon employees were unionized?

LO 12–4 Describe the tactics used by labor and management during conflicts, and discuss the role of unions in the future.

Tactics Used in Labor–Management Conflicts

If labor and management can't reach an agreement through collective bargaining, and negotiations break down, either side, or both, may use specific tactics to enhance its negotiating position and perhaps sway public opinion. Unions primarily use strikes and boycotts, as well as pickets and work slowdowns. Management may implement lockouts and injunctions and even hire strikebreakers. The following sections explain each tactic briefly.

Union Tactics

A **strike** occurs when workers collectively refuse to go to work. Strikes have been the most potent union tactic. They attract public attention to a labor dispute and can cause operations in a company to slow down or totally cease.[14] Besides refusing to work, strikers may also picket the company, walking around carrying signs and talking with the public and the media about the issues in the dispute.[15] Unions also often use picketing as an informational tool

Jason Redmond/AFP/Getty Images

strike

A union strategy in which workers refuse to go to work; the purpose is to further workers' objectives after an impasse in collective bargaining.

cooling-off period

When workers in a critical industry return to their jobs while the union and management continue negotiations.

primary boycott

When a union encourages both its members and the general public not to buy the products of a firm involved in a labor dispute.

secondary boycott

An attempt by labor to convince others to stop doing business with a firm that's the subject of a primary boycott; prohibited by the Taft-Hartley Act.

The conflict between NFL players and owners in 2011 resulted in the owners locking the players out of team facilities for months. What effects do you think lockouts have on professional athletes as well as sports fans?

before going on strike. Strikes sometimes lead to the resolution of a labor dispute; however, they also have generated violence and extended bitterness. Often after a strike is finally settled, labor and management remain openly hostile toward each other and mutual complaints of violations of the negotiated labor–management agreement continue.

Many states prohibit public safety workers (police and firefighters) and teachers from striking, even though they can be unionized. Employees of the federal government, such as postal workers, can unionize but are also denied the right to strike. When strikes are prohibited, however, public-sector workers sometimes display their frustrations by engaging in sickouts (often called the *blue flu*). That is, they arrange as a group to be absent from work and claim illness as the reason. In critical industries such as airlines and railroads, under the Taft-Hartley Act, the U.S. president can ask for a **cooling-off period**, during which workers return to their jobs while negotiations continue, to prevent a strike. The cooling-off period can last up to 80 days.

Unions also attempt boycotts as a means to obtain their objectives in a labor dispute. Boycotts can be classified as primary or secondary. A **primary boycott** occurs when labor encourages both its members and the general public not to buy the products or services of a firm engaged in a labor dispute. A **secondary boycott** is an attempt by labor to convince others to stop doing business with a firm that is the subject of a primary boycott. Labor unions can legally authorize primary boycotts, but the Taft-Hartley Act prohibits using secondary boycotts. For example, a union couldn't initiate a secondary boycott against a retail chain because its stores carry products of a company that's the target of a primary boycott.

Management Tactics

Like labor unions, management also uses specific tactics to achieve its workplace goals. A **lockout** is an attempt by management to put pressure on union workers by temporarily closing the business. When workers don't work, they don't get paid. Management rarely uses this tactic, but many fans remember the high-profile lockout of the National Basketball Association players imposed by the owners in the last decade. Management, however, most often uses injunctions and strikebreakers to counter labor demands it sees as excessive.

An **injunction** is a court order directing someone to do something or to refrain from doing something. Management has sought injunctions to order striking workers back to work, limit the number of pickets during a strike, or otherwise deal with any actions that could be considered detrimental to the public welfare. For a court to issue an injunction, management must show a just cause, such as the possibility of violence or destruction of private property.

Employers have had the right to replace striking workers since a 1938 Supreme Court ruling, but this tactic was used infrequently until the 1980s. Since then, the use of strikebreakers has been employed and has become a particular source of hostility and violence in labor relations. **Strikebreakers** (called *scabs* by unions) are workers hired to do the jobs of striking employees until the labor dispute is resolved. Be sure to read the Making Ethical Decisions box, which deals with this issue, and make your decision.

The Future of Unions and Labor–Management Relations

Organized labor continues at a crossroads. As noted earlier, 6.2 percent of workers in the private sector are unionized and nearly half of all union members work in the public sector, with union membership varying considerably by state (see Figure 12.6). Once-powerful unions like the United Auto Workers (UAW) have lost almost three-fourths of their membership since 1979.[16] Unions in the future will undoubtedly be quite different from those in the past. Today, the largest union in the United States is the National Education Association (NEA) with 3.2 million members. The Service Employees International Union (SEIU) with 2 million members

Leon T Switzer/Icon SMI/Corbis/Icon Sportswire/Getty Images

Walking a Fine Line

Your wallet is almost empty, and bills for college expenses, food, and other expenses keep piling up. You read last weekend that Shop-Till-You-Drop, a local grocery chain in your town, is looking for workers to replace striking members of United Food and Commercial Workers (UFCW) International Union. The workers are striking because of a reduction in health insurance benefits and reduced payment to their pensions.

Several classmates at your college are UFCW members employed at Shop-Till-You-Drop stores, and many other students at your college are supporting the strike. The stores also employ many people from your neighborhood whose families depend on the income and benefits. Shop-Till-You-Drop argues the company made a fair offer to the union workers, but with the increasing cost of health care and other benefits, the workers' demands are excessive and could force the company into bankruptcy.

Shop-Till-You-Drop is offering replacement workers an attractive wage rate and flexible schedules to cross the picket line and work during the strike. The company has even suggested the possibility of permanent employment, depending on the results of the strike. As a struggling student, you could use the job and the money for tuition and other expenses. Will you cross the picket line and apply? What could be the consequences of your decision? Is your choice ethical?

FIGURE 12.6 UNION MEMBERSHIP BY STATE

Source: Bureau of Labor Statistics, bls.gov, accessed March 2020

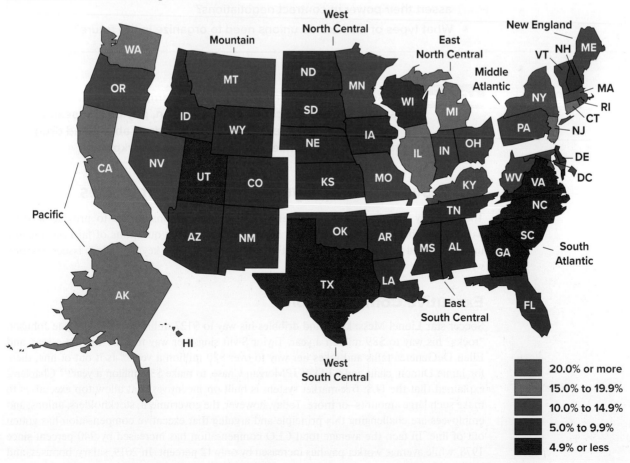

Legend:
- 20.0% or more
- 15.0% to 19.9%
- 10.0% to 14.9%
- 5.0% to 9.9%
- 4.9% or less

lockout

An attempt by management to put pressure on unions by temporarily closing the business.

injunction

A court order directing someone to do something or to refrain from doing something.

strikebreakers

Workers hired to do the jobs of striking workers until the labor dispute is resolved.

is second.[17] You might note that the NEA is a public-sector union and the SEIU's focus is on services. To grow, unions will have to include more white-collar, female, and foreign-born workers. The traditional manufacturing base that unions depended on for growth needs to give way to organizing efforts in industries like health care (over 16 million workers) and information technology (over 4 million workers). Perhaps what's even more concerning to labor unions is that union membership is highest among workers 45–64 years old and lowest among workers 18–25 years old.

Both public- and private-sector union members face challenges as they try to maintain remaining wage and fringe benefit gains achieved in past negotiations. With many states and cities facing continuous financial challenges, government officials are trying to cut costs, particularly labor costs. However, many states with public-sector unions face limited ability to cut labor costs because of prior agreements with the unions. With dwindling numbers, private-sector unions need to take on a new role in partnering with management in training workers, redesigning jobs, and assimilating members to the job requirements of the knowledge-work economy. Growing use of robotics and AI will test unions' relations with management. How organized labor handles these challenges may well define the future for labor unions. After the Test Prep, we will look at other workplace issues facing employees and managers in the 2020s.

?TESTPREP

- What are the major laws that affected union growth, and what does each one cover?
- How do changes in the economy affect the objectives of unions?
- What are the major tactics used by unions and by management to assert their power in contract negotiations?
- What types of workers do unions need to organize in the future?

LO 12–5 Assess some of today's controversial employee–management issues, such as executive compensation, pay equity, sexual harassment, child care and elder care, drug abuse and drug testing, and violence and bullying in the workplace.

Controversial Employee–Management Issues

Today, many questions persist concerning business's responsibilities to provide workers with certain benefits and assurances. Employees are raising questions of fairness, income inequality, and workplace security. Let's take a look at several key workplace issues, starting with executive compensation.

Executive Compensation

Soccer star Lionel Messi kicks and dribbles his way to $127 million a year, Dwayne Johnson "rocks" his way to $89 million a year, Taylor Swift sings her way to $185 million a year, and Ellen DeGeneres talks and jokes her way to over $80 million a year.[18] Is it out of line, then, for Jamie Dimon, chair and CEO of JPMorgan Chase, to make $31 million a year?[19] Chapter 2 explained that the U.S. free-market system is built on incentives that allow top executives to make such large amounts—or more. Today, however, the government, stockholders, unions, and employees are challenging this principle and arguing that executive compensation has gotten out of line. In fact, the average total CEO compensation has increased by 940 percent since 1978, while average worker pay has increased by only 12 percent. In 2019, salary, bonuses, and incentives at a major company were $17.2 million, compared to just over $56,000 for the average worker.[20] The Adapting to Change box looks at the disparity between what college head coaches (particularly in football and basketball) earn in salary and endorsements (millions) and what college athletes earn (zero).

In theory, CEO compensation and bonuses are determined by the firm's profitability or an increase in its stock price. The logic of this assumption was that as the fortunes of a company and its stockholders grew, so would the rewards of the CEO. Today, however, executives generally receive stock options (the ability to buy company stock at a set price at a later date) and restricted stock (stock issued directly to the CEO that can't be sold usually for three or four years) included as part of their compensation.[21] Today, stock and stock options account for over 50 percent of a CEO's compensation.

What's even more frustrating to those who question how much chief executives are paid is that CEOs are often rewarded richly even if their company doesn't meet expectations or if they leave under pressure. Ousted WeWork CEO Adam Neumann left the company after questions about his character, his personal dealings with the company, and his failure to take WeWork public. Neumann is expected to walk away with almost a billion dollars.[22] Many CEOs are also awarded large retainers, consulting contracts, and lavish perks when they retire.

Drew Angerer/Getty Images

Walmart CEO Doug McMillon earned more than $24 million in 2018 while the median Walmart worker brought in just $22,000. Corporate boards of directors determine executive compensation. Do you think this is a fair system of compensation for CEOs? Do you think workers should have input?

The late management guru Peter Drucker suggested that company CEOs shouldn't make more than 20 times the average salary at their company.[23] Noted economist Thomas Piketty agrees and believes this income inequality is harmful and unnecessary, "When you pay $10 million instead of $1 [million], you don't have necessarily better performance or much higher productivity. . . . So I think there is really very little evidence that we need to pay people 100 times or 200 times the average wage to get them to work."[24] Unfortunately, not many companies agree and few have placed such limits on executive compensation. Today, the average CEO of a *Fortune* 500 company makes over 287 times the average salary of workers in that same company.[25] Some pay differences can be staggering. For example, whereas restaurant and service workers push for a national minimum wage of $15 an hour, CEOs in those industries have huge pay packages. Consider that it takes less than a day for Starbucks CEO Kevin Johnson to make a typical employee's annual salary.[26]

As global competition intensifies, executive paychecks in Europe have increased, but European CEOs typically earn considerably less than what U.S. CEOs make. In some European countries, such as Germany, according to a system called *sozialpartnerschaft (social partnerships),* workers have a say in company management and are entitled to seats on the board of directors of major firms. Since boards set executive pay, this could be a reason why pay imbalances are less in Germany. This process, known as *co-determination,* calls for cooperation between management and workers in decision making. It's unlikely a similar system would be acceptable in the United States.[27]

Government and shareholder pressure for full disclosure of executive compensation has put U.S. boards of directors on notice that they aren't there simply to enrich CEOs or themselves. The passage of the Dodd-Frank Wall Street Reform and Consumer Protection Act was intended to give shareholders more say in compensation decisions and required more information about executive pay packages compared to average workers.[28] Still, it's important to remember that most U.S. executives are responsible for multibillion-dollar corporations, work 70-plus hours a week, and often travel excessively. Many have turned potential problems at companies into successes and reaped huge benefits for employees and stockholders as well as themselves. Furthermore, there are few seasoned, skilled professionals who can manage large companies, especially troubled companies looking for the right CEO to accomplish a turnaround. There's no easy answer to the question of what's fair compensation for executives, but it's a safe bet the controversy won't go away.

Pay Equity

The Equal Pay Act of 1963 requires companies to give equal pay to men and women who do the same job. For example, it's illegal to pay a female nurse less than a male nurse unless

Playing for Dollars or Degrees

With the stands packed and the television cameras rolling, there's no doubt that football is a huge profit center for top colleges (Division 1) in the National Collegiate Athletic Association (NCAA). Regional economies in college towns such as College Station, Texas; Auburn, Alabama; and South Bend, Indiana, also reap big benefits and revenues on football weekends. College basketball is no financial slacker either. Going to an NCAA basketball game does its part to help fill the coffers of the college. March Madness (a single-elimination tournament where schools compete for the national championship) is the biggest money-making event of the year for the NCAA. Before the COVID-19 pandemic forced the cancellation of the 2020 tournament, estimates were that it could generate almost a billion dollars in television and marketing rights. And let's not forget about top coaches in football and basketball. Today, over 50 coaches earn more than $3 million per year. Sounds like everyone is enjoying the good life.

Well, not exactly everyone. There's a major group of stakeholders who are noticeably left out

Mark LoMoglio/Icon Sportswire/Getty Images

of this financial windfall. College athletes aren't permitted to be paid a salary or receive gifts or compensation for their exploits on the gridiron or the court. True, many athletes are awarded scholarships that cover part or all of their tuition and room and board. However, today many fans and alumni are standing up and saying the players deserve a cut of the action.

It's possible that help may be on the way for college athletes to profit from the renown they

achieve in their sports. California has passed legislation that challenges the NCAA's ban on players having agents and signing endorsement deals. California's action has generated a bevy of responses from other states that are considering allowing athletes to receive some compensation for their efforts. However, it's too early for athletes to go out and buy a new car. The California law doesn't take effect until 2023. Plus, the NCAA promises to fight the California law, as well as other state efforts, fearing such actions could cause a patchwork of different rules across the country. Still, there is hope for student athletes. The NCAA has agreed it must modernize its rules and bylaws. However, no changes have been proposed or approved as of this writing.

Sources: Alan Blinder, "Should College Athletes Profit from Their Fame? Here's Where the Debate Stands," *The New York Times*, February 11, 2020; Dan Murphy, "Mark Emmert: 'Clear Consensus' on Need to Change Athlete Pay Rules," *ESPN*, espn. com, January 23, 2020; Dwight Jaynes, "Paying Colleges Athletes for Their Likeness Could Bring a Calamity of Unintended Consequences," *Yahoo! Sports*, February 18, 2020; Michael T. Nietzel, "Americans Now Overwhelmingly Support College Athletes Earning Endorsement and Sponsorship Money," *Forbes*, February 11, 2020; Laine Higgins, "When College Athletes Cash In," *The Wall Street Journal*, March 12, 2020.

factors such as seniority, merit pay, or performance incentives are involved. But *pay equity* goes beyond the concept of equal pay for equal work; it says people in jobs that require similar levels of education, training, or skills should receive equal pay.[29] Pay equity compares the value of a job like a hairstylist or librarian (traditionally women's jobs) with jobs like a plumber or welder (traditionally men's jobs). Such a comparison shows that "women's" jobs tend to pay less—sometimes much less. This disparity caused a brief reconsideration of a 1980s concept called *comparable worth* that suggested people in jobs requiring similar levels of education, training, or skills should receive equal pay. Evidence didn't support that comparable worth would lead to better market equilibrium, only more chaos and inequity.

In the United States today, women earn 81 percent of what men earn, although the disparity varies by profession, job experience and tenure, level of education, age, location, and other factors.[30] In the past, the primary explanation for this disparity was that women worked only 50 to 60 percent of their available years once they left school, whereas men normally worked all those years. This explanation doesn't have much substance today because fewer women leave the workforce for an extended time.

Today, women are competing financially with men in fields such as law, financial management, health care, biotechnology, information technology, and other knowledge-based jobs. Younger women are faring better than older women financially due to academic achievement. Today, women earn almost 60 percent of the bachelor's and master's degrees awarded and also earn more doctoral degrees than men.[31] However, even though more women are earning advanced business degrees, the wage gap begins to widen in their early thirties when they become underrepresented in managerial jobs.[32] Many workplace analysts suggest transparency in pay practices, which reveals how wages and salaries are set and how pay raises and bonuses are determined, assists in solving pay equity questions.[33] Companies including Cisco, Johnson & Johnson, PepsiCo, and Bank of America have committed to reviewing their hiring and promotion practices to protect against any pay or promotion disparities.[34] Still, Harvard professor Claudia Goldin, a longtime scholar on gender and pay, found that many companies tend to give larger financial rewards to managers that log the longest hours and are willing to job-hop often.[35] Unfortunately, women who tend to pull back for child rearing fall behind and never catch up. Women, especially women with children, still earn less, are less likely to go into business, and are more likely to live in poverty than men. There's no question that pay equity promises to remain a challenging employee–management issue.

Sexual Harassment

Sexual harassment refers to unwelcome sexual advances, requests for sexual favors, and other verbal or physical conduct of a sexual nature that creates a hostile work environment.[36] The Civil Rights Act of 1991 governs sexual harassment of both men and women. In 1997, the Supreme Court reinforced this fact when it said same-sex harassment also falls within the purview of sexual harassment law. Today, managers and workers are much more sensitive to sexual comments and behavior than they were in the past.[37] The number of complaints filed with the Equal Employment Opportunity Commission (EEOC) declined slightly over the past three years, yet EEOC statistics show sexual harassment still accounts for over 10 percent of the claims the EEOC receives.[38] Over 80 percent of the sexual harassment claims reported are filed by women.[39] Conduct on the job can be considered illegal under specific conditions:

- An employee's submission to such conduct is explicitly or implicitly made a term or condition of employment, or an employee's submission to or rejection of such conduct is used as the basis for employment decisions affecting the worker's status. A threat like "Go out with me or you're fired" or "Go out with me or you'll never be promoted here" constitutes *quid pro quo sexual harassment.*

- The conduct unreasonably interferes with a worker's job performance or creates an intimidating, hostile, or offensive work environment. This type of harassment is *hostile work environment sexual harassment.*

The Supreme Court broadened the scope of what can be considered a hostile work environment; the key word seemed to be *unwelcome,* a term for behavior that would offend a reasonable person. Companies and individuals have found that sexual harassment can be costly and can lead to the fall of top leadership at the company. In a highly publicized case that became a popular movie titled *Bombshell,* 21st Century Fox paid TV journalist Gretchen Carlson $20 million to settle sexual harassment charges against the late Fox News chief Roger Ailes.[40] Les Moonves, successful CEO of CBS, was forced to resign after charges of sexual misconduct surfaced at the television network.[41] Foreign companies doing business in the United States are also not immune to sexual harassment

sexual harassment
Unwelcome sexual advances, requests for sexual favors, and other conduct (verbal or physical) of a sexual nature that creates a hostile work environment.

> *Unwelcome sexual advances, requests for sexual favors, and other verbal or physical conduct are prohibited under the Civil Rights Act of 1991. The #MeToo movement brought further attention to these important issues after a number of prominent media figures were accused of harassment. What should companies do to reduce the risk of sexual misconduct in the workplace?*

Erik McGregor/LightRocket/Getty Images

charges as both Toyota and Nissan discovered. The number of reports of sexual harassment and assault in the military and at the military academies has risen sharply in recent years.

A key problem is that workers and managers often know a policy concerning sexual harassment exists but have no idea what it says. To remedy this, several states have taken the lead. California, Connecticut, Maine, Delaware, New York, and Illinois require companies to provide sexual harassment prevention training to supervisors and employees.[42] Most states require sexual harassment training only for employees in the government sector. Workers at small businesses often don't receive training regarding sexual harassment even though online tutorials are available. Fortunately, many companies today have responded proactively and established rapid, effective grievance procedures and reacted promptly when allegations of harassment were raised. Such efforts may save businesses millions of dollars in lawsuits and make the workplace more productive and harmonious. Nonetheless, as high-profile cases in the past few years have shown, there is a long way to go before sexual harassment as a key employee–management issue disappears.[43]

Child Care

Today, women make up the majority of the workforce in the United States.[44] Approximately three-fourths of women with children under 18 (including over two-thirds of mothers with children under age 6) are in the workforce.[45] Such statistics concern employers for two reasons: (1) absences related to child care cost U.S. businesses billions of dollars annually, and (2) the issue of who should pay for employee child care raises a question that often divides employees. Many co-workers oppose child care benefits for parents or single parents, arguing that single workers and single-income families shouldn't subsidize child care. Others contend that employers and the government have the responsibility to create child care systems to assist employees. Unfortunately federal assistance hasn't increased since passage of the Welfare Reform Act many years ago, and is very unlikely to be increased in the near future. This creates problems for many employees since the child care bill for a two-child household can exceed the cost of rent.[46] Thus, child care remains an important workplace issue.

A number of large companies offer child care as an employee benefit. *Working Mother* magazine compiles an annual list of the 100 best companies for working mothers.[47] IBM and Johnson & Johnson have made the list for 28 years and consistently rank in the top 10. The two companies offer on-site day care and have been praised as particularly sympathetic and cooperative with working mothers. Other large firms with extensive child care programs include American Express (which offers 20-week paid leave for all new parents), and Google and Intel, which provide online homework tutorial assistance for employees' children. Some additional child care benefits provided by employers include:

- Discount arrangements with national child care chains.

- Vouchers that offer payments toward child care the employee selects.

- Referral services that help identify high-quality child care facilities to employees.

- On-site child care centers at which parents can visit children at lunch or during lag times throughout the workday.

- Sick-child centers to care for moderately ill children.

Unfortunately, small businesses with fewer than 100 employees can't compete with big companies in providing assistance with child care.[48] Some small companies, however, have found that implementing creative child

On-site day care is still a relatively uncommon employee benefit in the United States today. Although it's often expensive to operate, it can pay big dividends in employee satisfaction and productivity. Who should pay for employee benefits like child care and elder care, the employee or the company?

Linda Davidson/The Washington Post/Getty Images

care programs can help them compete with larger organizations in hiring and retaining qualified employees.

Over 30 years ago, entrepreneurs Roger Brown and Linda Mason recognized the emerging need for child care as a benefit in the workplace. Today, their company is the leading provider in the corporate-sponsored child care market with more than 1,100 child care centers in approximately 400 companies. Bright Horizons today employs over 32,000 employees worldwide.[49] Haemonetics, a leading company in blood processing technology, attracts skilled employees by creating an employee-centered, work–life balance. The company uses the services of Bright Horizons to operate "Kid's Space at Haemonetics" where qualified early childhood educators develop daily activities for employees' children.

With large numbers of two-income households and over 12 million single-parent households in the United States, child care is sure to remain a key employee–management issue, even as businesses and employees face the growing challenge of elder care.[50]

Elder Care

Currently, there are approximately 56.4 million Americans over the age of 65. Over the next 20 years, the number of Americans over 65 is expected to grow to over 80 million; that will be approximately 22 percent of the U.S. population in 2040.[51] The likelihood that an American aged 65 will live to 85 has also increased significantly. What this means is that many workers will be confronted with how to care for older parents and other relatives. Today in the United States, over 43 million family caregivers provide unpaid care to an older person.[52] Over 75 percent of those caregivers report they needed to make some work accommodations due to their caregiving responsibilities.[53] According to the MetLife Mature Institute, such caregiving obligations cause employees to miss approximately 15 million days of work per year, costing companies an estimated $34 billion a year in reduced productivity, absenteeism, and turnover from employees responsible for aging relatives.[54] Elder care is a key workplace issue.

The U.S. Office of Personnel Management (OPM) suggests that employees with elder care responsibilities need information about medical, legal, and insurance issues, as well as the full support of their supervisors and company. The OPM also says such caregivers may require flextime, telecommuting, part-time employment, or job sharing. Many firms have responded and now offer employee assistance programs. JPMorgan Chase provides elder care management services that include a needs assessment program for the employee. Consulting firm Deloitte offers paid leave up to 16 weeks for employees providing elder care. UPS offers health-spending accounts in which employees can put aside pretax income for elder care expenses. However, the number of companies offering elder care benefits still lags behind the number offering child care benefits, and small businesses are far behind large companies in providing elder care benefits. Unfortunately, the government does not provide much relief. Both Medicare and Medicaid place heavy financial burdens for care on family caregivers.

According to the American Association of Retired Persons (AARP), as more experienced and high-ranking employees care for older parents and relatives, the costs to companies will rise even higher. This argument makes sense, since older, more experienced workers (who are most affected by elder care issues) often hold jobs more critical to a company than those held by younger workers. Many firms now face the fact that transfers and promotions are often out of the question for employees whose elderly parents or relatives need ongoing care. Unfortunately, as the nation gets older, the elder care situation will grow considerably worse, meaning this employee–management issue will persist well into the future.

Drug Abuse and Drug Testing

Alcohol and drug abuse remain serious workplace issues that touch many workers and stretch from factory floors to construction sites to the locker rooms of professional sports teams.

Alcohol is the most widely used drug in the workplace, with an estimated 6.4 percent of full-time U.S. employees believed to have an alcohol use disorder.[55] Approximately 40 percent of industrial injuries and fatalities can be linked to alcohol consumption.

Tony Freeman/PhotoEdit

Today, over 60 percent of major companies drug test new employees and 40 percent conduct random drug testing. Do you think these efforts are successful in reducing drug abuse in the workplace? Why or why not?

According to the Department of Health and Human Services' Substance Abuse & Mental Health Services Association, more than 8 percent of full-time workers aged 18–49 use illegal drugs.[56] In some industries, such as food services and construction, the percentage of workers using illegal drugs is much higher.[57]

Individuals who use illegal drugs are three and a half times more likely to be in workplace accidents and five times more likely to file a workers' compensation claim than other employees. According to the National Institute on Drug Abuse, employed drug users cost their employers about twice as much in medical and workers' compensation claims as do their drug-free co-workers. The U.S. Department of Labor projects that over a one-year period, drug abuse costs the U.S. economy $820 billion in lost work, health care costs, crime, traffic accidents, and other expenses, and over $120 billion in lost productivity.[58] The National Institutes of Health estimates each drug abuser can cost an employer approximately $10,000 annually. Drug abusers are associated with 55 percent on-the-job accident rates, 85 percent more injuries, 10 percent higher absenteeism, 30 percent more turnover, and more frequent workplace violence incidents.

Today, over 60 percent of major companies drug test new employees even though many now question the testing's effectiveness in improving safety or productivity.[59] Furthermore, 33 states and the District of Columbia have passed laws legalizing marijuana in some form that complicate the testing issue.[60] It's safe to say the issue of drug abuse and drug testing will remain an important and controversial employee–management issue in the future.

Violence and Bullying in the Workplace

The school shootings at Sandy Hook Elementary School shocked the nation. The tragedy also reminded businesses that even though workplace violence has declined over the past 30 years, the threat has in no way disappeared. Employers and managers must be vigilant about potential violence in the workplace. The Bureau of Labor Statistics reports that nearly two million Americans are impacted by workplace violence annually.[61] The Occupational Safety and Health Administration (OSHA) reports that homicides account for 9 percent of all workplace deaths, and are the number one cause of death for women in the workplace, accounting for 19 percent.[62]

Many companies have taken action to prevent problems before they occur. They have held focus groups that invite employee input, hired managers with strong interpersonal skills, and employed skilled consultants to deal with any growing potential for workplace violence. In many states employers can seek a temporary restraining order on behalf of workers experiencing threats or harassment. Such initiatives have helped curtail workplace violence. Unfortunately, as workplace violence has decreased, workplace bullying has increased.

According to the Workplace Bullying Institute (WBI), bullying at work involves "repeated, health-harming mistreatment of a person by one or more perpetrators. It is abusive conduct that is: threatening, humiliating, or intimidating, or work interference or sabotage which prevents work from getting done, or verbal abuse."[63] The WBI maintains bullying is almost four times more common than sexual harassment on the job.[64] Zogby International research estimates that 35 percent of workers have been bullied at work. Unfortunately, employers and managers often discount or deny bullying, and refer to it simply as personality conflicts or management styles. By trivializing bullying, an organization can suffer reduced employee morale and productivity, increased turnover, and, in some cases, even legal problems.

Although "schoolyard" bullying tends to be physical in nature, workplace bullying involves more psychological and verbal abuse. Also, the targets of workplace bullying are often the strongest employees (who are considered threats to the bully), not the weakest.

The majority of bullies are supervisors or managers but can also be fellow workers. Men far outnumber women as workplace bullies, but women tend to bully other women more frequently than men. Bullying is increasingly becoming a major problem in the workplace and can be directed at employees at all levels of the organization.

Firms that have healthy employee–management relations have a better chance to prosper than those that don't. Taking a proactive approach is the best way to ensure positive employee–management work environments. The proactive manager anticipates potential sensitive issues and works toward resolving them before they get out of hand—a good lesson for any manager.

TESTPREP

- How does top-executive pay in the United States compare with top-executive pay in other countries?
- What's the difference between pay equity and equal pay for equal work?
- How is the term *sexual harassment* defined, and when does sexual behavior become illegal?
- What are some of the issues companies are facing related to child care and elder care? How are companies addressing those issues?
- How can companies effectively address workplace violence and bullying?

SUMMARY

LO 12–1 Trace the history of organized labor in the United States.

- **What was the first union?**

  The cordwainers (shoemakers) organized a craft union of skilled specialists in 1792. The Knights of Labor, formed in 1869, was the first national labor organization.

- **How did the AFL-CIO evolve?**

  The American Federation of Labor (AFL), formed in 1886, was an organization of craft unions. The Congress of Industrial Organizations (CIO), a group of unskilled and semiskilled workers, broke off from the AFL in 1935. Over time, the two organizations saw the benefits of joining and became the AFL-CIO in 1955. The AFL-CIO is a federation of labor unions, not a national union.

LO 12–2 Discuss the major legislation affecting labor unions.

- **What are the provisions of the major legislation affecting labor unions?**

  See Figure 12.1.

LO 12–3 Outline the objectives of labor unions.

- **What topics typically appear in labor–management agreements?**

  See Figure 12.2.

LO 12–4 Describe the tactics used by labor and management during conflicts, and discuss the role of unions in the future.

- **What are the tactics used by unions and management in conflicts?**

Unions can use strikes and boycotts. Management can use strikebreakers, injunctions, and lockouts.

- **What will unions have to do to cope with continually declining membership?**

Unions are facing a changing workplace. The National Education Association is now the nation's largest union. The Service Employees International Union (SEIU), with two million members, is the second-largest union. Going forward, unions must adapt to an increasingly white-collar, female, and culturally diverse workforce. To help keep U.S. businesses competitive in global markets, many have taken on a new role in assisting management in training workers, redesigning jobs, and assimilating the changing workforce.

LO 12–5 Assess some of today's controversial employee–management issues, such as executive compensation, pay equity, sexual harassment, child care and elder care, drug abuse and drug testing, and violence and bullying in the workplace.

- **What is a fair wage for managers?**

The market and the businesses in it set managers' salaries. What is fair is open to debate.

- **How are equal pay and pay equity different?**

The Equal Pay Act of 1963 provides that workers receive equal pay for equal work (with exceptions for seniority, merit, or performance). Pay equity is the demand for equivalent pay for jobs requiring similar levels of education, training, and skills.

- **How are some companies addressing the child care issue?**

Responsive companies are providing child care on the premises, emergency care when scheduled care is interrupted, discounts with child care chains, vouchers to be used at the employee's chosen care center, and referral services.

- **What is elder care, and what problems do companies face with regard to this growing problem?**

Workers who need to provide elder care for dependent parents or others are generally more experienced and vital to the mission of the organization than younger workers are. The cost to business is very large and growing.

- **Why are more and more companies now testing workers and job applicants for substance abuse?**

Drug abuse costs the U.S. economy $820 billion in lost work, health care costs, crime, traffic accidents, and other expenses, and over $120 billion in lost productivity. Individuals who use drugs are three and a half times more likely to be in workplace accidents and five times more likely to file a workers' compensation claim than those who do not use drugs.

- **Why do managers need to be vigilant concerning violence and bullying in the workplace?**

Nearly two million workers are impacted by workplace violence yearly. Companies have been successful in taking action to protect against violence. Unfortunately, bullying in the workplace is growing.

KEY TERMS

CRITICAL THINKING

1. Do you believe that union shop agreements are violations of a worker's freedom of choice in the workplace? Do you think open shop agreements unfairly penalize workers who pay dues to unions they have elected to represent them in the workplace?

2. Some college football and basketball coaches earn huge incomes. Should college volleyball and swimming coaches be paid comparably? Should players in the Women's National Basketball Association (WNBA) be paid the same as their male counterparts in the National Basketball Association (NBA)? What role should market forces and government play in determining such wages?

3. If a company provides employer-paid child care services to workers with children, should those who don't have children or don't need child care services be paid extra?

PUTTING PRINCIPLES TO WORK

PURPOSE

To understand why workers choose to join unions and how unions have made differences in certain industries.

EXERCISE

Visit the AFL-CIO website (aflcio.org) and find information about why workers join unions and what the benefits have been.

1. Explain how union membership has affected minorities, women, older workers, and part-time workers.

2. The AFL-CIO site presents the union's perspective on labor issues. Look at the key issues and check sources such as the National Right to Work Legal Defense Foundation (nrtw.org) that support management's perspectives and compare their positions on these issues.

DEVELOPING CAREER SKILLS

KEY: ● Team   ★ Analytic   ▲ Communication   ◙ Technology

1. Check whether your state supports the right of public employees (police, firefighters, teachers) to unionize and collectively bargain. If not, should it? Should such workers be allowed to strike?   ★ ◙

2. Evaluate the following statement: "Labor unions are dinosaurs that have outlived their usefulness in today's knowledge-based economy." After your evaluation, take the position on this statement that differs from your own point of view and defend that position. Be sure to consider such questions as: Do unions serve a purpose in some industries? Do unions make the United States less competitive in global markets?   ★ ▲

3. Research federal and state legislation related to child care, parental leave, and elder care benefits for employees. Are specific trends emerging? Should companies be responsible   ★ ◙ ▲

for providing such workplace benefits, or should the government share some responsibility? Why?

 4. Compile a list of two or three employee–management issues not covered in the chapter. Compare your list with those of several classmates and see which issues you selected in common and which are unique to each individual. Pick an issue you all agree will be important in the future and discuss its likely effects and outcomes.

 5. Do businesses and government agencies have a duty to provide additional benefits to employees beyond fair pay and good working conditions? Propose a system you consider fair and equitable for employees and employers.

CAREER EXPLORATION

If you are interested in pursuing a career in employee-management relations, here are a few to consider. Find out about the tasks performed, skills needed, pay, and opportunity outlook in these fields in the *Occupational Outlook Handbook (OOH)* at bls.gov.

- **Labor relations specialist**—interprets and administers labor contracts regarding issues such as wages and salaries, health care, pensions, and union and management practices.

- **Human resource specialist**—recruits, screens, interviews, and places workers; handles other human resource work, such as those related to employee relations, compensation and benefits, and training.

- **Arbitrator and mediator**—facilitates negotiation and dialogue between disputing parties to help resolve conflicts outside of court.

VIDEO CASE   *Working with Unions at Freeman*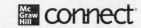

Because the number of workers in labor unions has declined dramatically over the years, you may be under the impression that unions aren't important today or that they have lost their passion for seeking fair treatment for workers. Not true. Although not all workers are members of labor unions, you probably encounter more union employees than you think. Of course, large numbers of truck drivers and construction workers belong to unions. However, actors, writers, and directors in the entertainment industry are union members, too. Even many college professors belong to a union.

Freeman XP, a brand experience company, organizes large events such as trade shows. Much like a large contractor on a construction site, it is Freeman's job to act as a general contractor for trade shows that are often complex in scope. The company coordinates all the vendors involved in an event and must make sure that all needed equipment (including high-tech devices) is working properly and available to show participants when needed. To accomplish this task, Freeman relies on the assistance of many different labor unions.

Union workers help make the trade show happen. In a typical trade show, Teamsters deliver and unload all the equipment into the building. Carpenters build the main structures while electricians make sure power is running throughout the entire show space and lighting is functioning where and when needed. In specific events such as restaurant shows, plumbers must supply water for demonstrations and ensure drainage for used water. Along with these construction-related union workers, Freeman also needs the services of the International Association of Theatrical Stage Employees (stage hands) to set up sound systems, video equipment, and special lighting. On a large-scale trade show, Freeman may easily rely on the work of 6 to 10 different labor unions to get the event fully operational.

Freeman believes a key benefit of using union workers is that no matter where it is setting up, the company can count on trained workers who have the necessary skills to make the show work from start to finish. Also, because Freeman sets up shows in many large convention venues throughout the United States, having skilled workers available when needed is vital. In fact, many large trade shows often require hundreds of workers to put together the event. To keep that many people permanently on the company payroll year-round would be cost prohibitive for Freeman.

By working with labor unions, the company can hire the needed workers for a limited period.

Unfortunately, the company admits, working with labor unions is not always a bed of roses. Union workers can be costly because their leadership works hard to get their members fair wages and safe working conditions. Labor unions also have different work rules pertaining to start and quit times, breaks, and voluntary versus involuntary overtime rules. Still, despite these challenges, Freeman believes that working with labor unions solves more problems than it creates. It's safe to say that not all companies in the United States feel the same.

Unions today are gathering momentum in nontraditional professions like nursing and teaching. They are also gaining support in low-paying jobs like fast food where the push is on for more equitable wages.

THINKING IT OVER

1. Why does Freeman use so many union workers? What are advantages and disadvantages of using union workers for Freeman? Describe how managing a project such as a trade show would be different if Freeman did not use union workers.

2. One of the primary concerns of traditional labor unions such as the steelworkers is the use of offshore outsourcing. Do you think American companies should be required to use steel that's made in the United States on major projects?

3. How has the government impacted the growth and stability of labor unions? Is your state a "right-to-work" state? Are there many union workers in your town or state? Do you see labor unions gaining strength or declining in your state in the future?

NOTES

1. Allen Smith, "Some Industries See an Increase in Unionization," Society for Human Resource Management, shrm.org, February 7, 2020; Margot Roosevelt, "The Number of Californians Represented by Unions Grows, as National Labor Organizing Stagnates," *The Los Angeles Times,* January 23, 2020.

2. U.S. Bureau of Labor Statistics, bls.gov, accessed February 2020; Lia Russell, "Public Sector Workers Continue to Drive Union Participation," *Federal Computer Week,* fcw.com, accessed February 2020; Eli Rosenberg, "Workers Are Fired Up," *The Washington Post,* January 23, 2020.

3. Lia Russell, "Public Sector Workers Continue to Drive Union Participation," *Federal Computer Week,* fcw.com, accessed February 2020; "Union Member Summary," U.S. Bureau of Labor Statistics, bls.gov, accessed February 2020.

4. "The Knights of Labor," Khan Academy, khanacademy.org, accessed February 2020; "Workers United: The Knights of Labor," Historical Society of Pennsylvania, hsp.org, accessed February 2020.

5. AFL-CIO, aflcio.com, accessed February 2020.

6. AFL-CIO, aflcio.com, accessed February 2020; Sharon Block and Benjamin Sachs, "Why U.S. Labor Laws Need to Be Revamped," *Harvard Gazette,* news.harvard.edu, January 23, 2020.

7. Eli Rosenberg, "Congress's Most Ambitious Attempt to Strengthen Unions in Years Is Set for a House Vote," *The Washington Post,* January 29, 2020; Alexander Hertel-Fernandez, "Labor Law Makes It Too Hard to Start Unions. Workers Deserve a Bigger Voice," *CNN,* cnn.com, January 29, 2020.

8. Tucker Higgins, "In a Blow to Public Sector Unions, Supreme Court Overturns 40-Year-Old Precedent," *CNBC,* cnbc.com, accessed February 2020.

9. Noah Smith, "Labor Unions Need All the Help They Can Get," *Yahoo! Finance,* finance.yahoo.com, February 14, 2020.

10. Ben Werschkul, "These 21 States Are Raising Their Minimum Wage in 2020," *Yahoo! Finance,* finance.yahoo.com, December 27, 2019; Paul Davidson, "Trump Touted Low-Wage Worker Pay Gains but Much of the Credit Goes to State Minimum Wage Hikes," *USA Today,* usatoday.com, February 9, 2020.

11. Katie Shonk, "How Mediation Can Help Resolve Pro Sports Disputes," *Harvard Law School Program on Negotiation,* pon.harvard.edu, accessed February 2020.

12. David Zabulowski, "Hader Loses to Brewers in Arbitration, Players Drop to 1-6," *Quad-City Times,* qctimes.com, February 14, 2020; Mike McCann, "What Will It Take to Stop Service Time Manipulation in MLB?," *Sports Illustrated,* si.com, February 4, 2020.

13. American Arbitration Association, adr.org, accessed February 2020.

14. Eric Morath and Noah Naughton, "Strikes, Lockouts Hit Highest Level since 2001," *The Wall Street Journal,* February 12, 2020.

15. Aidan Harper, "How Unions Can Flourish Again: Break Out of the Workplace and Think Local," *The Guardian,* theguardian.com, February 1, 2020.

16. Neal Boudette, "G.M. Workers Approve Contract and End U.A.W. Strike," *The New York Times,* October 25, 2019.

17. Service Employees International Union, seiu.org, accessed February 2020.

18. Laiba Omer, "The World's Highest Paid Celebrities," *Forbes,* forbes.com, February 13, 2020.

19. Jesse Pound and Hugh Son, "Jamie Dimon Gets Raise to $31.5 Million after Record 2019 Profit at JP Morgan," *CNBC,* cnbc.com, January 23, 2020; Sergei Klebnikov, "Jamie Dimon's Salary Rises to $31.5 Million in 2019, amid Record Bank Profits," *Forbes,* forbes.com, January 24, 2020; Laura Noonan, "Jamie Dimon's Pay Rose to $31.5 Million in 2019," *Financial Times,* January 24, 2020.

20. Nancy Skinner and Abigail Disney, "To Tackle Income Inequality, Tax Companies That Overpay CEOs and Underpay Workers," *The Sacramento Bee,* January 17, 2020.

21. Theo Francis, "CEOs' Take-Home Pay Exceeds Disclosures," *The Wall Street Journal,* August 26, 2019.

22. Polina Marinova, "WeWork's Other Co-founder Has a Plan to Save the Company. It's the Opposite of What Adam Neumann Envisioned," *Fortune,* January 22, 2020; Nicolas Vega, "Ex-WeWork CEO Adam Neumann Didn't Get a $1.7B Golden Parachute, Chairman Says," *The New York Post,* February 10, 2020.

23. Jason Wingard, "Yes Ms. Disney—CEOs Get Paid Too Much," *Forbes,* forbes.com, January 24, 2020.

24. "Measuring the 1%," *The Economist,* economist.com, November 30, 2019; "What's Wrong with Inequality?," *The Economist,* economist.com, February 13, 2020; Scott Lanman and Stephanie Flanders, "Thomas Piketty's New Book Is about a Lot More Than Capitalism," *Bloomberg,* February 10, 2020.

25. Ellen Wolf Mann, "The 19 Companies with CEOs Paid 1000X More Than the Median Employee," *Yahoo! Finance,* finance.yahoo.com, February 12, 2020; Jason Wingard, "Yes, Ms. Disney—CEOs Get Paid Too Much," *Forbes,* forbes.com, January 24, 2020.

26. Andy Kiersz, "We Did the Math to Calculate How Many Hours It Takes America's Top CEOs to Make What Their Workers Earn in One Year," *Business Insider,* businessinsider.com, February 9, 2020; "Disney CEO Bob Iger Was Paid $48 Million in 2019," *The Los Angeles Times,* latimes.com, January 17, 2020; Dawn Chmielewski, "Disney CEO Bob Iger's Compensation Drops Dramatically in 2019," *Forbes,* forbes.com, January 17, 2020.

27. "Most of the World Is Yet to Embrace Co-determination," *The Economist,* February 1, 2020; Marina N. Bolotnikova, "A Gut Renovation for U.S. Labor Law," *Harvard Magazine,* harvardmagazine.com, January 23, 2020; "What's American for Mitbestimmung?," *The Economist,* February 1, 2020.

28. Nana Ama Sarfo, "Pegging Taxes to Executive Pay Could Get Messy," *Forbes,* forbes.com, January 30, 2020.

29. "Pay Equity: What Is It and Why It's Important," Paycor, paycor.com, accessed March 2020; Scott Paywood, "Pay Equity Doesn't Mean Paying the Same for Everyone," *Workforce,* workforce.com, February 9, 2020; Robert O'Hara, "What Employers Don't Know about Pay Equity Can Hurt Them," Society for Human Resource Management, shrm.org, January 29, 2020.

30. Kathleen Elkins, "Here's How Much Women and Men Earn at Every Age," *CNBC,* cnbc.com, accessed March 2020; Andrew Sullivan, "Is There a Way to Acknowledge America's Progress?," *New York Magazine,* nymag.com, January 17, 2020.

31. Jenet Jacob Erickson, "More Women Are in the Workforce Than Men; Should We Celebrate or Be Concerned?," *Deseret News,* deseret.com, January 13, 2020; Kathy Petitte Novak, "Working Women Still Fighting Implicit Bias," *Ms.,* msmagazine.com, January 29, 2020.

32. Katherine Plumhoff, "Gender Inequality Starts at Work with Entry-Level Promotions," *Fast Company,* fastcompany. com, December 18, 2019.

33. Stephen Miller, "Transparency Shrinks Gender Pay Gap," Society for Human Resource Management, shrm.org, January 31, 2020; Courtney Connley, "Data Show Pay Transparency Could Be the No. 1 Solution to Closing the Gender Pay Gap," *CNBC,* cnbc.com, February 11, 2020.

34. Vanessa Fuhrmans, "Where Are All the Women CEOs?," *The Wall Street Journal,* wsj.com, February 6, 2020.

35. Howard R. Gold, "College Students Are Narrowing the Gender Wage Gap," University of Chicago Booth Review, review.chicagobooth.edu, January 23, 2020.

36. U.S. Equal Employment Opportunity Commission, eeoc. gov, accessed March 2020.

37. Steven Pearlman, "What the EEOC's New Data May Tell Us about the State of the #MeToo Movement," *Forbes,* forbes.com, February 2, 2020.

38. Allen Smith, "EEOC Harassment Charges Reflect #MeToo's Relevance," Society for Human Resource Management, shrm.org, January 24, 2020.

39. "Charges Alleging Sexual Harassment," U.S. Equal Employment Opportunity Commission, eeoc.gov, accessed March 2020.

40. Jessica Heslam, "Gretchen Carlson Takes Her Fight against Workplace Silence on Sexual Misconduct to Beacon Hill," *The Boston Herald,* bostonherald.com, January 27, 2020; "Ex-Fox Anchor Carlson to Highlight Nondisclosure Agreements," *U.S. News & World Report,* usnews.com, January 26, 2020; Emma Baker, "The Very True, Very Yikes, and Very Fascinating Story behind Bombshell," *Cosmopolitan,* cosmopolitan.com, February 4, 2020; Joan Vennochi, "From Fox News to Beacon Hill— the Buying of Women's Silence," *The Boston Globe,* January 29, 2020.

41. Tim Baysinger, "How George Cheeks Helps CBS Rid Itself of Les Moonves' Shadow," *Yahoo! Finance,* finance.yahoo. com, accessed March 2020; Edmund Lee, "CBS Replaces Its Top Executive as Dust Settles on Viacom Merger," *The New York Times,* January 31, 2020.

42. Sarah Gallo, "Sexual Harassment Prevention Training: State Update Requirements," *Training and Industry,* trainingindustry.com, February 5, 2020.

43. Deanna Paul, "Weinstein Jurors Asked to Set Aside #MeToo Emotions," *The Wall Street Journal,* wsj.com, January 17, 2020; Christie Brown, "Why the Women in the Weinstein Case Are So Believable," *Psychology Today,* psychologytoday.com, February 13, 2020; Linda Hirshman, "Prosecute Harvey Weinstein for Extortion Instead of Rape. It's Easier to Prove," *The Washington Post,* February 11, 2020; Deanna Paul, "Weinstein Accuser Details Sex Assault," *The Wall Street Journal,* February 2, 2020.

44. Aparna Mathur, "Women Are a Majority in the Workforce— but That's Not the Whole Story," *Yahoo! Finance,* finance.yahoo.com, February 2, 2020; Claire Cain Miller, "Women's Gains in the Workforce Conceal a Problem," *The New York Times,* nytimes.com, January 21, 2020; Pavithra Mohan, "Women Are Scooping Up High-Skill Jobs and Narrowing the Pay Gap," *Fast Company,* fastcompany.com, January 30, 2020.

45. Ashley Fetters, "The Working to Afford Child-Care Conundrum," *The Atlantic,* theatlantic.com, January 18, 2020; Carolyn Sun, "How to Make Money as a Stay-at-Home Mom," *Entrepreneur,* entrepreneur.com, January 19, 2020; U.S. Bureau of Labor Statistics, www.bls.gov, accessed March 2020.

46. Claire Cain Miller, "Why Mothers' Choices about Work and Family Often Feel Like No Choice at All," *The New York Times,* nytimes.com, January 17, 2020; Michelle Lerner, "High Child-Care Costs Are a Hurdle for First-Time Home Buyers," *The Washington Post,* February 12, 2020; Sue Shellenbarger, "The Challenges That Working Mothers Still Face," *The Wall Street Journal,* January 5, 2020.

47. Erin Delmore, "The Best Company for Working Moms Is . . . ," *NBC News,* nbcnews.com, September 24, 2019; "*Working Mother* Releases the 100 Best Companies of 2019," *MarketWatch,* marketwatch.com, September 24, 2019.

48. Jeffrey McKinney, "6 Child Care Options for Small Businesses to Consider to Support Employees," *Black Enterprise,* blackenterprise.com, February 3, 2020; Michael Guta, "Just 6% of Companies Offer Childcare Benefits to Workers," *Small Business Trends,* smallbiztrends.com, January 19, 2020.

49. Bright Horizons, brighthorizons.com, accessed March 2020.

50. U.S. Census Bureau, census.gov, accessed March 2020; Amanda Robert, "Why Elder Law Is a Growing, 'Anything Can Happen Practice,'" *American Bar Association Journal,* abajournal.com, January 30, 2020.

51. Dudley Poston, "3 Big Ways the U.S. Will Change over the Next Decade," *The Florida Times Union,* jacksonville.com, January 2, 2020; U.S. Census Bureau, census.gov, accessed March 2020; Administration for Community Living, acl.gov, accessed February 2020.

52. "Elder and Child Caregiving Statistics," Torchlight, torchlight.com, accessed March 2020; American Association of Retired Persons, aarp.com, accessed March 2020.

53. "Elder and Child Caregiving Statistics," Torchlight, torchlight.com, accessed March 2020; American Association of Retired Persons, aarp.com, accessed March 2020.

54. Lynn Feinberg and Rita Choula, "Understanding the Impact of Family Caregiving on Work," AARP Public Policy Institute, accessed March 2020; Veronica Woldt, "Solving Employee Elder Care Challenges," *Corporate Wellness Magazine,* corporatewellnessmagazine.com, accessed March 2020.

55. "Alcoholism & Treatment Statistics by Profession," Alcohol.org, alcohol.org, accessed March 2020.

56. Scot Thomas, "Alcohol and Drug Abuse Statistics," Substance Abuse and Mental Health Services Administration, samhsa.gov, accessed March 2020; "The Cost of Addiction in the Workplace," American Addiction Centers, americanaddictioncenters.org, February 3, 2020.

57. "Drugs and Alcohol in the Workplace," National Council on Alcoholism and Drug Dependence, ncaddms.org, accessed March 2020; National Drug-Free Workplace Alliance, ndwa.org, accessed March 2020.

58. "How Drug Use Affects Our Society," VeryWellMind, verywellmind.com, accessed March 2020.

59. Charisse Jones, "Weed, CBD, New Products, New Laws Are Causing Confusion in the Workplace," *USA Today,* January 21, 2020; Megan Gates, "The Science behind Marijuana Testing at Work," Society for Human Resource Management, shrm.org, February 5, 2020.

60. Jeremy Berke and Skye Gould, "Legal Marijuana Just Went on Sale in Illinois. Here Are All the States Where Cannabis Is Legal," *Business Insider,* businessinsider.com, January 1, 2020; Audrey McNamara, "These States Now Have Legal Weed, and Which States Could Follow Suit in 2020," *CBS News,* cbsnews.com, January 1, 2020.

61. "Assaults Fourth Leading Cause of Workplace Deaths," National Safety Council, nsc.org, accessed March 2020; U.S. Bureau of Labor Statistics, bls.gov, accessed March 2020.

62. Roy Maurer, "When Domestic Violence Comes to Work," Society for Human Resource Management, shrm.org, accessed March 2020; Occupational Safety and Health Administration, osha.gov, accessed March 2020.

63. Workplace Bullying Institute, workplacebullying.org, accessed March 2020; "Protect Your Employees: Have a Bullying Policy," *Business News Daily,* businessnewsdaily.com, February 3, 2020.

64. Jo Faragher, "Managers Swept Harassment under the Carpet, Says CIPD Report," *Personnel Today,* personneltoday.com, January 21, 2020; Heidi Lynn Kurtner, "5 Powerful Apps and Resources to Tackle Workplace Bullying and Harassment," *Forbes,* forbes.com, January 16, 2020.

13

Marketing: Helping Buyers Buy

LEARNING OBJECTIVES *After you have read and studied this chapter, you should be able to*

LO 13-1 Define *marketing,* and apply the marketing concept to both for-profit and nonprofit organizations.

LO 13-2 Describe the four Ps of marketing.

LO 13-3 Summarize the marketing research process.

LO 13-4 Show how marketers use environmental scanning to learn about the changing marketing environment.

LO 13-5 Explain how marketers apply the tools of market segmentation, relationship marketing, and the study of consumer behavior.

LO 13-6 Compare the business-to-business market and the consumer market.

Daniel Lubetzky, Founder of KIND

From granola to fruit-and-nuts to chocolate-packed treats, snack bars of all brands and varieties line the shelves at supermarkets across the country. Standing out in this crowd is no simple task, though, and requires companies to use clever marketing campaigns to distinguish themselves from the rest of the pack. That's how the snack brand KIND has managed to sell more than two billion bars since 2004. From the very beginning, founder Daniel Lubetzky has promoted KIND as a healthy alternative to sugary competitors while also emphasizing the company's commitment to good causes.

Born in Mexico City, Lubetzky learned early on about the immense power of kindness to fight against intolerance. His father was a Holocaust survivor who had been imprisoned in Dachau concentration camp as an adolescent. One day while he was standing dazed and starving against a fence, a passing German soldier quickly dropped half of a rotting potato at his feet. He credited this small but significant act of kindness with saving his life. "My mother thought I was too young to hear such things," said Lubetzky. "But it was important to my father to pass along how dark humanity can be, and how, in the midst of that darkness you can bring light." His father's experiences taught Lubetzky the value of acting unselfishly, a lesson he has depended on throughout his life and career.

He got his start in business at age 16 shortly after his family moved to San Antonio, Texas, to operate duty-free stores near the U.S.–Mexico border. Lubetzky purchased watches for wholesale prices from one of his father's suppliers, marked them up, and then sold them at a local flea market. He eventually upgraded to mall kiosks that he operated while attending Trinity University. Majoring in economics and international relations, Lubetzky wrote his senior thesis on using entrepreneurship to soothe tensions in the Israeli–Palestinian conflict. After graduating from law school, he moved to Israel to put his ideas into action but saw little success. "Nobody wanted this confused Mexican-Jewish attorney teaching them how to do business between Arabs and Israelis," said Lubetzky.

Still, his time abroad was far from a waste since it gave him the inspiration for a new business venture. He partnered with an Israeli entrepreneur who made sun-dried tomato spread but had to close up shop due to his complicated supply chain. Lubetzky realized he could save the business by sourcing from local suppliers while also bridging cultural and historical divides in the process. Soon he was shipping sun-dried tomatoes from Turks and olive oil from Palestinians in glass jars from Egyptians for his company called PeaceWorks. Lubetzky traveled across the world to develop more culturally collaborative brands, which is when he came up with the idea that would change his life.

During the course of his travels, he got tired of eating the same bland airport food no matter where he went. "I was crisscrossing the world, and everything tasted horrible," said Lubetzky. "I couldn't find anything that was wholesome, convenient, tasty and healthy. I just wanted to make something that I would want to eat." After a few years of perfecting recipes for his fruit-and-nut bars, he used profits from PeaceWorks to found KIND. He marketed the snacks as being healthier than the usual items on offer and relentlessly networked with suppliers to put them on store shelves. In 2007, Lubetzky managed to get KIND bars into Walmart, but the retailer dropped the company later in the year after some shipments went missing. With cash running low, he regretfully sold a third of his stake in KIND to the founders of Vitaminwater and a private equity firm.

These investors ended up providing Lubetzky with some key advice. Up to that point, KIND spent only about $800 annually on free samples of its bars. After his new partners suggested increasing that number, KIND raised the next year's budget for samples and field-marketing to $800,000. "It sounds like common sense in retrospect, but what we needed, really, was just for more people to try it," said Lubetzky. This strategy rapidly increased consumer awareness of the brand and sent sales skyrocketing. By 2014, KIND was doing so well that Lubetzky bought back his shares in the business. The company now spends $20 million per year on sampling in order to keep it among the top brands in snacks. Lubetzky also makes sure that the concept of kindness remains central to both the brand's marketing and the KIND Foundation, a nonprofit dedicated to creating more empathetic communities. "I've been given an incredible gift with KIND's growth and success," said Lubetzky. "Now I just want to incubate great ideas, great people and have maximum impact on the world."

In this chapter, you'll learn how master marketers like Daniel Lubetzky identify their audience and figure out how to reach them. Whether through distribution, advertising, or publicity, successful marketing makes a connection with customers that they won't soon forget.

Sources: Angel Au-Yeung, "Social Spin Doctor: Kind Bar's Daniel Lubetzky Builds a $1.5 Billion Fortune on Do-Gooder Rhetoric," *Forbes,* forbes.com, March 5, 2019; Francesca Fontana, "How the Kindness of Others Motivates KIND's Founder," *The Wall Street Journal,* wsj.com, January 10, 2020; Amelia Lucas, "Snack-Maker Kind Takes Its Bars to Refrigerators and Freezers," *CNBC,* cnbc.com, February 10, 2020; Mark Peruzzi, "Do the Kind Thing," First Descents, firstdescents.org, accessed February 2020; KIND, kindsnacks.com, accessed February 2020.

Let's talk business!
bit.ly/LetsTalkBusiness13

Brad Barket/Getty Images

THIS COMPANY HAS found success by studying the consumer market. While you may be familiar with its best-selling, typical product varieties, this firm slightly alters many of its recipes based on the location of its markets. Name that company. (Find the answer in the chapter.)

LO 13–1 Define *marketing,* and apply the marketing concept to both for-profit and nonprofit organizations.

What Is Marketing?

The term *marketing* means different things to different people. Many think of marketing as simply "selling" or "advertising." Yes, selling and advertising are part of marketing, but it's much more. The American Marketing Association has defined **marketing** as the activity, set of institutions, and processes for creating, communicating, delivering, and exchanging offerings that have value for customers, clients, partners, and society at large. We can also think of marketing, more simply, as the activities buyers and sellers perform to facilitate mutually satisfying exchanges.

In the past marketing focused almost entirely on helping the seller sell. That's why many people still think of it as mostly selling, advertising, and distribution from the seller to the buyer. Today, much of marketing is instead about helping the buyer buy. Let's take a look at a couple of examples.

Today, when people want to buy a new or used car, they often go online first. They go to a site like cars.com to search for the vehicle they want. Then they can navigate to other websites to compare prices and features. By the time they go to the dealer, they may know exactly which car they want and the best price available.

Websites have helped the buyer buy. Not only are customers spared searching one dealership after another to find the best price, but manufacturers and dealers are eager to participate so that they don't lose customers. The future of marketing is doing everything you can to help the buyer buy.[1] The easier a marketer makes the purchase decision process, the more that marketer will sell.

Let's look at another example. In the past, one of the few ways students and parents could find the college with the right "fit" was to travel from campus to campus, a tiring and expensive process. Today, colleges use virtual tours, live chats, and other interactive technologies to make on-campus visits less necessary. Such virtual tours help students and their parents buy.

Of course, helping the buyer buy also helps the seller sell. Think about that for a minute. In the vacation market, many people find the trip they want themselves. They go online to find the right spot, and then make choices, sometimes questioning potential sellers. In industries like this, the role of marketing is to make sure that a company's products or services are easily found online, and that the company responds effectively to potential customers. Sites like Expedia, Travelocity, and Priceline allow customers to find the best price or sometimes set their own.

These are only a few examples of the marketing trend toward helping buyers buy. Consumers today spend hours searching online for good deals. Wise marketers provide a wealth of information and even cultivate customer relationships using blogs and social media such as Facebook, Twitter, and Instagram.[2]

These online communities provide opportunities to observe people (customers and others) interacting with one another, expressing their own opinions, forming relationships,

marketing
The activity, set of institutions, and processes for creating, communicating, delivering, and exchanging offerings that have value for customers, clients, partners, and society at large.

and commenting on various goods and services. It is important for marketers to track what influencers are writing by searching feeds using key terms that define their market. Vendors who have text-mining tools can help companies measure conversations about their products and their personnel. Much of the future of marketing lies in mining such online conversations and responding appropriately. For example, marketers are learning why online shoppers will add goods to their shopping cart, but then leave the sale before they give their credit card information.[3]

The Evolution of Marketing

What marketers do at any particular time depends on what they need to do to fill customers' needs and wants, which are continually changing. Let's take a brief look at how those changes have influenced the evolution of marketing. Marketing in the United States has passed through four eras: (1) production, (2) selling, (3) marketing concept, and (4) customer relationship. Today, a new era is quickly emerging: mobile/on-demand marketing (see Figure 13.1).

The Production Era From the time the first European settlers began their struggle to survive in America until the early 1900s, the general philosophy of business was "Produce as much as you can, because there is a limitless market for it." Given the limited production capability and vast demand for products in those days, that production philosophy was both logical and profitable. Business owners were mostly farmers, carpenters, and trade workers. They needed to produce more and more, so their goals centered on production.

The Selling Era By the 1920s, businesses had developed mass-production techniques (such as automobile assembly lines), and production capacity often exceeded the immediate market demand. Therefore, the business philosophy turned from producing to selling. Most companies emphasized selling and advertising in an effort to persuade consumers to buy existing products; few offered extensive service after the sale.

The Marketing Concept Era After World War II ended in 1945, returning soldiers beginning new careers and starting families sparked a tremendous demand for goods and services. The postwar years launched the sudden increase in the birth rate that we now call the Baby Boom, and also a boom in consumer spending. Competition for the consumer's dollar was fierce. Businesses recognized that they needed to be responsive to consumers if they wanted to get their business, and a philosophy emerged in the 1950s called the marketing concept.

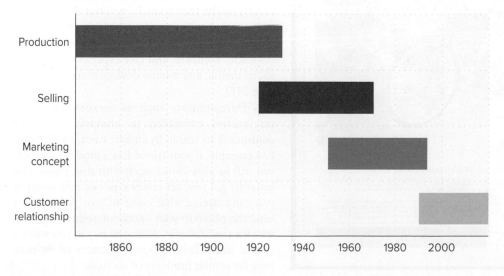

FIGURE 13.1
MARKETING ERAS
The evolution of marketing in the United States involved four eras: (1) production, (2) selling, (3) marketing concept, and (4) customer relationship. Today a new era is emerging: mobile/on-demand marketing.

marketing concept

A three-part business philosophy: (1) a customer orientation, (2) a service orientation, and (3) a profit orientation.

customer relationship management (CRM)

The process of learning as much as possible about customers and doing everything you can over time to satisfy them—or even exceed their expectations—with goods and services.

The **marketing concept** had three parts:

1. *A customer orientation.* Find out what consumers want and provide it for them. (Note the emphasis on meeting consumer needs rather than on promotion or sales.)

2. *A service orientation.* Make sure everyone in the organization has the same objective: customer satisfaction. This should be a total and integrated organizational effort. That is, everyone from the president of the company to the delivery people should be customer-oriented. Does that seem to be the norm today?

3. *A profit orientation.* Focus on those goods and services that will earn the most profit and enable the organization to survive and expand to serve more consumer wants and needs.

It took awhile for businesses to implement the marketing concept. The process went slowly during the 1960s and 1970s. During the 1980s, businesses began to apply the marketing concept more aggressively than they had done over the preceding 30 years. That led to a focus on customer relationship management (CRM) that has become very important today. We explore that concept next.

In the selling era, the focus of marketing was on selling, with little service afterward and less customization. What economic and social factors made this approach appropriate for the time?

The Customer Relationship Era In the 1990s and early 2000s, some managers extended the marketing concept by adopting the practice of customer relationship management. **Customer relationship management (CRM)** is the process of learning as much as possible about present customers and doing everything you can over time to satisfy them—or even to exceed their expectations—with goods and services.[4] The idea is to enhance customer satisfaction and stimulate long-term customer loyalty. For example, most airlines offer frequent-flier programs that reward loyal customers with free flights. The newest in customer relationship building, as mentioned earlier, involves social media and other online communities. Clearly, consumer dissatisfaction still exists, especially with services such as airlines and cell phone providers. This shows that marketers have a long way to go to create customer satisfaction and loyalty.

The Emerging Mobile/On-Demand Marketing Era The digital age is increasing consumers' power and pushing marketing toward being on demand, not just always "on." Consumers are demanding relevant information exactly when they want it, without all the noise of unwanted messages. Search technologies have made product information pervasive. Consumers share, compare, and rate experiences through social media; and mobile devices make it all available 24/7.[5]

Developments such as inexpensive microtransmitters embedded in products will allow consumers to search by image, voice, or gestures. For example, if your friend has a product you like, you will be able to just tap it with your phone and instantly get product reviews, prices, and so on. If you can't decide what color to buy, you can just send the photo to your Facebook friends who can vote for their favorite. After you buy it, you will get special offers from the manufacturer or its partners for similar products or services.

Universal Art Archive/Alamy Stock Photo

ADAPTING TO CHANGE

Sending the Very Best Online

Gone are the days of checking the mail and finding birthday cards. Even our grandmas don't even seem to send them anymore! Instead, they opt for a quick "Happy Birthday," an emoji or two, and—if we're lucky—a not too embarrassing photo on our Timeline. Social media has changed the way we send birthday cards and holiday greetings so much that e-mail card activity isn't tracked anymore.

So, what happens when a 110-year-old company, like Hallmark, sees this trend threatening to eat at its profits? It pivots. Hallmark is now shifting its focus from mass-produced paper cards to other retail products like gifts and home décor. Additionally, the Hallmark app helps users find products, directs them to nearby brick-and-mortar stores,

3rieart/Shutterstock

and helps them design personal cards. Creations made through the app are then sent directly through Hallmark. Instead of logging in to Facebook, you can send your grandma a picture of your pretty face through snail mail.

Changing the greeting card game isn't the end of it, though. Hallmark has embraced other elements of digital media. Hallmark owns Crown Media Networks, parent company of the Hallmark Channel and Hallmark Movies and Mysteries. Through constantly churning out feel-good movies and holiday specials, Hallmark is keeping its name out there and at the forefront of our minds when we want to connect with loved ones.

Sources: Sharon Terlep, "Hallmark Takes Most Greetings Online," *The Wall Street Journal,* January 30, 2020; Lisette Voytko, "Social Media and E-commerce Hurting Paper Greeting Card Sales, Critics Say," *Forbes,* January 30, 2020; Julia Sachs, "Hallmark Cards Cut around 400 Jobs This Year, but Its Business Is Growing," *Grit Daily,* February 14, 2020; Ron Charles, "Stationery Stores Are in Trouble, but Our Love for Valentine's Day Cards Burns Hotter Than Ever," *The Washington Post,* February 11, 2020.

As digital technology continues to grow, consumer demands are likely to rise in four areas:[6]

1. *Now.* Consumers want to interact anywhere, anytime.
2. *Can I?* They want to do new things with different kinds of information in ways that create value for them. For example, a couple wanting to know if they can afford to buy a house they walk by could simply snap a photo and instantly see the sale price and other property information; at the same, the device automatically accesses their financial information, contacts mortgagers, and obtains loan preapproval.
3. *For me.* Consumers expect all data stored about them to be used to personalize what they experience.
4. *Simple.* Consumers expect all interactions to be easy.

Companies will be looking for employees who can improve the business's handling of social media and customer experiences. The Adapting to Change box discusses a few of the challenges Hallmark faces as it transitions from focusing on greeting cards to an emphasis on digital media.

Nonprofit Organizations and Marketing

Even though the marketing concept emphasizes a profit orientation, marketing is a critical part of almost all organizations, including nonprofits. Charities use marketing to raise funds for combating world hunger, for instance, or to obtain other resources. The American Red Cross uses promotion to encourage people to donate blood when local or national supplies run low. Greenpeace uses marketing to promote ecologically safe technologies. Environmental groups use marketing to try to cut carbon emissions. Churches use marketing to attract new members and raise funds. Politicians use marketing to get votes.

Let's not

Party

Meet up

Bro-hug

Defy

Let's

Stay put

Binge watch

Video-happy-hour

Save lives

Visit **coronavirus.gov** for the latest tips and information from the CDC.

#AloneTogether

TOGETHER, WE CAN HELP SLOW THE SPREAD. ad CDC

The Ad Council sponsors many public service ads, such as this one that encouraged social distancing during the coronavirus pandemic. The idea is to make the public more aware of various issues and to encourage them to get engaged. Have you responded to any Ad Council advertisements?

marketing mix
The ingredients that go into a marketing program: product, price, place, and promotion.

FIGURE 13.2
MARKETING MANAGERS AND THE MARKETING MIX
Marketing managers must choose how to implement the four Ps of the marketing mix: product, price, place, and promotion. The goals are to please customers and make a profit.

States use marketing to attract new businesses and tourists. Many states, for example, have competed to get automobile companies from other countries to locate plants in their area. Schools use marketing to attract new students. Other organizations, such as arts groups, unions, and social groups, also use marketing. The Ad Council, for example, uses public service ads to create awareness and change attitudes on such issues as drunk driving, driving and texting, and fire prevention.

Organizations use marketing, in fact, to promote everything from environmentalism and crime prevention ("Take a Bite Out of Crime") to social issues ("Friends Don't Let Friends Drive Drunk").

LO 13–2 Describe the four Ps of marketing.

The Marketing Mix

We can divide much of what marketing managers do into four factors, called the four Ps to make them easy to remember. They are:

1. Product
2. Price
3. Place
4. Promotion

Managing the controllable parts of the marketing process means (1) designing a want-satisfying product, (2) setting a price for the product, (3) putting the product in a place where people will buy it, and (4) promoting the product. These four factors are called the **marketing mix** because businesses blend them together in a well-designed marketing program (see Figure 13.2).

Marketing Manager

Marketing mix

Product   **Price**   **Place**   **Promotion**

Applying the Marketing Process

The four Ps are a convenient way to remember the basics of marketing, but they don't necessarily include everything that goes into the marketing process for all products. One of the best ways to understand the entire marketing process is to take a product or a group of products and follow the process that led to their development and sale (see Figure 13.3).

Imagine, for example, that you and your friends want to start a moneymaking business near your college. Your preliminary research indicates some demand for fast, fresh, flavorful food that is preservative-free, chemical-free, cage-free, and antibiotic-free. You check the fast-food stores in the area and find that they offer little to no information about the meats and vegetables they use other than proclaiming them to be "fresh." And the vegetables are available only as salads.

You note the farm-to-table trend (documenting the food's path from its start at the farm to your plate on the table) has been growing nationwide. However, it appears in higher-level restaurants and some grocery stores in your area, but not in fast-food restaurants.

You've just performed the first few steps in the marketing process. You noticed an opportunity (a need for healthy, fresh, fast food, perhaps near campus). You conducted some preliminary research to see whether your idea had any merit. And then you identified groups of people who might be interested in your product. They will be your *target market* (the people you will try to persuade to come to your restaurant).

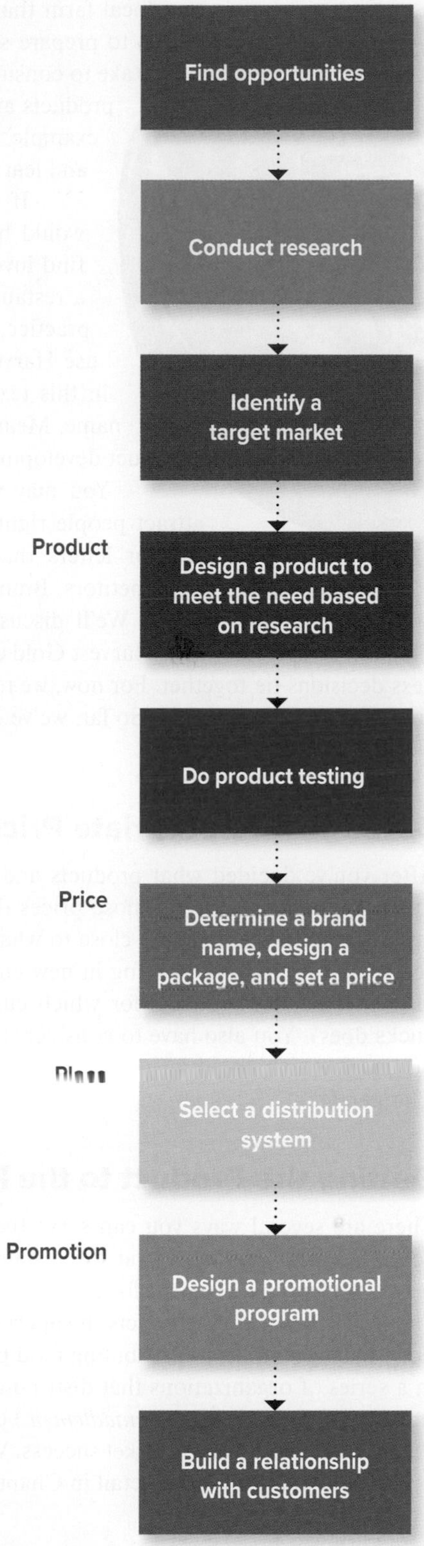

Designing a Product to Meet Consumer Needs

Once you've researched consumer needs and found a target market (which we'll discuss in more detail later) for your product, the four Ps of marketing come into play. You start by developing a product or products. A **product** is any physical good, service, or idea that satisfies a want or need, plus anything that would enhance the product in the eyes of consumers, such as the brand name. In this case, your proposed product is a restaurant that would serve different kinds of fresh, healthy meals at an affordable price.

It's a good idea at this point to do concept testing. That is, you develop an accurate description of your restaurant and ask people, in person or online, whether the idea of the restaurant and the kind of meals you intend to offer appeals to them. If it does, you might

FIGURE 13.3 THE MARKETING PROCESS WITH THE FOUR PS

Find opportunities

Conduct research

Identify a target market

Product

Design a product to meet the need based on research

Do product testing

Price

Determine a brand name, design a package, and set a price

Place

Select a distribution system

Promotion

Design a promotional program

Build a relationship with customers

McGraw Hill **connect**

▶ **iSeeit!** Need help understanding the marketing mix? Visit your Connect eBook to view a video for a brief animated explanation.

product
Any physical good, service, or idea that satisfies a want or need plus anything that would enhance the product in the eyes of consumers, such as the brand name.

A vegetarian restaurant might fill a popular need in the neighborhood of many college campuses today. Is there one near your school? What can you tell about its manager's application of the four Ps of marketing—product, price, place, and promotion?

test marketing
The process of testing products among potential users.

brand name
A word, letter, or group of words or letters that differentiates one seller's goods and services from those of competitors.

promotion
All the techniques sellers use to inform people about and motivate them to buy their products or services.

go to a local farm that offers chemical-free produce to get the ingredients to prepare samples of salads, wraps, and bowls that you can take to consumers to test their reactions. The process of testing products among potential users is called **test marketing**. For example, you can test market your preservative-free dishes and learn how best to prepare them.

If consumers like the products and agree they would buy them, you have the information you need to find investors and look for a convenient location to open a restaurant. You'll have to think of a catchy name. (For practice, stop for a minute and try to think of one.) We'll use Harvest Gold with the tagline "Fresh from the Farm" in this text, although we're sure you can think of a better name. Meanwhile, let's continue with the discussion of product development.

You may want to offer some well-known brand names to attract people right away. A **brand name** is a word, letter, or group of words or letters that differentiates one seller's goods and services from those of competitors. Brand names of clean, organic juice products include Odwalla, Suja, and Naked. We'll discuss the product development process in detail in Chapter 14, and follow the Harvest Gold case to show you how all marketing and other business decisions tie together. For now, we're simply sketching the whole marketing process to give you an overall picture. So far, we've covered the first P of the marketing mix: product. Next comes price.

Setting an Appropriate Price

After you've decided what products and services you want to offer consumers, you have to set appropriate prices. Those prices depend on a number of factors. In the restaurant business, the price could be close to what other restaurants charge to stay competitive. Or you might charge less to bring in new customers, especially at the beginning. Or you may offer high-quality products for which customers are willing to pay a little more (as Starbucks does). You also have to consider the costs of producing, distributing, and promoting the product, which all influence your price. We'll discuss pricing issues in more detail in Chapter 14.

Getting the Product to the Right Place

There are several ways you can serve the market for healthy meals. You can have people come in, sit down, and eat at the restaurant, but that's not the only alternative—think of pizza. You could deliver the food to customers' dorms, apartments, and student unions. You may want to sell your products in supermarkets or health-food stores, or through organizations that specialize in distributing food products. Such intermediaries are the middle links in a series of organizations that distribute goods from producers to consumers. (The more traditional word for them is *middlemen*.) Getting the product to consumers when and where they want it is critical to market success. We'll discuss the importance of marketing intermediaries and distribution in detail in Chapter 15.

Developing an Effective Promotional Strategy

The last of the four Ps of marketing is promotion. **Promotion** consists of all the techniques sellers use to inform people about and motivate them to buy their products or services. Promotion includes advertising; personal selling; public relations; publicity; word of mouth (viral marketing); and various sales promotion efforts, such as coupons, rebates, samples, and cents-off deals.

Promotion often includes relationship building with customers. Among other activities, that means responding to suggestions consumers make to improve the products or their marketing, including price and packaging. For Harvest Gold, post-purchase, or after-sale, service may include refusing payment for meals that weren't satisfactory and stocking additional healthy products customers say they would like. Listening to customers and responding to their needs is the key to the ongoing process that is marketing.

TEST**PREP**

- What does it mean to "help the buyer buy"?
- What are the three parts of the marketing concept?
- What are the four Ps of the marketing mix?

LO 13–3 Summarize the marketing research process.

Providing Marketers with Information

Every decision in the marketing process depends on information. When marketers conduct **marketing research**, they analyze markets to determine opportunities and challenges, and to find the information they need to make good decisions.

Marketing research helps identify what products customers have purchased in the past, and what changes have occurred to alter what they want now and what they're likely to want in the future. Marketers also conduct research on business trends, the ecological impact of their decisions, global trends, and more. Businesses need information to compete effectively, and marketing research is the activity that gathers it. You have learned, for example, how important research is when thinking of starting a healthy fast-food restaurant. Besides listening to customers, marketing researchers also pay attention to what employees, shareholders, dealers, consumer advocates, media representatives, and other stakeholders have to say. As noted earlier, much of that research is now being gathered online through social media. Despite all that research, however, marketers still have difficulty understanding their customers as well as they should.[7]

marketing research
The analysis of markets to determine opportunities and challenges, and to find the information needed to make good decisions.

The Marketing Research Process

A simplified marketing research process consists of at least four key steps:

1. Defining the question (the problem or opportunity) and determining the present situation.
2. Collecting research data.
3. Analyzing the research data.
4. Choosing the best solution and implementing it.

The following sections look at each of these steps.

Defining the Question and Determining the Present Situation Marketing researchers need the freedom to discover what the present situation is, what the problems or opportunities are, what the alternatives are, what information they need, and how to go about gathering and analyzing data.

secondary data

Information that has already been compiled by others and published in journals and books or made available online.

primary data

Data that you gather yourself (not from secondary sources such as books and magazines).

Collecting Data Usable information is vital to the marketing research process. Research can become quite expensive, however, so marketers must often make a trade-off between the need for information and the cost of obtaining it. Normally the least expensive method is to gather information already compiled by others and published in journals and books or made available online.

Such existing data are called **secondary data**, since you aren't the first one to gather them. Figure 13.4 lists the principal sources of secondary marketing research information. Despite the name, *secondary* data are what marketers should gather *first* to avoid incurring unnecessary expense. To find secondary data about the farm-to-table movement, go to 1000ecofarms.com.

Often, secondary data don't provide all the information managers need for important business decisions. To gather additional in-depth information, marketers must do their own research. The results of such *new studies* are called **primary data**. One way to gather primary data is to conduct a survey.

FIGURE 13.4 SELECTED SOURCES OF PRIMARY AND SECONDARY INFORMATION

PRIMARY SOURCES	SECONDARY SOURCES	
Interviews	**Government Publications**	*Census of Transportation*
Surveys	*Statistical Abstract of the United States*	*Annual Survey of Manufacturers*
Observation	*Survey of Current Business*	
Focus groups	*Census of Retail Trade*	
Online surveys		
Questionnaires		
Customer comments		
Letters from customers		
	Commercial Publications	
	Nielsen Company studies on retailing and media	
	J.D. Power offers consumer insights, data, analytics, and advisory services	
	Selling Areas—Marketing Inc. reports on food sales	
	Magazines	
	Entrepreneur *Journal of Retailing*	*Journal of Advertising Research*
	Bloomberg Businessweek *Journal of Consumer Research*	Trade magazines appropriate
	Fortune *Journal of Advertising*	to your industry such as
	Inc. *Journal of Marketing Research*	*Progressive Grocer*
	Ad Age *Marketing News*	Reports from various chambers
	Forbes *Hispanic Business Journal*	of commerce
	Harvard Business Review *Black Enterprise*	
	Journal of Marketing	
	Newspapers	
	The Wall Street Journal, Barron's, your local newspapers	
	Internal Sources	
	Company records Income statements	
	Balance sheets Prior research reports	
	General Sources	
	Internet searches Commercial databases	
	Google-type searches	

Christopher Weddle/Centre Daily Times/TNS/Getty Images

Surveys (online, phone, and mail) and personal interviews are the most common forms of primary data collection. Focus groups (defined below) are another popular method of surveying individuals.[8] What do you think would be the best way to survey students about your potential new restaurant? Would you do a different kind of survey after it had been open a few months? How could you help people find your restaurant? That is, how could you help your buyers buy? One question researchers pay close attention to is: "Would you recommend this product to a friend?"

A **focus group** is a group of people who meet under the direction of a discussion leader to communicate their opinions about an organization, its products, or other given issues. This textbook is updated periodically using many focus groups made up of faculty and students. They tell us, the authors, what subjects and examples they like and dislike, and we follow their suggestions for changes.

Marketers can now gather both secondary and primary data online. For example, we (the authors) do much research online, but we also gather data from books, articles, interviews, and other sources.

focus group

A small group of people who meet under the direction of a discussion leader to communicate their opinions about an organization, its products, or other given issues.

Analyzing the Research Data Marketers must turn the data they collect in the research process into useful information. Careful, honest interpretation of the data can help a company find useful alternatives to specific marketing challenges. For example, by doing primary research, Fresh Italy, a small Italian pizzeria, found that its pizza's taste was rated superior to that of the larger pizza chains. However, the company's sales lagged behind the competition's. Secondary research on the industry revealed that free delivery (which Fresh Italy did not offer) was more important to customers than taste. Fresh Italy now delivers—and has increased its market share.

Choosing the Best Solution and Implementing It After collecting and analyzing data, marketing researchers determine alternative strategies and make recommendations about which may be best and why. This final step in a research effort also includes following up on actions taken to see whether the results were what was expected. If not, the company can take corrective action and conduct new studies in its ongoing attempt to provide consumer satisfaction at the lowest cost. You can see, then, that marketing research is a continuous process of responding to changes in the marketplace and in consumer preferences.

LO 13–4   Show how marketers use environmental scanning to learn about the changing marketing environment.

The Marketing Environment

environmental scanning
The process of identifying the factors that can affect marketing success.

Marketing managers must be aware of the surrounding environment when making marketing mix decisions. **Environmental scanning** is the process of identifying factors that can affect marketing success. As you can see in Figure 13.5, they include global, technological, sociocultural, competitive, and economic influences. We discussed these factors in some detail in Chapter 1, but now let's review them from a strictly marketing perspective.[9]

Global Factors

By going online, businesses can reach many of the world's consumers relatively easily and carry on a dialogue with them about the goods and services they want. The globalization process puts more pressure on those whose responsibility it is to deliver products to these global customers.

Technological Factors

The most important technological changes also relate to the Internet. Using consumer databases, blogs, social media, and the like, companies can develop products and services that closely match consumers' needs.[10] As you read in Chapter 9, firms can now produce customized goods and services for about the same price as mass-produced goods. Thus, flexible manufacturing and mass customization are also major influences on marketers (check out the Spotlight on Small Business box). You can imagine, for example, using databases to help you devise custom-made salads and various dishes for your customers at Harvest Gold.

FIGURE 13.5
THE MARKETING ENVIRONMENT

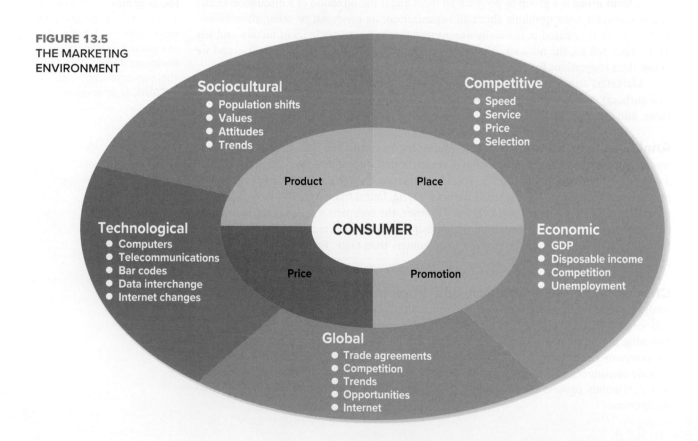

Creating Mass Appeal for a Custom Product

prose.com

Think of some of the most basic items you buy: toothpaste, shampoo, sports drinks, vitamins—the list can go on. It's likely you've bought the same products over and over. But what if you could have sports drinks for the specific way you sweat or a shampoo for your exact hair type? Would you make the switch?

More and more Americans already expect to have a personalized experience when shopping. In fact, 80 percent of customers are more likely to buy from a company that creates customized experiences by following product suggestions. If this process led to products specially made for each of us, marketers could experience huge growth.

Made-to-order hair care products company Prose asks customers 30 questions to better understand their individual needs. Every detail matters to Prose,

Orawan Pattarawimonchai/Shutterstock

not just your hair texture or curl pattern. Where you live, what you eat, your exercise routine, and your styling products all play a factor in what goes into your shampoo. From there, you can also specify if you're looking for vegan or silicone-free products.

This small-scale venture is hoping to grow to become a big business. Not only are these small businesses finding success, but large corporations like PepsiCo

and Procter & Gamble are also starting to break into customization. Maybe soon all of our products will be tailored to us.

Sources: Blake Morgan, "50 Stats Showing the Power of Personalization," *Forbes,* February 18, 2020; Ellen Byron, "We Now Live in a World with Customized Shampoo," *The Wall Street Journal,* April 18, 2019; Alice Chang, "Mastering a Customer-Centric Strategy in the Beauty Industry," *Forbes,* February 21, 2020; "The Vitamin Shoppe Introduces the fitfactor Weight Management System Brand," *Yahoo! Finance,* February 19, 2020; Prose, prose.com, accessed February 2020.

Sociocultural Factors

Marketers must monitor social trends to maintain their close relationship with customers, since population growth and changing demographics can have an effect on sales. One of the fastest-growing segments of the U.S. population is people over 65. The increase in the number of older adults creates growing demand for retirement communities, health care, prescription drugs, recreation, continuing education, and more. Do you see any evidence that older people would enjoy having more locally sourced, farm-fresh meals?

Other shifts in the U.S. population are creating new challenges for marketers as they adjust their products to meet the tastes and preferences of Hispanic, Asian, and other growing ethnicities. To appeal to diverse groups, marketers must listen better and be more responsive to unique ethnic needs. What might you do to appeal to specific groups with Harvest Gold?

Competitive Factors

Of course, marketers must pay attention to the dynamic competitive environment. Brick-and-mortar companies must stay aware of online competition. For example, in the book business Barnes & Noble had to adjust to the reality of Amazon's huge selection of books at good prices. Barnes & Noble answered the challenge from Amazon's Kindle with its own e-reader, the Nook. The company is still fighting to stay alive and trying to avoid the fate of other brick-and-mortar bookstores, such as Borders. Since consumers can literally search the world for the best buys online, marketers must continuously adjust their pricing, delivery, and services accordingly. What opportunities do you see for Harvest Gold to make use of the Internet and social media?

Economic Factors

Marketers must pay close attention to the economic environment. In the early 2000s, the United States was experiencing slow growth, and few customers were eager to buy the most expensive automobiles, watches, and vacations. As the economy slowed, marketers had to adapt by offering products that were less expensive and more tailored to consumers with modest incomes.

What economic changes are occurring around your school that might affect a new restaurant? How would an economic crisis or natural disaster, such as flood or drought, affect your area?

Two Different Markets: Consumer and Business-to-Business (B2B)

consumer market

All the individuals or households that want goods and services for personal consumption or use and have the resources to buy them.

business-to-business (B2B) market

All the individuals and organizations that want goods and services to use in producing other goods and services or to sell, rent, or supply goods to others.

Marketers must know as much as possible about the market they wish to serve. As we defined it in Chapter 6, a market consists of people with unsatisfied wants and needs who have both the resources and the willingness to buy. There are two major markets in business: the *consumer market* and the *business-to-business market*. The **consumer market** consists of all the individuals or households that want goods and services for personal consumption or use and have the resources to buy them.

The **business-to-business (B2B) market** consists of all the individuals and organizations that want goods and services to use in producing other goods and services or to sell, rent, or supply goods to others.[11] Oil-drilling bits, cash registers, display cases, office desks, public accounting audits, and business software are B2B goods and services. Traditionally, they have been known as *industrial* goods and services because they are used in industry.

The important thing to remember is that the buyer's reason for buying—that is, the end use of the product—determines whether a product is a consumer product or a B2B product. A cup of yogurt that a student buys for breakfast is a consumer product. However, when Harvest Gold purchases the same cup of yogurt to sell to its breakfast customers, it has purchased a B2B product. The following sections outline consumer and B2B markets.

?TESTPREP

- What are the four steps in the marketing research process?
- What is environmental scanning?
- What factors are included in environmental scanning?

The business-to-business (B2B) market consists of individuals and organizations that sell goods and services to other businesses. A manufacturer, for instance, buys its parts and supplies in the B2B market.

Luke Sharrett/Bloomberg Creative/Getty Images

LO 13–5 Explain how marketers apply the tools of market segmentation, relationship marketing, and the study of consumer behavior.

The Consumer Market

The total potential consumer market consists of the billions of people in global markets. Because consumer groups differ greatly by age, education level, income, and taste, a business usually can't fill the needs of every group. It must decide which groups to serve, and then develop products and services specially tailored to their needs.

Take the Campbell Soup Company, for example. You know Campbell for its traditional soups such as chicken noodle and tomato. You may also have noticed that Campbell has expanded its U.S. product line to appeal to a number of different tastes. Aware of population growth in the South and in Latino communities in cities across the nation, it introduced a Creole soup for the southern market and a red bean soup for the Latino market. In Texas and California, where people like their food with a bit of kick, Campbell makes its nacho cheese soup spicier than in other parts of the country. It's just one company that has had some success studying the consumer market, breaking it down into categories, and developing products for separate groups.

The process of dividing the total market into groups with similar characteristics is called **market segmentation**. Selecting which groups or segments an organization can serve profitably is **target marketing**. For example, a shoe store may choose to sell only women's shoes, only children's shoes, or only athletic shoes. The issue is finding the right *target market*—the most profitable segment—to serve.

Segmenting the Consumer Market

A firm can segment the consumer market several ways (see Figure 13.6). Rather than selling your product throughout the United States, you might focus on just one or two regions where you can be most successful, say, southern states such as Florida, Texas, and South Carolina. Dividing a market by cities, counties, states, or regions is **geographic segmentation**.

Alternatively, you could aim your product's promotions toward people aged 25 to 45 who have some college education and above-average incomes. Automobiles such as Lexus are often targeted to this audience. Age, income, and education level are criteria for **demographic segmentation**. So are religion, race, and occupation. Demographics are the most widely used segmentation variable, but not necessarily the best.

You may want your ads to portray a target group's lifestyle. To do that, you would study the group's personality, values, and lifestyle in a strategy called **psychographic segmentation**. If you want to target Millennials, you would do an in-depth study of their values and interests, like which shows they watch and which celebrities they like best.[12] With that information you would develop advertisements for those shows using those stars. Some marketers prefer ethnographic segmentation. Basically, using such segmentation resembles using psychographic segmentation in that marketers talk with consumers and learn about the product from their perspective. Often customers have an entirely different view of your product than you do.

In marketing for Harvest Gold, what benefits of fresh, organic food might you talk about? Should you emphasize health benefits, taste, or something else? Determining which product benefits your target market prefers and using those benefits to promote a product is **benefit segmentation**.

You can also determine who are the biggest eaters of healthy food. Does your restaurant seem to attract more men or more women? More students or more faculty members? Are your repeat customers from the local community or are they commuters? Separating the market by volume of product use is called **volume (or usage) segmentation**. Once you know who your customer base is, you can design your promotions to better appeal to that specific group or groups.

market segmentation
The process of dividing the total market into groups whose members have similar characteristics.

target marketing
Marketing directed toward those groups (market segments) an organization decides it can serve profitably.

geographic segmentation
Dividing the market by cities, counties, states, or regions.

demographic segmentation
Dividing the market by age, income, and education level.

psychographic segmentation
Dividing the market using the group's values, attitudes, and interests.

benefit segmentation
Dividing the market by determining which benefits of the product to talk about.

volume (or usage) segmentation
Dividing the market by usage (volume of use).

FIGURE 13.6 MARKET SEGMENTATION

This table shows some of the methods marketers use to divide the market. The aim of segmentation is to break the market into smaller units.

Main Dimension	Sample Variables	Typical Segments
Geographic segmentation	Region	Northeast, Midwest, South, West
	City or county size	Under 5,000; 5,000–10,999; 11,000–19,999; 20,000–49,999; 50,000 and up
	Density	Urban, suburban, rural
Demographic segmentation	Gender	Male, female
	Age	Under 5; 5–10; 11–18; 19–34; 35–49; 50–64; 65 and over
	Education	Some high school or less, high school graduate, some college, college graduate, postgraduate
	Race	Caucasian, African American, Asian, Hispanic
	Nationality	American, Asian, Eastern European, Japanese
	Life stage	Infant, preschool, child, teenager, collegiate, adult, senior
	Income	Under $15,000; $15,000–$24,999; $25,000–$44,999; $45,000–$74,999; $75,000 and over
	Household size	1; 2; 3–4; 5 or more
	Occupation	Professional, technical, clerical, sales supervisor, farmer, student, home-based business owner, retired, unemployed
Psychographic segmentation	Personality	Gregarious, compulsive, extroverted, aggressive, ambitious
	Values	Actualizers, fulfillers, achievers, experiencers, believers, strivers, makers, strugglers
	Lifestyle	Upscale, moderate
Benefit segmentation	Comfort Convenience Durability Economy Health Luxury Safety Status	(Benefit segmentation divides an already established market into smaller, more homogeneous segments. Those people who desire economy in a car would be an example. The benefit desired varies by product.)
Volume segmentation	Usage	Heavy users, light users, nonusers
	Loyalty status	None, medium, strong

The best segmentation strategy is to use all the variables to come up with a consumer profile that represents a sizable, reachable, and profitable target market. That may mean not segmenting the market at all and instead going after the total market (everyone). Or it may mean going after ever-smaller segments. We'll discuss that strategy next.

Reaching Smaller Market Segments

Niche marketing is identifying small but profitable market segments and designing or finding products for them. Because it so easily offers an unlimited choice of goods, online retail transformed a consumer culture once based on big hits and best sellers into one that supports more specialized niche products. With only 5 percent of Americans identifying themselves as vegetarians, what types of vegetarian options do you think Harvest Gold might sell to this niche market?

One-to-one marketing means developing a unique mix of goods and services for each individual customer. Travel agencies often develop such packages, including airline reservations, hotel reservations, rental cars, restaurants, and admission to museums and other attractions for individual customers. This is relatively easy to do in B2B markets where each customer may buy in huge volume. But one-to-one marketing is possible in consumer

iSeeit! Need help understanding how marketers segment target market? Visit your Connect eBook to view a video for a brief animated explanation.

niche marketing
The process of finding small but profitable market segments and designing or finding products for them.

one-to-one marketing
Developing a unique mix of goods and services for each individual customer.

Mia2you/Shutterstock

markets as well. Computer companies like HP, Dell, and Apple can produce a unique computer system for each customer. Can you envision designing special Harvest Gold menu items for individual customers?

Building Marketing Relationships

In the world of mass production following the Industrial Revolution, marketers responded by practicing mass marketing. **Mass marketing** means developing products and promotions to please large groups of people. That is, there is little market segmentation. The mass marketer tries to sell the same products to as many people as possible. That means using mass media such as TV, radio, and online ads to reach them. Although mass marketing led many firms to success, marketing managers often got so caught up with their products and competition that they became less responsive to the market.[13] Airlines, for example, are so intent on meeting competition that they often annoy their customers.

Relationship marketing tends to lead away from mass production and toward custom-made goods and services. The goal is to keep individual customers over time by offering them new products that exactly meet their requirements. Technology and social media enable sellers to work with individual buyers to determine their wants and needs and to develop goods and services specifically designed for them, like hand-tailored shirts and unique vacations. Take a look at the nearby Connecting through Social Media box to see how companies are using their interactions with the customer base to improve and tailor offerings to individuals.

Understanding consumers is so important to marketing that a whole area of marketing has emerged called the study of *consumer behavior.*[14] We explore that area next.

mass marketing
Developing products and promotions to please large groups of people.

relationship marketing
Marketing strategy with the goal of keeping individual customers over time by offering them products that exactly meet their requirements.

The Consumer Decision-Making Process

The first step in the consumer decision-making process is *problem recognition,* which may occur when your computer breaks down and you realize you need a new one. This leads to an *information search*—you look for ads about computers. You may consult a secondary data source like *CNET* or other online reviews from both experts and customers. And you'll likely seek advice from other people who have purchased computers.

After compiling all this information, you *evaluate alternatives* and make a *purchase decision.* But your buying process doesn't end there. After the purchase, you may ask the people you spoke to previously how their machines perform and then do other comparisons to your new computer.

Shuffling Your Style with Stitch Fix

stitchfix.com

It seems every time we use websites to search for information or products, we're asked to subscribe to the site's e-mail list or to provide small bits of information about who we are. Why is that? Marketers are finding that more contact with you and information gathered about you leads to a greater chance of satisfaction on your part and a far greater chance of sales.

The more you engage in discussions of clothing and accessories on Stitch Fix's Facebook page, the more likely you are to venture over to its site and subscribe to its box service. When interest is shown in the box service, customers are asked questions regarding their style and body types, and then they are shown a series of products. Customers then click whether

Sharaf Maksumov/Shutterstock

they like or dislike the different pieces shown. From there, Stitch Fix designs a box of clothing catered to your likes and what will work for you. But the interaction doesn't stop there. By using Style Shuffle, the company can easily collect billions of data points for its customers. This Tinder-like process helps make the shopping and styling process more efficient.

Getting users to make the jump into subscription is the hardest part. Marketers need to

know the difference between a person "liking" something and commenting and interacting with the content providers and other users. Research has shown that people who have a higher level of interaction feel more strongly committed to the company than those who "lurk" or passively consume the information. Online marketers need to design presentations in a way that gets more users into the conversation and thereby learn what their users want to see.

Sources: Adria Cimino, "Can Stitch Fix's 'Shop Your Looks' Become a Major Revenue Driver?," *The Motley Fool*, February 20, 2020; Steven Li, "The Stitch Fix Story: How a Unique Prioritization of Data Science Helped the Company Create Billions in Market Value," *Forbes*, February 17, 2020; Daniel Newman, "Stitch Fix: A Useful Case Study for Retail's Digital Transformation," *Forbes*, September 9, 2019; Dakota Shane, "How to Turn a Single Blog Post into a Month's Worth of Content Marketing," *Inc.*, February 26, 2019; Stitch Fix, stitchfix.com, accessed February 2020.

Marketing researchers investigate these consumer thought processes and behaviors at each stage in a purchase to determine the best way to help the buyer buy. As we mentioned, this area of study is called *consumer behavior.* Factors that affect consumer behavior include the following:

- *Learning* creates changes in an individual's behavior resulting from previous experiences and information. If you've tried a particular brand of shampoo and don't like it, you've learned not to buy it again.

- *Reference group* is the group an individual uses as a reference point in forming beliefs, attitudes, values, or behavior. A college student who carries a briefcase instead of a backpack may use businesspeople as a reference group.

- *Culture* is the set of values, attitudes, and ways of doing things transmitted from one generation to another in a given society. The U.S. culture emphasizes and transmits the values of education, freedom, and diversity.

- *Subculture* is the set of values, attitudes, and ways of doing things that results from belonging to a certain ethnic group, racial group, or other group with which one closely identifies (e.g., teenagers).

- *Cognitive dissonance* is a type of psychological conflict that can occur after a purchase. Consumers who make a major purchase may have doubts about whether they got the best product at the best price. Marketers must reassure such consumers after the sale that they made a good decision. An auto dealer, for example, may send positive press articles about the particular car a consumer purchased, offer product guarantees, and provide certain free services.

Many universities include courses in business-to-business marketing in their business curriculum. As you'll learn next, that market is a huge target for marketers.

iSeeit! Need help understanding the consumer buying process? Visit your Connect eBook to view a video for a brief animated explanation.

LO 13–6 Compare the business-to-business market and the consumer market.

The Business-to-Business Market

Business-to-business (B2B) marketers include manufacturers; intermediaries such as retailers; institutions like hospitals, schools, and nonprofits; and the government. The B2B market is larger than the consumer market because items are often sold and resold several times in the B2B process before they reach the final consumer. B2B marketing strategies also differ from consumer marketing because business buyers have their own decision-making process. Several factors make B2B marketing different, including these:

1. Customers in the B2B market are relatively few; there are just a few large construction firms or mining operations compared to the over 128 million households in the U.S. consumer market.[15]

2. Business customers are relatively large; that is, big organizations account for most of the employment in the production of various goods and services. Nonetheless, there are many small- to medium-sized firms in the United States that together make an attractive market.

3. B2B markets tend to be geographically concentrated. For example, oilfields are found throughout the Southwest and Canada. Thus B2B marketers can concentrate their efforts on a particular area and minimize distribution problems by locating warehouses near industrial centers.

4. Business buyers are generally more rational and less emotional than ultimate consumers; they use product specifications to guide buying choices and often more carefully weigh the total product offer, including quality, price, and service.

5. B2B sales tend to be direct, but not always. Tire manufacturers sell directly to auto manufacturers but use intermediaries, such as wholesalers and retailers, to sell to ultimate consumers.

6. Whereas consumer promotions are based more on *advertising,* B2B sales are based on *personal selling.* There are fewer customers and they usually demand more personal service.

Figure 13.7 shows some of the differences between buying behavior in the B2B and consumer markets. B2B buyers also use online stores to make purchases. You'll learn more about the business-to-business market in advanced marketing courses.

FIGURE 13.7
COMPARING BUSINESS-TO-BUSINESS AND CONSUMER BUYING BEHAVIOR

	Business-to-Business Market	Consumer Market
Market Structure	Relatively few potential customers	Many potential customers
	Larger purchases	Smaller purchases
	Geographically concentrated	Geographically dispersed
Products	Require technical, complex products	Require less technical products
	Frequently require customization	Sometimes require customization
	Frequently require technical advice, delivery, and after-sale service	Sometimes require technical advice, delivery, and after-sale service
	Buyers are trained	No special training
Buying Procedures	Negotiate details of most purchases	Accept standard terms for most purchases
	Follow objective standards	Use personal judgment
	Formal process involving specific employees	Informal process involving household members
	Closer relationships between marketers and buyers	Impersonal relationships between marketers and consumers
	Often buy from multiple sources	Rarely buy from multiple sources

Your Prospects in Marketing

There is a wider variety of careers in marketing than in most business disciplines. If you major in marketing, an array of career options will be available to you. You could become a manager in a retail store like Nordstrom or Target. You could do marketing research or work in product management. You could go into selling, advertising, sales promotion, or public relations. You could work in transportation, storage, or international distribution. You could design websites. These are just a few of the possibilities. Think, for example, of the many ways to use Facebook, Google, and other technologies in marketing. As you read through the following marketing chapters, consider whether a marketing career would interest you.

?TESTPREP

- Can you define the terms *consumer market* and *business-to-business market*?
- Can you name and describe five ways to segment the consumer market?
- What is niche marketing, and how does it differ from one-to-one marketing?
- What are four key factors that make B2B markets different from consumer markets?

SUMMARY

LO 13–1 Define *marketing,* and apply the marketing concept to both for-profit and nonprofit organizations.

- **What is marketing?**

  Marketing is the activity, set of institutions, and processes for creating, communicating, delivering, and exchanging offerings that have value for customers, clients, partners, and society at large.

- **How has marketing changed over time?**

  During the *production era,* marketing was largely a distribution function. Emphasis was on producing as many goods as possible and getting them to markets. By the early 1920s, during the *selling era,* the emphasis turned to selling and advertising to persuade customers to buy the existing goods produced by mass production. After World War II, the tremendous demand for goods and services led to the *marketing concept era,* when businesses recognized the need to be responsive to customers' needs. During the 1990s, marketing entered the *customer relationship era,* focusing on enhancing customer satisfaction and stimulating long-term customer loyalty. Today marketers are using mobile/on-demand marketing to engage customers.

- **What are the three parts of the marketing concept?**

  The three parts of the marketing concept are (1) a customer orientation, (2) a service orientation, and (3) a profit orientation (that is, marketing goods and services that will earn a profit and enable the firm to survive and expand).

- **What kinds of organizations are involved in marketing?**

  All kinds of organizations use marketing, including for-profit and nonprofit organizations like states, charities, churches, politicians, and schools.

LO 13–2 Describe the four Ps of marketing.

- **How do marketers implement the four Ps?**

  The idea behind the four Ps is to design a *product* people want, *price* it competitively, *place* it where consumers can find it easily, and *promote* it so consumers know it exists.

LO 13–3 Summarize the marketing research process.

- **What are the steps in conducting marketing research?**

  (1) Define the problem or opportunity and determine the present situation, (2) collect data, (3) analyze the data, and (4) choose the best solution.

LO 13–4 Show how marketers use environmental scanning to learn about the changing marketing environment.

- **What is environmental scanning?**

  Environmental scanning is the process of identifying factors that can affect marketing success. Marketers pay attention to all the environmental factors that create opportunities and threats.

- **What are some of the more important environmental trends in marketing?**

  The most important global and technological change is probably the growth of online and mobile marketing. Another is the growth of consumer databases, with which companies can develop products and services that closely match consumers' needs. Marketers must monitor social trends like population growth and shifts to maintain their close relationship with customers. They must also monitor the dynamic competitive and economic environments.

LO 13–5 Explain how marketers apply the tools of market segmentation, relationship marketing, and the study of consumer behavior.

- **What are some of the ways marketers segment the consumer market?**

  Geographic segmentation means dividing the market into different regions. Segmentation by age, income, and education level is *demographic segmentation*. We study a group's values, attitudes, and interests using *psychographic segmentation*. Determining which benefits customers prefer and using them to promote a product is *benefit segmentation*. Separating the market by usage is called *volume segmentation*. The best segmentation strategy is to use all the variables to come up with a consumer profile for a target market that's sizable, reachable, and profitable.

- **What is the difference between mass marketing and relationship marketing?**

  Mass marketing means developing products and promotions to please large groups of people. Relationship marketing tends to lead away from mass production and toward custom-made goods and services. Its goal is to keep individual customers over time by offering them products or services that meet their needs.

- **What are some of the factors that influence the consumer decision-making process?**

  Factors that influence the consumer decision-making process include learning, reference group, culture, subculture, and cognitive dissonance.

LO 13–6 Compare the business-to-business market and the consumer market.

- **What makes the business-to-business market different from the consumer market?**

  Customers in the B2B market are relatively few and large. B2B markets tend to be geographically concentrated, and industrial buyers generally are more rational than ultimate consumers in their selection of goods and services. B2B sales tend to be direct, and there is much more emphasis on personal selling than in consumer markets.

KEY TERMS

benefit segmentation 347
brand name 340
business-to-business (B2B)
  market 346
consumer market 346
customer relationship
  management (CRM) 336
demographic
  segmentation 347
environmental
  scanning 344
focus group 343

geographic
  segmentation 347
marketing 334
marketing concept 336
marketing mix 338
marketing research 341
market
  segmentation 347
mass marketing 349
niche marketing 348
one-to-one
  marketing 348

primary data 342
product 339
promotion 340
psychographic
  segmentation 347
relationship
  marketing 349
secondary data 342
target marketing 347
test marketing 340
volume (or usage)
  segmentation 347

CRITICAL THINKING

1. When businesses buy goods and services from other businesses, they usually buy in large volume. Salespeople in the business-to-business market usually are paid on a commission basis; that is, they earn a certain percentage of each sale they make. Why might B2B sales be a more financially rewarding career area than consumer sales?

2. Industrial companies sell goods such as steel, lumber, computers, engines, parts, and supplies. Name, or research, three such companies.

3. What environmental changes are occurring in your community? Is the community still feeling the impact of the economic crisis? What environmental changes in marketing are most likely to change your career prospects in the future? How can you learn more about those changes? What might you do to prepare for them?

4. Which of your needs are not being met by businesses and/or nonprofit organizations in your area? Are there enough people with similar needs to attract an organization that would meet those needs? How would you find out?

PUTTING PRINCIPLES TO WORK

PURPOSE

To demonstrate how the Internet can be used to enhance marketing relationships.

EXERCISE

Nike wants to help its customers add soul to their soles and express their individuality by customizing their own shoes. See for yourself at nike.com. Click "customize" and build a shoe that fits your style.

1. How does Nike's website help the company strengthen its relationships with its stakeholders? Give examples to support your answer.

2. How do the elements of the website reflect Nike's target market?

3. Does Nike invite comments from visitors to its website? If so, how does this affect its attempt to build positive relationships with its customers?

DEVELOPING CAREER SKILLS

KEY: ● **Team**   ★ **Analytic**   ▲ **Communication**   ▣ **Technology**

★ ▲ 1. Think of an effective marketing mix for a new electric car or a brushless car wash for your neighborhood. Be prepared to discuss your ideas in class.

● ★ ▲ 2. Working in teams of five, think of a product or service your friends want but cannot get on or near campus. You might ask your friends at other schools what's available there. What kind of product would fill that need? Discuss your results in class and how you might go about marketing that new product or service.

3. Business has fallen off greatly at your upscale restaurant because of the slow economy. List four things you can do to win back the loyalty of your past customers.

4. Working in teams of four or five, list as many brand names of pizza as you can, including from pizza shops, restaurants, supermarkets, and so on. Merge your list with the lists from other groups or classmates. Then try to identify the target market for each brand. Do they all seem to be after the same market, or are there different brands for different markets? What are the separate appeals?

5. Take a little time to review the concepts in this chapter as they apply to Harvest Gold, the restaurant we used as an example throughout. Have an open discussion in class about (*a*) a different name for the restaurant, (*b*) a location for the restaurant, (*c*) a promotional program, and (*d*) a way to establish a long-term relationship with customers.

CAREER EXPLORATION

If you are interested in pursuing a career in marketing, here are a few to consider. Find out about the tasks performed, skills needed, pay, and opportunity outlook in these fields in the *Occupational Outlook Handbook (OOH)* at bls.gov.

- **Marketing manager**—estimates the demand for a product and identifies markets, as well as develops pricing strategies.
- **Graphic designer**—creates visual concepts, using computer software or by hand, to communicate

ideas that inspire, inform, and captivate consumers; develops visuals for advertisements, brochures, magazines, and corporate reports.

- **Copywriter**—develops written content for advertisements, blogs, or other types of marketing media.
- **Sales manager**—directs sales teams, sets sales goals, analyzes data, and develops training programs for sales representatives.

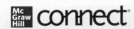 *National Park Service: Using the Four Ps to Help You Find Your Park*

VIDEO CASE

To celebrate its 100th birthday, the United States National Park Service (NPS) decided to host a big party at its 400 parks across the country. To make certain the party was successful, the park service wanted to invite as many Americans as possible to enjoy the festivities. The question NPS faced was, how do you get the word out to millions of Americans not familiar with the nation's parks? The answer: Marketing.

Interestingly, the National Park Service was founded with a public relations campaign created by Stephen Mather, one of the first leaders of NPS. His objective was to encourage Americans to visit the nation's beautiful parks and assist in preserving them for future generations. For many years, the park system was successful and essentially sold itself. During the 1950s and 1960s Americans flocked to the nation's parks and brought home memories and vacation slides that they shared with friends and family.

In the 1970s, the parks remained a destination for Americans to go on vacation. However, as time progressed, newer generations did not share the same experiences or perceptions of the parks. Younger generations, including Millennials and others, had little association with the national parks and instead traveled to many different locations and venues. As the centennial approached, NPS wanted to connect with a new audience of Americans that tended to shun the parks or had little understanding of their scope and majesty. It identified multicultural Millennials as a target audience that it wanted to pursue. The challenge was putting together a program that included a multimedia marketing campaign comprised of several forms of promotion.

The ultimate goal was to create the next generation of parkgoers. NPS also sought to increase the visibility of national parks beyond the most famous parks such as Yosemite and Yellowstone. The cornerstone of the campaign was the website FindYourPark.com. At the site, visitors could search for the parks based specifically on their interests or locations. An active public relations campaign also enhanced media coverage of the marketing plan. NPS was extremely concerned that the marketing campaign not only attract younger audiences, but also remain true to the spirit of NPS and the history it had built over 100 years.

The FindYourPark.com campaign was a resounding success, even beyond the expectations of NPS. Over the centennial year, NPS achieved 16.5 billion public relations impressions and 3 billion media impressions. The hashtag #findyourpark regularly trended on social media and developed 1.2 million followers. The service sold $10 million worth of merchandise and hosted more than 3,000 events across the country. The National Park Foundation raised $341 million in donations, a significant increase from NPS's initial goal of $100 million.

The National Park Service successfully achieved its objectives for celebrating its 100th year by using a full range of marketing activities, including the use of social media and marketing research to enhance its brand. This video highlights how marketing applied correctly can assist any organization in reaching its target market. As long as NPS remains committed to the four Ps of marketing, it can look forward to another century of success showing off the wonders of the U.S. parks.

THINKING IT OVER

1. Why was the use of social media critical in the marketing plan of the National Park Service?

2. Why did NPS limit its use of marketing during the 1960s and 1970s?

3. Why was it important to partner with a public relations firm to develop the marketing campaign?

NOTES

1. Paul Talbot, "Keeping Up with the Ever-Changing Language of Marketing," *Forbes,* February 21, 2020.
2. Forbes Communications Council, "13 Potentially Massive Social Media Trends (and How Marketers Can Use Them)," *Forbes,* February 13, 2020.
3. "10 Reasons Why Online Shoppers Abandon Their Carts," *Media Update,* February 21, 2020.
4. Paul Selby, "CRM: Service for a Bygone Era," *Business 2 Community,* February 21, 2020.
5. Mike de la Cruz, "AI Is Reshaping Consumers' Expectations for Customer Service," *Destination CRM,* February 20, 2020.
6. "Customer Expectations Hit All-Time Highs," Salesforce Research, salesforce.com, accessed February 2020.
7. Brett Dunst, "How Understanding Your Customers' Stories Can Help You Better Tell Your Own," *Forbes,* February 6, 2020.
8. Nick Chasinov, "Why It's a Mistake to Build a Content Strategy around Keywords," *MarTech Advisor,* January 27, 2020.
9. Alasdair Smith, "How to Prepare a Marketing Environmental Analysis," *Houston Chronicle,* chron.com, accessed February 2020.
10. Jessica Wong, "How to Get the Most out of Your Brand's Social Media Campaign," *Forbes,* February 11, 2020.
11. Mike Neumeier, "B2B Technology Marketing Trends to Watch for in 2020," *Forbes,* February 21, 2020.
12. Syed Balkhi, "4 Business Values That Appeal to the Millennial Market," *Ad Age,* January 31, 2020.
13. Suzie Ocie, "Niche to Mainstream: Industries Cracking the Mass Market," *Influencive,* February 23, 2020.
14. Kelly Dotson, "Consumer Behavior Matters More Than Sales Trends," *MarTech Advisor,* January 29, 2020; Alexandra Pastore, "New Study Analyzes Consumer Behavior at Point of Return," *Women's Wear Daily,* February 19, 2020.
15. U.S. Census Bureau, census.gov, accessed February 2020.

14

Developing and Pricing Goods and Services

After you have read and studied this chapter, you should be able to

LO 14–1 Describe a total product offer.

LO 14–2 Identify the various kinds of consumer and industrial goods.

LO 14–3 Summarize the functions of packaging.

LO 14–4 Contrast *brand, brand name,* and *trademark,* and show the value of brand equity.

LO 14–5 Explain the steps in the new-product development process.

LO 14–6 Describe the product life cycle.

LO 14–7 Identify various pricing objectives and strategies.

Katrina Lake, Founder of Stitch Fix

Since the early days of e-commerce, clothing companies have struggled to re-create the in-store shopping experience through their online retail platforms. After all, many consumers prefer to feel the fabric and try things on before making any purchasing decisions. Thanks to the entrepreneurial efforts of Katrina Lake, people who want a classic retail experience from the comfort of their homes can get exactly that through Stitch Fix. This start-up relies on an army of stylists and sophisticated algorithms to curate and ship personalized selections of clothing for millions of customers. People can buy the items they like and send the rest back, an innovative business model that has helped Stitch Fix sell more than $5 billion worth of clothes.

For most of her life Lake never thought that she would start a business. Growing up in San Francisco and Minnesota, she describes her personality as risk-averse but imaginative. "Creativity was definitely a big part of our household, and I remember always writing stories and being encouraged to be creative," said Lake. Enrolling at Stanford University for her undergraduate degree, she initially majored in premed studies with the goal of becoming a doctor. The idea of having a steady profession appealed to the naturally cautious Lake, but eventually she switched to economics after being drawn in by the vast possibilities offered by statistics and data. Once she earned her degree, Lake got a consulting job at the Parthenon Group, a firm that analyzes data for many businesses including restaurants and retailers.

Consulting allowed Lake to combine her creative skills with her analytical expertise in order to solve all sorts of problems facing modern companies. "I loved analyzing businesses and getting to understand how they worked," said Lake. "I thought there were so many interesting challenges in apparel retail. People were trying to figure out what is the role of stores in the future, and how does e-commerce fit in?" After consulting for two years, Lake got tired of advising innovative companies and instead wanted to work for one. She joined a venture capital firm hoping to "meet the entrepreneur creating the retailer of the future" but was disappointed to find that not many others shared her vision. In Lake's mind, the apparel market was due for a major shake-up since many retailers were failing to meet the current needs of their customers. "I was like, there's no way that the future of buying jeans is going to be spending a day at the mall or even searching online," said Lake. "Searching online for jeans is a ridiculously bad experience. And I realized that if I imagined a different future, I could create it, so I applied to business school."

Lake enrolled at Harvard Business School with the goal of developing a company that could combine the best aspects of online retail and physical stores in order to create a unique and effective shopping experience. "And if I wasn't able to do that, worst case scenario I'd have an MBA and I could go work at a great company," said Lake. "For me, that was a way to buy time and space to launch a business." With her bases carefully covered, Lake started Stitch Fix during her second year at Harvard as a personal shopping service for all types of consumers. In the beginning, she had her friends fill out style surveys that she then analyzed and used to buy clothing that they might like. Lake's recommendations worked, and soon her company began to grow. By 2011, a venture capitalist had enough faith in her idea to invest $750,000, allowing Lake to purchase office space and hire more staff.

Soon the company was sending out thousands of "fixes" per month, referring to the boxes of clothing that customers receive after filling out a style survey. The concept of Stitch Fix is simple to explain but exceedingly difficult to execute. In-house stylists use their own expertise plus data analytics to gather a selection of clothing that customers might like based on the results of their style survey. After receiving their "fix" in the mail, the customers then select which items they would like to buy and send back the rejects. Developing and perfecting this system required years of trial and error as Lake and her colleagues pored over ever-growing mountains of data. Still, this challenging road allowed Stitch Fix to grow into a powerful retail force that now serves more than three million clients and earns more than $1 billion annually. Lake says that the company's commitment to personalization will allow it to continue growing for years to come. "If Amazon is the everything store, we are in some ways almost the antithesis of that," said Lake. "I think our focus on personalization, our focus on apparel, our focus on recommendations . . . is what's going to differentiate us."

Like Katrina Lake, the entrepreneurs that command the business world are innovative pioneers. In this chapter, you'll learn all about how entrepreneurs develop and price new products and services. You will also learn about packaging, branding, and other elements of a total product offer.

Sources: Lauren Smiley, "Stitch Fix's Radical Data-Driven Way to Sell Clothes—$1.2 Billion Last Year—Is Reinventing Retail," *Fast Company,* fastcompany.com, February 19, 2019; Ana Colón, "How Going Viral Taught Katrina Lake to Embrace Being a 'Female CEO,'" *Glamour,* glamour.com, September 5, 2019; Layne Winn, "Stitch Fix Founder Katrina Lake on Shaking Up the Retail Apparel Industry," *ABC News,* abcnews.go.com, December 20, 2019; Sarah Spellings, "How I Get It Done: Stitch Fix CEO Katrina Lake," *The Cut,* thecut.com, December 30, 2019; Rebecca Jarvis and Taylor Dunn, "Why Stitch Fix CEO Katrina Lake Turned Down a Multimillion-Dollar Offer," *GMA,* goodmorningamerica.com, January 20, 2020; Stitch Fix, stitchfix.com, accessed March 2020; Tracey Lien, "How I Made It: Stitch Fix Founder Katrina Lake Built One of the Few Successful E-commerce Subscription Services," *Los Angeles Times,* June 9, 2017.

Let's talk business!
bit.ly/LetsTalkBusiness14

Dia Dipasupil/Getty Images

LO 14–1 Describe a total product offer.

Product Development and the Total Product Offer

Global managers will continue challenging U.S. managers with new products at low prices.[1] The best way to compete is to design and promote better products, meaning products that customers perceive to have the best **value**—good quality at a fair price. One of the American Marketing Association's definitions of marketing says it's "a set of processes for creating, communicating, and delivering *value* to customers." When consumers calculate the value of a product, they look at the benefits and then subtract the cost (price) to see whether the benefits exceed the costs, including the cost of driving to the store (or shipping fees if they buy the product online). You may have noticed many restaurants pushed value and dollar menus when the economy slowed. John Mackey of Whole Foods says that Trader Joe's offers customers great *value* every day rather than have frequent sales, as many retailers do.

Whether consumers perceive a product as the best value depends on many factors, including the benefits they seek and the service they receive. To satisfy consumers, marketers must learn to listen better and constantly adapt to changing market demands.[2] Marketers have learned that adapting products to new competition and new markets is an ongoing need. We're sure you've noticed menu changes at your local fast-food restaurants over time. An organization can't do a one-time survey of consumer wants and needs, design a group of products to meet those needs, put them in the stores, and then just relax. It must constantly monitor changing consumer wants and needs, and adapt products, policies, and services accordingly. For example, consumers are looking for healthier food choices today than in the past. Following customer requests for smaller portions, McDonald's now offers value meals with a choice of sandwich, fries, and drink sizes. It also transitioned some popular morning items into an all-day breakfast menu.

McDonald's and other restaurants are constantly trying new ideas. Are you ready to try *Snackin' Bacon* or *Beyond Meat's Sausage Breakfast Sandwich* at your local Dunkin'?[3] Many other restaurants have gotten into the plant-based meat game. Burger King and White Castle have rolled out *Impossible* offerings while McDonald's and Taco Bell are testing *Beyond* options.[4] Have you noticed any other fast-food restaurants offering plant-based menus?

Of course, McDonald's continues to try out more new ideas. For example, in Kokomo, Indiana, McDonald's tried using servers and a more varied menu. In New York, it offered Donut Sticks to compete with Krispy Kreme. In Hawaii, it tried a Spam breakfast platter, and in Columbus, Ohio, a mega-McDonald's had a karaoke booth. See the Connecting through Social Media box for an example of a company using Instagram to create new products.

McDonald's is challenging Starbucks and Dunkin' for the coffee market. What was Starbucks's answer to the new challenges? It began offering more food products. The expanded menu includes Starbucks's own pastries, egg bites, and juices. Oatmeal has become a huge

value
Good quality at a fair price. When consumers calculate the value of a product, they look at the benefits and then subtract the cost to see if the benefits exceed the costs.

Becoming Insta-Worthy Bridesmaids

birdygrey.com

VHarasymiv/Shutterstock

We're all guilty of spending a bit too much time scrolling Instagram throughout the day. What we might not be aware of, however, is how beneficial that can be for some businesses. While we're tapping through Stories and sliding through polls, companies like Birdy Grey are gathering data on what its customers *really* want.

The founders of Birdy Grey, Grace Lee and Monica Ashauer, have been bridesmaids more than a dozen times—they know a thing or two about what bridesmaids want and need. From dresses to accessories, these ladies have seen it all. They have also seen the changing trends and color palettes. Above all, they have seen money fly out of their bank accounts to buy all these items. They founded Birdy Grey to give

brides an affordable (every dress is $99), yet fashion-forward option to offer their bridesmaids.

By utilizing Instagram, Birdy Grey can figure out what colors brides were looking for and get input on what swatches are appealing and which are not. In 2018, Grace Lee reported getting tons of DMs asking for "dusty blue." But what shade of dusty blue

were they looking for? Lee used the polling feature in the company's Story to post several swatches and get feedback directly from the customers. Since employing this Instagram strategy, Birdy Grey has dressed over 100,000 bridesmaids and is starting to branch out into other bridal products—testing them on Instagram first, of course.

Sources: Katie Richards, "Birdy Grey Is Using Instagram Polls to Develop Some of Its Best-Selling Products," *Glossy,* February 25, 2020; Remi Rosmarin, "10 Cool Brands and Products We Were Introduced to by Social Media and Ended Up Loving in Real Life," *Business Insider,* February 5, 2020; Katie Richards, "How Birdy Grey Drove $2 Million in Revenue by Spending $10 a Day on Instagram," *Glossy,* December 19, 2019; Birdy Grey, birdygrey.com, accessed February 2020.

success there as well. Have you seen the Starbucks displays in your local supermarket? Starbucks is reaching out to many new distributors with its products.

Offerings may differ in various locations, according to the wants of the local community. In Iowa pork tenderloin is big, but in Oklahoma City it's tortilla scramblers. Globally, companies must adapt to local tastes. At Bob's Big Boy in Thailand, you can get Tropical Shrimp; at Carl's Jr. in Mexico, you can order the Machaca Burrito; and at Shakey's Pizza in the Philippines, you can get Cali Shandy, a Filipino beer. Product development, then, is a key activity in any modern business, anywhere in the world.

You can imagine what could happen when your product loses some of its appeal. Zippo lighters, for example, lost market strength as people turned away from smoking cigarettes to using e-cigarettes. Zippo, therefore, tried offering items such as knives, leather products, apparel, and candles.[5]

Who would have guessed that Budweiser could someday be available from a Keurig machine?[6] Anheuser-Busch InBev established a partnership with the coffeemaker to do just that. And who would have expected watchmakers, like Piaget and Swatch (Omega and Breguet), to push jewelry in their stores? It's all part of a movement across the world to offer consumers new products.

Distributed Product Development

The increase in outsourcing and alliance building has resulted in innovation efforts that often require using multiple organizations separated by cultural, geographic, and legal

distributed product development

Handing off various parts of your innovation process—often to companies overseas.

boundaries. **Distributed product development** is the term used to describe handing off various parts of your innovation process—often to companies overseas. It's difficult enough to coordinate processes within a firm, and it becomes substantially more difficult when trying to coordinate multi-firm processes. Great care must be taken to establish goals and procedures and standards before any such commitment is made. One company that has collaborated with many other firms to make innovative products is 3M Company. It has developed thousands of products from Scotch tape to Thinsulate, and many of those are embedded in other products such as the iPhone and Samsung Galaxy.[7]

total product offer

Everything that consumers evaluate when deciding whether to buy something; also called a *value package*.

Developing a Total Product Offer From a strategic marketing viewpoint, a product is more than just the physical good or service. A **total product offer** (also called a *value package*) consists of everything consumers evaluate when deciding whether to buy something. Thus, the basic product or service may be a washing machine, an insurance policy, or a beer, but the total product offer includes some or all of the *value enhancers* in Figure 14.1. You may hear some people call the basic product the "core product" and the total product offer the "augmented product." Can you see how sustainability can be part of the augmented product?[8]

When people buy a product, they may evaluate and compare total product offers on many dimensions. Some are tangible (the product itself and its package); others are intangible (the producer's reputation and the image created by advertising). A successful marketer must begin to think like a consumer and evaluate the total product offer as a collection of impressions created by all the factors listed in Figure 14.1. It's wise to talk with consumers to see which features and benefits are most important to them and which value enhancers they want or don't want in the final offering. Frito-Lay, for example, had to drop biodegradable bags in the United States because they were "too noisy." Who would think of such a thing when developing a product?

FIGURE 14.1 POTENTIAL COMPONENTS OF A TOTAL PRODUCT OFFER

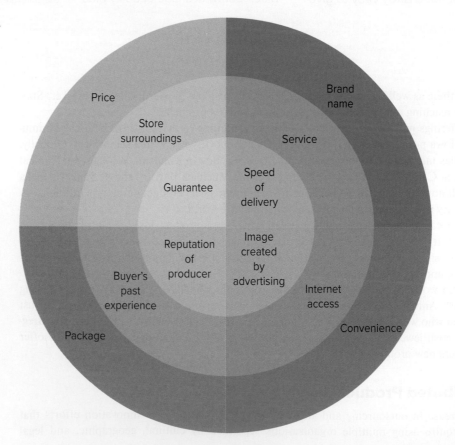

What questions might you ask consumers when developing the total product offer for Harvest Gold? (Recall the business idea we introduced in Chapter 13.) Remember, store surroundings are important in the restaurant business, as are the parking lot and the condition of bathrooms.

Sometimes an organization can use low prices to create an attractive total product offer. For example, outlet stores offer brand-name goods for less. Shoppers like getting high-quality goods and low prices, but they must be careful. Outlets also carry lower-quality products with similar but not exactly the same features as goods carried in regular stores. Different consumers may want different total product offers, so a company must develop a variety of offerings.

Westend61/Getty Images

Product Lines and the Product Mix

Companies usually don't sell just one product. A **product line** is a group of products that are physically similar or intended for a similar market. They usually face similar competition. In one product line, there may be several competing brands. Notice, for example, Diet Coke, Diet Coke with Splenda, Diet Coke with Lemon, Diet Coke with Lime, Diet Vanilla Coke, and Diet Cherry Coke. Now Coca-Cola is creating even more flavor options through its Coke Freestyle machines.[9] Makes it kind of hard to choose, doesn't it? Both Coke and Pepsi have added water and sports drinks to their product lines to meet new consumer tastes.

Procter & Gamble (P&G) has many brands in its laundry detergent product line, including Tide, Era, Downy, and Gain. P&G's product lines together make up its **product mix**, the combination of all product lines offered by a manufacturer. Have you noticed that there are more than 300 different types of toothpastes available in stores? Do you think that is too many or not?

Service providers have product lines and product mixes as well. A bank or credit union may offer a variety of services from savings accounts, automated teller machines, and computer banking to money market funds, safe deposit boxes, car loans, mortgages, online banking, and insurance.[10] AT&T combines services (communications) with goods (phones) in its product mix, with special emphasis on wireless products.

LO 14–2 Identify the various kinds of consumer and industrial goods.

Product Differentiation

Product differentiation is the creation of real or perceived product differences. Actual product differences are sometimes quite small, so marketers must use a creative mix of branding, pricing, advertising, and packaging (value enhancers) to create a unique, attractive image. Note the positive effect of developing brands like Peloton, Stitch Fix, and Shopify.[11] Various bottled water companies have successfully attempted product differentiation. The companies made their bottled waters so attractive through branding, pricing, packaging, and promotion that now restaurant customers often order water by brand name.

There's no reason why you couldn't create a similar attractive image for Harvest Gold, your farm-to-table restaurant. Small businesses can often win market share with creative product differentiation. One yearbook entrepreneur competes by offering multiple clothing changes, backgrounds, and poses along with special allowances, discounts, and guarantees. His small business has the advantage of being more flexible in adapting to customer needs and wants, and he's able to offer attractive product options. He has been so successful that companies use him as a speaker at photography conventions. How could you respond creatively to the consumer wants of your Harvest Gold customers? Note the success that companies have had using the term *organic* or *natural* in their promotions.

Apple, Samsung, and other smartphone makers are fighting for a greater share of the huge mobile market. Each continues to improve and add features hoping to win customers. What features would a smartphone company have to add to its product offer in order to convince you to switch phones or carriers?

 connect

 iSeeit! Need help understanding total product offer? Visit your Connect eBook to view a video for a brief animated explanation.

product line
A group of products that are physically similar or are intended for a similar market.

product mix
The combination of product lines offered by a manufacturer.

product differentiation
The creation of real or perceived product differences.

Marketing Different Classes of Consumer Goods and Services

One popular classification of consumer goods and services has four general categories—convenience, shopping, specialty, and unsought.

convenience goods and services

Products that the consumer wants to purchase frequently and with a minimum of effort.

1. **Convenience goods and services** are products the consumer wants to purchase frequently and with a minimum of effort, like candy, gum, milk, snacks, gas, and banking services. One store that sells mostly convenience goods is 7-Eleven. Location, brand awareness, and image are important for marketers of convenience goods and services. The Internet has taken convenience to a whole new level, especially for banks and other service companies.

shopping goods and services

Those products that the consumer buys only after comparing value, quality, price, and style from a variety of sellers.

2. **Shopping goods and services** are products the consumer buys only after comparing value, quality, price, and style from a variety of sellers. Target is one store that sells mostly shopping goods. Because many consumers carefully compare such products, marketers can emphasize price differences, quality differences, or some combination of the two. Think of how the Internet has helped you find the right shopping goods.[12] Think also of how people compare prices at competing wireless carriers.

specialty goods and services

Consumer products with unique characteristics and brand identity. Because these products are perceived as having no reasonable substitute, the consumer puts forth a special effort to purchase them.

3. **Specialty goods and services** are consumer products with unique characteristics and brand identity. Because consumers perceive that specialty goods have no reasonable substitute, they put forth a special effort to purchase them. Examples include fine watches, expensive wines, designer clothes, jewelry, imported chocolates, and services provided by medical specialists or business consultants. Specialty goods are often marketed through specialty magazines. Specialty skis may be sold through sports magazines and specialty foods through gourmet magazines. Again, the Internet helps buyers find specialty goods. In fact, some specialty goods can be sold exclusively online.

unsought goods and services

Products that consumers are unaware of, haven't necessarily thought of buying, or find that they need to solve an unexpected problem.

4. **Unsought goods and services** are products consumers are unaware of, haven't necessarily thought of buying, or suddenly find they need to solve an unexpected problem. They include emergency car-towing services, burial services, and insurance.

industrial goods

Products used in the production of other products. Sometimes called *business goods* or *B2B goods*.

When you're in a hurry and need something quickly, convenience stores offer a variety of goods that you can get in a pinch. What convenience goods do you buy, and where do you find them?

Sorbis/Shutterstock

The marketing task varies according to the category of product; convenience goods are marketed differently from specialty goods. The best way to promote convenience goods is to make them readily available and create the proper image. Some combination of price, quality, and service is the best appeal for shopping goods. Specialty goods rely on reaching special market segments through advertising. Unsought goods such as life insurance often rely on personal selling. Car towing relies heavily on online review sites, such as Yelp.

Whether a good or service falls into a particular class depends on the individual consumer. Coffee can be a shopping good for one consumer, while a gourmet roast is a specialty good for another. Some people shop around to compare different dry cleaners, so dry cleaning is a shopping service for them. Others go to the closest store, making it a convenience service. Marketers must carefully monitor their customer base to determine how consumers perceive their products.

Marketing Industrial Goods and Services

Many goods could be classified as consumer goods or industrial goods, based on their uses. A computer kept at home for personal use is clearly a consumer good. But in a commercial setting, such as an accounting firm or manufacturing plant, the same computer is an industrial good.

Industrial goods (sometimes called *business goods* or *B2B goods*) are products used in the production of other products. They are sold in the business-to-business (B2B) market. Some products can be both consumer and industrial goods.[13] We've just mentioned how computers fit in both categories. As a consumer good, a computer might be sold through electronics stores or configured by the end user online. Most of the promotion would be advertising. As an industrial good, personal computers are more likely to be sold through salespeople or online. Advertising is less of a factor when selling industrial goods. Thus, you can see that classifying goods by user category helps marketers determine the proper marketing mix strategy.

Figure 14.2 shows some categories of both consumer goods and industrial goods and services. *Installations* consist of major capital equipment such as new factories and heavy machinery. *Capital items* are expensive products that last a long time. A new factory building is both a capital item as well as an installation. *Accessory equipment* consists of capital items that are not quite as long-lasting or expensive as installations—like computers, copy machines, and various tools. Various categories of industrial goods are shown in the figure.

> Many goods could be classified as consumer goods or industrial goods, based on their uses. For example, a computer that a person uses at home for personal use would clearly be a consumer good. But that same computer used in a commercial setting, such as a farm, would be classified as an industrial good. What difference does it make how a good is classified?

pressmaster/123RF.com

Odua Images/Shutterstock

FIGURE 14.2 VARIOUS CATEGORIES OF CONSUMER AND INDUSTRIAL GOODS AND SERVICES

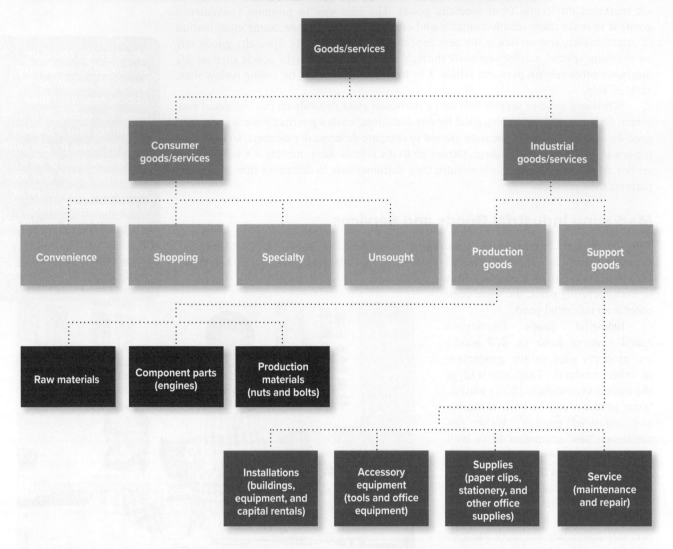

?TESTPREP

- What value enhancers may be included in a total product offer?
- What's the difference between a product line and a product mix?
- Name the four classes of consumer goods and services, and give examples of each.
- Describe three different types of industrial goods.

LO 14–3 Summarize the functions of packaging.

Packaging Changes the Product

We've said that consumers evaluate many aspects of the total product offer, including the brand. It's surprising how important packaging can be in such evaluations of various goods. Many companies have used packaging to change and improve their basic product. We have squeezable ketchup bottles that stand upside down; square paint cans with screw tops and integrated handles; plastic bottles for motor oil that eliminate the need for funnels; single-use packets of spices; and so forth. Another interesting trend is packaging designed to evoke emotions by prompting customers to think of homemade treats. The goal is to have the customers' warm feelings about the homemade product transfer to the commercial product. Peggy Jean's Pies uses jelly jars to ship its ready-to-eat pies, and cookies from Thelma's Treats come in a box resembling Grandma's oven.[14]

In each case, the package changed the product in consumers' minds and opened large new markets. Do you sometimes have difficulty opening plastic packaging? Which packaging innovations do you like best? Can you see some market potential in developing better packaging? Packaging has even become a profession. Check out the Michigan State University School of Packaging, for example. Packages must perform the following functions:[15]

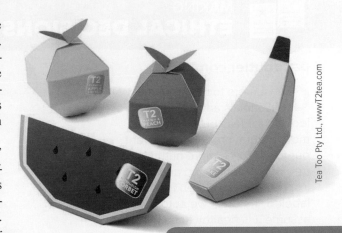

1. Attract the buyer's attention.
2. Protect the goods inside, stand up under handling and storage, be tamperproof, and deter theft.
3. Be easy to open and use.
4. Describe and give information about the contents.
5. Explain the benefits of the good inside.
6. Provide information on warranties, warnings, and other consumer matters.
7. Give some indication of price, value, and uses.

Innovative packaging can make a great product look even better, like these fruit snack boxes that look like pieces of fruit. Can you think of any other food brands that use interesting packaging?

Packaging can also make a product more attractive to retailers. The Universal Product Codes (UPCs) on many packages help stores control inventory. They combine a bar code and a preset number that gives the retailer information about the product's price, size, color, and other attributes. In short, packaging changes the product by changing its visibility, usefulness, or attractiveness.

One relatively new packaging technology for tracking products is the radio frequency identification (RFID) chip, especially the ones made with nanoparticle powder. When attached to a product, the chip sends out signals telling a company where the product is at all times. RFID chips carry more information than bar codes, don't have to be read one at a time (whole pallets can be read in an instant), and can be read at a distance.[16]

The Growing Importance of Packaging

Packaging has always been an important aspect of the product offer, but today it's carrying more of the promotional burden than in the past. Many products once sold by salespersons are now sold in self-service outlets, and the package has acquired more sales responsibility. The Fair Packaging and Labeling Act was passed to give consumers much more quantity and value information on product packaging. The Food and Drug Administration (FDA) recently changed its requirements for the nutrition labels on food products. In addition to the serving-size nutrition facts, there's now a breakdown of the nutritional value of the entire package. Focus was also put more on vitamin D, potassium, and the different types of fats in the product.[17] Proper labeling of food products has been a source of confusion for many American consumers. Not all we read on packaging may be quite what it seems (see the Making Ethical Decisions box).

Packaging may make use of a strategy called **bundling**, which combines goods and/or services for a single price. Icelandair has bundled layover tours with an Icelandair employee "stopover buddy" in its total product offer. In the incredibly popular program, transatlantic passengers can opt to spend their layover seeing the sights of Reykjavik instead of just the airport.[18] Financial institutions are offering everything from financial advice to help in purchasing insurance, stocks, bonds, mutual funds, and more. When combining goods

bundling

Grouping two or more products together and pricing them as a unit.

pacebutler.com

Consumers today, especially Millennials and Gen Zers, are looking for less processed and more natural products. We want our foods to be more nutritious, free of hormones and antibiotics, and healthy. When food is labeled "natural," we automatically assume it is healthy and nutritious. However, the term *natural* can often make our shopping more confusing. Currently, there are no federal regulations through the Food and Drug Administration (FDA) defining the word *natural* for manufacturers or consumers. That means some of the things we buy believing to be free of artificial preservatives or chemical compounds are not.

Investigative teams have found that products like "pure and 100% natural" vegetable oil and "natural" fruit cups were produced using genetically engineered soybeans or contained potassium sorbate, an artificial preservative. The phony "natural" label doesn't just encompass the stuff we put in our mouths; it also covers the products we use to clean our homes, including the

Keith Homan/Shutterstock

kitchen. Manufacturers of household cleaners are not yet required by law to list their ingredients. So that "green" cleaner you use on your countertops could be no different than the traditional spray left sitting on the store shelf.

The FDA is considering defining *natural* to eliminate consumer confusion and to give people the opportunity to really understand what they're buying. But in the meantime, people are left wondering if something is truly "natural." What if you found a popular product you were serving at Harvest Gold wasn't as "natural" as you thought? Would you still sell it as is? Would you relabel it and sell it? Or would you remove it from your store? What might be the consequences of each alternative?

Sources: Marty Gonzalez, "Take the Confusion out of Food Labels," *KRON4 News,* February 22, 2020; Ron Sterk, "Craving, Indulgence Drive Consumption Even as Consumers Seek to Avoid Sugar," *Food Business News,* February 26, 2020; Stephen Lamb, "Why We Need Mandatory Labeling of GMO Products," *STAT,* February 19, 2020; Melissa Erickson, "Food Labels vs. Marketing Claims," *Times-Herald Record,* January 21, 2020.

or services into one package, marketers must not include so much that the price gets too high. It's best to work with customers to develop value enhancers that meet their individual needs.

LO 14–4 Contrast *brand, brand name,* and *trademark,* and show the value of brand equity.

Branding and Brand Equity

brand

A name, symbol, or design (or combination thereof) that identifies the goods or services of one seller or group of sellers and distinguishes them from the goods and services of competitors.

A **brand** is a name, symbol, or design (or combination thereof) that identifies the goods or services of one seller or group of sellers and distinguishes them from the goods and services of competitors. The word *brand* includes practically all means of identifying a product. As we noted in Chapter 13, a *brand name* consists of a word, letter, or group of words or letters that differentiates one seller's goods and services from those of competitors. Brand names

REACHING BEYOND OUR BORDERS

What's in a Name?

oreo.com

So, you've developed a product and you're ready to take it on the market. What should you call it? America's favorite cookie, Oreo, is said to be a great name because the two O's nicely mirror the shape of the cookie itself. Could the name be part of the charm? Think of other names that come to your mind when you think of North American products: Coke, Nike, and Lululemon.

Canadian athleisure powerhouse Lululemon got its name when its founder was looking for a unique name that couldn't be easily replicated in foreign markets. By creating a name that could be difficult to say in some countries, he thought he could possibly avoid potential knockoffs. There is no Japanese phonetic sound for "L," so the three "L's" in *Lululemon* make it sound North American and authentic to Japanese consumers.

1989studio/Shutterstock

Have you ever thought about why Gap has such an unusual name? It's actually a reference to its largest customer base—those in the gap of being a kid and an adult. And what if you know nothing about the industry you're jumping into? Richard Branson went with *Virgin*.

At one time, creating a business name was relatively simple. Now, with a couple hundred countries on the cyber-platform, choosing

the right name is a global issue. For example, when Russian gas company Gazprom formed a joint venture with Nigeria's NNPC, the company was called NiGaz. Not a great name, we'd say.

Every once in a while, a successful name is created by accident. *Google* is a good example. The global search engine was supposed to be called *Googol* (a scientific name for 1 followed by 100 zeros). However, the founders made a typo when registering the domain name. The error resulted in a warm, catchy, human-sounding name. Some mistakes turn out to be luckier than others.

Sources: Phil Davis, "8 Mistakes to Avoid When Naming Your Business," *Entrepreneur,* January 14, 2020; Elaine Pofeldt, "Not Sure If You've Picked a Winning Name for Your Business? Here's How to Take the Risk out of Branding It," *Forbes,* September 30, 2019; Coeli Carr, "What's in a Name? A Business, It Turns Out," *Entrepreneur,* entrepreneur.com, accessed February 2020; Jeffrey Gabriel, "6 Things You Need to Consider When Appraising a Domain Name," *Forbes,* February 25, 2020.

you may be familiar with include Red Bull, Sony, Campbell's, Levi's, GE, Budweiser, Disney, and of course many more. Brand names give products a distinction that tends to make them attractive to consumers. Apple and Google now reign as brand champions—we're sure you understand why.[19] The Reaching beyond Our Borders box discusses product names in more depth.

A **trademark** is a brand that has exclusive legal protection for both its brand name and its design. Trademarks like McDonald's golden arches are widely recognized and help represent the company's reputation and image. McDonald's might sue to prevent a company from selling, say, McDonnel hamburgers. Did you know there once was a Starsbuck coffee shop in China? (Look closely at that name.)

People are often impressed by certain brand names, even though they say there's no difference between brands in a given product category. For example, even when people say all aspirin is alike, if you put two aspirin bottles in front of them—one with the Bayer label and one with an unknown name—most choose the one with the well-known brand name. Gasoline buyers often choose a brand name (e.g., Exxon) over price.

For the buyer, a brand name ensures quality, reduces search time, and adds prestige to purchases. For the seller, brand names facilitate new-product introductions, help promotional efforts, add to repeat purchases, and differentiate products so that prices can be set higher.[20] What brand-name products do you prefer?

trademark

A brand that has exclusive legal protection for both its brand name and its design.

manufacturers' (national) brands

The brand names of manufacturers that distribute products nationally.

dealer (private-label) brands

Products that don't carry the manufacturer's name but carry a distributor or retailer's name instead.

generic goods

Nonbranded products that usually sell at a sizable discount compared to national or private-label brands.

knockoff brands

Illegal copies of national brand-name goods.

brand equity

The value of the brand name and associated symbols.

brand loyalty

The degree to which customers are satisfied, like the brand, and are committed to further purchases.

Brand Categories

Several categories of brands are familiar to you. **Manufacturers' (national) brands** represent manufacturers that distribute products nationally—Xerox, Sony, and Dell, for example.

Dealer (private-label) brands are products that don't carry the manufacturer's name but carry a distributor or retailer's name instead. Kenmore and DieHard are dealer brands long associated with and sold by Sears. These brands are also known as *house brands* or *distributor brands*.[21]

Many manufacturers fear having their brand names become generic names. A *generic name* is the name for a whole product category. Did you know that aspirin and linoleum were once brand names? So were nylon, escalator, kerosene, and zipper. All those names became so popular, so identified with the product, that they lost their brand status and became generic. (Such issues are decided in the courts.) Their producers then had to come up with new names. The original Aspirin, for example, became Bayer aspirin. Companies working hard to protect their brand names today include Kleenex and Rollerblade.

Generic goods are nonbranded products that usually sell at a sizable discount compared to national or private-label brands. They feature basic packaging and are backed with little or no advertising. Some are of poor quality, but many come close to the same quality as the national brand-name goods they copy. There are generic tissues, generic cigarettes, generic drugs, and so on. Consumers today are buying large amounts of generic products because their overall quality has improved so much in recent years. What has been your experience trying generic products?

Knockoff brands are illegal copies of national brand-name goods. If you see an expensive brand-name item such as a D&G shirt or a Rolex watch for sale at a ridiculously low price, you can be pretty sure it's a knockoff. Often the brand name is just a little off, too, like Dolce & Banana (Dolce & Gabbana) or Bolex (Rolex). Look carefully. Zippo has taken to calling counterfeit copies "Rippos."

Generating Brand Equity and Loyalty

A major goal of marketers in the future will be to reestablish the notion of brand equity. **Brand equity** is the value of the brand name and associated symbols. Usually, a company cannot know the value of its brand until it sells it to another company. Brand names with high reported brand equity ratings include Reynolds Wrap aluminum foil and Ziploc food bags. What's the most valuable brand name today? It's Apple.[22]

The core of brand equity is **brand loyalty**, the degree to which customers are satisfied, like the brand, and are committed to further purchases. A loyal group of customers represents substantial value to a firm, and that value can be calculated. One way manufacturers are trying to create more brand loyalty is by focusing on sustainability.[23]

Companies try to boost their short-term performance by offering coupons and price discounts to move goods quickly. This can erode consumers' commitment to brand names, especially of grocery products. Many consumers complain when companies drop brand names like Astro Pops or Flex shampoo. Such complaints show the power of brand names. Now companies realize the value of brand equity and are trying harder to measure the earning power of strong brand names.

brand awareness

How quickly or easily a given brand name comes to mind when a product category is mentioned.

Brand awareness refers to how quickly or easily a given brand name comes to mind when someone mentions a product category. Advertising helps build strong brand awareness. Established brands, such as Coca-Cola and Pepsi, are usually among the highest in brand awareness. Sponsorship of events, like football's Orange Bowl and NASCAR's Cup Series, helps improve brand awareness. Simply being there over and over also increases brand awareness. That's one way Google became such a popular brand.

Perceived quality is an important part of brand equity. A product that's perceived as having better quality than its competitors can be priced accordingly. The key to creating a perception of quality is to identify what consumers look for in a high-quality product, and then use that information in every message the company sends out. Factors influencing the perception of quality include price, appearance, and reputation.

Consumers often develop *brand preference*—that is, they prefer one brand over another—because of such cues. When consumers reach the point of *brand insistence,* the product becomes a specialty good. For example, a consumer may insist on Goodyear tires for his or her car.

It's now so easy to copy a product's benefits that off-brand products can draw consumers away from brand-name goods. Brand-name manufacturers like Intel Corporation have to develop new products and new markets faster and promote their names better than ever before to hold off challenges from competitors.

Prisma Guitars

Creating Brand Associations

The name, symbol, and slogan a company uses can assist greatly in brand recognition for that company's products. **Brand association** is the linking of a brand to other favorable images, like famous product users, a popular celebrity, or a particular geographic area. Note, for example, how ads for Mercedes-Benz associate its company's cars with successful people who live luxurious lives. The person responsible for building brands is known as a brand manager or product manager. We'll discuss that position next.

Brand Management

A **brand manager** (known as a *product manager* in some firms) has direct responsibility for one brand or product line, and manages all the elements of its marketing mix: product, price, place, and promotion. Thus, you might think of the brand manager as the president of a one-product firm.

One reason many large consumer-product companies created this position was to have greater control over new-product development and product promotion. Some companies have brand-management *teams* to bolster the overall effort. In B2B companies, brand managers are often known as product managers.

Prisma Guitars cofounder Nick Pourfard began making guitars after a skateboarding injury left him immobile for six months. Now his company uses old skateboard decks to create colorful and sustainable instruments. Do you own any products made out of recycled materials?

brand association
The linking of a brand to other favorable images.

brand manager
A manager who has direct responsibility for one brand or one product line; called a product manager in some firms.

?TESTPREP

- What seven functions does packaging now perform?
- What's the difference between a brand name and a trademark?
- Can you explain the difference between a manufacturer's brand, a dealer brand, and a generic brand?
- What are the key components of brand equity?

LO 14–5 Explain the steps in the new-product development process.

The New-Product Development Process

The odds a new product will fail are high. Not delivering what is promised is a leading cause of new-product failure. Other causes include getting ready for marketing too late, poor positioning, too few differences from competitors, and poor packaging. As Figure 14.3 shows, new-product development for producers consists of six stages.

New products continue to pour into the market every year, and their profit potential looks tremendous. Think, for example, of 3D printing, streaming TV, virtual reality (VR) games and products, smartphones, tablets, and other innovations. Where do these ideas come from? How are they tested? What's the life span for an innovation? Let's look at these issues.

Generating New-Product Ideas

It now takes about seven ideas to generate one commercial product. Most ideas for new industrial products come from employee suggestions rather than research and development. Research and development, nonetheless, is a major source of new products. Employees are also a major source for new consumer-goods ideas. Firms should also listen to their suppliers for new-product ideas because suppliers are often exposed to new ideas. Present customers are also a good source for new-product ideas.[24] For example, brewers are focusing on "healthier" drinks after listening to their Millennial customers talk about their health-conscious lifestyles and their thirst for lower-calorie options to replace traditional beers and cocktails.[25]

Product Screening

Product screening reduces the number of new-product ideas a firm is working on at any one time so it can focus on the most promising. *Screening* applies criteria to determine whether the product fits well with present products, has good profit potential, and is marketable. The company may assign each of these factors a weight and compute a total score for each new product so that it can compare their potentials.

product screening
A process designed to reduce the number of new-product ideas being worked on at any one time.

Product Analysis

product analysis
Making cost estimates and sales forecasts to get a feeling for profitability of new-product ideas.

After product screening comes **product analysis**, or making cost estimates and sales forecasts to get a feeling for the profitability of new-product ideas. Products that don't meet the established criteria are withdrawn from consideration.

Product Development and Testing

If a product passes the screening and analysis phases, the firm begins to develop it further, testing many different product concepts or alternatives. A firm that makes packaged meat products may develop the concept of a chicken dog—a hot dog made of chicken that tastes like an all-beef hot dog. It will develop a prototype, or sample, so that consumers can try the taste.

concept testing
Taking a product idea to consumers to test their reactions.

Concept testing takes a product idea to consumers to test their reactions. Do they see the benefits of this new product? How frequently would they buy it? At what price? What features do they like and dislike? What changes in it would they make? *Crowdsourcing* is a newer tool companies can use to gather this information from consumers. Crowdsourcing platforms allow the public to give their opinions of potential products companies may offer. Crowd favorites are often moved on to the next steps in the process.[26] The firm tests samples using different packaging, branding, and ingredients until a product emerges that's desirable from both production and marketing perspectives. As you plan for Harvest Gold, can you see the importance of concept testing for new, healthy dishes?

Commercialization

Even if a product tests well, it may take quite awhile to achieve success in the market. Take the zipper, for example, the result of one of the longest development efforts on record for a consumer product. After Whitcomb Judson received the first patents for his clothing fastener in the early 1890s, it took more than 15 years to perfect the product—and even then consumers weren't interested. Judson's company suffered numerous financial setbacks, name changes, and relocations before settling in Meadville, Pennsylvania. Finally, the U.S. Navy started using zippers during World War I. Today, zippers are a $13 billion industry!

The example of the zipper shows why the marketing effort must include **commercialization**, which includes (1) promoting the product to distributors and retailers to get wide distribution, and (2) developing strong advertising and sales campaigns to generate and maintain interest in the product among distributors and consumers. New products are now getting rapid exposure to global markets through commercialization online and on social media. Websites enable consumers to view new products, ask questions, and make purchases easily and quickly.

commercialization
Promoting a product to distributors and retailers to get wide distribution, and developing strong advertising and sales campaigns to generate and maintain interest in the product among distributors and consumers.

> **LO 14–6** Describe the product life cycle.

The Product Life Cycle

Once a product has been developed and tested, it goes to market. There it may pass through a **product life cycle** of four stages: introduction, growth, maturity, and decline (see Figure 14.4). This cycle is a *theoretical* model of what happens to sales and profits for a *product class* over time. However, not all individual products follow the life cycle, and particular brands may act differently. For example, while frozen foods as a generic class may go through the entire cycle, one brand may never get beyond the introduction stage. Some product classes, such as microwave ovens, stay in the introductory stage for years. Some products, like ketchup, become classics and never experience decline.

product life cycle
A theoretical model of what happens to sales and profits for a product class over time; the four stages of the cycle are introduction, growth, maturity, and decline.

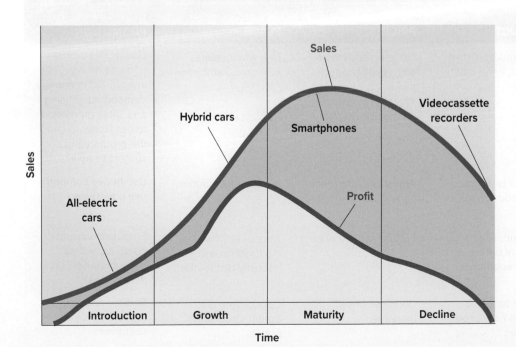

FIGURE 14.4 SALES AND PROFITS DURING THE PRODUCT LIFE CYCLE Note that profit levels start to fall *before* sales reach their peak. This is due to increasing price competition. When profits and sales start to decline, it's time to come out with a new product or to remodel the old one to maintain interest and profits.

Others, such as fad clothing, may go through the entire cycle in a few months. Still others may be withdrawn from the market altogether. Nonetheless, the product life cycle may provide some basis for anticipating future market developments and for planning marketing strategies.

Example of the Product Life Cycle

The product life cycle can give marketers valuable clues to successfully promoting a product over time. Some products, like crayons and sidewalk chalk, have very long product life cycles, change very little, and never seem to go into decline. Crayola has been successfully selling crayons for over 130 years. Mattel's Barbie is over 60 years old and is gearing up for another makeover.[27] How long do you think popular virtual reality games will last?

You can see how the theory works by looking at the classic product life cycle of instant coffee. When it was introduced, most people didn't like it as well as "regular" coffee, and it took several years for instant coffee to gain general acceptance (introduction stage). At one point, though, instant coffee grew rapidly in popularity, and many brands were introduced (growth stage). After a while, people became attached to one brand and sales leveled off (maturity stage). Sales then went into a slight decline when freeze-dried coffees were introduced (decline stage). Now freeze-dried coffee is, in turn, at the decline stage as consumers are buying bags of coffee from Starbucks and brewing them at home. It's extremely important for marketers to recognize what stage a product is in so that they can make intelligent and efficient marketing decisions about it.

Using the Product Life Cycle

Different stages in the product life cycle call for different marketing strategies. Figure 14.5 outlines the marketing mix decisions you might make. As you go through the figure, you'll see that each stage calls for multiple marketing mix changes. Remember, these concepts are largely theoretical and you should use them only as guidelines. We'll discuss the price strategies mentioned in the figure later in this chapter.

FIGURE 14.5 SAMPLE STRATEGIES FOLLOWED DURING THE PRODUCT LIFE CYCLE

LIFE CYCLE STAGE	MARKETING MIX ELEMENTS			
	PRODUCT	PRICE	PLACE	PROMOTION
Introduction	Offer market-tested product; keep mix small	Go after innovators with high introductory price (skimming strategy) or use penetration pricing	Use wholesalers, selective distribution	Use dealer promotion and heavy investment in primary demand advertising and sales promotion to get stores to carry the product and consumers to try it
Growth	Improve product; keep product mix limited	Adjust price to meet competition	Increase distribution	Use heavy competitive advertising
Maturity	Differentiate product to satisfy different market segments	Further reduce price	Take over wholesaling function and intensify distribution	Emphasize brand name as well as product benefits and differences
Decline	Cut product mix; develop new product ideas	Consider price increase	Consolidate distribution; drop some outlets	Reduce advertising to only loyal customers

LIFE CYCLE STAGE	SALES	PROFITS	COMPETITORS
Introduction	Low sales	Losses may occur	Few
Growth	Rapidly rising sales	Very high profits	Growing number
Maturity	Peak sales	Declining profits	Stable number, then declining
Decline	Falling sales	Profits may fall to become losses	Declining number

FIGURE 14.6 HOW SALES, PROFITS, AND COMPETITION VARY OVER THE PRODUCT LIFE CYCLE

Figure 14.6 shows in theory what happens to sales volume, profits, and competition during the product life cycle. Compare it to Figure 14.4. Both figures show that a product at the mature stage may reach the top in sales growth while profit is decreasing. At that stage, a marketing manager may decide to create a new image for the product to start a new growth cycle. You may have noticed how Arm & Hammer baking soda often gets a new image every few years to generate new sales. One year it's positioned as a deodorant for refrigerators and the next as a substitute for harsh chemicals in swimming pools. Knowing what stage in the cycle a product has reached helps marketing managers decide when such strategic changes are needed.

Theoretically, all products go through these stages at various times in their life cycle. What happens to sales as a product matures?

iSeeit! Need help understanding product life cycle? Visit your Connect eBook to view a video for a brief animated explanation.

TESTPREP

- What are the six steps in the new-product development process?
- What is the difference between product screening and product analysis?
- What are the two steps in commercialization?
- What is the theory of the product life cycle?

LO 14–7 Identify various pricing objectives and strategies.

Competitive Pricing

Pricing is so important to marketing and the development of total product offers that it has been singled out as one of the four Ps in the marketing mix, along with product, place, and promotion. It's one of the most difficult of the four Ps for a manager to control, however, because price is such a critical ingredient in consumer evaluations of the product. In this section, we'll explore price both as an ingredient of the total product offer and as a strategic marketing tool.

Pricing Objectives

A firm may have several objectives in mind when setting a pricing strategy. When pricing a new healthy meal offering for Harvest Gold, we may want to promote the product's image. If we price it *high* and use the right promotion, maybe we can make it the BMW of

jaminwell/Getty Images

Retailers around the world use sales to attract bargain-hunting customers. How many different ways can marketers appeal to shoppers' desires to find the lowest price? Do online retailers adopt different pricing strategies?

farm-to-table meals. We also might price it high to achieve a certain profit objective or return on investment. We could also price our product *lower* than its competitors, because we want lower-income customers (like students) to afford this healthy meal. That is, we could have some social or ethical goal in mind. Low pricing may also discourage competition because it reduces the profit potential, but it may help us capture a larger share of the market.

A firm may have several pricing objectives over time, and it must formulate these objectives clearly before developing an overall pricing strategy. Popular objectives include the following:

1. *Achieving a target return on investment or profit.* Ultimately, the goal of marketing is to make a profit by providing goods and services to others. Naturally, one long-run pricing objective of almost all firms is to optimize profit. One way companies have tried to increase profit is by reducing the amount of product provided to customers. Thus cereal companies have cut the amount of cereal in a box, toilet paper companies are making their products smaller, and so on. Have you noticed this happening for products you buy?

2. *Building traffic.* Supermarkets often advertise certain products at or below cost to attract people to the store. These products are called *loss leaders.* The long-run objective is to make profits by following the short-run objective of building a customer base.

3. *Achieving greater market share.* One way to capture a larger part of the market is to offer lower prices, low finance rates (like 0 percent financing), low lease rates, or rebates.

4. *Creating an image.* Certain watches, perfumes, and other socially visible products are priced high to give them an image of exclusivity and status.

5. *Furthering social objectives.* A firm may want to price a product low so people with little money can afford it. The government often subsidizes the price of farm products to keep basic necessities affordable.

A firm may have short-run objectives that differ greatly from its long-run objectives. Managers should understand both types at the beginning and put both into their strategic marketing plan. They should also set pricing objectives in the context of other marketing decisions about product design, packaging, branding, distribution, and promotion. All these marketing decisions are interrelated.

Intuition tells us the price charged for a product must bear some relationship to the cost of producing it. Prices usually *are* set somewhere above cost.[28] But as we'll see, price and cost aren't always related. In fact, there are three major approaches to pricing strategy: cost-based, demand-based (target costing), and competition-based.

Cost-Based Pricing

Producers often use cost as a primary basis for setting price. They develop elaborate cost accounting systems to measure production costs (including materials, labor, and overhead), add in a margin of profit, and come up with a price. Picture the process in terms of producing a car. You add up all the various components—engine parts, body, tires, radio, camera, door locks and windows, paint, and labor—add a profit margin, and come up with a price. The question is whether the price will be satisfactory to the market as well.[29] In the long run, the market—not the producer—determines what the price will be (see Chapter 2). Pricing should take into account costs, but it should also include the expected costs of product updates, the marketing objectives for each product, and competitor prices.

Demand-Based Pricing

Unlike cost-based pricing, **target costing** is demand-based.[30] That means we design a product so it not only satisfies customers but also meets the profit margins we've set. Target costing makes the final price an *input* to the product development process, not an outcome of it. You first estimate the selling price people would be willing to pay for a product and then subtract your desired profit margin. The result is your target cost of production, or what you can spend to profitably produce the item.

Competition-Based Pricing

Competition-based pricing is a strategy based on what all the other competitors are doing. The price can be at, above, or below competitors' prices. Pricing depends on customer loyalty, perceived differences, and the competitive climate. **Price leadership** is the strategy by which one or more dominant firms set pricing practices all competitors in an industry follow. You may have noticed that practice among oil companies and some fast-food companies.[31]

Break-Even Analysis

Before you begin selling a new sandwich at Harvest Gold, it may be wise to determine how many sandwiches you'd have to sell before making a profit. You'd then determine whether you could reach such a sales goal. **Break-even analysis** is the process used to determine profitability at various levels of sales. The break-even point is the point where revenues from sales equal all costs. The formula for calculating the break-even point is as follows:

$$\text{Break-even point (BEP)} = \frac{\text{Total fixed costs (FC)}}{\text{Price of one unit (P)} - \text{Variable costs (VC) of one unit}}$$

Total fixed costs are all the expenses that remain the same no matter how many products are made or sold. Among the expenses that make up fixed costs are the amount paid to own or rent a factory or warehouse and the amount paid for business insurance. **Variable costs** change according to the level of production. Included are the expenses for the materials used in making products and the direct costs of labor used in making those goods. For producing a specific product, let's say you have a fixed cost of $200,000 (for mortgage interest, real estate taxes, equipment, and so on). Your variable cost (e.g., labor and materials) per item is $2. If you sold the products for $4 each, the break-even point would be 100,000 items. In other words, you wouldn't make any money selling this product unless you sold more than 100,000 of them:

$$\text{BEP} = \frac{\text{FC}}{\text{P} - \text{VC}} = \frac{\$200,000}{\$4 - \$2} = \frac{\$200,000}{\$2} = 100,000 \text{ items}$$

Other Pricing Strategies

Let's say a firm has just developed a new line of products, such as VR headsets. The firm has to decide how to price these units at the introductory stage of the product life cycle. A **skimming price strategy** prices a new product high to recover research and development costs and make as much profit as possible while there's little competition. Of course, those large profits will eventually attract new competitors.

A second strategy is to price the new products low. Low prices will attract more buyers and discourage other companies from making similar products because profits are slim. This **penetration strategy** enables the firm to penetrate or capture a large share of the market quickly.

Retailers use several pricing strategies. **Everyday low pricing (EDLP)** is the choice of Home Depot and Walmart. They set prices lower than competitors and don't usually have special sales. The idea is to bring consumers to the store whenever they want a bargain rather than having them wait until there is a sale.

Department stores and some other retailers most often use a **high–low pricing strategy**. Regular prices are higher than at stores using EDLP, but during special sales they're lower.

target costing
Designing a product so that it satisfies customers and meets the profit margins desired by the firm.

competition-based pricing
A pricing strategy based on what all the other competitors are doing. The price can be set at, above, or below competitors' prices.

price leadership
The strategy by which one or more dominant firms set the pricing practices that all competitors in an industry follow.

break-even analysis
The process used to determine profitability at various levels of sales.

total fixed costs
All the expenses that remain the same no matter how many products are made or sold.

variable costs
Costs that change according to the level of production.

skimming price strategy
Strategy in which a new product is priced high to make optimum profit while there's little competition.

penetration strategy
Strategy in which a product is priced low to attract many customers and discourage competition.

everyday low pricing (EDLP)
Setting prices lower than competitors and then not having any special sales.

high–low pricing strategy
Setting prices that are higher than EDLP stores, but having many special sales where the prices are lower than competitors'.

Donato Sardella/Getty Images

psychological pricing

Pricing goods and services at price points that make the product appear less expensive than it is.

The problem with such pricing is that it encourages consumers to wait for sales, thus cutting into profits. One store that tried such pricing was JCPenney. When the store moved away from that strategy, sales fell off dramatically and may never recover, even though the store has since returned to that strategy. As online shopping has grown, you see fewer stores with a high–low strategy because consumers are able to find better prices online.

Retailers can use price as a major determinant of the goods they carry. Some promote goods that sell for only 99 cents, or for less than $5. Some of those 99-cent stores have raised their prices to over a dollar because of rising costs. On the other hand, Family Dollar Store is learning that, for low-income buyers, even $1 may be too expensive.

Psychological pricing means pricing goods and services at price points that make the product appear less expensive than it is. A house might be priced at $299,000 because that sounds like a lot less than $300,000. Gas stations almost always use psychological pricing.

How Market Forces Affect Pricing

Recognizing that different consumers may be willing to pay different prices, marketers sometimes price on the basis of consumer demand rather than cost or some other calculation. That's called *demand-oriented pricing,* and you can observe it at movie theaters with low rates for children and drugstores with discounts for senior citizens.

Today, marketers are facing a pricing problem: Most customers compare prices of goods and services online. Priceline introduced consumers to a "demand collection system," in which buyers post the prices they are willing to pay and invite sellers to accept or decline the price. Consumers can get great prices on airlines, hotels, and other products by naming their price. They can also get used goods online at places like Craigslist. Clearly, price competition is going to heat up as consumers have more access to price information from all around the world. As a result, nonprice competition is likely to increase.

Nonprice Competition

Marketers often compete on product attributes other than price. You may have noted that price differences are small for products like gasoline, candy bars, and even major products such as compact cars and private colleges.

You won't typically see price as a major promotional appeal on television. Instead, marketers tend to stress product images and consumer benefits such as comfort, style, convenience, and durability.

Many small organizations promote the services that accompany basic products rather than price in order to compete with bigger firms. Good service will enhance a relatively homogeneous product. Danny O'Neill, for example, is a small wholesaler who sells gourmet coffee to upscale restaurants. He has to watch competitors' prices *and* the services they offer so that he can charge the premium prices he wants. To charge high prices, he has to offer and then provide superior service. Larger companies often do the same thing. Some airlines stress friendliness, large "sleeping" seats, promptness, abundant flights, and other such services. Many hotels stress "no surprises," business services, health clubs, and other extras.

?TESTPREP

- Can you list two short-term and two long-term pricing objectives? Can the two be compatible?
- What are the limitations of a cost-based pricing strategy?
- What is psychological pricing?

SUMMARY

LO 14–1 Describe a total product offer.

- **What's included in a total product offer?**

A total product offer consists of everything consumers evaluate when deciding whether to buy something. It includes price, brand name, and satisfaction in use.

- **What's the difference between a product line and a product mix?**

A product line is a group of physically similar products with similar competitors. A product line of gum may include bubble gum and sugarless gum. A product mix is a company's combination of product lines. A manufacturer may offer lines of gum, candy bars, and breath mints in its product mix.

- **How do marketers create product differentiation for their goods and services?**

Marketers use a combination of pricing, advertising, and packaging to make their products seem unique and attractive.

LO 14–2 Identify the various kinds of consumer and industrial goods.

- **What are consumer goods?**

Consumer goods are sold to ultimate consumers like you and me for personal use.

- **What are the four classifications of consumer goods and services, and how are they marketed?**

There are convenience goods and services (requiring minimum shopping effort); shopping goods and services (for which people search and compare price and quality); specialty goods and services (which consumers go out of their way to get, and for which they often demand specific brands); and unsought goods and services (products consumers are unaware of, haven't thought of buying, or need to solve an unexpected problem). Convenience goods and services are best promoted by location, shopping goods and services by some price/quality appeal, and specialty goods and services by specialty magazines and interactive websites.

- **What are industrial goods, and how are they marketed differently from consumer goods?**

Industrial goods are products sold in the business-to-business (B2B) market and used in the production of other products. They're sold largely through salespeople and rely less on advertising.

LO 14–3 Summarize the functions of packaging.

- **What are the seven functions of packaging?**

Packaging must (1) attract the buyer's attention; (2) protect the goods inside, stand up under handling and storage, be tamperproof, and deter theft; (3) be easy to open and use; (4) describe the contents; (5) explain the benefits of the good inside; (6) provide information about warranties, warnings, and other consumer matters; and (7) indicate price, value, and uses. Bundling means grouping two or more products into a unit, through packaging, and charging one price for them.

LO 14–4 Contrast *brand, brand name,* and *trademark,* and show the value of brand equity.

- **Can you define *brand, brand name,* and *trademark*?**

A *brand* is a name, symbol, or design (or combination thereof) that identifies the goods or services of one seller or group of sellers and distinguishes them from the goods and services of competitors. The word *brand* includes all means of identifying a product. A *brand name* consists of a word, letter, or group of words or letters that differentiates one seller's goods and services from those of competitors. A *trademark* is a brand that has exclusive legal protection for both its brand name and design.

■ **What is brand equity, and how do managers create brand associations?**

Brand equity is the value of a brand name and associated symbols. Brand association is the linking of a brand to other favorable images such as product users, a popular celebrity, or a geographic area.

■ **What do brand managers do?**

Brand managers coordinate product, price, place, and promotion decisions for a particular product.

LO 14–5 Explain the steps in the new-product development process.

■ **What are the six steps of the product development process?**

The steps of product development are (1) generation of new-product ideas, (2) product screening, (3) product analysis, (4) development, (5) testing, and (6) commercialization.

LO 14–6 Describe the product life cycle.

■ **What is the product life cycle?**

The product life cycle is a theoretical model of what happens to sales and profits for a product class over time.

■ **What are the four stages in the product life cycle?**

The four product life cycle stages are introduction, growth, maturity, and decline.

LO 14–7 Identify various pricing objectives and strategies.

■ **What are pricing objectives?**

Pricing objectives include achieving a target profit, building traffic, increasing market share, creating an image, and meeting social goals.

■ **What strategies can marketers use to determine a product's price?**

A skimming strategy prices the product high to make big profits while there's little competition. A penetration strategy uses low price to attract more customers and discourage competitors. Demand-oriented pricing starts with consumer demand rather than cost. Competition-oriented pricing is based on all competitors' prices. Price leadership occurs when all competitors follow the pricing practice of one or more dominant companies.

■ **What is break-even analysis?**

Break-even analysis is the process used to determine profitability at various levels of sales. The break-even point is the point where revenues from sales equal all costs.

■ **Why do companies use nonprice strategies?**

Pricing is one of the easiest marketing strategies to copy. It's often not a good long-run competitive tool.

KEY TERMS

brand   368
brand association   371
brand awareness   370
brand equity   370
brand loyalty   370
brand manager   371
break-even analysis   377

bundling   367
commercialization   373
competition-based pricing   377
concept testing   372
convenience goods and services   364

dealer (private-label) brands   370
distributed product development   362
everyday low pricing (EDLP)   377
generic goods   370

CRITICAL THINKING

1. What value enhancers affected your choice of the school you attend? Did you consider size, location, price, reputation, WiFi services, library and research services, sports, and courses offered? What factors were most important? Why? What schools were your alternatives? Why didn't you choose them?

2. What could you do to enhance the product offer of Harvest Gold, other than changing the menu from time to time?

3. How could you use psychological pricing when making up the menu at Harvest Gold?

4. Are you impressed by the use of celebrities in product advertisements? What celebrity could you use to promote Harvest Gold?

PUTTING PRINCIPLES TO WORK

PURPOSE

To assess how consumers shop for the best deals for various goods online.

EXERCISE

Shopbots (short for *shopping robots*) are online sites for finding the best prices on goods you need. No shopbot searches the entire Internet, so it's a good idea to use more than one to get the best deals. Furthermore, not all shopbots quote shipping and handling costs. Imagine you want to buy a new headset and are considering investing in Beats. Go online to find reviews and prices. Here are some shopbots to try: MySimon.com, PriceGrabber.com, Shopping.com, and Shopzilla.com.

1. Which of the shopbots offers the most information? How helpful are the consumer reviews? The product descriptions?

2. Which shopbot is the easiest to use? The hardest? Why?

3. Write down some of the prices you find online and then go to a local store, such as Walmart or Target, and compare prices. Does either source (online or brick-and-mortar) consistently offer the best price?

4. Compare shopping online to shopping in stores. What are the advantages and disadvantages of each? Which has the best total product offer?

DEVELOPING CAREER SKILLS

KEY: ● **Team**   ★ **Analytic**   ▲ **Communication**   ▣ **Technology**

★▲ 1. Look around your classroom and notice the different types of shoes students are wearing. What product qualities were they looking for when they chose their shoes? How important were price, style, brand name, and color? Describe the product offerings you would feature in a new shoe store designed to appeal to college students.

●★▲ 2. A total product offer consists of everything consumers evaluate when choosing among products, including price, package, service, and reputation. Working in teams, compose a list of factors consumers might consider when evaluating the total product offer of a vacation resort, a smartphone, and a rental apartment.

★ 3. How important is price to you when buying the following: clothes, milk, computers, haircuts, rental cars? What nonprice factors, if any, are more important than price? How much time do you spend evaluating factors other than price when making such purchases?

★▲ 4. Go through several local stores of different types and note how often they use psychological pricing. Discuss the practice with the class to see whether students recognize the influence psychological pricing has on them.

CAREER EXPLORATION

If you are interested in working in product development and/or pricing, here are a few careers to consider. Find out about the tasks performed, skills needed, pay, and opportunity outlook in these fields in the *Occupational Outlook Handbook (OOH)* at bls.gov.

- **Marketing manager**—estimates the demand for a product and identifies markets, as well as develops pricing strategies.

- **Brand manager**—creates and directs brand assets for a company or product.

- **Industrial designer**—develops the concepts for manufactured products for everyday use.

- **Cost estimator**—collects and analyzes data in order to estimate the time, money, materials, and labor required to manufacture a product.

VIDEO CASE   *Developing New Products at Domino's*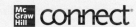

Domino's is the second-largest pizza chain in the world. Today, the company delivers its piping hot pizza to hungry customers everywhere from Columbus, Ohio, to Bombay, India. Domino's developed its reputation in the competitive pizza market by listening to consumers and creating a value proposition that is convenient, saves customers time, and provides a meal the whole family can enjoy. Developing new products and services is the heart of its business. That's why Domino's carefully looks at trends in diets, in foods, and in technology. By using focus groups, the company learns what customers like and don't like in pizza toppings, sandwiches, and appetizers. It also keeps a watchful eye on what competitors are doing.

When Domino's decided to add salads to its menu, it realized this would be a challenging expansion. The company had to answer several questions before adding salads.

One key issue was whether the company should assemble salads at its company stores or find a partner experienced in the salad business that could handle this task. It found a partner in Ready Pac Foods, a company with a solid reputation in the salad market. The company next had to decide what types of salads would become part of the Domino's menu. After lengthy taste testing and research from focus groups, the company decided on three variations: Classic Garden, Chicken Caesar, and Chicken Apple Pecan.

Whenever Domino's introduces a new product, it is careful to bring the new item along slowly in the market. The company introduced its salad offerings in about one-fifth of its 13,000 stores using a wide cross section of the country (large cities, small towns, north, south, etc.). Marketing of any new product is generally a key to its success. Domino's extensive use of advertising, social media, and in-store promotions helped introduce the product in the selected test markets to build consumer awareness of the new menu expansion. Acceptance of the new product in test markets is critical before the company makes any decision to fully commercialize it. Sometimes, Domino's has been surprised by customer feedback concerning goods and services. For example, many customers told the company how important Domino's was to them on their wedding day. Domino's used this feedback to create the Domino's Wedding Registry. The company has a complete marketing campaign with engaging photos of brides, grooms, and, of course, pizza.

Customers perceive value from a product by comparing the benefits they expect from the product and the cost of receiving those goods. The importance of listening to customers is critical to success in today's competitive marketplace. While Domino's is always willing to listen to customer suggestions concerning new products, it knows that not all product innovations are going to be a market success. In fact, the company lives by the standard "Failure Is an Option" when it evaluates new products. Like all successful companies, Domino's understands that delivering products that meet the changing needs of its customers is the path to long-term growth and success.

THINKING IT OVER

1. In what classification of consumer products would you consider Domino's Pizza? Why?

2. What are the steps in the new-product development process?

3. What stage of the product life cycle are salads in today? Why? Did Domino's make a wise decision expanding into salads?

NOTES

1. Rajesh Kalidindi, "How You Can Improve Your Company's New Product Introduction Process," *Forbes,* January 10, 2020.

2. Michelle Greenwald, "5 Key Trends Changing New Product and Service Development," *Forbes,* September 24, 2019.

3. Seren Morris, "Dunkin' Donuts Launches 'Snackin' Bacon' after Adding Matcha Latte to Menu," *Newsweek,* February 27, 2020.

4. Sophia Waterfield, "Meat-Free Fast Food: McDonald's, KFC, Starbucks and More Restaurants Are Selling Plant-Based Foods—but Are They Vegan?," *Newsweek,* February 19, 2020; Jeanette Settembre, "Taco Bell Considers Beyond Meat, Impossible Foods Plant-Based Menu Items," *Fox Business,* February 26, 2020.

5. Zippo, zippo.com, accessed February 2020.

6. Jade Scipioni, "K-Cups for Booze? Budweiser Owner, Keurig's Single-Serve Cocktail Machines Officially Roll Out," *Fox Business,* March 10, 2010; Scott Krather, "Experiencing Keurig's Cocktail Maker," *Forbes,* January 15, 2020.

7. "Thinsulate," 3M, 3m.com, accessed February 2020.

8. Suzanne Shelton, "How to Shape Your Sustainability Story," *Green Biz,* February 4, 2020.

9. Danielle Wiener-Bronner, "Cherry Vanilla Coke Has Been a Stealth Hit for Years. Now You Can Officially Get It at the Store," *CNN Business,* February 7, 2020.

10. "Personal Services," Bank of America, bankofamerica. com, accessed February 2020.

11. "The Most Innovative Companies of 2019," *Fast Company,* fastcompany.com, accessed February 2020.

12. Seb Joseph, "As Brand Concerns over Search Algorithm Escalate, Amazon Is Testing 'Stores' Results in Search," *Digiday,* February 19, 2020.

13. Sean Ross, "Capital vs. Consumer Goods: What's the Difference?," *Investopedia,* investopedia.com, accessed February 2020.

14. Peggy Jean's Pies, peggyjeanspies.com, accessed February 2020.

15. School of Packaging, Michigan State University, canr.msu. edu, accessed February 2020.

16. "What Is the Importance of RFID in Packaging and Shipping?," *CIO Review,* February 12, 2020.

17. "New Nutrition Labels Designed to Promote Healthier Food Choices," *KDKA Pittsburgh,* February 18, 2020;

"New Nutrition Labeling Regulations Help Fight Fat, Sugar and Deceptive Serving Sizes," *KOMO News,* February 10, 2020.

18. Pamela Vachon, "A Bite-Size Stop in Reykjavik, Iceland," *Chowhound,* December 21, 2019; Rivan V. Stinson, "22 Secrets to Save Money on Travel," *Yahoo! Finance,* February 28, 2020.

19. "The World's Most Valuable Brands," *Forbes,* forbes.com, accessed February 2020.

20. Aaron Hall, "Your Brand Is More Than a Name: 5 Overlooked Brand Elements to Invest In," *Ad Age,* February 27, 2020; "Psychology behind Developing Brand Loyalty," University of Southern California, usc.edu, accessed February 2020.

21. Lauren Thomas, "Macy's Says It Will Grow 4 of Its Private Brands to $1 Billion," *CNBC,* February 5, 2020.

22. "The World's Most Valuable Brands," *Forbes,* forbes.com, accessed February 2020.

23. Suzanne Shelton, "How to Shape Your Sustainability Story," *Green Biz,* February 4, 2020; Eliza Erskine, "Social Media as a Sustainability Tool," *Business 2 Community,* February 11, 2020.

24. Teresa Spangler, "How to Drive Innovation in 2020," *Forbes,* February 26, 2020.

25. Chris Furnari, "Chasing Michelob Ultra: Craft Brewers Unleash Wave of Low-Calorie Challenger Brands," *Forbes,* February 28, 2020.

26. Johanna Brunneder, Oguz A. Acar, Dirk Diechmann, et al., "A New Model for Crowdsourcing Innovation," *Harvard Business Review,* January 31, 2020.

27. Natalie Sherman, "Is Barbie's Makeover Working?," *BBC News,* December 21, 2019; Monica Chon, "Barbie Just Got a Makeover for Black History Month," *Yahoo! Lifestyle,* February 18, 2020.

28. "Huawei Learned Its Pricing Model from the IBM of Old," *The Wall Street Journal,* February 28, 2020.

29. Nora Naughton, "High Car Prices Are Locking Out Younger Shoppers," *The Wall Street Journal,* February 18, 2020.

30. Neil Kokemuller, "What Are the Benefits of Target Costing?," *Chron,* chron.com, accessed February 2020.

31. Rita Gunther McGrath, "The New Disrupters," *MIT Sloan Management Review,* February 17, 2020.

15

Distributing Products

LEARNING OBJECTIVES »

After you have read and studied this chapter, you should be able to

LO 15-1 Explain the concept of marketing channels and their value.

LO 15-2 Demonstrate how intermediaries perform the six marketing utilities.

LO 15-3 Identify the types of wholesale intermediaries in the distribution system.

LO 15-4 Compare the distribution strategies retailers use.

LO 15-5 Explain the various kinds of nonstore retailing.

LO 15-6 Explain the various ways to build cooperation in channel systems.

LO 15-7 Describe logistics, and outline how intermediaries manage the transportation and storage of goods.

Toby Johnson, Vice President of Sales Operations at Frito-Lay

For the brave men and women who serve in the U.S. military, the skills they learn during their time in service can yield rewards that continue to pay off throughout their careers. Just ask Toby Johnson, an army veteran who is currently vice president of sales operations at Frito-Lay, a subsidiary of the beverage giant PepsiCo.

Johnson was born in Syracuse, New York, and is the oldest of three sisters. From an early age, Johnson's parents taught her important lessons about serving others. Her father was a doctor while her mother worked in an operating room as a nurse, both of which are demanding professions that require lots of hard work and perseverance. Johnson took inspiration from her driven parents, applying herself to her schoolwork as well as to sports. An outstanding student and athlete, she turned down admission to several Ivy League schools and instead chose to accept an appointment to the United States Military Academy at West Point. She enrolled at West Point because she felt that the combination of rigorous training and high academic standards would make her a more well-rounded human being. Johnson held several leadership appointments while at the academy and was commissioned as a 2nd lieutenant in the U.S. Army Aviation Corps upon graduation. Deciding that she wanted to fly Longbow Apache attack helicopters, Johnson received an assignment to Fort Rucker in Alabama to begin training.

When she arrived at the base, Johnson realized immediately that she was the only woman among the 30 trainees. This made her feel out of place but no less motivated to succeed. "I initially felt that I had to represent all women," said Johnson. "Then there was my inclination to blend in with the guys and try not to stand out. In the end I had to accept the fact that I do not represent all women; I only represent myself." After two years at flight school, Johnson was assigned to the 18th Airborne Corps Rapid Deployment Force as a pilot, with her trainers describing her as a brilliant pilot and effective leader.

By 2003 Johnson had been deployed with the 3rd Infantry Division that was assigned to be the initial invasion force into Iraq. She served as part of the landing mission that traveled 400 miles from Kuwait across the desert to establish a base of operations at Baghdad International Airport. Johnson served almost a year in Iraq and then finished her military service stateside, serving seven years on active duty with the U.S. Army. Upon her discharge from the military, Johnson pursued a master of business administration (MBA) degree at Harvard University. She secured a summer internship with PepsiCo that helped her transition from the military to the private sector. After earning her MBA, Johnson accepted a position with PepsiCo managing a factory at the company's Frito-Lay subsidiary in Williamsport, Pennsylvania.

After assuming her new job at Frito-Lay, Johnson noticed some surprising similarities between the snack business and her time in the military, especially among workers. She found that her colleagues' concern for their workplace was very much like her troops' concern for their unit. Her success at Williamsport led to many new responsibilities over the next 12 years. During her tenure at PepsiCo, Johnson worked at multiple divisions where she attained broad experience managing teams throughout the company's value chain. Past duties include directing manufacturing operations, driving global productivity and Asian supply-chain distribution, analyzing consumer insights, developing supply-chain efficiencies and relationships, and performing other responsibilities.

Johnson is also one of the founders of Valor, PepsiCo's employee group for veterans. Established more than 10 years ago, Valor supports veterans and military families as they transition from service to civilian life. Thanks to the organization's efforts, veteran-hiring groups like RecruitMilitary and Military Friendly have praised PepsiCo for actively seeking out veterans for employment. Today, the company boasts 4,500 veterans who work at the company in various capacities. Along with providing key support to the Valor program, Johnson also works for the betterment of her fellow veterans as a speaker and board member with the USO of New York. "Veterans don't want to be seen as zoo animals," said Johnson. "They want to be seen just like a regular person."

The four Ps of marketing are product, price, place, and promotion. This chapter is all about place. The place function goes by many other names as well, including shipping, warehousing, distribution, logistics, and supply-chain management. At large consumer-products companies such as Pepsi and Frito-Lay, getting the product to the consumer at the right time and place is critical. We'll explore all these concepts in this chapter. At the end, you will have an understanding of the many steps required to get products from the producer to the consumer.

Sources: Dieter Holger, "PepsiCo Puts Military Veterans to Work," *The Wall Street Journal,* October 28, 2019; "Toby Johnson," Team Red, White, and Blue, teamrwb.org, accessed March 2020; "A Legacy of Veteran Hiring," PepsiCo, pepsico.com, accessed March 2020.

Let's talk business!
bit.ly/LetsTalkBusiness15

Laura Buckman

marketing intermediaries
Organizations that assist in moving goods and services from producers to businesses (B2B) and from businesses to consumers (B2C).

channel of distribution
A whole set of marketing intermediaries, such as agents, brokers, wholesalers, and retailers, that join together to transport and store goods in their path (or channel) from producers to consumers.

Distribution warehouses, such as Amazon's fulfillment centers, store goods until they are needed. What are the benefits of having food, household items, clothing, and other needed goods close at hand?

LO 15–1 Explain the concept of marketing channels and their value.

The Emergence of Marketing Intermediaries

It's easy to overlook distribution and storage in marketing, where the focus is often on advertising, selling, marketing research, and other functions. But it doesn't take much to realize how important distribution is. Imagine the challenge Adidas faces of getting raw materials together, making millions of pairs of shoes, and then distributing those shoes to stores throughout the world. That's what thousands of manufacturing firms—making everything from automobiles to furniture and toys—have to deal with every day. Imagine further that there has been a major volcano eruption or pandemic that has caused a disruption in the supply of goods. Such issues are commonplace for distribution managers.[1]

Fortunately there are hundreds of thousands of companies and individuals whose job it is to help move goods from the raw-material state to producers, and then on to consumers. Managing the flow of goods has become one of the most important managerial functions for many organizations.[2] Let's look at how this function is carried out.

Marketing intermediaries (once called *middlemen*) are organizations that assist in moving goods and services from producers to businesses (B2B) and from businesses to consumers (B2C). They're called intermediaries because they're in the middle of a series of organizations that join together to help distribute goods from producers to consumers. A **channel of distribution** consists of a whole set of marketing intermediaries, such as agents, brokers, wholesalers, and retailers, that join together to transport and store goods in their path (or channel) from producers to consumers. **Agents/brokers** are marketing intermediaries who bring buyers and sellers together and assist in negotiating an exchange but don't take title to the goods—that is, at no point do they own the goods. Think of real estate agents as an example.

A **wholesaler** is a marketing intermediary that sells to other organizations, such as retailers, manufacturers, and hospitals. Wholesalers are part of the B2B system. Because of high distribution costs, Walmart tries to eliminate independent wholesalers from its system and do the job itself. That is, Walmart provides its own warehouses and has its own trucks. It has

Uli Deck/picture alliance/Getty Images

over 150 distribution centers and 61,000 trailers to distribute goods to its thousands of stores and 260 million weekly customers.[3] Finally, a **retailer** is an organization that sells to ultimate consumers (people like you and me).

Channels of distribution help ensure communication flows *and* the flow of money and title to goods. They also help ensure that the right quantity and assortment of goods will be available when and where needed. Figure 15.1 shows selected channels of distribution for both consumer and industrial goods.

You can see the distribution system in the United States at work when you drive down any highway and see the thousands of trucks and trains moving goods from here to there. Less visible, however, are the many distribution warehouses that store goods until they are needed. Have you ever thought about the benefits of having food, furniture, and other needed goods close at hand? Have you seen distribution warehouses along the road as you drive from town to town?

agents/brokers
Marketing intermediaries who bring buyers and sellers together and assist in negotiating an exchange but don't take title to the goods.

wholesaler
A marketing intermediary that sells to other organizations.

retailer
An organization that sells to ultimate consumers.

FIGURE 15.1 SELECTED CHANNELS OF DISTRIBUTION FOR CONSUMER AND INDUSTRIAL GOODS AND SERVICES

Channels for consumer goods						Channels for industrial goods	
This channel is used by craftspeople and small farmers.	This channel is used for cars, furniture, and clothing.	This channel is the most common channel for consumer goods such as groceries, drugs, and cosmetics.	This is a common channel for food items such as produce.	This is a common channel for consumer services such as real estate, stocks and bonds, insurance, and nonprofit theater groups.	This is a common channel for nonprofit organizations that want to raise funds. Included are museums, government services, and zoos.	This is the common channel for industrial products such as glass, tires, and paint for automobiles.	This is the way that lower-cost items such as supplies are distributed. The wholesaler is called an industrial distributor.
Manufacturer	Manufacturer	Manufacturer	Farmer	Service organization	Nonprofit organization	Manufacturer	Manufacturer
		Wholesaler	Broker				Wholesaler
	Retailer		Wholesaler	Broker	Store		
		Retailer	Retailer				
Consumers						Industrial users	

iSeeit! Need help understanding distribution channels? Visit your Connect eBook to view a video for a brief animated explanation.

Why Marketing Needs Intermediaries

Figure 15.1 shows that some manufacturers sell directly to consumers. So why have marketing intermediaries at all? The answer is that intermediaries perform certain marketing tasks—such as transporting, storing, selling, advertising, and relationship building—faster and more cheaply than most manufacturers could. Here's a simple analogy: You could personally deliver packages to people anywhere in the world, but usually you don't. Why not? Because it's generally cheaper and faster to have them delivered by the U.S. Postal Service or a private firm such as UPS.

Similarly, you could sell your home by yourself or buy stock directly from individual companies, but you probably wouldn't. Why? Again, because agents and brokers are marketing intermediaries who make the exchange process easier and more efficient and profitable. In the next section, we'll explore how intermediaries improve the efficiency of various market exchanges.

How Intermediaries Create Exchange Efficiency

Here is an easy way to see the benefits of using marketing intermediaries. Suppose five manufacturers of various food products each tried to sell directly to five retailers. The number of exchange relationships needed to create this market is 5 times 5, or 25.

But picture what happens when a wholesaler enters the system. The five manufacturers each contact the wholesaler, establishing five exchange relationships. The wholesaler then establishes contact with the five retailers, creating five more exchange relationships. The wholesaler's existence reduces the number of exchanges from 25 to only 10. Figure 15.2 shows this process.

Some economists have said that intermediaries add *costs* and should be eliminated. Marketers say intermediaries add *value,* and that the *value greatly exceeds the cost.* Let's explore this debate and see what value intermediaries provide.

FIGURE 15.2 HOW INTERMEDIARIES CREATE EXCHANGE EFFICIENCY
This figure shows that adding a wholesaler to the channel of distribution cuts the number of contacts from 25 to 10. This improves the efficiency of distribution.

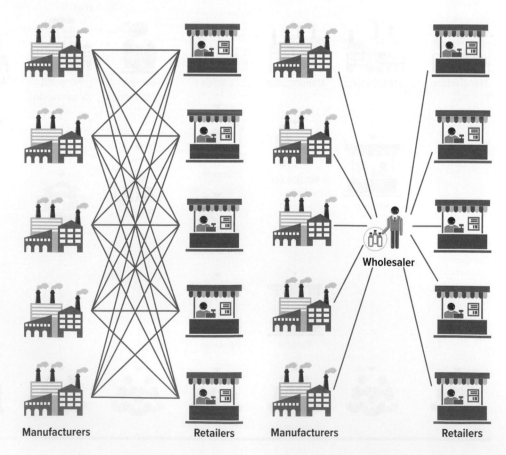

Manufacturers Retailers Manufacturers Retailers

Wholesaler

The Value versus the Cost of Intermediaries

The public has often viewed marketing intermediaries with a degree of suspicion. Some surveys show about half the cost of what we buy is marketing costs that go largely to pay for the work of intermediaries. If we could only get rid of intermediaries, people reason, we could greatly reduce the cost of everything we buy. Sounds good, but is the solution really that simple?

Take a box of cereal that sells for $4. How could we, as consumers, get the cereal for less? Well, we could all drive to Michigan, where some cereal is produced, and save shipping costs. But imagine millions of people getting in their cars and driving to Michigan just to buy cereal. No, it doesn't make sense. It's much cheaper to have intermediaries bring the cereal to major cities. That might make transportation and warehousing by wholesalers necessary. These steps add cost, don't they? Yes, but they add value as well—the value of not having to drive to Michigan.

The cereal is now in a warehouse somewhere on the outskirts of the city. We could all drive down to the wholesaler and pick it up. But that still isn't the most economical way to buy cereal. If we figure in the cost of gas and time, the cereal will again be too expensive. Instead, we prefer to have someone move the cereal from the warehouse to a truck, drive it to the corner supermarket, unload it, unpack it, price it, shelve it, and wait for us to come in to buy it. To make it even more convenient, the supermarket may stay open for 24 hours a day, seven days a week. Think of the costs. But think also of the value! For $4, we can get a box of cereal *when* we want it, and with little effort.

If we were to get rid of the retailer, we could buy a box of cereal for slightly less, but we'd have to drive farther and spend time in the warehouse looking through rows of cereals. If we got rid of the wholesaler, we could save a little more money, not counting our drive to Michigan. But a few cents here and there add up—to the point where distribution (marketing) may add up to 75 cents for every 25 cents in manufacturing costs. Figure 15.3 shows where your money goes in the food product distribution process. Note that only 3.5 cents goes to profit.

FIGURE 15.3
DISTRIBUTION'S EFFECT ON YOUR FOOD DOLLAR
Note that the farmer gets only 10.4 cents of your food dollar. The bulk of your money goes to intermediaries.

Source: USDA Economic Research Service, ers.usda.gov, accessed March 2020.

Total distribution costs

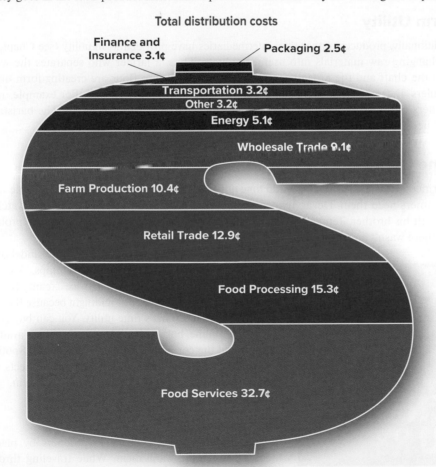

Finance and Insurance 3.1¢
Packaging 2.5¢
Transportation 3.2¢
Other 3.2¢
Energy 5.1¢
Wholesale Trade 9.1¢
Farm Production 10.4¢
Retail Trade 12.9¢
Food Processing 15.3¢
Food Services 32.7¢

Here are three basic points about intermediaries:

1. Marketing intermediaries can be eliminated, but their activities can't; that is, you can eliminate some wholesalers and retailers, but then consumers or someone else would have to perform the intermediaries' tasks, including transporting and storing goods, finding suppliers, and establishing communication with suppliers. Not all organizations use all the intermediaries. That doesn't mean an organization doesn't use intermediaries, such as retailers; it just means that some intermediary functions can be done in-house.

2. Intermediary organizations have survived because they perform marketing functions faster and more cheaply than others can. To maintain their competitive position in the channel, they now must adopt the latest technology. That includes using search engine optimization, monitoring social media sites, and analyzing website statistics to understand their customers better.

3. Intermediaries add costs to products, but these costs are usually more than offset by the values they create.

> **LO 15–2** Demonstrate how intermediaries perform the six marketing utilities.

The Utilities Created by Intermediaries

Utility, in economics, is the want-satisfying ability, or value, that organizations add to goods or services by making them more useful or accessible to consumers than they were before. The six kinds of utility are form, time, place, possession, information, and service. Although producers provide some utilities, marketing intermediaries provide most. Let's look at how.

Form Utility

Traditionally, producers rather than intermediaries have provided form utility (see Chapter 9) by changing raw materials into useful products. Thus, a farmer who separates the wheat from the chaff and the processor who turns the wheat into flour are creating form utility. Retailers and other marketers sometimes provide form utility as well. For example, retail butchers cut pork chops from a larger piece of meat and trim off the fat. The baristas at Starbucks make coffee just the way you want it.

Time Utility

Intermediaries, such as retailers, add **time utility** to products by making them available when consumers need them. Devar Tennent lives in Boston. One winter evening while watching TV with his brother, Tennent suddenly got the urge for a burger and a Coke. The problem was there wasn't any meat or Cokes in the house.

Tennent ran down to the corner store and bought some meat, buns, Cokes, and potato chips. He also bought some frozen strawberries and ice cream. Tennent was able to get these groceries at midnight because the store was open 24 hours. That's time utility. You can buy goods at any time online, but you can't beat having them available right around the corner *when you want them.* The Spotlight on Small Business box describes how Heal connects doctors to patients based on when customers need them.

Place Utility

Intermediaries add **place utility** to products by placing them *where* people want them. While traveling through the badlands of South Dakota, Rosa Reyes got hungry and

utility

In economics, the want-satisfying ability, or value, that organizations add to goods or services when the products are made more useful or accessible to consumers than they were before.

time utility

Adding value to products by making them available when they're needed.

place utility

Adding value to products by having them where people want them.

Think of how many stores provide time utility by making goods and services available to you 24 hours a day, seven days a week. Have you ever craved a late-night snack or needed to renew a prescription after normal hours? Can you see how time utility offers added value?

Andriy Blokhin/Shutterstock

SPOTLIGHT ON SMALL BUSINESS

Docs on Demand

heal.com

When you're sick, the last thing you want to do is to get out of your pajamas and go to the doctor's office or urgent care. On top of the inconvenience and the shortage of urgent care and emergency room doctors, many Americans don't want to waste hours waiting in the discomfort of an unfamiliar place. Luckily, technology is already changing the way Americans seek health care. Telehealth programs allow us to videoconference with a doctor or nurse who can tell us whether or not our problem warrants in-person care. But what if we do need in-person care and can't make it to the office?

In old movies, we see doctors making house calls and treating their patients in their own homes. Wouldn't it be nice if we could bring that back? Renee Dua and Nick Desai are trying to do just that. In 2014, the husband and wife duo created the Heal app. In fact, both their toddler daughter

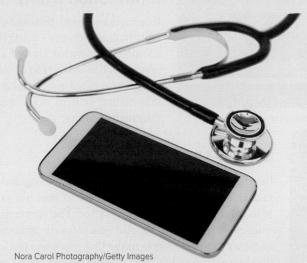

Nora Carol Photography/Getty Images

and aging parents are frequent Heal customers.

For a flat $90 fee, a doctor will visit to provide nearly any service regularly performed by a primary care physician. Doctors are available seven days a week between the hours of 8 a.m. and 8 p.m. The company provides the doctors with cars and a "Heal Hub" device to keep in households of patients

with chronic disease. The Heal Hub checks patients' vitals and has a two-way radio to connect patients with doctors at the push of a button. At the moment, Heal is still a growing company and operates in only a few large cities. In the near future, Dua and Desai believe the company will grow to provide healing services to 25 of the largest U.S. cities. That's a lot of people who won't have to get out of their pajamas.

Sources: Meeta Shah, "The Shortage of Physicians Can Be Deadly for Patients," *The Hill*, February 4, 2020; Heather Landi, "California House Call App Heal Acquires Doctors on Call, Expands to NYC Market," *Fierce Healthcare*, September 23, 2019; Susan Ladika, "Virtual Primary Care 'Visits'? That Future Is Already Here," *Managed Care Magazine*, February 7, 2020; Heal, heal.com, accessed March 2020.

---

thirsty. There are no stores for miles in this part of the country, but Rosa saw signs along the road saying a 7-Eleven was ahead. Following the signs, she stopped at the store for refreshments. She also bought some sunglasses and souvenir items there. The goods and services provided by 7-Eleven are in a convenient place for vacationers.

Throughout the United States, 7-Eleven stores remain popular because they are usually in easy-to-reach locations. They provide place utility. As more and more sales become global, place utility will grow in importance. Grocery stores have added pickup and delivery services, so that customers can order online and then pick up or receive their food at a convenient time and place.[4] This is just one more example of place utility.

Possession Utility

Intermediaries add **possession utility** by doing whatever is necessary to transfer ownership from one party to another, including providing credit. Activities associated with possession utility include delivery, installation, guarantees, and follow-up service. Larry Rosenberg wanted to buy a nice home in the suburbs. He found just what he wanted, but he didn't have the money he needed. So he went with the real estate broker to a local savings and loan and borrowed money to buy the home. Both the real estate broker and the savings and loan are marketing intermediaries that provide possession utility. For those

possession utility
Doing whatever is necessary to transfer ownership from one party to another, including providing credit, delivery, installation, guarantees, and follow-up service.

View Pictures/Universal Images Group/Getty Images

who don't want to own goods, possession utility makes it possible for them to use goods through renting or leasing.

Information Utility

Intermediaries add **information utility** by opening two-way flows of information between marketing participants. Jerome Washington couldn't decide what kind of TV to buy. He looked at various ads and reviews online and talked to salespeople at several stores. Newspapers, salespeople, libraries, websites, and government publications are all information sources made available by intermediaries. They provide information utility.

Service after the sale is one of the contributing factors to Apple's success. Customers can call to make an appointment with an Apple Genius who will help them learn how to use their computers, iPhones, or iPads. How does this service add value to Apple's products?

Service Utility

Intermediaries add **service utility** by providing fast, friendly service during and after the sale and by teaching customers how to best use products over time. Sze Leung bought a Mac from Apple for his home office. The Apple Store Leung used continues to offer help whenever he needs it. He also gets software updates to keep his computer up-to-date. What attracted Leung to Apple in the first place was the helpful, friendly service he received from the salesperson in the store and the service from the experts at the Genius Bar. Service utility is rapidly becoming the most important utility for many retailers, because without it they would lose business to direct marketing (e.g., marketing by catalog or online). Can you see how the Internet provides some forms of service utility?

TESTPREP

- What is a channel of distribution, and what intermediaries participate in it?
- Why do we need intermediaries? Illustrate how intermediaries create exchange efficiency.
- How would you defend intermediaries to someone who said getting rid of them would save consumers millions of dollars?
- Can you give examples of the utilities intermediaries create and how they provide them?

information utility
Adding value to products by opening two-way flows of information between marketing participants.

service utility
Adding value by providing fast, friendly service during and after the sale and by teaching customers how to best use products over time.

LO 15–3 Identify the types of wholesale intermediaries in the distribution system.

Wholesale Intermediaries

Let's stop for a minute and distinguish wholesaling from retailing and clearly define the functions of each. Some producers deal only with wholesalers and won't sell directly to retailers or to end users (consumers). Some producers deal with both wholesalers and retailers, but give wholesalers a bigger discount. In turn, some wholesalers sell to both retailers and consumers. The office superstore Staples is a good example. It sells office supplies to small businesses and to consumers as well. Warehouse clubs such as Sam's Club and Costco are other companies with both wholesale and retail functions.

The difference is this: A *retail sale* is the sale of goods and services to consumers *for their personal use.* A *wholesale sale* is the sale of goods and services to businesses and institutions, like schools or hospitals, *for use in the business,* or to wholesalers or retailers *for resale.*

Wholesalers make business-to-business sales. Most people are not as familiar with the various kinds of wholesalers as they are with retailers. So, let's explore some of these helpful wholesale intermediaries. Most of them provide a lot of marketing jobs and offer you a good career opportunity.

Merchant Wholesalers

Merchant wholesalers are independently owned firms that take title to the goods they handle. About 80 percent of wholesalers fall in this category.[5] There are two types of merchant wholesalers: full-service and limited-function.

Full-service wholesalers perform all the distribution functions. They provide a sales force to sell the goods, maintain inventory, communicate advertising deals, arrange the transportation of goods, and provide capital and market information, and they assume the risk for the goods. *Limited-function wholesalers,* on the other hand, perform select functions, but try to do them especially well. Three common types of limited-function wholesalers are rack jobbers, cash-and-carry wholesalers, and drop shippers.

Rack jobbers furnish racks or shelves full of merchandise, like music, toys, accessories, and health and beauty aids, to retailers. They display the products and sell them on consignment, meaning they keep title to the goods until they're sold and then share the profits with the retailer. Have you seen shelves at the supermarket full of magazines and related items? Rack jobbers likely put them there.

Cash-and-carry wholesalers serve mostly smaller retailers with a limited assortment of products. Traditionally, retailers went to such wholesalers, paid cash, and carried the goods back to their stores—thus the term *cash-and-carry.* Today, stores such as Staples allow retailers and others to use credit cards for wholesale purchases, so cash-and-carry is becoming obsolete for wholesalers.

Drop shippers solicit orders from retailers and other wholesalers and have the merchandise shipped directly from a producer to a buyer. They own the merchandise but don't handle, stock, or deliver it. That's done by the producer. Drop shippers tend to handle bulky products such as coal, lumber, and chemicals.

Agents and Brokers

Agents and brokers bring buyers and sellers together and assist in negotiating an exchange. However, unlike merchant wholesalers, agents and brokers never own the products. Usually they do not carry inventory, provide credit, or assume risks. While merchant wholesalers earn a profit from the sale of goods, agents and brokers earn commissions or fees based on a percentage of the sales revenues. Agents often maintain long-term relationships with the people they represent, whereas brokers are usually hired on a temporary basis.

Agents who represent producers are either *manufacturers' agents* or *sales agents.* As long as they do not carry competing products, manufacturers' agents may represent several manufacturers in a specific territory. They often work in the automotive supply, footwear, and fabricated steel industries. Sales agents represent a single producer in a typically larger territory.

Brokers have no continuous relationship with the buyer or seller. Once they negotiate a contract between the parties, their relationship ends. Producers of seasonal products like fruits and vegetables often use brokers, as does the real estate industry.

Noel Hendrickson/Getty Images

merchant wholesalers
Independently owned firms that take title to the goods they handle.

rack jobbers
Wholesalers that furnish racks or shelves full of merchandise to retailers, display products, and sell on consignment.

cash-and-carry wholesalers
Wholesalers that serve mostly smaller retailers with a limited assortment of products.

drop shippers
Wholesalers that solicit orders from retailers and other wholesalers and have the merchandise shipped directly from a producer to a buyer.

Agents and brokers are a familiar type of intermediary. Typically they don't take possession of the goods they sell. A real estate broker, for instance, facilitates the transaction between seller and buyer but never holds title to the house. What functions does a realtor provide in a home sale?

> **LO 15–4**   Compare the distribution strategies retailers use.

Retail Intermediaries

A retailer, remember, is a marketing intermediary, like a supermarket or a shoe store, that sells to ultimate consumers. The United States boasts more than 3.7 million retail stores. Retail organizations employ more than 42 million people and are one of the major employers of marketing graduates.[6] No doubt you're aware of the intense competition between retailers and Amazon. Retail stores and malls are fighting back by offering more entertainment, including indoor sports, and giving their stores major makeovers.[7] However, some say that Amazon will still win in the end. If so, what effect will Amazon's success have on the number of retail jobs?

Figure 15.4 lists, describes, and gives examples of various kinds of retailers. Have you shopped in each kind of store? What seem to be the advantages of each? Would you enjoy working in a retail store of some kind? Some retailers seem to compete mostly on price, but others, such as specialty stores, use variety as a competitive tool. Marketers use several strategies for retail distribution. We explain them next.

Retail Distribution Strategy

Because different products call for different retail distribution strategies, a major decision marketers must make is selecting the right retailers to sell their products. There are three categories of retail distribution: intensive, selective, and exclusive.

intensive distribution

Distribution that puts products into as many retail outlets as possible.

Intensive distribution puts products into as many retail outlets as possible, including vending machines. Products that need intensive distribution include convenience goods such as soft drinks, candy, gum, and popular magazines.

FIGURE 15.4 TYPES OF RETAIL STORES

TYPE	DESCRIPTION	EXAMPLE
Department store	Sells a wide variety of products (clothes, furniture, housewares) in separate departments	Macy's, JCPenney, Nordstrom
Discount store	Sells many different products at prices generally below those of department stores	Walmart, Target
Supermarket	Sells mostly food with other nonfood products such as detergent and paper products	Safeway, Kroger, Albertsons
Warehouse club	Sells food and general merchandise in facilities that are usually larger than supermarkets and offers discount prices; membership may be required	Costco, Sam's Club
Convenience store	Sells food and other often-needed items at convenient locations; may stay open all night	7-Eleven
Category killer	Sells a huge variety of one type of product to dominate that category of goods	Bass Pro Shops, Office Depot/OfficeMax
Outlet store	Sells general merchandise directly from the manufacturer at a discount; items may be discontinued or have flaws ("seconds")	Nordstrom Rack, Liz Claiborne, Nike, TJ Maxx
Specialty store	Sells a wide selection of goods in one category	Jewelry stores, shoe stores, bicycle shops

Selective distribution uses only a preferred group of the available retailers in an area. Such selection helps ensure producers of quality sales and service. Manufacturers of appliances, furniture, and clothing (shopping goods) use selective distribution.

Exclusive distribution is the use of only one retail outlet in a given geographic area. The retailer has exclusive rights to sell the product and is therefore likely to carry a large inventory, give exceptional service, and pay more attention to this brand than to others. Luxury auto manufacturers often use exclusive distribution, as do producers of specialty goods such as skydiving equipment.

selective distribution
Distribution that sends products to only a preferred group of retailers in an area.

exclusive distribution
Distribution that sends products to only one retail outlet in a given geographic area.

?TESTPREP

- Describe the activities of rack jobbers and drop shippers.
- What kinds of products would call for each of the different distribution strategies: intensive, selective, and exclusive?

LO 15–5 Explain the various kinds of nonstore retailing.

Online Retailing and Other Nonstore Retailing

Nothing else in retailing has received more attention than online retailing.[8] Online retailing (e.g., Amazon, Zappos, etc.) is just one form of nonstore retailing. Other categories include telemarketing; vending machines, kiosks, carts, and pop-ups; direct selling; multilevel marketing; and direct marketing. Small businesses can use nonstore retailing to open up new channels of distribution for their products.

Online Retailing

Online retailing consists of selling goods and services to ultimate consumers online. **Social commerce** is a form of electronic commerce that involves using social media, online media that support social interaction, and user contributions to assist in the online buying and selling of products and services (see Figure 15.5 for a list of different types of social commerce).

online retailing
Selling goods and services to ultimate customers (e.g., you and me) over the Internet.

social commerce
A form of electronic commerce that involves using social media, online media that support social interaction, and user contributions to assist in the online buying and selling of products and services.

FIGURE 15.5 TYPES OF SOCIAL COMMERCE

Social commerce denotes a wide range of shopping, recommending, and selling behaviors. As these models are tested and proven to increase sales and customer satisfaction, more will be introduced.

1. **Peer-to-peer sales platforms** (also known as *consumer-to-consumer* or *C2C marketing;* examples include eBay, Etsy, Amazon Marketplace, Getaround): Community-based marketplaces where individuals communicate and sell directly to each other.
2. **Social network shops and shopping apps** (Facebook Marketplace, Twitter, Instagram, Pinterest): Sales driven by referrals from established social platforms.
3. **Group buyings and daily deals** (Groupon, LivingSocial, Scoutmob): Products and services offered at a reduced rate if enough people agree to buy.
4. **Peer recommendations** (Amazon, Yelp): Sites that aggregate product or service reviews, recommend products based on others' purchasing history.
5. **User-curated shopping** (Fancy, Lyst): Shopping-focused sites where users create and share lists of products and services that others can shop from.
6. **Crowdfunding/crowdsourcing** (Threadless, Kickstarter, Indiegogo): Consumers become involved directly in the production process through voting, funding, and collaboratively designing products.
7. **Social shopping** (ModCloth, Fab, Fancy): Shopping sites that includes chat and forum features for people to discuss and exchange advice and opinions.

Sources: "The 7 Types of Social Commerce," *Conversity,* conversity.com, accessed March 2020; Megan DeGruttola, "8 Social Commerce Strategies to Win Consumers' Hearts and Wallets in 2020," *Social Media Today,* February 2, 2020.

Traveling by airplane in a post-COVID-19 world is considerably different as passengers must make sure to stock up on personal protective equipment like face masks and hand sanitizer. Thankfully, vending machines like this one provide travelers with a quick and clean way to obtain essential items before a flight. Can you think of any other useful products that could be sold from a vending machine?

Thanks to website improvements and discounting, online retail sales have risen dramatically.[9] But getting customers is only half the battle. The other half is delivering the goods, providing helpful service, and keeping your customers. When online retailers lack sufficient inventory or fail to deliver goods on time (especially at holidays and other busy periods), customers often give up and go back to brick-and-mortar stores.

Online retailers offer e-mail order confirmation. But sometimes they are not as good as stores at handling complaints, accepting returns, and providing personal help. Some online sellers are improving customer service by adding help buttons and consistently monitoring their social media accounts to give customers real-time online assistance from a human employee.

Brick-and-mortar stores that add online outlets are sometimes called brick-and-click stores. They allow customers to choose which shopping technique suits them best. Most companies that want to compete in the future will probably need both a real store and an online presence to provide consumers with all the options they want.[10]

Traditional retailers like Sears have learned that selling online calls for a new kind of distribution.[11] Sears's warehouses were accustomed to delivering truckloads of goods to the company's retail outlets. But they were not prepared to deliver to individual consumers, except for large orders like furniture and appliances. It turns out, therefore, that both traditional and online retailers have to develop new distribution systems to meet the demands of today's shoppers. It's often easy to sell goods on eBay, but there is always the need to distribute those goods. Most people outsource that function to FedEx or UPS, which have the needed expertise. Some brick-and-click stores offer their customers the option of saving on shipping costs by picking up their online purchases in a store, hoping they'll buy more while they're there.

Telemarketing

Telemarketing is the sale of goods and services by telephone. Many companies use it to supplement or replace in-store selling and complement online selling. Many send a catalog to consumers, who order by calling a toll-free number. Many electronic retailers provide a help feature online that serves the same function.

Vending Machines, Kiosks, Carts, and Pop-Ups

Vending machines dispense convenience goods when consumers deposit sufficient money. They carry the benefit of location—they're found in airports, office buildings, schools, service stations, and other areas where people want convenience items. In Japan, they sell everything from bandages and face cloths to salads and spiced seafood. Vending by machine will be an interesting area to watch as more innovations are introduced in the United States. U.S. vending machines are already selling iPods, Bose headphones, sneakers, digital cameras, and DVD movies. You can even find cars and trucks in some vending machines.[12] An ATM in Abu Dhabi dispenses gold.

Carts and kiosks have lower overhead costs than stores do, so they can offer lower prices on items such as T-shirts, purses, watches, and smartphones. You often see vending carts outside stores or along walkways in malls. Some mall owners love them because they're colorful and create a marketplace atmosphere. Kiosk workers often dispense coupons and helpful product information. You may have noticed airlines are using kiosks to speed the process of getting on the plane. Most provide a boarding pass and allow you to change your seat.

Pop-up stores are quickly gaining in popularity around the country. Pop-ups are temporary outlets that remain open for a short amount of time in small spaces and offer items not found in traditional stores. For online business owners they can drum up new business, allow customers to see their goods in person, save on shipping expenses, and even "test drive" operating a brick-and-mortar store. Building owners also benefit from pop-ups because they can generate rent on a currently empty space.[13]

Direct Selling

Direct selling reaches consumers in their homes or workplaces. Many businesses use direct selling to sell cosmetics, household goods, lingerie, clothes, and candles at house parties they sponsor. Because so many men and women work outside the home and aren't in during the day, companies that use direct selling are sponsoring parties at workplaces or at home on evenings and weekends. Some companies, however, have dropped most of their direct selling efforts in favor of online selling.

direct selling
Selling to consumers in their homes or where they work.

Multilevel Marketing

Many companies have had success using multilevel marketing (MLM) and salespeople who work as independent contractors. Some of the best-known MLM companies include Avon, Thirty-One, and Arbonne.[14] Salespeople earn commissions on their own sales, create commissions for the "upliners" who recruited them, and receive commissions from any "downliners" they recruit to sell. When you have hundreds of downliners—people recruited by the people you recruit—your commissions can be sizable. Some people make tens of thousands of dollars a month this way. The main attraction of multilevel marketing for employees, other than the potential for making money, is the low cost of entry. For a small investment, the average person can get started and begin recruiting others.

That doesn't mean you should get involved with such schemes.[15] Many people question MLM because some companies using it have acted unethically. More often than not, people at the bottom buy the products themselves and sell a bare minimum, if anything, to others. In other words, be careful of multilevel schemes as a seller and as a buyer. But do not dismiss them out of hand, because some are successful. Potential employees must be very careful to examine the practices of such firms.

Direct Marketing

Direct marketing includes any activity that directly links manufacturers or intermediaries with the ultimate consumer. It includes direct mail, catalog sales, and telemarketing as well as online marketing. Popular consumer catalog companies that use direct marketing include L.L.Bean and Lands' End. Direct marketing has created tremendous competition in some high-tech areas as well.

direct marketing
Any activity that directly links manufacturers or intermediaries with the ultimate consumer.

Direct marketing has become popular because shopping from home or work is more convenient for consumers than going to stores. Instead of driving to a mall, people can shop online. Or they can browse catalogs and advertising supplements in the newspaper and magazines and then buy by phone, mail, or online. Interactive online selling provides increasing competition for retail stores. For example, L.L.Bean put pressure on rivals by eliminating shipping charges. That made L.L.Bean even more attractive to people who like to shop by catalog or online.

Direct marketing took on a new dimension with interactive video. Companies that use interactive video have become major competitors for those who market through static paper catalogs. For example, customers watching a video of a model moving and turning around in a dress get a much better idea of the look and feel of the outfit than simply seeing it in a printed photo.

To offer consumers the maximum benefit, marketing intermediaries must work together to ensure a smooth flow of goods and services. There hasn't always been total harmony in the channel of distribution. As a result, channel members have created systems to make the flows more efficient. We'll discuss those next.

corporate distribution system

A distribution system in which all of the organizations in the channel of distribution are owned by one firm.

contractual distribution system

A distribution system in which members are bound to cooperate through contractual agreements.

administered distribution system

A distribution system in which producers manage all of the marketing functions at the retail level.

supply chain (value chain)

The sequence of linked activities that must be performed by various organizations to move goods from the sources of raw materials to ultimate consumers.

benedek/Getty Images

Franchisors like Edible Arrangements use a contractual distribution system that requires franchisees to follow the franchisors' rules and procedures. How does such a system ensure consistent quality and level of service?

> **LO 15–6**   Explain the various ways to build cooperation in channel systems.

Building Cooperation in Channel Systems

One way traditional retailers can compete with online retailers is to be so efficient that online retailers can't beat them on cost—given the need for customers to pay for delivery. That means manufacturers, wholesalers, and retailers must work closely to form a unified system.[16] How can manufacturers get wholesalers and retailers to cooperate in such a system? One way is to link the firms in a formal relationship. Four systems have emerged to tie firms together: corporate systems, contractual systems, administered systems, and supply chains.

Corporate Distribution Systems

In a **corporate distribution system** one firm owns all the organizations in the channel of distribution. If the manufacturer owns the retail firm, clearly it can maintain a great deal of control over its operations. Paint giant Sherwin-Williams engages in the manufacture, distribution, and sale of its products. It owns its own retail stores and coordinates everything: display, pricing, promotion, inventory control, and so on.

Contractual Distribution Systems

If a manufacturer can't buy retail stores, it can try to get retailers to sign a contract to cooperate with it. In a **contractual distribution system** members are bound to cooperate through contractual agreements. There are three forms of contractual systems:

1. *Franchise systems* such as McDonald's, Planet Fitness, Baskin-Robbins, and Dunkin'. The franchisee agrees to all the rules, regulations, and procedures established by the franchiser. This results in the consistent quality and level of service you find in most franchised organizations.

2. *Wholesaler-sponsored chains* such as Ace Hardware and IGA food stores. Each store signs an agreement to use the same name, participate in chain promotions, and cooperate as a unified system of stores, even though each is independently owned and managed.

3. *Retail cooperatives* such as Associated Grocers. This arrangement is much like a wholesaler-sponsored chain except it is initiated by the retailers. The same degree of cooperation exists, and the stores remain independent. Normally in such a system, retailers agree to focus their purchases on one wholesaler, but cooperative retailers could also purchase a wholesale organization to ensure better service.

Administered Distribution Systems

If you were a producer, what would you do if you couldn't get retailers to sign an agreement to cooperate? You might manage all the marketing functions yourself, including display, inventory control, pricing, and promotion. A system in which producers manage all the marketing functions at the retail level is called an **administered distribution system**. Kraft does that for its cheeses. Scotts does it for its seed and other lawn care products. Retailers cooperate with producers in such systems because they get a great deal of free help. All the retailer has to do is ring up the sale.

Supply Chains

A **supply chain (value chain)** consists of all the linked activities various organizations must perform to move goods and services from the sources of raw materials to ultimate consumers. A supply chain is longer than a channel of distribution because it includes links from

FIGURE 15.6 THE SUPPLY CHAIN

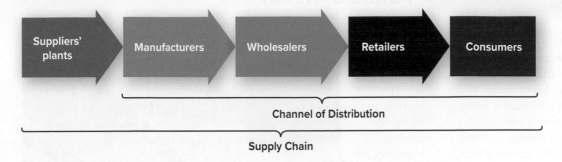

suppliers to manufacturers, whereas the channel of distribution begins with manufacturers. Channels of distribution are part of the overall supply chain (see Figure 15.6).

Included in the supply chain are farmers, miners, suppliers of all kinds (parts, equipment, supplies), manufacturers, wholesalers, and retailers. **Supply-chain management** is the process of managing the movement of raw materials, parts, work in progress, finished goods, and related information through all the organizations in the supply chain; managing the return of such goods if necessary; and recycling materials when appropriate. A key issue today is making the supply chain sustainable because so much of what affects the environment is caused by distribution.[17]

One complex supply chain is that for the automaker Kia's Sorento model. The Sorento is assembled in West Point, Georgia, and made of over 30,000 components from all over the world.[18] The shock and front-loading system is from German company ZF Sachs AG, the front-wheel drive is from BorgWarner, and the tires are from Michelin. Air bags are sometimes flown in from Swedish company Autoliv Inc., which makes them in Utah. As you can see, supply-chain management is interfirm and international.

Companies like SAP, i2, and Oracle have developed software to coordinate the movement of goods and information so that producers can translate consumer wants into products with the least amount of materials, inventory, and time. Firms can move parts and information so smoothly, they look like one firm. Naturally, the software systems are quite complex and expensive, but they can pay for themselves in the long run because of inventory savings, customer service improvement, and responsiveness to market changes. Because such systems are so effective and efficient, they are sometimes called *value chains* instead of supply chains. Starbucks has a value chain that includes a series of activities that claim to add value to its products at every step in the production process.[19]

Not all supply chains are as efficient as they can be. Some companies have struggled with high distribution costs, including the cost of disruptions, inefficient truck routes, and excess inventory. The complexity of supply-chain management often leads firms to outsource the whole process to experts who know how to integrate it. Imagine a company that does business in 125 countries with 37 different currencies. It may use services such as Oracle's PeopleSoft Supply Chain Management and Financial Management solutions. PeopleSoft provides financial help, making it easier and less expensive to ship goods anywhere in the world and be sure of payment.

Outsourcing supply-chain management is on the rise as more firms realize how complex distribution is. Outsourcing this function can have serious consequences, as companies learned when they found lead paint in toys and contaminants in the drug heparin.

supply-chain management
The process of managing the movement of raw materials, parts, work in progress, finished goods, and related information through all the organizations involved in the supply chain; managing the return of such goods, if necessary; and recycling materials when appropriate.

LO 15–7 Describe logistics, and outline how intermediaries manage the transportation and storage of goods.

Logistics: Getting Goods to Consumers Efficiently

Shipping costs have risen dramatically in recent years. It has been estimated that distribution makes up 8 percent of GDP.[20] When shipping from country to country, it is often

Walmart's Vision of the Future of Retail

Making a list, walking the aisles, filling a cart, and waiting in line—that's the traditional way we grocery shop, and Walmart knows all about it. However, Walmart, along with many other retailers, is always looking to know just a little bit more about its customers. Recently Walmart rolled out its future vision of retail, the Intelligent Retail Lab (IRL).

The store itself is smaller than the typical Walmart Supercenter we're familiar with. But that's not the only difference. The IRL is equipped with over 1,500 cameras to watch every move we make and monitor the inventory of each item in the store. Shelves have sensors that immediately let management know when an item has been moved from the shelf. This helps greatly with inventory control and preventing the frustration of customers when facing an empty shelf. This monitoring aids in pricing, reordering, and

lessening waste in Walmart's IRL. The store is so wired, the cabling alone could go up Mount Everest five times!

While it sounds great to not have to worry about product shortages or to always have the best-looking meat and produce out on display, customers are expected to give up quite a bit of their privacy. Walmart asserts that all cameras are directed toward food and used to monitor inventory. However, the cameras can also map customers as they roam the store. Would

Mark Lennihan/AP Images

you be okay letting Walmart monitor your shopping style if it made the experience better for you?

Sources: Joe Toscano, "Walmart Intelligent Retail Lab (IRL) Breaches Privacy Nightmares While Promising a Better Tomorrow," *Forbes,* February 17, 2020; Matt Smith, "Walmart's New Intelligent Retail Lab Shows a Glimpse into the Future of Retail, IRL," Walmart, April 25, 2019; Minda Zetlin, "Walmart Rolls Out Futuristic AI-Powered Concept Store, Hoping to Best Amazon Go," *Inc.,* April 27, 2019; Chris Albrecht, "Report: Walmart+ to Take On Amazon Prime," *The Spoon,* February 27, 2020.

logistics
The marketing activity that involves planning, implementing, and controlling the physical flow of materials, final goods, and related information from points of origin to points of consumption to meet customer requirements at a profit.

inbound logistics
The area of logistics that involves bringing raw materials, packaging, other goods and services, and information from suppliers to producers.

materials handling
The movement of goods within a warehouse, from warehouses to the factory floor, and from the factory floor to various workstations.

impossible to use trucks or trains because the goods have to travel over water. Shipping via air is often prohibitively expensive, which sometimes narrows the choice to moving goods by ship. But how do you get the goods to the ship—and from the ship to the buyer? How do you keep costs low enough to make exchanges beneficial for you and your customers? And how do you handle foreign trade duties and taxes? Distributing goods globally is complicated. As transportation and distribution have grown more complex, marketers have responded by developing more sophisticated systems.

To better manage customs problems, for instance, many turn to web-based trade compliance systems. Firms like TradePoint and Xporta determine what paperwork is needed, cross-checking their databases for information about foreign trade duties and taxes, U.S. labor law restrictions, and federal regulations from the Food and Drug Administration or the Bureau of Alcohol, Tobacco, Firearms and Explosives. In other words, they manage logistics.

Logistics is the planning, implementing, and controlling of the physical flow of materials, final goods, and related information from points of origin to points of consumption to meet customer requirements at a profit. Logistics describes how companies perform the 7 Rs: getting the right product to the right place, to the right customer, at the right time, in the right quantity, in the right condition, and at the right price.[21] The Adapting to Change box discusses the logistics issues Walmart faces in order to get fresh food to consumers. **Inbound logistics** brings raw materials, packaging, other goods and services, and information from suppliers to producers.

Materials handling is the movement of goods within a warehouse, from warehouses to the factory floor, and from the factory floor to various workstations. *Factory processes* change raw materials and parts and other inputs into outputs, such as finished goods like shoes, cars, and clothes.

Outbound logistics manages the flow of finished products and information to business buyers and ultimately to consumers like you and me. What do you think of Amazon's idea of using drones to deliver goods to your home? Even if the company does follow through, widespread use of delivery drones is still probably a bit into the future.[22] **Reverse logistics** brings goods back to the manufacturer because of defects or for recycling materials.[23]

Logistics is as much about the movement of *information* as it is about the movement of goods. Customer wants and needs must flow through the system all the way to suppliers and must do so in real time. Information must also flow down through the system with no delay. That, of course, demands sophisticated hardware and software.

Third-party logistics is the use of outside firms to help move goods from here to there. It is part of the trend to outsource functions your firm cannot do more efficiently than outside firms. The third-party logistics providers (3PLs) that have superior capability in business intelligence and are proactively sharing that knowledge are the ones who will grow in the future.

How do you get products to people around the world after the sale? What are your options? You could send goods by truck, train, ship, or pipeline. You could use a shipping specialist, such as UPS, FedEx, or the U.S. Postal Service, but often that is expensive, especially for large items. Nonetheless, some of the most sophisticated marketers outsource the distribution process to such specialists. All transportation modes can be evaluated on basic service criteria: cost, speed, dependability, flexibility, frequency, and reach. Figure 15.7 compares the various transportation modes on these criteria.

Trains Are Great for Large Shipments

The largest percentage of goods in the United States (by volume) is shipped by rail.[24] Railroad shipment is best for bulky items such as coal, wheat, automobiles, and heavy equipment. Railroads should continue to hold their own in competition with other modes of transportation.[25] They offer a relatively energy-efficient way to move goods and could experience significant gains especially if fuel prices climb again. Even short-line railroads (those that connect local branches of track to larger lines) will be growing.

A company may not ship enough goods to think of using a railroad. Such smaller manufacturers or marketers can get good rates and service by using a **freight forwarder**, which puts many small shipments together to create a single large one that can be transported cost-effectively by truck or train. Such shipments are known as less-than-carload (LCL) shipments. Some freight forwarders also offer warehousing, customs assistance, and other services along with pickup and delivery. You can see the benefits of such a company to a smaller seller. A freight forwarder is just one of many distribution specialists that have emerged to help marketers move goods from one place to another.

outbound logistics
The area of logistics that involves managing the flow of finished products and information to business buyers and ultimate consumers (people like you and me).

reverse logistics
The area of logistics that involves bringing goods back to the manufacturer because of defects or for recycling materials.

freight forwarder
An organization that puts many small shipments together to create a single large shipment that can be transported cost-effectively to the final destination.

FIGURE 15.7 COMPARING TRANSPORTATION MODES
Combining trucks with railroads lowers cost and increases the number of locations reached. The same is true when combining trucks with ships. Combining trucks with airlines speeds goods over long distances and gets them to almost any location.

MODE	COST	SPEED	ON-TIME DEPENDABILITY	FLEXIBILITY HANDLING PRODUCTS	FREQUENCY OF SHIPMENTS	REACH
Railroads	Medium	Slow	Medium	High	Low	High
Trucks	High	Fast	High	Medium	High	Highest
Pipelines	Low	Medium	Highest	Lowest	Highest	Lowest
Ships (water)	Lowest	Slowest	Lowest	Highest	Lowest	Low
Airplanes	Highest	Fastest	Low	Low	Medium	Medium

Railroads carry over a third of all goods shipped within the United States and are expected to remain a dominant transportation mode. What are some of the advantages of shipping by rail, both for large and small producers?

Digital Vision/Getty Images

Trucks Are Good for Small Shipments to Remote Locations

The second-largest surface transportation mode is motor vehicles (trucks and vans). As Figure 15.7 shows, trucks reach more locations than trains and can deliver almost any commodity door-to-door.

You could buy your own truck to make deliveries, but for widespread delivery you can't beat trucking specialists. Like freight forwarders, they have emerged to supply one important marketing function—transporting goods.

When fuel prices rise, trucking companies look for ways to cut costs. The newest measure of transportation from farm to consumer is the *carbon cost*. Some argue that the fewer miles food travels, the better for the environment.

Water Transportation Is Inexpensive but Slow

When sending goods overseas, often the least expensive way is by ship. Obviously, ships are slower than ground or air transportation, so water transportation isn't appropriate for goods that need to be delivered quickly. Water transport is local as well as international. If you live near the Mississippi River, you've likely seen towboats hauling as many as 30 barges at a time, with a cargo of up to 45,000 tons. On smaller rivers, towboats can haul about eight barges, carrying up to 20,000 tons—that's the equivalent of four 100-car railroad trains. Add to that Great Lakes shipping, shipping from coast to coast and along the coasts, and international shipments, and water transportation takes on a new dimension as a key transportation mode.

Pipelines Are Fast and Efficient

One transportation mode we don't often observe is pipelines. Pipelines primarily transport water, petroleum, and petroleum products—but a lot more products than you may imagine are shipped by pipelines. For example, coal can be sent by pipeline by first crushing it and mixing it with water. Today, there is a lot of discussion about shipping natural gas by pipeline. Much shale oil is now being shipped by rail, but recent accidents are leading companies to move to pipelines.[26] The battle between railroads and pipelines is going to be a huge one.

Air Transportation Is Fast but Expensive

Today, only a small proportion of shipping goes by air. Nonetheless, air transportation is a critical factor in many industries, carrying everything from small packages to luxury cars and elephants. Its primary benefit is speed. No firms know this better than FedEx and UPS. As just two of several competitors vying for the fast-delivery market, FedEx and UPS have used air transport to expand into global markets.

The air freight industry is starting to focus on global distribution. Emery, now part of UPS, has been an industry pioneer in establishing specialized sales and operations teams aimed at serving the distribution needs of specific industries. KLM Royal Dutch Airlines has cargo/passenger planes that handle high-profit items such as diplomatic pouches and medical supplies. Specializing in such cargo has enabled KLM to compete with FedEx and DHL.

Intermodal Shipping

Intermodal shipping uses multiple modes of transportation—highway, air, water, rail—to complete a single long-distance movement of freight. Services that specialize in intermodal shipping are known as intermodal marketing companies. Today, railroads are partnering with each other and with other transportation companies to offer intermodal distribution.[27]

Railroads joined with trucking firms to create a shipping process called *trailer on flat car (TOFC)* or *piggybacking*. A truck trailer is detached from the cab, loaded onto a railroad flatcar, and taken to a destination where it is offloaded, attached to a truck, and driven to the customer's plant. Today, intermodal shipping containers, which detach from the truck trailer's chassis, are widely used in place of truck trailers, and can be stacked two high on specially designed railcars called a double stack. This shipping process is called *container on flat car (COFC)*. When truck trailers are placed on ships to travel long distances at lower rates, it's called *fishyback*.

Picture an automobile made in Japan for sale in the United States. It's shipped by truck to a loading dock, and from there moved by ship to a port in the United States. It is then placed on another truck and taken to a railroad yard for loading on a train that will take it across the country, to again be loaded on a truck for delivery to a local dealer. Now imagine that one integrated shipping firm handled all that movement. That's what intermodal shipping is all about.

intermodal shipping
The use of multiple modes of transportation to complete a single long-distance movement of freight.

In order to transport heavy raw materials like timber from one country to another, trains and trucking companies bring logs to docks where huge cranes lift them onto a ship. Once the cargo has arrived at its destination, the ship must be unloaded and the logs transported to a processing plant. Why is managing the logistics process a key to survival in some industries?

The Storage Function

The preceding sections detailed the various ways of shipping goods once the company has sold them. But that's only the first step in understanding the system that moves goods from one point to another. Another important part of a complex logistics system is storage.

Buyers want goods delivered quickly. That means marketers must have goods available in various parts of the country ready to be shipped locally when ordered. Amazon builds warehouses all across the country in order to get goods to consumers faster.[28] A good percentage of the total cost of logistics is for storage. This includes the cost of the storage warehouse (distribution facility) and its operation, plus movement of goods within the warehouse.

m_albert/Shutterstock

Carlos Avila Gonzalez/The San
Francisco Chronicle/Getty Images

This retail robot named Tally manages inventory by scanning RFID tags on nearby racks of clothes and keeping track of items that a store has in stock. Can you think of any other uses for RFID tags?

Tracking Goods

There are two major kinds of warehouses: storage and distribution. A *storage warehouse* holds products for a relatively long time. Seasonal goods such as lawn mowers are kept in such a warehouse. *Distribution warehouses* are facilities used to gather and redistribute products. You can picture a distribution warehouse for FedEx or UPS handling thousands of packages in a very short time. The packages are picked up at places throughout the country and then processed for reshipment at these centers. Target's import warehouse in Savannah, Georgia, gives you a feel for how large such buildings can be. It measures 2 million square feet—that's enough to hold almost 30 football fields.[29]

How do producers keep track of where their goods are at any given time? As we noted in Chapter 14, some companies use Universal Product Codes—the familiar black-and-white bar codes and a preset number—to keep track of inventory. Bar codes got a big lift when smartphone apps made it possible to compare prices and read reviews about products from different suppliers.

Radio frequency identification (RFID), which we also mentioned earlier, tags merchandise so that it can be tracked from its arrival on the supplier's docks to its exit through the retailer's door.[30] Walmart, Target, and other organizations all plan to require suppliers to use RFID. The United States military uses RFID codes to track military equipment.

Few companies are more interested in tracking items than UPS, which uses a mix of Bluetooth's short-range radio capability and wireless receivers to track merchandise. It claims the system is even better than RFID. The U.S. State Department offers an electronic passport card as a substitute for passport books for use by U.S. citizens who travel often to Canada, Mexico, and the Caribbean. It uses an RFID chip to provide data about the user and is more convenient and less expensive than a passport book, though some people believe it can be easily altered.

What All This Means to Your Career

The life or death of a firm often depends on its ability to take orders, process orders, keep customers informed about the progress of their orders, get the goods out to customers quickly, handle returns, and manage any recycling issues. Some of the most exciting firms in the marketplace are those that assist in some aspect of supply-chain management.

What all this means to you is that many new jobs are becoming available in the exciting area of supply-chain management.[31] These include jobs in distribution: trains, airplanes, trucks, ships, and pipelines. It also means jobs handling information flows between and among companies, including website development. Other jobs include processing orders, keeping track of inventory, following the path of products as they move from seller to buyer and back, recycling goods, and much more. You can explore other careers in distribution in the Career Exploration section.

TESTPREP

- What four systems have evolved to tie together members of the channel of distribution?
- How does logistics differ from distribution?
- What are inbound logistics, outbound logistics, and reverse logistics?

SUMMARY

LO 15–1 Explain the concept of marketing channels and their value.

■ **What is a channel of distribution?**

A channel of distribution consists of a whole set of marketing intermediaries, such as agents, brokers, wholesalers, and retailers, that join together to transport and store goods in their path (or channel) from producers to consumers.

■ **How do marketing intermediaries add value?**

Intermediaries perform certain marketing tasks—such as transporting, storing, selling, advertising, and relationship building—faster and more cheaply than most manufacturers could. Channels of distribution ensure communication flows and the flow of money and title to goods. They also help ensure that the right quantity and assortment of goods will be available when and where needed.

■ **What are the principles behind the use of such intermediaries?**

Marketing intermediaries can be eliminated, but their activities can't. Without wholesalers and retailers, consumers would have to perform the tasks of transporting and storing goods, finding suppliers, and establishing communication with them. Intermediaries add costs to products, but these costs are usually more than offset by the values they create.

LO 15–2 Demonstrate how intermediaries perform the six marketing utilities.

■ **How do intermediaries perform the six marketing utilities?**

A retail grocer may cut or trim meat, providing some form utility. But marketers are more often responsible for the five other utilities. They provide time utility by having goods available *when* people want them, and place utility by having goods *where* people want them. Possession utility makes it possible for people to own things and includes credit, delivery, installation, guarantees, and anything else that completes the sale. Marketers also inform consumers of the availability of goods and services with advertising, publicity, and other means. That provides information utility. Finally, marketers provide fast, friendly, and efficient service during and after the sale (service utility).

LO 15–3 Identify the types of wholesale intermediaries in the distribution system.

■ **What is a wholesaler?**

A wholesaler is a marketing intermediary that sells to organizations and individuals, but not to final consumers.

■ **What are some wholesale organizations that assist in the movement of goods from manufacturers to consumers?**

Merchant wholesalers are independently owned firms that take title to the goods they handle. *Rack jobbers* furnish racks or shelves full of merchandise to retailers, display products, and sell on consignment. *Cash-and-carry wholesalers* serve mostly small retailers with a limited assortment of products. *Drop shippers* solicit orders from retailers and other wholesalers and have the merchandise shipped directly from a producer to a buyer.

LO 15–4 Compare the distribution strategies retailers use.

■ **What is a retailer?**

A retailer is an organization that sells to ultimate consumers. Marketers develop several strategies based on retailing.

- **What are three distribution strategies marketers use?**

  Marketers use three basic distribution strategies: intensive (putting products in as many places as possible), selective (choosing only a few stores in a chosen market), and exclusive (using only one store in each market area).

LO 15–5 Explain the various kinds of nonstore retailing.

- **What are some of the forms of nonstore retailing?**

  Nonstore retailing includes online retailing; telemarketing (marketing by phone); vending machines, kiosks, and pop-up stores (marketing by putting products in convenient locations, such as in the halls of shopping centers); direct selling (marketing by approaching consumers in their homes or places of work); multilevel marketing (marketing by setting up a system of salespeople who recruit other salespeople and help them sell directly to customers); and direct marketing (direct mail and catalog sales). Telemarketing and online marketing are also forms of direct marketing.

LO 15–6 Explain the various ways to build cooperation in channel systems.

- **What are the four types of distribution systems?**

  The four distribution systems that tie firms together are (1) *corporate systems,* in which all organizations in the channel are owned by one firm; (2) *contractual systems,* in which members are bound to cooperate through contractual agreements; (3) *administered systems,* in which all marketing functions at the retail level are managed by manufacturers; and (4) *supply chains,* in which the various firms in the supply chain are linked electronically to provide the most efficient movement of information and goods possible.

LO 15–7 Describe logistics, and outline how intermediaries manage the transportation and storage of goods.

- **What is logistics?**

  Logistics includes planning, implementing, and controlling the physical flow of materials, final goods, and related information from points of origin to points of consumption to meet customer requirements at a profit.

- **What is the difference between logistics and distribution?**

  Distribution generally means transportation. Logistics is more complex. *Inbound logistics* brings raw materials, packaging, other goods and services, and information from suppliers to producers. *Materials handling* is the moving of goods from warehouses to the factory floor and to various workstations. *Outbound logistics* manages the flow of finished products and information to business buyers and ultimate consumers (people like you and me). *Reverse logistics* brings goods back to the manufacturer because of defects or for recycling materials.

- **What are the various transportation modes?**

  Transportation modes include rail (for heavy shipments within the country or between bordering countries); trucks (for getting goods directly to consumers); ships (for slow, inexpensive movement of goods, often internationally); pipelines (for moving water, oil, and other such goods); and airplanes (for shipping goods quickly).

- **What is intermodal shipping?**

  Intermodal shipping uses multiple modes of transportation—truck, air, water, rail—to complete a single long-distance movement of freight.

- **What are the different kinds of warehouses?**

  A storage warehouse stores products for a relatively long time. Distribution warehouses are used to gather and redistribute products.

administered distribution
  system 398
agents/brokers 386
cash-and-carry
  wholesalers 393
channel of
  distribution 386
contractual distribution
  system 398
corporate distribution
  system 398
direct marketing 397
direct selling 397
drop shippers 393
exclusive distribution 395

freight forwarder 401
inbound logistics 400
information utility 392
intensive distribution 394
intermodal shipping 403
logistics 400
marketing
  intermediaries 386
materials handling 400
merchant
  wholesalers 393
online retailing 395
outbound logistics 401
place utility 390

possession utility 391
rack jobbers 393
retailer 387
reverse logistics 401
selective distribution 395
service utility 392
social commerce 395
supply chain
  (value chain) 398
supply-chain
  management 399
telemarketing 396
time utility 390
utility 390
wholesaler 386

1. Imagine that we have eliminated marketing intermediaries, and you need groceries and shoes. How would you find out where the shoes and groceries are? How far would you have to travel to get them? How much money do you think you'd save for your time and effort?

2. Which intermediary do you think is most important today and why? What changes are happening to companies in that area?

3. Many suggest that a scarce item in the future will be water. If you could think of an inexpensive way to get water from places of abundance to places where it is needed for drinking, farming, and other uses, such as fracking, you could become a wealthy marketing intermediary. Pipelines are an alternative, but could you also freeze the water and ship it by train or truck? Could you use ships to tow icebergs to warmer climates? What other means of transporting water might there be?

PURPOSE

To examine how small businesses can learn to distribute their products directly to customers online.

EXERCISE

Some small-business owners have no idea how to begin selling goods online. Online resources such as the *How to Sell Online?* guide (ecommerceguide.com/sell-online) can help them learn what their options are. Go to this site and answer the following questions:

1. What is the difference between hosted and self-hosted e-commerce platforms?

2. What are the advantages and disadvantages of the two types of e-commerce platforms?

3. Imagine Harvest Gold is such a success that you now want to expand your business by selling the ingredients for healthy meals online. Which platform would you use? Why?

DEVELOPING CAREER SKILLS

KEY: ● **Team** ★ **Analytic** ▲ **Communication** ▣ **Technology**

★ 1. The six utilities of marketing are form, time, place, possession, information, and service. Give examples of organizations in your area that perform each of these functions.

▲ ★ ● 2. Form small groups and diagram how Dole might get pineapples from a field in Thailand to a canning plant in California to a store near your college. Include the intermediaries and the forms of transportation each one might use.

★ 3. Compare the merits of buying and selling goods in brick-and-mortar stores and online. What advantages do physical stores have? Has anyone in the class tried to sell anything online? How did he or she ship the product?

▲ ★ 4. In class, discuss the differences between wholesaling and retailing and why retailing has more appeal for students considering jobs. Since fewer students seek jobs in wholesaling than in retailing, do you think wholesaling jobs may be easier to get?

▲ ★ ● 5. One part of retailing is using auction sites like eBay to sell new and used merchandise. Form small groups and discuss group members' experiences using eBay. What tips have they learned? How do eBay users minimize the problems associated with shipping?

CAREER EXPLORATION

If you are interested in working in product distribution, here are a few careers to consider. Find out about the tasks performed, skills needed, pay, and opportunity outlook in these fields in the *Occupational Outlook Handbook (OOH)* at bls.gov.

- **Purchasing manager**—plans, directs, and coordinates the buying of materials, products, or services for wholesalers, retailers, or organizations.

- **Logistician**—analyzes and coordinates an organization's supply chain including how a product is acquired, distributed, allocated, and delivered.

- **Wholesale and manufacturing sales representative**—sells goods for wholesalers or manufacturers to businesses, government agencies, and other organizations.

- **Railroad worker**—ensures that passenger and freight trains run on time and travel safely.

VIDEO CASE *Tuft & Needle*

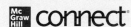

The Internet has had a tremendous impact on everyday life and business. Direct-to-consumer (D2C) businesses have literally exploded in the Internet age and have caused major shifts in traditional distribution channels. The efficiencies created by the Internet have allowed D2C companies to reduce or bypass the use of intermediaries in almost every industry. Intermediaries such as wholesalers, retailers, brokers, and agents are responsible for creating marketing utilities producers rely on to get their products to consumers in the most efficient manner. By eliminating such intermediaries, D2C companies needed to figure out how to assume the utility functions normally handled by them.

The Internet provides time utility by making products available for purchase at almost any time of day. However, some utilities are very difficult for companies to perform. Logistics (the planning and moving of materials and goods from one place to another) is a function that often has to be assumed by the D2C business itself. Tuft & Needle, a mattress company, found this out in 2012 when it tried to revolutionize the mattress industry.

J. T. Marino and Daehee Park decided to leave Silicon Valley jobs as software engineers and start their own business. After Marino had a bad experience purchasing a mattress, he and Park felt this could be a problem they could solve. Unfortunately, they found the mattress industry was a network essentially closed to new upstarts. Finally, they found a small manufacturer that agreed to produce their specialized mattresses. When they started business, Tuft & Needle would take the order and payment and then have the mattress made and ship it to customers. As business increased, the company had enough cash to carry inventory. The company also wanted to improve the form utility associated with its product. Tuft & Needle did this by designing its own foam for its mattresses and then shipping them directly to the factory. This reduced the role and cost of the mattress fabricator.

As a direct marketer, Tuft & Needle realized it needed to provide the greatest utility possible to customers. The company focused its objectives on three key categories: great customer service, fast delivery, and free returns. It knew that to provide great information utility the firm needed a great website. Tuft & Needle established a dedicated support page, live chat, YouTube channel, and customer service line. Shipment was handled through FedEx to ensure the product arrived promptly, providing time utility. The free-return policy proved the most challenging since FedEx charged over $600 to return a mattress to the company. The company decided to have customers donate returned mattresses to charities.

Though Tuft & Needle provided great service utility to its customers, the company found that many customers wanted to test out a mattress before buying one. Tuft & Needle opened its first retail store in 2016 and currently has expanded to six stores around the country. It also has agreements with major retailers such as Lowe's, Walmart, and Crate & Barrel where customers can try out the product. A decision was also made to sell mattresses on Amazon. This decision was made primarily so the firm could receive reviews from customers about its product and service. Today, out of over 8,000 reviews of the company, 75 percent have been five-star ratings, the highest possible rating.

As consumers shift and continue to buy more products online, more businesses will turn their efforts to D2C. The role of intermediaries will change and evolve to offer consumers the utilities they expect at prices that are acceptable.

THINKING IT OVER

1. What intermediaries are most threatened by the growth of direct-to-consumer (D2C) companies?

2. What products do you purchase from D2C companies? What products will you not purchase from D2Cs companies?

3. What's the value to a company in receiving very favorable customer reviews from a company such as Amazon?

NOTES

1. "Coronavirus Outbreak Deepens Its Toll on Global Business," *The New York Times,* February 21, 2020; Avi Salzman, "Coronavirus Is Disrupting Supply Chains. These Industries Are Most Vulnerable," *Barron's,* February 29, 2020; Pierre Haren and David Simchi-Levi, "How Coronavirus Could Impact the Global Supply Chain by Mid-March," *Harvard Business Review,* February 28, 2020.

2. Ronald Kleijwegt, "Protect against Disruption by Becoming a Better Partner," *Supply Chain Digital,* March 1, 2020; Premsai Sainathan and Ana Maria Gimenez, "Monitoring Supply Chain Returnable Packaging Made Simple," *Supply Chain Digital,* February 22, 2020.

3. Walmart, walmart.com, accessed March 2020.

4. Korin Miller, "Walmart Is Reportedly Launching a New Grocery Delivery Service with Some Big Perks," *Delish,* March 2, 2020.

5. U.S. Census Bureau, "Monthly Wholesale Trade: Sales and Inventories," census.gov, accessed March 2020.

6. National Retail Federation, nrf.com, accessed March 2020.

7. Patrick Sisson, "Dying Malls Seek Second Life as Entertainment Destinations," *Curbed Atlanta,* February 18, 2020.

8. Greg Sterling, "Amazon and Digital Commerce Top Traditional Retailers in Satisfaction Scores," *Marketing Land,* March 2, 2020; Sarah George, "How Online Retailing Is Allowing Fast Fashion to Thrive," *Edie,* February 26, 2020; Lance Lambert, "Target and Walmart Gain (a Little) Ground in the E-commerce War with Amazon," *Forbes,* February 3, 2020.

9. Samantha Ickes, "The Future of Groceries? Online Shopping on the Rise," *The Canton Repository,* February 22, 2020.

10. Ben Fox Rubin, "Amazon Now Operates Seven Different Kinds of Physical Stores. Here's Why," *CNET,* February 28, 2020.

11. Jason Schreiber, "Plan Would Bring 800,000-Square-Foot Distribution Center to Kingston," *New Hampshire Union Leader,* February 24, 2020.

12. "Enabling Retail Convenience with Vending Machines and Kiosks," *Pymnts,* March 2, 2020.

13. Chris Walton, "The Strategy behind Amazon Getting Back into Mall Pop-Up Stores," *Forbes,* February 3, 2020.

14. Casey Bond, "9 Signs That Exciting New Job Opportunity Is Really an MLM Scam," *HuffPost,* February 4, 2020.

15. Stephanie Asymkos, "How 'MLM' Schemes Turn Regular Lives Upside Down," *Yahoo! Finance,* February 29, 2020.

16. Jayson Derrick, "Walmart Pros Aren't Convinced It Can Beat Amazon at Its Own Game," *Yahoo! Finance,* March 2, 2020.

17. Marie Hugo, "Make Your Supply Chain a Sustainability Champion," *Logistics Viewpoints,* February 13, 2020; Peter Cook, "Redefining the Supply-Chain Approach to Sustainability," *Supply Chain Brain,* February 12, 2020.

18. "Kia's New Sorento to Be Manufactured at KMMG," *Times-News,* February 21, 2020.

19. Sean Galea-Pace, "Starbucks: Driving Big Data to Boost Business," *Supply Chain Digital,* February 21, 2020.

20. International Trade Administration, selectusa.gov, accessed March 2020.

21. C. Shane Hunt, John E. Mello, and George Deitz, *Marketing* (New York: McGraw-Hill Education, 2017).

22. Andy Pasztor, "FAA Moves toward Certifying Specific Drones for Package Deliveries," *The Wall Street Journal,* February 3, 2020.

23. Patrick Burnson, "Reverse Logistics Rides High on the Wave of E-commerce," *Logistics Management,* March 2, 2020.

24. "The Freight Transportation System," U.S. Department of Transportation, rita.dot.gov, accessed March 2020.

25. Jim Blaze, "Why HAL Freight Matters," *Railway Age,* February 27, 2020.

26. Andrew Baker, "Epic Crude Oil Pipeline Enters Service, Connecting Permian, Eagle Ford Supply with Gulf Coast Demand," *Natural Gas Intelligence,* February 26, 2020.

27. Laurence Gross, "Will US Intermodal Escape Another 'Annus Horribilis' in 2020?," *JOC,* January 2, 2020.

28. Jeffrey Dastin, "Amazon Adds Warehouse Network Closer to Cities to Speed Up Same-Day Delivery," *Yahoo! Finance,* March 3, 2020.

29. "Distribution Center," Target, target.com, accessed March 2020.

30. Bob Trebilcock, "GE Appliance: Pulling the Digital Thread," *Logistics Management,* March 2, 2020.

31. Rich Weissman, "How to Attract and Retain Supply Management Talent," *Supply Chain Dive,* February 6, 2020.

16

Using Effective Promotions

Neil Parikh, Cofounder and Chief Strategy Officer of Casper

Human beings spend about one-third of their lives asleep, but not everyone rests soundly through the night. The Centers for Disease Control and Prevention classifies sleep deprivation as a public health issue and estimates that tens of millions of Americans do not receive adequate rest. This is a state of affairs that entrepreneur Neil Parikh sought to change when he and four partners launched Casper, a mattress start-up that aims to become "the Nike of sleep." But in order to do that, the company needs to take on the $39 billion global mattress industry commanded by established brands like Tempur Sealy and Serta.

Although it's certainly a tough task, Parikh believes that Casper's commitment to making a strong connection with customers will allow it to compete against the big names. "Those companies don't understand that long term, consumers are investing in things that mean something bigger," said Parikh. "We're trying to shift the cultural norms so that hopefully, over time, when people pick a Casper, they're buying into something a lot bigger than just a slab of memory foam." Unlike traditional brands, Casper can ship mattresses directly to customers in mini-fridge-sized boxes. Once it's out of the packaging, the mattress stretches and expands in a captivating display that has been shared many times on social media. This consistent buzz coupled with some surprise celebrity endorsements have made Casper into a billion-dollar company with major plans for the future.

In some ways, Casper is the culmination of Parikh's lifelong fascination with science and slumber. Growing up in New Jersey, he learned a lot from his father who was a doctor specializing in the study of sleep. Parikh also demonstrated remarkable intelligence and excelled in school. Enrolling at Brown University at a young age, he launched an international nonprofit during his undergraduate years and was admitted to medical school at just 17 years old. After college, Parikh worked for a few years at NASA where he studied bacteria and coauthored three patents. Rather than pursue this promising future in the lab, however, Parikh continued studying medicine and planned to become a doctor like his father. Then his life changed forever after reconnecting with some old classmates from Brown.

All of a sudden, Parikh left medical school and moved to New York City in order to launch a business with his friends Philip Krim, Jeff Chapin, Luke Sherwin, and Gabriel Flateman. "It was the classic story," said Parikh. "Move to New York, have no money, share a room, that kind of stuff." Although everyone in the group came from entrepreneurial backgrounds with successful past ventures, they had trouble coming up with an idea that could make the most out of their collective skills. But inspiration struck one day when Parikh overheard somebody jokingly refer to Krim as a "mattress mogul." When they asked him what this meant, "He

told us the story about how he used to sell beds online, and the industry is a total racket," said Parikh. To his shock, he learned that mattress markups could run as high as 100 percent while customers endured unpleasant shopping experiences with pushy salespeople. At last, the group knew they had stumbled upon a concept that would bring out the best in all of them. While Krim, Flateman, and Sherwin knew the business side of selling mattresses online, Chapin was an engineer with industrial design skills and Parikh brought in plenty of expert contacts from his father. Soon they developed a prototype for a mattress-in-a-box named in honor of Sherwin's then roommate Kasper, a six-foot-six German man who unfortunately slept on a twin-sized bed.

Of course, the group changed the "K" to a "C" when they launched Casper in 2014 hoping to disrupt the sleep industry in the same way that Warby Parker upended eyewear a couple of years before. Despite receiving a number of rejections from potential investors, Casper proved the doubters wrong when it sold more than $1.8 million worth of mattresses in its first 60 days. The founders had not expected to reach that level for another year and scrambled to fulfill the influx of orders.

The viral unboxing videos served as the foundation of Casper's wide range of social media promotions. In fact, one of the company's greatest triumphs occurred in 2015 when Kylie Jenner posted a picture on Instagram of a her new Casper mattress to her audience of more than 140 million followers.

In this chapter we explore all the traditional and new elements of promotion. We'll explain how marketers use different media for promotion and the advantages and disadvantages of each. We'll also look at the role of public relations as well as the differences between B2C and B2B promotions. Finally, throughout the chapter we'll pay particular attention to the promotional uses of social media.

Sources: Daniel Rodic, "CEO of 'Bed in a Box' Start-Up Casper on Going from Zero to a $500 Million+ Company in 4 Years," *CNBC*, cnbc.com, June 14, 2017; Jonathan Ringen, "Why Casper Is the $750 Million Startup That Just Can't Rest," *Fast Company*, fastcompany.com, August 7, 2017; Tom Huddleston Jr., "How Casper's Founders Went from $100,000 in Debt to Building a Billion-Dollar Mattress Start-Up," *CNBC*, cnbc.com, April 5, 2019; Sheila Marikar, "Casper Dreams of Being Bigger Than Mattresses," *The New York Times*, September 13, 2019; "Most Creative People: Neil Parikh," *Fast Company*, fastcompany.com, accessed March 2020.

Let's talk business!
bit.ly/LetsTalkBusiness16

Brian Cahn/Zuma Press/Newscom

THIS COMPANY CAREFULLY CRAFTS its social media posts. It carefully times when its messages are posted so when people check their phones at specific times, they either want this company's products for breakfast or dinner. Name that company. (Find the answer in the chapter.)

LO 16–1 Identify the new and traditional tools that make up the promotion mix.

Promotion and the Promotion Mix

Promotion is one of the four Ps of marketing. As noted in Chapter 13, promotion consists of all the techniques sellers use to motivate people to buy their products or services. Both profit-making and nonprofit organizations use promotional techniques to communicate with people in their target markets about goods and services, and to persuade them to participate in a marketing exchange.[1] Marketers use many different tools to promote their products. Traditionally, those tools were advertising, personal selling, public relations, and sales promotion. Today they have grown to include e-mail, mobile, and social media promotions and advertising; blogging; podcasting; and more.[2]

The combination of promotional tools an organization uses is called its **promotion mix**; see Figure 16.1. We show the product in the middle of the figure to illustrate that the product itself can also be a promotional tool, such as when marketers give away free samples.

Integrated marketing communication (IMC) combines the promotional tools into one comprehensive, unified promotional strategy.[3] With IMC, marketers can create a positive brand image, meet the needs of the consumer, and meet the strategic marketing and promotional goals of the firm. Emphasis today is on integrating traditional media, like TV, with social media, or integrating print media with websites.[4]

Figure 16.2 shows the six steps in a typical promotional campaign. Let's begin exploring promotional tools by looking at advertising—the most visible tool.

promotion mix

The combination of promotional tools an organization uses.

integrated marketing communication (IMC)

A technique that combines all the promotional tools into one comprehensive and unified promotional strategy.

FIGURE 16.1 THE TRADITIONAL PROMOTION MIX

1. Identify a target market. (Refer back to Chapter 13 for a discussion of segmentation and target marketing.)
2. Define the objectives for each element of the promotion mix. Goals should be clear and measurable.
3. Determine a promotional budget. The budgeting process will clarify how much can be spent on advertising, personal selling, and other promotional efforts.
4. Develop a unifying message. The goal of an integrated promotional program is to have one clear message communicated by advertising, public relations, sales, and every other promotional effort.
5. Implement the plan. Advertisements, blogs, and other promotional efforts must be scheduled to complement efforts being made by public relations and sales promotion. Salespeople should have access to all materials to optimize the total effort.
6. Evaluate effectiveness. Measuring results depends greatly on clear objectives. Each element of the promotion mix should be evaluated separately, and an overall measure should be taken as well. It is important to learn what is working and what is not.

FIGURE 16.2 STEPS IN A PROMOTIONAL CAMPAIGN

iSeeit! Need help understanding integrated marketing communication? Visit your Connect eBook to view a video for a brief animated explanation.

LO 16–2 Contrast the advantages and disadvantages of various advertising media, including the Internet and social media.

Advertising: Informing, Persuading, and Reminding

Advertising is paid, nonpersonal communication through various media by organizations and individuals who are in some way *identified in the message.* Identification of the sender separates advertising from *propaganda,* which is nonpersonal communication that *does not have an identified sponsor.* Figure 16.3 lists various categories of advertising. Take a minute to look it over; you'll see there's a lot more to advertising than just print ads and television commercials.

advertising
Paid, nonpersonal communication through various media by organizations and individuals who are in some way identified in the advertising message.

FIGURE 16.3 MAJOR CATEGORIES OF ADVERTISING

Different kinds of advertising are used by various organizations to reach different target markets.

- *Retail advertising*—advertising to consumers by various retail stores such as supermarkets and shoe stores.
- *Trade advertising*—advertising to wholesalers and retailers by manufacturers to encourage them to carry their products.
- *Business-to-business advertising*—advertising from manufacturers to other manufacturers. A firm selling motors to automotive companies would use business-to-business advertising.
- *Institutional advertising*—advertising designed to create an attractive image for an organization rather than for a product. "We Care about You" at Giant Food is an example. "Virginia Is for Lovers" and "I ♥ New York" were two institutional campaigns by government agencies.
- *Product advertising*—advertising for a good or service to create interest among consumer, commercial, and industrial buyers.
- *Advocacy advertising*—advertising that supports a particular view of an issue (e.g., an ad against nuclear power plants). Such advertising is also known as cause advertising.
- *Comparison advertising*—advertising that compares competitive products. For example, an ad that compares two different cold care products' speed and benefits is a comparative ad.
- *Interactive advertising*—customer-oriented communication that enables customers to choose the information they receive, such as interactive video catalogs that let customers select which items to view.
- *Online advertising*—advertising messages that appear on computers as people visit different websites.
- *Mobile advertising*—advertising that reaches people on their smartphones.

FIGURE 16.4

ESTIMATED PERCENTAGE OF U.S. ADVERTISING SPENDING IN 2020 BY MEDIUM (IN BILLIONS OF DOLLARS)

Source: Erik Oster, "U.S. Advertising and Marketing Spend to Grow to Nearly $390 Billion in 2020," *Adweek*, January 17, 2020.

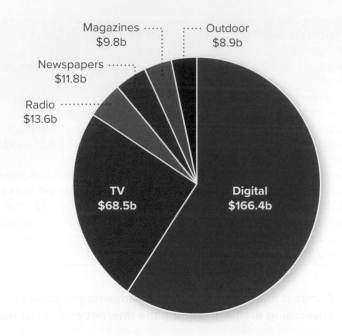

Magazines ······ $9.8b

Outdoor $8.9b

Newspapers ······· $11.8b

Radio ············· $13.6b

TV $68.5b

Digital $166.4b

It's also easy to appreciate the impact of advertising spending on the U.S. economy; see Figure 16.4. Total ad volume was estimated to be nearly $390 billion for 2020. Note that digital media is now the number one medium, with expenditures of over $166 billion.[5] Television reigned as number one until 2018.

How do we, as consumers, benefit from these advertising expenditures? Ads are informative. Direct mail is full of information about products, prices, features, store policies, and more; so is newspaper advertising.[6] Newspaper advertising is down because people are buying fewer newspapers.[7] Instead, they're choosing to get their news on mobile devices. Mobile advertising is growing very, very fast.[8]

Not only does advertising inform us, but the money advertisers spend for commercial time pays the production costs of TV and radio programs. Advertising also helps cover some of the costs of producing newspapers and magazines. Subscriptions and newsstand revenues may cover only mailing and promotional costs. Figure 16.5 compares the advantages and disadvantages for marketers of various advertising media. Note that newspapers, radio, and directories are usually attractive to local advertisers. As with national advertising, the trend for local advertisements is moving more toward digital outlets.

Marketers must choose which media will best reach the audience they desire. Radio advertising, for example, is less expensive than TV advertising and often reaches people when they have few other distractions, such as while they're driving. Research has revealed the effectiveness of radio as a traditional medium. Radio is especially effective at selling services people don't usually read about in print media—banking, mortgages, continuing education, and brokerage services, to name a few. On the other hand, radio has become so commercial-ridden that many people pay to switch to commercial-free premium services or stream on other devices. Marketers also search for other places to put

Advertising seems to be everywhere as we go about our daily lives. How many advertisements can you spot in this photo? Can the noise created by so many ads interfere with the messages the advertisers are trying to communicate?

S-F/Shutterstock

FIGURE 16.5 ADVANTAGES AND DISADVANTAGES OF VARIOUS ADVERTISING MEDIA
The most effective media are often very expensive. The inexpensive media may not reach your market. The goal is to use the medium that can reach your desired market most effectively and efficiently.

Medium	Advantages	Disadvantages
Newspapers	Good coverage of local markets; ads can be placed quickly; high consumer acceptance; ads can be clipped and saved.	Ads compete with other features in paper; poor color; ads get thrown away with paper (short life span).
Television	Uses sight, sound, and motion; reaches all audiences; high attention with no competition from other material.	High cost; short exposure time; takes time to prepare ads. Digital video recorders skip over ads.
Radio	Low cost; can target specific audiences; very flexible; good for local marketing.	People may not listen to ads; depends on one sense (hearing); short exposure time; audience can't keep ads.
Magazines	Can target specific audiences; good use of color; long life of ads; ads can be clipped and saved.	Inflexible; ads often must be placed weeks before publication; cost is relatively high.
Outdoor	High visibility and repeat exposures; low cost; local market focus.	Limited message; low selectivity of audience.
Direct mail	Best for targeting specific markets; very flexible; ads can be saved.	High cost; consumers may reject ads as junk mail; must conform to post office regulations.
Directories (Yellow Pages–type print and online advertising)	Great coverage of local markets; widely used by consumers.	Competition with other ads; cost may be too high for very small businesses.
Internet	Inexpensive global coverage; available at any time; interactive.	Customers may leave the site before buying.
Mobile advertising	Great reach among younger shoppers.	Easy to ignore, avoid.
Social media	Wonderful communication tools.	Time drain.

advertising, such as on video screens mounted on gas pumps. Have you noticed ads on park benches and grocery carts? You've certainly seen them on your favorite websites.

Mobile marketing started out mostly as text messages, but now stores like Starbucks can send signals to your phone as you approach the store. On many phones, your Starbucks card will show up on your home screen as you near the location. How's that for a reminder to grab a quick latte? Grocery chains have released apps to help customers create their meal plans and prepare their shopping lists—many giving aisle-by-aisle assistance. Most often, retailers use e-mail advertisements to build brand awareness and drive people to their stores or websites. Social media sites in general are growing so fast that some marketers can hardly keep up. In the next sections, we'll look in more depth at the various advertising media.

Television Advertising

Television offers many advantages to national advertisers, but it's expensive. Thirty seconds of advertising during the Super Bowl can cost more than $5.6 million.[9] That's not including the production costs of the ads. How many bottles of beer or cars must a company sell to pay for these commercials? A whole lot, but few media besides television allow advertisers to reach that many millions of people with such impact, although not all ads are equally effective.[10] Of course, advertisers can book cheaper airtime on other TV shows. For example, 30 seconds on the CW's *Riverdale* costs about $33,000 or on NBC's *This Is Us* just over $350,000.[11]

Advancing Past Traditional TV Ads

For decades, marketers have used television as a means to build awareness and air advertisements. It has long been the dominant medium for advertisers, and many thought it would stay that way forever. But lately, advertisers have been rethinking their strategies and moving toward advertising space on streaming services like Roku, Hulu, and Sling.

These services are sometimes referred to as "advanced TV." What makes it so much more "advanced" than traditional television advertising? It's the way marketers can tailor the advertising experience to each user. In traditional television advertising, marketers purchase an ad slot based on the typical demographics of a show's audience and geographic locations. But with "advanced TV," advertisers have access to more information, like

John Mantell/Shutterstock

browsing and purchase histories, income levels, and additional viewer data. Viewers watching the same show in the same neighborhood at the same time will each have different advertisements during the program—one may get a car commercial while the other may be learning about the newest luxury watches.

Traditional television ads are still very effective when it comes

to pushing an overall brand, like Campbell's Soup. Consumers are already familiar with the brand and have likely been buying their soups for as long as they can remember. Reaching specific audiences is not the main drive for marketers in this case. But if they want to push the higher-end Slow Kettle recipes, don't be surprised if those advertisements show themselves on Hulu.

Sources: Jon Lafayette, "49% of Viewers Say Streaming Ads Are More Relevant: Study," *Broadcasting + Cable,* March 5, 2020; Alexandra Bruell, "TV Advertising Directed at You," *The Wall Street Journal,* June 18, 2019; Hannah Blackiston, "90% of Media Buyers Placing Ads in Streaming Services, according to a New IAB Report," *Mumbrella,* February 28, 2020; Sahil Patel, "NBCUniversal Opens New Local Ads Business for Streaming TV," *The Wall Street Journal,* February 26, 2020.

Though digital advertising has taken over the top spot in terms of advertising dollars, TV advertising is still a dominant medium.[12] Of course, TV is helped by the fact that many people post about what they have recently watched, making social media "force multipliers" for TV. DVRs and on-demand services enable consumers to skip the ads during TV broadcasts. However, this may make TV less attractive to advertisers unless commercials get to the point that people *want* to watch them. Marketers are demanding better and more accurate measurements of the effectiveness of TV advertising, and many are switching to social media as a result. After all, 72 percent of U.S. consumers are active on social media.[13] Check out the Adapting to Change box to see how advertisements on streaming services are having an effect on traditional TV advertisements.

Product Placement

product placement
Putting products into TV shows and movies where they will be seen.

TV advertising isn't limited to traditional commercials; sometimes the products appear in the programs themselves. With **product placement**, advertisers pay to put their products into shows and movies where the audience will see them. One classic example of product placement is the trail of Reese's Pieces in the movie *E.T.* Nowadays we see *Sonic the Hedgehog*'s obsession for Olive Garden.[14] In Marvel's hit franchise *The Avengers,* the superheroes drive lots of different cars. Doctor Strange drives a Lamborghini Huracán, Black Widow tools around in a Chevrolet Corvette, and when Iron Man isn't flying, he's seen in an Audi R8.[15]

In addition to TV and movies, product placement is also used in video games. If you're a gamer, you've seen in-game ads, like ads around the court in basketball games. Technology

PictureLux/Netflix/The Hollywood Archive/Alamy Stock Photo

allows vending machines in racing games to be branded and rebranded over time, depending on whether Coke, Pepsi, Exxon, or Shell has purchased ad time. Do you think people are influenced by such exposure?

Infomercials

An **infomercial** is a full-length TV program devoted exclusively to promoting a particular good or service. Infomercials have been successful because they show the product and how it works in great detail. They are the equivalent of sending your very best salespeople to a person's home and having them use all of their techniques to make the sale: drama, demonstration, testimonials, graphics, and more.

Products that have earned hundreds of millions in sales through infomercials include Proactiv, MyPillow, P90X, the George Foreman Grill, and the Showtime Pro Rotisserie Oven.[16] Some products, such as personal development seminars, real estate programs, and workout tapes, are hard to sell without showing people a sample of their contents and using testimonials. Have you purchased any products that you saw in an infomercial?

Online Advertising

When marketers advertise on a search engine such as Google or Bing, they can reach the people they most want to reach—consumers looking for information about specific products. One goal of online advertising is to push potential customers to a website where they can learn more about the company and its products—and the company can learn more about them. If users click an ad to get to the website, the company has an opportunity to gather their names, addresses, opinions, and preferences. Online advertising thus brings customers and companies together. Another advantage is that it enables advertisers to see just how many people have clicked on an ad and how much of it each potential customer has read or watched.

E-mail marketing is a big component of online advertising. However, advertisers have to be careful not to overuse it because many customers don't like to see too much promotional e-mail in their in-boxes. Thus some companies use e-mail as an alert to send users to other social media such as Facebook, Twitter, or Instagram.

Interactive promotion allows marketers to go beyond a *monologue,* in which sellers try to persuade buyers to buy things, to a *dialogue,* in which buyers and sellers work together to create mutually beneficial exchange relationships. Technology has greatly improved customer communications and has fundamentally changed the way marketers work with customers. Notice we said *working with* rather than *promoting to.* Marketers now want to *build relationships* with customers over time. That means carefully listening to what consumers want, tracking their purchases, providing them with excellent service, and giving them access to a full range of information. Did you know Taco Bell carefully times when its messages will be posted to social media users? To sway people to choose Taco Bell for breakfast, the marketing team

infomercial
A full-length TV program devoted exclusively to promoting goods or services.

interactive promotion
Promotion process that allows marketers to go beyond a monologue, where sellers try to persuade buyers to buy things, to a dialogue in which buyers and sellers work together to create mutually beneficial exchange relationships.

will post a photo of breakfast items late at night. Then when people check their phones when they wake, they see Taco Bell's message.

Social Media Advertising

Oreo has millions of likes on Facebook. The company can then track and test users who follow "Milk's Favorite Cookie." The company can measure how many times a post is viewed, how many times it is shared, and what the user response is. Social media make it possible for organizations to test ads and other promotions before bringing them to traditional media, like TV, and to learn why people like and dislike messages.

It is best, if a company wants to establish a base with customers, to include top managers in the dialogue. For example, Sherry Chris, president of Better Homes & Gardens Real Estate, spends two hours each day reading and contributing to Twitter, Facebook, and LinkedIn. Such involvement with customers has become a major part of many companies' listening strategies. It may take time, but there is not a better way to learn about what customers are thinking and saying about your firm. McDonald's, for example, is mentioned every one to two seconds on social media. It has a global communications team on three continents constantly listening and interacting with potential customers.[17] We'll discuss more on social media and promotion later in the chapter.

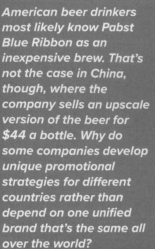

American beer drinkers most likely know Pabst Blue Ribbon as an inexpensive brew. That's not the case in China, though, where the company sells an upscale version of the beer for $44 a bottle. Why do some companies develop unique promotional strategies for different countries rather than depend on one unified brand that's the same all over the world?

Source: Pabst Brewing Company

Global Advertising

Global advertising requires the marketer to develop a single product and promotional strategy it can implement worldwide. Certainly global advertising that's the same everywhere can save companies money in research and design.[18] In some cases, however, promotions tailored to specific countries or regions may be more successful since each country or region has its own culture, language, and buying habits.

Some problems do arise when marketers use one campaign in all countries. When a Japanese company tried to use English words to name a popular drink, it came up with Pocari Sweat, not a good image for most English-speaking people. In England, the Ford Probe didn't go over too well because the word *probe* made people think of doctors' waiting rooms and medical examinations. People in the United States may have difficulty with Krapp toilet paper from Sweden. But perhaps worse was the translation of Coors's slogan "Turn it loose," which became "Suffer from diarrhea." Clairol introduced its curling iron, the Mist Stick, to the German market, not realizing *mist* in German can mean "manure." As you can see, getting the words right in international advertising is tricky and critical. So is understanding the culture, which calls for researching each country, designing appropriate ads, and testing them. The Reaching beyond Our Borders box discusses how a well-known company promotes products in foreign markets.

Many marketers today are moving from globalism (one ad for everyone in the world) to regionalism (specific ads for each country or for specific groups within a country). In the future, marketers will prepare more custom-designed promotions to reach even smaller audiences—audiences as small as one person.

LO 16–3   Illustrate the steps of the B2B and B2C selling processes.

Personal Selling: Providing Personal Attention

personal selling
The face-to-face presentation and promotion of goods and services.

Personal selling is the face-to-face presentation and promotion of goods and services, including the salesperson's search for new prospects and follow-up service after the sale. Effective selling isn't simply a matter of persuading others to buy. In fact, it's more accurately described today as helping others satisfy their wants and needs (again, helping the buyer buy).

REACHING BEYOND OUR BORDERS

More Than Milk's Favorite Cookie?

oreo.com

No matter our ages, we all know and grew up with Oreos. The double layers of crunchy cookie sandwiching a creamy vanilla center are classic. For many years, Nabisco, the maker of Oreos, followed the old adage "If it ain't broke, don't fix it." Today, however, if you visit the cookie aisle in your local supermarket, you find tons of variations of Oreos such as apple pie, chocolate berry, and even Peeps and glitter cream! If that isn't enough, you can also buy them chocolate-dipped, double stuffed, super thin, or even as a candy bar. Nabisco knew that to keep the brand vibrant and to reach different segments of the market, expanding its offerings was a good option.

It also knew it was a good decision to expand Oreos into global markets. Today, you can find

inkanya Anankitrojana/Shutterstock

Oreos in more than 100 countries around the world. However, Nabisco understood that globally consumer tastes vary just like in the United States. What some people consider mouthwatering in one country will be

frowned upon somewhere else. So with Oreos spanning the globe, additional variations on the original cookie-and-creme formula became even more extreme. China, for instance, has a mix of fruity and savory Oreos. Are you interested in trying the popular wasabi or hot wing options? In Dubai, consumers are leaning toward Tang-flavored Oreos. Argentines like their Oreos stuffed with banana and *dulce de leche,* a type of candied milk. What works overseas can even make its way back here to the United States. The popular Oreo Thins were first introduced in China.

Sources: Caitlyn Fitzpatrick, "Oreo Just Released a Trolls Cookie That Has a Glittery Pink Creme," *Yahoo! Lifestyle,* March 2, 2020; Sophie Caraan, "Oreo Introduces Orange Tang-Flavored Cookies in Dubai," *Hypebeast,* September 2, 2019; Sarah Poirier, "10 Awesome Oreo Flavors You Can Only Get in China," *Travel,* July 19, 2019; "Products," Oreo, oreo.com, accessed March 2020.

Given that perspective, you can see why salespeople use smartphones, tablets, and other technology to help customers search for information, design custom-made products, look over prices, and generally do everything it takes to complete the order. The benefit of personal selling is having a person help you complete a transaction. The salesperson should listen to your needs, help you reach a solution, and do everything possible to make accomplishing it smoother and easier.

It's costly for firms to provide customers with personal attention, so those companies that retain salespeople must train them to be especially effective, efficient, and helpful.[19] To attract new salespeople, companies are paying them quite well and providing necessary training.

Steps in the Selling Process

The best way to understand personal selling is to go through the selling process. Let's imagine you are a software salesperson whose job is to show business users the advantages of various products your firm markets. One product critically important to establishing long-term relationships with customers is customer relationship management (CRM) software, particularly social CRM that integrates social media to create a community-based relationship with customers. Let's go through the seven steps of the selling process to see what you can do to sell social CRM software.

Although this is a business-to-business (B2B) example, the process in consumer selling is similar, but less complex. In both cases the salesperson must have deep product knowledge—that is, he or she must know the product—and competitors' products—thoroughly.

Valerii Apetroaiei/Getty Images

You're familiar with all kinds of situations in which people do personal selling. They work in local department stores and sell all kinds of goods and services like automobiles, insurance, and real estate. What could they do to be more helpful to you, the customer?

prospecting
Researching potential buyers and choosing those most likely to buy.

qualifying
In the selling process, making sure that people have a need for the product, the authority to buy, and the willingness to listen to a sales message.

prospect
A person with the means to buy a product, the authority to buy, and the willingness to listen to a sales message.

trial close
A step in the selling process that consists of a question or statement that moves the selling process toward the actual close.

1. Prospect and Qualify   The first step in the selling process is **prospecting**, researching potential buyers and choosing those most likely to buy. The selection process is called **qualifying**. To qualify people means to make sure they have a need for the product, the authority to buy, and the willingness to listen to a sales message. Some people call prospecting and qualifying the process of *lead generation*.

A person who meets the qualifying criteria is called a **prospect**. Salespeople often meet prospects at trade shows, where they come to booths sponsored by manufacturers and ask questions. Others may visit your website looking for information. But often the best prospects are people recommended to you by others who use or know about your product. Salespeople often e-mail prospects with proposals to see whether there is any interest before making a formal visit.

2. Preapproach   The selling process may take a long time, and gathering information before you approach the customer is crucial. Before making a sales call, you must do some further research. In the preapproach phase, you learn as much as possible about customers and their wants and needs.[20] Before you try to sell the social CRM software, you'll want to know which people in the company are most likely to buy or use it. What kind of customers do they deal with? What kind of relationship strategies are they using now? How is their system set up, and what kind of improvements are they looking for? All that information should be in a database so that, if one representative leaves the firm, the company can provide important information about customers to the new salesperson.

3. Approach   "You don't have a second chance to make a good first impression." That's why the approach is so important. When you call on a customer for the first time, you want to give an impression of friendly professionalism, create rapport, build credibility, and start a business relationship. Often a company's decision to use a new software package is based on the buyer's perception of reliable service from the salesperson. In selling social CRM products, you can make it known from the start that you'll be available to help your customer, train its employees, and upgrade the package when necessary.

4. Make a Presentation   In your actual presentation of the software, you'll match the benefits of your value package to the client's needs. Since you've done your homework and know the prospect's wants and needs, you can tailor your sales presentation accordingly. The presentation is a great time to use testimonials, showing potential buyers that they're joining leaders in other firms who are using the product.

5. Answer Objections   Salespeople should anticipate any objections the prospect may raise and determine the proper responses.[21] They should think of questions as opportunities for creating better relationships, not as challenges to what they're saying. Customers may have legitimate doubts, and salespeople are there to resolve them. Successfully and honestly working with others helps build relationships based on trust. Often salespeople can introduce the customer to others in the firm who can answer their questions and provide them with anything they need. Using a tablet or other mobile device, salespeople may set up a virtual meeting in which the customer can chat with company colleagues and begin building a relationship.

6. Close the Sale   After a salesperson has answered questions and objections, he or she may present a **trial close**, a question or statement that moves the selling process toward the actual purchase. A salesperson might ask, "When would be the best time to train your staff to use the new software?" The final step is to ask for the order and show the client where to sign. Once a relationship is established, the goal of the sales call may be to get a testimonial from the customer.

7. Follow Up The selling process isn't over until the order is approved and the customer is happy. Salespeople need to be providers of solutions for their customers and to think about what happens after the sale. The follow-up step includes handling customer complaints, making sure the customer's questions are answered, and quickly supplying what the customer wants. Often, customer service is as important to the sale as the product itself. That's why most manufacturers have websites where customers can find information and get questions answered quickly and accurately. You can see why we describe selling as a process of establishing relationships, not just exchanging goods or services. The sales relationship may continue for years as the salesperson responds to new requests for information and provides new services.

Peathegee Inc/Getty Images

The selling process varies somewhat among different goods and services, but the general idea stays the same. The goals of a salesperson are to help the buyer buy and make sure the buyer is satisfied after the sale.

The Business-to-Consumer Sales Process

Most in-person sales to consumers take place in retail stores, where the role of the salesperson differs somewhat from that in B2B selling. In both cases, knowing the product comes first. However, in business-to-consumer (B2C) sales, the salesperson does not have to do much prospecting or qualifying. The seller assumes most people who come to the store are qualified to buy the merchandise (except in sales of expensive products, such as automobiles and furniture, during which salespeople may have to ask a few questions to qualify prospective customers before spending too much time with them).

Similarly, retail salespeople don't usually have to go through a preapproach step, although they should understand as much as possible about the type of people who shop at a given store. About 82 percent of the people who come to a store have already done some research online and know exactly what they want.[22] The salesperson does need to focus on the customer and refrain from talking to fellow salespeople—or, worse, to friends on the phone. Have you ever experienced such rude behavior from salespeople? What did you think? Did you complete the sale?

The first formal step in the B2C sales process is the approach. Too many salespeople begin with a line like "May I help you?" but the answer too often is "No." A better approach is "How can I help you?" or, simply, "Welcome to our store." The idea is to show the customer you are there to help and are friendly and knowledgeable.

Discover what the customer wants first, and then make a presentation. Salespeople should show customers how the company's products meet their needs and answer questions that help customers choose the right products for them.

As in B2B selling, it is important to make a trial close, like "Would you like me to put that on hold?" or "Will you be paying for that with your store credit card?" Selling is an art, and a salesperson must learn how to walk the fine line between being helpful and being pushy. Often individual buyers need some time alone to think about the purchase. The salesperson must respect that need but still be clearly available when needed.

After-sale follow-up is an important but often neglected step in B2C sales. If the product is to be delivered, the salesperson should follow up to be sure it is delivered on time. The same is true if the product has to be installed. There is often a chance to sell more merchandise when a salesperson follows up on a sale. Figure 16.6 shows the whole B2C selling process. Compare it to the seven-step process we outlined earlier for B2B selling.

> *Making the sale isn't the end of the salesperson's relationship with the customer. The salesperson should follow up on the sale to make sure the customer is happy and perhaps suggest something to complement what the customer purchased. Have salespeople been able to sell you more because they used effective follow-up procedures? How did they do it?*

FIGURE 16.6 STEPS IN THE BUSINESS-TO-CONSUMER (B2C) SELLING PROCESS

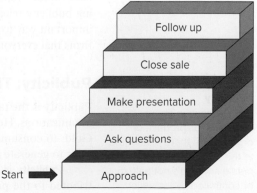

Follow up

Close sale

Make presentation

Ask questions

Start ➡ Approach

?TESTPREP

- What are the four traditional elements of the promotion mix?
- What are the three most important advertising media in order of dollars spent?
- What are the seven steps in the B2B selling process? How does it differ from the B2C selling process?

LO 16–4 Describe the role of the public relations department, and show how publicity fits in that role.

Public Relations: Building Relationships

public relations (PR)
The management function that evaluates public attitudes, changes policies and procedures in response to the public's requests, and executes a program of action and information to earn public understanding and acceptance.

Public relations (PR) is the function that evaluates public attitudes, changes policies and procedures in response to the public's requests, and executes a program of action and information to earn public understanding and acceptance. In other words, a good public relations program has three steps:

1. *Listen to the public.* Public relations starts with good marketing research to evaluate public attitudes. The best way to learn what the public wants is to listen to people often—in different forums, especially on social media. For example, Wendy's learned that consumers were searching for more fast-food breakfast options. In addition to creating a new breakfast service, Wendy's also started offering plant-based options.[23]

2. *Change policies and procedures.* Businesses earn understanding not by bombarding the public with propaganda but by creating programs and practices in the public interest. For example, Panera created a "No-No List" of ingredients and additives it would no longer use and reformulated over 100 ingredients to meet its needs when the company decided to go "clean."

3. *Inform people you're responsive to their needs.* It's not enough to simply have programs in the public interest. You have to *tell* the public about those programs. Public relations has more power to influence consumers than other corporate communications because the message comes via the media, a source usually perceived as trustworthy.

Recent events have emphasized the need for good public relations. Such events include Facebooks's user privacy scandal, Boeing's 737 Max aircraft problems, and the issues surrounding some politicians, popular actors, and sports personalities.[24]

The PR department maintains close ties with company stakeholders (customers, media, community leaders, government officials, and other corporate stakeholders). Marketers are looking for alternatives to advertising. Public relations is a good alternative. As newspapers cut back on their reporting staff, people are looking for other sources of news information, including publicity releases. Linking up with influencers, podcasters, and bloggers has become an important way to keep company names in the news. Public relations is so important to some firms that everyone in other departments beyond the PR department is participating as well.[25]

Publicity: The Talking Arm of PR

publicity
Any information about an individual, product, or organization that's distributed to the public through the media and that's not paid for or controlled by the seller.

Publicity is the talking arm of public relations and one of the major functions of almost all organizations. Here's how it works: Suppose you want to introduce your restaurant, Harvest Gold, to consumers, but you have little money to promote it. You need to get some initial sales to generate funds. One effective way to reach the public is through publicity.

Publicity is any information about an individual, product, or organization that's distributed to the public through the media and is not paid for or controlled by the seller. It takes skill to write interesting or compelling news releases that the media will want to publish. You may need to write different stories for different media.[26] One story may introduce the new owners. Another may describe some unusual meal offerings. If the stories are published, news about your restaurant will reach many potential consumers (and investors, distributors, and dealers) and you may be on your way to becoming a successful marketer. John D. Rockefeller (wealthy industrialist and philanthropist) once remarked, "Next to doing the right thing, the most important thing is to *let people know* that you are doing the right thing." What might Harvest Gold do to help the community and thus create more publicity?

Besides being free, publicity has several further advantages over other promotional tools like advertising. It may reach people who wouldn't read an ad. It may appear on the front page of a newspaper or in some other prominent position, or be given airtime on a television news show. Perhaps the greatest advantage of publicity is its believability. When a newspaper or magazine publishes a story as news, the reader treats that story as news—and news is more believable than advertising.

Publicity has several disadvantages as well. For example, marketers have no control over whether or how the media will use the story. The media aren't obligated to use a news release, most of which are thrown away. Furthermore, the media may alter the story so that it's not positive. There's good publicity (customers camp out all night to buy your products) and bad publicity (defective products are recalled). Also, once a story has run, it's not likely to be repeated. Advertising, in contrast, can be repeated as often as needed. One way to see that the media handle your publicity well is to establish a friendly relationship with media representatives and be open with them.

Nick Cammett/Diamond Images/Getty Images

Tens of thousands of people soaked themselves in freezing water to promote awareness for the disease ALS. From athletes and actors to ordinary people, videos of the Ice Bucket Challenge went viral for months and led to $115 million in donations to ALS research. What do you think made this promotion so successful?

LO 16–5 Assess the effectiveness of various forms of sales promotion, including sampling.

Sales Promotion: Giving Buyers Incentives

Sales promotion is the promotional tool that stimulates consumer purchasing and dealer interest by means of short-term activities. These activities include such things as displays, trade shows and exhibitions, event sponsorships, and contests. Figure 16.7 lists some B2B sales promotion techniques.

For consumer sales promotion activities, think of those free samples you get in the mail, cents-off coupons you clip in apps, contests that various retail stores sponsor, and prizes in cereal boxes (see Figure 16.7). Some experts, however, caution not to give away too

sales promotion
The promotional tool that stimulates consumer purchasing and dealer interest by means of short-term activities.

FIGURE 16.7 SALES PROMOTION TECHNIQUES

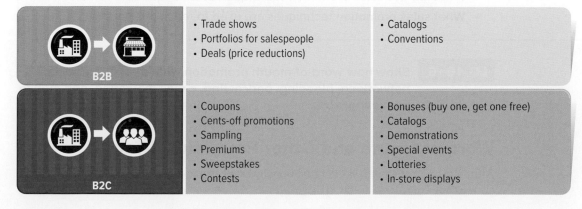

B2B
- Trade shows
- Portfolios for salespeople
- Deals (price reductions)
- Catalogs
- Conventions

B2C
- Coupons
- Cents-off promotions
- Sampling
- Premiums
- Sweepstakes
- Contests
- Bonuses (buy one, get one free)
- Catalogs
- Demonstrations
- Special events
- Lotteries
- In-store displays

Rob Kim/Amira Foods/Getty Images

Everyone likes a free sample. Sampling is a promotional strategy that lets people try a new product, often in a situation where they can buy it right away if they like it. What are some advantages of sampling food products that advertising can't duplicate?

sampling
A promotional tool in which a company lets consumers have a small sample of a product for no charge.

much during such promotions. For example, you can stimulate sales at Harvest Gold by putting half-off coupons in the school paper and dorm mailers. Do you see any problems that might emerge by using coupons or an outside source like Groupon to bring in customers?

Sales promotion programs are designed to supplement personal selling, advertising, public relations, and other promotional efforts by creating enthusiasm for the overall promotional program. Sales promotion can take place both within and outside the company. The most important internal sales promotion efforts are directed at salespeople and other customer-contact people, such as customer service representatives and clerks. Internal sales promotion efforts include (1) sales training, (2) the development of sales aids such as audiovisual presentations and videos, and (3) participation in trade shows where salespeople can get leads. Other employees who deal with the public may also receive special training to improve their awareness of the company's offerings and make them an integral part of the total promotional effort.

After generating enthusiasm internally, marketers want to make distributors and dealers eager to help promote the product. Trade shows allow marketing intermediaries to see products from many different sellers and make comparisons among them. Today, virtual trade shows online, often called webinars, enable buyers to see many products without leaving the office. Such promotions are usually interactive, so buyers can ask questions, and the information is available 24/7.

After the company's employees and intermediaries have been motivated by sales promotion efforts, the next step is to promote to final consumers using samples, coupons, cents-off deals, displays, store demonstrations, contests, rebates, and so on. Sales promotion is an ongoing effort to maintain enthusiasm, so sellers use different strategies over time to keep the ideas fresh. You could put food displays in your Harvest Gold restaurant to show customers how attractive the products look. You could also sponsor in-store cooking demonstrations to attract new customers.

One popular sales promotional tool is **sampling**—letting consumers have a small sample of the product for no charge. Because many consumers won't buy a new product unless they've had a chance to see it or try it, grocery stores often have people standing in the aisles handing out small portions of food and beverage products. Sampling is a quick, effective way of demonstrating a product's superiority when consumers are making a purchase decision. Standing outside Harvest Gold and giving out samples would surely attract attention.

Event marketing involves sponsoring events such as concerts or being at various events to promote products. When Pepsi introduced its SoBe product line (American teas, fruit-juice blends, and enhanced water beverages), it used a combination of sampling, event marketing, and a new website. Pepsi first sent samples to beach towns during spring break where students got to sample the drinks. Sampling and event marketing can be effective promotional tools used to introduce new products.

?TESTPREP

- What are the three steps in setting up a public relations program?
- What are five sales promotion techniques used to reach consumers?
- What sales promotion techniques are used to reach businesses?

LO 16–6 Show how word-of-mouth promotion, viral marketing, social networking, blogging, podcasting, e-mail marketing, and mobile marketing work.

Word of Mouth and Other Promotional Tools

Although word of mouth was not traditionally listed as one of the major promotional efforts (it was not considered to be manageable), it is now one of the most effective, especially online.[27] In **word-of-mouth promotion**, people tell other people about products they've purchased or services they've used. We've already discussed the role of social media in spreading word of mouth. Beyond word of mouth is customer participation, that is, getting customers to provide constructive suggestions and share their ideas on how to shape product and service offerings.[28]

Anything that encourages people to talk favorably about an organization can be effective word of mouth. Notice, for example, how stores use entertainers, banners, and other attention-getting devices to create word of mouth. Clever commercials can also generate word of mouth. The more people talk about your products and your brand name, the more easily customers remember them when they shop.

One especially effective strategy for spreading positive word of mouth is to send testimonials to current customers. Most companies use these only in promoting to new customers, but testimonials are also effective in confirming customers' belief that they chose the right company. Therefore, some companies make it a habit to ask customers for referrals.

Word-of-mouth promotion is so powerful that negative word of mouth can hurt a firm badly. Criticism of a product or company can spread through social media, websites, and other online forums. Addressing consumer complaints quickly and effectively is one of the best ways to reduce the effects of negative word of mouth.

You may enjoy brainstorming strategies for creating word of mouth about Harvest Gold. If your efforts are great, your message could "go viral" and be seen by millions of consumers.[29] **Viral marketing** includes any strategy that encourages people to pass on a marketing message to others, creating exponential growth in the message's influence as the message reaches thousands, or even millions. Many viral marketing programs give away free products or services, often in exchange for valuable social media profiles and e-mail addresses. Free attracts attention; once you have consumers' attention they can see other products or services you offer and buy those.

Social Networking

We briefly touched on the importance of social media and advertising earlier in the chapter. However, social media have a much greater role in promotion than just advertising. The majority of Americans are active on at least one social media platform, whether it be Facebook, Twitter, Instagram, or any of the many sites adding users daily. Marketers have quickly noticed how social media are changing the business environment. Companies utilize these tools to increase exposure for products or services, create loyalty among customers, drive traffic to the company website, and even to come up with new ideas.[30]

One of the greatest advantages of social media platforms is that they offer easier two-way communication between businesses and customers. For example, companies like Nabisco and Travelocity can be in constant contact with customers and entertain them along the way. Following the final episode of *Game of Thrones,* Nabisco capitalized on fans' excitement leading into the finale. It released #GameOfCookies, a 50-second video mirroring the opening credits of the show but made entirely of cookies. The video was also cut into smaller 15-second digital advertisements promoting its new *Game of Thrones* packaging. The video was shared millions of times on many social media platforms.[31] When people participate in these social media activities, they frequently continue interacting with the company and, more importantly, are likely to share branded content. Check out the Connecting through Social Media box to learn about how word-of-mouth promotion on Instagram and Facebook has its pros and cons.

Though all the "likes" and "shares" may seem as if they come easy for marketers, they often are the result of a detailed social media plan. The steps frequently used to launch a successful social media promotional campaign include:[32]

1. Get to know your customer base.
2. Create images your customers will *want* to see and post something new every day.
3. Develop fun, yet suitable, hashtags so your content is discovered by new users—but don't use too many.

word-of-mouth promotion
A promotional tool that involves people telling other people about products they've purchased.

viral marketing
The term now used to describe everything from paying customers to say positive things on the Internet to setting up multilevel selling schemes whereby consumers get commissions for directing friends to specific websites.

The Rise and Fall of Insta-influencers

SugarBearHair gummies, Byte aligners, FabFitFun boxes—we've seen them all . . . a lot. In fact, it's nearly impossible to scroll through an Instagram or Facebook feed and not see celebrities and social media influencers posting about these products and many others. This year, American advertisers are set to invest over $160 billion in digital advertising. More than half of that budget is likely to go toward social media ads.

In the past few years, tapping into influencers has been an incredibly successful marketing move. Endorsements appeared more genuine, consumers were more likely to trust these ads, and scores of users were reached in an instant. The power held by word-of-mouth promotion was proven by these influencers daily. However, as users have become more savvy, influencer engagement rates have been declining. In 2019, engagement dropped nearly 10 percent!

What's going on here? For starters, social media users have lost trust in these messages. They know they're advertisements and likely the influencer endorsing the product doesn't even use it. On top of that, feeds have become so saturated with these advertisements, users have stopped following major influencers or just trained their brains to skip over these posts. That doesn't mean influencer marketing is dead, though. Marketers can still boost brand recognition and increase sales using influencers. They just need to be more creative with their

Mykhailo Polenok/Alamy Stock Photo

content and increase engagement with users. This could help earn users' trust again and keep those dollars rolling in.

Sources: Nikki Carlson, "Why Your 2020 Marketing Strategy Should Include Influencers," *Forbes*, February 12, 2020; Suzanne Kapner and Sharon Terlep, "Advertisers Sour on Online Influencers," *The Wall Street Journal*, October 21, 2019; Barb Mosher Zinck, "Social Spending in 2020 Is Increasing, but Is It the Right Move?," *Diginomica*, February 5, 2020; Sean Hargrave, "Has Influencer Marketing Just Been Busted?," *MediaPost*, February 20, 2020.

4. Set up a publishing calendar to ensure consistency in posting.
5. Engage with your customers—offer contests and entertainment.
6. Follow back and reply to your commenters.
7. Familiarize yourself with new features the site may offer.
8. Measure the effectiveness of what you post and use what you learn for the future.

Blogging

There are hundreds of millions of blogs online. How do blogs affect marketing? Running a blog is great way to interact with customers. Businesses can attract new customers when they coordinate their social media profiles with their blogs. As people click to a company's blog through the social media profile, it helps improve the company's website ranking. People love to share content they find relevant. In order for a blog to succeed, a business must take time to post and respond to the customers that leave comments. They can use some of the comments to help create new posts. They have to post consistently in order to be recognized by the search engines, and to keep customers coming back to the blog for new information. If the blog isn't kept updated, it will lose traffic and, therefore, its power as a promotional tool.

Podcasting

podcasting
A means of distributing audio and video programs via the Internet that lets users subscribe to a number of files, also known as feeds, and then hear or view the material at the time they choose.

Podcasting is a means of distributing multimedia digital files online for downloading or streaming. Podcasts are important because they are a great way to capture your existing and prospective customers' attention for an extended period of time by giving them something of value that is easy for them to understand.[33] Of course, many companies have also found success in creating videos for YouTube.

E-mail Promotions

Uber has an e-mail marketing program designed to increase brand awareness and update subscribers on various deals or promotions. The e-mails are brightly colored, yet simple and to the point. A person can easily skim the e-mail and get most of the information he or she needs. If more information is needed than what appears in the main message, the subscriber can get expanded, illustrated instructions with an easy click at the bottom. In 2020, Lyft partnered with various organizations and used its e-mail subscribers' list to help its drivers and riders register to vote and get the newly registered voters to the polls on Election Day.[34]

Mobile Marketing

Most marketers make sure their media are viewable on mobile devices like tablets and smartphones. One key to success, therefore, is to keep the message brief because mobile users don't want to read through much text. With mobile media, marketers can use text messaging to promote sweepstakes, send customers news or sports alerts, and give them company information. Companies can determine where you are and send you messages about restaurants and other services in your vicinity.

Pawita Warasiri/EyeEm/Getty Images

Mobile media allow marketers to reach customers through text messaging. Have you received promotional messages? For which products are they most effective?

Managing the Promotion Mix: Putting It All Together

Each target group calls for a separate promotion mix. Advertising is most efficient for reaching large groups of consumers whose members share similar traits. Personal selling is best for selling to large organizations. To motivate people to buy now rather than later, marketers use sales promotions like sampling, coupons, discounts, special displays, and premiums. Publicity supports other efforts and can create a good impression among all consumers. Word of mouth is often the most powerful promotional tool. Generate it by listening, being responsive, and creating an impression worth passing on to others that you spread through social media, blogs, and podcasts.

Promotional Strategies

How do producers move products to consumers? In a **push strategy**, the producer uses advertising, personal selling, sales promotion, and all other promotional tools to convince wholesalers and retailers to stock and sell merchandise, *pushing* it through the distribution system to the stores. If the push strategy works, consumers will walk into a store, see the product, and buy it.

A **pull strategy** directs heavy advertising and sales promotion efforts toward *consumers*. If the pull strategy works, consumers will go to the store and ask for the products. The store owner will order them from the wholesaler, who in turn will order them from the producer. Products are thus *pulled* through the distribution system.

It has been important to make promotion part of a total systems approach to marketing. That is, promotion was part of supply-chain management. In such cases, retailers would work with producers and distributors to make the supply chain as efficient as possible. Then a promotional plan would be developed for the *whole system*. The idea would be to develop a total product offer that would appeal to everyone: manufacturers, distributors, retailers, and consumers.

push strategy
Promotional strategy in which the producer uses advertising, personal selling, sales promotion, and all other promotional tools to convince wholesalers and retailers to stock and sell merchandise.

pull strategy
Promotional strategy in which heavy advertising and sales promotion efforts are directed toward consumers so that they'll request the products from retailers.

While most bus shelter ads aren't too interesting, this one gives people a place to sit and potentially think about going on a skiing trip to Jackson Hole. Do you think providing subtle experiences like these is an effective way to inform consumers about a product or service?

Outdoor Advertising Association of America

?TEST**PREP**

- What is viral marketing?
- What are blogging and podcasting?
- Describe a push strategy and a pull strategy.

SUMMARY

LO 16–1 Identify the new and traditional tools that make up the promotion mix.

- **What is promotion?**

  Promotion is an effort by marketers to inform and remind people in the target market about products and to persuade them to participate in an exchange.

- **What are the four traditional promotional tools that make up the promotion mix?**

  The four traditional promotional tools are advertising, personal selling, public relations, and sales promotion. The product itself can also be a promotional tool—that's why it is shown in the middle of Figure 16.1.

LO 16–2 Contrast the advantages and disadvantages of various advertising media, including the Internet and social media.

- **What is advertising?**

Advertising is limited to paid, nonpersonal (not face-to-face) communication through various media by organizations and individuals who are in some way identified in the advertising message.

- **What are the advantages of using the various media?**

Review the advantages and disadvantages of the various advertising media in Figure 16.5.

- **Why is the use of infomercials, online advertising, and social media advertising growing?**

Infomercials are growing in importance because they show products in use and present testimonials to help sell goods and services. Online advertising pushes customers to a website where they can learn more about a company and its products. With social media advertising, companies can test ads and other promotions before bringing them to traditional media like TV.

LO 16–3 Illustrate the steps of the B2B and B2C selling processes.

- **What is personal selling?**

Personal selling is the face-to-face presentation and promotion of products and services. It includes the search for new prospects and follow-up service after the sale.

- **What are the seven steps of the B2B selling process?**

The steps of the selling process are (1) prospect and qualify, (2) preapproach, (3) approach, (4) make a presentation, (5) answer objections, (6) close the sale, and (7) follow up.

- **What are the steps in the B2C selling process?**

The steps are the approach, which includes asking questions; the presentation, which includes answering questions; the close; and the follow-up.

LO 16–4 Describe the role of the public relations department, and show how publicity fits in that role.

- **What is public relations?**

Public relations (PR) is the function that evaluates public attitudes, changes policies and procedures in response to the public's requests, and executes a program of action and information to earn public understanding and acceptance.

- **What are the three major steps in a good public relations program?**

(1) Listen to the public, (2) develop policies and procedures in the public interest, and (3) tell people you're being responsive to their needs.

- **What is publicity?**

Publicity is the talking arm of public relations; it is information distributed by the media that's not paid for, or controlled by, the seller. Publicity's greatest advantage is its believability.

LO 16–5 Assess the effectiveness of various forms of sales promotion, including sampling.

- **How are sales promotion activities used both within and outside the organization?**

Internal sales promotion efforts are directed at salespeople and other customer-contact people to keep them enthusiastic about the company. Internal sales promotion activities include sales training, sales aids, audiovisual displays, and trade shows. External sales promotions to consumers rely on samples, coupons, cents-off deals, displays, store demonstrators, premiums, and other incentives.

LO 16–6 Show how word-of-mouth promotion, viral marketing, social networking, blogging, podcasting, e-mail marketing, and mobile marketing work.

■ **Is word of mouth a major promotional tool?**

Word of mouth was not one of the traditional forms of promotion because it was not considered to be manageable, but it has always been an effective way of promoting goods and services.

■ **How is word of mouth used in promotion today?**

The goal of word of mouth is to get the company's message to as many people as possible. Viral marketing includes any strategy that encourages people to pass on a marketing message to others, creating exponential growth in the message's influence as the message reaches thousands to millions. Many viral marketing programs give away free products or services, often in exchange for valuable e-mail addresses.

■ **What other promotional tools can marketers use to promote products?**

Other promotional tools include social networking, blogging, podcasting, e-mail promotions, and mobile marketing.

■ **What are the major promotional strategies?**

In a *push strategy,* the producer uses advertising, personal selling, sales promotion, and all other promotional tools to convince wholesalers and retailers to stock and sell merchandise. In a *pull strategy,* heavy advertising and sales promotion efforts are directed toward consumers so they'll request the products from retailers.

KEY TERMS

advertising 415
infomercial 419
integrated marketing
   communication
   (IMC) 414
interactive promotion 419
personal selling 420
podcasting 428

product placement 418
promotion mix 414
prospect 422
prospecting 422
publicity 424
public relations
   (PR) 424
pull strategy 429

push strategy 429
qualifying 422
sales promotion 425
sampling 426
trial close 422
viral marketing 427
word-of-mouth
   promotion 427

CRITICAL THINKING

1. What kinds of problems can emerge if a firm doesn't communicate with environmentalists, the news media, and the local community? Do you know of any firms that aren't responsive to your community? What are the consequences?

2. How often do you buy online? If you don't actually buy, do you use the Internet to compare goods and prices? Do you or your friends take advantage of low prices on used goods on eBay or other online sites like Craigslist? Do you look at ads on the Internet? Do they seem to be effective?

3. As interactive communications between companies and customers grow, do you think traditional advertising will grow or decline? What will be the effect of growth or decline on the price we pay for TV programs, newspapers, and magazines?

4. How have blogging, podcasting, and social media affected other media you use, like newspapers or television? Do you read print newspapers now or do you get your news some other way? Do you watch programs on TV or on other devices? How has the move away from print and network television affected advertising?

PURPOSE

To learn how companies use live website chat to promote their products and services and build relationships with customers.

EXERCISE

Go to HubSpot at blog.hubspot.com and search for the post "9 Companies Using Live Website Chat in a Creative Way."

1. On what website does Petplan offer live chats? How does having the live chat on a website other than its own benefit the company and its customers?

2. SnapEngage offers live chats in a way that we wish more companies would. What is it, and how effective do you think it is in keeping viewers on its site instead of moving on somewhere else?

3. How do each of the companies' website chats help them develop stronger relationships with their customers?

KEY: ● **Team** ★ **Analytic** ▲ **Communication** ▣ **Technology**

1. Using at least two different media—a newspaper, magazine, television, radio, online—choose two ads you consider effective and two you find ineffective. Be prepared to explain your choices based on what you have learned in this chapter. ★ ▲

2. Scan your local newspaper or search online for examples of publicity (stories about new products) and sales promotion (coupons, contests, sweepstakes). Share your examples and discuss the effectiveness of such promotional efforts with the class. ▲ ★ ▣

3. Many students shy away from careers in selling, often because they think they are not outgoing enough or that salespeople are dishonest or pushy. Prepare a one-page document about your experience with salespeople and describe how they used one or more of the selling strategies covered in this chapter. ▲ ★

4. In small groups, discuss whether you are purchasing more goods using brick-and-mortar stores or online and why. If you shop at brick-and-mortar stores, do you look up information online before buying goods and services? How helpful are such searches? Present your findings to the class. ▲ ★ ●

5. In small groups, list six goods and services most students own or use and discuss promotional techniques that prompt you to buy them: advertising, personal selling, social media, publicity, sales promotion, or word of mouth. Which seems most effective for your group? Why? ▲ ★ ●

If you are interested in working in promotion, here are a few careers to consider. Find out about the tasks performed, skills needed, pay, and opportunity outlook in these fields in the *Occupational Outlook Handbook (OOH)* at bls.gov.

- **Advertising sales agent**—sells advertising space to businesses and individuals; contacts potential clients, makes sales presentations, and maintains client accounts.

- **Public relations specialist**—creates and maintains a favorable public image for the organization they represent; designs media releases to shape public perception of the organization and to increase awareness of its work and goals.

- **Fundraising manager**—designs and coordinates campaigns that attract donations for the organizations.

- **Web developer**—designs and creates websites.

VIDEO CASE *Getting Zapped by Promotion*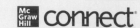

Back in 1999, when Nick Swinmurn couldn't find the pair of shoes he wanted in any shoe store, he figured the next step was to search online. To his surprise, he found that no major online retailer specialized in selling shoes. Like many successful entrepreneurs before him, he saw an opportunity and Zappos.com was born. While the idea of buying shoes online was certainly challenging, the company become successful by being the first online retailer that offered free shipping both ways. Fortunately, Swinmurn knew that being the first online retailer to offer such shipping benefits was not a guarantee of long-term success. He knew it was vital to create a corporate culture that was innovative and excelled at customer service.

He also knew that many of the firm's initial customers found the company by accidentally stumbling on its website. It primarily relied on word of mouth to build its customer base. While word of mouth is a very effective form of promotion, the company realized it had to expand and develop effective additional forms of promotion. As Zappos has grown, it has enlarged its promotion mix to include advertising, social media, public relations, sales promotions, and personal selling.

Advertising messages from Zappos have generally been low key and typically don't include traditional print or broadcast advertisements. Instead the company makes broad use of social media ads using interesting photography and video content to highlight the firm's products. The company also uses social media to inform customers what is going on in regard to special promotions, sales, and special events. Zappos also uses what it refers to as interest-based ads that are personally targeted to consumers based on their associations with the site.

Public relations (PR) activities include events, sponsorships, and other related personal involvement to increase awareness of products and services available from the company. PR attempts to improve the firm's image and helps it stay connected to current customers as well as attracting new ones. For example, at JFK airport in New York, the company partnered with JetBlue Airways and turned a baggage claim belt into a board game. Passenger bags that landed on a specific square on the belt won a prize such as shoes, a backpack, or a trip. The company attempted to bring a little pleasure to travelers on what is always a hectic and frustrating travel day.

A new promotional technique being employed by the company is the Zappos loyalty program. The program is part of an extensive sales promotion effort that communicates with customers their value to the company. The four-tiered loyalty program gives customers points for shopping at the site, and provides access to exclusive products and sales. It also offers free expedited shipping on all orders. In addition, the company makes use of coupons and discounts in an innovative way using special coupon codes. Sweepstakes are also part of its sales promotion efforts.

Zappos does not use personal selling in a traditional way. It does, however, operate a call center in Las Vegas that employs 500 representatives that are specifically trained in customer satisfaction. The call center team members don't use a fixed script in communicating with customers. Instead they talk candidly with consumers and are known to go to great lengths to provide customer satisfaction. Total customer service is an integral part of the Zappos company culture and marketing plan. It has been the primary booster of the powerful, favorable word of mouth the company enjoys. And in today's social media–driven world, a dependable word-of-mouth recommendation might be the most important type of promotion.

Today, the Zappos culture itself has become a promotional tool. Stories of how far the company is willing to go to satisfy customers have been unprecedented in the world of online commerce. Its corporate culture and carefully managed promotional program promise to keep Zappos providing the "shoe that fits" for a long time.

THINKING IT OVER

1. What are the differences between publicity and advertising?

2. How does a sales promotion activity such as the loyalty program help ensure continued customer support?

3. Is Zappos likely to increase or decrease its use of social media in its promotion mix? Why?

NOTES

1. Igor Sorokin, "How Marketing Agencies Can Help Not-for-Profits Thrive in 2020," *Forbes,* February 13, 2020.
2. Evan Varsamis, "How to Use Social Media to Promote Your Product," *Forbes,* February 12, 2020.
3. Laura Lake, "Why Integrated Marketing Communications Matters," *The Balance Small Business,* thebalancesmb.com, accessed March 2020.
4. Amy Gesenhues, "How Agencies Are Helping CMOs Break Down Barriers to Digital Transformation," *MarTech Today,* March 5, 2020.
5. Erik Oster, "U.S. Advertising and Marketing Spend to Grow to Nearly $390 Billion in 2020," *Adweek,* January 17, 2020.
6. Meghan King, "Why Direct Mail Still Matters in the Digital Age," *The Financial Brand,* February 13, 2020.

7. Sarah Fischer, "National Newspapers Thrive While Local Outlets Struggle to Survive," *Axios,* February 18, 2020; Elizabeth Grieco, "Fast Facts about the Newspaper Industry's Financial Struggles as McClatchy Files for Bankruptcy," Pew Research Center, February 14, 2020.

8. "What Do the Roaring 20s Have in Store for Mobile Advertising?," *Mobile Marketing Magazine,* February 24, 2020.

9. James Crabtree-Hannigan, "Super Bowl Commercials 2020: How Much Does an Ad Cost for Super Bowl 54?," *Sporting News,* sportingnews.com, February 2, 2020; Nick Swartz, "How Much Does a 2020 Super Bowl Commercial Cost?," *USA Today,* usatoday.com, February 2, 2020.

10. "Celebrity Saturation Fails in Super Bowl Ads," *WARC,* February 17, 2020.

11. Jeanine Poggi, "TV'S Most Expensive Commercials for the 2019-'20 Season," *Ad Age,* adage.com, accessed March 2020.

12. Brad Adgate, "TV Attribution: Keeping Ad Dollars in Television," *Forbes,* February 19, 2020.

13. "Social Media Fact Sheet," Pew Research Center, pewresearch.org, accessed March 2020.

14. Shane O'Neill, "Sonic the Hedgehog's Movie Is Obsessed with Olive Garden," *Screen Rant,* February 16, 2020.

15. Chris Flynn, "14 Epic Cars Hiding in These Superheroes' Garages," *The Things,* February 23, 2020.

16. Lia Sestric, "The Most Profitable 'As Seen on TV' Products of All Time," *Yahoo! Finance,* finance.yahoo.com, accessed March 2020.

17. "How McDonald's Handles Thousands of Social Mentions per Day," *Social Pros,* convinceandconvert.com, accessed March 2020.

18. Geoff De Weaver, "10 Steps to Global Advertising Success," *MediaPost,* February 22, 2020.

19. Shep Hyken, "A PSA for Sales Leaders: Ditch Your Sales Scripts," *Forbes,* March 1, 2020.

20. Andris A. Zoltners, Prabhakant Sinha, and Sally E. Lorimer, "How Sales Teams Can Thrive in a Digital World," *Harvard Business Review,* February 18, 2020.

21. Steli Efti, "Tired of Sales Rejections? Here's What You Need to Know," *Forbes,* December 3, 2019; Craig Wortman, "How to Turn Objections into a Powerful Sales Tool," *Inc.,* inc.com, February 26, 2020.

22. Erica Turner and Lee Raine, "Most Americans Rely on Their Own Research to Make Big Decisions, and That Often Means Online Searches," Pew Research Center, March 5, 2020.

23. Robert Williams, "Wendy's Cooks Up Social Media Buzz with New Breakfast Menu Campaign," *Mobile Marketer,* March 3, 2020.

24. Daney Parker, "The Biggest PR Disasters of 2019," *PR Moment,* December 5, 2019; Chris Isadore, "Boeing's Got Bigger Problems Than the 737 Max," *CNN Business,* cnn.com, February 11, 2020.

25. Anastasiya Golovatenko, "Six PR Trends That Will Impact Businesses in 2020," *Entrepreneur,* February 11, 2020; Seth Arenstein, "PR and Legal Are Collaborating on Regulatory Issues," *PR News,* February 21, 2020.

26. Donna St. Jean Conti, "The Press Release Is Alive and Well," *Business 2 Community,* March 5, 2020.

27. Amity Kapadia, "The Secrets of Word of Mouth Marketing Revealed," *Business 2 Community,* business2community.com, January 20, 2020.

28. Dianna Christie, "Jeep Leans on Fans, Multichannel Campaign to Build Off-Road Community," *Marketing Dive,* marketingdive.com, March 6, 2020.

29. Jessica Wong, "How to Get the Most Out of Your Brand's Social Media Campaign," *Forbes,* February 11, 2020.

30. Ralph DiBugnara, "Social Media Is the Biggest Factor in the New Real Estate Market," *Forbes,* March 5, 2020; Eric Peckham, "The Companies That Will Shape the Upcoming Multi-verse Era of Social Media," *TechCrunch,* March 2, 2020.

31. Brian Peters, "Top Social Media Campaigns of 2019," *Meltwater,* December 29, 2019.

32. "10 Fun, Competitive Ways Marketing Teams Can Promote Customer Engagement," *Forbes,* February 7, 2020; Ismael El Qudsi, "What to Expect for Influencer Marketing in 2020," *Forbes,* February 6, 2020.

33. Lynne Golodner, "How to Decide if a Podcast Is the Right Marketing Tool for You," *Forbes,* March 3, 2020.

34. Chris Burns, "Lyft Shows How to Get a Free Ride to Vote in 2020 Elections," *SlashGear,* February 18, 2020.

17

Understanding Accounting and Financial Information

LEARNING OBJECTIVES »

After you have read and studied this chapter, you should be able to

LO 17–1 Demonstrate the role that accounting and financial information play for a business and its stakeholders.

LO 17–2 List the steps in the accounting cycle, distinguish between accounting and bookkeeping, and explain how computers are used in accounting.

LO 17–3 Explain how the major financial statements differ.

LO 17–4 Demonstrate the application of ratio analysis in reporting financial information.

LO 17–5 Identify the different disciplines within the accounting profession.

Shelly Sun, CEO of BrightStar Care

Shelly Sun never expected to start her own company. As a certified public accountant (CPA) with a master's degree in accounting from the University of Colorado, by age 29 she was already a vice president at a major insurance firm. Then her life changed when her family was struggling to find quality in-home care for her ailing grandmother. They tried a series of in-home care agencies, but none of them lived up to the standards that the family expected. As their quest continued, it became evident they had uncovered a major gap in the health care sector: the need for better in-home care. It was then she decided to take the plunge and start her own business, BrightStar Care.

Thanks to her many years working in the corporate world as a CPA, Sun possessed the necessary skills to focus on the financial aspects of her new business. The hours were long, but she knew the hard work would be worth it if the company could offer people the level of service her own family once sought. After three years, BrightStar Care had opened three successful company-owned locations. Sun, however, believed the company's long-term success would come from franchising. Today, BrightStar Care has 340 locations that serve more than 15,000 families and in 2019 generated $500 million in systemwide revenue. The company remains on *Forbes* magazine's top-10 list of franchise opportunities under a $150,000 investment.

BrightStar Care's success has not caused Sun to slow down. She earned distinction as a Certified Franchise Executive and was named by the International Franchise Association (IFA) as Entrepreneur of the Year in 2009. In 2017, she was chairperson of the IFA's board of directors. She was featured on the CBS program *Undercover Boss* and published her first book, *Grow Smart, Risk Less,* in which she shares her lessons and experiences of building a successful franchise.

Shelly Sun credits her knowledge of accounting for helping BrightStar Care survive during the tough times of the Great Recession that started in 2008. By personally understanding and tackling her company's financial issues and working closely with franchisees to implement efficiencies and controls, the company survived the difficult times when franchise financing almost completely dried up. Sun strongly believes that developing a core competency such as accounting is a key to business or franchise success. As she readily admits, "Not a day goes by in running my company that I don't leverage some part of my accounting knowledge." Under her leadership, BrightStar Care has a goal to serve 100,000 families.

Controlling costs, managing cash flows, understanding profit margins and taxes, and reporting finances accurately are keys to survival for successful organizations like BrightStar

Care and small and medium-sized businesses. This chapter will introduce you to the accounting fundamentals and financial information critical to business success. The chapter also briefly explores the financial ratios that are essential in measuring business performance in a large or small business.

Sources: Kevin Kruse, "The Entrepreneur's Guide to Success with BrightStar Care CEO Shelly Sun," *Forbes,* January 17, 2018; Andrew Donlan, "BrightStar CEO, Shelly Sun Built a $500 Million Company—and She's Not Done Yet," *Home Health Care News,* January 8, 2020; BrightStar Care, brightstarcare.com, accessed March 2020; "Shelly Sun, CEO and Co-founder of BrightStar Care," *International Franchise Association,* franchising.org, accessed March 2020.

Let's talk business!
bit.ly/LetsTalkBusiness17

Courtesy of BrightStar Care and Shelly Sun

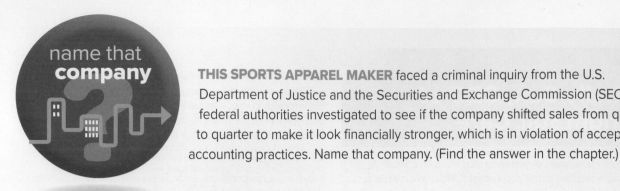
LO 17–1 Demonstrate the role that accounting and financial information play for a business and its stakeholders.

The Role of Accounting Information

Small and large businesses often survive or fail according to how well they handle financial procedures. Financial management is the heartbeat of competitive businesses, and accounting information helps keep the heartbeat stable. Accounting reports and financial statements reveal as much about a business's health as pulse and blood pressure readings tell us about a person's health.

You may think accounting is only for profit-seeking businesses. Nothing could be further from the truth. Accounting, often called the language of business, allows us to report financial information about nonprofit organizations such as churches, schools, hospitals, fraternities, and government agencies. Thus, you have to know something about accounting if you want to succeed in any type of business. It's almost impossible to understand business operations without being able to read, understand, and analyze accounting reports and financial statements.

By the end of the chapter, you should have a good idea what accounting is, how it works, and the value it offers businesses. You should also know some accounting terms and understand the purpose of accounting statements, as well as career opportunities in accounting. Your new understanding will pay off as you become more active in business, or will help you in simply understanding what's going on in the world of business and finance. Let's get started!

What Is Accounting?

accounting
The recording, classifying, summarizing, and interpreting of financial events and transactions to provide management and other interested parties the information they need to make good decisions.

Accounting is the recording, classifying, summarizing, and interpreting of financial events and transactions in an organization to provide management and other interested parties the financial information they need to make good decisions about its operation. Financial transactions include buying and selling goods and services, acquiring insurance, paying employees, and using supplies. Usually we group all purchases together, and all sales transactions together. The method we use to record and summarize accounting data into reports is an *accounting system* (see Figure 17.1).

A major purpose of accounting is to help managers make well-informed decisions. Another is to report financial information about the firm to interested stakeholders, such as employees, owners, creditors, suppliers, unions, community activists, investors, and the government (for tax purposes) (see Figure 17.2).

Accountants know it's vital for users of a firm's accounting information to be assured the information is accurate. The independent Financial Accounting Standards Board (FASB) defines the *generally accepted accounting principles (GAAP)* that accountants must

FIGURE 17.1 THE ACCOUNTING SYSTEM

The inputs to an accounting system include sales documents and other documents. The data is recorded, classified, and summarized. It is then put into summary financial statements such as the income statement and balance sheet and statement of cash flows.

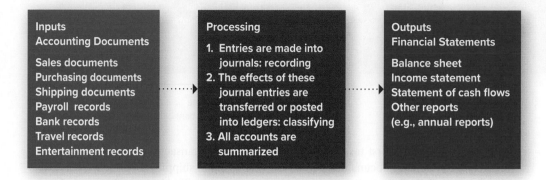

Inputs Accounting Documents	Processing	Outputs Financial Statements
Sales documents Purchasing documents Shipping documents Payroll records Bank records Travel records Entertainment records	1. Entries are made into journals: recording 2. The effects of these journal entries are transferred or posted into ledgers: classifying 3. All accounts are summarized	Balance sheet Income statement Statement of cash flows Other reports (e.g., annual reports)

FIGURE 17.2 USERS OF ACCOUNTING INFORMATION AND THE REQUIRED REPORTS

Many types of organizations use accounting information to make business decisions. The reports need to vary according to the information each user requires. An accountant must prepare the appropriate forms.

USERS	TYPE OF REPORT
• Government taxing authorities (e.g., the Internal Revenue Service)	• Tax returns
• Government regulatory agencies	• Required reports
• People interested in the organization's income and financial position (e.g., owners, creditors, financial analysts, suppliers)	• Financial statements found in annual reports (e.g., income statement, balance sheet, statement of cash flows)
• Managers of the firm	• Financial statements and various internally distributed financial reports

follow.[1] If accounting reports are prepared in accordance with GAAP, users can expect the information to meet standards upon which accounting professionals have agreed.[2]

LO 17-2 List the steps in the accounting cycle, distinguish between accounting and bookkeeping, and explain how computers are used in accounting.

The Accounting Cycle

The **accounting cycle** is a six-step procedure that results in the preparation and analysis of the major financial statements (see Figure 17.3). It relies on the work of both a bookkeeper and an accountant. **Bookkeeping**, the recording of business transactions, is a basic part of financial reporting. Accounting, however, goes far beyond the mere recording of financial information. Accountants classify and summarize financial data provided by bookkeepers, and then interpret the data and report the information to management. They also suggest strategies for improving the firm's financial condition and prepare financial analyses and income tax returns.

accounting cycle
A six-step procedure that results in the preparation and analysis of the major financial statements.

bookkeeping
The recording of business transactions.

FIGURE 17.3 STEPS IN THE ACCOUNTING CYCLE

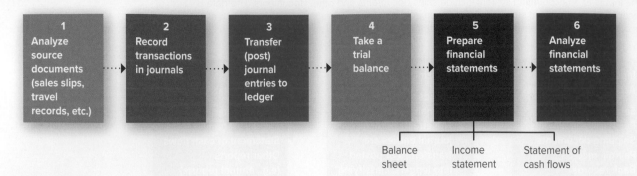

| 1 Analyze source documents (sales slips, travel records, etc.) | 2 Record transactions in journals | 3 Transfer (post) journal entries to ledger | 4 Take a trial balance | 5 Prepare financial statements | 6 Analyze financial statements |

Balance sheet   Income statement   Statement of cash flows

iSeeit! Need help understanding the accounting cycle? Visit your Connect eBook to view a video for a brief animated explanation.

journal

The record book or computer program where accounting data is first entered.

double-entry bookkeeping

The practice of writing every business transaction in two places.

ledger

A specialized accounting book or computer program in which information from accounting journals is accumulated into specific categories and posted so that managers can find all the information about one account in the same place.

trial balance

A summary of all the financial data in the account ledgers that ensures the figures are correct and balanced.

A bookkeeper's first task is to divide all the firm's transactions into meaningful categories, such as sales documents, purchasing receipts, and shipping documents, being very careful to keep the information organized and manageable. Bookkeepers then record financial data from the original transaction documents (sales slips and so forth) into a record book or computer program called a **journal**. The word *journal* comes from the French word *jour,* which means "day." Therefore, a journal is where the day's transactions are kept.

It's quite possible to make a mistake when recording financial transactions, like entering $10.98 as $10.89. That's why bookkeepers record all transactions in two places, so they can check one list of transactions against the other to make sure both add up to the same amount. If the amounts are not equal, the bookkeeper knows there is a mistake. The practice of writing every transaction in two places is called **double-entry bookkeeping**. It requires two entries in the journal and in the ledgers (discussed next) for each transaction.

Suppose a business wanted to determine how much it paid for office supplies in the first quarter of the year. Without a specific bookkeeping tool, that would be difficult—even with accurate accounting journals. Therefore, bookkeepers use a specialized accounting book or computer program called a **ledger**. In the ledger, they transfer (or post) information from accounting journals into specific categories so managers can find all the information about a single account, like office supplies or cash, in one place.

The next step in the accounting cycle is to prepare a **trial balance**, a summary of all the financial data in the account ledgers that ensures the figures are correct and balanced. If the information in the account ledgers is not accurate, the accountant must correct it before preparing the firm's financial statements. Using the correct information, the accountant then prepares the firm's financial statements—including a balance sheet, an income statement, and a statement of cash flows—according to generally accepted accounting principles (GAAP).

Using Technology in Accounting

A long while ago, accountants and bookkeepers needed to enter all of a firm's financial information by hand. The advent of adding machines and calculators made the job a bit simpler, but still generally required a paper entry. As we approached the 2000s, technology simplified the accounting process considerably. Today, computerized accounting programs can post information from journals instantaneously from remote locations to encrypted laptops or cell phones, making financial information available whenever the organization needs it. The company's sensitive financial information is safe and secure, but is in the accountant's hands when needed. Such assistance frees accountants' time for more important tasks such as financial analysis and financial forecasting.

Computerized accounting programs are particularly helpful to small-business owners, who don't often have the variety of accounting personnel within their companies that larger firms enjoy. Accounting software—such as Intuit's QuickBooks—addresses the specific needs of small businesses that are often significantly different from the needs of a major corporation.[3] Small-business owners, however, need to understand exactly which programs are best suited for their particular company needs.[4] That's one reason why entrepreneurs planning to start a business should either hire or consult with a trained accountant to identify the particular needs of their firm. They can then develop a specific accounting system that works with the accounting software they've chosen.

With sophisticated accounting software available and technology capabilities growing, you might wonder why you need to study and understand accounting. Without question technology has greatly assisted businesspeople and certainly helped ease the monotony of bookkeeping and accounting work. Unfortunately the work of an accountant requires training and very specific competencies that computers are not programmed to handle. It's the partnership of technology and an accountant's specialized knowledge that helps a firm make the right financial decisions. After the Test Prep, we'll explore the balance sheet, income statement, and statement of cash flows. It's from the information contained in these financial statements that the accountant analyzes and evaluates the financial condition of the firm.

?TESTPREP

- How is the job of the bookkeeper different from that of an accountant?
- What's the purpose of accounting journals and of a ledger?
- Why does a bookkeeper prepare a trial balance?
- How has computer software helped businesses in maintaining and compiling accounting information?

LO 17–3 Explain how the major financial statements differ.

Understanding Key Financial Statements

An accounting year is either a calendar or fiscal year. A calendar year begins January 1 and ends December 31. A fiscal year can begin at any date designated by the business. A **financial statement** is a summary of all the financial transactions that have occurred over a particular period. Financial statements indicate a firm's financial health and stability, and are key factors in management decision making.[5] That's why stockholders (the owners of the firm), bondholders and banks (people and institutions that lend money to the firm), labor unions, employees, and the Internal Revenue Service are all interested in a firm's financial statements. The key financial statements of a business are:

1. The *balance sheet,* which reports the firm's financial condition *on a specific date.*

2. The *income statement,* which summarizes revenues, cost of goods sold, and expenses (including taxes) for a specific period and highlights the total profit or loss the firm experienced *during that period.*

3. The *statement of cash flows,* which provides a summary of money coming into and going out of the firm. It tracks a company's cash receipts and cash payments.

The differences among the financial statements can best be summarized this way: The balance sheet details what the company owns and owes on a certain day; the income statement shows the revenue a firm earned selling its products compared to its selling costs (profit or loss) over a specific period of time; and the statement of cash flows highlights the difference between cash coming in and cash going out of a business. To fully understand this important financial information, you need to know the purpose of an organization's financial statements. To help with this task, we'll explain each statement in more detail next.

financial statement
A summary of all the transactions that have occurred over a particular period.

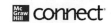

iSeeit! Need help understanding financial statements? Visit your Connect eBook to view a video for a brief animated explanation.

The Fundamental Accounting Equation

Imagine you don't owe anybody money. That is, you have no liabilities (debts). In this case, your assets (cash and so forth) are equal to what you *own* (your equity). However, if you borrow some money from a friend, you have incurred a liability. Your assets are now equal to what you *owe* plus what you own. Translated into business terms, Assets = Liabilities + Owners' equity.

In accounting, this equation must always be balanced. For example, suppose you have $50,000 in cash and decide to use that money to open a small coffee shop. Your business has assets of $50,000 and no debts. The accounting equation would look like this:

$$\text{Assets} = \text{Liabilities} + \text{Owners' equity}$$
$$\$50,000 = \$0 + \$50,000$$

You have $50,000 cash and $50,000 owners' equity (the amount of your investment in the business—sometimes referred to as net worth). However, before opening the business, you borrow $30,000 from a local bank; now the equation changes. You have $30,000 of additional cash, but you also have a debt (liability) of $30,000. (Remember, in double-entry bookkeeping we record each business transaction in two places.)

Your financial position within the business has changed. The equation is still balanced, but we change it to reflect the borrowing transaction:

$$\text{Assets} = \text{Liabilities} + \text{Owners' equity}$$
$$\$80,000 = \$30,000 + \$50,000$$

This **fundamental accounting equation** is the basis for the balance sheet.

Glossary (margin)

fundamental accounting equation

Assets = Liabilities + Owners' equity; this is the basis for the balance sheet.

balance sheet

Financial statement that reports a firm's financial condition at a specific time and is composed of three major accounts: assets, liabilities, and owners' equity.

assets

Economic resources (things of value) owned by a firm.

The Balance Sheet

A **balance sheet** is the financial statement that reports a firm's financial condition at a specific time. As highlighted in the sample balance sheet in Figure 17.4 (for our hypothetical restaurant, Harvest Gold, introduced in Chapter 13), assets are listed in a separate column from liabilities and owners' (or stockholders') equity. The assets are equal to, or *balanced* with, the liabilities and owners' (or stockholders') equity.[6] The balance sheet is that simple.

Let's say you want to know what your financial condition is at a given time. Maybe you want to buy a house or car and therefore need to calculate your available resources. One of the best measuring sticks is your balance sheet. First, add up everything you own—cash, property, and money owed you. These are your assets. Subtract from that the money you owe others—credit card debt, IOUs, car loan, student loans, and the like. These are your liabilities. The resulting figure is your net worth, or equity. This is fundamentally what companies do in preparing a balance sheet: they follow the procedures set in the fundamental accounting equation. In this preparation, any company that is publicly traded is required by the U.S. Securities and Exchange Commission to follow GAAP.

Since it's critical that you understand the financial information on the balance sheet, let's take a closer look at what is in a business's asset account and what is in its liabilities and owners' equity accounts.

Group4 Studio/Getty Images

Service businesses like dog groomers rely on the same set of financial statements as manufacturers like Ford and retailers like Macy's. What are some of the assets and liabilities a typical service business like this one would carry on its balance sheet?

Classifying Assets

Assets are economic resources (things of value) owned by a firm. Assets include productive, tangible items such as equipment, buildings, land, furniture, and motor vehicles that help generate income, as well as intangible items with value like patents, trademarks, copyrights, and goodwill. Goodwill represents the value attached to factors such as a firm's reputation, location, and superior products. Goodwill is included on a balance sheet only when one firm acquires another and pays more for it than the value of its tangible assets. Even though intangible assets such as brand names (Coca-Cola, Starbucks, etc.) can be among the firm's most valuable resources, they are not listed on a company's balance sheet if they were developed within the company.[7]

HARVEST GOLD Balance Sheet December 31, 2021		
Assets		
① Current assets		
Cash	$ 15,000	
Accounts receivable	200,000	
Notes receivable	50,000	
Inventory	335,000	
Total current assets		$600,000
② Fixed assets		
Land	$ 40,000	
Building and improvements	$200,000	
Less: Accumulated depreciation	−90,000	
	110,000	
Equipment and vehicles	$120,000	
Less: Accumulated depreciation	−80,000	
	40,000	
Furniture and fixtures	$ 26,000	
Less: Accumulated depreciation	−10,000	
	16,000	
Total fixed assets		206,000
③ Intangible assets		
Goodwill	$ 20,000	
Total intangible assets		20,000
Total assets		$826,000
Liabilities and Owners' Equity		
④ Current liabilities		
Accounts payable	$ 40,000	
Notes payable (due June 2022)	8,000	
Accrued taxes	150,000	
Accrued salaries	90,000	
Total current liabilities		$288,000
⑤ Long-term liabilities		
Notes payable (due Mar. 2024)	$ 35,000	
Bonds payable (due Dec. 2029)	290,000	
Total long-term liabilities		325,000
Total liabilities		$613,000
⑥ Owners' equity		
Common stock (1,000,000 shares)	$100,000	
Retained earnings	113,000	
Total owners' equity		213,000
Total liabilities & owners' equity		$826,000

FIGURE 14.4 SAMPLE HARVEST GOLD BALANCE SHEET

① Current assets: Items that can be converted to cash within one year.

② Fixed assets: Items such as land, buildings, and equipment that are relatively permanent.

③ Intangible assets: Items of value such as patents and copyrights that don't have a physical form.

④ Current liabilities: Payments that are due in one year or less.

⑤ Long-term liabilities: Payments that are not due for one year or longer.

⑥ Owners' equity: The value of what stockholders own in a firm (also called stockholders' equity).

Accountants list assets on the firm's balance sheet in order of their **liquidity**, or the ease with which they can convert them to cash. Speedier conversion means higher liquidity. For example, an *account receivable* is an amount of money owed to the firm that it expects to receive within one year. It is considered a *liquid* asset because it can be quickly converted to cash. Land, however, is not considered a liquid asset because it takes time, effort, and paperwork to convert it to cash. It is considered a fixed or long-term asset. Assets are thus divided into three categories according to how quickly they can be turned into cash:

1. **Current assets** are items that can or will be converted into cash within one year. They include cash, accounts receivable, and inventory.

liquidity

The ease with which an asset can be converted into cash.

current assets

Items that can or will be converted into cash within one year.

fixed assets

Assets that are relatively permanent, such as land, buildings, and equipment.

intangible assets

Long-term assets (e.g., patents, trademarks, copyrights) that have no real physical form but do have value.

liabilities

What the business owes to others (debts).

accounts payable

Current liabilities involving money owed to others for merchandise or services purchased on credit but not yet paid for.

notes payable

Short-term or long-term liabilities that a business promises to repay by a certain date.

bonds payable

Long-term liabilities that represent money lent to the firm that must be paid back.

owners' equity

The amount of the business that belongs to the owners minus any liabilities owed by the business.

retained earnings

The accumulated earnings from a firm's profitable operations that were reinvested in the business and not paid out to stockholders in dividends.

2. **Fixed assets** are long-term assets that are relatively permanent such as land, buildings, and equipment. (On the balance sheet we can also refer to these as property, plant, and equipment.)

3. **Intangible assets** are long-term assets that have no physical form but do have value. Patents, trademarks, copyrights, and goodwill are intangible assets.

Liabilities and Owners' Equity Accounts

Liabilities are what the business owes to others—its debts. *Current liabilities* are debts due in one year or less. *Long-term liabilities* are debts not due for one year or more. The following are common liability accounts recorded on a balance sheet (look at Figure 17.4. again):

1. **Accounts payable** are current liabilities or bills the company owes others for merchandise or services it purchased on credit but has not yet paid for.

2. **Notes payable** can be short-term or long-term liabilities (like loans from banks) that a business promises to repay by a certain date.

3. **Bonds payable** are long-term liabilities; money lent to the firm by bondholders that it must pay back.

As you saw in the fundamental accounting equation, the value of things you own (assets) minus the amount of money you owe others (liabilities) is called *equity*. The value of what stockholders own in a firm (minus liabilities) is called *stockholders' equity* or *shareholders' equity*. Because stockholders are the owners of a firm, we also call stockholders' equity **owners' equity**, or the amount of the business that belongs to the owners, minus any liabilities the business owes. The formula for owners' equity, then, is assets minus liabilities.

The owners' equity account will differ according to the type of organization. For sole proprietors and partners, owners' equity means the value of everything owned by the business minus any liabilities of the owner(s), such as bank loans. Owners' equity in these firms is called the *capital account*.

For corporations, the owners' equity account records the owners' claims to funds they have invested in the firm (such as stock), as well as retained earnings. **Retained earnings** are accumulated earnings from the firm's profitable operations that are reinvested in the business and not paid out to stockholders in distributions of company profits. (Distributions of profits, called dividends, are discussed in Chapter 19.) Take a few moments to look again at

FIGURE 17.5 YOU INCORPORATED

How do you think You Inc. stacks up financially? Let's take a little time to find out. You may be pleasantly surprised, or you may realize that you need to think hard about planning your financial future. Remember, your net worth is nothing more than the difference between what you own (assets) and what you owe (liabilities). Be honest, and do your best to give a fair evaluation of your private property's value.

ASSETS		LIABILITIES	
Cash	$ _____	Installment loans & interest	$ _____
Savings account	_____	Other loans & interest	_____
Checking account	_____	Credit card accounts	_____
Home	_____	Mortgage	_____
Stocks & bonds	_____	Taxes	_____
Automobile	_____	Cell phone service	_____
IRA or Keogh	_____		
Personal property	_____		
Other assets	_____		
Total assets	$ _____	Total liabilities	$ _____

Determine your net worth:

Total assets	$ _____
Total liabilities	− _____
Net worth	$ _____

Figure 17.4 and see what facts you can determine about our restaurant, Harvest Gold, from its balance sheet. After the Test Prep, have some fun and estimate your own personal net worth, following the directions in Figure 17.5.

?TESTPREP

- What do we call the formula for the balance sheet? What three accounts does it include?
- What does it mean to list assets according to liquidity?
- What's the difference between long-term and short-term liabilities on the balance sheet?
- What is owners' equity, and how is it determined?

The Income Statement

The financial statement that shows a firm's bottom line—that is, its profit (or loss) after costs, expenses, and taxes—is the **income statement**. The income statement summarizes all the resources, called *revenue,* that have come into the firm from operating activities, money resources the firm used up, expenses it incurred in doing business, and resources it has left after paying all costs and expenses, including taxes. The resources (revenue) left over or depleted are referred to as **net income or net loss** (see Figure 17.6).

The income statement reports the firm's financial operations over a particular period of time, usually a year, a quarter of a year, or a month. It's the financial statement that reveals whether the business is actually earning a profit or losing money. The income statement includes valuable financial information for stockholders, lenders, potential investors, employees, and, of course, the government. Because it's so valuable, let's take a quick look at how to compile the income statement. Then we will discuss what each element in it means.

	Revenue
−	Cost of goods sold
=	Gross profit (gross margin)
−	Operating expenses
=	Net income before taxes
−	Taxes
=	Net income or loss

Revenue

Revenue is the monetary value of what a firm received for goods sold, services rendered, and other payments (such as rents received, money paid to the firm for use of its patents, interest earned, etc.). Be sure not to confuse the terms *revenue* and *sales;* they are not the same thing.[8] True, most revenue a business earns does come from sales, but companies can also have other sources of revenue. Also, a quick glance at the income statement shows you that *gross sales* refers to the total of all sales the firm completed. *Net sales* are gross sales minus returns, discounts, and allowances.

Cost of Goods Sold

The **cost of goods sold (or cost of goods manufactured)** measures the cost of merchandise the firm sells or the cost of raw materials and supplies it used in producing items for resale. It makes sense to compare how much a business earned by selling merchandise and how much it spent to make or buy the merchandise. The cost of goods sold includes the purchase price plus any freight charges paid to transport goods, plus any costs associated with storing the goods.

income statement
The financial statement that shows a firm's profit after costs, expenses, and taxes; it summarizes all of the resources that have come into the firm (revenue), all the resources that have left the firm, expenses, and the resulting net income or net loss.

net income or net loss
Revenue left over after all costs and expenses, including taxes, are paid.

cost of goods sold (or cost of goods manufactured)
A measure of the cost of merchandise sold or cost of raw materials and supplies used for producing items for resale.

FIGURE 17.6 SAMPLE HARVEST GOLD INCOME STATEMENT

① Revenues: Value of what's received from goods sold, services rendered, and other financial sources.

② Cost of goods sold: Cost of merchandise sold or cost of raw materials or parts used for producing items for resale.

③ Gross profit: How much the firm earned by buying or selling merchandise.

④ Operating expenses: Cost incurred in operating a business.

⑤ Net income after taxes: Profit or loss over a specific period after subtracting all costs and expenses, including taxes.

gross profit (or gross margin)

How much a firm earned by buying (or making) and selling merchandise.

operating expenses

Costs involved in operating a business, such as rent, utilities, and salaries.

Most businesses incur operating expenses including rent, salaries, utilities, supplies, and insurance. What are some of the likely operating expenses for companies like Starbucks?

HARVEST GOLD
Income Statement
For the Year Ended December 31, 2021

① **Revenues**			
Gross sales		$720,000	
Less: Sales returns and allowances	$ 12,000		
Sales discounts	8,000	−20,000	
Net sales			$700,000
② **Cost of goods sold**			
Beginning inventory, Jan. 1		$200,000	
Merchandise purchases	$400,000		
Freight	40,000		
Net purchases		440,000	
Cost of goods available for sale	$640,000		
Less ending inventory, Dec. 31		−230,000	
Cost of goods sold			410,000
③ **Gross profit**			$290,000
④ **Operating expenses**			
Selling expenses			
Salaries for salespeople	$ 90,000		
Advertising	18,000		
Supplies	2,000		
Total selling expenses		$110,000	
General expenses			
Office salaries	$ 67,000		
Depreciation	1,500		
Insurance	1,500		
Rent	28,000		
Light, heat, and power	12,000		
Miscellaneous	2,000		
		112,000	
Total operating expenses			222,000
Net income before taxes			$ 68,000
Less: Income tax expense			19,000
⑤ **Net income after taxes**			$ 49,000

nyker/Shutterstock

In financial reporting, it doesn't matter when a firm places a particular item in its inventory, but it does matter how an accountant records the cost of the item when the firm sells it. Why? To understand, read the Spotlight on Small Business box about two different inventory valuation methods, *LIFO* and *FIFO*.

When we subtract the cost of goods sold from net sales, we get the firm's gross profit or gross margin. **Gross profit (or gross margin)** is how much a business earned by buying (or making) and selling merchandise. In a service firm, there may be no cost of goods sold; therefore, gross profit could *equal* net sales. Gross profit, however, does not tell you everything you need to know about the firm's financial performance. To get that, you must also subtract the business's expenses.

Operating Expenses

In selling goods or services, a business incurs certain **operating expenses** such as rent, salaries, supplies, utilities,

Generally accepted accounting principles (GAAP) sometimes permit an accountant to use different methods of accounting for a firm's inventory. Two of the most popular treatments are called FIFO and LIFO.

Let's look at a simple example. Say your college bookstore buys 100 copies of a particular textbook in July at $150 a copy. When classes begin in mid-August, the bookstore sells 50 copies of the text to students at $175 each. Since instructors intend to use the same book again next term, the bookstore places the 50 copies it did not sell in its inventory until then.

In late December, the bookstore orders 50 additional copies of the text to sell for the coming term. However, the publisher's price of the book to the bookstore has increased to $175 a copy due to inflation and other increased production and distribution costs. The bookstore now

has in its inventory 100 copies of the same textbook, purchased during two different buying cycles. If it sells 50 copies to students at $200 each at the beginning of the new term in January, what's the bookstore's cost of the book for accounting purposes? Actually, it depends.

The books sold are identical, but the accounting treatment could be different. If the bookstore uses a method called first in, first out (FIFO), the cost of goods sold is $150 for each textbook, because the textbook the store bought first—the first in—cost $150. The bookstore could use another method, however. Under last in, first out (LIFO), its last purchase

of the textbooks, at $175 each, determines the cost of each of the 50 textbooks sold.

If the book sells for $200, what is the difference in gross profit (margin) between using FIFO and using LIFO? As you can see, the inventory valuation method used makes a difference in the profit margin.

and insurance. Other operating expenses that appear on an income statement, like *depreciation,* are a bit more complex. For example, have you ever heard that a new car depreciates in market value as soon as you drive it off the dealer's lot? The same principle holds true for assets such as equipment and machinery. **Depreciation** is the systematic write-off of the cost of a tangible asset over its estimated useful life. Under accounting rules set by GAAP and the Internal Revenue Service (which are beyond the scope of this chapter), companies are permitted to recapture the cost of these assets (i.e., cars, computers, machinery, office and electronic equipment) over time by using depreciation as an operating expense.

We can classify operating expenses as either selling or general expenses. *Selling expenses* are related to the marketing and distribution of the firm's goods or services, such as advertising, salespeople's salaries, and supplies. *General expenses* are administrative expenses of the firm such as office salaries, insurance, and rent. Accountants are trained to help you record all applicable expenses and find other relevant expenses you can deduct from your taxable income as a part of doing business.

depreciation
The systematic write-off of the cost of a tangible asset over its estimated useful life.

Net Profit or Loss

After deducting all expenses, we can determine the firm's net income before taxes, also referred to as net earnings or net profit (see Figure 17.6 again). After allocating for taxes, we get to the *bottom line,* which is the net income (or perhaps net loss) the firm incurred from revenue

minus sales returns, costs, expenses, and taxes over a period of time. We can now answer the question, Did the business earn or lose money in the specific reporting period?

As you can see, the basic principles of the balance sheet and income statement are already familiar to you. You know how to keep track of costs and expenses when you prepare your own budget. If your rent and utilities exceed your earnings, you know you're in trouble. If you need more money, you may need to sell some of the things you own to meet your expenses. The same is true in business. Companies need to keep track of how much money they earn and spend, and how much cash they have on hand. The only difference is that they tend to have more complex problems and a good deal more information to record than you do.

Users of financial statements are interested in how a firm handles the flow of cash coming into a business and the cash flowing out of the business. Cash flow problems can plague both businesses and individuals. Keep this in mind as we look at the statement of cash flows next.

The Statement of Cash Flows

The **statement of cash flows** reports cash receipts and cash disbursements related to the three major activities of a firm:

- *Operations* are cash transactions associated with running the business.
- *Investments* are cash used in or provided by the firm's investment activities.
- *Financing* is cash raised by taking on new debt, or equity capital or cash used to pay business expenses, past debts, or company dividends.

Accountants analyze all changes in the firm's cash that have occurred from operating, investing, and financing in order to determine the firm's net cash position.[9] The statement of cash flows also gives the firm some insight into how to handle cash better so that no cash flow problems occur—such as having no cash on hand for immediate expenses.

Figure 17.7 shows a sample statement of cash flows, again using the example of our restaurant Harvest Gold. As you can see, the statement of cash flows answers such questions as: How much cash came into the business from current operations, such as buying and selling goods and services? Did the firm use cash to buy stocks, bonds, or other investments? Did it sell some investments that brought in cash? How much money did the firm take in from issuing stock?

We analyze these and other financial transactions to see their effect on the firm's cash position. Managing cash flow can mean success or failure of any business, which is why we analyze it in more depth in the next section.

The Need for Cash Flow Analysis

Cash flow, if not properly managed, can cause a business much concern. Understanding cash flow analysis is important and not difficult to understand. Let's say you borrow $100 from a friend to buy a used bike and agree to pay her back at the end of the week. You then sell the bike for $150 to someone else, who also agrees to pay you by the end of the week. Unfortunately, by the weekend your buyer does not have the money as promised, and says he will have to pay you next month. Meanwhile, your friend wants the $100 you agreed to pay her by the end of the week!

What seemed a great opportunity to make an easy $50 profit is now a cause for concern. You owe $100 and have no cash. What do you do? If you were a business, you might default on the loan and possibly go bankrupt, even though you had the potential for profit.

Lonnie McQuirter owns a gas station that works with local suppliers to provide customers with healthy, organic food instead of the typical convenience store fare. In 2007 he took out an $875,000 loan to purchase the property and gas pumps from BP. His business now brings in $11 million annually in gross revenue. What is the difference between revenue and profit?

statement of cash flows
Financial statement that reports cash receipts and disbursements related to a firm's three major activities: operations, investments, and financing.

HARVEST GOLD Statement of Cash Flows For the Year Ended December 31, 2021		
① Cash flows from operating activities		
Cash received from customers	$700,000	
Cash paid to suppliers and employees	(567,000)	
Interest paid	(64,000)	
Income tax paid	(19,000)	
Interest and dividends received	2,000	
Net cash provided by operating activities		$52,000
② Cash flows from investing activities		
Proceeds from sale of plant assets	$ 4,000	
Payments for purchase of equipment	(23,000)	
Net cash provided by investing activities		(19,000)
③ Cash flows from financing activities		
Proceeds from issuance of short-term debt	$ 2,000	
Payment of long-term debt	(8,000)	
Payment of dividends	(15,000)	
Net cash inflow from financing activities		(21,000)
Net change in cash and equivalents		$12,000
Cash balance (beginning of year)		3,000
Cash balance (end of year)		$15,000

FIGURE 17.7 SAMPLE HARVEST GOLD STATEMENT OF CASH FLOWS
① Cash receipts from sales, commissions, fees, interest, and dividends. Cash payments for salaries, inventories, operating expenses, interest, and taxes.
② Includes cash flows that are generated through a company's purchase or sale of long-term operational assets, investments in other companies, and its lending activities.
③ Cash inflows and outflows associated with the company's own equity transactions or its borrowing activities.

cash flow
The difference between cash coming in and cash going out of a business.

It's possible for a business to increase its sales and profits yet still suffer cash flow problems. **Cash flow** is simply the difference between cash coming in and cash going out of a business. Poor cash flow constitutes a major operating problem that many companies face. For example, fast-growing, innovative car manufacturer Tesla faced some formidable cash flow problems as the company was growing its operations.[10] Problems with cash flow are particularly difficult for small and seasonal businesses since they have less access to capital than large companies.[11] Cash flow also creates some tough ethical challenges for accountants in reporting the flow of funds into a business. Read the Making Ethical Decisions box to see how such an ethical dilemma can arise.

How do cash flow problems start? Often in order to meet the growing demands of customers, a business buys goods on credit (using no cash). If it then sells a large number of goods on credit (getting no cash), the company needs more credit from a lender (usually a bank) to pay its immediate bills. If a firm has reached its credit limit and can borrow no more, it has a severe cash flow problem. It has cash coming in at a later date, but no cash to pay current expenses. That problem could, unfortunately, force the firm into bankruptcy, even though sales may be strong—all because no cash was available when it was most needed. Cash flow analysis shows that a business's relationship with its lenders is critical to preventing cash flow problems.

Accountants provide valuable insight and advice to businesses in managing cash flow, suggesting whether they need cash and how much. They also ensure that the firm's financial statements—its balance sheet, income statement, and statement of cash flows—are properly prepared and form the basis for the firm's financial analyses. Accounting errors or misstatements can be costly for companies. Sports apparel maker Under Armour faced a criminal inquiry from federal authorities concerning its accounting practices. The U.S. Justice Department and the Securities and Exchange Commission (SEC) investigated the company to see if it shifted sales from quarter to quarter (called revenue recognition) to make the company look stronger financially, which is in violation of accepted accounting practices.[12] After the Test Prep, we will see how accountants advise companies by analyzing the financial statements using ratios.

Cash flow is the difference between money coming into and going out of a business. Careful cash flow management is a must for a business of any size, but it's particularly important for small businesses and for seasonal operations like ski resorts. Have you read about any firms that were forced into bankruptcy because of cash flow problems?

ultramarinfoto/Getty Images

LO 17–4 Demonstrate the application of ratio analysis in reporting financial information.

Analyzing Financial Performance Using Ratios

ratio analysis

The assessment of a firm's financial condition using calculations and interpretations of financial ratios developed from the firm's financial statements.

The firm's financial statements—its balance sheet, income statement, and statement of cash flows—form the basis for financial analyses performed by accountants inside and outside the firm. **Ratio analysis** is the assessment of a firm's financial condition, using calculations and financial ratios developed from the firm's financial statements. Financial ratios are especially useful in comparing the company's performance to its financial objectives and to the performance of other firms in its industry.[13]

You probably are already familiar with the use of ratios in sports. For example, in basketball we express the number of shots made from the foul line with a ratio: shots made to shots attempted. In baseball we use the ratio number of hits to the number of at bats. You don't want to foul a player who shoots 85 percent from the foul line or pitch to a .375 hitter in a close game.

Whether ratios measure an athlete's performance or the financial health of a business, they provide valuable information. Financial ratios provide key insights into how a firm compares to other firms in its industry on liquidity, amount of debt, profitability, and overall business activity. Understanding and interpreting business ratios is important to sound financial analysis. Let's look briefly at four key types of ratios businesses use to measure financial performance.

Liquidity Ratios

We've discussed that *liquidity* refers to how fast an asset can be converted to cash. Liquidity ratios measure a company's ability to turn assets into cash to pay its short-term debts (liabilities that must be repaid within one year). These short-term debts are of particular importance to the firm's lenders who expect to be paid on time. Two key liquidity ratios are the current ratio and the acid-test ratio.

The *current ratio* is the ratio of a firm's current assets to its current liabilities. This information appears on the firm's balance sheet. Look back at Figure 17.4, which details Harvest Gold's balance sheet. The company lists current assets of $600,000 and current liabilities of $288,000, yielding a current ratio of 2.08, which means Harvest Gold has $2.08 of current assets for every $1 of current liabilities. See the following calculation:

$$\text{Current ratio} = \frac{\text{Current assets}}{\text{Current liabilities}} = 2.08$$

The question the current ratio attempts to answer is: Is Harvest Gold financially secure for the short term (less than one year)? It depends! Usually a company with a current ratio of 2.0 or better is considered a safe risk for lenders granting short-term credit, since it appears to be performing in line with market expectations. However, lenders will also compare Harvest Gold's current ratio to that of competing firms in its industry and to its current ratio from the previous year to note any significant changes.

Another key liquidity ratio, called the *acid-test* or *quick ratio,* measures the cash, marketable securities (such as stocks and bonds), and receivables of a firm, compared to its current liabilities. Again, this information is on a firm's balance sheet.

$$\text{Acid-test ratio} = \frac{\text{Cash} + \text{Accounts receivable} + \text{Marketable securities}}{\text{Current liabilities}}$$

$$= \frac{\$265,000}{\$288,000} = 0.92$$

This ratio is particularly important to firms with difficulty converting inventory into quick cash. It helps answer such questions as: What if sales drop off and we can't sell our inventory? Can we still pay our short-term debt? Though ratios vary among industries, an acid-test ratio between 0.50 and 1.0 is usually considered satisfactory, but bordering on cash flow problems. Therefore, Harvest Gold's acid-test ratio of 0.92 could raise concerns that perhaps the firm may not meet its short-term debt and may have to go to a high-cost lender for financial assistance.

Leverage (Debt) Ratios

Leverage (debt) ratios measure the degree to which a firm relies on borrowed funds in its operations. A firm that takes on too much debt could experience problems repaying lenders or meeting promises made to stockholders. The *debt to owners' equity ratio* measures the degree to which the company is financed by borrowed funds that it must repay. Again, let's use Figure 17.4 to measure Harvest Gold's level of debt:

$$\text{Debt to owners' equity ratio} = \frac{\text{Total liabilities}}{\text{Owners' equity}} = \frac{\$613,000}{\$213,000} = 288\%$$

Anything above 100 percent shows a firm has more debt than equity. With a ratio of 288 percent, Harvest Gold has a rather high degree of debt compared to its equity, which implies that lenders and investors may perceive the firm to be quite risky. However, again *it's important to compare a firm's debt ratios to those of other firms in its industry,* because debt financing is more acceptable in some industries than in others. Comparisons with the same firm's past debt ratios can also identify possible trends within the firm or industry.

Profitability (Performance) Ratios

Profitability (performance) ratios measure how effectively a firm's managers are using its various resources to achieve profits. Three of the more important ratios are earnings per share (EPS), return on sales, and return on equity.

EPS is a revealing ratio because earnings help stimulate the firm's growth and provide for stockholders' dividends. The Financial Accounting Standards Board requires companies to report their quarterly EPS in two ways: basic and diluted. The *basic earnings per share (basic EPS) ratio* helps determine the amount of profit a company earned for each share of outstanding common stock. The *diluted earnings per share (diluted EPS) ratio* measures the amount of profit earned for each share of outstanding common stock, but also considers stock options, warrants, preferred stock, and convertible debt securities (see Chapter 19) the firm can convert into common stock. For simplicity's sake, we will compute only the basic EPS for Harvest Gold.

$$\text{Basic earnings per share} = \frac{\text{Net income after taxes}}{\text{Number of common stock shares outstanding}}$$

$$= \frac{\$49,000}{1,000,000 \text{ shares}} = \$0.049 \text{ per share}$$

Another reliable indicator of performance is *return on sales,* which tells us whether the firm is doing as well as its competitors in generating income from sales. We calculate it by comparing net income to total sales. Harvest Gold's return on sales is 7 percent, a figure we must measure against similar numbers for competing firms to judge Harvest Gold's performance:

$$\text{Return on sales} = \frac{\text{Net income}}{\text{Net sales}} = \frac{\$49,000}{\$700,000} = 7\%$$

The higher the risk of failure or loss in an industry, the higher the return investors expect on their investment; they expect to be well compensated for shouldering such odds. *Return on equity* indirectly measures risk by telling us how much a firm earned for each dollar invested by its owners. We calculate it by comparing a company's net income to its total owners' equity. Harvest Gold's return on equity looks reasonably sound since some believe anything over 15 percent is considered a reasonable return:

$$\text{Return on equity} = \frac{\text{Net income after tax}}{\text{Total owners' equity}} = \frac{\$49,000}{\$213,000} = 23\%$$

Remember that profits help companies like Harvest Gold grow. That's why profitability ratios are such closely watched measurements of company growth and management performance.

Activity Ratios

Converting the firm's inventory to profits is a key function of management. Activity ratios tell us how effectively management is turning over inventory.

The *inventory turnover ratio* measures the speed with which inventory moves through the firm and gets converted into sales. Idle inventory sitting in a warehouse earns nothing and costs money. The more efficiently a firm sells or turns over its inventory, the higher its revenue. We can measure the inventory turnover ratio for Harvest Gold as follows:

$$\text{Inventory turnover} = \frac{\text{Costs of goods sold}}{\text{Average inventory}} = \frac{\$410,000}{\$215,000} = 1.9 \text{ times}$$

Restaurant owners expect servers to turn over tables quickly so they can seat as many customers as possible. After all, more diners mean more money for the owner. Can you think of any other industries that depend on high rates of inventory turnover?

A lower-than-average inventory turnover ratio often indicates obsolete merchandise on hand or poor buying practices. Managers need to be aware of proper inventory control and anticipated inventory turnover to ensure proper performance. For example, have you ever worked as a food server in a restaurant like Harvest Gold? How many times did your employer expect you to *turn over* a table (keep changing customers at the table) in an evening? The more times a table turns, the higher the return to the owner. Of course, like other ratios, rates of inventory turnover vary from industry to industry.

Accountants and other finance professionals use several other specific ratios, in addition to the ones we've discussed. To review where the accounting information in ratio analysis comes from, see Figure 17.8 for a quick reference. Remember, financial analysis begins where the accounting financial statements end.

Juanmonino/Getty Images

FIGURE 17.8 ACCOUNTS IN THE BALANCE SHEET AND INCOME STATEMENT

BALANCE SHEET ACCOUNTS			INCOME STATEMENT ACCOUNTS			
Assets	**Liabilities**	**Owners' Equity**	**Revenues**	**Cost of Goods Sold**	**Expenses**	
Cash	Accounts payable	Capital stock	Sales revenue	Cost of buying goods	Wages	Interest
Accounts receivable	Notes payable	Retained earnings	Rental revenue	Cost of storing goods	Rent	Donations
Inventory	Bonds payable	Common stock	Commissions revenue		Repairs	Licenses
Investments	Taxes payable	Treasury stock	Royalty revenue		Travel	Fees
Equipment						
Land					Insurance	Supplies
Buildings					Utilities	Advertising
Motor vehicles					Entertainment	Taxes
Goodwill					Storage	

?TESTPREP

- What is the primary purpose of performing ratio analysis using the firm's financial statements?
- What are the four main categories of financial ratios?

LO 17–5   Identify the different disciplines within the accounting profession.

Accounting Disciplines

The accounting profession is divided into five key working areas: financial accounting, managerial accounting, auditing, tax accounting, and governmental and not-for-profit accounting. All five are important, and all create career opportunities. Let's look at each.

Financial Accounting

Financial accounting generates financial information and analyses for people primarily *outside* the organization. The information goes not only to company owners, managers, and employees, but also to creditors and lenders, employee unions, customers, suppliers, government agencies, and the general public. External users are interested in questions like: Is the organization profitable? Is it able to pay its bills? How much debt does it owe? These questions and others are often answered in the company's **annual report**, a yearly statement of the financial condition, progress, and expectations of an organization.

It's critical for firms to keep accurate financial information. Therefore, many organizations employ a **private accountant** who works for a single firm, government agency, or nonprofit organization. However, not all firms or nonprofit organizations want or need a full-time accountant. Fortunately, thousands of accounting firms in the United States provide the accounting services an organization needs through public accountants.

For a fee, a **public accountant** provides accounting services to individuals or businesses. Such services can include designing an accounting system, helping select the correct software

financial accounting
Accounting information and analyses prepared for people outside the organization.

annual report
A yearly statement of the financial condition, progress, and expectations of an organization.

private accountant
An accountant who works for a single firm, government agency, or nonprofit organization.

public accountant
An accountant who provides accounting services to individuals or businesses on a fee basis.

FIGURE 17.9 KEY PROVISIONS OF THE SARBANES-OXLEY ACT

- Prohibits accounting firms from providing certain nonauditing work (such as consulting services) to companies they audit.

- Strengthens the protection for whistleblowers who report wrongful actions of company officers.

- Requires company CEOs and CFOs to certify the accuracy of financial reports and imparts strict penalties for any violation of securities reporting (e.g., earnings misstatements).

- Prohibits corporate loans to directors and executives of the company.

- Establishes the five-member Public Company Accounting Oversight Board (PCAOB) under the Securities and Exchange Commission (SEC) to oversee the accounting industry.

- Stipulates that altering or destroying key audit documents will result in felony charges and significant criminal penalties.

certified public accountant (CPA)
An accountant who passes a series of examinations established by the American Institute of Certified Public Accountants (AICPA).

managerial accounting
Accounting used to provide information and analyses to managers within the organization to assist them in decision making.

Assembling a truck engine requires many tools, parts, raw materials, and other components as well as labor costs. Keeping these costs at a minimum and setting realistic production schedules is critical to a business's survival. What other internal departments must managerial accountants team with to ensure company competitiveness?

to run the system, and analyzing an organization's financial performance. An accountant who passes a series of examinations established by the American Institute of Certified Public Accountants (AICPA) and meets the state's requirement for education and experience is recognized as a **certified public accountant (CPA)**. CPAs find careers as private or public accountants and are often sought to fill other financial positions within organizations. Today, there are over 665,000 CPAs in the United States, 400,000 of whom are members of the AICPA.[14]

Unfortunately, the accounting profession suffered a dark period in the early 2000s when accounting scandals at WorldCom, Enron, and Tyco raised public suspicions about the profession and corporate integrity in general. Arthur Andersen, one of the nation's leading accounting firms, was forced out of business after being convicted of obstruction of justice for shredding records in the Enron case (the conviction was, however, later overturned by the U.S. Supreme Court).

Scrutiny of the accounting industry intensified, however, and resulted in the U.S. Congress's passage of the Sarbanes-Oxley Act (called Sarbox). This legislation created new government reporting standards for publicly traded companies. It also created the Public Company Accounting Oversight Board (PCAOB), which oversees the AICPA. Prior to the passage of Sarbox, the accounting profession was self-regulated. Today, critics have raised questions concerning relaxing the power of the PCAOB due to the burdens it places on small and medium-sized businesses.[15] Others believe limiting the power of the PCAOB would be a serious mistake. Figure 17.9 lists some of the major provisions of Sarbanes-Oxley.

The financial crisis that began in 2008 led Congress to pass the Dodd-Frank Wall Street Reform and Consumer Protection Act. The Dodd-Frank Act increased financial regulation affecting accounting by increasing the power of the PCAOB to oversee auditors of brokers and dealers in securities markets. Provisions of Dodd-Frank were called into question in 2018 and many regulations were relaxed.[16] We'll discuss the Dodd-Frank Act in more depth in Chapter 19.

The accounting profession understands that to be effective, accountants must be considered as professional as doctors or lawyers. Besides completing 150 hours of college coursework and a rigorous exam, CPAs on average take 20–40 hours of continuing education training a year, are subject to recertification, undergo ethics training requirements, and must pass an ethics exam.[17]

Managerial Accounting

Managerial accounting provides information and analysis to managers *inside* the organization to assist them in decision making.

Bill Pugliano/Getty Images

ADAPTING TO CHANGE

A Nose for Sniffing Out Problems

acfe.com

Fraud damages businesses both large and small. According to the Association of Certified Fraud Examiners, many large corporations lose almost 5 percent of their revenue each year due to fraud, and nearly half of all small businesses deal with financial fraud at some time in their business lives, often with very dire results. While the U.S. Securities and Exchange Commission (SEC) remains committed to fighting financial fraud and laws, such as Sarbanes-Oxley, promise stiff penalties, financial fraud marches on. The problem is that government and company auditors are not specifically trained in uncovering financial fraud. Their expertise is primarily to make sure accounting standards are being

applied correctly and company financial statements are fairly stated. If auditors and CPAs are not prepared to search for and identify signs of financial fraud, is losing 5 percent of revenue yearly a cost of doing business?

Fortunately, no. Luckily, forensic accountants are on call to come sniff out financial irregularities. Often called the Sherlock Holmes of the accounting industry, forensic accountants search for accounting errors by sifting through mountains of company information to put together a paper trail that identifies the company rogues responsible for fraud. Their work is often long and arduous and can involve investigating inflated sales figures, money laundering, and inventory fraud.

Richard Hutchings

Forensic accountants are often employed in law enforcement or as independent fraud examiners.

Forensic accountants generally need advanced training in investigation techniques and auditing. If forensic accounting interests you, many colleges offer advanced degrees and specialties in forensic accounting.

Sources: Association of Certified Fraud Examiners, acfe.com, accessed March 2020; "How to Spot the Red Flags for Employee Fraud," *Business News Daily,* businessnewsdaily.com, February 6, 2020; "How to Become a Forensic Accountant," Accounting.com, accounting.com, accessed March 2020.

Managerial accounting is concerned with measuring and reporting costs of production, marketing, and other functions; preparing budgets (planning); checking whether or not units are staying within their budgets (controlling); and designing strategies to minimize taxes. If you are a business major, you'll probably take a course in managerial accounting.

Auditing

Reviewing and evaluating the information used to prepare a company's financial statements is referred to as **auditing**. Private accountants within an organization often perform internal audits to guarantee that the organization is carrying out proper accounting procedures and financial reporting. Public accountants also conduct independent audits of accounting information and related records. An **independent audit** is an evaluation and unbiased opinion about the accuracy of a company's financial statements. Annual reports often include an auditor's unbiased written opinion.

After the accounting scandals of the early 2000s, the Sarbanes-Oxley Act put in place new rules about auditing and consulting to ensure the integrity of the auditing process. Auditing procedures, however, again came under fire in 2011, causing many to call for stricter controls over auditing procedures after analyzing the failure of Lehman Brothers in 2008 and the financial crisis that followed.[18]

In doing their job, auditors examine not only the financial health of an organization but also its operational efficiencies and effectiveness.[19] See the Adapting to Change box for a discussion of a forensic accountant, a special type of accountant trained to uncover financial fraud within an organization.

auditing
The job of reviewing and evaluating the information used to prepare a company's financial statements.

independent audit
An evaluation and unbiased opinion about the accuracy of a company's financial statements.

tax accountant
An accountant trained in tax law and responsible for preparing tax returns or developing tax strategies.

government and not-for-profit accounting
Accounting system for organizations whose purpose is not generating a profit but serving ratepayers, taxpayers, and others according to a duly approved budget.

Charlie Riedel/AP Images

With a workforce of more than 22,000 employees, the National Park Service maintains historical landmarks like Mount Rushmore. Such government organizations also employ accountants, auditors, and financial managers.

Tax Accounting

Taxes enable governments to fund roads, parks, schools, police protection, the military, and other functions. Federal, state, and local governments require individuals and organizations to file tax returns at specific times and in a precise format. A **tax accountant** is trained in tax law and is responsible for preparing tax returns, or developing tax strategies. Since governments often change tax policies according to specific needs or objectives, the job of the tax accountant is always challenging. As the burden of taxes grows in the economy, the role of the tax accountant becomes increasingly valuable to the organization, individual, or entrepreneur.

Government and Not-for-Profit Accounting

Government and not-for-profit accounting supports organizations whose purpose is not generating a profit, but serving ratepayers, taxpayers, and others according to a duly approved budget. Federal, state, and local governments require an accounting system that helps taxpayers, special interest groups, legislative bodies, and creditors ensure that the government is fulfilling its obligations, and making proper use of taxpayers' money. Government accounting standards are set by an organization called the Governmental Accounting Standards Board.[20] The Federal Bureau of Investigation, the Internal Revenue Service, the Missouri Department of Natural Resources, and the Cook County Department of Revenue are just a few of the many government agencies that offer career possibilities to accountants seeking to work in government accounting.

Not-for-profit organizations also require accounting professionals to ensure their financial results are correct and the organization is being well managed financially. Charities like the Salvation Army, Red Cross, museums, and hospitals all hire accountants to show contributors how their money is spent and that it is being spent properly. This is particularly important during tough economic times such as the Great Recession of 2008, when many businesses and individuals cut back on donations, making it more important than ever to account for every dollar contributed.

As you can see, financial and managerial accounting, auditing, tax accounting, and government and not-for-profit accounting each require specific training and skill. They also offer solid career opportunities. Looking ahead, the accounting profession is feeling the impact and challenge of the global market. The Reaching beyond Our Borders box discusses a movement to globalize accounting procedures. It's something that accountants will be following closely. Before leaving this chapter, it's worth saying once more that, as the language of business, accounting is a worthwhile language to learn.

?TESTPREP

- What is the key difference between managerial and financial accounting?
- How is the job of a private accountant different from that of a public accountant?
- What is the job of an auditor? What's an independent audit?

Speaking a Universal Accounting Language

You've read throughout the text about companies like Coca-Cola and IBM that earn the majority of their revenues from global markets. While such global good fortune adds to their bottom-line profits, they face considerable accounting headaches. The problem is there's no global accounting system. This means companies doing business around the globe must adapt their accounting procedures to different countries' accounting rules. Some suggest a solution might be at hand. The Financial Accounting Standards Board (FASB) in the United States and the London-based International Accounting Standards Board (IASB) want to explore if an agreement can be reached that's acceptable.

With over 110 countries permitting or requiring International Financial Reporting Standards (IFRS), the FASB proposed a possible integration of the U.S. accounting code with the IFRS used around the world. The U.S. Securities and Exchange Commission (SEC) seemed to support such a change and even suggested the IFRS might replace the long-standing generally accepted accounting principles (GAAP). However, the financial crisis of 2008 shifted the SEC's priorities to the financial rules required by the Dodd-Frank Act and away from an IFRS solution. At this time, the SEC's strategic plan does not offer a strong endorsement of moving to one global accounting standard. The agency also notes that a lack of strong support for the adoption of IFRS existed among accountants in the United States.

Nonetheless, many accountants continue to support the shift to global standards for accounting and applaud the efforts of the FASB and IASB to work at convergence between the two systems. Still, it appears that IFRS is coming later rather than sooner to accounting departments or accounting classes.

Sources: Barclay Palmer, "International Financial Reporting Standards (IFRS)," *Investopedia*, investopedia.com, January 29, 2020; "IFRS in the U.S.: The Importance of Being Financially Bilingual," PricewaterhouseCoopers, pwc.com, accessed February 2020; U.S. Securities and Exchange Commission, sec.gov, accessed March 2020; Danielle Smith, "What Are the Differences between IFRS and U.S. GAAP for Revenue Recognition?," *BizFluent*, bizfluent.com, January 21, 2020.

SUMMARY

LO 17–1 Demonstrate the role that accounting and financial information play for a business and its stakeholders.

- **What is accounting?**

  Accounting is the recording, classifying, summarizing, and interpreting of financial events and transactions that affect an organization. The methods we use to record and summarize accounting data into reports are called an accounting system.

LO 17–2 List the steps in the accounting cycle, distinguish between accounting and bookkeeping, and explain how computers are used in accounting.

- **What are the six steps of the accounting cycle?**

  The six steps of the accounting cycle are (1) analyzing documents; (2) recording information into journals; (3) posting that information into ledgers; (4) developing a trial balance; (5) preparing financial statements—the balance sheet, income statement, and statement of cash flows; and (6) analyzing financial statements.

- **What is the difference between bookkeeping and accounting?**

  Bookkeeping is part of accounting and includes the systematic recording of data. Accounting includes classifying, summarizing, interpreting, and reporting data to management.

- **What are journals and ledgers?**

  Journals are the first place bookkeepers record transactions. Bookkeepers then summarize journal entries by posting them to ledgers. Ledgers are specialized accounting books that arrange the transactions by homogeneous groups (accounts).

- **How do computers help accountants?**

  Computers can record and analyze data and provide financial reports. Software can continuously analyze and test accounting systems to be sure they are functioning correctly. Computers can help decision making by providing appropriate information, but they cannot themselves make good financial decisions. Accounting applications and creativity are still human functions.

LO 17–3   Explain how the major financial statements differ.

- **What is a balance sheet?**

  A balance sheet reports the financial position of a firm on a particular day. The fundamental accounting equation used to prepare the balance sheet is: Assets = Liabilities + Owners' equity.

- **What are the major accounts of the balance sheet?**

  Assets are economic resources owned by the firm, such as buildings and machinery. Liabilities are amounts the firm owes to creditors, bondholders, and others. Owners' equity is the value of everything the firm owns—its assets—minus any liabilities, thus: Owners' equity = Assets - Liabilities.

- **What is an income statement?**

  An income statement reports revenues, costs, and expenses for a specific period of time (say, the year ended December 31, 2021). The formulas we use in preparing the income statement are:

  - **Revenue – Cost of goods sold = Gross margin**
  - **Gross margin – Operating expenses = Net income before taxes**
  - **Net income before taxes – Taxes = Net income (or net loss).**

  Net income or loss is also called the bottom line.

- **What is a statement of cash flows?**

  Cash flow is the difference between cash receipts (money coming in) and cash disbursements (money going out). The statement of cash flows reports cash receipts and disbursements related to the firm's major activities: operations, investments, and financing.

LO 17–4   Demonstrate the application of ratio analysis in reporting financial information.

- **What are the four key categories of ratios?**

  The four key categories of ratios are liquidity ratios, leverage (debt) ratios, profitability (performance) ratios, and activity ratios.

- **What is the major value of ratio analysis to the firm?**

  Ratio analysis provides the firm with information about its financial position in key areas *for comparison to other firms in its industry and its own past performance.*

LO 17–5   Identify the different disciplines within the accounting profession.

- **How does financial accounting differ from managerial accounting?**

  Managerial accounting provides information and analyses to managers within the firm to assist them in decision making. Financial accounting provides information and analyses to external users of data such as creditors and lenders.

- **What is the job of an auditor?**

  Auditors review and evaluate the standards used to prepare a company's financial statements. An independent audit is conducted by a public accountant and is an evaluation and unbiased opinion about the accuracy of a company's financial statements.

- **What is the difference between a private accountant and a public accountant?**

  A public accountant provides services for a fee to a variety of companies, whereas a private accountant works for a single company. Private and public accountants do essentially the same things with the exception of independent audits. Private accountants do perform internal audits, but only public accountants supply independent audits.

CRITICAL THINKING

1. As a potential investor in a firm or perhaps the buyer of a particular business, would it be advisable for you to evaluate the company's financial statements? Why or why not? What key information would you seek from a firm's financial statements?

2. Why must accounting reports be prepared according to specific procedures (GAAP)? Would it be a good idea to allow businesses some flexibility or creativity in preparing financial statements? Why or why not?

3. Why is cash flow analysis more important to small and medium-sized businesses than to large multinational companies?

4. Why is it important for not-for-profit organizations to have top managers that have strong finance and accounting skills?

PUTTING PRINCIPLES TO WORK

PURPOSE

To evaluate career possibilities in accounting that meet your personal interests and future career expectations.

EXERCISE

Career opportunities in accounting can involve work in large or small firms, public or private accounting, various industries, and specific areas of specialization. In fact, there are so many career choices in accounting that it might feel overwhelming to know where to start. At aicpa.org, you can get an idea of the type of accounting careers that match your interests. Click the "Career Guidance" link and then, under "Becoming a CPA" click on "Choosing a career in accounting" and follow the path that fits you best.

1. What are the key differences in working for business, industry, or government as opposed to public accounting?

2. Does a large, international accounting firm seem appealing to you? What is the primary attraction of such firms? What's the major downside?

3. Summarize your personal career plan and offer a short explanation why you chose each option you selected.

DEVELOPING CAREER SKILLS

KEY: ● **Team** ★ **Analytic** ▲ **Communication** ▣ **Technology**

▲★ 1. Contact a CPA at a firm in your area, or talk with a CPA in your college's business department. Ask what challenges, changes, and opportunities he or she foresees in the accounting profession in the next five years. List the CPA's forecasts on a sheet of paper and then compare them with the information in this chapter.

▣★ 2. Go to the website of the American Institute of Certified Public Accountants (aicpa.org) and find the requirements for becoming a certified public accountant (CPA).

★▲ 3. Suppose you are a new board member for an emerging not-for-profit organization hoping to attract new donors. Contributors want to know how efficiently not-for-profit organizations use their donations. Unfortunately, your fellow board members see little value in financial reporting and analysis and believe the good works of the organization speak for themselves. Prepare a fact sheet convincing the board of the need for effective financial reporting with arguments about why it helps the organization's fundraising goals.

▣★ 4. Obtain a recent annual report for a company of your choice. (*Hints: The Wall Street Journal* has a free annual reports service, and virtually all major companies post their annual reports on their websites.) Look over the firm's financial statements and see whether they match the information in this chapter. Read the auditor's opinion (usually at the end of the report) and evaluate what you think are the most important conclusions of the auditors.

▣★ 5. Go back in time and read about the fraudulent accounting practices that led to passage of the Sarbanes-Oxley Act of 2002. Then travel forward and explore the causes of the financial crisis that began in 2008 that led Congress to pass the Dodd-Frank Wall Street Reform and Consumer Protection Act. Prepare a short explanation whether or not you believe these laws will stop such problems from happening again.

CAREER EXPLORATION

If you are interested in pursuing a career in accounting, here are a few to consider. Find out about the tasks performed, skills needed, pay, and opportunity outlook in these fields in the *Occupational Outlook Handbook (OOH)* at bls.gov.

- **Certified management accountant**—an accountant who has met educational and experience requirements, passed a qualifying exam, and has been certified by the Institute of Certified Management Accountants.

- **Certified internal auditor**—an accountant who has met educational and experience requirements, passed a qualifying exam, and has been certified by the Institute of Internal Auditors.

- **Tax examiner**—an accountant who ensures that federal, state, and local governments get tax money due from businesses and citizens by reviewing tax returns, conducting audits, and identifying taxes owed.

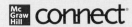

The Accounting Function at Goodwill Industries

Goodwill Industries is a major charitable organization that relies primarily on financial and nonfinancial donations and grants. It has retail operations that help sustain its financial operations so as to fulfill its mission to help train, support, and employ disadvantaged individuals and those with disabilities.

The video introduces the accounting function and the specific steps involved in the accounting cycle. The similarities and differences between for-profit and not-for-profit entities are discussed in detail. The importance of accounting in providing financial information and analysis is featured. Emphasis is placed on financial statements as well as ratio analysis in helping gauge the financial health of the organization.

Accounting is crucial for all organizations, whether they are a small business, large corporation, or a governmental or not-for-profit organization. The different types of accounting are discussed, including managerial, financial, tax, auditing, governmental, and not-for-profit. Balance sheets, income statements, and statements of cash flows provide important information for managers and others in the organization, helping demonstrate whether the organization is on budget or whether there are variances between projected and actual revenues. Costs and expenses have to be kept in line and are carefully monitored and analyzed by the accounting function.

Sufficient cash flow is critical to the sustainability of any organization, particularly the not-for-profit organization; in this case, Goodwill. Not-for-profit organizations utilize performance ratio analysis to gauge their overall financial performance. The results of these analyses help management assess the organization's performance against its plan or budget. They also help develop strategic plans for the future as well as benchmark against other similar companies.

THINKING IT OVER

1. What's the difference between assets and liabilities? Which of the key financial statements features these categories prominently?

2. Identify the six steps in the accounting cycle.

3. What are the key reasons that firms do ratio analysis?

NOTES

1. Sean Ross, "When and Why Were GAAP First Established?," *Investopedia,* investopedia.com, January 23, 2020; "About the Financial Accounting Standards Board," Financial Accounting Standards Board, fasb.com, accessed March 2020.

2. Stephanie Morrow, "Generally Accepted Accounting Principles or GAAP, What Does It Mean?," LegalZoom, legalzoom.com, accessed March 2020; Lauren Silva Laughlin, "Creative Accounting Measures Come at a Price," *The Wall Street Journal,* October 8, 2019; Justin Walton, "4 Must-Watch Movies for Accountants," *Investopedia,* investopedia.com, January 27, 2020.

3. Intuit QuickBooks, quickbooks.com, accessed March 2020; Shelley Elmblad, "Tips for Choosing Small Business Accounting Software," *The Balance Small Business,* thebalancesmb.com, February 1, 2020.

4. Crystalynn Shelton, "Intuit Quick Books Self-Employed: Cost and Features," *FitSmallBusiness,* fitsmallbusiness. com, March 8, 2019; Miriam Reimer, "Top 11 Small Business Accounting Tips to Save You Time and Money," *Fundera,* fundera.com, February 18, 2020; Kathy Yakal, "The Best Small Business Accounting Software for 2020," *PC Magazine,* pcmag.com, January 21, 2020.

5. "Preparing Financial Statements," U.S. Small Business Administration, sba.gov, accessed March 2020; "Beginners Guide to Financial Statements," U.S, Securities and Exchange Commission, sec.gov, accessed March 2020.

6. "The Critical Importance of an Accurate Balance Sheet," *AccountingHelper,* accountinghelper.org, accessed March 2020; "How to Prepare a Balance Sheet," *QuickBooks,* quickbooks.com, accessed March 2020; Derek Silva, "What Is a Balance Sheet, and How Do You Read One?," *Smart Asset,* smartasset.com, February 4, 2020.

7. Joshua Kennon, "Intangible Assets on the Balance Sheet," *Investopedia,* investopedia.com, January 28, 2020; "When Do Intangible Assets Appear on the Balance Sheet?," Accounting Tools, accountingtools.com, October 8, 2019; Jean Eaglesham, "Goodwill Sparks Deep Divisions, at Least on Balance Sheets," *The Wall Street Journal,* January 21, 2020; Jonathan Ford, "The U.S. Should Embrace Reform of Goodwill Accounting," *Financial Times,* January 26, 2020.

8. Joshua Kennon, "Analyzing Revenue and Sales on Your Income Statement," *The Balance,* thebalance.com, February 10, 2019; "The Difference between Gross Sales and Net Sales," *Accounting Tools,* accountingtools.com, January 7, 2019.

9. "Cash Flow Management: Techniques and Tools," *Business News Daily,* businessnewsdaily.com, February 4, 2020; Rosemary Carlson, "Is Cash Flow the Same as Profit?," *The Balance Small Business,* thebalancesmb. com, January 25, 2020; Nick Chandi, "Know the Difference between Cash Flow and Profit," *Forbes,* January 28, 2020; "How to Prepare a Cash Flow Statement," *QuickBooks,* quickbooks.intuit.com, accessed March 2020.

10. Al Root, "Tesla Just Solved Its Biggest Problem by Selling More Stock," *Barron's,* February 13, 2020; Emily Bary,

"Tesla's Earnings Win Praise Even from Doubters: 'We Fully Admit Things Are Better, Than We Expected,'" *MarketWatch,* marketwatch.com, February 1, 2020; Shawn Tully, "Tesla's Growth Problem—By the Numbers," *Fortune,* February 6, 2020; Jaime Powell, "Tesla's Shares Defy Skeptics, Short-Sellers, and Reason," *Financial Times,* February 7, 2020.

11. Sean Peek, "Cash Flow Problems and How to Solve Them," Business.com, February 7, 2020; "Cash Flow Financing: A Must-Read Guide for Business Owners," Funding Circle, fundingcircle.com, February 10, 2020.

12. Arwana Viswanatha and Khadeeja Safdar, "Under Armour Is Subject to Federal Accounting Probes," *The Wall Street Journal,* November 4, 2019; Steve Symington, "Buy Under Armour before North America Growth Turns for the Better," *The Motley Fool,* fool.com, January 23, 2020; Julie Dreswell and Kevin Draper, "How Under Armour Lost Its Edge," *The Wall Street Journal,* January 26, 2020; Michael Larkin, "Under Armour Dives on Weak Sales, Guidance, Coronavirus Warning," *Investor's Business Daily,* investors.com, February 11, 2020.

13. "Financial Ratios Explanation," Accounting Coach, accountingcoach.com, accessed October 2017.

14. National Association of State Boards of Accountancy, nasba.com, accessed March 2020; American Institute of Certified Public Accountants, aicpa.org, accessed March 2020.

15. "White House Proposal for SEC to Absorb Audit Watchdog Raises Concerns," Paycor, paycor.com, February 14, 2020; Francine McKenna, "Weakening the Oversight of U.S. Auditing Is a Very Bad Idea," *Financial Times,* February 17, 2020; Arthur Levitt, "Without an Independent Watchdog, Who Will Audit the Auditors?," *The Wall Street Journal,* February 19, 2020.

16. Kimberly Amadeo, "Dodd Frank Wall Street Reform Act, 8 Ways a Repeal Hurts You," *Investopedia,* investopedia.com, accessed March 2020; Gary Guthrie, "The Federal Reserve Wants to Relax Investment Rules for Banks," *Consumer Affairs,* consumeraffairs.com, January 31, 2020; Lara Crigger "Barney Frank: 'Forget Rhetoric, Look at Results'," *Yahoo! Finance,* finance.yahoo.com, January 24, 2020; Jesse Hamilton and Ben Bain, "Wall Street Venture-Fund Curbs to Be Eased in Volcker Revamp," *Boston Globe,* January 27, 2020.

17. "Maintaining a License," National Association of State Boards of Accountancy, nasba.org, accessed March 2020; "Overview of AICPA Membership Requirements," American Institute of Certified Public Accountants, aicpa.org, accessed March 2020.

18. Francine McKenna, "Weakening the Oversight of U.S. Auditing Is a Very Bad Idea," *Financial Times,* February 17, 2020; Nick K. Lioudis, "The Collapse of Lehman Brothers: A Case Study," *Investopedia,* investopedia.com, accessed March 2020; Gabrielle Olya, "Enron and the 24 Other Most Epic Corporate Downfalls of All Time," *Yahoo! Finance,* finance.yahoo.com, January 22, 2020.

19. Matt Danielson, "What Internal Auditors Do and How Much They Make," *Investopedia,* investopedia.com, January 28, 2020; Jean Eaglesham, "Auditor Sentenced in KPMG Case," *The Wall Street Journal,* September 12, 2019.

20. U.S. Governmental Accounting Standards Board, gasb.gov, accessed March 2020.

18

Financial Management

Dhivya Suryadevara, CFO of General Motors

Over the course of its more than 110-year history, General Motors grew into one of the world's largest automakers thanks to a roster of famous brands like Chevrolet, Buick, and Cadillac. Of course, the company has also hired plenty of talented people along the way to keep this enormous operation thriving. One of GM's latest recruits is Dhivya Suryadevara, a finance whiz who oversees billions of dollars in assets as the company's executive vice president and chief financial officer (CFO).

Long before she was brokering multibillion-dollar deals, Suryadevara grew up in the south Indian city of Chennai. "Growing up, the importance of education and working hard were drilled into my brain as the price of entry," Suryadevara said. "I still carry that with me." Suryadevara's strong upbringing eventually helped her succeed at the nearby University of Madras, where she earned a bachelor's and master's degree in commerce.

Suryadevara then decided to continue her education at Harvard University, a serious life change for someone who had never left India before. The risk proved to be worth it, though. She earned an MBA from Harvard's prestigious business school and soon landed an internship with the World Bank. From there, Suryadevara went on to work for the investment bank UBS. But at the age of 25, she made the fateful decision to accept a job as a senior financial analyst in the treasurer's office at GM. "It struck me right away that there was no shortage of interesting things to do there," said Suryadevara. "I saw that I was only limited by how much effort and time I wanted to put in, which is what made me want to work harder."

After about eight years at the company, Suryadevara's hard work paid off when she received a promotion to chief investment officer (CIO) of GM Asset Management. In this role, she oversaw more than $86 billion in company investments. Four years later, GM named Suryadevara vice president of corporate finance, where she took the lead on a number of major deals. Along with hammering out the details of GM's acquisition of the self-driving car company Cruise, she also played an integral role in the company's divestiture of Opel.

But Suryadevara's biggest opportunity arrived in 2018 when GM appointed her chief financial officer, the first woman to ever hold the post. As CFO, she leads GM's Global Finance organization and acts as a key representative dealing with the company's investors, lenders, and financial rating agencies. Her job is to take all the complicated pieces of GM's financial puzzle and create a financial plan that puts the company on the right path for the current year and the foreseeable future. She must also ensure GM has sufficient funds to invest in capital assets, brands, and other businesses to deliver on the company's long-term growth targets. Although it's a tough job for anybody to take on, Suryadevara is certainly up to the challenge.

Risk and uncertainty clearly define the role of financial management. In this chapter, you'll explore the role and critical importance of finance in business. We'll discuss the challenges and the tools top managers like Dhivya Suryadevara use to attain financial stability and growth.

Sources: Joann Muller, "Another Woman at the Top of GM: 39-Year-Old Finance Whiz Dhivya Suryadevara Is New CFO," *Forbes,* forbes.com, June 13, 2018; Maria Thomas, "A Chennai Girl's Rise from Madras University to General Motors's First Female CFO," *Quartz India,* qz.com, June 14, 2018; Lexi Churchill, "GM's New 39-Year-Old CFO Dhivya Suryadevara Is Making History," *CNBC,* cnbc.com, June 15, 2018; Matthew DeBord, "GM's First Female CFO Explains How She's Made It Her Mission to 'Slay Complexity' at the Largest US Automaker," *Business Insider,* businessinsider.com, November 1, 2019; General Motors, gm.com, accessed February 2020.

Let's talk business!
bit.ly/LetsTalkBusiness18

CJ Rivera/Getty Images

name that **company**

THIS GIANT TECH COMPANY WAS forced to lower its revenue expectations and adjust its financial plans due to the COVID-19 pandemic in 2020, which caused the global economy to slow down. Name that company. (Find the answer in the chapter.)

LO 18–1 Explain the role and responsibilities of financial managers.

The Role of Finance and Financial Managers

finance

The function in a business that acquires funds for the firm and manages those funds within the firm.

financial management

The job of managing a firm's resources so it can meet its goals and objectives.

financial managers

Managers who examine financial data prepared by accountants and recommend strategies for improving the financial performance of the firm.

The goal of this chapter is to answer two major questions: "What is finance?" and "What do financial managers do?" **Finance** is the function in a business that acquires funds for the firm and manages them within the firm. Finance activities include preparing budgets; doing cash flow analysis; and planning for the expenditure of funds on such assets as plant, equipment, new technology, and machinery. **Financial management** is the job of managing a firm's resources to meet its goals and objectives. Without a carefully calculated financial plan and sound financial management, a firm has little chance for survival, regardless of its product or marketing effectiveness. Let's briefly review the roles of accountants and financial managers.

We can compare an accountant to a skilled laboratory technician who takes blood samples and other measures of a person's health and writes the findings on a health report (in business, this process is the preparation of financial statements). A financial manager is like the doctor who interprets the report and makes recommendations that will improve the patient's health. In short, **financial managers** examine financial data prepared by accountants and recommend strategies for improving the financial performance of the firm.

Clearly financial managers can make sound financial decisions only if they understand accounting information. That's why we first examined accounting in Chapter 17. Similarly, since accounting and finance go together like a peanut butter and jelly sandwich, a good accountant needs to understand finance. In large and medium-sized organizations, both the accounting and finance functions are generally under the control of a chief financial officer (CFO). A CFO is generally the second-highest-paid person in an organization and CFOs often advance to the top job of CEO.[1] However, financial management could also be in the hands of a person who serves as company treasurer or vice president of finance. A comptroller is the chief *accounting* officer.

Figure 18.1 highlights a financial manager's tasks. As you can see, two key responsibilities are to obtain funds and to effectively control the use of those funds. Controlling funds includes

Michael Miller overhauled the underperforming Goodwill Industries operation in Portland, Oregon, by treating the nonprofit like a for-profit business. He trimmed operating expenses comparing sales by store, closing weak outlets and opening new ones in better locations, and cutting distribution costs. Sales soared from $4 million to over $135 million, eliminating the need for outside funding.

Jose A. Iglesias/Tribune Content Agency LLC/
Alamy Stock Photo

**FIGURE 18.1 WHAT
FINANCIAL MANAGERS DO**

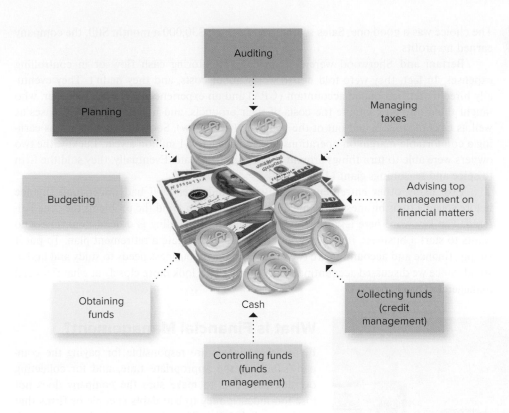

managing the firm's cash, credit accounts (accounts receivable), and inventory. Finance is a critical activity in both profit-seeking and nonprofit organizations.[2]

Financial management is important, no matter what the firm's size. As you may remember from Chapter 6, financing a small business is essential if the firm expects to survive its important first five years. But the need for careful financial management remains a continuing challenge that any business, large or small, must face throughout its existence.[3] This is a lesson many U.S. businesses learned when the financial crisis of 2008 and Great Recession that followed severely impacted the economy.[4]

The Value of Understanding Finance

Three of the most common reasons a firm fails financially are:

1. Undercapitalization (insufficient funds to start the business).
2. Poor control over cash flow.
3. Inadequate expense control.

You can see examples of all three in the following classic story:

Two friends, Elizabeth Bertani and Pat Sherwood, started a company called Parsley Patch on what can best be described as a shoestring budget. It began when Bertani prepared salt-free seasonings for her husband, who was on a no-salt diet. Her friend Sherwood thought the seasonings were good enough to sell. Bertani agreed, and Parsley Patch Inc. was born. The business began with an investment of $5,000 that was rapidly depleted on a logo and label design. Bertani and Sherwood quickly learned about the need for capital in getting a business going. Eventually, they invested more than $100,000 of their own money to keep the business from being undercapitalized.

Everything started well, and hundreds of gourmet shops adopted the product line. But when sales failed to meet expectations, the women decided the health-food market offered more potential because salt-free seasonings were a natural for people with restricted diets.

The choice was a good one. Sales soared, approaching $30,000 a month. Still, the company earned no profits.

Bertani and Sherwood weren't trained in monitoring cash flow or in controlling expenses. In fact, they were told not to worry about costs, and they hadn't. They eventually hired a certified public accountant (CPA) and an experienced financial manager, who taught them how to compute the costs of their products, and how to control expenses as well as cash moving in and out of the company (cash flow). Soon Parsley Patch was earning a comfortable margin on operations that ran close to $1 million a year. Luckily, the two owners were able to turn things around before it was too late. Eventually, they sold the firm to spice and seasonings giant McCormick.

Like many other entrepreneurs, if Bertani and Sherwood had understood finance before starting their business, they might have been able to avoid the problems they encountered. The key word here is *understood.* Financial understanding is crucial to anyone who wants to start a business, invest in stocks and bonds, or create a retirement plan. To put it simply, finance and accounting are two areas everyone in business needs to study and understand. Since we discussed accounting in Chapter 17, let's look more closely at what financial management is all about.

Martin Barraud/Getty Images

Most businesses have predictable day-to-day financial needs, like the need to buy fuel and pay employees. Financial management is the function that helps ensure firms have the funds they need when they need them. What would happen to the company providing the work in this photo if it couldn't buy fuel for its trucks?

What Is Financial Management?

Financial managers are responsible for paying the company's bills at the appropriate time, and for collecting overdue payments to make sure the company does not lose too much money to bad debts (people or firms that don't pay their bills). Therefore, finance functions, such as buying merchandise on credit (accounts payable) and collecting payment from customers (accounts receivable), are key components of the financial manager's job. While these functions are vital to all types of businesses, they are particularly critical to small and medium-sized businesses, which typically have smaller cash or credit cushions than large corporations.

It's also essential that financial managers stay abreast of changes or opportunities in finance, such as changes in tax law, since taxes represent an outflow of cash from the business. Financial managers must also analyze the tax implications of managerial decisions to help minimize the taxes the business must pay. Usually a member of the firm's finance department, the internal auditor, also checks the journals, ledgers, and financial statements the accounting department prepares, to make sure all transactions are in accordance with generally accepted accounting principles.[5] Without such audits, accounting statements would be less reliable. Therefore, it is important that internal auditors be objective and critical of any improprieties or deficiencies noted in their evaluation. Thorough internal audits assist the firm in financial planning, which we'll look at next.

LO 18–2   Outline the financial planning process, and explain the three key budgets in the financial plan.

Financial Planning

Financial planning means analyzing short-term and long-term money flows to and from the firm. Its overall objective is to optimize the firm's profitability and make the best use of its money. It has three steps: (1) forecasting the firm's short-term and long-term financial needs, (2) developing budgets to meet those needs, and (3) establishing financial controls to see whether the company is achieving its goals (see Figure 18.2). Let's look at each step and the role it plays in improving the organization's financial health.

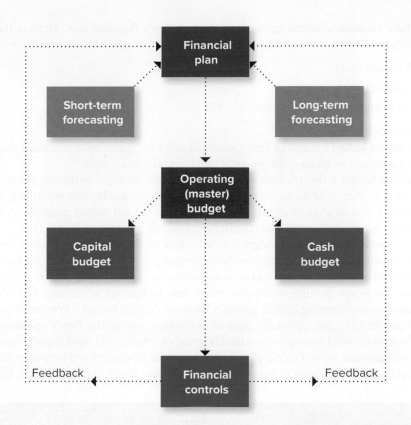

FIGURE 18.2 FINANCIAL
PLANNING

**FIGURE 18.2 FINANCIAL
PLANNING**
Note the close link between
financial planning and
budgeting.

iSeeit! Need help
understanding the key
aspects of financial
planning? Visit your
Connect eBook to
view a video for a brief
animated explanation.

Forecasting Financial Needs

Forecasting is an important part of any firm's financial plan. A *short-term forecast* predicts
revenues, costs, and expenses for a period of one year or less. Part of the short-term forecast
may be a **cash flow forecast**, which predicts the cash inflows and outflows in future periods,
usually months or quarters. The inflows and outflows of cash recorded in the cash flow
forecast are based on expected sales revenues and various costs and expenses incurred, as
well as when they are due for payment. The company's sales forecast estimates projected
sales for a particular period. A business often uses its past financial statements as a basis for
projecting expected sales and various costs and expenses.

    A *long-term forecast* predicts revenues, costs, and expenses for a period longer than
one year, sometimes as long as five years. This forecast plays a crucial part in the company's
long-term strategic plan, which asks questions such as: What business are we in? Should
we be in it five years from now? How much money should we invest in technology and new
plant and equipment over the next decade? Will we have cash available to meet long-term
obligations? Innovations in web-based software help financial managers address these long-
term forecasting questions.[6]

    The long-term financial forecast gives top management, as well as operations manag-
ers, some sense of the income or profit potential of different strategic plans. It also helps in
preparing company budgets.

Working with the Budget Process

A **budget** sets forth management's expectations for revenues and, on the basis of those
expectations, allocates the use of specific resources throughout the firm. As a financial
plan, it depends heavily on the accuracy of the firm's balance sheet, income statement,
statement of cash flows, and short-term and long-term financial forecasts, which all need
to be as accurate as possible. To effectively prepare budgets, financial managers must take
their forecasting responsibilities seriously. A budget becomes the primary guide for the
firm's financial operations and expected financial needs.

cash flow forecast
Forecast that predicts the
cash inflows and outflows
in future periods, usually
months or quarters.

budget
A financial plan that sets forth
management's expectations,
and, on the basis of those
expectations, allocates the
use of specific resources
throughout the firm.

capital budget

A budget that highlights a firm's spending plans for major asset purchases that often require large sums of money.

cash budget

A budget that estimates cash inflows and outflows during a particular period like a month or a quarter.

operating (or master) budget

The budget that ties together the firm's other budgets and summarizes its proposed financial activities.

There are usually several types of budgets in a firm's financial plan. Three of the most common are:

- A capital budget.
- A cash budget.
- An operating or master budget.

Let's look at each.

A **capital budget** forecasts a firm's spending plans for major asset purchases that often require large sums of money, like property, buildings, and equipment.

A **cash budget** estimates cash inflows and outflows during a particular period, like a month or a quarter. It helps managers anticipate borrowing needs, debt repayment, operating expenses, and short-term investments, and is often the last budget prepared. A sample cash budget for our restaurant example, Harvest Gold, is provided in Figure 18.3.

The **operating (or master) budget** is an aggregate of the firm's other budgets and summarizes its proposed financial activities. More formally, it is presented to all the company's managers and estimates the costs and expenses needed to run the business, given all projected revenues. The firm's spending on supplies, travel, rent, technology, advertising, and salaries is determined in the operating budget, generally the most detailed budget a firm prepares.

Financial planning obviously plays an important role in the firm's operations and often determines what long-term investments it makes, when it will need specific funds, and how it will generate them. Once a company forecasts its short-term and long-term financial needs and compiles budgets to show how it will allocate funds, the final step in financial

FIGURE 18.3 A SAMPLE CASH BUDGET FOR HARVEST GOLD

HARVEST GOLD Monthly Cash Budget			
	January	February	March
Sales forecast	$50,000	$45,000	$40,000
Collections			
Cash sales (20%)		$ 9,000	$ 8,000
Credit sales (80% of past month)		40,000	36,000
Monthly cash collection		$49,000	$44,000
Payments schedule			
Supplies and material		$11,000	$10,000
Salaries		12,000	12,000
Direct labor		9,000	9,000
Taxes		3,000	3,000
Other expenses		7,000	5,000
Monthly cash payments		$42,000	$39,000
Cash budget			
Cash flow		$ 7,000	$ 5,000
Beginning cash		−1,000	6,000
Total cash		$ 6,000	$11,000
Less minimum cash balance		−6,000	−6,000
Excess cash to market securities		$ 0	$ 5,000
Loans needed for minimum balance		0	0

planning is to establish financial controls. Before we talk about those, however, Figure 18.4 challenges you to check your personal financial planning skill by developing a monthly budget for You Inc.

Establishing Financial Controls

Financial control is a process in which a firm periodically compares its actual revenues, costs, and expenses with its budget. Most companies hold at least monthly financial reviews as a way to ensure financial control. Such control procedures help managers identify variances to the financial plan and allow them to take corrective action if necessary. Financial controls also help reveal which specific accounts, departments, and people are varying from

financial control
A process in which a firm periodically compares its actual revenues, costs, and expenses with its budget.

FIGURE 18.4 YOU INCORPORATED MONTHLY BUDGET
In Chapter 17, you compiled a sample balance sheet for You Inc. Now, let's develop a monthly budget for You Inc. Be honest and think of everything that needs to be included for an accurate monthly budget for You!

	Expected	Actual	Difference
Monthly income			
Wages (net pay after taxes)			
Savings account withdrawal			
Family support			
Loans			
Other sources			
Total monthly income			
Monthly expenses			
Fixed expenses			
Rent or mortgage			
Car payment			
Health insurance			
Life insurance			
Tuition or fees			
Other fixed expenses			
Subtotal of fixed expenses			
Variable expenses			
Food			
Clothing			
Entertainment			
Transportation			
Phone			
Utilities			
Publications			
Internet connection			
Cable television			
Other expenses			
Subtotal of variable expenses			
Total expenses			
Total income − Total expenses = Cash on hand/(Cash deficit)			

the financial plan. Finance managers can judge whether these variances are legitimate and thereby merit adjustments to the plan. Shifts in the economy, natural disasters, or volatility in global markets can also alter financial plans. For example, a slowdown in the U.S. housing market or unexpected events in the global economy can cause many companies to consider adjusting their financial plans. In 2020, the COVID-19 pandemic negatively impacted and slowed down the world economy. This caused companies such as Apple to lower their financial expectations.[7] After the Test Prep, we'll see why firms need readily available funds.

?TEST**PREP**

- Name three finance functions important to the firm's overall operations and performance.
- What three primary financial problems cause firms to fail?
- How do short-term and long-term financial forecasts differ?
- What is the purpose of preparing budgets in an organization? Can you identify three different types of budgets?

LO 18–3 Explain why firms need operating funds.

The Need for Operating Funds

In business, the need for operating funds never seems to end. That's why sound financial management is essential to all businesses. And like our personal financial needs, the capital needs of a business change over time. Remember the classic example of Parsley Patch to see why a small business's financial requirements can shift considerably. The same is true for large corporations such as Facebook, Johnson & Johnson, and Nike when they venture into new-product areas or new markets. Virtually all organizations have operational needs for which they need funds. Key areas include:

- Managing day-by-day needs of the business.
- Controlling credit operations.
- Acquiring needed inventory.
- Making capital expenditures.

Let's look carefully at the financial needs of these key areas, which affect both the smallest and the largest of businesses.

Managing Day-by-Day Needs of the Business

If workers expect to be paid on Friday, they don't want to wait until Monday for their paychecks. If tax payments are due on the 15th of the month, the government expects the money on time. If the interest payment on a business loan is due on the 30th of this month, the lender doesn't mean the 1st of next month. As you can see, funds have to be available to meet the daily operational costs of the business.

Financial managers must ensure that funds are available to meet daily cash needs without compromising the firm's opportunities to invest money for its future. Money has a *time value*.[8] In other words, if someone offered to give you $200 either today or one year from today, you would benefit by taking the $200 today. Why? It's very simple. You could invest the $200 you receive today and over a year's time it would grow. The same is true in business; the interest a firm gains on its investments is important in maximizing the profit it will gain. That's why financial managers often try to minimize cash expenditures to free up funds for investment in interest-bearing accounts. They suggest the company pay its bills as late as possible (unless a cash discount is available for early payment). They also advise companies to try to collect what's owed them as fast as possible, to maximize the investment potential of the firm's funds. Unfortunately, collecting funds as fast as possible can be particularly challenging, especially during times when the economy slows down. Efficient cash management is particularly important to small firms since their access to capital is much more limited than larger businesses.[9]

Creative Stock Studio/Shutterstock

Controlling Credit Operations

Financial managers know that in today's highly competitive business environment, making credit available helps keep current customers happy and helps attract new ones. Credit for customers can be especially important during tough financial times as was the case during the recession that began in 2008 when lenders were hesitant to make loans.

The problem with selling on credit is that as much as 25 percent of the business's assets could be tied up in its credit accounts (accounts receivable). This forces the firm to use its own funds to pay for goods or services sold to customers who bought on credit. Financial managers in such firms often develop efficient collection procedures, like offering cash or quantity discounts to buyers who pay their accounts by a certain time. They also scrutinize old and new credit customers to see whether they have a history of meeting credit obligations on time.

One convenient way to decrease the time and expense of collecting accounts receivable is to accept bank credit cards such as Mastercard or Visa. The banks that issue these cards have already established the customer's creditworthiness and are responsible for collections, which reduces the business's risk. Businesses must pay a fee to accept credit cards, but the costs are usually offset by the benefits. In an effort to reduce those credit card costs as well as speed up the transaction process, many businesses today accept mobile payments through services like Apple Pay and Android Pay.[10] For example, restaurants, supermarkets, and hotels have invested in mobile payment systems.[11] Mobile payment systems not only make transactions quick and simple, the processors usually charge lower fees than traditional credit card companies.

It's difficult to think of a business that doesn't make credit available to its customers. However, collecting accounts receivable can be time-consuming and expensive. Accepting credit cards such as Visa, Mastercard, and American Express can simplify transactions for sellers and guarantee payment. What types of products do you regularly purchase with a credit card?

Acquiring Needed Inventory

As we saw in Chapter 13, effective marketing requires focusing on the customer and providing high-quality service and readily available goods. A carefully constructed inventory policy helps manage the firm's available funds and maximize profitability. Doozle's, an ice-cream parlor in St. Louis, Missouri, deliberately ties up fewer funds in its inventory of ice cream in winter. It's obvious why: demand for ice cream is lower in winter in the Midwest.

Just-in-time inventory control (see Chapter 9) and other such methods can reduce the funds a firm must tie up in inventory. Carefully evaluating its inventory turnover ratio (see Chapter 17) can also help a firm control the outflow of cash for inventory. A business of any size must understand that poorly managed inventory can seriously affect cash flow and drain its finances dry. The Making Ethical Decisions box raises an interesting question about sound financial management and inventory control in a critical industry.

Making Capital Expenditures

Capital expenditures are major investments in either tangible long-term assets such as land, buildings, and equipment, or intangible assets such as patents, trademarks, and copyrights. In many organizations the purchase of major assets—such as land for future expansion, manufacturing plants to increase production capabilities, research to develop new-product ideas, and

capital expenditures
Major investments in either tangible long-term assets such as land, buildings, and equipment or intangible assets such as patents, trademarks, and copyrights.

After earning your business degree, you are hired as a hospital administrator at a small hospital. Having studied finance, you know that efficient cash management is important to all firms in all industries to meet the day-by-day operations. One way to ensure such efficiency is to use a carefully planned and managed inventory control system that reduces the amount of cash an organization

has tied up in inventory. You know that just-in-time inventory is a proven system that helps reduce the costs of managing inventory.

At a meeting of the hospital's executive committee, you recommend the hospital save money by using a just-in-time inventory system to manage its drug supply. You suggest discontinuing the hospital's large stockpile of expensive cancer treatment drugs

that tie up a great deal of the hospital's cash, and order them only when they are needed. Several board members like the idea, but the doctors in charge of the hospital's cancer center are outraged, claiming you are sacrificing patients' well-being for cash flow. After debate, the committee says the decision is up to you. What will you do? What could result from your decision?

equipment to maintain or exceed current levels of output—is essential. Expanding into new markets, however, can be expensive with no guarantee of success. Therefore, it's critical that companies weigh all possible options before committing a large portion of available resources.

Consider a firm that needs to expand its production capabilities due to increased customer demand. It could buy land and build a new plant, purchase an existing plant, or rent space. Can you think of financial and accounting considerations at play in this decision?

The need for operating funds raises several questions for financial managers: How does the firm obtain funds to finance operations and other business needs? Will it require specific funds in the long or the short term? How much will it cost (i.e., interest) to obtain these funds? Will they come from internal or external sources? We address these questions next.

Alternative Sources of Funds

We described finance earlier as the function in a business responsible for acquiring and managing funds. Sound financial management determines the amount of money needed and the most appropriate sources from which to obtain it. A firm can raise needed capital by borrowing money (debt), selling ownership (equity), or earning profits (retained earnings). **Debt financing** refers to funds raised through various forms of borrowing that must be repaid. **Equity financing** is money raised from within the firm, from operations or through the sale of ownership in the firm (stock). Firms can borrow funds either short-term or long-term. *Short-term financing* refers to funds needed for a year or less. *Long-term financing* covers funds needed for more than a year (usually 2 to 10 years). Figure 18.5 highlights reasons why firms may need short-term and long-term funds.

We'll explore the different sources of short- and long-term financing next. Let's first pause to check your understanding by doing the Test Prep.

⊳ iSeeit! Need help understanding equity financing and debt financing? Visit your Connect eBook to view a video for a brief animated explanation.

debt financing
Funds raised through various forms of borrowing that must be repaid.

equity financing
Money raised from within the firm, from operations or through the sale of ownership in the firm (stock or venture capital).

FIGURE 18.5 WHY FIRMS NEED FUNDS

SHORT-TERM FUNDS	LONG-TERM FUNDS
Monthly expenses	New-product development
Unanticipated emergencies	Replacement of capital equipment
Cash flow problems	Mergers or acquisitions
Expansion of current inventory	Expansion into new markets (domestic or global)
Temporary promotional programs	New facilities

- Money has time value. What does this mean?
- Why is accounts receivable a major financial concern to the firm?
- What's the primary reason an organization spends a good deal of its available funds on inventory and capital expenditures?
- What's the difference between debt and equity financing?

LO 18–4 Identify and describe different sources of short-term financing.

Obtaining Short-Term Financing

The bulk of a finance manager's job does not relate to obtaining long-term funds. In small businesses, for example, long-term financing is often out of the question. Instead, day-to-day operations call for the careful management of *short-term* financial needs. Firms may need to borrow short-term funds for purchasing additional inventory or for meeting bills that come due unexpectedly. Like an individual, a business, especially a small business, sometimes needs to secure short-term funds when its cash reserves are low. Let's see how it does so.

Trade Credit

Trade credit is the practice of buying goods or services now and paying for them later. It is the most widely used source of short-term funding, the least expensive, and the most convenient. Small businesses rely heavily on trade credit from firms such as United Parcel Service, as do large firms such as Target or Macy's. When a firm buys merchandise, it receives an invoice (a bill) much like the one you receive when you buy something with a credit card. As you'll see, however, the terms businesses receive are often different from those on your monthly statement.

Business invoices often contain terms such as *2/10, net 30*. This means the buyer can take a 2 percent discount for paying the invoice within 10 days. Otherwise the total bill (net) is due in 30 days. Finance managers pay close attention to such discounts because they create opportunities to reduce the firm's costs. Think about it for a moment: If the terms are 2/10, net 30, the customer will pay 2 percent more by waiting an extra 20 days to pay the invoice. If the firm *can* pay its bill within 10 days, it is needlessly increasing its costs by not doing so.

Some suppliers hesitate to give trade credit to an organization with a poor credit rating, no credit history, or a history of slow payment. They may insist the customer sign a **promissory note**, a written agreement with a promise to pay a supplier a specific sum of money at a definite time. Promissory notes are not as rigid as formal loan contracts and are negotiable. The supplier can sell them to a bank at a discount (the amount of the promissory note less a fee for the bank's services in collecting the amount due), and the business is then responsible for paying the bank.

trade credit
The practice of buying goods and services now and paying for them later.

promissory note
A written agreement with a promise to pay a supplier a specific sum of money at a definite time.

pogonici/Shutterstock

One thing you can never have too much of is cash. Financial managers must make certain there is enough cash available to meet daily financial needs and still have funds to invest in its future. What does it mean when we say cash has a time value?

Family and Friends

As we discussed in Chapter 17, firms often have several bills coming due at the same time with no sources of funds to pay them. Many small firms obtain short-term funds by borrowing money from family and friends. Such loans can create problems, however, if all parties do not understand cash flow. That's why it's sometimes better, when possible, to go to a commercial bank that fully understands the business's risk and can help analyze its future financial needs rather than borrow from friends or relatives.[12]

Entrepreneurs appear to be listening to this advice. According to the National Federation of Independent Business, entrepreneurs today are relying less on family and friends as a source of borrowed funds than they have in the past.[13] If an entrepreneur decides to ask family or friends for financial assistance, it's important that both parties (1) agree to specific loan terms, (2) put the agreement in writing, and (3) arrange for repayment in the same way they would for a bank loan. Such actions help keep family relationships and friendships intact.

Commercial Banks

Banks, being sensitive to risk, generally prefer to lend short-term money to larger, established businesses. Imagine the different types of businesspeople who go to banks for a loan, and you'll get a better idea of the requests bankers evaluate. Picture, for example, a farmer going to the bank in spring to borrow funds for seed, fertilizer, equipment, and other needs that will be repaid after the fall harvest. Or consider a local toy store buying merchandise for Christmas sales. The store borrows the money for such purchases in the summer and plans to pay it back after Christmas. Restaurants often borrow funds at the beginning of the month and pay at the end of the month.

How much a business borrows and for how long depends on the kind of business it is, and how quickly it can resell the merchandise it purchases with a bank loan or use it to generate funds. In a large business, specialists in a company's finance and accounting departments do a cash flow forecast. Small-business owners generally lack such specialists and must monitor cash flow themselves.

Did you ever wonder how retail stores get the money to buy all the treasures we splurge on during the holidays? Department stores and other large retailers make extensive use of commercial banks and other lenders to borrow the funds they need to buy merchandise and stock their shelves. How do stores benefit from using this type of financing?

Gao Jing/Xinhua/eyevine/Redux

During difficult economic times, bank loans can virtually disappear, even for well-organized small businesses. This was certainly the case during the Great Recession when bank loans were practically nonexistent. Since the recession ended, small-business lending has improved but only slightly.[14] That's why it's important for a small firm to remember if it gets a bank loan, the owner or person in charge of finance should keep in close touch with the bank and send regular financial statements to keep the bank up-to-date on its operations. The bank may spot cash flow problems early or be more willing to lend money in a crisis if the business has established a strong relationship built on trust and sound management.

Joni Hanebutt/Shutterstock

Different Forms of Short-Term Loans

Commercial banks offer different types of short-term loans. A **secured loan** is backed by *collateral,* something valuable such as property. If the borrower fails to pay the loan, the lender may take possession of the collateral. An automobile loan is a secured loan. If the borrower doesn't repay it, the lender will repossess the car. Inventory of raw materials like coal, copper, and steel often serves as collateral for business loans. Collateral removes some of the bank's risk in lending the money.

Accounts receivable are company assets often used as collateral for a loan; this process is called pledging and works as follows: A percentage of the value of a firm's accounts receivable pledged (usually about 75 percent) is advanced to the borrowing firm. As customers pay off their accounts, the funds received are forwarded to the lender in repayment of the funds that were advanced.

An **unsecured loan** is more difficult to obtain because it doesn't require any collateral. Normally, lenders give unsecured loans only to highly regarded customers—long-standing businesses or those considered financially stable.

If a business develops a strong relationship with a bank, the bank may open a **line of credit** for the firm, a given amount of unsecured short-term funds a bank will lend to a business, provided the funds are readily available. A line of credit is *not* guaranteed to a business. However, it speeds up the borrowing process since a firm does not have to apply for a new loan every time it needs funds.[15] As a business matures and becomes more financially secure, banks will often increase its line of credit.

If a business is unable to secure a short-term loan from a bank, the financial manager may seek short-term funds from *commercial finance companies.* These non deposit-type organizations make short-term loans to borrowers who offer tangible assets like property, plant, and equipment as collateral. Commercial finance companies will often make loans to businesses that cannot get short-term funds elsewhere. Since commercial finance companies assume higher degrees of risk than commercial banks, they usually charge higher interest rates. The Spotlight on Small Business box highlights the challenges small businesses face in securing short-term financing and choosing the best option for their business.

Factoring Accounts Receivable

One relatively expensive source of short-term funds for a firm is **factoring**, the process of selling accounts receivable for cash. Factoring dates as far back as 4,000 years, during the days of ancient Babylon. Here's how it works: Let's say a firm sells many of its products on credit to consumers and other businesses, creating a number of accounts receivable. Some buyers may be slow in paying their bills, so a large amount of money is due the firm. A *factor* is a market intermediary (usually a financial institution or a factoring company) that agrees to buy the firm's accounts receivable, at a discount, for cash.[16] The discount depends on the age of the accounts receivable, the nature of the business, and the condition of the economy. When it collects the accounts receivable that were originally owed to the firm, the factor keeps them or collects a fee.

A secured loan is backed by collateral, a tangible item of value. A car loan, for instance, is a secured loan in which the car itself is the collateral. What is the collateral in a mortgage loan?

secured loan
A loan backed by collateral (something valuable, such as property).

unsecured loan
A loan that doesn't require any collateral.

line of credit
A given amount of unsecured short-term funds a bank will lend to a business, provided the funds are readily available.

factoring
The process of selling accounts receivable for cash.

While factors charge more than banks' loan rates, remember many small businesses cannot qualify for a bank loan. So even though factoring is an expensive way of raising short-term funds, it is popular among small businesses. A company can often reduce its factoring cost if it agrees to reimburse the factor for slow-paying accounts, or to assume the risk for customers who don't pay at all. Remember, factoring is not a loan; it is the sale of a firm's asset (accounts receivable). Factoring is common in U.S. industries and in growing numbers of global trade ventures.

Commercial Paper

Commercial paper is a type of short-term financing available to large corporations that need funds for just a few months and prefer not to have to negotiate with a commercial bank. *Commercial paper* consists of *unsecured* promissory notes, in amounts of $100,000 and up, that mature or come due in 270 days or less. Commercial paper states a fixed amount of money the business agrees to repay to the lender (investor) on a specific date at a specified rate of interest.

Because commercial paper is unsecured, only financially stable firms (again, large corporations with excellent credit reputations) are able to sell it. Commercial paper can be a quick path to short-term funds at lower interest than charged by commercial banks. Since most commercial paper matures in 30 to 90 days, it can be an investment opportunity for lenders who can afford to put up cash for short periods to earn some interest on their money.

Credit Cards

According to a survey by the Federal Reserve, a large majority of businesses that apply for a traditional business loan are rejected. Estimates are 80 percent of small businesses are rejected for such loans.[17] That's why many businesses turn to short-term financing through credit cards. Credit cards provide a readily available line of credit that can save time and the likely embarrassment of being rejected for a bank loan.[18] The National Small Business Association (NSBA) estimates that one-third of all small firms now use credit cards to finance their businesses.[19]

Even though more businesses are turning to credit cards for financing, credit cards can be extremely risky and often costly. The Credit Card Responsibility Accountability and Disclosure Act reduced consumer interest rates and approved many protections for consumers against card company abuses. Unfortunately, rates for small-business and corporate credit cards did not fall under the protection of the law. That's why it's important to understand the penalties and perks that come with different credit cards.[20] Some credit card perks can help keep a small business afloat. For example, Christina Stembel used a cash-back card that helped put dollars back into her e-commerce company, Farmgirl Flowers. She used the cash-back funds to expand her marketing budget.[21] Today, she runs a $30 million business.

Still, when dealing with credit cards, remember it's an expensive way to borrow money and credit cards are probably best used very carefully. After the Test Prep questions, we'll look into long-term financing options.

TESTPREP

- What does an invoice containing the terms 2/10, net 30 mean?
- What's the difference between trade credit and a line of credit?
- What's the key difference between a secured and an unsecured loan?
- What is factoring?

LO 18–5 Identify and describe different sources of long-term financing.

Obtaining Long-Term Financing

In a financial plan, forecasting determines the amount of funding the firm will need over various periods and the most appropriate sources for obtaining those funds. In setting long-term financing objectives, financial managers generally ask three questions:

1. What are our organization's long-term goals and objectives?
2. What funds do we need to achieve the firm's long-term goals and objectives?
3. What sources of long-term funding (capital) are available, and which will best fit our needs?

Firms need long-term capital to purchase expensive assets such as plant and equipment, to develop new products, or perhaps finance their expansion. In major corporations, the board of directors and top management usually make decisions about long-term financing, along with finance and accounting executives. Merck, one of the world's largest research-based biomedical and pharmaceutical companies, spends over $9.8 billion a year researching and developing new products.[22] The development of a single new drug could take 10 years and cost the firm almost $2 billion before it brings in any profit.[23] Plus the company loses its patent protection on a drug after 20 years. It's easy to see why high-level managers make the long-term financing decisions at Merck. Owners of small and medium-sized businesses are almost always actively engaged in analyzing their long-term financing decisions. As we noted earlier, long-term funding comes from two major sources, debt financing and equity financing. Let's look at these sources next.

Debt Financing

Debt financing is borrowing money the company has a legal obligation to repay. Firms can borrow by either getting a loan from a lending institution or issuing bonds.

term-loan agreement
A promissory note that requires the borrower to repay the loan in specified installments.

risk/return trade-off
The principle that the greater the risk a lender takes in making a loan, the higher the interest rate required.

Debt Financing by Borrowing from Lending Institutions
Long-term loans are usually due within 3 to 7 years but may extend to 15 or 20 years. A **term-loan agreement** is a promissory note that requires the borrower to repay the loan with interest in specified monthly or annual installments. A major advantage is that the loan interest is tax-deductible.

Long-term loans are both larger and more expensive to the firm than short-term loans. Since the repayment period can be quite long, lenders assume more risk and usually require collateral, which may be real estate, machinery, equipment, company stock, or other items of value. Lenders may also require certain restrictions to force the firm to act responsibly. The interest rate is based on the adequacy of collateral, the firm's credit rating, and the general level of market interest rates. The greater the risk a lender takes in making a loan, the higher the rate of interest. This principle is known as the **risk/return trade-off**.

Debt Financing by Issuing Bonds
If an organization is unable to obtain its long-term financing needs by getting a loan from a lending institution such as a bank, it may try to issue bonds. To put it simply, a bond is like an IOU with a promise to repay the amount borrowed, with interest, on a certain date. The terms of the agreement in a bond issue are the indenture terms (discussed in Chapter 19). The types of organizations that can issue bonds include federal, state, and local governments; federal government agencies; foreign governments; and corporations.

You may already be familiar with bonds. You may own investments like U.S. government savings bonds, or perhaps you volunteered your time to help a local school district pass a bond issue. If your community is building a new stadium or cultural center, it may sell bonds to finance the project.[24] Businesses and governments compete for funds when issuing bonds. Potential investors (individuals and institutions) measure the risk of purchasing a bond against the return the bond promises to pay—the interest—and the issuer's ability to repay when promised.

Like other forms of long-term debt, bonds can be secured or unsecured. A *secured bond* is issued with some form of collateral, such as real estate, equipment, or other pledged assets. If the bond's indenture terms are violated (e.g., not paying interest payments), the bondholder can issue a claim on the collateral. An *unsecured bond,* called a debenture bond, is backed only by the reputation of the issuer. Investors in such bonds simply trust that the organization issuing the bond will make good on its financial commitments.

Bonds are a key means of long-term financing for many governments and corporations. They can also be valuable investments for private individuals or institutions. Given this importance, we will discuss bonds in more depth in Chapter 19.

Major League Baseball is a big business, and building a new stadium requires big dollars. When the Texas Rangers needed financing to replace their old stadium with a new state-of-the-art facility, the city of Arlington and the state issued bonds that helped finance the construction of the Rangers's new home. What organizations in your community have issued bonds, and for what purpose?

Tom Pennington/Getty Images

Equity Financing

If a firm cannot obtain a long-term loan from a lending institution or is unable to sell bonds to investors, it may seek equity financing. Equity financing makes funds available when the owners of the firm sell shares of ownership to outside investors in the form of stock, when they reinvest company earnings in the business, or when they obtain funds from venture capitalists.

Equity Financing by Selling Stock
The key thing to remember about stock is that stockholders become owners in the organization. Generally, the corporation's board of

directors decides the number of shares of stock that will be offered to investors for purchase. The first time a company offers to sell its stock to the general public is called an *initial public offering (IPO)*. Selling stock to the public to obtain funds is by no means easy or automatic. U.S. companies can issue stock for public purchase only if they meet requirements set by the U.S. Securities and Exchange Commission (SEC) and various state agencies. They can offer different types of stock such as common and preferred. We'll discuss IPOs and common and preferred stock in detail in Chapter 19.

©Jeff Clark Photography

Equity Financing from Retained Earnings You probably remember from Chapter 17 that the profits the company keeps and reinvests in the firm are called *retained earnings.* Retained earnings often are a major source of long-term funds, especially for small businesses since they often have fewer financing alternatives, such as selling stock or bonds, than large businesses do. However, large corporations also depend on retained earnings for needed long-term funding. In fact, retained earnings are usually the most favored source of meeting long-term capital needs. A company that uses its retained earnings saves interest payments, dividends (payments for investing in stock), and any possible underwriting fees for issuing bonds or stock. Retained earnings also create no new ownership in the firm, as stock does.

Suppose you wanted to buy an expensive personal asset such as a new car. Ideally you would go to your personal savings account and take out the necessary cash. No hassle! No interest! Unfortunately, few people have such large amounts of cash available. Most businesses are no different. Even though they would like to finance long-term needs from operations (retained earnings), few have the resources available to accomplish this.

Equity Financing from Venture Capital The hardest time for a business to raise money is when it is starting up or just beginning to expand. A start-up business typically has few assets and no market track record, so the chances of borrowing significant amounts of money from a bank or other lender are slim. **Venture capital** is money invested in new or emerging companies that some investors—venture capitalists—believe have great profit potential. Venture capital helped firms like Intel, Apple, Cisco, and Uber get started and helped Facebook and Google expand and grow. Venture capitalists invest in a company in return for part ownership and some control of the business. They expect higher-than-average returns and competent management performance for their investment.[25]

venture capital
Money that is invested in new or emerging companies that are perceived as having great profit potential.

The venture capital industry originally began as an alternative investment vehicle for wealthy families.[26] The Rockefeller family, for example (whose vast fortune came from John D. Rockefeller's Standard Oil Company, started in the 19th century), financed Sanford McDonnell when he was operating his company from an airplane hangar. That small venture eventually grew into McDonnell Douglas, a large aerospace and defense contractor that merged with Boeing Corporation in 1997. The venture capital industry grew significantly in the 1990s, especially in high-tech centers like California's Silicon Valley, where venture capitalists concentrated on Internet-related companies. Problems in the technology industry and a slowdown in the economy in the early 2000s reduced venture capital expenditures. The Great Recession caused venture capital spending to drop to new lows and did not start to recover until 2013. Today, venture capital is rising again with over $100 billion invested in 2020.[27] The Spotlight on Small Business talks about an innovative venture capital firm that hopes to assist in landing new investments.

Comparing Debt and Equity Financing

Figure 18.6 compares debt and equity financing options. Raising funds through borrowing to increase the firm's rate of return is referred to as **leverage**. Though debt increases risk because it creates a financial obligation that must be repaid, it also enhances the firm's

leverage
Raising needed funds through borrowing to increase a firm's rate of return.

ability to increase profits. Recall that two key jobs of the financial manager or CFO are forecasting the firm's need for borrowed funds and planning how to manage these funds once they are obtained.

Firms are very concerned with the cost of capital. **Cost of capital** is the rate of return a company must earn in order to meet the demands of its lenders and expectations of its equity holders (stockholders or venture capitalists). If the firm's earnings are larger than the interest payments on borrowed funds, business owners can realize a higher rate of return than if they used equity financing. Figure 18.7 describes an example, again involving our restaurant example, Harvest Gold (introduced in Chapter 13). If Harvest Gold needed $200,000 in new financing, it could consider debt by selling bonds or equity through offering stock. Comparing the two options in this situation, you can see that Harvest Gold would benefit by selling bonds since the company's earnings are greater than the interest paid on borrowed funds (bonds). However, if the firm's earnings were less than the interest paid on

cost of capital

The rate of return a company must earn in order to meet the demands of its lenders and expectations of its equity holders.

FIGURE 18.6

DIFFERENCES BETWEEN DEBT AND EQUITY FINANCING

Conditions	Type of Financing	
	Debt	**Equity**
Management influence	There's usually none unless special conditions have been agreed on.	Common stockholders have voting rights.
Repayment	Debt has a maturity date.	Stock has no maturity date.
	Principal must be repaid.	The company is never required to repay equity.
Yearly obligations	Payment of interest is a contractual obligation.	The firm isn't legally liable to pay dividends.
Tax benefits	Interest is tax-deductible.	Dividends are paid from after-tax income and aren't deductible.

Additional Debt		Additional Equity	
Stockholders' equity	$500,000	Stockholders' equity	$500,000
Additional equity	—	Additional equity	$200,000
Total equity	$500,000	Total equity	$700,000
Bond @ 8% interest	200,000	Bond interest	—
Total shareholder equity	$500,000	Total shareholder equity	$700,000
Year-End Earnings			
Gross profit	$100,000	Gross profit	$100,000
Less bond interest	−16,000	Less interest	—
Operating profit	$ 84,000	Operating profit	$100,000
Return on equity	16.8%	Return on equity	14.3%
($84,000 ÷ $500,000 = 16.8%)		($100,000 ÷ $700,000 = 14.3%)	

FIGURE 18.7 USING LEVERAGE (DEBT) VERSUS EQUITY FINANCING
Harvest Gold wants to raise $200,000 in new capital. Compare the firm's debt and equity options.

borrowed funds (bonds), Harvest Gold could lose money. It's also important to remember that bonds, like all debt, have to be repaid at a specific time.

Individual firms must determine exactly how to balance debt and equity financing by comparing the costs and benefits of each. Leverage ratios (discussed in Chapter 17) can also give companies an industry standard for this balance, to which they can compare themselves. Still debt varies considerably among major companies and industries. Social media leader Facebook, for example, has very little long-term debt and more than $50 billion in cash available. Similarly, tech companies like Microsoft, Apple, and Alphabet have very little debt and huge piles of cash. On the other hand, Exxon has over $45 billion in debt.[28] Smaller oil and gas companies have over $85 billion of debt on their balance sheets.[29] According to Standard & Poor's and Moody's Investors Service (firms that provide corporate and financial research), the debt of large industrial corporations and utilities typically ranges between 30 and 35 percent of the companies' total assets. The amount of debt obviously varies considerably from firm to firm and industry to industry.

Lessons Learned from the Financial Crisis and Great Recession

The financial crisis that began in 2008 caused financial markets to suffer their worst fall since the Great Depression of the 1920s and 1930s. The Great Recession that followed caused further deterioration in the economy that still impacts many areas in the United States.[30] Millennial and Gen X workers were particularly hit hard by the Great Recession.[31]

Many laid the collapse of financial markets at the feet of financial managers for failing to do their job effectively. Poor investment decisions and risky financial dealings (especially in real estate) caused long-standing financial firms such as Lehman Brothers to close their doors. The financial meltdown led the U.S. Congress to pass sweeping financial regulatory reform. The Dodd-Frank Wall Street Reform and Consumer Protection Act affected almost every aspect of the U.S. financial services industry. The government increased its involvement and intervention in financial markets, and made the requirements of financial institutions and financial managers more stringent. Today, there are some who question if the Dodd-Frank Act has gone too far in financial regulation and recommend it be amended.[32] Still, whether the law is modified or not, the job and responsibilities of the financial manager promise to become even more challenging in the future.

Financial managers have slowly regained the trust of the public. The financial crisis and Great Recession's severity called into question the integrity and good judgment of financial managers much like events in the early 2000s did the integrity and judgment of the accounting industry (see Chapter 17). Chapter 19 takes a close look at securities markets as a source of securing long-term financing for businesses and as a base for investment options for private investors. You will learn how securities exchanges work, how firms issue stocks and bonds, how to choose the right investment strategy, how to buy and sell stock, where to find up-to-date information about stocks and bonds, and more. Finance takes on a new dimension when you see how you can participate in financial markets yourself.

?TEST PREP

- What are the two major forms of debt financing available to a firm?
- How does debt financing differ from equity financing?
- What are the three major forms of equity financing available to a firm?
- What is leverage, and why do firms choose to use it?

SUMMARY

LO 18–1 Explain the role and responsibilities of financial managers.

What are the most common ways firms fail financially?

The most common financial problems are (1) undercapitalization, (2) poor control over cash flow, and (3) inadequate expense control.

What do financial managers do?

Financial managers plan, budget, control funds, obtain funds, collect funds, conduct audits, manage taxes, and advise top management on financial matters.

LO 18–2 Outline the financial planning process, and explain the three key budgets in the financial plan.

What are the three budgets in a financial plan?

The capital budget is the spending plan for expensive assets such as property, plant, and equipment. The cash budget is the projected cash balance at the end of a given period. The operating (master) budget summarizes the information in the other two budgets. It projects dollar allocations to various costs and expenses given various revenues.

LO 18–3 Explain why firms need operating funds.

What are firms' major financial needs?

Businesses need financing for four major tasks: (1) managing day-by-day operations, (2) controlling credit operations, (3) acquiring needed inventory, and (4) making capital expenditures.

What's the difference between debt financing and equity financing?

Debt financing raises funds by borrowing. Equity financing raises funds from within the firm through investment of retained earnings, sale of stock to investors, or sale of part ownership to venture capitalists.

What's the difference between short-term and long-term financing?

Short-term financing raises funds to be repaid in less than a year, whereas long-term financing raises funds to be repaid over a longer period.

LO 18–4 Identify and describe different sources of short-term financing.

■ **Why should businesses use trade credit?**

Trade credit is the least expensive and most convenient form of short-term financing. Businesses can buy goods today and pay for them sometime in the future.

■ **What is meant by a line of credit?**

A line of credit is an agreement by a bank to lend a specified amount of money to the business at any time, if the money is available.

■ **What's the difference between a secured loan and an unsecured loan?**

An unsecured loan has no collateral backing it. Secured loans have collateral backed by assets such as accounts receivable, inventory, or other property of value.

■ **Is factoring a form of secured loan?**

No, factoring means selling accounts receivable at a discounted rate to a factor (an intermediary that pays cash for those accounts and keeps the funds or charges a fee when it collects them).

■ **What's commercial paper?**

Commercial paper is a corporation's unsecured promissory note maturing in 270 days or less.

LO 18–5 Identify and describe different sources of long-term financing.

■ **What are the major sources of long-term financing?**

Debt financing is the sale of bonds to investors and long-term loans from banks and other financial institutions. Equity financing is obtained through the sale of company stock, from the firm's retained earnings, or from venture capital firms.

■ **What are the two major forms of debt financing?**

Debt financing comes from two sources: selling bonds and borrowing from individuals, banks, and other financial institutions. Bonds can be secured by some form of collateral or can be unsecured. The same is true of loans.

■ **What's leverage, and how do firms use it?**

Leverage is borrowing funds to invest in expansion, major asset purchases, or research and development. Firms measure the risk of borrowing against the potential for higher profits.

KEY TERMS

budget 469
capital budget 470
capital expenditures 473
cash budget 470
cash flow forecast 469
cost of capital 482
debt financing 474
equity financing 474
factoring 477

finance 466
financial control 471
financial management 466
financial managers 466
leverage 481
line of credit 477
operating (or master) budget 470

promissory note 475
risk/return trade-off 480
secured loan 477
term-loan agreement 480
trade credit 475
unsecured loan 477
venture capital 481

CRITICAL THINKING

1. What are the primary sources of short-term funds for new business owners? What are their major sources of long-term funds?

2. Why does a finance manager need to understand accounting information if the firm has a trained accountant on its staff?

3. Why do firms generally prefer to borrow funds to obtain long-term financing rather than issue shares of stock?

PUTTING PRINCIPLES TO WORK

PURPOSE

To identify which types of companies qualify for financing through the Small Business Administration.

EXERCISE

Many small-business owners have a difficult time finding financing to start or expand their business. The Small Business Administration is one potential source of financing for many types of small businesses, but there are also some businesses that do not qualify for SBA loans. Go to sba.gov, search for "7(a) loan program eligibility," and see whether the following businesses are eligible to apply for SBA financing:

1. Growing Like a Weed is a lawn-care business that needs funding to buy additional equipment in order to expand. Does it meet SBA criteria? Why or why not?
2. Glamour Galore is a cosmetic company that pays sales commissions based on a system that depends on salespeople recruiting additional salespeople. It needs funding to build a marketing campaign. Does it meet SBA criteria? Why or why not?
3. Glory Days is a day care center for older adults operated by a local church. It needs funding to remodel the center's kitchen and install an elevator to make the building accessible to those in wheelchairs. Does it meet SBA criteria? Why or why not?
4. Lettuce Entertain U is a company needing funding to remodel an old warehouse to house its latest vegan restaurant. Does it meet SBA criteria? Why or why not?

DEVELOPING CAREER SKILLS

KEY: ● Team ★ Analytic ▲ Communication ◙ Technology

◙ ★ 1. Go to your college's website and see whether its operating budget is online. If not, go to the campus library and see whether the reference librarian has a copy of your college's operating budget for the current year. Try to identify major capital expenditures your college has planned for the future.

★ ▲ ● 2. One of the most difficult concepts to get across to small-business owners is the need to take all the trade credit they can get. For example, the credit terms 2/10, net 30 can save businesses money if they pay their bills in the first 10 days. Work with a group of classmates to build a convincing financial argument for using trade credit.

◙ ★ 3. Go online and check the capitalization required to open a franchise of your choice, like Subway or McDonald's. Does the franchisor offer financial assistance to prospective franchisees? Evaluate the cost of the franchise versus its business potential using the risk/return trade-off discussed in the chapter.

◙ ★ 4. Contact a lending officer at a local bank in your community, or visit the bank's website, to check the bank's policies on providing a business a line of credit. Evaluate the chances that this bank will give a small business this form of short-term loan.

◙ ★ ▲ 5. Factoring accounts receivable is a form of financing used since the days of Babylonian King Hammurabi 4,000 years ago. Today it's still a source of short-term funds used by small businesses. Visit 21stfinancialsolutions.com to get more in-depth information about factoring and be prepared to discuss the pros and cons of factoring to the class.

If you are interested in pursuing a career in finance, here are a few to consider. Find out about the tasks performed, skills needed, pay, and opportunity outlook in these fields in the *Occupational Outlook Handbook (OOH)* at bls.gov.

- **Financial examiner**—ensures compliance with laws governing financial institutions and transactions; reviews balance sheets, evaluates the risk level of loans, and assesses bank management.

- **Tax preparer**—helps individual and small-business clients complete and file their tax returns; assists with tax planning.

- **Financial manager**—produces financial reports, directs investment activities, and develops strategies and plans for the long-term financial goals of the organization.

- **Cost estimator**—collects and analyzes data in order to estimate the time, money, materials, and labor required to manufacture a product, construct a building, or provide a service.

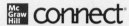

Threadless: Setting the Financial Design

VIDEO CASE

Searching for a T-shirt that fits your personality or sends a message you think needs sending? Unfortunately, your favorite retailer's stock of T-shirts won't always meet your objective. You might figure it's time to give up your search and accept the traditional T-shirt designs available for sale. Well take heart, your dilemma could be easily solved. Design your vision of the perfect T-shirt and then head over to Threadless.com and submit your design. At Threadless, viewers can vote on the design you present, and if your idea is a winner, the shirts will be printed and sold on the Threadless site.

Threadless is an e-commerce website founded in Chicago in 2002 by Jake Nickell. While in college, Nickell entered and won a T-shirt design contest that gave him personal recognition and satisfaction. It also prompted him to start his own online T-shirt competition to give others an equal opportunity to submit their designs. After seeing the quality of submitted designs, Nickell and his friend Jacob DeHart each invested $500 and began to print and sell winning designs. Today, Threadless sells T-shirts as well as hats, tote bags, iPhone cases, shower curtains, and other items all designed by artists who submitted designs to the Threadless website.

The Threadless business model of having individuals create designs and then having viewers vote on their favorites was an early form of crowdsourcing (gathering inputs and information by obtaining the services of a large number of people). By using the crowdsourcing approach to business, the company's working capital situation was always favorable. Nickell posted winning designs and took prepaid orders for the shirts up front. He didn't send a bulk order to a printer until after he received enough orders for a particular run of shirts. The company had no need to hire employees since all the shirts were shipped to Nickell's

apartment where he, DeHart, and his girlfriend packed and shipped them to consumers.

As profits began to grow, the partners decided to start printing shirts before they were sold. To do this, the company needed warehouse space for storage of finished shirts. This was the first fixed cost the company experienced. Fortunately, the firm's landlord owned several storage sites so Threadless could expand as needed. However, any expansion in storage space increases cost and that can drain finances. By the end of 2011, Threadless decided it needed better financial planning, and hired Jason Macatangay as vice president of finance.

Macatangay's experience prior to joining the firm was with a large manufacturing company. Moving to a smaller, online company like Threadless was challenging for him. His primary role at the firm was to monitor finances and make certain the company was operating efficiently without hindering the company's trademark creativity. He was well aware that at a small company it's impossible to implement every idea that surfaces due to a lack of funds. Planning and budgeting are vital at smaller firms like Threadless to ensure that expenses stay within reason as the firm attempts to expand its revenues and market share.

Under Macatangay's guidance, the company eliminated the cost of warehousing inventory by switching to a printing-on-demand process. This new technology allows Threadless to print one shirt at a time rather than having to wait for larger orders required by the old silk-screening process. Under silk screening, the company created a silk-screen and printed large quantities of shirts that needed to be warehoused before being shipped. Today, each order is transferred to a network of suppliers that produce a specific order and ship it directly to the customer. This leads to better customer satisfaction as well as better cash flow for the company. It also permits the company to focus on its online business rather than stocking inventory.

Today, 95 percent of the revenue earned by Threadless comes from its online business. The firm also earns additional revenue from licensing its artwork to other companies. The company has never had to rely on outside investors since its expenses are covered by sales income. Primary costs to the company today are payments to the artists and staff who maintain and market the firm's website. By improving and building online features, the company continues to improve user experiences on the website.

The story of Threadless is a story of innovation and growth. Financial management is a key to keeping these objectives intact and operational. The company has focused on keeping expenses in line since its inception in 2002.

Financial planning helps the firm allocate resources to the most important products the company offers and to add new products with the most market potential. Protecting the business financially without interfering with creativity is a fine line to walk, but one certainly worth walking.

THINKING IT OVER

1. What were the major financial challenges faced by Jason Macatangay when he became vice president of finance at Threadless?

2. Why is cash flow so important to a firm like Threadless?

3. Why hasn't the company ever needed to seek bank financing?

NOTES

1. "How to Become a CFO," *Indeed Career Guide,* indeed. com, February 4, 2020; "Financial Managers," U.S. Bureau of Labor Statistics, bls.gov, accessed March 2020; Laura Palmeiro and Delphine Gibassier, "Your Company's Next Leader on Climate . . . Is the CFO," *Harvard Business Review,* hbr.org, January 28, 2020.

2. Jennifer A. Barnes, "Four Best Practices for Helping Nonprofits Approach Profitability," *Forbes,* forbes.com, January 31, 2020; Nancy Master, "A Nonprofit's Success Story to Inspire You," *Sage Intacct,* sageintacct.com, February 5, 2020; Jeff Thomson, "Secrets of the Startup CFO: How to Be a High-Growth Company's First Finance Leader," *Forbes,* forbes.com, January 24, 2020.

3. Mark Maurer, "Company Finance Chiefs Fret over Geopolitical, Digital Risks," *The Wall Street Journal,* January 2, 2020; Richard F. Fischer, "Challenges Facing CFOs in 2020," *Philadelphia Business Journal,* bizjournals.com, February 1, 2020; "Middle Market CFOs Pursue Aggressive Agendas in 2020," *CFO,* cfo.com, accessed March 2020.

4. "CFOs' Biggest Challenges in 2020," Paycor, paycor.com, February 11, 2020; Kimberly Amadeo, "2008 Financial Crisis: The Causes and Costs of the Worst Crisis since the Great Depression," *The Balance,* thebalance.com, January 22, 2020.

5. Matt Danielsson, "What Internal Auditors Do—and How Much They Make," *Investopedia,* investopedia.com, January 28, 2020; Janelle Maregmen, "What Are the Top Risk Areas Internal Audits Should be Targeting in 2020?," AuditBoard, auditboard.com, January 29, 2020; David Lehmann and Michael Thor, "The Next Generation of Internal Audit," *CPA Journal,* cpajournal.com, February 2020.

6. "Best Business Plan Software for Financial Forecasting," *Business News Daily,* businessnewsdaily.com, February 19, 2020; "Budgeting and Forecasting Software Market Forecast 2020–2025, Latest Trends and Opportunities," *aeresearch,* aeresearch.com, January 22, 2020; Meredith Wood, "10 Sales Forecasting Methods for Your Business," *Fundera,* fundera.com, January 31, 2020.

7. Peter Goodman, "China's Coronavirus Has Revived Global Economic Fears," *The New York Times,* January 27,

2020; Ben Winck, "China May Cut 2020 Growth Forecast amid Coronavirus Fallout," *Markets Insider,* markets. businessinsider.com, February 3, 2020; Arjun Kharpal, "Apple Shares Slide after Coronavirus Guidance Warning as Its Global Suppliers Are Hammered," *CNBC,* cnbc. com, February 18, 2020; Tripp Mickle, "Apple to Fall Short of Projected Revenue Due to Coronavirus," *The Wall Street Journal,* February 17, 2020; Richard Waters, Patrick McGee, and Tim Bradshaw, "Coronavirus Forces Apple to Warn over iPhone Sales," *Financial Times,* February 17, 2020.

8. Rosemary Carlson, "How to Calculate the Present Value of a Single Amount," *The Balance Small Business,* thebalancesmb.com, February 6, 2020; James Chen, "Time Value of Money," *Investopedia,* investopedia.com, January 24, 2020.

9. Geri Stengal, "Closing the Small Business Financing Gap: The ABCs of Merchant Cash Advance," *Forbes,* forbes.com, January 29, 2020.

10. Julia Kagan, "Digital Wallet," *Investopedia,* investopedia. com, February 13, 2020; "Proximity Mobile Payment Transaction Value in the United States from 2018–2023," Statista, statista.com, accessed March 2020; Geoffrey Morrison, "A Case for Paying with Your Phone," *The New York Times,* February 5, 2020.

11. Aaron Klein, "Is Cash Still King? Reviewing the Rise of Mobile Payments," Brookings Institution, brookings.edu, January 30, 2020; Hayden Field, "How to Find the Right Payment System," *Entrepreneur,* entrepreneur.com, July 29, 2019; "'Dine and Dash' Redefined with New Clover Scan to Pay Feature," *Yahoo! Finance,* finance.yahoo.com, February 17, 2020.

12. Justin Pritchard, "How to Handle Lending and Borrowing Money with Family," *The Balance,* thebalance.com, February 18, 2020; Joyce Walsack, "Choosing the Best Lending Strategy for Your Business," U.S. Chamber of Commerce, uschamber.com, January 23, 2020.

13. National Federation of Independent Business, nfib.com, accessed March 2020.

14. Braden McCarthy, "Why Bank Lending to Small Business Isn't Recovering," *Fundera,* fundera.com, January 28, 2020; "Small Business Lending and the Great Recession," U.S.

Consumer Financial Protection Bureau, consumerfinance. gov, accessed March 2020.

15. Christina Majaski, "Loan vs. Line of Credit: What's the Difference?," *Investopedia,* investopedia.com, February 18, 2020.

16. Meredith Wood, "Factoring Receivables: Everything You Need to Know," *Fundera,* fundera.com, February 12, 2020; Geri Stengel, "Closing the Small Business Financing Gap: Invoice Factoring Basics," *Forbes,* forbes. com, January 20, 2020.

17. Braydon McCarthy, "Why Bank Lending to Small Business Isn't Recovering," *Fundera,* fundera.com, January 28, 2020; Rohit Arora, "3 Things to Do before Applying for a Small Business Loan in 2020," *Forbes,* forbes.com, February 17, 2020.

18. Alexandra White, "5 Benefits of Small Business Credit Cards," *CNBC,* cnbc.com, February 10, 2020; "The Basics of Using Credit Cards to Fund Your New Business," *Entrepreneur,* accessed March 2020; Sally French, "The Best Way to Use a Credit Card? Use It Like Cash," *The New York Times,* February 11, 2020.

19. "Credit Card Reform," National Small Business Association, nsba.biz, accessed March 2020.

20. Yvette Glover, "When Is Using Credit Cards to Fund Your Business Right?," *Fit Small Business,* fitsmallbusiness.com, February 3, 2020; Levi King, "How I Built $500 of Credit into $500,000," *Entrepreneur,* entrepreneur.com, March 24, 2019; Beverly Harzog, "Best Business Credit Cards," *U.S. News & World Report,* creditcards.usnews. com, February 13, 2020; Jared Hecht, "The 4 Things That Help Small Businesses Get More Financing," *Forbes,* forbes.com, January 31, 2020.

21. Brittany Galla, "Christina Stembel's Company Farmgirl Flowers Made $30M Last Year—Here's Her Success Secrets," *Parade,* parade.com, February 18, 2020; Emily McCormick, "Farmgirl Flowers Became a Multi-Million Dollar E-Commerce Startup without a Dime of Venture Capital," *Yahoo! Finance,* finance.yahoo.com, February 14, 2020.

22. "Merck Investing for Life," merck.com, accessed March 2020.

23. Sally Pipes, "Pelosi's Drug Price Controls Are Dangerous— but So Are Trump's," *Forbes,* forbes.com, January 29, 2020; "How Does Government Regulation Impact the Drug Sector?," *Investopedia,* investopedia.com, February 1, 2020.

24. Rochelle Olson, "Vikings, Charities, Lawmakers, Eye Growing Gambling Revenue Earmarked for U.S. Bank Stadium Debt," *Star Tribune,* startribune.com, February 14, 2020; Marq Burnett, "John Ingram's Soccer Team, MLS Blast Cooper over Stadium Delays," *Nashville Business Journal,* bizjournals.com, January 30, 2020; Michael McCann, "Nashville S.C., MLS's Legal and Political Battle Intensifies over Stadium Dispute with Mayor," *Sports Illustrated,* si.com, February 11, 2020.

25. Alex Gold, "Telltale Signs That You Shouldn't Be Raising Venture Capital," *Entrepreneur,* entrepreneur.com, January 24, 2020.

26. Nathan Heller, "Is Venture Capital Worth the Risk?," *The New Yorker,* newyorker.com, January 20, 2020.

27. Anne Spraders, "Private Equity Firms Are Sitting on $1.5 Trillion in Unspent Cash, and Looking to Raise More," *Fortune,* fortune.com, January 25, 2020.

28. Lawrence C. Strauss, "Exxon Has Raised Its Dividend for 37 Straight Years. Will That End?," *Barron's,* February 6, 2020; Rekha Khandelwal, "What Makes ExxonMobil Attractive," *Yahoo! Finance,* finance.yahoo.com, February 5, 2020.

29. Julia-Ambra Verlaine, "Energy Companies Face Looming Debt Burden," *The Wall Street Journal,* February 19, 2020; Joe Rennison, "Debt-Laden Energy Companies Are Taking Whatever Cash They Can Get," *Financial Times,* January 27, 2020; Robert Rapier, "Oil Bankruptcies Are Piling Up," *Forbes,* forbes.com, January 27, 2020; Laura Hurst, "BP Bucks Oil Industry Gloom," *Yahoo! Finance,* finance.yahoo.com, February 4, 2020.

30. Annie Lowery, "The Great Affordability Crisis Breaking America," *The Atlantic,* theatlantic.com, February 6, 2020; Lee DeVito, "The Recession Never Ended in These Michigan Communities," *Detroit Metro Times,* metrotimes. com, February 20, 2020.

31. Jessica Dickler, "Is Co-Living the New Craigslist?," *CNBC,* cnbc.com, February 2, 2020; Hillary Hoffower, "How the American Millennial Is Overcoming Debt, the Dollar, and the Economy They Were Handed," *Business Insider,* businessinsider.com, accessed March 2020; Jeanna Smialek, "How Millennials Could Make the Fed's Job Harder," *The New York Times,* February 17, 2020; Christopher Ingraham, "Millennials' Share of Housing Market Is Small and Shrinking," *The Washington Post,* January 26, 2020.

32. Jeanna Smialek and Emily Flitter, "The Fed Wants to Loosen Rules around Big Banks and Venture Capital," *The New York Times,* January 30, 2020; William Sprouse, "Fed Proposes Paring Back Volcker Rule," *CFO,* cfo.com, January 31, 2020; Greg Iacurci, "New Rules Are Gutting Consumer Watchdog Group from the Inside, Legal Experts Say," *CNBC,* cnbc.com, January 28, 2020.

19

Using Securities Markets for Financing and Investing Opportunities

LEARNING OBJECTIVES *After you have read and studied this chapter, you should be able to*

LO 19–1 Describe the roles of securities markets and of investment bankers.

LO 19–2 Identify the stock exchanges where securities are traded.

LO 19–3 Compare the advantages and disadvantages of equity financing by issuing stock, and detail the differences between common and preferred stock.

LO 19–4 Compare the advantages and disadvantages of obtaining debt financing by issuing bonds, and identify the classes and features of bonds.

LO 19–5 Explain how to invest in securities markets and set investment objectives such as long-term growth, income, cash, and protection from inflation.

LO 19–6 Analyze the opportunities stocks offer as investments.

LO 19–7 Analyze the opportunities bonds offer as investments.

LO 19–8 Explain the investment opportunities in mutual funds and exchange-traded funds (ETFs).

LO 19–9 Describe how indicators like the Dow Jones Industrial Average affect the market.

Warren Buffett, CEO of Berkshire Hathaway

Known as the "Oracle of Omaha," Warren Buffett is one of the most successful investors in world history. His company Berkshire Hathaway owns major brands like Geico, Fruit of the Loom, Duracell, and many more while also holding controlling interests in a number of others. Although Buffett has amassed an enormous fortune over the course of his legendary career, he lives modestly in the same home he purchased in the 1950s and has donated $46 billion to charity since 2000.

Buffett had a fascination with numbers and money when he was growing up in Omaha, Nebraska. The son of a stockbroker who also served in the U.S. Congress, he read his first books about the stock market at age 8 and purchased his first stock (Cities Service Preferred) at age 11. Buffett also began managing money early in his life, filing his first tax return at age 13, which included a $35 deduction for his bicycle. At 16 he enrolled at the University of Pennsylvania to study business before moving back to his home state and graduating from the University of Nebraska–Lincoln with a degree in business. He went on to earn a master's degree in economics from Columbia University where he studied under Benjamin Graham, a famed economist and author of the best-selling book *The Intelligent Investor.* The professor became Buffett's mentor and would have a profound effect on his life.

After working at Graham's investment partnership for a few years, Buffett moved back to Omaha and formed his own investment firm, Buffett Partnership Ltd. It was from Graham's book and tutelage that Buffett formed his rules for investing: the first rule is not to lose, and the second is not to forget the first rule. A turning point in his career came when he began investing heavily in a textile firm called Berkshire Hathaway. In just a few years, he had taken complete control of the company and began shifting its focus away from textiles and toward investments in media like *The Washington Post,* insurance firms like Geico, and other holdings. Despite achieving success with Buffett Partnership, he decided to dissolve the firm and direct his investing attention to Berkshire Hathaway.

This turned out to be the right decision as the value of the company's investments grew enormously over the decades, creating sizable fortunes for Buffett as well as the lucky people who purchased shares in the company. In fact, a $1,000 investment in Berkshire in 1965 would be worth $26.4 million today. Buffett guided Berkshire to its enormous success by investing in what he considered undervalued companies that had strong management. He injected money into struggling but cash-generating businesses that he believed could make strong financial comebacks. The money earned from these ventures allowed Buffett to buy large stakes in higher-quality brands such as Coca-Cola. Berkshire now controls 10 percent of the soft drink giant, making it among the firm's core holdings.

In recent years, Buffett has gone beyond investing small stakes in up-and-coming companies. Instead, he focuses on purchasing promising brands outright and adding them to the Berkshire empire. Geico is perhaps the crown jewel in its large portfolio of assets, with the company currently the second-largest provider of automobile insurance in the United States. Other major firms Berkshire has bought include battery maker Duracell, the grocery chain Kroger, and Dairy Queen. The company also holds stakes in many tech ventures and is the single largest shareholder in Apple. As of this writing, the company is sitting on over $120 billion in cash it can use for new purchases or investments.

With a net worth of more than $80 billion, Buffett has been one of the richest people on the planet for many years and plans to use his fortune to invest in good causes throughout the world. That's why Buffett has pledged to give away 99 percent of his fortune on his passing to philanthropic ventures, primarily to the Bill & Melinda Gates Foundation. In 2010, he co-founded the Giving Pledge whereby billionaires pledge to give away the majority of their wealth to charity upon their deaths. So far more than 200 billionaires have signed the Giving Pledge. Almost 90 years old, Buffett has entered what he calls the "urgent zone." He acknowledges he can't remain at Berkshire forever, but he has no plans to leave anytime soon. He also made a point to assure shareholders that "The company is 100% prepared for his departure." Until then, Buffett will remain on the hunt for quality businesses that fit his three essential criteria: they must earn good returns on capital, they must be run by able and honest managers, and they must be available at a sensible price.

To fully understand finance, you need to know the basics of securities markets, how they help businesses gain needed funding, and how investors can build their financial future like Warren Buffett. In this chapter you'll learn about how securities markets achieve both objectives.

Sources: Hillary Hoffower and Taylor Nicole Rogers, "How Frugal Billionaire Warren Buffett Spends $87.3 Billion Net Worth," *Business Insider,* businessinsider.com, July 1, 2019; Adam Sessell, "Valuation: How Warren Buffett Built Berkshire Hathaway—and What Might Happen When He Leaves," *Fortune,* February 21, 2020; "Berkshire Hathaway Is the World's Second Most Profitable Firm," *The Economist,* February 26, 2020; Taylor Locke, "The Advice from Warren Buffett That Inspired Bill and Melinda Gates," *CNBC,* cnbc.com, February 10, 2020; Bernhard Warner, "Warren Buffett Lays Out a Succession Plan for His Berkshire Shares," *Fortune,* February 22, 2020.

Let's talk business!
bit.ly/LetsTalkBusiness19

Frederic J. Brown/AFP/Getty Images

IF YOU ARE AN INVESTOR, IT'S LIKELY you would be thrilled if a company you own declares a stock split. Unfortunately, companies are never required to split their stock. In fact, this company has never declared a stock split, even when its stock price reached $312,000 for one share. Name that company. (Find the answer in the chapter.)

LO 19–1 Describe the roles of securities markets and of investment bankers.

The Function of Securities Markets

Securities markets—financial marketplaces for stocks, bonds, and other investments—serve two major functions. First, they assist businesses in finding long-term funding to finance capital needs, such as expanding operations, developing new products, or buying major goods and services. Second, they provide private investors a place to buy and sell securities (investments), such as stocks and bonds, that can help them build their financial future. In this chapter, we look at securities markets first from the perspective of funding for businesses and second as markets for private investors to buy and trade investments.

Securities markets are divided into primary and secondary markets. *Primary markets* handle the sale of *new* securities. This is an important point to understand. Corporations make money on the sale of their securities (stock) only once—when they sell it on the primary market.[1] The first public offering of a corporation's stock is called an **initial public offering (IPO)**. After that, the *secondary market* handles the trading of these securities between investors, with the proceeds of the sale going to the investor selling the stock, not to the corporation whose stock is sold. For example, imagine your restaurant, Harvest Gold, has grown into a chain and your products are available in many retail stores throughout the country. You want to raise additional funds to expand further. If you offer 1 million shares of stock in your company at $10 a share, you can raise $10 million at this initial offering. However, after the initial sale, if Shareholder Jones decides to sell 100 shares of her Harvest Gold stock to Investor Smith, Harvest Gold collects nothing from that transaction. Smith buys the stock from Jones, not from Harvest Gold. It is possible, however, for companies like Harvest Gold to offer additional shares of stock for sale to raise additional capital.

As mentioned in Chapter 18, we can't overemphasize the importance of long-term funding to businesses. Given a choice, businesses normally prefer to meet their long-term financial needs by using retained earnings or borrowing funds either from a lending institution (bank,

initial public offering (IPO)
The first public offering of a corporation's stock.

Casimiro/Alamy Stock Photo

pension fund, insurance company) or corporate bond issue. However, if long-term funds are not available from retained earnings or lenders, a company may be able to raise capital by issuing corporate stock. (Recall from Chapter 18 that selling stock in the corporation is a form of *equity financing* and issuing corporate bonds is a form of *debt financing.*) Visa's $18 billion IPO in 2008 was the largest U.S. IPO of the past 25 years until Alibaba's $21 billion IPO in 2014. These sources of equity and bond financing are not available to all companies, especially small businesses.

Let's imagine you need further long-term financing to *expand* operations at Harvest Gold. Your chief financial officer (CFO) says the company lacks sufficient retained earnings and she doesn't think it can secure the needed funds from a lending institution. She suggests that you offer shares of stock or issue corporate bonds to private investors to secure the funding. She warns, however, that issuing shares of stock or corporate bonds is not simple or automatic. To get approval for stock or bond issues you must make extensive financial disclosures and undergo detailed scrutiny by the U.S. Securities and Exchange Commission (SEC). Because of these requirements, your CFO recommends that the company turn to an investment banker for assistance. Let's see why.

The Role of Investment Bankers

Investment bankers are specialists who assist in the issue and sale of new securities. These large financial firms can help companies like Harvest Gold prepare the extensive financial analyses necessary to gain SEC approval for bond or stock issues. Investment bankers can also *underwrite* new issues of stocks or bonds.[2] That is, the investment banking firm buys the entire stock or bond issue at an agreed-on discount, which can be quite sizable, and then sells the issue to private or institutional investors at full price.

Institutional investors are large organizations—such as pension funds, mutual funds, and insurance companies—that invest their own funds or the funds of others. Because of their vast buying power, institutional investors are a powerful force in securities markets.

Before we look at stocks and bonds as long-term financing and investment opportunities in more depth, let's look at stock exchanges—the places where stocks and bonds are traded—and who regulates the industry.

LO 19–2   Identify the stock exchanges where securities are traded.

Stock Exchanges

As the name implies, a **stock exchange** is an organization whose members can buy and sell (exchange) securities on behalf of companies and individual investors. The New York Stock Exchange (NYSE) was founded in 1792 and was then primarily a floor-based exchange, which means trades physically took place on the floor of the stock exchange. Things changed in 2005 when the NYSE merged with Archipelago, a securities trading company that specialized in electronic trades. Two years later, it merged with Europe's Euronext exchange, and became the NYSE Euronext. In 2013, the Intercontinental Exchange (ICE) located in Atlanta purchased the NYSE Euronext for $8.2 billion.

Today, the once active floor of the NYSE is largely symbolic. Most trading takes place on computers that can transact thousands of stock trades within seconds. While the crowd on the floor may seem sparse, it isn't deserted. In 2017, the NYSE changed its rules and allowed trading of all U.S. stocks regardless of the exchange they are listed with on its historic floor. Prior to the change, only securities listed on the NYSE could be traded. Still, the bulk of the company's revenue comes from selling complex financial contracts (such as derivatives) and market data services to companies like Yahoo! and Google that offer stock quotes as a service on their websites.[3]

Not all securities are traded on registered stock exchanges. The **over-the-counter (OTC) market** provides companies and investors with a means to trade stocks not listed on the large securities exchanges. The OTC market is a network of several thousand brokers who

investment bankers
Specialists who assist in the issue and sale of new securities.

institutional investors
Large organizations—such as pension funds, mutual funds, and insurance companies—that invest their own funds or the funds of others.

stock exchange
An organization whose members can buy and sell (exchange) securities for companies and investors.

over-the-counter (OTC) market
Exchange that provides a means to trade stocks not listed on the national exchanges.

Ted Thai/The Life Picture Collection/Getty Images

Spencer Platt/Getty Images

The NYSE was once the largest floor-based exchange in the world. For years traders packed the floor to strike deals directly with other brokers. Today, stocks are bought and sold primarily on electronic networks. The photo on the right of the exchange floor today seems deserted compared to the old days.

NASDAQ

A nationwide electronic system that communicates over-the-counter trades to brokers.

maintain contact with one another and buy and sell securities through a nationwide electronic system. Trading is conducted between two parties directly, instead of through an exchange like the NYSE.

The **NASDAQ** (originally known as the National Association of Securities Dealers Automated Quotations) was the world's first electronic stock market. It evolved from the OTC market but is no longer part of it. The NASDAQ is an electronic-based network that links dealers so they can buy and sell securities electronically rather than in person. It is the largest U.S. electronic stock trading market and has more trading volume than any electronic exchange in the world. The NASDAQ originally dealt mostly with smaller firms, but today well-known companies such as Facebook, Microsoft, Intel, Google, and Starbucks trade their stock on the network.

Adding a company to an exchange is a highly competitive undertaking, and the battle between the stock exchanges for a stock listing is often fierce. The competition has intensified with the entry of new exchanges such as the Bats Global Markets (now owned by Cboe Global Markets) and IEX exchanges. You can find the requirements for registering (listing) stocks on the NYSE and NASDAQ on their websites at nyse.com and nasdaq.com. If a company fails to meet the listing requirements of an exchange, the stock can be delisted from the exchange.[4]

Securities Regulations and the Securities and Exchange Commission

Securities and Exchange Commission (SEC)

Federal agency that has responsibility for regulating the various exchanges.

The **Securities and Exchange Commission (SEC)** is the federal agency responsible for regulating the various stock exchanges. The Securities Act of 1933 helps protect investors by requiring full disclosure of financial information by firms selling bonds or stock. The U.S. Congress passed this legislation to deal with the free-for-all atmosphere that existed in the securities markets during the 1920s and the early 1930s that helped cause the Great Depression. The Securities and Exchange Act of 1934 created the SEC.

Companies trading on the national exchanges must register with the SEC and provide it with annual updates. The 1934 act also established specific guidelines that companies must follow when issuing financial securities, such as stocks or bonds. For example, before issuing either stocks or bonds for sale to the public, a company must file a detailed registration statement with the SEC that includes extensive economic and financial information. The condensed version of that registration document—called a **prospectus**—must be sent to prospective investors.

prospectus

A condensed version of economic and financial information that a company must file with the SEC before issuing stock; the prospectus must be sent to prospective investors.

The 1934 act also established guidelines to prevent insiders within the company from taking advantage of privileged information they may have. *Insider trading* is using knowledge or information that individuals gain through their position that allows them to benefit unfairly from fluctuations in security prices. The key words here are *benefit unfairly*. Insiders within a firm are permitted to buy and sell stock in the company they work for, so long as they do not take unfair advantage of information unknown to the public.

Insider trading involves buying or selling a stock on the basis of company information not available to the investing public. These hypothetical examples will give you an idea of what's legal and what's illegal. The answers are at the bottom of the figure.

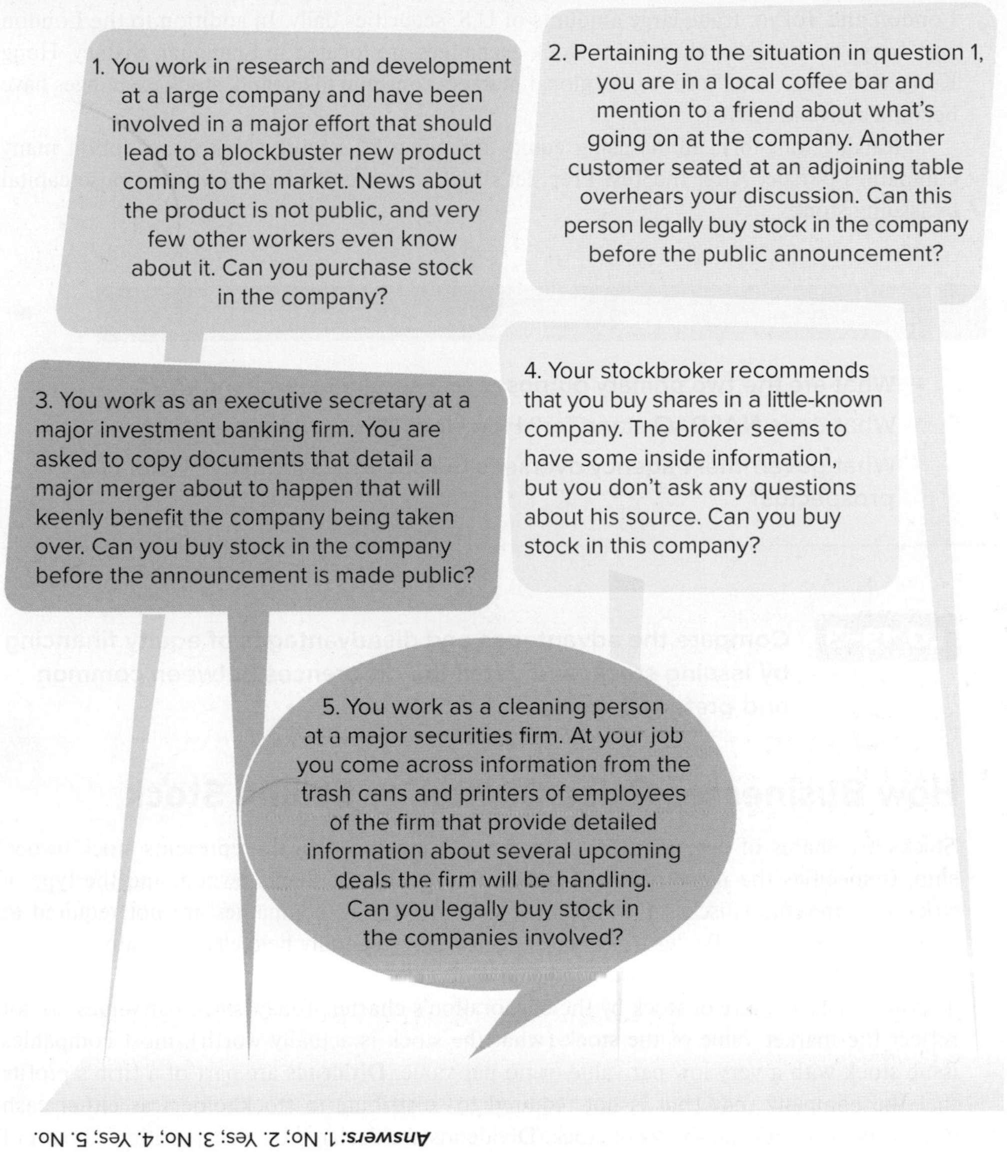

FIGURE 19.1 IS IT INSIDER TRADING OR NOT?

1. You work in research and development at a large company and have been involved in a major effort that should lead to a blockbuster new product coming to the market. News about the product is not public, and very few other workers even know about it. Can you purchase stock in the company?

2. Pertaining to the situation in question 1, you are in a local coffee bar and mention to a friend about what's going on at the company. Another customer seated at an adjoining table overhears your discussion. Can this person legally buy stock in the company before the public announcement?

3. You work as an executive secretary at a major investment banking firm. You are asked to copy documents that detail a major merger about to happen that will keenly benefit the company being taken over. Can you buy stock in the company before the announcement is made public?

4. Your stockbroker recommends that you buy shares in a little-known company. The broker seems to have some inside information, but you don't ask any questions about his source. Can you buy stock in this company?

5. You work as a cleaning person at a major securities firm. At your job you come across information from the trash cans and printers of employees of the firm that provide detailed information about several upcoming deals the firm will be handling. Can you legally buy stock in the companies involved?

Answers: 1. No; 2. Yes; 3. No; 4. No; 5. No.

Originally, the SEC defined the term *insider* rather narrowly as covering a company's directors and employees and their relatives. Today the term has been broadened to include just about anyone with securities information not available to the general public.[5] Let's say the CFO of Harvest Gold tells her next-door neighbor she is finalizing paperwork to sell the company to a large corporation, and the neighbor buys the stock based on this information. A court may well consider the purchase an insider trade. Penalties for insider trading can include hefty fines and imprisonment. SAC Capital portfolio manager Mathew Martoma was convicted in 2014 in the largest insider trading scheme ever. He was sentenced to nine years in prison and the company paid $1.8 billion in fines.[6] Look at Figure 19.1 and test your skill in identifying insider trading.

Foreign Stock Exchanges

Thanks to expanded communications and the relaxation of many legal barriers, investors can buy securities from companies almost anywhere in the world. If you uncover a foreign company you feel has great potential for growth, you can purchase shares of its stock with little difficulty from U.S. brokers who have access to foreign stock exchanges. Foreign investors can also invest in U.S. securities, and large foreign stock exchanges, like those in London and Tokyo, trade large amounts of U.S. securities daily. In addition to the London and Tokyo exchanges, other major stock exchanges are located in Shanghai, Sydney, Hong Kong, São Paolo, and Toronto. As global markets continue to expand, stock exchanges have become active in Africa.[7]

Raising long-term funds using equity financing by issuing stock is an option many companies pursue. After the Test Prep, let's look in more depth at how firms raise capital by issuing stock.

?TESTPREP

- What are the two primary purposes of a securities exchange?
- What does NASDAQ stand for? How does this exchange work?
- What government agency oversees the securities industry? What is a prospectus?

LO 19–3 Compare the advantages and disadvantages of equity financing by issuing stock, and detail the differences between common and preferred stock.

How Businesses Raise Capital by Selling Stock

stocks

Shares of ownership in a company.

stock certificate

Evidence of stock ownership that specifies the name of the company, the number of shares it represents, and the type of stock being issued.

dividends

Part of a firm's profits that the firm may distribute to stockholders as either cash payments or additional shares of stock.

Stocks are shares of ownership in a company. A **stock certificate** represents stock ownership. It specifies the name of the company, the number of shares owned, and the type of stock it represents (discussed in the next section). Today, companies are not required to issue paper stock certificates to owners since stock is generally held electronically.

Stock certificates sometimes indicate a stock's *par value*, which is a dollar amount assigned to each share of stock by the corporation's charter. Today, since par values do not reflect the market value of the stock (what the stock is actually worth), most companies issue stock with a very low par value or no par value. **Dividends** are part of a firm's profits that the company may (but is not required to) distribute to stockholders as either cash payments or additional shares of stock. Dividends are declared by a corporation's board of directors and are generally paid quarterly.[8]

Advantages and Disadvantages of Issuing Stock

Some advantages to a firm of issuing stock include:

- As owners of the business, stockholders never have to be repaid their investment.
- There's no legal obligation to pay dividends to stockholders; therefore, the firm can reinvest income (retained earnings) to finance future needs.
- Selling stock can improve the condition of a firm's balance sheet since issuing stock creates no debt. (A corporation may also buy back its stock to improve its balance sheet and stock price and make the company appear stronger financially.)[9]

Disadvantages of issuing stock include:

- As owners, stockholders (usually only holders of common stock) have the right to vote for the company's board of directors. (Typically, one vote is granted for each share of stock.) Issuing new shares of stock can thus alter the control of the firm.

- Dividends are paid from profit after taxes and are not tax-deductible.
- The need to keep stockholders happy can affect managers' decisions.

Companies can issue two classes of stock: common and preferred. Let's see how these two forms of equity financing differ.

Issuing Shares of Common Stock

Common stock is the most basic form of ownership in a firm. In fact, if a company issues only one type of stock, by law it must be common stock. Holders of common stock have the right to (1) elect members of the compa-

Johannes Eisele/AFP/Getty Images

ny's board of directors and vote on important issues affecting the company and (2) share in the firm's profits through dividends, if approved by the firm's board of directors. Having voting rights in a corporation allows common stockholders to influence corporate policy because the board members they elect choose the firm's top management and make major policy decisions. Common stockholders also have a *preemptive right* to purchase new shares of common stock before anyone else. This allows common stockholders to maintain their proportional share of ownership in the company.[10]

Issuing Shares of Preferred Stock

Owners of **preferred stock** are given preference in the payment of company dividends and must be paid their dividends in full before any common stock dividends can be distributed (hence the term *preferred*). They also have a prior claim on company assets if the firm is forced out of business and its assets sold, but preferred stockholders have no voting rights in the company.[11]

Preferred stock may be issued with a par value that becomes the base for a fixed dividend the firm is willing to pay.[12] For example, if a preferred stock's par value is $50 a share and its dividend rate is 4 percent, the dividend is $2 a share. An owner of 100 preferred shares receives a fixed yearly dividend of $200 if dividends are declared by the board of directors.

Preferred stock can have other special features that common stock doesn't have. For example it can be *callable,* which means preferred stockholders could be required to sell their shares back to the corporation. Preferred stock can also be converted to shares of common stock (but not the other way around), and it can be *cumulative.* That is, if one or more dividends are not paid when promised, they accumulate and the corporation must pay them in full at a later date before it can distribute any common stock dividends.

Companies often prefer to raise capital by debt financing. One debt funding option frequently used by larger firms is issuing corporate bonds. Let's look at what's involved with issuing corporate bonds and how they differ from issuing stock.

When Pinterest issued its initial public offering (IPO), the company raised approximately $1.4 billion from the sale. Can you see why issuing stock can be an appealing option for financing a company's growth?

common stock
The most basic form of ownership in a firm; it confers voting rights and the right to share in the firm's profits through dividends, if offered by the firm's board of directors.

preferred stock
Stock that gives its owners preference in the payment of dividends and an earlier claim on assets than common stockholders if the company is forced out of business and its assets sold.

?TESTPREP

- Name at least two advantages and two disadvantages of a company's issuing stock as a form of equity financing.
- What are the major differences between common stock and preferred stock?

LO 19–4   Compare the advantages and disadvantages of obtaining debt financing by issuing bonds, and identify the classes and features of bonds.

How Businesses Raise Capital by Issuing Bonds

bond

A corporate certificate indicating that a person has lent money to a firm.

A **bond** is a corporate certificate indicating that an investor has lent money to a firm (or a government). An organization that issues bonds has a legal obligation to make regular interest payments to investors and to repay the entire bond principal amount at a prescribed time. Let's further explore the language of bonds so you understand exactly how they work.

Learning the Language of Bonds

maturity date

The exact date the issuer of a bond must pay the principal to the bondholder.

interest

The payment the issuer of the bond makes to the bondholders for use of the borrowed money.

Corporate bonds are usually issued in units of $1,000 (government bonds can be in much larger amounts). The *principal* is the face value (dollar value) of a bond, which the issuing company is legally bound to repay in full to the bondholder on the bond's **maturity date**. **Interest** is the payment the bond issuer makes to the bondholders to compensate them for the use of their money. If Harvest Gold issues a $1,000 bond with an interest rate of 5 percent and a maturity date of 2028, it is agreeing to pay the bondholder a total of $50 interest each year until a specified date in 2028, when it must repay the full $1,000. Maturity dates can vary considerably. Firms such as Disney, IBM, and Coca-Cola have issued so-called century bonds with 100-year maturity dates.[13]

Bond interest is sometimes called the *coupon rate,* a term that dates back to when bonds were issued as *bearer* bonds. The holder, or bearer, was considered the bond's owner. Back then, the company issuing the bond kept no record of changes in ownership. Bond interest was paid to whoever clipped coupons attached to the bond and sent them to the issuing company for payment. Today, bonds are registered to specific owners and changes in ownership are recorded electronically.

The interest rate paid by U.S. government bonds influences the bond interest rate businesses must pay. U.S. government bonds are considered safe investments, so they can pay lower interest. Figure 19.2 describes several types of government bonds that compete with

FIGURE 19.2 TYPES OF GOVERNMENT SECURITIES THAT COMPETE WITH CORPORATE BONDS

U.S. government bond	Issued by the federal government; considered the safest type of bond investment
Treasury bill (T-bill)	Matures in less than a year; issued with a minimum denomination of $1,000
Treasury note	Matures in 10 years or less; sold in denominations of $1,000 up to $1,000,000
Treasury bond	Matures in 25 years or more; sold in denominations of $1,000 up to $1,000,000
Municipal bond	Issued by states, cities, counties, and other state and local government agencies; usually exempt from federal taxes
Yankee bond	Issued by a foreign government; payable in U.S. dollars

U.S. corporate bonds in securities markets. Bond interest rates also vary according to the state of the economy, the reputation of the issuing company, and the interest rate for bonds of similar companies. Though bond interest is quoted for an entire year, it is usually paid in two installments, and the rate generally cannot be changed.

Bond rating organizations assess the creditworthiness of a corporation's bond issues. Independent rating firms such as Standard & Poor's, Moody's Investors Service, and Fitch Ratings rate bonds according to their degree of risk.[14] Bonds can range from the highest quality to junk bonds (which we discuss later in this chapter). Figure 19.3 gives an example of the range of bond ratings issued by the ratings agencies.

Advantages and Disadvantages of Issuing Bonds

Bonds offer long-term financing advantages to an organization:

- Bondholders are creditors of the firm, not owners. They seldom vote on corporate matters; thus, management maintains control over the firm's operations.
- Bond interest is a business expense and tax-deductible to the firm (see Chapter 17).
- Bonds are a temporary source of funding. They're eventually repaid and the debt obligation is eliminated.
- Bonds can be repaid before the maturity date if they are *callable.* Bonds can also be converted to common stock. (We discuss both features below.)

Bonds also have financing drawbacks:

- Bonds increase debt (long-term liabilities) and may adversely affect the market's perception of the firm.
- Paying interest on bonds is a legal obligation. If interest is not paid, bondholders can take legal action to force payment.
- The face value of the bond must be repaid on the maturity date. Without careful planning, this obligation can cause cash flow problems when the repayment comes due.

Different Classes of Bonds

Corporations can issue two different classes of corporate bonds. *Unsecured bonds,* usually called **debenture bonds**, are not backed by any specific collateral (such as land or equipment). Only firms with excellent reputations and credit ratings can issue debenture bonds, due to the lack of security they provide investors. *Secured bonds,* sometimes called mortgage bonds, are backed by collateral such as land or buildings that is pledged to bondholders if interest or principal isn't paid when promised. A corporate bond issuer can choose to include different bond features. Let's look briefly at some special features.

debenture bonds
Bonds that are unsecured (i.e., not backed by any collateral such as equipment).

Bond Rating Agencies			
Moody's	**Standard & Poor's**	**Fitch Ratings**	**Descriptions**
Aaa	AAA	AAA	Highest quality (lowest default risk)
Aa	AA	AA	High quality
A	A	A	Upper medium grade
Baa	BBB	BBB	Medium grade
Ba	BB	BB	Lower medium grade
B	B	B	Speculative
Caa	CCC, CC	CCC	Poor (high default risk)
Ca	C	DDD	Highly speculative
C	D	D	Lowest grade

FIGURE 19.3 BOND RATINGS: MOODY'S INVESTORS SERVICE, STANDARD & POOR'S INVESTOR SERVICE, AND FITCH RATINGS

Special Bond Features

By now you should understand that bonds are issued with an interest rate, are unsecured or secured by some type of collateral, and must be repaid at their maturity date. This repayment requirement often leads companies (or governments) to establish a reserve account called a **sinking fund**. Its primary purpose is to ensure that enough money will be available to repay bondholders on the bond's maturity date. Firms issuing sinking-fund bonds periodically *retire* (set aside) some part of the principal they owe prior to maturity so that enough funds will accumulate by the maturity date to pay off the bond. Sinking funds are generally attractive to both issuing firms and investors for several reasons:

sinking fund
A reserve account in which the issuer of a bond periodically retires some part of the bond principal prior to maturity so that enough capital will be accumulated by the maturity date to pay off the bond.

- They provide for an orderly retirement (repayment) of a bond issue.
- They reduce the risk the bond will not be repaid.
- They support the market price of the bond because they reduce the risk the bond will not be repaid.

A *callable bond* permits the bond issuer to pay off the bond's principal before its maturity date. This gives companies some discretion in their long-term financial forecasting. Suppose Harvest Gold issued $10 million in 20-year bonds at 10 percent interest. Its yearly interest expense is $1 million ($10 million times 10 percent). If market conditions change and bonds of the same quality now pay only 7 percent, Harvest Gold will be paying 3 percent, or $300,000 ($10 million times 3 percent) in excess interest yearly. The company could benefit by *calling* in (paying off) the old bonds and issuing new bonds at the lower rate. If a company calls a bond before maturity, it often pays investors a price above the bond's face value.

Investors can convert *convertible bonds* into shares of common stock in the issuing company. This can be an incentive for an investor because common stock value tends to grow faster than a bond. Therefore, if the value of the firm's common stock grows sizably over time, bondholders can compare the value of continued bond interest earned with the potential profit of a specified number of shares of common stock into which the bonds can be converted.[15]

Now that you understand the advantages and disadvantages of stocks and bonds as a long-term financing tool from a company's perspective, let's explore the opportunities stocks, bonds, and other securities provide for *investors*. First, though, check your understanding with the Test Prep questions.

?TEST**PREP**

- Why are bonds considered a form of debt financing?
- What does it mean if a firm issues a 9 percent debenture bond due in 2028?
- Explain the difference between an unsecured and a secured bond.
- Why are convertible bonds attractive to investors?

LO 19–5 Explain how to invest in securities markets and set investment objectives such as long-term growth, income, cash, and protection from inflation.

How Investors Buy Securities

stockbroker
A registered representative who works as a market intermediary to buy and sell securities for clients.

Investing in stocks and bonds is not difficult. First, you decide what stock or bond you want to buy. After that, you find a brokerage firm authorized to trade securities to execute your order. A **stockbroker** is a registered representative who works for a brokerage firm as a market intermediary to buy and sell securities for clients. Stockbrokers place an order and negotiate a price. After the transaction is completed, the trade is reported to your broker,

How Independent Is Your Independent Advisor?

consumerfed.org

The independent financial advisory world is booming, as growing numbers of investors are turning to independent advisors to help them with financial planning. This is especially true for investors seeking future retirement income, financing education for their children, and managing student debt. Suspicions about large Wall Street firms not being fully committed to working in

PR Image Factory/Shutterstock

clients' best interest caused a stampede of investors to seek advice from small firms they feel are fully independent. After all, the word *independent* implies they will get unbiased advice, right? Well, maybe yes, maybe no!

Unfortunately, the word independent can be misused. According to Micah Hauptman of the Consumer Federation of America, "Just because a firm is independent doesn't mean it's free from the biases that other firms have." As some investors discovered, advisors at independent advisory firms can be just as conflicted as those working for a large Wall Street firm in recommending high-commission or risky investments. The major issue seems to be the term *best interests,* which is somewhat of a twisted phrase. If an advisor is a registered investment advisor (RIA), he or she is required to follow a "fiduciary" standard of advice, meaning the client's interests always must be placed ahead of the investment advisor's.

Confusion starts when advisors have dual registration as brokers and RIAs. With dual registration, advisors can recommend products for which they earn high commissions, then act as fiduciaries in other capacities.

The best advice is to take some time and learn about your advisor, the various investments available, and how they specifically fit your financial plans. Asking questions throughout your relationship is a must. Think about it. After all, you don't hesitate to ask your doctor questions about your health, so why should your financial health be any different? Financial advisors can be a valuable source in helping you reach your financial objectives. Just ensure you make the right choice.

Sources: Daren Fonda, "How Independent Is Your Independent Advisor?," *Barron's,* January 6, 2020; "How to Choose a Financial Advisor," *Sun Trust,* suntrust.com, accessed March 2020; Greg Iacurci, "Financial Advisors Must Find Their Niche to Survive over Next 5 to 10 Years," *CNBC,* cnbc.com, February 24, 2020; Coryanne Hicks, "What Is a Fiduciary Financial Advisor?," *U.S. News & World Report,* money.usnews.com, February 24, 2020; Jason Zweig, "The Puzzle of Your Adviser's Pay," *The Wall Street Journal,* March 7, 2020.

who notifies you. Today, large brokerage firms maintain automated order systems that allow brokers to enter your order the instant you make it. The order can be confirmed in seconds.

A stockbroker can also be a source of information about what investments would best meet your financial objectives. However, it's still important to learn about stocks and bonds on your own since stockbrokers' advice may not always meet your specific expectations and needs. Today, some investors are taking advantage of having their investment decisions being managed by independent advisors. The Spotlight on Small Business box, however, raises questions about the independence of independent advisors.

Investing through Online Brokers

Investors can also choose from multiple online trading services to buy and sell stocks and bonds. Charles Schwab, Interactive Brokers, and Fidelity are the leaders.[16] Investors who trade online are willing to do their own research and make investment decisions without the direct assistance of a broker. This allows online brokers the ability to charge zero trading fees. The leading online services do provide important market information, such as company financial data, price histories of a stock, and analysts' reports. Often the level of information services you receive depends on the size of your account and your level of trading.

MAKING ETHICAL DECISIONS

Invest or Pass on a Smoking Gun

You recently received news your Uncle Alex passed away after a long battle with lung cancer. To your surprise, he left you $25,000 in his will, saying you were his favorite nephew. You remember your uncle as a hardworking man who loved baseball and liked nothing better than to watch you pitch for your college team. Unfortunately, he started smoking as a young man and became a heavy chain-smoker. His doctors said that smoking was the primary cause of his lung cancer.

After receiving the inheritance, you wonder where to invest the money. Your old teammate, Jack, a financial advisor, recommends that you buy stock in a well-known multinational firm that offers a good dividend and has solid global growth potential. He tells you the firm's major revenue producer is tobacco and vaping products but assures you it has other products as well. You know Jack has your best interests at heart. You also believe your uncle would like to see the money he left to you grow. However, you wonder if a company that markets tobacco products is an appropriate place to invest your inheritance. What are the ethical alternatives in this situation? What are the consequences of the alternatives? What will you do?

Robo-advisors are automated online tools that use advanced algorithms to make investment suggestions, manage money, rebalance a client's portfolio, and perhaps even shift investments to save taxes. With robo investing, you tell the robots your risk tolerance and your financial goals, and the rest is handled by the robo-advisor's algorithms. In general, your account is invested in conservative exchange-traded funds (ETFs) and high-rated bond issues. However, the robo-advisor will rebalance your account and make beneficial trades to help minimize taxes.[17] At Wealthfront, robo-advisors charge no fees for the first $10,000 invested and then 0.25 percent on all investments after that. Traditional advisors often charge over 1 percent annually.

It's fair to say that robo-advisors cannot do all of the same work that human financial professionals can do. Human financial managers, especially certified financial planners (CFPs), are well schooled in estate planning, mortgage refinancing, and trust investments, as well as personal issues such as planning your children's education.

Whether you decide to use an online broker or to invest through a traditional stockbroker, remember that investing means committing your money with the hope of making a profit. The dot-com bubble in the early 2000s and the financial crisis that began in 2008 proved again that investing is a risky business. Therefore, the first step in any investment program is to analyze your level of risk tolerance. Other factors to consider include your desired income, cash requirements, and need to hedge against inflation, along with the investment's growth prospects. The Making Ethical Decisions box describes an interesting personal stock investment decision.

You are never too young or too old to invest, but you should first ask questions and consider investment alternatives. Let's take a look at several strategies.

Choosing the Right Investment Strategy

Investment objectives change over the course of a person's life. A young person can better afford to invest in high-risk investment options, such as stocks, than can a person nearing retirement. Younger investors generally look for significant growth in the value of their investments over time. If stocks go into a tailspin and decrease in value, as they did in 2008 (by 20 percent), a younger person has time to wait for stock values to rise again as they did in 2017. Older people, perhaps on a fixed income, lack the luxury of waiting and may be more inclined to invest in bonds that offer a steady return as a protection against inflation.

Consider five key criteria when selecting investment options:

1. *Investment risk.* The chance that an investment will be worth less at some future time than it's worth now.

2. *Yield.* The expected return on an investment, such as interest or dividends, usually over a period of one year.

3. *Duration.* The length of time your money is committed to an investment.

4. *Liquidity.* How quickly you can get back your invested funds in cash if you want or need them.

5. *Tax consequences.* How the investment will affect your tax situation.

What's important in any investment strategy is the risk/return trade-off. Setting investment objectives such as *growth* (choosing stocks you believe will increase in price) or *income* (choosing bonds that pay consistent interest or stocks that pay high dividends) should set the tone for your investment strategy.

Reducing Risk by Diversifying Investments

Diversification involves buying several different types of investments to spread the risk of investing. An investor may put 25 percent of his or her money into U.S. stocks that have relatively high risk but strong growth potential, another 25 percent in conservative government bonds, 25 percent in dividend-paying stocks that provide income, 10 percent in an international mutual fund (discussed later), and the rest in the bank for emergencies and other possible investment opportunities. By diversifying with such a *portfolio strategy* or *allocation model,* investors decrease the chance of losing everything they have invested.[18]

Both stockbrokers and certified financial planners (CFPs) are trained to give advice about the investment portfolio that would best fit each client's financial objectives. However, the more investors themselves read and study the market, the higher their potential for gain. A short course in investments can also be useful. Stocks and bonds are investment opportunities individuals can use to enhance their financial future. Before we look at investing in stocks and bonds in more depth, let's check your understanding with the Test Prep.

diversification
Buying several different investment alternatives to spread the risk of investing.

TESTPREP

- What is the key advantage of investing through online brokers? What is the primary disadvantage?
- What are three key factors to remember in establishing your investment strategy?
- What is the primary purpose of diversifying investments?

LO 19–6 Analyze the opportunities stocks offer as investments.

Investing in Stocks

Buying stock makes investors part owners of a company. This means that as stockholders they can participate in its success. Unfortunately, they can also lose money if a company does not do well or the overall stock market declines.

Stock investors are often called bulls or bears according to their perceptions of the market. *Bulls* believe that stock prices are going to rise; they buy stock in anticipation of the increase. A bull market is when overall stock prices are rising. *Bears* expect stock prices to decline and sell their stocks in anticipation of falling prices. That's why, when stock prices are declining, the market is called a bear market.

The market price and growth potential of most stock depends heavily on how well the corporation is meeting its business objectives. A company that achieves its objectives offers great potential for **capital gains**, the positive difference between the price at which you bought a stock and what you sell it for. For example, an investment of $2,250 in 100 shares of McDonald's when the company first offered its stock to the public in 1965 would have grown to 74,360 shares (after the company's 12 stock splits) worth almost $15 million as of the market close on March 2, 2020. Now that's a lot of Big Macs!

Investors often select stocks depending on their investment strategy. Stocks issued by higher-quality companies such as Coca-Cola, Johnson & Johnson, and IBM are referred to as *blue-chip stocks* (a term derived from poker where the highest value chip was the blue chip). These stocks generally pay regular dividends and experience consistent price appreciation.

Stocks of corporations in emerging fields such as technology, biotechnology, or Internet-related firms, whose earnings are expected to grow at a faster rate than other stocks, are referred to as *growth stocks*. While riskier, growth stocks may offer the potential for higher returns. Stocks of public utilities are considered *income stocks* because they usually offer investors a high dividend yield that generally keeps pace with inflation. There are even *penny stocks,* representing ownership in companies that compete in high-risk industries like oil exploration. Penny stocks sell for less than $2 (some analysts say less than $5) and are considered very risky investments.[19]

When purchasing stock, investors have choices when placing orders to buy. A *market order* tells a broker to buy or sell a stock immediately at the best price available. A *limit order* tells the broker to buy or sell a stock at a specific price, if that price becomes available. Let's say a stock is selling for $60 a share. You believe the price will eventually go higher but could drop to $52 first. You can place a limit order at $52, so your broker will buy the stock at $52 if it drops to that price. If the stock never falls to $52, the broker will not purchase it for you.

Stock Splits

High per-share prices can induce companies to declare **stock splits**, in which they issue two or more shares for every one that's outstanding. If Harvest Gold stock were selling for $100 a share, the firm could declare a two-for-one stock split. Investors who owned one share of Harvest Gold would now own two, each worth only $50 (half as much as before the split).

Stock splits cause no change in the firm's ownership structure and no immediate change in the investment's value. Investors generally approve of stock splits, however, because they believe demand for a stock may be greater at $50 than at $100, and the price may then go up in the near future. A company cannot be forced to split its stock, and today stock splits are becoming less common.[20] Legendary investor Warren Buffett's firm, Berkshire Hathaway, has never split its class A stock even when its per-share price surpassed $312,000.[21]

Buying Stock on Margin

Buying stock on margin means borrowing some of the stocks' purchase cost from the brokerage firm. The margin is the portion of the stocks' purchase price that investors must pay with their own money. The board of governors of the Federal Reserve System sets *margin rates* in the U.S. market. Briefly, if the margin rate is 50 percent, an investor who qualifies for a margin account may borrow up to 50 percent of the stock's purchase price from the broker.

Although buying on margin might sound like an easy way to buy more stocks, the downside is that investors must repay the credit extended by the broker, plus interest. If the investor's account goes down in value, the broker may issue a *margin call,* requiring the investor to come up with funds to cover the losses the account has suffered. If the investor is unable to fulfill the margin call, the broker can legally sell off shares of the investor's

capital gains

The positive difference between the purchase price of a stock and its sale price.

stock splits

An action by a company that gives stockholders two or more shares of stock for each one they own.

buying stock on margin

Purchasing stocks by borrowing some of the purchase cost from the brokerage firm.

account to reduce the broker's chance of loss. Margin calls can force an investor to repay a significant portion of his or her account's loss within days or even hours. Buying on margin is thus a risky way to invest in stocks.

Understanding Stock Quotations

Publications like *The Wall Street Journal, Barron's,* and *Investor's Business Daily* carry a wealth of information concerning stocks and other investments. Your local newspaper may carry similar information as well. Financial websites like MSN Money,

Lucky-photographer/Shutterstock

Yahoo! Finance, and CNBC carry up-to-the-minute information about companies that is much more detailed and only a click away. Take a look at Figure 19.4 to see an example of a stock quote from MSN Money for Microsoft. Microsoft trades on the NASDAQ exchange under the symbol MSFT. Preferred stock is identified by the letters *pf* following the company symbol. Remember, corporations can have several different preferred stock issues.

The information provided in the quote is easy to understand. It includes the highest and lowest price the stock traded for that day, the stock's high and low over the past 52 weeks, the dividend paid (if any), the stock's dividend yield (annual dividend as a percentage of the stock's price per share), important ratios like the price/earnings (P/E) ratio (the price of the stock divided by the firm's per-share earnings), and the earnings per share. Investors can also see the number of shares traded (volume) and the total market capitalization of the firm. More technical features, such as the stock's beta (which measures the degree of the stock's risk), may also appear. Figure 19.4 illustrates the stock's intraday

If you stroll through Times Square in New York City, you never have to wonder how stocks are performing on the NASDAQ exchange. The NASDAQ price wall continuously updates prices and the number of shares being traded. Originally, the NASDAQ dealt primarily with small companies; today, it competes with the NYSE for new stock listings.

FIGURE 19.4
UNDERSTANDING STOCK QUOTATIONS

Microsoft Corporation (MSFT)
NasdaqGS - NasdaqGS Real Time Price. Currency in USD

71.74 −0.74 (−1.01%)
As of 3:24PM EDT. Market open.

Previous Close	72.4700	Market Cap	552.559B
Open	71.90	Beta	1.44
Bid	71.94 × 100	PE Ratio (TTM)	31.66
Ask	71.94 × 3900	EPS (TTM)	2.27
Day's Range	71.56 - 72.19	Earnings Date	Oct 30, 2017
52 Week Range	55.6100 - 74.4200	Dividend & Yield	1.56 (2.14%)
Volume	15,191,793	Ex-Dividend Date	2017-08-15
Avg. Volume	25,006,690	1y Target Est	80.19

Trade prices are not sourced from all markets.

trading (trading throughout the current day), but you can also click to see charts for different time periods. Similar information about bonds, mutual funds, and other investments is also available online.

You might want to follow the market behavior of specific stocks that catch your interest, even if you lack the money to invest in them. Many successful investors started in college by building hypothetical portfolios of stocks and tracking their performance. The more you know about investing before you actually risk your money, the better. (The Developing Career Skills and Putting Principles to Work features at the end of this chapter have exercises you can use for practice.)

LO 19–7 Analyze the opportunities bonds offer as investments.

Investing in Bonds

Investors looking for guaranteed income and limited risk often turn to U.S. government bonds for a secure investment. These bonds have the financial backing and full faith and credit of the federal government. Municipal bonds are offered by local governments and often have advantages such as tax-free interest. Some may even be insured. Corporate bonds are a bit riskier and more challenging.

First-time corporate bond investors often ask two questions. The first is, "If I purchase a corporate bond, do I have to hold it until the maturity date?" No, you do not. Bonds are bought and sold daily on major securities exchanges (the secondary market we discussed earlier). However, if you decide to sell your bond to another investor before its maturity date, you may not get its face value. If your bond does not have features that make it attractive to other investors, like a high interest rate or early maturity, you may have to sell at a *discount,* that is, a price less than the bond's face value. But if other investors do highly value it, you may be able to sell your bond at a *premium,* a price above its face value. Bond prices generally fluctuate inversely with current market interest rates. This means *as interest rates go up, bond prices fall, and vice versa.* Like all investments, however, bonds have a degree of risk.

The second question is, "How can I evaluate the investment risk of a particular bond issue?"[22] Standard & Poor's, Moody's Investors Service, and Fitch Ratings rate the risk of many corporate and government bonds (look back at Figure 19.3). In evaluating the ratings, recall the risk/return trade-off: The higher the risk of a bond, the higher the interest rate the issuer must offer. Investors will invest in a bond considered risky only if the potential return (interest) is high enough. In fact, some will invest in bonds considered junk (discussed in the next section). The Adapting to Change box highlights a relatively new type of bond intended to deliver environmental as well as financial returns: green bonds.

Investing in High-Risk (Junk) Bonds

junk bonds
High-risk, high-interest bonds.

Although bonds are considered relatively safe investments, some investors look for higher returns through riskier high-yield bonds called **junk bonds**. Standard & Poor's, Moody's Investors Service, and Fitch Ratings define junk bonds as those with high risk *and* high default rates. Junk bonds pay investors interest as long as the value of the company's assets remains high and its cash flow stays strong.[23] Although the interest rates are attractive and often tempting, if the company can't pay off the bond, the investor is left with an investment that isn't worth more than the paper it's written on—in other words, junk.

Investing in Green Bonds, Not "Greenbacks"

Bonds provide companies long-term financing to fund capital needs in order to expand their business operations by promising to pay investors a fixed interest rate on the money they lend to the companies. Investors risk their money investing in bonds in order to earn a flow of "greenbacks" to help them reach their own financial objectives.

What are green bonds? A green bond is a fixed-income investment that is earmarked to raise money for climate and environmental objectives. The first green bond was issued by the World Bank (see Chapter 20) in 2009. These bonds have seen incredible growth over the past 10 years. In 2010, the market was under $5 billion; in 2020, that number is over $250 billion. Green bonds direct portions of the capital raised to environmental issues such as clean water, energy efficiency, habitat restoration, public transportation, and climate change impacts. The bonds are attractive to investors in two ways. Investors have the satisfaction of knowing that specific proceeds from their investment are being used in a socially responsible manner. The bonds are also a way to earn tax-free income.

Issuers of green bonds also enjoy key benefits. Investors in these bonds tend to be younger investors with whom the issuers may be able to cement a long-standing financial relationship. Also, as the demand for such bonds increases, it lowers the borrowing costs for the issuing company. With the success of green bonds, investment banks are looking at expanding offerings beyond just green bonds. They have begun

surassawadee/Shutterstock

to explore social bond fund programs that address health care issues, food security, equitable employment, and other social issues.

Sources: William Sokol, "Red Hot Year for Green Bonds," *ETF Trends,* etftrends.com, February 2, 2020; Thomas Kenny, "How Green Bonds Are a Cornerstone of Responsible Investing," *The Balance,* thebalance.com, February 4, 2020; Matt Wirz, "Green Bonds Branch Out with Record Sale," *The Wall Street Journal,* February 10, 2020; Nellie S. Huang and John Waggoner, "Investing in the Planet," *Kiplinger's Personal Finance,* April 2020.

LO 19–8 Explain the investment opportunities in mutual funds and exchange-traded funds (ETFs).

Investing in Mutual Funds and Exchange-Traded Funds

A **mutual fund** buys stocks, bonds, and other investments and then sells shares in those securities to the public. A mutual fund is like an investment company that pools investors' money and then buys stocks or bonds (for example) in many companies in accordance with the fund's specific purpose. Mutual fund managers are specialists who pick what they consider to be the best stocks and bonds available and help investors diversify their investments.

Mutual funds range from very conservative funds that invest only in government securities to others that specialize in emerging biotechnology firms, Internet companies, foreign companies, precious metals, and other investments with greater risk. Some funds will have a mix of investments like stocks and bonds. The size of the mutual fund industry today is staggering. For example, there were over 9,599 mutual funds handling over $19.9 trillion in investments for over 90 million Americans in 2019.[24] Figure 19.5 lists some of the mutual fund investment options.

mutual fund
An organization that buys stocks and bonds and then sells shares in those securities to the public.

FIGURE 19.5 MUTUAL FUND OBJECTIVES

Mutual funds have a wide array of investment categories. They range from low-risk, conservative funds to others that invest in high-risk industries. Listed here are abbreviations of funds and what these abbreviations stand for.

AB	Investment-grade corporate bonds	MP	Stock and bond fund
AU	Gold oriented	MT	Mortgage securities
BL	Balanced	MV	Mid-cap value
EI	Equity income	NM	Insured municipal bonds
EM	Emerging markets	NR	Natural resources
EU	European region	PR	Pacific region
GL	Global	SB	Short-term corporate bonds
GM	General municipal bond	SC	Small-cap core
GT	General taxable bonds	SE	Sector funds
HB	Health/biotech	SG	Small-cap growth
HC	High-yield bonds	SM	Short-term municipal bonds
HM	High-yield municipal bonds	SP	S&P 500
IB	Intermediate-term corporate bonds	SQ	Specialty
IG	Intermediate-term government bonds	SS	Single-state municipal bonds
IL	International	SU	Short-term government bonds
IM	Intermediate-term municipal bonds	SV	Small-cap value
LC	Large-cap core	TK	Science & technology
LG	Large-cap growth	UN	Unassigned
LT	Latin America	UT	Utility
LU	Long-term U.S. bonds	WB	World bonds
LV	Large-cap value	XC	Multi-cap core
MC	Mid-cap core	XG	Multi-cap growth
MG	Mid-cap growth	XV	Multi-cap value

Sources: *The Wall Street Journal* and *Investor's Business Daily.*

At one time, young or new investors were advised to buy a type of mutual fund called an index fund.[25] Index funds are constructed to match or track the components of a market index such as the Standard & Poor's 500 (S&P 500). The S&P 500 includes 500 leading companies and is considered the best market gauge of large-cap stocks. Index funds are very low cost, easy to obtain, and can be held by investors for a long period of time. Index funds have also matched or beat the performance of higher-priced funds managed by professional money managers. Today, index funds are recommended for all levels of investors. An index fund may focus on large companies, small companies, emerging countries, or real estate (real estate investment trusts or REITs). One way to diversify your investments is by investing in a variety of index funds. A stockbroker, certified financial planner (CFP), or banker can help you find the option that best fits your investment objectives. The *Morningstar Investor* newsletter is a good resource for evaluating mutual funds, as are business publications such as *Bloomberg Businessweek, Fortune, The Wall Street Journal, Forbes, Barron's, Investor's Business Daily,* and many others.

With mutual funds it's simple to change your investment objectives if your financial objectives change. For example, moving your money from a bond fund to a stock fund is no more difficult than making a phone call, clicking a mouse, or tapping your cell phone. Another advantage of mutual funds is that you can generally buy directly from the fund and avoid broker fees or commissions. It's important to check the long-term performance of the fund's managers; the more consistent the performance of the fund's management, the better. Also, check for fees and charges of the mutual fund because they can differ significantly.

FIGURE 19.6
COMPARING
INVESTMENTS

Investment	Degree of risk	Expected income	Possible growth (capital gain)
Bonds	Low	Secure	Little
Preferred stock	Medium	Steady	Little
Common stock	High	Variable	Good
Mutual funds	Medium	Variable	Good
ETFs	Medium	Variable	Good

A *load fund,* for example, charges investors a commission to buy or sell its shares; a *no-load fund* charges no commission. Mutual funds called *open-end funds* will accept the investments of any interested investors. *Closed-end funds,* however, limit the number of shares; once the fund reaches its target number, no new investors can buy into the fund.

Exchange-traded funds (ETFs) resemble both stocks and mutual funds. They are collections of stocks, bonds, and other investments that are traded on securities exchanges, but are traded more like individual stocks than like mutual funds. Mutual funds, for example, permit investors to buy and sell shares only at the close of the trading day. ETFs can be purchased or sold at any time during the trading day just like individual stocks. The number of exchange-traded funds has exploded over the past 12 years from 350 funds to 6,970 worldwide today.[26] Investors have invested over $6.1 trillion in ETFs.[27]

The key points to remember about mutual funds and ETFs is that they offer small investors a way to spread the risk of owning stocks, bonds, and other securities and have their investments managed by a financial specialist for a fee. Financial advisors put mutual funds and ETFs high on the list of recommended investments, particularly for small or first-time investors.

Figure 19.6 evaluates bonds, stocks, mutual funds, and ETFs according to risk, income, and possible investment growth (capital gain).

exchange-traded funds (ETFs)
Collections of stocks, bonds, and other investments that are traded on exchanges but are traded more like individual stocks than like mutual funds.

?TESTPREP

- What is a stock split? Why do companies sometimes split their stock?
- What does buying stock on margin mean?
- What are mutual funds and ETFs? How are they different?
- What is the key benefit to investors in investing in a mutual fund or ETF?

LO 19–9 Describe how indicators like the Dow Jones Industrial Average affect the market.

Understanding Stock Market Indicators

Investors today have an enormous wealth of investment information available to them. Newspapers like *The Wall Street Journal, Barron's,* and *Investor's Business Daily* provide vast amounts of information about companies and global markets. Television networks

Dow Jones Industrial Average (the Dow)

The average cost of 30 selected industrial stocks, used to give an indication of the direction (up or down) of the stock market over time.

like MSNBC and CNBC offer daily investment analysis and different viewpoints to assist investors. Websites like MSN Money and Yahoo! Finance offer financial information to investors free of charge that not long ago was available only to brokers for a hefty fee. But keep in mind that investing is an inexact science. Every time someone sells a stock, believing it will fall, someone else is buying it, believing its price will go higher.

You often hear business news reports include a comment like, "The Dow was up 90 points today in active trading." Ever wonder what that's all about? The **Dow Jones Industrial Average (the Dow)** is the average cost of 30 selected industrial stocks. The financial industry uses it to give an indication of the direction (up or down) of the stock market over time. Charles Dow began the practice of measuring stock averages in 1884, using the prices of 12 key stocks.[28] In 1982, the Dow was broadened to include 30 stocks. The 12 original and the 30 current stocks in the Dow are illustrated in Figure 19.7. Do you recognize any of the 12 original companies?

Today, Dow Jones & Company substitutes new stocks in the Dow when it's deemed appropriate. In 1991, Disney was added to reflect the increased economic importance of the service sector. In 1999, the Dow added Home Depot and SBC Communications along with its first NASDAQ stocks, Intel and Microsoft. In 2013, Visa, Goldman Sachs, and Nike replaced Alcoa, Bank of America, and Hewlett-Packard. In 2015, Apple replaced AT&T. In 2018, Walgreens Boots Alliance replaced General Electric.

Critics argue that the 30-company Dow sample is too small to get a good statistical representation of the direction of the market over time. Many investors and analysts prefer to follow stock indexes like the Standard & Poor's 500 (S&P 500), which tracks the performance of 400 industrial, 40 financial, 40 public utility, and 20 transportation stocks. Investors also closely follow the NASDAQ average, which is quoted each trading day to show trends in this important exchange.

Staying abreast of the market will help you decide what investments seem most appropriate to your needs and objectives. Remember two key investment realities: Your personal financial objectives and needs change over time, and markets can be rewarding but also can be volatile. Let's take a look at a short history of market volatility and how the securities industry responded to the challenges.

FIGURE 19.7 THE ORIGINAL DOW AND CURRENT DOW

THE ORIGINAL DOW 12	THE 30 CURRENT DOW COMPANIES	
American Cotton Oil	American Express	JPMorgan Chase
American Sugar Refining Co.	Amgen	McDonald's
American Tobacco	Apple	Merck
Chicago Gas	Boeing	Microsoft
Distilling & Cattle Feeding Co.	Caterpillar	3M
General Electric Co.	Chevron	Nike
Laclede Gas Light Co.	Cisco	Procter & Gamble
National Lead	Coca-Cola	Salesforce
North American Co.	Dow	Travelers
Tennessee Coal, Iron & Railroad Co.	Goldman Sachs	UnitedHealth Group
U.S. Leather	Home Depot	Verizon
U.S. Rubber Co.	Honeywell	Visa
	IBM	Walmart Inc.
	Intel	Walt Disney
	Johnson & Johnson	Walgreens Boots Alliance

fotog/Tetra Images/Getty Images

Riding the Market's Roller Coaster

Throughout the 1900s, the stock market had its ups and downs, spiced with several major tremors. The first major crash occurred on Tuesday, October 29, 1929 (called Black Tuesday), when the stock market lost almost 13 percent of its value in a single day. This day, and the deep depression that followed, reinforced the reality of market volatility, especially to those who bought stocks heavily on margin. On October 19, 1987, the stock market suffered the largest one-day drop in its history, losing over 22 percent of its value. On October 27, 1997, investors again felt the market's fury. Fears of an impending economic crisis in Asia caused panic and widespread losses. Luckily, the market regained its strength after a short downturn.

After regaining strength in the late 1990s, the market again suffered misfortune in the early 2000s. All told, investors lost $7 trillion in market value from 2000 through 2002 due to the burst of the tech stock bubble. A recovery that started in the mid-2000s was cut short in 2008, when the financial crisis fueled a massive exodus from the stock market, resulting in record losses. The Great Recession followed.

What caused the market turmoil of 1987, 1997, 2000–2002, and 2008? In 1987, many analysts agreed it was **program trading**, in which investors give their computers instructions to sell automatically to avoid potential losses if the price of their stock dips to a certain point. On October 19, 1987, computers' sell orders caused many stocks to fall to unbelievable depths. The crash prompted the U.S. exchanges to create mechanisms called *curbs* and *circuit breakers* to restrict program trading whenever the market moves up or down by a large number of points in a trading day. A key computer is turned off and program trading is halted. If you watch programming on CNBC or MSNBC, you'll see the phrase *curbs in* appear on the screen.

Circuit breakers are more drastic than curbs and are triggered when the Dow falls 10, 20, or 30 percent in a day. That happened on October 27, 1997, when the market suffered an approximate 7 percent decline and the market closed for the day at 3:30 p.m. instead of 4:00 p.m. Many believe the 1997 market drop (caused by the financial crisis in Asia) could have been much worse without the trading restrictions. Depending on the rate of decline and the time of day, circuit breakers will halt trading for half an hour to two hours so traders have time to assess the situation.

In the late 1990s, the stock market reached unparalleled heights only to collapse into a deep decline in 2000–2002. The bursting of the dot-com bubble was the primary reason. A bubble is caused when too many investors drive the price of something (in this case dot-com stocks) unrealistically high.

program trading

Giving instructions to computers to automatically sell if the price of a stock dips to a certain point to avoid potential losses.

Huge swings in the market cause a lot of anguish among Wall Street workers and people in general. What have we learned from market bubbles like those in technology and real estate?

The dot-com crash was, unfortunately, accompanied by disclosures of financial fraud at companies such as WorldCom, Enron, and Tyco. Investors trusted that the real value of these companies was fairly reflected in their financial statements. This trust was shattered when they found investment analysts often provided clients with wildly optimistic evaluations and recommendations about companies they knew were not worth their current prices.

After the financial downturn caused by the dot-com bubble, the stock market surged in the mid-2000s and set a new high. The market's growth was dramatic, especially in the real estate sector. From 2000 to 2006 prices of existing homes rose 50 percent; however, between 2006 and 2011, housing values fell $6.3 trillion. The real estate bubble was like the dot-com bubble before it: Investors believed that home prices would increase forever. Financial institutions reduced their lending requirements for buyers, homebuilders overbuilt, and buyers overspent, all sharing blame for the crisis. The government also contributed to the problem by requiring more mortgages be given to low- and moderate-income buyers, many with weak credit scores or no verification of income or assets. These *subprime* loans were pooled together and repackaged as mortgage-backed securities that were sold to investors (discussed in Chapter 20). What followed were huge numbers of foreclosures, the failure of government-sponsored mortgage giants Fannie Mae and Freddie Mac, and more than 350 bank failures.

The collapse of the real estate market caused the economy a combined loss of $8 trillion in housing and commercial property. Financial institutions, like Lehman Brothers, went out of business and Wall Street icon Merrill Lynch was purchased by Bank of America. With financial markets in the worst condition since the Great Depression and the economy in a deep recession, the federal government took action. Congress passed a $700 billion financial package called the Troubled Asset Relief Program (TARP) that allowed the Treasury Department to purchase or insure "troubled assets" to bolster banks and bail out the automotive industry and insurer American International Group (AIG). Unfortunately, in 2009 the economy recovered slowly and unemployment grew to double digits, causing Congress to pass an $800 billion economic stimulus package—a blend of tax cuts and increased government spending—that was intended to reduce unemployment and provide a "significant boost" to the crippled economy. In 2010, the government passed the Dodd-Frank Wall Street Reform and Consumer Protection Act that brought significant financial market regulation to the securities industry. Figure 19.8 highlights several regulations of Dodd-Frank designed to address some of the problems caused by the financial crisis.

Since 2009, the economy recovered steadily and the stock market experienced growth and again rallied to new highs. The Dow Jones Industrial Average closed at almost 30,000 for the first time in early 2020.[29] The high close was short-lived, though, due to the outbreak of the COVID-19 global pandemic that shook the market.[30]

FIGURE 19.8 CLEANING UP THE STREET

Key Dodd-Frank Provisions

- Gave the government power to seize and shutter large financial institutions on the verge of collapse.
- Put derivatives and complicated financial deals (including those that packaged subprime mortgages) under strict governmental oversight.
- Required hedge funds to register with the SEC and provide information about trades and portfolio holdings.
- Created the Consumer Financial Protection Bureau to watch over the interests of American consumers by reviewing and enforcing federal financial laws.

What should be obvious to you after reading the section above is the market undergoes frequent challenges and equally frequent periods of dramatic growth for investors. It's reasonable to assume that financial markets will likely experience additional changes in the future that will continue to heighten investor risk as well as heighten potential rewards.

What's important to remember is to diversify your investments, and be mindful of the risks of investing. Taking a long-term perspective is also a wise idea. There's no such thing as easy money or a sure thing. If you carefully research companies and industries, keep up with the news, and make use of investment resources—such as newspapers, magazines, newsletters, the Internet, TV programs, and college classes—the payoff can be rewarding over time.

TEST**PREP**

- What does the Dow Jones Industrial Average measure? Why is it important?
- Why do the 30 companies comprising the Dow change periodically?
- Explain program trading and the problems it can create.

SUMMARY

LO 19–1 Describe the roles of securities markets and of investment bankers.

- **What opportunities do securities markets provide businesses and individual investors?**

By issuing securities, businesses are able to raise much-needed funding to help finance their major expenses. Individual investors can share in the success and growth of emerging or established firms by investing in them.

- **What role do investment bankers play in securities markets?**

Investment bankers are specialists who assist in the issue and sale of new securities.

LO 19–2 Identify the stock exchanges where securities are traded.

- **What are stock exchanges?**

Stock exchanges are securities markets whose members are engaged in buying and selling securities such as stocks and bonds.

- **What are the different exchanges?**

The NYSE is the oldest and largest floor exchange but today does very little stock trading on its floor. The NASDAQ is a telecommunications network that links dealers across the nation so that they can buy and sell securities electronically rather than in person. It is the largest U.S. electronic stock trading market.

- **What is the over-the-counter (OTC) market?**

The OTC market is a system for exchanging stocks not listed on the national exchanges.

- **How are securities exchanges regulated?**

The Securities and Exchange Commission (SEC) regulates securities exchanges and requires companies that intend to sell bonds or stocks to provide a prospectus to potential investors.

- **What is insider trading?**

Insider trading is the use of information or knowledge that individuals gain that allows them to benefit unfairly from fluctuations in security prices.

LO 19–3 Compare the advantages and disadvantages of equity financing by issuing stock, and detail the differences between common and preferred stock.

- **What are the advantages and disadvantages to a firm of selling stock?**

  The advantages of selling stock include the following: (1) the stock price never has to be repaid to stockholders, since they become owners in the company; (2) there is no legal obligation to pay stock dividends; and (3) the company incurs no debt, so it may appear financially stronger. Disadvantages of selling stock include the following: (1) stockholders become owners of the firm and can affect its management by voting for the board of directors; (2) it is more costly to pay dividends since they are paid in after-tax profits; and (3) managers may be tempted to make stockholders happy in the short term rather than plan for long-term needs.

- **What are the differences between common and preferred stock?**

  Holders of common stock have voting rights in the company. In exchange for having no voting rights, preferred stockholders receive a fixed dividend that must be paid in full before common stockholders receive a dividend. Preferred stockholders are also paid back their investment before common stockholders if the company is forced out of business.

LO 19–4 Compare the advantages and disadvantages of obtaining debt financing by issuing bonds, and identify the classes and features of bonds.

- **What are the advantages and disadvantages of issuing bonds?**

  The advantages of issuing bonds include the following: (1) management retains control since bondholders cannot vote; (2) interest paid on bonds is tax-deductible; (3) bonds are only a temporary source of financing, and after they are paid off the debt is eliminated; (4) bonds can be paid back early if they are callable; and (5) sometimes bonds can be converted to common stock. The disadvantages of bonds include the following: (1) because bonds are an increase in debt, they may adversely affect the market's perception of the company; (2) the firm must pay interest on its bonds; and (3) the firm must repay the bond's face value on the maturity date.

- **What are the different types of bonds?**

  Unsecured (debenture) bonds are not supported by collateral, whereas secured bonds are backed by tangible assets such as mortgages, buildings, and equipment.

LO 19–5 Explain how to invest in securities markets and set investment objectives such as long-term growth, income, cash, and protection from inflation.

- **How do investors normally make purchases in securities markets?**

  Investors can purchase investments through market intermediaries called stockbrokers, who provide many different services. Online investing, however, has become extremely popular.

- **What are the criteria for selecting investments?**

  Investors should determine their overall financial objectives and evaluate investments according to (1) risk, (2) yield, (3) duration, (4) liquidity, and (5) tax consequences.

- **What is diversification?**

  Diversification means buying several different types of investments (government bonds, corporate bonds, preferred stock, common stock, global stock) with different degrees of risk. The purpose is to reduce the overall risk an investor would assume by investing in just one type of security.

LO 19–6 Analyze the opportunities stocks offer as investments.

- **What is a market order?**

  A market order tells a broker to buy or sell a security immediately at the best price available.

- **A limit order?**

  A limit order tells the broker to buy or sell if the stock reaches a specific price.

- **What does it mean when a stock splits?**

  When a stock splits, stockholders receive two (or more) shares of stock for each share they own. Each is worth half (or less) of the original share, so while the number of the shares increases, the total value of stockholders' holdings stays the same. Stockholders hope the lower per-share price that results may increase demand for the stock.

- **What does buying on margin mean?**

  An investor buying on margin borrows part (the percentage allowed to be borrowed is set by the Federal Reserve) of the cost of a stock from the broker to get shares of stock without immediately paying the full price.

- **What type of information do stock quotations give you?**

  Stock quotations provide the highest and lowest price in the last 52 weeks; the dividend yield; the price/earnings ratio; the total shares traded that day; and the closing price and net change in price from the previous day.

LO 19–7 Analyze the opportunities bonds offer as investments.

- **What is the difference between a bond selling at a discount and a bond selling at a premium?**

  In the secondary market a bond selling at a premium is priced above its face value. A bond selling at a discount sells below its face value.

- **What is a junk bond?**

  Junk bonds are high-risk (rated BB or below), high-interest debenture bonds that speculative investors often find attractive.

LO 19–8 Explain the investment opportunities in mutual funds and exchange-traded funds (ETFs).

- **How can mutual funds help individuals diversify their investments?**

  A mutual fund is an organization that buys stocks and bonds and then sells shares in those securities to the public, enabling individuals to invest in many more companies than they could otherwise afford. Index funds have become particularly popular among investors.

- **What are ETFs?**

  Like mutual funds, ETFs are collections of stocks that are traded on securities exchanges, but they are traded more like individual stocks.

LO 19–9 Describe how indicators like the Dow Jones Industrial Average affect the market.

- **What is the Dow Jones Industrial Average?**

  The Dow Jones Industrial Average is the average price of 30 specific stocks that analysts use to track the direction (up or down) of the stock market.

KEY TERMS

bond 498

buying stock on margin 504

capital gains 504

common stock 497

debenture bonds 499

diversification 503

dividends 496

Dow Jones Industrial Average (the Dow) 510

exchange-traded funds (ETFs) 509

initial public offering (IPO) 492

institutional investors 493

interest 498

investment bankers 493

junk bonds 506

maturity date 498

mutual fund 507

NASDAQ 494

over-the-counter (OTC) market 493

preferred stock 497

program trading 511

prospectus 494

Securities and Exchange Commission (SEC) 494

sinking fund 500

stockbroker 500

stock certificate 496

stock exchange 493

stocks 496

stock splits 504

CRITICAL THINKING

1. Imagine you inherited $50,000 and you want to invest it to meet two financial goals: (*a*) to save for your wedding, which you plan to have in two years; and (*b*) to save for your retirement several decades from now. How would you invest the money? Explain your answer.

2. If you are considering investing in the bond market, how could information provided by Standard & Poor's, Moody's Investors Service, and Fitch Ratings help you?

3. Why do companies like callable bonds? Why are investors generally not very fond of them?

4. If you were thinking about investing in the securities market, would you prefer individual stocks, mutual funds, or ETFs? Explain your choice by comparing the advantages and disadvantages of each.

PUTTING PRINCIPLES TO WORK

PURPOSE

To experience using online tools to gather stock information.

EXERCISE

Long gone are the days of paying a stockbroker to research stock information for you. Now you can readily find all the information you need online yourself. Go to Yahoo! Finance at finance.yahoo.com and click "Screeners" at the top of the screen, then click "Equity Screener." Create a screener that filters for U.S. stocks based on dividend yield. (*Hint:* Click on "Add another filter," then scroll down to section "Dividends and Splits" and choose "Dividend Yield %.")

1. Identify three stocks that pay a 5 percent or more dividend. To learn more about each stock, click on its ticker symbol. What is the dividend rate (yield) of each?

2. Find what financial analysts recommend for each of these stocks by clicking the Analysis tab. Do analysts recommend buying, holding, or selling each of your picks?

3. If you bought 100 shares of each of these stocks five years ago, how much would you have invested? How much would those stock holdings be worth today (if you didn't reinvest dividends)? (*Hint:* Click on "Historical Data," then "Time Period," then "5Y." Select monthly frequency. Base your calculations on the first and last days' closing prices.)

KEY: ● **Team**   ★ **Analytic**   ▲ **Communication**   ▣ **Technology**

1. Go to the websites of Charles Schwab (schwab.com), E*Trade (etrade.com), and Interactive Brokers (interactivebrokers.com). Investigate each of these brokerage companies to compare their fees and what they offer in terms of research and advice. Which firm seems most appropriate to your investment objectives? Be prepared to defend your choice to the class.   ▣ ★ ▲

2. Visit MSN Money or Yahoo! Finance and select six stocks for your portfolio—three from the NYSE and three from the NASDAQ. Track the stocks daily for three weeks using the graphs provided on the websites to see how market trends and information affected your stocks' performance. Report your observations.   ▣ ★ ▲

3. U.S. government bonds compete with corporations for investors' dollars. Check out the different types of bonds the federal government offers and list the types most appealing to you. (*Hint:* See treasurydirect.gov.) Be sure to check out TIPs and be able to explain how they work.   ▣ ★ ▲

4. See whether anyone in class is interested in forming an investment group. If so, each member should choose one stock and one mutual fund or ETF. Record each student's selections and the corresponding prices. In three weeks measure the percentage of change in the investments and discuss the results.   ● ▣ ★ ▲

5. Go to the website of Charles Schwab (schwab.com), E*Trade (etrade.com), or Interactive Brokers (interactivebrokers.com) and find two IPOs offered in the past year or two. Track the performance of each from its introduction to its present market price. Report your observations and conclusions about the stocks.   ▣ ★ ▲

If you are interested in pursuing a career in the securities industry, here are a few opportunities to consider. Make sure to find out about the tasks performed, skills needed, pay, and opportunity outlook in these fields in the *Occupational Outlook Handbook (OOH)* at bls.gov.

- **Personal financial advisor**—provides advice on investments, mortgages, insurance, college savings plans, estate planning, taxes, and retirement to help individuals manage their finances.

- **Investment banker**—connects businesses that need money to finance their operations with investors who are interested in providing that funding; assists with company mergers and acquisitions.

- **Stockbroker**—sells securities and commodities directly to individual clients; advises clients on appropriate investments based on their needs and financial understanding.

- **Financial analyst**—provides guidance to businesses and individuals making investment decisions; assesses the performance of stocks, bonds, and other types of investments.

VIDEO CASE   *Where Did All My Money Go?*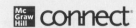

We all hear about the importance of investing, but how do you know what the best investments are? Is there an objective source you can use to get investment advice? The answer is, yes, you can get much helpful and unbiased information from a company called Morningstar.

Most people choose between stocks and bonds. When you buy stocks, you buy part ownership of a firm. You can choose from large firms like AT&T and Microsoft or smaller firms. Morningstar can help you choose from the thousands of firms available.

One way to spread the risk of investing in stock is to diversify. That is, you can buy stock in a variety of firms in a variety of sectors. For example, you can buy stock in firms from other countries, in service firms, manufacturing firms, health care firms, and so on. One easy way to diversify is to buy mutual funds. Such funds buy a whole range of stocks and then sell you a portion of that fund. ETFs, or exchange-traded funds, are much like mutual funds, but you buy and sell them through stock exchanges much like you would buy individual shares of stock.

In the long run, most investment advisors recommend investing in stock. Yes, the stock market goes up and down, but they say, in the long run, stocks usually go up. Since young people can wait for years to sell their stock, investment advisors like Morningstar would usually recommend stock (or mutual funds) to them.

Would Morningstar also be likely to recommend bonds? Sure. When you buy a bond, you are actually lending a company, the government, or some government agency money. The company (or the government) promises to return the money to you, plus interest. If the interest is high enough, such an investment makes sense. Of course, some companies are riskier than others, so the interest paid on bonds varies. Morningstar will help you choose bonds that are appropriate for you and your situation.

Almost everyone needs some investment advice. Morningstar has earned a reputation for being objective and helpful. This video is meant to reveal the benefits and drawbacks of investing. But stocks and bonds can earn you a nice return on your investment if you know what you are doing. If you don't know what you are doing, you can lose your savings rather quickly. Morningstar is just one source of information. You should explore as many sources as possible to learn about investing. Such sources include your textbook, your local newspaper, online publications such as *Money* and *Personal Finance,* and TV shows featuring financial news.

Everyone should have some money set aside (e.g., in a bank) for emergencies. Everyone should diversify their investments among stocks, bonds, real estate, and other investments, depending on their income and their willingness to assume risk.

Morningstar and other sources of advice are very important to your financial health. You have seen how some people believed that real estate could do nothing but go up. The 2008 real estate crash proved them wrong. The same is true of stocks, bonds, gold, oil, and other investments. They all involve risk, and expert advice is often wrong; but in any case, it pays to have the best, unbiased advice you can get, like that from Morningstar. It also helps to have several other sources of advice, including your own knowledge, gathered carefully over time.

THINKING IT OVER

1. Are you confident about investing in stocks, bonds, mutual funds, ETFs, and other investments? What sources of information would you use to make a decision about investments?

2. Should you totally rely on Morningstar or any other investment advice service or should you search out several sources of advice? How can you know what advice is best?

3. Given what you've read in this text and from other sources, would you recommend that your fellow students' first investment be in stocks, bonds, mutual funds, ETFs, real estate, or some other investments? Why?

NOTES

1. Eric Reed, "What Is a Capital Market?," *Yahoo! Finance,* finance.yahoo.com, February 19, 2020; Roger Wohlner, "How Are Stock Prices Determined?," *TheStreet,* thestreet.com, January 30, 2020.
2. Liz Smith, "Investment Banking Defined," SmartAsset, smartasset.com, February 6, 2020; Joshua Kennon, "What Are Market Makers and How Do They Make Money?," *The Balance,* thebalance.com, February 10, 2020; Laura Noonan, "Investment Banking Revenues Fall to the Lowest since 2008," *Financial Times,* ft.com, February 21, 2020; Matt Egan, "Ouch. Investment Banking Revenue Hasn't Been This Weak since 2008," *CNN,* cnn.com, February 25, 2020.

3. David R. Harper, "Getting to Know the Stock Exchanges," *Investopedia,* investopedia.com, February 6, 2020; Cara Lombardo and Carrie Driebusch, "NYSE Owner Intercontinental Exchange Makes Takeover Offer for eBay," *The Wall Street Journal,* February 4, 2020.

4. Maria Halkias, "J.C. Penney's under $1 Dollar Stock Price Has Put It Back at Risk for NYSE Delisting," *Dallas Morning News,* January 31, 2020.

5. Dori Zinn, "What Constitutes Insider Trading?," *Yahoo! Finance,* finance.yahoo.com, February 26, 2020; Matt Levine, "Everything Might Be Considered Insider Trading," *Bloomberg,* bloomberg.com, January 27, 2020; The Editorial Board, "U.S. Law Covering Insider Trading Is Ripe for Reform," *Financial Times,* ft.com, January 30, 2020; Russell G. Ryan, "Insider Trading Law Is Irreparably Broken," *The Washington Post,* January 27, 2020.

6. Bob Van Voris, "Analyst Who Tipped Off SAC Capital Wins Dismissal of Charges," *Bloomberg,* bloomberg.com, February 14, 2020; Jared Diamond and Gregory Zuckerman, "Hedge-Fund Billionaire's Deal for Mets Collapses," *The Wall Street Journal,* February 6, 2020.

7. Prableen Bajpai, "Interested in Investing in Africa? Here's How," *Investopedia,* investopedia.com, accessed March 2020.

8. Joshua Kennon, "What Is a Dividend?," *The Balance,* thebalance.com, February 17, 2020; J. D. Maverick, "What Causes Dividends per Share to Increase?," *Investopedia,* investopedia.com, February 16, 2020.

9. Brian O'Connell, "What Are Stock Buybacks and How Do They Work?," *TheStreet,* thestreet.com, February 12, 2020; Elvis Picardo, "Dividend vs. Buyback: What's the Difference?," *Investopedia,* investopedia. com, February 19, 2020; Mark Hulbert, "How to Use Stock Buybacks to Time the Market," *Barron's,* January 29, 2020; Shawn Tully, "3 Reasons Ballooning Stock Buybacks Are Worrisome," *Fortune,* February 12, 2020.

10. Joshua Kennon, "What Is the Preemptive Right?," *The Balance,* thebalance.com, accessed March 2020.

11. Adam Hayes, "Preferred versus Common Stock: What's the Difference?," *Investopedia,* investopedia. com, February 25, 2020; Dan Caplinger, "Beginner's Guide to Brokerages," *The Motley Fool,* fool.com, February 13, 2020.

12. "What Is Par Value?," Fincash, fincash.com, February 22, 2020.

13. Albert Phung, "Why Do Companies Issue 100-Year Bonds?," *Investopedia,* investopedia.com, June 25, 2019.

14. Cezary Podkul, "SEC Rethinks Approach to Conflicts among Bond-Rating Firms," *The Wall Street Journal,* February 24, 2020; Nellie S. Huang, "Is a Debt Bomb Ticking?," *Kiplinger Personal Finance,* kiplinger.com, January 30, 2020; Brian Chappatta, "The Credit-Ratings Business May Never Get Fixed," *Bloomberg,* bloomberg. com, February 6, 2020.

15. Sean Ross, "How Is Convertible Bond Valuation Different Than Traditional Bond Valuation?," *Investopedia,* investopedia.com, February 18, 2020; Eric Reed, "Hybrid Securities: Definitions and Examples," *Yahoo! Finance,* finance.yahoo.com, February 7, 2020; Andrew Bary, "Tesla Stock Is Powering the Convertible Bond Market," *Barron's,* February 5, 2020.

16. Eric Rosenberg, "The Best Online Stock Broker of 2020," *The Balance,* thebalance.com, accessed March 2020; Paul Katzeff, "Fidelity Brokerage Reclaims Top Rank in IBD Best Online Brokers Survey," *Investor's Business Daily,* investors.com, January 31, 2020; Matt Miller, "The Best Online Brokers Right Now—for Almost Every Kind of Investor," *Barron's,* www.barrons.com, February 21, 2020.

17. Bailey McCann, "Robo Advisers Keep Adding On Services," *The Wall Street Journal,* March 9, 2020.

18. Patrick B. Healey, "How a Multi-Asset Portfolio Investing Strategy Can Mitigate Risk," *Kiplinger,* kiplinger. com, February 27, 2020; Peter Tanous, "Here's Why Diversification Can Be an Investor's Worst Enemy," *CNBC,* cnbc.com, February 2, 2020.

19. Selena Maranjian, "Why You Should Avoid Penny Stocks Like the Plague," *The Motley Fool,* fool.com, February 24, 2020; David Saito-Chung, "Apple and Growth Stock: Why Most Penny Stocks Fail to Make Investor's Rich," *Investors Business Daily,* investors.com, August 8, 2019; Joshua Kennon, "Investing in Penny Stocks Is Almost Always a Bad Idea," *The Balance,* thebalance.com, January 27, 2020.

20. "Are Stock Splits a Thing of the Past?," Charles Schwab, schwab.com, February 16, 2018; Brett Owens, "How to Play Stock Splits for 3X Dividends and 200%+ Upside," *Forbes,* forbes.com, February 19, 2020.

21. Michael Larkin, "The Ultimate Warren Buffett Stock Is in the Buy Zone, but Should You Buy It?," *Investor's Business Daily,* investors.com, February 19, 2020; Andrew Bary, "Warren Buffett Made a Great Bet on Apple. Why Hasn't Berkshire Hathaway Stock Benefited?," *Barron's,* barrons.com, January 29, 2020; Adam Seessel, "Valuation: How Warren Buffett Built Berkshire Hathaway—and What Might Happen When He Leaves," *Fortune,* fortune.com, February 21, 2020.

22. Daniel Jark, "Don't Invest in Bonds without Asking These 7 Questions," *Investopedia,* investopedia.com, February 12, 2020.

23. Jeff Cox, "Junk Bond Scare Is Rising: No One Cares. People Are Buying Everything," *CNBC,* cnbc.com, February 7, 2020; Nir Kaissar, "If Value Stocks Are Toxic, Why Aren't Junk Bonds?," *Yahoo! Finance,* finance. yahoo.com, January 30, 2020; Karen Hube, "How to Build a Bond Portfolio for Stability in Uncertain Times," *Barron's,* January 30, 2020; Annalisa Esposito, "3 Questions to Ask before Buying High Yield Bonds," Morningstar, morningstar.com, February 25, 2020.

24. "Number of Mutual Funds in the United States from 1997 to 2018," Statista, statista.com, accessed March 2020; Sean Ross, "The 3 Biggest Mutual Fund Companies in the U.S.," *Investopedia,* investopedia.com, November 5, 2019; Nick Ravo, "The Buzz vs. the Beast," *The Wall Street Journal,* October 7, 2019.

25. Ty Bernicke, "Index Fund Pitfalls: What Investors Need to Know," *Forbes,* forbes.com, February 13, 2020; "What Is an Index Fund?," *The Motley Fool,* fool.com, accessed March 2020.

26. "Number of Exchange-Traded Funds (ETFs) Worldwide for 2003 to 2019," Statista, statista.com, accessed March 2020.

27. M. Szmigiera, "Worldwide ETF Assets under Management 2003 to 2019," Statista, statista.com, accessed March 2020.

28. "Dow Jones Industrial Average Fast Facts," *CNN,* cnn.com, accessed February 2020; "Dow Jones Today: Dow Stocks and Stock Market News," *Investor's Business Daily,* investors.com, accessed February 2020.

29. Kimberly Amadeo, "Dow Highest Closing Records," *The Balance,* thebalance.com, February 18, 2020.

30. David J. Lynch, Rachel Siegal, and Thomas Heath, "U.S. Markets Drop to Correction Territory, Extending Brutal Week of Losses," *The Washington Post,* February 27, 2020; Fred Imbert and Eustance Huang, "Dow Plunges 1,000 Points on Coronavirus Fears, 3.5% Drop Is Worst in Two Years," *CNBC,* cnbc.com, February 23, 2020; Jessica Menton, "Dow Plunges over 1,000 Points as Coronavirus Cases outside China Jump," *USA Today,* February 24, 2020; Karen Langley, Caitlin Ostroff, and Chong Koh Ping, "U.S. Stocks Slide into Correction as Virus Fears Show No Sign of Easing," *The Wall Street Journal,* February 27, 2020.

20

Money, Financial Institutions, and the Federal Reserve

LEARNING OBJECTIVES *After you have read and studied this chapter, you should be able to*

LO 20–1 Explain what money is and what makes money useful.

LO 20–2 Describe how the Federal Reserve controls the money supply.

LO 20–3 Trace the history of banking and the Federal Reserve System.

LO 20–4 Classify the various institutions in the U.S. banking system.

LO 20–5 Briefly trace the causes of the banking crisis of 2008, and explain how the government protects your funds during such crises.

LO 20–6 Describe how technology helps make banking more efficient.

LO 20–7 Evaluate the role and importance of international banking, the World Bank, and the International Monetary Fund.

Jerome (Jay) Powell, Chair of the Federal Reserve

The Federal Reserve (the Fed) is the central banking system of the United States. It is the agency in charge of the nation's monetary policy as well as the money supply and interest rates, which keeps its actions very much in the public eye. Jerome (Jay) Powell became chair of the Federal Reserve in 2018 after replacing Janet Yellen, the first woman to hold the position in the Fed's 100-year history. Along with being the wealthiest member of the Federal Reserve, Powell is also the first Fed chair in more than 40 years who does not have a degree in economics.

Powell grew up with his brother and four sisters in Washington, D.C., the son of a lawyer. After graduating from Princeton University with a bachelor's degree in politics, he decided to follow in his father's footsteps and study law. He earned a law degree from Georgetown University where he was also editor-in-chief of the *Georgetown Law Journal.* Powell then worked as a clerk for a federal appeals court judge before joining a major New York law firm. After a few years, though, Powell decided his father's career was not for him. So in 1984 he changed course and joined an investment banking firm.

Powell moved back to Washington in 1990 to become undersecretary for domestic finance in President George H. W. Bush's Treasury Department. Besides overseeing policy on financial institutions and the treasury debt market, he also assumed responsibility for untangling a series of bank failures. Following President Bush's reelection defeat in 1993, Powell returned to New York City and continued his banking career. In 1997 he again moved back to Washington and joined The Carlyle Group, a private equity investment firm. His work at Carlyle proved to be very rewarding as well as lucrative. In financial disclosures, Powell's net worth is estimated to exceed $112 million.

After spending years in the banking industry, Powell was eager to return to the public sector. He left Carlyle in 2005 to focus on public policy as a scholar at the Bipartisan Policy Center in Washington. While at the organization, he focused his research on federal and state fiscal matters and refused to take a salary. In 2011, Powell caught the eye of then Treasury Secretary Timothy Geithner who recommended him to President Obama for appointment to the Federal Reserve. His nomination was approved by the Senate in 2012, followed six years later by his appointment to Fed chair by President Trump. Colleagues describe Powell as an able collaborator who prefers a low public profile. And although he supports many of the regulations introduced by the Dodd-Frank reforms, he also feels that unnecessary burdens on the banking system can harm the economy. However, as Powell continues to lead the Fed during his time in charge, his direction and leadership will certainly have a major impact on the U.S economy today and for years to come.

You will learn more about money, the Federal Reserve, and the banking system in this chapter. Using that information, you can better understand key decisions involving monetary policy, interest rates, and unemployment. By reading this chapter, reading business publications, and listening to business reports, you can understand how the Fed's policies impact the U.S. economy.

Sources: Andrew Soergel, "Fed Chairman Jerome Powell Dismisses Negative Rates Despite Pressure from Trump," *U.S. News & World Report,* usnews.com, February 11, 2020; Federal Reserve, federalreserve.gov, accessed March 2020; Nick Timiraos, "Fed Chairman Heads to Capital Hill Facing New Questions over Growth Risks," *The Wall Street Journal,* February 10, 2020; Lisa Beilfuss, "Fed's Powell Opens the Door to a Cut in Interest Rates," *Barron's,* February 28, 2020.

Let's talk business!
bit.ly/LetsTalkBusiness20

Andrew Caballero-Reynolds/Getty images

LO 20–1 Explain what money is and what makes money useful.

Why Money Is Important

The Federal Reserve, or the Fed, is the organization in charge of money in the United States. You've probably heard about the Fed and perhaps are familiar with its current chair, Jay Powell. That is why we chose Powell to be the subject of the Getting to Know feature for this chapter. Once you have some understanding of the Federal Reserve, our goal in this chapter is to introduce you to the world of banking.[1]

Two of the most critical issues in the United States, economic growth and the creation of jobs, depend on the ready availability of money. Money is so important to the economy that many institutions have evolved to manage it and make it available when you need it. Today you can get cash from an automated teller machine (ATM) almost anywhere in the world, and most organizations will also accept a check, credit card, debit card, or smart card for purchases. Some businesses will even accept Bitcoins, an online version of money. Behind the scenes is a complex system of banking that makes the free flow of money possible. Each day, over $5 trillion is exchanged in the world's currency markets.[2] Therefore, what happens to any major country's economy has an effect on the U.S. economy and vice versa.

Let's start at the beginning by discussing exactly what the word *money* means and how the supply of money affects the prices you pay for goods and services.

What Is Money?

money
Anything that people generally accept as payment for goods and services.

Money is anything people generally accept as payment for goods and services. In the past, objects as diverse as salt, feathers, fur pelts, stones, rare shells, tea, and horses have served as money. In fact, until the 1880s, cowrie shells were one of the world's most popular currencies.

Newer engraved bills make counterfeiting much more difficult than in the past. The current bills look a little different than older ones and contain a variety of colors. If you owned a store, what would you do to make sure employees wouldn't accept counterfeit bills?

Bureau of Engraving and Printing, U.S. Department of the Treasury

524

Barter is the direct trading of goods or services for other goods or services. Though barter may sound like something from the past, many people have discovered the benefits of bartering online.[3] One entrepreneur describes his bartering experience as follows: "Last year we bartered the creation of a full-color graphic novel in exchange for a new website design. . . . The value of the trade was $50,000. We provided three months of writing services to provide the graphic novel story line . . . and then five months of illustration. In exchange, they helped us to define, design and then program our new website." [4]

Some people barter goods and services the old-fashioned way. In Siberia, for example, people have bought movie tickets with two eggs, and in Ukraine people have paid their energy bills with sausages and milk. Today you can go to a *barter exchange* where you can put goods or services into the system and get trade credits for other goods and services that you need.[5] The barter exchange makes it easier to barter because you don't have to find people with whom to barter. The exchange does that for you.

The problem with traditional barter is that eggs and milk are difficult to carry around. Most people need some object that's portable, divisible, durable, and stable so that they can trade goods and services without carrying the actual goods around with them. One solution is coins and paper bills. The five standards for a useful form of money are:

- *Portability.* Coins and paper money are a lot easier to take to market than pigs, eggs, milk, or other heavy products.

- *Divisibility.* Different-sized coins and bills can represent different values. Prior to 1963, a U.S. quarter had half as much silver content as a half-dollar coin, and a dollar had four times the silver of a quarter. Because silver is now too expensive, today's coins are made of other metals, but the accepted values remain.

- *Stability.* When everybody agrees on the value of coins, the value of money is relatively stable. In fact, U.S. money has become so stable that much of the world has used the U.S. dollar as the measure of value. If the value of the dollar fluctuates too rapidly, the world may turn to some other form of money for the measure of value.

- *Durability.* Coins last for thousands of years, even when they've sunk to the bottom of the ocean, as you've seen when divers find old coins in sunken ships.

- *Uniqueness.* It's hard to counterfeit, or copy, elaborately designed and minted coins. With the latest color copiers, people are able to duplicate the look of paper money relatively easily. Thus, the government has had to go to extra lengths to make sure *real* dollars are readily identifiable. That's why we have paper money with the picture slightly off center and with invisible lines that quickly show up when reviewed by banks and stores. On the $100 bill, for example, Ben Franklin shares space with colorful illustrations, hidden text, and pictographs that reveal themselves only when they are lit from behind or exposed to ultraviolet light. Coins and paper money simplified exchanges. Most countries have their own currencies, and they're all about equally portable, divisible, and durable. However, they're not always equally stable.

Electronic money (e-money) is a newer form of money. You can make online payments using PayPal, Google Wallet, or your bank's website or app. You can use Apple Pay on your smartphone to pay in brick-and-mortar stores. Cryptocurrencies like Bitcoin are digital versions of money that use cryptography for security, making it tougher to forge, easier to cut across international boundaries, and able to be stored on your hard drive instead of in a bank. However, the Bitcoin, which was launched in 2009, is not yet generally accepted and was the subject of over $4.5 billion in thefts in 2019 alone.[6] Nonetheless, efforts will likely continue to be made to create a cashless society using some other form of cryptocurrency than the bills and coins we use now.[7]

While no one knows when and what cryptocurrencies will succeed, no one can be sure of the future of our coins and currency either. The U.S. Mint is examining different

gosphotodesign/Shutterstock

Although people have long used barter to exchange goods without money, one problem is that products like fish are not as pleasant to carry around as a $10 bill. What other drawbacks does bartering have?

barter
The direct trading of goods or services for other goods or services.

Saying "See You" to the C-Note

choness/Getty Images

It's unlikely that you have a big wad of $100 bills stuffed in your wallet. Not surprising, the Benjamin Franklin–faced currency has been the largest U.S. bill since the $500, $1,000, and $5,000 bill were axed in 1969. What's strange is that the number of C-notes has eclipsed the $1 bill as the most widely distributed currency in the U.S. economy. Ten years ago that was not the case. Some economists suggest that since the financial crisis of 2008, many could be using it as a household savings vehicle for skeptics worried about another financial downturn. Others give a more dire speculation that the surge for the $100 bill is being driven by demand from the global underground economy. Some have suggested that the U.S. Treasury remove them from circulation, especially since the majority of the bills are not even present in the U.S. economy.

A paper published from Harvard's Center for Business and Government claimed that high-denomination notes such as the $100 bill are the "preferred payment mechanism" of criminals due to the lack of transaction record and ease with which they can be transported and moved. For example, $1 million in $20 bills would be bulky and weigh almost 70 pounds. $1 million in $100 bills weighs about 20 pounds and could easily be carried in a small case or shopping bag. Law enforcement agencies seem to be in agreement. Paper currency, especially large bills, facilitates crimes such as racketeering, extortion, money laundering, drug and human trafficking, corruption of public officials, and even terrorism. Large bills also facilitate tax evasion that costs federal, state, and local governments billions of dollars.

Professor Kenneth Rogoff of Harvard University has endorsed eliminating the $100 bill and would also like to see the $50 bill go. While not proposing a "cashless economy," he believes that moving to a "less cash" society, where cash is used primarily for small transactions, would be a boost to the economy.

He notes that as the level of purchases increases in price, consumers are more prone to use credit cards, debit cards, or checks rather than cash. For now, he agrees to let the $50 bill stay in circulation; but many are joining his call that it's time to get rid of all those Ben Franklins.

Sources: Taylor Telford and Jeanne Whalen, "$100 Bill Is Surging: Why So Many Benjamins?," *Chicago Tribune,* March 5, 2019; Aarthri Swaminathan, "There Are Now More $100 Bills Than $1 Bills in Circulation (and We're Not Sure Why)," *Yahoo! Finance,* finance.yahoo.com, February 27, 2019; Kate Rooney, "There's Been a Mysterious Surge in $100 Bills in Circulation, Possibly Linked to Global Corruption," *CNBC,* cnbc.com, February 27, 2019.

metals and alloys to bring down the production costs of the nickel, dime, and quarter. It now costs 1.99 cents to make a penny and 7.62 cents to make a nickel.[8] Someday you may find that your nickels and pennies are lighter and a different color. The Adapting to Change box discusses a question about why our largest-denomination bill is the most prevalent in circulation.

LO 20–2   Describe how the Federal Reserve controls the money supply.

The Federal Reserve is in control of the U.S. money supply. Two questions emerge from that sentence: What is the money supply? Why does it need to be controlled?

The **money supply** is the amount of money the Federal Reserve makes available for people to buy goods and services. And, yes, the Federal Reserve, in tandem with the U.S. Treasury, can create more money if it is needed. For example, some of the trillions of dollars that were spent after the Great Recession to get the economy moving again were printed with authorization from the Federal Reserve. The term *quantitative easing* was used quite a

money supply

The amount of money the Federal Reserve Bank makes available for people to buy goods and services.

bit. Quantitative easing (QE) means that the Fed can create more money when it believes that money is needed to get the economy moving again.[9] As the economy continued to grow after the Great Recession, the Fed reduced quantitative easing. We'll see how the Fed reacts as the economy moves forward into the 2020s.[10]

There are several ways of referring to the U.S. money supply. They're called M-1, M-2, and M-3. The *M* stands for "money," and the *1, 2,* and *3* stand for different definitions of the money supply. **M-1** includes coins and paper bills, money that's available by writing checks (demand deposits and share drafts), and money held in traveler's checks—that is, money that can be accessed quickly and easily. **M-2** includes everything in M-1 plus money in savings accounts, and money in money market accounts, mutual funds, certificates of deposit, and the like—that is, money that may take a little more time to obtain than coins and paper bills. M-2 is the most commonly used definition of money. **M-3** is M-2 plus big deposits like institutional money market funds.

Managing Inflation and the Money Supply

Imagine what would happen if governments (or in the case of the United States, the Federal Reserve, a nongovernmental organization) were to generate twice as much money as exists now. There would be twice as much money available, but still the same amount of goods and services. What would happen to prices? (*Hint:* Remember the laws of supply and demand from Chapter 2). Prices would go *up* because more people would try to buy goods and services with their money and bid up the price to get what they wanted. This rise in price is called *inflation,* which some people call "too much money chasing too few goods."

Then think about the opposite: What would happen if the Fed took money out of the economy, or put less money in? Prices would go down because there would be an oversupply of goods and services compared to the money available to buy them; this decrease in prices is called *deflation.*

Now we come to our second question about the money supply: Why does it need to be controlled? The reason is that doing so allows us to manage, somewhat, the prices of goods and services. The size of the money supply can also affect *employment* and *economic growth* or decline. That's why the Federal Reserve's role in the U.S. economy of keeping unemployment down and stabilizing prices is important.[11]

At this point, it is good for you to know that the global money supply is controlled by *central banks* like the Federal Reserve. What central banks do clearly affects the economies of the world. For example, the European Central Bank (ECB) enacted quantitative easing (increasing the money supply) to combat lackluster growth, low inflation, and political uncertainty that has plagued Europe.[12]

The Global Exchange of Money

A *falling dollar value* means that the amount of goods and services you can buy with a dollar in global markets decreases. A *rising dollar value* means that the amount of goods and services you can buy with a dollar goes up. Thus, the price in euros you pay for a German car will be lower if the U.S. dollar rises relative to the euro. However, if the euro rises relative to the dollar, the cost of cars from Germany will go up and U.S. consumers may buy fewer German cars.

What makes the dollar weak (falling value) or strong (rising value) is the position of the U.S. economy relative to other economies. When the economy is strong, the demand for dollars is high, and the value of the dollar rises. When the economy is perceived as weakening, however, the demand for dollars declines and the value of the dollar falls. The value of the dollar thus depends on a relatively strong economy. (See Chapter 3 for further discussion of effects of changes in currency values or exchange rates.) In the following section, we'll discuss in more detail the money supply and how it's managed. Then we'll explore the U.S. banking system and how it lends money to businesses and individuals, like you and me.

M-1

Money that can be accessed quickly and easily (coins and paper money, checks, traveler's checks, etc.).

M-2

Money included in M-1 plus money that may take a little more time to obtain (savings accounts, money market accounts, mutual funds, certificates of deposit, etc.).

M-3

M-2 plus big deposits like institutional money market funds.

Control of the Money Supply

Theoretically, with the proper monetary policy in place to control the money supply, one can keep the economy growing without causing inflation. (See Chapter 2 to review monetary policy.) Again, the Federal Reserve is the organization in charge of monetary policy.

Basics about the Federal Reserve

The Federal Reserve System consists of five major parts: (1) the board of governors, (2) the Federal Open Market Committee (FOMC), (3) 12 Federal Reserve banks, (4) three advisory councils, and (5) the member banks of the system. Figure 20.1 shows where the 12 Federal Reserve banks are located. (You should know that the Federal Reserve is *not* a part of the U.S. government, despite its name. It is a private firm not supported by taxpayer dollars.)[13]

The board of governors administers and supervises the 12 Federal Reserve banks. The 7 members of the board are appointed by the president and confirmed by the Senate. The board's primary function is to set monetary policy (again see Chapter 2). The Federal Open Market Committee (FOMC) has 12 voting members and is the policy-making body. The committee is made up of the 7-member board of governors plus the president of the New York reserve bank and 4 members who rotate in from the other reserve banks. The advisory councils represent the various banking districts, consumers, and member institutions, including banks, savings and loan institutions, and credit unions. They offer suggestions to the board and to the FOMC.

The Fed buys and sells foreign currencies, regulates various types of credit, supervises banks, and collects data on the money supply and other economic activity. As part of monetary policy, the Fed determines the *reserve requirement,* that is, the level of reserve funds all financial institutions must keep at one of the 12 Federal Reserve banks. It buys and sells government securities in *open-market operations.* Finally, it lends money to member banks at an interest rate called the *discount rate.*

As noted, the three basic tools the Fed uses to manage the money supply are reserve requirements, open-market operations, and the discount rate (see Figure 20.2). Let's explore how it administers each. Note how each move the Fed makes can impact the economy.

reserve requirement
A percentage of commercial banks' checking and savings accounts that must be physically kept in the bank.

The Reserve Requirement

The **reserve requirement** is a percentage of commercial banks' checking and savings accounts they must keep in the bank (as cash in the vault) or in a non-interest-bearing deposit at the local Federal Reserve district bank. The reserve requirement is one of the Fed's tools. When

FIGURE 20.1 THE 12 FEDERAL RESERVE DISTRICT BANKS

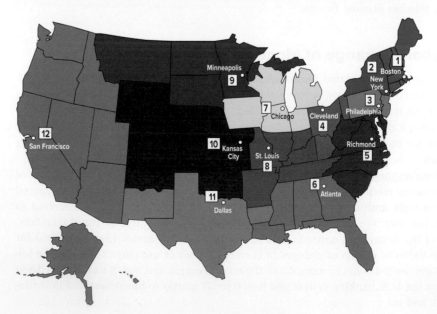

FIGURE 20.2 **HOW THE FEDERAL RESERVE CONTROLS THE MONEY SUPPLY**

Reserve Requirements

Control Method	Immediate Result	Long-Term Effect
A. Increase.	Banks put more money into the Fed, reducing money supply; thus, there is less money available to lend to customers.	Economy slows.
B. Decrease.	Banks put less money into the Fed, increasing the money supply; thus, there is more money available to lend to customers.	Economy speeds up.

Open-Market Operations

Control Method	Immediate Result	Long-Term Effect
A. Fed sells bonds.	Money flows from the economy to the Fed.	Economy slows.
B. Fed buys bonds.	Money flows into the economy from the Fed.	Economy speeds up.

Managing the Discount Rate

Control Method	Immediate Result	Long-Term Effect
A. Rate increases.	Banks borrow less from the Fed; thus, there is less money to lend.	Economy slows.
B. Rate decreases.	Banks borrow more from the Fed; thus, there is more money to lend.	Economy speeds up.

it increases the reserve requirement, money becomes scarcer, which in the long run tends to reduce inflation. For instance, if Omaha Security Bank holds deposits of $100 million and the reserve requirement is, say, 10 percent, then the bank must keep $10 million on reserve. If the Fed were to increase the reserve requirement to 11 percent, then the bank would have to put an additional $1 million on reserve, *reducing the amount it could lend out.* Since this increase in the reserve requirement would affect all banks, the money supply would be reduced and prices would likely fall.

A decrease of the reserve requirement, in contrast, *increases* the funds available to banks for loans, so they can make more loans, and money tends to become more readily available. An increase in the money supply can *stimulate the economy* to achieve higher growth rates, but it can also create inflationary pressures. That is, the prices of goods and services may go up. Can you see why the Fed may want to decrease the reserve requirement when the economy is in a recession? Can you also see the danger of inflation?

Open-Market Operations

Open-market operations consist of the buying and selling of government bonds. To decrease the money supply, the federal government sells U.S. government bonds to the public. The money it gets as payment for the bonds is no longer in circulation, decreasing the money supply. If the Fed wants to increase the money supply, it buys government bonds back from individuals, corporations, or organizations that are willing to sell. The money the Fed pays for these securities enters circulation, increasing the money supply. That's why in difficult financial times such as the Great Recession of 2008, the Fed bought bonds in an attempt to get the economy growing again.[14]

The Discount Rate

The Fed has often been called the bankers' bank because member banks can borrow money from the Fed and pass it on to their customers in the form of loans. The **discount rate** is the interest rate the Fed charges for loans to member banks. An increase in the discount

connect

iSeeit! Need help understanding how the Federal Reserve tries to stabilize the economy? Visit your Connect eBook to view a video for a brief animated explanation.

open-market operations
The buying and selling of U.S. government bonds by the Fed with the goal of regulating the money supply.

discount rate
The interest rate that the Fed charges for loans to member banks.

rate discourages banks from borrowing and reduces the number of available loans, decreasing the money supply. In contrast, lowering the discount rate encourages member banks to borrow money and increases the funds they have available for loans, which is supposed to increase the money supply. For seven years (from 2008 to 2015) the Fed lowered the discount rate to almost zero, hoping to increase bank lending. Since 2015, the Fed has gradually raised rates and reduced them as the economy has fluctuated.[15]

The discount rate is one of two interest rates the Fed controls. The other is the rate banks charge each other, called the *federal funds rate,* which is the interest rate financial institutions charge when they lend to other financial institutions overnight.[16]

The Federal Reserve's Check-Clearing Role

If you write a check to a local retailer that uses the same bank you do, it is a simple matter to reduce your account by the amount of the check and increase the amount in the retailer's account. But what happens if you write a check to a retailer in another state? That's where the Fed's check-clearing function comes into play.

That retailer will take the check to its bank. That bank will deposit the check for credit in the closest Federal Reserve bank. That bank will send the check to your local Federal Reserve bank for collection. The check will then be sent to your bank and the amount of the check will be withdrawn. Your bank will authorize the Federal Reserve bank in your area to deduct the amount of the check. That bank will pay the Federal Reserve bank that began the process in the first place. It will then credit the deposit account in the bank where the retailer has its account. That bank will then credit the account of the retailer. (See Figure 20.3 for a diagram of such an interstate transaction.) This detailed and involved process is a costly one for the Fed; therefore, banks have taken many measures to lessen the use of checks. Such efforts include the use of credit cards, debit cards, and other electronic transfers of money.

As you can see, the whole economy is affected by the Federal Reserve System's actions. Next, we'll briefly discuss the history of banking to give you some background about why the Fed came into existence about 100 years ago. Then we'll explore what's happening in banking today.

 TEST**PREP**

- What is money?
- What are the five characteristics of useful money?
- What is the money supply, and why is it important?
- How does the Federal Reserve control the money supply?
- What are the major functions of the Federal Reserve? What other functions does it perform?

LO 20–3   Trace the history of banking and the Federal Reserve System.

The History of Banking and the Need for the Fed

There was a time when there were no banks in the United States. Strict laws in Europe limited the number of coins people could bring to the colonies in the New World. Thus, colonists were forced to *barter* for goods; for example, they might trade cotton and tobacco for shoes and lumber.

Suppose Mr. Brown, a farmer from Quince Orchard, Maryland, purchases a tractor from a dealer in Austin, Texas.

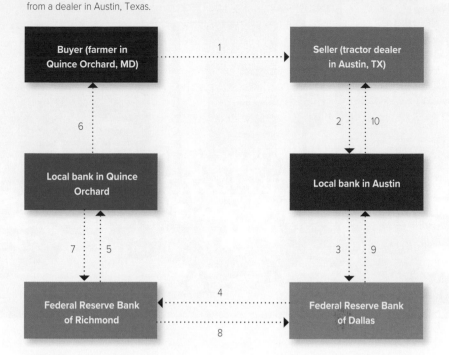

FIGURE 20.3 CHECK-CLEARING PROCESS THROUGH THE FEDERAL RESERVE BANK SYSTEM

1. Mr. Brown sends his check to the tractor dealer.
2. The dealer deposits the check in his account at a local bank in Austin.
3. The Austin bank deposits the check for credit in its account at the Federal Reserve Bank of Dallas.
4. The Federal Reserve Bank of Dallas sends the check to the Federal Reserve Bank of Richmond for collection.
5. The Federal Reserve Bank of Richmond forwards the check to the local bank in Quince Orchard, where Mr. Brown has his account.
6. The local bank in Quince Orchard deducts the check amount from Mr. Brown's account.
7. The Quince Orchard bank authorizes the Federal Reserve Bank of Richmond to deduct the check amount from its deposit account with the Federal Reserve Bank.
8. The Federal Reserve Bank of Richmond pays the Federal Reserve Bank of Dallas.
9. The Federal Reserve Bank of Dallas credits the Austin bank's deposit account.
10. The Austin bank credits the tractor dealer's account.

The demand for money was so great that Massachusetts issued its own paper money in 1690, and other colonies soon followed suit. But continental money, the first paper money printed in the United States, became worthless after a few years because people didn't trust its value.

Land banks were established to lend money to farmers. But Great Britain, still in charge of the colonies at that point, ended land banks by 1741. The colonies rebelled against these and other restrictions on their freedom, and a new bank was formed in Pennsylvania during the American Revolution to finance the war against England.

In 1791, after the United States gained independence, Alexander Hamilton persuaded Congress to form a *central bank* (a bank at which other banks could keep their funds and borrow funds if needed). This first version of a federal bank closed in 1811, only to be replaced in 1816 because state-chartered banks couldn't support the War of 1812. The battle between the Second (Central) Bank of the United States and state banks got hot in the 1830s. Several banks in Tennessee were hurt by pressure from the Central Bank. The fight ended when the Central Bank was closed in 1836. You can see that there was great resistance to a central bank, like the Federal Reserve, through much of U.S. history.

The Federal Reserve System was designed in 1913 to prevent the kind of run on banks that had occurred in 1907. Yet the stock market crash of 1929 caused depositors to make another run on their banks and take big withdrawals. Federal deposit insurance was established in 1933 to protect depositors' money. Do you think that these protections are enough?

Bettmann/Getty Images

By the time of the Civil War, the U.S. banking system was a mess. Different banks issued different kinds of currencies. People hoarded gold and silver coins because they were worth more as precious metal than as money. In any case, the chaos continued long after the war ended, reaching something of a climax in 1907, when many banks failed. People got nervous about the safety of banks and, in a run on the banks, attempted to withdraw their funds. Soon the cash was depleted and some banks had to refuse money to depositors. This caused people to distrust the banking system in general.

Despite the long history of opposition to a central bank, the cash shortage problems of 1907 led to the formation of an organization that could lend money to banks—the Federal Reserve System. It was to be a "lender of last resort" in such emergencies. Under the Federal Reserve Act of 1913, all federally chartered banks had to join the Federal Reserve. State banks could also join. The Federal Reserve became the bankers' bank. If banks had excess funds, they could deposit them in the Fed; if they needed extra money, they could borrow from the Fed. The Federal Reserve System has been intimately related to banking ever since, a link that has grown in recent years.

Banking and the Great Depression

The Federal Reserve System was designed to prevent a repeat of the 1907 panic. Nevertheless, the stock market crash of 1929 led to bank failures in the early 1930s. When the stock market began tumbling, people hurried to banks to withdraw cash. In spite of the Federal Reserve System, the banks ran out of money, and states were forced to close them. President Franklin D. Roosevelt extended the period of bank closings in 1933 to gain time to come up with a solution to the problem. In 1933 and 1935, Congress passed legislation to strengthen the banking system. The most important move was to establish federal deposit insurance to further protect the public from bank failures. As you can see, bank crises are nothing new; they often occur during a recession. From 1945 to 2009, the United States experienced 11 recessions. The average duration was 10 months; the longest recession was the Great Recession (2008–2009) that lasted 18 months. Now that you are familiar with the Federal Reserve, let's turn our attention to U.S. banks.

LO 20–4   Classify the various institutions in the U.S. banking system.

The U.S. Banking System

The U.S. banking system consists of commercial banks, savings and loan associations, and credit unions. In addition, there are various financial organizations, or nonbanks, that accept no deposits but offer many of the services of regular banks. Let's discuss the activities and services of each, starting with commercial banks.

Commercial Banks

The banks that are probably the most familiar to you are commercial banks. A **commercial bank** is a profit-seeking organization that receives deposits from individuals and businesses in the form of checking and savings accounts, and uses these funds to make loans. It has two types of customers—depositors and borrowers—and is equally responsible to both. A commercial bank makes a profit by efficiently using depositors' funds as inputs (on which it pays interest) to invest in interest-bearing loans to other customers. If the revenue generated by loans exceeds the interest paid to depositors plus operating expenses, the bank makes a profit.

commercial bank
A profit-seeking organization that receives deposits from individuals and corporations in the form of checking and savings accounts and then uses some of these funds to make loans.

Services Provided by Commercial Banks

Individuals and businesses that deposit money in a checking account can write personal checks to pay for almost any purchase or transaction. The technical name for a checking account is a **demand deposit** because the money is available on demand from the depositor. Some banks impose a service charge for check-writing privileges or demand a minimum deposit. They might also charge a small handling fee for each check written. For corporate depositors, the amount of the service charge often depends on the average daily balance in the checking account, the number of checks written, and the firm's credit rating and credit history. In the past, checking accounts paid no interest to depositors, but interest-bearing checking accounts are available today under certain conditions.[17]

demand deposit
The technical name for a checking account; the money in a demand deposit can be withdrawn anytime on demand from the depositor.

    Commercial banks also offer a variety of savings account options. A savings account is technically a **time deposit** because the bank can require a prior notice before you make a withdrawal. It would be wise for you to compare online and neighborhood banks to find where your money can earn the most interest. Unfortunately, over the past several years you haven't earned much interest on a time deposit in any bank. However, the low interest you receive in the United States is better than some depositors in Europe have experienced. The Reaching beyond our Borders box looks at how negative interest rates have turned traditional deposits upside down.

time deposit
The technical name for a savings account; the bank can require prior notice before the owner withdraws money from a time deposit.

    A **certificate of deposit (CD)** is a time-deposit (savings) account that earns interest, to be delivered on the certificate's maturity date. The depositor agrees not to withdraw any of the funds until then. CDs are now available for periods of months to years; usually the longer the period, the higher the interest rate. The interest rates also depend on economic conditions. At the present time, interest rates have rebounded a slight bit, but remain low.

certificate of deposit (CD)
A time-deposit (savings) account that earns interest to be delivered at the end of the certificate's maturity date.

    Commercial banks may also offer credit cards to creditworthy customers, life insurance, inexpensive brokerage services, financial counseling, automatic payment of bills, safe-deposit boxes, individual retirement accounts (IRAs), traveler's checks, trust departments,

Your Piggy Bank Could Pay Better Than a Bank

ecb.europa.eu

After saving some money from your new job, you are thinking about opening a savings account at your local bank. Probably your first question is, "How much interest will I earn on my deposit?" To your surprise, you find it's the bank that will earn the interest, not you. You literally have to pay the bank to hold your money. Sound crazy? Welcome to the upside-down world of negative interest rates that are taking hold in many parts of the global economy. Economist Olivia Mitchell, of the Wharton Business School at the University of Pennsylvania, believes that negative rates could be a feature of the global economy for years to come and will change the way people save and invest.

While U.S. banks bounced back strongly from the financial crisis in 2008, banks in Europe and Japan have struggled due to weak economies. Interest rates, therefore, have dropped below zero on some bank deposits as central

Georgios Kollidas/Shutterstock

banks, particularly in Japan and Germany, try to rejuvenate their lagging economies. The overall plan of the banks is to try to influence people about whether to save or invest their money. Investors tend to save when rates are high and invest and spend when it's cheaper to borrow. Spending

would be a boost to their economies.

In Germany, depositors have been informed they will have to pay the bank a prescribed rate for deposits instead of accruing interest. Currently, the charge applies only to large depositors with over a half-million dollars in deposits. Smaller investors so far are not being charged for their deposits. The low-rate environment, however, has raised concerns among smaller investors and has been very unpopular among Germans. It has particularly raised savers' concerns about preserving their wealth, especially for those saving for retirement or already retired. Rest assured, U.S. banks say they have no intention of following the path of banks in Japan and Europe.

Sources: David McHugh and Christopher Rugaber, "Negative Interest Rates Turn Saving, Borrowing Upside Down," *Yahoo! Finance*, finance.yahoo.com, February 14, 2020; Richa Rebello, "ECB Negative Rates Not Harmful, but Inflation Rise to Stay Elusive," *Bloomberg*, bloomberg.com, February 16, 2020.

automated teller machines (ATMs), and overdraft checking account privileges. The latter means preferred customers can automatically get loans when they've written checks exceeding their account balance.

Services to Borrowers

Commercial banks offer a variety of services to individuals and corporations in need of a loan. Since banks want to manage their funds effectively, loan applicants are screened carefully to ensure that the loan plus interest will be paid back on time. Generally, loans are given on the basis of the recipient's creditworthiness. Clearly banks failed to do that in the period leading up to the banking crisis in 2008. We will discuss why that happened later in the chapter. The nearby Making Ethical Decisions box explores an activity that could be an issue in banking.

Today, banks are continually trying to improve services to mobile users, especially Millennials. Having lived in an online world their entire lives, Millennials are very adept at mobile banking. They use technology to deposit checks, pay bills, track expenses, and transfer money, and over two-thirds make deposits by taking a photo of their checks.[18]

Savings and Loan Associations (S&Ls)

A **savings and loan association (S&L)** is a financial institution that accepts both savings and checking deposits, and provides home mortgage loans. S&Ls are often known as thrift institutions because their original purpose (starting in 1831) was to promote consumer thrift and home ownership. To help them encourage home ownership, thrifts were permitted for many years to offer slightly higher interest rates on savings deposits than banks. Those rates attracted a large pool of funds, which S&Ls used to offer long-term fixed-rate mortgages.

In their worst period, between 1986 and 1995, nearly 1,300 S&Ls failed. Reasons for the failures included the inflation of the 1970s, deregulation, regulatory failure (regulators allowed insolvent thrifts to stay open while their situations worsened), and fraud.[19] Today, S&Ls no longer offer better rates than banks because of changes in government laws, and many S&Ls have become banks. In 1980, there were almost 4,500 savings and loans in the United States. According to the FDIC, today there are about 754 savings and loan companies in the United States.[20]

savings and loan association (S&L)

A financial institution that accepts both savings and checking deposits and provides home mortgage loans.

Credit Unions

Credit unions are nonprofit, member-owned financial cooperatives that offer the full variety of banking services to their members—interest-bearing checking accounts at relatively high rates, short-term loans at relatively low rates, financial counseling, life insurance policies, and a limited number of home mortgage loans. They are organized by government agencies, corporations, unions, and professional associations. Today, credit unions are growing in popularity.

As nonprofit institutions, credit unions enjoy an exemption from federal income taxes. You might want to visit a local credit union to see whether you are eligible to belong, and then compare the rates to those at local banks. Credit unions often have fewer branches than banks and less access to ATMs and other services. It's best to determine what services you need, and then compare those services to the same services offered by banks. Today, credit unions are getting more ambitious in lending and are experiencing new growth in assets and number of institutions.[21] It's good to know that the money in credit union accounts (discussed later) is also insured for $250,000—as it is in your local bank.

credit unions

Nonprofit, member-owned financial cooperatives that offer the full variety of banking services to their members.

Other Financial Institutions (Nonbanks)

nonbanks

Financial organizations that accept no deposits but offer many of the services provided by regular banks (pension funds, insurance companies, commercial finance companies, consumer finance companies, and brokerage houses).

pension funds

Amounts of money put aside by corporations, nonprofit organizations, or unions to cover part of the financial needs of members when they retire.

Nonbanks are financial organizations that accept no deposits but offer many of the services provided by regular banks. Nonbanks include life insurance companies, pension funds, brokerage firms, commercial and consumer finance companies.

As competition between banks and nonbanks has increased, the dividing line between them has become less apparent. This is equally true in Europe, where U.S. companies compete with European banks. The diversity of financial services and investment alternatives nonbanks offer has led banks to expand their own services. In fact, many banks have merged with brokerage firms to offer full-service financial assistance.

Life insurance companies provide financial protection for policyholders, who periodically pay premiums. In addition, insurers invest the funds they receive from policyholders in corporate and government bonds. Today, insurance companies often provide long-term financing for real estate development projects.

Pension funds are monies put aside by corporations, nonprofit organizations, or unions to help fund their members' financial needs when they retire. Contributions to pension funds are made by employees, employers, or both. To generate additional income, pension funds typically invest in low-return but safe corporate stocks or other conservative investments, such as government securities and corporate bonds. Many financial services organizations that provide retirement and health benefits, such as TIAA, are a major force in U.S. financial markets. They also lend money directly to corporations. Unfortunately, after the long period of low interest rates over the past several years, many public and private pension funds are having problems meeting the expectations of their members.[22]

Brokerage firms have traditionally offered investment services in stock exchanges in the United States and abroad. They have also made serious inroads into regular banks' domain by offering high-yield combination savings and checking accounts. In addition, they offer money market accounts with check-writing privileges and allow investors to borrow, using their securities as collateral.

Commercial and consumer finance companies sometimes offer short-term loans to those who cannot meet the credit requirements of regular banks, such as new businesses, or who have exceeded their credit limit and need more funds. Be careful when borrowing from such institutions, however, because their interest rates can be quite high.

?TESTPREP

- Why did the United States need a Federal Reserve Bank?
- What are the differences among banks, savings and loan associations, and credit unions?
- What is a consumer finance company?

LO 20–5 Briefly trace the causes of the banking crisis of 2008, and explain how the government protects your funds during such crises.

The Banking Crisis of 2008 and How the Government Protects Your Money

In 2007–2008 the United States experienced a banking crisis that threatened to topple the economy. Who was responsible for the banking crisis? There is no simple answer. Some people believe the Federal Reserve was partly responsible because it kept the cost of borrowing so low that people were tempted to borrow more than they could afford to pay back.

Others blamed the U.S. Congress for pressuring banks, normally quite risk-averse, to make risky loans. The Community Reinvestment Act encouraged loans to families with questionable ability to repay. The intention was to create more "affordable housing," thus prodding banks to lend to people with minimal assets.

Banks learned they could avoid much of the risk of these questionable loans by dividing up their portfolios of mortgages and selling the mortgage-backed securities (MBSs) to other banks and other organizations all over the world. These securities seemed quite safe because they were backed by the homes that were mortgaged. Government-sponsored enterprises Fannie Mae and Freddie Mac seemed to guarantee the value of MBSs. Banks then sold more and more of such seemingly safe securities, hoping to make lots of money. Some banks were even accused of pushing loans onto naive consumers.

Photosbyjam/Getty Images

Meanwhile, the Federal Reserve and the Securities and Exchange Commission were accused of failing their regulatory duties by not issuing sufficient warnings. When the value of homes began to decline, people began defaulting on their loans (not paying them) and turned the properties back over to the banks. Almost 5 million households suffered through housing foreclosures when the housing bubble burst in 2008. Since the banks owned the mortgages on those homes, their profits declined dramatically, leading to a banking crisis—and the need for the government and the Fed to help out the banks. The long-term effects of that process are still being felt in the economy, especially for Millennials. Millennials' home-buying rate is 8 percent below that of their parents at a similar age.[23] Some even suggest that the United States is becoming a country of renters.

So whom do we blame for the banking crisis? The answer is that we could blame the Fed for suppressing interest rates, Congress for promoting questionable loans, the banks for making such loans and creating mortgage-backed securities that were not nearly as safe as promoted, government regulatory agencies for not doing their job, and people who took advantage of low interest rates to borrow money they couldn't reasonably hope to repay. No matter who was to blame, it was a painful period for the economy and its effect will linger on.

> *The bursting of the housing bubble in 2008 forced a sharp decline in home values. When homeowners discovered they owed more on their mortgages than their homes were worth, many stopped paying off their loans. As a result, the banks foreclosed on their houses. While home prices have since risen in many areas of the country, some areas have been slower to recover. How has the housing market fared in your hometown?*

Protecting Your Funds

The banking crisis that occurred in 2007–2008 was hardly the first economic crisis the nation has faced. The economy suffered similar problems during the Great Depression of the 1930s when many investors lost everything they had. To prevent investors from ever again being completely wiped out during an economic downturn, Congress created three major organizations to protect your money: the Federal Deposit Insurance Corporation (FDIC), the Savings Association Insurance Fund (SAIF), and the National Credit Union Administration (NCUA). All three insure deposits in individual accounts up to a certain amount. Because these organizations are so important to the safety of your money you have deposited, let's explore them individually in a bit more depth.

The Federal Deposit Insurance Corporation (FDIC) The **Federal Deposit Insurance Corporation (FDIC)** is an independent agency of the U.S. government that insures bank deposits. If a bank were to fail, the FDIC would arrange to have that bank's accounts transferred to another bank or reimburse depositors up to $250,000 per account. The FDIC covers many institutions, mostly commercial banks. Of course, one problem is that the government doesn't have unlimited money to cover all losses if too many banks should fail.

Federal Deposit Insurance Corporation (FDIC)
An independent agency of the U.S. government that insures bank deposits.

The Savings Association Insurance Fund (SAIF) The Savings Association Insurance Fund (SAIF) insures holders of accounts in savings and loan associations. A brief history will show why it was created. Some 1,700 bank and thrift institutions had failed during the early 1930s, and people were losing confidence in them. The FDIC and the Federal Savings and Loan Insurance Corporation (FSLIC) were designed (in 1933 and 1934, respectively) to create more confidence in banking institutions by protecting people's savings from loss. To get more control over the banking system in general, the government placed the FSLIC under the FDIC and gave it a new name: the Savings Association Insurance Fund (SAIF).

The National Credit Union Administration (NCUA) The National Credit Union Administration (NCUA) provides up to $250,000 coverage per individual depositor per institution. This coverage includes all accounts—checking accounts, savings accounts, money market accounts, and certificates of deposit. Depositors qualify for additional protection by holding accounts jointly or in trust. Individual retirement accounts (IRAs) are also separately insured up to $250,000. Credit unions, like banks, suffered from the banking crisis, and got money from the federal government to make more loans.

LO 20–6 Describe how technology helps make banking more efficient.

Using Technology to Make Banking More Efficient

Imagine the cost to a bank of approving a written check, physically processing it through the banking system, and mailing it back to you. It's expensive. Bankers long looked for ways to make the system more efficient.

One solution was to issue credit cards to reduce the flow of checks, but they too have their costs: there's still paper to process. Accepting credit cards costs retailers a bit over 2 percent of the amount charged. We'll continue to see much more electronic rather than physical exchange of money, because it is the most efficient way to transfer funds.

In an **electronic funds transfer (EFT) system**, messages about a transaction are sent from one computer to another. Thus, organizations can transfer funds more quickly and economically than with paper checks. EFT tools include electronic check conversion, debit cards, smart cards, direct deposits, and direct payments.

A **debit card** serves the same function as a check—it withdraws funds from a checking account. When the sale is recorded, the debit card sends an electronic signal to the bank, automatically transferring funds from your account to the seller's. A record of transactions immediately appears online. Debit transactions surpassed credit years ago and continue to grow.

Payroll debit cards are an efficient way for some firms to pay their workers, and are an alternative to cash for those who don't qualify for a credit or debit card—the so-called unbanked. Employees can access funds in their accounts immediately after they are posted, withdraw them from an ATM, pay bills online, or transfer funds to another cardholder. The system is much cheaper for companies than issuing checks, and more convenient for employees.[24] On the other hand, debit cards don't offer the same protection as credit cards. If someone steals your credit card, you are liable only for a certain amount. You are liable for everything when someone steals your debit card.

A **smart card** is an electronic funds transfer tool that combines a credit card, debit card, phone card, driver's license card, and more. Smart cards replace the typical magnetic strip on a credit or debit card with a microprocessor. The card can then store a variety of information, including the holder's bank balance. Merchants can use this information to check the card's validity and spending limits, and transactions can debit up to the amount on the card.

Some smart cards have embedded radio frequency identification (RFID) chips that make it possible to enter buildings and secure areas and to buy gas and other items with a swipe of the card. A biometric function lets you use your fingerprint to boot up your computer. Students are using smart cards to open locked doors to dorms and identify themselves to retailers near campus and online. The cards also serve as ATM cards.

For many, the ultimate convenience in banking is automatic transactions such as direct deposit and direct payments. A *direct deposit* is a credit made directly to a checking or savings account in place of a paycheck. The employer contacts the bank and orders it to transfer funds from the employer's account to the worker's account. Individuals can use direct deposits to transfer funds to other accounts, such as from a checking account to a savings or retirement account.

A *direct payment* is a preauthorized electronic payment. Customers sign a separate form for each company whose bill they would like to automatically pay from their checking or savings account on a specified date. The customer's bank completes each transaction and records it on the customer's monthly statement.

Courtesy of Pacsafe, www.pacsafe.com

RFID chips in credit cards allow consumers to pay for products with just a wave of a hand. But they're also easier for hackers to access, leading some people to keep their cards in RFID-blocking holders like this one. How do you make sure that your identity and finances are secure?

Online Banking

Almost all top U.S. retail banks allow customers to access their accounts online, and most have bill-paying capacity. Thus, you can complete all your financial transactions from home, using your telephone, computer, or mobile device to transfer funds from one account to another, pay your bills, and check the balance in each of your accounts. You can apply for a car loan or mortgage and get a response while you wait. Buying and selling stocks and bonds is equally easy.

Online banks such as Ally Bank offer online banking only, not physical branches. They can offer customers slightly higher interest rates and lower fees because they do not have the overhead costs traditional banks have. While many consumers are pleased with the savings and convenience, not all are happy with the service. Why? Some are nervous about security. People fear putting their financial information into cyberspace, where others may see it despite all the assurances of privacy.

LO 20–7 Evaluate the role and importance of international banking, the World Bank, and the International Monetary Fund.

International Banking and Banking Services

Banks help companies conduct business in other countries by providing three services: letters of credit, banker's acceptances, and money exchange. If a U.S. company wants to buy a product from Germany, the company could pay a bank to issue a letter of credit. A **letter of credit** is a promise by the bank to pay the seller a given amount if certain conditions are met. For example, the German company may not be paid until the goods have arrived at the U.S. company's warehouse. A **banker's acceptance** promises that the bank will pay some specified amount at a particular time. No conditions are imposed. Finally, a company can go to a bank and exchange U.S. dollars for euros to use in Germany; that's called *currency* or *money exchange*.

Banks have made buying goods and services globally easy for travelers and businesspeople. For example, automated teller machines provide yen, euros, and other foreign currencies through your personal Visa, Mastercard, Cirrus, or American Express card.

letter of credit
A promise by the bank to pay the seller a given amount if certain conditions are met.

banker's acceptance
A promise that the bank will pay some specified amount at a particular time.

The World Bank and the International Monetary Fund (IMF) are intergovernmental organizations that help support the global banking community. Both draw protests for their actions. Why?

Leaders in International Banking

It would be shortsighted to discuss the U.S. economy apart from the world economy. If the Federal Reserve decides to lower interest rates, within minutes foreign investors can withdraw their money from the United States and put it in countries with higher rates. Of course, the Fed's increasing of interest rates can draw money to the United States equally quickly.

Today's money markets thus form a global market system of which the United States is just a part. International bankers make investments in any country where they can get a maximum return for their money at a reasonable risk. About $5 trillion is traded daily![25] The net result of international banking and finance has been to link the economies of the world into one interrelated system with no regulatory control. U.S. firms must compete for funds with firms all over the world. An efficient firm in London or Tokyo is more likely to get international financing than a less efficient firm in Detroit or Chicago. Global markets mean that banks do not necessarily keep their money in their own countries. They make investments where they get the maximum return.

What this means for you is that banking is no longer a domestic issue; it's a global one. To understand the U.S. financial system, you must learn about the global financial system, including foreign central banks. To understand the state of the U.S. economy, you need to learn about the economic condition of countries throughout the world. In the world economy financed by international banks, the United States is a major player, but just one player. To continue being the global leader, the United States must stay financially secure and its businesses must stay competitive in world markets.

The World Bank and the International Monetary Fund

World Bank

The bank primarily responsible for financing economic development; also known as the International Bank for Reconstruction and Development.

The bank primarily responsible for financing economic development is the International Bank for Reconstruction and Development, or the **World Bank**. After World War II, it lent money to countries in Western Europe so they could rebuild. Today, it lends most of its money to developing nations to improve their productivity and help raise standards of living and quality of life.[26] That includes working to eliminate diseases that kill millions of people each year.

The World Bank has faced considerable criticism and protests around the world. Environmentalists charge that it finances projects damaging to the ecosystem. Human rights activists and unionists say the bank supports countries that restrict religious freedoms and tolerate sweatshops. AIDS activists complain that it does not do enough to get low-cost AIDS drugs to developing nations.

Despite its efforts to improve its image, the World Bank still has many critics.[27] Some want it to forgive the debts of developing countries and others want it to stop making such loans until the countries institute free markets and the right to own property. Some changes in World Bank policy may lie ahead.

In contrast to the World Bank, the **International Monetary Fund (IMF)** was established to foster cooperative monetary policies that stabilize the exchange of one national currency for another. About 189 countries are voluntary members of the IMF and allow their money to be freely exchanged for foreign money, keep the IMF informed about changes in monetary policy, and modify those policies on the advice of the IMF to accommodate the needs of the entire membership.[28]

The IMF is designed to oversee member countries' monetary and exchange rate policies.[29] Its goal is to maintain a global monetary system that works best for all nations and enhances world trade. While it is not primarily a lending institution like the World Bank, its members do contribute funds according to their ability, and those funds are available to countries in financial difficulty.

International Monetary Fund (IMF)

Organization that assists the smooth flow of money among nations.

?TEST**PREP**

- What is the role of the FDIC?
- How does a debit card differ from a credit card?
- What is the World Bank and what does it do?
- What is the IMF and what does it do?

SUMMARY

LO 20–1 Explain what money is and what makes money useful.

- **What is money?**

Money is anything people generally accept as payment for goods and services.

- **What are the five standards for a useful form of money?**

The five standards for a useful form of money are portability, divisibility, stability, durability, and uniqueness.

- **What are "Bitcoins," and can you buy things online with them?**

Bitcoins are a form of online money. Bitcoin has an online store that accepts the currency.

LO 20–2 Describe how the Federal Reserve controls the money supply.

- **How does the Federal Reserve control the money supply?**

The Federal Reserve makes financial institutions keep funds in the Federal Reserve System (reserve requirement), buys and sells government securities (open-market operations), and lends money to banks (the discount rate). To increase the money supply, the Fed can cut the reserve requirement, buy government bonds, and lower the discount rate.

LO 20–3 Trace the history of banking and the Federal Reserve System.

- **How did banking evolve in the United States?**

Massachusetts issued its own paper money in 1690; other colonies followed suit. British land banks lent money to farmers but ended such loans by 1741. After the American Revolution, there was much debate about the role of banking, and heated battles between the Central

Bank of the United States and state banks. Eventually, a federally chartered and state-chartered system was established, but chaos continued until many banks failed in 1907. The system was revived by the Federal Reserve only to fail again during the Great Depression. There have been 11 recessions since then, including the longest one in 2008.

LO 20–4   Classify the various institutions in the U.S. banking system.

■ What institutions make up the banking system?

Savings and loans, commercial banks, and credit unions are all part of the banking system.

■ How do they differ from one another?

Before deregulation in 1980, commercial banks were unique in that they handled both deposits and checking accounts. At that time, savings and loans couldn't offer checking services; their main function was to encourage thrift and home ownership by offering high interest rates on savings accounts and providing home mortgages. Deregulation closed the gaps between banks and S&Ls, and they now offer similar services.

■ What kinds of services do they offer?

Banks and thrifts offer such services as savings accounts, checking accounts, certificates of deposit, loans, individual retirement accounts (IRAs), safe-deposit boxes, online banking, life insurance, brokerage services, and traveler's checks.

■ What is a credit union?

A credit union is a member-owned cooperative that offers everything a bank does—it takes deposits, allows you to write checks, and makes loans. It also may sell life insurance and offer mortgages. Credit union interest rates are sometimes higher than those from banks, and loan rates are often lower.

■ What are some of the other financial institutions that make loans and perform banklike operations?

Nonbanks include life insurance companies that lend out their funds, pension funds that invest in stocks and bonds and make loans, brokerage firms that offer investment services, and commercial finance companies.

LO 20–5   Briefly trace the causes of the banking crisis of 2008, and explain how the government protects your funds during such crises.

■ What caused the banking crisis?

The goal was to have affordable housing, so the government urged banks to make loans to some who could not afford to repay. The banks wanted to minimize the risk of such loans, so they created mortgage-backed securities and sold them to other banks and organizations throughout the world. The government did not regulate these transactions well, and many banks failed because housing values fell and people defaulted on their loans. Many have been blamed for the loss: the Fed, Congress, bank managers, Fannie Mae, and Freddie Mac among them.

■ What agencies insure the money you put into a bank, S&L, or credit union?

Money deposited in banks is insured by the Federal Deposit Insurance Corporation (FDIC). Money in S&Ls is insured by another agency connected to the FDIC, the Savings Association Insurance Fund (SAIF). Money in credit unions is insured by the National Credit Union Administration (NCUA). Accounts are now insured to $250,000.

LO 20–6   Describe how technology helps make banking more efficient.

■ What are debit cards and smart cards?

A debit card looks like a credit card but withdraws money that is already in your account. When the sale is recorded, the debit card sends an electronic signal to the bank, automatically transferring funds from your account to the seller's. A smart card is an electronic funds transfer tool that combines a credit card, debit card, phone card, driver's license card, and more. Smart cards replace the typical magnetic strip on a credit or debit card with a microprocessor.

■ **What is the benefit of automatic transactions and online banking?**

A *direct deposit* is a credit made directly to a checking or savings account in place of a paycheck. A *direct payment* is a preauthorized electronic payment. Customers sign a separate form for each company whose bill they would like to automatically pay from their checking or savings account on a specified date. The customer's bank completes each transaction and records it on the customer's monthly statement. All top U.S. retail banks now allow customers to access their accounts online, and most have bill-paying capacity.

LO 20–7 **Evaluate the role and importance of international banking, the World Bank, and the International Monetary Fund.**

■ **What do we mean by global markets?**

Global markets mean that banks do not necessarily keep their money in their own countries. They make investments where they get the maximum return. What this means for you is that banking is no longer a domestic issue; it's a global one.

■ **What roles do the World Bank and the IMF play?**

The World Bank (also called the International Bank for Reconstruction and Development) is primarily responsible for financing economic development. The International Monetary Fund (IMF), in contrast, was established to assist the smooth flow of money among nations. It requires members (who join voluntarily) to allow their own money to be exchanged for foreign money freely, to keep the IMF informed about changes in monetary policy, and to modify those policies on the advice of the IMF to accommodate the needs of the entire membership.

KEY TERMS

banker's acceptance 539
barter 525
certificate of deposit (CD) 533
commercial bank 533
credit unions 535
debit card 538
demand deposit 533
discount rate 529
electronic funds transfer (EFT) system 538

Federal Deposit Insurance Corporation (FDIC) 537
International Monetary Fund (IMF) 541
letter of credit 539
M-1 527
M-2 527
M-3 527
money 524
money supply 526
nonbanks 536

open-market operations 529
pension funds 536
reserve requirement 528
savings and loan association (S&L) 535
Savings Association Insurance Fund (SAIF) 538
smart card 538
time deposit 533
World Bank 540

CRITICAL THINKING

1. If you were chairperson of the Federal Reserve, what economic figures might you use to determine how well you were doing? What role did the Federal Reserve play in the banking crisis of 2008–2009?

2. How much cash do you usually carry with you? What other means do you use to pay for items at the store or on the Internet? What trends do you see in such payments? How might those trends make your purchase experience more satisfactory?

3. If the value of the dollar declines relative to the euro, what will happen to the price of French wine sold in U.S. stores? Will people in France be more or less likely to buy a U.S.-made car? Why?

4. Do you keep your savings in a bank, an S&L, a credit union, or some combination? Have you compared the benefits you could receive from each? Where would you expect to find the best loan values?

PUTTING PRINCIPLES TO WORK

PURPOSE

To learn more about the banking crisis that began the Great Recession in 2008 and what has happened since.

EXERCISE

1. Search online for articles about the causes of the banking crisis that began in 2008. See if anyone in the class was directly affected by the banking crisis (i.e., lost their home). What organizations share the blame for the crisis?

2. Search for information about what has happened to banking in the United States and around the world since the banking crisis. What role did the Fed play in ending the crisis in the United States?

3. Search for information about what banking regulation changes the current president and Congress have proposed or passed. Do you think these changes will help or hurt the prevention of the problems that caused the 2008 crisis?

DEVELOPING CAREER SKILLS

KEY: ● **Team** ★ **Analytic** ▲ **Communication** ◎ **Technology**

●◎▲★ 1. In a small group, discuss the following: What services do you use from banks, S&Ls, or credit unions? How many of you use online banking? What seem to be its pluses and minuses? Use this opportunity to go online to compare the rates and services of various local banks, S&Ls, and credit unions.

▲★ 2. Poll the class to see who uses a bank and who uses a credit union. Have class members compare the services at each (interest rates on savings accounts, services available, loan rates). If anyone uses an online service, see how those rates compare. If no one uses a credit union or online bank, discuss the reasons why.

●▲★ 3. One role of the Federal Reserve is to help process your checks. In small groups discuss when and where you use checks, credit cards, debit cards, smartphones, and cash. Do you often write checks for small amounts? Would you stop if you calculated how much it costs to process such checks? Have you switched to debit cards as a result? Discuss your findings with the class.

●▲★ 4. Form several smaller groups and discuss the banking crisis of 2008–2009. Did it affect anyone in the class? What has happened to banks and the economy in general since the banking crisis? What have been the political implications of economic changes in recent years?

▲★ 5. Write a short report on the role of the World Bank and the International Monetary Fund in providing loans to countries. Is it important for U.S. citizens to lend money to people in other countries through such organizations? Why or why not? Be prepared to debate the value of these organizations in class.

CAREER EXPLORATION

If you are interested in pursuing a career in the banking industry, here are a few to consider. Find out about the tasks performed, skills needed, pay, and opportunity outlook in these fields in the *Occupational Outlook Handbook (OOH)* at bls.gov.

- **Loan officer**—evaluates, authorizes, or recommends approval of loan applications for people and businesses.

- **Foreign exchange trader**—focuses on foreign currency exchange markets; reviews the various factors that influence local rates of exchange and decides which currencies to buy and sell in the foreign exchange markets.

- **Credit counselor**—advises individuals and businesses about loans, financial goals, and debt; recommends different types of loans and payment plans to help with debt repayment.

McGraw Hill connect · *Understanding the Federal Reserve System* — VIDEO CASE

The Federal Reserve (also called the Fed) is the central bank of the United States. The Fed oversees the currency and money supply. The Fed system consists of five major parts: (1) the board of governors, (2) the Federal Open Market Committee, (3) 12 Federal Reserve banks, (4) three advisory councils, and (5) the 3,000 member banks in the system. The board of governors administers and supervises the 12 Federal Reserve banks. The 7 members of the board are appointed by the president of the United States and confirmed by the U.S. Senate. The Federal Open Market Committee has 12 voting members and is the policy-making body. The Federal Reserve is a private firm not supported by taxpayer dollars.

The Fed buys and sells foreign currencies, regulates various types of credit, supervises banks, and collects data on the money supply and other economic activity. The Fed's actions directly affect everyone in terms of credit card rates, consumer prices, and student loan rates. The Fed uses three processes for controlling the money supply that impacts the economy: the reserve requirement, open-market operations, and the discount rate.

The reserve requirement is a percentage of the money in commercial banks' checking and savings accounts that must be kept in the bank or in a non-interest-bearing deposit at the local Federal Reserve Bank. If a bank has $100 million in deposits and the reserve requirement is 10 percent, the bank must have $10 million on reserve.

The Fed also conducts open-market operations that involve the buying and selling of government bonds. There is a finite amount of bonds available in the economy. If the Fed sells bonds, the money received for them is no longer in circulation, which decreases the money supply. The

opposite occurs if the Fed is buying bonds. The money the Fed pays to buy the bonds is back in circulation, which increases the money supply.

The Federal Reserve is often referred to as the "banker's bank," because member banks can borrow money from the Fed and lend it out to customers in the form of loans. The discount rate is the interest rate the Fed charges for loans to member banks. If the rate goes up, banks don't borrow, thus less money is available for loans to businesses and consumers.

The Fed also acts as a clearinghouse in the banking system. The Fed clears transactions such as check cashing. The Fed sends payments back and forth among banks as the head of the Automatic Clearinghouse Network. The Fed also assumes the key role of managing the unemployment rate by keeping inflation at a level it deems acceptable. The Fed becomes extremely important during difficult economic times such as the Great Recession when unemployment accelerated and the Fed lowered the interest rate to almost zero hoping to encourage bank lending.

The entire economy is affected by the actions of the Federal Reserve. A simple piece of advice is to pay attention to the Fed and follow what it is doing.

THINKING IT OVER

1. Describe how the Federal Reserve can use its authority to stimulate the economy.

2. How does the Fed raising the reserve requirement affect the possibility of getting a business loan?

3. Why is monetary policy an important part of the Federal Reserve's mission?

NOTES

1. "About the Fed," Federal Reserve System, federalreserve. gov, accessed March 2020; Kimberly Amadeo, "The Federal Reserve and What It Does," *The Balance,* thebalance.com, January 27, 2020.

2. John Russell, "What Is a Forex Currency Trader?," *The Balance,* thebalance.com, February 5, 2020.

3. Hannah Wallace, "How to Barter Anything," *Real Simple,* realsimple.com, accessed March 2020; Victoria Fryer, "The History of Commerce: From the Silk Road to Modern Economics," *Big Commerce,* bigcommerce.com, accessed March 2020; James Chen, "Medium of Exchange Definition," *Investopedia,* investopedia.com, February 17, 2020.

4. J. D. Harrison, "Bartering Secrets," *The Washington Post,* March 6, 2013.

5. Jean Murray, "Barter Exchanges and How They Work," *The Balance Small Business,* thebalancesmb.com, August 2, 2019; Andrea Blackwell, "How to Barter for Goods & Services—Tips and Methods to Trade," *Money Crashers,* moneycrashers.com, accessed March 2020.

6. Gertrude Chavez-Dreyfuss, "Cryptocurrency Crime Losses More Than Double to $4.5 Billion in 2019, Report Finds," *U.S. News & World Report,* usnews.com, February 11, 2020.

7. "Cryptocurrency Opinion & Analysis," Investing.com, investing.com, accessed March 2020; Josh Nadeau, "Telegram, Facebook, and the Furious Fight over the Future of Cryptocurrency," *Fast Company,* fastcompany. com, February 21, 2020.

8. Mike Unser, "Penny Costs 1.99 Cents to Make in 2019, Nickel Costs 7.62 Cents," *Coin News,* coinnews.net, February 7, 2020.

9. Jeff Cox, "Market Pressure Heats Up on the Fed with at Least Three Price Cuts Now Priced in for 2020," *Yahoo! Finance,* finance.yahoo.com, February 27, 2020; Noah Smith, "QE Works. It's Just Not a Slam-Dunk Recession Stopper," *Bloomberg,* bloomberg.com, February 10, 2020.

10. Brian Cheung, "Economists Split over Whether Fed Policy Is 'Quantitative Easing,'" *Yahoo! Finance,* finance. yahoo.com, February 24, 2020; Greg Robb, "Powell Says Fed Will Aggressively Use QE to Fight Next Recession," *MarketWatch,* marketwatch.com, February 12, 2020; Howard Schneider and Ann Saphir, "In the Next Strong Downturn, Fed May Opt for Quick, Strong Action," *The New York Times,* February 21, 2020; Dominic White, "The Fed Is Not Doing QE., Here's Why That Matters," *Financial Times,* ft.com, February 5, 2020.

11. "Who's behind the Federal Reserve's Interest Rate Decisions?," *Fox Business,* foxbusiness.com, February 12, 2020; "What Are the Federal Reserve's Objectives in Conducting Monetary Policy?," Federal Reserve, federalreserve.com, accessed March 2020.

12. "The Culture Wars between Economists and Practitioners," *The Economist,* theeconomist.com, February 6, 2020; Dominic O'Neill, "ECB: Helicopter Money Could Lift the Mood in Europe," *Euromoney,* euromoney.com, February 13, 2020; Stephen Pope, "The ECB Wants to Hear from the Public; Will LaGarde Listen?," *Forbes,* forbes.com, February 24, 2020; John Ainger and Fergal O'Brien, "LaGarde Says ECB Running Out of Room to Fight Global Threats," *Bloomberg,* February 6, 2020.

13. "Making Sense of the Federal Reserve. Who Owns Reserve Banks?," Federal Reserve Bank of St. Louis, stlouisfed.org, accessed March 2020; "Is the Federal Reserve a Privately-Owned Corporation?," Federal Reserve Bank of San Francisco, frbsf.org, accessed March 2020; James Chen, "Federal Reserve System," *Investopedia,* investopedia.com, February 4, 2020; Joshua Kennon, "The Federal Reserve and Interest Rates," *The Balance,* thebalance.com, February 11, 2020; "Who Owns the Federal Reserve?," Federal Reserve, federalreserve.gov, accessed March 2020.

14. Jeanna Smialek, "'Now Is the Time:' A Fed Official Urges Congress to Plan for Recessions," *The New York Times,* February 21, 2020; Stan Choe and Christopher Rugaber, "Markets Want Fed to Save Them. Why Its Tools Might Not Work," *Star Tribune,* March 1, 2020; Larry Light, "A Fed Rate Cut Won't Cure What's Ailing the Stock Market," *Fortune,* March 2, 2020.

15. Jacob Sonenshine, "The Fed Is Ready to Cut Rates. But Debt Exceeds the Level of the Great Recession," *TheStreet,* thestreet.com, February 11, 2020; "Federal Reserve Makes Emergency Rate Cut to Offset Coronavirus Impact," *The Los Angeles Times,* March 3, 2020; Nick Timiraos, "Federal Reserve Cuts Interest Rates by Half Percentage Point," *The Wall Street Journal,* March 3, 2020.

16. "Fed Facts: Understanding the Federal Funds Rate," Federal Reserve, federalreserve.gov, February 18, 2020; Jeff Cox, "Fed Cuts Rates by Half a Percentage Point to Combat Coronavirus Slowdown," *CNBC,* cnbc.com, March 3, 2020; Heather Long, "Fed Cuts Interest Rate a Half Percentage Point, Largest Emergency Cut since the Financial Crisis," *The Washington Post,* March 3, 2020.

17. Dustin Clendenen, "What Is a High Yield Checking Account? Here's What You Need to Know," *Business Insider,* businessinsider.com, February 13, 2020; Rebecca Lake, "Checking vs. Savings Accounts," *Investopedia,* investopedia.com, February 11, 2020; "Best Checking Accounts of 2020," *Bankrate,* bankrate.com, accessed March 2020.

18. Mary Wisniewski, "Best Banks and Credit Unions for Mobile Banking," *Bankrate,* bankrate.com, February 5, 2020; Kate Ashford, "Best Online Banks of 2020—and How to Choose One," *Forbes,* forbes.com, February 28, 2020.

19. Federal Deposit Insurance Corporation, fdic.gov, accessed March 2020.

20. Priti Dhanuka, "Near-Term Prospects Look Gloomy for Savings & Loan Industry," *Yahoo! Finance,* finance.yahoo. com, February 28, 2020.

21. Ben Eisen, "Credit Unions Get More Ambitious," *The Wall Street Journal,* December 3, 2019; Ken McCarthy and Zain Tariq, "Credit Unions Growing Memberships but Challenges Still Abound," *S&P Global Market Intelligence,* spglobal.com, accessed March 2020.

22. "Public Pension Debt Burden Needs Reboot," *Boston Herald,* February 4, 2020; Heather Gillers, "Is Your City's Pension Fund a Little Short? Marijuana Might Help," *The Wall Street Journal,* February 4, 2020; Rick Wayman, "The Investing Risk of Underfunded Pension Funds," *Investopedia,* investopedia.com, February 28, 2020.

23. Annie Lowrey, "The Great Affordability Crisis Breaking America," *The Atlantic,* February 7, 2020; Maurie Backman, "Here's Why Ownership Might Be More Expensive for 70% of Millennial Buyers," *The Motley Fool,* fool.com, February 4, 2020; Daniel Bortz, "Here's How to Buy a Home If You Can't Save for a Down Payment," *Money,* money.com, February 17, 2020; Christopher Ingraham, "Millennials' Share of the U.S. Housing Market: Small and Shrinking," *Seattle Times,* February 18, 2020.

24. Scott Thompson, "How Does a Payroll Debit Card Work?," *Chron,* smallbusiness.chron.com, accessed March 2020; Justin Pritchard, "How to Set Up Direct Deposit," *The Balance,* thebalance.com, February 27, 2020.

25. John Russell, "What Is a Forex Currency Trader?," *The Balance,* thebalance.com, February 5, 2020; "Forex Market Overview," NASDAQ, nasdaq.com, accessed March 2020; Basia Hellwig, "How to Spot a Forex Scam," *Investopedia,* investopedia.com, February 21, 2020.

26. World Bank, worldbank.com, accessed March 2020.

27. Noah Smith, "When Development Aid Goes Awry," *Bloomberg,* bloomberg.com, February 24, 2020.

28. "List of Members," International Monetary Fund, imf.org, accessed March 2020.

29. "Structural Adjustment," *The Economist,* economist.com, February 15, 2020.

Working within the Legal Environment

LEARNING OBJECTIVES >>

After you have read and studied this bonus chapter, you should be able to

A–1 Define *business law,* distinguish between statutory and common law, and explain the role of administrative agencies.

A–2 Define *tort law* and explain the role of product liability in tort law.

A–3 Identify the purposes and conditions of patents, copyrights, and trademarks.

A–4 Describe warranties and negotiable instruments as covered in the Uniform Commercial Code.

A–5 List and describe the conditions necessary to make a legally enforceable contract, and describe the possible consequences if such a contract is violated.

A–6 Summarize several laws that regulate competition and protect consumers in the United States.

A–7 Explain the role of tax laws in generating income for the government and as a method of discouraging or encouraging certain behaviors among taxpayers.

A–8 Distinguish among the various types of bankruptcy as outlined by the Bankruptcy Code.

A–9 Explain the role of deregulation as a tool to encourage competition.

Jerome (Jerry) Schlichter, Attorney

For most attorneys, their typical day is a far cry from the legal acrobatics that lawyers perform in TV shows and movies. In reality, the majority of attorneys never have the opportunity to participate in a headline-grabbing case or landmark Supreme Court ruling that gets their names in national publications such as the *The New York Times* or *The Wall Street Journal*. That's not the case for Jerry Schlichter, though. Over the years, he has participated in more high-stakes trials than most attorneys could ever imagine.

Throughout his career, Schlichter has been a staunch defender of an individual's right to fair treatment. He has handled many precedent-setting class action and mass tort cases on behalf of employees and retirees against excessive fees charged by the 401(k) industry. In 2014 and 2015, Schlichter and his firm obtained two of the largest 401(k) excessive fee settlements in history against defense giants Lockheed Martin and Boeing. In 2015, he won a unanimous 9–0 decision from the U.S. Supreme Court in the first case dealing with fee charges in 401(k) plans. His actions led to dramatic changes in the 401(k) industry that have benefited employees and retirees across the country. In fact, *Investment News* once named him "public enemy no. 1 for 401(k) profiteers."

Before he ever entered the legal profession, though, Schlichter graduated with honors from the University of Illinois with a bachelor's degree in business administration. He attended law school at the University of California at Los Angeles where he was appointed associate editor of the *UCLA Law Review*. His work in personal injury and civil rights brought him from the West Coast to the Midwest where today he is managing partner of the law firm he founded, Schlichter Bogard & Denton. Here he has continued his work in civil rights and personal injury while also expanding his expertise into economic and environmental law. Over the course of his long career, he has earned the respect of the legal community and has repeatedly been selected as one of the best lawyers in the United States. To say he has been involved in many high-profile cases that altered the legal system would be an understatement.

Schlichter has also been instrumental in winning multiple judgments against railroads on behalf of employees. One such success was in obtaining an injunction against Union Pacific Railroad that barred the railroad from interfering with workers in their pursuit of injury claims. He also won a $27 million settlement for the widow and children of a St. Louis firefighter who died on duty due to a defective breathing apparatus. A defender of civil rights, Schlichter's firm handled a national class action employment discrimination case on behalf of female employees of Rent-A-Center that resulted in a $47 million verdict and a revamping of the company's policies. In a striking move, the trial judge in the case paid tribute to Schlichter's work by saying that "his advocacy was of the highest and noblest purpose, and accomplished a great public good."

Beyond his legal achievements, Schlichter's community initiatives have earned high praise. He and his wife, Sue, founded Mentor St. Louis, a nonprofit organization that provides disadvantaged students with guidance from adult mentors. Schlichter also helped lead Missouri's passage of the Rebuilding Communities Act, which is designed to attract businesses to distressed communities. His work on passing the Neighborhood Preservation Act led to improving housing in faltering neighborhoods in his community. Understanding the needs of entrepreneurs, Schlichter cofounded Arch Grants, a nationally recognized global business start-up competition that provides equity-free grants of $50,000 to emerging businesses in the St. Louis area. He has also been honored with the St. Louis Award, given to a person for countless contributions to the development of the community. Although Schlichter has accomplished a lot during his long career, his professional commitment to community and the fair application of the law is far from finished.

Legal issues affect almost every area of our lives and businesses. The United States has more lawyers than any other nation in the world and is clearly the world's most litigious society. In this bonus chapter, we will look briefly at the structure of the U.S. legal system. Then we will discuss key areas of business law such as torts, patents, copyrights, trademarks, sales law, contract law, laws to protect competition and consumers, tax law, and bankruptcy law. We will also look into the sometimes controversial topic of deregulation. It's unlikely you'll be able to go head-to-head with a lawyer of Jerry Schlichter's ability after reading this chapter, but you can use it as a foundation to the study of law. Who knows what your future might be?

Sources: Greg Edwards, "St. Louis Law Firm Wins $10.65 Million Settlement with Duke University," *St. Louis Business Journal,* bizjournals.com, January 18, 2019; David Nicklaus, "Marathon 401(k) Case Is Another Win for St. Louis Lawyer—and Workers," *St. Louis Post-Dispatch,* April 2, 2019; Brittney Wheeler, "Sue and Jerry Schlichter Receive Harris Award," *The Source,* source.wustl.edu, July 26, 2019; Schlichter Bogard & Denton, uselaws.com, accessed March 2020.

Let's talk business!
bit.ly/LetsTalkBusinessA

name that company

THESE COMPANIES WERE ORDERED to pay a university $1.1 billion for infringing on three of its WiFi patents. Name these companies. (Find the answer in the chapter.)

LO A–1 Define *business law,* distinguish between statutory and common law, and explain the role of administrative agencies.

The Case for Laws

Imagine a society without laws. Just think: no speed limits, no age restrictions on the consumption of alcohol, no limitations on who can practice law or medicine—a society where people are free to do whatever they choose, with no interference. Obviously, the more we consider this possibility, the more unrealistic we realize it is. Laws are an essential part of a civilized nation. Over time, though, the depth and scope of the body of laws must change to continue reflecting the needs of society. The **judiciary** is the branch of government chosen to oversee the legal system through a system of courts.

The U.S. court system is organized at the federal, state, and local levels. At both the federal and state levels, trial courts hear cases involving criminal and civil law. *Criminal law* defines crimes, establishes punishments, and regulates the investigation and prosecution of people accused of committing crimes. *Civil law* proceedings cover noncriminal acts—marriage, personal injury suits, and so on. Both federal and state systems have appellate courts that hear appeals from the losing party about decisions made at the trial-court level. Appellate courts can review and overturn these decisions.

The judiciary also governs the activities and operations of business, including hiring and firing practices, unpaid leave for family emergencies, environmental protection, worker safety, freedom from sexual harassment at work, and more. As you may suspect, businesspeople prefer to set their own standards of behavior and often complain that the government is overstepping its bounds in governing business. The financial crisis of 2008 highlighted that the U.S. business community did not follow acceptable standards, particularly in financial markets. This caused the government to expand its control and enforcement procedures.[1] This chapter will look at specific laws and regulations and how they affect businesses.

Business law refers to the rules, statutes, codes, and regulations that provide a legal framework for the conduct of business and that are enforceable by court action. A businessperson must be familiar with laws regarding product liability, sales, contracts, fair competition, consumer protection, taxes, and bankruptcy. Let's start by briefly discussing the foundations of law and what the legal system is all about.

Statutory and Common Law

Two major fields of law are important to businesspeople: statutory law and common law.

Statutory law includes state and federal constitutions, legislative enactments, treaties of the federal government, and ordinances—in short, written law. You can read the statutes that make up this body of law, but they are often written in language whose meaning must

judiciary
The branch of government chosen to oversee the legal system through the court system.

business law
Rules, statutes, codes, and regulations that are established to provide a legal framework within which business may be conducted and that are enforceable by court action.

statutory law
State and federal constitutions, legislative enactments, treaties of the federal government, and ordinances—in short, written law.

dcdebs/Getty Images

In the U.S. judicial system, judges are guided in their decisions by the precepts of common law (often called unwritten law because it is based on previous court decisions). Such decisions become precedent and assist other judges in making legal rulings. What are some practical benefits of this process?

be determined in court. With over 1.3 million licensed lawyers, the United States has more lawyers per citizen than any country in the world.[2]

Common law is the body of law that comes from decisions handed down by courts. We often call it *unwritten law* because it does not appear in any legislative enactment, treaty, or other written document. Under common law principles, what judges have decided in previous cases is very important in deciding today's cases. Such decisions are called **precedent**, and they guide judges in the handling of new cases. Common law evolves through decisions made in trial courts, appellate courts, and special courts (e.g., probate courts or bankruptcy courts). Lower courts (trial courts) must abide by the precedents set by higher courts (e.g., appellate courts) such as the U.S. Supreme Court.

Administrative Agencies

Administrative agencies are federal or state institutions and other government organizations created by Congress or state legislatures with delegated power to create rules and regulations within their given area of authority.

Legislative bodies can create administrative agencies and also terminate them. Some administrative agencies hold quasi-legislative, quasi-executive, and quasi-judicial powers. This means that an agency is allowed to pass rules and regulations within its area of authority, conduct investigations in cases of suspected rules violations, and hold hearings if it feels rules and regulations have been violated.

Administrative agencies issue more rulings affecting business and settle more business disputes than courts do.[3] Such agencies include the Securities and Exchange Commission (SEC), the Federal Communications Commission, and the Equal Employment Opportunity Commission (EEOC). Figure A.1 lists and describes the powers and functions of several administrative agencies at the federal, state, and local levels of government.

common law
The body of law that comes from decisions handed down by judges; also referred to as unwritten law.

precedent
Decisions judges have made in earlier cases that guide the handling of new cases.

administrative agencies
Federal or state institutions and other government organizations created by Congress or state legislatures with delegated power to pass rules and regulations within their mandated area of authority.

TEST**PREP**

- What is business law?
- What's the difference between statutory and common law?
- What is an administrative agency?

FIGURE A.1 EXAMPLES OF FEDERAL, STATE, AND LOCAL ADMINISTRATIVE AGENCIES

Federal Agencies	
Examples	**Powers and Functions**
Federal Trade Commission	Enforces laws and guidelines regarding unfair business practices and acts to stop false and deceptive advertising and labeling.
Food and Drug Administration	Enforces laws and regulations to prevent distribution of adulterated or misbranded foods, drugs, medical devices, cosmetics, and veterinary products, as well as any hazardous consumer products.

State Agencies	
Examples	**Powers and Functions**
Public utility commissions	Set rates that can be charged by various public utilities to prevent unfair pricing by regulated monopolies (e.g., natural gas, electric power companies).
State licensing boards	License various trades and professions within a state (e.g., state cosmetology board, state real estate commission).

Local Agencies	
Examples	**Powers and Functions**
Maricopa County Planning Commission	Oversees land-use proposals, long-term development objectives, and other long-range issues in Maricopa County, Arizona.
City of Chesterfield Zoning Board	Recommends policy regarding zoning of commercial and residential property in the city of Chesterfield, Missouri.

LO A–2 Define *tort law* and explain the role of product liability in tort law.

Tort Law

tort
A wrongful act that causes injury to another person's body, property, or reputation.

A **tort** is a wrongful act that causes injury to another person's body, property, or reputation. Although torts often are noncriminal acts, courts can award victims compensation if the conduct that caused the harm is considered intentional. Legally, an *intentional* tort is a willful act that results in injury. The question of intent was a major factor in the lawsuits against the U.S. tobacco industry. Courts had to decide whether tobacco makers intentionally withheld information from the public about the harmful effects of their products.

negligence
In tort law, behavior that causes unintentional harm or injury.

Negligence, in tort law, describes behavior that causes *unintentional* harm or injury. In a classic court finding of negligence, McDonald's lost a lawsuit to an older woman severely burned by hot coffee bought at a drive-through window. The jury felt that McDonald's failed to provide an adequate warning on the cup. The case became a flashpoint in the debate over product liability. Today, product liability remains a controversial area of tort law, so let's take a closer look at this issue.

Product Liability

product liability
Part of tort law that holds businesses liable for harm that results from the production, design, sale, or use of products they market.

Few issues in business law raise as much debate as product liability. Critics believe product liability laws have gone too far; others feel these laws should be expanded. **Product liability** holds businesses liable for harm that results from the production, design, or inadequate warnings of products they market. The average product liability case can cost businesses millions, including defense costs, out-of-court settlements, and jury awards.

At one time the legal standard for measuring product liability was whether a producer knowingly placed a hazardous product on the market. Today, many states have extended product liability to the level of **strict product liability**—legally meaning liability without regard to fault. That is, a company that places a defective product on the market can be held liable for damages—a monetary settlement awarded to a person injured by another's actions—even if the company did not know of the defect at the time of sale.

strict product liability

Legal responsibility for harm or injury caused by a product regardless of fault.

Strict product liability is a major concern for businesses. More than 100 companies have been forced into bankruptcy due to asbestos litigation and the issue is not yet closed.[4] Johnson & Johnson was ordered in a recent case to pay $4.6 billion to 22 women who alleged they suffered ovarian cancer from the company's talcum powder.[5] The company denies the claim and is appealing.[6] General Motors recalled more than 2.6 million cars and has paid more than $2.5 billion in penalties and settlements due to faulty ignition switches linked to 124 deaths.[7]

Some product liability cases have raised intriguing questions about responsibility. Gun manufacturers were sued by families of children killed in the Sandy Hook Elementary School massacre. Although a lower judge dismissed the legal claims, a higher court judge reinstated the case.[8] Cities including Chicago and Miami had previously sued for the costs of police work and medical care necessitated by gun violence. McDonald's faced a product liability suit (also dismissed) claiming that its food caused obesity, diabetes, and other health problems in children. Some communities, however, have banned trans fats in food, regulated menu information, and eliminated toys in children's products like McDonald's Happy Meals. San Francisco passed a law that requires health warnings on advertisements for soda and other sugar-added drinks. The American Beverage Association filed a civil complaint to block the law and currently an appeals court has blocked enforcement.[9] Many schools, however, have replaced soft drinks in vending machines with fruit juice and water.

Tort and product liability reform remains a key objective of business. Congress took action with passage of the Class Action Fairness Act in 2005, which expanded federal jurisdiction over many large class-action lawsuits. The legislation has been beneficial to some businesses since their cases were brought to federal court rather than state courts where awards were typically much higher. Still, businesses and insurance companies argue that more needs to be done to assist companies with product liability. Consumer protection groups disagree and feel not enough is being done to protect consumers. Figure A.2 highlights a brief history of several major product liability awards that have cost companies dearly over the years.

FIGURE A.2 MAJOR PRODUCT LIABILITY CASES

Company	Year	Settlement
Ford Motor Company	1978	$125 million in punitive damages awarded in the case of a 13-year-old boy severely burned in a rear-end collision involving a Ford Pinto
A. H. Robins	1987	Dalkon Shield intrauterine birth-control devices recalled after eight separate punitive-damage awards. Company settled over 6,900 cases for $200 million
Playtex Company	1988	Suffered a $10 million damage award in the case of a toxic shock syndrome fatality in Kansas. Forced to remove product from the market
Dow Corning	1998	Reached a settlement and agreed to pay $2 billion to customers who claimed silicone breast implants caused injury, even death
General Motors	1999	Suffered a $4.8 billion punitive award in a faulty fuel tank case
Major Tobacco Firms	2004	$130 billion sought by the federal government for smoking cessation programs
Toyota	2010	A safety feature known as "brake to idle fail safe" was not installed in many cars increasing the chances of an accident when the accelerator malfunctioned. Company settled for $1.1 billion

Sources: U.S. Department of Justice and American Trial Lawyers Association.

> **LO A–3** Identify the purposes and conditions of patents, copyrights, and trademarks.

Legally Protecting Ideas: Patents, Copyrights, and Trademarks

patent

A document that gives inventors exclusive rights to their inventions for 20 years.

copyright

A document that protects a creator's rights to materials such as books, articles, photos, and cartoons.

In 2011, Apple filed a lawsuit against Samsung claiming the Korean company had infringed on copyrights originally filed for the iPhone. The next year a U.S. court ruled in Apple's favor and ordered Samsung to pay $930 million in damages. The company quickly challenged the ruling and the case was finally settled in 2018 when both sides agreed on a $539 million settlement to Apple.

Have you ever invented a product you think may have commercial value? Many people have, and to protect their ideas they took the next step and applied for a patent. A **patent** is a document that gives inventors exclusive rights to their inventions for 20 years from the date they file the patent applications.

Patent applicants must make sure a product is truly unique and should seek the advice of an attorney.[10] How good are your chances of receiving a patent if you file for one? About 55 percent of patent applications received by the United States Patent and Trademarks Office (USPTO) are approved, with fees that vary according to the complexity of the patent.[11] A patent dealing with complex technology can cost anywhere from $10,000 to $30,000, whereas a patent dealing with simpler concepts (like a better mousetrap) will cost the inventor about $5,000 to $10,000.[12]

Patent owners have the right to sell or license the use of their patent to others. Foreign companies are also eligible to file for U.S. patents.[13] They account for nearly half the U.S. patents issued. Penalties for violating a patent (patent infringement) can be costly. In 2020, Apple and Broadcom were ordered to pay $1.1 billion to California Institute of Technology for infringing on three of the university's WiFi patents, which had helped Apple stay competitive in the mobile phone market.[14] The USPTO does not take action on behalf of patent holders if patent infringement occurs. The defense of patent rights is solely the job of the patent holder.

The American Inventors Protection Act was passed to require that patent applications be made public after 18 months regardless of whether a patent has been awarded. This law was passed in part to address critics who argued that some inventors intentionally delayed or dragged out a patent application because they expected others to eventually develop similar products or technology. Then when someone (usually a large company) filed for a similar patent, the inventor surfaced to claim the patent—referred to as a *submarine patent*—and demanded large royalties (fees) for its use. The late engineer Jerome Lemelson reportedly collected more than $1.3 billion in patent royalties for a series of long-delayed patents—including forerunners of the fax machine, industrial robots, and the bar-code scanner—from auto, computer, retail, and electronics companies.

Technology companies like Apple and Google have been the subject of lawsuits filed by "patent trolls" that license patents (or buy the licensed patents) and file infringement lawsuits against companies that often cost millions of dollars.[15] The trolls never intend to use the patents; their only intention is to file the lawsuits in the hopes of a financial settlement.[16] Verizon, Honda, IBM, Google, and Cisco are among companies that took action to defend themselves against patent infringement suits by joining Allied Security Trust, a nonprofit firm that acquires intellectual property of interest to its members.[17] The idea is to buy up patents that could impact their companies before they fall into the hands of others (mainly patent trolls) looking to pursue settlements or legal damages against the tech firms.

Just as a patent protects an inventor's right to a product or process, a **copyright** protects a creator's rights to materials such as books, articles, photos, paintings, and cartoons. Copyrights are filed with the Library of Congress and require a minimum of paperwork. They last for the lifetime of the author or artist plus 70 years and can be passed on to the creator's heirs. The Copyright Act of 1978, however, gives a special term of 75 years from publication to works published before January 1, 1978, whose copyrights had not expired by that date. The

Dado Ruvic/Reuters/Newscom

holder of a copyright can either prevent anyone from using the copyrighted material or charge a fee for using it. Author J. K. Rowling won a copyright violation suit against a fan who wanted to publish an unauthorized Harry Potter encyclopedia. If a work is created by an employee in the normal course of a job, the copyright belongs to the employer and lasts 95 years from publication or 120 years from creation, whichever comes first.

A *trademark* is a legally protected name, symbol, or design (or combination of these) that identifies the goods or services of one seller and distinguishes them from those of competitors. Trademarks generally belong to the owner forever, as long as they are properly registered and renewed every 10 years. Some well-known trademarks include the Aflac duck, Disney's Mickey Mouse, the Nike swoosh, and the golden arches of McDonald's. Like a patent, a trademark is protected against infringement. Businesses fight hard to protect trademarks, especially in global markets where trademark pirating can be extensive. They also work hard to gain the exclusive rights for a trademark. Coca-Cola, for example, attempted to trademark the rights to the word *Zero* for its diet brand drinks for nearly 13 years before gaining approval in 2016. Unfortunately for Coke, a federal appeals court overturned that decision in 2018.[18] (Chapter 14 discusses trademarks in more detail.)

?TESTPREP

- What is tort law?
- What is product liability? What is strict product liability?
- How many years is a patent protected from infringement?
- What is a copyright?

LO A–4 Describe warranties and negotiable instruments as covered in the Uniform Commercial Code.

Sales Law: The Uniform Commercial Code

At one time, laws governing businesses varied from state to state, making interstate trade extremely complicated. Today, all states have adopted the same commercial law. The **Uniform Commercial Code (UCC)** is a comprehensive commercial law that covers sales laws and other commercial laws. Since all 50 states have adopted the law (although it does not apply in certain sections of Louisiana), the UCC simplifies commercial transactions across state lines.

The UCC has 11 articles, which contain laws covering sales; commercial paper such as promissory notes and checks; bank deposits and collections; letters of credit; bulk transfers; warehouse receipts, bills of lading, and other documents of title; investment securities; and secured transactions. We do not have space in this text to discuss all 11 articles, but we will discuss 2: Article 2, which regulates warranties, and Article 3, which covers negotiable instruments.

Warranties

A *warranty* guarantees that the product sold will be acceptable for the purpose for which the buyer intends to use it. There are two types of warranties. **Express warranties** are specific representations by sellers that buyers rely on regarding the goods they purchase. The warranty you receive in the box with an iPad or a toaster is an express warranty.

Implied warranties are legally imposed on the seller, specifying that a product will conform to the customary standards of the trade or industry in which it competes. An implied

Uniform Commercial Code (UCC)
A comprehensive commercial law, adopted by every state in the United States, that covers sales laws and other commercial laws.

express warranties
Specific representations by the seller that buyers rely on regarding the goods they purchase.

implied warranties
Guarantees legally imposed on the seller.

Westend61/Getty Images

warranty entitles you to expect that materials and workmanship in an iPad will perform as expected when used according to published guidelines or your toaster will toast your bread to your desired degree (light, medium, dark).

Warranties can be either full or limited. A full warranty requires a seller to replace or repair a product at no charge if the product is not functioning or defective, whereas a limited warranty typically limits the defects or mechanical problems the seller covers. Companies often offer extended warranties that provide more coverage, but for a price, of course.[19] Many of the rights of buyers, including the right to accept or reject goods, are spelled out in Article 2 of the UCC.

Would you buy a new car if the dealer offered no warranty? How about an iPhone or a major kitchen appliance with no guarantee of performance? Warranties are an important part of a product and are generally of major concern to purchasers. It's important to check whether a product's warranty is full or limited. Should colleges offer students warranties with their degree programs?

Negotiable Instruments

Negotiable instruments are forms of commercial paper (such as checks) that are transferable among businesses and individuals; they represent a promise to pay a specified amount. Article 3 of the Uniform Commercial Code requires negotiable instruments to follow four conditions. They must (1) be written and signed by the maker or drawer, (2) be made payable on demand or at a certain time, (3) be made payable to the bearer (the person holding the instrument) or to specific order, and (4) contain an unconditional promise to pay a specified amount of money. Checks or other forms of negotiable instruments are transferred (negotiated for payment) when the payee signs the back. The payee's signature is called an *endorsement.*

LO A–5 List and describe the conditions necessary to make a legally enforceable contract, and describe the possible consequences if such a contract is violated.

Contract Law

If I offer to sell you my bike for $100 and later change my mind, can you force me to sell the bike by saying we had a contract? If I lose $120 to you in a poker game, can you sue in court to get your money? If I agree to sing at your wedding for free and back out at the last minute, can you claim I violated a contract? These are the kinds of questions contract law answers.

A **contract** is a legally enforceable agreement between two or more parties. **Contract law** specifies what constitutes a legally enforceable agreement. Basically, a contract is legally binding if the following conditions are met:

1. *An offer is made.* An offer to do something or sell something can be oral or written. If I agree to sell you my bike for $100, I have made an offer. That offer is not legally binding, however, until the following other conditions are met.

2. *There is a voluntary acceptance of the offer.* The principle of *mutual acceptance* means that both parties to a contract must agree on the terms. If I use duress—coercion through force or threat of force—in getting you to agree to buy my bike, the contract will not be legal. You couldn't use duress to get me to sell my bike, either. Even if we both agree, though, the contract is still not legally binding without the next four conditions.

3. *Both parties give consideration.* **Consideration** means something of value. If I agree to sell you my bike for $100, the bike and the $100 are consideration, and we have a legally binding contract. If I agree to sing at your wedding and you do not give me anything in return (consideration), we have no contract.

4. *Both parties are competent.* A person under the influence of alcohol or drugs, or a person of unsound mind (one who has been legally declared incompetent), cannot be held to a contract. In many cases, a minor may not be held to a contract either.

negotiable instruments
Forms of commercial paper (such as checks) that are transferable among businesses and individuals and represent a promise to pay a specified amount.

contract
A legally enforceable agreement between two or more parties.

contract law
Set of laws that specify what constitutes a legally enforceable agreement.

consideration
Something of value; consideration is one of the requirements of a legal contract.

If a 15-year-old agrees to pay $15,000 for a car, the seller will not be able to enforce the contract due to the buyer's lack of competence.

5. *The contract covers a legal act.* A contract covering the sale of illegal drugs or stolen merchandise is unenforceable since such sales are violations of criminal law. (If gambling is prohibited by state law in your state, you cannot sue to collect the poker debt.)

6. *The contract is in proper form.* An agreement for the sale of goods worth $500 or more must be in writing. Contracts that cannot be fulfilled within one year also must be put in writing. Contracts regarding real property (land and everything attached to it) must be in writing.

Breach of Contract

Both parties in a contract may voluntarily choose to end the agreement. **Breach of contract** occurs when one party fails to follow the terms of a contract. If that happens the following may occur:

1. *Specific performance.* The party who violated the contract may be required to live up to the agreement if money damages would not be adequate. If I legally offered to sell you a rare painting, I would have to sell you that painting.

2. *Payment of damages.* If I fail to live up to a contract, you can sue me for **damages**, usually the amount you would lose from my nonperformance. If we had a legally binding contract for me to sing at your wedding, for example, and I failed to come, you could sue me for the cost of hiring a new singer.

3. *Discharge of obligation.* If I fail to live up to my end of a contract, you can agree to drop the matter. Generally you would not have to live up to your end of the agreement either.

Lawyers would not be paid so handsomely if contract law were as simple as implied in these rules. That's why it's always best to put a contract in writing even though oral contracts can be enforceable under contract law. The contract should clearly specify the offer and consideration, and the parties to the contract should sign and date it. A contract does not have to be complicated as long as (1) it is in writing, (2) it specifies mutual consideration, and (3) it contains a clear offer and agreement.

breach of contract
When one party fails to follow the terms of a contract.

damages
The monetary settlement awarded to a person who is injured by a breach of contract.

?TEST**PREP**

- What is the purpose of the Universal Commercial Code (UCC)?
- Compare express and implied warranties.
- What are the four elements of a negotiable instrument specified in the UCC?
- What are the six conditions for a legally binding contract? What can happen if a contract is breached?

LO A–6 Summarize several laws that regulate competition and protect consumers in the United States.

Promoting Fair and Competitive Business Practices

Competition is a cornerstone of the free-market system (see Chapter 2). A key responsibility of legislators is to pass laws that ensure a competitive atmosphere among businesses and promote fair business practices. The U.S. Justice Department's antitrust division and other government agencies serve as watchdogs to guarantee competition in markets flows freely and new competitors have open access to the market. The government's power here is broad. The Justice Department's antitrust division has investigated the competitive practices of market giants such as Microsoft, Apple, Visa, Facebook, and Google.[20] Figure A.3 highlights several high-profile antitrust cases.

Antitrust oversight was not always the rule, however. Big businesses were once able to force smaller competitors out of business with little government resistance. The following brief history details how government responded to past problems and some new challenges government regulators face today.

The History of Antitrust Legislation

In the late 19th century, big oil companies, railroads, steel companies, and other industrial firms dominated the U.S. economy. Some feared that such large and powerful companies would be able to crush any competitors and then charge high prices. In that atmosphere, Congress passed the Sherman Antitrust Act in 1890 to prevent large organizations from stifling the competition of smaller or newer firms. The Sherman Act forbids (1) contracts, combinations, or conspiracies in restraint of trade; and (2) the creation of actual monopolies or attempts to monopolize any part of trade or commerce.

Because some of the language in the Sherman Act was vague, there was doubt about just what practices it prohibited. To clarify its intentions Congress enacted the following laws:

- *The Clayton Act of 1914.* The Clayton Act prohibits exclusive dealing, tying contracts, and interlocking directorates. It also prohibits buying large amounts of stock in competing corporations. *Exclusive dealing* is selling goods with the condition that the buyer will not buy from a competitor (when the effect lessens competition). A *tying contract* requires a buyer to purchase unwanted items in order to purchase desired ones. Let's say I wanted to purchase 20 cases of Pepsi-Cola per week to sell in my restaurant Harvest Gold. Pepsi, however, says it will sell me the 20 cases only if I also agree to buy 10 cases each of its Mountain Dew and Diet Pepsi products. My purchase of Pepsi-Cola would be *tied* to the purchase of the other two products. An *interlocking directorate* occurs when a company's board of directors includes members of the boards of competing corporations.

- *The Federal Trade Commission Act of 1914.* The Federal Trade Commission Act prohibits unfair methods of competition in commerce. This legislation set up the five-member Federal Trade Commission (FTC) to enforce compliance with the act.

FIGURE A.3 HISTORY OF HIGH-PROFILE ANTITRUST CASES

Case	Outcome
United States v. *Standard Oil* 1911	Standard Oil broken up into 34 companies; Amoco, Chevron, and ExxonMobil are results of the breakup
United States v. *American Tobacco* 1911	American Tobacco split into 16 companies; British Tobacco and R.J. Reynolds are results of the breakup
United States v. *E. I. du Pont de Nemours* 1961	DuPont ordered to divest its 23 percent ownership stake in General Motors
United States v. *AT&T* 1982	Settled after Ma Bell agreed to spin off its local telephone operations into seven regional operating companies
United States v. *Microsoft* 2000	Microsoft ordered to halt prior anticompetitive practices

Source: U.S. Department of Justice.

The FTC deals with a wide range of competitive issues—everything from preventing companies from making misleading "Made in the USA" claims to insisting funeral providers give consumers accurate, itemized price information about funeral goods and services. Along with the Department of Justice, the FTC has the added responsibility to oversee proposed mergers and acquisitions (Chapter 5) to prevent anticompetitive mergers or acquisitions that would "substantially reduce competition." The Wheeler-Lea Amendment of 1938 also gave the FTC additional jurisdiction over false or misleading advertising, along with the power to increase fines if its requirements are not met within 60 days.

- *The Robinson-Patman Act of 1936.* The Robinson-Patman Act prohibits price discrimination and applies to both sellers and buyers who knowingly induce or receive price discrimination. Certain types of price cutting are criminal offenses punishable by fine and imprisonment. That includes price differences that "substantially" weaken competition unless they can be justified by lower selling costs associated with larger purchases. The law also prohibits advertising and promotional allowances unless they are offered to *all* retailers, large and small. Remember, this legislation applies to business-to-business transactions and not to business-to-consumer transactions.

The change in U.S. business from manufacturing to knowledge-based technology has created new regulatory challenges for federal agencies. In the early 2000s, Microsoft's competitive practices were the focus of an intense antitrust investigation by the Justice Department. The government charged that Microsoft hindered competition by refusing to sell its Windows operating system to computer manufacturers that refused to sell Windows-based computers exclusively. The case ended with a settlement between the Justice Department and Microsoft that expired in 2011. Many antitrust advocates believe this case broadened the definition of anticompetitive behavior and proved the government's resolve in enforcing antitrust laws. It's safe to conclude, however, that antitrust issues will persist well into the future.

Justin Sullivan/Getty Images

Elizabeth Holmes founded the medical start-up Theranos in 2003 after claiming she developed a revolutionary new way to conduct blood tests. She eventually became one of Silicon Valley's brightest stars as the company began to earn multibillion-dollar valuations. But when an investigation found that Theranos's testing process did not work as advertised, Holmes's net worth quickly plummeted from $4 billion to zero.

Laws to Protect Consumers

Consumerism is a social movement that seeks to increase and strengthen the rights and powers of buyers in relationship to sellers. It is the people's way of getting a fair share and equitable treatment in marketing exchanges. The Public Company Accounting Reform and Investor Protection Act (better known as the Sarbanes-Oxley Act) was passed to allay concerns about falsified financial statements from companies like Enron and WorldCom in the early 2000s. The financial crisis of 2008 again fueled consumer anger, this time against the Treasury Department, Federal Reserve, and Securities and Exchange Commission (SEC) for their lack of oversight of the financial markets. The collapse of the real estate market, crisis in the banking industry, and failure of quasi-governmental mortgage agencies such as Fannie Mae and Freddie Mac led to passage of the Dodd-Frank Wall Street Reform and Consumer Protection Act. This legislation created the Consumer Financial Protection Bureau that provides government oversight involving consumers in areas such as online banking, home mortgage loans, and high-interest payday loans. Figure A.4 lists other major consumer protection laws.

LO A–7 Explain the role of tax laws in generating income for the government and as a method of discouraging or encouraging certain behaviors among taxpayers.

consumerism

A social movement that seeks to increase and strengthen the rights and powers of buyers in relation to sellers.

Tax Laws

Mention taxes and most people frown. **Taxes** are the way federal, state, and local governments raise money. They affect almost every individual and business in the United States.

Governments primarily use taxes as a source of funding for their operations and programs. Taxes can also help discourage or encourage certain behaviors among taxpayers.

taxes

How the government (federal, state, and local) raises money.

FIGURE A.4 CONSUMER PROTECTION LAWS

Fair Packaging and Labeling Act (1966)	Makes unfair or deceptive packaging or labeling of certain consumer commodities illegal.
Child Protection Act (1966)	Removes from sale potentially harmful toys and allows the FDA to pull dangerous products from the market.
Truth-in-Lending Act (1968)	Requires full disclosure of all finance charges on consumer credit agreements and in advertisements of credit plans.
Child Protection and Toy Safety Act (1969)	Protects children from toys and other products that contain thermal, electrical, or mechanical hazards.
Fair Credit Reporting Act (1970)	Requires that consumer credit reports contain only accurate, relevant, and recent information and are confidential unless a proper party requests them for an appropriate reason.
Consumer Product Safety Act (1972)	Created an independent agency to protect consumers from unreasonable risk of injury arising from consumer products and to set safety standards.
Magnuson Moss Warranty–Federal Trade Commission Improvements Act (1975)	Provides for minimum disclosure standards for written consumer product warranties and allows the FTC to prescribe interpretive rules and policy statements regarding unfair or deceptive practices.
Alcohol Labeling Legislation (1988)	Provides for warning labels on liquor saying that women shouldn't drink when pregnant and that alcohol impairs a person's abilities.
Nutrition Labeling and Education Act (1990)	Requires truthful and uniform nutritional labeling on every food the FDA regulates.
Consumer Credit Reporting Reform Act (1997)	Increases responsibility of credit issuers for accurate credit data and requires creditors to verify that disputed data are accurate. Consumer notification is necessary before reinstating the data.
Children's Online Privacy Protection Act (2000)	Gives parents control over what information is collected online from their children under age 13; requires website operators to maintain the confidentiality, security, and integrity of the personal information collected from children.
Country of Origin Labeling Law (2009)	Requires that the product label on most food products sold in U.S. supermarkets gives the product's country of origin.
Credit Card Accountability, Responsibility, and Disclosure (CARD) Act (2009)	Designed to protect consumers from unfair credit card practices.

If the government wishes to reduce consumer use of certain classes of products like cigarettes or liquor, it can pass *sin taxes* on them to raise their cost. Since the Great Recession, increasing sin taxes (i.e., taxes on things like liquor and cigarettes) has become a popular way for cash-starved states to raise revenue.[21] To date, 11 states and the District of Columbia have adopted laws legalizing marijuana for recreational use.[22] Expectations are the new taxes levied on recreational marijuana will help their economies.[23] In other situations, the government may encourage businesses to hire new employees or purchase new equipment by offering a *tax credit,* an amount firms can deduct from their tax bill.

FIGURE A.5 TYPES OF TAXES

Types of Taxes	
Type	**Purpose**
Income taxes	Taxes paid on the income received by businesses and individuals. Income taxes are the largest source of tax income received by the federal government.
Property taxes	Taxes paid on real and personal property. *Real property* is real estate owned by individuals and businesses. *Personal property* is a broader category that includes any movable property such as tangible items (wedding rings, equipment, etc.) or intangible items (stocks, checks, mortgages, etc.). Taxes are based on their assessed value.
Sales taxes	Taxes paid on merchandise sold at the retail level.
Excise taxes	Taxes paid on selected items such as tobacco, alcoholic beverages, airline travel, gasoline, and firearms. These are often referred to as *sin taxes*. Income generated from the tax goes toward a specifically designated purpose. For example, gasoline taxes often help the federal government and state governments pay for highway construction or improvements.

Taxes are levied from a variety of sources. Income taxes (personal and business), sales taxes, and property taxes are the major bases of tax revenue. The federal government receives its largest share of taxes from income. States and local communities make extensive use of sales taxes. School districts generally depend on property taxes.

The tax policies of states and cities are important considerations when businesses seek to locate operations. They also affect personal decisions such as retirement. As government revenues at all levels become more challenging, tax issues are debated. One such issue involves taxing Internet sales. Many states claimed they were losing billions in sales taxes by not collecting from Internet sales transactions. More than 30 states including California, New York, and Illinois have already taken action on Internet sales taxes.[24] The U.S. Supreme Court in 2018 opened the door to Internet sales tax collections wider when it ruled a retailer can be required to collect sales taxes even if it does not have a physical presence in the state. Some businesses want Congress to pass a law that would set uniform rules for sales tax collections. Figure A.5 highlights the primary types of taxes levied on individuals and businesses.

LO A–8 Distinguish among the various types of bankruptcy as outlined by the Bankruptcy Code.

Bankruptcy Laws

Bankruptcy is the legal process by which a person, business, or government entity, unable to meet financial obligations, is relieved of those debts by a court. Courts divide any of the debtor's assets among creditors, allowing them to recover at least part of their money and freeing the debtor to begin anew. The U.S. Constitution gives Congress the power to establish bankruptcy laws, and legislation has existed since the 1890s. Major amendments to the bankruptcy code include the Bankruptcy Amendments and Federal Judgeship Act of 1984, the Bankruptcy Reform Act of 1994, and the Bankruptcy Abuse Prevention and Consumer Protection Act of 2005.

The 1984 law allows a person who is bankrupt to keep part of the equity (ownership) in a house and car, and some other personal property. The 1994 act amended more than 45 sections of the bankruptcy code and created reforms to speed up and simplify the process. The Bankruptcy Abuse Prevention and Consumer Protection Act of 2005 was passed to reduce the total number of bankruptcy filings and to eliminate the perceived ease of filing for bankruptcy. The legislation increased the cost of filing and made it difficult for people (especially those with high incomes) to escape overwhelming debt from credit cards, medical bills, student loans, or other loans not secured through a home or other asset. It also requires debtors to receive credit counseling.

bankruptcy
The legal process by which a person, business, or government entity unable to meet financial obligations is relieved of those obligations by a court that divides any assets among creditors, allowing creditors to get at least part of their money and freeing the debtor to begin anew.

Toys"R"Us, once the largest toy retailer in the nation, filed for bankruptcy in 2017 and soon ceased operations altogether. Before liquidating, the chain operated nearly 1,600 stores and employed more than 64,000 people. Do you know of any other companies that have been forced into bankruptcy?

Jim Steinfeldt/Michael Ochs Archives/Getty Images

Bankruptcies started growing in the late 1980s and have increased tremendously since. Many attribute the increase to a lessening of the stigma of bankruptcy, an increase in understanding of bankruptcy law and its protections, and an increase in advertising by bankruptcy attorneys. Some suggest that the ease with which certain consumers could get credit contributed to the number of filings by allowing people to readily overspend. The 2005 reform helped reduce the annual number of bankruptcy filings to 600,000 from an average of 1.5 million between 2001 and 2004. However, the financial crisis of 2008 pushed the number of bankruptcies again to well over 1 million. As the economy slowly recovered, bankruptcies stayed over 1 million until 2015 when numbers began to decrease.[25] Although high-profile bankruptcies of businesses—such as Sears, Toys"R"Us, and Payless ShoeSource—tend to dominate the news, 97 percent of bankruptcy filings each year are by individuals.[26]

Bankruptcy can be either voluntary or involuntary. In **voluntary bankruptcy**, the debtor applies for bankruptcy; in **involuntary bankruptcy**, the creditors start legal action against the debtor. Most bankruptcies are voluntary, since creditors usually wait in hopes they will be paid all the money due them rather than settle for only part of it.

Bankruptcy procedures begin when a petition is filed with the court under one of the following sections of the Bankruptcy Code:

- Chapter 7—"straight bankruptcy" or liquidation (used by businesses and individuals).
- Chapter 11—reorganization (used almost exclusively by businesses).
- Chapter 13—repayment (used by individuals).

Chapter 7 is the most popular form of bankruptcy among small businesses. It requires the sale of nonexempt assets. States can choose different exemption statutes. When the sale of assets is over, creditors, including the government if taxes are owed, divide the remaining assets as stipulated by law. First, creditors with secured claims receive the collateral for their claims or repossess the claimed asset (such as an automobile, equipment, or building); then unsecured claims (backed by no asset) are paid in this order:

1. Costs of the bankruptcy case.
2. Any business costs incurred after bankruptcy was filed.
3. Wages, salaries, or commissions owed.

voluntary bankruptcy
Legal procedures initiated by a debtor.

involuntary bankruptcy
Bankruptcy procedures filed by a debtor's creditors.

4. Contributions to employee benefit plans.

5. Refunds to consumers who paid for products that weren't delivered.

6. Federal and state taxes.

Figure A.6 outlines the steps used in liquidating assets under Chapter 7.

In Chapter 11 bankruptcy, a company sued by creditors continues to operate under court protection while it tries to work out a plan for paying off its debts. Under certain conditions it may sell assets, borrow money, and change company officers to strengthen its market position. A court-appointed trustee supervises the proceedings and protects the creditors' interests.

A company does not have to be insolvent to file for relief under Chapter 11. In theory, it is a way for sick companies to recover, designed to help both debtors and creditors find the best solution. In reality, however, less than one-third of Chapter 11 companies survive— usually those with lots of cash available. The Bankruptcy Reform Act of 1994 provides a fast-track procedure for small businesses filing under Chapter 11. The Small Business Reorganization Act of 2019 (SBRA) came into effect in February 2020. The goal of SBRA is to simplify the bankruptcy process for small businesses by increasing efficiency, lowering costs, and easing the process.[27]

Chapter 13 permits individuals, including small-business owners, to pay back creditors over three to five years. Chapter 13 proceedings are less complicated and less expensive than Chapter 7 proceedings. The debtor files a proposed plan with the court for paying off debts. If the plan is approved, the debtor pays a court-appointed trustee in monthly installments as agreed on in the repayment plan. The trustee then pays each creditor.

LO A–9 Explain the role of deregulation as a tool to encourage competition.

Deregulation versus Regulation

The U.S. Constitution gives Congress the right "to regulate commerce." The debate concerning the degree of regulation, however, has been a source of disagreement for many years. At one time, the United States had laws and regulations covering almost every aspect of

FIGURE A.6 HOW ASSETS ARE DIVIDED IN BANKRUPTCY

This figure shows that the creditor (the person owed money) selects the trustee (the person or organization that handles the sale of assets). Note that the process may be started by the debtor or the creditors.

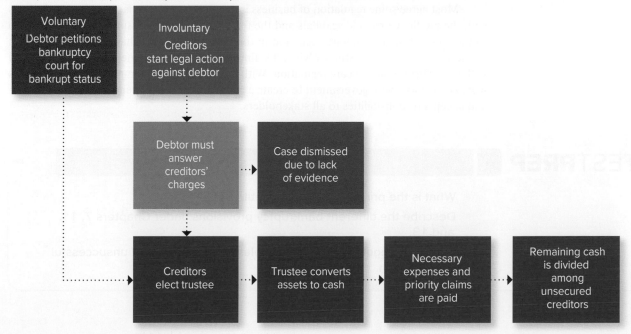

deregulation
Government withdrawal of certain laws and regulations that seem to hinder competition.

business. Some felt there were too many laws and regulations, costing the public too much money. A movement toward deregulation took hold. **Deregulation** means that the government withdraws certain laws and regulations that seem to hinder competition. The most publicized examples of deregulation first occurred in the airline and telecommunications industries.

Consumers clearly benefited from the Airline Deregulation Act of 1978 that ended federal control of commercial airlines. Before passage of the act, the government restricted where airlines could land and fly. When the restrictions were lifted, airlines began competing for different routes and charging lower prices. The skies were also opened to new competitors, such as Southwest and JetBlue, to take advantage of new opportunities.

Passage of the Telecommunications Act in 1996 brought similar deregulation to telecommunications and gave consumers a flood of options in local telephone service markets. There was also a significant increase in retail video competition. At one time, most homes received only four TV channels (the three major networks—NBC, CBS, and ABC—and public broadcasting). Today most households receive multiple over-the-air networks and hundreds more on cable, satellite, and online streaming services.

Deregulation efforts also occurred in the electric power industry. California was the first state to deregulate electric power in the late 1990s and experienced significant problems, especially with large-scale blackouts (loss of power). This caused other states to question the logic of deregulation. Today, however, 17 states have deregulated electric power with some success.[28]

The financial crisis reopened the question of how much deregulation is too much. Deregulation in the banking and investments industries had changed the nature of financial and mortgage markets and created huge problems. The Federal Reserve System's reluctance to toughen mortgage regulations and the government's insistence on providing more home loans to high-risk borrowers contributed to the collapse in the real estate market. The financial crisis that followed led to the passage of the most sweeping regulation of financial markets since the Great Depression.

In 2010, the U.S. Congress passed the Patient Protection and Affordable Care Act (PPACA), also known as Obamacare. The law, implemented in 2013, introduced a comprehensive system of health insurance for Americans not covered under an insurance plan. The law also provides for increased government regulation of the insurance industry. While the Affordable Care Act increased the number of people with health care insurance, it also increased prices for many consumers and caused other dissatisfaction.[29] At the time of this writing, the fate of Obamacare is uncertain. Congress repealed the mandate provision that required individuals to purchase health insurance if they didn't already have it, but the rest of the law is still being hotly debated.

Most agree some regulation of business is necessary to ensure fair and honest dealings with the public. Corporate scandals and the financial crisis led consumers and investors to call for increased government regulation in the financial sector. While the final evaluation of the health care law is still evolving, it's almost certain that businesses will need to deal with some form of health care regulation. With increasing global competition, U.S. business will need to work with government to create a competitive environment that is fair and open and accepts responsibilities to all stakeholders.

?TESTPREP

- What is the primary purpose of antitrust law?
- Describe the different bankruptcy provisions under Chapters 7, 11, and 13.
- What is deregulation? Give examples of successful and unsuccessful deregulation.

SUMMARY

LO A–1 Define *business law,* distinguish between statutory and common law, and explain the role of administrative agencies.

■ **What is the difference between statutory law and common law?**

Statutory law includes state and federal constitutions, legislative enactments, treaties of the federal government, and ordinances—in short, written law. Common law is the body of unwritten law that comes from decisions handed down by judges.

■ **What are administrative agencies?**

Administrative agencies are federal or state institutions and other government organizations created by Congress or state legislatures with power to create rules and regulations within their area of authority.

LO A–2 Define *tort law* and explain the role of product liability in tort law.

■ **What is an intentional tort?**

An intentional tort is a willful act that results in injury.

■ **What is negligence?**

Negligence, in tort law, is behavior that causes *unintentional* harm or injury. Findings of negligence can lead to huge judgments against businesses.

LO A–3 Identify the purposes and conditions of patents, copyrights, and trademarks.

■ **What are patents and copyrights?**

A patent is a document that gives inventors exclusive rights to their inventions for 20 years from the date they file the patent applications. A copyright protects a creator's rights to materials such as books, articles, photos, paintings, and cartoons.

■ **What is a trademark?**

A trademark is a legally protected name, symbol, or design (or combination of these) that identifies the goods or services of one seller and distinguishes them from those of competitors.

LO A–4 Describe warranties and negotiable instruments as covered in the Uniform Commercial Code.

■ **What does Article 2 of the UCC cover?**

Article 2 contains laws regarding warranties. Express warranties are guarantees made by the seller, whereas implied warranties are guarantees imposed on the seller by law.

■ **What does Article 3 of the UCC cover?**

Article 3 covers negotiable instruments such as checks. A negotiable instrument must (1) be written and signed by the maker or drawer, (2) be made payable on demand or at a certain time, (3) be made payable to the bearer (the person holding the instrument) or to specific order, and (4) contain an unconditional promise to pay a specified amount of money.

LO A–5 List and describe the conditions necessary to make a legally enforceable contract, and describe the possible consequences if such a contract is violated.

- **What makes a contract enforceable under the law?**

  An enforceable contract must meet six conditions: (1) an offer must be made, (2) the offer must be voluntarily accepted, (3) both parties must give consideration, (4) both parties must be competent, (5) the contract must be legal, and (6) the contract must be in proper form.

- **What are the possible consequences if a contract is violated?**

  If a contract is violated, one of the following may be required: (1) specific performance, (2) payment of damages, or (3) discharge of obligation.

LO A–6 Summarize several laws that regulate competition and protect consumers in the United States.

- **What does the Sherman Act cover?**

  The Sherman Act forbids contracts, combinations, or conspiracies in restraint of trade and actual monopolies or attempts to monopolize any part of trade or commerce.

- **What does the Clayton Act add?**

  The Clayton Act prohibits exclusive dealing, tying contracts, interlocking directorates, and buying large amounts of stock in competing corporations.

- **Which act regulates false and deceptive advertising?**

  The Federal Trade Commission Act prohibits unfair methods of competition in commerce, including deceptive advertising.

- **Which act prohibits price discrimination and demands proportional promotional allowances?**

  The Robinson-Patman Act applies to both sellers and buyers who knowingly induce or receive an unlawful discrimination in price.

LO A–7 Explain the role of tax laws in generating income for the government and as a method of discouraging or encouraging certain behaviors among taxpayers.

- **How does the government use taxes to encourage or discourage certain behavior among taxpayers?**

  If the government wishes to change citizens' behavior, it can reduce their use of certain classes of products (cigarettes, liquor) by passing *sin taxes* to raise their cost. In other situations, the government may offer tax credits to encourage businesses to hire new employees or purchase new equipment.

LO A–8 Distinguish among the various types of bankruptcy as outlined by the Bankruptcy Code.

- **What are the bankruptcy laws?**

  Chapter 7 calls for straight bankruptcy, in which all assets are divided among creditors after exemptions. Chapter 11 allows a firm to reorganize and continue operation after paying only a limited portion of its debts. Chapter 13 allows individuals to pay their creditors over an extended period of time.

LO A–9 Explain the role of deregulation as a tool to encourage competition.

- **What are a few of the most publicized examples of deregulation?**

  Perhaps the most publicized examples of deregulation have been those in the airline, telecommunications, electric power, financial services, and health care industries.

CRITICAL THINKING

1. Supporters of tort reform say it's unfair that plaintiffs (the parties bringing lawsuits) don't have to pay damages to the defendants (the parties subject to the lawsuits) if they lose the case. Should plaintiffs pay damages if they lose a case? Why or why not?

2. Go to the website of the U.S. Patent and Trademark Office (uspto.gov) and view the information about obtaining a patent. See whether you can estimate how long the process will take and what your cost will be.

3. Call your local real estate board or visit a realtor and obtain a copy of a real estate contract. Read it carefully to see how it meets the six requirements stated in the chapter for a contract to be legal and binding.

4. Has your state or a neighboring state implemented utility deregulation? How does it seem to be working?

PUTTING PRINCIPLES TO WORK

PURPOSE

You and several of your musician friends decide to start a band you want to call the Individual Mandates. You want to protect the band name and the new songs you've written so that other groups can't use them without your permission. Go to the U.S. Patent and Trademark Office's website (uspto.gov) to find out how to get the protection you seek.

EXERCISE

1. Do you need to apply for patents, copyrights, or trademarks, or some combination of these to protect your band name and songs?

2. When can you use the trademark symbols ™ and ®?

3. How can you secure a copyright for your songs?

4. What are the advantages of registering copyrights?

DEVELOPING CAREER SKILLS

KEY: ● **Team**   ★ **Analytic**   ▲ **Communication**   ◻ **Technology**

1. Do you think the laws that promote fair and competitive practices are effective in the United States? Why or why not? Provide evidence for your view.   ★▲

2. Increasing numbers of individuals and businesses file for bankruptcy each year. Do you think the U.S. Congress was correct in toughening the bankruptcy laws?   ★

● ★ ▲ 3. Divide the class into teams to debate the question: Should government action to deal with deceptive business practices increase, or should we count on business to regulate itself to prevent deceptive practices? Which solution is better for society and business in the long run?

● ★ ▲ 4. Go online to find the answers to the following questions: Does your state have an income tax? What percentage of your income do you have to pay in state income tax? What about property taxes and sales taxes? How do these taxes in your area compare to those in three other states and communities of your choice?

● ★ ▲ 5. Chapter 11 bankruptcy allows businesses to continue operating under court protection while they try to pay off their debts. Search online and find three companies that came back from Chapter 11 and regained their stature in the market. Explain why they were successful.

CAREER EXPLORATION

If you are interested in working in the legal environment, here are a few careers to consider. Find out about the tasks performed, skills needed, pay, and opportunity outlook in these fields in the *Occupational Outlook Handbook (OOH)* at bls.gov.

- **Arbitrator and mediator**—facilitate negotiation and dialogue between disputing parties to help resolve conflicts outside the court system.
- **Court reporter**—creates word-for-word transcriptions at trials, depositions, and other legal proceedings. Some court reporters provide captioning for television and real-time translation for people who are deaf or hearing impaired at public events, in business meetings, or in classrooms.
- **Lawyer**—advises and represents individuals, businesses, and government agencies on legal issues and disputes.
- **Paralegal and legal assistant**—perform a variety of tasks to support lawyers, including maintaining and organizing files, conducting legal research, and drafting documents.

NOTES

1. Neil Irwin, "How the Recession of 2020 Could Happen," *The New York Times,* nytimes.com, August 17, 2019; Kimberly Amadeo, "Causes of an Economic Recession," *Investopedia,* investopedia.com, February 18, 2020; "Key Government Regulations That Affect Investing in the Banking Sector," *Investopedia,* investopedia.com, February 5, 2020.
2. American Bar Association Market Research Department, americanbar.org, accessed March 2020.
3. Thomas Gleason, "The Power of Administrative Agencies and the Peril of Substantial Evidence Review," *The American Lawyer,* law.org, January 16, 2019; Corbin Barthold, "The Judiciary Can Corral the Administrative State, but Only the People Themselves Can Tame It," *Forbes,* January 17, 2019; Gillian E. Metzger, "The Roberts Court and Administrative Law," Columbia Law School, scholarship.law.columbia.edu, 2020.
4. "Asbestos Trust Funds Companies List," Mesothelioma Justice Center, asbestos.net, accessed October 2019; "Mesothelioma & Asbestos Trust Funds," Mesothelioma Fund, mesotheliomafund.com, accessed March 2020.
5. Tiffany Hsu and Roni Caryn Rabin, "Johnson & Johnson Recalls Baby Powder over Asbestos Worry," *The New York Times,* nytimes.com, October 18, 2019; Daniel Gala, "Talcum Powder Lawsuit Update," *The Law Firm,* thelawfirm.com, February 18, 2020.
6. Robert Rakers, "Summary of 2019 Talc Verdicts," *Technology, Manufacturing, and Transportation Industry Insider,* tmtindustryinsider.com, February 17, 2020.
7. "Testimony of Daniel Hinkle for the American Association for Justice [to the House Energy and Commerce Committee]," United States House of Representatives, docs.house.gov, February 11, 2020.
8. Ryan Lindsay, "Lawsuit by Sandy Hook Victims against Gun Manufacturer Allowed to Move Forward," National Public Radio, npr.org, March 14, 2019; Alison Frankel, "In Sandy Hook Massacre Case, Gunmaker Remington Wants Killer's Psych Records," Reuters, reuters.com, February 19, 2020.
9. Sara Geiser, "Ninth Circuit Strikes Down SF Soda Health Warning Law," *San Francisco Examiner,* January 31, 2019; Richard Gonzales, "Federal Appeals Court Blocks San

Francisco Law on Ad Warnings for Sugary Drinks," National Public Radio, npr.org, January 30, 2019; Alexei Koseff, "'Big Gulp Ban,' Soda Tax Coming before California Legislature," *San Francisco Chronicle,* February 19, 2019; "American Beverage Assoc. v. City and County of San Francisco," Justia Law, law.justia.com, accessed March 2020.

10. Sarah Pierce, "5 Steps for Turning Your Invention Ideas into a Product," *Entrepreneur,* entrepreneur.com, February 21, 2019; Alex Moss, "Design Patents Are Useless. So Why Are They Getting a Boost in DC?," Electrical Frontier Foundation, eff.org, January 29, 2020.

11. United States Patent and Trademark Office, uspto.gov, accessed March 2020.

12. Sarah Pierce, "5 Steps for Turning Your Invention Ideas into a Product," *Entrepreneur,* entrepreneur.com, February 21, 2019; Joe Runge, "How Much Does a Patent Cost?," LegalZoom, legalzoom.com, accessed March 2020; "How Much Does a Patent Cost: Everything You Need to Know," UpCounsel, upcounsel.com, accessed March 2020.

13. United States Patent and Trademark Office, uspto.gov, accessed March 2020.

14. Casey Tonkin, "Apple to Pay $1.25bn for Patent Infringement," *ACS Information Age,* ia.acs.org, February 3, 2020.

15. "The Enormous Toll of Patent Troll Litigation," Concord Law School, concordlawschool.org, June 12, 2019; Shawn Ambwani, "Rethinking the Patent System," *IPWatchdog,* ipwatchdog.com, February 19, 2020.

16. Tyler Smith, "Don't Feed the Trolls," Tyler Smith American Economic Association, aeaweb.org, February 10, 2020.

17. Allied Security Trust, ast.com, accessed March 2020.

18. Mehr Nadeem, "Coke's Bid for 'Zero' Trademark Tossed Back on Dr Pepper Appeal," *Bloomberg,* June 20, 2018; "Dr Pepper Wants Coke 'Zero' Case Ended 'Once and for All,'" *Law360,* law360.com, November 13, 2019.

19. Philip Reed, "Extended Car Warranties: When and How to Say No," *NerdWallet,* nerdwallet.com, February 19, 2020.

20. Jason Del Rey, "Why Congress's Antitrust Investigation Should Make Big Tech Nervous," Vox, vox.com, February 6, 2020; John D. McKinnon and Deepa Seetharaman, "FTC Expands Antitrust Investigation into Big Tech," *The Wall Street Journal,* wsj.com, February 11, 2020.

21. "Sin Taxes Are Sweeping the States!," Urban Institute, urban.org, February 12, 2020.

22. Jeremy Berke and Skye Gould, "Legal Marijuana Just Went on Sale in Illinois," *Business Insider,* businessinsider.com, January 1, 2020.

23. Ally Marotti, "Recreational Marijuana Sales in Illinois Generated More Than $10 Million in Tax Revenue in January," *Chicago Tribune,* chicagotribune.com, February 25, 2020; Tiney Ricciardi, "Colorado Marijuana Sales Hit a Record $1.75 Billion in 2019," *Denver Post,* denverpost.com, February 18, 2020.

24. "States with Internet Sales Tax 2020," World Population Review, worldpopulationreview.com, accessed March 2020.

25. United States Courts, uscourts.gov, accessed March 2020.

26. "Bankruptcy Statistics," Debt.org, debt.org, accessed March 2020.

27. "Three New Bankruptcy Amendments Become Law," JD Supra, jdsupra.com, accessed March 2020.

28. Kimberly Amadeo, "Deregulation Pros, Cons, and Examples," *The Balance,* thebalance.com, January 16, 2020; Jaclyn Brandt, "Electric Deregulation Bill Fails in Missouri Committee," *Daily Energy Insider,* dailyenergyinsider.com, January 30, 2020.

29. Kimberly Amadeo, "Obamacare Pros and Cons," *The Balance,* thebalance.com, December 19, 2019; "Viewpoints: Pros and Cons of Joe Biden's Ideas about Public Option," *Kaiser Health News,* khn.org, July 17, 2019; Kimberly Amadeo, "How Much Will Obamacare Cost Me?," *The Balance,* thebalance.com, December 28, 2019; Kimberly Amadeo, "Universal Health Care in Different Countries," *The Balance,* thebalance.com, January 10, 2020; Bruce Japsen, "Poll: Obamacare More Popular Than Ever," *Forbes,* forbes.com, February 21, 2020.

Using Technology to Manage Information

LEARNING OBJECTIVES »

After you have read and studied this bonus chapter, you should be able to

B–1 Outline the changing role of business technology.

B–2 List the types of business information, identify the characteristics of useful information, and discuss how data is stored and analyzed.

B–3 Compare the scope of the Internet, intranets, extranets, and virtual private networks, and explain how broadband technology and 5G enabled the evolution to Web 2.0 and 3.0.

B–4 Explain the differences between LAN and WAN and discuss the benefits and drawbacks of cloud computing.

B–5 Evaluate the human resource, security, privacy, and stability issues affected by information technology.

Jim Kavanaugh, CEO of World Wide Technology

To be a successful leader in today's tech-driven business world, it is important to be a team player as well as a fierce competitor. World Wide Technology CEO Jim Kavanaugh scores on both counts. An all-star athlete who successfully made the switch to business, he has built a multibillion-dollar company that helps firms around the country fulfill their technology needs.

Born and raised in a blue-collar family in St. Louis, Missouri, Kavanaugh began playing soccer as soon as he was able to kick a ball. After leading his high school to a state championship, he received a full athletic scholarship to attend St. Louis University. "If I didn't get a scholarship, there's probably a good chance I would have gone into construction," said Kavanaugh. Instead, he excelled both at school and sports during his college career. He was named to the U.S. Olympic and Pan American soccer teams and began his professional career as a member of the Los Angeles Lazers after graduation. Once the team traded him to the financially struggling St. Louis Steamers, though, Kavanaugh decided it was time to hang up his cleats.

With his business degree in hand, Kavanaugh responded to an ad from an electronics distributor where he was hired to sell computer chips and circuit board components. After a year on the job, he approached his boss about starting their own electronics distribution firm. His boss agreed as long as they also partnered with David Steward, a business executive and entrepreneur who had founded a number of successful ventures. Along with bringing in a wide range of expertise, Steward also invested some much-needed funds in order to get the company off the ground. Since Kavanaugh had no money to contribute himself, he had to prove his worth for a number of years before he earned a 15 percent stake in World Wide Technology (WWT).

As with most new businesses, the early years at WWT were difficult as the company fell behind on its line of credit. After a lot of hard work, WWT was able to secure government contracts that fueled the firm's early growth. Soon orders came pouring in from large government buyers like the departments of Defense, Transportation, and Agriculture. Its success with federal contractors was closely followed by interest from private-sector companies, causing WWT's revenue to climb to nearly $1 billion by 2001. Over time, Kavanaugh built the company's catalog to specialize in both hardware and software. WWT's ability to package a host of disparate tech products into a single system helped it stand out to buyers. WWT accomplished this by selecting products from suppliers such as Microsoft, Cisco, and Red Hat to create a comprehensive new program for customers. This helped the company differentiate itself from rivals who struggled to compete against WWT's ability to address its clients' specific technology needs.

Today, Kavanaugh's primary push is to expand the company's add-on tech services, which includes creating software such as apps and tools for websites. For example, the company recently revamped the mobile ordering platform for Jersey Mike's Sandwich Shops, created a ride-share app for Enterprise Rent-A-Car, and developed a curbside feature for Lowe's. Looking ahead, Kavanaugh hopes that services will grow to account for 50 percent of WWT's business. "The speed of new technology being introduced is at an all-time high," said Kavanaugh. "And isn't going to slow."

As industry leaders like Jim Kavanaugh and tech companies continue to change the face of the digital landscape, it's possible that even the most entrenched technologies could become obsolete in a few years. In this chapter you'll learn about how this ever-changing tech world affects business.

Sources: Lauren Debter, "The Billionaires behind the Secret Tech Mecca in America's Heartland," *Forbes,* August 8, 2019; Mark Haranas, "WWT CEO Jim Kavanaugh's 10 Boldest IT Bets and Myths for 2020," *CRN,* crn.com, January 17, 2020; World Wide Technology, wwt.com, accessed February 2020.

Let's talk business!
bit.ly/LetsTalkBusinessB

Ashley Gieseking

THIS FOOD COMPANY'S AnyWare platform allows customers to place orders on any social media platform and device imaginable. Along with providing convenience for customers, it also allows the company to collect a ton of data. Name that company. (Find the answer in the chapter.)

LO B–1 Outline the changing role of business technology.

The Role of Information Technology

The importance of business knowledge is nothing new—what is newer is the recognition of the need to manage it like any other asset. To manage knowledge, a company needs to share information efficiently throughout the organization and to implement systems for creating new knowledge. This need is constantly leading to new technologies that support the exchange of information among staff, suppliers, and customers. Studies have shown that data-driven decision making (i.e., collecting data, analyzing it, and using it to make crucial decisions, like whether to create a new product or service) can lift productivity 5 percent higher than decision making based on experience and intuition.[1]

Evolution from Data Processing to Business Intelligence

To understand technology today, it is helpful to review how we got here.

data processing (DP)
Name for business technology in the 1970s; included technology that supported an existing business and was primarily used to improve the flow of financial information.

database
An electronic storage file for information.

information systems (IS)
Technology that helps companies do business; includes such tools as automated teller machines (ATMs) and voice mail.

information technology (IT)
Technology used to store, retrieve, and send information efficiently.

- In the 1970s, business technology was known as **data processing (DP)**. (Although many people use the words *data* and *information* interchangeably, they mean different things. *Data* is raw, unanalyzed, and unorganized facts and figures. *Information* is processed and organized data that managers can use for decision making.) The primary purpose of data processing was to improve the flow of financial information. Data processing employees were support staff who rarely came in contact with customers. Instead, they were more likely to spend their time sorting information into a **database**, an electronic storage file for information.

- In the 1980s, business technology became known as **information systems (IS)** when it moved out of the back room and into the center of the business. Its role changed from *supporting* the business to *doing* business. Customers began to interact with a wide array of technological tools, from automated teller machines (ATMs) to voice mail. As business increased its use of information systems, it became more dependent on them.

- Until the late 1980s, business technology was just an addition to the existing way of doing business. Keeping up-to-date was a matter of using new technology on old methods. But things started to change when businesses applied new technology to new methods. Business technology then became known as **information technology (IT)**, and its role became to *change* business by storing, retrieving, and sending information efficiently.

- In the 1990s, the introduction of the World Wide Web changed the way that people interacted with one another and information. Online services such as Google offered a new way of accessing information. In addition, Bluetooth technology created conveniences by providing wireless communication systems to replace cables that typically connected devices, thus freeing people to access information wherever they wanted.

● In the 2000s, as this technology became more sophisticated, it became better known as **business intelligence (BI) or analytics**. BI refers to a variety of software applications used to analyze an organization's raw data and derive useful insights from it. BI activities include data mining (which we discuss later in this chapter), online analytical processes, querying, and reporting.[2] Knowledge is information charged with enough intelligence to make it relevant and useful. Knowledge technology adds a layer of intelligence to filter appropriate information and deliver it when it is needed.

Smith Collection/Gado/Getty Images

BI changed the traditional flow of information. Instead of an individual going to the database, the database comes to the individual. Managers can put a new employee at a workstation using BI training software and let the system take over everything from laying out a checklist of the tasks required on a shift to providing answers and insights that once would have taken up a supervisor's time.

BI helps businesspeople focus on what's important: deciding how to react to problems and opportunities. For example, imagine you're a sales rep who just closed a big deal. While you celebrate your success, the finance department is upset because your customer never pays on time, which costs the company a lot of money. BI could provide you that insight so that you could negotiate different payment terms with the customer, thus connecting sales activity to financial requirements in a seamless process.

Technology changes react with one another to create more change. Maintaining the flexibility to successfully integrate these changes is crucial to business survival. For instance, Kodak once dominated the camera industry but failed to compete effectively and lost market share. Even though it invented the first digital camera, the company was concerned that digital photography would eat into its traditional film business. So Kodak decided to continue focusing on film rather than digital cameras, a decision that eventually led to the company's bankruptcy.[3] Despite its size and money, Kodak wasn't flexible enough to adapt to changing trends.

Knowledge sharing is at the heart of keeping pace with change. Of course, it can be difficult to predict which new technologies will be successful. For a fun look at the worst tech predictions of all time, see Figure B.1.

Obviously, the role of the IT staff has changed as technology itself has improved and evolved. The chief information officer (CIO) has moved out of the back room and into the boardroom, and now spends less time worrying about keeping systems running and more time finding ways to boost business by applying technology to purchasing decisions, operational strategy, and marketing and sales. Today the role of the CIO is to help the business use technology to communicate better with others, while offering better service and lower costs.[4]

How Information Technology Changes Business

Time and place have always been at the center of business. After all, customers once had to visit a business during certain hours to satisfy their needs. For example, people shopped at department stores when they needed to buy clothes. They went to the bank to deposit checks and arrange for a loan. Businesses decided when and where they did business with customers. Today, IT allows businesses to deliver goods and services whenever and wherever the customer wants them. You can order books and clothes, arrange a home mortgage loan, or even buy a car online, anytime you choose.

Consider how IT has changed the entertainment industry. For decades people had to go to movie theaters if they wanted to see a movie. Then televisions became widely available and created the home video market. Rental outlets like Blockbuster soon began to hold a

The Amazon Echo is more than just an ordinary sound system: the hands-free device is powered by Alexa, Amazon's artificial intelligence software. All a user has to do is say "Alexa" and the device will start listening for a command. The user can then ask Alexa to play music, check the weather, or even order groceries. Do you think voice-activated appliances like this will become more popular in the future?

business intelligence (BI) or analytics

The use of data analytic tools to analyze an organization's raw data and derive useful insights from it.

"Television won't be able to hold onto any market it captures after the first six months. People will soon get tired of staring at a plywood box every night."
—Darryl Zanuck, executive at 20th Century Fox, 1946

"I predict the Internet will soon go spectacularly supernova and in 1996 catastrophically collapse."
—Robert Metcalfe, founder of 3Com, 1995

"Inventions have long since reached their limit, and I see no hope for further developments."
—Roman engineer Julius Sextus Frontinus, 10 A.D.

"This 'telephone' has too many shortcomings to be seriously considered as a means of communication."
— Western Union internal memo, 1876

"Who the hell wants to hear actors talk?"
—H. M. Warner, Warner Brothers, 1927

"I think there is a world market for maybe five computers."
—Thomas Watson, president of IBM, 1943

"Do not bother to sell your gas shares. The electric light has no future."
—Professor John Henry Pepper, scientist, 1870s

"Remote shopping, while entirely feasible, will flop."
—*Time*, 1966

"There is no reason anyone would want a computer in their home."
—Ken Olsen, founder of Digital Equipment Corporation, 1977

Sources: Chris Smith, "'We Have No Need for Phones' and 9 More Terrible Tech Predictions That Were Wide of the Mark," *British Telecommunications,* March 19, 2019; "17 Technology Quotes That Backfired Badly," *Global Business Intelligence,* globalbievents.com, accessed March 2020.

lot of sway over the industry, but their dominance disappeared with the rise of the Internet. Now consumers don't even have to leave the couch when they want to watch a movie. Video on demand from satellite, cable, or streaming services allows today's film buffs to watch movies whenever they want across a wide variety of devices.

As IT broke time and location barriers, it created new organizations and services that are independent of location. For example, NASDAQ is an electronic stock exchange without trading floors where buyers and sellers make trades by computer. Although the exchange started small, it is now home to more than 4,000 listings valued at approximately $15 trillion.[5] Smartphones, laptops, and tablets also grant you access to people and information as if you were in the office. That independence brings work to people instead of people to work.

The way people do business drastically changes when companies increase their technological capabilities. Electronic communications can provide substantial time savings. E-mail and texting have put an end to tedious games of telephone tag and are far faster than paper-based correspondence. Communicating on platforms like Slack allows team members to work on common documents without time-consuming meetings. See Figure B.2 for other examples of how information technology is changing business.

Organization
Technology is breaking down corporate barriers, allowing functional departments or product groups (including factory workers) to share critical information instantly.

Operations
Technology shrinks cycle times, reduces defects, and cuts waste. Service companies use technology to streamline ordering and communication with suppliers and customers.

Staffing
Technology eliminates layers of management and cuts the number of employees. Companies use computers and telecommunication equipment to create "virtual offices" with employees in various locations.

New products
Information technology cuts development cycles by feeding customer and marketing comments to product development teams quickly so that they can revive products and target specific customers.

Customer relations
Customer service representatives can solve customers' problems instantly by using company-wide databases to complete tasks from changing addresses to adjusting bills. Information gathered from customer service interactions can further strengthen customer relationships.

New markets
Since it is no longer necessary for customers to walk down the street to get to stores, online businesses can attract customers to whom they wouldn't otherwise have access.

FIGURE B.2 HOW INFORMATION TECHNOLOGY IS CHANGING BUSINESS This table shows a few ways that information technology is changing businesses, their employees, suppliers, and customers.

⁇ TESTPREP

- How has the role of information technology changed since the days when it was known as data processing?
- How has information technology changed the way we do business?

LO B-2 List the types of business information, identify the characteristics of useful information, and discuss how data is stored and analyzed.

Types of Information

Today, information flows into and through an organization from many different directions. The types of information available to businesses today include:

- *Business process information.* This includes all transaction data gathered at the point of sale as well as information gained through operations like enterprise resource planning, supply chain management, and customer relationship management systems.

Alex Wong/Getty Images

Biometric technology such as fingerprint sensors or retinal scanners allow organizations to identify people with near-perfect accuracy. For instance, some hospitals scan patients' fingerprints so that doctors can easily identify their medical histories. In the business world, retailers can use retinal scanners to track which products a customer looks at. Can you think of any other uses for biometric technology?

- *Physical-world observations.* These result from the use of radio frequency identification (RFID) devices, cameras, wireless access, global positioning systems, and sensor technology—all of which have to do with where people or items are located and what they are doing.

  These computer chips cost pennies apiece and can be found in a wide range of products, including credit cards, printer ink cartridges, baseballs, tire valves, running shoes, vacuum cleaners, and even coasters. That's right—you can buy a smart coaster that guides you through the steps to mix a cocktail. Just pour the ingredients into the glass until the light on the coaster turns green and you'll have a perfect drink every time.[6]

- *Biological data.* This includes the fingerprinting technology used on many smartphones as well as other biometric devices that scan retinas, recognize faces and voices, and analyze DNA. Although such information usually serves security purposes, it can also be used by companies for marketing research as well as by doctors to identify patients in busy hospitals.[7]

- *Public data.* Free and accessible, public data includes the electronic traces we leave when posting to social media, sending e-mail, and using search engines. More and more, public data is being stored, shared, or sold.

- *Data that indicates personal preferences or intentions.* Online shoppers leave a trail of information that can reveal personal likes and dislikes.

The volume and complexity of all the data and information is staggering. Computing systems can search through text, numbers, audio, and video—and identify, categorize, and refine relevant opinions on any topic imaginable.

Managing Information

Even before the use of computers, managers had to sift through mountains of information to find what they needed to help them make decisions. Today, businesspeople are faced with *infoglut,* an overabundance of data. Have you seen the classic scene from TV's *I Love Lucy* with Lucy and Ethel working in a factory on the candy line? (It's on YouTube in case you haven't seen it.) Everything was going OK until the candy started coming too fast for them. Then mayhem broke loose. That's what's happening for many managers today, only with information instead of candy. Too much information can confuse issues rather than clarify them.

How can managers keep from getting buried in the infoglut? Stepping back to gain perspective is the key. It is important to identify the four or five key goals you wish to reach, and eliminate information not related to them. That can cut the information flow by half. As we were gathering information for this chapter, we collected a huge number of articles from both print journals and online sources. Feeling the pressure of information overload, we identified the objectives we wanted the chapter to help you accomplish and eliminated all the articles that didn't address those objectives. As we further refined our objectives, the huge file gradually dropped to a manageable size.

Obviously, not all the information that ends up on your desk will be useful. The usefulness of management information depends on four characteristics:

1. *Quality.* Quality means that the information is accurate and reliable. When the clerk at a fast-food restaurant enters your order into the cash register, it may automatically transfer to a computer that calculates the day's sales and profits as soon as the store closes. The sales and expense data must be accurate, or the rest of the calculations will be wrong. Quality can be a real problem when a large number of calculations are based on questionable sales forecasts rather than actual sales.

2. *Completeness.* There must be enough information to allow you to make a decision, but not so much as to confuse the issue. Today, as we have noted, the problem is often too much information rather than too little.

3. *Timeliness.* Information must reach managers quickly. E-mail and texting can let marketing, engineering, and production know about a problem with a product the same day the salesperson hears about it, so customer complaints can be handled instantly if possible, or certainly within a day. Product changes can be made on the spot using computer-integrated manufacturing, as discussed in Chapter 9.

4. *Relevance.* Different managers have different information needs. Since information systems often provide too much data, managers must learn which questions to ask to get the answers they seek.

Remember, though, that you can never read everything available. Set objectives for yourself, and do the best you can.

Big Data and Data Analytics

Chances are that some program is keeping track of every click you make online, every movement you make as you shop in stores, every restaurant you go to for lunch—even what you eat. Collecting such data isn't enough; you have to derive meaning from it. And when you collect more data, you need more storage. How do businesses store and organize a data glut so that it eventually becomes useful information? The answer for many companies is data analytics. **Data analytics** is the process of collecting, organizing, storing, and analyzing large sets of data ("big data") in order to identify patterns and other information that is most useful to the business now and for making future decisions.[8]

One part of data analytics is *data mining,* a technique for looking for hidden patterns and previously unknown relationships in the data. Identifying these connections and profiting from them has become a key goal at many big companies.[9] For example, McDonald's gathers and analyzes all kinds of data about every single sale in real time. The fast-food chain uses high-tech algorithms and "machine learning" platforms to quickly crunch data such as recent sales, weather conditions, nearby events, and even local traffic. McDonald's then uses this data to push certain items on its digital menus. So if the computer notices that the weather seems unseasonably warm, it could offer customers an ice cream cone on the drive-thru screen. Thanks to this information, McDonald's has the opportunity to earn more money on each sale.[10]

The lesson here is that companies can gain a competitive advantage with high-quality data that supports management decisions. Companies can better target their goods and services, attract new customers, and adjust prices.[11] Figure B.3 offers a few examples of sectors that benefit from big data and data analytics.

Of course, data analytics is far from perfect. These human-built systems can sometimes make mistakes that lead to real-life harm. Just ask Sarah Wysocki, a middle school teacher who learned firsthand about the potential dangers of faulty analytics. Although both students and parents alike considered Wysocki to be a marvelous teacher, one day the school suddenly fired her after a computer algorithm judged her to be bad at her job. Astonished by the decision, Wysocki and her colleagues knew there had to be some flaw in the way the algorithm analyzed student performance data. The company that created the algorithm held a claim to proprietary secrecy, however, and she couldn't challenge her firing. Fortunately, Wysocki soon got another job in a school district that used humans to make decisions.[12]

Studies show that data analytics can also reflect the biases of its human creators, including sexist and racist views. For example, a beauty contest judged by an algorithm sparked controversy when viewers learned that the computer took off points if a contestant had dark skin. In another high-profile incident, Amazon scrapped an artificial intelligence–driven recruiting tool that turned out to be biased against women. The lesson to be learned here is that organizations must make certain that the applications they use to analyze data are not flawed.[13]

data analytics
The process of collecting, organizing, storing, and analyzing large sets of data ("big data") in order to identify patterns and other information that is most useful to the business now and for making future decisions.

FIGURE B.3 EXAMPLES OF SECTORS THAT BENEFIT FROM BIG DATA AND DATA ANALYTICS

E-commerce

Online sellers can analyze cart data to change prices for people who leave items behind in order to attract them back to the site to follow through on the purchase.

Retail

Stores such as Target can tell from a woman's previous purchases that she's pregnant. It can then send her coupons and other promotions for baby products. It can analyze the data a little more and promote similar products to the grandparents-to-be.

Real estate

Beach house rental agents can target vacation promotions to people who buy sunscreen frequently.

Law enforcement

Video cameras in light fixtures collect and feed data to software that can spot long lines, recognize license plates, and even identify suspicious activity, sending alerts to the appropriate staff. Sensors in the fixtures can pinpoint a gunshot, sense an earthquake or dangerous gas, or spot a person stopping at various cars in a parking lot.

Health care

Smartphones with motion sensors can detect early signs of Parkinson's disease.

Sources: Paul B. Ginsburg, Andres de Loera-Brust, Caitlin Brandt, et al., "The Opportunities and Challenges of Data Analytics in Health Care," Brookings Institute, November 1, 2018; Andrew Arnold, "Here's How Data and Analytics Can Benefit E-commerce Business Owners," *Forbes,* January 4, 2019; "How Big Data Analytics Can Be the Difference for Law Enforcement," *SAS,* accessed April 2019.

Using Information from Social Media

Every day billions of people share their thoughts and photos on social media.[14] This information doesn't go out just to their friends and followers, though. Businesses also keep a close eye on social networks to gather up-to-the-minute data about consumers. In fact, every day users across the Internet generate *quintillions* of bytes of data, with much of it coming from "unstructured" sources like social media. This wealth of topical information then helps companies develop new strategies to reach out to customers.[15]

Going back to McDonald's, the fast-food company closely studied eight years of social media data before it made the decision to offer breakfast menu items all day. Domino's Pizza is another tech-savvy restaurant chain that uses data to its advantage. Through its AnyWare platform, customers can order pizza on just about any device or social network imaginable. Whether it's by clicking a Domino's button on a smart TV or sending a pizza slice emoji on Twitter, AnyWare provides customers with convenience while allowing the company to collect all sorts of valuable data. Domino's GPS technology allows customers to follow the progress of their delivery from store to door. Domino's also obtains tons of data from its Points for Pies program, a promotion that lets customers earn rewards for taking pictures of any type of pizza, Domino's or not. Thanks to all this information, the company can continue to offer its customers quality food and reliable delivery service at a consistently low cost.[16]

?TESTPREP

- What types of information are available to businesses today?
- What are the four characteristics of information that make it useful?
- What is data mining and how do businesses use it?

LO B–3 Compare the scope of the Internet, intranets, extranets, and virtual private networks, and explain how broadband technology and 5G enabled the evolution to Web 2.0 and 3.0.

The Heart of Knowledge Management: The Internet

You already know the Internet is a network of computer networks that evolved from a one-to-one communications tool to a one-to-many broadcast communication tool. Today it is the *heart of knowledge management.* Internet users can point and click their way from site to site with complete freedom. But what if you don't want just anybody to have access to your website? You might create an intranet, extranet, or virtual private network.

An **intranet** is a companywide network, closed to public access, that uses Internet-type technology. To prevent unauthorized outsiders (particularly the competition) from accessing their sites, companies can construct a firewall between themselves and the outside world. A firewall can consist of hardware, software, or both. Firewalls allow only authorized users to access the intranet.[17]

Many businesses choose to open their intranets to other selected companies, and even customers, through the use of extranets. An **extranet** is a controlled private network that lets more than one company access the same information or allows people on different servers to collaborate and do so without granting access to the organization's entire network. Now almost all companies can use extranets for electronic data interchange (EDI) functions like sharing data and processing orders, specifications, invoices, and payments.[18]

A **virtual private network (VPN)** is a private data network that creates secure connections, or "tunnels," over regular Internet networks. VPNs use encryption to scramble data when it's sent over a WiFi network. Encryption makes the data unreadable, thus keeping the network secure. Another way to think of it is that a firewall protects your data on your computer and a VPN protects your data on the Internet. You probably use a VPN when you log on to your school's website. VPNs are commonplace in schools across the country that want to allow only affiliated students and faculty access to accounts like Blackboard (an online tool used to enhance teaching and learning, share course documentation, and register for courses). If you don't have access to a corporate VPN, you can easily set up an account at a public VPN provider like Norton Secure VPN, CyberGhost, and PureVPN.[19]

The challenge to the chief information officer (CIO) is to integrate resources, information, reports, and so on—all of which may be in a variety of places—so that they appear seamless to the user.

Broadband Technology

The more traffic on the Internet, the slower connections become. Tools to unlock these traffic jams include **broadband technology**, a continuous connection to the Internet that allows users to send and receive video, voice, and data files quickly. Broadband speed in the United States has improved over the last couple of years, with the nation now boasting an average speed of about 38 megabits per second (mbps). Still, it can't quite match the pace set by global leaders like Taiwan and Singapore, which average at about 85 mbps and 70 mbps, respectively.[20] As people use more and more bandwidth to stream video on services like Netflix or music on apps like Spotify, Internet service providers have begun to place caps on the amount of broadband consumers can use. Right now this isn't a problem for most users since average usage is well below the current caps, but as more mobile devices and services come online, the more likely broadband will become a consumption-based service (i.e., you pay for the broadband you use).

intranet
A companywide network, closed to public access, that uses Internet-type technology.

extranet
A semiprivate network that uses Internet technology and allows more than one company to access the same information or allows people on different servers to collaborate.

virtual private network (VPN)
A private data network that creates secure connections, or "tunnels," over regular Internet lines.

broadband technology
Technology that offers users a continuous connection to the Internet and allows them to send and receive mammoth files that include voice, video, and data much faster than ever before.

VPN providers like CyberGhost create secure connections over regular networks, allowing users to browse the Internet privately and safely. What are the benefits of using VPNs in schools and businesses?

CyberGhost

5G

There is a global race to see which country can roll out the next generation of wireless technology the fastest. 5G, short for fifth-generation wireless, is expected to be 100 times faster than today's 4G networks.[21] The sooner companies can access this more powerful technology, the better they can compete with companies across the globe. Of course, this means more jobs and higher profits. While the United States would like to be the winner of that race, it faces a number of roadblocks.

Roadblocks Slowing 5G Several parts of the government are at odds over how to assign space on the key public resource that 5G will need—the airwaves (also called the spectrum). Much of the space on the spectrum is already being used by many different organizations. For example, weather satellites use it to predict hurricanes and tornadoes, high-speed networks use it for education, satellites use it for TV broadcasts, automakers and utilities use it for safety and other purposes, cell phone companies use it for smartphones, transportation companies use it to track truck fleets and rental cars, and, of course, the Department of Defense uses it for radar. Carving out enough space on the spectrum for 5G is a challenge that policymakers hope to resolve soon so that they can explore the extraordinary possibilities offered by combining super-fast wireless tech with artificial intelligence.[22]

artificial intelligence (AI)
A term to describe machines programmed to think, work, and react like humans.

Artificial Intelligence Plus 5G **Artificial intelligence (AI)** describes machines programmed to think, work, and react like humans. AI can be classified as either narrow or general. *Narrow AI* involves training a device or software to perform a specific task like recognizing images. *General AI* involves technology that can evolve and improve any task. *Machine learning* involves training devices and software to perform a task and improve its capabilities by feeding it data and information so it can "learn" over time. For example, Amazon's recommendation engine collects data about your prior purchases and uses an algorithm to suggest other items you might like.[23]

As we saw with McDonald's earlier in the chapter, many companies now rely on advanced computer programs that can automatically sort through and analyze tons of data. These artificial intelligence–powered systems allow businesses to provide better service to their customers while also finding out more about them. For instance, every week millions of Spotify users receive their own personalized playlist compiled by the company's machine learning algorithms. Not only can this inform users about artists they've never heard before, but it also allows the music streaming platform to collect data on what their users are listening to.[24]

5G lets Internet-connected AI devices transmit more information faster than ever before. Here are just a few examples of how 5G and AI can work together:[25]

- Carlsberg A/S has a program called the Beer Fingerprinting Project, which developed sensors that can determine the ultimate flavor of yeast variants before the fermentation starts. Machine learning is used to analyze the data that the sensors produce and assemble it in a readable form. The current process requires months of research and thousands of variants before humans can taste the yeast and determine the one or two that might make the final cut. Carlsberg believes its sensors could have applications for the pharmaceutical and medical industries, such as detecting microbial contaminations.

- Neiman Marcus uses 5G and AI devices to gather new levels of customer intelligence and change the ways that shoppers browse its aisles. Sensors on store shelves can detect when customers pick up a product and put it back. If a product is picked up and returned often, the AI-enabled software and other analytics can help managers decide to reset prices or improve product displays. Using this technology, a retailer that arranges cosmetics by brand could discover that buyers prefer to shop by category such as fragrance, eye makeup, lipstick, and so on. Retailers using the tools report an average sales increase of 60 percent.

- The European Space Agency partnered with private companies and public-service agencies to explore how a combination of space-based technologies and AI might be able to track the spread of pandemics like the 2020 coronavirus. By collecting data about infection rates and analyzing it at the source, they combined this information with satellite images transmitted by 5G.

- Some hospitals use robots to help treat contagious patients. Remote communication helps patients avoid transmitting disease. Trusting robots to perform simple tasks like disinfecting rooms, taking vitals, and delivering medications saves time for health care workers. For example, in a hospital near Seattle, a robot carried a stethoscope and helped coronavirus patients communicate with medical staff while limiting staff exposure to the illness.

Net Neutrality

Today there is plenty of debate about "net neutrality" and the role the Federal Communications Commission (FCC) plays in regulating it.[26] Net neutrality is a concept that Internet service providers (ISPs) should provide the same level of access to all websites regardless of their content. So whether you're clicking "like" on a friend's Instagram post, looking up recipes on Epicurious, or watching videos on YouTube, your ISP must treat each site the same. Advocates claim that without net neutrality laws in place ISPs could eventually charge sites for faster access. That means while deep-pocketed companies like Amazon or Netflix could potentially afford to upgrade, smaller sites would be left behind. It is also possible that ISPs could charge people to visit certain websites; the more money you're willing to pay, the more sites you'll have access to. Rich customers and poor customers could get two different Internet experiences.

Internet2

Even with broadband technology, scientists and other scholars who access, transmit, and manipulate complex mathematical models, data sets, and other digital elements need a faster solution. Their answer? Create a private Internet reserved for research purposes only. **Internet2** runs the fastest network and supports heavy-duty applications such as videoconferencing, collaborative research, distance education, digital libraries, and full-body simulations known as tele-immersion.[27] The power of Internet2 makes it possible for a remote medical specialist to assist in an operation online without having the connection deteriorate due to millions of people watching Netflix at home.

Internet2 became available to only a few select organizations in late 1997, but there are now more than 550 member universities, government agencies, corporations, and laboratories representing over 100 countries.[28] Whereas the public Internet divides bandwidth equally among users (if there are 100 users, they each get to use 1 percent of the available bandwidth), Internet2 is more capitalistic. Users who are willing to pay more can use more bandwidth.

Web 2.0 and Social Media

Web 2.0 is the set of tools that allow people to build social and business connections, share information, and collaborate on projects online with user-generated sites like blogs, wikis, social networking sites and other online communities, and virtual worlds. In this context, *Web 1.0* consists only of static documents and read-only data such as corporate websites, while Web 2.0 is interactive and includes read-write capabilities. Social networking is the best example of Web 2.0. Facebook, YouTube, and Twitter are among the largest Web 2.0 businesses, where ordinary people create all the content.

How the existing broadband should be distributed and who should regulate the distribution are major concerns today. Why does it matter how broadband is divided and distributed? Some people are concerned that ISPs will charge customers to go to certain websites: the more money you're willing to pay, the more sites you'll have access to. Rich customers and poor customers could get two different versions of the Internet. Other people say that it's only fair that whoever uses the most broadband should pay the most. What do you think?

Internet2
The private Internet system that links government supercomputer centers and a select group of universities; it runs more than 22,000 times faster than today's public infrastructure and supports heavy-duty applications.

Web 2.0
The set of tools that allow people to build social and business connections, share information, and collaborate on projects online (including blogs, wikis, social networking sites and other online communities, and virtual worlds).

wildpixel/Getty Images

Social media platforms provide an array of opportunities and challenges for modern businesses. They are an inexpensive way to gain exposure in a crowded marketplace. Most importantly, they give businesses tools to collaborate with consumers on product development, service enhancement, and promotion. Successful companies develop social media ecosystems and comprehensive strategies where every part of the organization collaborates and where customers are part of the conversation instantly. Many businesses hire social media managers to oversee this increasingly complicated set of tasks.

As online ambassadors for a brand's image, social media managers must interact with customers daily while also creating content that can reach a wide audience. To achieve this goal, social media managers often coordinate with marketing teams on strategies like search engine optimization (SEO). This strategy centers on using common keywords or trending topics in order to appear higher in Google's search rankings, which can then drive traffic to a company's website or social media accounts. Social media managers must also be mindful of how they present content on different social media platforms. After all, posting a big block of text probably won't generate much interaction on an image-obsessed platform like Instagram.[29]

Some companies owe much of their success to social media marketing campaigns that went viral. Dollar Shave Club became a sensation thanks to a hilarious promotional video featuring founder and CEO Michael Dubin that was viewed millions of times. Then there are companies like JetBlue that use social media to expand their customer service capabilities. The airline employs a team of 25 people to keep constant watch over its social media channels, allowing JetBlue to respond to many customers within 10 minutes.[30]

Figure B.4 offers suggestions to consider when using social media in business. The most important thing to remember is that the social media have to serve a unique purpose and not be just gimmicky add-ons.

Mobile Web

Mobile devices like smartphones and tablets allow people to access and interact on the web no matter where they are located. Looking up a restaurant or shop in the area is

FIGURE B.4 TIPS FOR USING SOCIAL MEDIA TO PARTNER WITH CUSTOMERS
Using social media is about trusting your brand and identity to your customers, partners, and the world at large. The world is going to do things with your brand, whether or not you participate in the process. Here are some tips to keep in mind.

- **If your competition is using social media, you had better be using them too.** More than 50 percent of Twitter users say that they follow companies, brands, or products on social networks.

- **Let the network mature and develop a comprehensive social media strategy.** Provide unique content for each platform. It's important that you don't post the same thing across various platforms on a given day. Users visit different platforms in order to have unique experiences, so be sure to provide different visual strategies.

- **Take customers' comments seriously and establish two-way communication.** People expect to be listened to. If you respond, they'll keep coming back. Post questions and surveys.

- **Ask your customers to answer common questions.** Asking your most active fans and advocates to answer common questions is an effective way of acknowledging the value of loyal customers while adding credibility to information about your product or service.

- **Be authentic.** You have to talk directly with your customers, not just make an announcement as you would in a press release. Keep it authentic and you'll build a personality around your company and your brand.

- **Make your corporate site social.** Provide social sharing opportunities by offering share buttons, tweet widgets, and Facebook like buttons to make it easier to share across social networks.

Sources: Karen Neicy, "Perfecting Your Visual Strategy on Social Media," *Search Engine Journal,* searchenginejournal.com, March 4, 2020; Andrew Hutchinson, "10 Ways to Increase Your Social Media Reach and Engagement," *Social Media Today,* socialmediatoday.com, February 11, 2020; Ronn Torossian, "8 Tips to Increase Consumer Engagement on Social Media," *PR News,* prnewsonline.com, February 27, 2020.

simple thanks to location-based services that can instantly pinpoint a user's position. Many companies also use mobile apps for online ordering and loyalty programs, providing customers both convenience and frequent discounts. Because so many consumers switch between devices throughout the day, it is important for businesses to ensure that their apps and websites work across multiple platforms. That way users will be able to rely on consistent, high-quality access whether they're using a laptop, smartphone, or tablet. Users get frustrated or annoyed when they can't find what they need or where they were earlier.[31]

Immersive Internet

The immersive Internet includes virtual reality (VR), augmented reality, and 3D environments. The use of VR technology is expected to increase dramatically in education in the coming years. For example, Google Expeditions uses VR headsets to take students on trips to almost any place they can imagine. From the colorful coral of the Great Barrier Reef to the dusty surface of the moon, students can access it all with a free app and Google Cardboard, a VR headset that costs just $15.[32] Of course, not all VR systems are as affordable as this. After spending as much as $500 on an Oculus Rift or HTC Vive headset, users will also need a high-performance computer to run a VR system. Customers can end up spending thousands of dollars per unit if they don't already have the necessary hardware. Still, virtual reality costs are expected to drop as the technology potentially grows into a $25 billion industry.[33]

Internet of Things

The Internet connects more people faster than ever before, and mobile devices let people be online all of the time. However, it's not just phones and tablets that connect us to the Internet. There are so many other objects that connect us that the term the *Internet of Things (IoT)* has become popular in mainstream media. IoT refers to technology that enables ordinary objects to be connected to the Internet by using sensors, cameras, software, databases, and massive data centers.[34] There are WiFi-based home automation networks that automatically cool or heat your home, turn the lights on and off, and lock your doors, all from your smartphone or computer. People can also use voice-activated assistants like Amazon's Alexa or Google Home to accomplish these tasks and more. Wearables such as smart watches, exercise bands like Fitbit, or conductive fibers woven into the fabric of your workout clothes can monitor your breathing and heart rate, count your steps, and send the information to your phone. Companies like Walmart and Toyota use wearables with sensors that identify when a factory worker moves in a way that may cause him injury and notifies him in real time in order to keep him safe.[35]

Soon every part of our lives will be quantifiable, making us even more accountable for our decisions. For example, the life insurance company John Hancock offers its customers the option to wear a fitness tracker that collects information on their sleeping and exercise habits. If the Fitbit shows that the policyholders are living a healthy life, their insurance premiums go down. Experts expect that IoT technology like this will become even more widespread with the arrival of 5G wireless networks that could operate up to 20 times faster than previous data networks. This could allow factories to communicate with robot assembly lines through high-speed WiFi rather than through complicated networks of wires, increasing both efficiency and reliability. 5G networks could even be utilized to create "smart cities" by networking community data to improve traffic conditions and environmental sustainability.[36]

The start-up HerdDogg makes noninvasive ear tags for livestock that keep farmers constantly updated about their animals' health and activity. As wearable technology like this becomes more advanced, it may lead to major life changes for both animals and people. What do you think are the benefits and drawbacks of wearable tech?

Andy Cross/The Denver Post/Getty Images

Web 3.0—Moving toward Decentralization

Another generation of web innovators plans to expand the utility of the Internet by enabling an unprecedented level of decentralization and security. They refer to this emerging technology as **Web 3.0**. Their goal is to overcome the major problems created by Web 2.0, primarily (1) the fact that most of the data generated online is collected by big tech companies (i.e., Facebook, Google, Microsoft, etc.), and (2) the system is vulnerable to a variety of issues that could lead to losses of service and/or data.[37]

Most of the data generated on the web is consolidated by a few large companies, which severely limits the ability of new, smaller companies to compete. These tech giants make lots of money from all of the data they collect while giving the sources of that data (folks like you and me) little in exchange. Most of us have exchanged our privacy for the convenience of gadgets like smartphones, smart speakers (Amazon Echo, Google Home), and other devices that know where we are, what we say, and what we search for. Today, this data is commonly used to push ads for products and services that our browsing history indicates we might be willing to buy. Of course, we can think of more sinister applications it might be used for in the future.

It's not just users who are giving away valuable data. Consider the music industry for a moment. The Internet "freed" music from giant record labels and made it readily available on places like Spotify and Pandora. Sure, we can access music for pennies compared to what we used to pay for CDs, but what about the artists who created it? They get a fraction of those pennies, while the companies that played no role (or expense) in the music's creation add to their riches.

Instead of making users go through intermediaries that collect and profit from our data, Web 3.0 moves to a decentralized system in which users connect and collaborate directly with each other. The vision is for a more powerful peer-to-peer system than was used in the past. This is made possible through *blockchain,* which is a database that exists on many servers at the same time. The blockchain is constantly growing as new sets of recordings, or "blocks," are added to it. Each block contains a timestamp and a link to the previous block, so they actually form a chain. The data in each block can't be altered. This means data can't be lost since it exists on many independent servers at the same time and is not controlled by a central server.[38] The system can still go on if one server fails, unlike a centralized system in which the whole system goes down if the central server crashes. (Huge systems like Google don't have just one server but a network of many servers. However, that network is controlled by the central server.) The only way Web 3.0 could be changed is if there was a single computer that was as powerful as half of all the other computers on the network *combined*! Considering the millions or billions of computers that could be on the network, the odds of that happening are slim.

Who's the "Boss" of the Internet?

The U.S. Defense Department created the first computer network in the late 1960s; and Tim Berners-Lee, a software engineer in a physics lab in Switzerland, invented the World Wide Web in 1990. But who controls the Internet now? For years, the U.S. Commerce Department controlled the root server for the domain name system, a digital directory that tells your computer where to go when you type in a web address, including ".gov" or ".edu." This gave the U.S. hazy ownership rights to the Internet. The United States created the Internet Corporation for Assigned Names and Numbers (ICANN) in 1998 to keep the management of networks in the hands of a private-sector system of committees representing multiple stakeholders including companies, academics, and governments.

In 2016, the U.S. government agreed to give away its remaining ownership in ICANN, thus making the organization an entirely private entity. Some argue that America's withdrawal could upset the balance of power at ICANN, possibly convincing other countries to institute restrictive policies on the Internet.[39] So far, though, the United States has been successful in building a coalition of nations that agree the Internet should be free of government regulations or restrictions on free speech.[40] What does this mean to you? It could mean that someday the Internet would be very different than it is today; you may not be free to go where you want or say what you want on the Internet. On the other hand, the coalition will hopefully remain strong enough to keep the Internet open to everyone. Or perhaps the innovators working on Web 3.0 will meet their goals of creating an open, decentralized Internet controlled by users as Berners-Lee originally envisioned. We'll have to wait and see.

?TESTPREP

- How do computer networks change the way employees gather information?
- What is the Internet of Things?

LO B–4 Explain the differences between LAN and WAN and discuss the benefits and drawbacks of cloud computing.

Networks and Cloud Computing

There are many types of computer networks. Don't worry, we won't discuss all of them. For our purposes we'll mention only two major types: LAN and WAN.

A *local area network (LAN)* is a group of connected devices in one physical location, such as a home or office. A LAN can be small or large, ranging from a home network with one user to a large enterprise network with thousands of users and devices. A LAN may include both wired and wireless devices. Regardless of size, a LAN connects devices that are in a single, limited area.

A *wide area network (WAN)* is a network that extends over a large geographic area and connects individual users or multiple LANs. The Internet can be considered a WAN. Large organizations use WANs to connect their various sites, remote employees, suppliers, and data centers so they can run applications and access necessary data. WAN connectivity can involve leased lines, cellular connections, satellite links, and other means.[11]

Cloud networking (sometimes called cloud-based networking) involves the access of networking resources from a centralized third-party provider using WAN or Internet-based technologies. Cloud networking has spurred a trend of pushing more network management functions into the cloud, so that fewer customer devices are needed to manage the network.

Cloud networking is related to the concept of cloud computing, in which centralized computing resources are shared. **Cloud computing** is the delivery of computing services—including servers, storage, databases, networking, software, analytics, and intelligence—over the Internet ("the cloud").[42] The data isn't necessarily stored in a single data center; portions could be in a series of centers anywhere in the world. The data is easily accessible from any computer with an Internet connection. Vendors like Amazon, Google, Microsoft, and IBM offer cloud storage for a monthly pay-as-you-go fee.[43]

There are three types of cloud computing: (1) *private* clouds (wholly behind a firewall), (2) *public* clouds (run on remote computers), and (3) *hybrid* clouds (consist of a private cloud for essential tasks, but use a public cloud as needed).[44]

The advantages of cloud computing include:[45]

1. **Reduced software costs.** Most software is free because the service provider supplies it. No more paying for upgrades or spending time installing all those patches since they're installed in the cloud.

cloud computing
A form of virtualization in which a company's data and applications are stored at offsite data centers that are accessed over the Internet (the cloud).

Cloud computing changes the way people and businesses use technology. Since their data is stored in the cloud rather than locked on their computers, users are free to access files from anywhere with any device. How has cloud computing changed the way you access your programs and files?

shylendrahoode/Getty Images

2. **Improved security.** Offsite centers provide full and regular backups of data, which is something many small businesses fail to do regularly.

3. **Flexible capacity.** Sometimes businesses need large chunks of capacity during peak demand periods, but much less at other times. Cloud computing allows the company to rent only what it needs when it needs it. If its needs increase, it just rents more. This is especially important to growing businesses that don't know what their needs will be.

4. **Lower equipment costs.** Since applications run in the cloud and not on your desk, you don't need to buy expensive equipment.

5. **Easier access.** Since you access all of your documents in the cloud via the Internet, it is much easier to share documents and make sure that everyone is working with the latest version.

Of course, cloud computing has its disadvantages as well. Primarily these involve concerns about security, stability, and control of data. (We'll discuss these issues in more detail later in the chapter.) To prevent security breaches, the software company VMware provides a service that lets IT managers control the data on private and public clouds so they can enjoy the cost savings and flexibility of cloud services but still maintain control over security.

?TESTPREP

- What is the difference between LAN and WAN computer networks?
- What are the benefits and drawbacks of cloud computing?

LO B–5 Evaluate the human resource, security, privacy, and stability issues affected by information technology.

Effects of Information Technology on Management

The increase of information technology has affected management greatly and will continue to do so. Four major issues today are human resource changes, security threats, privacy concerns, and stability.

Human Resource Issues

We talked in Chapter 8 about tall versus flat organizational structures. Computers often eliminate middle-management functions and thus flatten organizational structures.

Human resource managers need to recruit employees who know how to use the new technology or train those who already work in the company. The speed at which technology has advanced has created a generational divide in terms of tech skills among different-aged workers. This creates greater challenges when it comes to recruitment and training. Companies frequently hire consultants instead of internal staff to address these concerns. Outsourcing technical training allows them to concentrate on their core businesses.

Perhaps the most revolutionary effect of computers and the Internet is telecommuting. Using computers linked to the company's network, mobile employees can transmit their work to the office from anywhere as easily as they can walk to the boss's office. Naturally, that decreases travel time and overall costs and often increases productivity. Having fewer employees in the office also means that a company can get by with a smaller, and therefore less expensive, office space than before.

Telecommuting enables men and women to work while staying home with small children or older adults. It has also been a tremendous boon for workers with disabilities.

Employees who have the option to work at home, rather than staying at the office, frequently report reduced stress and improved morale.[46] Telecommuting is most successful among people who are self-starters, who don't have home distractions, and whose work doesn't require face-to-face interaction with co-workers.

At the same time, electronic communication can never replace face-to-face communication for creating enthusiasm and team spirit. Even as telecommuting has grown in popularity, some telecommuters report that a consistent diet of long-distance work leaves them feeling dislocated or left out of the loop. Some miss the energy of social interaction or dislike the intrusion of work into what is normally a personal setting. Often people working from home don't know when to turn off the work.[47] Some companies are therefore using telecommuting only as a part-time alternative.

Figure B.5 illustrates how information technology changes the way managers and workers interact. For additional information about telecommuting and home-based workers, review Chapters 6 and 11.

Security Issues

"Secure" information may be at risk from hackers who break into companies' networks; from employees who steal it; or from companies' own incompetence, poor gatekeeping, or sloppy procedures. Computer security is more complicated today than ever, as smartphones and the networks they run on, social networks and online games, cloud storage databases, and USB storage devices (flash drives and memory cards) become hackers' targets. When information was processed on mainframes, the single data center was easier to control because there was limited access to it. Today, however, computers are accessible not only in all areas within the company but also in all areas of other companies with which the firm does business.

Viruses An ongoing security threat is the spread of computer viruses over the Internet. A **virus** is a piece of programming code inserted into other programming that usually lies

DaniloAndjus/Getty Images

Telecommuting is one of the biggest human resource boons of the wireless age, but some employees are better suited to its demands than others. Do you have what it takes?

virus
A piece of programming code inserted into other programming to cause some unexpected and, for the victim, usually undesirable event.

FIGURE B.5 WHEN INFORMATION TECHNOLOGY ALTERS THE WORKPLACE

MANAGERS MUST	WORKERS MUST
• Instill commitment in subordinates rather than rule by command and control.	• Become initiators, able to act without management direction.
• Become coaches, training workers in necessary job skills, making sure they have resources to accomplish objectives, and explaining links between a job and what happens elsewhere in the company.	• Become financially literate so that they can understand the business implications of what they do and changes they suggest.
• Give greater authority to workers over scheduling, priority setting, and even compensation.	• Learn group interaction skills, including how to resolve disputes within their work group and how to work with other functions across the company.
• Use new information technologies to measure workers' performance, possibly based on customer satisfaction or the accomplishment of specific objectives.	• Develop new math, technical, and analytical skills to use newly available information on their jobs.

dormant until triggered to cause some unexpected and, for the victim, usually undesirable event. Users pick up viruses by unknowingly downloading infected programming online or sharing an infected USB storage device. Often the source of the infected file is unaware of the virus. Viruses can be quite harmful erasing data or causing your hard drive to crash.[48] Programs such as McAfee and Norton AntiVirus inoculate your computer so that it doesn't catch a known virus. But because new viruses are being developed constantly, antivirus programs may have only limited success. Thus it is important to keep your antivirus protection up-to-date and, more important, practice safe computing by not downloading files from unknown sources.

Hackers If a business stores customer data, it is subject to laws and regulations regarding the proper protection of that data. Many smaller businesses that don't have the staff to handle security concerns might consider hiring a managed security services provider (MSSP) like Alert Logic or Perimeter E-Security.[49] MSSPs can install and manage firewalls, virtual private networks, web filtering and antispam programs, security intelligence services, and wireless and mobile functions. But even with all of this security protection, hackers can still find ways to get through. Yahoo! disclosed that more than three billion accounts became compromised when hackers breached the site and stole personal information like names and passwords. In 2018 the hotel chain Marriott International experienced a similar attack when hackers stole credit card information, addresses, and even passport numbers from more than 380 million guests.[50]

Even organizations charged with protecting your most vital information are vulnerable to hackers. In 2017, more than 145 million people had their Social Security numbers, birth dates, and other critical information stolen when hackers breached the consumer credit reporting agency Equifax. The hack exposed millions of people to great risk of having their identities stolen.[51] **Identity theft** is the obtaining of individuals' personal information, such as Social Security and credit card numbers, for illegal purposes. If you ever fall victim to identity theft, experts advise that you reset the passwords on all of your accounts and start using a password manager. They also recommend activating two-factor authentication, which is an additional layer of security, when possible, and using a VPN. Many employers even offer identity-theft protection as an employee benefit. This option may help the employers as much as employees since more than half of victims report that they needed to take off work to deal with the issue. As much as three-quarters of victims say that they suffer severe emotional distress as a result of identity theft.[52]

Some security experts advise businesses to assume that their systems have been breached and take the fight to the hackers. They recommend using methods that will frustrate the hackers and drive up their cost in order to deter them from future hacking. These methods include planting fake information on their systems to mislead data thieves, and creating decoys that gather information about intruders. If hackers try to access a company through one of these false gateways, IT workers can easily identify and take countermeasures against them.[53] Bottom line is that businesses that store data will need stronger and smarter tools to protect themselves from hackers.

identity theft
The obtaining of individuals' personal information, such as Social Security and credit card numbers, for illegal purposes.

In 2017 hackers breached the credit reporting agency Equifax and made off with personal information from nearly 148 million consumers. What can you do to protect yourself from loss when someone steals your vital information from a third party?

Jaap Arriens/NurPhoto/Getty Images

Phishing *Phishing* is another type of online security threat. A scammer will embellish an e-mail message with a stolen logo for a well-recognized brand such as eBay, PayPal, or Citibank that makes the message look authentic. Phishing messages often state something like "Account activation required" or "Your account will be canceled if you do not verify." When the victims click the link contained in the message, they are sent to a phony website that takes their personal information and uses it to commit fraud. The best way to avoid a phishing scam is never to access a website through a link in an e-mail message. Instead, open a new window and go to the home page of the company's website directly.

As the Internet continues to be at the center of many people's lives, the number of legal issues surrounding its use will likely increase. Today, copyright and obscenity laws are entering into the virtual world. Other legal questions relate to intellectual property and contract disputes, online sexual and racial harassment, and the use of electronic communication to promote crooked sales schemes. Cyber crimes are estimated to cost the world economy as much as $6 trillion by 2021.[54]

Ransomware Malicious software that holds data hostage is known as ransomware. Ransomware is like kidnapping: someone takes something valuable to you and then demands that you pay them in order to get it back. Like phishing, it typically works by infecting a computer with a virus that comes from a corrupted link or an e-mail attachment that looks real. One of the biggest cyber attacks in history occurred on May 12, 2017, when a ransomware named WannaCry stormed across the Internet. In the first few hours, 200,000 machines in 150 countries were infected and their owners were told to pay a ransom in order to unlock their data. Big organizations such as Renault and the UK's National Health Service were struck and crippled by the attack as were many hospitals and German and Russian railroads.[55]

Cyberterrorism Until September 11, 2001, corporate and government security officials worried mostly about online theft, credit card fraud, and hackers. Today, however, they are most concerned about the threat that *cyberterrorism* poses to the nation's communications infrastructure, money supply, electricity grids, and transportation systems. Recently, a group of large U.S. utility firms formed Grid Assurance, an organization that stockpiles key electrical equipment to be used in the event of a cyber attack or natural disaster. The idea is that if hackers knock out a portion of the electrical system, Grid Assurance can easily replace the broken parts without interrupting service for too long.[56]

The Critical Infrastructure Protection Board, part of the U.S. Department of Homeland Security, was created after September 11, 2001, to devise a plan for improving the security of critical infrastructure in the United States. The agency needs the cooperation of businesses across the country, because 85 percent of the system it needs to protect is in the private sector. Companies have been reluctant to file reports about security breaches, however, for fear the public will lose faith in their ability to protect their assets. To encourage the sharing of such information, Congress passed the Critical Infrastructure Information Act of 2002, assuring businesses that any information they provide the Department of Homeland Security will remain secret through an exemption from the Freedom of Information Act.

Privacy Issues

The increasing use of technology creates major concerns about privacy. In 2018, a whistleblower revealed that Facebook allowed an organization called Cambridge Analytica to collect private data from more than 50 million accounts. While the social network sometimes allows scholars to study its data, Cambridge Analytica was not a research institute. Instead, it was a political organization collecting information about potential voters. This revelation shocked the public and caused many to reconsider their trust in social networks like Facebook.[57]

As we mentioned earlier in the chapter, private industry is constantly keeping track of your clicks, swipes, and likes.[58] In addition, many U.S. companies scan employee e-mail regularly, and it's legal. They look for trade secrets, non-work-related traffic, harassing messages, and conflicts of interest. Any hacker with a desire to read your thoughts can also trap and read your messages, most of which are unencrypted. Some e-mail systems can encrypt e-mail to keep corporate messages private.[59]

The Internet presents increasing threats to your privacy as more personal information is stored in computers and more people are able to access it, legally or not. Some websites allow people to search for vehicle ownership from a license number or to find other individuals' real estate property records. This causes many people to ask the question, "Isn't this personal information already public anyway?" Civil libertarians have

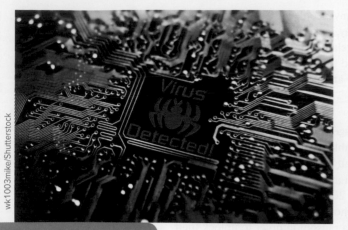

wk1003mike/Shutterstock

Do you know how many online and mobile apps track your whereabouts (both your physical location and where you go online) and share that information with third parties? Probably more than you think.

cookies

Pieces of information, such as registration data or user preferences, sent by a website over the Internet to a web browser that the browser software is expected to save and send back to the server whenever the user returns to that website.

long fought to keep certain kinds of information available to the public. If access to such data is restricted on the Internet, wouldn't we have to reevaluate our policies on all public records? Privacy advocates don't think so. After all, the difference is that the Internet makes obtaining personal information *too* easy. Would your neighbors or friends even consider going to the appropriate local agency and sorting through public documents to find your driving records or to see your divorce settlement? Probably not. But they might dig into your background if it's only a few clicks away.

Many web servers track the online movements of users willing to swap such personal details for free access to online information. Site owners can share your data with others without your permission. Websites also often send **cookies** to your computer that stay on your hard drive. These are pieces of information such as registration data (name and password) or user preferences that the browser sends back to the server whenever you return to that website. Some software, known as spyware, can be installed on your computer without your knowledge. The spyware can then infect your system with viruses and track your online behavior.

In this data-driven age, you need to decide how much personal information you are willing to give away. Remember, we are living in an information economy, and information is a commodity—that is, an economic good with a measurable value. All sorts of online entities want to know whatever they can about you, and unfortunately some of them don't have the best intentions in mind. To ensure that your data remains secure, experts recommend that users update their passwords frequently, use a password manager to store and protect their passwords, don't access financial sites on public WiFi, avoid suspicious links, and keep close watch on their credit card information.[60]

Stability Issues

Although technology can provide significant increases in productivity and efficiency, instability has a significant impact on business. Candy maker Hershey discovered the Halloween trick was on it one year when the company couldn't get its treats to stores on time. Failure of its new $115 million computer system disrupted shipments, and retailers were forced to order Halloween candy from other companies, leaving Hershey with a 12 percent decrease in sales that quarter.

What's to blame? Experts say it is a combination of computer error, human error, malfunctioning software, and an overly complex marriage of software, hardware, and networking equipment. Some systems are launched too quickly to be bug-proof, and some executives don't have the technical knowledge to challenge computer specialists. As critical as technology is to business, some of it is not built for rigorous engineering, and some people aren't properly trained to use it. As things get more complex, we will probably be prone to more errors.

Technology and You

As information technology eliminates old jobs while creating new ones, it will be up to you to learn and maintain the skills you need to be certain you aren't left behind. Keeping current with the latest technology can get complicated, so don't be afraid to seek help from experts when you need it. You can find many high-level IT professionals from major firms dispensing advice on social media platforms like Twitter or through YouTube videos. But as you've learned in this chapter, not everyone online can be trusted. Be mindful of misinformation and always seek out verifiable sources. If you learn about technology and how to use it responsibly, there's no limit to where you can go in today's hyperconnected world.

?**TEST**PREP

- How has information technology changed the way people work?
- What management issues have been affected by the growth of information technology?

SUMMARY

LO B–1 Outline the changing role of business technology.

- **What have been the various names and roles of business technology since 1970?**

In the 1970s, business technology was called data processing (DP) and its role was to support existing business. In the 1980s, its name became information systems (IS) and its role changed to doing business. In the 1990s, business technology became information technology (IT) and its role now is to change business. As technology became more sophisticated in the 2000s, it became known as business intelligence (or analytics) and includes data mining, online analytical processes, querying, and reporting.

- **How does information technology change business?**

Information technology has minimized the importance of time and place to businesses. Firms that are independent of time and location can deliver products and services whenever and wherever convenient for the customer. See Figure B.2 for examples of how information technology changes business.

- **What is business intelligence?**

Business intelligence refers to a variety of software applications that analyze an organization's raw data and take out useful insights from it.

LO B–2 List the types of business information, identify the characteristics of useful information, and discuss how data is stored and analyzed.

- **What types of information are available to businesses today?**

The types of information available to businesses today include (1) business process information, (2) physical-world observations, (3) biological data, (4) public data, and (5) data that indicates personal preferences or intentions.

- **How can you deal with information overload?**

The most important step in dealing with information overload is to identify your four or five key goals. Eliminate information that will not help you meet them.

- **What makes information useful?**

The usefulness of management information depends on four characteristics: quality, completeness, timeliness, and relevance.

- **What are data analytics and big data?**

Data analytics is the process of collecting, organizing, storing, and analyzing large sets of data ("big data") in order to identify patterns and other information that is most useful to the business now and for making future decisions. Data mining is the part of data analytics that involves looking for hidden patterns and previously unknown relationships among the data.

LO B–3 Compare the scope of the Internet, intranets, extranets, and virtual private networks, and explain how broadband technology and 5G enabled the evolution to Web 2.0 and 3.0.

- **What information technology is available to help business manage information?**

  The heart of information technology involves the Internet, intranets, extranets, and virtual private networks. The Internet is a massive network of thousands of smaller networks open to everyone with a computer and a modem. An intranet is a companywide network protected from unauthorized entry by outsiders. An extranet is a semiprivate network that allows more than one company to access the same information. A virtual private network is a private data network that creates secure connections, or "tunnels," over regular Internet lines.

- **What is Web 2.0?**

  Web 2.0 is the set of tools that allow people to build social and business connections, share information, and collaborate on projects online with user-generated sites like blogs, wikis, social networking sites and other online communities, and virtual worlds. YouTube and Twitter are among the largest Web 2.0 businesses, where ordinary people create all the content.

- **What is Web 3.0?**

  Web 3.0 is an emerging technology that is designed to expand the utility of the Internet by enabling an unprecedented level of decentralization and security.

- **What is the Internet of Things?**

  Internet of Things refers to technology that enables ordinary objects to be connected to the Internet by using sensors, cameras, software, databases, and massive data centers.

LO B–4 Explain the differences between LAN and WAN and discuss the benefits and drawbacks of cloud computing.

- **What is LAN?**

  A *local area network (LAN)* is a group of connected devices in one physical location, such as a home or office.

- **What is WAN?**

  A *wide area network (WAN)* is a network that extends over a large geographical area and connects individual users or multiple LANs. The Internet can be considered a WAN.

- **What is cloud computing and what are its benefits and drawbacks?**

  Cloud computing is the delivery of computing services—including servers, storage, databases, networking, software, analytics, and intelligence—over the Internet ("the cloud"). Its benefits are reduced software costs, improved security, flexible capacity, lower equipment costs, and easier access. The drawbacks of cloud computing are concerns about security, stability, and control of data.

LO B–5 Evaluate the human resource, security, privacy, and stability issues affected by information technology.

- **What effect has information technology had on business management?**

  Computers eliminate some middle-management functions and thus flatten organizational structures. Computers also allow employees to work from their own homes. On the negative side, computers sometimes allow information to fall into the wrong hands. Concern for privacy is an issue affected by the vast store of information available on the Internet. Finding the balance between freedom to access private information and individuals' right to maintain privacy will require continued debate.

artificial intelligence (AI) 580

broadband technology 579

business intelligence (BI) or analytics 573

cloud computing 585

cookies 590

data analytics 577

database 572

data processing (DP) 572

extranet 579

identity theft 588

information systems (IS) 572

information technology (IT) 572

Internet2 581

intranet 579

virtual private network (VPN) 579

virus 587

Web 2.0 581

Web 3.0 584

CRITICAL THINKING

1. What information, either from your personal life or for your job, would you like to receive exactly when and where you need it?

2. What are the implications for world trade given that firms and government organizations now have the ability to communicate across borders so easily?

3. How will the introduction and integration of more and more devices into the Internet of Things affect your life? Do you think they will widen or narrow the gap between the haves and have-nots (rich and poor people)?

PUTTING PRINCIPLES TO WORK

PURPOSE

To differentiate a good source of information from a bad source.

EXERCISE

There is so much information online. How do you know that you are using a reliable source? How do you know if a source is biased? Search online for the following article: "4 Ways to Differentiate a Good Source from a Bad Source." After reading this short article, go to mediabiasfactcheck.com. Explore the site and then answer the following questions.

1. Can you tell by the site's domain name (i.e., *.edu, .com, .org*, etc.) if it is reliable or not? Explain your answer.

2. Is *Wikipedia* a reliable source for accurate information? Why or why not? Explain the best way to use *Wikipedia* (if at all).

3. Do the following sources generally show bias?
   1. *The Wall Street Journal*
   2. Associated Press
   3. *The Economist*
   4. *The Guardian*
   5. American College of Pediatricians

DEVELOPING CAREER SKILLS

KEY: ● **Team** ★ **Analytic** ▲ **Communication** ▣ **Technology**

1. Imagine you have $2,000 to buy or upgrade a computer system for yourself. Research hardware and software in computer magazines and on websites such as ZDNet (zdnet.com). Visit a computer store or shop online to find the best value. List what you would buy, and write a summary explaining your choices.

2. Interview someone who recently bought a computer to use in his or her business. Ask why he or she bought that specific computer and how it is used. Ask about any problems that occurred during the purchase process or in installing and using the system. What would the buyer do differently next time? What software does he or she find especially useful?

3. Describe one technological glitch you've experienced and what you did to resolve it. Discuss the consequences of the interruption (lost data, decreased productivity, increased stress). What steps have you taken to prevent a recurrence of the problem you faced?

4. Choose a topic that interests you and use two search engines to find information about it online. Narrow your search using the tips offered by the search engine. Did both search engines find the same websites? If not, how were their results different? Which engine found the most appropriate information?

5. How does technology affect your relationship with specific businesses or organizations such as your bank, your school, and your favorite places to shop? Does it strengthen or weaken your relationship? Does technology affect your relationship with your family, friends, and community? Take a sheet of paper and write down how technology helps build your business and personal relationships on one side. On the other side, list how technology weakens those relationships. What can you and others do to use technology more effectively to reduce any negative impact?

CAREER EXPLORATION

If you are interested in pursuing a career in information technology, here are a few to consider. Find out about the tasks performed, skills needed, pay, and opportunity outlook in these fields in the *Occupational Outlook Handbook (OOH)* at bls.gov.

- **Information security analyst**—plans and carries out security measures to protect an organization's computer networks and systems.

- **Computer and information research scientist**—invents and designs new approaches to computing

technology and finds innovative uses for existing technology.

- **Computer network architect**—designs and builds data communication networks, including local area networks (LANs), wide area networks (WANs), and intranets.

- **Computer support specialist**—provides help and advice to people and organizations using computer software or equipment.

VIDEO CASE — *Applying Tech with World Wide Technology*

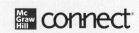

It's difficult to imagine going a single day without using some type of technology. This is especially true for today's businesses that depend on all sorts of information technology (IT). Along with storing and sending information, businesses use IT to manage resources, enhance company communication, and provide employee training. But simply buying the latest technology is not enough. Identifying the *right* technology, using it to effectively fit the organization's needs, and training employees how to use it are challenging tasks. Fortunately, World Wide Technology (WWT) can help with all these challenges.

With the help of its team of thousands of IT engineers, WWT collaborates with both public and private organizations

to discover, evaluate, build, and implement advanced technology systems. At the company's Advanced Technology Center (ATC), businesses can see product demonstrations firsthand or virtualized anywhere across the globe.

Much of WWT's work deals with big data, the massive amount of digital information that companies gather about their customer base. From health care providers to retailers, modern organizations generate enormous volumes of data that were not available in the past. Unfortunately, many companies cannot devote the time to analyze all that information. That's where WWT's experience and expertise comes to the rescue. WWT increases the value of unstructured data by making it accessible and useful. It also helps organizations protect the data through dependable security systems. Analysts at WWT always answer three questions when developing security systems: "What's on my network?," "What is it doing?," and "Should it be?"

Data security is especially critical when companies deal with the Internet of Things (IoT). This refers to technologies that enable objects to connect to the Internet using sensors, cameras, software, databases, and data centers. Examples of IoT range from smart watches and smart speakers to train track sensors that can prevent dangerous derailments. While such advancements can make our lives safer and more convenient, connected IoT devices also leave organizations more vulnerable to sabotage and theft.

Even with all the advancements in IT and data collection over the past few decades, we still cannot dispense with human reasoning. When we collect data, we need to be able to analyze that data and derive useful information

from it. Furthermore, when we allow new technologies to gather information about us, we need to know how to keep that information safe. According to WWT, you should always be smart about how you use your data, keep security in the front of your mind, and plan for security breaches. By staying safe, people can enjoy all the opportunities that innovative technologies have to offer.

THINKING IT OVER

1. Why is big data important in today's business environment?

2. Why do many companies need the services of companies like World Wide Technologies?

3. Do you think companies such as World Wide Technology will offer strong career opportunities in the next 10 years? Why or why not?

NOTES

1. Brent Dykes, "The Four Key Pillars to Fostering a Data-Driven Culture," *Forbes,* forbes.com, March 28, 2019; Nancy Smith, "What Does It Mean to Be Data-Driven as a Company?," *TechZone360,* techzone360.com, March 3, 2020; Eric Chi, Greg Layok, and Cameron Cross, "Data Driven Decision-Making—Better, Faster, and Cheaper—with Rapid Insights," West Monroe, westmonroepartners.com, February 11, 2020.

2. Chris Lukasiak, "What You Need to Know about Business Intelligence," *Forbes,* August 7, 2018; Tim Keary, "A Look at Data Analytics Trends for 2019," *Information Age,* information-age.com, March 26, 2019.

3. Ernest Werlin, "Role of Business in the American Economy," *Sarasota Herald-Tribune,* heraldtribune.com, March 2, 2020; Rich Duprey, "Is Eastman Kodak a Buy?," *The Motley Fool,* fool.com, May 9, 2019; Christopher Palmeri, "Kodak Is Having a Comeback Moment as Oscars Embrace Film," *Bloomberg,* bloomberg.com, February 6, 2020.

4. Lynden Tennison, "The 6 I's of the CIO Role," *The Wall Street Journal,* February 11, 2020.

5. Nasdaq, nasdaq.com, accessed March 2020.

6. "Can This Smart Coaster Make a Better Drink Than a Professional Bartender?," *InfoNews,* infonews.com, March 2, 2020.

7. Donna Marbury, "Why Biometrics Are the Future of Patient Care," *Medical Economics,* medialeconomics.com, February 6, 2020; "Border Control Biometrics Revenues to Reach $3.5B by 2025," *Security Sales Integration,* securitysales.com, February 6, 2020.

8. Tom O'Toole, "What's the Best Approach to Data Analytics?," *Harvard Business Review,* hbr.org, March 2, 2020.

9. Martine Paris, "Snowden Star Gordon-Levitt Slams YouTube and Instagram for Data Mining," *Forbes,* forbes.com, October 2, 2019; Jessica Kent, "Data Mining Techniques Could Improve Cancer Gene Therapies," *Health IT Analytics,* healthitanalytics.com, February 10, 2020.

10. Anthony Ha, "McDonald's Is Acquiring Dynamic Yield to Create a More Customized Drive-Thru," *TechCrunch,* techcrunch.com, March 25, 2019; Brian Barrett, "McDonald's Bites on Big Data with $300 Million Acquisition," *Wired,* March 25, 2019; Evan Jenkins, "I'm Loving' IT," *Bloomberg Businessweek,* bloomberg.com/businessweek, September 30, 2020.

11. "Benefits of Using Big Data," *Vents Magazine,* ventsmagazine.com, accessed March 2020.

12. Mark Buchanan, "Battling the Tyranny of Big Data," *Bloomberg,* January 13, 2017; Forbes Insights Team, "Managing the Ethics of Algorithms," *Forbes,* forbes.com, March 27, 2019.

13. Annie Brown, "Biased Algorithms Learn from Biased Data: 3 Kinds Biases Found in AI Datasets," *Forbes,* forbes.com, February 7, 2020.

14. "60 Social Media Statistics for 2020," *Influencer Marketing Hub,* influencermarketinghub.com, accessed March 2020.

15. Avantika Monnappa, "How Facebook Is Using Big Data—the Good, the Bad, and the Ugly," *Simpli Learn,* simplilearn.com, February 17, 2020; Dandan Tao, Pengkun Yang, and Hao Feng, "Utilization of Text Mining as a Big Data Analysis Tool for Food Science and Nutrition," *Comprehensive Reviews of Food Services and Food Safety,* February 16, 2020.

16. Greg Morabito, "Machiavellian Mega-Chain Domino's Wants to Trade Pizza for Data," *Eater,* eater.com, February 21, 2019; "Domino's® to Commemorate the Opening of Its 17,000th Store," *MarketWatch,* marketwatch.com, March 2, 2020; "Domino's Established US Restaurant Sales Rise 3.4 Pct," PYMNTS.COM, pymnts.com, February 20, 2020.

17. Hannah Unsworth, "10 Essentials for Creating an Intranet Employees Love," Unily, unily.com, accessed March 2020; Stuart Gentle, "Can a Better Intranet Improve Company Culture?," Onrec, onrec.com, February 20, 2020.

18. "What Is an Extranet? And Does Your Organization Need One?," *ThoughtFarmer,* thoughtfarmer.com, April 30, 2019.

19. "What Is a VPN?," Norton, norton.com, accessed March 2020.

20. "Worldwide Broadband Speed League 2019," cable.co.uk, accessed March 2020.

21. Ryan Tracy and Drew FitzGerald, "U.S. Government Is Tripping over Itself in 5G Race," *The Wall Street Journal*, November 12, 2019.

22. Drew FitzGerald, "5G Race Could Leave Personal Privacy in the Dust," *The Wall Street Journal*, November 12, 2019; Stu Woo, "Tensions Rise over the Sale of Spectrum," *The Wall Street Journal*, November 12, 2019.

23. "The Difference between AI, Machine Learning, and Robotics," Dell Technologies, delltechnologies.com, accessed March 2020; Daphne Leprince-Ringuet, "As 5G Arrives, the Biggest Impact Will Be on Business," *ZDNet*, zdnet.com, March 5, 2020.

24. Robert Safian, "5 Lessons of the AI Imperative, from Netflix to Spotify," *Fast Company*, September 11, 2018; David A. Teich, "Machine Learning and Artificial Intelligence in Business: Year in Review, 2018," *Forbes*, December 26, 2018; Aaron Pressman, "Spotify Nabs Top A.I. Expert from Netflix," *Fortune*, fortune.com, September 6, 2019.

25. James Rundle and Angus Loten, "The Power of 5G and AI Together," *The Wall Street Journal*, November 12, 2019; Lilly Smith, "Pentagram's Adaptive Identity for an Adaptive AI Company May Be the Most Meta Branding Ever," *Fast Company*, fastcompany.com, February 13, 2020; Rebecca Heilweil, "Coronavirus Is the First Big Test for Futuristic Tech That Can Prevent Pandemics," Vox, vox.com, February 27, 2020.

26. Klint Finley, "Here's Another Chance to Weigh In on the FCC's Net Neutrality Repeal," *Wired*, wired.com, February 21, 2020; Klint Finley, "A Court Says Repealing Net Neutrality Was (Mostly) OK," *Wired*, wired.com, October 1, 2019; Molly Wood, "We Need to Talk about 'Cloud Neutrality,'" *Wired*, wired.com, February 10, 2020.

27. Internet2, internet2.edu, accessed March 2020.

28. "The Internet2 Community: Enabling the Future," Internet2, internet2.edu, accessed March 2020.

29. Gary Vela, "When Should You Hire a Social Media Manager?," *Forbes*, forbes.com, February 25, 2020; Lilach Bullock, "These Are the Biggest SEO Trends of 2019," *Forbes*, January 10, 2019; Jeff Barrett, "Google's New Algorithm Update Means New SEO Best Practices for 2020," *Entrepreneur*, entrepreneur.com, March 5, 2020.

30. "How Millions of Views Put Dollar Shave Club on Course for a Billion-Dollar Sale," *CNBC*, cnbc.com, March 24, 2019; Jay Baer and Adam Brown, "How JetBlue Delivers Amazing Social Customer Service Working from Home," *Convince & Convert*, convinceandconvert.com, accessed March 2020; Lauryn Chamberlain, "How Airlines' Embrace of Social Media Is Evolving after a Decade of Learning," *Kambr Media*, kambr.media, February 25, 2020.

31. Erica Lovestrand, "The Importance of Mobile-Friendly Websites in 2019," August Ash, augustash.com, January 15, 2019; Adam C. Uzialko, "Why Your Website Needs to Be Google Mobile-Friendly," *Business News Daily*, businessnewsdaily.com, January 5, 2020.

32. Eli Zimmerman, "AR/VR in K–12: Schools Use Immersive Technology for Assistive Learning," *EdTech*, edtechmagazine.com, August 22, 2019; Google, edu.google.com, accessed March 2020.

33. Larry Alton, "Cheaper VR Is Coming: Will It Be Enough to Kick-Start Consumer Interest?," The Next Web, thenextweb.com, May 15, 2018; Mark Serrels, "At CES 2019, VR Feels Like a Dream Gathering Dust," *CNET*, cnet.com, January 8, 2019.

34. Brian O'Connell, "What Is the Internet of Things and Why Is It Essential in 2019?," *TheStreet*, thestreet.com, March 13, 2019; Andrew Meola, "The Critical Role of Internet of Things Infrastructure in Connecting All of Our Devices," *Business Insider*, businessinsider.com, February 20, 2020.

35. Katherine Bindley, "Blood Pressure, Baby's Pulse, Sperm Potency: Home Health Devices Are Tracking More Than Ever," *The Wall Street Journal*, January 6, 2019; Janet Morrissey, "The Race to Create the Coolest Smart Home Devices Is Hotter Than Ever," *The New York Times*, January 15, 2019; Katie Camero, "From Lab to Olympics: Scientists Work to Improve Athletic Gear," *The Wall Street Journal*, wsj.com, March 10, 2020; Jennifer Smith, "Wearable Devices Take Ergonomics to a New High-Tech Place," *The Wall Street Journal*, wsj.com, March 5, 2020.

36. Bernard Marr, "5 Internet of Things Trends Everyone Should Know About," *Forbes*, February 4, 2019; Drew FitzGerald and Sarah Krouse, "How 5G Will Change So Much More Than Your Phone," *The Wall Street Journal*, February 26, 2019; Sarah Jeong, "Insurers Want to Know How Many Steps You Took Today," *The New York Times*, April 10, 2019; Austen Hufford, "How 5G Will Transform the Factory Floor," *The Wall Street Journal*, wsj.com, March 5, 2020.

37. Juan Benet, "What Exactly Is Web 3.0?," Web3 Foundation, web3.foundation, accessed March 2020.

38. Nathan Reiff, "Blockchain Explained," *Investopedia*, investopedia.com, February 1, 2020; Siraj Raval, "Web 3.0 Explained," YouTube, youtube.com, March 21, 2018.

39. Kieren McCarthy, "US Govt Mulls Snatching Back Full Control of the Internet's Domain Name and IP Address Admin," *The Register*, theregister.co.uk, June 5, 2018.

40. Daniel Ortner, "Government Regulation of Social Media Would Kill the Internet—and Free Speech," *The Hill*, thehill.com, August 12, 2019; "Internet Policy," National Telecommunication and Information Administration, ntia.gov, accessed March 2020.

41. "What Is Computer Networking?," Cisco, cisco.net, accessed March 2020.

42. "What Is Cloud Computing?," Microsoft, azure.microsoft.com, accessed March 2020.

43. "How Corporate IT Is Entering the Multi-Cloud," *The Economist*, March 14, 2020.

44. Janakiram MSV, "Everything You Want to Know about Anthos—Google's Hybrid and Multi-Cloud Platform," *Forbes*, April 14, 2019; Blair Felter, "The Different Types of Cloud Computing and How They Differ," *Vxchnge*, vxchnge.com, February 6, 2020; "What Are Public, Private, and Hybrid Clouds?," Microsoft, azure.microsoft.com, accessed March 2020.

45. IBM, ibm.com, accessed March 2020.

46. Amar Hussain, "4 Reasons Why a Remote Workforce Is Better for Business," *Forbes*, forbes.com, March 29, 2019; Darren Menabney, "What You Need to Know to Start Working from Home," *Forbes*, forbes.com, March 6, 2020.

47. Kevin Roose, "Sorry, but Working from Home Is Overrated," *The New York Times*, nytimes.com, March 10, 2020.

48. Sara Morrison, "Apple's Malware Problem Is Getting Worse," Vox, vox.com, February 12, 2020.

49. Steve Morgan, "Directory of Managed Security Service Providers (MSSPs) to Watch in 2020," *Cybercrime Magazine*, cybersecurityadventures.com, February 20, 2020; Simon Quicke, "MSPs and MSSPs Being

Targeted by Ransomware Spreaders," *Microscope,* computerweekly.com, February 20, 2020.

50. "Biggest Cyber Attacks in History," *Fox Business,* foxbusiness.com, February 27, 2020; Shelby Brown, "Equifax, MGM Resorts and Beyond: Every Major Security Breach and Data Hack," *CNET,* cnet.com, February 20, 2020.

51. Bloomberg Editorial Board, "The Unfinished Business of the Equifax Hack," *Bloomberg,* bloomberg.com, January 29, 2019; Bev O'Shea, "Equifax Data Breach Settlement," *NerdWallet,* nerdwallet.com, March 2, 2020.

52. Scott Steinberg, "The Latest Ways Identity Thieves Are Targeting You—and What to Do If You Are a Victim," *CNBC,* cnbc.com, February 27, 2020; Levon Gasparian, "10 Steps to Protect against Identity Theft," *Forbes,* forbes.com, February 20, 2020.

53. "Researchers Use Fake Network to Analyze Hackers' Moves for Expected Olympic Cyber Attacks," *The Mainichi,* mainichi.jp, August 25, 2019; DefenseTalk, "System Uses Machine Learning, Curiosity-Driven 'Honeypots' to Stop Cyberattacks," *Cybersecurity Technology News,* defensetalk.com, February 21, 2020.

54. Tarek Ghoul, "Medium and Small Businesses Face Most Risk from Cyber Attacks," *Khaleej Times,* khaleejtimes.com, February 20, 2020.

55. Zack Whittaker, "Two Years after WannaCry, a Million Computers Remain at Risk," *TechCrunch,* techcrunch.com, May 12, 2019; Josh Fruhlinger, "Recent Ransomware Attacks Define the Malware's New Age," *CSO,* csoonline.com, February 20, 2020.

56. Grid Assurance, gridassurance.com, accessed March 2020.

57. Issie Lapowsky, "How Cambridge Analytica Sparked the Great Privacy Awakening," *Wired,* wired.com, March 17, 2019; Joe Humphreys, "Trust No One: The Cynical Logic of Social Media," *The Irish Times,* irishtimes.com, March 12, 2020.

58. Herb Weisbaum, "Who's Watching You Online?," *NBC News,* nbcnews.com, accessed October 2019; "Learn about Tracking Technologies, Market Structure and Data-Sharing on the Web," Who Tracks Me, whotracks.me, accessed March 2020.

59. "How to Encrypt Email (Complete Guide)," *Cactus VPN,* cactusvpn.com, accessed March 2020.

60. Tom Kellermann, "A Cybersecurity Chief's 8 Tips on How to Protect Yourself Online as Data Breaches Continue," *CNBC,* cnbc.com, September 27, 2019; Rebecca Lake, "How to Protect Your Online Banking Information," *Forbes,* March 13, 2020.

Managing Risk

Tricia Griffith, CEO of Progressive

When Tricia Griffith applied for a job as a claims adjuster trainee at Progressive more than 30 years ago, she did not plan to stay in the industry for long. "I really had no desire to work in insurance," said Griffith. "I went to school where State Farm is located and I was like, 'Ugh, who wants to be in insurance?'" Instead, she intended to train as a claims rep for just a few years until she completed her MBA. But the more Griffith learned about insurance, the more she fell in love with it, leading her to dedicate her career to Progressive. After a few decades, she ascended to the position of CEO, making her one of the rare people in business to rise from entry-level employee to head of the company.

Since becoming CEO, Griffith has guided Progressive's rapid growth in an industry that is not known for its innovation. Surprisingly, at times Progressive's sales growth has exceeded big-name companies such as Apple and Microsoft. Over a three-year span, the company grew from $20 billion in net premiums to $30 billion. In 2017, Progressive passed Allstate to become the nation's third-largest auto insurer behind only Geico and State Farm. That's a remarkable jump for a company that was founded in 1937 as a personal auto insurer specializing primarily in high-risk drivers. Under Griffith's leadership, the company has moved far beyond Progressive's roots by opening new markets and applying innovative technology.

In 2015, Progressive made a key decision to acquire home insurer ASI in an effort to convince consumers to bundle their auto and home insurance together. Progressive had seen little success in the home insurance market prior to the acquisition, so Griffith was chosen to lead the charge into the market. In just over two years, Progressive expanded its number of customers from 400,000 to 1 million. She also made the bold decision to bet on AI-powered technology. Under her direction, Progressive introduced a mobile app for its usage-based insurance program called Snapshot that employs AI to determine customers' premiums according to their driving behaviors. So far the company has collected more than 1.5 billion miles of driving data to measure distracted and risky driving based on specific variables. This information helps Progressive charge a higher rate for riskier drivers while retaining and rewarding safe drivers. Although other insurers have adopted similar programs, Progressive has remained the leader in innovative technology according to investors and analysts.

Griffith understands that leadership is not limited to a CEO's economic success. Coming up through the ranks at Progressive, she realized it's important to be accessible to staff and to create a culture that employees find both motivating and challenging. For example, the company's "innovation garage" serves as an employee think tank and experimental laboratory where employee ideas and suggestions are tested. Her workplace innovations and devotion to an inclusive culture have helped Progressive earn a spot on *Fortune* magazine's annual list of Best Places to Work. Accolades like this point to a bright future for Progressive, which Griffith is excited to tackle head-on: "I think we're going to be a bigger company, we're going to be well-run, and we're going to have a culture where people want to work here, want to stay here, want to have careers and where our customers want to stay because they get great service."

In this bonus chapter, you will learn something about risk management. The industry is so large and there is so much to learn that we only scratch the surface. Nonetheless, risk management has become such a huge part of every manager's responsibilities that you need to know the basics of risk management before you become involved in any type of business.

Sources: Aric Jenkins, "Meet the CEO of the Insurance Company Growing Faster Than Apple," *Fortune*, fortune.com, November 15, 2018; Sara Shookman, "Progressive Moves in 2019: One-on-One with CEO Tricia Griffith," *WKYC*, wkyc.com, February 20, 2019; Progressive, progressive.com, accessed March 2020.

Let's talk business!
bit.ly/LetsTalkBusinessC

Spencer Heyfron/Redux

COMPANIES OFTEN HAVE product liability insurance to protect against large jury awards in lawsuits. This company suffered multiple product liability lawsuit losses, with penalties that could add up to $20 billion. Plaintiffs claimed the company's talc powder caused them to suffer ovarian cancer. Name that company. (Find the answer in the chapter.)

LO C–1 Identify the environmental changes that have made risk management important.

Understanding Business Risks

No one knows better than Progressive CEO, Tricia Griffith, that managing risk is a challenge for businesses throughout the world. Almost every day we hear of a tornado, hurricane, earthquake, flood, fire, airplane crash, terrorist threat or attack, or car accident that destroyed property or injured or killed someone. The Insurance Institute for Business & Home Safety says that one out of four small businesses is forced to permanently close after a disaster.

Hackers and viruses are an increasing threat to computers, and identity theft is commonplace. Theft and fraud can destroy a small business. Business lawsuits in recent years have covered everything from job-related accidents to product liability.

Such reports are so much a part of the news that we tend to accept these events as part of everyday life. But the losses of property, equipment, transportation, communications, security, energy, and other resources mean a great deal to the people and organizations injured by them.[1] In some states, insurance against such loss is not available or is too expensive for high-risk businesses. New legislation in some areas aims to lessen some of these risks so that companies can obtain insurance coverage again at a reasonable price.

A recent report found that 80 percent of organizations either have or are in the process of developing an enterprise risk management (ERM) program.[2] An ERM program usually has a few well-defined goals, such as defining (1) which risks the program will manage; (2) what risk management processes, technologies, and investments will be required; and (3) how risk management efforts will be coordinated across the firm.

How Rapid Change Affects Risk Management

Risk goes beyond the obvious dangers of fire, theft, or accident. It is inherent in every decision a manager makes, and the prudent company assesses its exposure in all of them. Risk managers are expanding their expertise into human resources, information technology, security, legal, site construction, and more. Change is occurring so fast that it is difficult to identify new risks until they are upon us. Who can evaluate the risks of buying or selling products online or the risk of a cyber attack by hackers? How will currencies fluctuate in the next financial crisis, and how will their daily ups and downs affect the profits of global trade? How will climate change affect farms, cattle, and the price of food?[3] What would happen to the economy if there

Edward Snowden, former technical assistant for the CIA, leaked classified documents to the media regarding the NSA's tactics in tracking U.S. citizens, international governments, and companies. What strategies can help firms and even governments protect themselves against this type of pure risk?

The Guardian/Getty Images

were a new terrorist attack or another pandemic? What can we do to manage the risks of social unrest at home and abroad? Let's explore how companies go about managing risk. We'll begin by going over a few key terms.

LO C–2 Explain the four ways of managing risk, and distinguish between insurable and uninsurable risk.

Managing Risk

Risk is the chance of loss, the degree of probability of loss, and the amount of possible loss. There are two different kinds of risk:

- **Speculative risk** can result in *either* profit or loss. A firm takes on speculative risk by buying new machinery, acquiring more inventory or a new plant, and making other potentially profitable decisions in which the probability of loss may be relatively low and the amount of loss known. An entrepreneur's chance to make a profit is a speculative risk. Banks that bought mortgage-backed securities in 2008 were taking a speculative risk.

- **Pure risk** is the threat of loss with *no* chance for profit, such as the threat of fire, accident, or theft. If such events occur, a company loses money, but if they don't, the company gains nothing.

The risk that most concerns businesspeople is pure risk. It threatens the very existence of some firms. Once they identify pure risks, firms have several options:

1. Reduce the risk.
2. Avoid the risk.
3. Self-insure against the risk.
4. Buy insurance against the risk.

We'll discuss the option of buying insurance in detail later in this chapter. First we'll discuss each of the other alternatives for managing risk, which reduce the need for outside insurance.

Reducing Risk

A firm can reduce risk by establishing loss-prevention programs such as fire drills, health education, safety inspections, equipment maintenance, accident prevention programs, and so on. Many retail stores use mirrors, video cameras, and other devices to prevent shoplifting. Water sprinklers and smoke detectors help minimize fire loss. Most industrial machines have safety devices to protect workers' fingers, eyes, and so on.

Employees as well as managers can reduce risk. Truck drivers can wear seat belts to minimize injuries from accidents, operators of loud machinery can wear earplugs to reduce the chance of hearing loss, and those who lift heavy objects can wear back braces. Many companies have instituted wellness programs to keep employees healthy, active, and alert on the job.[4] The beginning of an effective risk management strategy is a good loss-prevention program. However, high insurance rates have forced some firms to go beyond merely preventing risks to avoiding them, in extreme cases by going out of business. Avoiding accidents is critical to the survival of the firm and its workers.

Avoiding Risk

We can't avoid every risk. There is always the chance of fire, theft, accident, or injury. But some companies are avoiding risk by not accepting hazardous jobs and by outsourcing shipping and other functions. The threat of lawsuits has driven some drug companies to stop manufacturing vaccines, and some consulting engineers refuse to work on hazardous sites. Some companies cannot attract members for their board of directors due to potential

---

risk
The chance of loss, the degree of probability of loss, and the amount of possible loss.

speculative risk
A chance of either profit or loss.

pure risk
The threat of loss with no chance for profit.

liability concerns that could develop from legal action against the firms they represent. Many companies have cut back on their investments to avoid the risk of financial losses.

Self-Insuring

self-insurance
The practice of setting aside money to cover routine claims and buying only "catastrophe" policies to cover big losses.

Self-insurance is the practice of setting aside money to cover routine claims, and buying only "catastrophe" insurance policies to cover big losses. It is most appropriate when a firm has several widely distributed facilities. Firms with a single huge facility, in which a major fire or earthquake could destroy the entire operation, usually turn to insurance companies to cover the risk of loss.

One of the riskier self-insurance strategies is for a company to "go bare," paying claims from its operating budget instead of from a special fund. The whole firm could go bankrupt over one claim if the damages are high enough. A less risky alternative is to form group-insurance pools that share similar risks.

Buying Insurance to Cover Risk

Although well-designed and enforced risk-prevention programs reduce the probability of claims, accidents do happen. Insurance is the armor individuals, businesses, and nonprofit organizations use to protect themselves from various financial risks. Together they spend about 10 percent of gross domestic product (GDP) on insurance premiums. The federal government provides some insurance protection (see Figure C.1), but individuals and businesses must cover most on their own.

To reduce the cost of insurance, some companies buy a business ownership policy (BOP)—a package that includes property and liability insurance. Let's continue our discussion of insurance by identifying the types of risks that are uninsurable and insurable.

What Risks Are Uninsurable?

uninsurable risk
A risk that no insurance company will cover.

Not all risks are insurable. An **uninsurable risk** is one that no insurance company will cover. Examples of things that you cannot insure include market risks (e.g., losses that occur because of price changes, style changes, or new products that make your product obsolete); political risks (e.g., losses from war or government restrictions on trade); some personal risks (such as loss of a job); and some risks of operation (e.g., strikes or inefficient machinery).

Businesses cannot accurately estimate damage from natural disasters like earthquakes before they occur. That's the reason for having insurance. Do you think most American businesses have insurance coverage for earthquake damage? Why or why not?

Ricardo Arduengo/AFP/Getty Images

FIGURE C.1 PUBLIC INSURANCE
State or federal government agencies that provide insurance protection.

Unemployment Compensation

Provides financial benefits, job counseling, and placement services for unemployed workers.

Social Security

Provides retirement benefits, life insurance, health insurance, and disability income insurance.

Federal Housing Administration (FHA)

Provides mortgage insurance to lenders to protect against default by home buyers.

National Flood Insurance Association

Provides compensation for damage caused by flooding and mudslides to properties located in flood-prone areas.

Federal Crime Insurance

Provides insurance to property owners in high-crime areas.

Federal Crop Insurance

Provides compensation for damaged crops.

Pension Benefit Guaranty Corporation

Insures pension plans to prevent loss to employees if the company declares bankruptcy or goes out of business.

What Risks Are Insurable?

An **insurable risk** is one the typical insurance company will cover, using the following guidelines:

1. The policyholder must have an **insurable interest**, which means the policyholder is the one at risk to suffer a loss. For example, you cannot buy fire insurance on your neighbor's house and collect if it burns down.

2. The loss must be measurable.

3. The chance of loss must be measurable.

4. The loss must be accidental.

5. The insurance company's risk should be dispersed; that is, spread among different geographic areas so a flood, tornado, hurricane, or other natural disaster in one area will not bankrupt the insurance company.

6. The insurance company must be able to set standards for accepting the risk.

insurable risk
A risk that the typical insurance company will cover.

insurable interest
The possibility of the policyholder to suffer a loss.

TESTPREP

- Why are companies more aware now of the need to manage risk?
- What is the difference between pure risk and speculative risk?
- What are the four major options for handling risk?
- What are some examples of an uninsurable risk?

LO C–3 Define insurance policies, and explain the law of large numbers and the rule of indemnity.

Understanding Insurance Policies

insurance policy
A written contract between the insured and an insurance company that promises to pay for all or part of a loss.

An **insurance policy** is a written contract between the insured, whether an individual or organization, and an insurance company that promises to pay for all or part of a loss by the insured. A **premium** is the fee the insurance company charges, the cost of the policy to the insured. A **claim** is a statement of loss that the insured sends to the insurance company to request payment.

premium
The fee charged by an insurance company for an insurance policy.

Like all private businesses, insurance companies are designed to make a profit. They therefore gather data to determine the extent of various risks. What makes it possible for insurance companies to accept risk and profit is the law of large numbers.

claim
A statement of loss that the insured sends to the insurance company to request payment.

The **law of large numbers** says that if a large number of people or organizations are exposed to the same risk, a predictable number of losses will occur during a given period of time. (For your information, the figures for homes are as follows: Over the course of a 30-year mortgage, a home has a 9 percent chance of catching fire and a 26 percent chance of flooding.) Once the insurance company predicts the number of losses likely to occur, it can determine the appropriate premiums for each policy it issues against that loss. The premium will be high enough to cover expected losses and yet earn a profit for the firm and its stockholders. Today, many insurance companies are charging businesses high premiums not for expected losses but for the costs they anticipate from the increasing number of lawsuits, court cases, and high damage awards.

law of large numbers
Principle that if a large number of people are exposed to the same risk, a predictable number of losses will occur during a given period of time.

Rule of Indemnity

rule of indemnity
Rule saying that an insured person or organization cannot collect more than the actual loss from an insurable risk.

The **rule of indemnity** says an insured person or organization cannot collect more than the actual loss from an insurable risk. Nor can you buy two insurance policies, even from two insurance companies, and collect from both for the same loss. You cannot gain from risk management; you can only minimize losses.

Almost everyone who drives is exposed to the risk of having an accident at some point. Insurance companies use the law of large numbers to predict the losses such accidents will cause and set their policy premiums high enough to cover the losses while earning a profit. How much do you pay for your auto policy?

Yellow Dog Productions/Getty Images

Types of Insurance Companies

There are two major types of insurance companies. A **stock insurance company** is owned by stockholders, just like any other investor-owned company. A **mutual insurance company** is an organization owned by its policyholders. It is a nonprofit organization, and any excess funds (over losses, expenses, and growth costs) go to the policyholders in the form of dividends or premium reductions. Prudential is one of the largest stock insurance companies in the United States, whereas New York Life is one of the largest U.S. mutual insurance companies.[5]

stock insurance company

A type of insurance company owned by stockholders.

mutual insurance company

A type of insurance company owned by its policyholders.

?TESTPREP

- What is the law of large numbers?
- What is the rule of indemnity?

LO C-4 Discuss the various types of insurance businesses can buy to manage risk.

Insurance Coverage for Various Kinds of Risk

There are many types of insurance to cover various losses: property and liability insurance, health insurance, and life insurance. Property losses result from fires, accidents, theft, or other perils. Liability losses result from property damage or injuries suffered by others for which the policyholder is held responsible. Figure C.2 lists the types of insurance available. Let's begin our exploration of insurance by looking at health insurance.

Health Insurance

The United States went through a period of major changes in health insurance with the implementation of the Affordable Care Act (ACA, also referred to as Obamacare). This legislation caused the government to be much more involved in the health insurance process. The law has been criticized and praised and its merits and failings have been debated since its passage. Because health insurance is so important to your future, you should keep up with any changes that might occur with the ACA. We are very likely to see many variations of health coverage in the future.

Health Savings Accounts

Health savings accounts (HSAs) (formerly called medical savings accounts) are tax-deferred savings accounts linked to low-cost, high-deductible health insurance policies. The idea is for your employer (or you) to take the money currently spent on high-cost, low-deductible health insurance and deposit it into a health savings account. You would use the money only for needed health care services.[6] At the end of the year, you get to keep the money you don't spend in the account for future medical coverage. One major benefit to you is that the money grows tax-free until you take it out. There are likely to be other such plans proposed to compete with the comprehensive national health care system now being offered.

health savings accounts (HSAs)

Tax-deferred savings accounts linked to low-cost, high-deductible health insurance policies.

Disability Insurance

Disability insurance replaces part of your income—usually 50 to 70 percent—if you become disabled and unable to work. You must usually be disabled for a certain period,

FIGURE C.2 PRIVATE
INSURANCE

Property and Liability

Fire	Covers losses to buildings and their contents from fire.
Automobile	Covers property damage, bodily injury, collision, fire, theft, vandalism, and other related vehicle losses.
Homeowner's	Covers the home, other structures on the premises, home contents, expenses if forced from the home because of an insured peril, third-party liability, and medical payments to others.
Computer coverage	Covers loss of equipment from fire, theft, and sometimes spills, power surges, and accidents.
Professional liability	Protects from suits stemming from mistakes made or bad advice given in a professional context.
Business interruption	Provides compensation for loss due to fire, theft, or similar disasters that close a business. Covers lost income, continuing expenses, and utility expenses.
Nonperformance loss protection	Protects from failure of a contractor, supplier, or other person to fulfill an obligation.
Criminal loss protection	Protects from loss due to theft, burglary, or robbery.
Commercial credit insurance	Protects manufacturers and wholesalers from credit losses due to insolvency or default.
Public liability insurance	Provides protection for businesses and individuals against losses resulting from personal injuries or damage to the property of others for which the insured is responsible.
Extended product liability insurance	Covers potentially toxic substances in products; environmental liability; and, for corporations, director and officer liability.
Fidelity bond	Protects employers from employee dishonesty.
Surety bond	Covers losses resulting from a second party's failure to fulfill a contract.
Title insurance	Protects buyers from losses resulting from a defect in title to property.
Cyber attack insurance	Helps protect companies from hackers.

Health Insurance

Basic health insurance	Covers losses due to sickness or accidents.
Major medical insurance	Protects against catastrophic losses by covering expenses beyond the limits of basic policies.
Hospitalization insurance	Pays for most hospital expenses.
Surgical and medical insurance	Pays costs of surgery and doctor's care while recuperating in a hospital.
Dental insurance	Pays a percentage of dental expenses.
Disability income insurance	Pays income while the insured is disabled as a result of accident or illness.
Vision insurance	Pays for eye exams, glasses, contacts, and sometimes vision correction surgery.

Life Insurance

Group life insurance	Covers all the employees of a firm or members of a group.
Owner or key executive insurance	Enables businesses of sole proprietors or partnerships to pay bills and continue operating, saving jobs for the employees. Enables corporations to hire and train or relocate another manager with no loss to the firm.
Retirement and pension plans	Provides employees with supplemental retirement and pension plans.
Credit life insurance	Pays the amount due on a loan if the debtor dies.

such as 60 days, before you can begin collecting. Insurance experts recommend getting disability insurance if your employer does not offer it, because the chances of becoming disabled by a disease or accident when you are young are much higher than the chance of dying. The premiums for disability insurance vary according to age, occupation, and income.

Workers' Compensation

Workers' compensation insurance guarantees payment of wages, medical care, and rehabilitation services, such as retraining, for employees injured on the job. Employers in every state are required to provide this insurance. It also pays benefits to the survivors of those who die as a result of work-related injuries. The cost of workers' compensation varies by the company's safety record, the size of its payroll, and the types of hazards its workers face. For example, it costs more to insure a steelworker than an accountant because the risk of injury is greater.

Liability Insurance

Professional liability insurance covers people found liable for professional negligence. If a lawyer gives advice carelessly and the client loses money, the client may sue the lawyer for an amount equal to that lost, and liability insurance will cover the lawyer's loss. Professional liability insurance is also known as *malpractice insurance.* That term may bring doctors and dentists to mind, but many other professionals, including mortgage brokers and real estate appraisers, buy professional liability insurance because of large lawsuits their colleagues have faced.[7]

Product liability insurance covers liability arising out of products sold (see Bonus Chapter A). A person injured by, say, a ladder, some other household good, or pharmaceutical product may sue the manufacturer for damages. For example, Johnson & Johnson is facing over 16,800 product liability lawsuits that claim its talc-based products caused ovarian cancer.[8] A New Jersey jury in 2020 awarded four plaintiffs $750 million. The decision is under appeal and the award is expected to be reduced. However, the lawsuits could eventually cost the company $20 billion. Insurance usually covers such product liability losses.

An employee with a work-related illness or injury can get workers' compensation benefits regardless of who was at fault. In exchange for these benefits, employees usually do not have the right to sue the employer for damages related to those injuries.

Fertnig/Getty Images

Life Insurance for Businesses

Regardless of how careful we are, we all face the prospect of death. To ensure that those left behind will be able to continue the business, entrepreneurs often buy life insurance that will pay partners and others what they need to keep the firm going.[9] The best kind of insurance to cover executives in the firm is term insurance, but dozens of new policies with interesting features are now available.

Insurance Coverage for Home-Based Businesses

Homeowner's policies usually don't have adequate protection for a home-based business. For example, they may have a limit for business equipment. For more coverage, you may need to add an endorsement, sometimes called a *rider,* to your homeowner's policy. If clients visit your office or if you receive deliveries regularly, you may need home-office insurance. It protects you from slip-and-fall lawsuits and other risks associated with visitors. For more elaborate businesses, such as custom cabinetry shops and other types of manufacturing or inventory-keeping businesses, you may need a business-owner policy. Unless you are an expert on insurance, you will need to consult an insurance agent about the best insurance for your home-based business needs.

The Risk of Damaging the Environment

Risk management now goes far beyond the protection of individuals, businesses, and non-profit organizations from known risks. It means the evaluation of worldwide risks with many unknowns, such as climate change. It also means prioritizing these risks so that international funds can be spent where they can do the most good. No insurance company can protect humanity from all such risks. These risks are the concern of businesses and governments throughout the world, with the assistance of the international scientific community. They should also be your concern as you study risk management in all its dimensions. For example, think of the risks that accompany the search for natural gas using fracking.[10] Now that such a search has gone global, companies throughout the world are examining the risks involved. That means more jobs and more interest in risk management in general.

Protection from Cyber Attacks

Often you will see articles in newspapers about a company being hacked by some outside (or inside) individuals or groups that steal your private information, such as Social Security numbers, address, and so on. Cyber risk insurance can help a business prepare for the worst.[11] For example, it will cover a company should its employees or customers decide to file a lawsuit against them in the event that their information is leaked.

TEST PREP

- Why should someone buy disability insurance?
- How many different kinds of private insurance can you name?

SUMMARY

LO C–1 Identify the environmental changes that have made risk management important.

- **What changes have made risk management more important?**

Hurricanes, floods, terrorist threats and attacks, identity theft, and an unstable economy have all contributed to additional risk and the need for more risk management.

LO C–2 Explain the four ways of managing risk, and distinguish between insurable and uninsurable risk.

- **What are the four major ways of managing risk?**

The major ways of managing risk are (1) reduce risk, (2) avoid risk, (3) self-insure, and (4) buy insurance.

- **What's the difference between insurable and uninsurable risk?**

An insurable risk is one the typical insurance company will cover. Generally, insurance companies use the following guidelines when evaluating whether a risk is insurable: (1) the policyholder must have an insurable interest, (2) the amount of loss should be measurable, (3) the chance of loss should be measurable, (4) the loss should be accidental, (5) the risk should be dispersed, and (6) the insurance company can set standards for accepting risks.

Uninsurable risk is risk that no insurance company will cover. Examples of things that you cannot insure include market risks, political risks, some personal risks (such as loss of a job), and some risks of operation (e.g., strikes or inefficient machinery).

LO C–3 Define insurance policies, and explain the law of large numbers and the rule of indemnity.

- **What is the rule of indemnity?**

The rule of indemnity says an insured person or organization cannot collect more than the actual loss from an insurable risk.

LO C–4 Discuss the various types of insurance businesses can buy to manage risk.

- **What are the two kinds of insurance companies?**

A stock insurance company is owned by stockholders, just like any other investor-owned company. A mutual insurance company is owned by its policyholders.

- **What kind of policies cover health risks?**

Health care and health insurance are topics that are heavily debated today. The government's role in health care and the role of private insurance will likely see changes going forward after much discussion and compromise. Health savings accounts (HSAs) enable you to pay for your health needs from a tax-deferred savings account and buy insurance for catastrophes.

- **What is workers' compensation insurance?**

Workers' compensation insurance guarantees payment of wages, medical care, and rehabilitation services like retraining for employees injured on the job. Employers in every state are required to provide this insurance. Professional liability insurance covers people found liable for professional negligence. Product liability insurance provides coverage against liability arising out of products sold. Most businesses also have some kind of life insurance for their key executives. Serving as a director on a corporate board carries with it great standing—and potential risk of liability. If you conduct business from home, you should also have some form of home-office insurance to cover liabilities.

■ **What are businesses doing to cover the risks of harming the environment?**

Many businesses are doing what they can to minimize damage to the environment. Such risks, however, are often beyond what businesses can manage. They are also the concern of governments around the world.

■ **Why do companies carry cyber risk insurance?**

Companies carry cyber risk insurance to protect against lawsuits that could be filed against them due to cyber attacks where personal information of employees, customers, and so on is compromised.

KEY TERMS

claim 604	law of large numbers 604	rule of indemnity 604
health savings accounts (HSAs) 605	mutual insurance company 605	self-insurance 602
insurable interest 603	premium 604	speculative risk 601
insurable risk 603	pure risk 601	stock insurance company 605
insurance policy 604	risk 601	uninsurable risk 602

CRITICAL THINKING

1. Are you self-insuring your residence and your assets? What have you done to reduce your risk? Have you done anything to avoid risk? How much would it cost to buy insurance for your dwelling and the contents?

2. What risks do you take that insurance cannot cover?

3. What actions have you taken to avoid risk?

4. What can you do to lower your personal risk of loss from natural disasters such as floods, hurricanes, and tornadoes?

PUTTING PRINCIPLES TO WORK

PURPOSE

To learn about insurance for your dwelling and property, and to examine the issue of liability.

EXERCISE

Go to the Insurance Information Institute's website (iii.org). Explore the site and then answer the following questions:

1. What is homeowner's insurance?

2. What is covered by a standard homeowner's policy?

3. What is renter's insurance?

DEVELOPING CAREER SKILLS

KEY: ● **Team**   ★ **Analytic**   ▲ **Communication**   ▣ **Technology**

★ ▲ 1. List the ways you could reduce risk in your life (such as not driving above the speed limit). Form small groups and share what you and others have written. Which of your classmates' suggestions can you adopt in your life?

2. You cannot insure yourself against speculative risk. However, you can minimize the risks you take when investing. Compare and contrast the risks of investing in stocks versus investing in bonds for the long term (refer to Chapter 19 for help).

3. Much of risk management consists of reducing risky behavior. What kinds of risky behavior have you observed among fellow college students? How can college students learn about and minimize these risks? Are they doing so? Discuss the merits of having a risk manager for education facilities.

4. Form small groups and discuss liability insurance, automobile insurance, health insurance, renter's insurance, life insurance, and disability insurance. Develop a list of questions to discuss openly in class so that everyone can contribute their thoughts about these issues. Do your fellow students understand all of these types of insurance?

5. Discuss with a group in your class the risks of a terrorist attack, a natural disaster, climate change, or major health disaster. Which risk do you perceive as most likely? Most dangerous? Discuss what you could do to warn others of such risks and motivate them to do something about them.

CAREER EXPLORATION

If you are interested in pursuing a career in risk management, here are a few to consider. Find out about the tasks performed, skills needed, pay, and opportunity outlook in these fields in the *Occupational Outlook Handbook (OOH)* at bls.gov.

- **Insurance underwriter**—decides whether to provide insurance and determines coverage amounts and premiums.

- **Emergency management director**—prepares plans and procedures for responding to natural disasters or other emergencies.

- **Insurance sales agent**—contacts potential customers and sells one or more types of insurance.

NOTES

1. Nicole Friedman and Leslie Scism, "Insurers Boost Rates for Businesses," *The Wall Street Journal,* February 12, 2020.
2. Michael Cohn, "COSO Offers Guidance on Enterprise Risk Management Value," *Accounting Today,* accountingtoday.com, February 5, 2020; Kevin Dancey, "Why Risk Management Should Be a Higher Priority," *CFO,* February 8, 2019; American Institute of Certified Public Accountants, aicpa.com, accessed March 2020.
3. Hanno Schoklitsch, "Climate Change Strategy Must Blend Policy, Tech," *Forbes,* forbes.com, February 24, 2020; Ivana Kottasova, "Climate Change Is the Biggest Risk to Business (and the World)," *CNN Business,* cnn.com, January 17, 2019; Alan Rappeport and Lisa Friedman, "Finance Ministers Grapple over Economic Threat of Climate Change," *The New York Times,* nytimes.com, February 23, 2020.
4. Gene Marks, "What Small Businesses Can Do to Reduce Employee Stress," *Philadelphia Inquirer,* inquirer.com, February 18, 2020; Julie Appleby, "How Well Do Workplace Wellness Programs Work?," NPR, NPR.com, April 16, 2019; Lauren Anderson, "Expanding Workplace Wellness to Mental Health," *BizTimes,* biztimes.com, March 2, 2020.
5. New York Life Insurance Company, newyorklife.com, accessed March 2020; Richard Rosen, "Mutual vs.

Stock Insurance Companies: What's the Difference?," *Investopedia,* investopedia.com, August 29, 2019; Marianne Bonner, "Stock Insurer versus Mutual Insurer," *The Balance,* thebalance.com, accessed March 2020.
6. Adelia Cellini Linecker, "Health Savings Account Facts: Check Out What's New and the Best HSA Accounts for 2020," *Investor's Business Daily,* investors.com, February 18, 2020; Dana Anspach, "Why You Might Want to Fund an HSA Instead of an IRA," *The Balance,* thebalance.com, March 2, 2020; Christine Benz, "HSAs Offer Path to Tax Deduction," *Morningstar,* morningstar.com, February 11, 2020.
7. "What Is Professional Liability Insurance?," *Insureon,* insureon.com, accessed March 2020; Ronna L. DeLoe, "What Kind of Insurance Does an LLC Need?," LegalZoom, legalzoom.com, accessed March 2020.
8. Peter Loftus, "N.J. Jury Orders J&J to Pay $750 Million in Punitive Damages in Latest Baby Powder Verdict," *The Wall Street Journal,* February 6, 2020; Joshua Bote, "Does Baby Powder Cause Cancer? A Jury Ordered Johnson & Johnson to Pay $750 Million," *USA Today,* usatoday.com, February 7, 2020; "Johnson & Johnson Hit with $750M Punitive Damages Verdict for Failing to Warn about Cancer-Causing Asbestos in Talc Products," *Yahoo! Finance,* finance.yahoo.com, February 7, 2020.

9. Anna Robaton, "The No. 1 Thing Every Business Owner Needs to Do to Protect Their Legacy," *CNBC,* cnbc.com, February 21, 2020; "Key Person Insurance," *Entrepreneur,* entrepreneur.com, accessed March 2020; Ed Leefeldt, "The Right Life Insurance for a Business Partner's Death," *Forbes,* forbes.com, March 3, 2020.

10. Ed Hirs, "The Arithmetic of Fracking," *Forbes,* forbes.com, February 21, 2020; J. B. Maverick, "How Has Fracking Decreased U.S. Dependence on Foreign Oil?," *Investopedia,* investopedia.com, February 14, 2020; "Should the Next U.S. President Ban Fracking?," *Philadelphia Inquirer,* inquirer.com, March 5, 2020; Jed Graham, "Is the U.S. Shale Boom Over? Four Major Threats to the Fracking Revolution," *Investors Business Daily,* investors.com, March 5, 2020.

11. Joyce M. Rosenberg, "Businesses Face Higher Cyber Risks via Mobile Devices—but Few Take Precautions," *Insurance Journal,* insurancejournal.com, March 5, 2020; "Cyber Insurance Market Size to Upsurge Owing to Increase in Incidences of Data Theft, Breach, and Cyberattacks: Radiant Insights, Inc.," *Yahoo! Finance,* finance.yahoo.com, February 18, 2020; Vishaal Hariprasad, "4 Steps to Improve Your Cyber Risk Management," *Forbes,* forbes.com, February 26, 2020.

Managing Personal Finances

LEARNING OBJECTIVES >>

After you have read and studied this bonus chapter, you should be able to

D–1 Outline the six steps for controlling your assets.

D–2 Explain how to build a financial base, including investing in real estate, saving money, and managing credit.

D–3 Explain how buying the appropriate insurance can protect your financial base.

D–4 Outline a strategy for retiring with enough money to last a lifetime.

Lauryn Williams, Founder of Worth Winning

For athletes who are talented enough to compete at a professional level, the roar of the crowds and substantial financial rewards can seem endless when times are good. But even the best in the game have to call it quits someday, and unfortunately some competitors are not ready for life after the final whistle. That's why three-time Olympic medalist Lauryn Williams started Worth Winning, a financial planning firm that helps both former athletes and young professionals manage their money responsibly. "Anybody who's looking for help deserves to have it," said Williams. "And that's why I started my firm."

After going pro in track and field at age 20, Williams qualified for the Olympics four times and made history in the process. She is the first American woman to win medals at both the Summer and Winter Olympics, winning gold for the 4 x 100 meter relay at London 2012 and silver in the two-woman bobsled at Sochi 2014. All of this success earned Williams a six-figure income thanks to lucrative sponsorships with brands like Nike. While this was more than anyone in her family had ever made, she knew that the big paydays would not last long. "Not all athletes earn at a rate that will allow them to retire forever when their sports career is over," said Williams. "The transition is extremely emotional. You don't want to have to jump into something to make a living while trying to get closure." Williams recognized that she needed to manage her money but had trouble finding experts she could trust. Over the course of her career, Williams hired and fired two financial advisors who did not take her long-term interests into account. Instead, they focused on risky investments that could have wiped out her earnings in an instant if things went wrong.

Although Williams knew enough about money management to get rid of these negligent advisors, taking control of her financial future still left her confused. "I knew there were responsible things to do [with money], but I didn't know what they were," said Williams. "I felt very disorganized with finances." She researched the specifics of financial planning and discovered that it was something she could possibly pursue as a career. After retiring from athletics in 2014, Williams started studying to become a financial advisor but soon found out that breaking into the profession would be just as challenging as sports. She failed the certification exam on her first try but did not allow this setback to diminish her confidence. In early 2017, Williams took the test again after months of intense studying and passed. "I didn't realize it was more like the bar exam," said Williams. "Being able to gracefully handle loss and dust yourself off is a good skill to have."

Williams's experience in professional sports taught her important lessons about financial responsibility that she passes on to all of her clients at Worth Winning. Based in Dallas, Texas, the firm helps clients budget their income as well as plan for retirement, something that Williams claims few of her young clients think about. She suggests that professionals should have three to six months' worth of their salary saved for emergencies. Meanwhile, Williams recommends that athletes have at least six months' to a year's worth of cash on hand just in case. She also helps her clients set up retirement accounts such as 401(k)s or IRAs, a necessity for people like athletes who have no company-provided retirement plans. "It feels good getting them on the right track and not getting into the situation I was in," said Williams.

In this chapter, you'll learn how to plan for your financial future so that you can follow the lead of Lauryn Williams and start preparing for tomorrow today.

Sources: Elizabeth O'Brien, "Meet the Record-Setting Olympian Who's Now a Certified Financial Planner for Broke Millennials," *Money*, money.com, February 27, 2019; Graison Dangor, "What's Harder: Training for the CFP Exam or the Olympics?," *Financial Planning*, financial-planning.com, April 16, 2019; Amy Fontinelle, "Financial Planning for Professional Athletes: An Inside Look," *Investopedia*, investopedia.com, October 30, 2019; Worth Winning, worth-winning.com, accessed March 2020.

Let's talk business!
bit.ly/LetsTalkBusinessD

ONE WAY TO GROW YOUR FINANCIAL BASE is to use a financial planner. Robo-advisors at this company automatically manage money for clients with as little as $5,000 to invest. The firm charges no fee for this service compared to 1 to 2 percent charged by other firms. Its robo-advisors use algorithms to help you reach your financial goals. Name that company. (Find the answer in the chapter.)

LO D–1 Outline the six steps for controlling your assets.

The Need for Personal Financial Planning

The United States is largely a capitalist country. It follows, then, that the secret to success in such a country is to have capital, or money. With capital, you can take nice vacations, raise a family, invest in stocks and bonds, buy the goods and services you want, give generously to others, and retire with enough money to see you through. Money management, however, is not easy. You have to earn the money in the first place. Your chances of becoming wealthy are much greater if you choose to become an entrepreneur. That's one of the reasons why we have put so much emphasis on entrepreneurship throughout the text, including a whole chapter on the subject. Of course, there are risks in starting a business, but the best time to take risks is when you are young. Would it help you to be more motivated if you knew that there are over 2,816 billionaires in the world and together they hold $11.2 trillion in wealth?[1] Not all billionaires are in the United States. For example, there are 799 billionaires in China compared to 626 in the United States.[2]

After you earn money, you have to learn to spend it wisely, save some, and insure yourself against the risks of serious accidents, illness, or death. With a bit of luck, you may be one of the millionaires or billionaires discussed in this book.

You'll likely need some help. A recent study showed that nearly two-thirds of those surveyed failed a test about finance principles encountered in everyday life, such as compound interest, inflation, risk and diversification, and retirement savings plans. Even people who are retired are finding that they don't know enough about such plans.[3] According to the Federal Reserve Board, 40 percent of U.S. adults don't have enough savings to cover a $400 emergency.[4]

This bonus chapter will give you the basics so that you'll be ahead of the game. Financial management is so important to your fiscal health that you may want to take a course on it. Check your school to see what is available. As Marsha Barnes, founder of The Finance Bar, reminds us, "No one will care about your financial success as much as you will. Learn as much as you can today."

Financial Planning Begins with Making Money

You already know that one of the secrets to finding a good-paying job is having a good education. That is still true, although what you major in does matter.[5] Throughout history, an investment in business education has paid off regardless of the state of the economy or political ups and downs. Benjamin Franklin said, "If a man empties his purse into his head, no one can take it away from him. An investment in knowledge always pays the best interest."[6] Education has become even more important since we entered the information age. One way to start to become a millionaire, therefore, is to finish college. Make sure you investigate all the financial help available to you.

Making money is one thing; saving, investing, and spending it wisely is something else. Following the advice in the next section will help you become one of those with enough to live in comfort throughout your life.

Six Steps to Controlling Your Assets

The only way to save enough money to do all the things you want to do in life is to spend less than you make. Although you may find it difficult to save today, it is not only possible but also imperative if you want to accumulate enough to be financially secure. The following are six steps you can take today to get control of your finances.

Step 1: Take an Inventory of Your Financial Assets To take inventory, you need to develop a balance sheet for yourself, like the one in Chapter 17. Remember, a balance sheet starts with the fundamental accounting equation: Assets = Liabilities + Owners' equity. List your tangible assets (such as a TV, iPad, computer, smartphone, bicycle, car, jewelry, clothes, and savings account) on one side, and your liabilities (including mortgage or rent, credit card debt, and auto and education loans) on the other.

Assign a dollar figure to each of your assets, based on its current value, not what you originally paid for it. If you have debts, subtract them from your assets to get your net worth. If you have no debts, your assets equal your net worth. If your liabilities exceed the value of your assets, you are not on the path to financial security. You may need more financial discipline in your life.

Let's also create an income statement for you. At the top of the statement is revenue (all the money you take in from your job, investments, and so on). Subtract all your costs and expenses (rent or mortgage, credit card and other loan payments, utilities, commuting costs, and so on) to get your net income or profit. Software programs like Quicken and websites like NerdWallet have a variety of tools that can easily help you with these calculations.

Now is also an excellent time to think about how much money you will need to accomplish all your goals. The more clearly you can visualize your goals, the easier it is to begin saving for them.

Step 2: Keep Track of All Your Expenses Do you occasionally find yourself running out of cash? If you experience a cash flow problem, the only way to trace where the money is going is to keep track of every cent you spend. Keeping records of your expenses can be tedious, but it's a necessary step if you want to learn discipline. Actually, it could turn out to be enjoyable because it gives you such a feeling of control.

Here's what to do: Use a free app like Mint or Wally to record *everything* you spend as you go through the day.[7]

Dean Mitchell/Getty Images

It might take a little time to balance your income with your expenses to make sure you have money left to save and invest, but the effort is worth it. People who don't take this step can reach retirement without enough funds to live on. How could you cut back your expenses?

Develop spending categories (accounts) to make your task easier and more informative. You can have a category called "Food" for all food you bought from the grocery or convenience store during the week. You might want a separate account for meals eaten away from home, because you can dramatically cut these costs if you make your meals at home.

Other accounts could include rent, insurance, automobile repairs and gasoline, clothing, utilities, toiletries, entertainment, and donations to charity. Most people also like to have a category called "Miscellaneous" for impulse items like latte, smoothies, and candy. You won't believe how much you fritter away on miscellaneous items unless you keep a *detailed* record for at least a couple of months.

Develop your accounts on the basis of what's most important to you or where you spend the most money. Once you have recorded all your expenses for a few months, you'll easily see where you are spending too much and what you have to do to save more. A venti caramel frappuccino at a coffee specialty shop may cost about $4.95. If you cut back from five to one a week, you'll save nearly $20 a week, or over $1,000 a year. Over 10 years, that could mean an extra $12,000 for retirement, if you invest the money wisely.

Step 3: Prepare a Budget Once you know your financial situation and your sources of revenue and expenses, you're ready to make a personal budget. Remember, budgets are financial plans and a recent survey showed a majority of American adults don't keep track of theirs![8] A household budget includes mortgage or rent, utilities, food, clothing, vehicles, furniture, life insurance, car insurance, medical care, and taxes.

You'll need to choose how much to allow for such expenses as eating out, entertainment, cell phone use, and so on. Keep in mind that what you spend now reduces what you can save later. Spending $5 or more a day for cigarettes or coffee adds up to about $35 a week, $140 a month, $1,700 a year. If you can save $5 a day, you'll have about $1,700 saved by the end of the year. Keep this up during four years of college and you'll have about $7,000 by graduation. And that's before adding any interest your money will earn. If you would invest the savings in a mutual fund earning 6 percent compounded annually, you would double your money every 12 years. The Rule of 72 says that your money doubles every 12 years at 6 percent. You do that calculation by dividing the percentage earned into 72 (72 divided by 6 = 12). Cost-saving choices you might consider to reach this goal are listed in Figure D.1.

FIGURE D.1 POSSIBLE COST-SAVING CHOICES

The choices you make today can have a dramatic impact on your financial future. Compare the differences these few choices you can make now would mean to your future net worth. If you would make the lower-cost choices five days a week during your four years of college, you'd have more than $8,300 by graduation. (*Note that the figures in this chart are based on 20 weekdays per month.*)

First Choice Cost per Month	Alternate Choice Cost per Month	Savings per Month
Starbucks tall caffè latte $3.00 for 20 days = $60.00	Service station cappuccino $0.70 for 20 days = $14.00	$ 46.00
Fast-food lunch of burger, fries, and soft drink $5.00 for 20 days = $100.00	Lunch brought from home $2.00 for 20 days = $40.00	60.00
Bottled water $1.50 for 20 days = $30.00	Refill water bottle $0 for 20 days = $0	30.00
Download album = $10.00	Listen to your old albums = $0.00	10.00
Banana Republic T-shirt = $40.00	Old Navy T-shirt = $12.00	28.00
	Total savings per month	$174.00
		× 48 months
	Total savings through 4 years of college	$8,352.00

Running a household is similar to running a small business. It takes the same careful record keeping, the same budget processes and forecasting, and the same control procedures. Sometimes it also creates the same need to borrow funds or rely on a credit card and become familiar with interest rates. The time you spend practicing budgeting techniques will benefit you throughout your life. You might start by going online to Mint.com. It will help you with your budgeting needs.

Step 4: Pay Off Your Debts

The first thing to do with the money remaining after you pay your monthly bills is to pay off your debts, starting with those carrying the highest interest rates. Credit card debt may be costing you 18 percent or more a year. A recent survey found that over a third of college seniors said they had been charged a fee for a late payment and 54 percent of those students were charged late fees more than once. It's better to pay off a debt that costs 21 percent than put the money in a bank account that earns, say, 2 percent or less.[9] Check credit card statements and other mailings carefully to make certain the charges are accurate.

Step 5: Start a Savings Plan

It's important to save some money each month in a separate account for large purchases you're likely to make (such as a car or house). Then, when it comes time to make that purchase, you'll have the needed cash. Save at least enough for a significant down payment so that you can reduce the finance charges you'll pay to borrow the rest.

Many people say they don't have any money left over at the end of the month to save. The best way to save money is to *pay yourself first.* When you get your paycheck, first take out money for savings and then plan what to do with the rest. You can arrange with your bank or mutual fund to deduct a certain amount for savings every month. You'll be pleasantly surprised when the money starts accumulating and earning interest over time. With some discipline, you can eventually reach your goal of becoming a millionaire. It's not as difficult as you may think. Figure D.2 shows how $5,000 grows over various periods at different rates of return.

Step 6: Borrow Only to Buy Assets That Increase in Value or Generate Income

Don't borrow money for ordinary expenses; you'll only get into more debt that way. If you have budgeted for emergencies, such as car repairs and health care costs, you should be able to stay financially secure. Most financial experts advise saving about six months of earnings for contingencies. Keep this money in highly liquid accounts, such as a bank account or money market fund.

Only the most unexpected of expenses should cause you to borrow. It is hard to wait until you have enough money to buy what you want, but learning to wait is a critical part of self-discipline. Of course, you can always try to produce more income by working overtime or by working on the side for extra revenue.

If you follow these six steps, not only will you have money for investment, but you'll have developed most of the financial techniques needed to become financially secure. If you find it hard to live within a budget at first, remember the payoff is well worth the effort.

¡Seeit! Need help understanding compound interest? Visit your Connect eBook to view a video for a brief animated explanation.

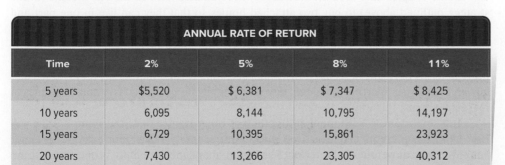

ANNUAL RATE OF RETURN				
Time	2%	5%	8%	11%
5 years	$5,520	$ 6,381	$ 7,347	$ 8,425
10 years	6,095	8,144	10,795	14,197
15 years	6,729	10,395	15,861	23,923
20 years	7,430	13,266	23,305	40,312
25 years	8,203	16,932	34,242	67,927

FIGURE D.2 HOW MONEY GROWS
This chart illustrates how $5,000 would grow at various rates of return. Recent savings account interest rates were very low (less than 2 percent), but in earlier years they've been over 5 percent.

LO D–2 Explain how to build a financial base, including investing in real estate, saving money, and managing credit.

Building Your Financial Base

The path to success in a capitalist system is to have capital to invest, yet many students today graduate with debt, sometimes sizable debt. As you've read, accumulating capital takes discipline and careful planning. With the money you save, however, you can become an entrepreneur, one of the fastest ways to wealth.

Living frugally is extremely difficult for the average person. Most people are eager to spend their money on a new car, furniture, electronics, clothes, entertainment, and the like. They look for a fancy apartment with all the amenities. A capital-generating strategy may require forgoing most (though not all) of these purchases to accumulate investment money. It might mean living like a frugal college student, in a relatively inexpensive apartment furnished in hand-me-downs from parents, friends, Craigslist, and resale shops.

For five or six years, you can manage with the old sound system, a used car, and a few nice clothes. The strategy is sacrifice, not luxury. It's important not to feel burdened by this plan; instead, feel happy knowing your financial future will be more secure. That's the way the majority of millionaires got their money. If living frugally seems too restrictive for you, you can still save at least a little. It's better to save a smaller amount than not to save at all.

It's wise to plan your financial future with the same excitement and dedication you bring to other aspects of your life. If you get married, for example, it is important to discuss financial issues with your spouse. Conflicts over money are a major cause of divorce, so agreeing on a financial strategy before marriage is very important.

A great strategy for couples is to try to live on one income and to save the other. The longer you wait to marry, the more likely it will be that one of you can be earning enough to do that—as a college graduate. If the second spouse makes $40,000 a year *after taxes,* saving that income for five years quickly adds up to $200,000 (plus interest).

What do you do with the money you accumulate? Your first investment might be a low-priced home. Why? The purpose of this investment is to lock in payments for your shelter at a fixed amount. Through the years, home ownership has been a wise investment, unlike renting, but that may be changing.

Real Estate: Historically, a Relatively Secure Investment

Paying for a home has historically been a good way of forcing yourself to save. You must make the payments every month. Those payments are an investment that could prove to be very rewarding over time. First, a home is the one investment that you can live in. Second, once you buy a home, your mortgage payments are relatively fixed (though taxes and utilities may go up, and there will be varying maintenance and repair costs). As your income rises, mortgage payments get easier to make, but renters often find that rents go up at least as fast as income. A home is also a good asset to use when applying for a business loan.

Some couples have used the seed money accumulated from saving one income (in the strategy outlined above) to buy two attached homes so that they can live in one part and rent out the other. The rent they earn covers a good part of the payments for both homes, so the couple can live comfortably, yet inexpensively, while their investment in a home appreciates. In this way they accumulate capital and, as they grow older, pull far ahead of their peers in terms of financial security. As capital accumulates and values rise, they can sell and buy an even larger apartment building or a single-family home. Many have made fortunes in real estate in just this way.

It is important to keep in mind that there is no guarantee that your home's value will rise. Unforeseen events may negatively affect your property values. For example, a major employer may move out of the region, leaving an abundance of empty properties with no one left to buy them. Therefore, it is important to research the stability of the areas where you are looking to buy.

Remember, three of the most important criteria in buying real estate are location, location, location. A home in the best part of town, near good schools, shopping, and work, is usually a sound financial investment. It's usually better, from a financial viewpoint, to buy a smaller home in a great location than a large home in a not-so-great setting where property values may rise more slowly.

The changes in home prices and rental rates have made it more important than ever for you to check whether it is better to own or rent. Since housing prices vary greatly from region to region, it is wise to use one of the many buy versus rent calculators available online to determine whether buying is better than renting in your area.

Today, many people are making additional income by renting unused housing space on Airbnb.[10] Of course, it all depends on how valuable your space is. A beachfront property may bring in some real income if you rent it while away. Such rentals are part of a "sharing economy" that is emerging. That is, people are learning to share cars, homes, bicycles, driveways, and tools as a way of saving some money.[11]

Once you understand the benefits of home ownership versus renting, you can decide whether those same principles apply to owning the premises where you set up your own business—or owning your own equipment, vehicles, and the like. Figure D.3 will give you some idea of how expensive a house you can afford, given your income. You can find current mortgage interest rates and mortgage calculators at Interest.com.

Fuse/Jupiter Images

Tax Deductions and Home Ownership

Buying a home is likely to be the largest and perhaps the most important investment you'll make. It's nice to know that the federal government is willing to help you with it. Here's how: Interest on your home mortgage payments is tax-deductible, as are your real estate taxes. (Starting in 2018, tax changes limited deductibility to interest on $750,000 of mortgage value

FIGURE D.3 HOW MUCH HOUSE CAN YOU AFFORD?

Monthly mortgage payments—including interest, principal, real estate taxes, and insurance—generally shouldn't amount to more than 28 percent of your monthly income. Here's how much people in various income categories can afford to pay for a home if they use a 30-year mortgage and make a 10 percent down payment.

		INTEREST RATES			
Income	Monthly Payment	5%	6%	7%	15%
$ 30,000	$ 700	$106,263	$ 98,303	$ 91,252	$ 56,870
50,000	1,167	180,291	167,081	155,376	98,606
80,000	1,867	287,213	266,056	247,308	155,916
100,000	2,333	361,240	334,832	311,433	198,013

Source: Federal Housing Finance Board.

Buying a home has usually been a very good and safe investment. But sometimes housing prices can rise fast, as they did between 2000 and 2007, and then fall, as they did between 2008 and 2012. Housing prices have been recovering since then in many areas. What has happened to housing prices in your area over the last few years?

and $10,000 of combined sales and real estate taxes.) Since virtually all your mortgage payments during the first few years are applied to the interest on your loan, almost all the early payments are tax-deductible—a tremendous benefit. If your payments are $1,000 a month and your income is in a 25 percent tax bracket, during the early years of your mortgage the government will, in effect, give you credit for about $250 of your payment, lowering your real cost. This makes home ownership much more competitive with renting than it may appear.

Learning to Manage Credit

Credit cards are an important element in your personal financial system, even if you rarely use them. First, you may have to own a credit card to buy certain goods or even rent a car, because some businesses require one for identification and to ensure payment. Second, you can use a credit card to keep track of purchases. A credit card gives you records of purchases over time for your income tax returns and financial planning purposes. Third, a credit card is more convenient than cash or checks. You can carry less cash and easily cancel a stolen card to protect your account. Fourth, paying off credit card balances *on time* can help you improve your credit score. Most of our phones have capabilities for managing data for your credit, debit, loyalty, membership, and gift cards through Apple Wallet and Android Pay. You can decide which card is best for you by comparing them at CardRatings.com or CreditCards.com. The most secure cards will be PIN and chip cards, since such cards are much less prone to identity theft.

If you do use a credit card, pay the balance in full during the period when no interest is charged. Finance charges on credit card purchases usually amount to, on average, 16 to over 20 percent annually.[12] If you finance a TV, home appliances, or other purchases with a credit card, you may end up spending much more than if you pay with cash. Not having to pay 16 percent or more in interest is as good as earning 16 percent tax-free. You may want to choose a card that pays you back in cash or offers credits toward the purchase of a car or frequent-flier miles. (Keep in mind that reward cards typically charge higher interest rates. So get one of these only if you will pay off the balance each month.) Some cards have no annual fees; others have lower interest rates. Do your research!

The danger of a credit card is the flip side of its convenience. It's too easy to buy things you wouldn't buy if you had to pay cash, or to pile up debts you can't repay.[13] If you aren't the type who can stick to a financial plan or household budget, *it may be better not to have*

Companies like Visa often encourage young people to apply for credit cards at student centers or even college sports events. Why are such companies so willing to give you a credit card?

Joe Robbins/Getty Images

a credit card at all. Imagine a customer who has a $10,000 balance on his or her credit card with a 16 percent interest rate and pays the minimum 4 percent monthly payment. How long will it take to pay off the debt, and what would the cost for interest be? The answers: 14 years and nearly $5,000—and that's without using the card again to purchase so much as a candy bar. Prior to 2006, the minimum payment was 2 percent. The lower minimum payment may have been enticing for the short term, but over time that same $10,000 balance would have taken over 30 years to repay and cost over $18,000 in interest if only the 2 percent minimum was paid.

Another danger of credit cards is the issue of hacking and credit card fraud. Stores like Target, Wendy's, and Home Depot have had credit card numbers stolen. This identity theft results in people getting access to your e-mail addresses, names, and account numbers. There are some things you can do to help protect yourself from credit card fraud:[14]

- Set up transaction alerts to let you know when charges have been made on your card.
- Cut up old cards.
- Limit the number of credit cards you have (the more you have, the greater chances one will be compromised).
- Only make online transactions on secure networks and websites.
- Never give your credit card number to someone who has called you (verify the business and phone number and call them).
- Be leery of social media quizzes (hackers can gather personal information similar to security questions from them).

Some people would be better off with a *debit* card only. Debit cards don't allow you to spend more than what you have in the bank, a great benefit for those who are not as careful with their spending as they should be. Furthermore, there are no interest payments or annual fees. Many people think a debit card can protect them from fraud better than a credit card. That's not true. While debit cards can protect you from overspending, a credit card offers greater consumer protection as the holder would be liable for only up to $50 in fraudulent charges.[15]

A recent credit card law created new consumer credit card protections. The law allows card issuers to increase interest rates for only a limited number of reasons and restricts increasing rates at all during the first year of a new card account. People must be at least 21 years old or get an adult to co-sign with them if they want new credit cards on their own. The Consumer Financial Protection Bureau regulates financial products and services, including mortgages, credit cards, student loans, and debt collection. You would be wise to explore what is available to you.

Where to Put Your Savings

Where are some other good places to save your money? For a young person, one of the *worst* places to keep long-term investments is a bank or savings and loan, or even a credit union. It is important to have savings equivalent to about six months of living expenses in the bank for emergencies, but the bank is not the best place to invest. Online banks usually pay higher interest than your local bank, but even their rates are relatively *low.*

One of the best places to invest over time has been the stock market. The stock market does tend to go up and down, but over a longer period of time it has proved to be one of the best investments. About half of U.S. households own stock and mutual funds.[16] Some financial experts believe the stock market may grow more slowly in the future than it has over the last 50 years. Still, the U.S. economy and stock market has always managed to rise up even after a financial crisis.

Remember, the greater the risk, usually the greater the return. When stock prices are low, that's the time to *buy.* When stocks collapse, that may be an opportunity to get into the stock market, not avoid it. The average investor buys when the market is high and sells when it's low. Clearly, that's not a good idea. It takes courage to buy when everyone else is selling.

contrarian approach
Buying stock when everyone else is selling or vice versa.

In the long run, however, this **contrarian approach** to investing is the way the rich get richer. (Of course, you'll need to do your research to determine the health and potential of any companies or sectors in which you're interested in investing.) After the Test Prep questions, we take a closer look at how to protect your financial base with insurance.

?TESTPREP

- What are the six steps you can take to control your finances?
- Why can real estate be a good investment?
- What are the advantages and disadvantages of using a credit card?

LO D–3 Explain how buying the appropriate insurance can protect your financial base.

Protecting your Financial Base: Buying Insurance

One of the last things young people think about is the idea that they may become sick, get injured, or die. It is not a pleasant thought, but the unexpected does happen every day. To protect your loved ones from the loss of your income, you should buy life insurance.

term insurance
Pure insurance protection for a given number of years.

The simplest and least expensive form of life insurance is **term insurance**. It is pure insurance protection for a given number of years that typically costs less the younger you buy it (see Figure D.4). Every few years, you might have to renew the policy, and the premium can then rise. Check prices through a service like SelectQuote or use one of Quicken's personal finance software packages to find the best rates and options.

Even stay-at-home parents should carry life insurance. It is estimated that a stay-at-home parent's work is equal to a $162,581 salary.[17] How much insurance do you need? It depends on your age, income, number of dependents, savings, debts, and how secure you want to leave your dependents. A general rule of thumb is to apportion your coverage so that a spouse earning 60 percent of the income carries 60 percent of the insurance.

Multiyear level-premium insurance guarantees that you'll pay the same premium for the life of the policy. Some companies allow you to switch your term policy for a more expensive whole or universal life policy.

whole life insurance
Life insurance that stays in effect until age 100.

Whole life insurance combines pure insurance and savings, so you are buying both insurance and a savings plan. This may be a good idea for those people who have trouble saving money. A universal life policy lets you choose how much of your payment should go to insurance and how much to investments. The investments in such plans traditionally are very conservative but pay a steady interest rate. Keep in mind they usually come with high costs.

FIGURE D.4 WHY BUY TERM INSURANCE?

INSURANCE NEEDS IN EARLY YEARS ARE HIGH	INSURANCE NEEDS DECLINE AS YOU GROW OLDER
1. Children are young and need money for education.	1. Children are grown.
2. Mortgage is high relative to income.	2. Mortgage is low or completely paid off.
3. Often there are auto payments and other bills to pay.	3. Debts are paid off.
4. Loss of income would be disastrous.	4. Insurance needs are few.
	5. Retirement income is needed.

Variable life insurance is a form of whole life insurance that invests the cash value of the policy in stocks or other high-yielding securities. Death benefits may thus vary, reflecting the performance of the investments.

Life insurance companies recognized people's desire to earn higher returns on their insurance (and to protect themselves against running out of money before they die) and began selling annuities. An **annuity** is a contract to make regular payments to a person for life or for a fixed period. With an annuity, you are guaranteed to have an income until you die (or for the agreed upon period). If you live a long life, you will continue to get income even if you've already received all the money you paid in. But if you die before your investment funds are depleted, the balance goes to the insurance company, not to your survivors (unless you've paid a steep additional fee for survivors' benefits).[18]

There are two kinds of annuities: fixed and variable. *Fixed annuities* are investments that pay the policyholder a specified interest rate. They are not as popular as *variable annuities,* which provide investment choices identical to mutual funds. Buyers must be careful in selecting an insurance company and choosing the investments made with their money. Companies charge sales commissions as high as 10 percent and other charges as high as 7 percent.

Consult a financial advisor who is not an insurance agent and who can help you make the wisest decision about insurance. You can also check out the insurance company through a rating service such as AM Best (ambest.com) or Moody's (moodys.com).

Health Insurance

The law called the Patient Protection and Affordable Care Act (PPACA) initially required nonexempt individuals to maintain a minimum level of health insurance or pay a tax penalty. In 2017, Congress passed a tax reform bill that removed the mandate beginning in 2019. At the time of this writing, the U.S. Supreme Court has agreed to hear a case dealing with the legality of the PPACA. The ruling will likely decide the future of the law.[19] It is important that you follow any changes as to how the law is implemented because almost everything to do with your health care could be affected.

You may already have health insurance coverage through your employer. If not, you can buy health insurance through the government's health care marketplace at healthcare.gov or directly from insurance companies like UnitedHealthcare or Blue Cross Blue Shield. One of the more popular health insurance alternatives is a health savings account (HSA), a tax-deferred savings account linked to a low-cost, high-deductible health insurance policy. The idea is to use the money that would have been spent on high-cost, low-deductible health insurance and deposit it in a health savings account. You can use the money in the HSA only for needed health care services. One major benefit to you is that the money grows tax-free until you withdraw it.

Disability Insurance

Your chances of becoming disabled at an early age are much higher than your chances of dying in an accident. It's dangerous financially not to have any health insurance. Hospital costs are simply too high to risk financial ruin by going uninsured. It is often a good idea to supplement health insurance policies with **disability insurance** that pays part of the cost of a long-term sickness or an accident. Disability insurance replaces part of your lost income, and, in some cases, pays disability-related costs not covered by health insurance. Call an insurance agent or check online for possible costs of such insurance. The cost is relatively low to protect yourself from losing your income for an extended period.

Homeowner's or Renter's Insurance

You may be surprised how much it would cost to replace all the things you own. As you begin to accumulate possessions, you may want to have apartment or homeowner's insurance that covers their loss. Specify that you want *guaranteed replacement cost.* That means the insurance

---

variable life insurance
Whole life insurance that invests the cash value of the policy in stocks or other high-yielding securities.

annuity
A contract to make regular payments to a person for life or for a fixed period.

disability insurance
Insurance that pays part of the cost of a long-term sickness or an accident.

company will give you whatever it costs to buy all those things *new*. It costs a little more than a policy without guaranteed replacement, but you will get a lot more if you have a loss.

The other option is insurance that covers the *depreciated cost* of the items. A sofa you bought five years ago for $600 may be worth only $150 now. That current value is what your insurance would pay you, not the $700 or more to buy a brand-new sofa. If your computer is stolen, you might get only a couple hundred dollars rather than its replacement cost.

Most policies don't cover expensive items like engagement and wedding rings. You can buy a *rider* to your policy to cover them at a reasonable cost.

Other Insurance

Most states require drivers to have automobile insurance; if your state doesn't, it's a good idea to buy it anyway. Be sure to insure against losses from uninsured motorists. Consider accepting a large deductible to keep the premiums low, and pay for small damages yourself.

You'll also need liability insurance to protect yourself against being sued by someone you accidentally injure. Often you can get a discount by buying all your insurance (life, health, homeowner's, automobile) with one company. Look for other discounts such as for safe driving, good grades, and more.

LO D–4 Outline a strategy for retiring with enough money to last a lifetime.

Planning Your Retirement

It may seem a bit early to be planning your retirement; however, not doing so would be a big mistake. Successful financial planning means long-range planning, and retirement is a critical phase of life. What you do now could make a world of difference in your quality of life after age 65, or whenever you retire. Presently, only half of workers say they or their spouses are currently saving for later life.[20] Fewer than 1 in 10 U.S. adults has accumulated enough money by retirement age to live comfortably, and of those who have, a large percentage are now planning to retire at a later age.[21] However, they may not be healthy enough to work when they are older, or there may not be jobs available that require their skills. Don't become one of the unfortunate ones left with little or no retirement funds.

Tim Pannell/Fuse/Getty Images

One purpose of planning your personal finances is to have enough money for retirement. If you plan to relax and travel when you retire, you need to begin saving now. What are your retirement goals, and what resources will you need to accomplish them?

Social Security

Social Security is the Old-Age, Survivors, and Disability Insurance Program established by the Social Security Act of 1935. It consists not of a fund of money but of a continuous flow of contributions in and payments out. The Social Security money you'll begin to receive when you retire will come directly from the Social Security taxes being paid by workers at that time. However, the number of people retiring and living longer is increasing dramatically, while the number paying into Social Security is declining. Maintaining Social Security may thus require reducing benefits, encouraging people to retire later, limiting cost-of-living adjustments (COLAs) made to benefits over time, and increasing Social Security taxes.[22]

Social Security will not provide you with ample funds for retirement. Plan now to save your own funds for your nonworking years. The government has established incentives to encourage you. Here are some specifics.

Individual Retirement Accounts (IRAs)

Traditionally, an **individual retirement account (IRA)** has been a tax-deferred investment plan that enables you (and your spouse, if you are married) to save part of your income for retirement. A traditional IRA allows people who qualify to deduct from their reported income the money they put into an account. **Tax-deferred contributions** are those for which you pay no current taxes, but the earnings gained in the IRA are taxed as income when they are withdrawn from your IRA after retirement.

Let's see why a traditional IRA is a good deal for an investor. The tremendous benefit is the fact that the invested money is not taxed. That means faster and higher returns for you. Say you put $6,000 into an IRA each year. (The maximum IRA contribution was $6,000 in 2020. If you're 50 or older, you can make an additional $1,000 "catch-up" contribution.) Normally you'd pay taxes on that $6,000 when you receive it as income. But because you put it into an IRA, you won't. If you're in the 22 percent tax bracket, that means you'll save $1,320 in taxes! Put another way, the $6,000 you save costs you only $4,680—a huge bargain.

The earlier you start saving, the better—because your money has a chance to double and double again. If you save $6,000 a year for 35 years in an IRA and earn 10 percent a year, you'll accumulate savings of more than $1.8 million. If you start when you're just out of school, you'll be a millionaire by the time you're 50. All you have to do is save $6,000 a year and earn 10 percent. You may be wise to use a Roth IRA instead (see the following).

If you increase your contribution to the maximum allowable each time it is raised, you can reach your million-dollar goal even earlier. The actual rate of return depends on the type of investments you choose. No one can predict future rates of return with certainty, and investments with higher rates of return also have higher risk. The actual rate of return on investments can vary widely over time (from the highest gain of 61 percent in 1983 to the lowest loss of –43 percent in 2008), but the average annual gain for the S&P 500 between 1970 and 2018 was 10.2 percent.[23] Some analysts predict returns could be lower in the coming years, so you may need to save more to reach the same goals.

The earlier you start saving, the better. Consider this: If you were to start contributing $6,000 to an IRA earning 10 percent when you're 22 years old and do so for only five years, you'd have about $43,000 by the time you're 27. Even if you *never added another penny* to the IRA, by the time you're 65 you'd have over $1.6 million. If you waited until you were 30 to start saving, you would need to save $6,000 every year for 33 years to have the same nest egg. And what would you have if you started saving at 22 *and* continued nonstop every year until 65? More than $3.9 million! Can you see why investment advisors often say that an IRA is the best way to invest in your retirement?

A second kind of IRA is the **Roth IRA.** You don't get up-front deductions from your taxes as with a traditional IRA, but earnings grow tax-free and are tax-free when withdrawn. *This is often the best deal for college-age students.* You can transfer money from a traditional IRA into a Roth IRA. You will have to pay taxes first, but the long-term benefits often make this exchange worthwhile if you believe your tax rate will be higher when you retire than it is now.

Social Security
The term used to describe the Old-Age, Survivors, and Disability Insurance Program established by the Social Security Act of 1935.

individual retirement account (IRA)
A tax-deferred investment plan that enables you (and your spouse, if you are married) to save part of your income for retirement; a traditional IRA allows people who qualify to deduct from their reported income the money they put into an account.

tax-deferred contributions
Retirement account deposits for which you pay no current taxes, but the earnings gained are taxed as regular income when they are withdrawn at retirement.

Roth IRA
An IRA where there are no up-front deductions on taxes as with a traditional IRA, but the earnings grow tax-free and are also tax-free when withdrawn.

Both types of IRA have advantages and disadvantages, so ask a financial advisor which is best for you. You may decide to have both.

You can't take money from either type of IRA until you are 59½ years old without paying a 10 percent penalty. That's a benefit for you, because it can keep you from tapping into your IRA in an emergency or when you're tempted to make a large impulse purchase. But the money is there if a real need or emergency arises. The government now allows you to take out some funds to invest in an education or a first home. But check the rules; they change over time.

Your local bank, savings and loan, and credit union all have different types of IRAs. Insurance companies offer them too. If you're looking for a higher return (and more risk), you can put your IRA funds into U.S. and international stocks, bonds, mutual funds, exchange-traded funds, or precious metals. You can switch from fund to fund or from investment to investment. You can even open several different IRAs as long as the total doesn't exceed the government's limit. Consider contributing to an IRA through payroll deductions to ensure that you invest the money before you're tempted to spend it.

If you are self-employed, you can look into a simplified employee pension IRA (SEP IRA). It's like an IRA for entrepreneurs. The annual contribution limit for SEP IRAs is $57,000, considerably higher than the $6,000 limit for traditional and Roth IRAs.

Simple IRAs

Companies with 100 or fewer workers can provide them with a simple IRA. Employees can contribute a larger part of their income annually than with a regular IRA (up to $13,000 versus $6,000), and the company matches their contribution. This plan enables people to save much more money over time and can help small companies compete for available workers.

401(k) Plans

401(k) plan
A savings plan that allows you to deposit pretax dollars and whose earnings compound tax-free until withdrawal, when the money is taxed at ordinary income tax rates.

A **401(k) plan** is an employer-sponsored savings plan that allows you to deposit a set amount of pretax dollars and collect compounded earnings tax-free until withdrawal, when the money is taxed at ordinary income tax rates. These or similar plans are the only pension many people have. Therefore, there have been several proposals for how to improve 401(k) plans.

If the value of your retirement account plunges, you may have to defer your dream of an early retirement. If you have already started to save for your retirement, is your portfolio well diversified?

FG Trade/Getty Images

The plans have three benefits: (1) your contributions reduce your present taxable income, (2) tax is deferred on the earnings, and (3) many employers will match your contributions, some even match 50 cents on a dollar. No investment will give you a better deal than an instant 50 percent return on your money. Not all companies have equally good programs, so be sure to check out what is available to you.

You should deposit at least as much as your employer matches, often up to 15 percent of your salary. You can usually select how the money in a 401(k) plan is invested: stocks, bonds, and in some cases real estate. Be careful not to invest all your money in the company where you work. It's always best to diversify your funds among different companies and among stocks, bonds, and real estate investment trusts.

Like the simple IRA, there is a simple 401(k) plan for those firms that employ 100 or fewer employees. Employees again are allowed to invest an amount (maximum of $13,500 in 2020, workers age 50 and older can add a catch-up of $3,000 for a total of $16,500) that is matched by the employer.[24] This is a rather new program, but it should also prove popular among small businesses in attracting new workers.

Qualified Retirement Plans (Keoghs)

Millions of small-business owners don't have the benefit of a corporate retirement system. Such people can contribute to an IRA, but the amount they can invest is limited. The alternative for all those doctors, lawyers, real estate agents, artists, writers, and other self-employed people is to establish their own qualified retirement plans (formerly called Keogh plans).

The advantage of qualified plans is that participants can invest up to $57,000 per year.[25] Like simple IRAs, qualified plan funds aren't taxed until they are withdrawn, nor are the returns the funds earn. Thus, a person in the 24 percent tax bracket who invests $10,000 yearly in a qualified plan saves $2,400 in taxes. That means, in essence, that the government is financing 24 percent of his or her retirement fund. As with an IRA, this is an excellent deal.

As with an IRA, there's a 10 percent penalty for early withdrawal. Also like an IRA, funds may be withdrawn in a lump sum or spread out over the years. However, the key decision is the one you make now—to begin early to put funds into an IRA, a qualified plan, or both so that the "magic" of compounding can turn that money into a sizable retirement fund.

Financial Planners

If the idea of developing a comprehensive financial plan for yourself or your business seems overwhelming, relax; help is available from financial planners. Be careful, though—anybody can claim to be a financial planner today. It's often best to find a certified financial planner (CFP) like Lauryn Williams—that is, a professional with a bachelor's degree who has completed a curriculum in personal financial planning, passed a 10-hour examination, and has at least three years of experience in financial planning.[26] Unfortunately, many so-called financial planners are simply insurance salespeople.

In the past few years, there has been an explosion in the number of companies offering other businesses financial services, sometimes called one-stop financial centers or financial supermarkets because they provide a variety of financial services, ranging from banking service to mutual funds, insurance, tax assistance, stocks, bonds, and real estate. It pays to shop around for the right financial advice. Find someone who understands your business and is willing to spend some time with you.

Financial planning covers all aspects of investing, from life and health insurance all the way to retirement and death. Today, robo-advisors such as Schwab Intelligent Portfolio, automatically manage money for clients with as little as $5,000 to invest. The firm charges no fee for this service, compared to 1 to 2 percent charged by other firms. You simply tell its robo-advisors your financial objectives and using financial algorithms they take over.

iSeeit! Need help understanding IRAs and 401(k) plans? Visit your Connect eBook to view a video for a brief animated explanation.

> *Your financial assets can protect your children and even your grandchildren far into the future, if you have taken the right steps through estate planning. What can you do now to make sure your assets are divided the way you would like them to be when you're gone?*

Ariel Skelley/Blend Images/Getty Images

Estate Planning

Your retirement may be far away, but it is never too early to begin thinking about estate planning, or making financial arrangements for those who will inherit from you. You may even help your parents or others to do such planning. An important first step is to select a guardian for your minor children. That person should have a genuine concern for your children as well as a parental style and moral beliefs you endorse.

Also ensure that you leave sufficient resources to raise your children, not only for living expenses but also for medical bills, college, and other major expenses. Often life insurance is a good way to ensure such a fund. Be sure to discuss all these issues with the guardian, and choose a contingent guardian in case the first choice is unable to perform the needed functions.

A second step is to prepare a **will**, a document that names the guardian for your children, states how you want your assets distributed, and names the executor for your estate. An **executor** assembles and values your estate, files income and other taxes, and distributes assets.

A third step is to prepare a durable power of attorney. This document gives an individual you name the power to take over your finances if you become incapacitated. A *durable power of attorney for health care* delegates power to a person you name to make health care decisions for you if you are unable to make such decisions yourself.

Other steps to follow are beyond the scope of this text. You may need to contact a financial planner/attorney to help you do the paperwork and planning to preserve and protect your investments for your children and spouse and others. But it all begins with a strong financial base.

will

A document that names the guardian for your children, states how you want your assets distributed, and names the executor for your estate.

executor

A person who assembles and values your estate, files income and other taxes, and distributes assets.

?TESTPREP

- What are the advantages of investing through an IRA? A qualified retirement plan? A 401(k) account?
- What are the main steps in estate planning?

SUMMARY

LO D–1 Outline the six steps for controlling your assets.

- **What are the six steps to managing personal assets?**

  (1) Take an inventory of your financial assets by developing a balance sheet for yourself with the fundamental accounting equation: Assets = Liabilities + Owners' equity; (2) keep track of all your expenses; (3) prepare a budget; (4) pay off your debts; (5) start a savings plan (the best way is to pay yourself first); and (6) if you must borrow, borrow only for assets that can increase in value or generate income.

LO D–2 Explain how to build a financial base, including investing in real estate, saving money, and managing credit.

- **How can I accumulate funds?**

  First, find a job. Try to live as frugally as possible. Invest your savings to generate even more capital. One such investment is a duplex home where the renter helps the owner pay the mortgage.

- **Why is real estate sometimes such a good investment?**

  First, a home is the one investment you can live in. Second, once you buy a home, the payments are relatively fixed (though taxes and utilities may go up). As your income rises, the house payments get easier to make, while rents tend to go up at least as fast as income.

- **How does the government help you buy real estate?**

  The government allows you to deduct interest payments on the mortgage, which lets you buy more home for the money.

- **Where is the best place to keep savings?**

  It is best, in the long run, to invest in stocks. Although they go up and down in value, in the long run stocks earn more than most other investments. Diversify among mutual funds and other investments.

- **What is a good way to handle credit cards?**

  Pay the balance in full during the period when no interest is charged. Not having to pay 16 percent interest is as good as earning 16 percent tax-free. Often a debit card is better than a credit card because it limits your spending to the amount you have in the bank.

LO D–3 Explain how buying the appropriate insurance can protect your financial base.

- **What is the role of insurance in protecting capital?**

  Insurance protects you from loss. If you were to die, your heirs would lose the income you would have earned. You can buy life insurance to make up for some or all of that loss.

- **Why is term insurance preferred?**

  Term insurance is pure insurance protection for a given number of years. You can buy much more term insurance than whole life insurance for the same amount of money.

- **Do I need other insurance?**

  It is important to have health insurance to protect against large medical bills. You also need car insurance (get a high deductible) and liability insurance in case you injure someone. You should also have homeowner's or renter's insurance. Often an umbrella policy will provide all your insurance protection for a lower cost.

LO D–4 Outline a strategy for retiring with enough money to last a lifetime.

- **Can I rely on Social Security to cover my retirement expenses?**

Social Security depends on payments from current workers to cover the needs of retired people. Fewer workers are paying into the system, so you can't rely on it to cover all your retirement expenses.

- **What are the basics of saving for retirement?**

Supplement Social Security with savings plans of your own. Everyone should have an IRA or some other retirement account. A Roth IRA is especially good for young people because your money grows tax-free and is tax-free when you withdraw it. For entrepreneurs, a qualified plan or simplified employee pension (SEP) IRA is wise. If you work for someone else, check out the 401(k) plan. Find a financial advisor who can recommend the best savings plan and help you make other investments.

- **What are the basics of estate planning?**

You need to choose a guardian for your children, prepare a will, and assign an executor for your estate. Sign a durable power of attorney to enable someone else to handle your finances if you are not capable. The same applies to a health durable power of attorney. Estate planning is complex and often calls for the aid of a financial planner/attorney, but the money is well spent to protect your assets.

KEY TERMS

annuity 625
contrarian
 approach 624
disability insurance 625
executor 630
401(k) plan 628

individual retirement
 account (IRA) 627
Roth IRA 627
Social Security 627
tax-deferred
 contributions 627

term insurance 624
variable life
 insurance 625
whole life
 insurance 624
will 630

CRITICAL THINKING

1. Housing prices in many parts of the United States have recovered from the losses during the financial crisis. What is the situation where you live? Would you encourage a college graduate in your area to buy a home or rent?

2. What kinds of questions must a person ask before considering the purchase of a home?

3. Imagine you inherited $50,000 and you want to invest it to meet two financial goals: (*a*) to save for your wedding, which you plan to have in two years; and (*b*) to save for your retirement several decades from now. How would you invest the money? Explain your answer.

4. Have you given any thought to becoming an entrepreneur? Do the statistics about millionaires in this chapter give you some courage to pursue such a venture?

5. What insurance coverage do you have? What type of insurance do you need to buy next?

PUTTING PRINCIPLES TO WORK

PURPOSE

To use online resources to make smart personal finance decisions.

EXERCISE

Use the calculators at Dinkytown.net to answer the following questions:

1. You need $5,000 for a trip to Europe in two years. How much would you have to deposit monthly in a savings account paying 1 percent in order to meet your goal?

2. Investing $1,000 at 6 percent for five years, what is the difference in purchasing power of your savings if inflation increases by 2 percent annually during that time? By 4 percent?

3. Starting today, how much would you need to save each month in order to become a millionaire before you retire?

4. You need a new car. What car can you afford if you have $1,500 for a down payment, can make monthly payments of $300, and get $1,000 for trading in your old clunker?

5. How much house can you afford if you earn $36,000 a year and have $10,000 savings for a down payment, a $6,000 car loan balance, and no credit card debts?

DEVELOPING CAREER SKILLS

KEY: ● **Team**   ★ **Analytic**   ▲ **Communication**   ▣ **Technology**

1. Check your local paper or use an online realtor to gather information regarding the cost to rent a two-bedroom apartment and to buy a two-bedroom condominium in your area. Go to Dinkytown.net and use the site's "rent-versus-buy calculator" to compare these costs. Discuss your findings in small groups.   ★ ▣ ▲

2. Talk with someone you know who has invested in a home. Has the value of the home appreciated or depreciated? What other benefits has the home brought? Create a list of the benefits and drawbacks of owning a home and real estate in general as an investment. Be prepared to make a short presentation on what you've learned.   ● ▣ ★ ▲

3. Go online and find out the cost of major medical/hospital treatments in your area. Ask some older friends or acquaintances about medical insurance and whether they have ever gone without any. What types of insurance do they recommend? Discuss your results with the class.   ★ ▣ ▲

4. The best time to start saving for the future is *now*. To prove this point to yourself, find a savings calculator online and calculate how much you will have at age 65 if you begin saving $100 a month now, versus $100 a month 10 years from now.   ★ ▣

5. Go online and check out the benefits and drawbacks of both traditional and Roth IRAs. Be prepared to make a two-minute presentation about each and to discuss your findings in class.   ★ ▣ ▲

CAREER EXPLORATION

If you are interested in working in personal finance, here are a few careers to consider. Find out about the tasks performed, skills needed, pay, and opportunity outlook in these fields in the *Occupational Outlook Handbook (OOH)* at bls.gov.

- **Personal financial planner**—provides advice on investments, insurance, mortgages, savings, estate planning, taxes, and retirement to help others manage their finances.

- **Accountant and auditor**—prepare and examine financial records. They also ensure that financial

records are accurate and that taxes are paid properly and on time.

- **Appraiser and assessor of real estate**—provide an estimate of the value of land and the buildings on the land usually before it is sold, mortgaged, taxed, insured, or developed.

- **Financial analyst**—provides guidance to individuals making investment decisions and assesses the performance of stocks, bonds, and other types of investments.

NOTES

1. Fang Block, "Global Billionaire Population Reaches Record; Jeff Bezos Remains No. 1," *Penta,* barrons.com, February 26, 2020; "Billionaires 2019," *Forbes,* forbes.com, March 2, 2020.

2. Fang Block, "Global Billionaire Population Reaches Record; Jeff Bezos Remains No. 1," *Penta,* barrons.com, February 26, 2020; Shi Jing, "Hurun Global Rich List 2020 Unveiled," *China Daily,* chinadaily.com.cn, February 2, 2020.

3. "National Financial Capability Study," FINRA Investor Education Foundation, usfinancialcapability.org, accessed March 2020; Bob Carlson, "What You Need to Know about Big Retirement Changes," *Forbes,* forbes.com, February 14, 2020; Kailey Hagan, "The Big Problem with Putting Off Retirement Planning until Your 40s," *The Motley Fool,* fool.com, February 20, 2020; Robert Exley Jr., "Here's What You'll Get for Retirement If You Make $50,000, Factoring in Social Security and Savings," *CNBC,* cnbc.com, February 7, 2020.

4. Kathleen Craig, "The State of Savings in America," *Forbes,* forbes.com, February 10, 2020; Shlomo Benartzi, "People Don't Save Enough for Emergencies, but There Are Ways to Fix That," *The Wall Street Journal,* wsj.com, February 17, 2020.

5. Greg McFarlane, "Top Paying Math-Related Careers," *Investopedia,* investopedia.com, March 3, 2020; Stacy Rapacon, "25 Best College Majors for a Lucrative Career," *Kiplinger,* kiplinger.com, February 5, 2019; Michael T. Nietzel, "The First College Rankings Based on Grad's Salary by Major Field," *Forbes,* forbes.com, February 7, 2020.

6. Benjamin Franklin (1706–1790).

7. Eric Rosenberg, "The 8 Best Budgeting Apps of 2020," *The Balance,* thebalance.com, January 15, 2020.

8. Matthew Goldberg, "How to Budget Money: Tackle Your Debt and Start Saving," *Bankrate,* bankrate.com, February 25, 2020; Megan Leonhardt, "Nearly 1 in 3 American Workers Run Out of Money before Payday—Even Those Earning over $100,000," *CNBC,* cnbc.com, February 12, 2020.

9. Oliver Isaacs, "8 Ways to Set Yourself Up for Financial Freedom in Your 20s," *Entrepreneur,* entrepreneur.com, February 20, 2020; Alexandria White, "Credit Card Debt in the U.S. Hits All-Time High of $930 Billion—Here's How to Tackle Yours with a Balance Transfer," *CNBC,* cnbc.com, March 6, 2020.

10. Erik Martin, "The Often-Overlooked Costs of Renting Your Home on Airbnb," *The Motley Fool,* fool.com, February 19, 2020; Gary Barker, "The Airbnb Effect on Housing and Rent," *Forbes,* forbes.com, February 21, 2020.

11. Paul Rosen, "The Self-Driving and Sharing Economy: How Regulation May Drive the Transportation Revolution in 2020 and Beyond," *Forbes,* forbes.com, February 12, 2020; Brian Martucci, "23 Best Sharing Economy Apps to Earn Extra Income," *Money Crashers,* moneycrashers.com, March 3, 2020; "6 Ways to Save and Earn Money by Sharing," *Entrepreneur,* entrepreneur.com, February 20, 2020.

12. Sienna Kossman, "Average Credit Card Interest Rate Is Now 21.21%," *The Balance,* thebalance.com, March 3, 2020; Matthew Frankel, "Here's the Average American's Credit Card Debt—and How Much It Costs Them,"

Nasdaq, nasdaq.com, February 17, 2020; Aimee Picchi, "Here's a Top Reason Americans Are Carrying an Average Credit Card Balance of over $6,200," *USA Today,* usatoday.com, February 12, 2020.

13. Yuka Hayashi, "Credit-Card Debt in U.S. Rises to Record $930 Billion," *The Wall Street Journal,* February 12, 2020.

14. "How Do Criminals Steal Your Credit Card Information?," *The Motley Fool,* fool.com, February 12, 2020; Latoya Irby, "10 Ways to Prevent, Detect, and Fight Identity Theft," *The Balance,* thebalance.com, February 29, 2020.

15. Alexandria White, "Credit Card vs. Debit Card: What's the Difference?," *CNBC,* cnbc.com, February 27, 2020.

16. Jessica Menton, "Trump Administration Considers Tax Incentive for More Americans to Buy Stocks, Report Says," *USA Today,* usatoday.com, February 28, 2020; Lydia Saad, "What Percentage of Americans Owns Stock?," *Gallup,* news.gallup.com, accessed March 2020.

17. Heather Marcoux, "Why America Needs to Consider Paying Stay-at-Home Parents," *Motherly,* motherly.com, February 10, 2020; Joelle Goldstein, "Mother Admits She Once Judged Stay-at-Home Moms—but Tearfully Reveals, 'I Get It Now,'" *People,* people.com, February 12, 2020.

18. Coryanne Hicks and Philip Moeller, "15 Things You Need to Know Now about Annuities," *USA Today Money,* money.usnews.com, February 18, 2020; Mark P. Kussen, "The Pros and Cons of Annuities," *Investopedia,* investopedia.com, February 7, 2020; Stan the Annuity Man, "What Is the Best Retirement Annuity?," *TheStreet,* thestreet.com, February 18, 2020; Matt Carey, "Fixed Annuity Details: What's a Market Value Adjustment?," *Forbes,* forbes.com, February 13, 2020.

19. Tucker Higgins, "Supreme Court Says It Will Again Decide Whether Obamacare Is Constitutional," *CNBC,* cbnc.com, March 2, 2020; Richard Wolf, "Supreme Court Once Again Will Decide the Fate of Affordable Care Act," *USA Today,* usatoday.com, March 2, 2020; Adam Liptak and Abby Goodnough, "Supreme Court to Hear Obamacare Appeal," *The New York Times,* nytimes.com, March 2, 2020.

20. Scott B. Van Voorhis, "How Much You Should Have in Savings at Each Life Stage," *MSN Money,* msn.com, February 13, 2020; Kristin Stoller, "How Much Should You Have Saved by Age?," *Forbes,* forbes.com, February 25, 2020; Maurie Backman, "You'll Be Shocked by How Many Americans Have No Retirement Savings at All," *The Motley Fool,* fool.com, February 19, 2020.

21. U.S. Senators Rob Portman and Ben Cardin, "Americans Deserve to Retire with Dignity. Here's How We'd Help Them Do It," *Barron's,* barrons.com, February 27, 2020; Alaina Tweddale, "27 Ugly Truths about Retirement," *Yahoo! Finance,* finance.yahoo.com, February 14, 2020; Jesse Pound, "As the Job Market Remains Strong, Older Workers Are Sticking Around," *CNBC,* cnbc.com, February 15, 2020.

22. Alicia Munnell, "There Are No Magic Fixes for Social Security," *MarketWatch,* marketwatch.com, March 5, 2020; Pamela Yellen, "How America's Retirement Dream Became a Nightmare," *Entrepreneur,* entrepreneur.com, February 12, 2020; Elena Botella, "Proposed Changes to Social Security Disability Insurance Could Undermine Your Retirement Security, Even if You're Not Currently Disabled," *Forbes,* forbes.com, February 9, 2020.

23. Standard & Poor's, standardandpoors.com, accessed March 2020; J. B. Maverick, "What Is the Average Annual Return for the S&P 500?," *Investopedia,* investopedia.com, February 19, 2020.

24. Internal Revenue Service, irs.gov, accessed March 2020; Rivan V. Stinson, "How Much Can You Contribute to a Simple IRA for 2020?," *Kiplinger,* kiplinger.com, February 24, 2020.

25. Internal Revenue Service, irs.gov, accessed March 2020.

26. Certified Financial Planner Board of Certification, cfp.net, accessed March 2020.

Getting the Job You Want

We hope that as you've read the text, you've developed an idea of the type of career you'd like to build for yourself. If so, how will you go about getting a job you want in your chosen field? That is what this epilogue is all about. Good luck—we hope you find a job doing something you love! Here are the topics we will be discussing in this section:

- Job Search Strategy
- Searching for Jobs Online
- Job Search Resources
- Writing Your Résumé
- Putting Your Résumé Online
- Writing a Cover Letter
- Preparing for Job Interviews
- Being Prepared to Change Careers

One of the most important goals of this book is to help you get the job you want. First, you have to decide what you want to do. So far we've helped you explore this decision by explaining what people do in the various business functions: management, human resource management, marketing, accounting, finance, and so on. There are many good books about finding the job you want, so we can only introduce the subject here.

If you are a returning student, you have both advantages and disadvantages that younger students do not have. First, you may have had a full-time job already. Second, you are more likely to know what kind of job you don't want. That is a real advantage. By exploring the various business careers in depth, you should be able to choose a career path that will meet your objectives.

If you have a full-time job right now, you already know that working while going to school requires juggling school and work responsibilities. Many older students must also balance family responsibilities in addition to those of school and work. But take heart. You have also acquired many skills from these experiences. Even if they were acquired in unrelated fields, these skills will be invaluable as you enter your new career. You can compete with younger students because you have the focus that comes with experience. Instructors enjoy having both kinds of students in class because they have different perspectives.

So, whether you're beginning your first career or your latest career, it's time to develop a strategy for finding and getting a personally satisfying job.

Do you look forward to saying "I got the job!" after your years of college study? Job fairs are among the many resources that can help you find the right job. Is it ever too early to start thinking about your career?

Job Search Strategy

It is never too early to begin thinking about a future career or careers. The following strategies will give you some guidance in that pursuit:

1. **Begin with self-analysis.** You might begin your career quest by completing a self-analysis inventory. You can refer to Figure E.1 for a sample of a simple assessment.

2. **Search for jobs you would enjoy.** Begin at your college's career planning office or website. Talk to people in various careers, even after you've found a job. Career progress demands continuous research.

3. **Begin the networking process.** Networking remains the number one way for new job seekers to get their foot in the door. You can start with your fellow students, family, relatives, neighbors, friends, professors, and local businesspeople. Be sure to keep a record of names, addresses, and phone numbers of contacts, including where they work, the person who recommended them to you, and the relationship between the source person and the contact. A great way to build contacts and make a good impression on employers is to do part-time work and summer internships for firms you find interesting.

4. **Use social media for help.** Many professionals use social networking sites like Facebook, Twitter, and LinkedIn to expand their networks and share industry news. If you haven't already, start profiles with these sites and start making connections. Don't sign up for a profile if you won't use it; employers will only think you don't finish what you start. When posting to these websites, be careful to include only information you would want a potential hiring agent to see and not something that might hurt your chances for landing a job.

5. **Prepare a good cover letter and résumé.** Once you know what you want to do and where you would like to work, you need to develop a good résumé and cover letter. Your résumé lists your education, work experience, and activities. We'll talk about these key job search tools in more detail. We'll also give you a list of resources you can use.

FIGURE E.1 A PERSONAL ASSESSMENT

Interests

1. How do I like to spend my time?
2. Do I enjoy being with people?
3. Do I like working with mechanical things?
4. Do I enjoy working with numbers?
5. Am I a member of many organizations?
6. Do I enjoy physical activities?
7. Do I like to read?

Abilities

1. Am I adept at working with numbers?
2. Am I adept at working with mechanical things?
3. Do I have good verbal and written communication skills?
4. What special talents do I have?
5. In which abilities do I wish I were more adept?

Education

1. Have I taken certain courses that have prepared me for a particular job?
2. In which subjects did I perform the best? The worst?
3. Which subjects did I enjoy the most? The least?
4. How have my extracurricular activities prepared me for a particular job?
5. Is my GPA an accurate picture of my academic ability? Why or why not?
6. Do I want a graduate degree? Do I want to earn it before beginning my job?
7. Why did I choose my major?

Experience

1. What previous jobs have I held? What were my responsibilities in each?
2. Were any of my jobs applicable to positions I may be seeking? How?
3. What did I like the most about my previous jobs? Like the least?
4. Why did I work in the jobs I did?
5. If I had to do it over again, would I work in these jobs? Why or why not?

Personality

1. What are my good and bad traits?
2. Am I competitive?
3. Do I work well with others?
4. Am I outspoken?
5. Am I a leader or a follower?
6. Do I work well under pressure?
7. Do I work quickly, or am I methodical?
8. Do I get along well with others?
9. Am I ambitious?
10. Do I work well independently of others?

Desired job environment

1. Am I willing to relocate? Why?
2. Do I have a geographic preference? Why?
3. Would I mind traveling in my job?
4. Do I have to work for a large, nationally known firm to be satisfied?
5. Must I have a job that initially offers a high salary?
6. Must the job I assume offer rapid promotion opportunities?
7. In what kind of job environment would I feel most comfortable?
8. If I could design my own job, what characteristics would it have?

Personal goals

1. What are my short- and long-term goals? Why?
2. Am I career-oriented, or do I have broader interests?
3. What are my career goals?
4. What jobs are likely to help me achieve my goals?
5. What do I hope to be doing in 5 years? In 10 years?
6. What do I want out of life?

6. **Develop interviewing skills.** Interviewers will be checking your appearance (clothes, haircut, fingernails, shoes); your attitude (friendly, engaged); your verbal ability (speaking clearly); and your motivation (enthusiasm, passion). Note also that interviewers want you to have been active outside of school and to have set goals. Have someone evaluate you on these qualities now to see if you have any weak points. You can then work on those weaknesses before you have any actual job interviews. We'll give you some clues on how to do this later.

7. **Follow up.** Write a thank-you e-mail after interviews, even if you think they didn't go well. You have a chance to make a lasting impression with a follow-up note. If you are interviewed by a group of people, ask for their business cards at the interview and e-mail them each separately. Let the company know you are still interested and

indicate your willingness to travel to be interviewed. Get to know people in the company and learn from them whom to contact and what qualifications to emphasize.

fizkes/Getty Images

Searching for Jobs Online

Social networking has become a powerful force in the job search. This should be no surprise; networking has always been the best way to hear about job leads, and networking online only makes it easier to connect and communicate with the people who could one day hire you.

Employers can use your online profiles to find your previous employers, learn more about your personality and interests, and gauge if you'd match the company's needs. Employers can also find red flags that could keep you from being hired, such as provocative photos, evidence of excessive drinking or drug use, bad-mouthing of previous employers, or discriminatory comments about race, age, gender, or other topics. The key is to build a professional yet genuine personality online, one you won't mind showing to your future boss.

Professional interview behavior includes writing a follow-up letter to thank the person or persons you met. What are your goals in writing such a letter?

You can be sure that a future employer will check out your social media personality before hiring you. Here are some social media sites you could utilize during your job search:

- Facebook: "Like" the company's page on Facebook and look through its posts, photos, and comments to get a sense for what the company does.

- Twitter: Follow people who work in the industries and positions you are applying for. Share links to interesting articles or updates, and "retweet," or repeat, interesting stories from other professionals.

- LinkedIn: Companies have always relied on current employees to find their best new employees, and with LinkedIn those connections become easier to make. Using LinkedIn, you may discover that your high school friend's old college roommate is hiring, and that connection could be enough to get you the job.

- Pinterest: Share photos or videos that showcase your skills, especially if your experiences are creative or visual. Or, just show employers your personality by sharing images you enjoy.

- YouTube: Show off your communication skills and personality by posting videos. If you don't have videos from your previous work experiences, consider starting a video blog where you share your opinions on topics relevant to your business.

- Blog/Personal website: While you should be careful about posting any personal information that could lead to identity theft on a public website, consider the value of writing regularly about a topic related to your career interests. A well-written blog can attract the attention of employers. However, if you create a blog, remember to proofread everything you post. Be sure to call attention to your blog posts by using Twitter and LinkedIn updates with links to what you write.

To find information about careers or internships online, try these sites (though keep in mind that addresses on the Internet are subject to sudden and frequent change):

- CareerBuilder.com
- Monster.com
- Indeed.com
- ZipRecruiter.com
- Glassdoor.com
- LinkUp.com
- Dice.com
- Idealist.org

Job Search Resources

Your school placement bureau's office and website are good places to begin learning about potential employers. On-campus interviewing is often a great source of jobs (see Figure E.2). Your library and the Internet may have annual reports and other resources that will give you even more information about your selected companies.

Other good sources of jobs include the want ads, job fairs, summer internships, placement bureaus, and sometimes walking into firms that appeal to you and asking for an interview. The *Occupational Outlook Handbook,* produced by the U.S. Department of Labor, says this about job hunting:

> *The skills that make a person employable are not so much the ones needed on the job as the ones needed to get the job, skills like the ability to find a job opening, complete an application, prepare the résumé, and survive an interview.*

Here are a few printed sources you can use for finding out about jobs, writing résumés and cover letters, and other career information:

1. U.S. Department of Labor, *Occupational Outlook Handbook* (2019–2020 edition)
2. Richard N. Bolles, *What Color Is Your Parachute? 2020: A Practical Manual for Job-Hunters and Career-Changers* (Ten Speed Press, 2019)
3. Dr. Dawn Graham, *Switchers: How Smart Professionals Change Careers and Seize Success* (AMACOM, 2018)
4. Robin Ryan, *60 Seconds and You're Hired!* (Penguin Books, 2016)
5. Amy Cudd, *Presence: Bringing Your Boldest Self to Your Biggest Challenges* (Little, Brown and Company, 2018)
6. Bill Barnett and Dave Evans, *Designing Your Life* (Alfred A. Knopf, 2018)
7. Paul D. Tieger, Barbara Barron, and Kelly Tieger, *Do What You Are: Discover the Perfect Career for You Through the Secrets of Personality Type* (Little, Brown and Company, 2014)
8. Wendy Enelow and Louise Kursmark, *Modernize Your Resume: Get Noticed . . . Get Hired* (Emerald Career Publishing, 2019)
9. Brenda Bernstein, *How to Write a KILLER LinkedIn Profile . . . and 18 Mistakes to Avoid (Updated)* (The Essay Expert, LLC, 2018)

It's never too early in your career to begin designing a résumé and thinking of cover letters. A quality résumé is both deep and wide: deep, meaning you had a strong commitment to your activities (leadership roles, responsibilities, long-term commitments), and wide, meaning you were active in several, varied areas (jobs, internships, clubs, volunteering).

By preparing a résumé now, you may find gaps that need to be filled before you can land the job you want. For example, if you discover that you haven't been involved in enough outside activities to impress an employer, join a club or volunteer your time. If you are weak on job experience, seek an internship or part-time job to fill in that gap.

It's never too soon to prepare a résumé, so let's discuss how.

FIGURE E.2 WHERE COLLEGE STUDENTS FIND JOBS

SOURCE OF JOB	
Online searches	College faculty/staff referrals
On-campus interviewing	Internship programs
Write-ins	High-demand major programs
Current employee referrals	Minority career programs
Job listings with placement office	Part-time employment
Responses from want ads	Unsolicited referrals from placement
Walk-ins	Women's career programs
Cooperative education programs	Job listings with employment agencies
Summer employment	Referrals from campus organizations

Writing Your Résumé

A résumé is a one-page document that lists information an employer would need to evaluate whether you qualify for that company's job opening. A résumé explains your immediate goals and career objectives as well as your educational background, experience, interests, and other relevant data. For example, experience working with teams is important to many companies. If you don't show an employer you have experience working with teams on your résumé, how can that employer decide if you should get an interview? Employers don't *read* résumés—they *scan* them, so use action words like those listed in Figure E.3 to grab an employer's attention quickly. You must be comprehensive and clear in your résumé if you are to communicate all your attributes.

Your résumé is an advertisement for you. If your ad is better than the other person's ad, you're more likely to get the interview. In this case, *better* means that your ad highlights your attributes more attractively. In discussing your education, for example, be sure to highlight your extracurricular activities such as part-time jobs, sports, and clubs. If you did well in school, include your grades. Be sure to describe your previous jobs, including your responsibilities, achievements, and special projects. If you include an interests section, don't just list your hobbies, but describe how deeply you are involved. If you organized the club, volunteered your time, or participated in an organization, make sure to say so in the résumé. The idea is to make yourself look as good on paper as you are in reality.

Here are some hints on preparing your résumé:

- Keep it simple. Put a summary of your skills and your objective at the top so that the reader can capture as much as possible in the first 30 seconds.

- If you e-mail your résumé, send it in the text of the message; don't just send it as an attachment. It takes too long for the receiver to open an attachment.

- Customize each mailing to that specific company. You may use a standard résumé, but add data to customize it and to introduce it.

- Use any advertised job title as the subject of your e-mail message, including any relevant job numbers.

See Figure E.4 for a sample résumé. Most companies prefer that you keep your résumé to one page unless you have many years of experience.

Putting Your Résumé Online

Many larger firms seek candidates on the Internet, and online tools can help you expand your résumé into a portfolio complete with links, work samples, and even video. An online résumé can thus allow you to reach the greatest number of potential employers with the least amount of effort.

But remember, thousands of other eager job hunters send résumés online, and the volume can overwhelm recruiters. That doesn't mean you shouldn't post your résumé online, but you can't just send a few hundred résumés into cyberspace and then sit back and wait for the phone to ring. Include online résumés as a tool in your job search process, but continue to use the more traditional tools, such as networking.

If you are sending a résumé through a career listing site like Monster.com, the company may be using a computer program to scan your résumé for keywords before actual

Administered	Directed	Investigated	Scheduled
Budgeted	Established	Managed	Served
Conducted	Handled	Operated	Supervised
Coordinated	Implemented	Organized	Teamed
Designed	Improved	Planned	Trained
Developed	Increased	Produced	Wrote

FIGURE E.3 SAMPLE ACTION WORDS

FIGURE E.4 SAMPLE
RÉSUMÉ

Yann Ng
345 Big Bend Boulevard
Kirkwood, MO, 63122
314-555-5385
yng@stilnet.com

Job objective: Sales representative in business-to-business marketing

Education: Earned 100 percent of college expenses working 35 hours per week

A.A. in Business, May 2019
St. Louis Community College at Meramec
Grade Point Average: 3.6

B.S. in Business, Marketing Major, expected May 2021
University of Missouri, St. Louis
Grade Point Average: 3.2 overall, 3.5 in major
Dean's List for two semesters

Experience

Schnuck's Supermarket, Des Peres, MO, 5/16 – present
- Responded to customer requests quickly as evening and weekend checkout cashier
- Trained new hires to build customer retention, loyalty, and service
- Learned on-the-job principles behind brand management, retail sales, and consumer product marketing

Mary Tuttle's Flowers, Kirkwood, MO, Summer 2015 and Summer 2016
- Created flower arrangements to customer specifications, managed sales transactions, and acted as an assistant to the manager
- Developed skills in customer relationship management
- Created window displays to enhance visual merchandising and retail marketing to consumers

Student Leadership

SLCC Student Representative Board: Created action plan for fundraising drive, which resulted in our largest donations ever to Habitat for Humanity
UMSL Student American Marketing Association: Ran team-building and recruitment activities, which resulted in a 10 percent increase in membership
UMSL Student Government Association: Ran focus groups to help prioritize goals, helping us target changes in the way we allocate student fees

Language Skills: Fluent in English, Vietnamese, and French

Computer Skills: Microsoft Office, Photoshop, and HTML/Web Publishing
- Developed own website (www.yng@stilnet.com)
- Created effective PowerPoint slides using Photoshop for Consumer Behavior class

humans get their hands on it. Computer programs look at résumés much differently than people do, so some people's perfectly executed, beautifully worded résumés don't pass the computer's test. If you are submitting a résumé online, you must understand what the computer is programmed to look for. Here are five ways to write an online résumé that will pass the computer scan with flying colors:

- Include as many of the keywords in the company's job description as possible. If you are applying for a sales management position, use the words *sales, managed,* and *manager* often in your résumé.

- Visit the employer's website. Are there any words they use to describe their corporate culture? If so, include those adjectives in your résumé as well.

- Keep your formatting simple and streamlined. Avoid underlining, italics, and boxes. You don't want to confuse the computer with fancy designs. Keep it simple and save your formatted résumé for the next stages in the process.

- List all the universities or colleges you've attended, even if it was just for a class or a semester. Some computer programs assign higher point values to prestigious universities.

- Don't ever lie, exaggerate, or cheat the system. You'll get caught, and you won't get the job.

Figure E.5 offers a sample online résumé, but you should also consult a résumé handbook to see what the latest résumés should look like.

FIGURE E.5 SAMPLE ONLINE RÉSUMÉ

Yann Ng
345 Big Bend Boulevard
Kirkwood, MO, 63122
314-555-5385
yng@stilnet.com

Job objective: Sales representative in business-to-business marketing

Education:
A.A. in Business, May 2019
St. Louis Community College at Meramec
Grade point average: 3.6

B.S. in Business, Marketing major, expected May 2021
University of Missouri, St. Louis
Grade point average: 3.2 overall, 3.5 in major
Dean's List for two semesters

Experience:
Schnuck's Supermarket, Des Peres, MO, 5/16–present Responded to customer requests quickly as evening and weekend checkout cashier. Trained new hires to build customer retention, loyalty, and service. Learned on-the-job principles behind brand management, retail sales, and consumer product marketing.

Mary Tuttle's Flowers, Kirkwood, MO, Summer 2015 and Summer 2016 Created flower arrangements to customer specifications, managed sales transactions, and acted as an assistant to the manager. Developed skills in customer relationship management. Created window displays to enhance visual merchandising and retail marketing to consumers.

Student Leadership
SLCC Student Representative Board: Created action plan for fundraising drive. UMSL Student American Marketing Association: Ran team-building and recruitment activities. UMSL Student Government Association: Ran focus groups to help prioritize goals.

Language Skills
English
Vietnamese
French

Computer Skills
Microsoft Office
Photoshop
HTML/Web Publishing

Posting résumés to online job sites can cause privacy nightmares for job seekers, who fear everything from identity theft to losing their current job when employers find out that they are looking for new jobs. Sometimes posted résumés are sold to other sites or individuals willing to pay for them. Scam artists posing as recruiters can download all the résumés they want and do virtually whatever they want with them. At worst, online résumés can give identity thieves a starting point to steal personal information.

Here are tips to protect your résumé and your identity:

- Never include highly private information, such as Social Security numbers and birthdays.
- Check job boards' privacy policies to see how information is used and resold.
- Post résumés directly to employers if possible.
- Date résumés and remove them promptly after finding a job.
- If possible, withhold confidential information such as telephone numbers and your name and use temporary e-mail addresses for contacts.

Some companies take résumés via Twitter before accepting full-page résumés by e-mail. Find a creative way to shorten your career objectives, experience, and interests to under 280 characters and share it with your connections.

Writing a Cover Letter

A cover letter is used to announce your availability and to introduce the résumé, but it also showcases your personality to an employer, often for the first time. The cover letter is probably one of the most important advertisements anyone will write in a lifetime—so it should be done right.

First, the cover letter should indicate that you've researched the organization and are interested in a job there. Let the organization know what sources you used and what you know in the first paragraph to get the attention of the reader and show your interest.

You may have heard people say, "What counts is not what you know, but who you know." If you don't know anyone, *get* to know someone. You can do this by calling the organization, visiting the offices, or reaching out on social media to talk to people who already have the kind of job you're hoping to get. Then, at the beginning of your cover letter, mention that you've talked with some of the firm's employees, showing the letter reader that you "know someone," if only casually, and that you're interested enough to actively pursue the organization. This is all part of networking.

Describe yourself in the next paragraph of your cover letter. Be sure to show how your experiences will benefit the organization. For example, don't just say, "I will be graduating with a degree in marketing." Say, "You will find that my college training in marketing and marketing research has prepared me to learn your marketing system quickly and begin making a contribution right away." The sample cover letter in Figure E.6 will give you a better feel for how this looks.

Use the last paragraph of your cover letter to say you are available for an interview at a time and place convenient for the interviewer. Offer to follow up with a phone call or e-mail if you don't hear from the employer after some time. Again, see the sample cover letter in Figure E.6 for guidance. Notice in this letter how the writer subtly shows that she reads business publications and draws attention to her résumé.

Principles to follow in writing a cover letter and preparing your résumé include:

- Be confident. List all your good qualities and attributes.
- Don't be apologetic or negative. Write as one professional to another, not as a humble student begging for a job.
- Describe how your experience and education can add value to the organization.

345 Big Bend Blvd.
Kirkwood, MO 63122
October 10, 2021

Mr. Carl Karlinski
Premier Designs
45 Apple Court
Chicago, IL 60536

Dear Mr. Karlinski: (Address the letter to a real person whenever possible.)

Recent articles in *Inc.* and *Success* praised your company for its innovative products and strong customer orientation. Having used your creative display materials at Mary Tuttle's Flowers, I'm familiar with your visually stimulating designs. Christie Bouchard, your local sales representative, told me all about your products and your sales training program at Premier Designs. Having talked with her about the kind of salespeople you are seeking, I believe I have the motivation and people skills to be successful.

Proven Sales Ability: For two summers, I created and sold flower arrangements at Mary Tuttle's Flowers, developing a loyal customer base. Also, for four years, I've practiced personable customer relations, based on the excellent customer-oriented training program that Schnuck's Supermarket delivers in the St. Louis region. I know our regular customers by name; they've told me that they first look for my station when they are checking out. I would bring this same attention to developing relationships in a business-to-business sales position.

Self-Motivation: I've worked 35 hours per week and every summer during my college years and have paid for 100 percent of my expenses. In addition, I've paid for trips to Asia, Europe, and the Americas.

Leadership: I've served actively in student governance both on the Student Representative Board at St. Louis Community College and as a part of the student government at the University of Missouri. I've always gotten to know other students to find out how I could make a difference through my student government work. I would take the initiative to not only serve customers well but also to help other new salespeople.

I will be in the Chicago area the week of January 4–9 and would appreciate the opportunity to meet with you to learn more about Premier's sales opportunities. I will phone your administrative assistant to check on your availability. Thank you for considering my application. I would work hard to maintain and expand the business-to-business relationships that have made Premier Designs so successful.

Sincerely,

Yann Ng

- Research every prospective employer thoroughly before writing anything. Use a rifle approach rather than a shotgun approach. That is, write effective marketing-oriented letters to a few select companies rather than general letters to a long list.
- Use printing services like FedEx Office if you do not have access to a reliable printer or high-quality paper.
- Have someone edit your materials for spelling, grammar, and style. Don't be like the student who sent out a second résumé to correct "some mixtakes." Or another who said, "I am acurite with numbers."
- Don't send the names of references until asked.

Preparing for Job Interviews

Companies use interviews to decide which qualified candidates are the best match for the job, so be prepared for your interviews. There are five stages of interview preparation:

1. **Do research about the prospective employers.** Learn what industry the firm is in, its competitors, the products or services it produces and their acceptance in the market, and the title of your desired position. You can find such information in the firm's annual reports, in Standard & Poor's, Hoover's, Moody's manuals, and various business publications such as *Fortune, Bloomberg, Barron's,* and *Forbes.* Ask your librarian for help or search the Internet. This important first step shows you have initiative and interest in the firm.

2. **Practice the interview.** Figure E.7 lists some of the more frequently asked questions in an interview. Practice answering these questions at the placement office and with your roommate, parents, or friends. Don't memorize your answers, but do be prepared—know what you're going to say. Interviewers will be impressed if you prepare questions for them about the products, job, company culture, and so on. Figure E.8 shows sample questions you might ask. Be sure you know who to contact, and write down the names of everyone you meet. Review the action words in Figure E.3 and try to fit them into your answers.

3. **Be professional during the interview.** You should look and sound professional throughout the interview. Dress appropriately. When you meet the interviewers, greet them by name, smile, and maintain good eye contact. Sit up straight in your chair and be alert and enthusiastic. If you have practiced, you should be able to relax

FIGURE E.7 FREQUENTLY ASKED QUESTIONS

- How would you describe yourself?
- What are your greatest strengths and weaknesses?
- How did you choose this company?
- What do you know about the company?
- What are your long-range career goals?
- What courses did you like best? Least?
- What are your hobbies?
- Do you prefer a specific geographic location?
- Are you willing to travel (or move)?
- Which accomplishments have given you the most satisfaction?
- What things are most important to you in a job?
- Why should I hire you?
- What experience have you had in this type of work?
- How much do you expect to earn?

FIGURE E.8 SAMPLE QUESTIONS TO ASK THE INTERVIEWER

- Who are your major competitors, and how would you rate their products and marketing relative to yours?
- How long does the training program last, and what is included?
- How soon after school would I be expected to start?
- What are the advantages of working for this firm?
- How much travel is normally expected?
- What managerial style should I expect in my area?
- How would you describe the working environment in my area?
- How would I be evaluated?
- What is the company's promotion policy?
- What is the corporate culture?
- What is the next step in the selection procedures?
- How soon should I expect to hear from you?
- What other information would you like about my background, experience, or education?
- What is your highest priority in the next six months and how could someone like me help?

and be confident. Other than that, be yourself, answer questions, and be friendly and responsive. Remember, the interview is not one-way communication; don't forget to ask the questions you've prepared before the interview. Do *not* ask about salary, however, until you've been offered a job. When you leave, thank the interviewers and, if you're still interested in the job, tell them so. If they don't tell you, ask them what the next step is. Maintain a positive attitude. Figures E.9 and E.10 outline what the interviewers will be evaluating.

4. **Follow up on the interview.** First, write down what you can remember from the interview: names of the interviewers and their titles, dates for training, and so forth, so you can send a follow-up letter, a letter of recommendation, or some other information to keep their interest. Your enthusiasm for working for the company could be a major factor in them hiring you.

5. **Be prepared to act.** Know what you want to say if you do get a job offer. You may not want the job once you know all the information. Don't expect to receive a job offer from everyone you meet, but do expect to learn something from every interview. With some practice and persistence, you should find a rewarding and challenging job.

FIGURE E.9 TRAITS RECRUITERS SEEK IN JOB PROSPECTS

1. **Ability to communicate.** Do you have the ability to organize your thoughts and ideas effectively? Can you express them clearly when speaking or writing? Can you present your ideas to others in a persuasive way?

2. **Intelligence.** Do you have the ability to understand the job assignment? Learn the details of operation? Contribute original ideas to your work?

3. **Self-confidence.** Do you demonstrate a sense of maturity that enables you to deal positively and effectively with situations and people?

4. **Willingness to accept responsibility.** Are you someone who recognizes what needs to be done and is willing to do it?

5. **Initiative.** Do you have the ability to identify the purpose of work and to take action?

6. **Leadership.** Can you guide and direct others to obtain the recognized objectives?

7. **Energy level.** Do you demonstrate a forcefulness and capacity to make things move ahead? Can you maintain your work effort at an above-average rate?

8. **Imagination.** Can you confront and deal with problems that may not have standard solutions?

9. **Flexibility.** Are you capable of changing and being receptive to new situations and ideas?

10. **Interpersonal skills.** Can you bring out the best efforts of individuals so they become effective, enthusiastic members of a team?

11. **Self-knowledge.** Can you realistically assess your own capabilities? See yourself as others see you? Clearly recognize your strengths and weaknesses?

12. **Ability to handle conflict.** Can you successfully contend with stress situations and antagonism?

13. **Competitiveness.** Do you have the capacity to compete with others and the willingness to be measured by your performance in relation to that of others?

14. **Goal achievement.** Do you have the ability to identify and work toward specific goals? Do such goals challenge your abilities?

15. **Vocational skills.** Do you possess the positive combination of education and skills required for the position you are seeking?

16. **Direction.** Have you defined your basic personal needs? Have you determined what type of position will satisfy your knowledge, skills, and goals?

Source: "So You're Looking for a Job?," The College Placement Council.

FIGURE E.10 INTERVIEW RATING SHEET

Candidate: "For each characteristic listed below there is a rating scale of 1 through 7, where '1' is generally the most unfavorable rating of the characteristic and '7' the most favorable. Rate each characteristic by *circling* just one number to represent the impression you gave in the interview that you have just completed."

Name of Candidate _____

1. **Appearance**

   Sloppy   1   2   3   4   5   6   7   Neat

2. **Attitude**

   Unfriendly   1   2   3   4   5   6   7   Friendly

3. **Assertiveness/Verbal Ability**

   a. Responded completely to questions asked

   Poor   1   2   3   4   5   6   7   Excellent

   b. Clarified personal background and related it to job opening and description

   Poor   1   2   3   4   5   6   7   Excellent

   c. Able to explain and sell job abilities

   Poor   1   2   3   4   5   6   7   Excellent

   d. Initiated questions regarding position and firm

   Poor   1   2   3   4   5   6   7   Excellent

   e. Expressed thorough knowledge of personal goals and abilities

   Poor   1   2   3   4   5   6   7   Excellent

4. **Motivation**

   Poor   1   2   3   4   5   6   7   High

5. **Subject/Academic Knowledge**

   Poor   1   2   3   4   5   6   7   Good

6. **Stability**

   Poor   1   2   3   4   5   6   7   Good

7. **Composure**

   Ill at ease   1   2   3   4   5   6   7   Relaxed

8. **Personal Involvement/Activities, Clubs, Etc.**

   Low   1   2   3   4   5   6   7   Very high

9. **Mental Impression**

   Dull   1   2   3   4   5   6   7   Alert

10. **Adaptability**

    Poor   1   2   3   4   5   6   7   Good

11. **Speech Pronunciation**

    Poor   1   2   3   4   5   6   7   Good

12. **Overall Impression**

    Unsatisfactory   1   2   3   4   5   6   7   Highly satisfactory

13. **Would you hire this individual if you were permitted to make a decision right now?**

All your efforts pay off when you land the job you want and take the first big step in your career. Go for it!

Winston Davidian/Getty Images

Being Prepared to Change Careers

If you're like most people, you'll follow several different career paths over your lifetime. This enables you to try different jobs and to stay fresh and enthusiastic. The key to moving forward and finding personal satisfaction in your career is a willingness to change and grow. This means that you'll have to write many cover letters and résumés and go through many interviews. Each time you change jobs, go through the steps in the section above to be sure you're fully prepared. Good luck!

GLOSSARY

401(k) plan (p. 628) A savings plan that allows you to deposit pretax dollars and whose earnings compound tax-free until withdrawal, when the money is taxed at ordinary income tax rates.

A

absolute advantage (p. 60) The advantage that exists when a country has a monopoly on producing a specific product or is able to produce it more efficiently than all other countries.

accounting (p. 438) The recording, classifying, summarizing, and interpreting of financial events and transactions to provide management and other interested parties the information they need to make good decisions.

accounting cycle (p. 439) A six-step procedure that results in the preparation and analysis of the major financial statements.

accounts payable (p. 444) Current liabilities involving money owed to others for merchandise or services purchased on credit but not yet paid for.

acquisition (p. 127) One company's purchase of the property and obligations of another company.

administered distribution system (p. 398) A distribution system in which producers manage all of the marketing functions at the retail level.

administrative agencies (p. 551) Federal or state institutions and other government organizations created by Congress or state legislatures with delegated power to pass rules and regulations within their mandated area of authority.

advertising (p. 415) Paid, nonpersonal communication through various media by organizations and individuals who are in some way identified in the advertising message.

affirmative action (p. 278) Employment activities intended to "right past wrongs" by increasing opportunities for minorities and women.

agency shop agreement (p. 313) Clause in a labor–management agreement that says employers may hire nonunion workers; employees aren't required to join the union but must pay a union fee.

agents/brokers (p. 386) Marketing intermediaries who bring buyers and sellers together and assist in negotiating an exchange but don't take title to the goods.

American Federation of Labor (AFL) (p. 309) An organization of craft unions that championed fundamental labor issues; founded in 1886.

annual report (p. 453) A yearly statement of the financial condition, progress, and expectations of an organization.

annuity (p. 625) A contract to make regular payments to a person for life or for a fixed period.

apprentice programs (p. 286) Training programs involving a period during which a learner works alongside an experienced employee to master the skills and procedures of a craft.

arbitration (p. 314) The agreement to bring in an impartial third party (a single arbitrator or a panel of arbitrators) to render a binding decision in a labor dispute.

artificial intelligence (AI) (p. 580) A term to describe machines programmed to think, work, and react like humans.

assembly process (p. 226) The part of the production process that puts together components.

assets (p. 442) Economic resources (things of value) owned by a firm.

auditing (p. 455) The job of reviewing and evaluating the information used to prepare a company's financial statements.

autocratic leadership (p. 183) Leadership style that involves making managerial decisions without consulting others.

B

balance of payments (p. 62) The difference between money coming into a country (from exports) and money leaving the country (for imports) plus money flows from other factors such as tourism, foreign aid, military expenditures, and foreign investment.

balance of trade (p. 62) The total value of a nation's exports compared to its imports over a particular period.

balance sheet (p. 442) Financial statement that reports a firm's financial condition at a specific time and is composed of three major accounts: assets, liabilities, and owners' equity.

banker's acceptance (p. 539) A promise that the bank will pay some specified amount at a particular time.

bankruptcy (p. 561) The legal process by which a person, business, or government entity unable to meet financial obligations is relieved of those obligations by a court that divides any assets among creditors, allowing creditors to get at least part of their money and freeing the debtor to begin anew.

bargaining zone (p. 314) The range of options between the initial and final offer that each party will consider before negotiations dissolve or reach an impasse.

barter (p. 525) The direct trading of goods or services for other goods or services.

benchmarking (p. 210) Comparing an organization's practices, processes, and products against the world's best.

benefit segmentation (p. 347) Dividing the market by determining which benefits of the product to talk about.

bond (p. 498) A corporate certificate indicating that a person has lent money to a firm.

bonds payable (p. 444) Long-term liabilities that represent money lent to the firm that must be paid back.

bookkeeping (p. 439) The recording of business transactions.

brain drain (p. 40) The loss of the best and brightest people to other countries.

brainstorming (p. 179) Coming up with as many solutions to a problem as possible in a short period of time with no censoring of ideas.

brand (p. 368) A name, symbol, or design (or combination thereof) that identifies the goods or services of one seller or group of sellers and distinguishes them from the goods and services of competitors.

brand association (p. 371) The linking of a brand to other favorable images.

brand awareness (p. 370) How quickly or easily a given brand name comes to mind when a product category is mentioned.

brand equity (p. 370) The value of the brand name and associated symbols.

brand loyalty (p. 370) The degree to which customers are satisfied, like the brand, and are committed to further purchases.

brand manager (p. 371) A manager who has direct responsibility for one brand or one product line; called a *product manager* in some firms.

brand name (p. 340) A word, letter, or group of words or letters that differentiates one seller's goods and services from those of competitors.

breach of contract (p. 557) When one party fails to follow the terms of a contract.

break-even analysis (p. 377) The process used to determine profitability at various levels of sales.

broadband technology (p. 579) Technology that offers users a continuous connection to the Internet and allows them to send and receive mammoth files that include voice, video, and data much faster than ever before.

budget (p. 469) A financial plan that sets forth management's expectations, and, on the basis of those expectations, allocates the use of specific resources throughout the firm.

bundling (p. 367) Grouping two or more products together and pricing them as a unit.

bureaucracy (p. 200) An organization with many layers of managers who set rules and regulations and oversee all decisions.

business (p. 4) Any activity that seeks to provide goods and services to others while operating at a profit.

business cycles (p. 47) The periodic rises and falls that occur in economies over time.

business environment (p. 9) The surrounding factors that either help or hinder the development of businesses.

business intelligence (BI) or analytics (p. 573) The use of data analytic tools to analyze an organization's raw data and derive useful insights from it.

business law (p. 550) Rules, statutes, codes, and regulations that are established to provide a legal framework within which business may be conducted and that are enforceable by court action.

business plan (p. 158) A detailed written statement that describes the nature of the business, the target market, the advantages the business will have in relation to competition, and the resources and qualifications of the owner(s).

business-to-business (B2B) market (p. 346) All the individuals and organizations that want goods and services to use in producing other goods and services or to sell, rent, or supply goods to others.

buying stock on margin (p. 504) Purchasing stocks by borrowing some of the purchase cost from the brokerage firm.

C

cafeteria-style fringe benefits (p. 293) Fringe benefits plan that allows employees to choose the benefits they want up to a certain dollar amount.

capital budget (p. 470) A budget that highlights a firm's spending plans for major asset purchases that often require large sums of money.

capital expenditures (p. 473) Major investments in either tangible long-term assets such as land, buildings, and equipment or intangible assets such as patents, trademarks, and copyrights.

capital gains (p. 504) The positive difference between the purchase price of a stock and its sale price.

capitalism (p. 34) An economic system in which all or most of the factors of production and distribution are privately owned and operated for profit.

cash-and-carry wholesalers (p. 393) Wholesalers that serve mostly smaller retailers with a limited assortment of products.

cash budget (p. 470) A budget that estimates cash inflows and outflows during a particular period like a month or a quarter.

cash flow (p. 449) The difference between cash coming in and cash going out of a business.

cash flow forecast (p. 469) Forecast that predicts the cash inflows and outflows in future periods, usually months or quarters.

centralized authority (p. 201) An organizational structure in which decision-making authority is maintained at the top level of management at the company's headquarters.

certificate of deposit (CD) (p. 533) A time-deposit (savings) account that earns interest to be delivered at the end of the certificate's maturity date.

certification (p. 311) Formal process whereby a union is recognized by the National Labor Relations Board (NLRB) as the bargaining agent for a group of employees.

certified public accountant (CPA) (p. 454) An accountant who passes a series of examinations established by the American Institute of Certified Public Accountants (AICPA).

chain of command (p. 200) The line of authority that moves from the top of a hierarchy to the lowest level.

channel of distribution (p. 386) A whole set of marketing intermediaries, such as agents, brokers, wholesalers, and retailers, that join together to transport and store goods in their path (or channel) from producers to consumers.

claim (p. 604) A statement of loss that the insured sends to the insurance company to request payment.

climate change (p. 17) The movement of the temperature of the planet up or down over time.

closed shop agreement (p. 313) Clause in a labor–management agreement that specified workers had to be members of a union before being hired (was outlawed by the Taft-Hartley Act in 1947).

cloud computing (p. 585) A form of virtualization in which a company's data and applications are stored at offsite data centers that are accessed over the Internet (the cloud).

collective bargaining (p. 311) The process whereby union and management representatives form a labor–management agreement, or contract, for workers.

command economies (p. 41) Economic systems in which the government largely decides what goods and services will be produced, who will get them, and how the economy will grow.

commercial bank (p. 533) A profit-seeking organization that receives deposits from individuals and corporations in the form of checking and savings accounts and then uses some of these funds to make loans.

commercialization (p. 373) Promoting a product to distributors and retailers to get wide distribution, and developing strong advertising and sales campaigns to generate and maintain interest in the product among distributors and consumers.

common law (p. 551) The body of law that comes from decisions handed down by judges; also referred to as unwritten law.

common market (p. 75) A regional group of countries that have a common external tariff, no internal tariffs, and a coordination of laws to facilitate exchange; also called a *trading bloc*. An example is the European Union.

common stock (p. 497) The most basic form of ownership in a firm; it confers voting rights and the right to share in the firm's profits through dividends, if offered by the firm's board of directors.

communism (p. 41) An economic and political system in which the government makes almost all economic decisions and owns almost all the major factors of production.

comparative advantage theory (p. 60) Theory that states that a country should sell to other countries those products that it produces most effectively and efficiently, and buy from other countries those products that it cannot produce as effectively or efficiently.

competition-based pricing (p. 377) A pricing strategy based on what all the other competitors are doing. The price can be set at, above, or below competitors' prices.

compliance-based ethics codes (p. 95) Ethical standards that emphasize preventing unlawful behavior by increasing control and by penalizing wrongdoers.

compressed workweek (p. 294) Work schedule that allows an employee to work a full number of hours per week but in fewer days.

computer-aided design (CAD) (p. 227) The use of computers in the design of products.

computer-aided manufacturing (CAM) (p. 227) The use of computers in the manufacturing of products.

computer-integrated manufacturing (CIM) (p. 227) The uniting of computer-aided design with computer-aided manufacturing.

concept testing (p. 372) Taking a product idea to consumers to test their reactions.

conceptual skills (p. 181) Skills that involve the ability to picture the organization as a whole and the relationships among its various parts.

conglomerate merger (p. 127) The joining of firms in completely unrelated industries.

Congress of Industrial Organizations (CIO) (p. 310) Union organization of unskilled workers; broke away from the American Federation of Labor (AFL) in 1935 and rejoined it in 1955.

consideration (p. 556) Something of value; consideration is one of the requirements of a legal contract.

consumerism (p. 559) A social movement that seeks to increase and strengthen the rights and powers of buyers in relation to sellers.

consumer market (p. 346) All the individuals or households that want goods and services for personal consumption or use and have the resources to buy them.

consumer price index (CPI) (p. 45) Monthly statistics that measure the pace of inflation or deflation.

contingency planning (p. 177) The process of preparing alternative courses of action that may be used if the primary plans don't achieve the organization's objectives.

contingent workers (p. 284) Workers who do not have the expectation of regular, full-time employment.

continuous process (p. 226) A production process in which long production runs turn out finished goods over time.

contract (p. 556) A legally enforceable agreement between two or more parties.

contract law (p. 556) Set of laws that specify what constitutes a legally enforceable agreement.

contract manufacturing (p. 66) A foreign company's production of private-label goods to which a domestic company then attaches its brand name or trademark; part of the broad category of outsourcing.

contractual distribution system (p. 398) A distribution system in which members are bound to cooperate through contractual agreements.

contrarian approach (p. 624) Buying stock when everyone else is selling or vice versa.

controlling (p. 174) A management function that involves establishing clear standards to determine whether or not an organization is progressing toward its goals and objectives, rewarding people for doing a good job, and taking corrective action if they are not.

convenience goods and services (p. 364) Products that the consumer wants to purchase frequently and with a minimum of effort.

conventional (C) corporation (p. 120) A state-chartered legal entity with authority to act and have liability separate from its owners.

cookies (p. 590) Pieces of information, such as registration data or user preferences, sent by a website over the Internet to a web browser that the browser software is expected to save and send back to the server whenever the user returns to that website.

cooling-off period (p. 316) When workers in a critical industry return to their jobs while the union and management continue negotiations.

cooperative (co-op) (p. 134) A business owned and controlled by the people who use it—producers, consumers, or workers with similar needs who pool their resources for mutual gain.

copyright (p. 554) A document that protects a creator's rights to materials such as books, articles, photos, and cartoons.

core competencies (p. 211) Those functions that the organization can do as well as or better than any other organization in the world.

core inflation (p. 45) CPI minus food and energy costs.

core time (p. 294) In a flextime plan, the period when all employees are expected to be at their job stations.

corporate distribution system (p. 398) A distribution system in which all of the organizations in the channel of distribution are owned by one firm.

corporate philanthropy (p. 98) The dimension of social responsibility that includes charitable donations.

corporate policy (p. 98) The dimension of social responsibility that refers to the position a firm takes on social and political issues.

corporate responsibility (p. 98) The dimension of social responsibility that includes everything from hiring minority workers to making safe products.

corporate social initiatives (p. 98) Enhanced forms of corporate philanthropy directly related to the company's competencies.

corporate social responsibility (CSR) (p. 97) A business's concern for the welfare of society.

corporation (p. 114) A legal entity with authority to act and have liability separate from its owners.

cost of capital (p. 482) The rate of return a company must earn in order to meet the demands of its lenders and expectations of its equity holders.

cost of goods sold (or cost of goods manufactured) (p. 445) A measure of the cost of merchandise sold or cost of raw materials and supplies used for producing items for resale.

countertrading (p. 72) A complex form of bartering in which several countries may be involved, each trading goods for goods or services for services.

craft union (p. 309) An organization of skilled specialists in a particular craft or trade.

credit unions (p. 535) Nonprofit, member-owned financial cooperatives that offer the full variety of banking services to their members.

critical path (p. 236) In a PERT network, the sequence of tasks that takes the longest time to complete.

cross-functional self-managed teams (p. 208) Groups of employees from different departments who work together on a long-term basis.

current assets (p. 443) Items that can or will be converted into cash within one year.

customer relationship management (CRM) (p. 336) The process of learning as much as possible about customers and doing everything you can over time to satisfy them—or even exceed their expectations—with goods and services.

D

damages (p. 557) The monetary settlement awarded to a person who is injured by a breach of contract.

data analytics (p. 577) The process of collecting, organizing, storing, and analyzing large sets of data ("big data") in order to identify patterns and other information that is most useful to the business now and for making future decisions.

database (pp. 13, 572) An electronic storage file for information.

data processing (DP) (p. 572) Name for business technology in the 1970s; included technology that supported an existing business and was primarily used to improve the flow of financial information.

dealer (private-label) brands (p. 370) Products that don't carry the manufacturer's name but carry a distributor or retailer's name instead.

debenture bonds (p. 499) Bonds that are unsecured (i.e., not backed by any collateral such as equipment).

debit card (p. 538) An electronic funds transfer tool that serves the same function as checks: it withdraws funds from a checking account.

debt financing (p. 474) Funds raised through various forms of borrowing that must be repaid.

decentralized authority (p. 201) An organizational structure in which decision-making authority is delegated to lower-level managers more familiar with local conditions than headquarters management could be.

decertification (p. 311) The process by which workers take away a union's right to represent them.

decision making (p. 178) Choosing among two or more alternatives.

deflation (p. 45) A situation in which prices are declining.

demand (p. 37) The quantity of products that people are willing to buy at different prices at a specific time.

demand deposit (p. 533) The technical name for a checking account; the money in a demand deposit can be withdrawn anytime on demand from the depositor.

demographic segmentation (p. 347) Dividing the market by age, income, and education level.

demography (p. 14) The statistical study of the human population with regard to its size, density, and other characteristics such as age, race, gender, and income.

departmentalization (p. 202) The dividing of organizational functions into separate units.

depreciation (p. 447) The systematic write-off of the cost of a tangible asset over its estimated useful life.

depression (p. 47) A severe recession, usually accompanied by deflation.

deregulation (p. 564) Government withdrawal of certain laws and regulations that seem to hinder competition.

devaluation (p. 71) Lowering the value of a nation's currency relative to other currencies.

digital natives (p. 211) Young people who have grown up using the Internet and social networking.

direct marketing (p. 397) Any activity that directly links manufacturers or intermediaries with the ultimate consumer.

direct selling (p. 397) Selling to consumers in their homes or where they work.

disability insurance (p. 625) Insurance that pays part of the cost of a long-term sickness or an accident.

discount rate (p. 529) The interest rate that the Fed charges for loans to member banks.

disinflation (p. 45) A situation in which price increases are slowing (the inflation rate is declining).

distributed product development (p. 362) Handing off various parts of your innovation process—often to companies overseas.

diversification (p. 503) Buying several different investment alternatives to spread the risk of investing.

dividends (p. 496) Part of a firm's profits that the firm may distribute to stockholders as either cash payments or additional shares of stock.

double-entry bookkeeping (p. 440) The practice of writing every business transaction in two places.

Dow Jones Industrial Average (the Dow) (p. 510) The average cost of 30 selected industrial stocks, used to give an indication of the direction (up or down) of the stock market over time.

drop shippers (p. 393) Wholesalers that solicit orders from retailers and other wholesalers and have the merchandise shipped directly from a producer to a buyer.

dumping (p. 63) Selling products in a foreign country at lower prices than those charged in the producing country.

E

e-commerce (p. 12) The buying and selling of goods over the Internet.

economics (p. 31) The study of how society chooses to employ resources to produce goods and services and distribute them for consumption among various competing groups and individuals.

economies of scale (p. 198) The situation in which companies can reduce their production costs if they can purchase raw materials in bulk; the average cost of goods goes down as production levels increase.

electronic funds transfer (EFT) system (p. 538) A computerized system that electronically performs financial transactions such as making purchases, paying bills, and receiving paychecks.

embargo (p. 74) A complete ban on the import or export of a certain product, or the stopping of all trade with a particular country.

empowerment (pp. 14, 185)   Giving frontline workers the responsibility, authority, freedom, training, and equipment they need to respond quickly to customer requests.

enabling (p. 185)   Giving workers the education and tools they need to make decisions.

enterprise resource planning (ERP) (p. 233)   A newer version of materials requirement planning (MRP) that combines the computerized functions of all the divisions and subsidiaries of the firm—such as finance, human resources, and order fulfillment—into a single integrated software program that uses a single database.

enterprise zones (p. 150)   Specific geographic areas to which governments try to attract private business investment by offering lower taxes and other government support.

entrepreneur (p. 4)   A person who risks time and money to start and manage a business.

entrepreneurial team (p. 147)   A group of experienced people from different areas of business who join together to form a managerial team with the skills needed to develop, make, and market a new product.

entrepreneurship (p. 144)   Accepting the risk of starting and running a business.

environmental scanning (p. 344)   The process of identifying the factors that can affect marketing success.

equity financing (p. 474)   Money raised from within the firm, from operations or through the sale of ownership in the firm (stock or venture capital).

equity theory (p. 256)   The idea that employees try to maintain equity between inputs and outputs compared to others in similar positions.

ethics (p. 92)   Standards of moral behavior; that is, behavior accepted by society as right versus wrong.

everyday low pricing (EDLP) (p. 377)   Setting prices lower than competitors and then not having any special sales.

exchange rate (p. 71)   The value of one nation's currency relative to the currencies of other countries.

exchange-traded funds (ETFs) (p. 509)   Collections of stocks that are traded on exchanges but are traded more like individual stocks than like mutual funds.

exclusive distribution (p. 395)   Distribution that sends products to only one retail outlet in a given geographic area.

executor (p. 630)   A person who assembles and values your estate, files income and other taxes, and distributes assets.

expectancy theory (p. 256)   Victor Vroom's theory that the amount of effort employees exert on a specific task depends on their expectations of the outcome.

exporting (p. 59)   Selling products to another country.

express warranties (p. 555)   Specific representations by the seller that buyers rely on regarding the goods they purchase.

external customers (p. 187)   Dealers, who buy products to sell to others, and ultimate customers (or end users), who buy products for their own personal use.

extranet (p. 579)   A semiprivate network that uses Internet technology and allows more than one company to access the same information or allows people on different servers to collaborate.

extrinsic reward (p. 247)   Something given to you by someone else as recognition for good work; extrinsic rewards include pay increases, praise, and promotions.

F

facility layout (p. 232)   The physical arrangement of resources (including people) in the production process.

facility location (p. 230)   The process of selecting a geographic location for a company's operations.

factoring (p. 477)   The process of selling accounts receivable for cash.

factors of production (p. 8)   The resources used to create wealth: land, labor, capital, entrepreneurship, and knowledge.

Federal Deposit Insurance Corporation (FDIC) (p. 537)   An independent agency of the U.S. government that insures bank deposits.

finance (p. 466)   The function in a business that acquires funds for the firm and manages those funds within the firm.

financial accounting (p. 453)   Accounting information and analyses prepared for people outside the organization.

financial control (p. 471)   A process in which a firm periodically compares its actual revenues, costs, and expenses with its budget.

financial management (p. 466)   The job of managing a firm's resources so it can meet its goals and objectives.

financial managers (p. 466)   Managers who examine financial data prepared by accountants and recommend strategies for improving the financial performance of the firm.

financial statement (p. 441)   A summary of all the transactions that have occurred over a particular period.

fiscal policy (p. 47)   The federal government's efforts to keep the economy stable by increasing or decreasing taxes or government spending.

fixed assets (p. 444)   Assets that are relatively permanent, such as land, buildings, and equipment.

flat organizational structure (p. 202)   An organizational structure that has few layers of management and a broad span of control.

flexible manufacturing (p. 227)   Designing machines to do multiple tasks so that they can produce a variety of products.

flextime plan (p. 294)   Work schedule that gives employees some freedom to choose when to work, as long as they work the required number of hours.

focus group (p. 343)   A small group of people who meet under the direction of a discussion leader to communicate their opinions about an organization, its products, or other given issues.

foreign direct investment (FDI) (p. 68)   The buying of permanent property and businesses in foreign nations.

foreign subsidiary (p. 68)   A company owned in a foreign country by another company, called the *parent company*.

form utility (p. 226)   The value producers add to materials in the creation of finished goods and services.

formal organization (p. 214)   The structure that details lines of responsibility, authority, and position; that is, the structure shown on organization charts.

franchise (p. 129)   The right to use a specific business's name and sell its products or services in a given territory.

franchise agreement (p. 129)   An arrangement whereby someone with a good idea for a business sells the rights to use the business name and sell a product or service to others in a given territory.

franchisee (p. 129)   A person who buys a franchise.

franchisor (p. 129)   A company that develops a product concept and sells others the rights to make and sell the products.

free-market economies (p. 41)   Economic systems in which the market largely determines what goods and services get produced, who gets them, and how the economy grows.

free-rein leadership (p. 184)   Leadership style that involves managers setting objectives and employees being relatively free to do whatever it takes to accomplish those objectives.

free trade (p. 60)   The movement of goods and services among nations without political or economic barriers.

freight forwarder (p. 401)   An organization that puts many small shipments together to create a single large shipment that can be transported cost-effectively to the final destination.

fringe benefits (p. 292)   Benefits such as sick-leave pay, vacation pay, pension plans, and health plans that represent additional compensation to employees beyond base wages.

fundamental accounting equation (p. 442)   Assets = Liabilities + Owners' equity; this is the basis for the balance sheet.

G

Gantt chart (p. 236)   Bar graph showing production managers what projects are being worked on and what stage they are in at any given time.

General Agreement on Tariffs and Trade (GATT) (p. 75)   A 1948 agreement that established an international forum for negotiating mutual reductions in trade restrictions.

general partner (p. 116)   An owner (partner) who has unlimited liability and is active in managing the firm.

general partnership (p. 116)   A partnership in which all owners share in operating the business and in assuming liability for the business's debts.

generic goods (p. 370)   Nonbranded products that usually sell at a sizable discount compared to national or private-label brands.

geographic segmentation (p. 347)   Dividing the market by cities, counties, states, or regions.

goals (p. 175)   The broad, long-term accomplishments an organization wishes to attain.

goal-setting theory (p. 255)   The idea that setting ambitious but attainable goals can motivate workers and improve performance if the goals are accepted, accompanied by feedback, and facilitated by organizational conditions.

goods (p. 4)   Tangible products such as computers, food, clothing, cars, and appliances.

government and not-for-profit accounting (p. 455)   Accounting system for organizations whose purpose is not generating a profit but serving ratepayers, taxpayers, and others according to a duly approved budget.

greening (p. 17)   The trend toward saving energy and producing products that cause less harm to the environment.

grievance (p. 314)   A charge by employees that management isn't abiding by the terms of the negotiated labor–management agreement.

gross domestic product (GDP) (p. 42)   The total value of final goods and services produced in a country in a given year.

gross output (GO) (p. 44)   A measure of total sales volume at all stages of production.

gross profit (or gross margin) (p. 446)   How much a firm earned by buying (or making) and selling merchandise.

H

Hawthorne effect (p. 249)   The tendency for people to behave differently when they know they are being studied.

health savings accounts (HSAs) (p. 605)   Tax-deferred savings accounts linked to low-cost, high-deductible health insurance policies.

hierarchy (p. 199)   A system in which one person is at the top of the organization and there is a ranked or sequential ordering from the top down of managers who are responsible to that person.

high–low pricing strategy (p. 377)   Setting prices that are higher than EDLP stores, but having many special sales where the prices are lower than competitors'.

horizontal merger (p. 127) The joining of two firms in the same industry.

human relations skills (p. 180) Skills that involve communication and motivation; they enable managers to work through and with people.

human resource management (HRM) (p. 274) The process of determining human resource needs and then recruiting, selecting, developing, motivating, evaluating, compensating, and scheduling employees to achieve organizational goals.

hygiene factors (p. 251) In Herzberg's theory of motivating factors, job factors that can cause dissatisfaction if missing but that do not necessarily motivate employees if increased.

I

identity theft (pp. 13, 588) The obtaining of individuals' personal information, such as Social Security and credit card numbers, for illegal purposes.

implied warranties (p. 555) Guarantees legally imposed on the seller.

importing (p. 59) Buying products from another country.

import quota (p. 74) A limit on the number of products in certain categories that a nation can import.

inbound logistics (p. 400) The area of logistics that involves bringing raw materials, packaging, other goods and services, and information from suppliers to producers.

income statement (p. 445) The financial statement that shows a firm's profit after costs, expenses, and taxes; it summarizes all of the resources that have come into the firm (revenue), all the resources that have left the firm, expenses, and the resulting net income or net loss.

incubators (p. 150) Centers that offer new businesses low-cost offices with basic business services.

independent audit (p. 455) An evaluation and unbiased opinion about the accuracy of a company's financial statements.

individual retirement account (IRA) (p. 627) A tax-deferred investment plan that enables you (and your spouse, if you are married) to save part of your income for retirement; a traditional IRA allows people who qualify to deduct from their reported income the money they put into an account.

industrial goods (p. 365) Products used in the production of other products. Sometimes called *business goods* or *B2B goods*.

industrial unions (p. 309) Labor organizations of unskilled and semiskilled workers in mass-production industries such as automobile manufacturing and mining.

inflation (p. 44) A general rise in the prices of goods and services over time.

infomercial (p. 419) A full-length TV program devoted exclusively to promoting goods or services.

informal organization (p. 214) The system that develops spontaneously as employees meet and form cliques, relationships, and lines of authority outside the formal organization; that is, the human side of the organization that does not appear on any organization chart.

information systems (IS) (p. 572) Technology that helps companies do business; includes such tools as automated teller machines (ATMs) and voice mail.

information technology (IT) (p. 572) Technology used to store, retrieve, and send information efficiently.

information utility (p. 392) Adding value to products by opening two-way flows of information between marketing participants.

initial public offering (IPO) (p. 492) The first public offering of a corporation's stock.

injunction (p. 316) A court order directing someone to do something or to refrain from doing something.

insider trading (p. 101) An unethical activity in which insiders use private company information to further their own fortunes or those of their family and friends.

institutional investors (p. 493) Large organizations—such as pension funds, mutual funds, and insurance companies—that invest their own funds or the funds of others.

insurable interest (p. 603) The possibility of the policyholder to suffer a loss.

insurable risk (p. 603) A risk that the typical insurance company will cover.

insurance policy (p. 604) A written contract between the insured and an insurance company that promises to pay for all or part of a loss.

intangible assets (p. 444) Long-term assets (e.g., patents, trademarks, copyrights) that have no real physical form but do have value.

integrated marketing communication (IMC) (p. 414) A technique that combines all the promotional tools into one comprehensive and unified promotional strategy.

integrity-based ethics codes (p. 95) Ethical standards that define the organization's guiding values, create an environment that supports ethically sound behavior, and stress a shared accountability among employees.

intensive distribution (p. 394) Distribution that puts products into as many retail outlets as possible.

interactive promotion (p. 419) Promotion process that allows marketers to go beyond a monologue, where sellers try to persuade buyers to buy things, to a dialogue in which buyers and sellers work together to create mutually beneficial exchange relationships.

interest (p. 498)   The payment the issuer of the bond makes to the bondholders for use of the borrowed money.

intermittent process (p. 226)   A production process in which the production run is short and the machines are changed frequently to make different products.

intermodal shipping (p. 403)   The use of multiple modes of transportation to complete a single long-distance movement of freight.

internal customers (p. 187)   Individuals and units within the firm that receive services from other individuals or units.

International Monetary Fund (IMF) (p. 541)   Organization that assists the smooth flow of money among nations.

Internet2 (p. 581)   The private Internet system that links government supercomputer centers and a select group of universities; it runs more than 22,000 times faster than today's public infrastructure and supports heavy-duty applications.

intranet (p. 579)   A companywide network, closed to public access, that uses Internet-type technology.

intrapreneurs (p. 147)   Creative people who work as entrepreneurs within corporations.

intrinsic reward (p. 247)   The personal satisfaction you feel when you perform well and complete goals.

inverted organization (p. 212)   An organization that has contact people at the top and the chief executive officer at the bottom of the organization chart.

investment bankers (p. 493)   Specialists who assist in the issue and sale of new securities.

invisible hand (p. 33)   A phrase coined by Adam Smith to describe the process that turns self-directed gain into social and economic benefits for all.

involuntary bankruptcy (p. 562)   Bankruptcy procedures filed by a debtor's creditors.

ISO 14001 (p. 235)   A collection of the best practices for managing an organization's impact on the environment.

ISO 9001 (p. 235)   The common name given to quality management and assurance standards.

J

job analysis (p. 279)   A study of what is done by employees who hold various job titles.

job description (p. 279)   A summary of the objectives of a job, the type of work to be done, the responsibilities and duties, the working conditions, and the relationship of the job to other functions.

job enlargement (p. 258)   A job enrichment strategy that involves combining a series of tasks into one challenging and interesting assignment.

job enrichment (p. 257)   A motivational strategy that emphasizes motivating the worker through the job itself.

job rotation (p. 258)   A job enrichment strategy that involves moving employees from one job to another.

job sharing (p. 297)   An arrangement whereby two part-time employees share one full-time job.

job simulation (p. 287)   The use of equipment that duplicates job conditions and tasks so that trainees can learn skills before attempting them on the job.

job specifications (p. 279)   A written summary of the minimum qualifications required of workers to do a particular job.

joint venture (p. 67)   A partnership in which two or more companies (often from different countries) join to undertake a major project.

journal (p. 440)   The record book or computer program where accounting data is first entered.

judiciary (p. 550)   The branch of government chosen to oversee the legal system through the court system.

junk bonds (p. 506)   High-risk, high-interest bonds.

just-in-time (JIT) inventory control (p. 234)   A production process in which a minimum of inventory is kept on the premises and parts, supplies, and other needs are delivered just in time to go on the assembly line.

K

Keynesian economic theory (p. 47)   The theory that a government policy of increasing spending and cutting taxes could stimulate the economy in a recession.

Knights of Labor (p. 309)   The first national labor union; formed in 1869.

knockoff brands (p. 370)   Illegal copies of national brand-name goods.

knowledge management (p. 185)   Finding the right information, keeping the information in a readily accessible place, and making the information known to everyone in the firm.

L

law of large numbers (p. 604)   Principle that if a large number of people are exposed to the same risk, a predictable number of losses will occur during a given period of time.

leading (p. 174)   Creating a vision for the organization and guiding, training, coaching, and motivating others to work effectively to achieve the organization's goals and objectives in a timely manner.

lean manufacturing (p. 228)   The production of goods using less of everything compared to mass production.

ledger (p. 440)   A specialized accounting book or computer program in which information from accounting journals is accumulated into specific categories and posted so that managers can find all the information about one account in the same place.

letter of credit (p. 539)   A promise by the bank to pay the seller a given amount if certain conditions are met.

leverage (p. 481)   Raising needed funds through borrowing to increase a firm's rate of return.

leveraged buyout (LBO) (p. 128)   An attempt by employees, management, or a group of investors to purchase an organization primarily through borrowing.

liabilities (p. 444)   What the business owes to others (debts).

licensing (p. 64)   A global strategy in which a firm (the licensor) allows a foreign company (the licensee) to produce its product in exchange for a fee (a royalty).

limited liability (p. 117)   The responsibility of a business's owners for losses only up to the amount they invest; limited partners and shareholders have limited liability.

limited liability company (LLC) (p. 125)   A company similar to an S corporation but without the special eligibility requirements.

limited liability partnership (LLP) (p. 117)   A partnership that limits partners' risk of losing their personal assets to only their own acts and omissions and to the acts and omissions of people under their supervision.

limited partner (p. 116)   An owner who invests money in the business but does not have any management responsibility or liability for losses beyond the investment.

limited partnership (p. 116)   A partnership with one or more general partners and one or more limited partners.

line of credit (p. 477)   A given amount of unsecured short-term funds a bank will lend to a business, provided the funds are readily available.

line organization (p. 205)   An organization that has direct two-way lines of responsibility, authority, and communication running from the top to the bottom of the organization, with all people reporting to only one supervisor.

line personnel (p. 206)   Employees who are part of the chain of command that is responsible for achieving organizational goals.

liquidity (p. 443)   The ease with which an asset can be converted into cash.

lockout (p. 316)   An attempt by management to put pressure on unions by temporarily closing the business.

logistics (p. 400)   The marketing activity that involves planning, implementing, and controlling the physical flow of materials, final goods, and related information from points of origin to points of consumption to meet customer requirements at a profit.

loss (p. 4)   When a business's expenses are more than its revenues.

M

M-1 (p. 527)   Money that can be accessed quickly and easily (coins and paper money, checks, traveler's checks, etc.).

M-2 (p. 527)   Money included in M-1 plus money that may take a little more time to obtain (savings accounts, money market accounts, mutual funds, certificates of deposit, etc.).

M-3 (p. 527)   M-2 plus big deposits like institutional money market funds.

macroeconomics (p. 31)   The part of economics study that looks at the operation of a nation's economy as a whole.

management (p. 173)   The process used to accomplish organizational goals through planning, organizing, leading, and controlling people and other organizational resources.

management by objectives (MBO) (p. 255)   Peter Drucker's system of goal-setting and implementation; it involves a cycle of discussion, review, and evaluation of objectives among top and middle-level managers, supervisors, and employees.

management development (p. 287)   The process of training and educating employees to become good managers and then monitoring the progress of their managerial skills over time.

managerial accounting (p. 454)   Accounting used to provide information and analyses to managers within the organization to assist them in decision making.

manufacturers' (national) brands (p. 370)   The brand names of manufacturers that distribute products nationally.

market (p. 160)   People with unsatisfied wants and needs who have both the resources and the willingness to buy.

marketing (p. 334)   The activity, set of institutions, and processes for creating, communicating, delivering, and exchanging offerings that have value for customers, clients, partners, and society at large.

marketing concept (p. 336)   A three-part business philosophy: (1) a customer orientation, (2) a service orientation, and (3) a profit orientation.

marketing intermediaries (p. 386)   Organizations that assist in moving goods and services from producers to businesses (B2B) and from businesses to consumers (B2C).

marketing mix (p. 338)   The ingredients that go into a marketing program: product, price, place, and promotion.

marketing research (p. 341)   The analysis of markets to determine opportunities and challenges, and to find the information needed to make good decisions.

market price (p. 37)   The price determined by supply and demand.

market segmentation (p. 347)   The process of dividing the total market into groups whose members have similar characteristics.

Maslow's hierarchy of needs (p. 249)   Theory of motivation based on unmet human needs from basic physiological needs to safety, social, and esteem needs to self-actualization needs.

mass customization (p. 228)   Tailoring products to meet the needs of a large number of individual customers.

mass marketing (p. 349)   Developing products and promotions to please large groups of people.

master limited partnership (MLP) (p. 117)   A partnership that looks much like a corporation (in that it acts like a corporation and is traded on a stock exchange) but is taxed like a partnership and thus avoids the corporate income tax.

materials handling (p. 400)   The movement of goods within a warehouse, from warehouses to the factory floor, and from the factory floor to various workstations.

materials requirement planning (MRP) (p. 232)   A computer-based operations management system that uses sales forecasts to make sure that needed parts and materials are available at the right time and place.

matrix organization (p. 207)   An organization in which specialists from different parts of the organization are brought together to work on specific projects but still remain part of a linc-and-staff structure.

maturity date (p. 498)   The exact date the issuer of a bond must pay the principal to the bondholder.

mediation (p. 314)   The use of a third party, called a mediator, who encourages both sides in a dispute to continue negotiating and often makes suggestions for resolving the dispute.

mentor (p. 288)   An experienced employee who supervises, coaches, and guides lower-level employees by introducing them to the right people and generally being their organizational sponsor.

merchant wholesalers (p. 393)   Independently owned firms that take title to the goods they handle.

merger (p. 127)   The result of two firms forming one company.

microeconomics (p. 31)   The part of economics study that looks at the behavior of people and organizations in particular markets.

micropreneurs (p. 148)   Entrepreneurs willing to accept the risk of starting and managing the type of business that remains small, lets them do the kind of work they want to do, and offers them a balanced lifestyle.

middle management (p. 180)   The level of management that includes general managers, division managers, and branch and plant managers who are responsible for tactical planning and controlling.

mission statement (p. 175)   An outline of the fundamental purposes of an organization.

mixed economies (p. 42)   Economic systems in which some allocation of resources is made by the market and some by the government.

monetary policy (p. 49)   The management of the money supply and interest rates by the Federal Reserve Bank.

money (p. 524)   Anything that people generally accept as payment for goods and services.

money supply (p. 526)   The amount of money the Federal Reserve Bank makes available for people to buy goods and services.

monopolistic competition (p. 38)   The degree of competition in which a large number of sellers produce very similar products that buyers nevertheless perceive as different.

monopoly (p. 38)   A degree of competition in which only one seller controls the total supply of a product or service, and sets the price.

motivators (p. 251)   In Herzberg's theory of motivating factors, job factors that cause employees to be productive and that give them satisfaction.

multinational corporation (p. 68)   An organization that manufactures and markets products in many different countries and has multinational stock ownership and multinational management.

mutual fund (p. 507)   An organization that buys stocks and bonds and then sells shares in those securities to the public.

mutual insurance company (p. 605)   A type of insurance company owned by its policyholders.

N

NASDAQ (p. 494)   A nationwide electronic system that communicates over-the-counter trades to brokers.

national debt (p. 48)   The sum of government deficits over time.

negligence (p. 552)   In tort law, behavior that causes unintentional harm or injury.

negotiable instruments (p. 556)   Forms of commercial paper (such as checks) that are transferable among businesses and individuals and represent a promise to pay a specified amount.

negotiated labor–management agreement (labor contract) (p. 312)   Agreement that sets the tone and clarifies the terms under which management and labor agree to function over a period of time.

net income or net loss (p. 445)   Revenue left over after all costs and expenses, including taxes, are paid.

networking (pp. 209, 288)   The process of establishing and maintaining contacts with key managers in one's own organization and other organizations and using those contacts to weave strong relationships that serve as informal development systems.

niche marketing (p. 348)   The process of finding small but profitable market segments and designing or finding products for them.

nonbanks (p. 536) Financial organizations that accept no deposits but offer many of the services provided by regular banks (pension funds, insurance companies, commercial finance companies, consumer finance companies, and brokerage houses).

nonprofit organization (p. 7) An organization whose goals do not include making a personal profit for its owners or organizers.

North American Free Trade Agreement (NAFTA) (p. 77) Agreement that created a free-trade area among the United States, Canada, and Mexico.

notes payable (p. 444) Short-term or long-term liabilities that a business promises to repay by a certain date.

O

objectives (p. 175) Specific, short-term statements detailing how to achieve the organization's goals.

off-the-job training (p. 286) Training that occurs away from the workplace and consists of internal or external programs to develop any of a variety of skills or to foster personal development.

oligopoly (p. 38) A degree of competition in which just a few sellers dominate the market.

one-to-one marketing (p. 348) Developing a unique mix of goods and services for each individual customer.

online retailing (p. 395) Selling goods and services to ultimate customers (e.g., you and me) over the Internet.

online training (p. 287) Training programs in which employees complete classes via the Internet.

on-the-job training (p. 286) Training at the workplace that lets the employee learn by doing or by watching others for a while and then imitating them.

open-market operations (p. 529) The buying and selling of U.S. government bonds by the Fed with the goal of regulating the money supply.

open shop agreement (p. 313) Agreement in right-to-work states that gives workers the option to join or not join a union, if one exists in their workplace.

operating expenses (p. 446) Costs involved in operating a business, such as rent, utilities, and salaries.

operating (or master) budget (p. 470) The budget that ties together the firm's other budgets and summarizes its proposed financial activities.

operational planning (p. 177) The process of setting work standards and schedules necessary to implement the company's tactical objectives.

operations management (p. 224) A specialized area in management that converts or transforms resources (including human resources) into goods and services.

organizational (or corporate) culture (p. 213) Widely shared values within an organization that provide unity and cooperation to achieve common goals.

organization chart (p. 200) A visual device that shows relationships among people and divides the organization's work; it shows who is accountable for the completion of specific work and who reports to whom.

organizing (p. 173) A management function that includes designing the structure of the organization and creating conditions and systems in which everyone and everything work together to achieve the organization's goals and objectives.

orientation (p. 286) The activity that introduces new employees to the organization; to fellow employees; to their immediate supervisors; and to the policies, practices, and objectives of the firm.

outbound logistics (p. 401) The area of logistics that involves managing the flow of finished products and information to business buyers and ultimate consumers (people like you and me).

outsourcing (pp. 6, 79) Contracting with other companies (often in other countries) to do some or all of the functions of a firm, like its production or accounting tasks.

over-the-counter (OTC) market (p. 493) Exchange that provides a means to trade stocks not listed on the national exchanges.

owners' equity (p. 444) The amount of the business that belongs to the owners minus any liabilities owed by the business.

P

participative (democratic) leadership (p. 183) Leadership style that consists of managers and employees working together to make decisions.

partnership (p. 114) A legal form of business with two or more owners.

patent (p. 554) A document that gives inventors exclusive rights to their inventions for 20 years.

penetration strategy (p. 377) Strategy in which a product is priced low to attract many customers and discourage competition.

pension funds (p. 536) Amounts of money put aside by corporations, nonprofit organizations, or unions to cover part of the financial needs of members when they retire.

perfect competition (p. 38) The degree of competition in which there are many sellers in a market and none is large enough to dictate the price of a product.

performance appraisal (p. 289) An evaluation that measures employee performance against established standards in order to make decisions about promotions, compensation, training, or termination.

personal selling (p. 420) The face-to-face presentation and promotion of goods and services.

place utility (p. 390) Adding value to products by having them where people want them.

planning (p. 173) A management function that includes anticipating trends and determining the best strategies and tactics to achieve organizational goals and objectives.

PMI (p. 179) Listing all the pluses for a solution in one column, all the minuses in another, and the implications in a third column.

podcasting (p. 428) A means of distributing audio and video programs via the Internet that lets users subscribe to a number of files, also known as feeds, and then hear or view the material at the time they choose.

possession utility (p. 391) Doing whatever is necessary to transfer ownership from one party to another, including providing credit, delivery, installation, guarantees, and follow-up service.

precedent (p. 551) Decisions judges have made in earlier cases that guide the handling of new cases.

preferred stock (p. 497) Stock that gives its owners preference in the payment of dividends and an earlier claim on assets than common stockholders if the company is forced out of business and its assets sold.

premium (p. 604) The fee charged by an insurance company for an insurance policy.

price leadership (p. 377) The strategy by which one or more dominant firms set the pricing practices that all competitors in an industry follow.

primary boycott (p. 316) When a union encourages both its members and the general public not to buy the products of a firm involved in a labor dispute.

primary data (p. 342) Data that you gather yourself (not from secondary sources such as books and magazines).

principle of motion economy (p. 248) Theory developed by Frank and Lillian Gilbreth that every job can be broken down into a series of elementary motions.

private accountant (p. 453) An accountant who works for a single firm, government agency, or nonprofit organization.

problem solving (p. 179) The process of solving the everyday problems that occur. Problem solving is less formal than decision making and usually calls for quicker action.

process manufacturing (p. 226) That part of the production process that physically or chemically changes materials.

producer price index (PPI) (p. 45) An index that measures the change in prices at the wholesale level.

product (p. 339) Any physical good, service, or idea that satisfies a want or need plus anything that would enhance the product in the eyes of consumers, such as the brand name.

product analysis (p. 372) Making cost estimates and sales forecasts to get a feeling for profitability of new-product ideas.

product differentiation (p. 363) The creation of real or perceived product differences.

production (p. 224) The creation of finished goods and services using the factors of production: land, labor, capital, entrepreneurship, and knowledge.

production management (p. 224) The term used to describe all the activities managers do to help their firms create goods.

productivity (p. 12) The amount of output you generate given the amount of input (e.g., hours worked).

product liability (p. 552) Part of tort law that holds businesses liable for harm that results from the production, design, sale, or use of products they market.

product life cycle (p. 373) A theoretical model of what happens to sales and profits for a product class over time; the four stages of the cycle are introduction, growth, maturity, and decline.

product line (p. 363) A group of products that are physically similar or are intended for a similar market.

product mix (p. 363) The combination of product lines offered by a manufacturer.

product placement (p. 418) Putting products into TV shows and movies where they will be seen.

product screening (p. 372) A process designed to reduce the number of new-product ideas being worked on at any one time.

profit (p. 4) The amount of money a business earns above and beyond what it spends for salaries and other expenses.

program evaluation and review technique (PERT) (p. 236) A method for analyzing the tasks involved in completing a given project, estimating the time needed to complete each task, and identifying the minimum time needed to complete the total project.

program trading (p. 511) Giving instructions to computers to automatically sell if the price of a stock dips to a certain point to avoid potential losses.

promissory note (p. 475) A written agreement with a promise to pay a supplier a specific sum of money at a definite time.

promotion (p. 340) All the techniques sellers use to inform people about and motivate them to buy their products or services.

promotion mix (p. 414) The combination of promotional tools an organization uses.

prospect (p. 422) A person with the means to buy a product, the authority to buy, and the willingness to listen to a sales message.

prospecting (p. 422) Researching potential buyers and choosing those most likely to buy.

prospectus (p. 494) A condensed version of economic and financial information that a company must file with the SEC before issuing stock; the prospectus must be sent to prospective investors.

psychographic segmentation (p. 347) Dividing the market using the group's values, attitudes, and interests.

psychological pricing (p. 378) Pricing goods and services at price points that make the product appear less expensive than it is.

public accountant (p. 453) An accountant who provides accounting services to individuals or businesses on a fee basis.

publicity (p. 424) Any information about an individual, product, or organization that's distributed to the public through the media and that's not paid for or controlled by the seller.

public relations (PR) (p. 424) The management function that evaluates public attitudes, changes policies and procedures in response to the public's requests, and executes a program of action and information to earn public understanding and acceptance.

pull strategy (p. 429) Promotional strategy in which heavy advertising and sales promotion efforts are directed toward consumers so that they'll request the products from retailers.

purchasing (p. 234) The function in a firm that searches for quality material resources, finds the best suppliers, and negotiates the best price for goods and services.

pure risk (p. 601) The threat of loss with no chance for profit.

push strategy (p. 429) Promotional strategy in which the producer uses advertising, personal selling, sales promotion, and all other promotional tools to convince wholesalers and retailers to stock and sell merchandise.

Q

qualifying (p. 422) In the selling process, making sure that people have a need for the product, the authority to buy, and the willingness to listen to a sales message.

quality (p. 234) Consistently producing what the customer wants while reducing errors before and after delivery to the customer.

quality of life (p. 5) The general well-being of a society in terms of its political freedom, natural environment, education, health care, safety, amount of leisure, and rewards that add to the satisfaction and joy that other goods and services provide.

R

rack jobbers (p. 393) Wholesalers that furnish racks or shelves full of merchandise to retailers, display products, and sell on consignment.

ratio analysis (p. 450) The assessment of a firm's financial condition using calculations and interpretations of financial ratios developed from the firm's financial statements.

real time (p. 209) The present moment or the actual time in which something takes place.

recession (p. 47) Two or more consecutive quarters of decline in the GDP.

recruitment (p. 280) The set of activities used to obtain a sufficient number of the right people at the right time.

relationship marketing (p. 349) Marketing strategy with the goal of keeping individual customers over time by offering them products that exactly meet their requirements.

reserve requirement (p. 528) A percentage of commercial banks' checking and savings accounts that must be physically kept in the bank.

resource development (p. 31) The study of how to increase resources and to create the conditions that will make better use of those resources.

restructuring (p. 212) Redesigning an organization so that it can more effectively and efficiently serve its customers.

retailer (p. 387) An organization that sells to ultimate consumers.

retained earnings (p. 444) The accumulated earnings from a firm's profitable operations that were reinvested in the business and not paid out to stockholders in dividends.

revenue (p. 4) The total amount of money a business takes in during a given period by selling goods and services.

reverse logistics (p. 401) The area of logistics that involves bringing goods back to the manufacturer because of defects or for recycling materials.

right-to-work laws (p. 313) Legislation that gives workers the right, under an open shop, to join or not join a union if it's present.

risk (pp. 5, 601) (1) The chance an entrepreneur takes of losing time and money on a business that may not prove profitable. (2) The chance of loss, the degree of probability of loss, and the amount of possible loss.

risk/return trade-off (p. 480) The principle that the greater the risk a lender takes in making a loan, the higher the interest rate required.

Roth IRA (p. 627) An IRA where there are no up-front deductions on taxes as with a traditional IRA, but the earnings grow tax-free and are also tax-free when withdrawn.

rule of indemnity (p. 604) Rule saying that an insured person or organization cannot collect more than the actual loss from an insurable risk.

S

sales promotion (p. 425) The promotional tool that stimulates consumer purchasing and dealer interest by means of short-term activities.

sampling (p. 426) A promotional tool in which a company lets consumers have a small sample of a product for no charge.

savings and loan association (S&L) (p. 535) A financial institution that accepts both savings and checking deposits and provides home mortgage loans.

Savings Association Insurance Fund (SAIF) (p. 538) The part of the FDIC that insures holders of accounts in savings and loan associations.

scientific management (p. 247) Studying workers to find the most efficient ways of doing things and then teaching people those techniques.

S corporation (p. 124) A unique government creation that looks like a corporation but is taxed like sole proprietorships and partnerships.

secondary boycott (p. 316) An attempt by labor to convince others to stop doing business with a firm that's the subject of a primary boycott; prohibited by the Taft-Hartley Act.

secondary data (p. 342) Information that has already been compiled by others and published in journals and books or made available online.

secured loan (p. 477) A loan backed by collateral (something valuable, such as property).

Securities and Exchange Commission (SEC) (p. 494) Federal agency that has responsibility for regulating the various exchanges.

selection (p. 281) The process of gathering information and deciding who should be hired, under legal guidelines, for the best interests of the individual and the organization.

selective distribution (p. 395) Distribution that sends products to only a preferred group of retailers in an area.

self-insurance (p. 602) The practice of setting aside money to cover routine claims and buying only "catastrophe" policies to cover big losses.

Service Corps of Retired Executives (SCORE) (p. 162) An SBA office with volunteers from industry, trade associations, and education who counsel small businesses at no cost (except for expenses).

services (p. 4) Intangible products (i.e., products that can't be held in your hand) such as education, health care, insurance, recreation, and travel and tourism.

service utility (p. 392) Adding value by providing fast, friendly service during and after the sale and by teaching customers how to best use products over time.

sexual harassment (p. 321) Unwelcome sexual advances, requests for sexual favors, and other conduct (verbal or physical) of a sexual nature that creates a hostile work environment.

shop stewards (p. 314) Union officials who work permanently in an organization and represent employee interests on a daily basis.

shopping goods and services (p. 364) Those products that the consumer buys only after comparing value, quality, price, and style from a variety of sellers.

sinking fund (p. 500) A reserve account in which the issuer of a bond periodically retires some part of the bond principal prior to maturity so that enough capital will be accumulated by the maturity date to pay off the bond.

Six Sigma quality (p. 234) A quality measure that allows only 3.4 defects per million opportunities.

skimming price strategy (p. 377) Strategy in which a new product is priced high to make optimum profit while there's little competition.

small business (p. 152) A business that is independently owned and operated, is not dominant in its field of operation, and meets certain standards of size (set by the Small Business Administration) in terms of employees or annual receipts.

Small Business Administration (SBA) (p. 159) A U.S. government agency that advises and assists small businesses by providing management training and financial advice and loans.

Small Business Investment Company (SBIC) Program (p. 160) A program through which private investment companies licensed by the Small Business Administration lend money to small businesses.

smart card (p. 538) An electronic funds transfer tool that is a combination credit card, debit card, phone card, driver's license card, and more.

social audit (p. 104) A systematic evaluation of an organization's progress toward implementing socially responsible and responsive programs.

social commerce (p. 395) A form of electronic commerce that involves using social media, online media that support social interaction, and user contributions to assist in the online buying and selling of products and services.

socialism (p. 40) An economic system based on the premise that some, if not most, basic businesses should be owned by the government so that profits can be more evenly distributed among the people.

Social Security (p. 627) The term used to describe the Old-Age, Survivors, and Disability Insurance Program established by the Social Security Act of 1935.

sole proprietorship (p. 114) A business that is owned, and usually managed, by one person.

sovereign wealth funds (SWFs) (p. 68) Investment funds controlled by governments holding large stakes in foreign companies.

span of control (p. 201) The optimum number of subordinates a manager supervises or should supervise.

specialty goods and services (p. 364) Consumer products with unique characteristics and brand identity. Because these products are perceived as having no reasonable substitute, the consumer puts forth a special effort to purchase them.

speculative risk (p. 601) A chance of either profit or loss.

staffing (p. 182) A management function that includes hiring, motivating, and retaining the best people available to accomplish the company's objectives.

staff personnel (p. 206) Employees who advise and assist line personnel in meeting their goals.

stagflation (p. 45) A situation when the economy is slowing but prices are going up anyhow.

stakeholders (p. 6) All the people who stand to gain or lose by the policies and activities of a business and whose concerns the business needs to address.

standard of living (p. 5) The amount of goods and services people can buy with the money they have.

state capitalism (p. 34) A combination of freer markets and some government control.

statement of cash flows (p. 448) Financial statement that reports cash receipts and disbursements related to a firm's three major activities: operations, investments, and financing.

statistical process control (SPC) (p. 235) The process of taking statistical samples of product components at each stage of the production process and plotting those results on a graph. Any variances from quality standards are recognized and can be corrected if beyond the set standards.

statistical quality control (SQC) (p. 234) The process some managers use to continually monitor all phases of the production process to ensure that quality is being built into the product from the beginning.

statutory law (p. 550) State and federal constitutions, legislative enactments, treaties of the federal government, and ordinances—in short, written law.

stockbroker (p. 500) A registered representative who works as a market intermediary to buy and sell securities for clients.

stock certificate (p. 496) Evidence of stock ownership that specifies the name of the company, the number of shares it represents, and the type of stock being issued.

stock exchange (p. 493) An organization whose members can buy and sell (exchange) securities for companies and investors.

stock insurance company (p. 605) A type of insurance company owned by stockholders.

stocks (p. 496) Shares of ownership in a company.

stock splits (p. 504) An action by a company that gives stockholders two or more shares of stock for each one they own.

strategic alliance (p. 67) A long-term partnership between two or more companies established to help each company build competitive market advantages.

strategic planning (p. 175) The process of determining the major goals of the organization and the policies and strategies for obtaining and using resources to achieve those goals.

strict product liability (p. 553) Legal responsibility for harm or injury caused by a product regardless of fault.

strike (p. 315) A union strategy in which workers refuse to go to work; the purpose is to further workers' objectives after an impasse in collective bargaining.

strikebreakers (p. 316) Workers hired to do the jobs of striking workers until the labor dispute is resolved.

supervisory management (p. 180) Managers who are directly responsible for supervising workers and evaluating their daily performance.

supply (p. 36) The quantity of products that manufacturers or owners are willing to sell at different prices at a specific time.

supply-chain management (p. 399) The process of managing the movement of raw materials, parts, work in progress, finished goods, and related information through all the organizations involved in the supply chain; managing the return of such goods, if necessary; and recycling materials when appropriate.

supply chain (value chain) (p. 398) The sequence of linked activities that must be performed by various organizations to move goods from the sources of raw materials to ultimate consumers.

SWOT analysis (p. 175) A planning tool used to analyze an organization's strengths, weaknesses, opportunities, and threats.

T

tactical planning (p. 177) The process of developing detailed, short-term statements about what is to be done, who is to do it, and how it is to be done.

tall organizational structure (p. 202) An organizational structure in which the pyramidal organization chart would be quite tall because of the various levels of management.

target costing (p. 377) Designing a product so that it satisfies customers and meets the profit margins desired by the firm.

target marketing (p. 347) Marketing directed toward those groups (market segments) an organization decides it can serve profitably.

tariff (p. 74) A tax imposed on imports.

tax accountant (p. 455) An accountant trained in tax law and responsible for preparing tax returns or developing tax strategies.

tax-deferred contributions (p. 627) Retirement account deposits for which you pay no current taxes, but the earnings gained are taxed as regular income when they are withdrawn at retirement.

taxes (p. 559) How the government (federal, state, and local) raises money.

technical skills (p. 180) Skills that involve the ability to perform tasks in a specific discipline or department.

technology (p. 11) Everything from phones to computers, mobile devices, medical imaging machines, robots, the Internet, social media, and the various software programs and apps that make business processes more effective, efficient, and productive.

telecommuting (p. 231) Working from home via computer and modem.

telemarketing (p. 396) The sale of goods and services by telephone.

term insurance (p. 624) Pure insurance protection for a given number of years.

term-loan agreement (p. 480) A promissory note that requires the borrower to repay the loan in specified installments.

test marketing (p. 340) The process of testing products among potential users.

time deposit (p. 533) The technical name for a savings account; the bank can require prior notice before the owner withdraws money from a time deposit.

time-motion studies (p. 247) Studies, begun by Frederick Taylor, of which tasks must be performed to complete a job and the time needed to do each task.

time utility (p. 390) Adding value to products by making them available when they're needed.

top management (p. 179) Highest level of management, consisting of the president and other key company executives who develop strategic plans.

tort (p. 552) A wrongful act that causes injury to another person's body, property, or reputation.

total fixed costs (p. 377) All the expenses that remain the same no matter how many products are made or sold.

total product offer (p. 362) Everything that consumers evaluate when deciding whether to buy something; also called a *value package*.

trade credit (p. 475) The practice of buying goods and services now and paying for them later.

trade deficit (p. 62) An unfavorable balance of trade; occurs when the value of a country's imports exceeds that of its exports.

trademark (p. 369) A brand that has exclusive legal protection for both its brand name and its design.

trade protectionism (p. 74) The use of government regulations to limit the import of goods and services.

trade surplus (p. 62) A favorable balance of trade; occurs when the value of a country's exports exceeds that of its imports.

training and development (p. 286) All attempts to improve productivity by increasing an employee's ability to perform. Training focuses on short-term skills, whereas development focuses on long-term abilities.

transparency (p. 183) The presentation of a company's facts and figures in a way that is clear and apparent to all stakeholders.

trial balance (p. 440) A summary of all the financial data in the account ledgers that ensures the figures are correct and balanced.

trial close (p. 422) A step in the selling process that consists of a question or statement that moves the selling process toward the actual close.

U

unemployment rate (p. 44) The number of civilians at least 16 years old who are unemployed and tried to find a job within the prior four weeks.

Uniform Commercial Code (UCC) (p. 555) A comprehensive commercial law, adopted by every state in the United States, that covers sales laws and other commercial laws.

uninsurable risk (p. 602) A risk that no insurance company will cover.

union (p. 308) An employee organization that has the main goal of representing members in employee–management bargaining over job-related issues.

union security clause (p. 313) Provision in a negotiated labor–management agreement that stipulates that employees who benefit from a union must either officially join or at least pay dues to the union.

union shop agreement (p. 313) Clause in a labor–management agreement that says workers don't have to be members of a union to be hired, but must agree to join the union within a prescribed period.

United States–Mexico–Canada Agreement (USMCA) (p. 77) Free-trade agreement among the United States, Mexico, and Canada that replaced NAFTA in an effort to create more balanced and reciprocal trade.

unlimited liability (p. 115) The responsibility of business owners for all of the debts of the business.

unsecured loan (p. 477) A loan that doesn't require any collateral.

unsought goods and services (p. 364) Products that consumers are unaware of, haven't necessarily thought of buying, or find that they need to solve an unexpected problem.

utility (p. 390) In economics, the want-satisfying ability, or value, that organizations add to goods or services when the products are made more useful or accessible to consumers than they were before.

V

value (p. 360) Good quality at a fair price. When consumers calculate the value of a product, they look at the benefits and then subtract the cost to see if the benefits exceed the costs.

variable costs (p. 377) Costs that change according to the level of production.

variable life insurance (p. 625) Whole life insurance that invests the cash value of the policy in stocks or other high-yielding securities.

venture capital (p. 481) Money that is invested in new or emerging companies that are perceived as having great profit potential.

venture capitalists (p. 159) Individuals or companies that invest in new businesses in exchange for partial ownership of those businesses.

vertical merger (p. 127) The joining of two companies involved in different stages of related businesses.

vestibule training (p. 287) Training done in classrooms where employees are taught on equipment similar to that used on the job.

viral marketing (p. 427) The term now used to describe everything from paying customers to say positive things on the Internet to setting up multilevel selling schemes whereby consumers get commissions for directing friends to specific websites.

virtual corporation (p. 210) A temporary networked organization made up of replaceable firms that join and leave as needed.

virtual private network (VPN) (p. 579) A private data network that creates secure connections, or "tunnels," over regular Internet lines.

virus (p. 587) A piece of programming code inserted into other programming to cause some unexpected and, for the victim, usually undesirable event.

vision (p. 174) An encompassing explanation of why the organization exists and where it is trying to go.

volume (or usage) segmentation (p. 347) Dividing the market by usage (volume of use).

voluntary bankruptcy (p. 562) Legal procedures initiated by a debtor.

W

Web 2.0 (p. 581) The set of tools that allow people to build social and business connections, share information, and collaborate on projects online (including blogs, wikis, social networking sites and other online communities, and virtual worlds).

Web 3.0 (p. 584) A combination of technologies that adds intelligence and changes how people interact with the web, and vice versa (consists of the semantic web, mobile web, and immersive Internet).

whistleblowers (p. 95) Insiders who report illegal or unethical behavior.

whole life insurance (p. 624) Life insurance that stays in effect until age 100.

wholesaler (p. 386) A marketing intermediary that sells to other organizations.

will (p. 630) A document that names the guardian for your children, states how you want your assets distributed, and names the executor for your estate.

word-of-mouth promotion (p. 427) A promotional tool that involves people telling other people about products they've purchased.

World Bank (p. 540) The bank primarily responsible for financing economic development; also known as the International Bank for Reconstruction and Development.

World Trade Organization (WTO) (p. 75) The international organization that replaced the General Agreement on Tariffs and Trade, and was assigned the duty to mediate trade disputes among nations.

Y

yellow-dog contract (p. 311) A type of contract that required employees to agree as a condition of employment not to join a union; prohibited by the Norris-LaGuardia Act in 1932.

NAME INDEX

ORGANIZATION INDEX

SUBJECT INDEX